1 MONTH OF
FREE
READING

at

www.ForgottenBooks.com

By purchasing this book you are eligible for one month membership to ForgottenBooks.com, giving you unlimited access to our entire collection of over 1,000,000 titles via our web site and mobile apps.

To claim your free month visit:

www.forgottenbooks.com/free1304272

ISBN 978-0-428-70422-3
PIBN 11304272

The

✺ AMERICAN ✺

FLORIST.

A WEEKLY JOURNAL FOR THE TRADE.

VOLUME XXI.

CHICAGO:
AMERICAN FLORIST COMPANY.
1904.

THE AMERICAN FLORIST.

VOLUME XXI.

August 1, 1903, to January 23, 1904.

CONTENTS.

Illustrations are indicated by an *

THE AMERICAN FLORIST

A WEEKLY JOURNAL FOR THE TRADE

America is "the Prow of the Vessel; there may be more comfort Amidships, but we are the first to touch Unknown Seas."

Vol. XXI. CHICAGO AND NEW YORK, AUGUST 1, 1903 No. 791.

THE AMERICAN FLORIST

NINETEENTH YEAR.

Copyright 1903, by American Florist Company
Entered as Second-Class Mail Matter.

PUBLISHED EVERY SATURDAY BY

AMERICAN FLORIST COMPANY,
324 Dearborn St., Chicago.

Eastern Office: 79 Milk St., Boston.

Subscription, $1.00 a year. To Europe, $2.00.
Subscriptions accepted only from the trade.
Volumes half-yearly from August, 1901.

SOCIETY OF AMERICAN FLORISTS AND
ORNAMENTAL HORTICULTURISTS.

OFFICERS.—JOHN BURTON, Philadelphia, Pa.,
president; C. C. POLLWORTH, Milwaukee, Wis.,
vice-president; WM. J. STEWART, 79 Milk Street,
Boston, Mass., secretary; H. B. BEATTY, Oil City,
Pa., treasurer.
Nineteenth annual meeting at Milwaukee, Wis.,
August 18-21, 1903.

THE AMERICAN CARNATION SOCIETY.

Annual convention at Detroit, Mich., March 2,
1904. ALBERT M. HERR, Lancaster, Pa., secretary.

AMERICAN ROSE SOCIETY.

Annual meeting and exhibition, Philadelphia,
March, 1904. LEONARD BARRON, 136 Liberty St.,
New York, secretary.

CHRYSANTHEMUM SOCIETY OF AMERICA

Annual convention and exhibition, New York,
November 10-12, 1903. FRED H. LEMON, Richmond,
Ind., secretary.

THIS ISSUE 36 PAGES WITH COVERS.

Palms and Ferns.

INSECT PESTS.

There exists an idea that at the midsummer season the palm grower may calmly sit down and watch his stock grow into money, an idea that is not entirely borne out by facts, although there is a slack period of a month or more at that time of the year. One of the greatest sources of anxiety to the grower during the hot weather is found in the attacks of insects. These pests increase with wonderful rapidity if allowed to go on unchecked, among those most likely to appear being mealy bugs, thrips and the various scale insects.

There is a possibility, of materially reducing the quantity of insects in a palm house during the winter, by frequent and careful vaporizing with nicotine, but after the artificial heat is done away with and summer puts in an appearance, this vaporizing is generally stopped and the insects that have been hiding away in the axils of the leaves and other protected corners, soon discover the change of atmosphere and proceed to business.

The mealy bug is highly objectionable on palms, owing to its comparatively large size and noticeable color, though the injury it does to the plants is not so great as that worked by several other noxious insects, and in addition to this there is no very great difficulty in keeping this insect within bounds by the use of aphis punk. This preparation may be used in greater proportion than is specified in the directions without doing any harm to palms, and indeed needs to be used more freely in order to kill the majority of the mealy bugs. The instructions advise the use of three rolls of the preparation in a house 20x100 feet in size, but the plants will not be injured by using five to six of the rolls in the same space, and the remedy will be much more effective. The liquid preparations of nicotine that are used by vaporizing, are also effective for destroying mealy bugs, but the cost is so much greater as to be almost prohibitive. I have also experimented with formaldehyde as an insect destroyer, but so far as my experiments were concerned it was not a success, the plants being more injured than the insects by the use o fthis gas.

Another troublesome pest in the palm house and one that attacks any species without discrimination is thrips, and of the members of this insect family the minute yellow thrips is the most troublesome, this being so small an insect that one has to watch closely to find it. Vigorous syringing will doubtless dislodge the thrips, though but few will be killed in that way, and as the plants dry off again the thrips will crawl up and resume their work. Strong smoking with aphis punk, tobacco dust or tobacco stems is the surest remedy to use for thrips, but needs to be repeated two or three evenings in succession in order to catch the stragglers. Areca lutescens is especially liable to be attacked by the yellow thrips during the hot weather, the first intimation of the presence of the insect being found in the form of patches of slightly lighter color on portions of the leaflets, this being caused by the sucking of the insects on the lower side of the leaf, which if permitted to continue, will soon become a permanent injury to the foliage. The common black thrips is not unusual upon the foliage of the kentias, but with plenty of moisture and thorough syringing this insect seldom gives much trouble. Owing to the system of growing these palms under comparatively high temperature and having insufficient appliances for syringing with strong pressure, on some of the European establishments, the marks of thrips are frequently found on the foliage of the imported kentias, and from which is drawn the inference that there are still some weak spots in European practice, just as we are frequently finding out that there are vulnerable points in our own methods.

Red spider does not give so much trouble in the palm houses during the summer as it does in the winter, for during the latter season there are frequently cold and dark days when it is scarcely wise to syringe very freely, and yet the fire heat is drying out the atmosphere to the degree that the red spider flourishes and spreads rapidly. A dip in a moderately strong solution of some good sulphur soap is a good remedy, or a solution of whale oil soap and tobacco extract, being especially applicable to small plants such as are difficult to syringe among. Tobacco extract used in moderation seems to do little harm to kentias and arecas, but is far from being beneficial to the palms of the livistona group, hardy as some of these species are, and it is therefore suggested that a dip be used on Latania borbonica, should be weaker in tobacco than when it is to be applied to Kentia Forsteriana, and for Livistona rotundifolia a less quantity of both soap and tobacco is advisable.

The scale insects are the most troublesome we have to contend with on palms, and with these eternal vigilance is no doubt the price of success. With the exception of the soft brown scale that sometimes appears on various palms, most of these unwelcome visitors are too well protected when fully grown, to suffer from any spray or dip that is not strong enough to do injury to the tender foliage. Young scale insects that are traveling about on the plant may be affected by vapors and dips, but the adult insect is too thoroughly covered to feel such applications and it usually becomes necessary to do more or less sponging to cleanse these plants properly, notwithstanding all the vapors and solutions that have been brought forward of late years. The conditions are so different to those by which the vegetable grower or the orchardist is surrounded, that in some cases the plant grower must necessarily adopt these slow processes. A slight injury to a fruit tree, caused by an overstrong solution counts for little, but if one cripples two or three of the best leaves on a fine palm by such means, the plant may be completely ruined, or else may be only used for rough decorating or filling in. It is hard to say which scale is the worst to have on palms, for all are highly injurious, and the only way to keep these insects down is to watch the stock closely and pick out and clean out any that are affected.   W. H. TAPLIN.

The Late Henry Burt.

The will of the late Henry Burt, whose death was noted in the AMERICAN FLORIST of July 25, was read July 23, the heirs being present at the reading, although the matter was informal. The widow is given a life estate in the home and all other property and the daughter is to receive the homestead on Cortland avenue after the death of her mother. The estate is valued at $45,000, being mostly personal property. Alfred Burt, who was his father's right hand man for years, will conduct the business as formerly.   R. H. C. B.

St. Louis World's Fair.

The department of horticulture at the St. Louis World's Fair has just issued a circular of forty pages which gives very complete information with regard to every possible question which may arise with relation to that department.

A part of the pamphlet is devoted to a statement as to the importance of placing a large amount of fruit in cold storage this fall in order that the space to be assigned any state may be covered at the opening of the exposition and kept covered during its entire period. Accompanying this are very full instructions for collecting, packing, wrapping and handling the fruit, in order that the best results may be obtained. Those who have given the subject no thought will be surprised when they study it to learn the great advance which has been made along this line within the past ten years. As a matter of fact the refrigeration of fruit in a commercial way may be said to have grown up within that very brief period. The information contained in the pamphlet is all new and is brought together at a considerable expenditure of labor in order that every person interested may be able to participate in an intelligent way in the fruit exhibit at St. Louis.

The chief of the department of horticulture will be glad to mail a copy of this pamphlet to any one who asks for it. Requests should be addressed to Frederic W. Taylor, Department of Horticulture, World's Fair, St. Louis, Mo.

The Carnation.

DORNER'S NOVELTIES.

The F. Dorner & Sons Company, of Lafayette, Ind., has two new carnations, the names of which are Lady Bountiful and The Belle. The former has a pure, glistening, white color and measures from three to three and one half inches in diameter with a stem of twenty-four inches or more. The Belle is a companion to Lady Bountiful, having

The Late Henry Burt.

equally strong points to bring it into popular favor. Both are early and easy propagators.

CULTURAL REMINDERS.

As the stock recovers from the check of transplanting, which can be readily determined from the return of the rich bloom and the foliage taking on a crisp, succulent appearance, the palliative measures adopted to tide them through this stage should be gradually reduced and the plants given as near the winter treatment as weather conditions will permit. Watering at the roots may be increased, but great care is still necessary not to sour the soil by over-watering.

In syringing, special attention should be paid to the prevention of red spider. From now on until October 1, it will be safe to syringe the plants every sunny day, from both sides of the bench alternately, with a sharp, fine spray. In addition to this they should be showered and the house cooled off as often as may be necessary to keep the temperature within proper bounds. After the date mentioned a good syringing once a week will be sufficient to keep the pest in subjection. This pest, as well as all others, is best handled before it makes its appearance, for when once it becomes firmly

established it will take ten times the worry and time to eradicate it than would be expended in judicious preventive measures at the proper time. So while the sunny weather lasts, which dries off the foliage rapidly, see that no sign of this pest appears, and the road will be easy to travel after that.

The same holds true with green fly. After the plants have resumed an active growth a light fumigation once a week with strong tobacco stems should be given. A good time for this operation is after sundown or after a good rain in the evening. The house should be kept closed until the fumes have become entirely spent, which will take from two to three hours, when the ventilators should be adjusted at the proper height for the night, which will for some weeks to come be as high as they can be raised, except when squally weather is anticipated. In no case should they be left closed tightly over night.

Make it a hobby to have as much air as possible at all times; a volume could be written on the value of pure air in promoting a healthy growth. The value of ventilation consists not alone in regulating the temperature, but pure air is absolutely necessary to enable the plants to carry on the processes of building up new tissue and tearing down the old. A vitiated atmosphere arrests the functions of the organs and the plants soon become laden with dead and half starved tissue, becoming at the same time a prey to all manner of disease germs. Growth is much faster in summer than in the winter months and the forces consumed in its production multiply by the square of the rate of increase.

The dying of old leaves is often caused by improper ventilation and by the presence of moisture over night. If proper attention is paid to all the little details of cultivation, it will seldom be necessary to remove old leaves from the plants. In case they are affected by disease, they should of course be removed, but the longer a healthy leaf can be left on the better it will be for the plant. Cleaning the plants is no longer the arduous job that it was before we understood what caused the necessity of an elaborate cleaning process, and spraying has been almost entirely done away with for the same reason. Just as men have the power to get along without the use of drugs, so are plants endowed with the same powers under favorable conditions.

The cultivator should be kept going in the field and topping will require regular attention. Let me again mention the danger of topping too severely at this time, lest a valuable crop of blooms be destroyed. It is sometimes difficult to tell whether a shoot is about to run up to a bud before the first stage in this direction is well advanced. It is the safest plan at this time to cut back only such shoots as have the bud distinctly set and the future tendency to produce blooms in crop can be partly obviated by topping frequently and little at a time. This, however, cannot be relied upon to entirely transform a habitual cropper into a continuous bloomer.

There will be no necessity for feeding stock on the benches for some time, to come, except it be in case a bench was planted in rather poor soil early in May. An ordinarily rich soil will in most cases run the plants for four or five months without the addition of any extra fertilizers. A very light top-dressing of bone meal or pulverized sheep manure will supply all the needed elements early in the season.

Planting should go forward as rapidly as possible from now on and hot weather should not hold back this work unless the soil in the field is too dry for digging.

It is not too early to think of the soil pile for next year. If sod is scarce in your locality any chance to obtain a load or two at odd times should not be neglected. If you have a piece of ground which has been used for farm crops for several years, a good plan is to manure heavily about the last of August and sow to winter rye. In good fall weather this rye will make a good growth before settled cold weather sets in. Just about that time the ground will be quite wet, much wetter than would be safe to handle in spring. It should then be plowed, throwing the furrows up into ridges as much as possible to allow thorough freezing. In spring the necessary fertilizers and manures are spread broadcast and it is again plowed and carted into a convenient place for subsequent handling. Sod intended for next year should commence rotting as soon as possible and should therefore be turned down or carted into a pile as soon as it can be done. Carting soil into a large pile in the fall has little to recommend it. It is much better to have it lying exposed to the elements through the winter, and as space counts for nothing at that season, there is everything to gain and nothing to lose by that plan.   J.

Florists' Plant Notes.

OXALIS.

The bulbs of Bermuda oxalis should be set into 3-inch pots as soon as possible. A sandy soil is what they want and until the bulbs start it is best to give them a slightly shaded place to prevent the sun from drying them out too fast. If any bulbs were left over from the previous season, which are now resting under the bench they can be shaken out and also placed into 3-inch pots, handling them just as the new bulbs are being treated. Later on a shift to a 4-inch size is necessary.

GERANIUMS.

While it is too early to take the main batch of geranium cuttings, it might be found desirable to increase the stock of a few choice varieties, if only a limited quantity of stock plants of these varieties are at hand. A batch of cuttings taken from the plants now will leave plenty of time to produce another crop of cuttings by September 1, when the main batch is taken. Whenever possible leave an eye at the base of the cutting to facilitate rooting. Pot them off as soon as possible into 2¼-inch pots in sandy soil, pressing the soil firmly around the cuttings. Water them well immediately after potting, but after that be more sparing with water until they are rooted. Shading with newspapers during the hot hours of the day is necessary for the first few days, and a light wash on the glass overhead will be found beneficial.

MIGNONETTE.

It is now the proper time to sow the mignonette seed for winter cutting. Either a solid bed or a raised bench with about five inches of soil and plenty of light and head room will grow them nicely. Three parts of a good heavy soil with one part of well rotted cow manure is what they want. Sow a few seeds in spots twelve inches apart each way and when of sufficient size thin them out to one strong plant for each spot. Until the seed germinates it is a good plan to cover the bed with sheets of newspaper to hold the moisture and prevent the sun

from baking the soil. Keep a sharp lookout for slugs and woodlice which trouble the plant when small, as well as the little yellow butterfly that deposits the eggs of the destructive cabbage worm. When the plants are about three inches high, they will commence to branch and four of the strongest shoots should then be selected and the rest pinched out. The laterals should be removed from the leading shoots, which will require staking later on, one stake being sufficient to support three or four branches. Ventilate freely on every possible occasion to produce strong heavy spikes, and give them a temperature of 45° to 50° at night.

If pot plants of mignonette are desired for Easter sales, sow a few seeds into 5-inch pots, covering the seed to a depth of a quarter of an inch, and later thin out to one strong plant for each pot. If they show signs of coming into bloom too early, stop them once or twice, but no topping should be done within three months of the time when they are wanted in bloom. In every other respect, with regard to temperature, etc., they require the same conditions as those growing in the bed. It pays to get the best seed; we consider Machet to be the best for pots and prefer the Defiance strain for cutting.
                                        G.

New Trees and Shrubs.

All of the following have been introduced to J. Veitch & Sons' nurseries from Central China by their collector, Mr. E. H. Wilson.

Davidia involucrata.—This Chinese tree is not definitely classified yet, for some botanists place it with hamamelis, others with cornus. It is a most exceptional tree, of rare characteristics and therefore to be a subject in every ornamental plantation when it becomes well known, and a sufficient stock is raised. It grows twenty to thirty feet high in its native habitat, and produces twin bracts, each the size of one's hand, pure white in color, at the tips of the branches, and these bracts surround or enclose a distinctive bunch of red stamens.

Itea ilicifolia.—This holly-leaved itea is very different from I. Virginica, a fairly well known shrub in gardens. It is remarkable also for the length of its flower racemes, which are fully fifteen inches long and very slender.

Schizophragma integrifolia.—A semi-scandent shrub with pure white bracts, these being the size and shape of plum leaves. The inconspicuous flowers are in whorls.

Populus lasiocarpa.—This is the largest leaved poplar known, these being eight inches long by five inches broad.

Dipteronia Sinensis.—A new monotypic (?) genus, described by Dr. Augustine Henry. It is allied to acer, but differs in this that the wings are carried all around the seed instead of being on one side, as is the case in the maples.

Rhododendron auriculatum.—This is so named from the ear-like lobes of the base of the leaves. The flowers are blush-white, borne in trusses.

Rhododendron micranthum.—A species bearing, possibly, the smallest flowers of any member of the genus; these are like those of a small daphne, and blush-white. From the province of West Hupeh, Central China.

Rubus Henryi.—This can be used like vines for training to pillars. It has trilobed leaves, three inches long and the same in breadth. The specific name is in honor of Dr. Henry.

Viburnum rhytidophylla.—Leaves nine to ten inches long, two inches broad, with white, wooly under-surface. The inflorescence is a whitish mass. West Hupeh, Central China.

Lonicera tragophylla.—This has opposite leaves and long, tubular flowers, yellow with a reddish base.

Quercus cleistocarpa.—The acorns are "hidden," that is, they are so tightly encased in a hard, woody cup that it is difficult to conceive how they ever escape.
—*Journal of Horticulture.*

An Old Subscriber's Opinion.

Am. Florist Co.:—Enclosed please find subscription price for one year, for which send me the old, good and true AMERICAN FLORIST, a paper which I have read since the early days of its infancy, except during the past eighteen months. I find on again perusing its columns that for news items and instructive articles it has not only kept up its high standard of excellence as a florist's paper, but has otherwise vastly improved and shall gladly welcome my old friend again when it arrives with the mail.
                                ANDREW MEYER.

WRECKED PLANT OF HENRY SCHWEITZER, MENDOTA, ILL.
(See issue of July 25, page 956.)

RETAIL STORES OF MILWAUKEE.

MILWAUKEE — Provides Work For Many Busy Florists.

ERY few persons who are not directly connected with the florists' business could come anywhere near giving a correct estimate of the number of retail and wholesale floral establishments in the Cream City, and if the casual passer-by, who never has interested himself in a flower store except when it was necessary to make a purchase in that line, should be informed that the retail stores of the city of Milwaukee buy stock from the wholesalers to the amount of $200,-000 per annum, he would perhaps question the veracity of the person who volunteered the information. Nevertheless the craft in Milwaukee has no small reason to feel gratified as it forms an important as well as useful element, and one that the city could not very well dispense with. Although Milwaukee cannot boast of any extraordinary greatness in area, it has so many other good points to its credit that the size is hardly taken into consideration. In proportion it is no doubt the greatest city from a social standpoint in this part of the country and as flowers of all descriptions play an important part with society folk it means prosperity for the florist and such is most certainly enjoyed here.

There is quite a variation in the amount of business handled by the different members of the craft, which is due to the different classes of trade catered to and the part of the city in which the firm is located. For some reason or other the east side of town has always taken the lead in all lines of the business and there was a time when it was even necessary for west side growers to bring their stock over to the east side to find an outlet for it, this being perhaps the reason that the wholesale market was established in the latter named part of the city.

The C. C. Pollworth Company recently moved to City Hall square, leaving Holton & Hunkel sole proprietors as it were of what had for so long been considered the wholesale block.

Although Currie Brothers' store is located on Wisconsin street, the concern is generally considered as being of the west side, as all the greenhouses are located there. While it may seem strange, it is nevertheless true that the east side has not now and never did have a greenhouse within its boundaries, even though the bulk of the city's flower business is conducted there.

James Chacona, on Wisconsin street, puts up quite a show at his place and handles a considerable amount of trade in connection with his confectionery, which proves the fact that sweetmeats and flowers, although differing widely in substance, can still be handled together to advantage. Mr. Chacona caters more especially to transient trade, which is very extensive at times.

The latest addition to Wisconsin street is P. Kapsalis & Company, who have somehow always maintained some of the finest displays in the flower line. Their store is elaborately equipped with beautiful fixtures of tasteful and original design, while their window is one of the most attractive in Milwaukee, making it

MILWAUKEE PUBLIC LIBRARY AND ART GALLERY, LATTER AT BOTTOM.

well worth a person's while to stop and look at it.

The Ellis Floral Company has the Wells building just about all to itself as far as any other florists are concerned. As the building is a small sized town in itself it could hardly be noticed that a floral concern inhabited part of it unless a person went inside. The company is getting along nicely here, however, and has no kick coming.

A nicely arranged store is that of the M. A. McKenney Company, on Milwaukee street, which is patronized by the better class of customers.

In spite of the fact that J. M. Fox, at 414 Milwaukee street, pays very little attention to outside display, the business

done at his place is something extraordinary. This is explained, however, by the promptness and care in filling orders that has always been one of Mr. Fox's set principals, so that he is deserving of all the business he can get.

Home Brothers, on Mason street, are among the late comers and have not been in the business for any extended period, but nevertheless have been making an excellent showing so far, and their future appears gratifyingly bright.

In another section of the east side, in the old German market, S. E. Hoppenrath, J. C. Rost and John Arnold have enjoyed a most prosperous season and wait on numerous customers from day to day.

While the west side cannot as yet compare with the east side, it is nevertheless of a great deal more importance than it was ten years ago.

Mrs. F. Ennis, who conducts a stand in the Plankinton house, is handling large quantities of cut flowers, although she has not much use for plants. Mrs. Ennis is a hustler and her place of business rarely closes at all.

The Baumgarten Floral Company, on upper West Water street, does not get much transient trade, but is very freely patronized by the more wealthy German element, with whom the company is most popular through the first-class treatment and courtesy that has always been shown its buyers.

William Edlefsen, at 349 Third street, serves all kinds of flowers to all kinds and classes all over the city and is doing well.

On upper Third street is a locality which differs from all the others in the city, ably taken care of by Edward H. Stewart, Emil Welke and E. Haasch, and which has always made a first-class showing in the way of flower traffic.

The Reitz Floral Company and Wm. Brauch hold sway in a most creditable manner at the upper end of Vliet street.

Although the south side handles an extensive trade, all the growers doing more or less retailing, the most important establishments belong to A. B. Loofbourow, 376 Grove street; successor to Fred. Schmeling; F. Hesse, 392 Grove street, and M. H. Moore.

The above brothers in the craft, as well as others who are not mentioned, have all the warm congeniality that is characteristic of the city in which they live, and any visiting members can always be assured of the best possible treatment. For a proof of this, one need only inquire of those who have been there. C. B. W.

Chicago.

MARKET STILL QUIET.—CARNATIONS AND ROSES FALLING OFF.—ASTERS IN PLENTY. —ABUNDANCE OF GOOD GLADIOLI.— SWEET PEAS SMALL IN SUPPLY AND DEMAND.—COMING NUPTIAL.—A LINE OR TWO OF NEWS.

The market is still quiet but good stock is nevertheless hardly sufficient to fill out-of-town orders, which are coming in very nicely, considering the season. Asters are now very conspicuous everywhere and they have gone down a little in price, good white stock now bringing $2 per hundred, although $3 was the price on July 18, there being a tremendous demand for white flowers of all kinds on that day, due to the funeral of Inspector Shea, of the Chicago police department. Gladioli are in great abundance at this time and command from $2 to $4 per hundred. Carnations are easier than last week. Roses can hardly be noticed and what there are do not look well as a rule. No considerable quantity of sweet peas confronts the commission men and they are not bringing much either, there not being much call for them.

Albert Fuchs, of North Halsted street, is getting his stock into shape. He will make a specialty of palms, ferns, cycas, pandanus, etc., and has made good headway since he took his place back again last November, out of the hands of Retzer & Company, who went bankrupt at that time.

Alex. Newett, of J. B. Deamud's place, will take an extended fishing trip through Illinois. If his luck should happen to be poor we will probably never know of it, as he will take along sufficient cash and if necessary will buy fish enough to make a showing.

L. Coatworth, of Benthey & Company, has just returned from a trip to the company's establishment at New Castle, Ind. He reports things progressing nicely at that place. The firm will begin cutting American Beauty stock next week.

Edson Haas and Miss Linna Hutchinson, of Austin, Ill., will be married on August 5, after which the young couple will take a tour of two or three weeks through the eastern states. They will be at home after November 1.

J. N. Mangel has quite a collection of bay trees, and other shrubs and plants in front of his store on Wabash avenue. Gus. Lange, who has been suffering with rheumatism for some time, left July 29 for the springs at Mt. Clemens, Mich. Chas. Zafe, of J. A. Budlong's place, begins his vacation on Monday, and will absent himself for a couple of weeks.

Ed. Hauswirth and wife have been spending a part of their vacation at The Dells, Wisconsin.

H. Manheim has just returned to his post at J. A. Budlong's from a fishing trip.

Magnus Froberg, of Poehlman Brothers, is rusticating for a spell.

J. A. Budlong had a nice lot of roses at his place the other day.

Visitors: J. D. Carmody, Evansville, Ind.; S. Alfred Baur, Erie, Pa.; F. Baller, Bloomington, Ill.; F. D. Rennison, Waterloo, Neb.; Geo. Souster, Elgin, Ill.; D. E. Law, Butte, Mont., returning from the east.

OGDEN, UTAH.—The condition of business in this locality is good this season. H. H. Holbrook has returned to his old location which had been leased to another party for a year.

New York.

A SUPERABUNDANCE OF GLADIOLI IN THE MARKET, NOT DESIRABLE FOR DECORATIVE WORK.—ASTERS MAKE AN APPEARANCE IN QUANTITY.—ROSES VERY SMALL. —ARRANGEMENTS FOR THE MILWAUKEE TRIP.—NEW STORE ON TWENTY-NINTH STREET.—SOME NEWS ITEMS.

A heavy influx of gladioli has struck the flower market this week. If they were of the white or light pink varieties they would find a much better sale. As it is the majority are of the tawny dun and purple shades, which are anything but pleasing to the eye. Examined individually, close to, the markings are pretty and the tints sensationally odd, but for decorative effect, used in mass, the effect is muddy and disappointing and one

The Late A. H. Hews.
(See obituary, page 8.)

turns with a better appreciation to the common old Gandavensis, which, although lacking in almost every other quality, yet is brilliantly effective in decorative work. Flowers of the Shakespeare class, however, bring five or six times the price, and these are what the growers should provide if they want to make money in gladiolus blooms. Asters are also beginning to appear in quantity. As a rule the blooms are of quite ordinary grade, but a few fine ones appear here and there and will soon be due in quantity. Large numbers of roses—if such they may be called—are coming in. They are not much larger than beans, a hundred being easily grasped in one hand, and do not bring much, but the young plants are all the better for having them picked off, and there is a little profit left after commissions and express charges have been deducted. There are many lilies coming in and they sell well. Charlie Millang, who handles quantities of them, has been getting twelve dollars a hundred for some specially choice ones, and thinks that doing pretty well for July. A record has also been made at Young & Nugent's this week, where some magnificent specimens of Cattleya Hardyana were sold for $1 a bloom. These and other instances of a similar sort would indicate that, notwithstanding the very evident summer inactivity, there is still "something doing" in the cut flower trade.

The itinerary of the representatives of the New York Florists' Club who will

make the trip to Milwaukee is now issued in a four-page folder, giving all information regarding the excursion and stating that the arrangements will be under the personal management of Mr. Lou. Hafner, of the West Shore Railroad, and that means that everybody's comfort will be well provided for. The train will leave Franklin street station at 1 p. m. and West Forty-second street at 1:15 p. m. on Sunday, August 16, arriving at Chicago at 4 p. m. Monday. Fare for the round trip to Milwaukee, $27.40:

N. Lecakes & Company have now, in their Twenty-ninth street store, the lightest and most attractive establishment in the city devoted to the "greens" specialty. Their business is rapidly assuming large proportions.

Wm. R. Wilcox, commissioner of public parks, sailed July 21 on the Kaiser Wilhelm II. for Europe, where he will study the small park systems and playgrounds of London and Glasgow.

Charlie Carlin, indispensable man at Thorley's, is just back from a vacation session at Cornwall-on-Hudson and Brighton Beach.

J. K. Allen has taken to the woods. He will soon return, however, with fish stories from the favorite Candian hunting resorts.

George V. Nash, superintendent of the New York botanical garden, sailed July 25 for Hayti on a botanical exploration. Miss H. Walreich, A. J. Guttman's industrious bookkeeper, has just come back from a vacation at Cook's Falls.

Mr. Trumpore, leading man at Small's, and Mrs. Trumpore left on Friday for a two weeks' stay in the Adirondacks.

Elwood Brant is sending in some extra nice roses for the season from the old T. G. Slaughter place at Madison.

Visitors: M. T. Bailey, Tannersville, N. Y.; R. H. James, Bermuda; Arnold Ringier, of Barnard's, Chicago.

Boston.

NO PERCEPTIBLE CHANGE IN CUT FLOWER BUSINESS. — POPULARITY OF FOSTER FERN.—EXHIBITION AT HORTICULTURAL HALL.—CHAS. EVANS RETURNED FROM EUROPE.—VISITORS.

L. H. Foster and daughter will attend the Milwaukee meeting of the S. A. F., going first to Duluth by the lake route. Mr. Foster is much elated over the immense sale he has found for his fern. Not only over the entire United States, but in Canada, England, Germany and elsewhere has the Foster fern found an eager call and the appreciative letters received indicate that it is proving all that the buyers expected from its description. Mr. Foster has another sport under propagation, of which he has confidant hopes.

The cut flower trade continues about as last outlined. The receipts are not heavy in any line at present and the demand is at low ebb. Asters are beginning to appear but are small of flower and short of stem as yet. Carnations are dwindling in diameter. Kaiserin and Carnot are the most desirable roses offered.

On Saturday evening, July 25, Mr. and Mrs. D. T. Mellis, of Flatbush, slid quietly into Boston on their homeward route from the Thousand Islands and other picturesque Canadian resorts and the White Mountains. After a brief glance at Boston's highways and byways they proceeded to Newport.

The regular exhibition at Horticultural hall, on July 25, brought out a fine display of garden flowers in which the

Blue Hill nursery especially excelled. Wm. Whitman, Mrs. Gill, Mrs. G. Duncan and others were also contributors in this section. Miss Fay was represented by another excellent table of hardy roses and M. H. Walsh showed bloom of his Lady Gay, a lovely double pink Crimson Rambler hybrid. Mrs. J. L. Gardner showed a tank of choice aquatics. Hydrangeas were on the prize schedule but nobody competed. ·

F. J. Geist, son of J. Geist, of Melrose, died on July 21, after a long illness, at the age of 26. He had been associated in business with his father, but was obliged to give up work several months ago on account of failing health.

Charles Evans has just returned on the steamship Saxonia from a visit to his old home in Wales, bringing with him his nephew, a young man whom he hopes to make into a good Yankee.

In town this week: Hon. Dan. Macrorie, South Orange, N. J.

Philadelphia.

TRADE QUIET IN THE STORES EXCEPT FOR FUNERAL ORDERS.—A WHOLESALER HAS THRILLING EXPERIENCE.—GLASS COMES DOWN IN PRICE.—DOINGS OF THE LOCAL CLUB.—NEWS NOTES.

Horace Dumont, the wholesale florist of Filbert street, is, to say the least, a trifle above the average in physical appearance and would be set down by the visiting stranger as one of our four hundred. Some time back, however, just before the strenuous Easter period, after being shadowed about his place of business and his home for a period of two days by an energetic and semi-professional sleuth, he was caught "red handed" in his office in the presence of his father and foreman and other employes and carried off to the city hall to answer the charge of assault and battery with robbery thrown in. His captors would listen to no explanation to the effect that he was not the man named in the warrant. They knew their business, and so Horace endured a nerve-racking half hour, by which time he was released and then the other fellows, whose explanation was that "He looked like the man they wanted," had the tables turned on them and are now trying to make peace with Mr. Dumont with as little financial trouble as possible. And now Horace says, "What's the use."

At the next meeting of the Florists' Club of Philadelphia, Tuesday, August 4, an exhibit of cannas will be a feature. Introducers of new varieties will have an opportunity to display their flowers and have them passed upon by the club committee if sent, express prepaid, to the hall, to arrive any time on the day of the meeting. Last year's symposium was very successful and this season's collection, together with Antoine Wintzer's paper on "Up to Date Varieties," should prove very interesting. Convention matters are now the current topic and quite a large delegation is sure from this neighborhood. Just how the crowd will go is not yet decided, or at least it will not be known until the night of the meeting, when the committee will make its report. The price of the ticket, round trip, will be about $35.

Things are quiet in the stores, although there is the usual amount of business for the season and some quite large funeral orders, on account of the deaths of prominent persons, have been received, asters, white roses and lily of the valley being the principal flowers used. Asters are now in fine form and some very good

stock is seen, 75 cents to $1 per hundred being the price. White roses are very scarce and are grabbed up as fast as they are unpacked in the commission houses; $5 to $8 is about the price asked for these. There are still a few carnations but the quality is poor, and as asters make a better showing for the money, they have the call. Lily of the valley is scarce, the price being as usual, $3 to $4.

The growers who were struck by the hail are still busy with the repairs and it will probably be a month or more before everything is cleaned up. Wm. C. Smith says he was not hit so hard as reported, as $50 will cover his loss. Glass men, when they found the storm was not general, came down in their prices and were around offering to make orders at low figures. Julius Koehler & Sons are making a much needed improvement by erecting a store and show house on the Frankford road front of their property. This was necessitated by the increase in their retail trade, which is growing rapidly.

S. S. Pennock is carrying some nice American Beauty roses from new crop. They command $2 to $4 per dozen.

K.

Cleveland.

HIGH SCHOOL GRADUATES RUIN TREES.— GENERAL RUN OF STOCK POOR.—ADVENT OF A TEN-POUND FLORIST.—NEWS.

The desire to lay up shekels now, to the detriment of future business, seems to be the only aim some people have. Some young men just graduated from our high schools, with no more knowledge of forestry than what is taught in the text books, recently made a house-to-house canvass, soliciting orders for spraying trees. Strange to relate, they received many orders and immediately did the work, charging and getting exorbitant prices, where a reputable experienced man couldn't touch the job. However, instead of helping to keep down insects, etc, they have killed the trees in every instance and spoiled chances for an honest, capable man. Such things should be looked into and prohibited if possible for the protection of reliable florists and nurserymen, who make spraying and the care of trees one of their specialties.

Last week Miss Jennie Coder and mother of Marysville, O., visited Cleveland, getting new ideas on decorative and design work. She was much impressed with the commercial activity shown in the fine condition of our greenhouses. Miss Coder is a florist of no mean ability, and has now five large houses, contemplating the erection of others. Her specialty is carnations and she grows some first-class stock.

The general run of stock is very poor. It is, however, all used up in funeral designs, a great deal of that kind of work being handled. Chrysanthemums are all in the benches and are looking well.

Henry Eichoff has just finished building a fine dwelling house on his Herald street place. It is adjacent to his greenhouses, making it very convenient for him.

John Kirchner, of Kirchner Brothers, is the proud father of a bouncing 10-pound baby boy.

The F. R. Williams Company is cutting the best Kaiserins in the city.

Bate Brothers are cutting some fine carnations.

O. G.

PLAINFIELD, N. J.—Charles L. Stanley, is building a boiler room at his conservatories on South avenue.

Cincinnati.

FLORISTS' OUTING AT CONEY ISLAND.— EXCITING GAMES OF QUOITS AND BASEBALL.—MARKET ENLIVENED BY LARGE FUNERAL.—GUS. ADRIAN'S PLACE HAS BEEN REBUILT.

The annual outing of the florists of Cincinnati and vicinity was held at Coney Island, Thursday, July 23. The weather was all that could be desired to make it a success, which it certainly was. The morning was enjoyably passed by both ladies and gentlemen in games of quoits. The gentlemen's contest was the first on the programme, eight teams going after the honors. Ed. and Rob. Murphy were awarded the first prize, a box of good cigars, and Ben. George and George Henning received a box of stogies as second prize. Four teams competed for the ladies' prize and in the final pitch-off, there was great excitement, Mrs. Henry Konzelman and Mrs. Gus. Adrian both pitching nip and tuck. Mrs. Konzelman won by one point only and was awarded a handsome fan as first prize. Mrs. Gus. Adrian received a silver salt shaker as second prize. After the quoits all adjourned for the midday meal, after which the baseball game took place, Jim Allen and Frank Dellar acting as captains. The game was a hot one and was finally won by Jim Allen's team with a score of 18 to 17. The winning side was awarded a prize of $15, the losing side $5.

Trade during the past week was all that could be expected for this time of year. Bride roses and white carnations were in excellent demand, and white flowers of all kinds were short in supply. An immense amount of flowers were used for the funeral of Sid Holder, police court clerk, and all the florists seemed to get their share of the work. Asters in this locality seem to be a little late and the few that come into the wholesale houses are grabbed on sight. A good many growers in this vicinity report that asters are doing poorly and all the growers would welcome a hard rain, as a good many are not in position to give stock the water it is in need of.

Gus Adrian, whose place was recently destroyed by fire, has rebuilt the same. Gus is certainly a hustler. · ALEX.

Denver.

A meeting of the Colorado Society of Floriculturists was held at the commissioner's office on Thursday, July 23, at which several new members were taken in. The constitution was adopted and a schedule for the flower show, which will be held in connection with the state fair at Pueblo in September, was distributed. Miss Gertrude Page, who has been visiting in the east, in company with Mrs. J. A. Valentine, returned last week. After an absence of ten weeks. They went to Galveston and thence by boat to New York. Both returned much benefited by the trip.

L. C. Waterbury, formerly engaged in the growing business at University Park, opened a commission house here last week. The venture looks good and it is hoped that Mr. Waterbury will make it a success.

Phil. Scott is happy over the arrival of a baby girl on July 20. Buffalo boys please sing "Guess that'll hold you for a while."

John Berry, of the Park Floral Company, is away on a vacation, fishing somewhere along the Platte river.

Manager Bush, of Daniels & Fisher's flower department, is on a summer outing trip. B.

THE AMERICAN FLORIST

NINETEENTH YEAR.

Subscription, $1.00 a year. To Europe, $2.00.
Subscriptions accepted only from those
in the trade.

Advertisements, on all except cover pages,
10 Cents a Line, Agate; $1.00 per inch,
Cash with Order.

No Special Position Guaranteed.

Discounts are allowed only on consecutive insertions, as follows—6 times, 5 per cent; 13 times,
10 per cent; 26 times, 20 per cent;
52 times, 30 per cent.

Cover space sold only on yearly contract at
$1.00 per inch, net, in the case of the two
front pages, regular discounts applying only to the back pages.

The Advertising Department of the AMERICAN
FLORIST is for florists, seedsmen and nurserymen
and dealers in wares pertaining to those lines only.

Orders for less than one-half inch space not accepted.

Advertisements must reach us by Wednesday to
secure insertion in the issue for the following
Saturday. Address

AMERICAN FLORIST CO., Chicago.

WITH this issue the AMERICAN FLORIST
enters upon its nineteenth year.

IN a recent issue of Moller's Deutsche
Gartner-Zeitung we find a large standard
plant of metrosideros semperflorens illustrated. The plant is in a tub and in this
form looks rather attractive.

CHIEF TAYLOR, of the World's Fair
department of horticulture, reports that
construction work on the building of the
department has been begun and that he
expects it will be entirely finished before
cold weather.

Hail Notes.

John G. Esler, secretary of the Florists'
Hail Association, writes that the follow-
ing members of the association lost glass
by hail in Philadelphia and vicinity last
week: August Lutz, W. K. Harris, Geo.
F. Christie, C. and G. L. Pennock, A. J.
Pennock, J. W. Colflesh, Richard C.
Smith, Geo. R. Geiger and Philip Fulmer.

Chicago to Milwaukee.

The transportation committee of the
Chicago Florists' Club has selected the
Chicago, Milwaukee & St. Paul railroad
as the official route to the convention
city. Those who propose to reach Milwaukee by way of Chicago should
procure tickets over the above road.
Arrangements will be made for all necessary special trains between these two
points.

Hotels of Milwaukee.

The following hotels are recommended
as desirable and convenient at the following rates per day:

	American	European
Pfister	$3 00 to $5.00	$1.50 to $1.50
Plankinton	2.5- to 5.00	1.00 to 3.50
Republican	2.00 to 3.50	
St. Charles	3.00 to 3.50	1.50 to 1.00
Kirby House	3.00 to 3.50	1.00
S-bilts		75 to 2.50
Blatz		1.00 to 2.50
Davidson		1.00 to $2.50

Society of American Florists.

AMERICAN BULBS AT MILWAUKEE.

Arrangements have been made whereby
American growers of any forcing bulbs,
plants or seeds hitherto supplied mainly
from foreign sources, or dealers controlling stocks of such goods, may exhibit
samples of their product in the trade
exhibition free of charge. The bulbs so
exhibited are to become the property of
the society for testing purposes as to

their forcing qualities and the results of
said testing and awards for quality to
be published the following season.
Entries in this department should be
made with the secretary.

WM. J. STEWART, Sec'y.

St. Louis.

MARKET CONDITIONS HAVE NOT CHANGED
PERCEPTIBLY. — A LOCAL ESTABLISH-
MENT CHANGES HANDS.—ANNUAL PICNIC
AT PRIEST'S PARK.—DIRECTOR OF THE
BOTANICAL GARDEN LEAVES FOR MEXICO.
—NOTES FROM VARIOUS PARTS OF THE
CITY.

The picnic given at Priest's Park,
Illinois, by the St. Louis Florists' Club,
on July 25, was well attended, although
not as many were out as last year.
However every one came away happy.
Music was furnished by a colored orchestra, the members of which, after indulg-
ing in a little Missouri "hospitality" and
Illinois "atmosphere," were equal to the
occasion. Several athletic events took
place, but whether any records were
broken has not been reported.

The market conditions are about as
usual. Good stock, nearly all of which is
received from outside growers, is in
demand, but hard to get. A few good roses
are seen occasionally and bring first prices.
The carnations offered are small and
short-stemmed but of clear color. Sweet
peas are too numerous to mention. China
asters are not of the best owing, no
doub., to weather conditions. Single
tuberoses are commencing to come in.

There is much going on at the Koenig
Floral Company's establishment. A fine
modern show house, 25x100 feet, is being
built, the office is being remodeled and
new equipment installed. The season
has been a most favorable one for the
firm.

The next meeting of the St. Louis
Florists' Club will be held at A. Jablonsky's, at Wellston, Mo., on August 13,
at 2 p m. Take the Suburban Park car,
get off at Suburban Garden, where
wagons will be in waiting.

Shaw's garden has a fine collection of
gladioli, about 250 species and varieties
being grown. It offers a good opportunity to the florist to note the better
strains. Why not take advantage of it?

E. H. Michel, of the Michel Plant and
Bulb Company, has disposed of his
Maryland avenue store to Geo. Wagner,
a former employe, who will continue the
business.

Dr. Wm. Trelease, director of the
Missouri botanical garden, left for
Mexico on July 29 to continue his studies
of the native flora of that country.

Conn. Winthers, gardener at Bellefontaine cemetery, returned to the city
Thursday from a tour of duty with the
state militia at St. Joseph, Mo.

Approximately thirty-five or forty
members of the craft from here will
attend the S. A. F. convention at Milwaukee.

John L. Koenig and bride have returned
from a three weeks' honeymoon in the
eastern states.

Otto G. Koenig and family are getting
ready and will be at the Milwaukee convention.   F. K. B.

Nolens Volens.

AMERICAN FLORIST CO.:—I like your
paper best of all. I subscribed for the
—— because they persisted in sending me
free sample copies, though I never wrote
them in my life.

Salem, Ind.   O. P. FORDYCE, Florist.

Minneapolis.

CONDITION OF LOCAL MARKET REMAINS
UNCHANGED.—FLORISTS' CLUB HAS ENJOY-
ABLE OUTING.—NEWS NOTES.

The Minneapolis Florists' Club gave
its first annual picnic at Excelsior on
Lake Minnetonka, Wednesday, July 22.
It was a success in every way. A trip of
three hour's duration was enjoyed on the
lake, touching all the prominent points,
directly after arrival at Excelsior. Following the excursion were the games and
different contests. Dancing was enjoyed
in the evening and the party returned
home late at night well satisfied with the
result. All wish to thank the committee
in general for the well arranged programme.

The market conditions remain the
same as they were a week ago. Stock is
in quantity sufficient to meet all demands
excepting carnations, there being a
scarcity of benched stock. Mildew is
prevalent on tea roses, which makes
them of a second quality and a product
hard to dispose of.

C. F. Rice and wife have returned from
a trip east. They spent a number of
days at Kalamazoo, Mich., where Mr.
Rice's father died after a sickness of about
twelve weeks.

Ted. Nagel and wife, of E. Nagel &
Company, are away on a vacation trip
as are also a great many others in the
trade.

Arrangements, rates, etc., for the Milwaukee convention will be discussed at
the next meeting of the local club.

     C. F. R.

Obituary.

A. H. HEWS.

A. H. Hews, head of the firm of A. H.
Hews & Company, potters, of North
Cambridge, Mass., died at his old home
in Weston, Mass., on Wednesday, July
8, aged 59 years. Mr. Hews had been in
bad health for some months and was
obliged finally to go to the hospital and
undergo an operation, which he survived
but two weeks. Mr. Hews was a business man of the highest character and
unwavering integrity. His public-spirited
generosity was well demonstrated at the
time of the S. A. F. convention in Boston,
when he entertained the visiting ladies
and their escorts, assisted by Mrs. Hews.

FREDERICK DILLEMUTH.

On Thursday, July 22, Frederick Dillemuth, aged 57 years, who was general
manager and a stockholder in the Pittsburg Rose & Carnation Company,
Bakerstown, Pa., met his death through
drowning in one of the reservoirs on the
company's premises. For some time
past he had experienced a great deal of
trouble in keeping the pumps in operation, and, while endeavoring to locate
the source of the trouble, it is said that
in walking out on the plank leading to
the flood gate, he lost his balance and
fell into the water. As Mr. Dillemuth
did not return for supper that evening,
his wife and son Harry, the latter being
on a visit from Toronto, went to search
for him, first at the greenhouses and
later at the gas well, but discovered no
trace of him. It was very dark by this
time and a number of the hired men were
called, and securing lanterns the party
went to the pump house where Mr. Dillemuth's coat was found. There was no
response to the calling of his name
and it was then discovered that the
large iron key to the flood gate was
missing from its usual place. Grappling

hooks were secured and the search for the body was begun. The key was fished out first, with which the floodgate was opened and at 10 o'clock, the water having receded from the reservoir, the body was found.

Mr. Dillemuth had always been held in high esteem. He always saw the bright side of everything and in his daily pursuits was earnest and sincere, being guided in all things by his conscience. His capabilities were most evident by his success in every business enterprise with which he associated. He was a member of the Order of United Workmen and an organizer, charter member and director of the German Beneficial Union. Mr. Dillemuth leaves a wife, daughter and three sons. One of the sons, Harry, is manager for J. H. Dunlop, of Toronto, Canada.

The funeral services took place from the German Lutheran church, of which he was a member, on Sunday, July 26. The services were conducted in German and English, and attended by many of the foremost business men of the community.   E. L. M.

SITUATIONS, WANTS, FOR SALE.

One Cent Per Word.

Cash with the Adv.

Situation Wanted—By a florist and gardener; single; ten years' experience. Good references. Florist, care American Florist.

Situation Wanted—By first-class grower of flowers, fruit and vegetables under glass or outside; good references; married; no family. F. F. GARDENER, Box 425, Bangor, Mich.

Situation Wanted—As head gardener on private place by a good all-around man with practical experience; English; age 32; abstainer; good references.   C C, care American Florist.

Situation Wanted—By orchid grower on private place, has been with most of the best firms in Europe; first-class education. State number of houses. Further particulars and references. Address   S T, American Florist.

Situation Wanted—By an all-around florist; 13 years' experience in growing out flowers and general greenhouse stock. Best of references; age 26; married; private or commercial place. Address   A F B, care American Florist.

Situation Wanted—Dutchman, single, 38 years, speaks English, as head gardener on private place or in reliable commercial establishment. Good grower of stove and greenhouse plants; also understands forcing; 15 years' European experience; can furnish good references. Preference given to New York or vicinity. Please state wages.   W O, care American Florist.

Help Wanted—Experienced greenhouse man; single. E. HELD, 928 N. Cambell Ave, Chicago.

Help Wanted—Good handy man for general outdoor garden work. Address   F, care American Florist.

Help Wanted—Good young florist; general greenhouse work.   H. N. BRUNS, 1409 W. Madison St., Chicago.

Help Wanted—Experienced, unmarried gardener for my private greenhouse, garden, etc. W. H. CHADWICK, 532 Rialto Bldg., Chicago.

Help Wanted—Florist as assistant in place of 15,000 feet where only cut flowers are grown. Good chance for man who can show good references.   H. BORNHORST, Tipton, Ind.

Help Wanted—Wanted a sober and reliable florist; must have experience in pot plants. No other need apply.   ORCHAIN BROS., 1688 W. Madison St., Chicago.

Help Wanted—Competent store man. Must be able to decorate and make up; $60 per month; references. Address   CENTRAL GREENHOUSES, Sandusky, Ohio.

Help Wanted—Young man experienced in handling palms and ferns in greenhouse, also competent to wait on customers. Address   H. F. HALLE, 848 W. Madison St., Chicago.

Help Wanted—Four or five young men wanted for rose and carnation section, with or without experience.   J. M. GASSER CO., 234 Euclid Ave., Cleveland, O.

Help Wanted—Young man with some experience in general greenhouse work, to work under foreman. State wages and send reference to   ALFRED BROMAN, Independence, Mo.

Help Wanted—Wanted a good carnation grower; sober and. single man that will take interest in his stock. Vicinity Chicago. State wages and experience. Address   HIGH GRADE, care American Florist.

Help Wanted—Florist-fireman wanted; good, reliable man as night fireman on large place. Steam. Must be willing to turn a hand to potting, propaga ing. and general greenhouse work in the mild months. Address   W. E. GULLETT & SONS, Lincoln, Ill.

Help Wanted—Wanted a good all-around gardener for new retail greenhouses. 5,000 feet of glass. Must understand the growing of pot plants, bulbs and everything required for that class of trade. Also be able to make up designs etc. None but a faithful, sober man, need apply. State wages and references. Address   OPPORTUNITY, care American Florist.

Wanted—Second-hand small hot water heater. F. M. PRICE, Nokomis, Ind.

Wanted—To exchange the new edition of Galloway's "Violet Culture" (just out) for a copy of the first edition. Address   VIOLETS, care American Florist.

Wanted—Partner. The writer wishes to correspond with an energetic young man, one who has executive ability and thorough knowledge of the growing of plants and cut flowers and who can furnish some capital to join advertiser in developing a first-class opportunity. We have a beautiful stoce well equipped and doing good business and wish to increase the growing end of the business. Address   W G, care American Florist.

For Sale—Ballard's Greenhouse, Perry, Iowa. Cause poor health.

For Rent—Sixty-foot greenhouse, 8 room house, two lots, $25 per month; 3181 Elston Ave. DR. BANOS, 554 N. Robey St., Chicago.

For Rent or Sale—Small greenhouse business cheap. Established 28 years. Address   E. HELD, 923 N. Campbell Ave., Chicago.

For Sale—One builer 4x14 feet, steam pipe fittines, glass; one closed florist wagon.   1817 N. Michigan Ave., Saginaw City, Mich.

For Sale—No. 8 Furman Hot Water Boiler in running order. Is heating 5,000 feet of glass. Make us cash offer F. O. B.   WISS BROS., East Aurora, N. Y.

For Rent—12 acres of land with 17 hot houses, house, barn, coal shed; all in fair condition, about ½-mile south of Blue Island, Ill. Will rent from one to five years. Address   F. W. HEITMAN, 331 E. 63rd St., Chicago.

For Sale—Five greenhouses located in Minneapolis. Over 7,000 feet of glass with steam heat. This is a snap; $600 takes them. For further particulars apply to   MRS. A. CHANEY, 3630-32½ Avenue So., Minneapolis, Minn.

For Sale—$3,500 ft. 4-inch cast iron pipe with fittings; 1,500 ft. 3-inch wrought iron pipe with fittings; 1 boiler, heating capacity 4,000 ft., 4-inch pipe; 1 boiler, heating capacity 1,9 0 ft., 4-inch pipe; glass, 8x10 and 10x16; 50,000 pots, all sizes; sash bars. General plant stock cheap.   W. L. SMITH, Aurora, Ill.

For Sale or Rent—Three places with stock. Established with stock for florist and nursery. 17 greenhouses, all in good order; plenty of stock to fill for winter; city water; well established. Come and see. 45 minutes from New York City; trolley passes the door. Good business; established in 1864. Cause of sale, retiring from business. Apply to   SEA CLIFF NURSERY, box Cliff, N. Y.

FOR SALE.

10,000 feet of greenhouses with a beautiful store attached and with living rooms well equipped above. Steam heated, located in a fine residence section of one of our largest northern cities. Has a well established trade both in cut flowers and plants. A young pushing American of German descent would step into a lucrative business. Price of land and buildings, $15,000.00; a bargain. For further particulars address   A B C, care American Florist.

For Sale—Four large size Gorton side feed boilers (for hard or soft coal). $50 each; one small Gorton side feed, $25; one large sectional Florida heater, $50; one small coil-boiler, hot water, in use two winters, will heat 3,000 square feet of glass, $20. Boilers taken out to put in larger one. Write for particulars.   F. FALLON, Roanoke, Va.

TO LEASE....

To lease for a term of years. 4 greenhouses, each 25 ft. x 100 ft., heat'ed by hot water, well stocked, with 4 acres of land; located in Malden, Mass. (40 000 inhabitants), four miles from Boston. Trolley cars to Boston every five minutes. Address

MRS. R. H. HALEY,
106 Avon Street,   Malden, Mass.

For Sale and Exchange.

We want a god second-hand sectional hot water boiler and wish to exchange field-grown Mrs. T. W. Lawson carnations, a big lot of them ready August 1, and later. $5.00 and $6.00 per 100. Have you any drip grown rafters you want to exchange?

S. T. DANLEY, McComb, Ill.

NOTICE TO BUILDERS.

Will build one 20x100 ft. Greenhouse, 16x24 in. double thick No. 1 glass, complete, $500.00. One 12x100 ft., $225.00. Material on hand. Address

J R,   care American Florist.

FOR SALE.

Store fixtures complete, consisting of refrigerator 8x8x8 feet, plate glass front, double plate glass doors, box made to order after original design, desk with mirror 5x6 feet, mantel shelf with mirror 5x6 feet, all glass and mirrors beveled plate. counter table 10x4 feet, plant table 8x8 feet, zinc lined, other shelving and fixtures all made to order of select birch, stained mahogany, cost $800, used six months; will sell at $500. Address

AUGUST S. SWANSON, St. Paul, Minn.

Gardeners' and Florists' Union 10,615 Chicago, Ill.

Next meeting Wednesday, Aug. 12. All members are earnestly requested to attend, as matters of great importance will be taken up.

Gardeners' and Florists' Union 10,615
106. E. Randolph St., CHICAGO.

NOTICE
—OF—
STOCKHOLDERS' MEETING.

CHICAGO, July 9, 1903.

Stockholders of the American Florist Company:
You are hereby notified that the annual meeting of the Stockholders of the American Florist Company will be held in the Plankinton House Milwaukee, Wis., Wednesday, August 19, 1903, at 3 o'clock p. m., for the purpose of electing directors and officers for the ensuing term, and for the transaction of such other business as may come before the meeting.   J. C. VAUGHAN, Pres.
M. BARKER, Sec'y.

Pittsburg.

SLIGHT IMPROVEMENT IN MARKET CONDI-
TIONS.—SAD DEATH TROUGH DROWNING.
—TRIPLETS IN THE CRAFT.—GENERAL
NOTES.

Business conditions are slightly
improved over last week, and yet not
to that extent that we can claim it
good. We continue to have difficulty in
securing a small quantity of good stock,
and have as much trouble in getting any
reasonable amount of second class stock.
Carnations have been very backward,
and no wonder, as weather conditions
have been greatly against them. Very
few good asters are to be had, gladioli
in general are very poor and contain few
open flowers, lily of the valley is very
scarce, sweet peas very fine and greens
plentiful.

John Scott, an employe of Wm. Turner,
of Williamsburg, is the father of triplets,
two sons and a daughter, born on Monday, July 27. They are said to be healthy
and will live. No race suicide here.

Harry Dillemuth, of Toronto, expected
to return to his home a number of days
ago, but owing to the sad death of his
father, will remain here until about
Thursday.

Frederick Dillemuth, Sr., died suddenly
July 24, on the farm of his brother-in-law,
Frederick Burki. Mr. Dillemuth had
charge of the farm up to the time of his
death.

The Pittsburg Cut Flower Company is
having no troubles with surplus stock
these days with the exception of gladiolus.

Al. Sheppard is making fine progress
with his farm, and his appearance indicates that farm life agrees with him.

Mr. Langhans is getting ready to
reduce the fish population of Lake
Chatauqua.

Jim Orr, a former florist, has accepted
a position with the department of public
works.

Tom Uhlan has had a big week in
funeral work.

John Bader has had an extraordinary
run on palms.   E. L. M.

BEADLING, PA.—John S. Smith was seriously injured at his home, July 26, by
being kicked on the leg by a horse, causing a compound fracture.

Wholesale Flower Markets

MILWAUKEE, July 30.

Roses, Beauty, med. per doz.	1.50
" short "	.75@1.00
" Liberty	4.00@ 6.00
" Bride, Bridesmaid	4.00@ 6.00
" Meteor, Golden Gate	4.00@ 6.00
" Perle	4.00@ 6.00
Carnations	1.00@ 2.00
Sweet peas	.15
Smilax	10.00@12.50
Asparagus	50.00

PITTSBURG, July 30.

Roses, Beauty, specials, per doz. 2.50@3.50	
" " extra	1.00@2.00
" " No. 1 "	75@1.00
" " No. 2 "	3.00@ 5.00
" Bride, Bridesmaid	1.00@ 6 UU
" Meteor	2.00@ 4.00
" Kaiserin	2.00@ 6.00
" Liberties	2.00@ 6.00
Carnations	.50@ 1.5)
Lily of the Valley	2.00@ 4.00
Sweet peas	.20@ .30
Smilax	5.00@12.50
Adiantum	.75@ 1.25
Asparagus, strings	2.00@50.00
" Sprengeri	2.00@ 4.00
Gladioli	1.00@ 4.00
Easter lilies	8.00@12.50

CINCINNATI, July 30.

Roses, Beauty	10.00@35.00
" Bride, Bridesmaid	3.00@ 6.00
" Liberty	3.00@ 6.00
" Meteor, Golden Gate	3.00@ 6.00
Carnations	1.00@ 3.00
Lily of the valley	3.00@ 4.00
Asparagus	50.00
Smilax	12.50@15.00
Sweet peas	.15@ .25
Adiantum	1.00
Gladioli	4.00
Asters	1.50@ 2.0J

ST. LOUIS, July 30.

Roses, Beauty, long stem	15.00@25.00
" Beauty, medium stem	8.00@12.50
" Beauty, short stem	1.00@ 6.00
" Bride, Bridesmaid	3.00@ 4.00
" Golden Gate, Meteor	3.00@ 4.00
" Perle	1.00@ 3.00
Carnations	.50@ 1.50
Sweet peas	.15
Lily of the valley	3.00@ 4.00
Smilax	12.50@15.00
Asparagus Sprengeri	1.00@ 1.50
Plumosus	25.00@50.00
Gladioli	2.00@ 5.00
Ferns	per 1000 1.50
China Asters	.50@ 2.00

PIQUA, O.—There is at present nothing
doing in the way of business. Carnations
in the field are doing well considering the
long dry spell to which they have been
subjected. Frank H. Frisch is rebuilding
three houses to be 15, 18 and 20x66 feet.

INTERNATIONAL FLOWER DELIVERY.

PLEASE MENTION US TO OUR ADVERTISERS.

INTERNATIONAL FLOWER DELIVERY.

STEAMSHIPS LEAVE FOREIGN PORTS.

FROM	TO	STEAMER	*LINE	DAY	DUE ABOUT
Liverpool	Boston	Saxonia	1	Tues. Aug. 11,	Aug. 18
Liverpool	"	Campania	1	Tues. Aug. 8,	Aug. 14
Liverpool	"	Umbria	1	Tues. Aug. 15,	Aug. 21
Liverpool	"	Majestic	7	Wed. Aug. 5, 5:00 p. m.	
Liverpool	"	Celtic	7	Fri. Aug. 7, 5:00 p. m.	
Liverpool	"	Oceanic	7	Wed. Aug. 12, 5:00 p. m.	Aug. 19
Liverpool	"	Cymbric	7	Fri. Aug. 14, 5:00 p. m.	Aug. 20
Liverpool	Montreal	Canada	15	Wed. Aug. 5,	
Liverpool	"	Kensington	15	Wed. Aug. 12,	
Liverpool	Boston	Columbus	15	Thur. Aug. 6,	
Liverpool	"	Commonwealth	15	Thur. Aug. 13,	Aug. 20
Liverpool	"	Devonian	16	Fri. Aug. 7,	
Liverpool	"	Winifredian	16	Fri. Aug. 14,	
Liverpool	Montreal	Bavarian	19	Thur. Aug. 6,	
Liverpool	"	Ionian	19	Thur. Aug. 13,	
Glasgow	New York	Columbia	5	Sat. Aug. 8,	
Glasgow	"	Ethiopia	5	Thur. Aug. 13,	
Glasgow	"	Mongolian	3	Sat. Aug. 15,	Aug. 24
Genoa	"	Sardegna	12	Mon. Aug. 3,	
Genoa	"	Citta di Napoli	12	Mon. Aug. 10,	Aug. 27
Genoa	"	Liguria	12	Mon. Aug. 17,	
Genoa	Boston	Vancouver	15	Sat. Aug. 8,	
Southampton	New York	St. Louis	8	Sat. Aug. 8, Noon.	
Southampton	"	New York	8	Sat. Aug. 15, Noon.	
Southampton	"	Manitou	8	Wed. Aug. 12,	
London	"	Minnetonka	6	Sat. Aug. 8,	
London	"	Minneapolis	6	Sat. Aug. 15,	Aug. 24
Antwerp	"	Vaderland	9	Sat. Aug. 8, 1:00 p. m.	
Antwerp	"	Kroonland	9	Sat. Aug. 15, 3:00 p. m.	Aug. 24
Hamburg	"	Bluecher	3	Thur. Aug. 6,	
Hamburg	"	Patricia	3	Sat. Aug. 8,	Aug. 17
Hamburg	"	Auguste Victoria	3	Thur. Aug. 13,	
Havre	"	La Savoie	10	Sat. Aug. 8,	
Havre	"	La Bretagne	10	Sat. Aug. 15,	Aug. 23
Copenhagen	"	Oscar II	4	Wed. Aug. 12,	
Rotterdam	"	Noordam	11	Sat. Aug. 8,	
Rotterdam	"	Rotterdam	11	Sat. Aug. 15,	
Sidney	SanFrancisco	Sonoma	18	Mon. Aug. 17,	Sept. 7
Hongkong	Yokohama	Gaelic	17	Tues. Aug. 4,	Aug. 15
Hongkong	"	Hongkong Maru	17	Fri. Aug. 14,	Aug. 25
Hongkong	"	Empress of China	20	Wed. Aug. 5,	Aug. 14
Hongkong	"	Athenian	20	Wed. Aug. 12,	Aug. 22
Hongkong	"	Iyo Maru	22	Tues. Aug. 11,	Aug. 24
Yokohama	Seattle	Riojun Maru	22	Tues. Aug. 11,	Aug. 26
Sidney	Vancouver	Moana	20	Mon. Aug. 10,	Sept. 3
Bremen	New York	Kaiser Wilh. II	13	Tues. Aug. 11,	Aug. 18
Bremen	"	Koenigin Louise	13	Sat. Aug. 8,	Aug. 18
Genoa	"	Hohenzollern	13	Thur. Aug. 13,	Aug. 26

* See steamship list on opposite page.

CHRYSANTHEMUMS.

ESTELLE, (Altick)..............................$1.50 per dozen; $10.00 per 100
Lady Fitzwygram, white and yellow, Lady Harriet..................... 4.00 per 100
Willowbrook, Timothy Eaton and Col. Appleton..................... 3.00 per 100
From 2-inch pots.

Carnation Cuttings in the New and Standard Varieties.

E. T. GRAVE,
RICHMOND, IND.

Please mention the American Florist when writing.

PRIMROSES.
Per 100
Chinese, 2-inch pots. July......................$2.00
Obconica, Alba and Rosea.....................2.00
Forbesi, "Baby"...................................2.00
Paper White Narcissus Grandiflora, Sept. 1.. 1.00
CASH.

ASPARAGUS.
Per 100
Sprengeri, 3-inch pots, Ready August 20th...$2.00
Plumosus Nanus.....................................2.50
Pansy Seed, Non Plus Ultra, ready August
1st, per oz..$4.00

JOS. N. CUNNINGHAM, Delaware, O.

The F. R. WILLIAMS CO.
Wholesale Florists,
CLEVELAND, - OHIO.

When writing to any of the advertisers on this page please mention the American Florist.

25,000 CANNAS, Field Clumps for fall. Low,
Best Sorts. Write for prices. 25,000 Violets for
Fall, Pot and Field Stock, $3 and $4 per 100. $5,000
Shrubs, Vines and Bulbs for catalogue trade. Send
for list. BENJ. CONNELL, West Grove, Pa

THE SEED TRADE.

AMERICAN SEED TRADE ASSOCIATION.
S. F. Willard, Pres.; J. Charles McCullough,
First Vice-Pres.; C. E. Kendel, Cleveland, O.,
Sec'y and Treas.
Twenty-second annual convention St. Louis,
Mo., June, 1904.

Onion Sets at Chicago.

Hail did practically no damage to this
crop, there being no acreage in the path
of the storm. Pulling the crop is now in
active progress and the sets look good
and of excellent size.

Budlong & Company, the largest
growers at Chicago, report a larger
crop than usual and do not anticipate
any advance over prices of an average
season.

Holland Seed Crop Conditions.

SPECIAL, JULY 18, 1903.
Cauliflower, all very good.
Cabbage, the white sorts, medium, the
late sorts are bad, the early ones some-
what better; red, medium; Savoy, fair.
Brussels sprouts and kale, good.
Turnip, almost total failure.
Swedes, fairly good.
Kohlrabi, little planted, crop medium.
Mangel wurzel, little planted, crop good.
Beet, Crosby, small crop; Early
Egyptian, half the usual amount planted,
but that is good.
Carrot, good.
Parsnip, good.
Borage, middling.
Corn salad, fair.
Parsley, good.
Sorrel, bad.
Salsify, fair.
Radish, early and summer sorts,
medium; winter varieties, very small.
Celeriac, middling.
Thyme, fair.
Spinach, three-fourths of a crop, no
seed carried over.
Peas very good. Beans, very back-
ward; Broad Windsor, middling.

FLOWER SEEDS.
Nasturtium, dwarf mixed, short.
Mignonette, short.
Myosotis, short.
Candytuft, mixed, probably short.
Pansy, all colors. mixed, good.

Meeting of D. Landreth & Sons' Creditors.

Philadelphia, July 24.—A meeting of
the creditors of the firm of D. Landreth
& Sons was held July 20 and a committee
of three, representing the creditor banks
and merchandise creditors, was appointed
to investigate the books and affairs of
the firm and to make a report of its condition as well as to suggest and recommend such plan of settlement as might in
their judgment be for the best interest of
all the creditors without distinction or
preference, and by which more could be
realized than by proceedings under the
insolvent laws or in bankruptcy. The
committee respectfully reports that it has
made an examination of the books of the
firm and an investigation of its condition,
which it respectfully submits. The following assets are submitted:

As a going concern..............$134,197.36
Estimated value at forced sale... 53,946.98
Liabilities, unsecured 122,946.04

Real estate consisting of farm lands in Pennsylvania, New Jersey and Virginia, mortgaged for
$155,000, not considered of greater value than
would cover the mortgaged indebtedness.

The committee is of the opinion, upon
all facts, that if the firm of D. Landreth
& Sons is forced into bankruptcy there

cannot be realized for creditors more than
fifteen to twenty per cent of their claims,
while if allowed to continue on the plan
recommended are of the opinion that fifty
per cent will be realized on the settlement
notes. The committee therefore recommends that the creditors accept in settlement fifty per cent of their respective
claims in four notes of the firm, to be
dated the first day of August, 1903, payable without interest as follows.

Twenty per cent payable April 1. 1904.
Ten per cent payable October 1. 1904.
Ten per cent payable April 1. 1905.
Ten per cent payable July 15, 1905.

The report of the committee is further
endorsed by the following letter:

PHILADELPHIA, July 23, 1903.
We have been informed of the condition of the
financial affairs of the old seed establishment of
David Landreth & Sons, and believe the plan that
firm suggests of settling their debts on a basis of
fifty per cent, without interest, by four notes—
twenty per cent on 1st April and ten per cent on
1st October, 1st April and 12th July—to be the
most practical settlement which can be offered
by them, as also by far the most satisfactory,
because the most profitable settlement the creditors can obtain.

As seed merchants and creditors ourselves we,
without any legal or moral obligations as to the
plan, suggest its prompt acceptance by all concerned.

J. M. THORBURN & CO., New York.
JOSEPH H. BRECK & SONS, Boston.
W. ATLEE BURPEE & CO., Philadelphia.
JOHNSON & STOKES, Philadelphia.
T. W. WOOD & SONS, Richmond, Va.
J. M. McCULLOUGH'S SONS, Cincinnati, O.,
J. B. RICE SEED CO., Cambridge, N. Y.

The attorneys representing D. Landreth & Sons urge that the creditors accept
the recommendation of the committee at
once, as the carrying out of the proposed
settlement is dependent on its immediate
acceptance by the creditors.

COUNCIL BLUFFS, IA.—Defective water
pipes on the second floor of the Shugart
& Ouren Seed Company's building, at
the corner of Broadway and Bryant
street, caused a small loss a few days
ago. The rear part of the first floor was
entirely flooded. The water started running through the night and was not discovered until the store was opened in the
morning.

MANITOWOC, WIS.—Plans have been
accepted by the Manitowoc Seed Company for a new brick building which will
have a frontage of sixty feet and will be
used as a warehouse and for the offices
of the company.

J. E. WOODBRIDGE TRACY, of the United
States Agricultural Department, will
return to England when he has
"explored" the continent.

PORTLAND, ORE.—The capital stock of
the Portland Seed Company has been
increased to $75,000.

FAVORABLE rains have fallen in the
Minnesota potato districts since our last
issue.

THE NURSERY TRADE.

AM. ASSOCIATION OF NURSERYMEN.
N. W. HALE, Knoxville, Tenn.. Pres.; FRANK
A. WEBER, St. Louis, Mo., Vice-Pres.; GEORGE C.
SEAGER, Rochester, N. Y., Sec'y.
Twenty-ninth annual convention, Atlanta, Ga.,
June, 1904.

WALPOLE, MASS.—S. L. Miller, superintendent of the Walpole electric works, was arraigned in the district court on July 13 charged by the tree warden, Edward Grover, with defacing and injuring shade trees.

A. F. MILLER, of Portland, Ore., has been appointed commissioner of agriculture and horticulture for the state of Oregon at the St. Louis exposition. Mr. Miller was forestry commissioner at the Chicago World's Fair, preparing a display of 120 varieties of Oregon woods for the occasion.

PLANS are in progress under the general direction of Governor Bates for restoring the forests of Massachusetts by the work of convict camps. The work, which is the first experiment of the kind in the United States, will be done on a large scale, many thousand acres of land now considered valueless being taken by right of eminent domain.

SPRINGFIELD, O.—W. H., Frank J. and George W. Smith, who were in the nursery business at this place, recently filed their petitions for bankruptcy in the United States court. The liabilities of each include those of the partnership, as well as the individual debts. The liabilities of W. H. Smith are $46,780, those of Frank $37,760 and those of George W. $20,067.

Geneva, N. Y.

William Smith, the nurseryman, will, it is announced, found and endow a college for women, to be known as the William Smith College for Women. The institution will be on a site of thirty acres in one of the most beautiful sections in the outskirts of the city. The plans call for one building to cost $150,000.

Mr. Smith has made large donations to public institutions and also maintains the Smith observatory.

Helena, Mont.

STATE NURSERY COMPANY HAS ANNUAL
PICNIC. — DELIGHTFUL COACH RIDE
THROUGH THE MOUNTAINS.—PLEASANT
STEAMER TRIP.

The annual picnic given by the State Nursery Company for its employes with families took place on Sunday, july 26. Three four-horse coaches took the party to Hilger's, a drive of twenty miles to the Missouri river, where the steamer Rose of Helena was boarded and a delightful ride enjoyed through the canyon, where lunch was served. Caves were explored, etc., and wild strawberries found in abundance. The return trip up the river was very interesting, the banks being lined with wild syringa and blue and white clematis. Rock formations could be seen that resembled famous and noble men but nary a one that looked like a florist. An exciting game of baseball was played, lasting until supper time, when ample justice was done to fried chicken and mountain trout, to say nothing of the other good things too numerous to mention. The ride home through the mountains was delightful, the only thing to mar the complete enjoyment being a noise from the rear coach in which rode the gentlemen from Germantown, Penn., and Boston, who unfortunately brought their voices with them.   A. J.

NILES, MICH.—The Michigan Central Railroad will at once begin the erection of four large greenhouses at this place for the purpose of growing flowers on an extensive scale for through passengers.

PENDLETON, IND.—The Indiana Horticultural Society will hold its annual meeting at this place on August 4 and 5. Among the papers to be discussed is "Some Things Learned from Experience in Spraying," by Joseph A. Burton, of Orleans.

NOON HOUR AT THE STATE NURSERY COMPANY'S, HELENA, MONT.

("A Fish Story From Boston.")

OUR PASTIMES.

S. A. F. COMMITTEE ON SPORTS.

P. J. Hauswirth. 227 Michigan avenue. Chicago; C. C. Pollworth and F. Schmeling, Milwaukee.

Announcements of coming contests or other events of interests to our bowling, shooting and sporting readers are solicited and will be given place in this column.

Address all correspondence for this department to Wm. J. Stewart, 79 Milk St., Boston. Mass.; Robt. Kift, 1725 Chestnut St., Philadelphia, Pa.; or to the American Florist Co.. 324 Dearborn St., Chicago, Ill.

At Chicago.

The game between the regular team and the "Has-been's," played at Mussey's alleys, July 28, resulted in three straight victories for the regulars. Some very poor scores were made on both sides. The scores were as follows:

REGULARS.	1st	2d	3d
Balluff	188	133	134
Lambros	115	118	
F. Stollery	126	192	174
Scott	119	134	144
Asmus	162	171	145
G. Stollery	189	147	145
Total	861	800	743
HAS-BEENS.	1st	2d	3d
Hauswirth	130	180	153
Bentley	96	136	130
Sterrett	119	130	182
Kreitling	56	101	111
Kohler	105	93	
Winterson	128	167	165
Total	684	807	740

Omaha.

ANNUAL OUTING AT COURTLAND BEACH.—BATHING, BOWLING, ETC.—THE LADIES BREAK ALL RECORDS FOR LOW BOWLING SCORES.—TRADE QUIET BUT PRICES HOLD UP WELL.—CARNATIONS SOON TO BE BENCHED.

An event which many of the florists of this locality will remember for many days has come and gone, namely the third annual picnic. This was held at Courtland Beach, East Omaha, on Thursday, July 23, and from every point of view was a decided success. Many attractions outside of the picnic itself drew an extra large attendance, and the day being perfect, bathing on the sandy beach was indulged in by many. A lunch by the

Nebraska Florists' Club was served at 7:15 p. m., after which a match game at bowling was in order, Lewis Henderson's side being defeated. The ladies also indulged in this pastime, and the competition was a close one as to who could make the lowest score, in which Miss Clara Hildebrand, of Hess & Swoboda, won the prize by making a score of 24 in ten frames. After the games a steamer ride and the vaudeville circus were enjoyed and at 11:30 p. m. the party started for home, all having enjoyed the event to the fullest extent. The president of the club is in Berlin at present, and the writer is sure he will regret having missed the outing.

Trade is of a very quiet order, but prices hold up better than a year ago. Owing to very favorable weather the carnations in the field are making splendid growth. Benching will start about August 1. GRIPPE, JR.

Indianapolis.

John Bertermann, who always shows due regard for his outer appearance, recently invested in a panama hat, and to avoid giving it a drenching the other night remained on the owl car and passed by his home four times, traveling sixteen miles between Irvington and Mount Jackson. When he finally arrived home, the electric light shone on some other person's 98-cent straw hat which he had been wearing instead of his own expensive headpiece.

The wedding of Clarence R. Green and Miss Elizabeth C. Stephens took place July 22. Mr. Green and wife will be at home after September 1 at 3507 N. Senate avenue.

John Bertermann and family, together with I. Bertermann and wife, will leave for Michigan next week.

Wm. Billingsly will carry destruction to the fish in the Kankakee river.

John Riemann and family will spend the summer at Broad Ripple.

Ed. Bertermann is enjoying his vacation in some rustic place.

F. Conway has returned from a trip to his old Kentucky home.

Mr. Hasselman and family have gone to the lakes. H. J.

Seattle, Wash.

A PROMINENT BUSINESS PLACE CHANGED HANDS.—NEW PLANS OF MALMO & COMPANY.

The retail store at 916 Second avenue, for the past ten years operated by the Malmo Seed and Floral Company, has been sold to the Pacific Seed and Floral Company. The new firm is under the management of A. L. Aabling and J. Anthon. whose success is assured on account of their long and extensive business experience in the same line, who will in the future continue the business as heretofore conducted under the able management of C. Malmo, the founder. The well-known florist and seedsman, C. Malmo, under the firm name of Malmo & Company, retains the extensive wholesale business and mailing trade, together with the warehouses, nurseries and greenhouses on the corner of East Pike and Broadway, to which place the main office, as well as the mailing department, has been moved, and where, with superior facilities, orders can be executed even to better satisfaction than heretofore.

Peoria, Ill.

The weather here has been very hot and dry for the last two weeks, but recently there was a welcome rain, which will be a great benefit to all outdoor stock, especially carnations. All the florists report a good trade for the last year and are now busy getting everything ready for the coming season. The carnations in the field are looking fine, the rose stock is all planted and doing well and everyone is looking forward to a good run of trade.

C. Loveridge has moved from 321 Main street to 402 Main street, in the Florist block, and has a much better stand than before. All the flower stores in Peoria are now in the one block.

Cole Brothers are remodeling nearly all of their houses, replacing their old ones with short-span structures.

J. C. Murray is talking of building two new houses for carnations. H. G.

WINAMAC, IND.—Mary J. Wittmer has bought out Mrs. Burgel.

OUTING OF THE STATE FLORISTS' ASSOCIATION OF INDIANA.

Louisville, Ky.

KENTUCKY FLORISTS MEET AT RIVERVIEW PARK DURING THE SUMMER.—NUMEROUS FUNERAL ORDERS.—GOOD STOCK SCARCE. —LESS BUILDING THAN USUAL.—NOTES OF LOCAL INTEREST.

Funeral work has been very good this summer. At the funeral of Pulaski Leeds, of the Louisville & Nashville Railroad, many large and expensive designs were used and the Falls City Wire Works worked all night getting designs ready for the florists.

The Kentucky Society of Florists is holding its monthly meetings at Riverview Park during the summer, where the members have an enjoyable time. The meeting usually lasts from 2 p. m, until about 9 p. m., supper being taken at the park.

Mrs. C. B. Thompson is erecting a 23x60-foot greenhouse in the rear of her store, where she will keep plants for sale and palms to be used in decorating.

Jacob Schultz has moved into temporary quarters until his new store is completed. He is now building a greenhouse measuring 20x60 feet.

Henry Fuchs recently hurt his hand by cutting it with glass and was laid up, but is now out again. He is building a house 35x125 feet.

E. G. Reimes is erecting five greenhouses to grow bedding plants in, measuring 17x65 feet each.

Mr. Creighton, representing Henry Dreer, was in Louisville a few days ago.

There will not be as much building in this vicinity this season as last year.

Herbert G. Walker is building a residence on Grand boulevard.

Good stock is scarce and finds ready sale. H. G. W.

Baltimore.

Business has slackened very perceptibly since the Elks' convention, which was, however, a great success. Good stock is very scarce at present. The city will spend $3,000 for bulbs, to be used as a spring display in the various parks and public squares. The park board has advertised in the daily papers and the municipal board of awards will make the contract. So far it does not seem as though this locality will be very strongly represented at the Milwaukee convention.

RETAIL STORES OF MILWAUKEE.

Troy, N. Y.

WORK ON NEW CITY PARK PROGRESSING RAPIDLY.—A FIRM DISCONTINUES BUSINESS ON ACCOUNT OF LOSS FROM FIRE.—A NEW FLOWER STORE.—AN ALBANY VISITOR HAS ACCIDENT.

Work on Prospect Park, the new pleasure ground acquired by the city, is being pushed rapidly and much has already been accomplished. A retaining wall has been erected along Congress street, new roads built, and much grading done. Civil Engineer Baltimore, who has charge of the work, recently returned from a trip to various eastern cities, where he inspected the parks in order to obtain information and suggestions for the laying out and maintenance of the park under his charge. Of the $164,000 appropriated by the common council for the purchase of the park property and its improvement, only a small balance of about $1,000 remains unexpended.

Louis Menand, Jr., son of the well known florist on Cemetery avenue, Albany, while in the city a short time ago, stumbled on the sidewalk and dislocated his shoulder. The many friends of young Menand hope for his speedy recovery.

The firm of Boardman & Smith, at 7 Third street, has discontinued business, having suffered a bad loss through fire a few weeks ago.

John H. Duke has opened a flower store at 2006 Fifth avenue in connection with his place on Lake avenue.   R. D.

Madison, N. J.

L. A. Noe, first base, and one of the best players in the Madison base ball fraternity, evidently knows something of the abilities of the Chatham warriors, and when they come to town for a tussle with their Madison friends his money and his sympathy occasionally take divergent paths. Elwood Brant is also a base ball enthusiast of no mean abilities.

Toledo, O.

LOCAL JOURNAL SPEAKS HIGHLY OF THE FLORISTS.—SAYS THAT G. A. HEINL CONTRIBUTES TO COMMERCIAL LEADERSHIP OF CITY.—A PUFF OR TWO FOR S. N. PECK.

"No one has contributed more to the commercial leadership of this city than the leading florist, George A. Heinl," says the Toledo *Times*. "His business operations have always been active, progressive and successful in the highest sense, in so far as they have harmonized with a proper conception of public wants and needs. Mr. Heinl's floral establishment is the result of requisite competency, fruitful enterprise and a business management prosecuted with reference to individual benefit and public credit. Mr. Heinl founded his floral business on broad, liberal lines, and with a paramount purpose. It too often happens that a business is established with no thought excepting of self. Such may flourish for a while, but eventually there comes to them proper condemnation. It is the business that was started and maintained with the thought that its success must needs depend on public patronage that will live to grow and prosper; hence to win public regard and gain desirable recognition it is necessary that the masses of the people are pleased and satisfied. This is the secret of Mr. Heinl's success. His house was established right and managed from first to last with a due regard for Toledo's commercial supremacy. The Heinl greenhouses at West Toledo are all that modern improvements and careful management can make them. They represent a mastery in their line which is indeed creditable alike to the wisdom and watchfulness of the founder and the public judgment which, in the beginning, gave its seal of commendation."

In glowing terms does the same paper speak of S. N. Peck: "The greenhouses of S. N. Peck, 1707 Broadway, are among the active and fast growing business establishments of the city. Their extensive trade and flourishing condition indicate a public appreciation desirable and quite general. A new house is being built which will be utilized for growing carnations. Mr. Peck may be styled a born florist. His natural talents are indicated in his artistic work for weddings, funerals and many other occasions. He takes delight in his business and is happiest when art makes its strongest appeals to him. He is a member of the Society of American Florists and attends all of its annual meetings, getting all the newest and best ideas in floral work and decorations. Mr. Peck established his floral business nearly eight years ago. He started with nothing but a love for plants and flowers, and for growing them, as well as an abundance of patience. He began industriously and from the first has been successful."

Canton, O.

The American Carnation Society, in view of the benefits it will derive as a result of the establishment of the McKinley Carnation League, has offered to raise a florists' fund which will be turned over to the committee having charge of the erection of a monument at this city to the late president. The matter will be taken up at the Milwaukee meeting in August.

EAST HAMPTON, MASS.—James Morrison has purchased the buildings and floral business of E. A. Brainard.

Worcester, Mass.

FUNERAL WORK THE MAIN FACTOR AT PRESENT.—SUMMER FLOWERS PLENTIFUL.—CARNATIONS IN FIELD ARE FINE. —WORK ON WORCESTER CONSERVATORIES PROGRESSING RAPIDLY.—NOTES.

Funeral work and an occasional belated wedding decoration make up the bulk of business at the present time. Summer flowers, such as sweet peas, gladioli, asters, dahlias, etc., are plentiful and of exceptionally good quality. Carnations still hold out, and on account of the cool weather are very good for so late in the season. Summer roses as a rule are off crop, with the exception of Souvenir du President Carnot. Carnations in the field are in fine condition and give promise of good returns next season. Outside vegetation, with the exception of geraniums is in good condition, as we have had plenty of rain and cool weather.

Work on the Worcester conservatories is progressing rapidly now, two houses being already planted with roses and five in various stages of completion. One will be planted to carnations and the balance with roses. Four 100 h. p. Cunningham boilers are ready to be installed and the if the weather remains favorable the plant should be completed by September.

The weekly exhibitions of the Worcester County Horticultural Society are being well attended and some very fine displays are being made.

A Philip Powers, clerk at H. F. A. Lange's store, has a badly sprained wrist, the result of a trolley car accident last week.

W. J. Stewart stopped off and said "Howdy" on his way to New York.

F. B. Madaus is passing around the cigars—it's a boy. A. H. L.

Boiler Tubes

For Greenhousemen.

Second-Hand, in Good Condition.

For many years past we have been selling these tubes to the greenhouse men of this country.

They are economical and practical, and make a first-class pipe line.

We clean and paint them and their appearance and quality is first-class. With these tubes we furnish without additional charge, sleeve or jacket couplings; also oakum and cement to make a tight joint. They come in long straight lengths. Note our prices:

Outside Dia. meter In.	Weight Per Ft.	Price Per Ft.
2	1.9	4c
2¼	2.2	5c
3½	4.4	8c
4	5.5	11c
6	10.5	21c

We also carry a complete stock of standard galvanized and black water and steam pipe at low prices.

Ask For Catalogue No. 47.

Boilers, Heating Apparatus, Glass, Pipe, Hose, Etc., Etc., Etc.

Chicago House Wrecking Co,
WEST 35th & IRON STS.,
CHICAGO, ILL.

NOT every man that runs a mill is an expert judge of lumber. Fewer still are familiar with the peculiar requirements of greenhouse construction. We have made it a special study and know exactly what to furnish. You are welcome to the benefits of our wide experience. If you contemplate building, write us.

JOHN C. MONINGER COMPANY.
GREENHOUSE MATERIAL
111 TO 115 BLACKHAWK ST. CHICAGO ILL.
SELLING AGENTS FOR
GARLAND IRON GUTTERS.

The Wolf

IMPROVED SYSTEM
Greenhouse Ventilating Apparatus.

Operates long houses from either the end or center. One machine does the work of two or three other makes. The most durable, economical and time saving machine on the market. They have been thoroughly tested and we offer as references over

Over 100 Long Distance Machines

now in use operating long lines of sash, averaging 260 ft. to each machine. Prices 10 to 30 per cent cheaper, with a ten-year guarantee. Send for catalogue and list of long houses operated by these machines.

A. Q. WOLF & BRO.,
Office: 329 River Street, ...DAYTON, O.

WATER.

Rider and Ericsson Hot Air Pumping Engines

If water is required for Household use, Lawns, Flower Beds or Stable, no pump in the world will pump it so safely, cheaply and reliably. No danger, as from steam. No complication, as in gasoline engines. No uncertainty, as in windmills.

Prices Reduced. Catalogue "A3" on Application.

RIDER-ERICSSON ENGINE CO.

35 Warren St., NEW YORK. 40 Dearborn St., CHICAGO. 40 North 7th St., PHILADELPHIA. 239 Franklin St., BOSTON. 692 Craig St., MONTREAL, P. Q. Teniente-Rey 71, HAVANA, CUBA.

EUREKA GREENHOUSES
——SOLD BY——
DILLON GREENHOUSE MFG. CO. Bloomsburg, Penna.

Can be erected by any mechanical person Practical, reasonable in cost. Most durable. Send for circular, blue prints and plain directions.

Always mention the......

American Florist

when you write to an advertiser.

THE AMERICAN FLORIST

A WEEKLY JOURNAL FOR THE TRADE

America is "the Prow of the Vessel; there may be more comfort Amidships, but we are the first to touch Unknown Seas."

Vol. XXI. CHICAGO AND NEW YORK, AUGUST 8, 1903. No, 792.

THE AMERICAN FLORIST

NINETEENTH YEAR.

Copyright 1903, by American Florist Company
Entered as Second-Class Mail Matter.

PUBLISHED EVERY SATURDAY BY

AMERICAN FLORIST COMPANY,
324 Dearborn St., Chicago.

Eastern Office: 79 Milk St., Boston.

Subscription, $1.00 a year. To Europe, $2.00.
Subscriptions accepted only from the trade.
Volumes half-yearly from August, 1901.

SOCIETY OF AMERICAN FLORISTS AND
ORNAMENTAL HORTICULTURISTS.

Officers—John Burton, Philadelphia, Pa.,
president; C. C. Pollworth, Milwaukee, Wis.,
vice-president; Wm. J. Stewart, 79 Milk Street,
Boston, Mass., secretary; H. B. Beatty, Oil City,
Pa., treasurer.
Nineteenth annual meeting at Milwaukee, Wis.,
August 18-21, 1903.

THE AMERICAN CARNATION SOCIETY.

Annual convention at Detroit, Mich., March 3,
1904. Albert M. Herr, Lancaster, Pa., secretary.

AMERICAN ROSE SOCIETY.

Annual meeting and exhibition, Philadelphia,
March, 1904. Leonard Barron, 136 Liberty St.,
New York, secretary.

CHRYSANTHEMUM SOCIETY OF AMERICA

Annual convention and exhibition, New York,
November 10-13, 1903. Fred H. Lemon, Richmond,
Ind., secretary.

THIS ISSUE 36 PAGES WITH COVERS.

CONTENTS.

Cannas to Date.

(Read before the Florists Club of Philadelphia,
August 4, 1903, by Antoine Wintzer, West Grove,
Pa.)

Two decades ago the canna was used
in bedding mainly as a decorative plant
for its beautiful and effective foliage. At
that time the flowers were so small and
and insignificant that they were not considered an important factor. Nicholson
in his "Dictionary of Gardening" gives
us a list of twenty-eight varieties, only
two or three of which are now catalogued by a few firms in this country.
In 1885 Cannell & Sons, England, listed
sixty-six varieties. Of this list Ehemannii,
Noutoine, Discolor and one or two others
are now offered by a few American firms.
A few years later M. Crozy sent out his
famous Mme. Crozy and several other
fine varieties, these being so much in
advance in size and earliness of bloom
that they created a great sensation
among canna growers.

The cannas exhibited at the World's
Fair in Chicago in 1893 by leading
American canna growers were a great
factor in bringing them to the notice of
the people, placing them in the front
rank as effective ornamental decorative
plants for massing, and the leading varieties exhibited at that time are now
among the most popular, and are generally catalogued by the leading firms
to-day. At that time American growers
and breeders began to take up the canna
and send out new varieties of American
production. As the French and other
European growers were sending out anywhere from thirty to fifty new varieties
annually, it was rather difficult to find
room for all the new comers. It looked
for awhile as if the American varieties
would be crowded out of the market
through sheer force of numbers. It soon
became a race of the survival of the fittest
with the Americans in the rear at the
start. Let us see if they stand in the
rear to-day. Without going too much
into detail let us now try to get at the
result.

The writer has glanced over the lists of
fourteen leading American catalogues to
see what they are doing in the canna
line. The first thing noticed was that
long lists of varieties are not in favor
with them, the average being less than
fifty varieties. This indicates a healthy
condition, showing that worthless varieties are being discarded. The next thing
noticed was that our American varieties
have made prodigious strides, and if we
are to judge them on their merits alone,
it now appears they will soon leave for-

eign productions in the rear. In the following table a list is given of the varieties catalogued by the above mentioned
fourteen firms. Only varieties are noted
that are listed by no less than four different firms. To note all would make this
paper too long.

4 Admiral Avellan.		4 J. D. Cabos.	
4 Alphonse Bouvier		4 L. Patray	
11 Allemania.		9 Luray.	
11 Alsace.		11 Mme. Crozy.	
5 America.		4 Maiden's Blush.	
4 Ami Pichou.		5 Martha Washington.	
11 Austria.		4 Mlle. Berat.	
8 Beaute Poitevine.		8 Mrs. Kate Gray.	
5 Betsy Ross.		4 Paul Marquant.	
10 Black Beauty.		9 Pennsylvania.	
5 Black Prince.		6 Philadelphia.	
4 Brandywine.		8 President Carnot.	
8 Burbank.		8 President Cleveland.	
4 Buttercup.		11 President McKinley.	
11 Chas. Henderson.		12 Queen Charlotte.	
10 Chicago.		4 R bert Christie.	
5 Comte de Bouchaud.		4 Robusta.	
5 David Harum.		8 Rosemawr.	
10 Duke of Marlboro		8 Sam. Trelease.	
11 Egandale.		11 Secrétaire Chabanne.	
4 Flamingo.		4 Shenandoah.	
12 Florence Vaughan.		11 Souvenir de Antoine	
8 Gloriosa.		Crozy.	
13 Italia.		4 Victory.	

The combined number of varieties in
the fourteen catalogues would run the
list of varieties close to three hundred.
Of the forty-seven varieties mentioned
above, twenty-four were originated and
and grown by American breeders. Three
others of the most popular varieties were
introduced by American firms. The
largest, or orchid flowering varieties as
they are now generally known, first
came from Italy seven or eight years ago
and American buyers paid $5 per root
for them The writer potted seventeen
roots of Austria himself in an enterprising Philadelphia house with instructions
to grow all he could. Three years later
half of the stock was thrown on the
dump. The flowers of this breed, while
the largest and most perfect in form, lack
substance, which causes them to wilt
after a few hours of strong sunlight.
This class will soon be superseded by
such varieties as Mrs. Kate Gray and
Pennsylvania, both American hybrids,
the latter being the nearest to scarlet in
this class introduced to date.

In the creation of new colors and
shades American breeders have enriched
the collection by such varieties as Duke
of Marlboro, Cherokee, Philadelphia and
others. In the production of pink colors
and shades they have given the world
such cannas as Martha Washington,
Luray, Betsy Ross and many others; in
yellow colors they have given us Buttercup, Coronet and others, while Alsace
and Mont Blanc are among the shades
of white. Then why should a production

of American breeders be listed as a Crozy or French canna in some of our leading catalogues? Or why should our noble parks be deprived of our beautiful American cannas and made the dumping ground for a lot of rubbish that our best American breeders would not tolerate in their common mixed lots? The same can be said of our railroads, along which good canna beds are the exception, not the rule. The majority of them are filled with very inferior varieties.

In conclusion the writer would remark that the cannas at the famous Biltmore estate were a disgrace to the name of cannas as they exist at the present time. Would a millionaire fill his house with a lot of cheap, inferior paintings, and ignore the work of the world's famous artists? Show me the artist who can produce the shades and colors of say twenty of our best cannas, the product of ten years' work by artists in nature's art gallery. The one produces his ideal with the brush. His highest ambition is to produce a painting as good as the master minds produced hundreds of years before he was born. If he succeeds, his painting is sold to some millionaire (probably American) for a few thousand. The plant artist also has an ideal, but he has no model to draw from. He pollinates a flower, it produces a seed. The seed is planted, sprouts and grows. He watches for days, weeks, months. Why? He is looking for a new shade or color to give the world something better than ever before produced. He may be working to create a better carnation, rose, chrysanthemum or canna, and his ambition is always the same, to do better than the man who lived before his day and generation. His work will endure for all time. Coming millions will see and admire the flowers that brightened his eye. * * * * * *

Then will they look over this beautiful city of brotherly love and admire the glories of its Fairmount park, fair with the finest products of the floral world, gorgeous with its beautiful beds of American cannas. This happy event will come to pass when the people cease to be the tools of politicians, and when all "grafting" except the grafting performed by our horticulturists shall be unknown.

Paris Letter.

ORCHIDS IN LEAF SOIL.

Considerable interest has been shown lately in the new process of cultivating orchids in leaf soil. A Belgian horticulturist, De Langhe-Vervaene, of Brussels, was first in using that method, commencing four or five years ago. He has been followed since by several French horticulturists, among whom is noted Leon Duval, of Versailles, the well-known hybridizer of bromelias, orchids and anthuriums. Mr. Duval is to-day a great advocate of the leaf soil, growing all his orchids in it with remarkable results. Odontoglossum crispum, Pacho strain, grown in this compost is simply unique. However, a few amateurs who have tried the method dispute its efficiency. G. Magne and Mr. Opoix, the head gardener of the Paris Luxembourg park, went back to the old system of culture in sphagnum moss, which fact created a great controversy in the horticultural papers.

It may be that both sides are right. The orchid specialists grow their plants in distinct houses especially suited to groups of like requirements and consequently they are more easily given the

needed care and attention. With amateurs the case is different, as the latter often grow in the same house a large number of species requiring entirely different treatment. The keystone to success with leaf soil is to water often but very sparingly all the plants of the same house at the same time. The moisture should never be stagnant. The use of sphagnum moss is a guarantee against any excess of moisture after watering and against a too quick absorption, but so far this conclusion does not seem to have been suggested by the French papers, the only point on which they agree being that the cypripediums do not thrive in leaf soil.

OWNERSHIP OF NOVELTIES.

The question of the ownership of horticultural novelties was raised last year

Joseph Steckler.
(President New Orleans Horticultural Society.)

by J. Pernet-Ducher at the congress held at Marseilles, and some views were exchanged at the recent meeting at Angers. Mr. Pernet favors a law assuring to the introducer the exclusive ownership of his novelties during four years, but other horticulturists do not consider such a law practical. The horticultural press dealt with the matter, and the question was placed before the Horticultural Congress of Paris as well as at the rose growers' meeting at Angers, but nowhere has it been debated. The only paper on the subject which was presented in Paris was that of N. Severi, of Rome, Italy, and the chairman speaking of it said "Hum! Hum! the matter is very serious, let it be taken up at another session."

JAPANESE DWARFED TREES.

The business which is now being done in dwarfed Japanese trees by one of our tradesmen in Chinese and Japanese articles, namely, Mr. Bing, of Paris, is noteworthy. Every season Mr. Bing imports a lot of these trees, which are sold at auction at this time of the year. Fine specimens were shown in the Japanese section of the Paris exposition of 1900 and have also been exhibited at various horticultural shows. The display last year was very important and attracted a great deal of attention. The English and French press have described the process of dwarfing the trees, which consists especially in selecting the smallest seed-

lings grown from seeds of specimens which have already been twisted and stunted, and in frequent removal of the large roots, placing the plants in shallow pots in order to induce the upper part of the root to grow above the surface of the soil. Such a process requires many years of patient work and some of the specimens are several hundred years old. This alone will be sufficient to prevent the specialist from bringing such curiosities into fashion, the labor here being too expensive to make the venture pay, and I believe that when present purchasers attend two or three auction sales they will discontinue to admire the monstrosities.

ETHERIZATION AND REFRIGERATION.

French horticulturists are beginning to take great interest in the various processes of the refrigeration of flowers and fruit and of the etherization of plants. Refrigeration would enable the flower merchants to delay the flowering season until the time when flowers, being scarcer, command better prices, and would also afford the fruit growers an opportunity to dispose of their crops in the same way. The success of the well known English grower, Thomas Rochford, and the fine appearance of American apples on their arrival in Europe awakened paramount attention. But most of our horticultural establishments are not important enough to go to the expense of a new and costly installation. The cold storage system can therefore be practiced only by co-operation, unless some large corporations take it in hand. The basement of the Bourse Du Commerce, Paris, has just been fitted with cold storage appliances and the compartments are rented to the shippers. We shall soon know the result of the venture. Etherization, the object of which is the forcing of the plants after abridging considerably the natural period of rest, will soon be put into practice. The experiments of Professor Johannsen, of Copenhagen, along this line are now daily used by German horticulturists, among whom may be mentioned Fred. Harms, of Hamburg. In France Messrs. Leblanc, of Nancy, and Aymard, of Montpellier, obtained good results in their trials and will shortly use the system on a practical scale. They will no doubt have followers as its establishment is not costly or complicated. German lilacs forced by etherization have given that country an advantage in competition, which has been very keen of late, and it is time that our French forcers adopted their method. SEER.

Joseph Steckler.

Joseph Steckler, president-elect of the New Orleans Horticultural Society, was born February 18, 1870, in Iberia parish on a farm near the town of New Iberia. His father, Henry Steckler, Jr., was a merchant and planter in that section for forty years. At the age of twelve years he went to New Orleans with his uncle, Richard Frotscher, the veteran seedsman of the south, and was in his employ until the time of his death. Having come to New Orleans at this age, and not having had facilities for education at home, he worked with his uncle in the store by day and took lessons at night for four or five years, receiving a compensation for his work that enabled him to keep up his studies. After the death of Mr. Frotscher, he, with his present associates, viz., Miss M. T. Frotscher and his brother, R. P. Steckler, bought what was called "Branch Store of Richard Frotscher" and with hard work and energy have made the business what it is to-day, the largest house of its kind in the south. The warehouse and sales department occupy a space of 150 feet front and 150 feet deep, with thirty employes and the nurseries, greenhouses and poultry farms of the firm are second to none in that kind of business. Mr. Steckler is a member of numerous social and trade organizations, the latter including the Gardeners' Mutual Protective Association, American Seed Trade Association, New Orleans Park Commission, etc.

Florists' Plant Notes.

ALTERNANTHERAS.

It is a good plan to propagate A. paronychioides major Kuntzii during the early part of this month. The cuttings will root readily in flats of sand and soil, mixed half and half, and can be wintered on shelves in a warm light house. The other varieties can be handled better and more cheaply by lifting a few plants in the fall and planting them in two inches of light soil in flats, and carried through the winter in the same manner as the above. In March the cuttings are taken and the old plants divided. P. major, however, should be attended to soon, for the old plants grow little if any during winter, and produce very few good cuttings.

CINERARIAS.

It is time now to sow the last batch of cineraria seed for Easter plants. Use light soil mixed with sand and leaf mould and cover the seed pan with glass or paper for a few days until the seeds have germinated. When of sufficient size give them small pots, and later a shift to a 4-inch size. We always aim to have the Easter flowering plants in their 6-inch blooming pots by the first of the year. Those sown earlier in the season for Christmas blooming, or shortly after, should be in 4-inch pots by this time. Keep fresh tobacco stems scattered between the pots to hold green fly in check, and use them frequent syringing. See that the drainage is perfect, so as to allow the water to pass through the soil freely.

POINSETTIAS.

Poinsettias can be propagated until the middle of August, these later struck cuttings making dwarfed, stocky plants in 4-inch or 5-inch pots by Christmas, but propagated later than this they will be too small to be of any use. Keep the sand well watered until the cuttings are rooted, and shade them from the sun with cheese cloth or a [newspaper to prevent wilting. Give them 2½-inch

pots when rooted, and a shift to 4-inch or 5-inch when ready. Those propagated earlier in the season should never be allowed to stop growing for want of pot room; keep them shifted along, using rich soil, and draining the pots with potsherds. Syringe them several times a day to hold red spider and mealy bug in check, and give them all the light and air possible. Support the plants, as they require it, tying with raffia. Be sure to have the plants shifted into their flowering pots by the first of October as they cannot bear to have their roots disturbed after that time. Being a tropical plant it requires a warm place and should never be subjected to a temperature less than 60° at night. Too often around Christmas, when they should be in their glory, we see plants with yellow, drooping leaves, or no leaves at all, with the fiery bracts at the end a bare stem. This is invariably caused either by too low a temperature, starvation at the root by using poor soil, allowing them to become pot-bound, or by disturbing the roots after the plants begin to form their bracts, which is usually around October 1. If extra large bracts are desired for cutting, plant out some strong young plants on a bench, in rich soil, during August. The old stock plants can be shifted to a size larger pot during September, and will make a quantity of smaller bracts if given the proper temperature.   G.

The Carnation.

WATERING.

Much has been written in these notes about watering carnations, but brief allusions now and then give but a faint insight into a subject which taxes the skill of the best growers. This most important subject in carnation growing is certainly deserving of separate and exhaustive treatment, and yet one hesitates to approach it. It is one thing to know how to water a house of carnations and quite another to tell others how to do it. Besides, each individual case is a problem in itself, soil, climate and variety each bearing a separate influence or requiring the adjustment of conditions to that particular case. A grower may be thoroughly familiar with the requirements of a particular locality and so long as he remains in that place he may be successful with many varieties of carnations and attain a reasonable degree of success in his profession, but such a man does not reap the best that is in the business, and if accident removes him to another field or if weather conditions become extremely unfavorable, he is often at sea as to what

course to pursue. A careful study, therefore, of the requirements of the plant is of as great importance as a knowledge of the results of past experiments. A man who can truthfully be called a gardener will be successful in his business whether he is constantly located in one place or whether chance throws him from one part of the country to another far removed, and dominated by a climate which greatly differs from that of the former in vital points, because he knows what his plants require and quickly sees whether or not the natural climate and soil conditions are favorable to the subject to be treated. If they are not favorable he knows what measures to pursue to mitigate the effect of any adverse influence. Experience will, of course, always be a most powerful teacher, but a reasonable conception of embryonic possibilities is an invaluable aid in determining beforehand the value of an experiment and recognizing the value of results when they mature.

Of experience, theory and imagination, experience may be the most tangible and least fickle, but neither can work to its fullest capacity without the aid of the other two. So, in watering carnations, it is well for each individual to be guided by the immediate surroundings and explore in theory and imagination whatever possibilities may not appear upon the surface. A few rules can be safely followed and made the foundation of a system more or less elaborate, whether surface watering or sub-irrigation is the method employed. The texture of the soil, the variety to be treated and in what stage of growth it may happen to be must all be taken into account.

A light soil dries out faster than a heavy one and as the soil takes the larger than is the case with a heavy soil, giving it correspondingly less root contact, it will be readily seen that there is less danger of overwatering and that not only will it be necessary to water oftener, but that the actual amount of moisture present should be greater with the same variety, other environments being the same. A good rule to follow is to water only when the plants need it and then give a good soaking, which, however, should not approach the point of saturation. This does not mean that the plants should be actually thirsting for water before any is given, but the soil should be as near as possible at that degree of moisture at which the balance between root and foliage is exactly stationary. The condition of the plants will enter largely into determining this. It is easy to carry the plants along with far less soil moisture than is necessary to produce a normal growth. The result of

this is seen in short stemmed and small flowers and a dwarfing of the whole plant. So it is necessary to strive to accustom the plants to just so much water as is required to produce a high grade of blooms. If the soil is kept just well moistened, but not by any means saturated at any time, the desired result will be obtained. It is a good thing to allow the soil to come well on to the dry side occasionally to prevent souring. How far it will be safe to go in this direction will depend some upon external conditions. In winter, when the atmospheric conditions are well under control and when the sun is weak, it will be safe to carry this farther than at more active seasons of the year. At such times the balance between root and foliage can often be maintained without harm for a day or two by a thorough syringing after the soil is ready for a good watering.

The greatest care is necessary from the time the plants are benched until after the turn of the season, about February 1, in order to prevent stagnation and

sourness, and at the same time to supply sufficient water to support the growth both above and below the surface of the soil. During that time the skill of the grower is taxed to the utmost and the man who keeps his plants in robust growth throughout this critical period can truly say that he has mastered the art of watering. An alert mind, energy and patience are dominant characteristics of such a man and it is not strange that the florist business is not overstocked with such, considering the abundant opportunities for quick advancement in other branches of industry. He will examine the soil thoroughly every day and water only such benches or parts of benches as may require it, having an eye to preparing the whole bench for a good soaking, making sure in that case that the water penetrates clear to the bottom. After a thorough watering the soil is again watched for a few days for dry places until the entire bench is in condition to require another soaking. After about February 1, if the plants have made a good growth, there is not much

danger, with reasonable care, of over-watering and from then on it will be possible to keep the soil at about a uniform degree of moisture without danger of souring, and as the season advances the degree of moisture maintained can be proportionately increased, still guarding, however, against saturation, which is always dangerous.

Wetting the foliage must be avoided in applying water to the roots. Syringing should be made an entirely separate operation and should be performed only on a sunny day. A man who is careful and turns on only a small stream of water may be trusted to water at almost any time of the day, for he will keep the foliage dry. It is best, however, to do all watering early in the forenoon, just about the time the sun warms the house up and when ventilation begins. If it is necessary to water and syringe on the same day, do the watering first and the syringing afterwards, otherwise it is hard to detect dry places.   J.

A Chicago Funeral Design.

The accompanying illustration shows a funeral piece made by Walter Kreitling & Company and tendered at the obsequies of the late Charles Long, base ball player and bowler, who was buried July 11. White carnations, Lilum auratum, smilax, galax, Asparagus Sprengeri and fern were used.

Growers of Milwaukee.

A very small portion of the flowers handled in Milwaukee are grown in the city, the wholesale market being supplied with stock mostly from other points. But many local growers do an extensive business direct from their greenhouses, as shown in the two full-page illustrations in this issue.   C. B. W.

Society of American Florists.

DEPARTMENT OF PLANT REGISTRATION.

The Conard & Jones Company, West Grove, Pa., submits for registration, rose, Northern Light. Climbing, very vigorous, perfectly hardy, foliage large and leathery, of deep glossy green. Flowers produced in large clusters of from fifty to seventy-five, single flowers measuring about two inches, very double, fragrant; color variable, pink, some on the same cluster half pink, others white. The same company also submits for registration, rose, Leo XIII. Plant very vigorous, flowers pure white, large, quite double. First blooms open about May 20 and continues in bloom all summer and fall. This variety is as hardy as the single Rugosa.   WM. J. STEWART, Sec'y.

Recent Publications.

CHRYSANTHEMUM SOCIETY REPORT.— This pamphlet of about seventy pages contains the proceedings of the first annual meeting of the Chrysanthemum Society of America, held at Chicago, November 12, 1902, and the papers presented thereat. There are sixteen of these papers, any one of which is well worth the annual membership fee of $1.

GUIDE TO HARDY FRUITS AND ORNAMENTALS.—By T. J. Dwyer. Fifty cents. —There are many useful suggestions in this paper bound book of 125 pages. It is freely illustrated and the selections of varieties should prove useful to beginners.

CONVENTION SOUVENIR.—The souvenir issued by the Milwaukee Florists' Club in compliment to the S. A. F. convention visitors is a very handsome affair, amply fitting to the great occasion. Attend the meeting and secure a copy.

FUNERAL DESIGN FOR A BOWLER.
(Artists, Walter Kreitling Company, Chicago.)

MILWAUKEE GROWERS' ESTABLISHMENTS.

1. Fred Schmeling. 2. Carl Johannes. 3. Wm. Helwig. 4. Mrs. J. Freytag. 5. Rudolph Preuse. 6. Pohl & Kraure. 7. H. Schweise. 8. Fred Menger. 9. Archie Middlemass. 10. Heitman & Baertman 11. Wm. Edlefsen.

Chicago.

BUSINESS SOMEWHAT BRISK FOR A FEW DAYS.—NOT MUCH GOOD STOCK OUTSIDE OF GARDEN FLOWERS.—SUPPLY INADEQUATE FOR SHIPPING ORDERS.—SOME RAINY WEATHER.—SOME NEW AMERICAN BEAUTY ROSES MAKE AN APPEARANCE.—ASTERS IN ABUNDANCE.—NOTES OF THE TOWN.—VISITORS.

Although trade was quite brisk for a number of days, about Wednesday a general slacking was noticed in all lines. Outside of garden flowers there is not much good stock to be had and a great deal of trouble is experienced in filling out-of-town orders that are still coming in all out of proportion to the available supply at the wholesale markets. The rainy weather that has prevailed for the past couple of weeks has affected stock to a certain extent. A few new American Beauty roses are being cut and make a very nice appearance. There is a super-abundance of asters everywhere, but prices for them seem to hold up well as they brought as high as $2 per hundred this week. Large quantities of very fine gladioli are still being received. Auratum lilies appear to hold their own. Greens of all kinds are very plentiful, although the demand for such material is not very great.

J. B. Deamud has become vice-president of the Chicago-Kansas Oil & Gas Company, a new corporation which owns 1,500 acres of oil land in the Buffalo fields near Chanute, Kas. He has just returned from a tour of inspection and feels highly elated over the prospects in view. We wish him luck in his enterprise.

The J. C. Moninger Company recently received among other orders a contract for four greenhouses at Niles, Mich., from the Michigan Central Railway Company, and an order for three 200-foot houses from the Miami Floral Company, Dayton, O.

Joseph Brooks assumes charge as foreman for Weiland & Risch at their greenhouses, Evanston, Ill. Mr. Brooks has for several years been in the employ of Poehlmann Brothers as foreman, and is considered a very capable man.

Miss Cassie M. Arnold, of Omaha, Neb., who has been spending her vacation in the east, passed through the city this week, having been called home by the illness of her father, who was stricken with paralysis.

Leonard Kill recently umpired a hot game of ball on the west side, and according to reports he will not officiate again for some time to come.

O. P. Bassett and wife have gone to Lake Minnetonka, Minn., where they will remain for three or four weeks at the Lafayette Hotel.

Sinner Brothers have housed nearly all of their carnation stock and their young roses are coming in in good shape.

George H. Peiser, of Kennicott Brothers, has just returned from a tour through the country in his automobile.

G. H. Peiser, secretary of the Kennicott Brothers Company, is now sojourning at Lakewood, Wis.

Harry Lubliner, of the Consumer's Floral Company, has returned from the woods.

A new ice box, measuring 18x18 feet, has been installed at the Growers' Exchange.

J. B. Deamud has been getting his share of first-class gladiolus stock the past week.

J. C. Enders, of Poehlmann Brothers, left August 1 for an extended northern trip.

J. A. Budlong received some excellent carnations the other day.

E. C. Amling went fishing for a few days this week at Antioch, Ill.

A. C. Kohlbrand, of Amling's, has returned from his outing.

Kennicott Brothers are shipping some fine lilies of the valley.

Visitors: F. E. Dorner, Lafayette, Ind.; A. Washburn, Bloomington, Ill.; H. Villiers Stuart, representing the Kentucky Tobacco Product Company, Louisville, Ky.

New York.

PRESENT SUMMER SEASON ABOUT THE SAME AS IN PREVIOUS YEARS.—ASTERS INCREASE IN QUANTITY. — GENERAL ABSENCE OF HIGHER NOTICES IN STOCK.—REGARDING THE MILWAUKEE TRIP.—BROADWAY FLORISTS PROTEST AGAINST TEARING UP STREET.—COLD STORAGE PLANT GIVES SATISFACTION.—HIGHER PRICES FOR DUTCH BULBS.—NEW SPECIMENS AT BOTANICAL GARDEN.

The situation in the cut flower trade at present is one of extreme lassitude. August is always a very dull month in New York city and this year is assiduously following precedent. There is but little variation in the mid-summer trade from year to year and the best thing that can be said of the present season is that it is no better than its predecessors. As to the stock in market it is noted that asters are increasing in quantity from day to day. Sweet peas are doing the same act, but those received at present are generally short of stem. In tea roses the majority are also short of stem, but happily mildew is usually absent—a rather unusual summer condition. The quality of American Beauty varies; some are really good but many are imperfect. The demand for them is not constant but the best of them find a fairly regular sale to out-of-town buyers. There is a variety of roses with good stems and flowers to be obtained when one is seriously bent on finding them. Those steadfast summer favorites, Kaiserin, Testout and Carnot are in the front rank and there are some good Meteors, as well as some unnamed kinds. Of carnations there is a sufficient number on hand to supply the limited demand.

It is expected that the interest manifested here in the S. A. F. convention will result in a good representation going from New York, which will also be swelled by the Boston members who will join us at Rotterdam Junction. W. F. Sheridan, 39 West Twenty-eighth street, has charge of the transportation arrangements and desires every one who can go with the New York Florists' Club party to make application at once for sleeping car berths, if they want to get in on the ground floor. The train leaves New York, Sunday, August 16, at 1 o'clock, over the West Shore road.

W. H. Siebrecht's cold storage equipment is giving good satisfaction and with its use there seems no limit as to the date at which bulbous stock of any kind may be brought into bloom. All through the early summer he had very fine double daffodils but the experiment was not fully satisfactory as to prices realized, the public manifestly caring little for yellow flowers in June or July. Mr. Siebrecht's place is one of the regular sources of supply for lily of the valley flowers the year around and the grade is always excellent. A good proportion of the pips used are home grown.

Broadway florists are participating in a protest against the digging up of that thoroughfare for the Broadway extension of the underground railroad. Frank Hunter, of Small & Sons, appeared as a remonstrant at a meeting of storekeepers and hotel men and expressed the views of the florists as to the loss of business they would suffer in consequence of the street's being torn up.

There is a prospect of higher prices on Dutch bulbs the coming season, as it is understood that the hyacinth crop is not up to the average and red tulips are decidedly scarce. Narcissus in all varieties remains about stationary as to supply and price.

The collection at the New York Botanical Garden has recently been enriched by gifts of many large specimen palms from Miss Helen Gould and Walter Hunnewell.

Philadelphia.

FLORISTS' CLUB HOLDS AN INTERESTING SESSION.—PAPER ON CANNAS DISCUSSED.—CONVENTION TOPICS.—CONDITION OF MARKET.—NEW MUSHROOM HOUSE AT SECANE.—GENERAL NOTES.

The meeting of the Florists' Club of Philadelphia, on August 4, was well attended in spite of the very hot weather. A feature of the occasion was the show of canna varieties, which, considering the earliness of the season, was very good. The displays of the Conard & Jones Company, of West Grove, and that of H. A. Drter, each staging over twenty-five varieties, all fine sorts and most of them new, were much admired. Other exhibitors were the H. E. Newbury Company, of Magnolia, N. C., a seedling; Gustav Obermeyer, Parkersburg, W. Va.; Henry Morris, Syracuse, N. Y., and John Watler, who entered a wine-colored seedling. Antoine Wintzer, of West Grove, read a very interesting paper on "Cannas Up to Date." In the discussion following he stated that it was the ambition of most canna growers to always get something better, either in foliage or flower, than existing varieties, and if the seedlings did not size up with the old kinds they most resembled they were immediately discarded. The transportation committee has concluded to go to the convention via the Pennsylvania route. The train will leave Broad street at 8:40 a. m. Monday, August 17, and is due to arrive in Chicago at 7:35 a. m. Tuesday, and Milwaukee at 11 a. m. A Pullman car will be engaged if thirty-five delegates send in their names. Hurry them along, as "First come first served" will be the case. The fare is $20.80. John Westcott, the commissary, has reserved the drawing room for his department, so that no one will be likely to suffer from hunger or thirst enroute. An invitation is hereby extended to all whose route brings them in this direction to travel in company with the club, as ample accommodations can be secured by notifying John Westcott or David Rust of the transportation committee, Horticultural Hall, Broad street. Lemonade and "Florists' Club" punch of the Westcott brew were served at the meeting, which were much enjoyed. The punch was served from the beautiful silver punch bowl won by the bowling team in the city league contest last winter. The next meeting is to be enlivened by reports of the convention from J. W. Colflesh, Thos. B. Meehan, Robert Kift and Edward Reid from the grower's, nurseryman's, florist's and commission man's standpoint.

Business the past week has been very quiet. Roses are more plentiful, the Kaiserin houses now producing at a great rate with prices away down. New crop American Beauty is coming in.

Bridesmaid and Liberty are to be seen but stems are short. Asters are plentiful. Lily of the valley is in good supply again.

The Philadelphia Carnation Company, at its place at Secane, is erecting a mushroom house, 40x150 feet, which will give them 12,000 square feet of space. They are now cutting field carnations, aurateum lilies and fine gladioli.

Thos. Meehan & Sons have recently fitted up an office and packing shed that is said to be one of the finest in the country. Their business the past spring was a record breaker.

Wm. Graham has taken a store at 108 South Twelfth street, two doors below the old business of his brother, Hugh Graham.

A. H. Lanser, of Wayne, has something fine in the heliotrope line and is cutting trusses ten inches in diameter.

Ed. Reid has just returned from a southern trip into Georgia and reports all hands prosperous.

John Westcott and family are now at their Waretown cottage on Barnegat Bay.

John N. May was a recent visitor. K.

Boston.

MARKET IN BETTER CONDITION THAN LAST YEAR AT THIS TIME.—HEAVY SHIPMENTS OF ASTERS.—OLD AMERICAN BEAUTY STOCK IS FADED IN APPEARANCE.— WEEKLY EXHIBITION AT HORTICULTURAL HALL.—A DEATH.—ITEMS OF INTEREST.

The most conspicuous change in the stock of flowers in market this week is the great increase in receipts of asters. Shipments are already very heavy considering the date and are multiplying daily, with the natural result of diminishing values. The usual effect on carnations is already apparent and prices on these are also weakening. Carnations are just now in better size than the summer average, the cool weather of this week helping them greatly. In roses, Kaiserin is easily the best variety available. Some growers are producing splendid flowers of this. Liberty, on the other hand, is now at its worst, thin and undesirable. Teas as a rule are poor, most of the stock being small buds from young plants. American Beauty from old bushes presents generally a faded appearance and abundant evidence of the severe enervating effect of the high July temperatures. Lily of the valley is in excellent quality and enjoying a fairly good sale. On the whole the market seems to be in better condition as to activity than it was at the same time last year and conditions are in the main satisfactory.

The weekly show at Horticultural Hall on Saturday, August 1, was notable for some exceptionally fine orchids of which J. E. Rothwell made a large and comprehensive display for this date, and the Ames estate, W. N. Craig, gardener, showed a seedling, Cypripedium Chamberlaino-Rothschildsianum, for which a silver medal was awarded. The sweet pea displays from E. L. Lewis, A. F. Estabrook and Wm. Whitman were excellent. George Hollis showed seventeen hardy phloxes.

The affairs of George A. Sutherland have been amicably settled with his creditors, most of whom have already accepted a compromise which permits of the business going on without interruption. A very friendly spirit has been displayed by all interested parties.

Mr. and Mrs. D. F. Roy, of Malden, are

mourning the loss of their youngest daughter, Ida, a bright, sweet little child of five years, who died on Sunday, August 2. The funeral services on Tuesday were attended by a number of gardeners and florists.

Pavia macrostachya is making a fine show at present at Franklin park, where Mr. Pettigrew has planted some effective groups.

St. Louis.

NO MATERIAL CHANGE IN MARKET CONDITIONS.—SOME NEW SEEDLING NYMPHÆAS. —LARGE NUMBER OF WORLD'S FAIR EMPLOYES LAID OFF.—CLUB DECIDES THAT NOTHING IS GAINED BY EARLY PLANTING.—SOME VISITORS.

The market has not changed materially since last week, good stock, more especially roses, being still hard to get. A few short stemmed American Beauties are seen now and then, but long and medium are not to be found. Meteor and Perle are not offered, Liberty taking the place of Meteor. Geo. Waldbart says that he has not seen business so dull in twenty-five years as it is at present. The weather has been so warm that it is no wonder trade is dull. Things ought to become livelier from now on, however, rain storm a few days since.

James Gurney, superintendent of Tower Grove park, has a fine lot of seedling nymphæas, hybrids of his own creation, which he hopes will show an improvement over anything now offered. Already he has blooms that are decidedly better than N. O'Marana and N. Devoniensis.

At the last meeting of the St. Louis Florists' Club a lively discussion was held in regard to early and late planting of carnations in this locality. On account of the hot weather it was decided that there is nothing to gain by early planting.

R. J. Mohr has left the employ of the World's Fair people and will embark in business for himself, giving especial attention to landscape gardening as pertaining to World's Fair exhibits. He may be found at 1220 Olive street.

One hundred and fifty or more employes in the horticultural and landscape departments at the World's Fair have been laid off for four weeks. Lack of funds is given as the cause.

F. J. Fillmore is busily engaged in painting and renovating his carnation houses. He will plant later than usual this season.

Howard M. Earl, representing W. Atlee Burpee & Company, stopped a few hours in St. Louis enroute to Texas.

Mr. Siebrecht, Jr., of Siebrecht & Son, New York, was in the city recently on World's Fair business.

Walter Gilles has returned to work after a week's illness. F. K. B.

Minneapolis.

CLUB MEETING HELD EARLIER THAN USUAL.—COMMITTEE REPORT ON PICNIC. CONVENTION RATES.—PRIZE WINNERS IN BOWLING CONTEST.—TRADE STILL DULL. —VISITORS.

The Minneapolis Florists' Club held its regular meeting Thursday, July 30, instead of on the first Thursday in August, which would have been of August 6, as the picnic committee had a report to make and the convention rate to Milwaukee had to be taken under consideration. The meeting took place at A. S. Swanson's greenhouses at St. Anthony Park and was well attended.

About twenty-five florists of this city will attend the convention. The club was more than pleased at the result of the picnic, and the way in which the florists and prominent business people contributed to the prize list. The bowling contests at the festival were entered with great zest. In the men's game the first prize, a beautiful clock, donated by Wm. Donaldson & Company, was won by Joseph Mitton; second prize, $3 in cash, Will Toppel; third prize, box Havanna cigars, donated by California Fruit Company, Oscar Carlson. The first prize in the ladies' bowling contest was a silk umbrella, won by Mrs. Wm. Desmond; second prize, $3 cash, Miss Minnie Busch; third prize, a cut glass flower vase, donated by Miss H. B. Whitted, Mrs. J. Jacobson.

Trade still continues the same as for some time past, there being not much doing and not much to do with. Carnations are about exhausted, and what the market does afford is very poor. Asters, gladioli and other summer stock is abundant.

In its issue of August 2, the Minneapolis *Journal* devoted a full page in color to its sweet pea exhibition poster.

E. P. Lord, of Owatonna, and T. J. Larkin, of ribbon letter fame of New York, were recent visitors. A. F. R.

Abilene, Kan.

Mrs. S. H. Bagley died at her home in this city July 29, after a long illness, and was buried in the Abilene cemetery on July 31. She started the Abilene greenhouses over twenty years ago, beginning on a small scale, and at the time of her death was handling a large business, with five houses. She gave her entire time to the care of her flowers, and no one could wish for neater houses, or cleaner plants. "Honesty in business" was her life motto. C. H. B.

Milwaukee.

The convention programme does not schedule Whitefish Bay as among the places to be visited, reports to the contrary notwithstanding.

The C. C. Pollworth Company will build two additional houses, each 23x256 feet, at its new establishment.

Heitman & Baerman will add three new carnation houses, each 15x200 feet, on the Dietsch plan.

The S. A. F. souvenir has been mailed and convention preparations are well advanced.

Peoria, Ill.

Cole Brothers are rebuilding half their greenhouse range and putting in new boilers. James Cole, Sr., 80 years of age, is superintending the work. The new houses will be modern in every respect.

Henry Baer's outdoor carnations and stock in general are in splendid shape this season. He ships everything to C. A. Kuehn, of St. Louis.

LOCKPORT, N. Y.—The King Construction Company is getting its new works started here. Among the orders on hand are six houses, each 150 feet in length, for P. R. Quinlan, of Syracuse, N. Y., two houses 200 feet in length for Salter Brothers, of Rochester, N. Y. The firm is also supplying one of its patented water tube steam boilers for the latter firm.

THE AMERICAN FLORIST.

NINETEENTH YEAR.

Subscription, $1.00 a year. To Europe, $2.00.
Subscriptions accepted only from those
in the trade.
Advertisements, on all except cover pages,
10 Cents a Line, Agate; $1.00 per inch.
Cash with Order.
No Special Position Guaranteed.

Discounts are allowed only on consecutive insertions, as follows—6 times, 5 per cent; 13 times,
10 per cent; 26 times, 20 per cent;
52 times, 30 per cent.

Cover space sold only on yearly contract at
$1.00 per inch, net, in the case of the two
front pages, regular discounts applying only to the back pages.

The Advertising Department of the AMERICAN
FLORIST is for florists, seedsmen and nurserymen
and dealers in wares pertaining to those lines only.

Orders for less than one-half inch space not accepted.

Advertisements must reach us by Wednesday to
secure insertion in the issue for the following
Saturday. Address

AMERICAN FLORIST CO., Chicago.

Our readers are hereby cautioned
against the payment of subscriptions
or other moneys to unknown parties.

IN EUROPE: F. L. Atkins, of Bobbink
& Atkins, Rutherford, N. J.; Mr. Stroh-
lein, of Henry A. Dreer's, Philadelphia,
Pa.

ALFRED W. CRAWFORD, colored, for-
merly in the florist business at Meriden,
Conn., has been appointed professor of
floriculture and landscape gardening at
Tuskegee University under Booker T.
Washington.

Hotels of Milwaukee.

The following hotels are recommended
as desirable and convenient at the following rates per day:

	American		European	
Pfister	$3.00 to $5.00	$1.50 to $3.50
Plankinton	3.50 to 5.00	1.00 to 3.50
Republican	2.00 to 3.50	
St. Charles	2.00 to 3.50	1.00 to 2.50
Kirby House	2.00 to 2.50	.50 to 1.00
Schlitz		.75 to 2.50
Blatz		1.00 to 2.50
Davidson		1.00 to $2.50

The Price of Glass.

There has been no decline in price on
the part of the larger manufacturers,
according to Patton's Monthly, but
sundry stock lists have been sacrificed,
and in many sections jobbers have been
unloading glass at what seems ridiculously low prices, in view of the wage
settlement. There is almost certain to be a
brisk demand in the early fall for certain
sizes, as stocks of glass in the hands of
consumers are very light, and consequently poorly assorted, but in the
absence of any understanding between
the jobbers and the manufacturers the
market seems likely to drift and for some
time be unprofitable to all concerned, but
it would not take much of a demand to
radically change these conditions.

Chicago to Milwaukee.

Arrangements have been completed
with the Chicago, Milwaukee and St.
Paul railway for a special train of solid
vestibule cars, including buffet-composite
car, to leave Chicago from Union Passenger Station, Canal and Adams streets,
at 10 o'clock Tuesday morning, August
18. The equipment throughout will be
the newest that the road can furnish.
Special will arrive in Milwaukee at 11:50
a. m., three hours before the time set for
the opening of the convention. Special
rate of one fare and a third for the round
trip on certificate plan has been granted
all those attending this convention.
The Milwaukee entertainment committee

---

has arranged for return movement, Milwaukee to Chicago, by steamer for those
wishing to make the lake trip. When
purchasing your ticket to Milwaukee be
sure that it reads via the Chicago, Milwaukee and St. Paul railway, also ask
ticket agent to furnish you with a certificate receipt, as this insures you a
return ticket at one-third fare, should
you decide to return by rail. Tickets can
be purchased at city ticket office, 95
Adams street, or at Union Passenger
Station, Chicago.

New York to Milwaukee.

The transportation committee of the
New York Florists' Club has chosen the
West Shore, Wabash and Chicago, Milwaukee and St. Paul railways as the
official route from New York and state
points, and arrangements have been perfected for the running of a special train
(if number warrants) consisting of Pullman vestibule sleeping cars. Departure
will be from West Shore station, Franklin street, N. R., at 1 p. m., and from
foot of West Forty-second street, N. R.,
at 1:15 p. m., Sunday, August 16, arriving in Chicago at 4 p. m. the following
afternoon, leaving there at 5 p. m., due
in Milwaukee at 7 o'clock Monday evening, August 17. The rate authorized is
one and one-third fare on the certificate
plan, viz., full fare going, and on presentation of certificate to the agent in
Milwaukee (obtained from agent when
purchasing ticket), members will be furnished with tickets at one-third fare,
returning.
The fare from New York to Milwaukee,
Wis., is $20.55 per capita, one-third or
$6.85 returning, making the round trip
rate from New York to Milwaukee, Wis.,
and return $27.40. Sleepers from New
York to Chicago, Ill., $5 per berth and
$18 for stateroom. If party is large
enough, arrangements have been made
to run sleepers through to Milwaukee,
thus avoiding a transfer in Chicago, at
rate of $5.50 per berth and $20 for state-
room from New York direct to Milwaukee.
Members from New York state points
who will join the party will kindly note
the following: When purchasing tickets
be sure and ask the agent for a certificate, which must be deposited with the
secretary of the S. A. F. in the convention hall. This must be done, otherwise
one-third fare will not be granted.
Members from New York and vicinity
will be furnished with tickets and certificates on the train by Louis Hafner, passenger agent of the West Shore railroad,
who will also look after the comfort and
welfare of the party.

Obituary.

THEODORE RICHTER.

In a recent storm at the World's Fair
grounds, St. Louis, Mo., Theodore
Richter, of Kirkwood, Mo., was instantly
killed by a flying plank while seeking
shelter.

J. W. ARNOLD.

J. W. Arnold, the well known pioneer
florist of Omaha, Neb., died August 3
after an illness of but short duration, the
result of a paralytic stroke. His daughter
Cassie, who was summoned from Boston,
Mass., did not arrive until the fifth.

WM. T. HARDING.

William T. Harding died at Mount
Holly, N. J., on July 27, at an advanced
age. Mr. Harding was a very entertaining writer on horticultural topics. A

---

generation ago he contributed many
interesting articles for the Gardeners'
Monthly on travels in Australia and
elsewhere. He has been living in retirement for a number of years, devoting his
time entirely to literature. He is said to
have laid out the upper part of Fairmount park, Philadelphia.

Montreal.

CLUB MEETING WELL ATTENDED. — AN
AMENDMENT TO BY-LAWS.—UNIVERSAL
QUIET STILL PREVAILS.—NOTES OF THE
LOCALITY.

The meeting of the craft on August 4
was one of the largest ever held in this
city, although but little business was
transacted. A written invitation from
Thomas Manton, president of the Canadian Horticultural Association, to the
members of the local club to attend the
convention in Toronto was received with
much pleasure, and a number of the boys
will go. The membership is steadily
increasing, and M. G. Copperthwaite, of
Outremont, was elected a member at this
meeting. John Pidduck favored the
assembly with a little essay on outdoor
flowers, after which a taxation clause
was inserted in the by-laws to the effect
that all the members be assessed pro
rata, for tributes of condolence, as provided in the by-laws.

The condition of trade is very quiet at
present. Some good asters are being cut,
although in some quarters disease is
affecting them as was the case in past
years, while in other places not a single
plant seems to suffer. The source of the
trouble is said to be the careless selection
of the seed.

P. McKenna & Son, of Cote des Neiges,
have finished their new house which is
planted with chrysanthemums and smilax. They are tearing down the old
houses, moving the barns and have
opened their new store at Guy and St.
Catherine streets.

Jos. Bennett is the only grower in this
vicinity that has a portion of his carnations planted indoors. They are doing
as well as the outdoor stock and the
neatness of his place is commendable.

S. S. Bain is erecting a double carnation
house, 40x200 feet, with iron gutters.
His American Beauty and chrysanthemum stock is looking fine.

Hall & Robinson, of Outremont, are
building two small houses of King construction. They recently shipped some
fine ferns.   G. V.

HOLYOKE, MASS.—E. D. Shaw, of E. D.
Shaw & Company, has sold out his business to Miss Georgia Humphreys, who
has been for some time in his employ.

Wholesale Flower Markets

MILWAUKEE, Aug. 6.	
Roses, Beauty, med, per doz.	1.50
" short	.75@1.00
" Liberty	4.00@ 6.00
" Bride, Bridesmaid	4.00@ 6.00
" Meteor, Golden Gate	4.00@ 6.00
" Perle	4.00@ 6.00
Carnations	1.00@ 3.00
Sweet peas	.15
Smilax	10.0@12.50
Asparagus	50.00
Gladioli	3.00@ 4.00
Asters	1.00@ 2.00

PITTSBURG, Aug. 6.	
Roses, Beauty, specials, per doz.	2.50@3.50
" extras "	1.00@2.00
" No. 1 "	.75@1.00
" No. 2 "	2.00@ 5.00
" Bride, Bridesmaid	1.00@ 6.00
" Liberty	2.00@ 6.00
" Meteor	2.00@ 4.00
" Kaiserin	2.00@ 6.00
" Liberties	2.00@ 6.00
Carnations	.50@ 1.5)
Lily of the Valley	2.00@ 4.00
Sweet peas	.20@ .40
Smilax	8.00@12.00
Adiantum	.75@ 1.25
Asparagus, strings	30.00@50.00
" Sprengeri	2.00@ 4.00
Gladioli	1.00@ 4 00
Easter lilies	8.00@12.00
Asters	.50@ 1.50

CINCINNATI, Aug. 6.	
Roses, Beauty	10.00@35.00
" Bride, Bridesmaid	2.00@ 6.00
" Liberty	3.00@ 6.
" Meteor, Golden Gate	3.00@ 6.
Carnations	1.00@ 2.
Lily of the valley	3.00@ 4.
Asparagus	
Smilax	12.50@15
Adiantum	1.00@ 1.
Gladioli	3.00@ 4.
Asters	1.00@ 2 00
Lilium Album and Rubrum	4.00

ST. LOUIS, Aug. 6.	
Roses, Beauty, long stem	—
" Beauty, medium stem	—
" Beauty, short stem	5.00@ 8.00
" Liberty	2.00@ 4.00
" Bride, Bridesmaid	2.00@ 8.00
" Golden Gate	2.00@ 8.00
Carnations	1.00@ 2.00
Smilax	12.50
Asparagus Sprengeri	1.00@ 1.50
" Plumosus	25.00@50.00
Gladioli	1.00@ 3.00
Ferns	per 1000 15)
China Asters	1.00
Tuberoses	4.00

KANSAS CITY, MO.—It has been decided
definitely that there will be no flower
show here this season, but Fred. S.
Doggett, president of the convention hall
directorate, expects to have a record
breaker next year.

INTERNATIONAL FLOWER DELIVERY.

PASSENGER STEAMSHIP MOVEMENTS.

The table herewith give the scheduled time of departure of ocean steamships carrying first-class passengers from the principal American and foreign ports, covering the space of two weeks from date of this issue of the AMERICAN FLORIST. Much disappointment often results from attempts to forward flowers for steamer delivery by express, to the care of the ship's steward or otherwise. The carriers of these packages are not infrequently refused admission on board and even those delivered on board are not always certain to reach the parties for whom they were intended. Hence florists in interior cities having orders for the delivery of flowers to passengers on out-going steamers are advised to intrust the filling of such orders to some reliable florist in the port of departure, who understands the necessary details and formalities and has the facilities for attending to it properly. For the addresses of such firms we refer our readers to the advertisements on this page:

FROM	TO	STEAMER	*LINE	DAY	DUE ABOUT
New York	Liverpool	Etruria	1	Sat. Aug. 13, 10:00 a. m.	Aug. 21
New York	"	Campania	1	Sat. Aug. 13, 9:00 p. m.	Aug. 28
New York	Glasgow	Laurentian	3	Thur. Aug. 13, 1:00 p. m.	Aug. 23
New York	"	Numidian	3	Thur. Aug. 20, 2:00 p. m.	Aug. 31
New York	Hamburg	Bluecher	3	Thur. Aug. 20, 3:00 p. m.	
New York	"	Pennsylvania	3	Sat. Aug. 22, 4:15 p. m.	Sept. 1
New York	Copenhagen	Hellig Olav	4	Wed. Aug. 19,	
New York	Glasgow	Astoria	5	Sat. Aug. 15, Noon.	
New York	"	Columbia	5	Sat. Aug. 22, 9:00 a. m.	
New York	Southampton	Marquette	6	Fri. Aug. 14, 9:00 a. m.	
New York	London	Minnetonka	6	Sat. Aug. 22, 8:00 a. m.	
New York	Liverpool	Cedric	7	Fri. Aug. 14, 9:00 a. m.	Aug. 24
New York	"	Majestic	7	Wed. Aug. 19, Noon.	
New York	"	Celtic	7	Fri. Aug. 21, 4:00 p. m.	
New York	Southampton	Philadelphia	8	Sat. Aug. 15, 10:00 a. m.	
New York	"	St. Louis	8	Wed. Aug. 19, 10:00 a. m.	
New York	Antwerp	Finland	9	Sat. Aug. 15, 10:00 a. m.	Aug. 24
New York	"	Vaderland	9	Sat. Aug. 22, 10:00 a. m.	
New York	Havre	La Champagne	10	Thur. Aug. 13, 10:00 a. m.	
New York	"	La Savoie	10	Thur. Aug. 20, 10:00 a. m.	
New York	Rotterdam	Statendam	11	Wed. Aug. 12, 10:00 a. m.	
New York	"	Ryndam	11	Wed. Aug. 19, 10:00 a. m.	Aug. 28
New York	Genoa	Lombardia	12	Tues. Aug. 11, 11:00 a. m.	
New York	"	Nord America	12	Tues. Aug. 18, 11:00 a. m.	
New York	Bremen	Kronprinz Wilh.	13	Tues. Aug. 11, 7:00 a. m.	Aug. 18
New York	"	Grosser Kurfuerst	13	Thur. Aug. 13, Noon.	Aug. 23
New York	"	Bremen	13	Sat. Aug. 20, 9:00 p. m.	Aug. 30
New York	Genoa	Lahn	13	Sat. Aug. 15, 11:00 a. m.	Aug. 27
Boston	Liverpool	Columbus	15	Thur. Aug. 20, 8:00 a. m.	
Boston	"	Mayflower	15	Sat. Aug. 15, 1:00 p. m.	Aug. 30
Boston	"	Ivernia	1	Tues. Aug. 11, 11:30 a. m.	Aug. 17
Montreal	"	Canada	15	Sat. Aug. 22, Daylight.	
Montreal	"	Cestrian	16	Sat. Aug. 15, 2:30 p. m.	
Boston	"	Devonian	16	Sat. Aug. 22, 9:00 a. m.	
San Francisco	Yokohama	Uoptic	17	Tues. Aug. 18, 1:00 p. m.	Sept. 6
San Francisco	Hongkong	Coptic	17	Tues. Aug. 18, 1:00 p. m.	Sept. 17
Vancouver	Yokohama	Empress of Japan	20	Mon. Aug. 17,	Aug. 1
Vancouver	Sidney	Aorangi	20	Fri. Aug. 21,	Sept. 16
Montreal	Glasgow	Corinthian	19	Wed. Aug. 19, Daylight.	
Montreal	Liverpool	Bavarian	19	Sat. Aug. 22, 5:00 a. m.	
San Francisco	Honolulu	Alameda	18	Wed. Aug. 12, 11:00 a. m.	
San Francisco	Tahiti	Mariposa	18	Sat. Aug. 15, 11:00 a. m.	Aug. 27
Tacoma	Yokohama	Tacoma	21	Thur. Aug. 13,	Aug. 46
Seattle	"	Kaga Maru	22	Sat. Aug. 22, a. m.	Sept. 7

*1 Cunard; 2 Allen-State; 3 Hamburg-American; 4 Scandinavian-American; 5 Anchor Line; 6 Atlantic Transport; 7 White Star; 8 American; 9 Red Star; 10 French; 11 Holland-American; 12 Italian Royal Mail; 13 North German Lloyd; 14 Fabre; 15 Dominion; 16 Leyland; 17 Occidental and Oriental; 18 Oceanic; 19 Allan; 20 Can. Pacific Ry.; 21 N. Pacific Ry.; 22 Hongkong-Seattle.

PLEASE MENTION US TO OUR ADVERTISERS.

INTERNATIONAL FLOWER DELIVERY.

STEAMSHIPS LEAVE FOREIGN PORTS.

FROM	TO	STEAMER	*LINE	DAY	DUE ABOUT
Liverpool	New York	Umbria	1	Sat. Aug. 15,	Aug. 21
Liverpool	"	Lucania	1	Sat. Aug. 22,	Aug. 26
Liverpool	"	Oceanic	7	Wed. Aug. 12, 5:00 p. m.	Aug. 19
Liverpool	"	Cymbric	7	Fri. Aug. 14, 5:00 p. m.	Aug. 30
Liverpool	"	Teutonic	7	Wed. Aug. 19, 5:00 p. m.	Aug. 26
Liverpool	"	Arabic	7	Fri. Aug. 21, 5:00 p. m.	
Liverpool	Boston	Saxonia	1	Tues. Aug. 11,	Aug. 17
Liverpool	"	Commonwealth	15	Thur. Aug. 13,	Aug. 20
Liverpool	"	New England	15	Thur. Aug. 20,	Aug. 27
Liverpool	"	Winifredian	16	Fri. Aug. 14,	
Liverpool	"	Bohemian	16	Fri. Aug. 28,	
Liverpool	Montreal	Kensington	15	Wed. Aug. 12,	
Liverpool	"	Dominion	15	Wed. Aug. 19,	
Liverpool	"	Ionian	19	Thur. Aug. 13,	
Liverpool	"	Tunisian	19	Thur. Aug. 20,	
Glasgow	New York	Ethiopia	5	Thur. Aug. 13,	
Glasgow	"	Anchoria	5	Thur. Aug. 20,	Aug. 31
Glasgow	"	Mongolia	2	Sat. Aug. 15,	Aug. 24
Genoa	"	Citta di Napoli	12	Mon. Aug. 10,	Aug. 27
Genoa	"	Liguria	12	Mon. Aug. 17,	
Southampton	"	New York	8	Sat. Aug. 15,	
Southampton	"	Philadelphia	8	Sat. Aug. 22,	
Southampton	"	Manitou	6	Wed. Aug. 12,	
London	"	Minneapolis	6	Sat. Aug. 15,	Aug. 24
London	"	Minnehaha	6	Sat. Aug. 22,	Sept. 1
Antwerp	"	Kroonland	8	Sat. Aug. 15, 2:00 p. m.	Aug. 24
Antwerp	"	Zeeland	9	Sat. Aug. 22, Noon.	Aug. 31
Hamburg	"	Auguste Victoria	3	Thur. Aug. 13,	
Hamburg	"	Moltke	3	Thur. Aug. 20,	
Hamburg	"	Pretoria	3	Sat. Aug. 22,	
Havre	"	La Bretagne	10	Sat. Aug. 15,	Aug. 23
Havre	"	La Lorraine	10	Sat. Aug. 22,	
Copenhagen	"	Oscar II	4	Wed. Aug. 12,	
Rotterdam	"	Rotterdam	11	Sat. Aug. 15,	Aug. 31
Rotterdam	"	Potsdam	11	Sat. Aug. 22,	Aug. 26
Genoa	"	Hohenzollern	13	Thur. Aug. 13,	Aug. 25
Bremen	"	K. Wil. Der Grosse	13	Tues. Aug. 18,	Aug. 25
Bremen	"	Frdk. Der Grosse	13	Sat. Aug. 22,	Aug. 25
Sidney	SanFrancisco	Sonoma	23	Mon. Aug. 17,	Sept. 7
Sidney	Vancouver	Moana	20	Mon. Aug. 10,	Sept. 3
Hongkong	"	Athenian	20	Wed. Aug. 12,	Sept. 5
Hongkong	SanFrancisco	Hongkong Maru	17	Fri. Aug. 14,	Sept. 11
Hongkong	"	China	17	Sat. Aug. 22,	Sept. 19
Hongkong	Yokohama	Iyo Maru	22	Tues. Aug. 11, p. m.	Aug. 24
Hongkong	Seattle	Iyo Maru	22	Tues. Aug. 11, p. m.	Sept. 9
Yokohama	"	Riojun Maru	22	Tues. Aug. 11, p. m.	Aug. 26

* See steamship list on opposite page.

CHRYSANTHEMUMS.

ESTELLE, (Altick)............................$1.50 per dozen; $10.00 per 100
Lady Fitzwygram, white and yellow, Lady Harriet................ 4.00 per 100
Willowbrook, Timothy Eaton and Col. Appleton................ 3.00 per 100
From 2-inch pots.

Carnation Cuttings in the New and Standard Varieties.

E. T. GRAVE,
RICHMOND, IND.

Please mention the American Florist when writing.

PRIMROSES.
Per 100
Chinese, 2-inch pots. July.....................$2.00
Obconica, Alba and Roses................... 2.00
Forbesi, "Baby"........................... 2.00
Paper White Narcissus Grandiflora, Sept. 1.. 1.00
CASH.

ASPARAGUS.
Per 100
Sprengeri, 2-inch pots, Ready August 20th..$2.00
Plumosus Nanus........................... 2.50
Pansy Seed, Non Plus Ultra, ready August
1st, per oz...............................$4.00

JOS. M. CUNNINGHAM, Delaware, O.

The F. R. WILLIAMS CO.
Wholesale Florists,
CLEVELAND, - OHIO.

When writing to any of the advertisers on this page please mention the American Florist.

THE SEED TRADE.

AMERICAN SEED TRADE ASSOCIATION.
S. F. Willard, Pres.; J. Charles McCullough, First Vice-Pres.; C. E. Kendel, Cleveland, O., Sec'y and Treas.
Twenty-second annual convention St. Louis, Mo., June, 1904.

THE sweet pea crop in California is turning out a little worse than first expected.

THE government pea seed trials at Cheboygan, Mich., were almost a complete failure.

J. R. RATEKIN & SON, of Shenandoah, Ia., are making extensive additions to their building.

RAVENNA, OHIO.—The Ford Seed Company is offering its creditors thirty per cent in its settlement.

BRANTFORD, ONT.—The American Seeding Company, of Springfield, O., will establish a factory here.

HOLLAND bulb prices, wholesale, advanced generally ten per cent during July. The most decided advance was in hyacinths.

WALLA WALLA, WASH.—A branch house of Lilly, Bogardus & Company, of Seattle, will shortly be established in Walla Walla.

JESSE E. NORTHRUP is still in the hospital with his bad leg. The ligaments were so strained that the injury was almost as bad as a broken bone.

It is reported that the Holland bulb growers are buying heavily of English grown narcissi this season on account of shortage in their own crops.

A. H. GOODWIN, of the Goodwin, Harries Company, Chicago, expects to spend Sunday, the 9th inst., with Jesse E. Northrup, at Minneapolis, Minn.

THE new rot in cabbages is active at Racine, Wis., 200 acres having been ruined. One man has lost forty acres. This disease has been described by Erwin Smith in a bulletin of the United States Department of Agriculture.

FRENCH bulb prices are slowly coming to a settlement and growers and jobbers are now closing deals. It is believed in a general way that the basis reached is ten to fifteen per cent lower than the first demands made by the growers.

VISITED CHICAGO: C. W. Crossman, Rochester, N. Y.; Howard M. Earl, with W. Atlee Burpee & Company, Philadelphia, Pa., passed through the city July 31; A. J. Brown, Grand Rapids, Mich.; Wm. Kuehn, Farmer Seed Company, Faribault, Minn.

Peas, Beans and Corn.

One of our well informed correspondents writes as follows concerning above seed crops, date August 5: "Since the middle of June the season has been fairly favorable to the growth of peas. The frost at that time cut the early varieties in northern Wisconsin from twenty to thirty per cent. Medium early promises an average crop. Late varieties not so good and much depends on the weather conditions for the next two weeks. Reports from northern Michigan indicate a full average crop. Beans have a good stand, and promise well, but the critical

season for beans has yet to come. Corn, both sweet and field, is very late. Nothing can insure even a fair crop except a warm September and belated frosts."

Nebraska Seed Crops.

The outlook for vine seeds is not very favorable. Very many crops are small and late and there is hardly a field of seasonable growth and many fields are very weedy, owing to the wet weather, preventing cultivation.
Sweet corn.—Very hard to estimate; some fields fair, others small and late. Can hardly mature without favorable weather and long delayed frosts.
Cucumber.—If the lice keep off there should be a fair crop.
Watermelon. — There will be many shortages.
Muskmelon.—Same as watermelon.
Squash.—Late sorts, same as above.

Columbus, O.

DEATH AND FUNERAL OF WELL KNOWN CEMETERY SUPERINTENDENT.—THE PAST WEEK A BUSY ONE, THERE BEING MORE THAN THE USUAL AMOUNT OF FUNERAL WORK.

The death of Adam Stephens came as a shock to us. Although he was past 78 years of age he was very robust and had only been sick one week. For over thirty years Mr. Stephens acted as superintendent of Greenlawn cemetery, which in its grandeur to-day displays the handiwork of this grand old gentleman. Mr. Stephens officiated personally at the burial of nearly every one of the 50,000 who to-day sleep in the cemetery, where he has joined them. His funeral was the largest ever held in this city, being only another evidence of the esteem in which he was held by Columbus society. He leaves three sons and two daughters to mourn his loss, Sherman F. Stephens, proprietor and manager of the Clover Hill Greenhouses, being especially well known to the trade.
The week just closed was a very busy one, as there never has been such a demand for funeral work at this season as last week and, strange to say, the supply held out remarkably well. Asters and lilies, of which there was a good supply were used in great quantities with very good effect.
                                        CARL.

SOUTHINGTON, CONN.—The heirs of the Dwight Twitchell estate have transferred to C. W. Blatchley the greenhouse property on Main street.

TURNER'S FALLS, MASS.—The Turner's Falls Company offers the town the most sightly piece of land in the town, overlooking the river valley and on the line of the electric cars, for a public park.

Florists' Stock Now in Season.

Below we give names which may suggest to the readers articles needed by them for summer use. All of these are supplied by us of the best make and closest possible prices.

GLAZING POINTS, all kinds.
HOSE, Electric, the best.
HOSE COUPLERS.
HOSE MENDERS.
INSECTICIDE, Tobacco, Extract Rose Leaf.
   " Nicoticide.
   " Nikoteen.
   " Aphis Punk.
   " Slug Shot.
MASTICA, much or little.
PLANT STAKES, Cane.
   " Galvanized.
PLANT TUBS.
PRUNERS, Knives.
   " Shears.
   " Saws.
PUTTY, Twemlow's Semi-Liquid.
PUTTY BULBS.
SPHAGNUM MOSS.
TOBACCO STEMS.

WRITE FOR ALL OUR CATALOGUES, FREE.

VAUGHAN'S PERFECTION GLAZING POINTS.

PERFECTION POINT

| SIZE 2 | SIZE 2¼ |

Per 1000......55c
Per 10000......50c

Vaughan's Rose Grower Bone Meal.

This is a special brand we have put up for our trade. It is ground fine, hence acts quickly. It is made from bone accumulated in large slaughter houses, and should not be compared with Bone Meal made from cattle heads and feet gathered on the western prairies.

ANALYSIS.—Ammonia, 4¼ to 5¼ per cent. Total phosphoric acid, 22 to 25 per cent. Total bone phosphate, 48 to 54 per cent.

☞Price F. O. B. Chicago. 100 lbs. $2.00; 500 lbs. $8.00; 1000 lbs., $15.00; 2000 lbs., $30.00.

F. O. B. New York, 100 lbs. $2.50; 500 lbs., $9.75; 1000 lbs., $18.50; 2000 lbs., $36.00.

BONE SHAVINGS.

This is a very choice article, the refuse of the best hard white bone from a knife handle factory. It is lasting and especially recommended for use in palm soil and on other plants which are not shifted very often and where a continuous and lasting supply of plant food is required. Price 5 lbs., 25c; 10 lbs., 45c; 25 lbs., $1.00; 100 lbs., $3.00.

TOBACCO DUST.

One of the best remedies for green and black, aphis, fleas, beetles, etc. 100 lbs., $2.25.

Mushroom Spawn. Fresh Importation.

FERTILE, PRODUCTIVE.
ENGLISH in bricks, per 100 lbs., $6.50 f. o. b. New York; $7.00 f. o. b. Chicago.
Write for prices on quantity.

French Bulbs.

Prices Ready.
Quality Right.
Prices Right.

"INTERNATIONAL" PANSY MIXTURE.

THE WORLD'S BEST. This is a combination of as many separate colors, types, blendings and unique kinds as can be found in the world. It has been made up and sold by us for fourteen years; it is the best general mixture in existence, and is most widely known and popular. It is used by most florists. It received the highest award at the Columbian Exposition and was awarded the gold medal at Omaha in 1898, and a medal at the Buffalo exposition. We beat the world on Pansies. Price, per oz., $10.00; ¼ oz., $5.00; ⅛ oz., $1.50; trade pkt., 50c.

"Giant Pansy Mixture."

This mixture includes the richest reds, coppers and bronzes, together with the most delicate rose and dark shadings, all the distinct colors of "Odmardesus, the splendid Cassier strain with its delicate veinings. We have spared no expense to secure the newest, richest and finest sorts. Price, ¾ lb., $14.00; oz., $4.00; 60c; trade pkt., 25c.

"International" Primula Mixture.

Unquestionably the best mixture of Chinese Primroses. It contains the largest variety of the best selling colors. Flowers large, beautifully fringed, borne in large clusters well above the rich green leaves. Pkt., (250 seeds), 50c; 5 pkts., $2.00.

THE "ASMUS" MIGNONETTE.

This seed is saved from selected plants and in the greenhouse only. There is to our knowledge no seed in the market of a strain of Mignonette that compares with the "Asmus." Large pkt. (about 800 seeds), 50c; ¼ oz. (about 5,000 seeds), $3.00. Full cultural instructions furnished with each package.

Ten per cent discount on flower seed orders amounting to $3.00 and over for Cash with Order.
Send for our Mid-Summer List of Pansy Seed in separate colors and complete list of Hardy Perennials.

ROSES

	2½-inch Per 100	3-½-inch Per 100
Ivory		$10.00
Bride	$8.50	8.00
Bridesmaid	3.50	8.00
Golden Gate	3.5¼	8.00
Meteor	3.50	
Souvenir de Pierre Notting	8.00	12.00

HARRISII.

Our stock now being shipped has been grown, rogued, and packed by one firm of Bermuda growers, whose entire output we control. It is as clean stock as can be found on the island and is uniform in type and grading. Order now. Our grades are 5 to 7, 6 to 7, 7 to 9, 9 to 11 and 11 to 13.

Special Harrisii (Dooli)
Size 6 to 7-inch.

This type is one of the cleanest and truest to type of all the Bermuda Lilies. It is a little later than true Harrisii but makes up in healthiness. We can make a very special price on select 6 to 7-inch bulbs of these of $4.00 per 100; $33.50 per 1000. They will pay a big profit on the investment.

Bermuda Freesias.
This is the purest strain of White Flowered Freesias in existence. Ready.

	Per 100	Per 1000
CHOICE	$ .85	$7.50

Oxalis Buttercup.

	Per 100	Per 1000
MAMMOTH	$1.00	$9.90
STRONG	.85	7.50

EXTRA STRONG STOCK.

	2½-inch Per 100	3½-inch Per 100
		$5.00
Franz Deegen	$5.00	$10.00
Pres. Carnot		8.00
Perle des Jardins	4.00	14.00
American Beauty	7.00	
Hermosa	3.00	
Clothilde Soupert, strong, 3-in.	5.00	

	Per 100
ASPARAGUS PLUMOSUS SEEDLINGS	$2.00
" 2-inch, strong	3.00
FERNS, assorted for Fern Dishes	4.00
SMILAX, 2-inch, strong	3.00

Chicago. Vaughan's Seed Store, New York.

THE NURSERY TRADE.

AM. ASSOCIATION OF NURSERYMEN.
N. W. HALE, Knoxville, Tenn., Pres.; FRANK
A. WEBER, St. Louis, Mo., Vice-Pres.; GEORGE C.
SEAGER, Rochester, N. Y., Sec'y.
Twenty-ninth annual convention, Atlanta, Ga.,
June, 1904.

TOPEKA, KAN.—The city park was
damaged to the extent of about $300 by
the recent flood.

OWATONNA, MINN—The Clinton Falls
Nursery Company has been incorporated
with a capital stock of $100,000.

PROF. JOHN CRAIG has succeeded Prof.
L. H. Bailey as head of the horticultural
department of Cornell University, Ithaca,
N. Y.

NORTH ABINGTON, MASS. — Wm. H.
Record, nurseryman, has filed a bankruptcy petition, liabilities $2741.46,
assets $103.50.

NEWPORT, R. I.—The beautiful villa
and grounds known as Stone Acre, on
Bellevue avenue, has been purchased by
Edward R. Thomas, of New York.

HARTFORD, CONN.—The trees in Bushnell park have all been labelled recently
under the supervision of Superintendent
Wirth. The common as well as the
botanical names are given.

NEW HAVEN, CONN.—A nursery of considerable extent is in operation at East
Rock park under the direction of Superintendent Amrhyn and contains a fine
stock of ornamental shrubbery and trees.

BRUNSWICK, ME.—The gale which prevailed on Monday, July 27, damaged
many of the handsome shade trees which
abound here. Large limbs were torn
from street trees and several of the famous
college pines were blown down.

CARTHAGE, MO.—John C. Teas recently
received a letter from his old employe, B.
F. Mahorney, who was arrested here two
weeks ago on a charge of fraud supposed
to have been perpetrated in Oklahoma,

which says that he easily cleared himself
of the charge and will soon be back here
to his work.

SPRINGFIELD, MASS. — City Forester
Gale states that the elm-leaf beetle has
been unusually destructive this year in
Springfield, especially in territory which
has not been sprayed in the past.

AMHERST, MASS.—George A. Drew has
resigned his position as superintendent
of the horticultural department at the
agricultural college to take the management of the Convers farm at Greenwich,
Conn.

Cincinnati.

FUNERAL WORK THE MAIN FEATURE AT
THIS TIME.—GOOD WRITE ASTERS MOVE
READILY.—GLADIOLI A GLUT.—NOTES.

Funeral work during the past week
has been keeping the boys fairly busy and
white flowers of all kinds were in good
demand. Good white asters bring about
$2 per hundred, while pink, purple and
lavender are not moving very well. The
majority of the carnations coming into
this market are small and about $1 per
hundred is the price obtained for them.
Dark colored gladioli are a glut on the
market, the light colored moving a little
better at $2 and $3 per hundred.

The Ohio Cut Flower Company, which
occupied quarters at Third and Main
streets, has removed to 129 East Third
street.

Albert Sunderbruch, of J. M. McCullough's Sons, is on a month's vacation.
He will take in the Milwaukee convention.

Thomas Windrum has torn down one
of his small houses and is erecting three
new houses 22x150 feet.

Clarence J. Ohmer, of E. G. Gillett's, is
spending a two weeks' vacation at his
old home in Dayton, O.   ALEX.

OIL CITY, PA.—Fred. C. Crane is building three 140-foot houses of Dietsch
short-roof construction. Mr. Crane was
formerly with W. M. Deyoe, of this place.

PANSY FIELD OF PETER BROWN, LANCASTER, PA.

OUR PASTIMES.

S. A. F. COMMITTEE ON SPORTS.
P. J. Hauswirth, 237 Michigan avenue, Chicago;
C. C. Pollworth and F. Schmeling, Milwaukee.
Announcements of coming contests or other
events of interests to our bowling, shooting and
sporting readers are solicited and will be given
place in this column.
Address all correspondence for this department
to Wm. J. Stewart, 79 Milk St., Boston, Mass.;
Robt. Kift, 1725 Chestnut St., Philadelphia, Pa.;
or to the American Florist Co., 324 Dearborn St.,
Chicago, Ill.

At Chicago.

The scores for the practice game on
Tuesday, August 4, were as follows:

Player	1st	2d	3d	4th	T'l
G. Stollery	136	130	145	112	523
F. Stollery	135	130	158	202	630
Lambros	144	123	163	119	549
W. Kreitling	104	145	80	156	483
Balluff	154	145	169	189	657
Asmus	189	166	145	175	635
Winterson	135	135	184	128	582
Sterrett	120	194	149	148	611
Hauswirth	147	191	167	503	

At Natick, Mass.

On Saturday, August 1, the Waban
Rose Conservatory base ball club, in
defeating the Boston Flower Market
team by a score of 14 to 3, obtained
revenge for its defeat at the hands of
the latter earlier in the season. The visitors were unable to connect at critical
moments with the speedy delivery of R.
Montgomery, who as usual had a long
line of strikeouts to his credit. He
received excellent support from Casey, a
new man behind the bat for the home
team, and Gallagher, who held down
second base, also covered himself with
glory. The batting of the Wabans was
much improved compared with their
efforts in former games. For the Boston
team, Lane, who had been knocked out
of the box by the Waban boys, redeemed
himself by putting up a good exhibition
of fielding in the left garden, while the
heavy hitting of Malloy, the second base-
man, was a terror to the spectators.
Another game has been arranged for
August 15, when it is expected that both
teams will be prepared to fight to a
finish.

Cricket at Philadelphia.

A cricket match between eleven selected
from the Florists' Club of Philadelphia
and the employes of John G. Gardner, of
the Montgomery Nurseries, was played
at Villa Nova on Saturday, August 1,
resulting in a victory for the home eleven
with five wickets to spare. The features
of the game were the brilliant batting of
Mr. Gardner for the Montgomery side
and the bowling of S. B. Lohman for the
florists. C. H. Eimerman, the crack
bowler of the florists' club, made a grand
stand finish in the second inning and a
sensational catch in the first. If all had
done as well for their side the Montgom-
eries would not have had such an easy
thing of it. Edward Campbell and William K. Harris acted as umpires and
their decisions were something scandal-
ous, some of them being enough to turn
a person's hair. After the match a colla-
tion was served to the visitors on the
lawn under the able superintendence of
Mrs. Gardner and Miss Ethel Gardner.
The Montgomery fife and drum corps
made things lively after the moon rose
and a most enjoyable evening was spent.
It was ten of the clock before the last
guest had departed and all went home
with a feeling of gratitude to their kind
entertainers. The return match will be
played on the grounds of the Florists'

BILLIARD ROOM AT THE OLYMPIA BOWLING ALLEYS, MILWAUKEE.

Gun Club at Wissinoming, on Saturday,
August 8.   G. C. W.

Convention Bowling Prizes.

We are advised that the following prizes
have been offered in bowling and other
contests; complete list next week.
Milwaukee Florists' Club, six gold
medals for members of winning team.
C. C. Pollworth Company, Milwaukee,
six scarf pins for members of second team;
and gold medal to florist coming the
greatest distance.
John A. Evans, Quaker City Machine
Works, Richmond, Ind., $10 gold medal.
John F. Wilcox, Council Bluffs, Ia.,
$10 umbrella.
Prizes are also offered by Milwaukee
Citizens' Business League; F. Pollworth
& Brother, Milwaukee; Henry Weber,
park commissioner, Milwaukee; Brunswick-Balke Company, Chicago.
E. F. Winterson Company, Chicago,
silver cup for highest individual total in
three games.
W. P. Mussey, Chicago, $25 gold
badge for best individual bowler, under
special regulations.

With Philadelphia Gunners.

The two tie scores of Huttenlock and
Anderson were the features of the semi-
monthly target shoot of the Philadelphia
Florists' Gun Club at Wissinoming, July
28. While the field was small the competition for the special prize offered by
the club was keen. Both Anderson and
Huttenlock outdistanced the rest of the
shooters, and at the termination of the
fifty targets they stood on even footing,
with a total score of fifty-six. Anderson
made the best actual score of the two,
with forty-nine breaks out of fifty, while
Huttenlock broke forty-four out of fifty.
The club has arranged an elaborate
programme to be shot on its grounds at
Wissinoming on Saturday, August 8.
This shoot is practically a preliminary
test for the open amateur tournament
which will be shot on September 30 and
October 1 and 2. The conditions for
August 8 are 100 targets, speed handicap, sweepstake, entrance $5, targets
$1.50.

Hartford, Conn.

No better evidence of the destructive
power of hail can be seen than the condition of the greenhouses in this city and
the suburbs following the storm last
week. Charles K. Swenson estimates
his damage at $1,000, nearly all the
glass in the roofs of his greenhouses
being shattered. J. Coombes estimates
that $200 will cover the damage to their
greenhouse on Benton street, where
about 300 panes of glass were broken.
H. Palmer, in West Hartford had nearly
every pane of glass in his houses broken
and A. Whiting, on Whiting lane, will
require seventy-five to 100 boxes of glass
to put his greenhouses in good repair.
Two hundred to 300 lights of glass were
smashed in the new houses and the old
houses were completely riddled. No
damage was done to either George
Osborne's houses at Atwood and Ser-
geant streets or to those belonging to
Drake & Carlson at Bushnell and Otis
streets, the Campfield greenhouses.
These are built of small panes of heavy
glass, which resisted the impact of the
blocks of hail.

Boise, Idaho.

Business in this vicinity is extremely
dull just now but there was an excellent
demand for roses and carnations during
the season. We use the irrigation system
here and the growing of flowers is merely
a matter of planting the seed, turning
the water into the furrows and nature
does the rest.
Wm. Bayhouse is engaged in erecting a
six-span ridge and furrow house, each
span measuring 15x115 feet, which is
now about ready for piping. A Carmody
boiler and hot water heating system will
be used. In addition to the new building, the firm has two houses measuring
28x80 feet.
The Boise Floral Company is erecting
a five-span ridge and furrow house which
will be heated by hot water. Two of the
spans have been completed, are now
under glass and have been planted with
roses.
                                    W. B.

St. Paul.

A VISIT TO LAKEVILLE.—TRADE HOLDS FAIR IN 'SPITE OF HOT WEATHER.— GROWERS ATTEND TO PLANTING AND REPAIRING.—BAD HAIL STORM VISITS CITY.—FLORISTS' PICNIC TO BE HELD AT WILDWOOD.—SOME BIRTHS IN THE TRADE. —NOTES.

Quite a severe wind and hail storm visited this section shortly after midnight July 27. R. C. Seeger, the principal sufferer, lost about 1,000 square feet of glass, while Keiper & Powles' place was also struck quite heavily. Mr. Seeger had hail insurance, but Keiper & Powles had none. Carl Peterson's place in the same section escaped damage. Trees and shrubbery were demolished in different parts of the city.

H. L. Pattbey, manager of the Minneapolis sweet pea show, is very hopeful for a successful exhibit. The prizes are open to amateurs only, but any florists having anything nice for exhibition in either annuals or perennials will be accorded space and duly credited with what they send. All contributions should be sent by express prepaid to Mr. Patthey at the Dayton building, 710 Nicollet avenue, Minneapolis.

There will be quite a delegation to the convention when they are all rounded up. C. C. Pollworth of Milwaukee, made us a hurried call last week. He was brim full of convention enthusiasm and has infused some of it into St. Paul and Minneapolis florists, so that a good attendance may be expected from the North Star state.

Trade has kept up fairly well, notwithstanding the heat and the dull season in floral lines. Roses and carnations have been scarce with stock of all grades from poorest to best. Sweet peas have been quite scarce but are plentiful now, the wholesale price being $1.50 per 1000. The growers are all busy planting and repairing.

Gust. Colberg, the genial clerk in L. L. May & Company's retail store, smiles blandly and tells everyone it was a 10½-pound boy. Frank Gustafson, of the same firm, is rejoicing over the arrival of a girl a few weeks since.

The St. Paul florists will picnic at Wildwood, on White Bear Lake, Wednesday, August 5. A full programme of sports has been arranged and everybody is expected to be present.

L. L. May & Company are making some much needed repairs to their oldest range and repainting their entire plant.

Recent rains have helped out all vegetation and some of the growers will be benching carnations this week.

Aug. S. Swanson is a perennial builder, his latest addition consisting of a nice large rose house.

Christ Hansen is cutting some choice long stemmed Liberty roses from old plants.

L. L. May & Company are bringing in some beautiful perennials from their nurseries.

Holm & Olson are building a new plant house.

Visitors: H. E. Philpott, of Winnipeg, with his perennial smile; Mr. Creighton, representing H. A. Dreer; E. G. Hill, of Richmond, Ind., who never grows old, dropped in some time ago.   FELIX.

DANVILLE, PA.—Hitchings & Company are about to erect a capacious curvilinear palm house for John R. Bennett. Lawrence Cotter, formerly of Boston, is now in charge of this place and under his skillful management great things are expected of it.

MILWAUKEE GROWERS' ESTABLISHMENTS.

1. N. Zweifel.   2. Benj. Gregory.   J. C. Howard.   4. Aug. Burmeister & Co.   5. Frank P. Dilger.   6. Heitman & Baerman.   7. Currie Bros.
8. A. F. Kaiser.   9. Chas. Zepnick.   10. Otto Tietbohl.   11. Hans Bartels.

Lowell, Mass.

A FATAL EXPLOSION PROVIDES MUCH FUNERAL WORK.—STOCK ON HAND OF INFERIOR QUALITY.—NEWS.

The last week of July was a busy one with funeral work, greatly due te a sad accident in which twenty people were killed through the explosion of some powder magazines. Although numerous panes of plate glass were broken by the explosion, all the greenhouses escaped uninjured, strange as it may seem.

There is a great deal of inferior stock on hand, although good asters are beginning to appear. The rose supply has practically gone to pieces and what Brides and Bridesmaids there are present a rusty appearance.

John Gale, of Tewksbury, who is connected with Patten, surprised everybody by taking a vacation and at the same time getting married.

Geo. W. Patten and wife left recently for a month's vacation among the Green Mountains of Vermont.

Geo. A. Sanders, of Patten's, has returned home after spending a vacation at Newport.

Visitors: Geo. E. Buxton, and Rudolph Gaedeke, Nashua, N. H.; Walter Morse with J. W. Howard, Somerville, Mass.
A. M.

VIOLETS

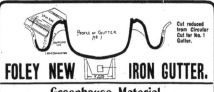

Saratoga Springs, N. Y.

Saratoga will have no floral fete this year, this decision being arrived at during a session of the committee last week. The reasons given are lack of interest on the part of those who in past years labored for its success, together with the lateness of the season. In past years the floral fete, held during the first week of September, brought large numbers of people from surrounding places to view the pageant. It may be resumed after this year.   R. D.

DEERFIELD, N. Y.—A clam bake and picnic at Buchanan's Grove is to be held by the florists on August 12.

NEW HAVEN, CONN.—Edward J. Morse has purchased sixteen acres of land on Townsend avenue from Henry Burg, of Morristown, N. J.

BARGAINS
For Greenhousemen.

Boiler Tubes.

In good condition. We have been selling them for many years past to greenhouse men. They are economical and practical, and make a first-class pipe line. We clean and paint them. We furnish without additional charge sleeve or jacket couplings; also oakum and cement to make tight joints. They are in straight, long lengths. Note our prices:

2-inch, per foot	4c
2¼-inch, per foot	5c
3½-inch, "	9c
4-inch, per foot	11a
6-inch, "	21c

Pipes.

Our stock of good standard black second-hand pipe with guaranteed threads and couplings as follows:

100,000 ft. 1-inch, per foot	3½c
200,000 ft. 1¼-inch, "	4½c
50,000 ft. 2-inch, "	7½c
200,000 ft. 2½-inch, "	10 c
50,000 ft. 1-inch, extra heavy, per foot	4 c
55,000 ft. 1¼-inch, "	5½c

Radiation.

100,000 ft. second-hand, cast iron radiation, per foot...........................18c.
200,000 ft. second-hand, wrought iron radiation, per foot........................18c.
Also valves, heaters and all necessary apparatus.

Roofing Glass.

16-inch, thick ribbed roofing glass from the Pan-American Exposition Buildings. Per square foot 5c.

Valves.

250 iron body, brass trimmed, Gate, Check, Globe and Angle valves, ranging in sizes from 1 to 16 inches. They are second-hand, overhauled and in first-class condition. Write us your wants. Also all kinds of fittings.

Boilers.

Over 350 good boilers in stock. Can furnish anything you may require in the line.

Hot Bed Sash.

Several jobs to offer. Write us your wants.

Hose.

All kinds of garden and water-conducting hose for sale at low prices.

WRITE FOR OUR CATALOGUE NO. 47.

We handle building material, plumbing material, hardware and stocks of every kind.

Chicago House Wrecking Co,
WEST 35th & IRON STS.,
CHICAGO, ILL.

Always mention the AMERICAN FLORIST
when writing to advertisers.

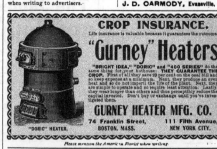

THE AMERICAN FLORIST

A WEEKLY JOURNAL FOR THE TRADE

America is "the Prow of the Vessel; there may be more comfort Amidships, but we are the first to touch Unknown Seas."

Vol. XXI.　　　　CHICAGO AND NEW YORK, AUGUST 15, 1903.　　　　No. 793.

THE AMERICAN FLORIST

NINETEENTH YEAR.

Copyright 1903, by American Florist Company
Entered as Second-Class Mail Matter.

PUBLISHED EVERY SATURDAY BY

AMERICAN FLORIST COMPANY,
324 Dearborn St., Chicago.
Eastern Office: 79 Milk St., Boston.

Subscription, $1.00 a year.　To Europe, $2 00.
Subscriptions accepted only from the trade.
Volumes half-yearly from August, 1901.

SOCIETY OF AMERICAN FLORISTS AND
ORNAMENTAL HORTICULTURISTS.

OFFICERS—JOHN BURTON, Philadelphia, Pa.,
president; C. C. POLLWORTH, Milwaukee, Wis.,
vice-president; WM. J. STEWART, 79 Milk Street,
Boston, Mass., secretary; H. B. BEATTY, Oil City,
Pa., treasurer.
Nineteenth annual meeting at Milwaukee, Wis.,
August 18-21, 1903.

Convention Pointers.

If you have occasion to enquire your way to the convention headquarters enquire for "the Exposition Building," that is the name of building. The distance is but a few blocks from most of the hotels, but if you wish to take a street car, the one labeled "State Street" is the one which passes the north end of building.

Secretary Stewart's headquarters are in the Exhibition building, near the entrance.

There will be a spacious passage across the main floor to a large room at west side of building selected for auditorium where the business sessions of the convention are to be held. South of this are the two toilet rooms.

The southwest corner room is a restaurant. Refreshments can be had without leaving the building.

TUESDAY EVENING.

President Burton's reception will take place in auditorium. As you enter take stairs to balcony. This is a large promenade entirely around the trade exhibit, affording you a view of everything that may be going on. The reception will take place at south end.

This trade exhibit is the largest and the greatest floor space of any convention on record. The view from this balcony will interest you.

The writing room of Milwaukee Florist Club will be near the restaurant.

The AMERICAN FLORIST will be at the Plankinton and in Exhibition Building.

• Forcing Lilacs in France. •

Lilac Forcing.

PART I.

The lilac (Syringa vulgaris) was introduced to western Europe from Turkey about the middle of the XVI century. Botanists are widely at variance regarding its native habitat, which is not known with any degree of certainty. Most of the old authors, including Linnæus, mention it as being a native of Persia or western Asia, which is, however, considered as inaccurate. In late years the plant was found, by several botanists, to occur wild in the mountainous regions of Central Europe. Hungaria, Servia and the Balkan Hills and the prevailing belief, strengthened by these discoveries, is now that it may be of European origin.

The lilac is one of the noblest shrubs and is represented in every garden, however uninteresting it may be. It is, however, not as a garden shrub that the plant interests us in the present notes, but as the most favorite and most popular of our forcing plants. It has been said by one of our authorities that the forced lilac is of such paramount importance to the Parisian florist trade that were our florists deprived during winter of its delicate, white trusses, so profusely used at that time in the composition of wreaths, bouquets and sprays, it would be very hard, if not impossible, to find a substitute for them.

From October until the flowering season of the open air lilac, and even later, immense quantities of forced lilac trusses are brought every morning to the Central Market, Paris, the trade in which amounts to several millions of francs a year. The forcing requires pretty close attention, constant vigilance and some skill which is the outcome of practical experience. Each forcer claims to have little knacks only known to him; they are in most cases of small importance, but may account for the difficulty encountered in getting admittance to the forcing houses of some of our large forcers. If the French forcers rank first in the production of fine flower spikes so much prized on all the European flower markets, it is due to several causes, and particularly to their extended experience. It is now about a century since Mathiew, a grower at Belleville, a section now prom-

inent as a residence district for working men of Paris, but which had been for some time the home of the lilac, commenced the forcing of this plant.

Lilac growers. The center of the production of the plants used for forcing is in 1903, Vitry-sur-Seine, near Paris, and in that place alone some 600 to 700 acres of land, producing about 12,000 plants per acre, are devoted to growing lilacs. The plants not being ready for forcing until five to seven years old, we may reckon that about one-fifth or 125 acres furnishing one and a half million of plants are worked upon every year. Prominent among the growers is Mr. Abel Chatenay, Vitry, the sympathetic secretary of the French National Horticultural Society, whose family from father to son has been growing lilacs for upwards of a century; they have materially aided us in illustrating the present notes.

The soil about Vitry, aided by our Parisian climate, seems better suited to the formation of the flower buds of the lilacs grown for forcing, than those of any other section. Forcers consider that if a plant gives, for example, fifteen buds when grown by our good growers at Vitry, it is liable to produce only from five to ten flowers when grown in other parts of the country.

The plants thrive under the best conditions for forcing, when rather dry weather prevails at the time of the formation of the buds in the fields; a month of June with too much rain is often conducive to the production of leaves instead of buds. This accounts to some extent for the fact that in some seasons less than half the flower buds will open, while in others, like last year, fully nine-tenths will throw the desired white trusses. To obtain best results in the forcing house, it is highly essential that the plants should be pruned in the fields, by the growers early enough in the summer to prevent growth of suckers at the expense of flower buds. Careful growers, therefore, cut off, before the end of June, not only all the suckers on the plants, but also the spray growth and all branches or shoots not likely, to produce good flower buds.

Lilac Forcers. There are about a score of forcers around Paris, located principally at Montrouge, Montreuil, Belleville and Vitry and utilising some 350 glass houses or other structures. Some of these forcers use little less than 100,000 plants in improved houses—while others do not force more than 25,000 to 30,000 plants a year in rudimentary structures. We do not take into account the horticulturist or market gardener who occasionally forces lilacs during winter in their heated frames or sashes.

As is well known, it is the colored lilac named Marly which is the best and most generally used by the Parisian forcers for cut flowers, whether the flowers are to come white or colored. The Marly lilac is the most vigorous kind, forces readily and yields slender, light, graceful, white panicles, which, when produced by our best forcers, are unsurpassed. The plants are dug from the fields in the fall, delivered by the growers to the forcers with a

Lilac Flowers Ready for Market.

ball of earth and with the flower buds well set and ripened but in an acquiescent state.

Before taking them into the forcing house, the forcer allows the plants a period of rest in which the flower buds are made to suffer from thirst. To that effect he places the plants in a covered, dry shade without watering them for about two weeks. At the end of that time the balls are quite dry and ready to undergo the process of forcing. The resting period is the keystone of success.

Once in the forcing house, the plants are covered with about four inches of soil, which will as much contribute to keep them erect as to retain moisture and are given a good soaking. The light is then obstructed by covering the glass with straw mats, all apertures are hermetically shut and the heat, during the first five days rises to about 75° Fahr. At least three, but better four or five syringings should be given daily, using water of the same temperature as the atmosphere in the houses. Moisture and heat being the chief aids to success, one need not be afraid of watering the pipes

to create evaporation. Towards the second or third day vegetation starts, the scales of the buds widen to give passage to the tip of the panicle. At the end of the first week, the sap is on full circulation and the inflorescences from one-half to nearly an inch long. The heat is then increased to 77°–86° Fahr. during the day, with about 9° Fahr. lower at night and the syringings are only applied to the stems or shoots and not to the trusses, which otherwise are liable to blacken or rot. It sometimes happens that a house is spoiled by improper watering. It is also necessary to pinch the superfluous leaf shoots which might hinder the development of the panicles. The flowering shoots being often terminated by three buds, the middle one is usually removed in order to make room and improve the two other buds; should the branches or shoots carry several flowering shoots the two upper ones, which are usually the largest, are retained, or in case the two upper buds are not the best, they might be cut back to the two lower, finer ones. At the end of the second week, when the panicles are fully developed and the lower florets begin to unfold, partial light should be let in for a couple of hours daily by uncovering slightly from the forcing house which, up to that time, has been kept dark. The light hardens off the etiolated, apparently faded panicles and makes them stronger, weather permitting a little air might also be given to ensure better keeping qualities. Should it perchance happen that the panicles instead of being entirely white take on some pinkish spots, cover and shut the house immediately to prevent the access of the light and air, raise the heat to 95° or even 105° Fahr. and syringe abundantly the flowers and the pipes.

The cost and expense of forcing a lilac plant averages thirty to forty cents, and the returns from forty to fifty.

Cutting. Under proper treatment the first panicles are ready to be cut in fifteen days and the last on the eighteenth or twentieth day. They may be cut at any time of the day, but better in the afternoon, keeping them during night in cold water in a cool room from which frost is excluded. Thus prepared, the panicles are said to be more enduring and keep

well for five or six days. The finest panicles are cut with a stem from two to three feet long; eight or ten of them fastened together, some leaf shoots passed around and sold, according to the market value, at from $1.30 to $2. The medium and small panicles are cut with a stem from twelve to fifteen inches long, and the way in which a large bunch is made up with only eight of these panicles is an example of Parisian ingenuity. The procedure is as follows: A handful of straw is folded in the form of a mushroom coming out as illustrated. For hiding the straw and part of the stems some lilac leaf shoots or a fringe of ivy or box sprays are fastened around, thus providing a large but loose appearing bunch. The retail price of a medium-sized bunch varies from forty to sixty cents. It is about "All Saints'" day, Christmas and New Year that lilac flowers bring the highest prices.

Period of Forcing. Some years ago forcing was only practiced during eight or nine months, from September to April, but now it is done the whole twelve months. Our florists shopmen prefer the forced lilac, which is a better white and better suited for fine bouquet work to the open air grown and always pay a better price for it. Our large forcers now succeed by various methods and especially the "retarding process," in supplying bloom during May, june and even July. The skill of some of the forcers has, in some cases even enabled them to show us in August forced trusses grown from the flower-buds developed in the same year, which means an advance of nine months over the open air lilac. The methods used vary with the forcers and according to the object to be attained.

Mr. Crousse, the well-known nurseryman of Nancy, staged a few years ago, in the middle of May, some splendid white trusses from the colored Marly lilac which were much admired. According to the Revue Horticole, the trusses were obtained by the following procedure: After trimming up the plants as if they had to undergo the ordinary forcing, Mr. Crousse dug them up in November—December with an earthball, leaving them after digging in the open ground.

PARISIAN.

DORMANT LILAC PLANTS IN STORAGE SHED.

FORCED LILAC, POT GROWN FOR EXHIBITION.

Sweet Pea Society of England.

One of the latest organizations established in London for the development of a particular class of flower is the National Sweet Pea Society. This was founded about three years ago and has just held its annual exhibition at Earls Court. This was in many ways a great improvement on the Royal Aquarium, where horticultural shows of all kinds had been held until the Aquarium was purchased by the Wesleyan community. The exhibition this year was quite up to the standard of its predecessors and appeared to much better advantage as it could be all seen at once. Notwithstanding the wretched season, the blossoms were of first rate quality taken all around. Most of the older varieties were of course in evidence, and represented all the well known shades, varying from pure white to the deepest maroon, through pale and deep rose to salmon and lilac to heliotrope and purple.

Although the sweet pea is an abundant bloomer still it is difficult to find a variety that shows a tendency to produce more than three blossoms on a spray. There are any number of varieties having two flowers and a fairly large number with three, but those with four or five are few and far between. If it were only possible to obtain as many blossoms on the annual varieties as it is on such a fine perennial as Lathyrus latifolius albus grandiflorus, which was shown by Hobbies of Dereham, it would indeed be a triumph to be proud of. Amongst the white varieties the honors were divided among Sadie Burpee and a new form called Dorothy Eckford, the last-named being, if anything, the better of the two.

New Rose Urania.

Salopian and Mars were the best of the crimsons, and Lord Roseberry the finest of the rose and crimson class.

There is not a really good first-class yellow sweet pea in cultivation, but the one nearest approaching this honor is the Hon. Mrs. E. Kenyon. A variety called Lovely is well named, as it is a really lovely rich pink. Lady Grisel Hamilton (lavender), Black Knight and Boreatton (maroon), Coccinea (cerise) Miss Willmott (orange-scarlet), and America (flaked), all attracted universal attention. But the finest variety in the show was undoubtedly the new one called Scarlet Gem. The flowers were of a brilliant scarlet crimson without any tinge of mauve so often seen in such colors. Close upon this variety came another called King Edward VII., which was very fine but had a tinge of mauve in the blossoms. It should be mentioned that Scarlet Gem was awarded a silver medal and a first-class certificate, the latter honor also going to King Edward VII. These two varieties stood out so distinctly from all the others that it is but their due to receive special mention. If there should be a good crop this year, both kinds will be put into commerce next year, so that they will have a chance of being proved in many gardens at the same time. W.

New Rose Urania.

This new rose, which is shown in the accompanying illustration, is one of the productions of M. H. Walsh of Woods Holl, Mass. A seedling of American Beauty crossed with Mlle. Susanna Marie Rodocanachi, it has all the good characteristics of the American Beauty except ing the strong characteristic fragrance, and is of a lighter and much more glowing color. The foliage is heavy and waxy.

Florists' Plant Notes.

PERENNIALS.

It is a good time now to sow the seed of various hardy perennials, such as hollyhocks, aquilegia, gaillardia, coreopsis and others. One of the most beautiful of the aquilegias, a variety not known so well nor grown as extensively as it should be, is the Rocky Mountain columbine, or Aquilegia cœrulea, a pale violet and white variety. Sow the seed in flats and when the plants are large enough to handle transplant them a couple of inches apart in cold frames, and cover with sash during the winter. In early spring, as soon as the ground is dry enough to be worked, transplant them into the border or the garden. Sown now, most of the varieties will bloom the following season.

CALLAS.

Callas which are now resting out of doors should have the old soil shaken out and started into growth again in the same size pot, as soon as possible. They require very rich soil, and for the first few weeks after repotting may be left outside, where copious waterings and frequent syringings are necessary. Before the first frost move them into the greenhouse; they will thrive in places where it is difficult to grow anything else, although they are quick to respond to better treatment. They will do well in a temperature of 55° at night, with no shading on the glass until spring.

If extra flowers are wanted, they can be planted out on benches in very rich soil, allowing about eighteen inches of space between the plants. Solid beds are not desirable because the plants run to foliage too much; in fact, we prefer to grow them in pots the year round, being more easily handled with equally good results. Heavy feeding with liquid manure is necessary after the pots are filled with roots. If any young plants were planted out of doors in a frame and grown along all summer, they should now be carefully lifted without disturbing the roots too much, and given six or seven-inch pots as required. Keep them lightly shaded and well syringed for a few days and they will soon become established in their new quarters.

PANSIES.

It is now time to sow the seed of pansies for next spring's sales. Get the best seed, and if the seed has been raised on the place from strains of your own selection, so much the better; otherwise, get the best the market affords. A good mixture may be all right for the average florist, but it is also good policy to sow separate colors, especially the giant yellow and Lord Beaconsfield. Use good soil to which plenty of old hotbed manure has been added in which to sow the seed. Sow in drills, covering the seed a quarter of an inch, and cover the frame with sash. Until the seed has germinated, keep the sash lightly shaded, but as soon as the seed is up, remove the sash entirely and give the plants the benefit of all the light and air possible. About the middle of September, as soon as the plants are large enough to handle, transplant them into cold frames, placing them four inches apart, and using rich soil in which to grow them. No protection is required from the elements until winter sets in, about the first of December. After that time they should be covered with sash, although we have wintered them successfully without protection of any kind. It is best to be on the safe side, however,

and protect them from extremely cold weather with sash or an inch or two of straw.

These early sown plants will come into bloom much earlier than those sown inside later in the season, and will make stronger and sturdier specimens. If any are desired for cutting during the winter, sow them at once, and when of sufficient size transplant them to a bench in the greenhouse, using rich but not too heavy soil. Give them a light place and plenty of water and ventilation. A temperature of 45° to 50° at night suits them, and to increase the size of the flowers feed with liquid manure when the buds are set.   G.

BALTIMORE.—A steel greenhouse is nearing completion in Riverside park, South Baltimore, under the direction of J. Frederick Wessier, superintendent of parks in the southern district, which it is thought will be finished in about a month at a cost of $3,000.

SNOWBALL IN BLOOM IN FORCING HOUSE (AT VITRY.)

Palms and Ferns.

SHADING.

As the summer wears away so should the shading on the palm and fern houses, and it is good practice to allow the shading to become thin on the east sides of the houses by the end of August or beginning of September. But from the fact that September frequently gives us some very warm days, it is not wise to have too thin a shade on the west side of a palm house at that season, the plants being mostly in a well-rooted condition by that time, and liable to get just a little off color when exposed to too much sunshine. Such a condition will do no harm to the plants that are to be used for decorating, in fact it will make them more tough in texture and give the foliage more endurance under adverse conditions, but the retail buyer does not fully understand these fine points, and demands only dark colored areas and other palms of deepest hue, the explanation that Areca lutescens gets its specific name from its yellow stems being non-persuasive in most instances, while the plant with green stems and dark foliage,

even though over-sappy, is the one that will be chosen in nine cases out of ten. Of course a kentia should be deep colored in the foliage, and to display such a color does not argue that the plant is soft and sappy, as may be the case with the areca.

Judging from the location on their native island at which the three so-called kentias are found, one would infer that Kentia Fosteriana would require the most heat for its development, from the fact that this palm is found at quite a low elevation near the coast, Kentia Belmoreana growing considerably higher up on the hills, and Kentia Canterburyana (now called Hedyscepe) being located still higher, the latter being said not to be found lower than 900 feet above sea level. In ordinary practice, however, we grow the two first mentioned under the same conditions of heat and moisture, though constantly proving that K. Belmoreana cannot be satisfactorily forced into growth by strong heat. K. Canterburyana has much the larger

seeds, among these three palms from Lord Howe's Island, and germinates and grows but slowly, the seedlings being of very dwarf and compact habit. The graceful foliage and short-jointed appearance of the palm in question makes it a most attractive specimen, and also one that endures exposure very well, but the slowness of its growth while in the juvenile state make K. Canterburyana somewhat unpopular in the trade, in addition to which the seed is more expensive than that of its more popular relatives.

The Rhapis is among the most serviceable palms for decorative purposes, and likewise does not require much heat for its best development, R. flabelliformis keeping in good condition during the winter in a temperature of 50° to 55°. No seeds of this useful palm are offered in the trade, and consequently propagation by division is the usual resort, a great many of the plants offered being raised by those painstaking gardeners, the Japanese, and exported to Europe and America in great quantities each season, the circumstances of their production naturally tending to keep the price up.

GREENHOUSES, PALM HOUSES AND STORE OF HOLTON & HUNKEL, MILWAUKEE.

Rhapis humilis is also sent over from Japan quite freely, and although not quite so strong in growth and foliage as the former, is also an admirable palm for decorating with, and will endure considerable exposure without injury. Both of these Rhapis may prove hardy along the coast, possibly to North Carolina, but I do not know if any extensive experiments have been made in this direction. It may possibly have been noted by some observant persons that the hardiest palms we have all show indications of tesselated venation, that is, that the veins of the leaflets are laid out in blocks, so to speak, rather than running through the leaf in straight lines, and while this rule may have exceptions, yet this system of veining seems to have something to do with the hardiness and endurance of the plants in question.

A similar condition is pointed out by Freeman-Mitford in regard to the hardiness of bamboos, this authority on the bamboos declaring that all of the hardiest of those plants were species with tesslated leaves. But perhaps we had better not flounder around among systems of venation or some of us may be lost, and the thought comes to us that these cool summers, comfortable though they be, sometimes disarrange our plans to some extent. We find that there must be a little judgment shown in the matter of watering, else there will be so much moisture hanging about through the night that some of the lower foliage may suffer, especially where the plants are crowded to some extent on the bench.

Such an excess of moisture combined with a low temperature often causes the tips of some leaves to decay. To avoid such a condition do all watering in the forenoon, between 9 and 11 o'clock, which is a good time for this operation, the rule applying with equal force to the fern houses.

Sometimes a handful of fern fronds other than Adiantum cuneatum are very useful to the retailer, and a small section of bench may well be spared for such a purpose. The ferns of free growth and good texture are the kind to have for cutting from, and there are more of these to be found among the pteris than in any other common family of ferns. Pteris serrulata, P. cretica albo-lineata and P. cretica magnifica are among the most lasting that I have tested in water under ordinary conditions in a dwelling, and as these species and varieties are among the easiest of all to raise or to buy, there is no difficulty in getting a stock. Plant them out on the bench in about four to five inches of decayed sod compost, giving plenty of water after they become established, and only moderate shading. There will seldom be a time when some fronds may not be had for some tasty design work.

These ferns may also be grown under the benches, but such a plan is not to be recommended as many of the leaves will become so soiled that they will not be fit for use, and in addition to this the foliage will be too soft to give entire satisfaction. Small Boston ferns for stock may still be taken up from the bench and

potted, there being quite a good length of growing weather before them yet. Well rooted young plants from 4-inch pots shifted on into 6-inch during the early part of September should make some useful plants for the holiday trade, for singular as it may seem when one takes into consideration the vast number last season, there is not now an oversupply of Boston ferns that were disposed of of this excellent house plant, and a prophet might remark that by next spring the dealers will be on the hunt for good stock of this fern.

There are still a great many Boston ferns grown by the planting out system, but the best and most satisfactory for the dealer to handle are those that are pot-grown throughout the season, such plants being in much better condition to endure hardship than are those recently dug up from a bench and only half established.   W. H. TAPLIN.

Asphaltum Paint.

Asphaltum paint should be used to paint every tool used in outdoor work, applying it in the fall when outdoor operations have practically come to a close. This includes mowing machines and all field tools. Every florist should have a note in his diary for each of the fall months to see that all tools not in use are painted with this material, which preserves the iron or paint from rust. It is wanton extravagance to put away tools or machinery of any kind before they have been thoroughly cleaned and painted with some such preservative.

SOME COMMITTEEMEN AT MILWAUKEE CONVENTION.—See page 81

With the Growers.

ROBERT CRAIG & SON, PHILADELPHIA, PA.

Calling on Robert Craig July 25, I found him in the midst of repair work on account of the recent disastrous hail storm which, he calculates, will cost at least $2,000. He was fortunate in saving his stock, very few of the plants being injured. The single thick small panes in the older houses, on the side facing the storm, fared the worst while the larger sizes seemed more flexible and the hail bounced off without doing much damage. Mr. Craig had just been congratulating himself that the summer work had been progressing so nicely and was nearly done, but now all is confusion and it will take several weeks to get the place straightened out, as all the plants have to be handled in order to get the broken glass gathered up. While this loss is severe, that of May 9 in the early 70's was more so, at that time the greater part of the stock grown being bedding plants, and as nearly all the glass was broken the plants were all hammered down and stripped of their leaves. It was a great blow to the growers, coming, as it did, just at the the beginning of their selling season.

One of the houses that was badly hit in the recent storm, contained a fine lot of ardisias, as promising a lot as I have ever seen. They are of this season's importation, just now setting a large crop of berries and Mr. Craig regards them as one of the best of the Christmas plants. A large house of the Pierson fern with some specimen as well as 2,000 plants in 6-inch pots, all looking vigorous and strong, made a pretty picture. Mr. Craig said, "I like this fern very much. I think it is the best novelty of recent years and I believe it will have a great sale. When I think of how popular the old Boston has become and that even now it is scarce, I believe that nearly everyone who has a Boston will want to try one of these. I think the Piersoni has elegance and dignity, but neither is the new Foster fern lacking in favor, the latter being between the Pierson and the Boston and making a fine specimen in larger sizes, as the fronds are long and graceful."

Several houses of kentias and arecas in various sizes were seen. They were vigorous, stocky plants, many of which were made up, as is the present popular way of growing. Mr. Craig said this was the quickest method for immediate results but that he preferred the single plant grown on into a specimen that would branch naturally. When asked about insects he said that prevention was better than cure, and that if the houses were fumigated twice a week and the plants syringed faithfully with a good strong stream there would be very little scale. For fumigating he uses tobacco dust burnt in pans, about two quarts to a pan, these pans being set about twenty feet apart in the walks and the fire started with a table-spoonful of coal oil. This is done when the house is closed for the night and smolders until all the tobacco is consumed, he uses evaporating pans when the steam is on.

When asked if there was any advantage in planting palm seed in individual pots or a few together, so as to avoid as much as possible the danger of injury to the roots from being separated, as is the case when quantities are grown together, he said that he had only tried cocos in this way and while the results were good, it was a great deal of trouble and he questioned whether it paid or not.

There are several houses of chrysanthemums to be seen, which have been planted but a short time. Marie Liger and Yellow Eaton are leading varieties, although all the good new ones are given a trial in smaller quantities.

A 200-foot house of crotons were in the best possible condition and according to Mr. Craig they were easily the best lot he had ever had. I have heard it said that this is the best collection in the world; it is certainly number one in this country. Among the new kinds is Lord Bellhaven, a very large leaved as well as magnificently colored variety. BeCompt is a striking new sort as is also Moonlight, Gloriosum and Fascination. A lot of seedlings, some of them raised by Edwin Lonsdale and the stock purchased by Mr. Craig, will certainly attract attention when sent out. Propagation is accomplished with cuttings and by rooting the shoots on the plant as is done with the rubber. Some grown

GREENHOUSES AND STORE OF C. C. POLLWORTH & CO., MILWAUKEE.

O. P. Bassett.

J. B. Deamud.
State Vice-President S. A. F. (Illinois.)

Peter Reinberg.

C. M. Dickinson.

F. F. Benthey.

Edgar F. Winterson.

Jas. S. Wilson.
(Vaughan's Greenhouses.)

James Hartshorne.

Flint Kennicott.

PROMINENT MEN OF THE CHICAGO TRADE.

E. C. Amling.   P. J. Foley.   John Poehlmann.

L. Coatsworth.   C. L. Washburn.   Leonard Kill. With Peter Reinberg.

John P. Risch.   A. Dietsch.   E. E. Pieser.

PROMINENT MEN OF THE CHICAGO TRADE.

three in a pot make nice bushy stock and should sell well. Mr. Craig said they had a great call for the croton in the fall for window decoration, its brilliant coloring of autumn tints being seasonable and arranging well with the chrysanthemum.

Outside in long frames were 9,000 cyclamen plants, which showed great strength and vigor and were as large now as they were last season when ready to take into the house. The point in growing cyclamens is to have them well ripened by exposure to the sun in the fall so that they will throw quantities of flowers at once, they being very salable in such condition.

Some roses in an adjoining frame prompted Mr. Craig to say that there has been a great demand the past spring for pot roses. Ramblers particularly had had a great sale and they now seemed more popular than before. He thought department store selling of

trifle overdone but .that it had such a hold on popular favor that it would always be in reasonable demand. In reference to the cost of palms and whether we would be able, on account of the stock raised here, to stop importing, be said that it pays to bring over large stock when the supply runs short, but that small sizes were cheaper here than in Belgium. He spoke of the growing popularity of the phoenix for hotel purposes on account of its lasting qualities.

One advantage they have in Belgium is that they charge the cost of preparing goods for shipment, which seems fair enough, but is not done here. The cost of boxes and packing is a very important item on a large place. When goods are sold to a florist in this city they are put on a wagon and delivered without extra expense, but the same goods sold at the same price to a florist out of town costs considerable in boxes, packing and labor, which under the present conditions are

The plants should be kept as clean as possible of all yellow and rotted leaves, as well as those affected with spots, even if it be necessary to go over them every few days. After they are once thoroughly cleaned they ought not to require much attention to keep them so. Dead leaves, bad blooms or rubbish of any nature should never be left in the path, as it tends to foul the air in the house.

On or about November 1 the plants should receive a ¼-inch mulch of good leaf mould. Where the leaf mould is not available, some well rotted manure applied to the same depth will answer. The soil in the beds in which violet plants are grown should never be stirred after the early part of November, as it does no good and will only be the cause of dirty flowers. Where the proper mulch cannot be obtained. an occasional dose of liquid manure will answer fairly well. From February 1 until Easter it is well to keep the night temperature 45° to 50°

PANSY BED AT MRS. PATTERSON'S, PHILADELPHIA, EDWARD KULP, GARDENER.

imported roses had not hurt the sale of home grown stock, as this latter had sold better than ever.

Several frames of azaleas, treated in the same manner as in Belgium, were noticed, the plants looking equal in vigor and color of foliage, to any foreign stock. They were planted out in beds of peat and leaf mold and given plenty of water. Mr. Craig thought that with the advantage of the tariff it would pay some one to take up the cultivation of the azalea in this country, that he felt confident a large and profitable business could be built up.

In other frames with a little bottom heat were seen growing dracænas and crotons, while in the new carnation ranges were some of the more recent varieties planted out on the tables. Enchantress, McKinley, Lawson and others growing nicely.

A lot of Begonia Gloire de Lorraine was being potted up, which Mr. Craig thinks a most excellent Christmas plant. He says it will hold its flowers if prepared for market by being grown cold and that it should have plenty of light and air and a temperature of 55° when ready to flower.

When asked about the rubber plant he stated that he thought it had been a

all furnished gratis. A movement started last year to have all shippers charge for the actual cost of this work met with some encouragement and should, I think, be taken up by the S. A. F., as it would at least be a good subject for discussion.

When asked about the best kind of fuel Mr. Craig said that bituminous was considerably cheaper than any other coal tried and could be put in their bins at about $3.65 per ton.   ROBT. KIFT.

The Violet.

SEASONABLE NOTES.

Violets, in order to do well and make a good growth, should be housed about August 15. They should be planted in a good rich compost, and after the first thorough watering should be moistened sparingly for two or three weeks until a good supply of roots has been started, after which they should never be allowed to suffer for lack of water. A night temperature of 40° to 45° and a day temperature of 60° to 65° should be maintained to avoid yellow and spotted leaves. As violets are better suited to a pure, sweet atmosphere, a good circulation of air should be maintained on bright days. ·· ···

and the day temperature 65° to 70°, as prices are generally good at that time and it is desirable to get as many flowers as possible from the plants. Shortly after Easter, when prices as a rule drop out of sight, the plants may be divided and cuttings taken for the next season's stock.   FRANK P. BRIGHAM.

Sweet Peas for Exhibition.

At the recent exhibition of the National Sweet Pea Society of England the following were used in the premier exhibit of the great open class of thirty-six bunches in distinct varieties: Lord Rosebery, Agnes Johnson, America, Blanche Burpee, Emily Eckford, Lady Mary Currie, Navy Blue, Gorgeous, Countess of Radnor, Mrs. Eckford, Lottie Hutchins, Her Majesty, Jeannie Gordon, Shasada, Gracie Greenwood, Monarch, Prince Edward of York, Salopian, Captain of the Blues, Hon. Mrs. Kenyon, Lottie Eckford, Colonist, Triumph, Lady Grisel Hamilton, Duchess of Sutherland, Miss Willmott, Princess of Wales, Black Knight, Duke of Westminster, Coccinea, Dorothy Eckford, Prince of Wales, Countess of Lathom, Countess Cadogan, Lovely and King Edward VII.

William Currie.
Chairman Reception Committee.

P. J. Hauswirth.
Chairman National Sports Committee.

W. A. Kennedy.
Milwaukee Bowling Committee.

A Good Pansy Bed.

About a month ago, when looking through the garden of Mrs. C. Stuart Patterson, Chestnut Hill, Philadelphia, a pansy bed in full bloom was one of the most attractive features of this very interesting garden, where hardy plants are the most popular and are given the right of way. This particular bed was the result of seed sown August 15, 1901, and planted the last week of the following March, and the plants have been blooming more or less ever since, save and excepting, of course, during the dead of the winter season. The accompanying illustration shows the profusion of bloom and the individual pansy blossoms to good advantage, and if they can be transferred to the pages of your valuable journal with something like the appearance they have in the garden and on the photograph, some idea of the beauty of the bed may be realized.

The beds of hybrid tea and hybrid perpetual roses were also very healthy, much more so than roses generally growing outdoors. The foliage was clean—no mildew and no insects—and the stems were longer than are usually seen outdoors in this part of the country. Edward Kulp has charge of this garden, and he deserves great credit for the evidences of care and intelligence in the cultivation of plants. E. L.

[The foregoing communication was received at this office June 25.—ED.]

Chrysanthemums.

NOTES ON AUTUMN TREATMENT.

Chrysanthemums being grown for single stem cut blooms, whether for exhibition or commercial purposes, are now arriving at a critical period of their growth. At this date (August 10) many varieties, especially the early planted, are forming early crown buds. This is altogether too early to select a bud and such should be removed as soon as the shoots on each side are large enough to handle without bruising. The strongest of these side shoots, if left to grow on, will in most cases form another bud between August 25 and September 10, which is the bud we depend on for our exhibition bloom. It is very important that these

shoots be taken in time and not allowed to make a growth of three or four inches, as some varieties will form clusters of growth and another bud on the end of these shoots, which will ruin chances for fine exhibition flowers.

Early planted stock will need a mulching at this time, the soil being now well filled with roots that should be in condition to be greatly benefited by using partly rotted cow manure if it can be obtained. Do not use manure that is too fresh or when in a wet condition, as it may form a crust that will prevent the water from penetrating the soil evenly.

The foliage on the plants is getting thicker and more dense every day, which means that extra judgment in watering and syringing must be used. It sometimes happens that the edges of the benches need water when the center will be in an entirely different condition. Also when syringing from the front side of the bench the other side will derive very little benefit. This is where red spider is most likely to get a foothold and now is the time to keep this pest in check or it will cause lots of trouble when the blooms begin to expand as well as ruin many a fine flower.

If the glowing description of some of the new novelties for this season proves to be a reality there should be some startling blooms at the exhibition this fall, and according to reports they are well distributed all over the country. What they will amount to in bloom remains to be seen, but among the several we are trying here there are. some wonderful growers.

Convention Hall is doing well and we like the growth of this, the best of any we have had for some time. It is clean and stocky and throws very few side shoots. Mlle. Marie Liger will make a fine companion for Convention Hall and be just right to grow on the same bench. Henry Barnes, an English red, has already made five and one-half feet of clean, heavy growth and is certainly stronger than any other red variety. Mrs. T. W. Pockett and Mrs. E. Thirkell are right there with Col. D. Appleton at four and one-half feet, clean and healthy. Both are splendid growers, though we are inclined to think Mrs. Thirkell will run away to a long neck, unless we are

careful. C. J. Salter and Mrs. Harry Emmerton are both of dwarfed growth, but still not stunted. P. J. Taggart and Mme. Nicollaud are both becoming quite tall, also being a little shy on foliage. H. W. Buckbee and Columbia are making a nice growth, standing about four feet at this date. Godfrey's King and Queen Alexandra are making a better showing than last season, the one fault with the King being that it wants to bloom so often. Matthew Smith lacks several points as a grower with us, but may make it up in bloom. Thos. Humphreys and Matchless, two other imported reds, are both. ideal growers. Bluebeard is most stubborn, and we have so far only managed to get sixteen inches of stem, although it is in the best of health. Among the very latest importations we are pleased with the growth and actions of Don McLeod, Wm. Duckham, Harrison Dick, S. T. Wright and Lælia Filkins. There are several others, but these at present take our fancy.

C. W. JOHNSON.

Crude Drugs from a New Source.

A number of common plants, occuring in some cases as weeds, furnish, when properly collected and cured, crude drugs such as are now imported in large part from Europe and elsewhere. The Bureau of Plant Industry of the United States Department of Agriculture is now engaged in the preparation of a bulletin pointing out the desirability of satisfying the demand for these drugs from domestic sources. The bulletin will contain descriptions and cuts of the plants and methods of collecting, handling and curing will be given.

In order to increase the effectiveness of the bulletin it is thought necessary to bring the prospective collector in touch with buyers. Therefore circular letters are being sent to dealers in drugs asking if they wish to be included in the list of firms to whom the bureau is authorized to direct those wishing to submit samples and get prices.

SPOKANE, WASH.—The annual sweet pea show was successfully held here on July 29.

The Schizanthuses.

Although the several varieties of schizanthus are tolerably well known as garden annuals, and succeed well with a minimum of care, it is as pot plants that they are particularly valuable, when bulbous subjects, herbaceous calceolarias, cinerarias and other greenhouse plants are on the wane, and before pelargoniums, gloxinias or tuberous begonias are fit to use as decorative plants.

We sow our seeds in 2½-inch pots about September 15, placing two or three seeds in a pot. The seeds quickly germinate and fill the little pots with roots and are shifted into larger pots before the roots become matted. A cold frame is the best place for them as long as frost can be excluded, after that a cold, airy house where the plants can be well up to the light; so long as no actual freezing occurs, the colder the house is the better.

The plants are shifted into their flowering pots about January 1. We use 10-inch pots for most of the plants, although we find a few in 6-inch pots useful for decorative purposes, and the variety Wisetonensis does not require pots over 6 inches to 8 inches in diameter, being a less rampant grower than the other sorts.

Schizanthuses are not fastidious as to comfort and for the final shift, some well decayed cow manure and loam with a dash of fine bone or Clay's fertilizer is suitable. Liquid manure can be freely used as soon as the plants are well

rooted. As these plants are rather rampant growers, staking, or at least some support is necessary when they are a few inches high. Many growers use balloon frames for them and they are very good, provided the plants are not tied down too formally. We use a number of wire stakes and tie the shoots round and round these until flowers appear, when they are allowed to grow naturally. Such varieties as S. pinnatus and S. papilionaceus oculatus grow three to four feet in height. S. Wisetonensis does not exceed one and one-half feet.

Schizanthuses mix well with nearly all other plants, but a group of themselves, with their fairy, butterfly-like flowers, produced in thousands, in a number of beautiful shades makes a delightful picture. For piazza decoration they are splendid. If the tall darker colored sorts are arranged in groups, bordered with white marguerites or Golden Gem calceolaria they make a very pretty effect. Schizanthuses are rarely heard of as cut flowers but sprays of S. pinnatus roseus and S. retusus albus cut of any desired length make as beautiful a center piece for a dining table, or as pretty an individual vase as any one could wish, for their lasting qualities are good for such airy, frail-looking flowers.

Of the several varieties in general cultivation we find S. grandiflorus oculatus makes the finest specimens. S. pinnatus with its varieties roseus and candidissimus are also good. The last named is the finest pure white variety, although S.

retusus albus is also worth forcing; it produces large pure white flowers, blotched with bright golden yellow. S. Wisetonensis, introduced a few years ago by Hugh Low & Company, Bush Hill Park, London, Eng, is a decided acquisition. The plant is rather dwarfish and flowers finely in smaller-sized pots than the other varieties, the colors vary from white to crimson. A few of our plants were of a beautiful pink color this season. This variety unfortunately is a very shy seeder. The seed is consequently expensive and this year it is unprocurable. There are some few other varieties of this pretty annual but the foregoing we find are the most desirable. Schizanthuses are at their best during the last half of April and the whole of the following month.

W. N. CRAIG.

Either Way We Win.

Florists are shaking their heads ominously and saying that because of the lack of rain, flowers will be dear this season. Last year they shook their heads and said that flowers would be dear because there was too much rain. Either way they win.—Worcester (Mass.) Telegram.

STERLING, NEB. — Mrs. Hoeger has opened in the flower business with a nice variety of plants.

WEST HOBOKEN, N. J.—Mr. E. G. Asmus is on his vacation and will not be able to attend the Milwaukee convention.

SCHIZANTHUSES AS GROWN BY W. N. CRAIG, NORTH EASTON, MASS.

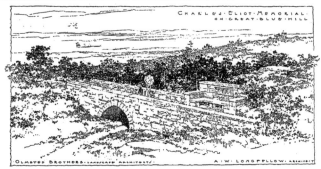

CHARLES ELIOT MEMORIAL ON GREAT BLUE HILL

OLMSTED BROTHERS · LANDSCAPE ARCHITECTS ·   A · W · LONGFELLOW · ARCHITECT

PROPOSED CHARLES ELIOT MEMORIAL.

Charles Eliot Memorial.

The following circular with reference to a memorial of the late Charles Eliot, the well known landscape architect, was issued at Boston, Mass., last June. The honor is well merited and the form it is proposed to give the memorial, most commendable:

The metropolitan park system conceived by Charles Eliot, exemplifying, as it does, his foresight and skill, is in itself the noblest of monuments to him, but it is fitting that the people of his own time should leave some visible record that they appreciated the man and what he accomplished in his too brief career. Such a memorial is called for not only because of his leading part in securing for the people these great public domains, but because of his still wider service in arousing an intelligent general interest in the opportunities for making the earth beautiful instead of ugly when adapting it to the use of man.

To erect any mere monument, in the ordinary sense of the term, within the public domain which he planned, would violate the principle which he so strongly argued for, that no structure or object, however beautiful or commendable in itself, should be introduced into these reservations unless it tends to serve directly the uses for which alone they were created—to provide permanently rural and sylvan landscape for the enjoyment of the people.

It has accordingly been decided, after careful deliberation on the part of the Metropolitan Park Commission, and the undersigned committee, that a "Charles Eliot Path" should be constructed encircling the summit of Great Blue Hill, on the line from which the best views are successively commanded in the most enjoyable manner; views for the preservation of which he labored, and views over the whole district where will live the future millions dependent upon these lands for rest and recreation. In the course of the path a little ravine must be crossed at a point overlooking the long range of wooded summits and valleys of the Blue Hills reservation. Here it is proposed to build a simple stone foot-bridge, whence those who use the path will command this view effectively, and against a rock forming the abutment of its parapet to place a tablet of bronze, dedicating to the memory of Charles Eliot the bridge, the path which it carries, and the landscape he loved, a monument of a grandeur unapproachable by any human construction.

The Park Commission has no funds which it can devote to a distinctly memorial work, but has undertaken to make a practicable path on the desired line and to improve it from time to time as funds permit, while the undersigned committee proposes at once to erect the memorial bridge and tablet. To do this simply, unostentatiously, but in a thoroughly permanent manner, will require three thousand dollars.

Of this amount some of Charles Eliot's personal friends have contributed nearly half, but his life was so eminently devoted to the public welfare, and this memorial will so strongly express the public character of his services, that it ought to be built by a wider contribution, and it is felt that many who were not personally acquainted with Charles Eliot will welcome this opportunity of expressing their appreciation of the ends to which he so successfully devoted his life.

Contributions should be sent to Charles S. Rackemann, treasurer, 23 Court street, Boston, Mass.

HENRY P. WALCOTT,
E. H. FAY,
(Signed) GEORGE C. MANN, } Committee.
WILLIAM L. PUTNAM,
CHARLES S. RACKEMANN.

The Carnation.

SUPPORTS.

Of the many different methods of supporting carnations but three or four have passed into common use; the rest are only occasionally met with here and there. Simplicity, efficiency and cheapness have been potent elements in bringing to the front the few standard ideas upon which every method, which has any claim to distinction, is founded, and the same elements have quickly relegated to obscurity any unproductive or cumbersome feature of any method. The writer is a crank on simplicity and efficiency and if cheapness can be obtained along with this is the spirit of the age, of the ambition to rise to the top ranks of the profession.

The method which we have adopted combines these three elements in a very satisfactory manner, although it is not claimed that there is no other method just as good. It consists simply of a set of tiers of wire and string netting placed one above the other at proper heights to support the plants and flowering shoots. The first tier is placed six inches above the soil and each successive tier six inches above the one below it. With ordinary varieties two tiers are sufficient, while with extra tall growing varieties that do not possess sufficient rigidity of stem to hold the flowers erect until fully matured, the third tier will be found necessary. This should, however, be left out until late in the season, for any unnecessary encumbrance to disbudding and cutting the blooms will be very annoying and cause a great waste of time. Two tiers, the higher of which is only a foot above the soil, may to some seem inadequate to meet the needs of most tall growing varieties, but experience has proven that this is not the case.

If the base of the flowering shoot is properly supported the bloom will be held erect without extra support.

A variety to receive any recognition of merit nowadays is usually seen on exhibition tables in many sections of the country before dissemination, and any weak points are bound to be observed and put down to its discredit. A variety must be strong indeed in all other qualities if a weak stem does not condemn it on the spot. After some decades of this process of selecting the best we have produced a set of standard varieties with stems strong enough from the base up to hold the flowers erect. Improvements along this line are noticeable with each year's introductions, and while we need hardly look for a race of carnations that will not need any support, I believe that it is safe to say the present standard of strong stems will not be lowered. This enables us to have the supports well down in the body of the plants and have the flowering shoots where they can be conveniently reached for disbudding and cutting.

The construction of the system of tiers is so simple and has been so often described that it seems like warming over an old dish to elaborate upon it again. But for those who may have just recently entered the ranks of the carnation fraternity some allowance must be made, and the following remarks will probably be helpful to such. On each end of the bench a strong framework of wood or iron pipe, out both combined, is securely fastened. The materials used should be as light as possible; 1-inch iron pipe is strong enough, or, if wood is used, 1x3-inch will do for the uprights and braces and 2x2-inch for the cross-pieces upon which the wires are fastened. A strand of wire is stretched between each row of plants lengthwise of the bench and on the outside of each edge row. These wires are drawn as tight as possible to hold them rigid and they are supported, to keep them from sagging, at intervals of about fifteen feet throughout the length of the bench, by a light framework, the uprights of which are fastened to the side boards of the bench. Plaster laths will be heavy enough for these. When the wires of the lower tiers are in place the cross-strings are put in, one on each side of each row of plants, leaving a space of about three inches between each row to serve for an air passage. The strings are fastened securely to the outside wires with a knot that will not slip and around the inside wires they are given a simple twist.

The plants are thus enclosed each in its own space and no further work is necessary, where this system is used, outside of keeping the plants from straying from their allotted spaces. It is easily removed at the end of the season by cutting out the strings and hanging the wires up overhead, and replacing when again needed is very simple and speedily accomplished. Some growers fasten the strings diagonally across the bench, forming a series of diamonds instead of rectangles, as described above. By this method the plants are not held as firmly nor is the space which each plant should occupy so well defined.

Individual supports, that is, a separate framework for each plant, have been placed upon the market from time to time and the best are still advertised, showing that they possess some degree of popularity. Those that have survived the commercial tests are very good, and the first cost is probably the reason why they are not more extensively used. A method of individual supports, not covered by a patent, which should be comparatively cheap in first cost, consists of two wire arches crossing each other at right angles. The lower ends are buried in the soil and wabbling is reduced to a minimum by the firm hold secured. Strings are fastened around the uprights at proper heights to support the plants and flowering shoots. A simple wrap around each upright will keep the string from slipping up or down. No. 10 wire is a good size and the arches should be about twenty-two inches high, allowing for four inches to go into the soil and eighteen inches above the soil. This system is easily taken apart and stored when not in use, the only disadvantage being its obstruction to a free access to the soil after it is in place.

The primitive method of tying each plant to a simple upright stake no longer finds favor among up-to-date growers. Some growers who use the wire and string netting first described prefer to use a ∧-shaped piece of wire netting between each row across the bench, in conjunction with this. This may be all right, but has never been considered of much value by the writer, and there are very few growers who use it extensively. The simple method which we have adopted, if put in in proper time, fills the bill admirably and leaves little to be desired in the way of improvement.

J.

The Watsonias.

Ed. Am. Florist:—I cannot too highly commend the new white watsonias described on pages 827–828 of your issue of June 27. I have grown them since their first importation in 1899, and have been thoroughly convinced of their attractiveness and decorative value, but have never been able to winter the corms in a dormant condition without greatly lowering their vitality. They seem best grown cool under glass and have here never failed to give profuse blooms if started in September and allowed to come on gradually in a carnation temperature. I have grown watsonia species for over fifteen years and have made many efforts, by starting seedlings at different times, to change the blooming and resting periods so as to carry the corms dormant through the winter months, but with very limited success.

The white watsonias, Ardernei and O'Brieni, are splendid additions to our forcing bulbs, certain to attain great popularity as they become known. The main point in their culture is to use sound fibrous loam, excluding all raw animal manures, for potting soil and avoid high temperatures at the start. When the bloom spike shows, weak liquid manures greatly stimulate the development of the flowers. The corms keep best in the soil where grown until growth starts again, when they may be separated and replanted. With this treatment they get very strong and increase at a fair rate. The colored species and varieties of watsonia are handsome and interesting plants for amateurs, but do not possess many qualities desired by florists.

W. Van Fleet.

Want Glass Importations Stopped.

The union glass workers are strongly opposed to the importation of window glass, as we judge from the tenor of some comments recently made by a correspondent of one of their trade publications, indicated by the following:

"The enormous importations should be checked. The thousands of boxes of foreign glass shipped into this country monthly are unpalatable propositions to the average window (glass) worker, and while we have been averse to making the small size, it is reasonable to assume that every thrifty member of the craft would rather make the imported sizes than be idle seven months in the year."

THE COLISEUM, CHICAGO, WHERE THE NEXT FLOWER SHOW MAY BE HELD.

American Carnation Society.

DEPARTMENT OF REGISTRATION.

Geo. E. Buxton, Nashua, N. H., registers the Marion Buxton, a seedling of 1900 and the result of a cross between Flora Hill and Wm. Scott; color a soft shade of pink, similar to Mrs. James Dean; bloom three to three and one-half inches in diameter, born on long, stiff stems, averaging eighteen inches in length; it is very prolific and a good keeper.

Fred. Dorner & Sons Company, Lafayette, Ind., registers The Belle, the color of which is pure white; size three to three and one-half inches; form rounding, petals well arranged and fine finish; stem twenty-four inches and over, stiff and straight; fragrance spicy and very strong; calyx perfect and substance a splendid keeper; habit strong, clean, healthy, upright growth, makes a quick growth and a well formed plant; blooming qualities of the best. This is the earliest of all white carnations, being very free and continuous and one of the easiest to propagate.

ALBERT M. HERR, Sec'y.

MEETING AT MILWAUKEE.

A meeting of the board of directors of the society will be held at Milwaukee immediately after the adjournment of the S. A. F. evening session on Wednesday, August 19, at which a number of important matters will be taken up.

Chicago.

MARKET SOMEWHAT UNEASY.—ALL GOOD STOCK SELLS EASILY.—NEW ROSE STOCK COMING IN.—SHIPMENTS OF CARNATIONS ON THE INCREASE.—COLORED ASTERS IN PLENTY.—DAHLIAS MAKE AN APPEARANCE.—DOINGS OF THE LOCAL TRADE.—VISITORS.

The market is now undergoing its usual annual period of restlessness, as there is no longer any old stock available and the new material has not yet begun to come in very large quantities. Wholesalers are daily teased with nice big orders that can not possibly be filled and the thought that the growers will not be able to afford them any material relief for some time does not help matters much. The season is probably no worse than those of former years, but as most of the craft are living in the present, not in the past, it certainly appears to be the worst ever. Some very nice American Beauty roses are beginning to appear although the stems have no length to speak of, but such as they are they find ready sale, being grabbed up on sight. It is not uncommon these days to see buyers wandering aimlessly, some of them piteously, about from store to store, looking for something that they won't find yet a while. Almost all a florist can do at this time is to slumber through the long quiet days and dream of what is coming to him when the fall business commences. The cool weather seems to retard Brides and Bridesmaids, there being more Kaiserins and Golden Gates. Shipments of field grown carnations, although not great, are increasing right along.

The aster is quite a prominent flower just now; colored are being received in large quantities and are a great help in funeral work, although white asters are scarce. The quality on an average is not very good. Dahlias have made their appearance, although not very plentiful so far, but there will doubtless be enough of them later on. Gladioli still occupy a prominent place on the tables and the general run of out-door flowers are seen

in plenty at the establishments where such are handled.

A new chimney has just recently been completed at A. J. Budlong's greenhouses, which is said to be the largest of its kind in the country, 200 tons of brick having been used in the construction. It is 125 feet in height and has a flue seven feet in diameter. The steam heating system of the establishment is centrally located, which makes it possible to have only one chimney. Two new boilers are to be installed, and will bring the total horse power up to 800.

J. A. Budlong is returning from Providence, R. I., on his wheel. He left that city on August 8 after a stay of about a month's duration.

Benthey & Company are cutting good American Beauty, Liberty and Sunrise roses and say that their stock is increasing every day.

Herman Pennock, convicted of the murder of his brother-in-law, Oscar Kreitling, was granted a new trial on August 8.

Peter Reinberg and wife, together with Geo. Weiland and P. Olinger and wife, have taken a trip to New Castle, Ind

John Deamuds place has just undergone a thorough cleaning and has been painted and calcimined.

Bassett & Washburn are cutting some fine though short-stemmed Brides and Bridesmaids.

The gardens surrounding the county hospital look very attractive just at present.

Weiland & Risch have equipped their place with several new flower tables.

J. C. Enders, of Poehlmann Brothers, has returned from his vacation.

Kennicott Brothers are having their annual house cleaning.

Visitors: Fred Breitmeyer, Detroit; D. B. Hazen, Wheaton, Ill.; Mr. Mathews, Dayton Floral Company, Dayton, Ohio; Mrs. A. L. Glaser, Dubuque, Ia.; J. N. McIntire, Fulton, Mo.

An Invitation.

Messrs. Bassett & Washburn and Vaughan's Greenhouses are out with a joint invitation to all returning convention visitors to visit these two establishments on Saturday, August 22. Luncheon will be served at the latter place from 1 to 2 p. m. Trains run both ways hourly.

Philadelphia.

FUNERAL WORK THE PRINCIPAL FACTOR JUST NOW.—ROSES IN GOOD CONDITION.—DAHLIAS COMING IN.—BUILDING AND RENOVATING.—GENERAL NOTES.—VISITORS IN TOWN.

With the exception of flowers for the dead there is but little doing in the way of business. Flowers are becoming more plentiful, there being in fact too many offered to bring anything like fair returns. Roses are in good condition; the continued cool weather being a great help to them. Bridesmaids are of good size and color, something unusual for the season. Very fine Kaiserins are seen and offered at $2 to $6 per hundred. American Beauty stock is going down in price as it becomes more plentiful, $2 per dozen now buying 30 inch stems with $3 for the longest. Asters are very plentiful; Semple's, are now coming in and taking the place of the earlier kinds at 50 cents to $1 per hundred. Outside carnations are offered at 75 cents per hundred. Greens of all kinds are almost a drug and bunches of

asparagus are offered at from 25 cents to 50 cents. Just a few dahlias are shown.

M. Rice & Company say the season is opening up in great shape as they have already had to cable to Europe for renewals of stock. They are making a specialty of wicker vases and pedestals in large sizes of their own designs, made in their own factory. A line of pedestals made strong and shaped like standing wheat sheaves look like winners. Another novelty is a line of wicker screens. These, with a little green and a cluster of flowers can be made very decorative and will be useful to cover doorways or conceal orchestras, etc.

John C. Gracey, the florist of 2028 Columbia avenue and also of 1230 North Twenty-sixth street, has purchased the property three doors above his Columbia avenue establishment and is fitting up a first-class store with a greenhouse in the rear. It will be thoroughly up to date when finished, about October 1. Mr. Gracey is a thorough painstaking and obliging gentleman and deserves the success he is having.

Edward Reid has been refitting his establishment. There is a new cooling room in the basement with an opening which allows the outside air to do the work in winter weather. Although his accommodations are nearly twice as large as last year he is getting pushed for room and fears he will have to expand some more before the season is over.

S. S. Pennock and wife sail from this city on the steamer Heverford, Saturday, August 15, for a six weeks' trip abroad. The tour is partly for recreation and in Mr. Pennock's case to escape his annual attack of hay fever, to which he is unfortunately subject at this time.

The "S. S. Pennock Athletic Association"—what other wholesale house boasts of such a luxury?—is dated to play King Peacock's subjects a game of ball on August 21.

The Philadelphia Carnation Company is sending out some good Scott carnations, also gladioli and Japan lilies.

Ralph Shrigley, for several years with S. S. Pennock, is now with Leo Niessen.

Robt. Craig & Son are offering good roseum lilies in quantity.

G. Anderson is cutting some nice Carnot stock at $4 to $5.

Visitors in town: Ernest Zeiger, Mrs. E. A. Williams, of Pittsburg; Chas. Wagner, Cleveland; M. Warnecke, Detroit; Lloyd Blick, Norfolk, Va. K.

New York.

Business is exceedingly dull here, nothing going on in any line and very little prospect of any improvement in the immediate future. On Sunday the Milwaukee party takes its departure and convention news will be the topic of interest for the time being.

August Rhotert sailed for Europe on Tuesday, August 11, on the Kronprinz Wilhelm.

Wm. Ford was last seen boarding a train bearing a fish pole and sundry parcels.

Mrs. C. B. Weathered is mourning the loss of her father, who died on Friday, August 7.

Visitors: W. R. Smith, Washington; Robt. E. Berry, Philadelphia, Pa.

POUGHKEEPSIE, N. Y.—The Dutchess County Horticultural Society held an interesting meeting in Rhinebeck, August 8, and the violet industry at that place was inspected.

Pittsburg.

CONVENTION TOPICS DISCUSSED AT CLUB MEETING.—THEY THAT WILL GO TO MILWAUKEE.—BUSINESS DOWN TO BED ROCK. —THE NEW ELECTRIC RAILWAY WILL IMPROVE SHIPPING FACILITIES.—NEWSY ITEMS.—A VISITOR.

Business is almost extinct and the weather continues cool and showery. A very poor quality of rose stock is received, much of it coming in badly mildewed. Carnations are a little more plentiful than usual and are fair in quality. Some fine asters and gladioli are acceptable factors at this time.

The last meeting of the Pittsburg and Allegheny Florists' and Gardeners' Club was fairly well attended and information regarding the Milwaukee convention was given out. B. C. Reinaman and Earnest Ludwig were appointed a committee to secure twenty signatures for a Pullman car to the convention and return. No decision has yet been reached as to what road the Pittsburgers will travel. The rate is $2 cheaper over the Pittsburg & Lake Erie Railroad, yet it seems that the majority are desirous of going via the Pennsylvania Railroad. The arrangements will be completed with the view of leaving Pittsburg on Monday morning, August 17. The names of those that will go are as follows: C. Reiger and wife, E. Ludwig and family, E. Reinaman and wife, Samuel Gass and wife, G. Ludwig and family, Julius Ludwig and wife, John Bader, Frederick Burki, George Blind, Joseph Kletzley of Natrona, Pa., Casper Limbach, Thomas Mayberry, B. L. Elliott and others. Mr. Negley displayed a new scarlet seedling canna with brownish petals which was the object of much interest.

Preparations for the regular autumn planting of trees in Schenly park are now under way. The entire contents of the park nursery will be used in beautifying the park with additional trees and shrubbery. During the year many of the old trees along the line of the Junction Railroad- and that part of the park nearest the Jones & Laughlins Company's steel plant died. The cause is attributed to the effects of the large amount of ore dust and gas in the air.

The Stark Electric Railway Company is vigorously pushing its work in connecting many important towns in eastern Ohio, which will greatly improve the shipping service between Akron, Alliance, Canton, Salem and Beloit. The florists in those communities will be greatly benefited by this project.

A recent letter from Phil Langhans, who is fishing on Lake Chautauqua, states that he caught 780 pounds of fish in two hours, and had to charter the largest boat operating in those waters to bring in the day's catch. Mr. Langhans will furnish affidavits upon request.

Charles T. Siebert visited his friends in the city recently. He is looking well, although extremely nervous, and may go to the convention if conditions permit.

Graves & Risch, of Beloit, O., are sending some exceptionally fine asters to this mart, white and purple Queen of the Market being their best productions.

Billy Hall and John Baldinger know all about Buffalo, Niagara Falls and Fort Erie, as they spent two pleasant weeks at those places.

Howard Carney, financial secretary of the Whittaker Fire Brigade, is actively engaged with the firemen's convention at Latrobe this week.

H. W. Breitenstein, of Breitenstein & Flemm, has gone to Sugar Island,

Canada, to attend the American Canoe Association meet.

The city of Pittsburg will ask for bids next week for about 5,000 trees and 2,000 young shrubs to be planted in the park nursery.

Karl Klinke, bookkeeper for the Pittsburg Cut Flower Company, is visiting his brother in Muncie, Ind.

B. Eschner, of M. Rice & Company, Philadelphia, Pa., was a recent visitor.

P. S. Randolph and family are spending their vacation at Cambridge Springs.

L. I. Neff is showing some remarkably fine specimens of gladioli. E. L. M.

Boston.

TRADE EXPERIENCES A POOR WEEK. — ASTERS AND SWEET PEAS OF POOR QUALITY.—ROSES IN GENERAL INFERIOR AND SMALL.—CARNATIONS IMPROVE DURING WET WEATHER.—FINE SPECIMENS OF GLADIOLI—MILL-BOARD LAW ACCEPTED BY POSTER PEOPLE.—WEEKLY EXHIBIT AT HORTICULTURAL HALL.—NEWS NOTES. —VISITORS.

The week since last report has been a poor one, partly because of the very inclement weather which cut off all enthusiasm at the summer resorts and at the same time cut into the quality of most of the stock offered in the market. At the present time the market is demoralized—in fact "broke." Asters continue to multiply, likewise sweet peas, both of these summer specialties suffering from the heavy rains and also from a very scanty demand. Roses are inferior as a rule, most of the stock in all varieties being very small. White roses find the best sale but there are more than enough for all purposes. Carnations are the exception so far as quality is concerned, they having perceptibly improved during the wet weather. There is a moderate supply of Shakespeare gladioli in sight, of splendid quality and they bring from $3 to $5 a hundred, while the customary market assortment is moved with difficulty at $5 a thousand. It is said that these fine specimens are grown in sandy soil. However, the individual blooms are almost equal to candidum lilies and are available for the same uses, such as funeral work. Altogether it may be said that the season is still fully up to the average from the stand point of both wholesale and retail trade. The wholesalers are finding a pretty good legitimate call for most of the goods received and are not forced to depend upon the street fakir to carry away the stock as has been the case oftentimes in the past.

The bill-board law and resultant rules adopted by the Boston park commission, prohibiting offensive advertising signs and bill-boards within a certain distance of city parks or parkways, has been accepted with good grace by the poster people and the park commission's rules will be obeyed without protest.

The Saturday show at Horticultural Hall on August 8 was a splendid display of hardy phloxes and old-fashioned garden flowers from numerous exhibitors. Prizes were awarded to T. C. Thurlow, Geo. Hollis, Blue Hill Nurseries and Wm. Whitman for phloxes. Blue Hill Nurseries were given a certificate of merit for new variety "Blue Hills."

The Massachusetts Horticultural Society has changed the date of the annual fall exhibition of plants and flowers to September 24–27 inclusive, and the annual fruit and vegetable show will be combined with it.

The annual convention and exhibition of the American Pomological Society will

be held in Horticultural Hall, September 10—11—12.

George H. Walsh has leased the Haley greenhouses at Malden for one year.

Kenneth Finlayson and wife sailed for England on the Ivernia, August 11.

John D. Twombly is just recovering from a five-weeks' illness.

Visitors: George Brown, Quebec, Canada; F. F. Goode, New York; J. J. Long; Turners' Falls, Mass.; W. R. Smith, Washington, D. C.; Hugh M. Hughes, Norristown, Pa.

Detroit.

LOCAL CLUB ELECTS OFFICERS.—REPORTS OF SECRETARY AND TREASURER.—PREPARATIONS FOR CONVENTION TRIP.—BOWLERS FOR MILWAUKEE. — SOME NOTES.—VISITORS.

The meeting of the Detroit Florists' Club on Wednesday, August 5, brought out an attendance of about forty members and the annual election of officers was the chief business of the evening. The most intense interest was manifested by all present and the nominations and voting for candidates was very spirited, resulting as follows: President, Robert Flowerday; vice-president, Robert Watson; treasurer, B. Schroeter; secretary, J. F. Sullivan. The latter two officers were unanimously re-elected. The treasurer's report was read, showing the financial condition of the club to be very satisfactory and the treasurer promised to soon add materially to the goodly sum now on hand. The secretary's report showed a steadily increasing active membership, which at present numbers over one hundred, there being in addition fifteen honorary members, the latter evincing much interest in the work of the club. Another application for membership was presented at the meeting. Philip Breitmeyer, who recently returned from an extended visit in the east, related his observations of eastern trade matters. Owing to the probable absence from the city of many members during the S. A. F. convention week, it was announced that there would be no meeting of the club on the next regular meeting date, August 19. About forty members have already signified their intentions of attending the convention and it is altogether likely that there will be many more. The route will be via the Grand Trunk railway, leaving Detroit at 5 p. m. (standard time) Monday, August 17, arriving Grand Haven at 10:30 p. m., leaving there by boat at 10:45 p. m. and arriving Milwaukee at 6 o'clock Tuesday morning, the opening day of the convention. The round trip fare will be $9.62 on the certificate plan, including berths on the boat both ways. An invitation is hereby extended to all florists from points adjacent to Detroit to join our party here.

The bowlers have been in active practice for the past few weeks and a strong team from here will enter the contest at Milwaukee. The team will probably consist of Frank Holznagle, Philip Breitmeyer, Robert Watson, Frank Beard, John Dunn and Norman Sullivan.

A. J. Stahelin is about to build a boiler shed and one greenhouse, 24x200 feet, on Grand River road, near Greenfield. He will grow vegetables the present season and carnations later.

Henry Flammer, John Carey and James Taylor, with their wives, are enjoying the breezes of Put-in-Bay this week.

William Dilger made a short visit to his old home in Sandusky, O., last week. Visitors: A. L. Glaser, Dubuque, Ia.; Henry A. Siebrecht, New York; G. H. Harrison, Cheboygan, Mich. J. F. S.

Cleveland.

MEETING OF LOCAL CLUB WELL ATTENDED.—COMMITTEE APPOINTED FOR PICNIC.—IMPROVEMENTS AND BUILDING.—FUNERAL WORK KEEPS STOCK MOVING.

The last regular meeting of the Cleveland Florists' Club was very well attended and considerable enthusiasm was displayed over the project of a picnic, one that is to be a regular old howler, so to speak. The following members were appointed on the committee to determine the date and place: A. Schmitt, Isaac Kennedy, A. Graham, William Brinker and Lincoln Brown. Six new members were elected. Between forty and fifty members of the club are going to the convention.

There is a great deal of funeral work being done, which keeps the stock down very close, although the general run of material is very poor. Some very good rubrum, album and auratum lilies are coming in as well as light colored gladioli. There are lots of asters on the market, which come in very handy for funeral work.

Gordon Gray, John Kelly and John Kirchner drove out to Isaac Kennedy's place one day last week and found that worthy gentleman hard at work fitting pipe. They say his houses are very fine. Brides and Bridesmaids being the specialties.

F. W. Ziechmann contemplates extensive improvements at his place on Quincy street. The houses facing Cemetery street will be torn down and the new one built farther back. Other improvements on Quincy street will be made.

The Market Gardeners' and Producers' Association will hold its first annual basket picnic at Euclid beach Wednesday, August 12, and a general good time is anticipated.

Fred. Ehrbar, the Lorain street florist, is continually originating new ideas, his latest move being to dress his delivery men in uniforms of gray and gold.

J. J. Kirchner is going to Atlantic City, and on his return will stop off at New York and Pittsburg, visiting all the large commercial places.

J. Mollenkopf, of Glenville, is erecting several houses 20x100 feet to meet the increasing demand.   O. G.

St. Louis.

PLANTING WILL SOON BE IN ORDER.—REBUILDING.—RAILROAD WANTS.—FLORIST'S PROPERTY.—DEMAND FOR STOCK SAME AS LAST WEEK.—MILWAUKEE TALK.

The Connon Floral Company will soon begin planting carnations to which four houses will be given. Mr. Connon does not approve of late planting, as the plants can be given closer attention when under cover. Two houses will be planted with roses. The violets are coming on nicely and the tuberose section is supplying hundreds of flowers. The gladioli turned out to be mostly dark colors, so that next year a new supply will be secured. Connections are being made with the city water pipes, a steam pump being formerly used.

Max Herzog is having his ups and downs with the St. Louis and San Francisco Railroad, which is badly in need of his property in order to enlarge switching facilities. No acceptable proposition has so far been made and Mr. Herzog is still managing the florist business.

H. G. Berning is preparing to move into the next block west on Pine street as soon as he returns from the convention. The new place is much better fitted for his purpose, as it has greater floor space, a large basement and everything can be arranged to suit.

Out at Henry F. Aue's establishment in Lindenwood everyone is busy. The carpenters are enlarging the big house sixteen feet and the steam heating system is being changed to hot water. Two houses are used for smilax and one for carnations.

The demand for stock is no greater than last week. A few roses are offered of better quality, but not enough to meet the demand for such. Carnations are about the same. Wholesale men say that "everything is quiet."

Everyone expects to have a right royal time at Milwaukee. The bowling club, if able to take the full team, is anxious to compete, as the members have been making high scores recently.

Nearly all the growers in the vicinity of St. Louis supply Chas. Beyer with stock.   F. K. B.

Buffalo.

OUTING OF FLORISTS' CLUB.—RESULTS OF THE VARIOUS CONTESTS.—MATRIMONIAL NEWS.—OTHER ITEMS.—VISITORS.

The Buffalo Florists' Club outing was postponed from Tuesday, August 4, until Wednesday, owing to the severe rain storm. About 125 were in attendance and a few of the stores were closed, but business is now such that it is rather hard to close entirely, so that some had to remain on duty. There were twelve events on the programme, which extended well into the evening before all were seated at the supper table. The grounds were very fine and conveniently situated, being only about an hour's ride from the city on the street cars. The prize winners of the various contests were as follows: Old men's race, Geo. McClure first, Wm. Waring second, M. Berrimen third; hundred-yard dash, A. J. Rerchert first, J. Wiese second, C. Reichert third; potato race, A. Reichert first, W. Grever second, J. Speidel third; sack race, W. B. Scott first, W. Waring, Jr., second, E. Slattery third; three-legged race, J. Wiese and A. Reichert first, Longby and Hestler second, W. B. Scott and L. H. Neubeck third; all-four race, J. Neubeck first, J. Wiese second, E. Slattery third; standing-jump, D. J. Scott first, C. Reichert second; onelegged race, E. Slattery first, L. Neubeck second; ladies' race, Mrs. Beiler first, Mrs. Kasting second, Mrs. Kircher third; shoe race for boys, A. Voak first, G. Klokow second, C. Scott third; hop-skip-and jump, W. Grever first, D. J. Scott second, C. Keitsch third. The base ball game was really the best thing on the programme, and lasted five innings, between the east and west side, the score being six and seven respectively. W. F. Kasting very ably umpired the game, and for a wonder he gave good satisfaction and left the field without the help of an officer. Mr. Kasting entered the sack race and made a good attempt but fell by the wayside, and for his efforts a special prize was given by Mr. Scott in the shape of a combination rattle and thermometer. The committee in charge was composed of H. Keitsch, W. A. Adams, E. Brucker, R. Cloudsley and F. G. Lewis. All had an elegant time. Geo. W. Golden, of Reed & Keller, New York, was a visitor and ably assisted the committee in its work. There were a great many ladies present, which was one of the factors that made the day a success, and President Scott very ably thanked them for their being with us to keep the young and frisky, such as Buxton, Cowell, Braik, Hewson and himself, in a subdued mood.

The wedding of Joseph Sangster and Miss Emma C. Schmidt, both valued employes of S. A. Anderson, took place at the home the bride's mother on. Wednesday, August 5. The house was very prettily decorated with palms and cut flowers and the marquee on the lawn prettily lighted with Chinese lanterns, the whole effect being very pretty. The young couple departed on the evening train for a short trip west. At home after September 1, 66 West Genesee street. The congratulations of all are extended to them.

The Milwaukee delegation will leave in all probability on Sunday, and a very good crowd is going. We hope to do something in the bowling line. C. H. Keitsch, New York state vice-president of the S. A. F., has been busy circulating convention literature, and if the attendance is not large from his district it will not be his fault.

The writer recently visited Toronto and called on J. H. Dunlop at his greenhouses, which are all being replanted. The whole place looked well and there is every prospect of a good crop of American Beauty, Meteor, Bride and Brides. maid and Sunrise for this fall and winter.

Cool weather and slow trade are what we have just now. Gladioli are coming in in fine shape as are also asters. Lilium roseum is now very good.

Recent visitors: Arnold Ringier, Chicago; Geo. W. Golden, New York City; Richard Ludwig, Cromwell, Conn.; Jerry Brookins, of Orchard Park, are sending in some very fine asters.   BISON.

Baltimore.

Trade has been very dull during the past week and there is a great deal of inferior stock on the market.

According to the present outlook there will be no delegation from here to the convention this year.

Our public parks never looked as beautiful as this season.

R. Vincent is now in Paris, after having visited Scotland and England, and is about to start for home.

The Florists' Club of Baltimore, held a well attended meeting on August 10.   C. L. S.

Minneapolis.

The sweet pea show, held in this city August 5-7, was a decided success. The hall in which the exhibition was held was tastefully decorated with palms and ferns. The long list of liberal prizes brought many exhibitors and all the tables were crowded to their fullest capacity.

Trade conditions are about the same as last report. The only flower in abundance is the aster, which finds ready sale on account of scarcity of other stock. Tea roses are in limited supply and bring from $3 to $5 per hundred. Carnations can be counted by the dozen instead of by the hundred these days.

A Milwaukee Group.

Key to group on page 70.

1. Miss Zweifel.
2. W. E. Dallwig.
3. Fred. H. Holton, Supt. Exhibits.
5. Albert Enge.
6. C. C. Pollworth, President.
7. F. S. Schmeling.
8. William Branch.
9. John M. Dunlop, Vice-President.
10. W. H. Ellis.
11. H. V. Hunkel, Secretary.
12. C. B. Whitnall, Treasurer.

THE AMERICAN FLORIST

NINETEENTH YEAR.

Subscription, $1.00 a Year. To Europe, $2.00.
Subscriptions accepted only from those
in the trade.

Advertisements, on all except cover pages,
10 Cents a Line, Agate; $1.00 per inch.
Cash with Order.

No Special Position Guaranteed.

Discounts are allowed only on consecutive insertions, as follows—6 times, 5 per cent; 13 times,
10 per cent; 26 times. 20 per cent;
52 times. 30 per cent.

Cover space sold only on yearly contract at
$1.00 per inch, net, in the case of the two
front pages, regular discounts applying only to the back pages.

The Advertising Department of the AMERICAN
FLORIST is for florists, Seedsmen and nurserymen
and dealers in wares pertaining to those lines only.

Orders for less than one-half inch space not accepted.

Advertisements must reach us by Wednesday to
secure insertion in the issue for the following
Saturday. Address

AMERICAN FLORIST CO., Chicago.

THIS ISSUE 80 PAGES WITH COVERS.

CONTENTS.

SEVERAL portraits of representative
men were received too late for this issue,
because of early press work required on
this large Convention Number.

HOLLAND reports wet weather July 31
and indications are that Dutch bulbs will
be shipped this season a week or ten
days later than usual, owing to the difficulty in drying out the bulbs.

VAN TUBERGEN, of Haarlem, Holland,
is said to have a good new bulbous plant
in Allium albopilosum. The deep lilac
flowers, with a metallic sheen, are nearly
two inches across and they are borne in
umbels eight inches in diameter.

THE failure of the French bulb growers
and dealers to agree on prices until the
first week in August will make late arrival
of the bulk of this stock. They will not
come in quantity before September 5 to
10. French cable advices, August 11,

indicate firmer prices on French bulbs in
the growing district.

On to Milwaukee.

The florists of the eastern, southern and
central states voted last August to visit
Milwaukee at this time. These visitors
are now starting on their annual journey
and many travel far at no little expense.
They are the invited guests not only of
Milwaukee but of the whole northwest.
This great section, not generally so
thickly populated by our trade as the
eastern states, has been honored by the
selection of this meeting place in our
midst. It is a tribute from our older
brethren to our pioneer efforts in the new
country. The benefit of such gatherings,
while not always calculable in dollars
and cents, is incalculable in its inspiration to all members and its general influence on the public. The growth of our
business carries with it responsibilities
which we owe as a body and which we
must meet and consider as an organization.

It is, therefore, especially fitting that
the florists of the west be present at Milwaukee to welcome them. Let the west
then meet its duty as hosts and as florist
citizens. The location is convenient; to
many and a more opportune occasion
will not soon come. Let the cry be,
"On to Milwaukee."

Special Train Chicago to Milwaukee.

The special train to Milwaukee via the
Chicago, Milwaukee & St. Paul railroad
leaves Chicago 10 o'clock Tuesday morning, August 18, making a fast run to
that city. The train and car equipments
will be the finest in the west. Many
visiting delegates are likely to be on this
train. It is desired that the Chicago
florists, seedsmen and their friends take
this special and meet the other delegates
and make up an enjoyable party.

A Correction.

ED. AM. FLORIST:—The Milwaukee
souvenir is in error. Mr. W. R. Beattie
is the man who is to read the essay that
the souvenir attributes to me. Mr.
Beattie has made a study of this subject
and at my suggestion he was finally
selected. What I may say on the subject
will entirely depend upon what Mr.
Beattie says, and as I believe he will
fully cover the ground I have not even
outlined what my remarks may be, for I
realize that if he covers a few facts he
will entirely steal my thunder.
Respectfully yours,   JOHN G. ESLER.
P. S. Mr. Beattie is of the agricultural
department of the U. S. government.

Nephrolepis Piersoni.

In the report of the Massachusetts
Horticultural Society for 1902, its plant
committee gives a most careful description of this new fern, following same with
very favorable comment as to its value
commercially.

Greenhouse Building.

Southington, Conn.—C. W. Blatchley,
two houses.
Kingston, N. Y.—Henry A. Stone, violet house, 24x250.
Waterbury, Conn.—Alex. Dallas, house
150 feet long.
Upland, Pa.—John P. Crozer, vegetable
house.
Valley Falls, R. I.—J. J. Kelley, one
house.

Hotels of Milwaukee.

The following hotels are recommended
as desirable and convenient at the following rates per day:

SITUATIONS, WANTS, FOR SALE.

One Cent Per Word.

Cash with the Adv.

Plant Advs. NOT admitted under this head.

Every paid subscriber to the AMERICAN FLORIST
for the year 1903 is entitled to a five-line WANT
ADV. (situations only) free, to be used at any
time during the year.

Situation Wanted—By experienced grower of
cut flowers, as manager of small place. Address
MANAGER, care American Florist.

Situation Wanted—By experienced gardener,
single, to take charge of medium sized private
place. Address   THOS. CALLAHAN,
Glen Cove, N. Y.

Situation Wanted—By an experienced foreman
in good establishment where good wages are paid;
married; English.   S T, Mount Airy P. O.,
Germantown, Phila.

Situation Wanted—By first-class florist and
gardener as head gardener in private place. Best
references. Address
B P. care American Florist.

Situation Wanted—This fall, as head gardener
on private or public institutions; 21 years' experience; age 36; married. For further particulars
address   P G F. care American Florist.

Situation Wanted—Young man; 28 married, 10
years' experience, capable of taking full charge
of glazing and painting range of greenhouses,
desires steady situation.   JOSEPH OHRMUS,
163 Potter Ave., Long Island City, N. Y.

Situation Wanted—Foreman, propagator and
grower of roses, carnations, 'mums and the general routine of a commercial place. Thorough
recommendations as to ability; age 30.
A. L. STEVENS, 311 Chestnut St., Amble, Pa.

Situation Wanted—By orchid grower on private
place, has been with most of the best firms in
Europe; first-class education. State number of
houses. Further particulars and references.
Address   S T, American Florist.

Situation Wanted—By an all-around florist;
13 years' experience in growing cut flowers and
general greenhouse stock; best of references;
age 36; married; private or commercial place.
Address   R G B, care American Florist.

Situation Wanted—By first-class florist with
good taste, knowledge and business ability,
wishes to take charge of store or plant department in same in any city. First-class references.
Western city preferred. Address
W, care American Florist.

Situation Wanted—Take charge or second man
on private place; good propagator and grower of
cut flowers, pot and bedding plants; landscape
work; all-around gardener, farmer, poultryman.
Married; age 35; life experience; good references.
Address   GARDENES, Cowesett, R. I.

Situation Wanted—An Englishman wants a
position as gardener on a private place or grower of roses and carnations and violets on commercial place. Have good references from the last
two places where I worked 19 years. Private
place preferred. Address
J H. care American Florist.

Situation Wanted—Dutchman, single, 28 years,
speaks English, as head gardener on private place
or in reliable commercial establishment. Good
grower of roses and greenhouse plants; also
understands forcing; 18 years' European experience; can furnish good references. Preference
given to New York or vicinity. Please state
wages.   W O, care American Florist.

Help Wanted—Rose growers.
SOUTH PARK FLORAL CO., New Castle, Ind.

Help Wanted—At once, young all-around florist. State wages.   P G, care American Florist.

Help Wanted—All-around man for general
greenhouse work. Address
T. N. YATES & CO., Mt. Airy, Phila., Pa.

Newport.

NEWPORT SEASON IN FULL BLAST.—DECORATIONS FOR MRS. ASTOR.—NEW CONSERVATORY.—DAHLIA SHOW THIS FALL.

At a recent function given by Mrs. Astor the decorations by Hodgson were rich rather than elaborate, in keeping with the house. Throughout the house were many handsome palms and foliage plants, many of which were from the extensive greenhouses on the Astor estate, and others specially selected from the florist's greenhouses. The entrance hall was lined with roses on either side around the doorway and staircase, the newel posts being elaborately decorated with these flowers. In the hall, dining and reception rooms were many tall vases of seasonable flowers with ornamental grasses. The large piazza on the cliff side of the house, from which an uninterrupted view of the ocean could be had, was made unusually attractive by the use of palms, hydrangeas and other flowering plants, passion vines in full flower being a prominent feature of the display. The sun parlor adjoining was similarly treated.

The Newport season is now in full swing. J. M. Hodgson, Siebrecht & Son, Wadley & Smythe, from New York, and Gibson Brothers and S. Fadden, of Newport, are handling most of the decorations. Outdoor flowers are plentiful and masses of hollyhock, gladioli and asters are being used. American Beauty roses, of which Carl Jurgens grows a great quantity, are used for table decorations. Italian gardens are now the fashion here, about a dozen of the large estates have adopted them and more are being laid out.

A greenhouse 22x50 feet has been built for Mrs. Rose Grosvenor by the Philips Manufacturing Company, of Newark, N. J. The potting shed is built of rustic logwood. The genial gardener, Henry C. Hogan, will grow carnations, gardenias and bulbous flowering plants.

The Newport Horticultural Society will hold a dahlia show this fall. P. L. Z.

Wholesale Flower Markets

MILWAUKEE, Aug. 13.	
Roses, Beauty, med. per doz.	1.50
" " short "	.75@1.00
" Liberty	4.00@ 6.00
" Bride, Bridesmaid	4.00@ 6.00
" Meteor, Golden Gate	4.00@ 6.00
" Perle	4.00@ 6.00
Carnations	1.00@ 2.00
Sweet peas	.15
Smilax	10.00@12.50
Asparagus	50.00
Gladioli	3.00@ 4.50
Asters	1.50@ 2.00

PITTSBURG, Aug. 13.	
Roses, Beauty, specials, per doz.	2.50@3.50
" " extras	1.00@2.00
" " No. 1 "	.75@1.00
" " No. 2 "	.50@ .75
" Bride, Bridesmaid	1.00@ 6.00
" Meteor	3.00@ 4.00
" Kaiserin	2.00@ 6.00
" Liberties	2.00@ 6.00
Carnations	.50@ 1.50
Lily of the Valley	3.00@ 4.00
Sweet peas	.30@ .50
Smilax	8.00@12.00
Adiantum	.75@ 1.25
Asparagus, strings	40.00@50.00
" Sprengeri	2.00@ 4.00
Gladioli	1.00@ 4.00
Flower lilies	8.00@14.00
Asters	.50@ 1.50

CINCINNATI, Aug. 13.	
Roses, Beauty	10.00@35.00
" Bride, Bridesmaid	3.00@ 6.00
" Liberty	3.00@ 8.00
" Meteor, Golden Gate	3.00@ 6.00
Carnations	1.00@ 2.00
Asparagus	50.00
Smilax	12.50@15.00
Adiantum	1.00@ 1.50
Gladioli	3.00
Asters	1.00@ 2.00
Lilium Album and Rubrum	4.00

ST. LOUIS, Aug. 13.	
Roses, Beauty, long stem	3.00
" Beauty, medium stem	1.50
" Beauty, short stem	4.00@ 6.00
" Lib'ty	2.00@ 6.00
" Bride, Bridesmaid	2.00@ 4.00
" Golden Gate	3.00@ 4.00
Carnations	1.00@ 1.50
Smilax	12.50
Asparagus Sprengeri	1.00@ 1.50
" Plumosus	18.00@30.00
Gladioli	1.00@ 4.00
Ferns	per 1000 1.50
China Asters	1.00@ 2.00
Tuber'es	4.00

INTERNATIONAL FLOWER DELIVERY.

INTERNATIONAL FLOWER DELIVERY.

STEAMSHIPS LEAVE FOREIGN PORTS.

FROM	TO	STEAMER	*LINE	DAY		DUE ABOUT
Liverpool	New York	Lucania	1	Sat. Aug. 22,		Aug. 30
Liverpool	"	Etruria	1	Sat. Aug. 29,		Sept. 4
Liverpool	"	Teutonic	7	Wed. Aug. 19, 5:00 p. m.		Aug. 26
Liverpool	"	Arabic	7	Fri. Aug. 21, 5:00 p. m.		Aug. 29
Liverpool	"	Germanic	7	Wed. Aug. 26, 5:00 p. m.		Sept. 2
Liverpool	"	Cedric	7	Fri. Aug. 28, 5:00 p. m.		Sept. 3
Liverpool	Boston	Ivernia	1	Tues. Aug. 25,		Sept. 2
Liverpool	"	New England	15	Thur. Aug. 20,		Aug. 27
Liverpool	"	Mayflower	16	Thur. Aug. 27,		Sept. 3
Liverpool	"	Bohemian	16	Fri. Aug. 21,		
Liverpool	"	Canadian	16	Fri. Aug. 28,		
Liverpool	Montreal	Dominion	15	Wed. Aug. 19,		
Liverpool	"	Southwark	15	Wed. Aug. 26,		
Liverpool	"	Tunisian	19	Thur. Aug. 20,		
Liverpool	"	Parisian	19	Thur. Aug. 27,		
Glasgow	New York	Anchoria	5	Thur. Aug. 20,		Aug. 31
Glasgow	"	Furnessia	5	Thur. Aug. 27,		
Glasgow	"	Laurentian	5	Sat. Aug. 29,		Sept. 8
Genoa	"	Liguria	12	Mon. Aug. 17,		
Genoa	"	Citta di Milano	12	Mon. Aug. 24,		
Genoa	"	Princess Irene	13	Thur. Aug. 27,		Sept. 9
Genoa	"	Cambroman	15	Sat. Aug. 29,		
Southampton	"	Philadelphia	8	Sat. Aug. 22, Noon.		Sept. 2
Southampton	"	St. Paul	8	Wed. Aug. 26, Noon.		Sept. 2
Southampton	"	St. Louis	8	Sat. Aug. 29, Noon.		Sept. 5
Southampton	"	Menominee	6	Wed. Aug. 26,		Sept. 5
London	"	Minnehaha	6	Sat. Aug. 22,		Sept. 1
London	"	Mesaba	6	Sat. Aug. 29,		
Antwerp	"	Zeeland	9	Sat. Aug. 22, Noon.		Aug. 31
Antwerp	"	Finland	9	Sat. Aug. 29, 3:00 p. m.		Sept. 7
Hamburg	"	Moltke	3	Thur. Aug. 20,		Aug. 27
Hamburg	"	Pretoria	3	Sat. Aug. 22,		
Hamburg	"	Furst Bismarck	3	Thur. Aug. 27,		Sept. 4
Havre	"	La Lorraine	10	Sat. Aug. 22,		Aug. 29
Havre	"	La Touraine	10	Sat. Aug. 29,		Sept. 5
Copenhagen	"	United States	4	Wed. Aug. 26,		
Rotterdam	"	Potsdam	11	Sat. Aug. 22,		Aug. 31
Rotterdam	"	Statendam	11	Sat. Aug. 29,		
Bremen	"	Kronprinz Wilhelm	13	Tues. Aug. 25,		Sept. 1
Bremen	"	Barbarossa	13	Sat. Aug. 22,		Sept. 1
Bremen	"	Grosser Kurfuerst	13	Sat. Aug. 29,		Sept. 7
Sidney	San Francisco	Sonoma	18	Mon. Aug. 17,		Sept. 1
Hongkong	"	China	17	Sat. Aug. 22,		Sept. 18
Hongkong	Vancouver	Empress of India	20	Wed. Aug. 26,		Sept. 16
Hongkong	Yokohama	Aki Maru	22	Tues. Aug. 25, p. m.		Sept. 9
Hongkong	Seattle	Aki Maru	22	Tues. Aug. 25, p. m.		Sept. 23
Yokohama	"	Iyo Maru	22	Tues. Aug. 25, p. m.		Sept. 9
Naples	New York	Roma	14	Thur. Aug. 27,		Sept. 8

* See steamship list on opposite page.

Hardy Cut Ferns

First Quality, 60c per 1000.

FANCY DAGGER ALSO DEALER IN

CHRISTMAS TREES, Baled Spruce for Cemetery Use,
Bouquet Green, Sphagnum Moss, Etc.

L. B. BRAGUE, Hinsdale, Mass.

Mr. Brague will have an exhibit at Milwaukee Convention.

PRIMROSES.

Per 100
Chinese, 2-inch pots, July $2.00
Obconica. Alba and Rosea 2.00
Forbesi, "Baby" 2.00
Paper White Narcissus Grandiflora, Sept. 1 .. 1.00

CASH.

ASPARAGUS.

Per 100
Sprengeri, 2-inch pots, Ready August 20th...$2.00
Plumosus Nanus 2.50
Panay Seed, Non Plus Ultra, ready August
1st, per oz..$4.00

JOS. H. CUNNINGHAM, Delaware, O.

The F. R. WILLIAMS CO.

Wholesale Florists,

CLEVELAND,   OHIO.

SMILAX PLANTS.
700, 2¼-inch and 3½-inch, strong, out back,
$1.50 per 100. Cash.
M. M. LATHROP, Courtland, N. Y.

25,000 CANNAS, Field Clumps for fall. Low,
Best Sorts. Write for prices. 25,000 Violets for
Fall, Pot and Field Stock, 83 and $4 per 100. 25,000
Shrubs, Vines and Bulbs for catalogue trade. Send
for list. BENJ. CONNELL, West Grove, Pa

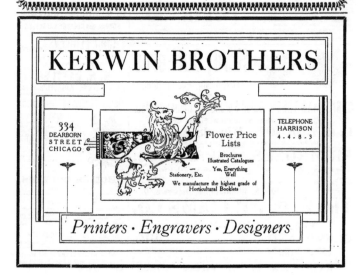

THE SEED TRADE.

AMERICAN SEED TRADE ASSOCIATION.
S. F. Willard, Pres ; J. Charles McCullough, First Vice-Pres.; C. E. Kendel, Cleveland, O., Sec'y and Treas.
Twenty-second annual convention St. Louis, Mo., June, 1904.

FURTHER news from Holland, July 28, reports the hyacinth crop very poor.

VISITED CHICAGO: J. C. Robinson, Waterloo, Neb.; S. J. Lee, Fort Smith, Ark.

ALSIKE clover in Canada is a good crop and prices, will be lower than last year.

TORONTO, ONT.—Thos. Rennie and wife have returned safely from their Pacific coast trip.

LOUISVILLE reports a sixty-five per cent onion set crop, but the average is fairly large.

THE southeastern Wisconsin onion set districts report crops of sets in fine condition and medium in size.

THE sweet corn outlook in the vicinity of Rochester, N. Y., is rather poor, the majority of crops not yet being in tassel.

RED top onion sets (the true summer variety) have been harvested and the yield is good; prices $1.50 to $1.75 per bushel at first hand.

Wm. Sim, Cliftondale, has entered suit against several seed houses for damages alleged to have been sustained by using a certain insecticide.

THE cucumber pickle crop about Chicago is reported badly injured by an insect which has killed the plants at the root. Some fields are reported plowed under.

CLASS ADVERTISING for July contains an exceedingly interesting, illustrated article regarding the Atlantic City seed trade convention and prominent members who attended it.

SPEAKING of the French bulb market, one dealer ingenuously remarks: "Purchases are very difficult, the growers do not wish to conform to the prices that we have fixed for them." Strange!

F. BARTELDES & COMPANY report, August 13: "We are handling in Kansas a large crop of meadow fescue and prices will rule low. Timothy is also good. The alfalfa crop is not yet made, but the acreage is large."

SEATTLE, WASH.—Malmo & Company have sold their retail store at 916 Second avenue, but retain their wholesale business, nursery and greenhouses, with store at East Pike and Broadway, where their office will also be located.

CONNECTICUT sweet corn growers report the average crop there large, and, although the crop is backward, if the season proves favorable from now on there should be considerable corn for sale which has not been contracted.

THE Livingston Seed Company writes "Indications are not very assuring for a large tomato seed crop. In the first place, plants went out late owing to the cold, late spring. Now the weather is very dry, and development is being much retarded. It all depends upon how late frosts hold off."

C. C. MORSE & COMPANY report, August 10: Crops generally with us are good. This does not apply, however, to the sweet pea crop, which is considerably less than an average one. About thirty per cent of the sweet pea list will be short, and the surplus on the few varieties which will be filled in full will be extremely limited. Excepting sweet peas we expect to have fewer items to report short this year than for many years past.

EVERETT B. CLARK, president of the Everett B. Clark Seed Company, Milford, Conn., writes August 11. "It is very hard to give an intelligent report regarding our seed crops. We had expected our late ripening crops would come in better, but as the season advances our weather conditions continue to be unfavorable, wet and cold instead of heat and sunshine. We will hardly get at best more than half a crop of carrot, parsnip, beet, onion and sweet corn, and even to reach that result we must have a late fall with plenty of sunshine for a month to come."

J. B. RICE & COMPANY write a very interesting letter dated, Cambridge, August 6. "Regarding seed crops here in Washington county, New York, there are quite a few hundred acres under cultivation, seeds which are not yet harvested, principally vine seeds and sweet corn.

"Owing to continuous dry weather, over fifty days in early springtime, planting was somewhat delayed on this account and many crops that were planted did not germinate satisfactorily. For this reason we have a stand which is very uneven and which is quite variable in forwardness, as you can imagine.

"All crops are three or four weeks later than they ought to be at this season of the year, and, while most crops are coming forward and look very well at this time, so much depends upon the fall and the holding off of the frost that it is quite unsafe to prophesy now what our crop will be.

"It can be said that if we have a very favorable fall and freedom from frost we will get a fair average crop of both vines and sweet corn. This is the best we can say at present. Present conditions of weather are cool, cloudy and unfavorable."

"Other parts of the country are in line with Washington county, pretty good show of cucumber vines but few fruits as yet set on them.—ED.]

PANSY—MASTERPIECE.   CHINESE PRIMROSE—TYPE OF INTERNATIONAL STRAIN.   CINERARIA.

THE NURSERY TRADE.

AM. ASSOCIATION OF NURSERYMEN.
N. W. HALE, Knoxville, Tenn. Pres.; FRANK
A. WEBER, St. Louis, Mo., Vice-Pres.; GEORGE C.
SEAGER, Rochester, N. Y., Sec'y.
Twenty-ninth annual convention, Atlanta, Ga.,
June, 1904.

SANTA ROSA, CAL.—Luther Burbank's
experimental grounds were recently visited by a party of Texan horticulturists.

GERANIUM MME. A. CHEVRELIERRE, in
the opinion of W. N. Rudd, is the best
double white to date.

MUNCIE, IND.—On July 30 work was
commenced on the beautifying of McCulloch park, donated to the city by George
McCulloch, of Indianapolis.

AMPELOPSIS QUINQUEFOLIA, in that
common form which does not produce
supporting disks freely, is very useful as
a summer hedge plant, trained over
wires.

ROSA RUGOSA hybrids Belle Poitevine
and Blanc Double De Coubert are the
best for the west. The former has semi-
double flowers of a deep rose shade while
in the latter the blooms are double, pure
white and very fragrant.

WELLESLEY, MASS.—C. E. Dana, the
billboard man, refuses to recognize the
authority of the town park commission
in their regulations regarding the maintenance of billboards contiguous to the
public parks and the question may be
carried to the courts for determination.

PITTSBURG.—Lawrenceville will soon
have a public park as the Schoenberger
tracts of between seven and eight acres
in the seventeenth ward, occupying the
block between Butler, Forty-sixth, Lawrence and Forty-seventh streets, has been
purchased for the purpose at a cost of
$46,516.

MONTPELIER, VT.—The late John E.
Hubbard bequeathed a fine tract of land
to Montpelier to be used as a public park.
Plans are on foot to call a special city
meeting for the purpose of formally
accepting the gift and providing for its
care.

HUNTINGTON, N. Y.—A movement is on
foot for the formation of a horticultural
and agricultural society and a very general interest is manifested in the project
by · professional and amateur plant
lovers.

A TRACT of 320 acres in Fitzwilliam,
N. H., has been given to the Appalachian
Club of Boston by Miss Mary L. Ware.
This includes a magnificent grove of
Rhododendron maximum, eleven acres in
extent, famed as the only growth of
these of any size east of the Allegheny
mountains. The intent of the gift is to
insure the preservation of the rhododendrons from removal or destruction. G.
W. Putnam has been appointed superintendent.

Raffia.

Raffia grows in several parts of the
world but the best quality for nurserymen's use comes from Madagascar.
When raffia first came to this country,
about twenty-five years ago, it was an
unknown quantity. The first consignment was shipped· to a commission
merchant in New York who handled
fibers used in the manufacture of paper,
and as near as we can learn, the

first lot of raffia was sold as "paper
stock" at about 2 cents a pound.
Within a few years the asparagus
growers in the vicinity of New York City
began using raffia for tying asparagus in
bunches ready for market, then nurserymen began using it for tying buds, and
now is is used by nurserymen everywhere.
A few years ago the wholesale millinery
houses offered hats made from raffia and
to-day you can buy a raffia hat in almost
any town in the country. Raffia is also
used for fancy or "Indian" baskets,
pillow covers, table covers, belts, slippers,
etc., and it can be bought in many colors.
There is no specific, dependable grade of
raffia, as is the case with most articles of
merchandise, and the "best" from one firm
may not be near as good as the "best"
from another firm.

Colorado Springs, Colo.

THE HORTICULTURAL SOCIETY COMPLETES
ARRANGEMENTS FOR FLOWER SHOW. —
LULL IN BUSINESS STILL CONTINUES.—
NOTES.

At the regular meeting of the El Paso
County Horticultural Society, held at
the offices of W. W. Williamson, final
arrangements were made with respect to
the flower show to be held in North park
from August 19 to 21 inclusive. Every
detail has been carefully planned and the
management has promised to put up the
best show ever held by the society. The
gate receipts are expected to cover a
great part of the expense connected with
the exhibition. These shows have been
well patronized in former years by residents and visitors of the city and the
regular admission fee of 25 cents is cheerfully paid by the public. The prizes,
which will this year consist of about
$1,200 in cash and a number of cups and
other souvenirs, are taken out of a. fund
made up by subscription. The school
children's department is of special interest and the distribution of patronage
among all classes always creates an active
interest on the part of all citizens and
secures their hearty co-operation.
There is little to report in the way of
trade news, the lull in business reported
at last writing still continuing to an
extent quite unusual to this section.
Trade has seldom slackened up much in
this city during the summer months in
former years, owing to the constant
stream of tourists stopping here for a
few days on their way to California and
back, but now flowers seem to have lost
their charm over tourists hustling
through strenuous vacations.
Wm. Clark has overhauled his heating
system at the Roswell place and erected
wooden benches in place of the solid
beds used last season.
Stock benched for A. J. Baur's cut
flowers looks very promising, as also
does the supply of flowering plants,
palms, ferns, etc.
S. S.

LACOMBE, ALTA, N. W. T.—Grace Gibberson, daughter of C. A. Gibberson, was
married recently to Robt. Ritchie. Business is light in this vicinity. Some building will be done this fall.

MENDOTA, ILL. — Henry Schweitzer
states that he has received many offers of
material to re-stock his place but so far
has no house in which to care for it. The
hail insurance has been paid, however,
and Mr. Schweitzer will soon be in a
position to handle anything which sym-
pathizers may send him.

OUR PASTIMES.

S. A. F. COMMITTEE ON SPORTS.

P. J. Hauswirth, 227 Michigan avenue, Chicago; C. C. Pollworth and F. Schmeling, Milwaukee. Announcements of coming contests or other events of interests to our bowling, shooting and sporting readers are solicited and will be given place in this column.

Address all correspondence for this department to Wm. J. Stewart, 79 Milk St., Boston, Mass.; Robt. Kift, 1725 Chestnut St., Philadelphia, Pa.; or to the American Florist Co., 324 Dearborn St., Chicago, Ill.

At Chicago.

The members of the Chicago bowling club will hold a meeting at Ed. Winterson's place, Sunday, August 16, at 3 o'clock, when they will definitely decide regarding matters at Milwaukee.

Cricket at Philadelphia.

The return cricket match between the Florists' Club of Philadelphia and Montgomery eleven's took place at Wissinoming on August 8. It was a much closer contest than the first and the florists had the game by a margin of five runs at the end of the first inning, but lost their lead in the second and were beaten by two runs and one wicket to spare. After the game lunch was served on the porch of the club house, the florists being the hosts on this occasion.

William K. Harris and Edward Campbell acted as umpires and succeeded in getting themselves so cordially disliked as umpires usually do—which is equivalent to saying that they did their duty and did it well. Commodore Westcott did not attend this match, having a pressing engagement at Waretown but he sent some of his special brew of "Florists' Club punch" and that was the next best to having John himself. Bats have now been laid away for the season with Montgomery victor for this year. The score follows:

FLORISTS.	1st	2d
S. Hammond	7	5
W. Robertson	14	7
J. Cullen	0	5
Jas. Campbell	1	0
Geo. Campbell	4	0
H. Warner	6	0
W. Falck	1	0
G. C. Watson	0	1
T. Councillor	0	0
C. W. Cox	2	1
Totals	34	16

MONTGOMERY.	1st	2d
J. G. Gardner	5	1
Neil Gardner	0	15
P. P. Ewing	6	0
C. Peacock	1	1
C. Pollicott	5	2
C. Dumont	3	4
T. Archbold	5	3
T. Cummings	2	2
Jas. Brett	2	
W. Carey	0	1
Totals	29	26

G. C. W.

Convention Bowling Prizes.

We are advised that the following prizes have been offered in bowling and other contests; complete list next week.

Milwaukee Florists' Club, six gold medals for members of winning team.

C. C. Pollworth Company, Milwaukee, six scarf pins for members of second team; and gold medal to florist coming the greatest distance.

John A. Evans, Quaker City Machine Works, Richmond, Ind., $10 gold medal. John F. Wilcox, Council Bluffs, Ia., $10 umbrella.

Prizes are also offered by Milwaukee Citizens' Business League; F. Pollworth & Brother, Milwaukee; Henry Weber,

park commissioner, Milwaukee; Brunswick-Balke Company, Chicago. E. F. Winterson Company, Chicago, silver cup for highest individual total in three games. W. P. Mussey, Chicago, $25 gold badge for best individual bowler, under special regulations.

At Philadelphia.

The convention team has had several matches with good teams on outside alleys which have resulted more or less disastrously. These games are, however, good practice and have helped in more ways than one. The difference between the surface of the club alleys and the very smooth surface of the more modern kind now being built is a great handicap to the club players, as the balls do not grip the floor and the action is entirely different. This is even more apparent when strangers play in matches at the club, as the home team is almost always the winner. An estimate to plane down or resurface the alleys has been obtained from the Brunswick Balke Company and

it looks as if something will be done to bring things up to date. The score rolled Thursday, August 6, was as follows:

Player	1st	2d	3d	T'l
Moss	157	191	164	512
Yates	196	180	156	532
Robertson	138	144	187	469
Connor	148	156	200	505
Kift	114	134	158	406
Petties	195	148	134	477

K.

Joliet, Ill.

The J. D. Thompson Carnation Company has finished building and planting for the season. A new steam heated boarding house was the latest addition to the establishment. J. E. Jenson, foreman for the company, has just returned from a trip through the east. Among the carnations planted are the Nelson Fisher and Mrs. Patten varieties, the latter being variegated. Both are seedlings of Peter Fisher, of Ellis, Mass., and the firm believes them to be the two best carnations that will be disseminated in in 1904. Judging from the record of Enchantress, this company would not recommend anything but the best.

THE AMERICAN FLORIST

A WEEKLY JOURNAL FOR THE TRADE

America is "the Prow of the Vessel; there may be more comfort Amidships, but we are the first to touch Unknown Seas."

Vol. XXI.   CHICAGO AND NEW YORK, AUGUST 22, 1903.   No. 794.

THE AMERICAN FLORIST

NINETEENTH YEAR.

Copyright 1903, by American Florist Company
Entered as Second-Class Mail Matter.

PUBLISHED EVERY SATURDAY BY

AMERICAN FLORIST COMPANY,
324 Dearborn St., Chicago.
Eastern Office: 79 Milk St., Boston.

Subscription, $1.00 a year.   To Europe, $2.00.
Subscriptions accepted only from the trade.
Volumes half-yearly from August, 1901.

THE AMERICAN CARNATION SOCIETY.
Annual convention at Detroit, Mich., March 2,
1904. ALBERT M. HERR, Lancaster, Pa., secretary.

AMERICAN ROSE SOCIETY.
Annual meeting and exhibition, Philadelphia,
March, 1904. LEONARD BARRON, 136 Liberty St.,
New York, secretary.

CHRYSANTHEMUM SOCIETY OF AMERICA
Annual convention and exhibition, New York,
November 10-13, 1903. FRED H. LEMON, Richmond,
Ind., secretary.

THIS ISSUE 52 PAGES WITH COVER.

THE MILWAUKEE CONVENTION.

Next Convention at St. Louis.

BREITMEYER, President.

The nineteenth annual meeting of the Society of American Florists was in every way a pronounced success. The attendance, perhaps was not so large as might have been expected in a location so central, but it was very satisfactory nevertheless. The exhibition made a very fine appearance and compared favorably with the best ever held under the auspices of the society. Much credit is due to Superintendent Holton and his assistants for their excellent work in this department. On Tuesday morning there remained nothing to do but to receive the visitors in the exhibition hall three hours before the time appointed for the opening of the first session. This is probably without precedent.

Except on the first day the weather was all that could be desired and the local trade and citizens were most hospitable in their attentions. At the meetings much good work was accomplished in every department and we can safely say that the society is keeping well abreast of similar institutions in other lines of industry. But there is much to be done and the necessity of united and spirited educational and missionary work appears to grow as the trade develops. The recent programme of valuable and timely papers and discussions assures us that the officers of the society have these facts well in mind.

The opening session was a record breaker in the attendance, and standing room only was obtainable in the convention hall when Chairman C. C. Pollworth, of the Milwaukee Florists' Club, formally greeted the visitors.

Mayor David S. Rose, in welcoming the convention, which he characterized as a splendid demonstration far exceeding his anticipations, remarked: "You might as well say that sunshine is not necessary to human life and human happiness as to say that flowers do not contribute to accomplish both results. In those sections of the country where Milwaukee is not known it is recognized as the city of beer; but, ladies and gentlemen, you will agree with me, after visiting our residential sections, that ours is entitled to the distinction of the city of flowers."

Assuming that his hearers were interested in knowing something of the city, the mayor explained that its population of 325,000, that that of any other city in the nation; that the value of its manufactured products last year exceeded $230,000,000, that its manufacturing interests gave employment to upwards of 80,000 pairs of willing and industrious hands, and that its wholesale jobbing trade exceeded $340,000,000 last year. He then spoke of the city's splendid public institutions, its commodious city hall which cost $1,000,000, its public library and museum, one of the great educational institutions of the middle west; its unapproachable public school system which, as a part of the general system, had contributed to place the Badger State among the foremost of the states from an educational standpoint; its musical conservatories, art galleries and societies, and its system of small public parks which afforded the poor a luxury that only the rich enjoy in many of the large cities. The excellent police department, he said, was instructed to perform the functions of members of the Red Cross societies when visitors were in town. (Laughter.)

The mayor declared that there was no tenement house district in Milwaukee, but the people owned their own homes and, wherever a patch of ground was found, there was to be seen verdure and fragrant flowers. "Take the esthetic attributes out of man's nature," he exclaimed, "and we would have no man left. (Applause.) We are located but 85 miles from the wickedest city on God's earth (laughter), and yet ours is the most orderly. With us life and property are always secure. Your ladies may go, at mid-day or midnight, through

Robert Kift.
Sergeant-at-Arms.

any section of our city without fear of interference. They tell me that you have brought your champion bowlers, marksmen and sportsmen with you. Let me warn you now that you don't know what you're up against. Milwaukee has more high grade bowling alleys and more champion bowlers to the square inch than any other city in this whole land, and if any of you florists who profess to be experts in this very manly sport desire to take issue with me upon that proposition you may pick your bowling team, and I will pick one, and we'll put you to sleep in the first round. (Laughter.) I spoke of that product which has served to make Milwaukee famous. You needn't be afraid of it. We feed it to our babies and, if you want to know the result, just observe our handsome women and our strong, sturdy men passing along the street." The mayor closed by urging the visitors to avail themselves of the pleasures afforded by the Cream City so that they might preserve happy memories of their visit.

Ex-President Adam Graham, of Cleveland, made a humorous response and three hearty cheers were given his honor upon his retirement from the hall. President John Burton, of Philadelphia, then delivered his annual address, which was much applauded.

President Burton's Address.

To THE SOCIETY OF AMERICAN FLORISTS —LADIES AND GENTLEMEN:—Most of you are aware, I suppose, that I am not a believer in long addresses, and it will be my aim in the few remarks I have to make to you at this, our nineteenth annual convention, to say what I have to say in the fewest possible words. From all sections of the country I hear good news of a prosperous business during the past season. The black cloud which hung over many of us during the fall and early winter, the strike in the hard coal regions of Pennsylvania, was happily dispelled before it had spelt absolute ruin to our business. The subsequent good prices and brisk demand largely compensated for losses sustained in the majority of cases, but we regret the misfortune and extend our fullest sympathy to those who suffered so

severely, many of whom were almost ruined by this calamity. Another black cloud which threatened our business last season in addition to the calamity of the coal strike, was the arbitrary action of the express companies in advancing rates on the shipment of cut flowers, to an exorbitant and almost prohibitory extent. The trade was greatly alarmed and a storm of protest arose in all sections of the country. Florists' clubs, local committees and private individuals, all took an energetic hand in resisting the exactions, and the national society gives full acknowledgement to all this assistance in securing the victory which it happily gained after several months of energetic effort. Special acknowledgement is also due to the valuable and faithful work performed in this connection by the society's special committee, Messrs. May, O'Mara and Sheridan. On the whole the past year has been one of progress and prosperity, and there seems every reason to believe that the upward tendency will continue. I am not going to preach to you about the inevitable reaction which they say is

J. J. Beneke.
Vice-President elect of the S. A. F.

bound to come sometime, but will content myself with a word of caution to hold something in reserve. During a season of remarkable expansion the excitement is apt to carry us further than is wise or expedient and in this, as in all other things it is best not to be as expansive as we can but to stop short before we reach the extreme of our ability or endurance. This remark is inspired by the way things are developing in the middle west. Glass is being erected so fast and general business is expanding at such a rate in that section as almost to make an easterner's head swim. I have travelled considerably over the western section in the past year, and have to acknowledge that we in the east have but the faintest conception of how things have been developing, especially in the production of cut flowers. It is simply astonishing and we must extend our congratulations and endeavor to sit as gracefully as we can on the back seat hereafter. I may remark, however, that the development in the culture of foliage

and flowering plants does not seem to have kept pace with that of cut flowers. Plants will probably be the next department taken up by our enterprising friends in the west and will tend to diversify and steady the business.

Looking back over the development of the past nineteen years, we must all feel that progress would have been much slower if there had been no Society of American Florists with its annual conventions, its discussions of timely topics, the swapping of ideas among the members, each member giving and receiving inspiration for further progress, giving and receiving counsel of untold value and laying the foundations of success, not only for themselves, but for all those of their neighbors who in turn profited by their good example. Those pioneers of progress who attended the conventions in days gone by, came from all sections of the country and when they went home and put their new ideas into effect, all their neighbors saw it and went and did likewise. And so the good work went on all over the land, quietly and unostentatiously, but none the less surely, until we see the remarkable expansion of the present day. And, yet how few of those stay-at-homes ever give the society the credit for all the priceless benefits they thus received from it.

Every member of the trade owes a debt of gratitude to the society beyond money and beyond price, and they owe it to their profession to do their share for the general advancement. One's first duty is to look after his own interests, of course, but there are other duties beside that of one's family and one's business; one of which is the duty which each of us owes to his profession. I do not attribute neglect of this higher duty altogether to mere selfishness. I think a great deal of it comes from want of reflection. If all would reflect on the great silent work the society has been doing for the past nineteen years we would never hear the question, "What has the society done?" and instead of grudging the three dollars annual dues they would put their hand in their pockets cheerfully to the last man, for that small sum and also find the time to attend conventions, and so pay the debt to the society at least that much. We

Frank P. Dilger.
The ladies' favorite at Milwaukee.

have made great strides so far, but there are great questions in front of us yet and we need the combined strength of the whole trade to tackle them.

While reflecting on my visits among my compeers in different parts of the country, there is one point that has struck me very forcibly, namely, that the place where packing sheds are clean and tidy and orderly, where the walks are smooth and free from rubbish, where the beds are without weeds, where paint and repairs are in evidence all round, there is the place where the prosperous man holds out, showing very clearly that the old fashioned virtues of industry and thrift are not dead letters in this modern age of improvement and invention but are still the difficult and narrow paths that lead to success. I admire hard work aided by brains, but I do not forget that hard work comes first, brains after. Brains will never do anything in this world unless there be some push behind them. An industrious and thrifty worker will beat the born-tired genius every time. In our business it is not the genius we want so much as the fellow who will take hold with a will and do his share of the daily grubbing, confident that in the long run that is the way to become competent and be able to hold his end up in the race for life. Not that I object to genius; about one in five thousand, perhaps, will be a genius and we can look on and wonder when he comes along; what we have to consider now is that we want the other four thousand, nine hundred and ninety nine to be competent and industrious hewers of wood and drawers of water. If the whole five thousand are aided and abetted by higher education into thinking themselves geniuses, life will be half over for most of them before they realize their mistake. Let us start them out right.

We heard something recently about the help forming a union, which may be a good thing for the business and then again it may not. For myself I have grave doubts about it if the same spirit of antagonism and selfishness animates it as seems to be the case in other businesses. I have no objection to any good workman bettering his condition if he can, and I think merit should always be promptly recognized, but I cannot see any good in boosting the incompetent man at the expense of his fellows. If a workman's union will devote itself to improving the quality of our help it will be doing a good work and if the help are bound to have a union we ought to minimize the evil of same by encouraging them along that line. Most of you have had experience of what a coal strike means and you can realize the damage that a body of irresponsible, bull-headed men could do on a greenhouse establishment at a critical time. For damage of that kind there seems to be no protection and we will have to prepare ourselves as best we may against this threatened trouble. A factory or mine can shut down without much direct loss but the florist has to keep going or be ruined.

Among the few remarks which I had the honor of presenting to the society for its consideration last year, I included a suggestion for a plan to knit our organization more closely together when special work was required on any particular flower. The method previously followed had been to form a separate society, and I agreed with nearly every president before me in thinking that way was not the best that could be devised, and suggested that a committee with power to add to its numbers should be appointed,

PHILIP BREITMEYER.
President elect Society of American Florists.

say on the peony as a starter; not that that was the only flower on which good work could be done best, but because the interest in it was on the increase and its possibilities in the florists' business seemed capable of being stimulated for the benefit of the members of our society. The suggestion having been adopted, it devolved on me to appoint the committee and in that I found some difficulty. I had to cover quite a large field and occupy several months before I could find nine men to serve on that committee. As finally made up the committee consisted of the following: Patrick O'Mara, Carl Cropp, G. C. Watson, John Farquhar, Edwin Lonsdale, J. T. Temple, Peter Bisset, S. M. Meehan and W. R. Smith.

That committee will no doubt make its report to you in due course. I understand there has been a question raised as to the committees power to add to its number from the omission of that clause from the motion, although the said motion was intended to give effect to my suggestion—"that a committee with power to add to its numbers be appointed." This may have hampered the committee, but if the society wishes to continue the work of the committee the defect can easily be remedied at this meeting. A year will not make a great deal of difference to a committee whose work will be continuous and permanent.

The difficulty of securing a committee on the peony arose from two reasons, first, the peony being a specialty, second, because several of the more prominent peony specialists had already pledged themselves to another organization. While disclaiming all thought of rivalry, we recognize that there is work of a special nature from the florists' standpoint, which our organization can do for us better than the other, which seems to be under the wing of the nurserymen's society.

I would also suggest for consideration at this meeting, the wisdom of appointing similar committees for the iris and the phlox. Both of these families have a future before them and we want all the information we can get that will help the florist in extending his business along these lines.

In regard to nomenclature I would again suggest the advisability of reviving that committee. This matter was recommended by the executive committee at its meeting in Milwaukee. The good work accomplished in the past, leads to the belief that such a committee has a permanent function in our society both preventive and remedial, and I would strongly recommend to the individual members to call the attention of this committee (if appointed) to all instances of duplication or renaming that come to their knowledge. It is very little encouragement to a committee of this kind to be told they have not corrected an abuse when the individuals who suffered never took the trouble to call their attention to the matter.

The executive committee had several important matters before it at the annual meeting in Milwaukee, which will come

our society to the families and friends of those of our members who have been called from amongst us during the past year. We feel the loss of their able assistance and wise counsels in the work we are now doing; what they have done is graven on our memories and in the records of the society and we will ever hold in affectionate remembrance.

Class : D, Greenhouse Appliances and Flower Pots.—J. S. Wilson, W. A. Kennedy, H. M. Altick.

Class E, Supplies.—W. F. Kasting, C. Samuelson, John Westcott.

Class F, Bulbs.—Wm. Currie, A. Poehlman, J. K. M. L. Farquhar.

Secretary Stewart then presented and read his report as follows:

GREENHOUSE BUILDING DEPARTMENT MILWAUKEE EXHIBITION.

before you in the regular order. Of special importance I consider the arrangement instituted for the meeting of state vice-presidents for the purpose of getting in closer touch with each other, and with the society. The wishes of each state as to next incumbent can be more readily ascertained by this means also, and I look for good results in various ways from this innovation and trust each vice-president will be on hand.

Another important subject discussed was how to have the business sessions better attended. This resulted in the appointment of a sergeant-at-arms, who with his assistants is required to see that all members who can do so be induced to attend the meetings and postpone the discussion of personal or business matters to a more opportune time. This is no new problem, being as old as civilization. We read of the scheme which the ancient Greeks adopted, a rope covered with wet paint stretched from side to side of the street in the hands of two stalwart officers, to compel the crowd to attend the public meetings, and even in more modern times among our colonial fathers the pains and penalties for lounging instead of going to church were severe, but while we are not going to be so drastic, perhaps, in our case, we still mean in all seriousness to make an earnest effort to do justice to the able gentlemen, who have come so far and who have prepared themselves at great pains to address us. The executive committee wish it clearly understood that the rule as to having the exhibition hall cleared during sessions is to be strictly enforced; that it is no mere whim of the sergeant-at-arms, but an iron-clad rule that must be obeyed by all, by exhibitors as well as by visitors.

In conclusion, I take this opportunity of extending sympathy as official head of

Appointment of Judges.

The following were appointed judges to pass upon the exhibits in the trade display:

Class A, Plants.—A. Ferguson, Herman Junge, W. L. Palinski, Harry Papworth, Otto Speidel.

Class B, Cut Flowers.—A. H Langjahr John Sibson, E. G. Gillett, A. F. Barbe.

Class C, Boilers.—Lemuel Ball, J. M. Gasser, John T. Temple.

Report of the Secretary.

Again we assemble, as a society, to sum up the doings and experiences of another year, to draw conclusions therefrom and determine lines of future activity; as individuals to meet congenial friends and renew old friendships, to gain knowledge and enlarge our minds by contact and intercourse with the foremost representatives of our profession.

It becomes my duty to make report to you of our transactions and our progress as an organization since the hour of our adjournment one year ago, when we said goodbye to beautiful Biltmore and voiced in vociferous chorus our gratitude to the good and faithful friends we had found in Dixie land.

The story of our Asheville convention is told in a book of 210 pages—the largest annual volume ever issued by the society. Its contents established the fact that our meeting in the south compared favorably in all respects with its predecessors, that the accompanying exhibition, although of moderate size, was comprehensive and creditable and that the customary pastimes and entertainments were fully enjoyed.

The list of the year's plant introductions in America as recorded in the annual report comprised nineteen cannas, seventeen carnations, forty-seven chrysanthemums, ten roses, four geraniums and eighteen miscellaneous plants—doubtless a very incomplete list, but the best possible with the data at hand. Unquestionably full and authentic statistics on this line would prove of great service for future reference.

During the past year our florists have

SUPPLIES DEPARTMENT MILWAUKEE EXHIBITION.

GENERAL VIEW OF PLANT DEPARTMENT MILWAUKEE EXHIBITION.

been confronted with an unusual measure of harassing conditions demanding alert vigilance on the part of the national society. The extortionate prices exacted for greenhouse glass, the notorious coal famine and the advance in express tariff on flowers may be cited in particular as inflicting direct injury upon the florists' industry. On two of these matters special committee reports are due, hence a brief reference to them will suffice here. Numerous letters from the secretary's office to influential florists, seeking to stir up a movement in favor of congressional action on the glass question, met with a depressingly scant response. A remarkable evidence of indifference on the part of the florist trade outside of the society's membership, which I feel should go on permanent record as a modern repetition of an oft-told story, was furnished after our successful encounter with the express companies. Immediately upon the rescinding of the high rates letters were written by your secretary to the numerous florists throughout the country —who had been appealing to the S. A. F., through trade papers, petitions, protests and letters, for relief—announcing to them the happy outcome of our agitation, reminding them that this could not have been accomplished without organized effort and asking that they become members and supporters of the organization in recognition of its substantial services to them. Just one response was the net result.

The executive committee met in Milwaukee on March 17 and 18, seven members being in attendance, and their reception by the Chicago and Milwaukee brethren was generous and cordial. The various departments of the society's affairs were scrutinized, suggestions as to our future welfare fully discussed and progressive measures adopted with a view to bringing every feature of the Milwaukee meeting up to the highest standard. An innovation which will doubtless find occasion to speak for itself and demonstrate its utility during the next three days is the appointment of a

sergeant-at-arms with two sturdy assistants whose functions are to see to the enforcement of the rules appertaining to the exhibition and maintain order in and about the hall and ante-rooms while the society's deliberations are in progress.

The list of plants registered in the secretary's office has been added to during the year as follows:

August 26, 1902, Carnations Wingold and Biltmore, by J. B. Trudo.
September 20, 1902, Geraniums Double Dryden, James S. Wilson, Little Red Riding Hood, Governor Stone, Cleopatra and Goliath, by Henry Eichholz.
September 23, 1902, Rose Beauty of Rosemawr, by Conard & Jones Company.
October 20, 1902, Rose Ideal, by Jacob Becker.
October 27, 1902, Carnation Mrs. Phoebe Hearst, by Leonard J. Stankowicz.
November 10, 1902, Carnation Governor Lowndes, by H. Weber & Son.
November 10, 1902, Rose Canadian Queen by the H. Dale Estate.
November 17, 1902, Canna Hiawatha, Chautauqua, Gladiator and Louise, by the Conard & Jones Company.
November 19, 1902, Roses Prof. C. S. Sargent, Wm. F. Dreer, Wm. K. Harris, Robert Craig, Edwin Lonsdale and John Burton, by Hoopes Brothers & Thomas.
January 31, 1903, Adiantum Cuneatum Crowesnum, by Peter Crowe.
March 26, 1903 Herbaceous peonies Rosalind, Mequsa, Crown on Crown, Originality, Harlequin, Daybreak, Cascade, Delight, Felicity, Cathedral, Sunrise, Dragon's Head, Flamboyant, Bonfire, Ebony, Crystal Queen, Fantasy, Marble Fawn, Apple Blossom, Mayflower, Cashmere, Cherub, Bacchus, Diana, Gypsy, Fascination and Fireball, Tree peonies Achievement, Wistaria, Icicles, Red Cape, Morning Glory, Panorama, Pink Silver, Red Riding Hood, Frigallity, Red Cloud, Blushing Bride, Coral, Snowstorm, Jacqueminot, White Dragon, Eternity, Meteor, Purple Crown, Rose Queen, Dawn, Pink Perfection, Mars, Celestial, Purple Cloud, Serenade, Croesus and Abbess, by Suekt & Ida.
April 20, 1903 Rose Climbing Pillar of Gold, by the Good & Reese Company.
July 14, 1903, Canna Lord Charles Beresford, by Henry Morris.
August 1, 1903, Roses Leo XIII. and Northern Light, by Conard & Jones Company.
August 4, 1903, Geranium The Mascotte, by E. Worden.
August 8, 1903, Manda's Golden Privet, by W. A. Manda.

Medals have been awarded since last report as follows:
November 8, 1902, through the Cincinnati Florists' Society, a silver medal to George A Allen for Adiantum cuneatum Georgdi.
December 8, 1901, through the New Haven County Horticultural Society, a silver medal to David Kydd for Begonia Kydii.

December 4, 1902, through the Horticultura Society of Chicago, a silver medal to Fred. Dorner & Sons Company for Carnation Fiancee and a bronze medal to Nathan Smith & Son for Chrysanthemum F. J. Taggard.
December 14, 1902, through the New York Florists' club, a silver medal to F. R. Pierson Company for Nephrolepis exaltata Piersoni and a bronze medal to the H. Dale estate for Rose Canadian Queen.
December 29, 1902, through the Chrysanthemum Society of America, to L. G. Hill Company, a silver medal for Chrysanthemum R. E. Richardson and a bronze medal to Nathan Smith & Son for Chrysanthemum H. W. Buckbee.
March 3 1903, through the American Carnation Society, a silver medal to L. E. Marquisee for Carnation Flamingo, and a bronze medal to Peter Fisher for Carnation Mrs. M. A. Patten.

Our total membership as per the printed list for 1902 was fifty-eight life and 830 annual, fifty-three less than for 1901. Nine annual members have since taken out life memberships. Seven have been taken from us by death since our last meeting. Deaths are recorded as follows:
W. A. Bock, Cambridge, Mass., August 19, 1902.
J. J. Harris, Philadelphia, Pa., November 25.
1902.
F. L. Harris, Wellesley, Mass., January 11, 1903.
A. Wollgers, Brooklyn, N. Y., February 25, 1903.
J. W. Withers, New York City, April 13, 1903.
Charles Zeller, Brooklyn, N. Y., June 26, 1903.
A. H. Hews, Cambridge, Mass., July 5, 1903.

The number of new and reinstated members added during the year 1902 was 107, of whom three are life members. In these additions the various states were represented as follows:
Connecticut, Kentucky, Minnesota, New Jersey, Wisconsin, Louisiana, Texas and Ontario one each; Michigan, Rhode Island, Tennessee and Indiana, two each; District of Columbia, Florida, Maryland and Massachusetts, three each; Alabama, California, Maine, New York and Virginia, four each; South Carolina, five; Georgia, seven; Ohio and Illinois, eight each; Pennsylvania, fifteen; North Carolina, sixteen.

From the foregoing it will be seen that, notwithstanding the disadvantage of having moved our center of activity from the thronged Pan-American to remote Asheville with its scattered constituency, our society is in fairly prosperous circumstances as to funds, membership and general activity along legitimate lines. It is especially gratifying to note that the life membership list is steadily lengthening and its permanent fund approaching dimensions where the accruing annual interest amounts to a substantial sum.

We should not, however, lose sight of the fact that, considering the number of people engaged in horticultural pursuits in the United States, our membership is disappointingly small and our sphere of usefulness consequently limited. We should have a life membership of at least one thousand and an annual list of twice that number. How shall we attain it? Thus far all expedients for acquiring the consistent allegiance of the thousands of prosperous florists of our country have produced but minor results, and when such services as we have been able to give this year prove ineffectual whither shall we turn?

In closing this report permit me to express the hope that the results of this convention shall justify all the unselfish, faithful preparatory work which has been done by society officials and the energetic members of the local florists' club, whose favored guests we are to-day.

WM. J. STEWART, Sec'y.

On motion of Alex. Wallace, of New York, action on that part of the report referring to the registering of the tree and Japanese peonies was deferred until it could be ascertained whether the said registration applies to new plants as provided by the constitution of the S. A. F. The remainder of the report was accepted and ordered filed.

The report of Treasurer H. B. Beatty, of Oil City, Pa., was presented and read. It was accepted and ordered filed.

Numerous reports from state vice-presidents were presented without being read and ordered published in the official report.

John N. May, of Summit, N. J., presented and read a report from the committee on legislation reciting that efforts had been successful in securing from the express companies a restoration of the old express rates.

Geo. C. Watson, of Philadelphia, presented the report of the peony committee. He prefaced it with the statement that, as there had been no recent meeting of the committee, he made the report upon his own responsibility as secretary.

Report of the Peony Committee.

In view of the fact that the peony committee went to work under the idea that they were constituted according to the suggestion of the president of the society "with power to add to their numbers," and as it appeared after the publication of the minutes that they did not have that power, it follows that all that they did under a wrong impression remains inoperative. A good deal of preliminary work was done in the way of establishing communication with foreign peony growers as well as with those interested in the peony in this country. Arrangements were made for a public testing ground in Fairmount park, Philadelphia, and a commencement made with a collection of fifty-four varieties. It was publicly announced through the press and otherwise that any member of the S. A. F. could add himself to the peony committee without cost, and all that an outsider had to do was to become a member of the S. A. F. to qualify for membership on the peony committee. The "power to add" proviso on the constitution of the committee naturally suggested the idea of associating all those who were interested in the peony, and the word "Association" was used to designate the fact that the peony committee was more than an ordinary committee as usually under-

stood. After the flaw in the constitution of the committee was discovered, it was thought best not to go ahead any further, but to wait for whatever action the society might take at the annual meeting. If the society should validate the "power to add" proviso, the work can be taken up at the point where it now stands. If the society decides on some other plan to carry out the work, the members of the present committee will no doubt be glad to do all in their power to help things along.

GEORGE C. WATSON, Sec'y.

On the motion of P. O'Mara, of New York, the report was received and the committee continued with power to add to their members.

Wm. Scott, of Buffalo, N. Y., reported from the committee on closer relations

Breitmeyer's New Rose.

This new pink seedling rose, which has received much favorable notice in all the cut flower sections of the west, is to be introduced later by John Breitmeyer's Sons, Detroit. The illustration shows the rose exploited by Frederick Breitmeyer, Jr. Master Breitmeyer is 6 years old and four feet high.

with kindred societies an amendment to the constitution providing for the organization of such societies as sections of the S. A. F.

On the motion of W. N. Rudd, of Chicago, the report was sent to the executive committee with instructions to report thereon, if that body approved the scheme, at the next annual meeting.

President's Reception.

The president's reception, in the exposition building, on Tuesday evening, was a delightful social affair under the auspices of the Milwaukee Florists' Club. It was well attended by the members of the society, accompanied with their ladies,

and many of the leading families of the city were cremated.

President Burton was assisted in receiving by Secretary Stewart, who presented the visitors, and by Mr. and Mrs. H. B. Beatty, Ex-Presidents Craig, Smith and Graham, Messrs. Pollworth and Whitnall, of the local club and ladies of the family of the latter. The guests formed in line, and each in turn, upon making the acquaintance of the host and his genial associates, was cordially greeted and afforded an opportunity for a social chat and a brief interchange of sentiments of mutual regard. The remainder of the evening was spent in renewing old friendships and forming new ones. Vocal and instrumental music enlivened the occasion, a number of selections being admirably rendered by Miss Fulmar, the Milwaukee Glee Club and Bach's Quartette. Later refreshments were served.

Wednesday's Proceedings.

The convention took up, as the first business, the reports of the exhibition judges, a number of which were then presented.

The selection of a meeting place for 1904 resulted in the unanimous choice of St. Louis, the claims of which were presented by J. T. Ammann.

R. F. Tesson, of St. Louis, read an interesting paper on "A System of Accounts for Greenhouses and Forms for Determining Cost of Production," and received a vote of thanks from the convention for his able effort.

The only other business of the morning session was the nomination of officers for 1904. The following were named in complimentary speeches: For president, John F. Cowell, of Buffalo, N. Y.; C. C. Pollworth, of Milwaukee; J. T. Temple, of Davenport, Ia.; Philip Breitmeyer, of Detroit, Mich.

For vice-president, J. J. Beneke, of St. Louis, was nominated. Secretary Stewart and Treasurer Beatty were the only nominees for their positions.

The ladies' outing in the afternoon was taken advantage of by a large number and proved very enjoyable.

Thursday's Proceedings.

At the opening session the reports of the judges in classes A and D were read.

In the election of officers for 1904, which followed, Philip Breitmeyer, of Detroit, was chosen president by a vote of 203 in a total of 334. J. F. Cowell, of Buffalo, received fifty-two votes; C. C. Pollworth, of Milwaukee, fifty-five, and John T. Temple, of Davenport, Iowa, twenty-four. H. Beneke, of St. Louis, was elected vice-president, and Secretary Stewart and Treasurer Beatty were re-elected without opposition.

H. Altick, of Dayton, Ohio, briefly addressed the convention upon the propriety of the florists of the country observing each recurring 29th of January as Carnation day in memory of the late President McKinley. He spoke of the lamented president's love for that flower and of what was due to him from the florists because of his influence in their behalf. He thought it would be a good idea for every man in the business to wear a carnation in his coat lapel on that day. Aside from its patriotic feature he said he regarded the proposition as a good one from a business standpoint, as the memorial day would stimulate the sale of carnations and had already had

Henry Wietor.   George Wittbold.   George Reinberg.

G. H. Pieser.   J. D. Thompson, President Chicago Florists' Club.   Emil Buettner.

John Weiland.   A. H. Budlong.   Louis Wittbold.

PROMINENT MEN OF THE CHICAGO TRADE.

that effect when it was observed by the Carnation League of Canton, Ohio. He also made an appeal for individual subscriptions to the McKinley monument fund.

W. T. Gude, of Washington, D. C., expressed his appreciation of kindnesses shown the society by President McKinley and his cabinet, and promised his co-operation in any movement intended to honor the memory of that great president.

D. J. Carmody, of Evansville, Ind., expressed a like sentiment and advocated the adoption of the carnation as the national flower of America.

Further discussion was cut short by routine business and no action on the matter was taken.

Prof. Corbett, of the Bureau of Plant Industry, at Washington, D. C., stated that during the last few years the Agricultural Department had acquired a tract of about 500 acres across the Potomac, opposite Washington, and it was intended to devote some thirty acres of this not exactly as a botanical garden, but one for all our native plants worthy of cultivation for ornamental purposes. Greenhouses would be erected there in which to house all new plants brought from different parts of the world. It was contemplated also to build houses in which to experiment in nutrition, propagation and the keeping of plants.

The convention, after a brief discussion, voted its endorsement of the bill pending in congress for a parcels post law.

Committees were appointed to report, next year, upon methods of grading pot plants and upon sizes of cut flowers and bulbs.

A paper on "Modern Methods in Floral Decoration," prepared by Alex. McConnell, of New York, was then read by Wm. Scott.

Wm. Scott, of Buffalo, N. Y., said that while the national government was expending millions for the benefit of the farmer and the orchardist, it had done nothing of practical value for the grower. He understood that it was proposed to embellish some thirty acres of a strip in the District of Columbia with flowers and he thought that if an appeal were made to congressmen, with the endorsement of this society, a moderate appropriation would be made to build a plant in which actual experiments could be made for the benefit of the florists. He therefore offered the following, which was unanimously adopted:

Resolved, That inasmuch as the interests which the S. A. F. and O. H. represent have many millions of dollars at stake, and inasmuch as there are problems in plant nutrition, plant propagation and plant culture which now perplex and hamper our interests, and which we believe are capable of solution, but which require time and equipment not at the disposal of the practical grower, it is the sense of this convention that Congress be requested to appropriate sufficient funds to enable the secretary of agriculture to undertake the study and solution of the florists' problems.

G. F. Crabb, of Grand Rapids, Mich., presented and read an interesting paper on "Violet Culture in the West."

On motion of E. H. Cushman, of Sylvania, Ohio, that portion of Secretary Stewart's report referring to tree and herbaceous peonies was referred to the peony committee.

The proposed amendment to the constitution offered by J. K. L. M. Farquhar, of Boston, Mass., regulating plant registration and defining the status of the secretary in relation thereto was adopted without objection.

At the evening session a scientific paper on "Substitutes for Coal and their Com-

parative Efficiency," was read by W. R. Beattie, of the U. S. Dept. of Agriculture, followed by the roll call of states, when J. D. Carmody, of Evansville, Ind., gave a most entertaining address under the title of the "Humorous Side of the Florists' Business."

A pleasant incident of the closing session was the presentation to Ex-President Wm. R. Smith of a handsome gold watch and masonic charm to replace those stolen from him in the convention city. The presentation speech was made by Robert Craig in his usual felicitous style and Mr. Smith replied very feelingly. Similarly pleasing was the presentation of a gold watch to President Burton, by Wm. Currie, of Milwaukee, on behalf of the members of the society.

On Friday the visitors were guests of the Milwaukee Florists' Club on a lake trip to Chicago, where they were taken in hand by local members of the florists' and allied trades, closing the day with dinner at the Auditorium, followed in the evening with the music of the Brooks band at the Coliseum.

During dinner at the Auditorium, W. N. Rudd in fitting terms presented J. C. Vaughan with a diamond ring, as a token of the high esteem in which he is held by the Chicago trade.

The Trade Exhibition.

The trade exhibition was a success in every respect, every foot of floor space in the exhibition hall being occupied. Many of the exhibits were very extensive and elaborate showings were made. The majority of opinions were to the effect that it was the grandest affair of its kind ever held at a convention of the S. A. F. The exhibiting firms and their specialties were as follows:

C. C. Pollworth Company, Milwaukee, decorative plants and florists' supplies.

Vaughan's Seed Store, Chicago, seeds, bulbs and decorative plants.

Holton & Hunkel Company, Milwaukee, palms and ferns.

N. A. Manda, South Orange, N. J., imported orchids and flowers

Robt. Craig & Son, Philadelphia, decorative plants.

Albert Fuchs, Chicago, palms and ferns.

Siebrecht & Son, New Rochelle, N. Y., palms and other decorative plants.

P. J. Berckman's Company, Augusta, Ga., Biota aurea nana and palms.

Julius Roehrs, Rutherford, N. Y., begonias, palms and rubber plants.

A. C. Oelsching, Savannah, Ga., rubber plants.

Geo. Wittbold Company, Chicago, palms and ferns.

Chas. D. Ball, Philadelphia, palms and ferns.

Geo. A. Kuhl, Pekin, Ill., Boston and Piersoni ferns.

Joseph Heacock, Wyncote, Pa., palms.

H. A. Dreer, Philadelphia, glazing points, plant food and general decorative stock.

M. Rice & Company, florist's supplies.

J. A. Peterson, Cincinnati, decorative plants.

Lemuel Ball, Philadelphia, palms and decorative plants.

F. R. Pierson Company, the new Pierson fern.

Ionia Pottery Company, Ionia, Mich., pots.

John C. Meyer & Company, Boston, Mass., silkaline.

B. H. Hunt, Chicago, florists supplies.

Stern & Company, Philadelphia, wax flowers and florists' supplies.

A. Hermann, New York, metal floral designs and other supplies.

Sigmund Geller, New York, florists' supplies.

J. W. Sefton Manufacturing Company, Anderson, Ind. and Chicago, florists' boxes.

Roseville Pottery Company, Zanesville, O., Rozane art jardinieres.

Reed & Keller, New York, miscellaneous florists' supplies.

W. F. Kasting, Buffalo, general line of supplies.

H. Bayersdorfer & Company, Philadelphia, basket novelties and supplies.

S. S. Pennock, Philadelphia, ribbons and supplies.

L. Baumann, Chicago, decorative articles, metallic and artificial floral designs.

Dayton Paper Company, Dayton, O., flower boxes.

Thomas Meehan & Sons, Dreshertown, Pa., raffia.

H. Thaden, Atlanta, Ga., wire tendril.

Schloss Brothers, New York, ribbons and novelties.

J. G. & A. Esler, Saddle River, N. J., hose.

E. P. Winterson Co., Chicago, florists' supplies.

A. Klokner, Milwaukee, high vase flat.

C. E. Finley, Joliet, Ill., flower pot washer.

Edwards & Docker Company, Philadelphia, boxes.

W. C. Krick, Brooklyn, immortelles, letters, etc.

Arthur Cowee, Berlin, N. Y., Groff's gladioli.

Foley Manufacturing Company, Chicago, greenhouse material.

John C. Moninger Company, Chicago, greenhouse material.

Kroeschell Brothers Company, Chicago, boilers.

Lord & Burnham Company, New York, greenhouse material.

Herendeen Manufacturing Company, Geneva, N. Y., hot water boilers.

Kramer & Son, Cedar Rapids, Ia., iron greenhouse material and pot hangers.

Henry F. Michell Company, Philadelphia, zinc glazing points.

Chadborn Manufacturing Company, Newburgh, N. Y., ventilating device.

Quaker City Machine Company, Richmond, Ind., ventilating machinery.

A. Dietsch & Company, Chicago, short roof houses and new round gutter.

Dillon Greenhouse Manufacturing Company, Bloomsburg, Pa., greenhouse material.

H. J. Smith, Hinsdale, Mass., ferns.

Thomas Collins, Hinsdale, Mass., ever. greens.

B. Rosens, Brooklyn, N. Y., bells, stars and novelties.

Benthey & Company, Chicago, new aster Benthey's Perfection.

Chester A. Olmstead, East Bloomfield, N. Y., new white aster.

Cushman Gladiolus Company, Sylvania, G., gladiolus bulbs.

Poat Brothers, Chicago, bulbs.

Peter Crowe, Utica, N. Y., Adiantum Croweanum.

Lager & Hurrell, Summit, N. J., orchids.

Engineering & Power Company, Jamestown N. Y., soil conveyor.

Jos. Kift & Son, Philadelphia, Pa., vase stands.

J. Stern, Philadelphia, Pa., baskets.

Caldwell, The Woodsman Company, Evergreen, Ala., wild smilax.

H. W. Koener, Milwaukee, Wis., gail. lardias, etc.

Henri Beaulieu, Woodhaven, N. Y., hose supporters.

The following subscribed for advertising space around the exhibition hall: Bassett & Washburn, Benthey & Co., Wietor Brothers, Peter Reinberg, Weiland & Risch, Kennicott Brothers Company, Poehlmann Brothers, E. C. Amling, Foley Manufacturing Co., George Reinberg, E. F. Winterson Co., J. B. Deamud, W. W. Barnard & Company, Chicago; C. C. Pollworth Company, W. E. Dallwig, Patek Brothers, Milwaukee; H. G. Berning, St. Louis; Chicago Carnation Company, Thompson Carnation Company, Joliet, Ill: Michigan Cut Flower Exchange, Detroit, Mich.

Reports of the Judges.

Awards were made by the judges as follows:

CUT FLOWERS.

Cushman Gladiolus Company, exhibit of gladioli. For collection of blue ribbon mixture, certificate of merit.

Chester A. Olmstead, for the new aster, Olmstead's Commercial White, certificate of merit.

Arthur Cowee, for collection of gladioli, honorable mention. For new varieties Princeps and Merceria, certificate of merit.

BOILERS AND HEATING APPARATUS.

The Herendeen Manufacturing Company makes an exhibit of three Furman new sectional boilers, also one conical boiler. Highly recommended.

The Lord & Burnham Company exhibits one round boiler, also new sectional boiler. Honorable mention.

Kroeschell Brothers' Company exhibits one return tubular steel boiler for hot water. Certificate of merit.

SUPPLIES.

M. Rice & Company.—Exhibit very large and complete. Many new and meritorious features. Certificate on general line of special supplies.

H. Bayersdorfer & Company.—Exhibit very large and complete. Many new and meritorious features. Certificate on general line of special supplies.

Sig. Geller.—A very creditable display of florists' supplies. Honorable mention.

E. H. Hunt.—A very creditable display of florists' supplies. Honorable mention.

J. Stern & Company. — Wax flowers and designs.

A. Herrmann & Company. — Metal designs and other florists' supplies. Honorable mention.

Reed & Keller.—General line of supplies. Adjustable plant stand. Very useful for decorative purposes. Honorable mention.

E. F. Winterson Company.—Florists' supplies. Highly commended.

C. C. Pollworth Company.—Original wire design. Honorable mention.

L. Baumann & Company.—Artificial palms and plants. Highly commended.

Robt. Kift.—Adjustable flower holder. Very effective for decorating. Honorable mention.

Alex. Klokner.—Vase for table decorating. Highly commended.

S. S. Pennock.—Ribbon and novelties. A very creditable display of ribbons adapted for florists' use. A large and complete line. Honorable mention.

Schloss Brothers.—Ribbons. Highly commended.

M. Rice & Company.—Highly commended for display of ribbons.

Dayton Paper Novelty Company.—A very creditable display of florists' folding boxes.

Edwards & Docker.—A very creditable display of florists' folding boxes.

J. W. Sefton Manufacturing Company. —Corrugated box. Deserves special mention. Also folding boxes.

Lord's folding shipping box for plants. Looks very useful for the purpose.

H. J. Smith.—Moss, ferns, evergreens.

Thos Collins.—Wreathing.

J. E. Esler.—Exhibit of hose.

J. Meyer.—Display of silkaline.

Thos. Meehan.—Display of raffia.

D. B. Long.—Floral albums, shipping tags and florists' stationery. Honorable mention.

Roseville Pottery.—A very fine and ornamental display of jardiniers and pedestals. Honorable mention.

Ionia Pottery Company.—Display of pots.

W. J. Cowee.—Display of wired toothpicks.

B. Rosens.—Exhibit of Christmas bells.

Wm. F. Kasting, Chenille and immortelle Christmas bells. Very pretty and artistic. Also a tin enameled cemetery vase and floral shears.

BULBS.

E. H. Hunt exhibited bulbs of Lilium Harrisii, Freesia refracta alba and Chinese narcissus—the last produced in California. Were of good size and very solid.

The Misses Wilson exhibited bulbs of large-flowered Paper White Polyanthus narcissus, which were of fair size and clean appearance.

The Cushman Gladiolus Company exhibited two plates of well matured gladiolus bulbs from early flowered stock.

The largest collection of bulbs came from Vaughn's Seed Store. It included very fine Dutch hyacinths, Emperor and double Von Sion narcissus, which attracted special attention. Tulips and other stock were of good quality. Two cases of Lilium lancifolium rubrum from cold storage were solid and well preserved.

Clucas & Boddington Company exhibited a lot of Lilium Harrisii and longiflorum which were of very clean appearance and thoroughly ripened. The exhibit included good bulbs of Amaryllis Johnsonii and gladioli from Bermuda, also remarkably well kept bulbs of Lilium longiflorum from cold storage.

PLANTS.

Siebrecht & Son.—Large collection of decorative plants, in all sizes, including palms, dracænas, pandanus; also a very pretty plant of Phoenix Roebelinii, Phoenicophorium Sechellarium, Ananassa sativa fol. var. and Kentia Wendtlandii. Certificate of merit.

Albert Fuchs.—Collection of well grown decorative plants, including small ferns, pandanus and a good specimen of Nephrolepis Bostoniensis. Honorable mention.

Peter Crowe.—Exhibits two specimen plants from benches; also a large quantity of cut fronds of Adiantum Croweanum. The committee thinks this adiantum will prove a very valuable variety as a cut fern and a distinct variety of great promise. The committee strongly recommends a certificate of merit.

P. J. Berckman's Co.—The exhibit consists of well grown clean plants of Biota aurea nana and small sizes of Kentia Belmoreana. Highly commended.

J. A. Peterson.—Besides a collection of ferns and pandanus, Mr. Peterson shows some well grown specimens of Begonia Gloire de Lorraine and Adiantum Farleyense. Certificate of merit.

R. & J. Farquhar & Co.—Exhibit consists of Begonia Gloire de Lorraine and B. Gloire de Lorraine nana compacta in small pots. Honorable mention.

Lemuel Ball.—Collection of well grown palms, dracænas, arecas and ferns; the latter including Cibotium Schiedei. Certificate of merit.

Julius Roehrs.—A very creditable exhibit of araucarias, crotons, aspidistras, oranges, ardisias, dracænas and palms in variety. Certificate of merit.

Robert Craig & Son.—This firm exhibits a very good collection of decorative plants, such as kentias, pandanus and dracænas. This collection includes a good specimen of Thrinax elegans, some Dracæna Goldieana; also Maranta roseolineata, ferns in variety and a very highly colored specimen of Ananassa sativa fol. var. They also show some samples of promising Cyclamen Persicum. Their collection of crotons, especially the new variety Craigii, proved the center of attraction in this line. Certificate of merit.

A. C. Oelschig.—Well grown Ficus elastica var. in 3-inch pots, also the type. Highly commended.

Holton & Hunkel Co.—Exhibit of kentias, araucarias, fine plants of Cocos Weddelliana and a collection of small ferns and asparagus. Honorable mention.

George A Kuhl.—A collection of well grown specimen plants of Boston ferns. Honorable mention.

Mrs. R. Mauff—A nice specimen of supposed sport of the Boston fern. Highly commended.

Joseph Heacock.—A collection of well grown commercial palms. Honorable mention.

Chas. D. Ball.—This firm exhibits, as usual, its well grown decorative stock. Certificate of merit.

L. H. Foster.—A collection of Nephrolepis Anna Foster. This variety appears well as a specimen plant. Certificate of merit.

C. C. Pollworth Co.—Exhibits a well arranged group of plants such as palms, ferns, also Araucaria plumosa—considered a novelty. Certificate of merit.

J. B. Heiss.—A well grown collection of small palms. Honorable mention.

Vaughan's.—Exhibit some large commercial plants of made-up kentias, also small specimens of Nephrolepis Anna Foster, Piersoni and Bostoniensis, also a nice plant of Adiantum Farleyense. Certificate of merit.

George Wittbold Co.—Exhibits a collection of decorative plants of all sizes, including two grand specimens of Cocos Bonneti. Certificate of merit.

W. A. Manda.—Exhibits a table of very valuable plants. In orchids are shown Lælia elegans, also Cypripedium Josephianum, good forms of cattleyas, dendrobiums, oncidiums and others. He also exhibits a nice collection of stove plants. A novelty in his collection is a variegated privet which, should it prove hardy and retain its color, will prove a valuable plant. The firm also exhibits some specimens of well grown evergreens. Certificate of merit for collection of plants, also certificate of merit for golden leaved privet.

H. A. Dreer.—As usual this firm makes a large and creditable display of palms in all sizes, a well grown collection of araucarias, also a large collection of small ferns, some Eurya latifolia, well colored, and some Kentia Sanderiana very promising. In ferns, Gymnogramma chrysophylla superba, highly colored. Certificate of merit.

H. A. Dreer.—Novelties. Asparagus myriocladus, a distinct form. It appears to be a cross between A. Sprengeri and A. decumbens and a great improvement over both. Certificate of merit. Asparagus plumosus compactus. A chance hybrid between A. plumosus nanus and A. plumosus tenuissimus. A valuable plant if it retains its character. Certificate of merit. New fancy caladiums, Countess of Warwick, Undulatum, L'Ami Schwartz, Mrs. Oliver Ames. These are representatives of a new dwarf type. Honorable mention.

F. R. Pierson Co.—A magnificent lot of Nephrolepis Piersoni, which was awarded the gold medal of this society last year, at Asheville. As it has already received the highest award possible in the gift of this society your committee can make no additional award at this time, but they wish to say that another year has only further demonstrated its great value commercially and confirmed the judgment of the Asheville committee in awarding it the first and only gold medal so far given by this society for any new plant.

Lager & Hurrell.—Exhibit a table of orchids, established and unestablished plants. This collection represents some very valuable varieties, including Cypripedium Harrisiannum superbum, Lælia elegans, Cattleya Leopoldii, Vanda cærulea, and many other valuable species. Certificate of merit.

Those Present.

ALABAMA.—Miss Anna K. Luffman, Birmingham; G. Caldwell, Evergreen.
COLORADO.—Frank F. Crump, Robert Kurth, Colorado Springs; W. A. Benson, A. E. Mauff, Phil. Scott, Denver.
CONNECTICUT.—George H. Traendly, Rowayton.
DELAWARE.—Chas. Simon, Jr., Wilmington.
DIS'T. OF COLUMBIA.—L. C. Corbett, W. H. Ernest, Albert F. Esch, A. Gude, W. F. Gude, wife and daughter, A. J. Gude, E. C. Loeffler, Poehlman. C. Ponnet, Geo. C. Shaffer, W. R. Smith, Washington.
GEORGIA.—C. S. Critchell, H. Thaden, Atlanta; L. H. Berckmans, Augusta; J. E. Jackson, Jamesville.
ILLINOIS.—Jos. M. Smely, Aurora; E. W. Guy, Belleville; A. Edwin Washburn, F. L. Washburn, Bloomington; E. C. Amling, Geo. Asmus, C. M. Balluff, Chas. Balluff, Michael Barker, F. F. Benthey, H. N. Bruns and wife, J. B. Deamud, Jas. Foerster, Philip J. Foley, H. B. Gerhardt, P. J. Hauswirth, M. G. Holdings, R. Johnstone, Aug. Jurgens, Leonard Kill, Walter Kreitling and wife, Misses Ludlow, A. P. Matthews, S. W. McKellar, W. L. Palinsky, Peter Pearson, Peter Reinberg, A. Ringer, N. J. Rupp, A. H. Schneider, C. W. Scott, Geo. R. Scott, J. A. Sheppard, John Sinner, Fred Stollery, Geo. Stollery, Anton Then, J. C. Vaughan and wife, N. J. Wietor, Hugh Wood, Chicago; H. H. Schwiemann, Danvers; G. M. Garland, Desplaines; O. L. Baird, Dixon; J. F. Ammann, Edwardsville; G Swensen, Elmhurst; Geo. Weiland, Evanston; John McDonald, Farmer City; Fritz Bahr, Highland Park; Andrew Benson, A. C. Benson, Hinsdale; Emil R. Petake, Hixton, Jas. Hartshorne, Jos. Labo, J. D. Thompson, Joliet; L. L. Fry, LeRoy; Albert Amling, Maywood; F. Hunt, Mt. Greenwood; J. F. Klimmer, Oak Park; John Hillins, Painesville; Emil Buettner, Park Ridge; G. A. Kuhl, Pekin; Andrew Peterson, Paxton; Chas. W. Johnson, Rockford; H. L. Phelps, Springfield; Jas. S. Wilson, Albert Heyst, Arthur Hay, Western Springs.
INDIANA.—Mrs. E. W. Bullocks, H. D. Seele, Elkhart; J. D. Carmody, G. H. Blackman, Evansville; F. J. Knecht, Fort Wayne; John Bertermann, Wm. Billings-

ley, H. Junge, Indianapolis; Fred. Dorner, Jr., Theo. A. Dorner, Lafayette; E. G. Hill, Richmond.
IOWA.—J. A. Kramer, Cedar Rapids; W. H. Wetherbee, Charles City; J. F. Wilcox, Roy F. Wilcox, Council Bluffs; W. B. Perry and wife, Cresco; Leo. L. Ewoldt, J. T. Temple, Davenport; W. T. Simonds and wife, Decorah; J. T. D. Fulmer, W. Greene, Des Moines; A. L. Glaser, G. A. Heyne, Dubuque; P. L. Larson, Fort Dodge; W. J. Springer, New Hampton; Walter S. Hall, Osage; John Christiany, Sheldon; J. C. Rennison, Sioux City; E. C. Keck, Washington.
KANSAS.—Ansel H. Whitcomb, Lawrence; Chas. P. Mueller, Wichita.
KENTUCKY.—F. D. White, Lexington; A. R. Banmer. Henry Nanz, Jacob Schulz, Louisville; E. R. Hall, Shelbyville.
LOUISIANA.—P. A. Chopin, M. Cook, Harry Papworth, W. Rehm, E. Valdejo, E. J. Virgin, New Orleans.
MASSACHUSETTS.—John K. M. L. Farquhar, L. H. Foster, Wm. J. Stewart, Patrick Welch, Boston; C. Warburton, Fall River; L. B. Brague, Thos. Collins, H. J. Smith, Hinsdale; F. R. Mathison, Waltham.
MICHIGAN.—C. H. Maynard, Mrs. C. H. Maynard, Allen; A. G. Boehringer, Bay City; Harry Balsley, Frank H. Beard, Philip Breitmeyer, Wm. Dilger, John Dunn, A. Ferguson, J. A. Priscoe, Geo. A. Rackham, J. F. Sullivan, Norman Sullivan, Walter G. Taepke, Chas. Warneke, Robt. Watson, Detroit; A. Peterson, Escanaba; Thos. F. Browne, Greenfield; Geo. Reynolds, Harry G. Smith, Grosse Point; H. C. Fruck, Grosse Point Farms; A. M. York, Hancock; Frank Holznagle, Highland Park; C. B. Derthick, Ionia; W. C. Cook. Kalamazoo; J. A. Bissinger, Lansing; Engelman Cohn, Manistee; Mrs. L. H. Stafford, Marquette; Chas. Schulz, Menominee; J. B. Carey, Jas. Taylor, Mount Clemens; John Gipner, Niles; A. Creuse, Chas. Fruck, Ed. A. Grohman, C. L. Roethke, Saginaw.
MINNESOTA.—D. O. Pratt, Anoka; Pauline Windmiller, Mankato; T. H. Hall, H. L. Patthey, H. B. Whitted, Minneapolis; L. P. Lord, Owattona, Christ Hansen, August S. Swanson, St. Paul John Wunder, Winona.
MISSOURI.—J. Steidle, Central; A. F. Barbe, Chas. E. Heite, Arthur Newell, Kansas City; Geo. M. Kellogg, Pleasant Hill; W. F. Adels, Jr., J. J. Beneke, Chas. Beyer, H. G. Berning, John M. Connell, J. H. Hadkinson, C. A. Junge and wife, Otto G. Koenig, C. A. Kuehn, Theo. Miller, F. H. Meinhart and wife, Emil Schray, Geo. Waldbart, F. C. Weber, R. F. Tesson, F. W. Taylor, St. Louis.
NEBRASKA.—Lewis Henderson, Omaha.
NORTH CAROLINA.—Mrs. J. B. Deake, J. W. C. Deake, Asheville.
NEW HAMPSHIRE.—E. R. Shaw, Nashua.
NEW JERSEY.—C. W. Turnley, Haddonfield; Emil Lenley, West Hoboken; Julius Roehrs, Rutherford; W. B. Du Rie, Rahway; John G. Esler, Saddle River; D. MacKorie, South Orange; John N. May, Geo. F. Struck, Summit.
NEW YORK.—G. S. Hatcher, Amsterdam; Wm. H. Siebrecht, Astoria; W. J. Cowee, Berlin; A. H. Langgahr, W. C. Krick, Brooklyn; F. P. Baum, J. F. Cowell, W. F. Kasting and wife, Chas. H. Kietsch, Daniel B. Long, Carl Risch, David J. Scott, William Scott, Jas. P. Braik, L. Wallace, Wm. Weber, Buffalo; A. D. Carpenter, Cohoes; R. E. Berger, Eggertsville; Julius Kretschman, Platbush, L. I.; Chas. Lenker, Freeport, L. I.; W. L. Herendon, Geneva; C. H. Roney, E. Worden, Jamestown; Thos. Mans-

field, W. H. Mansfield, Lockport; Leopold Oesternei, New Rochelle; Harry A. Bunyard, Lyman B. Craw, A. T. De La Mare, Victor S. Doval, A. J. Guttman, Theo. J. Lang, J. B. Nugent, Jr., Leopold Osternei, Emil Schloss, J. A. Shaw, Walter F. Sheridan, Emil Steffens, F. H. Traendley, Alex. Wallace, R. M. Ward, Wm. Wilson, New York; J. R. Fotheringham, Tarrytown; Peter Crowe, Utica.
OHIO.—L. L. Lamborn, H. S. Miller, Alliance; E. G. Gillett and wife, J. A. Peterson, J. W. Rodgers, Albert Sunderbruch, F. C. Bartels, James Eadie, E. A. Fetters and wife, J. M. Gasser, Robert Kegg, J. C. Kelley, G. M. Naumann, Geo. W. Smith, Mrs. Geo. W. Smith, L. Warnke and wife, Cleveland; Jos. J. Hellenthal, J. R. Hellenthal, Columbus; H. M. Altick, J. B. Heiss, Dayton; E. R. Sackett, Fostoria; Henry Kuns, Fred Ponting, A. Schmitt and wife, Glenville; Ed Berno, Mansfield; Philip Hagenburger, J. Merkel, Mentor; E. B. George. Painesville; E. H. Cushman, Sylvania; L. B. Pierce, Tallmadge; Lewis Ulbricht, Tiffin; F. J. Peck, S. N. Peck, W. E. Snider, Toledo; E. Sheppard, Youngstown; J. D. Imlay, H. Schwab, Zanesville.
PENNSYLVANIA.—E. C. Ludwig, Gus Ludwig, J. W. Ludwig, Allegheny; J. L. Dillon, Max Dillon, Bloomsburg; J. A. Valentine, Denver; V. L. Schlwab, Erie; J. F. Sibson, Germantown; Chas. D. Ball, W. H. Taplin, Holmesburg; Albert M. Herr and wife, Lancaster; Abraham Hostetter, Manheim; M. A. Krueger, M. A. Krueger, Jr., Meadville; Henry P. Moon, Morrisville; Chas. D. Ball, Miss Clara Ball, Lemuel Ball, Jno. E. Burton, D. T. Connor, Robt. Craig, F. W. Creighton, Edward Ellinger, B. Eschner, Wm. Falek, E. J. Fancourt, G. S. Ford, James Karins, Rupert Kienle, Robt. Kift, Jno. Kuhn, A. H. Lanser, Fred Michell, Jas. Michell, F. J. Michell, Felix H. Myers, Leo. Niessen, Frank Polites, Edw. Reid, Wm. Robertson, Jno. T. Sibson, Mrs. Sibson, C. Simon, F. S. Simpson, S. S. Skidelsky, James F. Smith, Turnley, W. Ludwig, George C. Watson, John Westcott and wife, Julius Wolff, Mrs. Wolff, J. Wolff, Jr., Walker Yates, Philadelphia; H. B. Beatty, Geo. D. Blind, H. L. Blind, Casper Limbach, Wm. Loew, E. C. Reineman, Christ. Rieger and wife, Pittsburg; Frank Adelberger, A. H. Lanser, Wayne; A. Wintzer, West Grove; Jos. Heacock, Wyncote.
RHODE ISLAND.—John F. Wood, Providence; Albert Gaedke, Scotland.
VIRGINIA.—Hugh L. Aumann; Lloyd G. Blick, Norfolk.
WISCONSIN.—F. C. Smith, Ashland; A. Helfrich and wife, Burlington; Edw. Amerpohl, Janesville; Mrs. A. Guillaume, C. E. Schaller, La Crosse; Geo. Vatter, Marinette; F. P. Dilger, W. Edlefsen, Herman V. Huckel, Milwaukee; A. Joban. son, North Milwaukee; Otto Speidel, Oconomowoc; A. J. Jewett, Miriam Jewett, Sparta; Christ Lund, Wausau; Albert Loeffler, Wm. J. Stuebe, Watertown.

Notes and Incidents.

Emil Leuly, of West Hoboken, N. J., made a run on his wheel of 900 odd miles to the convention, taking twelve days to do it, getting to Port Jarvis, crossing Pike county, Pennsylvania, and then finding it hilly lost time by bad roads. Crossing into Canada at Buffalo the level land and easy grade made a good gait possible; reaching Sarnia, crossing to Port Huron, then across Michigan to St. Joe. He says this beats twentieth century limited trains if you want to get acquainted and see the country. Last year he wheeled nearly all the way to Asheville. Emil is good company, with a kind, friendly word for everyone he meets.

President-elect Breitmeyer was treated to a ride on the "Elephant" into the convention hall. "Phil" was the quiet, unassuming gentleman throughout the active canvass made by his friends, and the "robbery" was a good card if not a pleasant experience.

A. Kruger and wife, with Superintendent Roney, of the Lakeview Rose Gardens, at Jamestown, N. Y., came over the Erie road. Their train was delayed three hours by an accident to the engine and so they missed the convention train at Chicago.

The AMERICAN FLORIST, says a man who had run his advertising in forty-seven different papers, brings him more inquiries for the lines he advertises in this paper than he gets in any other trade journal in or out of the florist line.

The exhibition, says a life member who has attended seventeen conventions, was one of the best if not the best of all the trade exhibitions I have seen. The display of material was excellent.

F. W. Taylor, who at Providence was the means of carrying the convention to Omaha, was in evidence in soliciting favorable consideration for St. Louis. He had an easier job this time.

The convention is growing more and more as a set meeting place for business acquaintances to meet once a year to compare notes, make deals, and make fresh and new acquaintances.

Says F. R. Pierson: I do not think that there is as much professional courtesy in any known trade than you will find among the flower growers of this country.

Many old ladies were present and all of them enjoyed themselves hugely. One old lady with white hair remarked: "Why, it did me lots of good; I feel young again."

Frank P. Dilger, as chairman of the ladies' day committee was the right man in the right place. He was very popular with the fair sex throughout the meeting.

Isaac Kennedy and P. J. Foley failed to act as sergeants-at-arms, but their places were well supplied by Robert Kift and his able assistant, John Reardon.

The cowboy delegation headed by Valentine, of Denver, cut a unique appearance in their white felt broad brims.

The Convention Special from Chicago to Milwaukee was a whopper.

The lake sail Milwaukee to Chicago was very pleasant.

Mayor Rose has extravagant ideas of morality.

Etiquette of Bridal Bouquets.

West end florists do not agree with the opinion expressed by the judge of the Lambeth county court that pink tinted roses and oak leaves are not inappropriate constituents of a bridal bouquet, says the Daily Mail, of London, Eng.

The bridal bouquet of a spinster is, it appears, invariably composed of fine white flowers relieved by asparagus fern or other delicate foliage, with a sprig of white heather for luck.

A widow, on the other hand, usually carries at her second wedding a bouquet containing a few colored flowers. Furthermore, she does not wear or include in the bouquet orange blossom. That ornament, like the white, long-trained bridal gown, is the exclusive privilege of the spinster.

Modern Methods in Floral Decorations.

BY ALEXANDER M'CONNELL, NEW YORK.

The artistic arrangement of floral decorations for best effect is an important factor and well deserving the study of the professional florist, especially the younger generation, who are ambitious to become proficient in their chosen profession.

A progressive movement in the arrangement of floral effect has been manifest to all observing admirers of the blending of color and the graceful clustering of nature's most beautiful gifts.

The incongruous massing of flowers, regardless of harmony of color, ignoring surroundings where it is desirous to produce an artistic effect, is frequently the cause of failure and disappointing results.

Church weddings of the present day, where the decorator has been given carte blanche, or a liberal remuneration for his material and artistic skill, are certainly an improvement on the decorations of auld lang syne; no reflection on the ability and refined taste of the operator of the past. Lacking the material from which to select for pleasing and beautiful effects, set designs of decapitated flowers entered largely into the arrangements. Specimens of the graceful and stately kentia with its rich, dark foliage, contrasting in color and characteristic habit with Areca lutescens; the expansive foliage of Latania Borbonica and other natives of the tropics could not then be obtained in stately specimens, as today.

One of the most important factors in church wedding embellishment is the proper grouping of the magnificent palms, elevated to the proper height, not in a conglomerated mass, but grouped to show individuality and graceful habit.

In the floral arrangements, cut flowers with long stems are now, and should be, used wherever most effective; the sacred altar and chancel decorated with a tasteful profusion of white flowers and Asparagus plumosus; columns or arches garlanded with the same attractive green, or perhaps, which is more pleasing in a large hall or church, the glossy foliage of southern smilax, introduced in the north a few years ago, and now almost indispensable to the floral decorator.

The lycopodium or Christmas green roping, which was considered very essential in days of yore, is almost obsolete, excepting for Christmas festivities.

The decorators should ever bear in mind, to obtain a successful result, the treatment of the church should be as pleasing and effective on entering the holy edifice as at the altar.

The decoration of the home for the wedding festivities has been somewhat revolutionized. We seldom behold flowers contorted in such emblems as cupid's darts, bow and arrow, or balls of flowers massed in solids and suspended in some prominent place in the drawing rooms. The ancient wedding bell appears to be the only reminiscence of "ye olden time," and its apparent fascinating influence on the fair sex justifies the belief that the emblem may continue to ring joyfully for many moons to come.

In modern treatment of the house, the same conditions may be adhered to as in the church or hall. The grouping of the plants, artistically arranged in the parlors in a selected corner, forming a bower, giving sufficient space for the per-

formance of the wedding ceremony and for the bridal party to receive their congratulations. The wire frame in the shape of a canopy, covered with green and wired flowers, has lost its popularity and is now supplanted by the dignified palm.

The banked mantels of growing adiantum, interspersed with roses of one color, arranged in a loose and natural habit, is much more attractive than the ancient formal stereotyped arrangement, where so much wood and wire entered into the construction. Garlands of Asparagus plumosus or smilax entwined on mirrors and wherever effective, orchids with stems in water contained in small glass tubes to prevent wilting, vases of long stemmed cut flowers of distinct color, harmonizing with decorations of the different rooms to be treated, are more preferable and artistic than the former every day basket arrangement, even if the durability of the flowers were the only consideration. It is gratifying to observe there is less ribbon used in conjunction with floral decorations than formerly. While ribbon embellishment is not objectionable sometimes on floral designs, it is somewhat out of character garlanded with flowers and smilax in the drawing room decorations.

The construction or arrangement of the bridal bouquets of previous years was formal and compact. I will not reflect so far to the past as to refer to the camellia and tuberose bouquets of 35 years ago, with a border of bristol board paper surmounted by an edging of silk fringe, but contrast the progress in floriculture of later years.

The introduction and growing of improved varieties of roses, orchids and novelties of every family in Flora, all assist the artist in forming the beautiful and graceful bouquets of the times.

Flowers are never more admired, nor do they appeal to us more favorably in decorations of any kind, than when arrayed as near as possible to nature's handiwork.

The treatment of the residence for receptions or dinner entertainments is somewhat similar to decorations for the wedding celebration.

Illustrating the decoration for a modern festivity, we cannot do better than describe in detail one of the many which came under our own consideration.

Groups of palms arranged for best effect relieved by cut branches of Forsythia Fortunei, Spiraea prunifolia and Pyrus Japonica, forced for the occasion, loosely arranged in concealed vases of water. Mantels and mirrors were banked and treated with same flowering shrubs, all producing a very pleasing effect. Stairways were profusely garlanded with Asparagus plumosus and forsythia descending to the main floor where the dining room, library, parlors and conservatory were thrown into one great dining room. The tables, which seated 300 guests, were constructed to order, the center portion built separately, six inches below the outer sides for the placing of growing orchids in pots. With tubs concealed under the tables, the trunks coming through twelve feet apart, specimens of Dicksonia Antarctica eight feet in height were utilized, their tropical and graceful fronds producing an admirable and tasteful decoration. Hidden and suspended in the fronds by flexible wires were many glass tubes of water, each containing sprays of cattleyas. Growing orchids embellished the mantels, festoons of Asparagus plumosus interspersed · with cattleyas beautified the mirrors and the conservatory in the back ground, in brilliant colors of potted azaleas, sheltered as it were by the over-hanging branches of tropical foliage, completed one of the most original and elaborate decorations of the season.

Now, as to the accomplishment of success in these "modern methods," it must be remembered that these results can be attained, so far as artistic effects and charming designs are concerned, without any expensive and elaborate process, and with even limited means at one's disposal.

If one has the love of flowers and the soul of the artist within him, as every florist worthy of the name should have, the "modern methods" become a delight, and the development of a satisfactory contract an easy possibility. Any intelligent florist can succeed who gives proper thought and study to his decorative department, and realizes that herein lies the greatest opportunities for his own development and the certain growth of his business.

One must be alert, progressive, ambitious and a student, to achieve lasting success in these modern days. With the growth of capital comes greater demands and larger opportunities, and to fill the demands of the wealthy, originality, tact, and ability to advise must be continually cultivated. There is no limitation to the growth of the taste for and elaborateness of floral decoration. Its future will be a "giant" in comparison with what has been accomplished in the past,—there is no "method" of the present that does not admit of improvement, and to be "modern" we must live in the future and grow upward to its inevitable demands.

Should time permit, it would be interesting to look at another side of our subject, and that is the achievement of our time in the decorations of immense buildings, for national events, such as the inauguration of a president or the graceful testimonies of respect and grief when a hero is buried. But this opens up a field that our limited time forbids us to enter. Again, another demonstration of "floral decoration" flashes across our vision, and we behold what art and nature combined to produce in the glorious floral effects at the World's Fair in Chicago. Now comes another exposition, building at St. Louis, by "modern methods," grander results than were even imagined ten short years ago, and demonstrating to all the world, as it will, that Flora is the American Queen, and that in our devotion to her, and in ability to utilize her handiwork we lead the nations.

It would be an interesting study to consider how, under efficient supervision, the modern method will be utilized in working out the perfected accomplishments in decorative, floral and horticultural achievements that will make our glorious country in this respect the admiration of the centuries.

Thank Superintendent Holton.

At a meeting of exhibitors, held August 20, at the exposition building, the following resolution has been unanimously adopted: "That the thanks of the trade exhibitors be extended to Mr. F. H. Holton for his uniform courtesy and untiring efforts in making the present exhibiton one of the best in the history of the S. A. F. THE EXHIBITORS.

The Humorous Side of the Florists' Business.

BY J. D. CARMODY, EVANSVILLE, IND.

Everything possessing animal life is more or less endowed with a sense of humor, though it is said it takes a surgical operation to get a joke into an Englishman.

It is a well known fact that horses laugh, hyenas smile, and mankind has learned many monkey-shines and a lot of frolicsome capers from their quadruped companions. The feathered tribe indulge in many merry antics, and even flies and fleas seem to take delight in playing tag on our bald heads, and tickling us mortals in out of the way places. Lambs gambol on the green, and it is said that men also delight to gamble on the green, (cloth) ofttimes till the small hours of the morning.

Being endowed with a higher order of intellect, and possessing the gift of speech, mankind has more scope for emotional demonstration than the rest of the brute creation, and often takes the one step which reaches from the sublime to the ridiculous, in that step frequently drying tears of sorrow with breezes of laughter. In all walks of life incidents both serious and humorous lie along our pathway in parallel lines to darken or illumine our existence, and in my experience I have found the florist's vocation one that affords an abundant opportunity for the development of these antipode conditions. The florist's vocation leads him into close relation with both rich and poor. His business calls him alike to the palace of wealth and the chamber of mourning. He decks the funeral bier and the banquet table. He weaves the chaplet of roses that crowns the bride as well as the wreath of forgetmenots that illumine the face of the dead. He goes hand in hand with joy and sorrow, and it becomes his privilege to dispel sadness with buds of promise that bloom into flowers of peace and gladness. In the monotony of daily business the florist's surroundings are such that humorous incidents are of frequent occurrence, and both salesroom and potting shed are alike arenas of mirth.

No florist but what has had in his employ queer characters (as well as cranky customers) who furnish numerous examples of the ridiculous. One source of levity is the mangling of plant names. I had at one time an "Oirishman" in my employ, one O'Neil by name, who was a good workman and a well posted grower, but absolutely indifferent as to the names of plants. When asked the name of any plant out of common line by visiting customers, it was sure to be a Rorum Snoram Grandiflorum, a Japanese Jincum, a Rodus Sidibus or some other outlandish cognomen of which he had a large vocabulary. A Gloire de Dijon rose with him was a Glory to John. When I would take him to task for these pranks he would say: "Sure begorry I grows plants, I don't grow names; and if I did know the right names and give it to them spalpeens straight they would be none the wiser. A divel a hate o' gud it 'ud do 'em."

I was once asked for a sweet jureen by a colored "gemman." He said he wanted it "fur his Ginney." I found out after some investigation he wanted a rose geranium. An exquisite little lady customer called for a Maiden Prayer fern. She said it was a very rare plant; a friend of hers had the only one she had ever seen. I later discovered it was an adian-

tum or maiden-hair fern she wished to see.

A tall, awkward looking countryman, from Posey county, came into my greenhouse one day, and after looking around for an hour or more, his attention was centered on a peculiar looking specimen plant, which seemed to excite his curiosity. Calling to me, he said: "I say, stranger, what in the dickens is that thar thing?" That is a Bryophyllum calycinum, said I, and a very unusual plant. "Well," replied he, "I never seed anything like it afore, but that are just what I thought it wor."

One season I had for a fireman, hostler and all-around work, a native of east Tennessee, very illiterate and with very little memory for anything. One day a clergyman and his wife visited the greenhouse, and being attracted by the beauty of a double-flowering begonia, inquired the name of the plant of this man, who at the time was the only person present. His reply was, "Well, now, I ain't real certain sure, but I thinks as how it are a specimen of some sort or another."

I had a boy, we will call him John, whom I took to teach me how to run my business. Well, he was a case never to be forgotten. The monkey-tricks that boy played would often lay the real thing in the shade. He soon learned the peculiar properties of a certain plant, namely, Caladium aboreum odoratum. The smallest piece of the leaf stem taken in the mouth has the effect of the Indian turnip, producing a sensation as if one has swallowed a galvanic battery and all the chemicals. He dosed the boys that came around the potting shed with this plant, getting them to eat it under the name of "Mexican Sugar Cane," and at times would have a gang of them all spitting and drooling and vieing with each other in making uncomplimentary remarks regarding John and his sugar cane. It was fun for John, but tough on the boys.

One bright spring day John was plunging pot plants in a spent hotbed which was full of immense fat angle worms. Near him, seated on the upper edge of the frame, was a good, big girl chinning him for a bouquet. Becoming tired of her importunities, and wanting a little fun, John picked up a fine plump wiggler, the size of a small garter snake, and with the remark, "Does birdie want a worm?" gave it a toss in her direction with an aim so true that it dropped down between the girl's high collar and the back of her neck. Up into the air went 150 pounds of girl, with a yell like a Comanche Indian; then a streak of calico and ribbon made a rush for the potting shed, which was the nearest cover, with a squeal at every jump, while John cut all sorts of capers over the poor girls antics. I think a disrobing took place, but don't know, as I thought her not to follow the girl. But John said he found some ribbon and pieces of corset string after she had left.

In the florist's business there is great chance of misrepresentation and swindling the public, and there are many unscrupulous people that make it their business to sell all sorts of imaginary things backed up with gaudy colored pictures, and give next to nothing in exchange for good money. One early spring a fine looking woman canvassed our city selling red, white, yellow and blue tuberoses. A lady customer of mine, who had patronized her, told me of the rare purchase she had made and wanted me to grow her tuberoses on shares. You may well know I was very much amused, but told her I would do so if she would take the colored ones and let me keep all the white for myself. This she readily assented to. The result was I got all the bulbs and she had nothing but experience.

Two years ago I was out in Colorado at a small town about 40 miles from Denver, and calling at the house of a friend I found the lady bargaining with a well dressed man for some plants and roots done up in paper and pieces of rags, which he represented as fine clematis and choice shrubs from a Denver nursery. The lady had already made purchase to the amount of $5 or more. After the gentlemen had left she asked me, knowing I was a florist, what I thought of the plants. I told her that there was no clematis in the lot and the whole bunch I thought was a collection of weeds and shrubs pulled up from the ravine not far from her house. "Oh, no!" said she, "that could not be, he was too much of a gentleman to do such a thing." The following season I was back at the same place and asked the lady if her clematis had bloomed yet. She gave me a sickly smile and said, "You guessed the character of the man, as all I got was worthless weeds." Yes, of course, I laughed and said, "I told you so," with that air of superiority which belongs to us florists.

In the early days of my connection with the florists' business our customers had little idea of the value of cut flowers. During the holidays one winter, a girl of about 13 years came into my flower store bringing with her a good sized market basket. She broke loose at once with, "Ma's in a hurry and wants 15 cents worth of orchards, and if yer ain't got any orchards she said give her some sturdions and schinele roses, and put in some fern leaves and 5 cents worth of smilax." I told the little lady my 15-cent orchids were not in bloom yet, and 15 cents would buy just half of a Marechal Niel rose. She looked quite dazed, and when I further told her roses were worth $2 per dozen, she went away muttering something about stingy folks. I thought she had reference to her mother.

It was a common practice for my patrons to endeavor to impress upon my mind that they were buying flowers to give away, therefore I should sell them at reduced rates. My reply generally was, that is the difference between you and I. You are the giver and I am the seller; you must not expect me to be giver and seller both. The more you pay for them the greater the gift, and the greater the satisfaction you should feel in giving. .

Close dealing in those days was a rule, as per example: A lady came to my place one day in quest of a floral tribute for her daughter, who was about to graduate at the high school opening. · When I told her it would cost from $1 to $5 she lost her breath and came near fainting. As she regained consciousness she gasped in smothered tones, "I wouldn't mind 25 or even 50 cents if I could get some nice carnations and roses and a lily or two in a good sized basket, but I reckon I'll have to make her some paper flowers as I can't afford such extravagance." My sleeves were full of laughter, but I kept a straight face and casually remarked, as it is a literary entertainment and your daughter has a paper to read, perhaps paper flowers would be appropriate, but thought she had better ask her daughter which she would prefer. She said my advice was good and so

departed in good humor. Then the fun that was up my sleeve burst out and I laughed good and long.

I am not a professional mind reader, but I felt there would be a hot house where that woman lived that night, and sure enough the next day the lady came back looking very meek, for with her came the daughter, a tall strawberry blonde with hazel eyes full of fire, denoting an up-to-date girl of the period. The first thing she said was, "Mr. C—— did you advise my ma to get me a paper flower boquet for the commencement tomorrow night?" "Certainly not, Miss, I simply advised her to consult with you regarding the matter." "There, ma, what did I tell you? Paper flowers,' she hissed out in disgust, "for me, a graduate with high honors. Ma, ain't you ashamed of yourself? Would you wish me to appear so ridiculous?" Mr. C—— you make the nicest basket of flowers you can for $5, and if ma don't pay for it I will." When left alone I laughed again and patted myself on the back for being an expert diplomat, as well as mind reader.

Many very funny things occur in connection with floral tributes at most funeral occasions. You have all heard the relative beauty of different floral offerings discussed, and the character of the giver will generally come in for comments. "The stingy things, it seems to me they might have given something better than that," or another will whisper, "just see what extravagance in them getting such a fine piece as that big pillar. They'll go hungry for a week if the florist gets his money."

An amusing story is told of an "Oirish" lady whose late husband was receiving the honors of a dacint wake. They had commenced life at the bottom of the ladder, but by Dennis getting into politics and other jobs he had attained the position of alderman of his ward, and the wealth that generally goes with the position. As a natural result many and beautiful were the floral offerings the widow had to inspect and comment upon as they arrived one after another. "Och a hone, arn't they beautiful jist? See that great cross of the blessed Savior, and the wreath made with roses so pure and beautiful, just like Dinny, dear. An' thet swate harp iv Oierland an the gates ajar; sure Dinny darlint has passed Peter's gates and is in heaven playing a harp this minute. Peace to his soul." All at once a change came over the tearful face of the woman as a handsome anchor was brought in for inspection. Her tears were at once dried by the fire of wrath. "Holy mother, just look at that thing. Bad scan to the provoking divil that sent that pick. Och sure and don't Oi wish Dinny was aloive here fur a few minutes jist to bate the divil out of the blaggard who sent that pick, just because poor Dinny used to work on the strate. May old nick fly away with him. Who is the spalpane? Lave me get at him, Oi'l scratch his two eyes into one." When it was explained to the enraged widow that the emblem was an anchor of hope, instead of the symbol of labor she had in her mind, she was quickly appeased, harmony reigned again and Dinny was dacintly interred.

The demand for special funeral emblems applicable to the vocation of the deceased oftimes taxes the inventive genius of the florist, and some of the pieces suggested by the surviving friends frequently seem very ridiculous. A butcher in our vicinity, being in condition for a funeral, one of

his intimate friends came to order a floral offering and insisted on its being in the form of a cleaver. It occurred to me that such an implement was hardly the proper thing. But no one could tell the road he went or the conditions he would encounter at the end of his route. Perhaps it was the very thing he would need.

A commercial traveler having been assigned a new territory, in the unknown world, I was asked to make a floral grip for his funeral ornamentation, by some of his friends. Did he die of the grip, I asked. Oh, no! but as his satchel was his constant companion, one said, we thought it would be a very appropriate emblem for this sad occasion. Alright, I replied, it shall be made, but will I fill it with light underwear, or do you think something heavier would be needed. Not knowing his destination, they failed to advise, so as a precaution, the man being an acquaintance of mine, I filled the grip with wet moss, which you know has a very cooling effect.

To an Englishman I am indebted for the following story, in illustrating a case of ignorance with the nomenclature of plants: A get-rich-quick lady in England was possessed of a hobby for the cultivation of choice plants, the names of which she was apt to distort and garble in the most ridiculous manner. A nobleman, whom she was showing through the conservatory, observing her weakness and wishing to have some fun at her expense, asked if she had ever had a specimen of the Scabies septannis. "Oh, no," she replied, "I used to have it very fine, but I gave it to the Dutchess of Sutherland, and I know her grace would oblige, if you expressed a desire for it." When you comprehend Scabies septannis is a name for the seven-year-itch you will be apt to enjoy the story, unless you are too English to draw the proper conclusion.

We might continue these stories to a great extent, but we have taken enough of your time in this manner for this occasion, and think these will suffice to prove that few vocations afford greater opportunity for enjoyment than does the florist's profession. Now, let me add that to woman—God bless her—we are wholly indebted for the very existence of our profession. They are really our sole patrons, for what they do not buy, men buy because of them. It is my opinion flowers were the after-thought of the Creator and were made for woman's especial pleasure and adornment. I doubt if flowers were in existence prior to the advent of women, for there was no demand for them; but God having made woman to please man, flowers were then made to please woman. There is no woman who is not fond of flowers and gems for adornment of her person, and flowers are nature's own gems with which she beautifies the earth.

F lowers are but Nature's gems
L oaned to us of mortal realms
O urselves with them we'll beautify,
'R ound our homes we'll multiply.
A ll their bright entrancing gleams,
L ighting up our waking dreams.

G ems are they, for though they fade,
E ach bloom has its history made,
M emories are immortal.

Yes flowers are the radiant gems
That deck the fields when spring returns;
They nature weaves fair diadems
Of blossoms sweet and emerald ferns.

Pearls and rubies together meet
When dew drops rest on roses red;
Diamond glints in vain compete
With gems which glow from Flora's bed.

In the civilised world the .florist is the honored attendant and companion of his fellow-man, from the cradle to the grave. He is at the christening of the infant, at stated periods of the youth's education he is called for, and when the young man steps to the front, a graduate, on the platform of some high school or college and shy's his castor into the arena of public life to do battle in the world of business, he finds encouragement in the florists' handiwork, tossed him by loving hands.

In love-making the florist is Cupid's right bower and ofttimes the joker to trump the best card of a lover, with flowers from a rival who knows the value of the florists' art. At the wedding he lights the fire on Hymen's altar and twines the garland of roses that bind two loving hearts together for life, (unless separated by the scissors of divorce) and when death enters the door, he mitigates sorrow with the sweet incense of flowers which rises to the soul that's fled.

To conclude, there should be no pessimist in the florist's profession. The Creator has made you his chosen people to carry on his divine work of creation. The building of cities and labor in the channels of commercial pursuits is man's work, but they who make nature a study, and in obedience with her laws plant and propagate to bring from mother earth new beauties to cheer the souls of their fellow-men are doing God's work in completing this world left by the Creator in an unfinished state. Every park with its lakelets and drives, its beautiful landscape scenery, and beds of flowers and its terraces are all in the line of God's work left for man to accomplish. Every flower that blooms under your care is a smile of recognition of your labor. Keep on with your good work of creation and decoration, also learn to cultivate happiness as you go through life, and when grief turns sorrow into gladness. Beautify that part of this world over which you have control, and when you slide off this earth may you light somewhere on a bed of roses, spiritual flowers of your own cultivation, gone before, awaiting to welcome with their sweet perfume your entrance into that land where all is joy and gladness.

Flowers at Funerals.

We are indebted to A. Gude & Brother, Washington, D. C., for the following sensible comment on this matter in the New Century of recent date, a religious journal:

A correspondent asks us, "to attack" the custom of lavishly displaying garlands and "set pieces" of flowers at funerals. We should be glad to oblige our correspondent if we thought "attacks" on this sort of thing ever did any good.

It is natural enough that bereaved friends, kindly acquaintances and sympathetic neighbors should wish to offer some beautiful tribute to the dead, and flowers are the most appropriate possible symbols of love and hope. It is not true that the offering of flowers in memory of the dead is a "pagan custom," as our friend says, in an objectionable sense. Everything in paganism was not antagonistic to christian sentiment. If the rose was a symbol of Venus, christians have made it a symbol of the Blessed Virgin, and it is no unusual thing, in christian symbolical pictures, as she ascends to heaven. Whether a man be pagan or christian, the natural desire to reverence the dead, to show love for them, springs in his heart, it must take some form, and in all ages, especially in the case of the young, it has taken the form of a tribute of flowers.

The offering of flowers at the grave of the dead is a beautiful and human custom. It is perfunctory. If it becomes a mere matter of fashion; if it loses its simplicity and takes those who can not afford it, then its abuse ought to be restrained by those whose position ought to make them an example to others.

Convention Bowling Contests.

The Milwaukee Bowling tournament on the Olympia alleys was a great success from every point of view. The accommodations were all that could be desired, and the master of ceremonies, Philip J. Hauswirth, did himself proud in the way in which the affair was managed. He was always on hand to settle disputed points, of which there were but few, and had all about the scores at his finger ends for the interested parties. Before the individual championship, the last match on the programme, was over, he had all the other results figured out and who won the strike and spare prize and other intricate matters were all reduced to black and white. He certainly was the right man in the right place and we all take off our hats to the old Chicago captain.

The principal event, the club contest, was started at 2:30 p. m., the teams being paired as follows: New York and St. Louis, Denver and Chicago, Buffalo and Washington and Milwaukee and Cleveland. As they finished their first games they moved over to the next pair of alleys, each game being rolled on a different set. Chicago's first game was great, with a score of 1024, the best ever made in an S. A. F. tournament up to this time, and they were much elated. St. Louis was second with 949, and Buffalo third with 930. In the second game Buffalo came up strong with 1001, Chicago second, 919, and St. Louis third, 898. Buffalo's spirits now ran high as they were but 12 pins behind Chicago. In the third game, however, they could not keep the pace, while Chicago took a spurt and scored another 1000 game, making 1019 to Buffalo's 908. This gave the Chicago boys a total of 2962, against 2839 for Buffalo, who was next to them. It now seemed as though all was over with exception of the shouting for the Chicago boys, who had already begun to celebrate. After the alleys had been cleared Philadelphia and Detroit, who had drawn last places, had their little tussle. The Quaker City boys started badly and it took them some time to work off their case of rattles, their first game being only 871, beating Detroit by but 5 pins. It looked like a hopeless task to catch Chicago with a handicap of 153 pins, but they buckled down to it and the way they made the pins fly was a caution. When the ten frames were cleared up they had the fine total of 1102, an average of 188⅔ per man. Adelberger was first with 226, which proved to be the high game of the tournament, beating by 5 pins Foerster of the Chicago's high game of 221. This placed Philadelphia 30 pins ahead of Chicago in the total of the two games. But there was the last game on which the Hitchings trophy depended. Chicago had made 1019 and it would be hard to beat it. They went to work, however, with a will, and inspired by the large "gallery" that had gotten back from supper they finished with 1062, making a total in the three games of 3035. This gives them the championship for another year and cut the string on the Hitchings trophy, which is now their property.

In the bowling of the high men of the teams to decide the individual champion-ship of the S. A. F., Foerster, of Chicago, won out in the last few frames from Pollworth, of Milwaukee, with a score of 549. Pollworth was but one pin ahead of Wilcox, of Council Bluffs, with ascore of 534. Mr. Wilcox's score being 533. Mr. Foerster is an ideal bowler; his delivery is simply perfect, and

there is no reason why he should not get the coveted twelve strikes straight some of these days and obtain what to all the rest of us is but an ambitious dream.

The individual tournament for all comers was a strenuous affair, and while some good scores were made, the getting away of the ball was in some cases worth going miles to see.

A very interesting feature was the ladies' tournament, which took place in the morning. Some really good scores were made. While many of the fair con testants showed they were novices, yet all displayed such interest that this will no doubt hereafter be made a permanent feature. Over forty ladies took part.

At the meeting of the National Florists' Bowling Association Wm. Scott was re-elected president; J. J. Beneke, of St. Louis, treasurer, and P. J. Hauswirth secretary. It was decided to leave the matter of loaded balls and all other things pertaining to the game to be governed entirely by the rules of the National Bowling Congress. It was also decided that in the future the teams shall consist of only five men each and that but one strike can be counted in the last frame when figuring for the total number made for a prize. Also that a member of a florists' club can legally play on that club's team even if he does not reside in their city but is a member because it is the club most convenient to his place of residence.

TEAM SCORES.

Player	PHILADELPHIA.	1st	2d	3d	T'l
Connor		159	160	186	505
Yates		176	169	199	520
Robinson		146	173	199	518
Kift		195	173	173	471
Adelberger		137	226	196	559
Polites		134	169	156	459
Total		871	1102	1062	3036

Player	CHICAGO.	1st	2d	3d	T'l
G. Stollery		158	170	199	517
F. Stollery		173	153	177	503
Lambros		178	125	168	471
Asmus		179	162	177	518
Balluff		118	190	110	367
Foerster		221	170	196	586
Total		1024	919	1019	2962

Player	BUFFALO.	1st	2d	3d	T'l
Kasting		196	168	176	539
McClure		166	207	181	508
Weber		148	164	151	463
D. Scott		195	172	196	433
Wallace		147	118	183	448
Risch		144	177	157	478
Total		930	1009	908	2839

Player	MILWAUKEE.	1st	2d	3d	T'l
Hunkel		146	173	134	453
Edlefsen		170	199	174	477
Zweifel		150	196	161	458
Kennedy		134	114	168	416
Holton		160	157	195	481
Pollworth		147	163	193	503
Total		915	972	969	2756

Player	ST. LOUIS.	1st	2d	3d	T'l
Beneke		148	161	166	475
Beyer		148	312	184	459
Miller		166	147	157	472
Adles		194	116	150	460
Guy		176	133	130	418
Kohn		186	139	160	425
Total		949	898	898	2745

Player	DENVER.	1st	2d	3d	T'l
A. L. Muell		161	186	134	437
R. Karh		133	145	113	391
J. A. Valentine		114	151	144	409
Frank Cramp		174	1	0	132	376
G. Benson		167	133	206	424
Total		200	163	153	515
Total		889	869	936	2694

Player	DETROI.r.	1st	2d	3d	T'l
Ferguson		117	168	134	437
Beard		127	119	138	384
Breitmeyer		179	173	146	498
Sullivan		158	150	138	439
Hasmann		145	140	130	301
Holznagle		163	145	148	454
Total		896	898	831	2598

CLEVELAND.

Player	1st	2d	3d	T'l
F. Pouting	105	92	107	305
A. Graham	148	129	105	393
J. Eadie	147	161	184	492
J. Keeley	124	169	161	496
H. Kuzz	99	157	197	448
C. Graham	179	156	188	523
Total	803	869	915	2587

WASHINGTON.

Player	1st	2d	3d	T'l
Ernst	166	153	155	474
A. Gude	89	195	111	395
Schaffer	117	112	146	375
W. J. Gude	133	135	127	395
Esch	100	85	136	321
Leoffler	98	109	149	356
Total	703	779	824	2306

NEW YORK.

Player	1st	2d	3d	T'l
O'Mara	166	181	194	473
Traendly	157	140	157	454
Bunyard	107	184	126	387
Guttman	97	109	85	291
Siebrecht	104	100	78	282
Lang	109	214	164	377
Total	632	878	734	2244

FINAL INDIVIDUAL CHAMPIONSHIP.

Player	1st	2d	3d	T'l
Foerster	189	185	175	549
Pollworth	190	131	313	534
Wilcox	146	207	180	533

TEAM CONTESTS.

Teams	1	2	3	Total
Philadelphia	971	1102	1062	3035
Chicago	1024	919	1019	2962
Buffalo	930	1001	908	2839
Milwaukee	915	872	960	2756
St. Louis	949	808	898	2746
Detroit	889	869	936	2694
Detroit	866	808	831	2505
Cleveland	803	869	915	2587
New York	878	878	734	2444
Washington	703	779	824	2306

The prize winners of the team contest
were as follows: Gold medal to each
member of team scoring highest total,
Philadelphia, 3,035 pins; Citizens' Business League prize, six steins to second
high team in three games, Chicago, 2962
pins; C. C. Pollworth Company prize,
scarf pins to third team, Buffalo, 2839;
Henry J. Webr prize, 100 cigars to fourth
highest team, Milwaukee, 2769; Hitchings cup, team scoring highest total in
three games, Philadelphia, 1092; E. F.
Winterson Co. prize, silver cup, highest
total by individual bowler in team or individual bowling; J. A. Foerster, Chicago
team, 586; W. J. Stewart prize, field
glass to member scoring highest in three
games, Theodore Lang, 577; Henry
Weber prize, cut glass bowl, third highest
in three games, F. Adelberger, Philadelphia, 558; Sargeant's prize, gold medal to
bowler making most strikes, F. Adelberger, 14 strikes; Sargeant's prize, gold
medal to bowler making most spares in
three games, George Stollery, 20 spares.

INDIVIDUAL BOWLING CONTEST.

Player	1	2	3	T'l
George Wenith	108	120	131	359
John Evans	127	154	113	394
H. M. Altick	98	157	164	359
C. Critchell	107	110	150	367
Baumser	144	180	151	446
G. R. Scott	133	153	132	403
A. Chew링	167	101	86	354
L. Poehlmann	104	93	111	308
Wm. Scott	113	138	147	395
J. F. Wilcox	179	151	172	502
R. F. Wilcox	113	118	100	330
J. S. Wilson	125	145	114	384
J. Taylor	141	138	134	363
J. Meckel	137	94	118	348
J. B. Goetz	93	182	108	383
B. Bartels	101	82	90	273
Dunn	143	137	113	393
W. Kreitling	108	94		395
Straub	144	100		341
Roney	107	82		189
McRoble	134	122		262
Freytag	161	143	157	461
Klockner	134	137	150	421
Geo. Watson	146	101	112	359
Hauswirth	137	160	143	440

Prize winners in the individual contest
were as follows: Evans medal, highest
total in three games, J. F. Wilcox, 502;
John Weber prize, gold medal, second
high individual in three games, M. Frey-

tag, 461; J. F. Wilcox prize, silk umbrella,
third highest total, Mr. Baumner, 445;
Kuntz Brothers' prize, umbrella, fourth
highest total in three games, J. S. Wilson,
Chicago; Brunswick Balke Company
prize, bowling ball, fifth highest total,
P. J. Hauswirth, 440; F. Pollworth &
Brother prize, pair cuff buttons to sixth
highest total, M. Rodgers, 437.

Following are the winners of the
miscellaneous prizes: Western Bowling
Journal, highest single score during entire
tournament, F. Adelberger 226; Steve
Gouroux prize, umbrella, second highest
single score, Jos. Foerster, 221; Citizens'
Business League prize, fishing pole, third
highest, Carl Meyer, 212; Sam Kindt &
Brother prize, box of cigars, fourth
highest, G. McClure 207; Mussey grand
special prize for championship of S. A. F.,
J. Foerster 549.

LADIES' INDIVIDUAL CONTEST.

Player	1	2	T'l
Mrs. S. Reinberg, first, 85 g 1d piece..	122	113	235
Mrs. Kreitling, second, sofa pillow	104	101	205
Mrs. Keppley, third, bottle perfumery.	120	55	175
Mrs. Smith, fourth, box stationery	63	110	173
Mrs. Johanseau, fifth, h'd k'f case	90	69	159
Mrs. F. C. Weber, sixth, h'd k'f Cuke..	89	88	157
Mrs. L. Meinhardt, seventh, box candy	72	84	156
Mrs. Hauswirth, eighth, bottle ginger	78	75	153
Mrs. Reinhardt, nine, box candy	62	84	146
Mrs. F. Stollery	53	81	133
Mrs. Kasting	73	70	143
Miss Ritterback	47	72	119
Miss Sendler	57	74	141
Miss F. Mienhardt	32	31	63
Miss Hebel	57	70	137
Miss Sleidel	52	96	
Mrs. Guy	40	34	83
Mrs. Meinhardt	33	70	103
Miss Kleismer	48	56	104
Mrs. Hoff	41	45	85
Mrs. Zender	54	59	113
Mrs. Heneke	54	57	111
Mrs. Zweifel	42	62	104
Mrs. Ellis	35	31	67
Miss Folsom	30	67	97
Mrs. Haliiday	50	59	119
Mrs. Hofman	66	39	105
Mrs. McKellar	65	44	109
Mrs. Hunkel	47	46	93

Some special prizes were awarded in
the ladies' individual contest. Highest
single score, bowling ball, Mrs. P. Reinberg; most strikes, pocket book, Mrs.
Smith; most spares, ebony hair brush,
Mrs. F. C. Weber.

Presentation to Philip J. Hauswirth.

John Westcott on behalf of the Philadelphia Florists' Club gave an impromptu
reception to the captains of the bowling
teams last Thursday evening at the
Hotel Pfister. It was held in the large
club room and was a most enjoyable
affair. In addition to the captains invitations had also been extended to President Burton, President-elect Philip Breitmeyer and all the ex-presidents present
in the city, as well as a few personal
friends. The Hitchings loving cup, now
the property of the Quaker City bowlers,
was filled with Florists' Club punch and
many words of good will and well
wishes for the host and his club were
made as the cup was passed around.

Bowling as an adjunct for the good of
the society was agreed to by all and
efforts to increase the interest in the
game were talked over in an informal
way.

Mr. Kastings, of Buffalo, offered to
donate a solid silver trophy to be a perpetual challenge prize that will go with
the championship and be awarded the
team making the highest total score each
year. This was accepted with general
acclamation. The feature of the evening
was the presentation of a silver tea set
to Mr. and Mrs. Philip J. Hauswirth by
their Philadelphia friends as a recognition of the faithful and very efficient
manner in which he managed the contest.

Mr. Hauswirth was taken completely
by surprise, but made a neat speech,
accepting the gift on behalf of his good
lady and himself. K.

Lake Geneva Gardens.

SUMMER HOME OF H. H. PORTER.

The summer home of H. H. Porter is
one of the leading estates along the
north shore of Lake Geneva and through
many years of persistent energy on the
part of Supt. John Tiplady, is a picture
of neatness. The park consists of fourteen acres. The large imposing residence is
set well back from the water on a prominent rise, commanding a good view of
the lake and the large well kept lawn,
which is judiciously planted with fine
specimens of both native and foreign
trees, each one free and well developed.
Some of the elms, twenty to thirty toes
in weight, were transplanted two years
ago and are doing well. Among the finer
specimens are ash, butternut, black walnut, cut-leaved birch, catalpa, elm, horse
chestnut, hickory, linden, several species
of oak, cut-leaved maple, sugar maple,
poplar, purple beech, picea alba glauca,
P. excelsa, P. pungens and P. Nordmann-
iana, and Thuya occidentalis. Near the
shore are Wisconsin weeping and several
other species of willow interspersed in
the openings with shrubbery.

All objectionable features about the
grounds have been carefully obscured by
judicious planting and the native grape,
northwestern honeysuckle, blackberry
and Virginia creeper have been used freely
for screening and covering fences.

The shrubbery is extensive and is carried around the outlines of the estate and
about the residence, massed irregularly
or grouped in species in which all of the
better native kinds have been brought
into use and others, Syringa Josikæa, S.
Pekinensis, S. Chinensis, S. vulgaris,
Tamarix Gallica, Viburnum Opulus, V.
acerifolium, V. dentatum, V. Lentago
and Xanthoxylum Americanum.

Mr. Tiplady makes a specialty of
native flowers and has brought together
the ferns, orchids and other wild flowers
from the surrounding country. By careful study he has selected suitable natural
locations and introduced them among
the shrubbery and beneath the trees,
which would otherwise look bare and
unsightly.

Producing pretty and interesting
results, quantities of Aquilegia Canadensis are planted along the shore for early
spring effect. Patches of native adiantum, asplenium, cypripedium, dodeca-
theon, geranium, eupatorium, helianthus,
hepatica, iris, monarda, orchis, osmunda,
pteris, rudbeckia and violet are massed
among or bordering the shrubbery,
enhancing the effect and prolonging the
flowering season. These are assisted by
a host of hybrid aquilegias, delphiniums,
dianthuses, campanulas, hemerocallis,
myosotis, peonies, new French phlox,
papaver and others. Lysimachia and
glechoma are much used for carpeting
beneath the trees.

A good part of the lawn was replanted
two years ago and its success was due to
careful selection of grasses adapted to
the native soil which is a heavy sandy
loam impregnated with clay. The mixture of seed used is equal parts of red top,
Rhode Island bent, June, and Kentucky
blue grass with the addition of one-
eighth part white clover.

The greenhouses are devoted to ferns,
asparagus, bedding plants and carnations and the soil seems favorable to
Joost, Lawson and Norway.

THE AMERICAN FLORIST

NINETEENTH YEAR.

Subscription, $1.00 a Year. To Europe, $2.00.
Subscriptions accepted only from those in the trade.

Advertisements, on all except cover pages,
10 Cents a Line. Agate; $1.00 per inch.
Cash with Order.

No Special Position Guaranteed.

Discounts are allowed only on consecutive insertions, as follows:—6 times, 5 per cent; 13 times,
10 per cent; 26 times, 20 per cent;
52 times, 30 per cent.

Cover space sold only on yearly contract at
$1.00 per inch, net, in the case of the two
front pages, regular discounts applying only to the back pages.

The Advertising Department of the AMERICAN
FLORIST is for florists, seedsmen and nurserymen
and dealers in wares pertaining to those lines only.

Orders for less than one-half inch space not accepted.

Advertisements must reach us by Wednesday to
secure insertion in the issue for the following
Saturday. Address

AMERICAN FLORIST CO., Chicago.

IN W. L. Smith's advertisement of last
week, glass was offered in 8x19 and
19x16 sizes, when 8x10 and 10x16 were
were intended.

WE are in receipt of a copy of the proceedings of the twelfth annual meeting of
the American Carnation Society. In
addition to the usual account of the
meeting, the report contains an excellent
portrait of C. W. Ward, the president of
the society.

John G. Esler.

Members of the Florists' Hail Association will be interested to know that John
G. Esler, the secretary, will be away
from home, at Chicago, August 22–29.

Florists' Hail Association.

At the meeting of the stockholders of
this association, held August 20, the
following were chosen directors to serve
for term of three years: Stephen D.
Horan, Joseph Heacock and F. E. Dorner,
Jr.

At the directors' meeting the former
officers were re-elected, as follows: J. C.
Vaughan, president; E. G. Hill, Vice-
president; A. M. Herr, treasurer; J. G.
Esler, secretary.

The fourteenth annual assessment was
levied, payable March 1.

Society of American Florists.

DEPARTMENT OF PLANT REGISTRATION.

E. Worden, Jamestown, N. Y., offers
for registration Geranium The Mascotte.
Color, delicate light rose without any
salmon or magenta tint. Flowers semi-
double, center blooms remain till cluster
is fully developed. Habit, bedder.
W. A. Manda, South Orange, N. J.,
submits for registration Manda's Golden
privet, a strikingly-variegated sport
from the California privet, Ligustrum
ovalifolium. WM. J. STEWART, Sec'y.

American Carnation Society.

At a meeting of the American Carnation Society, held at the Plankinton
House, Milwaukee, August 19, during
the progress of the S. A. F. convention,
the prize list drawn up at Detroit was
formally adopted. H. M. Altick, chairman
of the McKinley Memorial Society, made
some reference to this matter. It was
arranged that President Burton, of the
S. A. F., be requested to introduce the
subject at one of the meetings of the
latter association.

It was decided at this meeting of the
Carnation Society that a sweepstakes of

$25 be divided into two prizes—$15 for
the best vase in class A and $10 for the
best vase in class B. The premium of
$50 offered by C. H. Rooney, of the Lake-
view Rose Gardens, Jamestown, N. Y.,
was accepted, the awarding of the same
to be subject to the donor's suggestion.
Much progress was made with the programme for the next annual meeting.

The Window Glass Market.

The New York window glass market
was dull during the past week and the
trade continued to adopt the hand-to-
mouth policy in making their purchases,
according to a leading glass trade journal
of August 15. The tone of the market
was steadier, however, as a result of
outside concerns being less disposed to
shade prices, and the fact that foreign
competition has decreased to a considerable extent.

Western advices are to the effect that
indications point to a brisk demand in
the early fall, as supplies of glass in the
hands of consumers are reported as being
very light. All authorities on window
glass are of the opinion that prices will
go up within the next two months, as
the increase in the wage rate will make a
step of this kind necessary.

Pipe for Greenhouse Heating.

ED. AM. FLORIST:—Kindly give some
suggestions as to the piping of a carnation house, 18x60 feet, south gutter 6½
feet to ground, north gutter five feet to
ground, also a rose house, 11x63 feet,
lean-to against shed; thirty-eight feet of
the latter house is exposed, the balance
adjoining another house. Would like to
use 4-inch pipe and hot water flows rising
to rear of house. B. J.

The carnation house can be heated
with six runs of 4-inch pipe, while five
will answer for the rose house.
L. R. TAFT.

Greenhouse Piping.

ED. AM. FLORIST:—Kindly inform me
as to the pipes required for an even span
carnation house, 30x100 feet, 4-foot
walls, 11-foot ridge, solid benches.
How many runs of 1-inch pipe will it
take to insure an inside temperature of
56° when the mercury outside drops to
15° below zero, steam heat to be used?
H. G. D.

To heat a house such as described
above to 56°, six and one-half square
feet of steam radiation will be required
for each foot in length. To furnish this,
twenty 1-inch pipes will be needed.
Another method will be to use two 2-inch
flow pipes, either on the walls or the
purlin posts. If these are used, sixteen
1-inch pipes will be needed in the coils.
While these may be on the walls it is
advisable to have a part of them distributed through the house.
L. R. TAFT.

Hot Water Heating.

ED. AM. FLORIST:—I shall be pleased to
have you advise me through your columns as to the best method of heating
with hot water the plant shown in the
enclosed sketch, using 2-inch pipe for
returns. B. J. A.

The plan shows one house 16x75 feet
and another 18x72 feet with a passageway between. A temperature of 55° is
desired in zero weather. The boiler shed
is at one end of the 16x75-foot house and
a palm house 14x21 feet is at the other.

The east end of the palm house connects
with the 18x72-foot house. The 16x75-
foot house has eighteen inches of glass in
the sides and there are thirty inches of
glass in the sides of the 18x72-foot house.
For the 18x72-foot house run a 4-inch
flow through the 16x75-foot and palm
house and with it supply fifteen 2-inch
returns. For the other houses run two
2½-inch pipes as flows to the farther side
of the palm house and with each of them
feed a coil of four 2-inch pipes running on
the walls back to the boiler. If there is
any glass in the walls of the palm house
put in an additional pipe in each coil for
every two feet of glass. L. R. TAFT.

Heating Greenhouses.

ED. AM. FLORIST:—Last winter I had a
hard time keeping a new greenhouse
warm. First I tried a single pipe system,
with a rise of ten inches to the 100 feet,
starting at the end nearest the boiler,
which gave fair results. I was advised
to put in a smaller pipe, using steam,
with an air cock at the farther end of the
house. Finding that this was not practical, I connected all pipes at farther end
and put in a return pipe from there
equipped with an air valve, with unsatisfactory results. Next I tried dropping
the pipes from the nearest to the farther-
est end of the house, which had its disadvantage as the pipes could not be cleared
of air. I then ran a 1½-inch pipe overhead through center of house to the farthest end from boiler with a down slope
of about one foot. I also put in two
1-inch pipes under middle bench, sloping
them down toward the boiler, where
they were about twelve inches above the
water level. In this case I was obliged
to shut off the return water in order to
let out the cold air, otherwise the water
would force out. I now have on hand
two small steam boilers and about 115
feet of 2½-inch, 70 feet of 2-inch and 110
feet of 1½-inch pipe, together with a lot
of 1-inch and 1¼-inch pipe. Can the second-hand boiler, of which I enclose a
sketch, be made to answer for a steam
plant by adding a steam dome or something similar, or would it be more advisable to change the eighteen 3-inch flues
to hot water heating? Could I use the
1-inch and 1¼-inch pipe for hot water
and would one of my small steam boilers
do for heating the house spring and fall,
or would you advise me to buy a new
steam boiler in place of the old one mentioned above? Will a steam trap be of
any use? P. S. W.

The principal trouble with the steam
piping seems to be that the coils are too
nearly on a level with the boiler, but
without knowing more about the size of
the house and the arrangement of the
piping. The connections of the return
pipe with the boiler may be too small.
Placing the air valve at the upper end of
a relief pipe two feet in height will probably correct the difficulty. The boiler
will probably answer as it is for either
steam or hot water. Except for short
runs or when the coils are several feet
above the boiler it is not advisable to use
pipe smaller than 1½-inch for hot water.
The boilers will probably heat 600 to 800
square feet of steam radiation.
L. R. TAFT.

Boiler for Greenhouse Heating.

ED. AM. FLORIST:—Would you recommend a steam or a hot water boiler to
heat two 100-foot houses, soft coal being
used for fuel, more houses to be added
later? Would an ordinary tubular boiler

give as- good satisfaction as a regular cast iron greenhouse boiler, especially for steam? Is soft coal a suitable fuel where hot water is used, or will it be apt to create too much sweating in the tubes? With a good boiler well bricked in, how long could steam be kept up without attention with soft coal? E. D. C.

For plants of medium size hot water will give the best results, firing and fuel alone being considered. On the other hand the cost of the pipe will be nearly twice as much for hot water as for steam. Having the pipe for steam radiation, it will probably be most satisfactory. to put in a steam boiler, if the enlarged plant will require 2,000 square feet of radiation or more. Tubular boilers are not as durable as those made of cast iron, but they cost less, are quite economical of fuel and give good results for large plants especially. With good care they often last fifteen or twenty years. With a large boiler and a grate of ample size steam could be kept up four or five hours with a good grade of soft coal.
L. R. TAFT.

HANNIBAL, Mo.—David Whisler was killed in a runaway on August 6. The deceased is survived by a widow, a daughter, Miss Maude, and one son, Harry Whisler. The latter recently moved here from Quincy to engage in business with his father.

SITUATIONS, WANTS, FOR SALE.

One Cent Per Word.

Cash with the Adv.

Plant Advs. NOT admitted under this head.

Every paid subscriber to the AMERICAN FLORIST for the year 1903 is entitled to a five-line WANT ADV. (situations only) free, to be used at any time during the year.

Situation Wanted—By experienced grower of cut flowers, as manager of small place. Address MANAGER, care American Florist.

Situation Wanted—By experienced gardener, single, to take charge of medium sized private place. Address THOS. CALLAHAN, Glen Cove, N. Y.

Situation Wanted—By an experienced foreman in good establishment where good wages are paid; married; English. S T, Mount Airy P. O., Germantown, Phila.

Situation Wanted—At once, by an up-to-date store man. Expert designer and decorator. Best references. Work cheap to begin. Address WILLIAM, care American Florist.

Situation Wanted—This (all, as head gardener on private or public institution; 21 years' experience; age 36; married. For further particulars address P G F, care American Florist.

Situation Wanted—By experienced grower of cut flowers. Carnations and 'mums a specialty. Competent to take full charge; temperate; best references; married. Address RELIABLE, care American Florist.

Situation Wanted—By a florist, 25 years' experience on commercial places; grower of general stock; capable to take charge; state of Pennsylvania preferred. When answering please state wages. E E, care American Florist.

Situation Wanted—American. 23 years of age; 4 years' experience in the growing business; desires position as traveler (no experience); of good appearance, character. etc. Can furnish references. TRAVELER, care American Florist.

Situation Wanted—As head landscape gardener as superintendent or manager of large private estate or park. Experience and ability only first-class; best references. Small places need not answer. Address F W, care American Florist.

Situation Wanted—By a reliable and up-to-date grower of Beauties, teas, carnations, 'mums and violets; 18 years' experience. Position as foreman or assistant, where first-class stock is wanted. Good wages expected. State wages and conditions in first letter. Address BEAUTY, care American Florist.

Help Wanted—Rose growers. SOUTH PARK FLORAL CO., New Castle, Ind.

Help Wanted—All-around man for general greenhouse work. Address T. N. YATES & CO., Mt. Airy, Phila., Pa.

Help Wanted—Experienced, unmarried gardener for my private greenhouse, garden, etc. W. H. CHADWICK, 632 Rialto Bldg., Chicago.

Help Wanted—As assistant in place of 15,000 feet where only cut flowers are grown. Good chance for man who can show good references. H. BORNHOEFT, Tipton, Ind.

Help Wanted—A grower of general greenhouse stock, carnation, bedding plants, etc., by September 1. Please state wages. Address L. A. RIKE & SON, LeRoy, Ill.

Help Wanted—A man experienced in packing roses for shipping. We have a good position for a reliable man that understands the business. SOUTH PARK FLORAL CO., New Castle, Ind.

Help Wanted—We have opening for a young gardener with park experience at $60 per month, with a future, in state of Washington. Apply by letter, stating full particulars. VAUGHAN'S SEED STORE, Chicago.

Help Wanted—A good all-around florist to accept a permanent situation in the south. For particulars call Sunday next at 53 Wabash Ave., Chicago, or at J. B. Deamud's, 51 Wabash Ave. Must have best of references.

Help Wanted—Experienced florist to take charge, grow cut flowers and general stock; 8,000 feet of glass; $60, board and room to start with; give description, also good reference required. Address J. C. STEINHAUSER, Pittsburg, Kans.

Help Wanted—An experienced carnation grower. First year $45 per month. If ability is proven an increase will be made. Houses all planted; about 3 miles from Cleveland, O.; single man preferred. Address M. BLOY, Essex Greenhouses, North Olmstead, Ohio.

Help Wanted—Young man with some general greenhouse experience, to assist in establishment of 30,000 feet of glass, growing general stock. City of 15,000. Want an ambitious young man, willing to work. Good prospects for advancement. Reasonable salary to start on. ILLINOIS GROWER, care American Florist.

Help Wanted—An experienced salesman and decorator for an up-to-date retail store, catering to the best trade. Must be experienced in store work and decorating, not afraid to work and come well recommended. A good salary and chance for advancement to the right party. Address with full particulars RANDOLPH & MCCLEMENTS, 5 Highland Ave. and Baum St., Pittsburg, Pa.

Wanted—Second-hand small hot water heater. F. E. PRICE, Nokomis, Ill.

Wanted—Some second-hand cast-iron pipe and fittings. Must be in good condition. Address W. P. RANSON, Junction City, Kans.

For Sale or Rent—Greenhouses, 6,000 feet of glass, fine location, 722 North 64th Ave. Address FRANK JUNE, Oak Park.

For Sale—House and barn, frame, two greenhouses, stock, with stock complete. A bargain. MILO W. BROWN, Spirit Lake, Iowa.

For Rent—Sixty-foot greenhouse, 8 room house, two lots, $25 per month. 3181 Elston Ave. DR. BANGS, 654 N. Robey St., Chicago.

For Sale—One No. 30 Wilks hot water boiler with stock complete, used only three months. A bargain for cash. JAMES W. DUNFORD, R. R. No. 1, Clayton, Mo.

For Sale—Fine old establishment of about 10,000 square feet of glass, one acre of land or ground with or without good dwelling. A bargain. Investigate most if interested. Address OHIO, care American Florist.

For Sale—In the World's Fair city, three-room house, two greenhouses, one 14x80, one 18x80, one acre of ground; heated by steam; plenty of water. Price $1,200; $800 cash. LEO EBERENZ, Webster Grove, Mo.

FOR SALE. A good home and greenhouses well stocked with up-to-date stock for retail trade; established 20 years. Splendid opening for a party here offered. Reason, the death of Mrs. S. H. Bagley. C. H. Bagley, Abilene, Kan.

For Sale—Four large size Gorton side feed boilers (for hard or soft coal), $60 each; one small Gorton side feed, $25; one large sectional Florida heater, $60; one small coll-boiler, hot water, in use two winters, will heat 3,000 square feet of glass, $20. Boilers taken out to put in larger one. Write for particulars. F. FALLON, Roanoke, Va.

Chicago.

THE PAST WEEK IS PRONOUNCED THE DULLEST OF THE SEASON.—ROSES OF POOR QUALITY AND CHEAP.—OUTDOOR FLOWERS IN GREAT PLENTY.—GENERAL NOTES.

Some of the wholesalers say that the past week was the worst one experienced this summer and there is no doubt ample ground for their complaints as business has been practically dead, with exception of on Monday, when some stock was disposed of. There is very little to do at the flower market except the monotonous changing of water, cutting of stems and the subsequent transporting of the unsalable flowers to the dump. The dump is certainly working overtime these days. There is one consolation, however, if such it may be called, and that is that whatever happens, it will be for the better, as we have without a doubt struck bed rock at last. Some of the retail stores are handling large quantities of roses at extremely low figures, these being probably some from old stock that has not yet been dried off. Roses from new stock are coming in quite lively but are as yet of poor quality, and the weather being warm with practically no demand, prices are as a consequence low. A few very good American Beauty roses are noticed. Hydrangeas, asters and gladioli are coming in in better shape than a week ago, although not so plentiful. Auratum lilies are seen in abundance and are of good quality, but there is no demand for them.

Alex. Newell, of John Deamud's establishment has a refrigerator car-load of fish to dispose of as a result of his recent pilgrimage to the southern part of the state.

Weiland & Risch's American Beauty stock is coming along in elegant shape, their carnations being better than ever.

The downtown office of Peter Reinberg is undergoing a thorough overhauling and cleaning.

Oscar Friedman is giving all his employes two weeks off.

John Deamud is handling some nice American Beauty roses.

Joe Curran at Friedman's is on a two weeks' vacation.

Wholesale Flower Markets

MILWAUKEE, Aug. 20.
Roses, Beauty, med. per doz.	1.50
" " short "	.75@1.00
" Liberty	4.00@ 6.00
" Bride, Bridesmaid	4.00@ 6.00
" Meteor, Golden Gate	4.00@ 6.00
" Perle	4.00@ 6.00
Carnations	1.00@ 2.00
Sweet peas	.15
Smilax	10.0C@12.50
Asparagus	50.00
Gladioli	3.00@ 4.00
Asters	1.00@ 2.00

PITTSBURG, Aug. 20.
Roses, Beauty, specials, per doz.	2.50@3.50
" " extras "	1.00@2.00
" " No. 1 "	.75@1.00
" " No. 2 "	2.00@ 5.00
" Bride, Bridesmaid	1.00@ 6.00
" Meteor	2.00@ 4.00
" Kaiserin	2.00@ 6.00
" Liberties	3.00@ 8.00
Carnations	.50@ 1.5
Lily of the Valley	2.00@ 4.00
Sweet peas	.30@ .50
Smilax	8.00@12.00
Adiantum	.75@ 1.25
Asparagus, strings	30.00@50.00
" Sprengeri	2.00@ 4.00
Gladioli	1.00@ 4.00
Easter lilies	8.00@12.00
Asters	.50@ 1.50

CINCINNATI, Aug. 20.
Roses, Beauty	10.00@25.00
" Bride, Bridesmaid	3.00@ 5.00
" Liberty	3.00@ 5.00
" Meteor, Golden Gate	3.00@ 5.00
Carnations	1.00@ 2.00
Lily of the valley	3.00@ 4.00
Asparagus	50.00
Smilax	12.50@15.00
Adiantum	1.00@ 1.50
Gladioli	3.00
Asters	1.00@ 2.00
Lilium Album and Rubrum	4.00

ST. LOUIS, Aug. 20.
Roses, Beauty, long stem	3.00
" Beauty, medium stem	12.50
" Beauty, short stem	4.00@ 6.00
" Liberty	3.00@ 6.00
" Bride, Bridesmaid	2.00@ 4.00
" Golden Gate	2.00@ 4.00
Carnations	1.00@ 1.50
Smilax	12.50
Asparagus Sprengeri	1.00@ 1.50
" Plumosus	18.00@20.00
Gladioli	1.00@ 3.00
Ferns	per 1000 1.50
China Asters	1.00@ 3.00
Tuberoses	4.00

Pittsburg Cut Flower Co., Ltd

WHOLESALE FLORISTS.

————Pittsburg, Pa.

INTERNATIONAL FLOWER DELIVERY.

PASSENGER STEAMSHIP MOVEMENTS.

The table s herewith give the scheduled time of departure of ocean steamships carrying first-class passengers from the principal American and foreign ports, covering the space of two weeks from date of this issue of the AMERICAN FLORIST. Much disappointment often results from attempts to forward flowers for steamer delivery by express, to the care of the ship's steward or otherwise. The carriers of these packages are not infrequently refused admission on board and even those delivered on board are not always certain to reach the parties for whom they were intended. Hence florists in interior cities having orders for the delivery of flowers to passengers on out-going steamers are advised to intrust the filling of such orders to some reliable florist in the port of departure, who understands the necessary details and formalities and has the facilities for attending to it properly. For the addresses of such firms we refer our readers to the advertisements on this page:

FROM	TO	STEAMER	*LINE	DAY	DUE ABOUT
New York	Liverpool	Umbria	1	Sat. Aug. 29, 10:00 a. m.	Sept. 4
New York	"	Lucania	1	Sat. Sept. 5, 2:00 p. m.	Sept. 11
New York	Glasgow	Mongolian	2	Thur. Sept. 3, 8:00 p. m.	Sept. 12
New York	Hamburg	Augusta Victoria	3	Thur. Aug. 27, 10:00 a. m.	
New York	"	Patricia	3	Sat. Aug. 29, 10:30 a. m.	Sept. 10
New York	"	Moltke	3	Thur. Sept. 3, 3:30 p. m.	Sept. 10
New York	Copenhagen	Oscar II	4	Wed. Sept. 2,	
New York	Glasgow	Ethiopia	5	Sat. Aug. 29, Noon.	
New York	"	Anchoria	5	Sat. Sept. 5, Noon.	Sept. 16
New York	Southampton	Manitou	6	Fri. Aug. 28, 9:00 a. m.	
New York	London	Minneapolis	6	Sat. Aug. 29, 10:00 a. m.	Sept. 7
New York	"	Minnehaha	6	Sat. Sept. 5, 4:00 p. m.	Sept. 15
New York	Liverpool	Oceanic	7	Wed. Aug. 26, 8:00 a. m.	Sept. 2
New York	"	Cymbric	7	Fri. Aug. 28, 9:30 a. m.	Sept. 8
New York	"	Teutonic	7	Wed. Sept. 2, Noon.	Sept. 9
New York	"	Arabic	7	Fri. Sept. 4, 4:00 p. m.	Sept. 16
New York	Southampton	New York	8	Wed. Aug. 26, 10:00 a. m.	Sept. 1
New York	"	Philadelphia	8	Wed. Sept. 2, 10:00 a. m.	
New York	"	St. Paul	8	Sat. Sept. 5, 10:00 a. m.	
New York	Antwerp	Kroonland	9	Sat. Aug. 29, 10:00 a. m.	Sept. 7
New York	"	Zeeland	9	Sat. Sept. 5, 10:00 a. m.	Sept. 14
New York	Havre	La Bretagne	10	Thur. Aug. 27, 10:00 a. m.	Sept. 4
New York	"	La Lorraine	10	Thur. Sept. 3, 10:00 a. m.	
New York	Rotterdam	Noordam	11	Wed. Aug. 26, 10:00 a. m.	
New York	"	Rotterdam	11	Wed. Sept. 2, 10:00 a. m.	
New York	Genoa	Sardegna	12	Tues. Aug. 25, 11:00 a. m.	
New York	"	Citta di Napoli	12	Tues. Sept. 1, 11:00 a. m.	Sept. 18
New York	"	Hohenzollern	13	Sat. Aug. 29, 11:00 a. m.	Sept. 11
New York	Bremen	Kaiser Wilh. II	13	Tues. Aug. 26, 7:30 a. m.	Sept. 1
New York	"	Koelligin Luise	13	Thur. Aug. 27, 1:00 p. m.	Sept. 6
New York	"	K. Wil. Der Grosse	13	Tues. Sept. 1, 10:00 a. m.	Sept. 8
New York	"	Prdk. Der Grosse	13	Thur. Sept. 3, 2:00 p. m.	Sept. 12
New York	Naples	Germania	14	Tues. Aug. 25,	Sept. 8
Boston	Genoa	Vancouver	15	Sat. Aug. 29, 3:00 p. m.	
Boston	Liverpool	Commonwealth	15	Sat. Aug. 27, 1:00 p. m.	Sept. 3
Boston	"	New England	15	Thur. Sept. 3, 8:00 p. m.	Sept. 10
Boston	"	Saxonia	15	Tues. Aug. 25, 11:30 a. m.	Sept. 1
Boston	"	Winifredian	15	Sat. Aug. 29, 3:00 p. m.	
Boston	"	Bohemian	15	Sat. Sept. 5, 9:30 a. m.	
Montreal	"	Kensington	15	Sat. Aug. 29, Daylight.	
Montreal	"	Dominion	15	Sat. Sept. 5, Daylight.	
Montreal	"	Ionian	15	Sat. Aug. 29, 4:00 a. m.	
Montreal	"	Tunisian	15	Sat. Sept. 5, 4:00 a. m.	
San Francisco	Yokohama	America Maru	17	Wed. Aug. 26, 1:00 p. m.	Sept. 14
San Francisco	"	Korea	17	Thur. Sept. 3, 1:00 p. m.	Sept. 20
San Francisco	Honolulu	Sierra	18	Thur. Aug. 27, 2:00 p. m.	Sept. 1
San Francisco	"	Alameda	18	Sat. Sept. 5, 11:00 a. m.	Sept. 1
San Francisco	Yokohama	Sierra	18	Thur. Aug. 27, 2:00 p. m.	Sept. 18
Vancouver	"	Tartar	20	Mon. Aug. 24,	Sept. 10
Vancouver	"	Empress of China	20	Mon. Sept. 7,	Sept. 21
Vancouver	Hongkong	Tartar	20	Mon. Aug. 24,	Sept. 10
Vancouver	"	Empress of China	20	Mon. Sept. 7,	Sept. 21
Seattle	Yokohama	Riojun Maru	22	Sat. Sept. 5, a. m.	Sept. 21
Seattle	Hongkong	"	22	Sat. Sept. 5, a. m.	Oct. 6

*1 Cunard; 2 Allen-State; 3 Hamburg-American; 4 Scandinavian-American; 5 Anchor Line; 6 Atlantic Transport; 7 White Star; 8 American; 9 Red Star; 10 French; 11 Holland-American; 12 Italian Royal Mail; 13 North German Lloyd; 14 Fabre; 15 Dominion; 16 Leyland; 17 Occidental and Oriental; 18 Oceanic; 19 Allan; 20 Can. Pacific Ry.; 21 N. Pacific Ry.; 22 Hongkong-Seattle.

INTERNATIONAL FLOWER DELIVERY.

STEAMSHIPS LEAVE FOREIGN PORTS.

FROM	TO	STEAMER	*LINE	DAY	DUE ABOUT
Liverpool........	New York	Etruria	1	Sat. Aug. 29,	Sept. 4
Liverpool........	"	Campania	1	Sat. Sept. 5,	Sept. 11
Liverpool........	"	Germanic	7	Wed. Aug. 26, 5:00 p. m.	Sept. 3
Liverpool........	"	Cedric	7	Fri. Aug. 28, 5:00 p. m.	
Liverpool........	"	Majestic	7	Wed. Sept. 2, 5:00 p. m.	
Liverpool........	"	Celtic	7	Fri. Sept. 4, 5:00 p. m.	
Liverpool........	Boston	Ivernia	1	Tues. Aug. 25,	Sept. 2
Liverpool........	"	Mayflower	15	Thur. Aug. 27,	Sept. 3
Liverpool........	"	Columbus	15	Thur. Sept. 3,	
Liverpool........	"	Canadian	16	Fri. Aug. 28,	
Liverpool........	"	Cestrian	16	Fri. Sept. 4,	
Liverpool........	Montreal	Southwark	15	Wed. Aug. 26,	
Liverpool........	"	Parisian	19	Thur. Aug. 27,	
Glasgow........	New York	Furnessia	5	Thur. Aug. 27,	
Glasgow........	"	Laurentian	18	Sat. Aug. 29,	Sept. 8
Glasgow........	"	Numidian	2	Sat. Sept. 5,	Sept. 16
Genoa	"	Citta di Milano	12	Mon. Aug. 24,	
Genoa	"	Lombardia	12	Mon. Sept. 7,	
Southampton...	"	St. Paul	8	Wed. Aug. 26, Noon.	
Southampton...	"	St. Louis	8	Sat. Aug. 29, Noon.	
Southampton...	"	New York	8	Sat. Sept. 5, Noon.	Sept. 12
Southampton...	"	Menominee	6	Wed. Aug. 26,	Sept. 5
London.........	"	Mesaba	6	Sat. Aug. 29,	
London.........	"	Minnetonka	6	Sat. Sept. 5,	
Antwerp........	"	Finland	8	Sat. Aug. 29, 3:00 p. m.	Sept. 7
Antwerp........	"	Vaderland	9	Sat. Sept. 5, Noon.	Sept. 14
Hamburg........	"	Furst Bismarck	3	Thur. Aug. 27,	Sept. 4
Hamburg........	"	Graf Waldersee	3	Sat. Aug. 29,	Sept. 11
Hamburg........	"	Deutschland	3	Tues. Sept. 1,	
Hamburg........	"	Bluecher	3	Thur. Sept. 3,	Sept. 10
Havre	"	La Touraine	10	Sat. Aug. 29,	Sept. 5
Havre	"	La Savoie	10	Sat. Sept. 5,	
Copenhagen	"	United States	4	Wed. Aug. 26,	
Rotterdam	"	Statendam	11	Sat. Aug. 29,	
Rotterdam	"	Ryndam	11	Sat. Sept. 5,	Sep'. 14
Bremen.........	"	Grosser Kurfuerst	13	Sat. Aug. 29,	Sept. 7
Bremen.........	"	Prinzess Irene	13	Thur. Aug. 27,	Sept. 9
Genoa	"	Lahn	13	Thur. Sept. 3,	Sept. 15
Sidney..........	SanFrancisco	Ventura	13	Mon. Sept. 7,	Sept. 28
Sidney..........	Vancouver	Miowera	20	Mon. Sept. 7,	
Hongkong.......	"	Empress of India	20	Wed. Aug. 26,	Sept. 16
Tahiti	SanFrancisco	Mariposa	17	Mon. Aug. 31,	Sept. 12
Hongkong.......	"	Doric	17	Tues. Sept. 1,	Sept. 26
Hongkong.......	Seattle	Aki Maru	22	Tues. Aug. 25, p. m.	Sept. 23

* See steamship list on opposite page.

NEXT SEASON'S BUSINESS

can be started now by advertising in this journal. Don't delay in commencing next winter's business. The best orders are placed early with advertisers in

TRY THIS PLAN.   **THE AMERICAN FLORIST**

THE SEED TRADE.

AMERICAN SEED TRADE ASSOCIATION.
S. F. Willard, Pres.; J. Charles McCullough, First Vice-Pres.; C. E. Kendel, Cleveland, O., Sec'y and Treas.
Twenty-second annual convention St. Louis, Mo., June, 1904.

MINNEAPOLIS.—James Lynes, of Northrup, King & Company, who was recently called to New York, is again at his post.

WALTHAM, MASS.—E. N. Pierce, the lily grower, is in Bermuda superintending the packing of his Harrisii bulbs. He uses stock dug fairly late.

NORTHERN Michigan pea growers report a pretty full crop with possibly a slight shortage on Stratagem, Notts, Wonders and Gems. Beans in western New York are doing fairly well considering their very late start.

VISITED CHICAGO: Jesse E. Northrup, of Minneapolis, Minn. Mr. Northrup and A. H. Goodwin, of the Goodwin, Harries Co., have gone to Ottawa Beach to spend Sunday, August 23, with A. J. Brown, of Grand Rapids, Mich.

NEW YORK.—Charles A. V. Frith, of Hamilton, Bermuda, arrived here August 10; on the steamer Trinidad and left a week later for a several months' trip to Europe, accompanied by his wife. Mr. and Mrs. Henry also came on the same steamer.

ALFRED J. BROWN SEED CO., Grand Rapids, Mich., writes August 6: "Regarding beans we have had very unfavorable weather, but in spite of this the beans have made considerable headway during the past few weeks and if we should have favorable weather the balance of this month and do not get an early frost in September, there is prospect of a fairly good crop, but it is entirely too early to say anything definite."

J. M. LUPTON, Mattituck, L. I., writes August 7: "The Long Island seed crops of this season, cabbage, kale and spinach, are all below an average yield, but in consequence of the large crop of last year there is less demand for large quantities, and there will be no serious inconvenience experienced by the trade, except on a few items where we have a complete failure. On most standard varieties the crop harvested, while not large, is still sufficient for the demands of trade this season."

W. J. FOSGATE, Santa Clara, Cal., writes August 9: "My crop of onion is good, but lettuce very light, carrot very fine, radish not good. The month of July was very cool, except the first few days, when a hot wind burned a good many crops, but fortunately mine escaped. But I suffered from a flood which did me great damage about the first of April. I believe onion seed will be of excellent quality as it did not ripen fast and the heads are filled underneath all around the stalk. I have seventy-five Chinamen cutting onion and will be threshing about September 1."

THE JOHN H. ALLAN SEED CO., Sheboygan, Wis., writes, August 5: "Peas, early sorts are nearly all harvested in this section, with some lots already threshed. Weather was favorable to saving in good condition until recently frequent rains have delayed harvest and caused some damage north of here. In northern Wisconsin lice have appeared in great numbers over large sections, but up to pres-

ent advices do not seem to have done any great damage. In Canada frequent and abundant rains have damaged late peas to some extent." Beans, although planted late are looking well in this section and central New York. In northern New York rains have damaged the pea and bean crop materially."

French Seed Trade.

Crops have improved to an incredible extent during the last few months and are now in splendid condition in France. Instead of the great scarcity expected and predicted at the close of the winter, we now find all around encouraging prospects for the new yield and prices, as an average, will rule lower than last season.

Mr. d'Estienne, brother-in-law of Philippe De Vilmorin and a member of the great seed firm, will sail August 30 in company with Alfred Emerich on a tour of the United States.

Nebraska Seed Crops.

One of our correspondents writes as follows August 8: "Both sweet and field corn have made an abnormally rapid growth during the past week, and with a few possible exceptions, it is estimated the crop will be fully up to the average. These exceptions relate especially to late varieties that were damaged by floods and hail, but which may yet make better crops than anticipated, if frost holds off until the latter part of September, and as the average killing frost date for Nebraska for the past ten years is September 27, it is to be hoped we will be favored with at least the full average growing and maturing season. Last season the ground was saturated with the excessive rainfall of August, and we experienced a killing freeze September 13. Thus far this month we have had an excessive rainfall, and there is therefore a reasonable possibility of a repetition of last year's early frost, if present conditions continue.

"The melon aphis has made its appearance at Waterloo and in other vine seed growing localities, as a result of the prevailing showers, followed by hot, muggy weather of pronounced humidity, and if these conditions continue, it is only a question of a very short time when last season's failure of vine seed crops in the west will be repeated this year. Several storms, some of them accompanied with hail, in different sections of Nebraska and Colorado have damaged vine seed crops, but to what extent cannot be fully determined for some days, until it can be seen if the crops can recover. It is a foregone conclusion that the damage suffered will certainly reduce prospective full deliveries on contract orders for musk and watermelon crops to a considerable extent, but which cannot be determined until later."

Massachusetts Crops.

James J. Gregory writes August 10: "In my more than forty years of experience I cannot recall a season so backward for all beat-loving crops, such as corn, squash, cucumbers, melons and tomatoes. Without an exceptionally hot and late fall a well ripened tract of field corn promises to be a curiosity. The extremely dry weather of early spring hindered the vegetation of much of the seed planted at that time, and the other extreme of wetness which followed rotted much of the later planted. The heat early

in the season prevented peas from rooting well and consequently we had a poor crop. It also made the potato vine spindling and the later weather has brought the rust on many pieces. Onions were never more generally eaten by the maggot and rarely so badly. The squash crop never in my remembrance had less promise in it. Many pieces have been plowed up and more ought to be, for at this late day there are many pieces that have hardly pushed a runner. As this is the third consecutive year; we have had a poor crop, our market farmers who practice planting largely of the vegetable, have serious faces. As a rule the fields planted to sweet corn are very thinly populated. Though this season has had much to do with this, the exceptional coolness of the last season should have credit also, for then we had about an average English summer and though much of the sweet corn looked fair to the eye the fact is that the chit had not ripened as well as usually. Consequently much of it failed to vegetate when planted.

A canner wrote me yesterday for quotation for two varieties of sweet corn. I wrote him in reply that I was so far from being able to supply them that I expected to have to pay $5 in gold about fair time for the privilege of looking at a well ripened ear of either variety. Grass thickened up wonderfully after the heavy rain of June and though some of the upland had got beyond recovery much of the low land is very heavy, so that on the whole the hay crop in quantity will not in this section fall much behind the average. There are no peaches or plums in this region and but few winter apples."

Nebraska Seed Crop.

WATERLOO, NEB., August 12.—C. P. Coy & Son write: "The weather for the past ten days has been very bad. We need hot dry weather to bring forward the late crops, but on the contrary the thermometer stands at 50° to 70° and there are frequent heavy rains. Ground is wet and cold and many crops are not making much headway toward maturity.

"Cucumber—The bulk of the acreage is doing fairly well, but some fields have been attacked by a blight and have been at a standstill for more than a week. No lice working. Estimate crop at seventy-five to ninety per cent on the acreage planted.

"Muskmelons—A good many failures and shortages, fields vary greatly in stand and condition. Yields will probably run from fifty to seventy-five per cent.

"Watermelon—Same as muskmelon.

"Summer Squash—Looking well, but acreage reduced from amount originally arranged for. Yields will probably run from seventy-five per cent up.

"Winter Squash—Acreage greatly reduced and crops are small and late; estimated at forty to seventy-five per cent according to season and frost.

"Pumpkins—Same as winter squash.

"Early Sweet Corn—Good fair crops in sight.

"Late Sweet Corn—Pieces vary greatly in size and condition. A portion of the area will probably ripen all right, but we would consider that more than one-half the acreage is too late to mature, with frost at the usual date. Yields will probably run from fifty to eighty per cent, according to circumstances.

"So far as our own crops are concerned we have lost heavily, by hail, among growers along the northern and southern edges of this district in central Nebraska and eastern Iowa.

"Thermometer 60° as we write, and at 50° at 10 o'clock last night. Very heavy rain this morning."

Melon Growing.

Pinch the main shoots of musk melon vines when eighteen inches long. This makes them bear much earlier, yield more and bear fewer culls. As a result of pinching these shoots laterals are thrown out and then set fruits. Do not pinch the laterals. When the other main vines start out from the center of the hill they are pinched also as were the first.

CHINESE PRIMROSE—TYPE OF INTERNATIONAL STRAIN.

PANSIES.
Vaughan's "International"
Received the only reward for Mixed Pansies at the World's Fair. It is to-day better and more complete than ever. It contains the cream of the stock of 10 Pansy specialists. There is no better mixture in existence as all the florists who saw or used it can tell you. Price per oz., $10.00; ¼-oz., $3.00; ⅛-oz., $1.50; trade pkt., 50c.

Vaughan's "Giant Mixture."
This mixture is specially made by us from all the separate colors of Giant Trimardeau, the Giant Bugnot and Cassier and several special strains which can not be had any other way. If your trade demands large flowers there is no better mixture. Price ¼-lb., $14.00; oz., $4.00; ¼-oz., 60c; trade pkt., 25c.

CHICAGO.

"INTERNATIONAL" Primula Mixture.
Unquestionably the best mixture of Chinese Primroses. It contains the largest variety of of the best selling colors. Flowers large, beautifully fringed, borne in large clusters well above the rich green leaves. Pkt. (250 seeds), $1.00; 5 Pkts., $4.00.

CHINESE PRIMULA, Chiswick, red, Alba Magnifica, white, blue, pink, striped. Each per pkt. of 250 seeds, 50c; 1000 seeds, $1.75.

DOUBLE CHINESE PRIMULA, white, pink, red, or mixed per pkt. 50c.

CINERARIA.

Cineraria.
Vaughan's Columbian Mixture.
Consists of a mixture made up by ourselves of the choicest English, French and German strains and cannot be excelled in variety of colors, size, shape and substance of flowers and perfect habit of plant. Strictly fresh seeds, just received. Trade pkt., (1000 seeds), 50c.; 3 pkts. $1.25.

Calceolaria Hybrida.
Choicest mixture, pkt., 50c.

VAUGHAN'S SEED STORE, NEW YORK.

THE NURSERY TRADE.

GUTHRIE, OKLA.—At a meeting of the board of World's Fair commissioners at Oklahoma City, Tuesday, July 14, C. A. McNabb, of Oklahoma county, was elected to have charge of the preparations of the horticultural exhibit to be made by Oklahoma at the St. Louis World's Fair.

St. Louis.

LOCAL CLUB HOLDS INTERESTING MEETING—A MARRIAGE IN THE TRADE—TRADE CONDITIONS—NOTES FROM HERE AND THERE.

At the meeting of the St. Louis Florists' Club on Thursday, August 13, twenty-four members and one visitor were present which was a creditable attendance considering the inclement weather. The annual reports of the several officers were read and approved. In summarizing the attendance for the year it was found that the average number at each meeting was fifteen—not a very large per cent when one realises the importance of the club. The election of officers resulted as follows: J. J. Beneke, president; William Winters, of Kirkwood, vice-president; Emil Schray, secretary and Otto Koenig, treasurer. For trustees: Fred Ammann, Edwardsville, Ill.; Dr. Halstead, Belleville, Ill., and J. W. Dunford, St. Louis. Robt. Frau, Mr. Hauser, and Mr. Furber were elected to full membership. H. G. Ude and F. W. Ude, both former members, were reinstated. F. K. Balthis' name was proposed for membership. Final arrangements were then made for the Milwaukee convention after which a delicious luncheon was served by A. Jablonsky. The September meeting was decided upon and will be held at Fred. Ammann's place in Edwardsville.

The marriage of Alice Dunford, a sister of James Dunford of the J. W. Dunford Carnation Company, and Clyde Blankenship was solemnized at the home of the bride at 8 p. m., on Friday, August 14. Mr. Blankenship is a graduate of the Missouri botanical garden. Only members of the family and a few intimate friends witnessed the ceremony which was quite informal. The rooms were tastefully decorated with palms and cut flowers. Light refreshments were served. Mr. and Mrs. Blankenship will reside near Corpus Christi, Texas, where Mr. B. is making a survey for the St. Louis & San Francisco railroad.

There is no change in the market since last week. American Beauty roses are quoted at $20, but it would be difficult to obtain very many at one time. The petals fall very soon after shipments are received, so that unless offered as short stems there would be no demand. Prices on other roses are stationary, with a scarcity of good stock. Owing to the cold weather the color in roses and carnations is becoming much better. Some fine tuberoses are coming in from Kirkwood and vicinity.

S. H. Thorwegen was making the rounds last week. He stopped with your correspondent long enough to subscribe for the AMERICAN FLORIST, which, he said, he needed badly—as everyone else does. His place of some ten acres is located one and one-half miles southwest of Forest Park. Fruit trees, ornamental trees and shrubs, roses, hardy perennials, etc., are grown.

Dr. J. N. Rose of the Smithsonian Institute was a visitor at Shaw's garden last week. He has recently completed a monograph of the echeverias of the United States.

The grounds at the Compton Heights water tower are in fine condition at present. The season has been most favorable for the trees and shrubs.

The workmen at C. Young & Son's are busy with repair work and cleaning up the houses.

The Michel Plant & Bulb Company has a fine lot of rubbers (Ficus elastica) in the field.   F. K. B.

St. Paul.

FLORISTS' OUTING AT WILDWOOD.—PLEASANT TROLLEY RIDE.—EXCITING RACES.— SIDE-SPLITTING PIE-EATING CONTEST.— TUG OF WAR.—STEAMER RIDE.—DANCING.—ATTENDING VISITORS.

The outing of the St. Paul florists is now a thing of the past and everybody seems to have enjoyed the event, the ladies and children especially, as the committee in charge made it a point to entertain them this year. The grounds selected were at Wildwood, and a better place for a picnic would be very hard to find, with all the accommodations and amusements, such as bathing, dancing, boating, bowling and a hundred and one other things. The weather appeared quite threatening in the morning, which probably kept a few from going out early in the day, but about nine o'clock the sun put in an appearance and it turned out to be an almost perfect picnic day.

First of all was the delightful trolley ride of ten miles in a large special car and after all were settled the races began. The first event was the boys' race, which was won by young Bussjaeger, the first prize being a fine pocket knife. The girls' race was won by Frances Herman, who received a fine pair of slippers. Next came the young ladies' turn in a potato race, and Frances Bussjaeger showed herself to be the best potato picker, for which she received a fine silver-mounted pocketbook. Some of the young ladies were a trifle modest and did not enter, but are probably sorry now as there were some very nice prizes. The men's 100-yard dash, next to bowling, was the main

event, the first prize being a ton of hard coal, which will help keep Ole Olson's home warm this coming winter; Christ Hansen, Jr., took second prize and Willie Swanson came in third. The married ladies' race, as usual, was quite interesting, the first prize being an elegant mirror and won by Mrs. Skooghin; Mrs. Holm was second and Mrs. G. F. Franke third. In the fat men's race Pete Holm could not be beat, Otto Nordquist was second and Carl Peterson, who thought he had it so easy that he started to roll in, came in third.

This being the first time that a pie-eating contest had been put on the 'programme, everybody was eager either to look or get into the game, and what a hungry lot of florists there were. To a spectator it looked as though they had been starving themselves for weeks. All had their arms tied behind their backs; the pie was set on a table in front of each contestant and at the word go everyone dived into the soft lemon pie which was covered with lots of sticky frosting. Such a sight as they made when they were through; one could not tell one from the other. Johnny Freeberg's face was covered back to the ears and Willie Swanson managed to get some of the frosting into his hair. Ludwig Anderson had frosting all over his face and under his chin, while Joe Herrog got his nose and eyes full. Carl Hansen had been practicing ever since programme came out, but he wasn't in it except with his face. Gilbert Jensvold was the lucky one, as he swallowed the pie whole.

In the target shoot Peter Hansen proved himself to be the best shot, Wm. Swanson second and Carl Haugen third.

Then came the tug of war between the married and single men, which, contrary to expectation, proved to be a very close match, the Benedicts winning after a very hard pull, but not until the best single man had strained a leg. The final event was the bowling, in which everybody was sure they would get first prize, but after it was all over Willie Swanson had proved himself to be the best bowler, winning a ton of hard coal, while O. J. Olson, second, received 1,000 4-inch pots and Henry Puvogel, third, got a box of fine cigars.

The steamboat ride of two and one-half hours around beautiful White Bear lake was enjoyed immensely, taking in the whole lake.   O.

OUR PASTIMES.

Announcements of coming contests or other events of interests to our bowling, shooting and sporting readers are solicited and will be given place in this column.
Address all correspondence for this department to Wm. J. Stewart, 79 Milk St., Boston, Mass.; Robt. Kift, 1725 Chestnut St., Philadelphia, Pa.; or to the American Florist Co., 324 Dearborn St., Chicago, Ill.

JOHN BURTON, one of the most prominent sportsmen in the trade, prefers rabbits (Welsh) for breakfast.

Chicago vs. St. Louis.

In a match game between teams representing Chicago and St. Louis, at the Geroux alleys, August 17, the former team won by a total of 261 points. The scores are given below:

CHICAGO.	1st	2d	3d	T'l
G. Stollery	184	149	195	524
F. Stollery	177	145	170	495
Hauswirth	150	180	148	478
Asmus	180	153	187	503
Winterson	143	157	151	451
Foerster	108	197	212	517
Totals	998	981	1043	3,22
ST. LOUIS.	1st	2d	3d	T'l
Beneke	193	173	177	483
Miller	99	125	129	353
Guy	159	183	182	524
Meyer	171	167	163	501
Adles	127	156	151	434
Kuehn	144	127	185	406
Totals	833	941	987	2761

At Natick, Mass.

A rather unexpected turn was given to baseball matters in this vicinity when on Saturday, August 15, by a score of 13 to 4, the Waban Rose Conservatories baseball club was defeated by the combined forces of the Boston Flower Market and the Dennison Tag Manufacturing Company of South Framingham. The arrangement of the Boston team, whereby the captain and several of the regular players of the visiting faction were compelled to view the game from the grand stand, proved most unfortunate for the home nine. The features of the game were the unusually poor work of a part of the Waban infield, and the reversible, double action decisions of the umpire which were handed out with strict impartiality to both of the opposing teams. The battery work of the home team was as usual first-class, and from a spectator's point of view there were enough good plays on both sides to keep up the interest to the end of the game. It is likely that the Waban team will now disband for the season, as the leading spirit, Capt. Dunn, who has served the team faithfully for the past two seasons, has severed his connection with the conservatories.

Cleveland.

COMMUNITY SUFFERS FROM DROUGHT.—ROSES AND CARNATIONS ALTHOUGH POOR ARE EXTENSIVELY USED IN FUNERAL WORK.—AN OUTING.—THE GARDENERS' PICNIC.

We need rain badly in this district and stock planted in the open fields is suffering for want of water. Continued warm weather keeps roses and carnations at the same low standard, but they are eagerly sought for in funeral work, of which there is still any amount being done. Some good sweet peas, asters and hardy phloxes are still seen among the cut flowers. Several of the stores are having quite a run on rudbeckias, which is very good stock and does well for decorations. . . . .

Recently a party of eighteen people, among whom were D. S. Livingston, the Crawford Road florist, Geo. Bate and wife and F. W. Griffin and wife, visited some very beautiful lakes in Canada the names of which sound like a good sneeze and breath perfumer, lakes Couchiching and Sin Sin. Hunting, fishing and killing Indians were among the pastimes.
The market gardeners had a fine time at their picnic, one of the special features being the rube's band, which rendered some fine selections.　　　　O. G.

Toronto.

CONDITION OF MARKET SHOWS IMPROVEMENT.—MILDEW DISAPPEARING.—ROSES IN GOOD CONDITION.—CARNATIONS ARE RATHER POOR.—NEWS NOTES FROM THE VICINITY.

The past two weeks have seen a decided improvement in business as well as in quality of stock. Very good blooms are now being cut from this season's young stock, the cool weather with which we have lately been favored having proved very beneficial. Mildew, which was so prominent, is now disappearing and it is surprising how good the roses are for the season of the year. Most notable among the roses is the Kaiserin, being exceptionally fine in bloom, stem and foliage. Some choice American Beauty stock is being cut and some very good long-stemmed Meteors are coming in. Brides, Bridesmaids and Perles are all coming along very nicely. There are very few good carnation blooms to be had, the old stock being about exhausted and the young stock not far enough along, but present indications predict some very good flowers in the near future. Lily of the valley is quite prominent in all the stores; our local growers are going more extensively into cold storage each season and the quality seems to get better each year. Lilies in general are quite plentiful and helpful in the funeral work, which is about the only thing which keeps the stores moving at this season.
Chas. Turp has added several hundred feet to each of his four houses the past season. He has painted one house with roses, from which he has started to make cuttings, and they will be quite up to the mark. His carnations have been planted and some fairly good flowers are being cut from this young stock, although the stems are rather short.
Jno. Milligan has taken over the lease for the greenhouses at the Mimico Industrial School. He has quite a large range of glass, and will the stock he intends growing it should prove quite a favorable venture. Carnations, violets and bedding stock will be grown. This place for the last seven or eight years has been occupied by W. J. Lawrence.
Wm. McKay has recently purchased a piece of ground on Dundas street and is overhauling the house and transferring the glass, which he formerly had at Toronto Island. This new place is quite handy to the city and will afford him a m ch easier market than he had heretofore.
Miss Nesbitt, who for the past eight years has been a clerk at Dunlop's retail store, was quietly married on Wednesday, August 12, to Jack Robson, a fine fellow, and whom we hope will make a good husband. The happy couple have the best wishes of the local craft.
The Queen City Floral Company, of Queen street west, has been purchased by R. Collins, who was formerly gardener for F. Nichols. He has been prospering and will no doubt do a very fine business.

The doctors have ordered Edgar Buckland, who formerly looked after George Hollis's greenhouses, to a northern climate for his health and he has left for Moose Jaw, N. W. T.
Jno. Hand, for the past ten years engineer, steam-fitter and night watchman at J. H. Dunlop's, is seriously ill with heart trouble. His condition at present is very critical.　　　H. G. D.

Columbus, O.

Quite a few carnations are being housed at present on account of the dry weather, which is preventing further development in the field. Lorna and Queen Louise are two of the best whites for our soil and climate. Local growers speak highly of the growth Enchantress made in the field and are in hopes this variety will do as well when staged. Boston ferns are more plentiful again, as quite a number of growers have taken up their stock from benches and potted it ready for market. Mr. Drobisch seems to have the finest supply of this stock in this locality.
A pathetic letter was received from unfortunate brother Schweitzer, of Mendota, Ill., by one of our local florists, who contributed a little to the support of Schweitzer's family. Not an inch of glass is left on Mr. Schweitzer's place, and as he is entirely penniless he is not able to build and place himself in a position to take care of donations in stock. Mr. Schweitzer has labored for twenty years to gain what has been swept away in a single moment, and as he is worthy, let us help him.
Frank A. Brigel, corner of 11th and Fields avenues, has about completed his range of four houses. He will use his space mostly for bedding stock, for which he has a great demand, and depend on others for his roses and carnations.
　　　　　　　　　　　　　　CARL.

Dallas, Tex.

Superintendent Beach, of the Haskell Avenue Floral Company, is busy resoiling his carnation houses for this fall's planting. It is too hot under glass here to plant in August, so we plant the bulk of stock in September, and have better results than by early planting. Young roses are growing finely and the cuttings now being potted are rooted to perfection. Two houses are being run to rose cuttings alone and turn out a batch every three weeks. This firm will not do any building this season but is making arrangements for the addition of a large range next season, which will be used for roses alone.
Business is very quiet, with exception of funeral work. Flowers are scarce and of poor quality, the dry weather the past few weeks having cut the home production very perceptibly. Light showers the past two days have helped somewhat, but we need a good rain to put growing stuff on the move.
A park fever has struck Dallas, and if one-half of what is proposed materializes, we shall have the best line of pleasure grounds in the south. We need them and trust the promoters will not grow weary in well-doing.
Otto Lang is doing a good deal of repairing at his plant and making preparations for a big trade the coming season, and when Lang doesn't get there something is wrong, for Lang is a hustler.
Ernest Nitsche and wife are expected home this week from their trip to Germany. . . . 　　　LONE STAR.

STUDER OFFERS

Fine healthy plants ready for a shift.

Ferns, Bostons, 5-in., 40 cts.; 7-in., 75 cts.; **Davalloides Furcans** 4-in., 20 cts.; 5-in., 30 cts.; 7-in., 75 cts. **Cordata and Phillippenais,** 5-in., 30 cts.; mixed ferns, 3½-in., 3 cts. **Alsophila Australis,** large specimen plants, 11-inch pots, $3 each. **Washingtoniensis,** 7-in., $1.00. **Lomaria Gibba,** extra fine, 4-in., 15 cts.; 5-in., 30 cts.; 6-in., 40 cts. Pot-grown better than from benches, need no nursing.

Rubbers, 5-in., 35 cts. **Palms, Latanias,** 7-in., $1. **Lantanas, Phœnix, Caryota Urens, Chamærops Excelsa,** ready for 4-inch pots, 6 cts. Plants for fern pans, etc. **Selaginella, Asparagus Sprengeri, Sansevieria, Marantas, Carex Japonica, Cyperus Alternifolius, Anthuriums, Dieffenbachias, Alocasias,** 3 to 5 cents. **Fine cut Roses, Bridesmaids, Ivory. Gates,** 3 cts.; **Meteor,** 5 cts.; **Beauty,** 10 cts. **30,000 Field-Grown Roses, Hybrids, Hybrid Teas, Monthly, Moss, Hardy and Tender Climbers.** Ready October and November. Also any quantity of Bedding Plants, Rooted Cuttings, etc. Will exchange any plants for Field-Grown Carnations. Ten per cent discount per 100. Cash with order.

N. STUDER, Anacostia, D. C.

Please mention the American Florist when writing.

LARGEST STOCK OF

Jessamines

IN THE COUNTRY.

Grand Duke, Triplicate, Sambac— Per 100
2-inch pots.................................$3.00
3-inch pots.................................5.00
4-inch pots.................................8.00
BEGONIA REX, in assortment, 3-inch pots . . 6.00
ROSES, American Beauties, 3-inch pots 8.00
   La Franco, 3-inch pots 6.00
ENGLISH IVIES, strong, 3-inch pots 2.00

FIELD GROWN CARNATIONS,

Ready September 1st. Send us your list.

Nanz & Neuner,
Louisville, Ky.

Please mention the American Florist when writing.

LOOK!
Don't Miss These Berried Plants For Christmas.

SOLANUM CILIATUM or Adam's Apple, large bright red berries from 3-inch pots, 5c; 4-in. pots 10c. **SOLANUM ARMUUM** or Celestial Peppers, 4-inch 10c each. **SOLANUM CAPSICASTRUM** or Jerusalem Cherry, large Var., 3-inch pots 8c. **STEVIA,** 1¾-inch pots, 2½c; 4-inch pots 6c each. **STEVIA VARIEGATA,** 3-inch pots 5c each. **HYDRANEGA OTAKSA,** Pink or blue, 3-in. pots 5c; 4in. pots 8c. **ENGLISH IVY,** 2¼-inch pots 5c.

Strong, clean plants ready to shift. Cash. Satisfaction assured.

M. F. LaROCHE, Collingsdale, Pa.

Cut Gladioli
UNTIL FROST.

For prices apply to

CUSHMAN
Gladiolus Co.,
Sylvania, Ohio.

Gladioli by the Million.

Lilies, Pæonias, Clematis Paniculata, Oxalis, Dahlias, Asparagus, Rhubarb, Shrubs, Shade Trees, etc.

——PRICE LIST FREE.——

E. Y. TEAS, Centerville, Ind.

LILIUM CANDIDUM.

If your wants are not covered on Paper Whites, Roman Hyacinths or Dutch Stock write for Prices.

PANSIES.

Herr's Strain, known to be strictly high-grade. Plants ready in September, at 75c per 100; $4.00 per 1000.

GERANIUMS.

From small pots, at $2.00 per 100; $15.00 per 1000. LaFavorite, Jaulin, Harrison, Perkins, Viaud, Heteranthe, Poitevine and Landry. .

Send for list of Rooted Cuttings......

Smilax and Sprengeri.

Smilax, $1.50 per 100; $12.50 per 1000. Sprengeri, $2 per 100; $15 per 1000.

ALBERT M. HERR, Lancaster, Pa.

PERENNIAL PHLOX,

A fine lot of mixed phlox consisting of 15 choice varieties 3-inch pots, extra strong plants, $5.00 per 100.

Wagner Park Conservatories, Sidney, O.

PÆONIAS.

In 10 distinct, named kinds, selected for florists' use. Earliest to latest, all colors. $1.50 per dozen; $10.00 per 100. **Poet's Narcissus,** double and single, home grown, blooming bulbs, 75c per 100; $5.00 per 1000.

F. BALLER, Bloomington, Ill.

Paeonias...

OUR SPECIALTY: Best Collections.

P. Festiva Maxima. P. Off. Mutabilis. Strong plants. True to name. Catalogues free.

A. DESSERT, CHENONCEAUX, FRANCE.

PEONIES.

PEONY HUMEI, very large and fine pink, one of the best bloomers, $7.00 per 100. Mixed varieties, $6.00 per 100. Sample root free.

S. J. GALLOWAY, Eaton, Ohio.

Paeonias Double Pink, $8.00 per 100. **VIOLETS,** field-grown, $6 per 100. **Meteor Roses,** large plants for late planting, cheap.
L. COLE, Battle Creek, Mich.

LILIUM CANDIDUM

An Improvement on the common variety. Wider flowers, of more substance, can be forced.

Mammoth Bulbs, per 100, $6.00; per 1000, $50.00
Select Bulbs, ... per 100, $5.00; per 1000, $45.00

LILIUM HARRISII.

Our stock of late dug bulbs now being shipped has been grown, rogued, and packed by one firm of Bermuda growers, whose entire output we control. It is as clean stock as can be found on the island and is uniform in type and grading. Order now. Our grades are 5 to 6, 6 to 7, 7 to 9, 9 to 11 and 11 to 13.

SPECIAL HARRISII (Ocell.)

Size 6 to 7-inch.

This type is one of the cleanest and truest to type of all the Bermuda Lilies. It is a little later than true Harrisii but makes up in healthiness. We can make a very special price on select 6 to 7-inch bulbs of these of $4.00 per 100; $33.50 per 1000. They will pay a big profit on the investment.

Vaughans Seed Store,
CHICAGO. NEW YORK.

3,000 FINE SURPLUS STOCK

Of 2½-inch 'Mums, including Wedding, Reiman, Chadwick, Estelle, Morel, Appleton and many others, $20.00 per 1000.

3,000 extra nice, 2½-inch **Maids,** $40.00 per 1000. Liger and Richardson, the two new **Pinks,** fine 2½-inch stock, $5.00 per 100.

Poehlmann Bros. Co., Morton Grove, Ill.

Forcing Lilacs.

Best French de Marly, and best German pot-grown, special forcing stock, imported to order. For particulars and prices, address

AUGUST RÖLKER & SONS,
NEW YORK, 31 Barclay St., P. O. Box 752.

AMERICAN FLORIST COMPANY'S

DIRECTORY

FOR 1903.

THIS 1903 Trade Directory is fully revised to date, with thousands of new names and changes of addresses. It contains 416 pages, including complete lists of the Florists, Seedsmen and Nurserymen of the United States and Canada. These lists are arranged both by states and all alphabetically. It also contains lists of Private Gardeners, Firms that issue catalogues, Horticultural Supply Concerns, Parks, Cemeteries, Landscape Architects, Experiment Station Horticulturists, Botanical Gardens, and much other conveniently indexed and valuable trade information.

PRICE $2.00 POSTPAID.

THE AMERICAN FLORIST CO.
324 Dearborn Street,
CHICAGO, ILL., U. S. A.

PLEASE mention the AMERICAN FLORIST every time you write to an advertiser.

Washington.

FLORIST IN VICINITY HAS TERRIBLE LOSS. —CHILD BURNED TO DEATH. — CLUB MEETING.

Florence Bissett, the two-year-old daughter of Mr. and Mrs. David Bissett, was burned to death at their home in Garrett Park, Md., on August 2. The fire which caused her death occurred at about 12:30 p. m. and resulted in the total destruction of their home and greenhouses. Mrs. Bissett, who was ill in bed at the time, is in a precarious condition. One of the unfortunate features of the fire was the fact that a large tank of water on the Bissett place was located directly over the kitchen, where the fire started, and was not accessible from the start; had it been possible to get at it the fire could have been checked in the kitchen and the house saved.

On August 5 the Florists' Club held its monthly meeting and President J. R. Freeman being absent, Vice-president George Field took the chair. After routine business was disposed of, Wm. F. Gude read an extract from *The New Century*, a local paper of which D. I. Murphy is the publisher, giving his views editorially on the use and abuse of flowers at funerals. His criticism on this subject was very just and well expressed. George C. Shaffer gave full details in connection with the convention at Milwaukee. A letter of condolence was sent to David Bissett. Wm. F. Gude asked for and obtained a generous voluntary contribution to aid Mr. Bissett in his present difficulties. The annual election of officers was postponed until the September meeting.   P. .G

Livonia, N. Y.

The fifth annual exhibition of the Livonia Floral Society took place on August 6. There were fifty classes with about 250 entries. The display of gladioli was very good.

CONCORD, N. H.—Frank A. Main and wife are away on a vacation at York Beach.

Violet Plants
FOR SALE.

Strong, healthy Lady Campbell plants, field grown for sale. Ready now. $15.00 per 1000.

CASH WITH ORDER.

Address all orders to

G. H. Branham, Jr.,

Waldrop P. O,   Louisa County, Va.

MARIE LOUISE VIOLETS

Clean and strong plants from frames

$15.00 per 1000, $2.00 per 100.

H. N. HOFFMAN.   Elmira, N. Y.

New White Canna
MONT BLANC.

THE GREATEST NOVELTY IN CANNAS.

Potted plants 75c each; $7.50 per dozen. $50.00 per 100.

The Conard & Jones Co.,   WEST GROVE, PA.

Diseased Sweet Peas.

ED. AM. FLORIST:—Please state cause of sweet peas dying, as shown by enclosed specimen. I planted the peas in trenches, mixed in well rotted horse manure, and after they came up sprinkled them with a little hen manure. E. R. L.

The bit of sweet pea vine you send has the old familiar look. They turn yellow and go to straw, either before they reach the blooming stage or as soon as the first discouraged blossoms open, the trouble being a root denuded of fibrous matter which does not allow a sufficient supply of the life fluid. It is not an insect trouble, nor a fungus, nor a disease, but is about the same phenomenon as the "yellows" in asters. I hold that in both cases it is the price paid for trying to make nature do more than she is able to do. Nobody can get a normal sweet pea root to-day. Those who have the best success get but a quarter of a root, with a small amount of fibrous matter. If they get a fairly good season of bloom, it is because they have conditions that are peculiarly favorable, or because they know just how to supply food and drink in some semi-artificial way. I hope "E. R. L." put the horse manure well below the seed, and firmed the soil in the trench. If he has facilities for watering, a good soaking once a week seems now almost indispensable, and it is better to reserve all additional doses of fertilizer until the vines begin to show buds, when a wash of liquid manure, cow manure being preferable, should be used once in two weeks. I also hope he did not sprinkle dry hen manure around the vines. During the drought I let my hose run right into mine every few days until they were soaked, working in some liquid hen manure at the same time. The result was a growth that at first I feared would be too rank, but they are perfectly green, and at a height of from three to three and one-half feet are just beginning to bud freely. I knew better than to use such fertilizer at that stage, but it was a case of thoughtless impatience.

Regarding the "yellows" on the sweet peas, my judgement is that it is a kind of natural reaction after a period of high pressure, and at the present time the whole seed stock of sweet peas behaves in this way. Even if the vines hold green, the imperfect root plays all sorts of tricks with the buds. If it rains, it starts a sudden spurt of vine growth and every bud will blast; if the buds have half way developed, the neck of the flowering stem wilts and that blights them; if a hot day strikes them, the root cannot support the evaporation, and if you have aphis and turn the hose on the foliage, you stimulate a growth of foliage greater than the root can stand. All these intermittent weaknesses are due to lack of sufficient fibrous matter on the root, and the best we can get is a shortened season of bloom. I am convinced there is no cure for this at present, but a season of rest, or of less unreasonable demand on nature will doubtless restore the old equilibrium. Any flower that is subjected to the high pressure methods of development and of large popular demand for seed will sooner or later tell this same story. It may be that "E. R. L." will save some of his vines, and if they do pull through the first hard place, they may throw out a secondary root and go up to a height of ten feet.

W. T. HUTCHINS.

MASON, MICH.—Miss Effie Beach will build an addition to her greenhouse.

Annual Report of the Florists' Hail Association of America.

REPORT OF THE SECRETARY.

The following subdivision by states represents the glass insured by the 1,187 members of the F. H. A.; also the amount of losses in the various states for the year from August 1, 1902, to August 1, 1903:

STATES.	Single thick glass.	Double thick glass.	Extra one-half single thick glass.	Extra one-half double thick glass.	Extra whole single thick glass.	Extra whole double thick glass.	Amount paid for losses from Aug. 1, 1902, to Aug. 1, 1903.
Arkansas	13,765	7,700	......	......	2,965	1,400	......
Colorado	271,186	237,381	60,211	11,056	92,020	175,900	$ 75.04
Connecticut	7,540	76,841	......	43,986	......	5,355	......
Delaware	38,498	13,986	270	608	......	4,200	......
Georgia	2,736	3,360	......	......	......	......	......
Illinois	233,539	1,670,158	74,910	187,544	55,652	276,673	126.86
Indiana	221,420	501,280	26,180	65,960	31,810	139,836	165.54
Indian Ter.	......	2,000	......	......	......	2,000	......
Iowa	292,060	528,644	50,267	174,314	101,646	141,420	1,478.46
Kansas	226,572	123,173	31,137	16,480	125,050	76,562	235.88
Kentucky	93,090	101,521	1,500	......	46,466	17,425	412.55
Louisiana	6,150	......	......	......	3,150	......	......
Maine	7,470	21,021	......	......	......	......	......
Maryland	110,945	82,807	5,860	......	8,900	20,750	6.26
Massachusetts	44,090	128,464	......	15,000	......	......	......
Michigan	662,848	199,022	......	......	8,782	49,650	10.54
Minnesota	103,148	544,165	8,760	1,830	7,695	280,167	127.90
Missouri	507,042	703,377	59,965	21,831	272,851	515,170	1,336.21
Montana	81,670	3,460	......	......	......	......	54.00
Nebraska	255,299	58,477	50,688	2,100	77,471	12,006	53.12
New Hampshire	1,500	18,150	600	13,400	......	......	......
New Jersey	44,509	906,733	......	208,901	......	23,870	......
New Mexico	1,030	20,234	......	13,734	1,030	......	64.20
North Carolina	8,680	......	......	......	......	......	......
North Dakota	7,425	5,385	......	1,492	7,425	2,475	......
New York	165,842	553,745	9,462	11,810	13,500	57,610	......
Ohio	541,529	1,173,285	53,946	54,298	96,890	282,163	397.14
Oklahoma Ter.	3,845	15,595	1,080	......	1,265	15,595	......
Pennsylvania	430,660	1,668,169	24,738	121,182	48,914	587,849	6.54
Rhode Island	400	19,035	400	985	......	9,950	......
So. Carolina	8,000	8,800	......	......	......	......	......
South Dakota	7,765	11,240	1,200	......	8,075	1,400	......
Tennessee	......	6,680	......	......	......	6,680	......
Texas	32,323	25,821	......	......	8,911	10,403	......
Virginia	40,200	31,302	......	......	......	18,782	17.55
West Virginia	28,480	6,050	......	......	7,000	6,050	35.70
Wisconsin	115,577	187,192	21,734	5,390	9,107	5,160	19.85
Wyoming	3,000	......	......	......	......	......	......
Dist. of Colum	1,317	6,671	400	3,888	......	......	......
Canada	5,506	7,168	......	......	......	......	......
	4,026,665	9,678,092	483,308	975,789	1,036,575	2,746,501	$4,623.34

The above being equivalent to 18,217,381 square feet of glass insured. The amount paid for losses during the year is below the average, but at the time of making this report upwards of forty losses are in various stages of adjustment. These losses will require at least $5,000 of the reported emergency fund to liquidate them.

The receipts for the year ending August 1, 1903, have been: From thirteenth assessment, $10,678.86; from new business, as per Treasurer's report, $2,685.48; from interest on investment, $550.62; from reinsurance of glass broken by hail, $72.27; from repayment of loan, $2,000.00; from Tri-State B. and L. Association, $2,200. Total receipts for the year, $18,187.23.

The expenditures for the year are $4,623.34 for losses, $1,741.93 for expenses, $5,177.50, for account of reserve fund. Total, $11,542.77. The cash balance on hand at the close of the year is $12,761.26, of which $742.01 belongs to the reserve fund, leaving $12,019.25 available for use in the emergency fund. To this should be added $4,000 which has been invested upon call, making a total of $16,019.25 on hand for the payment of losses.

The reserve fund now consists of $10,400, invested, as per Treasurer's report, and $742.01 cash in hand, making the total reserve fund on hand August 1, 1903, $11,142.01.

Fifty-nine thousand seven hundred and forty-eight square feet of single and 18,290 square feet of double-thick glass have been broken by hail and paid for by this association during the past year.

Since the organization of the Florists' Hail Assocaton, on June 1, 1887, 680 losses have been paid, involving an expenditure of $58,000.

The following table may prove interesting to the student of statistics:

STATES.	No. of losses paid for year ending Aug. 1, 1903.	No. of hailstorms for year ending Aug. 1, 1903.	No. of losses paid from June 1, 1887, to Aug. 1, 1903.	No. of hailstorms from June 1, 1887, to Aug. 1, 1903.
California	1	..	1	..
Maine	3	..	..	..
Vermont	3	..	..	..
New Hampshire	7	1	..	..
Rhode Island	3	..	..	..
Connecticut	10	1	1	..
Massachusetts	10	..	..	..
New York	80	11	3	..
New Jersey	54	9	2	..
Pennsylvania	65	30	6	1
Delaware	3	1	1	..
Ohio	62	47	8	4
Indiana	27	17	8	7
Illinois	74	55	5	3
Michigan	17	6	3	1
Wisconsin	27	29	1	2
Minnesota	30	32	2	1
Iowa	64	79	12	16
Missouri	55	93	5	13
Kansas	65	99	9	15
Nebraska	44	58	3	3
Arkansas	2	..	..	..
Colorado	36	46	3	1
North Dakota	0	1	..	..
South Dakota	11	5	3	1
Montana	2	1	1	1
Wyoming	3	3	..	..
Maryland	11	6	1	1
Virginia	5	2	2	1
West Virginia	12	4	1	1
North Carolina	5	1	1	..
Kentucky	13	9	3	5
Georgia	3	..	..	..
Texas	11	6	5	..
Louisiana	2	..	..	..
Tennessee	2	1	..	..
Florida	1	..	..	..
Mississippi	1	..	..	..
Oklahoma Territory	9	7	2	..
Indian Territory	1	..	..	..
District of Columbia	4	..	..	..
Canada	4	4	2	..
New Mexico	2	3	..	1
South Carolina	1	..	1	..

The constantly improving financial condition of this association is a monument to the wisdom of the originators of the plan of hail insurance. Besides a reserve fund of $11,142.01, a handsome balance will remain in the emergency fund after the payment of all unadjusted losses.

The careful management of the affairs of the Florists' Hail Association by its officers and directors deserves the commendation of those who have intrusted their money to the hands of these officials for disbursement and investment.

JOHN G. ESLER, Secretary.

REPORT OF THE TREASURER.

Received from Thirteenth Assessment	$10,678.86
Received from Membership Fee	1,048.86
Received from New Assessments	601.22
Received from Additional Assessments	615.67
Received from Extra One-half	95.41
Received from Extra Whole	324.32
Received from Re-insurance	72.27
Interest from Orville B. & L. (Call Loan)	187.12
Interest from Tri-State B. & L.	55.00
Interest from Certificates of Deposits	136.00
Interest from Government Bonds	15.00
Interest from Chicago School Bonds	20.00
Interest from Orville Twp. Bonds	50.00
Interest from Milwaukee Bonds	87.50
Tri-State B. & L.	2,200.00
Orville B. & L.	2,000.00
Total	$18,187.23

LOSSES.

1902.		
Aug. 3.	John Nichols, Scottdale, Pa	$ 6.54
Aug. 11.	Raymond Miller, Abilene, Kan	7.50
Aug. 12.	Mrs. M. E. Jehu, Estherville, Iowa	25.34
Sept. 1.	Grant Newport, Cedar Rapids, Iowa	3.80
Sept. 1.	Mathew Krons, Great Falls, Mont	54.00
Sept. 4.	Mrs. Margaret Ballard, Perry, Iowa	19.00
Sept. 4.	J. T. Holmes, Kansas City, Mo	93.98
Sept. 4.	A. L. Harmon, Iola, Kan	7.58
Sept. 12.	C. A. & A. P. Krebs, Cedar Rapids, Iowa	6.51
Oct. 8.	Salineville Floral Co., Salineville, Ohio	23.50
Oct. 13.	D. Grimes, Denver, Colo	75.04
Oct. 27.	C. Hutchinson, Des Moines, Iowa	22.90
Oct. 27.	Mrs. Margaret Ballard, Perry, Iowa	5.96
Oct. 27.	Mrs. M. D. Eggling, St. Louis, Mo	560.10
Oct. 27.	Wm. Mackie, St. Louis, Mo	105.26
Nov. 3.	Chas. A. Juengel, St. Louis, Mo	25.50
Nov. 3.	Henry Eggert, East St. Louis, Ill	27.58
Nov. 3.	Michel Plant & Bulb Co., St. Louis, Mo	155.70
Nov. 3.	Henry Johann, Collinsville, Ill	82.20
Nov. 5.	Fred Huke, St. Louis, Mo	17.80
Nov. 5.	J. R. Oughton, St. Louis, Mo	31.43
Nov. 5.	Missouri Bot. Gardens, St. Louis, Mo	122.64
Nov. 10.	Sunenschmitt & Junge, Indianapolis, Ind	8.72
Nov. 13.	Anthony Wiegand, Indianapolis, Ind	87.82
Dec. 15.	O. R. Demler, Eau Claire, Wis	13.40
Dec. 15.	Bertermann Bros., Indianapolis, Ind	6.65
1903.		
Jan. 1.	Greensburg Floral Co., Greensburg, Ind	31.85
Mar. 2.	Henry Schnell, Glasgow, Mo	97.30
Apr. 15.	F. A. Blake, Columbus, Kan	26.00
Apr. 27.	Paul Goebel, Grand Rapids, Mich	10.54
Apr. 27.	Mrs. Elizabeth Kuntz, Frankfort, Ind	15.75
May 2.	C. H. Kunzmann, Louisville, Ky	53.30
May 4.	Chas. Schleeter, Louisville, Ky	13.13
May 4.	Julius Buser, Louisville, Ky	252.92
May 6.	Fred. Summerfield, Springfield, Mo	58.20
May 8.	Edward F. Wetstein, Louisville, Ky	55.60
May 8.	Chas. Raynor, Anchorage, Ky	37.60
May 18.	F. E. Blake, Columbus, Kan	22.40
May 18.	R. M. Nugent, Columbus, Kan	11.00
May 21.	A. Kinsman & Co., Austin, Minn	127.90
June 1.	Geo. H. Staton, Columbus, Kan	12.30
June 4.	J. O. Rennison, Sioux City, Iowa	267.81
June 4.	Sunderbruch & Meir, Cincinnati, Ohio	41.48
June 4.	D. G. Noble, Columbus City, Ind	7.40
June 4.	Fred. Bishop, Sioux City, Iowa	33.37
June 6.	Schmalz & Huber, Marysville, Kan	4.35
June 8.	Thomas Wilson, Kimmswick, Mo	17.50
June 8.	L. A. Smith, Wheeling, W. Va	35.70
June 8.	M. K. Bishop, Sioux City, Iowa	166.65
June 12.	W. Murphy, Cincinnati, Ohio	58.60
June 12.	Henry R. Brown, Seneca, Kan	27.24
June 12.	A. C. Anderson, Columbus, Neb	9.24
June 12.	John R. Elder, Sioux City, Iowa	654.14
June 16.	Henry Moore, Manhattan, Kan	26.90
June 16.	John Lester, Ottawa, Kan	24.00
June 22.	E. R. Sackett, Fostoria, Ohio	273.56
June 24.	Mrs. S. H. Bagley, Abilene, Kan	3.80
June 24.	C. J. Lampe, Concordia, Kan	5.66
June 25.	Conrad Hess, Baltimore, Md	6.26
June 25.	E. H. Zimmer, Woodbine, Iowa	3.10
June 25.	Bertermann Bros., Indianapolis, Ind	7.35
June 29.	W. A. Lankford, Charlottsville, Va	17.55
July 3.	S. R. Faulkner, Omaha, Neb	16.73
July 3.	Chas. Pfeiffer, Sedalia, Mo	20.50
July 6.	Raymond Miller, Abilene, Kan	10.00
July 10.	Mrs. R. B. Church, Roswell, New Mexico	64.20
July 16.	E. H. Zimmer, Woodbine, Iowa	3.35
July 28.	Wheeler Floral Co., Mason City, Iowa	15.19
July 20.	E. F. Walter, Wakefield, Kan	5.85

ANNUAL REPORT OF THE FLORISTS' HAIL ASSOCIATION OF AMERICA.—Continued.

July 20. Palmer Greenhouses, Cherokee, Iowa	19.05	
July 20. Franklin E. Keefe, Eau Claire, Wis.	6.45	
July 22. Mrs. B. Buckl, Salina, Kan.	41.30	
July 30. John Christiancy, Sheldon, Iowa	128.70	
July 30. W. J. Hesser, Plattsmouth, Neb.	27.15	
July 30. E. A. Lowatech, Chicago, Ill.	17.08	
July 31. E. A. Barnhart, Clinton, Mo.	39.30	
July 31. Nichols Bros., Atlantic, Iowa	103.80	
Total	$ 4,623.34	

EXPENSES.

1902.	
Aug. 11. Dewitt Trimble & Co., bonds	$ 2,058.75
Aug. 28. Florists' Publishing Co., advertising	4.00
Aug. 28. A. T. De La Mare Co., printing	3.25
Sept. 1. Gardening Co., advertising	1.50
Sept. 12. Addressograph Co., plates	21.95
Sept. 12. American Florist Co., advertising	14.00
Sept. 15. A. T. De La Mare Co., printing	5.00
Oct. 27. A. T. De La Mare Co., printing	50.40
Nov. 5. American Gardening, advertising	4.00
Dec. 15. Addressograph Co., plates	2.54
Dec. 19. A. T. De La Mare Co., printing	3.75
Dec. 19. Dewitt Trimble Co., bonds	3,118.75
1903.	
Jan. 5. J. G. Esler, part salary	300.00
Jan. 28. A. T. De La Mare Co., printing	5.00
Jan. 29. Wilson Humphreys, books	16.00
Feb. 18. Raynor & Perkins, envelopes	5.10
Feb. 16. A. T. De La Mare Co., printing	5.25
Mar. 10. J. G. Esler, postage, etc.	36.83
Mar. 23. F. J. Faesig, printing	3.50
Mar. 23. A. M. Herr, postage	60.33
Mar. 23. A. T. De La Mare Co., printing	8.75
Apr. 21. A. T. De La Mare Co., printing	3.72
May 4. A. T. De La Mare Co., printing	2.63
May 27. A. T. De La Mare Co., printing	3.35
July 1. Florists' Publishing Co., advertising	15.00
July 16. J. G, Esler, postage	23.18
July 16. American Gardening Co., advertising	7.50
July 20. American Florist, advertising	15.00
July 20. Gardening Co., advertising	7.50
July 20. J. C. Vaughan, salary	125.75
July 20. J. C. Vaughan, postage	7.50
July 20. A. M. Herr, salary	362.00

July 20. J. G. Esler, salary	605.00	
July 20. A. T. De La Mare Co., advertising	12.00	
July 27. A. T. De La Mare Co., printing	2.65	
Total	$ 6,919.43	

DISBURSEMENTS ON ACCOUNT OF LOANS.

Aug. 11. Dewitt Trimble & Co., Milwaukee Bonds for Reserve Fund	$ 2,058.75
Dec. 19. Dewitt Trimble & Co., Milwaukee Bonds for Reserve Fund	3,118.75
Total	$ 5,177.50

RECEIPTS—LOANS PAID.

Tri-State Bldg. and Loan Asso, Reserve Fund	$ 2,200.00
Orvil Bldg. and Loan Asso. Call Loan, Emergency Fund	2,000.00
Total	$ 4,200.00

RESERVE FUND INVESTMENTS.

Certificate of Deposit with the Lancaster Trust Co.	$ 3,400.00
Chicago School Bond	500.00
United States Government Bond	500.00
Orvil Township Bonds (two)	1,000.00
City of Milwaukee Bonds (five)	5,000.00
Total	$10,400.00

EMERGENCY FUND INVESTMENT.

Call loan to the Orville Building and Loan Association	$ 4,000.00
Total investments	$14,400.00

RECAPITULATION.

To balance on hand August 1, 1902	$ 6,116.80
To total receipts for year ending August 1, 1903	18,187.23
	$24,304.03
By dues paid for year ending August 1, 1903	$ 4,623.34
By expenses and investments	6,919.43
By balance	12,761.26
	$24,304.03

ALBERT M. HERR, Treasurer.

DREER'S PALMS

Why not lay in your supply of Palms for the Fall and
Winter trades now, while shipments can be made with reasonable safety by freight and at the same time gain the benefit of
the Summer's growth in your own houses.

KENTIA.

AREOA LUTESCENS.

	In. high	Per doz.	Per 100	Per 1000
2-in. pots, 1 plant in pot	6 to 8	$ .75	$ 6.00	$ 50.00
4 " 3 "	12 to 15	1.25	10.00	75.00
5 " 3 "	15 to 18	3.00	20.00	100.00
5 " 3 "	18 to 24	5.00	40 00	350.00
6 " 3 "	28 to 30	$1.00 each.		
7 " 3 "	30 to 36	1.50 "		
8 " 3 "	36	2.50 "		
10 " 3 "	48 to 54	10.00 "		

COCOS WEDDELIANA.

A good lot of 3-inch pots, ready now. 10 to 12 inches high, $2.00 per doz.; $15.00 per 100.

KENTIA SANDERIANA.

A comparatively new Palm which, when it becomes more plentiful and can be sold at a lower
price, will become a popular standard variety on account of its graceful habit of growth. 3-inch
pots, 15 inches high, 50c each; 6-inch pots, 24 inches high, $2.50 each; 4-inch pots, 3 plants in a
pot, 16 to 18 inches high, $1.25 each.

KENTIA BELMOREANA.

	Per doz.	Per 100	Per 1000
2¼-in. pots, 4 leaves, 8 to 10 in. high	$1.25	$10.00	$ 90.00
3 " 5 " 12 to 15 "	2.00	15.00	140.00
4 " 5 to 6 " 15 to 18 "	4.50	35.00	325.00
5 " 5 to 6 " 18 to 20 "	7.50	60.00	
5 " 5 to 6 " 20 to 24 "	9.00	70.00	

		Each
6 " 6 " 20 to 22 "		$1.00
6 " 6 " 28 to 30 "		1.25
6 " 6 to 7 " 30 to 36 "		1.50
7 " 6 to 7 " 30 to 36 "		2.00
8 " 6 to 7 " 36 "		2.50
8 " 6 to 7 " 38 to 42 "		3.50
8 " 6 to 7 " 42 "		4.00
9 " 6 to 7 " 42 to 48 "		5.00

KENTIA FORSTERIANA.

	Per doz.	Per 100	Per 1000
2¼-in. pots, 4 leaves, 8 to 10 in. high	$1.25	$10.00	$ 90.00
3 " 5 " 12 to 15 "	2.00	15.00	140.00
4 " 5 to 6 " 15 to 18 "	4.50	35.00	325.00
5 " 5 to 6 " 18 to 20 "	7.50		

		Each
6 " 6 " 28 to 30 "		$1.00
6 " 6 " 30 to 36 "		1.25
7 " 6 " 32 to 36 "		1.50
7 " 6 " 36 "		2.00
8 " 6 " 42 "		2.50
8 " 6 to 7 " 42 "		3.00
8 " 6 to 7 " 4 ft. high "		4.00
8 " 6 to 7 " 4 to 4½ "		5.00

KENTIA FORSTERIANA.

		Each
9-in. pots, 6 leaves, 5½ to 6 ft. high		$ 6.00
10 " 6 to 7 " 5½ to 6 "		7.50
10 " 6 to 7 " 6 "		10 00
10 " 6 to 7 " 6 "		12.50
12-in. tubs, 6 to 7 leaves, 6 ft. high		20.00
12 " 6 to 7 " 7 to 8 ft. high		25.00

MADE-UP KENTIA FORSTERIANA.

All of these are extra good value.
4-in. pots, 4 plants in a pot, 1. to 18 in. high, pretty stock for retailing,
per doz., $6.00.

		Each
5-in. pots, 4 plants in a pot	4 ft. high	$ .50
8 " 3 to 3 "		2.50
9-in. tubs, 3 "	3½ "	6.00
10 " 4 "	4½ "	7.50
9-in. tubs, 3 "	4½ "	9.00
10-in. tubs, 3 " 5½ to 6 "		12. 0
12 " 3 " 7 "		15.00
		20.00

LATANIA BORBONICA.

	Per doz.	Per 100	Per 1000
2-in. pots	$ .50	$ 4.00	$30.00
3-in. pots, 5 leaves	1.00	6.00	40.00
3-in. pots, 5 to 6 leaves, 12 to 15 in. high	1.00		
4 " 5 to 6 " 15 "	3.50	20.00	
6 " 5 to 6 " 18 to 20 "	6.00	50.00	

		Each
8 " 6 to 7 " 28 to 30 "		$1.50
9 " 6 to 7 " 7 to 8 " 30 to 36 "		2.50

For a complete list of Palms, as well as for all other Decorative Stock, also Bulbs and Seasonable Flower Seeds, see our current Wholesale List.

HENRY A. DREER, Philadelphia.

Palms, Ferns, Etc.

WE OFFER GOOD VALUES, SAVING IN EXPRESS AND FREIGHT TO BUYERS WEST OF OHIO. SAMPLES AT MILWAUKEE.

KENTIA BELMOREANA.

Size pots	Leaves	Height		Each	Doz.	100
3-inch	4 to 5	12 to 15 inches.....$		.20	$ 2.00	$15.00
4-inch	5 to 6	15 to 18 "	......	.40	4.50	35.00
5-inch	5 to 6	18 to 20 "	......	.60	7.00	50.00
5-inch	6	20 to 22 "	......	.75	9.00	70.00
6-inch	6	24 "	......	1.00	12.00	
6-inch	6	28 "	......	1.25	15.00	
6-inch	6 to 7	30 "	......	1.50	18.00	
7-inch	6 to 7	32 to 34 "	......	2.00		
7-inch	6 to 7	36 "	......	2.50		
8-inch	6 to 7	38 "	......	3.00		
8-inch	7	40 " heavy		5.00		
9-inch	7	42 "	"	6.00		
9-inch	7	60 "	......	10.00		
12-inch	7	65 to 70 "	......	25.00		

KENTIA FORSTERIANA.

Size pots	Leaves	Height		Each	Doz.	100
3-inch		8 to 10 inches.....$		$ 1.80	$15.00	
3½-inch	3 to 4	15 to 16 "	......		3.00	25.00
4-inch	5	18 to 20 "	......	.40	4.50	35.00
4-inch	5	22 to 24 "	......	.50	6.00	
5-inch	5 to 6	24 to 28 "	......	.75	9.00	
5-inch	5 to 6	30 to 32 "	......	1.00	12.00	
6-inch	6	34 "	......	1.25		
6-inch	6 to 7	34 to 36 "	......	1.50		
7-inch	6	40 "	......	2.00		
7-inch	6	44 "	......	2.50		
8-inch	5 to 6	48 "	......	3.00		
8-inch	6	50 to 54 "	......	4.00		
9-inch	6	60 "	......	5.00		
9-inch	6 to 7	65 "	......	6.00		
10-inch	6 to 7	70 "	......	7.50		
10-inch	6 to 7	6 feet	......	15.00		
12-inch tubs, 6 to 7 7 feet			......	25.00		

ARAUCARIA EXCELSA.

Size pots	Height	Whorls		Each
4-inch	8 to 10 inches	3..............................		$ .60
5-inch	12 "	3 to 4..............................		.75
6-inch	20 "	4..............................		1.25
6-inch	24 "	4 to 5..............................		1.50

The New Fern, Nephrolepis Piersoni.

We have a fine stock of this beautiful Fern, all pot-grown plants ready for September delivery.

2½-inch pot plants............................		..each	$ .35
4-inch	"	"	.75
5-inch	"	"	1.00
6-inch	"	"	1.50
7-inch	"	"	2.50
8-inch	"	"	3.00

If you are a buyer of Palms, Ferns, etc., a personal visit of inspection to our Greenhouses at Western Springs, Ill., (one-half hour's ride from Chicago), will pay you. — Long Distance Telephone No. 221 Western Springs, Ill.

BOSTON FERNS.

Nephrolepis Exaltata Bostoniensis.

We have the finest stock in the West. All our plants are pot-grown, bushy stock, well furnished with fronds from the pot up, and cannot be compared with the cheap, long-drawn-up, lifted stock from the bench. A sample shipment will convince you of our superior stock. **STOCK READY LAST OF AUGUST.**

		Each	Per doz.	Per 100
2½ inch pot plants.......................$			$ .60	$ 5.00
3 " " "			1.50	10.00
4 " " "			2.50	20.00
5 " " "		.50	5.00	40.00
6 " pans "		.75	8.00	60.00
7 " " "		1.00	10.00	75.00
8 " " "		1.50	15.00	
9 " " "		$2.00 to	2.50	
10 " " "		3.00 to	3.50	
12 " " "		4.00 to	5.00	
8 " wire hanging baskets, full and bushy..............................				
10 " wire hanging baskets, full and bushy.......................1.50				
12 " wire hanging baskets, full and bushy..............,$4.00 to 5.00			2.50	

Anna Foster, the New Nephrolepis.

Size pots		Each	Doz.	100
2½-inch.............................$			$ 1.00	$ 8.00
3-inch..............................			2.00	15.00
4-inch..............................			3.50	25.00
5-inch..............................		.60	6.00	50.00
6-inch..............................		.75	9.00	
7-inch..............................		1.25	12.00	
8-inch..............................		1.75	18.00	
9-inch..............................		2.50		
10-inch..............................		4.00		
12-inch..............................		6.00		

Asparagus Plumosus Nanus.

We are headquarters.

2½-inch pots..............................per doz., 75; per 100, $5.00
3-inch pots..............................per doz., $1.00; per 100, 8.00
ASPARAGUS PLUMOSUS SEEDLINGS......................per 100, $2.00

CELESTIAL PEPPER.

One of the very best of Christmas plants. The plants are covered with bright colored, cone-shaped fruit at Christmas.
Strong plants, ...per doz., $1.50; per 100, $12.00

Chicago. Vaughan's Greenhouses, Western Springs.

Please mention the American Florist when writing.

Syracuse, N. Y.

BUILDING AT ONONDAGA VALLEY.—WILL OF HENRY BURT CONTESTED.—ASTERS SUPERSEDE CARNATIONS.—SWEET PEAS IN DEMAND.

P. R. Quinlan & Company have purchased the Hurd property at Onondaga Valley, consisting of nearly twenty acres, and will utilize it for the erection of greenhouses. The company will at once spend $10,000, and when the whole plant is completed it will cost in the neighborhood of $30,000, the plan being to eventually remove all the business from West Genesee and Geddes streets to the new site, with the possible exception of a storehouse that will be located near the center of the city. A portion of the property is being graded and will be used at once for the erection of six greenhouses, each to be 150 feet long and so built that an additional 150 feet may be added in the future. The contract has been let to the King Construction Company, of Lockport, N. Y. While the houses will have the appearance of individual houses they will be so connected as to make one continuous building. These buildings will be completed in six weeks and will be used for the cultivation of carnations. When the plant is finished it will be the largest in central and western New York. The present site of the company will probably be cut up in building lots, the location being a very desirable one. The new property contains two dwelling houses, one of which will be occupied by W. J. Quinlan, brother of P. R. Quinlan. Mr. Quinlan has been looking for a site for two years and the one decided upon has a south and east aspect and is sheltered from north and west winds by hills. The will of Henry Burt, who died recently and left the bulk of his estate of $40,000 to his widow, will be contested by Albert Burt, a son. Neither of the sons, Albert nor Alfred Burt, were mentioned in the will. The surrogate has appointed Mrs. Louisa Light temporary administrator of the will and she will continue to manage the retail store in East Genesee street. It was stated that most of the personal estate, consisting of $40,000, was in growing plants. The contest is on the ground of undue influence and testamentary incompetence.

Asters are beginning to take the place of carnations as cut flowers in this vicinity and a great demand is reported for sweet peas.

L. E. Marquisee is getting in his carnations and refilling his houses with earth.

A. J. B.

HADLEY FALLS, MASS.—One of the closing features of the celebration of this town's 150th anniversary was a "floral" parade, on July 30, two miles long. Unfortunately the greater part of the "flowers" were made of paper.

Pittsburg.

NO PERCEPTIBLE CHANGE IN BUSINESS CONDITIONS.—RETAIL BUSINESS THIS SUMMER DOES NOT COME UP TO LAST YEAR'S MARK.—PROPOSED BOND ISSUE FOR PARK IMPROVEMENTS.—NEWS.

There is practically no change in business conditions over last week and none is expected for some time to come. The general weakness of trade during this season clearly indicates that the gross amount of retail business will be far below last summer's record, which was an exceptionally good one. Poor qualities and insufficient supplies of stock have been in a great measure responsible for this condition. In roses American Beauty and Meteor are the best. Small quantities of good Brides and Bridesmaids are obtainable. Gladioli are piling up and unless something happens soon they will become a glut. Asters are good while carnations are very poor and small.

Director McElvain, of Allegheny, is preparing an ordinance providing for a bond issue of $100,000 for the improvement of the city parks. The passing of this ordinance will mean the purchase of a liberal quantity of trees, shrubbery, etc.

H. Bayersdorfer & Company's representative states that he is selling lots of immortelle Christmas bells and it looks as though there will be a shortage in the supply of this Christmas novelty.

Owing to the absence of so many club members, a postponement of the regular meeting for a week or two may be necessary. Regular notices will be sent around preceding the meeting.

Frank Banning, of Kinsman, O., is shipping some fine gladioli. His new pink seedling is one of remarkable beauty.

J. F. Smith, of Edwards & Docker discussed the box question at the convention.

Mr. McCollum, of the Pittsburg Cut Flower Company, is visiting at Du Bois, Pa.

G. & J. Ludwig, of Allegheny, are doing a heavy business in funeral work.

J. B. Murdock & Company are cutting a large quantity of fine smilax.

E. C. Ludwig, of Allegheny, is making a fine display of gladioli.

Julius Ludwig displayed his skill in bowling at Milwaukee. E. L. M.

We Make Paint For Two Gentlemen Only

"UNCLE SAM" AND "MR. PARTICULAR."

MAN COPPER ROOF PAINT is used on Government Buildings under rigid inspection.
Your good judgement demands the "BEST" when length of service is considered.

Superior to diamond; turret holder; 6 cutters; sample 50c; $4.00 per dozen, postpaid. Send for wholesale quotations on paints.

AMERICAN PAINT AND ROOFING WORKS.

GEO. N. HOLLAND, Distributor, Washington, D. C.

Kramer's Pot Hangers

THE neatest, simplest, most convenient and only practical device for converting ordinary flower pots into hanging baskets. They fit all standard made pots from 3 to 10 inches in diameter. The illustration shows how they are attached. Just the thing for hanging up ferns, begonias, etc. You can make room and money by their use. Try them. For Sale by

Vaughan's Seed Store, Chicago and New York.
E. F. Winterson Co., Chicago.
C. C. Pollworth Co., Milwaukee, Wis.

Price with wire chain as shown in cut, $1.00 per dozen by express. Sample dozen by mail, $1.25.

I. N. KRAMER & SON, Cedar Rapids, Iowa.

WHY NOT BUY
RED POTS
OF US?
Standard Size
Quality—No Better.
Carefully Packed in Small Crates. Easy to Handle.
Price List Free.

Syracuse Pottery Co.,
Syracuse, N. Y.

BEST POT IN THE MARKET

THOSE RED POTS
"STANDARDS"
FULL SIZE AND WIDE BOTTOMS.
BULB PANS AND AZALEA POTS.

DETROIT FLOWER POT M'F'Y.
HARRY BALSLEY, DETROIT, MICH.
Rep. 490 Howard St.

RED POTS
SAMPLE POT AND PRICE LIST ON APPLICATION.

C. C. POLLWORTH CO., MILWAUKEE, WIS......

EUREKA GREENHOUSES

MANUFACTURED BY

Dillon Greenhouse Mfg. Co:

BLOOMSBURG, PENNSYLVANIA.

Are Practical, Durable and Reasonable in Cost.

THEY CAN BE ERECTED BY ANY PRACTICAL MAN AND WILL GIVE SATISFACTION. IF YOU WISH TO BUILD A GREENHOUSE THAT WILL LAST A LIFETIME. WRITE US.

MYERS & CO.
Established 1849.

Greenhouse
Boilers.

GREENHOUSE ARCHITECTS : BUILDERS
HEATING ENGINEERS.
116 South 17th St., Philadelphia, Pa.
Send For Catalogue and Latest Prices.

Use our Patent
IRON BENCH
FITTINGS and
Roof Supports.

THE JENNINGS IMPROVED
IRON GUTTER.

IMPROVED VAPORIZING PANS
For Tobacco Extracts, Etc. Send for Circulars.

VENTILATING
APPARATUS,

DILLER, CASKEY & CO., SUCCESSORS TO JENNINGS BROS.,
S. W. Cor. Sixth and Berk Sts., PHILADELPHIA.

GEO. M. GARLAND,
DES PLAINES, ILL.
IRON GUTTERS and POSTS.
Patented Dec. 27, 1898.

GARLAND'S IRON GUTTERS and POSTS, PIPE FITTINGS, GRATE BARS, ANGLE IRON, PURLINS, Etc.

Kansas City, Mo.

At a recent meeting of the Directors of Convention Hall it was decided that no Flower Show would be held this fall, for the reason that a great many of the business men who had supported the Flower Shows of 1901-02 were for the most part heavy losers in the recent flood, and without their subscriptions the directors did not feel justified in shouldering the proposition.

Summer resort weather has prevailed in and around Kansas City for the past week, the thermometer dropping as low as 60°, making it very pleasant for planting in late carnations. Most growers report their field stock in fine condition, brought about principally by an abundance of rainy weather. Asters are an exception; in almost every instance they were a complete failure.

The W. L. Rock Flower Company has recently completed its addition of three 28x200-foot houses and have them planted to roses and carnations. They are now building a 75-foot brick stack, and putting in one more 80-horse-power boiler and will build one more house, 20x150 feet, for propagating purposes.

James Payne, one of our pioneer florists, has bought out the late Paul Ducret's greenhouses. May better success follow him in his new venture is the hearty wish of all the craft.

Store men report an exceptionally good trade for the month of July, but cannot say as much for first part of August. With the present quality of stock to be had, very little trade can be expected.

Report is out that Ed. Ellsworth, formerly with Murray, will take full charge of Geo. Kellogg's Kansas City store.

The following stores are closed for July, August and September: A. F. Barbe, Mrs. Edgar, John Schneider and John Ross.

Wm. Wade, Ed. Day, M. Carter, clerks, and L. Westervelt, bookkeeper, from Rock's, are all off on their vacation.

A. Newell, Geo. Kellogg and Chas. E. Heite are about all that will attend the convention from here.   W.

SACO, ME.—Alonzo Hill was married to Mrs. C. Y. Foss, August 1.

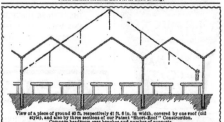

Springfield, Mass.

Business is fair, there being quite a little funeral work, which helps to keep things moving. Fairly good roses are plentiful. Asters are abundant and good, although the disease seems to be as bad as in former years. Chrysanthemums are in fine shape and need a great deal of attention. Ferns, callas, cyclamen, primulas and cinerarias, of which quite a lot are grown in this vicinity, are doing nicely. Outside stock, such as feverfew, rudbeckias, candytuft and dahlias are plentiful and are used for indoor decoration, also helping out in many other ways.

Mark Aitken is visiting New York and Philadelphia looking up stock and novelties for fall trade.   A. B.

PEORIA, ILL.—J. C. Murray is on the sick list again.

BARGAINS
For Greenhousemen.

Boiler Tubes.

In good condition. We have been selling them for many years past to greenhouse men. They are economical and practical, and make a first-class pipe line. We clean and paint them. We furnish without additional charge sleeve or jacket couplings; also oakum and cement to make tight joints. They are in straight, long lengths. Note our prices:

2-inch, per foot 4c
2¼-inch, per foot 5c
3½-inch, " 8c
4-inch, per foot 11c
6-inch, " 21c

Pipes.

Our stock of good standard black second-hand pipe with guaranteed threads and couplings as follows:

100,000 ft. 1-inch, per foot 2¼c
200,000 ft. 1¼-inch, " 4¼c
50,000 ft. 2-inch, " 7¼c
200,000 ft. 3½-inch, " .... 10 c
80,000 ft. 1-inch, extra heavy, per foot.... 4 c
55,003 ft. 1¼-inch, " 5½c

Radiation.

100,000 ft. second-hand, cast iron radiation, per foot, ... 18c.
200,00 ft. second-hand, wrought iron radiation, per foot, ... 16c.
Also Valves, heaters and all necessary apparatus.

Roofing Glass.

¼-inch. thick ribbed roofing glass from the Pan-American Exposition Buildings. Per square foot 5c.

Valves.

250 iron body, brass trimmed Gate, Check, Globe and Angle valves, ranging in sizes from 3 to 10 inches. They are second-hand, overhauled and in first-class condition. Write us your wants. Also all kinds of fittings.

Boilers.

Over 250 good boilers in stock. Can furnish anything you may require in the line.

Hot Bed Sash.

Several jobs to offer. Write us your wants.

Hose.

All kinds of garden and water-conducting hose for sale at low prices.

WRITE FOR OUR CATALOGUE NO. 47.

We handle building material, plumbing material, hardware and stocks of every kind.

Chicago House Wrecking Co.,
WEST 35th & IRON STS.,
CHICAGO, ILL.

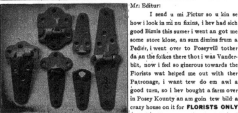

THE EVERLASTIN HINGE.

Mr: Editur:

I send u mi .Pictur so u kin se how i look in mi nu fixins, i hev had sich good Biznis this sumer i went an got me some store klose, an sum dimins frum a Pedler, i went over to Poseyvill tother da an the folkes there thot i was Vander-bilt, now i feel so ginerous towards the Florists wat helped me out with ther Patronage, i want tew do em awl a good turn, so i hev bought a farm over in Posey Kounty an am goin tew bild a crazy house on it for **FLORISTS ONLY** wot git nutty a worryin about butted gias an laped gias an short span nort! an short span south, an this kind uv bug an tuther kind uf Bug an mikrobes an sich things, an then kum to the Kon-venshin an kuss an dis-kuss till awl git daffey. So tel Florists to send tew me fur a Kat-a-loge what tels awl about mi **BILER an HINGES an VENTILATIN CONTRAPSHINS** an say if tha By uv me tha ma be helpin to bild a home fur thereselves in the future. Mi name is

THE "NEW DEPARTURE." VENTILATING APPLIANCE.

J. D. CARMODY,

an i live in **EVANSVILLE, IND.**
whitch is klose tew Posey Kounty.

AMERICAN CHAMPION BILER.

American Florist Ads. always do business,
At Home and Abroad.

THE AMERICAN FLORIST

America is "the Prow of the Vessel; there may be more comfort Amidships, but we are the first to touch Unknown Seas."

Vol. XXI.　　　　CHICAGO AND NEW YORK, AUGUST 29, 1903.　　　　No. 795.

THE AMERICAN FLORIST

NINETEENTH YEAR.

Copyright 1903, by American Florist Company
Entered as Second-Class Mail Matter.

PUBLISHED EVERY SATURDAY BY

AMERICAN FLORIST COMPANY,
324 Dearborn St., Chicago.
Eastern Office: 79 Milk St., Boston.

Subscription, $1.00 a year.　To Europe, $2.00.
Subscriptions accepted only from the trade.
Volumes half-yearly from August, 1901.

SOCIETY OF AMERICAN FLORISTS AND
ORNAMENTAL HORTICULTURISTS.
OFFICERS—JOHN BURTON, Philadelphia, Pa.,
president; C. C. POLLWORTH, Milwaukee, Wis.,
vice-president; WM. J. STEWART, 79 Milk Street,
Boston, Mass., secretary; H. B. BEATTY, Oil City,
Pa., treasurer.
OFFICERS-ELECT—PHILIP BREITMEYER, presi
dent; J. J. BENEKE, Vice-president; secretary and
treasurer as before. Twentieth annual meeting
at St. Louis, Mo., August, 1904.

THE AMERICAN CARNATION SOCIETY.
Annual convention at Detroit, Mich., March 3,
1904. ALBERT M. HERR, Lancaster, Pa., secretary.

AMERICAN ROSE SOCIETY.
Annual meeting and exhibition, Philadelphia,
March, 1904. LEONARD BARRON, 136 Liberty St.,
New York, secretary.

CHRYSANTHEMUM SOCIETY OF AMERICA
Annual convention and exhibition, New York,
November 10-13, 1903. FRED H. LEMON, Richmond,
Ind., secretary.

THIS ISSUE 40 PAGES WITH COVER.

MILWAUKEE CONVENTION.

AUGUST 18-21, 1903.

Modern Greenhouse Construction.

BY JOHN N. MAY, SUMMIT, N. J.

Why I have been chosen to talk to you on this subject is a conundrum to me. When your secretary wrote me some two months ago, asking me to prepare a paper on this subject, I told him that I was not in a position to do justice to it, as I have not any of the so-called modern houses of my own, and have not had time to investigate them properly in other places; and so declined to handle it. One week ago I received another letter from him reading somewhat like this: "I like to see your name on the programme and am going to put it there, and trust to Providence and you, as I have done more than once before, so fire away. Yours, Stewart." Now the weather is a little too warm to need fire at the present time, besides I do not like the stoke hole well enough to go down there to make fires; coal is also too expensive to burn it unnecessarily. Regarding the words "trust to Providence" here, he is off his base and the umpire should declare him out, because if he had given this subject to one of the florists of that fine old city of Rhode Island, you might have had an interesting and instructive paper prepared, instead of a running talk as must always be the result of anything written on a train going at something less than forty miles an hour, particularly, when that train is practically full of florists out for a royal good time. So under these circumstances, I trust you will not be too severe in your criticisms of my shortcomings in what I may have to say about modern greenhouse construction, because this word "modern" applies to all sorts and sizes of greenhouses, ranging from one of 6 x 8 feet all the way to others 50 feet wide by 400, 500 or 600 feet long, and each and all of these have their especial use and claim to modern construction. Some are built of practically all iron, or rather steel, others a combination of iron and wood, others again nearly all wood; which of these are the most desirable, all things considered, is yet an open question.

For the general florist, the first question in building a greenhouse to be considered is the cost, and with many, this is a very important matter, as every additional dollar expended on it means additional yearly cost in interest on the investment; for no matter how you figure it, the money put into any kind of a business should be charged with the interest yearly, whether it may be borrowed money or ready cash on hand. This brings us face to face with the different kinds of greenhouse most desirable to build. In deciding this point, the next question that comes up is that of durability in conjunction with first cost. If a house, say, of any given size, costing fifty per cent more when built of the most expensive materials than another built of a cheaper grade of material, but with the same quality of glass in each; can be safely guaranteed to stand in good order for twice the length of time than the cheaper one will, then it would be a safe investment to adopt the higher priced one as a general rule. But this is another open question, which I, for one, would not like to venture an opinion on. Many of our younger florists will have ample opportunity to judge of this in a few years.

That there have been improvements made in greenhouse building within the last twenty years, no one will deny; but not all the changes made in construction can, I think, be called improvements. The adoption of much larger glass with a corresponding lighter grade of woodwork, producing, as it does, a much brighter light in the interior of the greenhouse, is, unquestionably, an improvement in producing a better and larger quantity of cut flowers during the dull cloudy months of winter. But, are such extra light houses any benefit for general plant culture? As a general rule I think not.

Another point of improvement, considered so at least by many, is the size of the greenhouse. It is an undisputed fact that a large volume of air enclosed in a greenhouse, can be maintained at a more even temperature much easier than a small volume; in other words, a house, say, 30 feet wide by 100 feet long, can be kept at a much more even temperature than two houses 15 feet wide each by 100 feet long, the two having the same relative amount of glass and volume of air as the one larger one. This is an advantage, especially as the consumption of coal is less to maintain an equal heat in the large house than in the two small ones; hence, the reason why some of our live florists are building much larger houses than formerly.

Some will probably ask, what is the best form or style of house to build? This is purely a matter of choice with each one contemplating building, because there are so many different forms in use, and all have their advocates; and as far as my limited observation goes, almost all of them will produce good flowers in quantity. The system of ridge and furrow built house without any partitions, leaving a very large clear open space, or in other words, a large area, covered with glass, certainly has many features to commend it. In a little trip around among the florists' establishments last winter, I was particularly struck with the fine healthy growth and abundance of bloom (roses) which I saw in one such range of greenhouses near Chicago. I considered it at that time, the best I saw in my whole trip. There are also very large establishments, practically all built in this style, around Toronto, Canada.

In other sections, I saw what is known as the short span to the south style of houses. These never struck me as favorable for rose growing especially; in fact, I have yet to see where any advantage is gained for any class of flowers or plants by this method of construction, and it is certainly the most expensive to heat of any system I know of, having much the largest area of glass exposed to the north, and it has long been clearly demonstrated that glass exposed to the north will require twenty-five to thirty per cent more fuel to maintain a given temperature under it, than it does for glass facing south, and in cold hard weather with the wind blowing from the north or northwest, the difference is much greater still.

Another style of house, which is gaining in favor to a large degree, is the very wide house with equal span, each being a separate structure. These are very light and have many points of advantage over the others named above and for certain varieties of roses, such as American Beauty, they are certainly much better adapted when the side walls are made high enough to allow the walk next to the side wall and with low benches or raised beds from the surface of even height all throughout the house.

Such very wide houses should have a double row of ventilators at the ridge and side ventilation also to give ample circulation of air in hot weather and, as far as my observation and experience goes should have a pitch of the roof of 34° to 36° or, in other words, a fall of from 7½ to 8 inches to the foot. This applies to all and every class of greenhouse, whether large or small for the production of cut flowers in winter.

In conclusion I would suggest to those contemplating adding new greenhouses to carefully investigate each of the different classes of buildings before deciding in every case. I think it would well repay them to see the houses several times and under different conditions of weather, to enable them to form a fair and correct opinion of which particular style of house will best suit their purpose and remember that soil and location of the greenhouse, combined with proper management, is a very large factor in producing the best quality of flowers.

HITCHCOCK, TEXAS.—Business at a standstill with most of the trade in Galveston. One new greenhouse since the storm. Cape jasmines, chrysanthemums and roses do well through the whole year. Carnations do not thrive here. Oleanders, palms and ferns are at home with us.

How to Grow Violets In the West.

BY GEORGE F. CRABB, GRAND RAPIDS, MICH.

The cultivation of the violet is a fascinating vocation, pleasant and profitable, should the crop prove a success, disappointing and expensive when failure is the result. There are so many trials and tribulations to go through before a successful crop is assured that many a grower has abandoned the cultivation of violets in sheer despair for some other more certain crop; yet, with healthy plants, careful cultivation, proper soil and good constant care there is no reason why the violet cannot be as sure a crop as any other variety of plants. There are not many growers who can positively say: "My crop will be a success," for experience teaches us that no matter how great our success last season, we can fail miserably this. Yet these failures help to guard against a repetition of the same mistakes.

Our first set-back was the black fly; it was our first acquaintance. He was allowed to get too strong a foothold before his identity was discovered, and then, while every effort was made to dislodge the enemy, it was too late; the damage was done. The next season we kept the fly in check, but had a different mishap. For covering the cracks on the bottom of the benches we used inverted

Gordon Whitnall.
(Our Errand Boy at the Milwaukee Convention.)

sod. It turned out to be quack sod. The quack grass grew and we set the men to work pulling it out. They found it easier to pull when wet, so they kept the beds soaked with water. No sooner were the beds in that condition than a rainy week set in. The soil would not dry off, the plants having what we term wet feet, and immediately we had the most beautiful crop of black spot imaginable, the crop being ruined. We finally dried the soil out, and with proper care the plants out free from spot, and, in fine shape; but instead of picking 40,000 blooms at Christmas we had to be content with a quarter of that number and vowing we would never get caught that way again.

The last set-back (and may it remain

the last) occurred at a time when most growers have more or less trouble from the same causes, and under similar conditions, and find it hard to determine just what was the matter. We were attending the Chicago chrysanthemum show; our violets were fine. They were blooming freely and selling at a good price. Like many other florists, similarly situated, we were building air castles of what we would do with the profits of our promising crop, and how many more houses we would put to violets next season. The weather during show week was warm, the thermometer standing at 55° to 60° at night. The wind blew and the rain poured down and was blown in mist through the ventilators and over the plants. It was so warm the hands decided, it best to leave the ventilators up, at least until my return. Oh, what a sight I beheld. Eight hands still picking the spotted leaves off those magnificent plants that but a few days previous we were banking on so high; they were so checked that it was not until towards spring they fully recovered. Had the ventilators been closed the crop would have been saved. I have mentioned our principal failures as possibly they might be of value in preventing others from failing into the same costly mistakes.

Propagation.—We propagate our stock the last of March and through April in two ways, by divisions and sand rooted cuttings. For divisions we select the strongest runners, remove from the plant and pot in 2-inch pots. It is immaterial whether the divisions when potted have roots or not. The sand-rooted cuttings are also put in 2-inch pots and all covered with long strips of cotton until thoroughly rooted, when the use of cotton is discontinued. Newspapers would for small quantities answer just as well. We are careful to put the covering on before the sun strikes the plants in the morning and remove immediately after the sun's rays no longer strike house, giving as much light as possible while not letting the sun get at the plants to wilt them. As soon as the plants have filled the pots with roots they are ready for planting; those we cannot plant until later in the season we put in 3-inch pots and grow them on. A well rooted violet plant from a 3-inch pot we prefer to a field grown plant; one thing, it does not suffer a check when planted. We plant direct to the bench, our plants being grown wholly under glass the year around. Very few field grown plants are used in this vicinity, unless it is the Princess of Wales, single.

Preparation of the Soil.—We prefer of a clay loam about three parts, two parts muck sod and two parts well rotted cow manure, all thoroughly mixed and chopped fine. Under no circumstances is old soil ever used. We plant eight inches between the plants, ten inches between the rows, and by the first of October we have robust, bushy plants with foliage touching and covered with buds. Picking begins about the first of October and in a couple of weeks is under full headway.

Varieties.—The principal variety grown is the Lady Campbell, as being the least liable to disease, the strongest grower, freest bloomer, producing three flowers to one of the dark varieties. Swanley White is successfully grown with Lady Campbell, but in limited quantity. In dark violets Imperial is the best. While requiring the same treatment as Marie Louise, it has a larger flower, stronger stem and is a little hardier in its consti-

AT THE S. A. F. CONVENTION, MILWAUKEE, AUGUST 18-21, 1903.

tution than Marie Louise. Farquhar is no longer grown here.

Temperature.—Lady Campbell and Swanley White both require 45° to 50° night temperature; 10° higher in daytime. The dark varieties 38° to 40° at night; 5° to 8° higher during the day. The warmer varieties require a steadier temperature than the dark. The latter, if the temperature occasionally dropped to 33° would be uninjured; with the former it would check the flowers and prevent them from opening.

Ventilation.—At all times give all the air your conveniences will allow. It is an invigorating stimulant to the health of the plant, and an antidote of disease. Let the wind, even if cold, blow on the plants. If they are healthy do not be afraid if you see the leaves moving with the breeze; they are drinking in a deep breath of fresh air, for you know you cannot properly grow violets in a close, ill-ventilated house. Such a one is apt to be damp and muggy, right conditions for spot.

Watering.—From the time of planting until about the middle of October the plants should be kept on the wet side; from that date on they should be kept on the dry side. This period to the middle of December being the critical time of their existence, if you get through till then, or even till the first of December you can then reasonably bank on what kind of a crop you will have for the season.

Cultivation.—Keep the soil constantly stirred, so as to let the light penetrate to the roots, pick off all decayed and dead leaves. Remove all runners on Lady Campbell and Swanley White as fast as they appear, retaining the one center crown. On the dark violets the same process should be gone through with, although better results are claimed for the system that retains three or four crowns, pinching the strongest runners about three inches from the plant for this purpose; longer stems and more flowers will result. Keep the atmosphere in the houses dry at all times, even at the risk of getting the houses too warm; turn on a little steam, even if no longer than to take off that raw, chilly dampness. Particularly is this true when early fall rains set in. The neglect of these precautions frequently allows spot to put in an appearance. A hand rake is used for stirring the soil, but better still, if the man in charge knows how to stir soil with his fingers; it is much better, and he never has to hunt for his rake, it is always by him.

Black Spot.—It is frequently caused by overwatering, wet feet we call it. In mild weather, while ventilation is all open and a warm rain sets in, before you really seem to be aware what is going on, the wind switches the rain over the foliage in the form of mist, which is very distasteful to the sweet capricious beauty. Again, a close, ill-ventilated house should be avoided, as it is sure to breed spot.

Red Spider.—Frequent syringings on bright mornings will serve to keep this insidious enemy down. If you have been taking care of your plants you will have very little trouble with spider.

Eel Worms.—These are a rarity in this vicinity. As soon as a plant stops growing, ceases to have that bright gloss inseparable from a healthy plant, pull it out and replant from a stock that should be kept on hand in 3-inch or 4-inch pots for that purpose. This disposes of the worm, or any other trouble that may ail the plant. There are other enemies, insects and diseases, with which we are yet unfamiliar.

Watering.—Great care should be exercised in watering not to get the soil too wet, as it will then become sour and in winter it is hard to again get it in healthy growing condition. Morning is the best time to water, and in cloudy weather and fall, judgment should be used so as to select such time when watering that the foliage will dry out before night.

Style of House.—Narrow 10-foot to 12-foot houses grow good violets, but on account of the sash ventilators are harder to handle during the critical period. Large houses from 100 to 300 feet long, 29 feet wide, containing four 5-foot benches, with ventilators 3x4½ feet, all on the north side of the house, half opening at the ridge, the other alternating sash hinged at the ridge and opening at cross-bar, houses running east and west. These houses admit of more air and light and less liability of a sudden fall of rain getting in before ventilation is closed, as it is easier to close the ventilators with the Evans machine than to let down a lot of sash.

The successful growing of violets may be summed up in four words, "take care of them.".

Presentations.

An impressive incident of the closing session at Milwaukee was the presentation to ex-President Wm. R. Smith, of a handsome gold watch and masonic charm to replace the watch and charm which had been stolen from him, and which had been presented to him by the society some years ago.

Mr. Robert Craig made the presentation speech. He said:

Mr. President, I am about to speak to you on a matter of great importance to our good friend, Wm. R. Smith of Washington and any matter of importance to him certainly is interesting to all of us. We look upon him as one of the greatest friends of horticulture and floriculture that America has ever had. For nearly half a century he has been in the forward ranks of those who have labored to elevate our profession to a higher plane, and he has been eminently successful. We all value his counsel in our meetings; we know how valuable a friend he has been to this society from its inception; we delight to listen to him, as he enjoys telling us of the growth of floriculture from its very early beginning, and to listen to him when he tells of the arrival of the first plant of Pandanus Veitchii in this country, the first Latania Borbonica and those plants so rare in those days but which are now within the reach of all in the decoration of their homes. When we learned that our good friend

had, on his journey to the convention, fallen into the hands of the Phillistines and been robbed of his purse, we were very much concerned. It didn't seem to concern him much that he had lost his money; he seemed to think that "he who steals my purse steals trash," but when he got to this city and in his room at night was robbed of his watch which had come to him as a token of esteem from his friends in this city, then all could see that he had met with a loss, that something he valued highly had been taken from him.

This robbery of Mr. Smith came as a great shock. I know the mayor of Milwaukee has had detectives at work and has done all he could to find the watch and has not found it. But I am glad to say that the florists themselves, working along other lines, have recovered the watch. I am sure you will all join with

Thomas Manton.
(President Canadian Hortleultural Association.)

me in the pleasure I have in restoring to Mr. Smith the property which he valued so highly. We have the watch here, the Masonic charm and the ring just as he lost them.

Mr. Smith rose to respond but found it difficult to give expression to his emotions. He looked rather than voiced his feelings. He assured the society of his appreciation of their kindness and said the circumstances made the gifts doubly

valuable to him. He incidentally remarked that he was proud of his labors in assisting to secure the society's national charter, and he hoped to be spared a few more years of life and to meet annually the florist friends whose faces had become so familiar to him.

A presentation of a gold watch to President Burton was then made, on behalf of many friends in the society by Wm. Currie, of Milwaukee. After the usual preliminaries, Mr. Currie said: We all know Mr. Burton and have known him, most of us for a considerable number of years and to know him is to love him. We regret that at the last meeting he was unable to be present because of a family bereavement, and this is the first opportunity that we have had to express to him personally our sympathy. It is my duty and pleasure to present him with this little gift from his friends in the society and to convey the assurance of their wishes that he may live long to enjoy it.

President Burton received the gift and thanking the donors asked to be excused from saying more. He assured them that he would treasure the beautiful present as long as he lived and that it would be equally valued by his children.

A pleasant feature of the dinner at the Auditorium on Friday evening, August 21, was the presentation to Mr. Vaughan of a diamond ring by the Chicago florists in recognition of his efficient services in the excellent preparations that had been made for the reception and entertainment of the visiting S. A. F. members. W. N. Rudd made the presentation speech. Mr. Rudd said:

Ladies and gentlemen: It has been said that a prophet is not without honor save in his own country. It has also been said that "exceptions prove the rule to-night by an exception. We have here, in Chicago, a man who has been associated with the Society of American Florists from the very day of its birth down to the present time, who has always been in the front rank, who has invariably been identified with every move in the way of progress—a man whom you all know and one who has taken a back seat, on occasions,' to advance the interests of the society and to promote the interests of other men.

Tonight is, with me, a night for plain speaking. We have with us here the founders of the Society of American Florists, and yet I want to say to you that there is none among them all who has done more for the Society of American Florists than our worthy and honored leader in Chicago, Mr. J. C. Vaughan.

NEW RANGE OF PETER REINBERG, CHICAGO.

TORONTO EXHIBITION BUILDING.

(Where the Canadian Horticultural Association Meeting and Exhibition will be held.)

And in proof of our appreciation of the work that he has done, members of the craft in the city of Chicago were unanimous in securing a small ornament as a token of their esteem for that gentleman and have honored me by requesting me to present it to him with assurances of their sincere admiration and regard. (cheers.)

I want to say further, that we realize that the value of this little token is as a drop in the bucket in comparison with the debt we owe to Mr. Vaughan and that there are many of us who, if we contributed to the joy of this occasion in proportion to our indebtedness to him, would go home to-night bankrupt.

Mr. Vaughan briefly expressed his thanks for the gift and his appreciation of the kindly motives that had suggested it. Concluding he said: We must not close without extending to the florists of Milwaukee the thanks of our committee and I believe of all here for their courtesy and co-operation, by which this gathering was made possible.

Report of the Treasurer.

Treasurer Beatty's report showed that the balance on hand on January 1, 1902, of $2,111.11 had been increased during the year by $2,519.82, making a total of $4,630.93. The disbursements amounted to $1,920.16, making the cash on hand, January 1, 1903, $2,710.77.

The life membership fund had been increased, during 1902, by $349.88, making the amount in the permanent fund, on January 1, 1903, $1,924.56.

The receipts from January to July 31 of the present year were $1,255.00 and the disbursements $1,492.70, leaving cash on hand, $2,473.07. Nine additional life members were reported for this year and the permanent fund has now reached $2,223.04.

Mr. Beatty stated that the permanent fund is drawing four per cent in the Germania Savings Bank of Pittsburg, Pa.

Convention Notes.

The soil carrying machine is the talk of the day.

The veterans of the society were out in strong force.

The meeting was a record breaker for new members.

Craig's crotons are much admired by the westerners.

J. A. Shaw, the mirth provoker, and his assistant were there.

Some of the best houses in the trade have entered orders for Finley's pot washer.

Alexander Wallace, the authority (?) on peony names and legislation, was singularly silent.

The trade drummers worked hard throughout the meeting and it is said that the returns in business were good.

The firm of A. Herrmann was erroneously given as A. Herrmann & Company in our issue of August 22, under the heading "Supplies" on page 141.

Dan McRorie, who was a very busy man in the interests of his house all through the Milwaukee convention, has been confined to his room at the Palmer house, Chicago, with malaria, since August 22. He is now progressing very favorably.

Adiantum Croweanum in frond and plant was exhibited by Peter Crowe, of Utica, N. Y. Mr. Crowe, for comparison, exhibited some plants of Adiantum hybridum, which to us appears to be altogether different from A. Croweanum. We have no hesitation in saying that there is a great future for A. Croweanum. For comparison with hybridum in this issue illustrations of A. Croweanum and A. hybridum.

On Saturday, August 22, a party of 247 conventionites visited the greenhouses of J. C. Vaughan and Bassett & Washburn, at Western Springs and Hinsdale respectively. The company was well taken care of by Messrs. Bassett, Washburn, Vaughan, Cropp and Wilson. Refreshments were served and the day was most pleasantly spent. Bohmanville, Rosehill, Forest Glen, Joliet and other establishments in the vicinity were visited by many.

Palms and Ferns.

FERNS FOR VARIOUS PURPOSES.

In addition to the extremely popular Boston ferns and other species and varieties of nephrolepis, there are some few species that often prove salable for the retail dealer, and which may be procured from some of the large growers, in quantity, if desired. One of these, which has attracted much attention of late years and which has also caused much favorable comment, is one of the tree ferns, Cibotium Schiedei, a remarkably graceful

species, and one that has proved to be very durable under trying conditions. From the fact that this cibotium is quite a large growing variety, it is not of special value to those who have no outlet for large plants, for this fern requires to be grown to at least a 6-inch pot size in order to demonstrate fully its great beauty. But once having reached such a size it is bound to attract, and with only reasonable care will long continue in good condition.

This fern may be grown under much the same conditions as the Boston fern, except that it is preferable to give the cibotium a somewhat lighter soil, a rather open compost, of which one-third should be of peat, such compost being better adapted to the needs of the tree ferns in general, the latter being usually found growing in a spongy and well drained soil rather than in clay. Cibotium Schiedei will absorb a large quantity of water once it is well established, but at the time of repotting it is well to be just a little cautious with water until the roots are again active. As to the production of this fine fern from spores, it will perhaps be more profitable to leave that portion of the work to those having the facilities and the experience to handle it properly and to purchase the young plants for growing on. Not only is there great risk in purchasing tree fern spores but it is also not the easiest thing in the business to germinate them.

Another fern of the arboreal section that is frequently grown for the retail trade is Dicksonia Antarctica, a fern that does not grow to quite so large a size as the cibotium noted above, although developing a stem or trunk much sooner. Dicksonia antarctica as a small plant forms a compact specimen with finely divided leaves of firm texture, and being found in the temperate portions of Australia does not require a very high temperature for its best development. Our hot summers are just a little trying for these cool house ferns, and moderately heavy shading and abundant moisture are quite necessary for their welfare. Thrips is the most likely pest to attack the dicksonias during the summer, and indeed most tree ferns are liable to this trouble if kept too warm and dry, the best preventive being a moderate syringing overhead on each bright day through the summer months.

In its native country this dicksonia often produces a stem over twenty feet in height and about one foot in diameter, this being surmounted by a magnificent

ADIANTUM CROWEANUM.

ing good results. The pots need to be well drained, and I have found it more satisfactory when shifting A. Farleyense not to ram the soil too hard, and also to have the soil rather dry at the time of potting. Then water the plants carefully until the roots get into active work, after which these plants will dispose of a considerable quantity of water in bright weather. A temperature of 70° and a shaded house, in which a fresh atmosphere is maintained by means of regular ventilation without direct draughts, are the conditions favorable for results with this fern. As to what we mean by results, it may be said that with proper attention one may grow the fern in question from a 2½-inch pot to a 10-inch pan, well furnished, within nine months.

Fern balls formed of the rhizomes of davallias have been quite common for several years past, and it might make a profitable change to work up a few fern baskets by way of variety. Of course there is not a large opening for these in the average market, but such baskets may be made into very beautiful objects without being very costly to produce. One of the quickest growing ferns for basket work is that singular maidenhair, Adiantum dolabriforme, a species with long slender fronds that are simply pinnate, having the characteristic of producing young plants at the tips of the mature frond, these in turn throwing out similarly proliferous fronds, which may be pinned down to the surface of the basket and thus form a complete covering, in a short time, of these apparently delicate but wiry fronds.

Adiantum Edgeworthii is another species of similar habit and also of rapid growth, though quite distinct in appearance from the foregoing. The baskets to be used for this purpose should be of gal-

crown of fronds, each of which may be ten feet long, but in cultivation it is unusual to find fronds more than six feet in length. One of the first large importations of dicksonia stems to this country was that sent to the Centennial exposition in Philadelphia in 1876, but nearly all of the stems in question were dead upon their arrival, as was also the case with many of those sent to the World's Fair in Chicago in 1892–93. Many of these were particularly fine stems and it was greatly to be regretted that they should not have survived the journey.

Blechnum Brasiliense is also a tree fern of easy culture and rapid growth, and is readily suited in the matter of soil. A light open loam with about one-sixth part of short stable manure added will answer very well for this fern, provided it is given plenty of water and a night temperature of 60° maintained. Both the blechnum and the dicksonia will germinate quite freely from fresh spores and may be grown on with reasonable rapidity.

It may be well to recall the fact once more that when using stable manure in the compost for ferns, it should always be old and well rotted, as fresh manure is liable to contain too much ammonia for this class of plants and may do them injury. Dry cow manure that is broken up fine, forms a very good fertilizer for many ferns, among those that are especially benefitted by its use being Adiantum Farleyense, a fern that has been much more successfully grown of late years since its needs have been better understood. This adiantum is one that enjoys a rather strong soil, a stiff fibrous sod with one-fifth to one-fourth part of dry cow dung mixed in it frequently giv-

JOHN H. LEY'S ADIANTUM HYBRIDUM.

vanized wire, and may either be the common flat baskets or ox muzzles, each of which may be purchased for a few cents. These baskets should be lined with either green flake moss or sphagnum in order to retain the soil, the latter being any light and peaty or sandy mixture that may be convenient, and in this three or four small plants of A. dolabriforme or A. Edgeworthii should be planted. The baskets should be hung in a warm and shaded greenhouse, and the soil kept continually moist, after which but little attention will be required beyond occasionally pinning down the tips of the fronds as they show indications of becoming proliferous, and in a few months the basket should become a perfect mass of graceful foliage, and doubtless would prove quite a revelation to some customers. W. H. TAPLIN

Adiantum Hybridum.

Adiantum hybridum was raised and introduced to commerce by John H. Ley, Good Hope, D. C., several years ago, but it is totally barren of spores, and Mr. Ley says stock was long limited to a few hundred specimens. It is a very rapid grower, the specimen (about four feet through as illustrated) being planted on the bench from a 2-inch pot in June, and potted into a 10-inch pan in September; fifty plants fill 600 feet of bench room. Fronds are very valuable for cutting and realize a high price in the market. It is said to be a distinct cross between A. decorum and A. amabile.

The Carnation.

BURSTING CALYXES.

A very small proportion of the varieties of carnations in cultivation are free from this bad habit, and to get at the remedy the question must be viewed from several sides. Anyone who is familiar with the subject knows that our race of monthly carnations is still in the infancy of its development, and that many years must elapse before ideality is reached. Great strides have indeed been made in some directions, as the improvement in form, color, size, stem and other qualities over those of older varieties will attest, but in the pressing demand for improvement in some qualities other qualities, for the improvement of which there seemed to be a less pressing demand, were bound to suffer.

The almost entire absence of fragrance in many popular varieties is perhaps the most conspicuous reminder that a good quality not used gradually wears away and will not again come forward until there is a chance of its benefiting those upon whose patronage it depends for an existence.

The carnation in its present stage of development in all its qualities depends upon man for its existence and is ever ready to court his patronage and contribute its share to his physical and spiritual needs, for nature realizes that any one of her subjects must serve a useful purpose in order to exist or its elements must decompose and become available for the nourishment of some useful form of life. In all nature there can be no such thing as a useless growth.

All living things depend for their existence upon other forms of life and must return that which they receive in some other form or be forever banished from a system in which permanent waste is unknown. And thus, looking at all the qualities of our monthly carnation, we fail to see a single one which does not contribute directly or indirectly to the benefit of man whose needs called it into the present stage of its development. He admired its divine color, and lo, it rivals the rainbow's hues. The cravings of his vision demanded a wealth of fine-textured petals upon which to feast, and straightway they unfolded with the richest luster. The demands of commerce dictated an ever increasing quantity of flowers from a given space, and the response was not lacking in the spirit of obedience.

All these changes have not been made in a single day, but have come about slowly through evolution based mainly upon the principle of artificial selection along the lines of man's own artificial development. If, therefore, we would improve any quality it must be through the channels freely opened by nature, and given the desire to improve and the knowledge of how to improve, there is no visible limit to what can be done. The demand for a good calyx will produce it in our coming varieties as surely

RECENT FUNERAL DESIGNS BY THE NUNNALLY COMPANY, OF ATLANTA, GA.

as was produced a well-formed system of petals and a stem strong enough to hold the flower up to view. The breeder of new varieties has taken the problem in hand and we can safely trust that he will in time reward our patience.

But in the meantime there is much that we can do to reduce the loss that must result from bad cases of bursting. Among the contributory causes of bursting are low temperature, deficient light, improper watering and other checks of various characters. The question of temperature requires adjustment according to the peculiarities of each variety. Some varieties are far more sensitive to extreme variations in temperature and watering than others, so that each variety will need careful study in these particulars. Many growers are apt to allow the night temperature to drop too low and strive to make up a fair average degree of heat by carrying the day temperature too high. A large proportion of split calyxes invariably accompanies this treatment. Then, again, there are

those who carry both the day and night temperature too low in order to increase the size of the flower. While it is true that the size of the flower can be materially increased by this treatment, the proportion of split calyxes and smaller quantity of flowers cut will far outweigh anything gained in size by the low temperature.

The propensity to burst is in many cases the sole factor in determining the temperature in which a variety should be grown. This is seen in the case of Lawson, which usually bursts badly in a night temperature lower than 55°. There can be no doubt that there would be a material increase in the size of the flower if grown at 50°, and the plants certainly would not suffer by it. In White Cloud we have a variety that is remarkably free from this habit, and so we can grow it profitably in a temperature of 50°. These remarks apply, of course, to the darker months.

During spring and fall the calyx is not so sensitive to changes and allowance can often be made. The length of the day in spring and the amount of sunshine give the plants a buoyancy of vitality that easily surmounts slight drops in the night temperature. After Easter, when it comes rather late, it is often a question whether or not it will pay to keep up the fires. An increase in the proportion of burst calyxes is about the only objection to discontinuing firing at that time, and the amount of loss suffered through imperfect flowers will, of course, determine the financial side of the question.

In fall it is well to adhere strictly to winter treatment. The days are much shorter than in spring, and besides the plants are not so firmly established, and a few cloudy days in succession with cool nights will often severely check them. The result is not only seen in bursting, but the vitality of the plants suffers by it. Through September, which is usually a sunny month, firing can be dispensed with, except on the coolest nights, but after that the grower's skill in keeping up proper atmospheric conditions will be put to the test.

In these notes the writer has on several occasions discussed the soil question, and there is often an intimate connection between a case of bursting and the kind of soil used. I will simply mention that habitual bursters want a lighter soil, as a rule, and what may be called light treatment—no solid beds, a sunny situation, careful watering, a high temperature, etc. A good dusting of air-slacked lime over the soil about once a month will help to correct evils traceable to overwatering.

Some varieties will burst in spite of anything, but most varieties respond liberally to the right treatment. Some growers use a small rubber band : on bursted flowers, which is put on sometimes after the flowers are cut and sometimes before the bud shows color. The latter way seems the more sensible, and in obstinate cases these rubber bands prevent much loss. But the ideal way, as has been suggested in the first part of this article, is to correct the evil through proper selection in the raising of new varieties. J.

A Prize Hydrangea.

The fine specimen hydrangea illustrated herewith was grown by William Robertson, gardener to John W. Pepper, of Jenkintown, Pa. Mr. Robertson gives the following particulars with regard to culture: "I find the best way to grow hydrangeas is to flower them every other year. The plants flowered last year I take out of the pots, shake most of the soil away from the roots and plant out in the field in good rich soil, pruning them well back. I lift the plants about the end of September and find in this way that almost every shoot flowers."

Florists' Plant Notes.

ANTIRRHINUM.

A bench of white antirrhinum, or snapdragon, planted up now will produce an abundance of flowers during the winter and spring months. Used in designs and for mixing with other flowers the white

are quite useful, although the colored varieties are of little importance to the florist. Lift them with a good ball of earth and plant them in rich soil about a foot apart, cutting off all the old flowers and seed pods before transplanting. A carnation house temperature will grow them, although 5° warmer is all the better. They require copious waterings and heavy feeding after the plants are established, as the soil will soon be filled with a mass of roots.

AZALEAS.

Azaleas summered over should be in good condition by this time. If they were properly handled during the past few months with respect to watering and syringing, they should be strong well-formed plants with the foliage dark and green and the buds well set. They must be removed to the greenhouse before the slightest frost touches them, as the first frost blasts the buds and renders them useless for the following winter. A cool house with a temperature of about 40° at night is about right in which to winter them. The old plants can be forced into flower much earlier than those imported this coming fall. Given a good heat, four weeks is ample time in which to force such varieties as Vervaeneana, Deutsche Perle, Simon Mardner and Mme. Van der Cruysen.

GERANIUMS.

About September 1 is the proper time to propagate the main batch of geraniums for the spring trade. It is safe to say that fully half the geraniums used for bedding are scarlet and crimson varieties. S. A. Nutt, crimson, and Alphonse Riccard, scarlet, are two of the best double varieties in cultivation, while Queen of the West for scarlet and Glory of Lyons for crimson are good single sorts. Other good double ones useful in smaller quantities are La Favorite and Countess of Harcourt, white; Beaute Poitevine, fine salmon; Mme. Jaulin, light pink; Marquis de Castellane, maroon; Frances Perkins, pink; Jean Viaud, shell pink. The best single varieties are Mrs. E. G. Hill, salmon; L'Aube, white; Mme. Bruant, white veined with carmine and Dryden, brilliant red. The variegated

types, such as Mrs. Pollock, Mount of Snow and Mme. Salleroi are also best propagated at this time.

Select strong end cuttings, leaving an eye at the base, and pot off at once into 2¼-inch pots. A little wilting does no harm perhaps, but neither will it do any good, so after the first good watering shade them from the bright sun with newspapers for a few days after potting. Hold them a little on the dry side until rooted, and do not sprinkle them as in the case of other cuttings, or fungus is sure to start. The soil should be a sandy loam, not too rich, for they are not expected to grow very much before the first of the year. A light, dry house of about 50° at night is what they require during the winter and spring. ·

Rose geraniums and . the ivy-leaved varieties do not root as easily as the others, and are best started in sand in the propagating house. . Use clean, fresh sand and hold them on the dry side until rooted. The old stock plants can be left outside a few weeks longer, but before heavy frost comes they should be lifted and placed into 4-inch pots, trimming the roots a little and cutting back the top to within four or five inches from the pots. If wanted for stock from which to propagate during the winter, grow them right along in an ordinary temperature, otherwise keep them on the dry side until about February 1, when a shift to a 5-inch size is necessary.

HELIOTROPE.

A bench of heliotrope planted at this time will yield good returns during the winter. Use rich soil and give them a light place with a temperature of about 55°. Plants for this purpose should have been grown along in pots all summer, as they do not sit so well when grown outside. In the absence of pot plants, however, it is possible to transfer them from the outside if they are lifted carefully and cut back to within six inches of the g ound, keeping them close and shaded for a few days. They can stand plenty of liquid manure when well established.

ROMAN HYACINTHS. .

The first consignment of Roman hyacinths will soon arrive and a batch should be started at once for early forcing. It is a good plan to start them at intervals of two or three weeks until late into the fall, as it is more difficult and sometimes impossible to keep them from coming along too fast in spring if they are all started early. Any old carnation soil may be used. Plant them in flats of a convenient size for one man to handle, 3x12x16 inches being about the right dimensions. The bulbs should be set about one-half inch apart. Give them a thorough soaking after planting and cover the boxes with about one-eighth of an inch of sand before putting on the covering of soil. The purpose of the sand is to allow the soil on the boxes to be easily removed when the bulbs are brought inside for forcing. Three inches of soil covering is sufficient. An occasional watering may be necessary unless rain supplies the needed moisture.

CYCLAMENS.

The seed of Cyclamen Persicum should be sown as soon as possible for next year's stock. They can be sown up to the first of the year, although the later sown plants will not be as satisfactory, coming into bloom quite late. Use light soil in which to sow them, press the seed into the surface and cover slightly with light, sandy soil. Keep moderately

PRIZE HYDRANGEA GROWN BY WM. ROBERTSON, PHILADELPHIA, PA.

THE S. A. F. VISITORS AT VAUGHAN'S GREENHOUSES, WESTERN SPRINGS, ILL., AUGUST, 22.

moist and shaded from the sun until the seed germinates, which it will in about four weeks. As soon as the little plants have formed bulbs about the size of a small pea, give them 3-inch pots and place them on a light bench in a temperature of about 55°. It is a serious mistake to neglect these little plants at any time during the winter and the spring rush, for they must never be stunted during their growing period.

Plants to be used this coming Christmas should be given their flowering pots, a 6, 7 or 8-inch size. Use good soil mixed with leaf mould and sand, and above all, see that the drainage in the pots is perfect. A handful of charcoal, or several potsherds in the bottom of the pots will serve the purpose. Pot them just deep enough to have the top of the bulb even with or a little above the surface of the soil. If they are growing outside in a frame, syringe them well several times a day, and protect from the sun during the hot hours of the day by stretching a cheesecloth over the frame. A free circulation all around the plants is necessary, and plenty of room is required to permit the leaves to develop properly. To keep down aphis, scatter tobacco stems between the pots, renewing about once a month. Where fumigation is possible, this should be done regularly once a week. All the plants should be brought inside by the middle of September, and given a light place in a temperature of 55° at night. Standing them on inverted pots to bring them nearer the glass is a good plan. G.

CHESTER, PA.—Edward Delahunt, one of the pioneer florists of this place died on August 5.

POMFRET, CONN.—A. J. Newell, who has been in charge of the J. S. Bailey place at West Roxbury, Mass., is to succeed Thos. Beattie at Mrs. Clarke's place here.

Worms in Carnation Benches.

ED. AM. FLORIST:—Kindly inform me what I can do to eradicate worms that are now infesting the soil in my carnation benches and eating into the buds as per sample enclosed herewith. The soil used was taken from an old asparagus bed that has been heavily manured for the past thirty years, spaded, but never plowed up. Is there any solution that can be used to spray the buds without injuring same or that will soak the ground properly without detriment to the roots? There is no injury done to the roots apparently. They appear only at night, eating into the heart of the buds. J. S.

The sample of worms received is a common form of millipedes often found among decaying vegetable matter. The writer has never known this insect to stray far from the soil in quest of food and is therefore inclined to doubt whether some other pest is not to blame for the trouble. Suspicion will point to cut worms rather than to millipedes, for it is their habit to come forth at night and climb up among the tender growths to feed, hiding among the loose soil at the base of the plants during the day. They often escape notice, unless a vigorous search is instituted, being of a dark brown color, very near the color of the soil. There is nothing that could be sprayed upon the plants or the soil that would dispose of the worms in just the way that "J. S." has in mind, without injuring the plants.

Chewing insects must be reached from within, through their digesting apparatus, not from without, with a poison such as Paris green, Dalmatian powder or hellebore. Paris green is best diluted at the rate of a teaspoonful to a gallon of water and sprayed on the parts of the plants attacked. Dalmatian powder and hellebore are dusted on with an ordinary bellows at the rate of a pound to about 1,000 plants. Smoking would no doubt prove of some benefit, but should be done

in the dead of night, when the insects are out feeding. For the millipedes trapping would be helpful. Cut up some potatoes and lay them all over the benches, cut side down, and, examine early in the morning, removing whatever worms may be hiding under them. Two or three of these methods persistently carried out in conjunction will dispose of the millipedes and cut worms, if there are any. J.

Painted Tomatoes.

State Dairy and Food Commissioner Warren, of Pennsylvania, has announced that retail grocers here recently have received among the orders for canned tomatoes, packages which, upon close examination, proved to be a miscellaneous assortment of vegetables, including a few green tomatoes and red paint, the whole having the appearance of ripe tomatoes.

Agents detailed to investigate found that red paint was used to a great extent in coloring worthless and unripe tomatoes and that other coloring matter also was used to give a ripe appearance to worthless canned vegetables of various kinds.

Forcing Lilium Longiflorum.

A very successful grower of Japanese longiflorum lilies says: "Keep the bulbs cool and unsprouted, planting about the first week in October. Bulbs so treated seem to come on faster than those planted a month earlier and have been successfully bloomed for Easter. The bulbs should be set deep in the pots so that the top of each bulb is covered with two inches of soil. Two 7 to 9-inch bulbs may be put in a 6-inch pot. The object in covering so deep with soil is to get a good growth of feeding roots which sprout out of the flower stalk just at the top of the bulb. It seems that no grower succeeds well with lilies who does not secure a good growth of these upper feeding roots.

St. Louis.

NO PERCEPTIBLE CHANGE IN MARKET.—
ST. LOUIS THE NEXT CONVENTION CITY.
—DAHLIAS AT SHAW'S GARDEN.—MEET-
ING OF BOWLING CLUB.—CITY NEWS.

One might say of the market conditions
here, "It's the same old news" and in
truth that is so. Prices remain the same
except for gladioli and tuberoses, which
are quoted at a lower figure, as so many
are sent in. American Beauty roses, as
well as other varieties are showing an
improvement in quality with each shipment. Carnations continue small and
short stemmed with color better. Tuberoses are of first quality with enough
energy in to meet any demand. Some
fine Semple asters are offered in lots sufficient to supply the immediate demand.

Now that St. Louis has been selected
by the S. A. F. as the convention city for
1904 the sooner plans are formulated
and put in execution the more successful
the meeting will be. The St. Louis florists
have much to do, but by bending every
energy there will be no doubt of the
outcome. J. J. Beneke, vice-president of
the society, says that he fully appreciates
the amount of work necessary, and that
he intends to appoint the necessary committees as soon as possible.

There are some people who believe that
dahlias cannot be grown successfully in
this vicinity. A visit to Shaw's garden
would do much toward dispelling that
idea, as a most notable collection is
coming into flower. The plants are full
of buds, heavy with foliage, and of good
vigorous growth. The collection consists of about 150 species and varieties.
Is it not a good opportunity to take
notes?

It is evident from the expressions heard
about town, that those who attended
the convention had a big time. Everyone says, "You missed it by not going."
But wait until next year. Why our side
attraction, the World's Fair, will more
than compensate for coming.

The bowling club will meet as usual on
Monday night. The box of cigars won
—perhaps lost, as it was a consolation
prize—at Milwaukee will be "on tap."
All the men who can be present ought to
do so as the club needs new material.

Lyster H. Dewey, botanist in charge of
fiber plants at the U. S. department of
agriculture passed through the city Monday enroute to Washington, D. C. He
has been investigating the fiber plants of
Mexico.

There are no better caladiums—now
known as Colocasia Antiquorum, var.,
esculenta—anywhere than one sees at
Tower Grove Park. Some are more than
seven feet high and still growing.

Geo. S. McClure, of Buffalo, N. Y., has
been stopping with his son, G. E. Mc-
Clure, for a few days. He is on his way
home from Milwaukee, where he has
been attending the convention.

W. H. Gullett, of Lincoln, Ill., is supplying the St. Louis market with good
American Beauty roses.

W. F. Kasting, of Buffalo, N. Y., is
shipping some fine Semple asters to the
St. Louis market.

F. J. Foster says that this has been the
most profitable season since he engaged
in business.

Con. Winter visited with friends in
Sedalia, Mo., on Sunday, August 23.
                                    T. K. B.

PORTSMOUTH, N. H.—All the stock in
the Greenhouses at the Frank Jones
estate is to be sold off and the houses
shut down.

Philadelphia.

ANOTHER QUIET WEEK FOR THE TRADE.—
ROSES PLENTIFUL.—PHILADELPHIA FLO-
RISTS RETURNED FROM MILWAUKEE.—
COMMENTS.—ANOTHER PRIZE FOR ADEL-
BERGER.—NEW FIRM.

Nearly all of the local tradesmen have
returned from the convention and report
having had a great time. They did not
get to see as much of Milwaukee as they
would have liked, as the two days,
Wednesday and Thursday, were so taken
up with the convention and the departure on Friday was so early that most of
the sight-seeing was done in Chicago.
The steamer excursion to Chicago was a
real pleasure and the destination was
reached all too soon. The banquet at
the Auditorium and the concert at the
Coliseum came as a surprise. The western boys certainly know now to do
things and the warmth of their hospitality will ever be remembered.

Business during the past week has been
very quiet and stock is accumulating.
Asters move slowly at from 50 cents to
$1 per hundred. Carnations command
about the same price as asters, being
mostly field grown. Roses are plentiful,
American Beauty, with extra long stems
selling at $2 per dozen, while those with
from eighteen inches to two feet of stem
are sold at from 75 cents to $1 per dozen.
Japanese lilies at $3 per hundred are dis-
posed of slowly.

The J. Wolff Moore Company will succeed Mrs. Julius Wolff, who for so many
years has conducted an establishment on
Columbia avenue above Broad street.
The new firm will be managed by Mrs.
Wolff's son-in-law and a new store will
be opened almost across the street, corner of Carlisle and Columbia avenues
about September 1.

Godfrey Aschmann, with his son
Howard, sailed for Antwerp on the
steamer Ryndam August 19. Mr. Aschmann will visit the different growers in
Holland and vicinity and purchase plants
in the interest of his business. During
his absence the business will be conducted
by his sons.

The bowlers are being congratulated
and welcomed with open arms. Adelberger, who was high man and won four
prizes found another one on his return
home. The stork had left him an eight
and one-half-pound boy. This makes
seven in all.   K.

Syracuse, N. Y.

SUMMER QUIET STILL HOLDS SWAY.—
BRIGHT OUTLOOK FOR SEPTEMBER.—
HENRY MORRIS RECEIVES VOTE OF
THANKS FOR CANNA SPECIMENS.—SOME
LOCAL FLORISTS ATTEND PICNIC.

Several Syracuse florists attended the
annual picnic of the Utica Florists at
Buchanan's grove Wednesday, August
12. There were also florists present from
Ilion, Little Falls, Canajoharie, Schenec-
tady and Rome. The Syracuse party
consisted of W. J. Quinlan, Robert H. C.
Bard, A. H. Davis, John F. Dunn, T. D.
Grenmann, David Campbell, superintendent of city parks, William Burt, J.
M. Dutton, John F. Dow, J. H. Huller,
S. F. Ham and S. F. Ham, Jr. Aside
from a clambake a programme of sports
was held where prizes offered by Syracuse
and Utica merchants were competed for.
Utica beat Syracuse 11 to 5 in the ball
game.

At the meeting of the Florists' Club of
Philadelphia a vote of thanks was
tendered Henry Morris of this city for
the specimens of the Cannas Lord Beresc-

ford and Sir Thomas Lipton which he
sent to the exhibition at Horticultural
Hall in Philadelphia. Mr. Morris is also
in receipt of a personal letter from Edwin
Lonsdale of the club, formerly of this
city, telling his experience in the matter
of finding sports from cannas. Mr.
Lonsdale found some sports from Robusta
although some experts deny that cannas
will sport. Mr. Morris' cannas were
found among Robusta and he believes
that they are bona fide sports.

The usual lull in business is now on
but florists are looking forward to September with more than usual interest.
The first week in September brings the
National Association of Letter Carriers
here for their annual convention and the
second week has the New York state
fair when President Roosevelt will be in
the city. The floral exhibition at the
state fair will be larger and more varied
than usual. Asters and golden glow
are the popular flowers at present. The
asters are especially good this year.
There is a large trade in golden glow
roots. Carnations are scarce and roses
are poor.

W. S. Wheadon, of P. R. Quinlan &
Company has plans for some new
designs that ought to attract a great
deal of attention at the state fair next
month.   A. J. B.

Buffalo.

TRADE SLOW EXCEPT FOR FUNERAL WORK.
—A NOVEL WINDOW DESIGN.—RETURN OF
MILWAUKEE CROWD.—VARIOUS ITEMS OF
INTEREST.

L. H. Neubeck has all his houses down
and has started to rebuild on his former
site at Main and High streets, where he
has a long lease. A modern store and
some greenhouses will be erected. Louie
is to be congratulated on his success in
his short business career.

The Milwaukee delegation has returned
and all say it was a great convention.
While we should have liked to see our
Prof. Cowell president, our congratulations go heartily to Phil. Breitmeyer,
who will certainly fill the office in a most
able manner.

S. A. Anderson had a very pretty
window for the national yacht races, it
being a yacht under sail, a good breeze
keeping the sails full at all times. It was
named Reliance and again Shamrock,
but for the time being will be called
Reliance.

Trade has been rather slow until the
last of the week, when the death of a
very prominent mason and an alderman
gave all plenty of work. The different
designs were very fine, Palmer, Rebstock
and Anderson handling the largest
orders.

We were all agreeably surprised to have
Philip Scott, from Denver, Colo., drop in
on us Saturday, and only hope that he
can remain a week or more to renew old
acquaintances, but that baby is home
and papa must be there.

J. H. Rebstock has secured the services
of Wm. J. Pufpaff, formerly with Burge-
vin Brothers, Kingston, N. Y., as foreman
in his greenhouses. The former foreman
has bought out Louis Rapin, of Pine
Hill.

The consecration of the new Roman
catholic bishop of Buffalo caused all the
principal buildings to be decorated a few
days ago and a great many palms and
gladioli were used.

W. J. Palmer is very busy at his Lancaster greenhouses with new building
and the like. He is only at the store a
very short time each day.

Next week will see elaborate decorations in flowers, palms and flags, it being the conclave of the Knight Templars of New York state and 10,000 persons are expected here.

Now that the convention is over, active work will be resumed in the club to help along the chrysanthemum show.

J. H. Rebstock has been removed to his home and is fast improving from his recent injury.

S. A. Anderson and family are at Crystal beach for a week.

Two good rains have brightened things considerably. BISON.

Toronto.

CANADIAN CONVENTION DISCUSSED AT A MEETING OF LOCAL ASSOCIATION.—WEDDINGS AND SOCIAL FUNCTIONS HELP BUSINESS SOMEWHAT.—STOCK IN GOOD SHAPE BUT MUCH GOES TO WASTE.—LOCAL NEWS NOTES.

A fairly well attended meeting of the Toronto Gardeners' and Florists' Association was held in St. George's hall on Tuesday, August 18. Business relating to the coming convention occupied the time and ways and means were considered for the entertainment of the many visitors that are expected. President Manton, of the Canadian Horticultural Association has been unceasing in his efforts to have a large assembly of florists gathered here, and from present indications it is expected the attendance will be much larger than at any of the previous conventions. All the intending exhibitors will have no trouble in getting their goods in to or out of the exhibition grounds, as there will be a customs officer on the grounds, and while the goods are exhibited they will be practically the same as if they were in a bonded warehouse. If these goods are returned there will be no difficulty whatever, or if they should be sold on the grounds the customs officer will release them after the payment of the necessary duties. The space already taken up by the intending exhibitors is large, and this section alone will compensate many visitors who will come miles to see the new things.

There has been a number of small weddings and social affairs which is helping out the retailers, although the volume of business is not sufficient to relieve the growers of the quantities of roses that are cut at the present time. The quality of stock continues to get better and there are good blooms of nearly all varieties of roses, but many of them are going to waste. Carnations are picking up and several growers are cutting some fair young stock. Lilies continue to be plentiful, sweet peas are of better quality and the later varieties of asters are now coming in and are very good.

Geo. Hollis has been making a quality of gladioli. He has been cutting very large flowers of Burpee's double flowering helianthus, which proves attractive in the window and finds ready sale. His greenhouses are in better shape than they have been for some years. Chrysanthemums are looking very good and some good blooms are expected.

John Hand, who was reported in so critical a condition in my last report, died on Friday night, August 21. His family in their bereavement has the sincere sympathy of the many florists who had the pleasure of John's acquaintance.

The harvesters' excursion to the great northwest, which took so many from

our midst, also gathered in Ed. Sinclair, who has gone to Manitoba, the attractions of the floral business seeming insufficient to keep him here.

H. Waters, of Norway, is spending a few holidays in Brampton. His health has been bad, but by the change it is expected that he will go back much improved.

Grobba & Wandrey, of Mimico, are the first this season to arrive with freesias. It is a rare occurence to have these flowers sent in so early.

The first chrysanthemums have been cut by R. Jennings, of Brampton.
H. G. D.

Los Angeles.

SCARCITY OF GOOD GROWERS IN THIS VICINITY.—TWO NEW ESTABLISHMENTS. — AMERICAN BEAUTY EXPERIMENT.— CARNATIONS AT GRACE HILL NURSERIES. —EXPRESS RATE BROUGHT BACK TO OLD SCALE.—SOME ITEMS OF INTEREST.

The greatest trouble growers have in this country is their inability to secure good men who will accept a position and stay with it. An eastern grower is not worth his salt until he has been on a place for two or three years, and his experiments are costly; by that time his employer has lost all patience and lets him go. There is a dearth of good men who are acquainted with the conditions and who are capable of producing the goods. I do not know one single man in Southern California who is capable of going to a nursery and doing everything as it properly should be done. There is plenty of opportunity for good conscientious men who want steady positions at good wages, who are capable growers of roses, carnations and general stock.

Two thoroughly new and up to date florists' establishments are the latest additions to the craft in this city. Vawter's new wholesale and retail store on South Spring street, is as its name implies, and the American Florist is the name of the other. If the latter does as well as its namesake in its line it will be a credit. The proprietor is a brother of O. A. Saakes, proprietor of the Central Park Floral Company.

Geo. Watson, superintendent of the Grace Hill Nurseries, reports that he now has eight houses full of carnations about equally divided among the following varieties: Enchantress, Lawson, Roosevelt, Queen Louise, Norway and Estelle. The success that he has attained with these eastern varieties in so short a time in a climate which is to them new and supposedly undesirable, is something remarkable.

The American Beauty experiment is still going on. One house, 200 feet long, at the Redondo Floral Company's gardens, is devoted to them and they are branching out beautifully and showing a splendidly healthy growth. It is predicted that they will be a success this year, and if they are, the growth of this magnificent rose will become general in these parts and San Francisco will be the loser thereby.

Through a united effort made by the florists of this city the express rate which was increased to one and one-half merchandise has been restored to the general special and as a result happiness reigns. Of course their rule only applies to shipments among the trade. Individuals must pay the excess rate.

Carnations are very poor at present, owing to the heat, and all being outdoor stock. They retail at 25 cents per dozen. Asters are a drug. Amaryllis Belladona

is plentiful but sells readily at $1 per dozen, and none are wasted. Roses are scarce, very few being found at any price.

A. F. Borden, manager of the Redondo Floral Company, spent his vacation at Catalina Island and says he did not catch any big fish.

I understand that H. H. Friend, the design maker at the Redondo Floral Company is about to become a Benedict.

Morris Goldenson, the Third Street florist, is spending a well earned vacation at San Francisco.

This is renovation week and the various stores are getting a coat of paint and paper. POPPY.

Spokane, Wash.

Virgil T. Case, of V. T. Case & Company, wholesale and retail dealers in hay, grain and mill feed, contemplates the opening soon of a wholesale and retail seed store, where he expects to conduct an up-to-date establishment. Mr. Case has been managing his present business for the past seven years and the success with which he has met, can best be appreciated by dropping around to the corner of Mill street and First avenue. Mr. Case has placed an order for a carload of seed for a starter, to be delivered this winter, when he will be open for business. He has associated with him Zenas A. Pfile, who has quite an extensive practical experience in horticulture and floriculture. We anticipate for them a successful establishment and one that will merit the confidence of the community.

It Is to Laugh.

WHAT THE WIND HEARD.

"So you are really going to 'leave,' are you?"

As will readily be guessed, it was the stately old chestnut that spoke.

"No," replied the stately oak. "Too much trouble to pack my trunk. Do you twig?"

Amid the stillness that followed nothing was heard but the sound of the weeping willow.—*Chicago Tribune.*

NEWPORT, VT.—J. F. Farrant will occupy handsome new quarters in the new Pratt building.

SPRINGFIELD, MO.—W. A. Chalfant is adding to his range three houses of Dietsch short-roof construction.

DOWNER'S GROVE, ILL.—Gelion & Wolf are making improvements in their greenhouse on North Washington street.

SIOUX CITY, IA.—J. C. Rennison lost about 3,000 square feet of glass by hail August 16, covered by insurance.

GRAND RAPIDS, MICH.—James Schols is adding 1,000 feet of glass. He grows Campbell and Imperial violets exclusively.

STROUDWATER, ME.—Fred. Waterhouse, a well known market gardener, died suddenly on August 10, aged 65 years.

ROCHESTER, N. Y.—The E. R. Fry Company has made a general assignment for the benefit of it's creditors. The stock and other assets were turned over to Attorney A. Mosher.

ATHOL, MASS.—George W. Sutherland is remodeling the entire establishment of the late James Sutherland, Jr., taking out the five hot-water heaters and replacing them by a 75-horse-power steam boiler.

THE AMERICAN FLORIST

NINETEENTH YEAR.

Subscription, $1.00 a year. To Europe, $2.00.
Subscriptions accepted only from those
in the trade.

Advertisements, on all-except cover pages.
10 Cents a Line. Agate; $1.00 per inch.
Cash with Order.

No Special Position Guaranteed.

Discounts are allowed only on consecutive insertions, as follows:—6 times, 5 per cent; 13 times,
10 per cent; 26 times, 20 per cent;
52 times, 30 per cent.

Cover space sold only on yearly contract at
$1.00 per inch, net, in the case of the two
front pages, regular discounts applying only to the back pages.

The Advertising Department of the AMERICAN
FLORIST is for florists, seedsmen and nurserymen
and dealers in wares pertaining to those lines only.

Orders for less than one-half inch space not accepted.

Advertisements must reach us by Wednesday to
secure insertion in the issue for the following
Saturday.   Address
AMERICAN FLORIST CO., Chicago.

MONTANA florists with glass figure on
making $1 per square foot, but expenses
run high.

Nolens Volens.

AMERICAN FLORIST CO.:—I like your
paper best of all. I subscribed for the
—— b-cause they persisted in sending me
free sample copies, though I never wrote
them in my life.
Salem, Ind.   O. P. FORNVCE, Florist.

Steam Boiler for Heating.

ED. AM. FLORIST:—I have a horizontal
tubular steam boiler, the inside dimensions of which are 2½x8 feet, with
twenty-eight 1¾-inch flues. Firebox
measures 2x2½x3 feet; top of the boiler
is nineteen inches below paths in greenhouse, which slope one and one-half feet
up to the end farthest from boiler. The
greenhouse is 23x150 feet and a temperature of 55° to 60° is desired. Can the
above boiler be made to answer the purpose if hot water is used instead of steam?
Kindly inform me as to size and arrangement of pipes, also the best kind of fuel
to use.   H. L.
It will be well to use three 3-inch flow
pipes and nine 2½-inch returns. The
boiler is rather small for economical
firing but will work with hot water even
better than with steam. A good grade
of steam lump coal should be used.
                                L. R. TAFT.

Greenhouse Piping.

ED. AM. FLORIST:—We are building
three houses, measuring 17x190 feet,
gutters seven feet from ground, eleven
feet to ridge. Range runs north and
south. The three houses are to be planted
as follows: First or west house, roses;
second, carnations, and third, general
plants. There will be no glass in ends of
the buildings, but the first house will
have three feet of glass in the side. Two
forty horse-power tubular boilers will be
placed at north end of range. We have
1½-inch pipe for coils. Shall feed into
coils at north end, and at south end run
the drain into a trap placed in the southwest corner. The first and second houses
will have two solid beds, eighteen inches
high. How many runs of pipe would it
be necessary to use in each house for
coils?   W. & C.
For the rose house use nine pipes, if the
glass is in one side only and ten if there
is glass in both sides. For the carnation
house use seven pipes and put eight in

the third house. One 40-H. P. boiler
will readily heat these houses, but the
second boiler will be desirable in case of
an accident.   L. R. TAFT.

Boiler Heating Capacity.

ED. AM. FLORIST:—Have two boilers,
one measuring 5x14 feet with forty
4-inch flues and the other 3½x12 feet
with forty-four 3-inch flues. How many
feet of 1¼-inch pipe will the above boilers
heat respectively, main pipes being covered with asbestos moulded covering,
chimneys high with good draft and burning Pocahontas coal?   J.
The larger boiler is perhaps of sixty-
horse-power and will handle about 6,000
square feet of radiation or 13,500 feet of
1¼-inch pipe. The other is of about
forty-horse-power, and has a capacity of
4,000 square feet of steam radiation or
9,000 feet of 1¼-inch pipe. While this is
the usual method of estimating steam
radiation, it is always well to make an
allowance of twenty-five per cent and
11,000 and 6,500 square feet respectively
will be a safer estimate.   L. R. TAFT.

Pipe for Greenhouse Heating.

ED. AM. FLORIST:—We have one even
span house, measuring 20x100 feet and
will add two more of the same size. One-
half of the old house will be planted to
carnations and the other half to mixed
stock and both new houses to bedding
plants. Have enough 3-inch wrought
iron pipe for four runs and a quantity of
2½-inch pipe. Please give arrangement
of pipes for these houses. Will one 4-inch
flow from boiler supply these three
houses? Would a smaller size of pipes
for returns be any more economical?
                               E. E. S.
For the old house use two 2½-inch
flows and eight 2½-inch returns. In the
new houses use two 3-inch flows and
eight or nine 2½-inch returns, according
to the temperature desired. One flow
can be on each plate or on the purlin
posts, and the returns can be either on
the side walls or under the benches.
There should be a 4-inch flow and return
to each of the houses. If 2½-inch pipe is
on hand it can be used to good advantage.   L. R. TAFT.

Greenhouse Building.

Waterbury, Conn.—M. Hemingway, one
house.
Northumberland, Pa.—E. H. Luck-
hart, one house.
Philadelphia, Pa. — Overbrook Sem-
inary, two conservatories.
Warren, Ohio.—Gaskill's Greenhouses,
rebuilding two houses and adding one
house.
Newton Center, Mass.—Frederick Ayer,
conservatory.
Trenton, N. J.—R. Abbott, conservatory.
Greenfield, Mich.—A. J. Stahelin, a
boiler shed and one greenhouse, 24x200.
Woburn, Mass.—J. T. Maloney, range
of vegetable houses.
Ashland, Mass.—Fales & Company,
range of houses.
Johnstown, N. Y.—T. Barson, range of
commercial houses.
Madison, N. J.—Jeff. Doremus, three
rose houses, each 100 feet long.
Mystic, Conn.—H. M. Fitch, one house.
Towanda, Pa.—G. H. Cox, one house.
Wyomissing, N. Y.—G. H. Hoskin, one
house.

Silverdale, Pa.—W. Allabough, one
tomato house.
Lincoln, Mass.—Flint Brothers, range
of cucumber houses.
Baldwinville, Mass.—H. Graham, one
cucumber house.
Malden, Mass.—J. J. McCormack,
range of houses.
Plainfield, N. J.—Mrs. G. H. Babcock,
conservatory.
Baltimore, Md.—Riverside Park, palm
house and two wings.
Maspeth, N. Y.— Herman Maenner,
steel frame house.
Mason, Mich.—Addition to greenhouse.
Lacombe, Alta, N. W. T.—C. A. Giber-
son, an additional house.
Ft. Madison, Ia.—J. M. Auge, one car-
nation house.
Fall River, Mass.—John Lannagan, a
house 25x79.
Byfield, Mass.—M. Graham, one cucum-.
ber house.
Northampton, Mass.—R. B. Graves,
one house.
West Hoboken, N. J.—John Birnie, two
houses.
North Salem, Mass.—G. E. Ward &
Sons, one violet house.
Lynn, Mass.—F. J. Delanski, range of
houses.
Burgettstown, Pa.—Goodwin & Sons,
one house 20x100 and one 20x90.
College Point, N. Y.—G. Golsner's Sons,
four houses.
Valley Falls, R. I.—John J. Kelly, one
house, 25x132.
Utica, N. Y.—W. P. Pfiefer, a carnation
house, 30x125.
Exeter, N. H.—Geo. W. Hillard, a rose
house, 34x150.
North Beverly, Mass.—Geo. W. Gilnes,
two cucumber houses.
Norwalk, Conn.—R. G. Hanford, a car-
nation house, 20x140.
Fruitvale, Cal. — A. Galloway, one
house 26x135.
Gloucester, Mass.—A. B. Tuck, one
house.
Danbury, Conn.—T. Harrison Judd,
one house.
Maynard, Mass.—Arthur Silloway, one
house.
Durham, N. H.—State Agricultural
College, range of houses.
Pittsburg, Pa.—A. R. Peacock, one
greenhouse.
Essex, Conn.—Frederick Scholes, two
houses.
Ashland, Pa.—C. E. Nelson, two lettuce
houses, each 30x300.
Lenox, Mass.—R. W. Patterson, range
of conservatories.
Richford, Vt.—H. C. Thayer, one house.
Peoria, Ill.—J. C. Murray, one house.
Cincinnati, O.—Thomas Windrum,
three houses 22x150 feet.

Chicago.

MARKET ABOUT THE SAME AS LAST WEEK.
— GOOD AMERICAN BEAUTY STOCK
APPEARS.—FAKIRS SELL ROSES CHEAP.
—SAD DEATH OF LITTLE RAYMOND RHIN-
BERG.—LOCAL NEWS OF THE DAY.

Market conditions are about the same
as they were last week, perhaps a little
better, if anything, although growers
are still getting very poor returns for the
stock shipped in. If the present cool
weather continues, it will perhaps help
matters to some extent. The extreme
dullness in business was not noticed so
much during the past couple of weeks on
account of the convention, but the convention now being a thing of the past,
"where no man goes except on the wings
of his dreams," all are brought' more
forcibly to realise the condition of affairs

and it is to be hoped that the fall activity will not be long in making its appearance. Some very good new American Beauty stock is being cut, which is an agreeable change from the monotonous sight of the abundant outdoor flowers that have greeted the vision all summer. Asters are still to be had in any quantity but they are getting poor and many go to waste. There seem to be more Brides than Bridesmaids in sight just at present although neither are overpientiful. Outdoor carnations are holding up well but are not very abundant and some cuttings from greenhouse stock are beginning to be made. Lilies of the valley are looking cool and fresh. Outside summer flowers are an old story but one that is still here. Some of the street fakirs are handling old rose stock at extremely low figures but their dreams of fortune will soon be dispelled, when the trade awakens from its summer nap.

The friends of George Reinberg will be shocked and grieved to learn that his little two-year-old son was drowned in a water tank not far from the house on Saturday, August 22. After the boy was missed and a search was made for him, one of the men accidentally dropped a wrench into the tank and on raking the bottom for the lost tool found the child.

Michael Winandy has made an addition of ten houses to his range. They will be planted chiefly to carnations. He expects to erect nine more houses, in which will be planted carnation stock for spring cutting. A new chimney and boiler room have been completed.

C. L. Washburn the other day again hied himself to the cool shade of the Wisconsin pine woods, only for a brief stay, however, as he will return Monday, August 31.

Carl Netschert, at 187 South Clark street, has purchased the interest of his brother Frank Netschert in the artificial flower trade and will continue the business.

Geo. Piegrass, with Benthey & Company, is very ill and was taken to the Mercy hospital on Wednesday, August 26. We all hope for his speedy recovery.

G. H. Peiser, of the Kennicott Brothers' Company has returned from his extensive tour through the northern part of Wisconsin.

Weiter Brothers have . been cutting some nice American Beauty roses all summer, being very fortunate with this stock.

Miss W. E. Horton, the cheerful cashier at Bassett & Washburn's has returned to her desk after a pleasantly spent vacation.

E. A. Asmus, of E. Buettner & Company, is mending and will take a vacation in the Wisconsin woods.

A more or less general tendency to stomach trouble has been noticed since the Milwaukee episode.

R. Rocklin, with E. H. Hunt, will·take up the matrimonial yoke some time during the coming week.

SITUATIONS, WANTS, FOR SALE.

One Cent Per Word.

Cash with the Adv.

Plant Advs. NOT admitted under this head.

Every paid subscriber to the AMERICAN FLORIST for the year 1903 is entitled to a five-line WANT ADV. (situations only) free, to be used at any time during the year.

Situation Wanted—By experienced grower of cut flowers, as manager of small place. Address
MANAGER, care American Florist.

Situation Wanted—By a single man, as assistant in general greenhouse work. State wages in first letter. A B, care Am. Florist.

Situation Wanted—By experienced gardener, single, to take charge of medium sized private place. Address. THOS. CALLAHAN,
Glen Cove, N. Y.

Help Wanted—Rose growers.
SOUTH PARK FLORAL CO., New Castle, Ind.

For Rent—Sixty-foot greenhouse, 8 room house, two lots, $25 per month; 3181 Elston Ave.
DR. BANGS, 854 N. Robey St., Chicago.

Help Wanted—All-around man for general greenhouse work. Address
T. N. YATES & CO., Mt. Airy, Phila., Pa.

Help Wanted—Assistant in the packing department. Must have experience in filling and packing orders. E. G. HILL CO., Richmond, Ind.

Help Wanted—Florist as assistant in place of 15,000 feet where only cut flowers are grown. Good chance for man who can show good references.
H. HORNBOFF, Tipton, Ind.

Help Wanted—Night fireman, steam boilers, state wages; references required. Address
C. C. POLLWORTH CO.,
454 E. Water St., Milwaukee, Wis.

Help Wanted—An assistant florist on a retail place. State experience and wages expected with board and room. Send references.
I. L. PILLSBURY, Galesburg, Ill.

Help Wanted—Florist: sober, industrious, for general greenhouse work. Send references and wages expected to
W. W. STERTZING, Maplewood Sta., St. Louis.

Help Wanted—A man experienced in packing roses for shipping. We have a good position for a reliable man that understands the business.
SOUTH PARK FLORAL CO., New Castle, Ind.

Help Wanted—Single man competent to grow carnations, roses, bedding stock and general line of plants for town of 12,000 inhabitants. English, Scotch, Swedish, Dutch or German. Room and board. Address
COSMOPOLITAN, care American Florist.

Help Wanted—Young man about 20 to 25 years of age, to do general greenhouse work. This is a good opening for a young man. State wages expected with bed and board. This place is 25 miles from Pittsburgh, Pa. Address-
T. M. FITZGERALD, Beaver, Beaver·Co., Pa.

Help Wanted—An experienced carnation grower. First year $45 per month. If 'ability is proven an increase will be made. Houses all planted; about 3 miles from Cleveland, O.; single man preferred. Address M. BLOT,
Essex Greenhouses, North Olmstead, Ohio.

Wanted—Goldfish. Send prices on all ornamental fish in quantity at once to
THE HULSIKER CO., Des Moines, Ia.

Wanted—Partner. An Italian gardener; must be single and come well recommended and desire engagement for tropical country. Address
ANDY V. FROLEASE,
No. 8303 59th St., New York.

For Sale—Two No. 6, Furman boilers, one brick set, one portable. Prices on application.
J. E. LONG, Holliston, Mass.

For Sale—One No. 30 Wilks hot water boiler with stack complete, used only three months. A bargain for cash. JAMES W. DUNFORD,
R. R. No. 1. Clayton, Mo.

For Sale—Fine old establishment of about 10,000 square feet of glass, one acre or more of ground with or without good dwelling. A bargain. Investigate now if interested. Address
OHIO, care American Florist.

For Sale—In the World's Fair city, three-room house, two greenhouses, one 14x80, one 18x80, one acre of ground; heated by steam; plenty of water. Price $1,300; $600 cash.
LEO EHRERNZ, Webster Grove, Mo.

For Sale or Lease—A nicely located place in the Borough of the Bronx, consisting of t greenhouses: (no stock), hot water heating, windmill, barn, dwelling house and about 2 acres of ground. J. RINGLER, 723 3rd Ave., New York City.

For Sale—Four large size Gorton side feed boilers (for hard or soft coal), 250 caudr size small Gorton side feed, 825; one-pipe sectional Florida heater, 860; one-and a half, 1,000 square feet of glass, 830. Boilers taken out to put in larger one. Write for particulars.
F. FALLON, Roanoke, Va.

Pittsburg.

BUSINESS CONTINUES DULL,—RETURN OF THE MILWAUKEE PARTY.—COMING NUPTIAL.—ITEMS OF LOCAL INTEREST.

Excessively hot weather together with electrical and rain storms help break the monotony while waiting for the business that does not seem to come. Roses are improving nicely; American Beauty is very good and Meteor, Bride, Bridesmaid and Kaiserin are becoming more plentiful. Carnations are much improved. Asters and gladioli are moving very slowly. Greens are abundant.

The Pittsburgers who attended the convention at Milwaukee, arrived home early Wednesday morning, August 26. Their anticipations were more than realized and the entire party unanimously agreed that Milwaukee has established a record for entertaining that will be hard to beat.

The wedding of Gilbert Weaklin and Miss Patten will take place early in September. Mr. Weaklin is held in high esteem by his employers, Randolph & McClements, and his warm friends in the craft, who extend their congratulations and good wishes.

John Bader is making active preparations for his incoming stock of palms and plants. Mr. Bader is an extensive importer and has a very large plant trade throughout western Pennsylvania, eastern Ohio, West Virginia and Virginia.

William Turner, Jr., of Williamsburg, has been selected by the citizens' party to become the candidate for the office of county poor director.

P. S. Randolph, of Randolph & McClements, is visiting the east for the purpose of purchasing palms and decorative plants.

Mr. Campbell, of Castle Shannon, has been cutting some very fine gladioli in spite of the unfavorable weather conditions.

Great consternation continues among the fish in Lake Chatauqua for Phil. Langhans is still there.

The Pittsburg Cut Flower Company is feeling the full force of the prevailing business relaxation.

The Oakwood Rose Gardens, of Oil City, continue to ship in a fine quality of roses.   B. L. M.

Wholesale Flower Markets

MILWAUKEE, Aug. 27.

Roses, Beauty, med. per doz.	1.50	
" short "	.75@1.00	
" Liberty	4.00@ 6	
" Bride, Bridesmaid	4.00@ 6.	
" Meteor, Golden Gate	4.00@ 6	
" Perle	4.00@ 2	
Carnations	1.00@ 2	
Sweet peas		
Smilax	10.00@12.	
Asparagus		50
Gladioli	2.00@ 4.00	
Asters	1.00@ 1.00	

PITTSBURG, Aug. 27

Roses, Beauty, specials, per doz.	2.50@3.50	
" extras "	1.00@2.00	
" No. 1 "	.75@1.00	
" No. 2 "	2.00@ 5.	
" Bride, Bridesmaid	3.00@ 6.	
" Meteor	3.00@ 6.	
" Kaiserin	3.00@ 6.	
" Liberties	3.00@ 6.	
Carnations	1.00@ 1.	
Sweet peas	.50	
Smilax	8.00@12.	
Adiantum	.75@ 1	
Asparagus, strings	30.00@50.	
" Sprengeri	1.00@ 4	
Gladioli	1.00@ 3	
Easter lilies	8.00@12.00	
Asters	.50@ 1.00	

CINCINNATI, Aug. 27.

Roses, Beauty	10.00@35.00	
" Bride, Bridesmaid	3.00@ 6.00	
" Liberty	3.00@ 6.00	
" Meteor, Golden Gate	1.00@ 6.00	
Lily of the valley	3.00@ 4.00	
Asparagus		50.00
Smilax	12.50@15.00	
Gladioli	1.00@ 1.50	
Asters		8.00
Lilium Album and Rubrum	1.00@ 2.00	
		4.00

ST. LOUIS, Aug. 27.

Roses, Beauty, long stem		8.00
" Beauty, medium stem		12.50
" Beauty, short stem	4.	6.
" Liberty	4.	6.
" Bride, Bridesmaid	2.	4.
" Golden Gate	3.00@ 4.	
Carnations	1.	1
Smilax		12
Asparagus Sprengeri	1.	
" Plumosus	1.00@50.00	
Gladioli	1.00@ 3.00	
Ferns	per 1000 1.50	
China Asters	1.00@ 2.00	
Tuberoses	2.00@ 8.10	

Pittsburg Cut Flower Co., Ltd
WHOLESALE FLORISTS.
—————Pittsburg, Pa.

INTERNATIONAL FLOWER DELIVERY.

PASSENGER STEAMSHIP MOVEMENTS.

The tables herewith give the scheduled time of departure of ocean steamships carrying first-class passengers from the principal American and foreign ports, covering the space of two weeks from date of this issue of the AMERICAN FLORIST. Much disappointment often results from attempts to forward flowers for steamer delivery by express, to the care of the ship's steward or otherwise. The carriers of these packages are not infrequently refused admission on board and even those delivered on board are not always certain to reach the parties for whom they were intended. Hence florists in interior cities having orders for the delivery of flowers to passengers on out-going steamers are advised to intrust the filling of such orders to some reliable florist in the port of departure, who understands the necessary details and formalities and has the facilities for attending to it properly. For the addresses of such firms we refer our readers to the advertisements on this page:

FROM	TO	STEAMER	*LINE	DAY	DUE ABOUT
New York	Liverpool	Lucania	1	Sat. Sept. 6, 2:00 p.m.	Sept. 11
New York	"	Etruria	1	Sat. Sept. 13, 9:00 a.m.	Sept. 18
New York	Glasgow	Mongolian	2	Thur. Sept. 3, 2:00 p.m.	Sept. 10
New York	Hamburg	Molike	3	Thur. Sept. 3, 2:30 p.m.	Sept. 10
New York	"	Furst Bismarck	3	Thur. Sept. 10, 10:00 a.m.	Sept. 16
New York	"	Pretoria	3	Sat. Sept. 12, 8:30 a.m.	
New York	Copenhagen	Oscar II	4	Wed. Sept. 2,	
New York	Glasgow	Anchoria	4	Sat. Sept. 5, Noon.	Sept. 16
New York	"	Furnessia	4	Sat. Sept. 12, Noon.	
New York	Southampton	Menominee	5	Fri. Sept. 11, 8:00 a.m.	Sept. 21
New York	"	Philadelphia	5	Wed. Sept. 2, 10:00 a.m.	
New York	"	St. Paul	5	Sat. Sept. 5, 10:00 a.m.	
New York	"	St. Louis	5	Wed. Sept. 9, 10:00 a.m.	
New York	Liverpool	Teutonic	7	Wed. Sept. 2, Noon.	Sept. 9
New York	"	Arabic	7	Wed. Sept. 4, 4:00 p.m.	Sept. 12
New York	"	Germanic	7	Wed. Sept. 9, Noon.	Sept. 17
New York	"	Cedric	7	Fri. Sept. 11, 8:00 a.m.	
New York	London	Minnehaha	6	Sat. Sept. 5, 4:00 p.m.	Sept. 13
New York	"	Mesaba	6	Sat. Sept. 12, 9:00 a.m.	
New York	Antwerp	Zeeland	8	Sat. Sept. 5, 10:00 a.m.	Sept. 14
New York	"	Finland	9	Sat. Sept. 12, 10:00 a.m.	Sept. 21
New York	Havre	La Lorraine	10	Thur. Sept. 3, 10:00 a.m.	
New York	"	La Touraine	10	Thur. Sept. 10, 10:00 a.m.	Sept. 17
New York	Rotterdam	Rotterdam	11	Wed. Sept. 2, 10:00 a.m.	
New York	"	Potsdam	11	Sat. Sept. 9, 10:00 a.m.	Sept. 18
New York	Bremen	K. Wil. Der Grosse	12	Tues. Sept. 1, 10:00 a.m.	Sept. 8
New York	"	Frdk. Der Grosse	12	Thur. Sept. 3, 2:00 p.m.	Sept. 13
New York	"	Kronprinz Wilh.	12	Tues. Sept. 4, 6:30 a.m.	Sept. 15
New York	"	Barbarossa	12	Thur. Sept. 10, Noon.	Sept. 21
New York	Genoa	Printess Irene	12	Sat. Sept. 12, 11:00 a.m.	Sept. 22
New York	"	Citta di Napoli	12	Tues. Sept. 1, 11:00 a.m.	Sept. 18
New York	"	Liguria	12	Tues. Sept. 6, 11:00 a.m.	
Boston	Liverpool	Ivernia	1	Tues. Sept. 8, 10:00 a.m.	Sept. 14
Boston	"	New England	15	Thur. Sept. 6, 8:00 a.m.	Sept. 10
Boston	"	Mayflower	15	Thur. Sept. 10, Noon	Sept. 17
Boston	"	Bohemian	16	Sat. Sept. 5, 8:30 a.m.	
Boston	"	Canadian	16	Sat. Sept. 12, 8:00 a.m.	
Montreal	"	Dominion	16	Sat. Sept. 5, Daylight.	
Montreal	"	Southwark	16	Sat. Sept. 12, Daylight.	
San Francisco	Yokohama	Korea	17	Thur. Sept. 3, 1:00 p.m.	Sept. 22
San Francisco	"	Gaelic	17	Fri. Sept. 11, 1:00 p.m.	Sept. 30
Vancouver	"	Empress of China	19	Mon. Sept. 7,	Sept. 21
Montreal	Liverpool	Tunisian	19	Sat. Sept. 5, 9:30 a.m.	
Montreal	"	Parisian	19	Sat. Sept. 12, 9:30 a.m.	
San Francisco	Honolulu	Alameda	18	Sat. Sept. 5, 11:00 a.m.	Sept. 11
Seattle	Yokohama	Riojun Maru	22	Sat. Sept. 5, a.m.	Sept. 21
Seattle	Hongkong	"	22	Sat. Sept. 5, a.m.	Oct. 6

*1 Cunard; 2 Allen-State; 3 Hamburg-American; 4 Scandinavian-American; 5 Anchor Line; 6 Atlantic Transport; 7 White Star; 8 American; 9 Red Star; 10 French; 11 Holland-American; 12 Italian Royal Mail; 13 North German Lloyd; 14 Fabre; 15 Dominion; 16 Leyland; 17 Occidental and Oriental; 18 Oceanic; 19 Allan; 20 Can. Pacific Ry.; 21 N. Pacific Ry.; 22 Hongkong-Seattle.

INTERNATIONAL FLOWER DELIVERY.

STEAMSHIPS LEAVE FOREIGN PORTS.

FROM	TO	STEAMER	*LINE	DAY	DUE ABOUT
Liverpool	New York	Campania	1	Sat. Sept. 5,	Sept. 11
Liverpool	"	Umbria	1	Sat. Sept. 12,	Sept. 18
Liverpool	"	Majestic	7	Wed. Sept. 2, 5:00 p. m.	
Liverpool	"	Celtic	7	Fri. Sept. 4, 3:00 p. m.	
Liverpool	"	Oceanic	7	Wed. Sept. 9, 4:00 p. m.	Sept. 16
Liverpool	"	Cymbric	7	Fri. Sept. 11, 3:00 p. m.	Sept. 19
Liverpool	Boston	Saxonia	1	Tues. Sept. 8,	Sept. 14
Liverpool	"	Columbus	15	Thur. Sept. 3,	
Liverpool	"	Commonwealth	16	Thur. Sept. 10,	Sept. 17
Liverpool	"	Cestrian	16	Fri. Sept. 4,	
Liverpool	"	Devonian	16	Fri. Sept. 11,	
Liverpool	Montreal	Canada	15	Wed. Sept. 9,	
Liverpool	"	Pretorian	19	Thur. Sept. 3,	
Glasgow	New York	Columbia	5	Sat. Sept. 5,	
Glasgow	"	Astoria	5	Thur. Sept. 10,	
Glasgow	"	Numidian	2	Sat. Sept. 12,	Sept. 22
Genoa	"	Lombardia	12	Mon. Sept. 7,	
Genoa	"	Nord America	12	Mon. Sept. 14,	
Genoa	"	Lahn	13	Thur. Sept. 3,	Sept. 15
Southampton	"	New York	8	Sat. Sept. 5, Noon.	Sept. 12
Southampton	"	Philadelphia	8	Sat. Sept. 12, Noon.	
Southampton	"	Marquette	6	Wed. Sept. 9,	
London	"	Minnetonka	6	Sat. Sept. 5,	
London	"	Minneapolis	6	Sat. Sept. 12,	Sept. 21
Antwerp	"	Vaderland	9	Sat. Sept. 5, Noon.	Sept. 14
Antwerp	"	Kroonland	9	Sat. Sept. 12, 3:00 p. m.	Sept. 21
Hamburg	"	Deutschland	3	Tues. Sept. 1,	
Hamburg	"	Bluecher	3	Thur. Sept. 3,	Sept. 10
Hamburg	"	Auguste Victoria	3	Thur. Sept. 10,	
Hamburg	"	Pennsylvania	3	Sat Sept. 12,	Sept. 22
Havre	"	La Savoie	10	Sat. Sept. 5,	
Havre	"	La Bretagne	10	Sat. Sept. 12,	Sept. 20
Copenhagen	"	Hellig Olav	4	Wed. Sept. 9,	
Rotterdam	"	Ryndam	11	Sat. Sept. 5,	Sept. 14
Rotterdam	"	Noordam	11	Sat. Sept. 12,	
Bremen	"	Kaiser Wilh. II	13	Tues. Sept. 8,	Sept. 15
Bremen	"	Koenig Albert	13	Sat. Sept. 5,	Sept. 14
Sidney	Vancouver	Miowera	20	Mon. Sept. 7,	Oct. 1
Sidney	SanFrancisco	Ventura	8	Mon. Sept. 7,	Sept. 29
Tahiti	"	Mariposa	18	Mon. Aug. 31,	Sept. 12
Hongkong	"	Doric	17	Tues. Sept. 1,	Sept. 28
Hongkong	"	Nippon Maru	17	Tues. Sept. 9,	Oct. 5
Hongkong	Seattle	Shinano Maru	22	Tues. Sept. 8,	Oct. 5

* See steamship list on opposite page.

THE SEED TRADE.

AMERICAN SEED TRADE ASSOCIATION.
S. F. Willard, Pres.; J. Charles McCullough,
First Vice-Pres.; C. E. Kendel, Cleveland, O.;
Sec'y and Treas.
Twenty-second annual convention St. Louis,
Mo., June, 1904.

MERGER & MITCHELL, of New Zealand, are offering new crop cocksfoot.

VISITED CHICAGO: C. R. Root, of Barteldes & Company, Denver, Col.

VAUGHAN'S SEED STORE, Chicago, will introduce a white dwarf nasturtium in the spring of 1904.

MILFORD, CONN.—Albertus N. Clark lost his seed barns by fire the night of August 20, loss approximately $10,000.

As stated in our recent issue nearly all French bulbs will be late this year and hints are also heard of short deliveries.

THE present market price for French Roman hyacinths, twelve to fifteen centimeters, is reported to be about $26 per 1,000. The grade larger than this, twelve to fifteen centimeters and up, is scarce but if to be had will probably be worth $2 more.

Don't Want Beans.

A San Francisco firm cornered the bean crop of that state and then made the discovery that nobody wanted beans. The firm is now among the "has beens."
—*Ohio State Journal.*

Free Advertising.

Many of the newspapers appear anxious to help along the government seed shops with gratuitous advertising. The latest example, from the *Kansas City Journal* of recent date, is reproduced herewith:

Many requests for garden seeds are being received by Delegate Bird S. McGuire. Oklahoma's quota of seeds is 15,000 packages of five packages each, and Mr. McGuire is planning to have this number increased after reaching Washington. All applications should be sent to him at Pawnee as soon as possible, for there may not be enough to supply everybody, and it is desired as many as possible be served, and that as soon as practicable.

A Model Seed Store.

The accompanying illustration is from a photograph of the interior of the new store of the Holmes Seed Company, Harrisburg, Pa. The store is 163 feet deep by forty feet in breadth, which allows easy access in shipping in the rear, the elevator being located in that part of the building. The basement is lathed and plastered, of the same dimensions as the street floor, with a ten-foot ceiling and a cemented floor, which is capable of holding forty cars or more of seed. This is used for the storage of heavy goods, such as beans and peas. The first floor is used for retail business and the rear for wholesale, the second floor being employed for the storage of onion sets and light seeds. The building is centrally located, within five minutes of any railroad station, which gives easy access in shipping. H. L. Holmes, the manager, says that the mail business has increased about 100 per cent, retail business about 100 per cent and wholesale about 140 per cent since they entered the new building. They handle in the retail department ornamental plants, and so

forth, as well as seeds and all requisites for the garden.

Nebraska Seed Crops.

One of our well known and reliable correspondents writes August 25 as follows:

"Our seed crops are not in shape as yet to make any definite reports on, but the general outlook is fair. Some crops promise as well today as any I have ever seen growing, while many others look poor, owing to the land having remained too wet. We never had a nicer acreage arranged for than we had this season. High water and excessive rains, however, disarranged our crop plans, and in many instances prevented proper acreages being planted, while in other cases the crops were finally planted, some of them being fairly mudded in. The result now shows in the vine growths; the dry land has given an excellent growth, while the wet fields are weedy and inferior. They are also rusted a little and in a few instances affected with a root disease. We, however, have no aphis or lice, except in half a dozen instances, where a hill or two has been found affected.

"Cucumbers will average fair. It now looks as though contract orders on most kinds will be filled, with little or no surplus in sight.

"It has been too wet for melons, and they will be very spotted, many entire failures and more shortages.

"Summer squash promise good as do some fields of winter squash. In fact the latter are very good, but acreage is small, owing to backsets and discouragements early in the season.

"The early varieties of corn are coming out well, but the later kinds are yet uncertain, and will depend on weather in September."

Catalogues in Foreign Languages.

A report by the British vice-consul at Aden has been received at the British Foreign Office from which the following extract has been made:

I am glad to say that I have recently received catalogues from British houses in the French language and the French comparative weights and measures, which is a step in the right direction. I would strongly advise our traders to send a card with name, address and business before troubling so much expensive trade circulars and catalogues to consulates. In case a sale exists idea of what trade they can expect all over the world. By the present system no reply reaches them unless a definite question is asked, and remaining in doubt, they continue to send catalogues, many of which must necessarily be of no use whatever in certain parts of the world.

Longfoot Cabbage.

"A very hardy acclimatized variety of the common cabbage is found occasionally in the West Indies, chiefly in negro provision grounds," says a *Garden* correspondent. "It has bright green leaves without the glaucous bloom usually found on some cabbages. It is said to thrive anywhere, and is evidently well suited to dry acrid conditions, where no other kind of cabbage will grow. The negro name of Longfoot at once suggested that it was not unlikely to be closely related to the cabbage grown in the Channel Islands and in the Canary Islands for the purpose of making walking sticks from its stems. This is evidently the case. The growth of the stem is promoted by constantly stripping off the lower leaves. Some specimens

have been known to attain a height of ten feet. The Longfoot cabbage may, however, have other uses, and that is to supply green food for man and beast in time of scarcity. We, therefore, commend this hardy and apparently neglected vegetable to the attention of those living in remote and acrid localities. It is easily propagated by cuttings."

It is to Laugh.

ABOUT THE LIMIT.

The following is a literal copy of an order received by a certain seed dealer, 20 cents being enclosed:

"I want you to send me some flower seeds.

"Aster dwarf german twelve colors
mixed .... 5c.
"Love lies bleeding...................... 5c.
"Canterbury bell......................... 5c.
"Chrysanthemum or a plant a purpose for a crock I want you to
send me .... 5c.
"You never give me a Christmas gift yet. I want you to send me one seed of Marquis of brone cucumber for a present thankey. I want to know if they live out of door all winter. Send soon, good by. S—. J—. S—."

Worcester, Mass.

Business conditions are very satisfactory for this time of the year, as we consider the month of August the dullest of the season. Funeral work, of which there has been considerable, has been the main outlet for stock. Good flowers are plentiful, asters, sweet peas, dahlias and gladioli making up the bulk of the supply. Carnots and Kaiserins are coming in in fair quantity and Liberties and Bridesmaids from early plantings are commencing to appear. Housing carnations is going on briskly and the end of this week will see the majority of the stock planted. Carnations have done very well this season and very little stem-rot has been noticed. Enchantress has made a good growth and looks promising. Chrysanthemums are in fine condition and give promise of splendid blooms later on.

F. B. Madaus has the sympathy of the craft in the loss of his youngest child and the continued illness of the mother.

H. F. A. Lange is making an addition to his boiler house, which will give him a capacity of over 500 tons of coal.

H. F. Littlefield has made several improvements in his store, adding an office and renovating generally.

The Worcester Conservatories have finished planting six houses to roses.

Will A. Lewis, chief clerk for Lange, is in Maine on a two weeks' vacation.
A. H. L.

LIVONIA, N. Y.—The fifth annual exhibition of the Livonia Floral Society took place on August 6.

NEW CASTLE, IND.—Herbert Heller and his mother are spending their vacation at Battle Creek, Mich.

PEKIN, ILL.—Geo. A. Kuhl and wife, together with their son Edward, are at Lake Geneva, Wis., where they will spend a month.

Something Invaluable.

ED. AM. FLORIST:—Enclosed please find $1 in payment for another year's subscription of the AMERICAN FLORIST. It has been invaluable to me during this my first year in the florist business. MARY.E. TRUMBLE.

The Nursery Trade.

AM. ASSOCIATION OF NURSERYMEN.

N. W. Hale, Knoxville, Tenn., Pres.; Frank A. Weber, St. Louis, Mo., Vice-Pres.; George C. Seager, Rochester, N. Y., Sec'y.

Twenty-ninth annual convention, Atlanta, Ga., June, 1904.

Los Angeles, Cal.—The board of park commissioners has requested of the city a general increase of salaries in the park department amounting to $7,572 a year.

Hartford, Conn.—Theodore Wirth, superintendent of the Hartford park system, has been selected to have charge of the layout and embellishment of the Connecticut grounds at the St. Louis exposition. The engagement has been announced of Herbert D. Hemenway, director of the school of horticulture, and Miss Myrtle Hawley of Amherst, Mass.

A newspaper of Toulon, France, "Le Petit Var," prints a letter dated August 11, which claims that the syndicate of growers has practically succeeded in securing the prices demanded by it for most of its members. At a future meeting it is proposed to unify the organization, some members not having definitely expressed themselves at the previous meeting.

Chelsea and Its Nurseries.

The nursery gardens in King's road, which have been so long a feature and ornament of Chelsea, have of late become considerably reduced in area," says the London *Leader*. "They tend to be less and less nurseries, and to become more and more horticultural exhibitions. Last winter Messrs. Veitch tranferred a large portion of their conservatories to Feltham, and most of their growing is now carried on at this and their other country nurseries." About two and one-half acres, however, are still covered by glass and are used by Messrs. Veitch as a show place for plants. Originally their Chelsea nursery covered about five acres. London smoke and fog, which have been gradually increasing their hold on the district, are to blame for this exodus of plants.

Destruction of Woodlice.

The number of lauded preparations for the destruction of the woodlouse is pretty considerable; each orchardist possesses his own favorite remedy, more efficacious, doubtless, than all the others; nevertheless, the woodlouse continues to work havoc. A recent French writer, according to a correspondent of the *Garden*, mentions a process which has given very satisfactory results. In an orchard where he had a free hand to do anything to destroy this pest, M. Mangin had tried a large number of recipes; all of them yielded negative results. At last he hit upon a mixture by means of which he has destroyed whole masses of woodlice. This mixture consists simply of a varnish composed of a light gum-lake mixed with five to ten per cent of lysol. The "body" of this varnish, being constituted of alcohol, moistens and penetrates the parts which shelter certain species of woodlice. All of the parts invaded by the pest are painted over with a brush or powdered, but this must be done only in very dry weather. The alcohol evaporates and the gum-lake "fixes" the wood-

lice, preventing them from escaping by flight from the toxic action of the lysol. At the end of two or three paintings the lice will be entirely destroyed, not only upon the branches, but also upon the green parts of the tree. The preparation of this product is very simple. A quantity of light-colored varnish is procured, such as is in common use among cabinet-makers and polishers, and this is mixed with once or twice its volume of denatured alcohol and with five to ten per cent of lysol. A remedy so easily prepared, and which has been used with successful results in France, should be worth a trial.

Propagating Roses From Outdoor Wood.

Ed. Am. Florist:—Please give some instructions on the propagating of roses from outdoor wood. We have plenty of wood outdoors but none under glass.

W.

If "W," will take the young soft wood of his outdoor roses and make suitable cuttings, they can be rooted in frames during August very nicely; at least a very large percentage will root if careful attention is given to the watering, shading, etc.

In preparing the frame for the reception of cuttings, two methods are available, one of which is cold-frame propagation. Have an ordinary 3x6-foot box frame tightly made, the back of which should be about one foot higher than the front, in order to throw off rain. Place this on ground that is well drained and cover the bottom with several inches of short dry moss or excelsior refuse. Press this firmly, after which cover it evenly all over with from three to four inches of clean sharp sand, when it should be pressed or beaten quite firm. After giving the whole a good soaking of water it is ready for the cuttings.

The frame should be placed so that the slope faces the north and, if slightly shaded by nearby trees, so much the better. The cuttings should be pressed very firmly into the sand and the sash of the frame closed as soon as the cuttings are in position and a good watering given them. They must be kept shaded from bright sun, but on calm, warm nights, after the first ten days, the sash can be removed altogether, replacing it again early in the morning. Water the cuttings as required until they show signs of starting new growth, when they can be gradually exposed to more air and light and in time the sash removed altogether. As soon as the roots are one-half inch long, they should be potted into small pots, using good, firm soil, and placed in the frame again, at which time watering, shading, etc., should be handled in a similar manner as for the cuttings. When they have fairly taken hold of the soil the shading can be gradually removed and the cuttings placed in the greenhouse and grown on in the usual way.

The other method is to make a bed of manure and leaves or some similar material, that will produce a slight, steady bottom heat for three or four weeks. On this bed place the frame in the same position as for cold-frame propagating and insert the cuttings in the same manner as stated above; treat them generally in about the same way. This last method will give rooted cuttings three or four weeks quicker than the other, but they require more careful attention and watering. As a rule, however, the latter system will give a much better percentage of rooted plants. John N. May.

OUR PASTIMES.

Announcements of coming contests or other events of interests to our bowling, shooting and sporting readers are solicited and will be given place in this column.

Address all correspondence for this department to Wm. J. Stewart, 79 Milk St., Boston, Mass.; Robt. Kift, 1725 Chestnut St., Philadelphia, Pa.; or to the American Florist Co., 324 Dearborn St., Chicago, Ill.

Gunning at Milwaukee.

F. Schmeling, of the committee on the shooting contest Thursday afternoon, August 20, sends the following report of prize winners: Forty-bird race, indi-

J. Foerster of Chicago.
(The Champion Bowler.)

vidual, H. M. Altick, Dayton, O., first; Hippard, Youngstown, O., second; James Eadie, Cleveland, third; Ed. Reid, Philadelphia, fourth; Braik, fifth; Kirschner, Milwaukee, sixth. In the twenty-bird race, ten pairs, Eadie, first; Reid, second; Braik, third; Altick, fourth. About 150 spectators were on hand and the event was most interesting.

It is to Laugh.

OF HIS OWN RAISING.

Tommy (mysteriously)—"I shall have lots of cake this summer, all for myself."
Mother—"O! Has aunty promised you some?"
Tommy (with withering scorn)—"No, I've planted seed cake in the garden."—Punch.

New Orleans.

WARM WEATHER AND POOR BUSINESS.—HORTICULTURAL SOCIETY MEETS.—ASTERS AND DAHLIAS EXHIBITED.—CONVENTIONITES.—NOTES.

Warm weather and dull times have been the order of the day for some time past, but the last meeting of the New Orleans Horticultural Society was nevertheless well attended, and the merits of a number of flowers were discussed. The summer cultivation of the aster is a new thing in this vicinity, but gives good results, judging from the plants that were exhibited by Paul Abele. R. Eichling thinks that the cultivation of the dahlia during the summer would be a paying proposition and exhibited some superior specimens of the white variety Storm King. D. Newsham, secretary of the society, is well satisfied with the collection of plants he has so far secured for the World's Fair.. Everyone reported chrysanthemum stock coming along finely for the season.

W. G. Eichling, after having disposed of all his old stock at auction, has opened a new establishment on Magazine street.

H. H. Papeworth, U. J. Virgin, E. Valdejo and P. A. Chopin were visitors at the Milwaukee convention, stopping at Cincinnati.   M.M.L.

Thoughtlessness of Youth.

I have no patience with people who talk about the "thoughtlessness of youth" indulgently. I had infinitely rather hear of thoughtless old age and the indulgence due to that. When a man has done his work, and nothing can any way be materially altered in his fate, let him forget his toil and jest with his fate, if he will; but what excuse can you find for wilfulness of thought at the very time when every crisis of future fortune hangs on your decision? A youth thoughtless! when all the happiness of his home forever depends on the chances, or the passions, of an hour! A youth thoughtless! when the career of all his days depends on the opportunity of a moment! A youth thoughtless! when his every act is as a torch to the laid train of future conduct, and every imagination a fountain of life or death! Be thoughtless in any after years rather than now—though, indeed, there is only one place where a man may be nobly thoughtless—his deathbed. No thinking should ever be left to be done there.—*John Ruskin.*

IOLA, KANS.—A. L. Harmon has located at Pasadena, Cal., where he intends to establish a floral business.

Lake Geneva Gardens.

ESTATE OF J. C. FLEMING.

The summer estate of J. C. Fleming is situated five miles or more west of the village of Lake Geneva, Wis., on the south shore of the lake and is one of the largest in that section. The residence, a modern frame structure with a wide veranda, is located well back on a prominent rise, commanding good views in every direction. Large broad winding steps with landings at short intervals and a broad walk lead to the lake pier. At each of the landings, above the stone coping are large vases filled with foliage and flowering plants while behind the coping and along the walk leading to the beach is a shrubbery composed of aralia, berberis, cornus, philadelphus, sambucus, spiræa, syringa, etc.

At the base of the steps on either side are terraced mounds several feet in height, planted with cannas, S. A. Nutt geraniums and coleus, while several large beds of geraniums, consisting principally of the S. A. Nutt and Pride of the West, are laid out in prominent positions along the walks.

The large lawns, sloping toward the beach, are studded here and there with specimen trees such as cut-leaved birch, catalpa, Weirs' cut-leaved and Schwedler's ler's maple, silver willow, while towards the west, along a broad gravel walk leading to a rustic summer house near the lake, are planted singly, or loosely grouped along the slope, a number of golden thuya, blue, Norway and Nordman spruce, Austrian and Mugho pine and juniperus, the contrast in color being very effective.

Further along a large bed of double Persian yellow roses in bloom (June 8) were equally striking.

The estate south of the residence is still under a native growth of oak, grouped among which are Austrian and white pine, Norway and white spruce, while here and there large catalpas and maples have been introduced and the margins of the shaded avenues are planted with specimen American lindens, which are at present twenty to twenty-five feet in height.

Mr. Fleming's property is under the care of Christopher Krabby, and could not be kept in finer condition.

ROCHESTER, N. Y.—The schedule in the assignment of E. R. Fry Company shows liabilities of $7,737.43 and assets amounting to $2,368.57. A. A. Mosher is trustee.

NEW ORLEANS, LA.—Abele Brothers are busy erecting a new greenhouse with office attached. The house measures 15x50 feet. A general stock will be handled.

Columbus, O.

STATE FAIR ON NEXT WEEK.—VISITING FLORISTS INVITED TO INSPECT LOCAL ESTABLISHMENTS.—HOT DRY WEATHER STILL PREVAILS.

There will be an exhibition at the Ohio State Fair during the week beginning August 31, and the florists will have a good showing. The visiting members of the craft are invited to inspect the establishments of our local growers and dealers, where they will perhaps be able to find something of interest. Since all but one can be conveniently reached by electric cars there is no reason why any should be slighted. To reach the establishments of Gus. Drobisch, J. R. Hellenthal and E. Metzmeyer take South High street car; Underwood Brothers, M. Evans and Franklin Park Floral Company, Oak street car; Fifth Avenue Floral Company and Smith Floral Company, Neil avenue car; S. F. Stephens, Cemetery car. The Livingston Seed Company's greenhouses are the only ones not in reach of the car lines, but provision will be made to accommodate all those who apply at the company's store, corner High and Long streets. To see the cannas will alone justify a trip to this place. Any of the visitors wishing further information while in the city can obtain it by calling at the centrally located cut flower stores.

Drought and heat still continue to ruin our aster fields, causing a shortage of all cut flowers, and the few carnations that still remain in the field will soon be entirely gone if not housed in the near future. The earth used in filling benches is as dust and necessitates thorough drenching before planting.   CARL.

ALBERT LEA, MINN.—P. Clausen & Son, proprietors of the Lake Shore greenhouses, have added one carnation house, 26x125 feet, and one violet house, 14x45 feet. About 10,000 carnations have been planted.

MANCHESTER, MASS.—The North Shore Horticultural Society held its annual sweet pea show July 31. The blooms were not equal to those of previous seasons, owing to the unfavorable weather. Most of the noted gardens of Beverly, Manchester and other summer resorts were represented in the displays.

THE AMERICAN FLORIST

America is "the Prow of the Vessel; there may be more comfort Amidships, but we are the first to touch Unknown Seas."

Vol. XXI.   CHICAGO AND NEW YORK, SEPTEMBER 5, 1903.   No. 796.

THE AMERICAN FLORIST

NINETEENTH YEAR.
Copyright 1903, by American Florist Company
Entered as Second-Class Mail Matter.
PUBLISHED EVERY SATURDAY BY
AMERICAN FLORIST COMPANY,
334 Dearborn St., Chicago.
Eastern Office: 79 Milk St., Boston.
Subscription, $1.00 a year.   To Europe, $2.00.
Subscriptions accepted only from the trade.
Volumes half-yearly from August, 1901.

SOCIETY OF AMERICAN FLORISTS AND
ORNAMENTAL HORTICULTURISTS.
OFFICERS—JOHN BURTON, Philadelphia, Pa.,
president; C. C. POLLWORTH, Milwaukee, Wis.,
vice-president; WM. J. STEWART, 79 Milk Street,
Boston, Mass., secretary; H. B. BEATTY, Oil City,
Pa., treasurer.
OFFICERS-ELECT—PHILIP BREITMEYER, president; J. J. BENEKE, Vice-president; secretary and
treasurer as before. Twentieth annual meeting
at St. Louis, Mo., August, 1904.

THE AMERICAN CARNATION SOCIETY.
Annual convention at Detroit, Mich., March 2,
1904. ALBERT M. HERR, Lancaster, Pa., secretary.

AMERICAN ROSE SOCIETY.
Annual meeting and exhibition, Philadelphia,
March, 1904. LEONARD BARRON, 136 Liberty St.,
New York, secretary.

CHRYSANTHEMUM SOCIETY OF AMERICA
Annual convention and exhibition, New York,
November 10-12, 1903. FRED H. LEMON, Richmond,
Ind., secretary.

THIS ISSUE 36 PAGES WITH COVER.

CONTENTS.

Cold storage systems......................... 217
Frederick Law Olmst d (portrait)............. 218
Some prominent Canadians (portraits)........ 218
Cana lian Horticultural association.......... 219
Floral display at Toronto exhibition........ 2 9
Cincinnati 220
Decoration of home grounds (illus.).......... 220
Chicago 222
New York 222
Boston 222
Philadelphia 223
Hons—y's apostrophe to horticulturists...... 223
Western expansion 224
The carnation as a national flower.......... 224
Society of horticultural science............ 224
Lake Geneva gardens 224
Obituary - Jules Ponch 224
—E. H. Swan 224
Indianapolis 226
The seed trade 232
—Nebraska as d'crops......................... 233
—State of Hol an s Seed Co. (illus.)......... 234
The nursery trade 234
—Boston park notes 234
—Transplanting large trees.................. 234
O r pastimes 234
St. Louis 236
Detroit...................................... 236
Minneapolis 242
Cleveland 234
Montreal 2 2
Parkersburg, W. Va........................... 244
Washington, Pa............................... 244
Lowell, Mass 246

Cold Storage Systems.

In the development of commercial floriculture from an insignificant industry
dependent largely upon weather and
season to its present prominence, many
unforeseen problems have presented themselves to the enterprising cultivator.
Flowers "out of season" on a scale of
any magnitude is so recent an achievement that many of us can remember the
time when such was something of a
marvel to the average person; nowadays
the public has become so accustomed to
indulgence in that direction that nothing
in this line causes any surprise; rather are
they surprised to hear that there is any
possible limitation to the production of
anything and everything on any and all
days of the year. Soil and climate conditions have not changed; but the stimulus of a greedy market at remunerative
rates has awakened the ingenuity of our
flower growers, as it has that of fruit
and vegetable growers, to the development of what is now becoming one of the
most important features of the flower
industry—the retarding of the growth of
roots and bulbs by cold storage methods
so that they may be brought into bloom
at option and their flowering period
extended over an indefinite time.

The primitive methods of ice storage,
while successful to a limited extent in
favorable latitudes, were too uncertain
and carried too many possibilities of
failure and loss to induce ventures of any
magnitude, but since the introduction of
mechanical refrigeration by means of the
various modifications of the ammonia-
compression principle it is now possible
for a grower so to control the development of lilies, daffodils and such stock
that he can bring in a crop of flowers at
any season of the year. The only limitation is that the market shall stand a
price sufficient to defray the cost and
compensate for the inevitable proportion
of loss of vitality and productive power
in the bulbs so stored.

To cool a substance and keep it at a
set temperature it is necessary to take
from it its own surplus heat and protect
it against additional heat from any other
source. The expansion of any substance
being always accompanied by absorption
of heat, ammonia gas, which is capable

of being greatly reduced in volume by
compression, has been found to be well
adapted for this use. When compressed
and then admitted to pipes coiled directly
about the storage room or through tanks
of brine which when chilled is pumped
through the coils, the expansion of the
gas quickly withdraws the heat from the
air or surrounding brine. This gas after
traversing the pipes is returned to the
condenser and compresser, where it is
again made ready for repeating the process. The first mentioned method is
known as the direct expansion system
and the latter the brine system. Of equal
importance with the cooling room is the
matter of so insulating it as to prevent
so far as possible the absorption of any
heat from outside sources. No absolutely
perfect material for this purpose has yet
been found, and although much ingenuity
has been displayed in this direction, the
work of insulation is the most expensive
part of the outfit.

The Waban Rose Conservatories at
Natick, Mass., are operating successfully
a direct ammonia equipment, and W. H.
Siebrecht, of Long Island City, N. Y., has
an extensive outfit on the brine system,
and in each case entire economy is
expressed.

Mr. Siebrecht has many visitors, to
whom he courteously explains his system.
The ammonia compresser is operated by
a 10-horse-power pump driven by an
electric motor. From the compresser the
ammonia passes through extra-heavy
ball-inch steel pipe to the condenser
which is filled with hydrant water. After
liquefaction the ammonia enters a small
reservoir whence it passes as a gas to
coils of 1¼-inch pipe immersed in brine,
which is thus rapidly chilled. This cold
brine is then pumped through a coil of
¾-inch pipe, which is run in four lines
through the cold storage rooms, the
pumping being done by a 1-horse-power
pump operated by an electric motor. Mr.
Siebrecht finds that about fifteen pounds
pressure gives the best results in the compresser. All the pipes are exhausted under
fifty pounds vacuum gauge register before
the ammonia is admitted. Two of Mr.
Siebrecht's storage rooms are under
ground. The temperature at which they

may be kept is merely a matter of coils and equipment. For lily of the valley pips he keeps the thermometer at 25° to 30°. The machine is not kept continuously at work, about two hours a day on an average being all that is necessary to keep the brine at the required temperature.

At the Waban Rose Conservatories the cooling process is used not only to keep bulbs but to maintain a cool room in which to hold flowers before shipment. The entire refrigerated space is about 26x36 feet in area. This is divided into three rooms, a freezing room for bulbs 12x12 feet, a cold room for flowers 12x14 feet and a packing room 14x36 feet, all being ten feet in height Insulation is secured by means of ¼-inch corrugated straw-board encased between sheets of paper which had previously been dipped in a solution of silicate of soda, which was allowed to dry on the surface of the paper. These sheets, four feet square, are nailed to the walls with pieces of cheese cloth dipped in silicate of soda fastened over the joinings. There are sixteen thicknesses of this material, there being also between each thickness air spaces 12x24 inches, formed by strips of ¼-inch lathing. These walls are finished on the inside with ⅞-inch spruce flooring shell-laced. Doors are built in the same manner and windows are provided with five sashes. One of the advantages claimed for the use of the silicate of soda is that this material is vermin and fire-proof.

As above stated, the direct expansion of ammonia is used here. The refrigerating pumps are located in the boiler house and are in charge of the man operating the boilers, steam being used to drive the pumps. One-inch pipe is used in the coils about the cooling rooms, and the connecting pipe from the boiler house is ½-inch, laid in earthen tile pipe in the ground. The return pipe to the pump is placed alongside the return drip steam pipes through the greenhouses and archways. The condenser is a round tank of iron in which iron coils are submerged, the water from this tank flowing to the manure pits.

A temperature of 17° is maintained in the bulb room for the first fourteen days after the bulbs are stored, and afterward it is permitted to rise to 24°, where it remains until all the bulbs are used. Thermometers are so placed, with a bent tube running through the insulation, that the temperature can be read without going into the refrigerator. All the valves are in the shipping room and either room can be carried at any desired temperature by opening or closing a valve.

Frederick Law Olmsted.

Frederick Law Olmsted, the noted landscape architect, died at a sanitarium in Waverly, Mass., on August 28, aged 81 years and 4 months.

Thus passes away a man whose memory America will honor for all time. He stood indisputably the foremost exponent of one of the noblest professions followed by men. Comprehensive, conscientious, unassuming, his was a rare personality, the impress of whose beneficent influence shall never depart so long as lovers of outdoor beauty and friends of humanity exist.

A native of Connecticut, Frederick Law Olmsted first became known to the public through a series of books in which he gave his impressions obtained during several long horseback journeys through the Atlantic slave states and from Texas to Carolina. These books gave to the people of the north their first authentic information concerning much of the southern country, and to most of them their first idea of the true workings of the slave system, and exerted a powerful influence in rousing the public opinion which finally produced the war of secession and the freedom of the slaves.

Later Mr. Olmsted became a farmer on Staten Island, and in 1852, when a successful movement was made in New York to secure a great public park for that city, Mr. Olmsted, in association with Calvin Vaux, a young English architect who had been brought to this country by Downing to plan country houses, presented in competition the plan for Central Park which was adopted and afterward executed. This plan was a

The Late Frederick Law Olmsted.

work of genius remarkable in the fact that the author had had no special preparation for it except in his inherent love of nature which he had cultivated in his long horseback journeys through the south and in a journey which he had made through rural England on foot. The plan was remarkable, too, in the forethought which the author displayed for the then hardly suspected park requirements of the people of a great city, and in the arrangements made to enable its traffic to go on uninterruptedly across the park without interfering with its rural character. All things considered, Mr. Olmsted has never surpassed his first efforts at park making, and Central Park must stand as the best expression of his creative genius. Mr. Olmsted subsequently designed Prospect Park in Brooklyn, which is usually considered more beautiful, but this beauty is due largely to natural advantages of topography and to the existence of fine natural woods.

During the war Mr. Olmsted did the country good service as secretary of the United States Sanitary Commission, and in the years immediately following the war he was able further to gratify his love for nature in California, where he resided near the Yosemite Valley as agent for the owners of the lands embraced in the Fremont grant. Returning to the east, he continued his profession as landscape gardener, and made plans more or less elaborate for parks in many of the principal cities of the United States.

Among these may be mentioned Golden Gate Park, San Francisco; South Park, Chicago; Niagara Falls Reservation; Capitol Grounds at Washington and the park systems of Buffalo, Trenton, Louisville, Wilmington, Rochester, Bridgeport, Montreal and Des Moines.

In 1875, having been invited to prepare a scheme for a system of parks for the city of Boston, he moved to Cambridge and then to Brookline, where he has continued to reside and where some of his most important work has been planned. In this latter period Mr. Olmsted developed the unrivalled Boston park system, the Biltmore estate, the property of George W. Vanderbilt, with its four thousand acres of home grounds, and the Columbian Exposition at Chicago. The beauty and success of this last enterprise was chiefly due to Mr. Olmsted, who placed the buildings and laid out and developed the grounds and waterways which surrounded them.

Eight years ago age and infirmities compelled Mr. Olmsted to retire from the active practice of his profession and the business has been carried on by John L. and F. L. Olmsted, Jr.

In accordance with his expressed wish, the body was cremated at Mt. Auburn cemetery, August 31.

An appreciative writer has the following in the Chicago *Tribune* of August 30:

> There his works stand! Central park in New York, the south side parks in Chicago, Prospect park in Brooklyn, Biltmore in North Carolina, and many others. Frederick Law Olmsted himself is gone. "One generation shall praise his works to another."
>
> He had the advantage those artists have who work in the visible, the concrete, and the large. It will not be necessary to go to libraries and hunt through dusty volumes for what Mr. Olmsted did. It will not be necessary to go to concert halls and depend upon orchestras for the resurrection of his efforts. He did not deal with words and sounds. He dealt with things. Go to Washington or Jackson park. There, visible, concrete, large, tangible, obvious, is what Mr. Olmsted did for all of us. One can't get away from it. There it is all about one.
>
> The glory of being the creator of such things is subjective as well as objective. Whatever satisfaction Mr. Olmsted may have had in other men's appreciation of his works must have been completely obscured by his own joy in leaving behind him such monuments to his power and his energy.
>
> Mr. Olmsted had not only technical dexterity and practical effectiveness but creative genius. He was among those men who not only know what beauty is but can make beauty. They see beauty grow under their hands. There are not many such men. That Mr. Olmsted was one of them means that most of the "great ones of the earth" seem small beside him.

Some Prominent Canadians.

Wm. Algie is a prominent manufacturer residing at Alton, about twenty-three miles distant from Brampton, Ont. Mr. Algie is the father-in-law of the late H. Dale's eldest daughter and being one of the executors of the estate visits the establishment every Saturday to supervise any building operations that may be going on, as well as to assist in any matter of special importance.

T. W. DUGGAN.

T. W. Duggan, of Brampton, Ont., has been connected with the well known H. Dale Estate at that place since 1895, at which time the late H. Dale requested him to take charge and endeavor to better the financial condition of the concern. After a couple of years Mr. Duggan took permanent charge with power of attorney giving him sole general management of the business part of the firm. Shortly before Mr. Dale's death in July, 1900, that gentleman made a will in which he named T. W. Duggan and Wm. Algie as executors and gave instructions to the

Wm Algie, Brampton, Ont. L. W. Duggan. H. G. Dillemuth.

SOME PROMINENT MEN IN THE CANADIAN TRADE.

effect that Mr. Duggan should have the general management of the business until the estate was wound up, the limit for which is 1914 when the youngest child of Mr. Dale becomes of age. At Mr. Dale's death Mr. Duggan took complete charge as managing executor, which position he has most ably filled up to the present time.

H. G. DILLEMUTH.

H. G. Dillemuth, is the able manager of Dunlop's retail stores, Toronto. At the age of 26, he has had the management of this place for four years, where those in a position to know can see with what splendid progress he has succeeded in this department. He originally came from Pittsburg, where he was connected with Patterson Brothers and A. M. Murdock, with whom he started his career.

Canadian Horticultural Association.

The sixth annual convention of the Canadian Horticultural Association was opened in St. George's hall, Sept. 2. Mayor Urquhart and President Thos. Manton welcomed the delegates to the meeting. In his address of welcome the mayor hoped the convention would be a success and thought every person should be interested in horticulture, inasmuch as it brought all so closely in touch with nature; he spoke highly of the improvement of the various parks in this country, a predominant factor in the beautifying of all centers; he was very profuse in his eloquence on the horticultural display of the exhibition and of the interest taken by the general public. In conclusion he addressed the Montreal delegates, thanking them in behalf of the city council of Montreal for the valued assistance given Toronto recently in defense of municipal rights at Ottawa. Mr. Walsh, of Montreal, in response, was thankful for the mayor's reference to this beautiful convention city adding that Montreal was continually learning lessons from Toronto.

President Manton then made his address and raised several live issues, touching especially the relationship of employers and employed, and referred to the poor salaries received by many first-class gardeners working on private

establishments, who are not receiving the salaries many junior clerks on leaving a business college receive, with little or no responsibility entailed, while they have devoted their best years to floriculture with a multitude of responsibilities of which only a good gardener has any knowledge. The gardener, he said, was usually so occupied with his plants that little leisure time was left him for the acquiring of practical knowledge which is sometimes so necessary in his vocation. He spoke of a fast freight service to facilitate foreign shipments to this country; and referring to the customs officers inability to place proper values on florists' plants, etc., he suggested that an appraiser acquainted with the stock should be placed at all the principal ports. Personally Mr. Manton does not believe that a duty should be placed on florists' stock, but as the duty was put on it should be handled by someone with a technical knowledge of horticulture.

In the discussion which followed instances were given in which thousands of packages of seeds were passed as palms, where bronze galax leaves were held under the impression that they were metallically bronzed and numerous other incidents which were ridiculously humorous to the full fledged florist. The opinion was unanimous that the executive committe should ask the Dominion government to appoint a special officer at Toronto, the Montreal delegates being fairly satisfied with conditions at their city. London and Ottawa coincided with Toronto. The meeting then adjourned until 2:30 p. m.

The Steele, Briggs Seed Company entertained the convention visitors at luncheon at their spacious grounds. Mr. Steele made some appropriate remarks on the progress of the business along the several lines of the trade represented by the delegates present which were highly appreciated, for they were cleverly portrayed by a scholar and a speaker.

FLORAL DISPLAY AT THE TORONTO EXHIBITION.

The delegates then returned by the special cars which the Steele people had provided and the afternoon session was taken in hand. A very gratifying report from the treasurer showed the following: Balance on hand August 30, 1902, $64.15; revenue from advertising in official programme of that year, $29.50; dues $96 and interest 90 cents, making the total receipts $190.55. The secretary's expenses, printing, postage, etc., amounted to $99 85, leaving a balance on hand of $90.70.

An essay and practical demonstration on "Floral Art and Values" were given by H. G. Dillemuth, who pointed out many details connected with the retail florist establishment. The essay was only a minor part of Mr. Dillemuth's section of the programme, as the practical illustration of making designs, wiring flowers and combining colors were interesting to the many retail men who were present. This closed the afternoon session and an adjournment was made until 7:30 p. m.

On Wednesday evening A. Gibb, of Montreal, read a most creditable paper on "Public Parks and Squares," and R. W. King, of the King Construction Company, Toronto, delivered an essay, "Construction of Greenhouses and Operation."

Thursday morning the delegates were entertained at the hands of the Toronto city council by drives through the various parks and driveways, lunch being provided for the company at High park. An invitation of the Kenzie Seed Company was then accepted and the drive continued to that establishment, where light refreshments were served, after which the party was transported to the exhibition grounds for the afternoon business, the session having been delayed two hours.

It was decided that application should be made to the government for a practical appraiser to value florists' importations and the azalea was selected as the favorite plant to be used in an appeal to relieve duties, and if the appeal is successful other varieties will follow.

The officers elected were the following: President, E. J. Mepstead, Ottawa; first vice-president, Geo. Robinson, Montreal; second vice-president, Mr. Suckling, Truro, N. S.; secretary, A. H. Ewing, Woodstock; treasurer, Herman Simmers, Toronto. The members of the executive committee: J. H. Dunlop, Toronto; Robert Wright, Ottawa; Wm. Gammage, London. The retiring president was presented with a handsome writing desk by E. J. Mepstead on behalf of the members of the association.   H. G. D.

Cincinnati.

Trade has been very quiet during the past week, although a little funeral work has helped to relieve the monotony of things. Asters have dropped a little in price and quite a few find their way to the barrel. Roses are faring better at $2 to $4 per hundred. Gladioli are finding a poor market and the only way they can be disposed of is in job lots. The majority of the carnations coming into this market are poor.

George & Allan were the principal prizewinners at the Oakley fair of the Hamilton County Agricultural Society, August 20. The display was very good.

A recent heavy storm broke the 8x12-foot plate-glass window of the Walnut Hills Floral Bazaar.

Visitors: L. Baumann, Chicago; Martin Rheukauff, B. Eschner, Philadelphia.

The Decoration of Home Grounds.
BY C. B. WHITNALL, MILWAUKEE, WIS.

We present herewith some extracts from Mr. Whitnall's valuable address on the "Decoration of Home Grounds," delivered before the Society of American Florists at the Milwaukee Convention, August 19, 1903.

"Although there may be much in nature lacking beauty, nothing can be beautiful unless it conforms to the requirements of nature. What can you do for an English family living in a Swiss cottage situated on an Illinois prairie? There you have a shelter which has been the outcome of the ingenuity and acquired characteristics of a people living in a mountainous country. To an English family it will be a misfit, and the prairie with its monotony will cause the building and the family to appear like awkward intruders. The attempt of a gardener to harmonize these differences can only be a compromise, which in time may gradually evolve into a new order of things and become natural; then it may be beautiful, not before.

"Did it ever occur to you that paths are always beautiful, while walks laid out by a single individual seldom are? Sometimes a manufactured walk becomes a path, an occurrence too rare. The principal reason why the country is considered more beautiful than the city is due to the more natural method of adopting and maintaining the highways and byways, yet they are constantly being obliterated by what is called improvements. I am sorry that the landscape gardener finds it necessary to follow in the wake of the improvement agitator. Of course, it may be argued that there is where he is most needed, the same as the army surgeon follows the destructive army, but I do hope the time is not far distant when the landscape gardener, as a subdivision of the department of forestry, together with the co-operation of our health department, will be given precedence over the ordinary architect and grading contractor. It does seem a pity that we begin some of our most important efforts at the roof and work down to the foundation, struggling so long with innumerable complications necessarily arising during such procedure, with disasters outnumbering successes, until nature, untiring, never

No. 1. THE DECORATION OF HOME GROUNDS.

missing an opportunity of setting a good example, very quietly and gently transforms our failures into beauty spots. Many a millionaire's residence becomes beautiful after the owner has lost his fortune; many a town site, once beautiful, destroyed by man's ambition, returns to beauty after man acknowledges himself a failure.

"The effort to lay out a town in squares is a fatal mistake that cannot be overcome in our efforts to beautify our homes; the distance alone is not all the waste, the travel of squares forces us on to hills and into holes, and acting on the theory that two wrongs make a right we cut down the hills to fill the holes, the natural contour of the land is destroyed, the natural beauty is sacrificed for an imaginary necessity or false economy.

"Of course roads should be built, but build them to accommodate our natural desires. Many cross roads make cross people, while short cuts always give relief to whoever may have occasion to use them, and the main channels of travel will have our unanimous approval if our natural inclinations and necessities be the governing influence in building them.

"A person who lays out a road or walk without understanding and conforming to these characteristics of humanity insures a contest with the public; every sign 'Keep off the grass,' 'No trespassing,' every barrier put up to divert travel and every corner or projection of a lawn or garden trampled down in opposition to the manifest desires of the designer is conclusive evidence that the contest is on.

"The landscape gardener, engineer or architect should never lose sight of the fact that utility is the foundation of beauty. Fads and fashions may create a ripple of enthusiasm where ingenuity is paid a high price for tickling vanity, but common sense never leaves the utility idea, and fashionmongers are obliged to return to it continually, from whence they make a fresh start. A landscape gardener should wear the word 'utility' in his hat. He should understand that to maintain a very large specimen of a tree, sheltered protection from direct influence of sun and wind must be provided, its feeders should reach to one or more secluded nooks where the deposit of vegetable matter is continuously supplied and moisture conserved. He should appreciate the utility of the hundreds of perennial rooted subjects which succeed each other in their short period of attractiveness, where one comes up early and protects its neighbor while it is awakening, then goes to sleep for the balance of the year, folding its dry leaves around the stems of its neighbor which now, having reached the climax of its attractiveness, requires just that much of a mulch, each one attracting its favorite insect or variety of animal life in some form or another to aid in the fertilization and distribution of its seeds.

"While women wear birds, abhor the sight of the earth worm, admire the torture of grass spread out in front of the house with its lungs cut out, and allow trees to be treated like telegraph poles, and must have all effects immediately after an impulse is felt, and while their husbands measure the desirability of all things by the cash value put upon it, it is no wonder that homes are not better decorated.

"I have spoken to you about the influence of character upon the vegetation surrounding the owner's home, perhaps many of you have not noticed how true this is. If you look at a horse and wagon you can imagine what the driver is, or you can make a very good guess at what kind of a home a dog has, but you have not been in the habit of judging people by what they have encouraged and have seen fit to let grow about them. You might, for instance look at two elms upon a farm. Do you see any happiness, harmony or content there, or anything well done? Do you find within you any desire for the owner's acquaintance? And now let us also look at two other elms on another farm; you are passing such differences every day, not only do you pass them but you begin to make them. You would not be afraid to stop over night with the family who spend their leisure hours under these trees.

Do you remember how thousands of people sent from all over the country for a vine seedling gathered in our southern swamps? Most all had better material at home but didn't know it, or even know that they wanted anything. It's the energy of the catalogue man in disseminating the desire for something to plant and look at, that we thank him for, even when he resorts to humbugging, as some do; it has not been barren of some good results. A certain spiræa might possibly be a beautiful shrub for ten days, but don't you see that it came by express and was planted without regard to its fitness for the situation? Elsewhere we see a shrub that appears to have been understood. The forsythia, covered with its yellow bell-shaped flowers in April, can easily be grown up the side or corner of a house as if it were a vine. A tree agent called and talked a man into buying a double flowered crab tree; when it was delivered it was decided to select for it a convenient place most out of the way, but it has since attracted the admiration of the neighborhood. Others have been somewhat enthused and they begin to look over fences to see who has anything better than they have; that tree agent planted seed that are germinating. These lonesome plantings suggest a comparison to the state of affairs described by Mark Twain in speaking of the missionaries distributing clothing among the Sandwich Islanders, after which they came to church, one wearing a hat, another a collar and tie, another a coat, etc.

"The aralia and the ailanthus are two of the most beautiful and satisfactory trees there are for house decoration. There has been an unwritten law come into recognition which I want to break. It seems to prevent people from allowing

No. 8. THE DECORATION OF HOME GROUNDS.

anything to form part of the house embellishment but vines. We want vines to tie together, to hold and intertwine, to 'weave nature's mantle of shelter, lending grace and protection to the tree in compensation for its strength of support and endurance. The tree and vine have evolved together, and we want to continue them so. The clematis is showy and thrifty, and the porch railing is a tolerable substitute for a natural support, but the house is still bare or bleak; if this little bashful tree would move up to the base of steps and assist the vine in draping the porch roof, and if close by the bay window a graceful canopy of the ailanthus tree was suspended, we would feel that the owner was more companionable with nature, and that her soothing influences were being exerted for his peace and tranquility. Another example will show you such a condition in an early stage of development; there both the aralia and the ailanthus and the vines just making each other's acquaintance. Some shrubs set out last fall along the base have failed, a few castor beans have been enlisted for temporary assistance. If in four years from now this place will look as though no gardener ever touched it, it will be beautiful, because nature will have found a congenial spot on which to vegetate.

"I wish now to speak of a very important difficulty frequently met with in successfully beautifying homes by planting. It is a matter more carefully considered by the forester than the gardener. You must know that you may expose yourself to a strong wind of a prairie and suffer no harm, but you may sit by a crack in the wall and be killed with the same air under even less pressure; you know how you blow a spoon of soup to cool it, and how you breathe on your hands to warm them, the difference in temperature being caused by the formation of your lips. Now trees suffer from draughts, and everything which naturally grows under and about trees suffers from the same causes. If you go in the woods during a blizzard, you can see the disturbance overhead, but the snow falls about you as fitting the pictures of fairyland; even if you cut away the forest, leaving only a square section of trees standing exposed on all sides, the outer edges will be filled by accelerated growth in three seasons. Unfortunately, however, in the city these remedies are not permitted; just look at this state of affairs. Currents of air, not doing much harm where they enter, but considerable where they go out, and the combination of shade and wind is in conflict with the acquired characteristics of things which we must make use of. A plant which is adapted for shade cannot endure a drying wind, and a plant grown to withstand wind is an open air plant. You can't get along with all large trees or all small trees. We come across places where we are careful, yet make a failure. I have barely finished one experience that has bothered me more than a little for two seasons. Dahlias were desired; I picked out a place quite suitable as I thought. I was careful to get a choice assortment and pick out the best tubers; the broken pieces and some decayed ones were thrown on the compost heap; that compost heap got to look beautiful, but the mass of dahlias turned out to be a mess of dahlias. There is a current of air which constantly comes down between two buildings, no matter whether the wind blows north, south or west. It's always worrying those dahlias. You can notice

in the winter there are places where there are always snow-piles, and other places where it never lodges; you will come across them when you least expect them."

REFERENCES TO ILLUSTRATIONS.

No. 1,—Clematis Jackmani is pretty anywhere, but is more easily admired when grown on or between trees. When desirable to have it close to a house, the use of trees that are suitable for its support is preferred rather than the limited scope of a trellis.

No. 2.—This view shows how trees may be utilized for screening. The willows in the distance grow up rapidly and hang over neighboring sheds with a much prettier effect than that of vines. Trees are effective, particularly at corners of buildings.

good asters are still to be had, but many are now beginning to show their centers and the only sellers are the white varieties. Gladioli are still coming in and comfortably fill all orders, the supply being just about right.

Albert Fuchs is remodeling his establishment. He will have a new and up-to-date office and will add a stenographer and cashier to his staff. Mr. Fuchs is installing large plate glass windows in the fronts of all the houses in his range that face the street. He has just completed his residence, which is adjacent to the greenhouses.

C. L. Washburn returned to the city Wednesday, September 2, from the Wisconsin pine woods. His family, who had been sojourning in that region all summer, accompanied him home.

No. 3. THE DECORATION OF HOME GROUNDS.

No. 3.—Bocconias are beautiful when in their prime, but all perennials require companions, some to grow ahead and shelter the late growers and then mulch their roots, while others to cover the early varieties with their best efforts, each one assisting the other in some essential point. Combined they keep the garden in dress from winter to winter.

Chicago.

There was a decided improvement in market conditions the past week. Stock has not come in quite as plentiful as a week ago, and while the material shipped in does not warrant very high prices, values are becoming steadier. There has been a good demand on the rose stock, which was, however, shortened by the prevailing cool weather, and it has not been possible to fill orders in a satisfactory manner. Some short-stemmed Golden Gate roses that a week ago would have been condemned to the dump were sold at very fair prices. Inside carnation stock is increasing each day, although short-stemmed. Some

Geo. Piepgrass, with Benthey & Company, who was taken to the Mercy hospital August 26, successfully underwent an operation and is said to be recovering.

Geo. Weiland, of Evanston, Ill., will, on October 8, marry Miss Louise Sontag. Miss Sontag is a sister-in-law of John Risch, of the firm of Weiland & Risch.

A number of the wholesale establishments began closing at 6:30 p. m. last week, and it is to be the general rule, beginning Monday, September 7.

E. H. Hunt issued his first weekly price list of the season on Saturday, August 29.

F. Lautenschlager, of Albert Fuch's establishment, is away on a vacation.

P. J. Hauswirth will leave for Atlantic City on Wednesday, September 9.

Miss Florence Emmett, of John Deamud's, is on her vacation.

E. C. Amling began Monday, August 31, closing at 6:30 p. m.

Weiland & Risch are enjoying a good shipping business.

In town: H. E. Philpott, Winnipeg, Manitoba; Geo. A. Kuhl, Pekin, Ill.; F. C. Smith, Ashland, Wis.

New York.

MARKET SHOWS AN IMPROVEMENT OVER PREVIOUS WEEK.—ROSES TAKE TURN FOR THE BETTER.—CARNATIONS POOR. —A DEATH.—NEWS NOTES.

Last week was pronounced by old campaigners the deadest period ever recorded in the cut flower trade at this or any other season of the year. Even the street men found nothing open to their enterprise. Monday of this week, however, saw a pronounced change for the better, not so much in regard to amount of business but as to values. Roses especially, have taken an upward turn, owing largely to the cold, rainy weather, which has retarded the blooming and made havoc with the color and other characteristics of a saleable article. There is a demand for good asters. Last week these were abundant and unsaleable, but this week they are arriving in bad condition generally, all out-door stock being water soaked. Carnations are few and poor.

Mr. Reed, of Reed & Keller, is well pleased with his business and pleasure trip to Milwaukee. He, and, in fact all the boys wish the time limit could have been extended, as they could not see or do as much of that city as they would have liked, owing to the pressing invitations, and hospitality extended to them by that great city, Chicago.

Those having carnation plants to sell would do well to advertise same, as there is a great demand and seems to be a short supply here about. Do not forget to name the quality of same as well as the price.

B. S. Slinn with the New York Cut Flower Co., will form a partnership in the wholesale flower business with Mr. Walker, former salesman for J. Snydam.

Mr. Benj. Dorrance of Dorrancetown, Pa., passed through town on his way to the wilds of Canada on a fishing and hunting trip.

Information has been received of the death of Mrs. Edward W. Hitchings, wife of the president of Hitchings & Co.

Carnation growers, are about through planting. Prospects are considered good for quantities of flowers this winter.

Moore, Hents & Nash are receiving heavy shipments of roses from the Floral Exchange, of Edgely, Pa.

Chas. Millang will begin next week to handle some of the best asters coming in to New York.

A new wholesale establishment is reported as about to open in twenty-eighth street.

J. K. Allen, has greatly improved the appearance of his place with a coat of paint.

Gladioli and asters are the chief flowers in the florists' windows just now.

Boston.

LAST WEEK STARTED POORLY BUT IMPROVEMENT IS NOTICED.—AMERICAN BEAUTY ROSES NOT SELLING WELL AT SUMMER PRICES.—OUTDOOR FLOWERS ABOUT BOSTON.—A MARRIAGE.—NEWS.— A VISITOR.

The present week came in with a dismal outlook for the flower growers for mildew was knocking at the door and the only relief was to fire up. Low temperature and rain continued for three days. The situation was little better for the dealer, who began the week with a big stock held over from last week's unmovable surplus. Luckily, the situation has improved very decidedly. The overstock has been placed and the

reduced receipts have favored an upward turn of prices. This especially refers to roses; there are no carnations worth mentioning. Asters are off in quality on account of the rain and very few presentable flowers are seen; while sweet peas are actually rotten when received. American Beauty is not holding its own at the summer resorts this season. Economy seems to be the order of the day with the festive sojourners.

Hardy phloxes are a complete failure in most of the gardens about Boston, the result of mildew. Cannas, which started off all right, are at present in bad shape owing to the recent low temperature and rain. Dahlias have never appeared to better advantage. They began flowering early and have made a sturdy growth and unless an early frost should interfere they will make a glorious display show on all sides as they have been more generally planted than ever before, the cactus-flowered varieties especially.

At the exhibition on Saturday, August 29 there was again a magnificent display of dahlias, asters, gladioli and cannas from a number of exhibitors. A. F. Schenkelburger was awarded a certificate of merit for gladiolus White Lady.

The marriage of Miss Blanche Arline, daughter of the late Edmund Mc. Wood, to Mr. Clyde P. Pitman, of Alamogordo, New Mexico, will take place at Natick, Mass., on September 9.

W. J. Maloney, brother-in-law of the Welch Bros., died on August 29, of pneumonia, having been ill but three days.

Among this week's visitors was Hans Ringier, representing Bobbink & Atkins, Rutherford, N. J.

Philadelphia.

SEPTEMBER MEETING OF FLORISTS' CLUB. —CONVENTION MATTERS DISCUSSED.— BUSINESS IS SLOW.—CURRENT EVENTS.

The September meeting of the Florists' Club of Philadelphia was all that could be desired in attendance and interest. The convention as it appeared to the various branches of the trade was the topic for discussion. Robert Craig spoke for the growers, and said that society was getting to be a great factor in the land. When first organized as several a man as Peter Henderson said "You will never get the men to attend," but the next year he said he was mistaken and it was sure to be a success and it has continued to grow from that time. The exhibition feature had been a special success this year and all exhibitors had done well. Young men just starting in business had a great chance in these exhibitions as any choice showings come before the best buyers of the land and they could establish a reputation at once, that would take a long time in any other way. He cited an instance of a man who with a few samples sold a stock of nearly a thousand plants in a few hours at the New York convention. After speaking of the achievements of the society in reducing express rates and along other lines, he said he hoped to see a better union of the minor societies with the S. A. F. as their success would be much greater than if carried on independently. The educational features of the going and coming journey must not be forgotten and the opportunity to see the large Chicago growers was freely commented on. Their great success was due to the great market which extended so far in every direction. He wondered if fifteen or twenty years hence this would

be taken away by the home production of the various cities. New York had at one time a great shipping trade but this has nearly all gone, as all towns of importance are now well supplied from local growers.

Leo Niessen said that the wholesale business in Chicago was conducted on a large scale but there is not the variety of stock to be found there as in the east. He was very glad he had attended the convention and felt himself well repaid as he had made new friends and stored away ideas for future use. Fred Michell for the seedsmen spoke of the great good it had done him to visit the convention and of the ideas he had obtained on the side trips coming back. He thought it the greatest meeting he had as yet attended. Robert Kift thought the retail merchants derived more benefit than almost any other branch of the trade, as all the supply dealers were there with their newest goods and the very latest things in ribbons, baskets and other supplies were spread out and displayed as could be seen nowhere else. This was also the case with plants, of which there were no such variety and comparison of prices anywhere as could be found there. The chance to see what the best men of other cities were doing was also afforded and in many other ways the stock of knowledge to be gained was invaluable. A feature of the evening was the presentation of a "log" book to John Westcott for his Waretown Rod and Gun Club, also to Mr. and Mrs. Westcott a silver tea set as a recognition of the many favors received at their hands by those who had enjoyed the hospitalities of the club house. As the meeting was about to adjourn, the Hitchings cup, just won in Detroit, was filled with Westcott's celebrated brew and many were the congratulatory words extended to the victorious team and wishes for their future success.

The Wm. Graham Company; incorporated, Wm. Graham, president and George N. Bainbridge, secretary and treasurer, will open its store at 108 South Thirteenth street in a few days. An ice box and new store fittings have been put in and these with the interior of the store are all finished in white. They have a fine stock of electric fixtures, rugs, furniture, etc., and are prepared to do business on a large scale.

Business is very slow and flowers are as a consequence plentiful. Prices are about the same as last week. American Beauty roses, 75c to $2 per dozen; Kaiserins, $4 to $6 per hundred; Brides and Maids, $3 to $4; Liberty, $4 to $8. Carnations command 75c to $1.50; asters, 75c to $1.50; lily of the valley, $3 to $4; gladioli and tuberoses, $2 to $3 per hundred.

H. Bayersdorfer & Co., are having a great time housing their importations. Another large warehouse is being added, which together with their present facilities makes one wonder where all the stock goes to. Harry only smiles and says: "Our principle trouble is to get the orders out as fast as they come in."

Wm. Gibson, with Pennock Brothers has been spending his vacation in Canada and reports having seen some fine stores in Toronto and the stock seemed to be better than anything offered here.

John Habermehl and wife are spending a month at Wildwood, N. J. George Faulkner and wife and Samuel Dunlop have just returned from the same place.

Fred Chyecwsky now smiles all over. Little girl last Saturday.   K.

THE AMERICAN FLORIST

NINETEENTH YEAR.

Subscription, $1.00 a year. To Europe, $2.00.
Subscriptions accepted only from those
in the trade.

Advertisements, on all except cover pages,
10 Cents a Line, Agate; $1.00 per inch.
Cash with Order.

No Special Position Guaranteed.

Discounts are allowed only on consecutive insertions, as follows—6 times, 5 per cent; 13 times,
10 per cent; 26 times, 20 per cent;
52 times, 30 per cent.

Cover space sold only on yearly contract at
$1.00 per inch, net, in the case of the two
front pages, regular discounts applying only to the back pages.

The Advertising Department of the AMERICAN
FLORIST is for florists, seedsmen and nurserymen
and dealers in wares pertaining to those lines only.

Orders for less than one-half inch space not accepted.

Advertisements must reach us by Wednesday to
secure insertion in the issue for the following
Saturday. Address

AMERICAN FLORIST CO., Chicago.

Bonney's Apostrophe to Horticulturists.

"Friends of the seed, the flower, the
fruit, fair trinity of potency and beauty
and use," said the late C. C. Bonney at the
World's Horticultural Congress, Chicago,
1893. (Mr. Bonney died Aug. 23, 1903.)

ARE your coal contracts made.

FROST may be expected in three weeks.

PLANT Lilium candidum and move the
peonies now.

KEEP working on the compost heap;
there's little doing there in cold weather.

LAWN GRASS can be sown now, remind
your customers who have new or thin
lawns.

FILL in low places on lawns and walks
so that frost and water do not work
damage during the winter.

WATERING the dahlia plants, where
practical, in the early morning will prevent injury from early frosts.

ARE the heating arrangements in order
for work the first cool nights? Don't let
Jack Frost steal a march on you.

Don't forget to water thoroughly all
bulbous stock when planted in flats or
in pots and set away for root growth.

FIND the men now who said they
wanted some good tulip beds next spring.
There is profit in the sales and such displays advertise your business.

PRESIDENT BREITMEYER, in accepting
the presidency of the S. A. F. invited the
co-operation of every wearer of its badge.
While the lessons of the 1903 convention
are fresh in your mind, drop him a suggestion or two. Philip Breitmeyer,
Gratiot and Miami avenues, Detroit,
Mich.

ACER NEGUNDO VARIEGATUM is used
extensively for decorations in London,
Eng. The plants range from five to nine
feet high and are in small pots. The
plants should be lifted one year before
they are sold (in Holland) the heavy
roots chopped down and planted another
year so as to secure fibrous roots.

A STORY was told at Milwaukee when
discussing Mr. Tesson's paper which
tended to belittle bookkeeping methods.
It appealed to the galleries and created
a laugh, but thoughtful men say they are
constantly aiming for accurate figures on
the result of their work and that representatives of large establishments may
well recommend such methods to beginners. The pen and pencil can be used to

advantage by him who handles the spade
and trowel.

Western Expansion.

It is interesting to note that President
Burton in his address at the Milwaukee
convention made the following comment
with regard to the development of the
business in the west:

During a season of remarkable expansion the
excitement is apt to carry us further than is wise
or expedient and in this, as in all other things it
is best not to be as expansive as we can but to
stop short before we reach the extreme of our
ability and endurance. This remark is inspired
by the way things are developing in the middle
west. Glass is being erected, so fast and general
business is expanding at such a rate in that section as almost to make an easterner's head swim.

The Carnation as National Flower.

VIEWS OF SOME NEWSPAPER WRITERS.

The Society of American Florists in
session at Milwaukee, is hearing several
propositions about the carnation. One
is that each member of the association
become a member of the McKinley Carnation League, that fantastic organization started in Ohio some months ago.
This is a matter entirely for the association to settle for itself, as each member
has the inalienable right to join anything
he pleases that does not collide with the
law. But when it is proposed to make
the carnation the national flower the
association might desist with much propriety. Just when the choice of a
national flower was committed to the
florists is unknown, and when it comes
to forcing a nation to elevate some one
man to the position of its highest product, and of commemorating him by a
flower as the emblem of the nation, perhaps another than Mr. McKinley, great
and good though he was, would be the
selection of the people of the United
States. A good many people prefer roses
to pinks, anyhow, and some would
choose sunflowers or hollyhocks.—Pittsburg Post, August 21, 1903.

The annual convention of American
florists rejected a resolution to make the
carnation the national flower. The reason
for doing so is right. The carnation is a
beautiful flower, but it is imported and
in this country can be grown only by
being cultivated. If we are to have a
regularly adopted national flower, let it
be one that is native to this country.
That is the view of the American florists
and it is all right.—Wilkesbarre Record,
August 24, 1903.

Society for Horticultural Science.

Prof. S. A. Beach, of Geneva, N. Y., has
issued the following circular with regard
to the proposed society for horticultural
science, dated August 7, 1903:

The organization of the society for Horticultural Science, proposed in my circular letter of
June 30 has been decided on. The proposition
met with a wide and enthusiastic and almost
unanimously favorable reception among not only
horticulturists but also a considerable number of
botanists and other scientists. The need of the
society is keenly felt, and the time appears ripe
for inaugurating the new movement. An attendance of at least thirty of those interested is
assured for the Boston meeting, and Professor
L. H. Bailey has consented to preside at the first
meeting.
The circular letter has elicited various and
often divergent expressions of opinion as to the
organization, affiliation and policy of the society,
especially as to its affiliation. In order that the
whole subject may be gone over thoroughly and
deliberately a preliminary meeting for organization and conference will be held in the rooms of
the Massachusetts Horticultural Society Wednesday afternoon, September 9, at 2 o'clock. It is
hoped to have the fullest possible attendance at
this meeting. The headquarters of the society
will be the same as those of the American Pomological Society.

On account of the time that will be required to
discuss matters of organization it will be impracticable to present a scientific programme.

GEORGE M. GARLAND, of iron gutter
fame, writes stating that he "can not
take any more fitting orders for awhile."
Labor and iron must be scarce.

BROWN BROTHERS COMPANY, of Rochester, N. Y., will probably offer the new
rose Mme. Norbert Levavasseur in the fall
of 1904 or spring of 1905.

Greenhouse Building.

Lawndale, Philadelphia, Pa.—Theodore Kirnzie, one house.

Georgetown, Mass.—Ira Wood, one
cucumber house.

Newburyport. Mass.—E. W. Pearson,
house 30x250.

Erie, Pa.—S. Alfred Bauer, seven houses
each 30x150 and one boiler house.

Sterling, Mass.—Ole Nelson, two houses.

Norton, Mass.—T. P. Leonard, range
of houses.

Baldwinville, Mass.—C. C. Streeter,
one cucumber house.

Cortland, N. Y.—Adolph Frost, two
houses each 25x55. Remodelling three
others each 25x75.

Gardner, Mass.—C. L. Peirce & A. L.
Hawkes, two cucumber houses.

Westfield, Mass.—E. DeWitt Herrick,
one conservatory.

Philadelphia, Pa.—E. R. Clark, one
conservatory.

Hampton Falls, N. H.—J. A. Dow &
Son, one house.

Georgetown, Mass.—Herbert Graham,
range of cucumber houses.

North Attleboro, Mass.—John J. Nolan,
one house.

Philadelphia, Pa.—Rothacker & Lang,
house 19x100. Robt. N. Neely, house
17x125.

South Tacoma, Wash.—James Harrison, one house 20x85.

Lake Geneva Gardens.

ED. AM. FLORIST:—Your correspondent
from Lake Geneva, Wis., states that elm
and maple are only prevalent on the
north shore, which statement is an error.
Although elm is not plentiful anywhere
around the lake except on the slopes
toward Lake Como, maple is quite plentiful on the south shore where the shore is
heavily wooded. I have found the prettiest groves of maples (Acer saccharinum
and Acer rubrum) here.

A new enemy has appeared in the Lake
Geneva region since I wrote my article in
the Forester on the dying out of the oak,
the dreaded agrilus. So far I have only
located this voracious borer on the south
shore, but expect during the summer to
examine the oaks on the north shore.
The prevalence of the agrilus is best
detected in the latter part of July and
during August, at which time the foliage
of the attacked trees suddenly withers as
if struck by blight. As this borer feeds
on the cambium layers it is easily found
by removing the bark of the attacked
trees.

An important matter your correspondent did not mention is that the hills
consist of gravel or very gravelly clay
(packing gravel), which almost everywhere comes up to the surface, especially
on steep slopes or high elevations. It is
only the lower levels that, benefited by
washouts, contain a better top soil.

I also desire to mention that the pin
oak (Quercus palustris) is very rare. this
locality being perhaps its northern limit.

JENS JENSEN.

Obituary.

JULES POSTH.

Jules Posth, for many years connected with the firm of Messrs. Vilmorin-Andrieux & Company, Paris, France, passed away on August 14 at the age of 70 years.

E. H. SWAN.

E. H. Swan, an amateur rose enthusiast, died at his home on Cove Neck, Long Island, N. Y., on August 30, aged 76 years. He had many acres of his vast estate devoted to rose cultivation.

Eine absolute Rothwendigkeit!

Hiermit $1.00 für mein Abonnement. Es ist die Pflicht eines Jeden prompt für den „American Florist" zu bezahlen, weil dieser eine absolute Rothwendigkeit für jeden Blumenzüchter ist.

Carl Roegner, Alabama.

SITUATIONS, WANTS, FOR SALE.

One Cent Per Word.

Cash with the Adv.

Plant Adv. NOT admitted under this head.

Every paid subscriber to the AMERICAN FLORIST for the year 1903 is entitled to a five-line WANT ADV. (situations only) free, to be used at any time during the year.

Situation Wanted—By experienced grower of cut flowers, as manager of small place. Address MANAGER, care American Florist.

Situation Wanted—By practical, experienced, and well recommended. PROPAGATOR, care AM. Florist.

Situation Wanted—By experienced gardener, single, to take charge of medium sized private place. Address THOS. CALLAHAN, Glen Cove, N. Y.

Situation Wanted—As foreman; by a strictly competent and all-round grower. Age 31. Life experience in all branches. Address Z, Newtown Square, Dwl. Co., Pa.

Situation Wanted—In St. Louis, Mo., by experienced gardener, 25, experienced in Germany, England and America. Commercial or private place. H V H, care American Florist.

Situation Wanted—By an American; position in first-class cut flower store as clerk. Six years' experience. Good recommendations. East preferred. Address EAST, care American Florist.

Situation Wanted—As working foreman by first-class growers of cut flowers and general stock. Roses a specialty. Only first-class place wanted. Chicago preferred. Address A B, care American Florist.

Situation Wanted—Young man, 19 years of age, wishes a position in City of New York, as assistant in general greenhouse work. Been with the best firms. Am a resident of New York City. E. H. C. M. Y., 1375 Boston Road, N. Y.

Situation Wanted—As head gardener; experienced in every branch of horticulture and management of a first-class place. English, married. Good references. GEO. STANDEN, South Millbrook, care J L Powell, N. Y.

Situation Wanted—As working foreman; carnations, roses, violets and general stock or decorator and designer. 16 years' experience. Near Boston preferred. Address I M, 419 Auburn St., Auburndale, Mass.

Situation Wanted—In or near Boston, by experienced grower of roses, carnations and chrysanthemums. Manager in last place for nine years. Best of references. Address JOHN PRITCHARD, Newtonville Av., Newtonville, Mass.

Situation Wanted—By practical florist. A No. 1 grower, capable of taking charge; single and can furnish best of references as to ability and sobriety. Well posted in almost all the lines of business. Age 29. Please state wages. Can come at once. Address EDWARD TATRO, Cleveland, Ohio.

Help Wanted—Rose growers. SOUTH PARK FLORAL CO., New Castle, Ind.

Help Wanted—A good steady man, for general greenhouse work. Apply to C. LOVERIDGE, Peoria, Ill.

Help Wanted—Florist as assistant in place of 15,000 feet where only cut flowers are grown. Good chance for man who can show good references. H. HORNBOEFT, Tipton, Ind.

Help Wanted—For flower store; a lady with some experience; also a man for carnations. State experience and wages expected. Address C R, care American Florist.

Help Wanted—At once; a sober, reliable, all-around man for commercial place. Single and German preferred. Reference required. BOEHRINGER BROS., Bay City, Mich.

Help Wanted—A man experienced in packing roses for shipping. We have a good position for a reliable man that understands the business. SOUTH PARK FLORAL CO., New Castle, Ind.

Help Wanted—At once, assistant rose grower, a man who can make himself useful. Good wages; steady work; send references. Address JAMES C. MURRAY, 403 Main St., Peoria, Ill.

Help Wanted—A good, steady man at once; single. To grow roses. Must have 3 years' experience. $80.00 per month, room and board. KRANZ FLORAL CO., 107 N. Market St., Ottumwa, Ia.

Help Wanted—First-class rose grower to take charge of section, good references as to ability, character and sobriety; wages $60.00 per month. THE J. A. BUDLONG & SON CO., 564 Pontiac Ave., Auburn, R. I.

Help Wanted—Good, bright, energetic young man for a first-class retail store, one who understands green house work, decorating and cut flower work thoroughly. State salary wanted and give references. World's Fair City. Address St. LOUIS, care American Florist.

For Rent—Sixty-foot greenhouse, 8 room house, two lots, $25 per month; 3181 Elston Ave. DR. BANGS, 554 N. Robey St., Chicago.

For Sale—One No. 30 Wilks hot water boiler with stack complete, used only three months. A bargain for cash. JAMES W. DUNFORD, R. R. No. 1, Clayton, Mo.

For Sale or Rent—On easy terms, 5,000 feet of glass in a good factory town of 5,000. Established seven years. No competition. Other business. J. R. JOHNSTONE, Dunkirk, Ind.

For Sale—House and barn, 4 greenhouses, about 4,000 ft. of glass, 9 hot water boilers, 2 vacant lots for growing plants. Stock enough to fill the houses. No competition. Address JOHN GEDDES, Girard, O.

For Sale—Fine old establishment of about 10,000 square feet of glass, one acre or more of ground with or without good dwelling. A bargain. Investigate soon if interested. Address OHIO, care American Florist.

For Sale—In the World's Fair city, three-room house, two greenhouses, one 14x80, one 18x80, one acre of ground; heated by steam; plenty of water. Price $1,900; $600 cash. LEO ESBRENZ, Webster Grove, Mo.

For Sale or Lease—A finely located place in the Borough of the Bronx, consisting of 11 greenhouses, (no stock), hot water heating, windmill, barn, dwelling house and about 2 acres of ground. J. RINGLER, 728 3rd Ave., New York City.

For Sale—Four large size Gorton side feed boilers (for hard or soft coal), 850 radiating surface each; one large sectional Florida heater, $50; one small coil-boiler, hot water in use two winters, will heat 3,000 square feet of glass, $20. Boilers taken out to put in larger one. Write for particulars. F. FALLON, Roanoke, Va.

FOR SALE. A good home and greenhouses well stocked with up-to-date stock for retail trade; established 20 years. Splendid opportunity is here offered. Reason, the death of Mrs. S. H. Bagley. C. H. Bagley, Abilene, Kan.

For Sale—Retail greenhouse establishment of about 3,300 feet glass, connected with two tenement dwellings; first-class reputation; good trade; center of town of about 9,000 people, growing rapidly. Must sell, low for cash. Reason, death of proprietor. One minute from depot; two railroads. Address THE N. A. CHASE GREENHOUSES, Winsted, Conn.

FOR SALE.

In a thriving Ohio town of about 22,000 inhabitants, fine greenhouse plant, consisting of 8 greenhouses, ranging in size from 12x100 to 20x130, also fine work shed and modern up-to-date office and store room attached. For particulars address

S. S. SKIDELSKY,
708 North 16th St.   PHILADELPHIA.

FOR SALE.

One set of Bailey's Cyclopedia of American Horticulture. One set of Nicholson's Dictionary of Gardening, four volumes, A to Z and supplement. No reasonable offer refused. Address

E. ASMUS, 1860-70 Evanston Avenue, CHICAGO.

For Sale.

40 HORSE-POWER STEAM BOILER. This boiler is in fair condition with exception of the back, one of which leaks a little in the fire box around the flues. New flues put in two years ago. Boiler has been in use 14 years. We ran it at a low pressure, 15 to 20 pounds of steam. It should heat 8,000 to 10,000 feet of glass. Size of smoke stack opening, 18 x 24 inches. No stack goes with the boiler. Price (includes grate bars, steam and water gauge with valves. Weight of boiler 4 to 5 tons. Cost to load on cars here $75.00. We had a patch put on one side last year, which now is as good as new. This is a cheap boiler with a little expense can be put in good shape.

Price on the ground here $50.00
Price on board cars 65.00

Vaughan's Greenhouses,
WESTERN SPRINGS, ILL.

A Rare Chance

For a good grower to go into business. The plant of the Morton Grove Greenhouses, (incorporated) is for sale. It is situated 14 miles from Chicago courthouse and consists of 38,000 feet of glass, ½ being new glass 16x20 put up in 1900. Four acres of tiled land. Excellent soil. 2,000 Peonies 2 years old. Steam heat, 3 boilers, one a 100 H. P. Kroeschell make, virtually new. 800 tons washed coal in shed. Have planted, 7,500 Roses, 16,000 Carnations, all first stock. Old established trade. Plant in A1 condition excepting the old range, for which no charge will be made. Will sell at a very attractive figure and on easy terms, with or without a 6 room dwelling on a 60 foot lot across the street. The rebuilding of the old range will give you an up-to-date plant. Might rent or sell half-interest with option of future purchase to a responsible grower, who must take full charge as the proprietor's interests are now entirely away from the city.

Address until Sept. 17th care UNITED STATES GAGE CO., 37 Spruce St., New York. After that care of same Company, Milwaukee, Wis.

PAUL KREISMAN.

*Horses, wagons, tools, etc., everything complete.

†No special hurry to sell. Transfer may be made at any time between now and spring.

ALWAYS mention the AMERICAN FLORIST when writing to advertisers.

For Sale.

A well established and profitable plant-growing establishment. Full equipment and everything in perfect order. Close to the city and enjoying a large patronage from the leading retail establishments in the Metropolis. For a man or firm with fair cash capital this is a chance to step in to a money-making business. Address

J W, care JULIUS LANG,
53 W. 30th Street, NEW YORK CITY.

Indianapolis.

STATE ASSOCIATION MEETING.—LIGHTNING STRIKES BARN.—GENERAL NEWS NOTES.

—VISITORS.

Baur & Smith's barn was struck by lightening a few days since. The bolt passed through the roof and the hay beneath it, hit a bale of straw on the ground floor and narrowly missed five gallons of gasoline. The damage done was comparatively small.

The September meeting of the State Florists' Association of Indiana was well attended, which is one sign that everybody is getting ready for work and the winter season.

Martin Brandlein is now at home in his new residence, recently bought. His new property is conveniently situated near his greenhouses.

Irvin Bertermann has announced his intention to call on the trade for contributions to the chrysanthemum show—Johnny get your gun.

Bert Stanley recently treated his rose bed with bisolphid of carbon against grub worms. He put the fluid too close to the plants and lost quite a number of them.

Gunnar Teilmann, of Marion, who visited our city recently, has a family record that runs back to the sixteenth century.

John Hartje is cutting fine blooms from his new white carnation Moonlight; a good name and a grand variety.

A number of the boys will go to Marion in the near future. They will be chaperoned by Fred Hukriede.

Wm. Billingsley recently took a trip to the lakes by order of his physician.

H. W. Riemann is recovering from an attack of appendicitis.

Most of our florist friends are back from their vacations.

Charles Wheatcraft left on a southern trip last week.

John Heidenreich is down with the hay fever.

Visitors: Charles Wester, of Little Rock, Ark., and J. A. E. Haugh, of Anderson, Ind.   H. J.

SOUTH SALEM, CONN.—Pinchbeck Brothers have started here with 5,000 feet of glass for carnation growing.

Wholesale Flower Markets

	MILWAUKEE, Sept. 3.	
Roses, Beauty, med. per doz.		1.50
" " short "		.75@1.00
" Liberty		4.00@ 6.00
" Bridesmaid		4.00@ 6.00
" Meteor, Golden Gate		4.00@ 6.00
" Perle		1.00@ 2.00
Carnations		.15
Sweet peas		.10.0C@12.50
Smilax		
Asparagus		60.00
Gladioli		3.00@ 4.00
Asters		1.00@ 2.00

	PITTSBURG, Sept. 3.	
Roses, Beauty, specials, per doz.	3 50@3.50	
" " extra	1.00@2.00	
" " No. 1	.75@1.00	
" " No. 3	3.00@ 5.00	
" Bride, Bridesmaid	1.00@ 6.00	
" Meteor	2.00@ 4.00	
" Kaiserin, Liberties	3.00@ 6.00	
Carnations	.50@ 1.00	
Lily of the Valley	3.00@ 4.00	
Sweet peas	.30	
Smilax	8.00@12.00	
Adiantum	.75@ 1.25	
Asparagus, strings	30.00@60.00	
" Sprengeri	2.00@ 4.00	
Gladioli	1.00@ 3.00	
Easter lilies	8.00@12.00	
Asters	.25@ 1.25	
L. Album and Rossum	2.00@ 3.00	

	CINCINNATI, Sept. 3.	
Roses, Beauty	10.00@35.00	
" Bride, Bridesmaid	3.00@ 6.00	
" Liberty	3.00@ 6.00	
" Meteor, Golden Gate	3.00@ 6.00	
Carnations	1.00@ 2.00	
Lily of the Valley	3.00@ 4.00	
Smilax	12.50@15.00	
Adiantum	1.00@ 1.50	
Gladioli	3.00	
Asters	.75@ 2.00	
Lilium Album and Rubrum	4.00	

	ST. LOUIS, Sep'. 3.	
Roses, Beauty, long stem	2.00	
" Beauty, medium stem	1.50	
" Beauty, short stem	4.00@ 6.00	
" Liberty	3.00@ 6.00	
" Bride, Bridesmaid	2.00@ 3.00	
" Golden Gate	2.00@ 4.00	
Carnations	1.00@ 1.50	
Smilax	12.50	
Asparagus Sprengeri	1.00@ 1.50	
Gladioli	1.00@ 2.00	
Ferns per 1000	1.85	
China Asters	1.00@ 2.00	
Tuberoses	3.00	

Pittsburg Cut Flower Co., Ltd

WHOLESALE FLORISTS.

——————Pittsburg, Pa.

INTERNATIONAL FLOWER DELIVERY.

PASSENGER STEAMSHIP MOVEMENTS.

The tables herewith give the scheduled time of departure of ocean steamships carrying first-class passengers from the principal American and foreign ports, covering the space of two weeks from date of this issue of the AMERICAN FLORIST. Much disappointment often results from attempts to forward flowers for steamer delivery by express, to the care of the ship's steward or otherwise. The carriers of these packages are not infrequently refused admission on board and even those delivered on board are not always certain to reach the parties for whom they were intended. Hence florists in interior cities having orders for the delivery of flowers to passengers on out-going steamers are advised to intrust the filling of such orders to some reliable florist in the port of departure, who understands the necessary details and formalities and has the facilities for attending to it properly. For the addresses of such firms we refer our readers to the advertisements on this page:

FROM	TO	STEAMER	*LINE	DAY	DUE ABOUT
New York	Liverpool	Etruria	1	Sat. Sept. 12, 3:00 a. m.	Sept. 18
New York	"	Campania	1	Sat. Sept. 19, 3:00 p. m.	Sept. 26
New York	Glasgow	Laurentian	2	Thur. Sept. 17, Noon.	Sept. 27
New York	Hamburg	Furst Bismarck	3	Thur. Sept. 10, 10:00 a. m.	Sept. 18
New York	"	Pretoria	3	Sat. Sept. 12, 8:00 a. m.	
New York	"	Deutschland	3	Tues. Sept. 15, 11:00 a. m.	
New York	"	Bluecher	3	Thur. Sept. 17, 1:30 p. m.	Sept. 24
New York	Copenhagen	United States	4	Wed. Sept. 16.	
New York	Glasgow	Furnessia	5	Sat. Sept. 12, Noon.	
New York	"	Columbia	5	Sat. Sept. 19, 3:00 p. m.	
New York	Southampton	Menominee	6	Fri. Sept. 11, 9:00 a. m.	Sept. 21
New York	"	St. Louis	6	Wed. Sept. 9, 10:00 a. m.	
New York	"	New York	6	Sat. Sept. 16, 10:00 a. m.	Sept. 23
New York	Liverpool	Germanic	7	Wed. Sept. 9, Noon.	Sept. 17
New York	"	Cedric	7	Fri. Sept. 11, 8:00 a. m.	Sept. 19
New York	"	Majestic	7	Wed. Sept. 16, Noon.	
New York	"	Celtic	7	Sat. Sept. 12, 3:00 p. m.	
New York	London	Mesaba	6	Sat. Sept. 12, 9:00 a. m.	
New York	"	Minnetonka	6	Sat. Sept. 19, 4:00 p. m.	
New York	Antwerp	Finland	9	Sat. Sept. 12, 10:00 a. m.	Sept. 22
New York	"	Vaderland	9	Sat. Sept. 19, 10:00 a. m.	Sept. 28
New York	Havre	La Touraine	10	Thur. Sept. 10, 10:00 a. m.	Sept. 17
New York	"	La SaVoie	10	Thur. Sept. 17, 10:00 a. m.	
New York	Rotterdam	Potsdam	11	Wed. Sept. 9, 10:00 a. m.	Sept. 18
New York	"	Statendam	11	Wed. Sept. 16, 10:00 a. m.	
New York	Genoa	Liguria	12	Tues. Sept. 8, 11:00 a. m.	
New York	"	Citta di Milano	12	Tues. Sept. 15, 11:00 a. m.	
New York	"	Princess Irene	13	Sat. Sept. 12, 11:00 a. m.	Sept. 25
New York	Bremen	Kronprinz Wilh.	13	Tues. Sept. 8, 9:00 a. m.	Sept. 15
New York	"	Barbarossa	13	Thur. Sept. 10, Noon	Sept. 21
New York	"	Grosser Kurfuerst	13	Thur. Sept. 17, 1:00 p. m.	
Boston	Liverpool	Ivernia	1	Tues. Sept. 8, 10:30 a. m.	Sept. 14
Boston	"	Mayflower	15	Thur. Sept. 10, Noon.	Sept. 17
Boston	"	Columbus	15	Thur. Sept. 17, 7:00 a. m.	
Boston	"	Canadian	16	Sat. Sept. 12, 1:30 p. m.	
Boston	"	Cestrian	15	Sat. Sept. 19, 11:00 a. m.	
Montreal	"	Southwark	15	Sat. Sept. 12, Daylight.	
Montreal	"	Parisian	19	Sat. Sept. 12, 8:30 a. m.	
San Francisco	Yokohama	Gaelic	17	Fri. Sept. 11, 1:00 p. m.	Sept. 30
San Francisco	"	Hongkong Maru	17	Sat. Sept. 19, 1:00 p. m.	Oct. 5
San Francisco	Hongkong	Gaelic	17	Fri. Sept. 11, 1:00 p. m.	Oct. 10
San Francisco	"	Hongkong Maru	17	Sat. Sept. 19, 1:00 p. m.	Oct. 20
San Francisco	Sydney	Sonoma	18	Thur. Sept. 17, 8:00 p. m.	Oct. 9
San Francisco	Tahiti	Mariposa	18	Sun. Sept. 20, 11:00 a. m.	Oct. 2
Vancouver	Hongkong	Empress of China	20	Mon. Sept. 7.	Sept. 29
Vancouver	"	Athenian	20	Mon. Sept. 21.	Oct. 19
Seattle	"	Iyo Maru	22	Sat. Sept. 19, a. m.	Oct. 20
New York	Naples	Roma	14	Tues. Sept. 15,	Sept. 27

*1 Cunard; 2 Allen-State; 3 Hamburg-American; 4 Scandinavian-American; 5 Anchor Line; 6 Atlantic Transport; 7 White Star; 8 American; 9 Red Star; 16 French; 11 Holland-American; 13 Italian Royal Mail; 13 North German Lloyd; 14 Fabre; 15 Dominion; 16 Leyland; 17 Occidental and Oriental; 18 Oceanic; 19 Allan; 20 Can, Pacific Ry.; 21 N. Pacific Ry.; 22 Hongkong-Seattle.

INTERNATIONAL FLOWER DELIVERY.

STEAMSHIPS LEAVE FOREIGN PORTS.

FROM	TO	STEAMER	*LINE	DAY	DUE ABOUT
Liverpool	New York	Umbria	1	Sat. Sept. 12,	Sept. 18
Liverpool	"	Lucania	1	Sat. Sept. 19,	Sept. 25
Liverpool	"	Cymbric	7	Fri. Sept. 11, 5:00 p. m.	Sept. 19
Liverpool	"	Teutonic	7	Wed. Sept. 16, 5:00 p. m.	Sept. 23
Liverpool	"	Arabic	7	Fri. Sept. 11, 5:00 p. m.	Sept. 26
Liverpool	Boston	Saxonia	1	Tues. Sept. 8,	Sept. 15
Liverpool	"	Commonwealth	15	Thur. Sept. 10,	Sept. 17
Liverpool	"	New England	15	Thur. Sept. 17,	Sept. 24
Liverpool	"	Devonian	16	Fri. Sept. 11,	
Liverpool	"	Winifredian	16	Fri. Sept. 18,	
Liverpool	Montreal	Canada	18	Wed. Sept. 9,	
Liverpool	"	Kensington	15	Wed. Sept. 16,	
Glasgow	New York	Astoria	5	Thur. Sept. 10,	
Glasgow	"	Ethiopia	5	Thur. Sept. 17,	
Glasgow	"	Numidian	2	Sat. Sept. 12,	Sept. 23
Glasgow	"	Mongolian	2	Sat. Sept. 19,	Sept. 26
Genoa	"	Lombardia	12	Mon. Sept. 7,	
Genoa	"	Nord America	12	Mon. Sept. 14,	
Genoa	"	Sardegna	12	Mon. Sept. 21,	
Genoa	"	Hohenzollern	12	Thur. Sept. 17,	Sept. 30
Southampton	"	Philadelphia	8	Sat. Sept. 12, Noon.	
Southampton	"	St. Paul	8	Wed. Sept. 16, Noon.	
Southampton	"	St. Louis	8	Sat. Sept. 19, Noon.	
Southampton	"	Marquette	6	Wed. Sept. 9,	
London	"	Minneapolis	6	Sat. Sept. 12,	Sept. 21
London	"	Minnehaha	6	Sat. Sept. 19,	Sept. 29
Antwerp	"	Kroonland	9	Sat. Sept. 12, 2:00 p. m.	Sept. 21
Antwerp	"	Zeeland	9	Sat. Sept. 19, 11:00 a. m.	Sept. 29
Hamburg	"	Auguste Victoria	3	Thur. Sept. 10,	
Hamburg	"	Pennsylvania	3	Sat. Sept. 12,	Sept. 22
Hamburg	"	Moltke	3	Thur. Sept. 17,	Sept. 26
Hamburg	"	Patricia	3	Sat. Sept. 19,	O.t. 1
Havre	"	La Bretagne	10	Sat. Sept. 12,	Sept. 20
Havre	"	La Lorraine	10	Sat. Sept. 19,	
Copenhagen	"	Hellig Olav	4	Wed. Sept. 9,	
Rotterdam	"	Noordam	11	Sat. Sept. 12,	
Rotterdam	"	Rotterdam	11	Sat. Sept. 19,	
Bremen	"	Kaiser Wilh. II	13	Tues. Sept. 8,	Sept. 15
Bremen	"	Bremen	13	Sat. Sept. 12,	Sept. 21
Bremen	"	K. Wil. Der Grosse	13	Tues. Sept. 15,	Sept. 22
Sidney	Vancouver	Miowera	20	Mon. Sept. 7,	Oct. 1
Sidney	San Francisco	Ventura	18	Mon. Sept. 7,	Sept. 28
Hongkong	"	Nippon Maru	17	Tues. Sept. 8,	Sept. 15
Hongkong	"	Siberia	17	Wed. Sept. 16,	Oct. 13
Hongkong	Tacoma	Olympia	21	Thur. Sept. 10,	Oct. 9
Hongkong	Seattle	Shinano Maru	22	Tues. Sept. 8, p. m.	Oct. 8
Naples	New York	Germania	14	Thur. Sept. 17,	Sept. 26

* See steamship list on opposite page.

THE SEED TRADE.

AMERICAN SEED TRADE ASSOCIATION.
S. F. Willard, Pres.; J. Charles McCullough, First Vice-Pres.; C. E. Kendel, Cleveland, O., Sec'y and Treas.
Twenty-second annual convention St. Louis; Mo., June, 1904.

DEATH of M. Jules Posth. See page 225.

A. H. GOODWIN is making an eastern trip.

EARLY spring cabbage is a fifty per cent crop on Long Island.

LONDON.—N. Sherwood, of Hurst & Son, will make a tour of the world, going first to New Zealand.

CATALOGUE makers should be looking for photographs of plants, vegetables, fruits and flowers now.

S. B. DICKS is reported ill with appendicitis in a Boston hospital; his son will come on to make his American trip.

ONION set buyers are holding off on fall contracts expecting the lower prices towards spring which have prevailed the past two seasons.

THE Chicago *Tribune* of August 30 gives an interesting half page article (illustrated) on the Budlong onion set and pickle farm—largest in the world, they say.

IF the recommendations of the newly appointed bulb committee of the S. A. F. on grading of gladioli could be made public soon the benefits might be secured a year sooner than otherwise.

J. COMONT, with James Carter, Dunnett & Beale, is in his forty-fifth year of service with that firm. Mr. Comont is making his twenty-first annual American trip, and is in Chicago to-day.

WATERLOO, NEB, August 30, 1903.— C. P. Coy & Son report serious flood with three feet of water, in Waterloo many fields have been flooded along the Platte, Elkhorn and Rawhide rivers.

System.

We read in these days a great deal about system, and we cannot question the fact that system has done much to facilitate the work of the world. The successful business enterprises of the country, the successful schools and colleges, are definitely systematic. Yet every educator knows that real education depends upon the man behind the system, and the most ardent friends of education are advocating greater individual development. I do not believe the schools can teach success in advertising. Many of the details we can learn from each other, but the true elements of success are not written in the books. The great advertising successes of the country have been characterized by individuality. We believe in system, but it must be a system of sufficient elasticity to enable the man at the head of the business to change it in a day if conditions change.—*Frank B. Long in Agricultural Advertising, July.*

Nebraska Seed Crop.

A well known grower writes as follows August 26:

"Have had about ten days of sunshine, accompanied with warm nights, representing excellent conditions for promoting the growth of corn and vine seeds west of the Missouri river, and growers by watching their crops and destroying the vines that gave evidence of being attacked by the melon aphis have checked this evil from spreading, in accomplishing which the clear, warm weather has been of material assistance.

"We are having to-day a continuous heavy rain that extends generally throughout the state, and which will

STORE OF HOLMES SEED CO., HARRISBURG, PA.
(See issue of August 29, 1903.)

check the maturing of corn and vine seed crops and encourage their continuous growth. This condition will be of great value, providing the season subsequently proves to be favorable for the ripening and maturing of crops.

"Of course, many crops are already beyond redemption, having been unable to withstand the wet weather or recover from damage sustained by hail. As heavy rains in September are generally followed by frost we would very much prefer to have them come at this time than later on."

St. Paul.

Mr. Crossland, manager for Steele, Briggs Seed Company, Winnipeg, Manitoba, was a recent caller.

W. Utterman, of L. L. May & Company, has gone to the Pacific coast. A. W. Martin, of the same firm, will return from his European trip this week.

With favorable weather and no frost till October 1, corn should make a crop in this section.

The Albert Dickinson Company, of Chicago, is about to erect a warehouse and elevator in the Midway district.

FELIX.

Cleveland.

It is possible that stores handling Dutch bulbs will get their stock from Holland before the Romans and Paper Whites get in; they are expected to be ready to be hauled up from the depots September 1.   O. G.

Milwaukee.

The Milwaukee Florists' Club held a meeting at the St. Charles hotel on Friday, August 28. The election of officers resulted as follows: C. C. Pollworth, president; W. A. Kennedy, vice-president; H. V. Hunkel, secretary and C. Dallwig, treasurer.

The Water Hyacinth Nuisance.

A successful method for destroying the water hyacinth, which seriously obstructs navigation in southern rivers, has been tried on the St. Johns, where some wharves have been abandoned because of it, according to the Boston *Transcript*. A boat filled with a laboratory and force-pump sprays a swath ninety feet wide with a chemical which causes them to die to the roots.

THE NURSERY TRADE.

AM. ASSOCIATION OF NURSERYMEN.
N. W. HALE, KnoxVille, Tenn., Pres.; FRANK
A. WEBER, St. Louis, Mo., Vice-Pres.; GEORGE C.
SEAGER, Rochester, N. Y., Sec'y.
Twenty-ninth annual convention, Atlanta, Ga.,
June, 1904.

WE are in receipt of the report of the twenty-eighth annual meeting of the American Association of Nurserymen, held at Detroit, Mich., June 10-12, also a copy of the nurserymen's telegraphic code.

Boston Park Notes.

The American elms on Commonwealth avenue and elsewhere are beginning to show the effects of the severe drought experienced last May. While the foliage of the English elms is still of the richest dark green, the foliage of the Americans is matured and already beginning to fall. From Dartmouth street to the Fens entrance a majority of the trees in the avenue are Scotch elms, inferior in all respects to the campestris or English species. Moreover the original planting was badly arranged and the soil is as poor as it possibly could be and support anything, there being but eight or ten inches of loam on top of a bed of stony gravel. Superintendent J. A. Pettigrew is now opening up holes, twenty feet square by four feet in depth, at regular intervals through the center of each grass plot and filling in with rich loam and manure. Grafted English elms will be set out in these prepared beds next spring and as they grow existing trees will be taken away as soon as they interfere with them. The English elm is very variable as to habit and other characteristics and in order to secure the requisite uniformity for such a plantation, grafted stock has been prepared, all from one tree. These were done in England, and the young trees have now been one year in the nursery grounds here.

Norway maples throughout the park are suffering severely this season from the attacks of greenfly. The leaves are dropping and the trees have a dejected look that suggests a serious outlook for the future. Conifers of all kinds are giving more or less trouble, each year increasingly so, as has been the experience in every city where an attempt has been made to grow evergreens, and without some method of abating the smoke nuisance Mr. Pettigrew is of the opinion that twenty-five years from now will see practically the extermination of the conifers within the city limits. Another pest which has been unusually active this year is red spider. It swarms on and over everything.

A large amount of water-side planting has been done during the past season along both shores of the river way. Wild rice grass, whose hardiness for this latitude has heretofore been questioned is now well established and waves its graceful plumes here and there along the water's edge. Azaleas such as viscosa, calendulacea and Vaseyi and ferns, hibiscus, cardinal flower, pontederia, sagittaria, lythrum, alisma, hardy asters, Iris versicolor, Asclepias incarnata and a variety of sedges and rushes are fast filling in a beautiful fringe along the banks, making a charming effect.

The ornamental unfruited shrubs are now attracting attention. The barberries are veritable fountains of vivid scarlet and the cranberry trees and other viburnums are glorious masses of color.

Symphoricarpos with its waxy white berries, wild roses with their red hips, Pyrus nigra with shining black fruit and a multitude of thorns with fruit of changing color all are now in their prime, while the euonymuses and celastruses with an unusually heavy crop are beginning to open their pods and disclose the brilliant arils.

Transplanting Large Trees.

I have had some experience in transplanting large trees, on one occasion planting about seventy elms of from six to fourteen inches in diameter. About half of the number were frozen balls of roots. The remainder were dug after the frost left the ground with as long roots as possible, the roots being followed, and after digging being bagged and kept moist. The latter method is the better of the two, and is the one adopted by O. C. Simonds with the large elms transplanted into Graceland cemetery, Chicago, of which Mr. Olmsted speaks. In the case I refer to, roots often twenty feet long were procured, and the trees planted in clumps on the surface of well prepared ground. The roots were carefully laid out, the trees guyed, and loam wheeled in to cover. Not one tree so treated was lost; on the contrary, all grew well. This work was done under the best possible conditions, the trees being selected in summer from open pasture lands, carefully dug, the roots kept moist, and carefully planted and mulched.

Now while such good results may be had in transplanting elms, willows or soft maples, there are no other trees, in my experience, from which as good results might be expected. I have seen hundreds of thousands of dollars spent in the planting of large trees in Chicago, and I think nearly all wasted. The same amount of money spent in a proper preparation of the ground, with the planting of young nursery stock would have been infinitely better.

There are times when the horticulturist has to do violence to his better judgment; and in such case, in the transplanting of large trees, I would recommend the getting of all roots possible; never mind the ball of earth if you can get roots and keep them moist. Thin out a portion of the branches but do it without seeming to have done it. Thoroughly prepare the bed for the tree; and, I repeat it all, only attempt it with the trees I have previously enumerated, with the possible inclusion of red and hard maples.

I hope that Mr. Hemingway may not find that he is crowing before he is out of the woods. Conifers of fifteen or twenty-five feet in height are so little things to transplant. If successful it will be a feather in his cap, and a tribute to his careful methods. In answer to his query as to what trees it is better to transplant in fall and which in spring, I have found it best to leave oaks, beeches, magnolias tulips, thorns and Cornus florida for spring planting.—J. A. Pettigrew in Bulletin New England Park Superintendents.

PEORIA, ILL.—James C. Murray will build a greenhouse on Perry avenue.

OUR PASTIMES.

Announcements of coming contests or other events of interests to our bowling, shooting and sporting readers are solicited and will be given place in this column.
Address all correspondence for this department to Wm. J. Stewart, 79 Milk St., Boston, Mass.; Robt. Kift, 1725 Chestnut St., Philadelphia, Pa.; or to the American Florist Co., 324 Dearborn St., Chicago, Ill.

At Philadelphia.

There was a lively game on the home alleys Wednesday evening, September 2. A match had been arranged between the Asheville team of last year and the Milwaukee champions. Those who bowled on both teams had their scores counted for each side so the contest was really between four men, except that the five lowest had to pay for the games and refreshments. The first game had a Milwaukee flavor to it, but after that the boys seemed to get tired. Still the average was not so bad, being within two pins of 166 to a man, the total 2986 defeating Chicago's convention score of 2962 by 24 pins.
The Asheville team, although defeated by 202 pins, is not satisfied and there will be another game next Wednesday. The score follows:

PHILADELPHIA.	1st	2d	3d	T'l
Connor	161	177	196	534
Polites	210	168	162	543
Robertson	182	149	158	489
Yates	168	154	147	463
Adelberger	197	138	170	505
Kift	152	150	153	455
Total	1061	986	986	2986
ASHEVILLE.	1st	2d	3d	T'l
Moss	184	171	193	548
Starkey	160	132	184	480
Kift	156	180	153	495
Anderson	143	125	134	401
Watson	132	148	131	411
Robertson	162	149	158	489
Total	953	885	947	2784

St. Louis.

The meeting of the Florists' club will be held at Fred. Ammann's, Edwardsville, Ill., on Thursday, September 10. An enjoyable and profitable meeting is sure to be had as Mr. Ammann is an entertaining host. Meet on the west side of Eads bridge.
The Michel Plant and Bulb Company will dispose of its surplus stock by auction on Tuesday, September 8. Mr. Michel holds a sale each autumn, which enables him to dispose of stock left over.
R. J. Mahn, who has recently started business, has been awarded the contract for grading and planting the grounds surrounding the Jerusalem exhibit at the World's Fair.
Chas. Beyer is busy propagating rubbers this week. His carnation houses are all filled and cleaned up. He says business is improving slowly.
F. J. Fillmore is on jury service. His carnations and roses are doing well. The painting and repairing is about finished at his place.
Dr. Wm. Trelease has returned from Mexico.
Visitors: Dr. Schafferneck, St. Charles, Mo.; also Wm. Bastien, Pleasant Hill, Mo.　　　　　　F. K. B.

CARNATIONS.

Strong, healthy plants, guaranteed first-class, at $4.00 per 100.
MARQUIS, CRANE, GLAZIER, JOOST, W. CLOUD, DOROTHY, Q. LOUISE, M. GLORY, ARMAZINDY.

G. VanBochove & Bro., Kalamazoo, Mich.

Detroit.

MILWAUKEE CONVENTION DISCUSSED AT MEETING OF FLORISTS' CLUB.

The meeting Wednesday evening of the Detroit Florists' Club was one of special interest to the thirty members present: Robt. Flowerday, the newly elected president of the club, presided and the efficiency of his ruling made it plain that no mistake was made by electing him. Philip Breitmeyer, the president elect of the S. A. F. was greeted by all with expressions of joy over his success at Milwaukee. In his address to the club he thanked his many friends for their loyal support and promised his continued devotion to the interests of the S. A. F. whose membership he hoped to raise to a thousand for the St. Louis convention. In referring to the benefits accruing to the members he attached more importance to the social features of the society, which are being more and more appreciated by those regularly attending the conventions.

Many of the Detroit visitors at the convention gave their impressions of the various features of the meeting. All were loud in their praise of Milwaukee and Chicago florists' hospitality and the genial spirit shown throughout. A resolution was passed thanking them for the kindness and consideration shown, and the secretary was instructed to apprise them of the action of the club.   J. F. S.

Minneapolis.

The market has been in an unsettled state during the past week, the weather having much to do with same as most of the present production is from outside. The new cut of roses has helped considerably in filling orders and has brought fair returns, although the American Beauty stock is short-stemmed and of an inferior quality.

The Minneapolis boys who attended the Milwaukee convention report, having the time of their lives and many relate of the glorious trip to Chicago and their entertainment by the trade of that city. Rice Brothers furnished the wild smilax used at the opening of Wm. Donaldson & Company. It was the first smilax of the season and of a fancy quality.

A. S. Swanson had a cut bloom of Philodendron pertusum which attracted much attention.   C. F. R.

Cleveland.

The club meeting was very well attended on Monday night, August 24, as all members who did not go to the convention, were anxious to hear the news. A. Graham spoke at some length on general topics, of the convention and its broadening influence, etc. The Cleveland florists were very enthusiastic over the way the Chicago boys entertained them and voted them royal good fellows. They claim that they were never treated better.

Retail trade is somewhat slack these very hot days. Gladioli and rudbeckias are somewhat tiring to the constant buyers, but the demand for flowers for funeral work is as heavy as ever. There has been an early demand for callas.   O. G.

EAST ORANGE, N. J.—The T. W. Lowden & Sons Company has been incorporated to do a florist, seed and landscape gardening business with capital stock fixed at $50,000.

Carnations.

Norway, Crane, G. Lord, $4.00 per 100.
Flora Hill, Prosperity, Lawson, $5.00 per 100.
Also a few hundred very fine plants of our new red Alice Kennicott at $6.00 per 100.

Boston Ferns

All sizes pot and bench grown.
All of the above are good values and if not satisfactory may be returned. Cash with order.

DAVIS BROS.,   Geneva, Ill.

FINE FIELD-GROWN
Carnation Plants.

This is very nice and healthy stock.
Flora Hill, Queen Louise. Marquis, Morning Glory, first size $4.00; second size, $3.00. Joost, McGowan, $3.00.

SUNNYSIDE GREENHOUSES,   Owosso, Mich.

STRONG, HEALTHY, FIELD GROWN

CARNATION PLANTS.

Enchantress and Adonis, $20.00 per 100. Flora Hill, Queen Louise, Prosperity, Lawson, Crane, $6.00 per 100; $50 00 per 1000. Lord, Ine, Joost, Sport, Marquis, $5.00 per 100; $35.00 per 1000.

Mrs. A. M. SCHAFER,   229 Balmoral Ave. CHICAGO, ILL.

CARNATIONS.

Rooted cuttings of all the leading varieties now ready. Also rooted runners of Lady Campbell, Swanley White and Princess of Wales Violets. Send me a list of what you want and get prices. Stock in fine condition. Address

Chas. Chadwick, L. Box II, Grand Rapids, Mich.

All The Best Carnations Cheap

The Leading Novelties of 1903.
The Best Varieties of 1902.
All the Standard Sorts.
Order your Field-Grown Plants NOW.

GEO. HANCOCK & SON, GRAND HAVEN, MICH.

SURPLUS CARNATIONS

1,000 QUEEN LOUISE.   500 ESTELLE.
500 DOROTHY.   100 DAYBREAK.
CASH WITH ORDER.

W. SABRANSKY, Kenton, O.

A1 Carnation Plants.

Prosperity .... 8c each
Mrs. Thomas Lawson, Gov. Roosevelt..... 6c each
Crane, White Cloud, Flora Hill, Marquis. 5c each
Daybreak, Portia .... 4c each
Field Grown—Fine Plants.

FRANK BERRY, Stillwater, Minn.

CARNATIONS

We have the following varieties to offer:
Ethel Crocker, per 1000....$35.00; per 100......$8.00
G. Lord, per 100............................. 3.25
Avondale, per 100............................ 8.00
America, per 100............................. 4.00
Crane, per 100............................... 4.00
White Cloud, per 100......................... 4.00
Queen Louise, (second size).................. 3.00

W. W. COLES, Kokomo. Ind.

SPECIALTIES

ROSES, from 3-inch pots,   In Best
CARNATIONS, for all delivery,
CHRYSANTHEMUMS,   Varieties
SMILAX, VIOLETS.
Prices Low. Send for List.

WOOD BROTHERS, Fishkill, N. Y.

Montreal.

It was a pleasure for the boys of Montreal to visit their friends at Lachine on the occasion of the fourth annual exhibition of the Lachine Horticultural Society, which was a credit to the society. The exhibits of the professionals were better than in former years, with more entries and better qualities; on the other hand the amateur section was a very large one, showing a keen competition. The society received many compliments on the fine showing from prominent members of the Montreal Gardeners' and Florists' Club. The principal prize winners among the professional growers were Tom. McHugh, of the Forest and Stream Club, at Dorval, C. A. Smith, Gabriel Vrengde, Ed. Gernaey, Jos. Lefebore, Thomas Pewtress and Ed. Derynck.

James Jansen, of Berlin, Ont., was in the city recently.

PUEBLO, COLO.—G. Fleischer has completed a new and up-to-date flower store which is in charge of Sam. Lundy, formerly of the Park Floral Company at Denver. G. V.

Lowell, Mass.

The quality and supply of flowers is considerably below last year's record on account of the frequent cold rains, which have retarded growth. All outdoor stock is water-soaked and in a bad condition. There has been a great deal of funeral work.

During the past two months the florists all agreed with the other merchants to close up their establishments every Thursday at 12:30 o'clock, but found that it was hard for some to adhere to the agreement.

H. B. Greene left us Monday, August 31, to be gone six weeks. He will visit all the large cities as far west as St. Louis in the interest of his book on pressed flowers from the holy lands.

George W. Patten, who was stricken with a slight shock of paralysis several weeks ago while sojourning in Vermont, arrived home a few days ago very much improved in health.

James J. McManmon, who has been spending his vacation at Atlantic City, New York and Philadelphia, arrived home August 29 after a very enjoyable trip.

Backer & Company, of Billerica, have been very busy the past few months erecting a new carnation house, 30x250, to be filled with all the latest varieties.

Gilbert Wentworth, for several years with A. Roper, of Tewksbury, severed his connection with the above to go to his old position with Patten.

M. A. Patten with his wife and family have returned home after spending two weeks at Plum Island.

Peter McManmon started on his annual vacation August 31. He will spend two weeks in Washington.   A. M.

LE ROY, N. Y.—W. H. Baxter, the Lathrop Avenue florist, wishes to announce to his friends and patrons that he will continue to do business as heretofore.

Standard Pumping Engines.
GAS OR GASOLENE.

No hot air; no fuss; no uncertainty. If you really want water, at pressure enough to do good work, let us tell you what we can do for you.

THE STANDARD PUMP AND ENGINE CO., Cleveland, O.

THE Regan Printing House
Nursery
Seed   CATALOGUES
Florists'
87-91 Plymouth Place,   CHICAGO.

THE AMERICAN FLORIST

A WEEKLY JOURNAL FOR THE TRADE

America is "the Prow of the Vessel; there may be more comfort Amidships, but we are the first to touch Unknown Seas."

Vol. XXI.　　CHICAGO AND NEW YORK. SEPTEMBER 12, 1903.　　No. 797.

THE AMERICAN FLORIST

NINETEENTH YEAR.

Copyright 1903, by American Florist Company
Entered as Second-Class Mail Matter.

PUBLISHED EVERY SATURDAY BY

AMERICAN FLORIST COMPANY,
324 Dearborn St., Chicago.

Eastern Office: 79 Milk St., Boston.

Subscription, $1.00 a year.　To Europe, $2.00.
Subscriptions accepted only from the trade.
Volumes half-yearly from August, 1901.

SOCIETY OF AMERICAN FLORISTS AND
ORNAMENTAL HORTICULTURISTS.
Officers—JOHN BURTON, Philadelphia, Pa.,
president; C. C. POLLWORTH, Milwaukee, Wis.,
vice-president; WM. J. STEWART, 79 Milk Street,
Boston, Mass., secretary; H. B. BEATTY, Oil City,
Pa., treasurer.
OFFICERS-ELECT—PHILIP BREITMEYER, president; J. K. M. L. FARQUHAR, vice-president; secretary and
treasurer as before. Twentieth annual meeting
at St. Louis, Mo., August, 1904.

THE AMERICAN CARNATION SOCIETY.
Annual convention at Detroit, Mich., March 2,
1904. ALBERT M. HERR, Lancaster, Pa., secretary.

AMERICAN ROSE SOCIETY.
Annual meeting and exhibition, Philadelphia,
March, 1904. LEONARD BARRON, 136 Liberty St.,
New York, secretary.

CHRYSANTHEMUM SOCIETY OF AMERICA
Annual convention and exhibition, New York,
November 10-13, 1903. FRED H. LEMON, Richmond,
Ind., secretary.

THIS ISSUE 40 PAGES WITH COVER.

CONTENTS.

Convention Afterthoughts.

While the annual meeting of our craft in convention is still fresh in our minds it is a good thing to note down our impressions and give honest expression to our praise and our criticism.

The recent meeting of the S. A. F. in the Cream City was, in many respects, one of the most successful of its kind and no words are too emphatic in commendation of those on whom the management devolved. To our Milwaukee friends we owe a debt for their endeavors to make our stay with them both pleasant and profitable. This is not said in an attempt to curry favor.

It is pleasant to know that Chicago is no longer the western limit of our successful operation, and the large attendance this year promises well for our next meeting at St. Louis.

The development of the business in the middle west during the last decade has been phenomenal, and no one who took occasion to visit the immense establishments in the vicinity of Chicago can doubt that the center of activity is steadily moving westward.

It strikes me that the trade exhibit was unusually attractive, due more, perhaps, to the abundant light and tasteful arrangement of the wares, than to size or variety of exhibits.

The supply men were evidently working a profitable field, and, judging by the display, metal wreaths and other gorgeous "contrapshuns" are more appreciated west of Lake Michigan than in some other localities.

Considering the fact that the exhibition and the business meetings were both held in the same building, almost in the same room in fact, the noninterference is worthy of remark. This was no doubt due in great measure to the very efficient sergeant-at-arms, and proves the wisdom of the appointment of such an officer, and the insight that selected the appointee.

The present system of conducting the exhibition seems, to one who looks at it from the outside, to be nearly perfect. Everything seems harmonious and in every way admirable, as far as it goes. Besides its uses as a show room it makes an excellent place for renewing acquaintances or for forming new ones, the crowd being more concentrated than in the lobbies of the hotels or in the canteens.

Speaking of the canteen, it is pleasing to note how very inconspicuous a figure it cut in Milwaukee, notwithstanding the fact that Milwaukee is noted for its mild exhilarants, and that its manufactories thereof were both numerous and large. It would be hard to find, I think, a more orderly crowd than the florists, even when under the excitement of their great outing.

As I remarked before, the exhibition hall is a good place to renew acquaintances, but it is not as easy to form new ones as it ought to be. Is it not about time that we had some simple identification scheme? A numbered button to be given to members as they register, and an extra sheet to be attached to the programme giving the names and local stopping place with corresponding number are all that would be necessary. The expense would be very small, and the benefits great. The plan works well in other societies, why not in ours? It would save a great deal of embarrassment, mortification, white lies and bluff and would prove an inestimable blessing to those who, like myself, have a short memory for names and a long memory for faces. I brought this matter up some years ago but there were objectors at that time, and it miscarried as some other aspirations of mine have done. Now I hereby resign all political honors and devote myself to the propagation of the identification idea. Will the executive committee please take notice?

Good examples of modern martyrs could be seen in abundance in the meeting room during the reading of several papers.

The man who will sit quietly in his seat for an hour or so, respectfully pretending to appreciate what he can not possibly hear has my admiration and sympathy, and is entitled to a crown. Either a megaphone should be employed or else only those blessed with siren-like voices should attempt to read, in the average convention hall.

Do we not have too much reading anyway? Is it not a mistake to have any papers read that are not of a character to bring out a spirited discussion? Or one that depends upon accessories in the way of illustration for its proper understanding? All essays, lectures and sermons other than as above should be read by title only and printed as is already the custom in the proceedings of the society. Then while we are waiting for our winter fires to catch up with the increasing cold outside, we can read them with pleasure and profit. Time at the convention is too valuable to be used in that way.

Everybody says, and so it must be true, that the great value of our annual gathering is in the personal contact with others of our craft who are not within reach at ordinary times; to rub up against kindred spirits and saturate ourselves with an inspiration to sustain us for the ensuing year. In these informal meetings it is easier to apply the suction pump, and there is no stern presiding officer to close the debate.

Of course it is necessary to have a programme embracing papers on various subjects of interest to the craft. Many of them are of great value and worthy of being preserved, as they are, in our printed volume. But what we want in something thoroughly alive and sociable and as informal as possible for our open meetings.

We have wisely put upon our executive committee a great deal of the routine work of the society, which is a great relief. Would it not be possible to relieve the annual meeting a little more?

Life is too short for repetition of dry details. It is results we are after.

Yes. There was a report on closer relations with the kindred societies, apparently not quite satisfactory, although showing earnest endeavor on the part of the committee in charge. The doctors disagree, so I suppose the decision must be left to the laity. Possibly the kindred societies may solve the problem. Personally I doubt if anything satisfactory can be brought about without having all the members of the auxiliary organizations members of the S. A. F., and full members at that. Then the S. A. F. could set aside sufficient funds to take care of the affiliated bodies. There would be a gain in economy of administration and secretarial work, as well as in publication and other matters. The specialist in carnations, chrysanthemums or roses cannot afford to leave the S. A. F., for the rank and file of that society are his best customers.

While it is true that the exhibitions of these other societies must be held at another time of year than that of our mid-summer conventions, yet perhaps it is possible to combine a number of these exhibitions in one. Anyone who attended the chrysanthemum show at Chicago last November, must admit that it is possible to show good carnations and roses at that time of year. Would it not be possible for the S. A. F. to hold or authorize the holding of such combined exhibitions every year? I will throw it out as a suggestion for the consideration of the executive committee at their next meeting.

It would be nice if we could make our regular summer exhibition a little broader. There have, I am aware, been one or two attempts to do this. Perhaps we might offer, regularly, inducements that would bring out a good display of other seasonable flowers than gladiolus. It is too late for the peony society, but how about the dahlia society? We certainly ought to be able to make a good showing of dahlias, asters, geraniums and seasonable hardy perennials. It would add largely to the interest of the exhibition and be of educational value. J. F. COWELL.

SYLVANIA, OHIO.—Last month the Toledo Daily Blade contained an illustrated account of E. H. Cushman's gladiolus business.

Floriculture at the St. Louis Exhibition.

Frederick W. Taylor, chief of the department of horticulture at the World's Fair, St. Louis, was called upon for some remarks at the Wednesday evening session. Apologizing for introducing the subject of the World's Fair when the audience were waiting to hear Mr. Whitnall's lecture, he promised not to occupy more than a few minutes. After referring to his appearance just after St. Louis had been selected as the next meeting place of the society, he continued:

"I want to speak more particularly to those who may be interested in sending exhibits to the exhibition and who desire to know what provision is being made for their flowers, bedding plants and other things they may present. A month or so ago the head of another department of the exhibition asked our department if we would be able to plant a good deal of bedding material and plants outside the buildings. I told him that if he would put that in the hands of the horticultural department we would agree that every tree, flower and spear of grass should come there as it existed. In promising that, I felt that those who had been with me in other exhibitions where I had a department could be depended upon to make good my word. I am happy to say tonight there is every indication of their doing so. There are now on file applications for two-thirds of the space which is available for the horticultural exhibits. We have almost fifty acres, a considerably greater amount of space than was available for all the exhibits and all the gardens at the last great world's fair. It is beautifully located about the great agricultural and horticultural buildings, which are upon a hill by themselves. There will be grouped upon that hill every possible form of agricultural and horticultural exhibits. The two great buildings cover twenty-six acres of ground. This is actual floor space; galleries not being figured in that area, as they have been in other exhibitions. The interior of the buildings, in addition to being beautified with live plants, will contain every accommodation for man or beast in the way of eating or drinking. Immediately surrounding them are the areas of nearly fifty acres which are available for those who desire to plant outdoor exhibits. This ground has already been laid off in a very artistic way—a way which has met the approval of some of the best florists and horticulturists, who have been there to look the ground over. It was pleasant to hear their words of commendation of the arrangements we are making there to take care of their interests.

"We propose to receive all material of that kind which we find ourselves able to use, expecting you always to send us the cream of what you have and to pay the freight. We will do the rest, except in the case of live plants and grasses. We prefer that you attend to your own planting of these in order that you may not stay later on, if this or that thing you sent there has not succeeded, that it was the fault of the unfortunate chief or the badly trained gardener who was in charge of the work at the exposition. After they have been planted we will assume the responsibility. When the time comes to send them home we will take them up and will expect you to pay the freight.

"I have outlined this perhaps low view of the matter to give you an idea of the financial conditions surrounding the exhibiting of plants at the exhibition. We propose to make these forty-five or fifty acres of outside space a veritable garden. We have already planted about ten thousand roses. This was done in May and June, and the have been very successful. These are the hardy plants, which will go through the winter in good shape and be ready to start out next spring. Within one month from this time every acre of that space will be in fit condition for planting, so that all of you who have perennials or shrubs or anything which had better be planted during the coming season can arrange for that to be done. We will then be ready to start out, in the early spring, planting everything which can be planted out early and following this along with the handling of plants which come to us.

"The provision made at this exhibition for horticulture and agriculture is the best ever made at any exhibition in the world's history. This is fitting because St. Louis is practically the center of that great territory, which was acquired a hundred years ago and the acquisition of which is to be celebrated. It is a wonderful territory in many respects and most wonderful of all in its resources from an agricultural and horticultural standpoint."

Mr. Taylor went on to say that only in recent years had the love of the artistic and beautiful in gardening received a decided impetus; that, with their greater wealth, the people of the west, following what the east had been doing for many years in planting, in the growing of better flowers and in the higher type of landscape gardening, were beginning to show results more worthy of themselves. He thought that the opportunity for horticulturists to give their help and incidentally to benefit themselves by coming to St. Louis was one which they should not fail to appreciate. He earnestly urged that all florists who could do so should lend the exhibition any material that they thought could be used in decorating the grounds. He continued:

"We are delighted that you are to meet with us next year. A splendid hall is being built at the south end of the agricultural building, only a hundred yards from the horticultural building, which will be placed at your disposal. Adjoining this is a large room where your trade display may be held. There is a room for the officers and committees of the society and a library which will contain all the current horticultural literature you will be likely to want. All this is within the grounds and may be had without cost. You are most cordially welcome to it, on our part. It is only a part of that which we have tried to provide for you. There will be a great hotel on the grounds where you can get accommodations at very low prices and where you can stay within three or four hundred yards of the place for your meetings. Conveniences and facilities for your meeting together have been proxided for at my own request, and these were suggested by my observations at former exhibitions.

"I bring you the greeting of the exposition and am glad to be here to improve this opportunity to ask you to help us. I hope you will respond."

WESTFIELD, N. J.—W. B. Woodruff is conducting an up-to-date establishment, growing for retail and wholesale.

Mr. Supiot, Philadelphia.   Mr. Chatenay, Vitry.   "Parisian."
LILAC GROWING AT VITRY. . THREE YEAR OLD PLANTS.

Lilac Forcing in France.

PART II. CONCLUDED.

At the end of the winter, in February—March, according to the year, when the sap shows signs of being ready to flow and before the buds are swelling, the plants are moved to whatever structure, cellar or shed is at hand, but exposed in preference to the north. Every aperture is then hermetically closed to secure complete darkness; the plants remain until the expanding of the panicles in the dark, which place is cooled every evening by a northern window or aperture, opened during the night but shut before dawn, to deprive the plants of light. By this ridiculously simple process the plants may be "retarded" a good deal.

The experiment of Mr. Jassin, at his establishment near Nice, in southern France, is also worth recording. Mr. Jassin had unsatisfactory results from his first lots of lilacs forced for Christmas, while the later forced plants did well. He consequently conceived last year the idea of utilising an ice factory close at hand in order to obtain a better ripening of the wood, favoring a quicker expanding of the panicles. To that end he placed his first lilacs in a dark shed, close together, about the middle of November, surrounded by a pile of ice blocks four or five feet high. The ambient temperature of the shed ranged between 33 and 35° Fahr. above zero. On December 3 the lilacs were taken to the forcing house and subjected to ordinary forcing. Along with them twenty plants, which had not been in contact with ice, were submitted to the same treatment. On December 21 the panicles could be cut from the iced plants, on which nine out of ten buds were already expanded

while the other plants did not flower until a week later and very sparingly—only one panicle out of ten being fully developed. The results are surely gratifying to our southern forcers.

A brief mention must also be made of etherisation, which shortens materially the natural resting period of lilac and other forcing plants. It is a well known fact now that by exposing the plants for a short period, usually not exceeding forty-eight hours, to the evaporation of ether in a given quantity (four grains to each ten litres of space, according to the season) in a hermetically sealed tank or room, plants throw forth their pure white panicles in a much shorter time than by the ordinary process. Professor Johannsen, the Danish physiologist describes the process minutely and the practical experiments of some German forcers, closely followed now by our own forcers, have been attended with great success.

It is now generally admitted that darkness is not absolutely necessary to obtain white flowers by means of the colored lilac, provided the forcing is crowded forward in a temperature of 65° or 75° Fahr. and in a confined atmosphere. The formation of the coloring principle appears to take place only between special limits of temperature and these are exceeded in cases of rapid forcing. White lilac can be produced in glass houses briskly heated under the direct rays of the sun, provided the houses be hermetically closed.

This, however, is of little amount, as it will always found advantageous to cover forcing houses with thick mats, which however superfluous they may be as light excluders, will be most useful in prevent-

ing the loss of heat by radiation. By the latter process the plants are much longer in recovering than when forced in the full light, yet they are of little value, being thrown away after forcing.

The late experiments conducted by Mr. Harancourt, however, tend to show that even with as low a temperature as 62° Fahr. and uninterrupted light, day and night, white lilacs can be obtained from the colored Marly in fifteen days. After lifting the plants in the fall, when the leaves are shed, and trimming them of their useless growth, Mr. Harancourt plants them in a corner of his glass house. They then get one good soaking, not more. An electric lamp of 18-candle power is placed above them, the heat raised the first day to 60° Fahr., the second day to 62° Fahr., and from the third to the end of the forcing to 68° Fahr., which latter is never exceeded. Syringings are given with water of the temperature of the house every couple of hours, except during night, until the flower shoots are well developed. From that time on the plants are only syringed three or four times during the day and twice in the evening. All day long the lilacs are exposed to the solar light, and when the latter decreases, at about 4 p. m., it is replaced by the electric light, the glass house is, of course, covered with straw mats as long as the electric light is on.

Mr. Harancourt's experiments are of paramount importance in so far as they show that the high temperature claimed by the forcers of 68° to 77° Fahr. at the start raised to 77° to 86° Fahr. from the time the flower buds appear until the end of the forcing may not be absolutely necessary to obtain, within a very short time, in full light, white panicles from the colored lilac.

Knowing, as we now do, that the complete exclusion of light makes a colored lilac produce white flowers, it is possible, by a clever gradation of light, to produce curious variations of tints, such as those that are often admired in the shop windows of our large florists. These results are brought about by forcing the Marly lilac as described, admitting the light progressively until uncovering the whole house. In two to three days entirely white flowers will turn rose or pink. When darker tints are required, the forcing should take place at a slow rate, in gentle heat of 54° to 60° Fahr. with plenty of light, giving air as often as weather will permit and syringing only twice a day, morning and evening. It needs twice as much time, or from forty to forty five days, to produce such colored lilacs, but they sell at double the price of white. The Charles X. is often recommended for producing colored blooms.

We have seen in these notes that the Marly lilac is the best kind and that most to be recommended for cut flowers, although the Charles X. and a few others are sometimes forced.

For forcing in pots a greater number of varieties may be used. Mr. Boucher, 164 Avenue d' Italie, Paris, one one of the best forcers of show plants in pots, usually grows his plants in a temperature of 60° to 65° Fahr., giving occasionally some dry blood manure. It requires about six weeks to force them into bloom in such a temperature. At the February exhibition he staged the following pot grown varieties:

Marie Legreye,
Alba Magnifica, } Single white.
Mme. Moser,
Ville de Troyes, } Single rose.
Macrostachya, }
Louis Van Houtte, single violet red.
President Carnot, double lilac.
Senateur Volland, double violet red.
Emile Lemoine, double rose.
Mrs. Lemoine, } Double white.
Mrs. Casimir Perrier, }
Michael Buchner, double pale lilac.
President Grevy, double violet mauve.
which make up a splendid group.

The lilac is so tractable that pot grown plants with the flowerbuds well set, as

they are usually delivered by the growers, are easily bloomed in a few weeks by placing them in a bay window or room not too much heated, far from the fire, exposed to full light, giving plenty of water and syringing often the stems and leaves.

The sorts to be recommended to amateurs in that case are Alba Virginalis, Charles X and Persica.

Before closing the subject, reference must also be made to the artificial aniline dyeing of the lilacs which some years ago was brought under notice, but does not seem to have continued in favor to judge from the few dyed blooms now seen either in the streets or on our market.

The Revue Horticole in 1894 published a splendid colored plate of the curious tints obtained and then mentioned the

Lilac After Fifteen Days Forcing.

metholene blue as producing light azure blue flowers; methyl violet produced salmon red flowers; methyl orange produced golden yellow and sulphur colored flowers; eosin produced carmine red flowers; with slightly different dyes for coloring the stems.

The dyeing is said to be easily effected by crushing or bruising the ends of the flower stems by a slight hammer blow, then plunging them for a couple of hours in a small bottle holding one-third of an ounce, in which one-sixth of the desired dye has been previously poured. After taking the flowers out, the bruised parts are cut off and the stems placed for two or three hours in fresh, clean water.

The writer has tried to make his notes as plain as possible and hope they will be understood by every one.

It may take some years before the lilac will be as fully appreciated for winter blooming in the United States as it is in France, England and Germany, but the writer is confident that when forcing is once well understood and fine bloom produced, it will not take very long to popularize this beautiful flower.

Most of the plants prepared for forcing being imported into the United States, it may interest your readers to know that upon their arrival such plants are to be removed from the cases to a covered, dry storeroom shed and kept dry until forcing has been started. Should the plants have been frozen, put them in a sheltered place where the temperature will enable them to thaw out very gradually.

Lilacs do not suffer as long as the thermometer does not go farther down than 4° below zero Fahr., and even then the balls of earth protect the more tender.

Some forcers also produce during three or four months forced snowballs or viburnums, as per illustration in part 1 of this article. The treatment is about the same as for forcing the lilac but is practiced in the full light.

The snowball requires less heat and it takes about four weeks to force it into bloom.　　　　PARISIAN.

Lilac After Five Days Forcing.

LILAC FORCING HOUSES OF M. GRAINDORGE, VITRY.

LILACS TRIMMED FOR FORCING AFTER SIX YEARS' GROWTH.
(M. Boucher in the foreground.)

Chicago Through Eastern Eyes.

The first view of this great western city is disappointing to the visitor, whether arriving by rail or boat. A huge smoky haze reaches from midway of the tall buildings apparently to the clouds above, concealing that sky line and sharp architectural profile which is so noticeably a feature of the landscape view of New York city. Chicago should spend a million of dollars or more each year until a method is found that will effectually eliminate the smoke nuisance; then the architects and the people can get at least a glimpse of that heavenly region they are trying so hard to reach. But this is merely incidental. It was flowers and the way they raised and sold them that attracted us during our short stay when homeward bound from the convention.

Peter Reinberg's:—This establishment is a veritable ocean of glass, amounting about in round numbers to one million square feet. The houses are all built on the same general plan, that is, a number built together with no dividing walls, gutters raised high enough to walk underneath without stooping. As range after range, all connected, is passed through, the improvement in construction is noticed, large wooden posts and gutters giving way to new iron devices and greater height of eaves, until in the newest block of about 200,000 feet, completed the past spring, the iron gutters are eight feet six inches high, not more than eight inches wide, supported on stout iron posts, about every third of

which screws into the gutter and carries the water off into the main drain underneath the houses. There is also a narrow drip-pan along the entire length of each side of gutter, which discharges into the larger outlets, to carry away the condensation.

The stock is all growing on benches about three feet from the ground. In many of the houses it is in its second year, the beds having been dried off and the plants cut back. All without exception looked well and in the most forward houses the growth was luxuriant. Large blocks of Perle, Sunrise and M. Chatenay were seen; the latter variety, although generally discarded in the east, is well thought of here and is claimed to be one of the most profitable sellers, owing to its productiveness and good selling qualities. Brides and Bridesmaids are also grown in large quantities, as are Golden Gates. Of course the American Beauty is also in evidence and is done well in quantity. This variety is not tried the second year, new plants being set out each season.

Immense blocks of carnations are also grown. The range of Lawson looked like a two-acre field and must be a grand sight when in full flower. There were also large blocks of other standard kinds. Wires are stretched the length of the tables as soon as planted, which, by the way, had all been done several weeks. As the plants grow, these are raised and strings attached to them run across between the plants, giving them the necessary support. This is probably the most simple form of staking and is said to be very effective.

The erection of this immense range of glass was commenced about seventeen

years ago with four small houses in which lettuce was forced, which in one year brought in $4,000, enough to pay the cost of construction. This vegetable gave way in a short time to roses and carnations, and as the profits accumulated, new and improved ranges were added until now the tract of sixteen acres of farm land which was the original capital of Mr. Reinberg is almost entirely covered and another tract of some fifty acres has been purchased for, well, perhaps to be covered with some more ranges.

The soil item is important as it has now to be hauled a distance of two miles or over.

The product of this immense place is shipped twice a day to the city and is handled by Mr. Reinberg's own force in the commission district. About 90 per cent is shipped out of town, so the market is a very large one, and in spite of the immense stock, quite frequently in the busy season it is difficult to fill all the orders.

Steam pumps keep up a constant pressure of water so that all the rose and carnation beds, which appear about four feet wide, get a thorough hoseing. All sides of the beds are accessible as there are none built against the sides of the houses, a walk always intervening.

Mr. Reinberg is a very pleasant and affable gentleman on the sunny side of fifty and takes pleasure in answering questions and showing visitors about his immense establishment. Everything seems to work smoothly, his system being such that he could apparently manage twice as large a place without much more trouble to himself.

ROBERT KIFT.

The Carnation.

CULTURAL REMINDERS.

Summer blooming stock will by this time be producing heavily and the cut should be of good quality. Flowers produced on growth started in the open air are just about starting to come in, and the quality of flowers produced on such growths is much nearer perfection than those produced on growths started indoors. The amount of returns received from a batch of summer blooming plants depends much upon the fall weather. It is a pity that the plants should often be ruined by frost just about the time when they are coming into their heaviest crop, but this is a condition for which no remedy has as yet been found. It would hardly pay to erect a protecting framework over the plants for the short season in which it would be in use. If the plants are growing in frames it might pay to cover on frosty nights with sash, or a cheese cloth might be stretched over the plants, to be removed during the day, as has been suggested by a contemporary. Cheese cloth is extensively used in growing fine tobacco and pineapples, and the time may not be far off when florists will find it profitable to use in connection with the growing of some plants outdoors.

Next years' supply of blooming plants is an important thing to look out for during the fall months. There is nothing to be gained by making cuttings much before October 1, so far as the resulting plants are concerned, but it is often difficult to find enough good cuttings to work up a good supply of plants, and so it is well to begin as early as possible to propagate. Cuttings taken from plants growing in the field (if you are able to root them) will materially help out any possible deficiency later on. These cuttings must be taken before severe frost has made its appearance, and even a light frost will greatly diminish the chance of a good strike with rare varieties. In order to root these cuttings successfully, they must be in a cool situation and shading and watering will have to be handled with the season in mind.

If the bench is well drained (as it should be) it will be safe to soak the sand every morning for the first two weeks. After that the degree of moisture should be gradually reduced until the cuttings are rooted. There should be a substantial shade on the glass above the cuttings, and in addition to this newspapers should be used during the day, not only to protect from the sun, but also to exclude draughts that will be strong when ventilation must be free in order to keep down the temperature. The newspapers should be sprinkled several times a day while the sun is on them. Cover early in the morning and do not uncover until near sundown, which will often be long after the sun has ceased to shine on the cutting bench.

Trim the cuttings the same as in winter, being sure to leave the heel on, and with a sharp knife remove the tail that sometimes hangs on the base. Take great care in removing the cuttings from the plants not to bruise the base of the cuttings, and to get all there is to it, clear down to where it connects onto the parent stem. Nature has wisely provided for accidents in plant growth and made extra provision for roots to form where breaks are most apt to occur. After the benched plants have resumed an active growth, cuttings taken from these will root readily.

It is well at this season to use only such cuttings as have the best possible chance to root. All cuttings should be well developed and ready to go ahead on their own resources; they should be past that stage at which they depend upon the parent stem for digested nourishment.

It will be some weeks yet before much firing will be needed, but we may as well be ready when the time comes and not shove off preparations until the last minute. A thorough inspection of the heating apparatus at this time will be well worth the trouble. It is seldom that a winters' firing does not develop some chronic defect which will require more than a simple patch to repair it. These should be attended to, and after the whole apparatus has received a thorough cleaning it is well to raise steam and try all the pipes about as severely as they will be used during heavy firing. If there are any pipes hanging in a position where they are apt to evaporate drip or standing water, they should be placed so as to do away with this. A dry atmosphere is essential to success with carnations.

The shoots will be running up on early planted stock about this time, and with such no time should be lost in putting in the supports. Clear the benches of all stray weeds first and carefully remove whatever dead leaves that may be on the plants. Be very careful not to injure the bark of the plants in this operation by taking each leaf singly and pulling upwards and sideways, as you would do in removing cuttings, steadying the plant with one hand, so that there will be no danger of loosening it from the soil and tearing the roots. J.

Miltonia Vexillaria.

My miltonias this year have been finer than ever, large flowers and exquisite coloring and not wishing to enjoy this alone I send you a photograph, which may also interest your readers. I also enclose photograph of Phalænopsis amabilis; the plants I brought with me from the Philippines last year. I have hundreds of these and the show all spring was a grand one. Phalænopsis Ludde. manniana is now in full flower and of this variety I have about 100 plants. I am daily expecting another 1,000 of Phalænopsis in variety, which I collected on my recent trip to the Philippines.
R. SCHIFFMANN.

MILTONIA VEXILLARIA.

Florists' Plant Notes.

STEVIAS.

Stevias should be brought into the greenhouse before the slightest frost touches them. They will now need a final shift to 7-inch pots; any old carnation soil will grow them without further enrichment. Give each plant a stake and place them in a moderately cool house with a temperature of 45° to 50°. No more topping should be done after this date.

SWEET ALYSSUM.

A few small plants of sweet alyssum planted along the edge of a carnation bench will produce an abundance of flowers for design work during the winter. Planted two or three feet apart they will not interfere with the carnations till late in spring. The little yellow butterfly, which deposits the eggs of the destructive cabbage worm, relishes alyssum, so when this pest makes its appearance, which it usually does in spring, the best thing to do is to destroy the alyssum plants, insects and all.

BOUGAINVILLEA.

Bougainvillea Sanderiana should be brought inside as soon as possible. If it was planted out in the open ground, lift carefully and give 7-inch or 8-inch pots, according to size. They require rich, medium heavy soil, and should be given a night temperature of about 45° until January 1. No forcing should be attempted before that time.

PROPAGATING.

A number of different plants should now be propagated for stock. Cuttings of verbena, German ivy, ageratum, coleus, achyranthes, petunia and others should be put into the sand at once. Use clean sand, not too coarse, and white-wash the bench thoroughly before filling in the sand. It may be necessary to apply a light wash to the glass, but unless the sun is very strong, it is best not to do so at this time of the year. Shade the cuttings with newspapers during the warm hours of the day, not only to protect them from the sun, but also to prevent the air from wilting them. Until firing commences and regular bottom heat can be had, there is danger of keeping the sand too moist, resulting in the cuttings rotting off. Sprinkle them several times a day but be sure to have them dry at night or fungus is liable to set in.

PRIMULAS.

Primula sinensis for Christmas should now be ready for a shift to its flowering pot, a 5-inch size. Use rather light soil, with a third part of leaf mould added and drain the pots with charcoal or broken potsherds. Pot them deeply enough, not only to furnish nourishment for the roots forming at the base of the plant, but also to prevent the plant from wobbling. Care must be taken, however, not to place them too deeply in the pot, or the crown will rot. These plants can be left outside in the frames for another month, where they should have the benefit of all the air possible. Before the first frost, however, it is best to close in the skeleton above the frame with temporary curtains of carpet or matting, which can be removed in the day time. By October 15 or November 1, they should all be housed; a temperature of 45° at night in a cool light house is sufficient to grow them. After they commence to flower, overhead watering should be discontinued. Stand them on inverted 5-inch pots, giving each plant

sufficient room to allow the foliage to develop properly. In watering turn on the water slowly and pass the end of the hose between the pots, watering each plant carefully. They are sometimes, though rarely troubled with greenfly, in which case fumigation must be properly attended to.

Bedding Plants, September Work.

It is important just at this time of the year that we look over our bedding plants and mark those wanted for next year's stock. Nothing but the best and healthiest plants should be selected for this purpose. During this month all bedding plants such as geraniums, coleuses, cannas, etc, are at their best, so that there can be no excuse for selecting poor ones. Where we propagate year after year from the same plants the strain is very apt to deteriorate. This can be overcome if special attention is given to selection. Whenever we notice that the plants we have are not so good as they were the previous year, we begin to lose interest in them, and with a lack of interest no gardener can be successful for any length of time. Therefore I say pay close attention each season to selecting your stock, and so long as the plants are good the pleasure in growing them will not cease. No one tires of anything that is really well done.

He who is careless regarding his stock, plants and propagation, can be sure in time to have the poorest collection in his community.

New plants and new varieties always interest us and in examining our beds at this time if any plant be found that is even a little better than its neighbor or shows a variation of apparent value, stock and label it at once. If neglected it may become mixed with the others and later lost, when the cold weather and rains make the foliage and flowers of all look alike.

Advances in bedding plants may be discovered by carefully looking over the flower beds, with the question always in mind, which plant is an improvement over the others? A notable example of this was the discovery of Ageratum Stella Gurney. In examining a batch of young seedling plants. James Gurney noticed one, and only one, among them of more compact habit and distinct color than the others. Had a more careless observer than Mr. Gurney grown this flower, this beautiful variety might have been lost to commerce. Every grower can cite similar instances of new kinds which have been brought into commerce from time to time.

There is trouble with mixed plants every spring, especially with cannas. In most cases this occurs because the plants were not carefully gone over in September and correctly labelled. This is the time to label them; for we are now so close to frost time that there is little danger of misplacing the labels, as occasionally occurs when labeled earlier.

Make cuttings now of coleuses, rose geraniums, verbenas and other bedding plants that will suffer by the first frost. Give a day now to stock selection and cutting up the plants, and you will have put in that day which saves nine at any other time of the year for this purpose.

KAN.

MOUNT CLEMENS, MICH.—Thomas Gordon is about to move his place of business from the old location on Cass avenue to the corner of North Gratiot avenue and Market street.

The Rose.

CARE OF YOUNG STOCK.

The care of the young stock is a very important matter at this time. The soil must be kept in good condition and the plants tied as soon as they need it. Do not allow the plants to be left without tying until the growth becomes crooked as the results will never be the same as they would have been had this been attended to at the proper time. As soon as the young stock has started to grow the pits around the plants should be levelled off and the soil made firm. Whenever the surface of the beds becomes crusted or green it should be broken up and allowed to dry out well, thereby keeping the soil from becoming sour.

At this time of the year, when there is heavy watering, there is always a danger that the beds become too wet and sour. To avoid this condition it is well to allow them to dry out well at intervals and then follow by giving a watering which you are sure will leave no dry soil in the bottom of the beds. If it has not been attended to before, this is a good time to remove all plants which have become mixed. Very often when the cutting commences it is found that a few plants have been under the wrong label, and as it is too late to change, they are left in over winter. As soon as these appear they should be marked or the result will be that the young stock will be badly mixed the following year. If there are any stray ones in the houses which are being carried over, it is a very easy matter to remove them and substitute the proper variety before all the old plants are thrown out.

With the cool weather we are having it will be possible to harden the young stock somewhat, and whenever it is possible it should be taken advantage of, as the mildew will be checked thereby. Attend carefully to the ventilation and avoid a dose of mildew or black spot that may prove serious. R. I.

LIBERTY ROSES.

ED. AM. FLORIST:—Will Liberty roses grow and produce good results in the same house with American Beauty? W. C. C.

There are no reasons whatever why Liberty and American Beauty roses cannot be successfully grown in the same house together, as both are benefited by a little additional heat more than ordinary tea varieties. The best method is to plant the American Beauty in the center benches and the Liberty on the side benches.

JOHN N. MAY.

Missouri Botanic Garden.

The Missouri Botanic Garden was never more beautiful than at present, as it has been such a favorable year for plant life. Among other points of interest at this time is a large specimen of the sisal hemp plant (Agave rigida, sisalana) with a flowering stem about four feet high. The collection of dahlias is superb. Victoria crusiana is in good trim, growing alongside of which is the royal water lily, or Victoria regia. This year two long carpet beds inside the gate entrance attract much attention. B.

SOUTH TACOMA, WASH.—James Harrison is building a carnation house measuring 20x85 feet.

Palms and Ferns.

CULTURE AND DISEASES.

The months of August, September and October cover a season of very active growth among the palms; for during the bright and warm days that usually prevail at that season the palms will root freely and push up leaves with great rapidity. It is, therefore, particularly necessary that the plants should not be allowed to get dry at the root, nor should the syringing be neglected on every bright day, though it is preferable not to syringe too late in the day from this time forward, or there may be just a little too much moisture condensed on the foliage during the following night. Some dew will surely appear upon the foliage during the night, and the plants will not be affected by it, but an excess of water on the foliage and a few cold nights at the same time will sometimes show its effects on the foliage of Areca lutescens in spotting the leaves or making the tips rusty.

As a general practice I do not find it necessary to use liquid manure on palms, there being no difficulty in getting young stock to grow on with reasonable rapidity without any undue forcing. But most establishments count among their stock some old plants that may be used for conservatory decoration or on a special occasion, and it being out of the question to shift on or repot these large plants every season, it is needful to supply them some extra food from time to time in order to keep up the color of the foliage. A topdressing of good stable manure and a watering with liquid manure once or twice a week will help these starved plants very greatly, whether they stand outdoors under a lath shelter or are kept in the greenhouse, and will encourage the formation of strong foliage.

The lath shelter referred to is a very useful adjunct during the warm weather, there being no better place for the storage of some large decorative plants at that time, provided there is a good force of water to be had for syringing and that proper attention is paid to the watering.

During the last summer months it is much the better practice to keep a moderate amount of ventilation on the palm houses throughout the night, thus disposing of some of the surplus moisture and at the same time keeping the foliage harder, this method being continued until the nights become too cold to permit it. In the vicinity of Philadelphia it is seldom necessary to resort to fire heat in the palm houses before October 1, and some seasons it is fully two weeks later than that before the fires are requisite, but the weather being such a variable quantity it is impossible to lay down any hard and fast rule, and it is much the better plan to start a little fire when the thermometer registers 50° and thus avoid the possibility of a check to the stock.

Insects have been frequently referred to in these notes, the reason being that insects in some form or other are one of the greatest troubles the palm grower has to contend with, and during the month of August there usually appears a fresh outbreak of these pests, and one that should be watched for. In going through a house of plants any observant grower will quickly note the dirty plants, should there be any, and the best time to cope with the insects is in the beginning of the outbreak, when the cleaning of a few plants may postpone or prevent a lot of trouble in the future. It is also a

wise plan to fumigate the houses at intervals during the summer on general principles, some of the nicotine preparations being very valuable for such fumigations and being quite harmless to the palms unless used in unreasonable quantities.

There are also some few fungous diseases that attack our common palms, though seldom causing severe loss. Among the latter is that singular trouble that attacks the kentias at times and, seeming to enter the stem just at the surface of the ground, frequently causes the stem of the plant to rot off before the roots have had time to stop growing. A specific for this trouble is one of the discoveries of the future, there being apparently no positive remedy as yet, and the most reasonable treatment seems to be

Century Plant in Bloom at Hinsdale, Ill.

to keep the houses just as sweet and clean as possible, to remove all decayed wood and decayed leaves, to paint benches and side walls with hot lime wash once or twice a year, and in short to adopt modern sanitary ideas so far as is compatible with greenhouse practice. There have seldom been great losses from this disease, but it has sometimes become sufficiently plentiful to cause anxiety to the growers, and in some cases has carried off some hundreds of plants of various sizes from 4-inch to 8-inch pots, and occasionally even some few larger than that.

There is also another form of stem rot

that sometimes appears among the kentias, in this case attacking the stems of the individual leaves rather than the plant as a whole, and causing an ugly black canker on the stem, that sometimes extends for a length of several inches and usually results in the loss of the affected leaf. This trouble seldom spreads beyond a few plants, except in rare instances, and I have sometimes had some doubts as to whether the bruising of the plants by careless cleaning or the use of some strong insecticide was not at the foundation of the evil, though were this disfigurement to appear to any great extent I should be inclined to try Bordeaux mixture on it.

Arecas that have shown signs of the "yellows" in the early spring will frequently outgrow this weakness during the warm weather, though when the plants have been seriously affected in this way they seldom fully recover and the bilious tint of the foliage is liable to return during the winter or just as soon as the growth becomes less active. There are differences of opinion among growers as to the origin of this latter trouble among the arecas, and one primary safeguard is found in the selection of healthy seedlings, it being a waste of time and labor to pot off a lot of weak and diseased seedlings such as are occasionally found. Granted, however, that one starts out with a batch of healthy young plants it is, in the opinion of the writer, largely a matter of culture, the avoidance of extremes of heat and cold and dryness and moisture having much to do with the welfare of such a lot of plants.

Excessive watering was once credited with causing the "yellows" in Areca lutescens, but it seems more probable that excessive dryness was the true cause, this checking the tender tips of the roots with the result that the roots then failed to do their work properly and the soil becoming sodden from repeated waterings, the blame for the bad condition of the plant was credited to the wrong cause.

This unhealthy appearance of some arecas does not come about in a few days, but is a progressive disease, and the cause must be looked for beyond the mere fact that the soil looks sodden and the roots are few and watery in appearance. It may also be worthy of mention that seldom, if ever, does one find a yellow areca where a plant stands in such a position as to catch a drip from the roof and is thus continuously moist, though it is hoped that this sentence will not be taken as an argument for the use of leaky houses for palm growing.

W. H. TAPLIN.

A Century Plant in Bloom.

A century plant, eighty-five years old, is in full bloom at the Oak Forest cemetery, Hinsdale. It is the property of G. K. Wright, president of the cemetery company. The plant came originally from Mexico, and is said to be the largest growing away from its native soil. The leaves at the base are nine feet across and the foliage and blooms rise to a height of thirty feet.

Rose Lady Gay.

The rose Lady Gay here with illustrated is one of the best of the hardy climbers originated by M. H. Walsh. It is a Crimson Rambler cross, of beautiful pink color, the flowers full double and borne on trusses of from twenty to forty blooms.

The Retail Trade.

HAS the shop received its fall coat of paint and varnish? Don't put it off another week.

MAKE it a rule not to keep a plant displayed in your store for sale that you would not willingly buy yourself.

A LITTLE advertisement for a couple of weeks now in your local newspaper will tell your customers who are returned from summer vacations that your palms, ferns and bulbs are ready.

VACATION customers are returning and a sense of brisker business is in the cooler autumn air. Print and mail a folder anticipating the needs of buyers of fall plants and flowers and proving that you are the man.

YOU have plenty of gladiolus, dahlias and other showy flowers to spare now. Send a good bunch every third day to the railroad and express agent, the doctor and the editor. The bread will return later, butter side up.

A COLLECTION of fall bulbs of sorts not readily mixed may be displayed now, profiting you and interesting your customers. The end of a counter, a window or a corner will suffice. The unsold stock November 10 may be planted or disposed of at cost.

DECORATIONS AT NEWPORT.

Mrs. Herman Oelrichs gave at Rosecliff, September 2, her largest party of the season and one of the most novel entertainments in many years. The entire estate was lavishly decorated and illuminated. The dinner was served by Berger on twelve tables placed on the terraces and lawn overlooking the Cliffs under a canopy of flowers and electric lights. In the center was a large fountain which was throwing its sprays at all times during the dinner, the water being illuminated with hundreds of small electric lights.

The color scheme of the table decorations was pink, the flowers being placed in gilded baskets tied with pink ribbon and suspended from long garlands by white doves, which, apparently flying in the air, held the long graceful handles in their mouths. On the handles of the baskets and among the flowers were myriads of tiny electric lights, and from the canopy shone many other twinkling lights, giving the appearance of stars in the sky. Other baskets were placed on the tables and at their bases small articles representing rustic life.

Trinity church was decorated for the Brooks-Thayer wedding, September 3. This church, famous for aristocratic weddings, has rarely been more artistically decorated for a wedding ceremony than it was that day. The scheme, arranged and successfully carried out by Hodgson, was well adapted to the stately colonial architecture of the church. The general color scheme was white with green, pleasingly relieved by touches of pink. As a background for the flowers, long garlands of bay leaves were hung in graceful folds along the side wall above the galleries, on either side and across the front of the organ gallery. Beneath these garlands were clusters of pale green and light pink flowers, which hung with wide sash ribbons of pink from the face of the galleries and organ loft. On each of the large white pillars supporting the galleries were large placques of pink and white flowers, with variegated grasses

rising nearly to the columns at the roof, and from these placques were tied long knots of broad white ribbons. At regular intervals on either side of the aisles were tall standards wound with white satin ribbon, on which were large bunches of white roses with full bows of broad white satin ribbons.

The chancel was a mass of handsome palms and garlands of white roses, while the altar was banked with choice white roses. Along the altar rail were garlands of white roses, lilies of the valley and white orchids, with soft green foliage. The pulpit was a special feature in pink and white flowers, marking a step in transition from the severe white and green of the chancel to the more delicate treatment of the body of the church in pink and green. The general impression was of a massing of flowers and plants in profusion, but so distributed as to practically cover the whole interior.

The reception was held at 1 o'clock and a wedding breakfast was served immediately afterwards, Mr. and Mrs. Thayer receiving beneath a charming arrangement of strands of white roses and lilies

New Rose Lady Gay.

of the valley and before a background of palms. The breakfast tent on the lawn, reaching far out on the cliffs, covered a floor 60x80 feet, and there was another, 25x50, adjoining on the east.

The decorations of the tents were a groundwork of red and white stripes from the ridge down to the side walls, the latter being hung with solid red curtains looped up to give a view of the cliffs and the water, and the centerpoles covered with oak boughs with long white ribbon streamers from the top of the poles to the side walls. The side poles were treated with large white satin bows.

Wadley & Smythe had the subscription ball. Garlands of laurel were festooned in the high arches of the ballroom and twined in graceful curves around the massive white pillars and statuary and side tables, on which were large vases filled with American Beauty roses. The broad steps and corridor leading to the ballroom were grouped with tall Australian tree ferns, their long, graceful foliage mingling with imitation trees of American Beauty roses in full bloom. Banks of tree ferns, palms and American Beauty roses were arranged most effectively across the front of the stage, completely screening the musicians and giving the effect of a bank of roses. Z.

Violets.

I wish to differ a little from Mr. Brigham in your issue of August 15. We have grown Marie Louise for twelve years and have not had one unsuccessful season in all that time. We always plant about the middle of June and keep the stock well watered for two weeks; our compost is well rotted loam sod, with as much good manure added as can be well stirred in. A good mulch is laid on about September 15, just after the plants start in bloom. We always use well rotted horse or cow manure, but never give leaf mould a second trial, as it holds the moisture too long during the winter months, while manure will dry on the surface and prevent spot.

Important in violet culture is fumigation; and great care must be taken to do it properly. Our method is not followed by all the florists in this vicinity, but many wonder why our plants appear so green and clean. The cause is careful fumigation. For our purpose we use a pipe about fifteen inches high and eight inches wide; on the bottom we place a newspaper and a good handful of dry stems, wetting the other stems down for about an hour before using. We make it a practice to smoke the house about 8 o'clock at night, when the plants are hardened and the pores closed. Allow no wind to blow through the house, otherwise the smoke will fill but one end. We use about one-half bushel of stems to a house 16x100 feet with excellent results.

Place one of these lighted cans at a point twenty-five feet from each end of the house to be fumigated. When they are through smoking take a little look in the door and see if the smoke is thick enough. If not, be ready to put a third lighted can in the middle of the house. But do not, when inspecting, be satisfied to say that is "good enough," for to my mind no fumigating in violet culture is good enough that is not the best that can be done. This is equally true of most of the florist's other daily labors. Do not water too freely now, or the growth will be so soft that diseases or spot may find a lodging place. For a time at this season we keep the surface as dry as possible, allowing the soil to dry out once in a while and stir it to make the surface sweet and clean. We stir the soil again thoroughly, about the end of January. We run our violet houses at from 40° to 43° Fahr. at night, 60° to 65° on clear days and from 55° to 58° on dark days. We never raise the temperature to 75° at the holidays, as we believe it injures the market for the balance of the season. The misguided ambition of some growers to exceed their neighbors results, by such high forcing, in placing inferior stock on the market. In the end such schemes are detected and those who practice them go down and out. ALEX. A. LAUB.

A Look at German Florists.

J. J. Hess of Hess & Swoboda, Omaha, passed through Chicago, September 5, returning from Europe. Mr. Hess found much to admire in the effective use of foliage and bedding plants in the cities of Berlin, Frankfort and Potsdam. He found the flower shops in Berlin to excel those of Paris, both in artistic and volume of business. The lavish use of large and showy plants out of doors, many kinds not well adapted to his section of the United States, was such as to cause astonishment and admiration.

He found one German grower raising cut carnations of American varieties and in Yankee fashion and selling and shipping in a large way cut blooms of these, out door grown at 6 cents each! The summer has been cold and rainy, unpleasant to get about, still he admits the trip was not without its pleasures.

New England News Items.

E. W. Breed, of Clinton, Mass., who for the past twenty years has very successfully conducted a retail florist business, contemplates devoting his entire time and attention in the future to landscape gardening. Here is an unusual opportunity for some young florist of industry and enterprise to step in and succeed to a well established trade.

At Pawtucket, R. I., arrangements are being made for an exhibition on September 12 and 13 at the hall of the Fair Lawn Improvement Society. William Stephenson, 145 Owen avenue, is the secretary.

We hear of many so-called floral parades at the various summer resorts this year. Interest fades, however, when we realize that most of the decorative material in these affairs is made of paper.

The annual exhibition of the Houghton Horticultural Society will be held at Odd Fellow's Hall, Lynn, Mass., on September 15 and 16, to be followed on the next day by the annual festival.

The American Horticultural Society held its fall meeting in Odd Fellows' Building, September 4. Vice-President L. D. Robinson presided. The gladiolus was the subject for discussion.

The N. A. Chase greenhouses at Winsted, Conn., are to be closed. George F. Chase, who has managed the business since his sister, Miss Nettie Chase, died will remove to Milbury, Mass.

A new flower store has been opened at 205 South Main street, Waterbury, Conn., by John Saxe. There was a public opening on September 2, the decorations being very handsome.

C. A. Pringle, of the University of Vermont, has gone to Mexico on a botanical exploration and will spend the coming autumn and winter in the Andes of southern Mexico.

At the weekly exhibition in Worcester, Mass., on August 27, William Anderson, gardener for Bayard Thayer, of South Lancaster, showed a large tank of very fine aquatic flowers.

Dahlias and perennial phloxes were the leading features of the exhibition at Horticultural Hall in Boston on August 22. T. C. Thurlow's display of phloxes was superb.

Alex. Dallas' newly renovated store at Waterbury, Conn., is very attractive. The exterior has been painted white and electric lights have been installed.

E. L. Brown, a prominent citizen of Dalton, Mass., an enthusiastic expert in farming and landscape gardening, died on August 15, aged 42 years.

An appropriation for the purpose of purchasing shade trees for the public streets is being considered by the city council of Central Falls, R. I.

Gladiolus princeps, exhibited by A. F. Estabrook, was honored with a first-class certificate of merit at Horticultural Hall, Boston, on August 15.

One of the most complete collections of the native ferns of New England is to be seen at the home of Mrs. F. B. Horton, Brattleboro, Vt.

Jas. E. Bishop, the well-known florist of Thomaston, Conn., is critically ill at his home on Elm street.

Chicago.

MARKET ABOUT THE SAME AS LAST WEEK. —EXECUTIVE COMMITTEE OF HORTICULTURAL SOCIETY TO MEET.—DOINGS ABOUT TOWN.—VISITORS.

Some of the wholesalers report business slightly better than last week, but with the majority there has been no perceptible change. Some very warm weather during the week brought out large quantities of more or less inferior stock, but having turned cool again, the supply of such material will doubtless be shortened. Some high grade American Beauty roses are beginning to show themselves and command very fair prices. At some of the marts large quantities of Kaiserins, Brides and Bridesmaids are noticed, which are as a rule, however, from old stock and very poor. Carnations are coming in quite lively and are not very hard to dispose of. Asters appear to be slowing up a little although the white still continue to command satisfactory figures, the colored not holding up so well. Gladioli continue to do very nicely. Tuberoses are becoming quite plentiful at some establishments. Lily of the valley is present in large quantities.

The gardeners' and florists' union here purpose having an organ of their own. The suggestion is to model it on the plan of the German Gartner Verein. It will be an eight-page sheet devoted to the interests of working gardeners and contain favorable notices of well grown stock wherever seen.

Meuret & Stange have taken John Hoeft's Park Ridge establishment. Edw. H. Meuret, the senior member of the firm, has been for several years carnation grower with Emil Buettner. W. I. Stange was formerly in the advertising line.

A meeting of the executive committee of the Horticultural Society at Chicago is due soon and then reports of committee on hall and fall show; pending the action of the committees comment is hardly in order.

J. A. Budlong has now some chrysanthemums, about the first of the season, and from the outlook will have a nice lot of stock by October.

Henry Payne, at Hinsdale, has now 45,000 feet of glass, all devoted to Asparagus plumosus, Sprengeri and adiantum.

Two more growers have made their headquarters at the Growers' Market, Matson & Kron and G. Gunderman.

W. N. Rudd is at Rochester, N. Y., attending the national convention of cemetery superintendents.

Joseph Lang, Melrose and Robey streets, is tearing down his two greenhouses at that location.

J. P. Foley has returned from Seattle and the west and will join his brother in the building line.

A new retail establishment will be opened at 33 State street by H. P. Klunder next week.

Dan. MacRorie, who has been ill here since the convention is now able to be about again.

The Fleischman Floral Company is kept quite busy with out-of-town wedding orders.

A. Lange has a pulsating electric sign which illumines State and Monroe street.

Vaughan's seed store took in two carloads of Dutch bulbs this week.

Kennicott Brothers handled some good gladioli stock during the week.

C. A. Alles, with Wietor Brothers is building a $3,500 residence.

J. B. Deamud received some first-class shipments of smilax.

Miss N. Wolfe, of J. A. Budlong's office is on a vacation.

John Degnan is now with Ed. F. Winterson.

Visitors: Wm. Graff, Columbus; J. Sandstrom, Momence, Ill.; H. C. Irish, St. Louis; L. C. Waterbury, Denver; Wm. Young of C. Young & Sons, St. Louis, returning from a Michigan vacation; J. J. Curran, with G. Von Bochove Bro., Kalamazoo.

New York.

MARKET FAIR BUT DECLINES THE LATTER PART OF THE WEEK.—THE CUT FLOWER COMPANY INSTALLS SPECIAL TELEPHONE SERVICE.—LOCAL NOTES.

Good prices prevailed during the week until Wednesday; on Thursday values declined materially and to-day, Friday, all stock is very dull except carnations. A good demand exists for white roses and they are scarce. Lily of the valley and smilax both dull. The quality of asters has improved but prices are lower. All retail stores complain of dullness and no evidence yet of fall business having set in.

I. Nash of Moore, Hentz & Nash, is the latest arrival from Europe, and is looking ten years younger. He visited France and England. He is very enthusiastic over the methods of selling cut flowers in London, but says their roses were not to be compared with ours. Brunners with them, however, were fair.

The New York Cut Flower Company has installed a private telephone exchange in its office which connects directly with the establishments of each of its members.

Three thousand carnations and fifteen hundred gladioli spikes were used at Siegel, Cooper & Company's restaurant, recently opened.

Geo. Matthew's carnations are so fine that they are often sold in advance before delivery at the cut flower exchange.

Frank and Joe Millang made a fine appearance in the volunteer firemens' parade at Flushing.

Charles Thorley secured judgment against F. Ziegfield, husband of Anna Held, for $390.

The New Jersey Cut Flower Company will open here in a wholesale way September 15.

Geo. M. Stumpp and family sailed from Bremen September 8.

August Millang is the glad father of a son and heir.

John Einsel of Stumpp's is again on duty.

Boston.

Business is at present in a state of tranquility. The month of August, just passed, gave us the lowest temperature on record for the season, and the effect has been decidedly unfavorable that ordinarily enjoys a good patronage from the many New England summer resorts throughout August and sometimes well into September. This year the cool weather has driven the visitors home, and so the florists keep company with hotel keepers in misfortune. The quality of stock coming to wholesale markets is decidedly inferior. Roses are well below the standard. Carnations are conspicuously absent, but asters more than fill their place. Carnation growers generally are well advanced in the work of housing their plants.

Jackson Dawson's family has been peculiarly unfortunate ever since Mrs. Dawson's death, three of Mr. Dawson's sons being sick. Chas. J. is just convalescing from a four weeks' siege of pneumonia, Walter has been a victim of tonsilitis and Fred. left a week ago last Saturday on a European voyage for his health by order of his physician.

This week we have the biennial convention of the American Pomological Society at Horticultural Hall, opening on Thursday. The accompanying exhibition is expected to excel anything ever seen in the line of fruit displays.

Among recent visitors was Charles Thoriey, of New York, whose daughter is seriously ill here; Percy Rogers, of St. Johnsbury.

Tidings from Prof. C. S. Sargent have been received, he having safely completed the somewhat perilous journey across Siberia.

Detroit.

MORE HONORS TO PRESIDENT PHIL. BREITMEYER.—MICHIGAN STATE FAIR NEWS.

On Thursday evening, September 3, a party of about forty florist friends of Philip Breitmeyer, president-elect of S. A. F., assembled at the Rusch House, on Grosse Pointe road, where a banquet was held and a presentation of a beautiful gold watch, chain and charm made to Mr. Breitmeyer, who was lured to the place and totally surprised by his friends. The watch was inscribed "To Philip Breitmeyer from his many florist friends, September 1, 1903." The charm was a miniature water can made of pearl with gold trimmings. After the feast, which was a sumptuous one, Geo. Reynolds, who presided as toastmaster, called first upon Mr. Breitmeyer, who was most overcome by the happy event. His response was full of gratitude to his many friends and he referred feelingly to their efforts to make the event a memorable one. Addresses were made by Robt. Flowerday, president-elect of the Detroit Florists' Club, Chas. W. Ward, Chas. Fruch, Edward Collins, Geo. Browne, E. A. Scribner, Thos. F. Browne and J. F. Sullivan. The festivities closed at a late hour with singing of "Auld Lang Syne" and "Home Sweet Home." The out of town visitors were Chas. W. Ward, New York, and Chas. Fruch, Saginaw.

C. W. Ward, of New York, at our last meeting, made a masterly address on the value of trade organizations and referred particularly to the achievements of the S. A. F. and also of the American Carnation Society and urged all who were not already members to join their ranks. His remarks were received with rounds of applause.

E. B. Schroeter and Chas. Warncke were the only Detroit florists exhibiting at the state fair at Pontiac this week. Other florists making extensive exhibits were A. B. Lewis, Pontiac, and Otto A. Stoll, Oxford, Pa. Mr. Schroeter took first premiums on all of his eight separate exhibits.

W. J. Pearce, of Pontiac, Mich., mysteriously disappeared August 18, and was last heard of at a hotel in Detroit. The family, is unable to find out anything of him but so far without avail. His greenhouse establishment was operated under the name of Pontiac Floral Company.
J. F. S.

BAYONNE, N. J.—P. Stier has a fine house of cyclamen.

DETROIT FLORISTS' GATHERING AT GROSSE POINTE, SEPTEMBER 3.

Philadelphia.

Quite a change has taken place since last week and flowers are much scarcer. But this does not mean that New York and other cities are to take notice, as there is still enough for our scanty wants, even if we do hustle a bit to get suited. American Beauty roses are getting better and Bridesmaid, Kaiserin and Liberty are also improving. Asters are getting scarcer. Carnations are all outdoor grown stock and fairly good. Dahlias are now to be had in fairly good variety and will still fill in nicely for awhile. They are really useful and the public is taking to using them for table decoration. The colors are so brilliant and varied that there is scarcely a room that some of them will not beautify.

The wholesale market up on Cherry street has a natural or rather unnatural appearance these mornings, as it seems that quite a few growers are starting in and propose to fight it out here for the coming season. Keep it up, gentlemen, and at the same time do a little missionary work with your more timid colleagues. Manager Meehan says the shipping business is growing and when a few more of the out-of-town folks get to find out the good quality of the stock handled, he will make some of the commission men hustle to keep up with the market.

W. P. Peacock, whose eighty-acre farm at Atco, N. Y., is now a harlequin of color, is sending some fine dahlias to S. S. Pennock. His cut last year was enormous, but with the additional acreage of this year he promises to far eclipse that record.

Robt. Craig & Son have some fine Longiflorum lilies. These are from cold storage bulbs and while fine are hardly profitable, averaging only about one flower to a bulb.

At Ed. Reid's flower market things are growing lively, although the moving spirit is still out in Dakota. Thirteen orders in one mail is not so bad for this season.

Fred. Ehret, the up-town commission man, reports an excellent business the past week, there being a rush of funeral work in his district.

Ralph Shrigley is back to his old love having returned to S. S. Pennock's.
K.

St. Louis.

Business is slowly improving although of the past week and the condition of trade. The quality of most stock is better than it has been for some time. American Beauty roses are coming in rapidly, other stock being about the same as last week.

Sunday, September 6, was open Sunday at Shaw's Garden and 10,699 visitors passed through the gates. The garden is increasing in popularity each year and but for the changeable weather the attendance would have been twice as great.

Owing to the inclement weather there were not many in attendance at the recent plant sale of the Michel Plant and Bulb Company, although bids were lively.

H. C. Irish, assistant director of the Missouri Botanic Garden, is away for a two-weeks' vacation.

T. L. Mead, of Oviedo, Fla., was visiting in St. Louis on Tuesday, September 8. Geo. Waldbart has had a busy week with funeral work.

In the notes last week R. J. Mohr was erroneously printed R. J. Mahn.
B.

Des Moines.

The state fair has been the interesting event of the past week and competition in cut flowers, design work and plants was pretty sharp. In flower design Blair was first with a flower cushion, Morris second with a flower cradle with a sleeping doll labeled "Don't wake the baby," Lozier third with a large flower air-ship. I. W. Lozier received first on the only general exhibit of greenhouse plants. W. L. Morris received first for palms, cannas, carnations and tuberous begonias.

Carnation plants made a good field growth and are mostly housed. The rain and cold weather were favorable. Roses are mostly mildewed. Cut flower business has been quiet the whole summer, but prospects are now more promising. Raining daily, weather cold.

W. L. Morris has moved his plant to Thirty-fifth and Ingersoll avenue and is grouping his glass together hereafter.
M.

THE AMERICAN FLORIST

NINETEENTH YEAR.

Subscription, $1.00 a year. To Europe, $2.00.
  Subscriptions accepted only from those
  in the trade.
Advertisements, on all except cover pages,
  10 Cents a Line, Agate; $1.00 per inch.
        Cash with Order.

No Special Position Guaranteed.

Discounts are allowed only on consecutive insertions, as follows—6 times, 5 per cent; 13 times,
  10 per cent; 26 times, 20 per cent;
        52 times, 30 per cent.

Cover space sold only on yearly contract at
  $1.00 per inch, net, in the case of the two
  front pages, regular discounts applying only to the back pages.

The Advertising Department of the AMERICAN
FLORIST is for florists, seedsmen and nurserymen
and dealers in wares pertaining to those lines only.

Orders for less than one-half inch space not accepted.

Advertisements must reach us by Wednesday to
secure insertion in the issue for the following
Saturday. Address
        AMERICAN FLORIST CO., Chicago.

"FRIENDS of the seed, the flower, the
fruit, fair trinity of potency and beauty
and use."—C. C. Bonney, Hort. Congress. 1893.

FROST in a fortnight.

ARE the tools not in use covered with
asphalt paint.

A FEW seasonable notes for retailers
will be found in this issue.

ALEX. A. LAUB in this issue writes
straight from the shoulder about violets.

SURELY there are no broken lights of
glass in any of your houses at this date.

FERTILIZING of fields or grounds, neglected in the spring should be done now.

FRUITS will be cared for by special
refrigeration at the St. Louis Fair. Why
not care for flowers the same way?

OUTDOOR flowers can often be saved for
three or four weeks' blooming by covering with papers or other protection the
first one or two frosty nights; it is worth
trying.

BOOKKEEPING and account forms for
same by R. F. Tesson, as read at the
Milwaukee convention will be printed in
pamphlet form by the AMERICAN FLORIST
and mailed FREE on request to any
florist and extra copies to employers
wishing the same to distribute among
their employes. The address is of much
permanent value and well worth studying by our young men.

DAHLIA is the September flower, says
S. S. Pennock.

H. A. DREER is offering seed of Stokesia
cyanea, the cornflower aster. with
illustrated circular.

PETER HENDERSON & CO. have a striking and effective cover on their retail
fall catalogue, combining the commercial and the artistic in a happy way.

C. S. Harrison on the Paeonia.

Near most of our towns and cities a peony
garden could be established, and while you wait
for the roots to grow you can harvest a crop of
flowers.   In Nebraska and Kansas they are on
time for Decoration Day, and if there is not a
home demand for all, florists in the Dakotas and
Minnesota will gladly take the surplus. A Chicago firm last year sold over 100,000 blooms after
Decoration Day. They are usually 70 cents per
dozen, but the choice ones brought $2.00 a dozen.

Better Than Dinner.

Had rather miss Sunday dinner than
the weekly issue of the FLORIST.
        OKLAHOMA FLORAL CO.

Re-echoes of Convention Thoughts.

It takes a popular man to win a
majority with four candidates in the
field.

        Such a face and such a mien,
        As to be lov'd needs only to be seen.

The basket-lunch on the Virginia was
an object lesson in the science of crowd-
feeding.

Whatever is worth doing at all, is worth doing
well.

As usual, the secretary's headquarters
was a magnet for the gallants of the
society.

        Alas! our young affections run to waste.
        Or water but the desert.

Did Rudd take the floor and hold it?

        A plain blunt man,
        I speak right on.

Copies of the constitution were in brisk
demand on the morning of election day,
but they were not needed.

        For this relief much thanks.

Philadelphia, as usual, took her time,
and Chicago's pride was of short duration.

        When fortune flatters she does it to betray.

Geo. C. WATSON's peony report was a
gem of diplomacy.

        Stands Scotland where it did?

Theodore Lang might use that new
field-glass to search for New York's van-
ished bowling glories.

        On fortune's cap we are not the very button.

John Westcott's florists' club punch is
the most remarkable harmonizer ever
invented.

        The wheels o' life gae down hill scrievin'
        Wi' rattlin' glee.

Has the ginger jar been swapped for a
honey-pot?

        'Tis not in mortals to command success,
        But we'll do more, Sempronius—we'll deserve it.

A Correction.

ED. AM. FLORIST:—In my recent article on cyclamens in "Florists' Plant
Notes," the sentence, "As soon as the
little plants have formed bulbs about the
size of a small pea, give them three-inch
pots, etc.," should read, "As soon as the
little plants have formed bulbs about the
size of a small pea, give them thumb
pots,"   G.

Adiantum Hybridum.

In our issue of August 29 we failed to
state clearly that in Mr. Ley's opinion
Adiantum hybridum is totally barren of
spores. The executive of the S. A. F. has
the plant under technical observation
with regard to this matter, and the
report will be made in due course.

A Prompt Adjustment.

ED. AM. FLORIST:—Permit us to express
through your widely circulated journal
our thanks and appreciation for the
prompt and satisfactory adjustment by
the Florists' Hail Association of our loss
by hail of July 24. We have had other
losses in the past eight years and all
have been promptly and satisfactorily
adjusted. We wish to recommend the
association to all florists in the country.
Very truly yours,
        COLFAX AVENUE FLORAL CO.
        By Bernard Beer, President.

Can Valley Be Stored at 15° F.?

ED. AM. FLORIST:—Can lily of the valley
be kept in cold storage at a temperature
of 15° Far., or is this temperature too
low and would it injure the vitality of
the pips?   H.

Canadian Convention Notes.

A. H. Ewing was unanimously re-elected
secretary, having filled that office most
acceptably. Herman Simmer's practical
knowledge of finance assured him the
treasurership.

The banquet given by the local club
taxed the dining hall to its utmost capacity. The mayor informed the guests
that a percentage of the present tax rate,
amounting to about $800,000, would be
set aside during the next five years for
the extension of parks and public playgrounds. Toasts were responded to by
Messrs. Manton, Suckling, Dunlop and
Leslie. Songs were given to W. J.
Lawrence, of Toronto, and Mr. Stephens,
of London. F. .R. Pierson's paper was
badly missed.

The trade exhibits were somewhat disappointing, yet on the whole creditable.
Among these were Julius Roehrs, of Rutherford, N. J., orchids; Hall & Robinson,
of Montreal, ferns and palms; J. Gammage & Sons, of London, cyclamens,
ferns and other plants; Webster Brothers,
of Hamilton, ferns and palms; Wm. Jay
& Sons, general collection of plants; W.
J. Lawrence, ferns, palms and gladiolus
blooms; J. Simmers, florists supplies;
Steele, Briggs Seed Company, florists'
supplies; John Davis & Son, pottery.
Prize winners at Horticultural Association: Exhibition Park, 19 prizes; George
White, gardener for Pellat & Pellat, 10;
Horticultural Gardens, 11; George Graham, government greenhouse, 10; Manton Brothers, 10; Mr. Houston, of Central prison, 12; Messrs. Jay & Son, 4;
Messrs. C. Hodge, of Woodstock and L.
G. Stone and C. A. Stone of Toronto,
were also prize winners.   H. G. D.

Fire Insurance.

ED. AM. FLORIST:—Can you give me
any information in regard to fire insurance on greenhouses, boiler room and
packing shed.   JOSEPH BOCK.

Thanks.

Henry Schweitzer, of Mendota, Ill.,
who met with the terrible loss of all his
property by hail some time ago, recently
received $25 from the Detroit Florists'
Club and $19 from the Indianapolis
florists. Mr. Schweitzer wishes to give
his sincere thanks through the columns
of this paper for the kindness shown him.

Greenhouse Building.

Lawrence, Mass.—A. H. Wagland, one
palm house.
North Beverly, Mass.—Geo. W. Glines,
two houses.
Bull's Head, N. Y.—W. Pink, one house.
Woburn, Mass.—A. Porter, one cucum-
ber house.
North Cambridge, Mass.—J. McKinzie,
two houses, each 12x120.
Westerly, R. I.—S. J. Reuter, one house
35x500.
West Springfield, Mass.—A. L. Pease,
one cucumber house.
Aurora, Mo.—John Werdien, rebuilding
houses.
Hyde Park, Pa.—Wm. Kern, one house.
Oconto, Wis.—J. Sylvester, one house
16x160.
Clinton, Mass.—F. P. Sawyer, house
22x122.

BRIQUETTED fuel (coal dust, etc., made
into bricks), is described in U. S. Consular reports, Vol. XXVI.

SITUATIONS, WANTS, FOR SALE.

One Cent Per Word.

Cash with the Adv.

Plant Advs. NOT admitted under this head.

Every paid subscriber to the AMERICAN FLORIST
for the year 1903 is entitled to a five-line WANT
ADV. (situations only) free, to be used at any
time during the year.

Situation Wanted—By an experienced grower
of carnations, violets and 'mums. Competent to
take charge. Best references. Single.
P L M, care American Florist.

Situation Wanted—Steady, by sober, reliable
man, u-ed to cut flowers, bedding plants, etc.
Address with particulars.
WM. HOLST, General Delivery, Troy, N. Y.

Situation Wanted—I want work as landscape
engineer, draftsman, foreman, grower, designer,
maker up. Private or commercial. Best references. F. A. HAHN ELMAN, Fostoria, Ohio.

Situation Wanted—Position together for 2 single men as 1st and 2nd gardeners, one English
and one Swede, age 37 and 25. Very best of
references. GARDENER, care American Florist.

Situation Wanted—By an experienced grower,
in first-class cut flower store as Clerk. Six years'
experience. Good recommendations. East, preferred. Address EAST, care American Florist.

Situation Wanted—As working foreman or
extra man by first-class cut flower grower. 8
years with one of the leading growers of the
East. Chicago preferred. Address
N S, care American Florist.

Situation Wanted—As working foreman by
first-class growers of cut flowers and general
stock. Roses a specialty. Only first-class place
wanted. Chicago preferred. Address
A B, care American Florist.

Situation Wanted—As head gardener or superintendent on private place, park or institution,
new place and the west preferred. Single, German, 28 years of age. Satisfactory references.
Will be at liberty Oct. 15. Address
J W, care American Florist.

Situation Wanted—In or near Boston, by expe-
rienced grower of roses, carnations and chrysan-
themums. Manager in last place for nine years.
Best of references. Address
JOHN PRITCHARD,
Newtonville Ave., Newtonville, Mass.

Situation Wanted—By single man as gardener
in private place. Thoroughly practical in all
branches. Best of references from England and
U. S. At present in charge of a large private
estate of over 300 acres. Address
GARDENER, care American Florist.

Situation Wanted—Foreman, single, 34 years
of age, expert grower of cut flowers and pot
plants, 20 years' experience, wishes position in
up-to-date establishment by Oct. 1. Please state
wages paid and full particulars. Address
J. F. GODFREY, care Robert Binder,
7th & Grant, Pittsburg, Pa.

Situation Wanted—As head gardener on private place, single, age 32, thoroughly experienced
in growing palms, ferns, orchids, fruits and vegetables, under glass and outdoor, drawing plans and
laying out new grounds. Used to handle plenty
help. Address SWEN, Lockbox 8,
Flatbush Sta., Brooklyn, N. Y.

Help Wanted—Gardener, for private place;
young man; single, sober and industrious. Apply
MRS. WILCE, cor. Marshfield Ave. and
Harrison Street, Chicago.

Help Wanted—At once; a sober, reliable, all-
around man for Commercial place. Single and
German preferred. References required.
BOEHRINGER BROS., Bay City, Mich.

Help Wanted—Florist; competent to take
charge of 6,000 feet of glass, grow cut flowers and
general stock. State wages with reference, etc.
J. C. STEINHAUSER, Pittsburg, Kansas.

Help Wanted—2 young men with some experience in the retail florist business. Address stating
salary expected
C. A. SAMUELSON, 2129 Michigan Ave., Chicago.

Help Wanted—A man experienced in packing
roses for shipping. We have a good position for
a reliable man that understands the business.
SOUTH PARK FLORAL CO., New Castle, Ind.

Help Wanted—A good, steady, single German
florist for general greenhouse work. Address with
references. Jos. F. KLIMMER,
Desplaines Ave. & Harrison St., Oak Park, Ill.

Help Wanted—At once; a sober, reliable man
for general greenhouse work. Good wages and
a steady position the year around to the right
man. References required. Address
J. A. BISSINGER, Lansing, Mich.

For Rent—Sixty-foot greenhouse, 8 room house,
two lots, $25 per month; 3181 Elston Ave.
DR. BANGS, 554 N. Robey St., Chicago.

For Sale—One No. 30 Wilks hot water boiler
with stack complete, used only three months. A
bargain for cash. JAMES W. DUNFORD,
R. R. No. 1, Clayton, Mo.

For Sale—Well established, good greenhouse
at a bargain. Fine opening for a single man with
small capital. Write soon if you are looking for
a snap and mean business. Address
BUCKEYE, care American Florist.

For Rent—Greenhouse plant, 17 hot houses,
barn, coal shed, dwelling house; including 12
acres of land, located one-quarter mile south of
Blue Island, Ill. For particulars inquire at
F. W. HEITMAN, 334 E. 59d St., Chicago.

For Sale or Lease—A finely located place in
the Borough of the Bronx, consisting of 11 greenhouses. (no stock), hot water heating, windmill,
barn, dwelling house and about 3 acres of ground.
J. RINGLER, 723 3rd Ave., New York City.

FOR SALE. A good home and greenhouses
well stocked with up-to-date
stock for retail trade; established 20 years. Splendid opportunity is here offered. Reason, the death
of Mrs. S. H. Bagley. C. H. Bagley, Abilene Kan.

For Sale—Fire box boiler, length 11 ft., diameter 3 ft. 25 3-inch flues; put in new last year. Has
been heating 6,000 sq. ft. of glass to hot water,
but could be used for steam. Have added 19 000
sq. ft. of glass and put in larger boiler. Price
$80.00 f. o. b. cars. Decatur.
JESSE A. ERNSBERGER, Decatur, Ind.

For Sale—Four large size Gorton side feed
boilers (for hard or soft coal), $50 each; one small
Gorton side feed, $25; one large sectional Florida
heater, $80; one small coil-boiler, hot water, in
use two winters, will heat 3,000 square feet of
glass, $20. Boilers taken out to put in larger one.
Write for particulars.
F. FALLON, Roanoke, Va.

FOREMAN WANTED...

Must be a first-class grower of cut flowers and
plants; one capable of managing 75,000 square
feet of glass, devoted to both wholesale and retail
trade. Good wages, steady position. References
required. Address

Crabb & Hunter, Grand Rapids, Mich.

For Sale—Retail greenhouse establishment
about 3,0 0 feet glass, connected with two tenement dwellings; first-class reputation; good
trade; center of town of about 9,000 people, growing rapidly. Must sell, low for cash. Reason,
death of proprietor. One minute from depot; two
railroads. Address
THE N. A. CHASE GREENHOUSES, Winsted, Conn.

WANTED.

A great nurseryman in Holland, wishing to
extend business in America asks an active
person acquainted with the trade, to sell his
goods, (especially weeping, ornamental and
forest trees, shrubs, conifers, etc.,) under personal responsibility. Send solicitations with
references to

NURSERYMAN, care Am. Florist.

Traveling Salesman Wanted.

A traveling representative, for a house, of
highest commercial standing. None but
those of experience and good general knowledge of seeds, bulbs and plants, and well
recommended, need apply.
Energetic, care Bonnot Bros.,
Cut Flower Exchange, Coogan Bldg., N. Y.

FOR SALE.

In a thriving Ohio town of about 22,000 inhabitants, fine greenhouse plant, consisting of 8
greenhouses, ranging in size from 18x100 to
30x180, also fine work shed and modern up-to-
date office and store room attached. For particulars address

S. S. SKIDELSKY,
708 North 16th St.,   PHILADELPHIA.

A Rare Chance

For a good grower to go into business. The
plant of the Morton Grove Greenhouses, (incorporated) is for sale. It is situated 14 miles from
Chicago courthouse and consists of 28,000 feet of
glass, ¼ being new glass 16x20 put up in 1900.
Four acres of tiled land. Excellent soil. 3,000
Peonies 2 years old. Steam heat 3 boilers, one a
100 H. P. Kroeschell make, virtually new. 500 tons
washed coal in shed. Have planted, 7,500 Roses,
16,000 Carnations, all best stock. **Old established
trade.** Plant in A1 condition excepting the old
range, for which no charge will be made. Will
sell at a very attractive figure and on easy terms,
with or without a 6 room dwelling on a 60 foot lot
across the street. The rebuilding of the old range
will give you an up-to-date plant. We prefer to
sell ha't-interest with option of future purchase
to a responsible grower, who must take full
charge as the proprietors' interests are now
entirely away from the city.
Address until Sept. 17th care UNITED STATES
GLUE CO., 37 Spruce St., New York. After that
care of same Company, Milwaukee, Wis.
PAUL KREISMAN.

•Horses, wagons, tools, etc., everything complete.
•No special hurry to sell. Transfer may be
made at any time between now and spring.

UNUSUAL OPPORTUNITY

FOR SALE AT A BARGAIN

In a good Wisconsin city, the establishment shown
above. For price, terms and full particulars, address

C. B. WHITNALL, care Central Trust Co., Milwaukee, Wis.

Milwaukee.

Messrs. Riemer & Radmer, of this city, are erecting a hot water plant in the new greenhouses now being built for H. G. Selfridge, Lake Geneva, Wis. This firm has also received contracts for the heating of several greenhouses in Michigan, and are extending their reputation very largely in this particular class of heating work. Furman new sectional boilers are used in all their work. Up to the present time Riemer & Radmer have successfully heated over 155,000 square feet of glass. L. H. S.

Floral Decorations of Royalty.

The floral decorations at the ball given by the Prince and Princess of Wales at Marlboro House were on a lavish scale, and in the best possible taste. On the walls of the ball-room large panels of silky material of a myrtle shade of green were formed, and upon them light wooden trellises of white, enamelled wood were fixed. Over these lattices immense trails of natural ivy were trained, and alternating at short distances were long mirrors draped with green. Further color was given by the liberal use of flowers, which were not only arranged at the foot of the mirrors and round the recesses, but were used in profusion in festoons over the frieze connecting the capitals of the columns. For this purpose the flowers of pink ivy-leaf pelargoniums were employed, and Covent Garden had to strain its utmost resources to supply the vast quantities required. Three varieties, each of a slightly different color, namely Souvenir de Charles Turner, Constance and Galilee were entwined with delightful gradations of color, the design being that of a thick, deep festoon. At the points at which it was caught up a great medallion formed of the same flowers with ferns and light foliage was fixed, and from this depended a hanging basket to correspond. Malmaison carnations from Sandringham (royal gardens) were freely used in the decoration of the supper tables.—*Gardeners' Magazine.*

TOLEDO, O.—Henry Krueger, of Krueger Brothers, and Miss Agnes Smith were married Monday, August 31.

Wholesale Flower Markets

Pittsburg Cut Flower Co. Ltd

WHOLESALE FLORISTS.

Pittsburg, Pa.

INTERNATIONAL FLOWER DELIVERY.

PASSENGER STEAMSHIP MOVEMENTS.

The table herewith give the scheduled time of departure of ocean steamships carrying first-class passengers from the principal American and foreign ports, covering the space of two weeks from date of this issue of the AMERICAN FLORIST. Much disappointment often results from attempts to forward flowers for steamer delivery by express, to the care of the ship's steward or otherwise. The carriers of these packages are not infrequently refused admission on board and even those delivered on board are not always certain to reach the parties for whom they were intended. Hence florists in interior cities having orders for the delivery of flowers to passengers on out-going steamers are advised to intrust the filling of such orders to some reliable florist in the port of departure, who understands the necessary details and formalities and has the facilities for attending to it properly. For the addresses of such firms we refer our readers to the advertisements on this page.

FROM	TO	STEAMER	*LINE	DAY	DUE ABOUT
New York	Liverpool	Campania	1	Sat. Sept. 19, 2:00 p. m.	Sept. 25
New York	"	Umbria	1	Sat. Sept. 26, 9:00 a. m.	Sept. 21
New York	Glasgow	Laurentian	2	Thur. Sept. 17, Noon.	Sept. 27
New York	"	Deutschland	3	Tues. Sept. 15, 11:00 a. m.	
New York	"	Bluecher	3	Thur. Sept. 17, 1:30 p. m.	Sept. 24
New York	"	Graf Waldersee	3	Sat. Sept. 19, 3:00 p. m.	Oct. 1
New York	"	Auguste Victoria	3	Thur. Sept. 24, 10:00 a. m.	
New York	Copenhagen	United States	4	Wed. Sept. 16,	
New York	Glasgow	Columbia	2	Sat. Sept. 19, 3:00 p. m.	
New York	"	Astoria	5	Sat. Sept. 26.	
New York	London	Minnetonka	6	Sat. Sept. 19, 4:00 p. m.	
New York	"	Minneapolis	6	Sat. Sept. 26, 9:00 a. m.	Oct. 4
New York	Southampton	Marquette	6	Fri. Se.t. 25, 9:00 a. m.	
New York	"	New York	8	Sat. Sept. 16, 10:00 a. m.	Sept. 22
New York	"	Philadelphia	8	Wed. Sept. 23, 10:00 a. m.	
New York	"	St. Louis	8	Wed. Sept. 30, 10:00 a. m.	
New York	Liverpool	Majestic	7	Wed. Sept. 16, Noon.	
New York	"	Celtic	7	Fri. Sept. 18, 3:00 p. m.	
New York	"	Oceanic	7	Wed. Sept. 23, 7:00 a. m.	Sept. 30
New York	"	Cymbric	7	Fri. Sept. 25, 8:00 a. m.	Oct. 3
New York	"	Teutonic	7	Wed. Sept. 30, Noon.	Oct. 6
New York	Antwerp	Vaderland	9	Sat. Sept. 19, 10:00 a. m.	Sept. 28
New York	"	Kroonland	9	Sat. Sept. 26, 10:00 a. m.	Oct. 5
New York	Havre	La Savoie	10	Thur. Sept. 17, 10:00 a. m.	
New York	"	La Bretagne	10	Thur. Sept. 24, 10:00 a. m.	Oct. 1
New York	Rotterdam	Statendam	11	Wed. Sept. 16, 10:00 a. m.	
New York	"	Ryndam	11	Wed. Sept. 23, 10:00 a. m.	Oct. 1
New York	"	Noordam	11	Wed. Sept. 30, 10:00 a. m.	
New York	Genoa	Citta di Milano	12	Tues. Sept. 15, 11:00 a. m.	
New York	"	Lombardia	12	Tues. Sept. 29, 11:00 a. m.	
New York	"	Lahn	13	Sat. Sept. 26, 11:00 a. m.	Oct. 6
New York	Naples	Roma	14	Sat. Sept. 15.	Sept. 27
New York	Bremen	Grosser Kurfuerst	13	Thur. Sept. 17, 1:00 p. m.	Sept. 27
New York	"	Kaiser Wilh. II	13	Tues. Sept. 22, 6:30 a. m.	Sept. 29
New York	"	Koenig Albert	13	Sat. Sept. 26, Noon.	Oct. 4
New York	"	K. Wil. Der Grosse	13	Tues. Sept. 29, 10:00 a. m.	Oct. 6
Boston	Liverpool	Saxonia	1	Tues. Sept. 22, 10:30 a. m.	Sept. 29
Boston	"	Columbus	15	Tues. Sept. 17, 7:00 a. m.	
Boston	"	Commonwealth	15	Thur. Sept. 24, Noon.	Sept. 31
Boston	"	Cestrian	16	Sat. Sept. 19, 1:00 a. m.	
Boston	"	Devonian	16	Sat. Sept. 26, 1:30 p. m.	
Montreal	"	Canada	16	Sat. Sept. 26, Daylight.	
San Francisco	Hongkong	Hongkong Maru	17	Sat. Sept. 19, 1:00 p. m.	Oct. 20
San Francisco	Yokohama	Hongkong Maru	17	Sat. Sept. 19, 1:00 p. m.	Oct. 5
San Francisco	Sydney	Sonoma	18	Thur. Sept. 17, 2:00 p. m.	Oct. 9
San Francisco	Honolulu	Alameda	18	Tues. Sept. 29, 2:00 p. m.	Oct. 2
San Francisco	Tahiti	Mariposa	18	Sun. Sept. 20, 11:00 a. m.	Oct. 2
Vancouver	Sydney	Moana	20	Fri. Sept. 18,	Oct. 13
Vancouver	Hongkong	Athenian	20	Mon. Sept. 21,	Oct. 20
Seattle	"	Iyo Maru	22	Sat. Sept. 19, a. m.	Oct. 20

*1 Cunard; 2 Allen-State; 3 Hamburg-American; 4 Scandinavian-American; 5 Anchor Line; 6 Atlantic Transport; 7 White Star; 8 American; 9 Red Star; 10 French; 11 Holland-American; 12 Italian Royal Mail; 13 North German Lloyd; 14 Fabre; 15 Dominion; 16 Leyland; 17 Occidental and Oriental; 18 Oceanic; 19 Allan; 20 Can. Pacific Ry.; 21 N. Pacific Ry.; 22 Hongkong-Seattle.

INTERNATIONAL FLOWER DELIVERY.

STEAMSHIPS LEAVE FOREIGN PORTS.

FROM	TO	STEAMER	*LINE	DAY	DUE ABOUT
Liverpool	New York	Lucania	1	Sat. Sept. 19,	Sept. 25
Liverpool	"	Etruria	1	Sat. Sept. 26,	Sept. 31
Liverpool	"	Teutonic	7	Wed. Sept. 16, 5:00 p. m.	Sept. 23
Liverpool	"	Arabic	7	Fri. Sept. 18, 5:00 p. m.	Sept. 26
Liverpool	"	Germanic	7	Wed. Sept. 33, 5:00 p. m.	Sept. 31
Liverpool	"	Cedric	7	Fri. Sept. 24, 5:00 p. m.	
Liverpool	Boston	Ivernia	1	Tues. Sept. 22,	Sept. 28
Liverpool	"	New England	15	Thur. Sept. 17,	Sept. 24
Liverpool	"	Winfredian	16	Fri. Sept. 18,	
Liverpool	"	Bohemian	16	Fri. Sept. 25,	
Liverpool	Montreal	Kensington	15	Wed. Sept. 16,	
Liverpool	"	Dominion	15	Wed. Sept. 23,	
Glasgow	New York	Ethiopia	6	Thur. Sept. 17,	
Glasgow	"	Anchoria	5	Thur. Sept. 24,	Oct. 2
Glasgow	"	Mongolian	2	Sat. Sept. 19,	Sept. 28
Genoa	"	Nord America	12	Mon. Sept. 14,	
Genoa	"	Sardegna	12	Mon. Sept. 21,	
Genoa	"	Citta di Napoli	12	Mon. Sept. 28,	Oct. 14
Genoa	"	Hohenzollern	12	Thur. Sept. 17,	Sept. 30
Southampton	"	St. Paul	3	Wed. Sept. 16, Noon.	
Southampton	"	St. Louis	3	Sat. Sept. 19, Noon.	Oct. 2
Southampton	"	New York	3	Sat. Sept. 26, Noon.	
Southampton	"	Manitou	6	Wed. Sept. 23,	
London	"	Minnehaha	6	Sat. Sept. 19,	Sept. 29
London	"	Mesaba	6	Sat. Sept. 26,	
Antwerp	"	Zeeland	9	Sat. Sept. 19, 11:00 a. m.	Sept. 28
Antwerp	"	Finland	9	Sat. Sept. 26, 2:00 p. m.	Oct. 8
Hamburg	"	Moltke	3	Thur. Sept. 17,	Sept. 24
Hamburg	"	Patricia	3	Sat. Sept. 19,	Sept. 31
Hamburg	"	Furst Bismarck	3	Thur. Sept. 24,	Oct. 1
Havre	"	La Lorraine	10	Sat. Sept. 19,	
Havre	"	La Touraine	10	Sat. Sept. 26,	Oct. 2
Copenhagen	"	Oscar II	4	Wed. Sept. 23,	
Rotterdam	"	Rotterdam	11	Sat. Sept. 19,	
Rotterdam	"	Potsdam	11	Sat. Sept. 26,	Oct. 3
Bremen	"	K. Wil. Der Grosse	13	Tues. Sept. 15,	Sept. 22
Bremen	"	Frdk. Der Grosse	13	Sat. Sept. 19,	Sept. 28
Bremen	"	Kronprinz Wilh.	13	Tues. Sept. 22,	Sept. 29
Bremen	"	Barbarossa	13	Sat. Sept. 26,	Oct. 6
Naples	"	Germania	14	Thur. Sept. 17,	Sept. 27
Hongkong	Vancouver	Empress of Japan	20	Wed. Sept. 23,	Oct. 14
Hongkong	SanFrancisco	Siberia	3	Sat. Sept. 19,	Oct. 13
Hongkong	"	Coptic	17	Sat. Sept. 26,	Oct. 23
Hongkong	Tacoma	Tacoma	21	Thur. Sept. 24,	Oct. 23
Hongkong	Seattle	Tosa Maru	22	Tues. Sept. 22,	Oct. 22
Sidney	SanFrancisco	Sierra	18	Mon. Sept. 28,	Oct. 19

* See steamship list on opposite page.

THE SEED TRADE.

AMERICAN SEED TRADE ASSOCIATION.
S. F. Willard, Pres : J. Charles McCullough, First Vice-Pres.; C. E. Kendel, Cleveland, O., Sec'y and Treas.
Twenty-second annual convention St. Louis, Mo., June, 1904.

ELGIN, ILL.—F. Stumme, grocer and seed dealer, is in bankruptcy.

JOBBERS are trying to get in early with carload orders for evergreen sweet corn, but the same are not accepted.

SLATTED cases are used by some Dutch bulb shippers. Possibly danger of heating is thereby avoided to some extent.

IRON cowpea, a variety said to be resistant to root-knot and wilt, is exploited by the Department of Agriculture.

WASHINGTON, D. C.—Contracts were let last week for the new Department of Agriculture building. The appropriation for same is $1,500,000.

PAINESVILLE, O.—The crop of local grown onion seed here is a good one, the acreage being larger than usual. Yellow and red globe are grown here.

THE Minnesota Field Seed Growers' association has been formed with the following officers: President, C. C. Thompson, Farmington; secretary, W. M. Hayes; treasurer, E. L. Jenks.

MILFORD, CONN.—Corn prospects are still unfavorable. We must have a warm September and freedom from frosts to secure a fair crop. The acreage planted is unusual.

PARTIES who have visited Louisville say the onion set crop is about one-half of a normal one in number of bushels and about one-third of last year's big crop. Chillicothe about the same. Smut is found in the whites at both places.

CINCINNATI. — Fire injured the retail department of J. Charles McCullough to the amount of about $20,000 by smoke and water, but fortunately their main stocks are carried at their wholesale warehouse which is in no way affected, and business will go on uninterrupted.

VISITED CHICAGO.—F. W. Maas, of Plant Seed Company, Adolph Corneli, of Schisler, Corneli Seed Company, St. Louis; R. H. Shumway, Jr., Rockford, Ill.; James McKellar, of Livingston Seed Company, Columbus; E. D. Funk, of Funk Brothers' Seed Company, Bloomington, Ill.; G. L. Bissell, of Ottumwa (Ia.) Seed Company.

WATERLOO, NEB.—It is a critical time for corn. Crops are late and for ten days the weather has been very unfavorable for ripening. It is making progress, but has not yet commenced to dry down as it should. We are watching days and nights. Every little change in weather creates talk and every rain puts us back. It is really a critical time.

BOSTON.—R. & J. Farquhar & Company maintain on their counter a daily exhibition of flowers of annuals and garden perennials in their blooming season, all neatly labelled. The number of customers who take advantage of the opportunity to place their order for seed or plants for next spring, of flowers which appeal to their fancy, is very large and Messrs. Farquhar find the plan both pleasing and profitable.

THE French Syndicate for the Defence of Agriculture, a combination of French bulb growers at and near Toulon in southern France, reports recently that its managers have sold for cash, to or through Messrs. Flower and Deprat, its remaining stock of flower bulbs for this season. The close of the season will be celebrated by the members of the syndicate with a banquet about September 15. The syndicate congratulates itself on the work done this season and trusts that it has laid the foundation for successful results for the next campaign.

Seed Crop Report—German.

FLOWER.

VARIETIES.	CONDITION, Sept. 1.
Aster, early,	good.
Aster, medium early,	good.
Aster, late,	salable.
Stocks,	good.
Pansy,	short crop.
Phlox,	not good.
Nasturtium,	good.
Lathyrus odoratus,	good.
Mignonette,	good.

VEGETABLE.

Beet, sugar,	below middling.
Beet, table,	good.
Mangel Wurzel,	below middling.
Radish, early, summer, winter,	good.
Lettuce,	good.
Beans, pole,	late, not good.
Beans, bush,	middling.
Carrot,	fair.
Parsnip,	fair.
Parsley,	fair.
Cucumber,	total failure.
Onion,	middling.
Turnip,	good.
Rutabaga,	good.

1. Lilium Harrisii 2. Lilium Docii.

New Lily, Stephens' Hybrid.

P. W. Stephens of Bermuda, successful grower of true Harrisii lily bulbs and in touch with the needs of the forcing florist has for several years past been experi-

menting with seedlings of the best Bermuda grown Lilium longiflorum, pollenized from selected Harrisii, aiming to get a bulb which would retain the the health and evenness of the former, while it took on the earliness and freedom of the true Harrisii strain. He has this year succeeded in raising two bulbs of fifteen inches circumference, the picture of health, and as much alike as two twins, as the photograph will show,

Stephens Hybrid. (New).

the product of two four-inch bulblets of last fall's planting. The scars at the top of stems show that each had thirteen flowers and by comparing them with the accompanying illustrations of L. Harrisii and L. Docii (which is the best and earliest longiflorum hitherto) it will be seen that they have intermediate characteristics of foliage and bulb. Especially noticeable is the pronouncedly pointed, free and somewhat twisted petalage of the new bulbs, promising extra early forcing quality.

Mr. Stephens will grow the scales of these two bulbs in special ground this coming season and expects to raise a carefully segregated lot of bulbs true to this new type, which he will in due time exhibit, and, if successful, introduce, as Stephens' Hybrid.   PAN.

Nature's Garden.

We are so pre-Raphælite as to admire Nature. She weaves her mats much as do the Persians, without much apparent thought of the result. She does not ask whether such and such colors will blend or contrast, but simply puts them together. Should we attempt to imitate either the oriental or the Good Mother, the chances are that we might have to chronicle a conspicuous failure. There is perhaps a subtle design under a kaleidoscopic effect.
—Dr. W. Whitman Bailey.

THE NURSERY TRADE.

AM. ASSOCIATION OF NURSERYMEN.

N. W. HALE, Knoxville, Tenn.. Pres.; FRANK A. WEBER, St. Louis, Mo., Vice-Pres.; GEORGE C. SEAGER, Rochester, N. Y., Sec'y. Twenty-ninth annual convention. Atlanta, Ga., June, 1904.

BAMBOOS in the United States are interestingly described in the August number. of *Forestry and Irrigation.*

THE growing season, says W. A. Peterson, has been ideal at Chicago for the growth of nursery stock.

NEWCASTLE, PA.—The Nature Study Club made a large exhibition of wild flowers at its monthly meeting September 3.

RIPON, WIS.—The South Woods Park Association has purchased twenty acres for a public park. The association's flower show was held September 2.

GRAND HAVEN, MICH.—Z. L. Bliss of the National Bureau of Forestry, Washington, D. C., has been studying the sand hills of the lake shore. The government purposes to experiment with beach growing grasses and trees to cover the bleak sand hills with verdure.

ROCHESTER, N. Y.—The seventeenth annual convention of American Cemetery Superintendents was held here September 8-10. The printed programme was followed. The lunch served by Ellwanger & Barry on the hill top in their trial grounds, with a view of miles of the Genesee valley, was a notable feature, and the presence of the elder Ellwanger delighted all. John C. Dix of Cleveland was elected president and the next meeting will be at Chicago.

Orchids at St. Paul.

A call at Dr. Schiffman's found everything about the establishment in its usual "spick and span" condition. His latest acquisition is a case of cattleyas from Brazil, which arrived in good condition and are now being potted up. His collection of well established Phalaenopsis is said to be the largest and finest in the world. These were obtained from the Philippines two years ago. The genial doctor is a most enthusiastic collector, sparing no time, means or expense in procuring stocks. He grows them for the love he bears them and the amusement they afford. Each year he imports several hundred plants in the hope of procuring one or two good specimens and each year he sells a number of good commercial plants to make room for others. By careful selection and hybridizing he hopes to have in time the most valuable collection in America. Mr. Whatton, a noted English grower, intends the growing and is most successful with all varieties. In addition to the orchids here I noted a new and valuable variety of asparagus—A. myriocladus, a nice round, bushy, decorative plant with finely cut foliage. It is new to this country and should prove valuable for commercial growers.   FELIX.

CAMBRIDGE, MASS.—Edward J. O'Brien, manager for the business of his brother, J. F. O'Brien, died at his home in this city on September 4, at the age of 45 years. He has been associated with his brother in business for twenty-three years.

White Ants.

ED. AM. FLORIST:—Can you advise me of some way to get rid of white ants? I have a fine batch of chrysanthemums, several of which are being killed each week by the ant entering at the root and boring up the center. Sometimes I find a dozen or more at one root and sometimes only one.   SUBSCRIBER.

I think there is very little doubt that the damage described is due to the white ant (Termes flavipes). In addition to the better known and more serious damage, which they often cause to buildings or to books and papers, they occasionally become a distinct pest in greenhouses and conservatories, attacking cuttings and the roots and stems of plants. The source of the termite in greenhouses is usually the woodwork of the building, or plant benches, which, when somewhat moistened and partly decayed, are especially attractive to these insects. From such locations they carry their galleries to the roots of plants. In one instance the termites were found working on the label sticks, the removal of which gave immediate relief. The remedy is not always easy, unless the old wooden framework of the benches and propagating beds be removed and replaced with a framing of gas pipe and stone plates. The individuals about the plants can often be killed by injecting into the ground about the plants kerosene emulsion or bisulphide of carbon, using the latter, however, in very small quantities and not too near the plants, otherwise the death of the latter will result. All such remedies are merely palliative for unless the woodwork in which these creatures are breeding is examined and corrected they will continually re-introduce themselves among the plants. Creosote is an effectual preventive. The means of controlling this pest are given in detail in circular No. 50, second series, of the U. S. Department of Agriculture, Washington, D. C.   C. L. MARLATT.

Catalogues Received.

John Peed & Son, London, England, bulbs; C S Harrison, York, Neb., peonies; H. H. Berger & Company, New York, bulbs; Walker & Pratt Manufacturing Company, Boston, Mass., boilers; Samuel McGredy & Son, Portadown, Ireland, St. Brigid's anemone; Barr & Sons, Covent Garden, London, England, daffodils; Alexander Seed Company, Augusta, Ga , seeds; A Klokner, Milwaukee, Wis., high vase flat; Lindgren Chemical Company, Grand Rapids, Mich., thistlebine; J. W. Sefton Manufacturing Company, Anderson, Ind., florists' boxes; Peter Henderson & Company, New York, bulbs; Weeber & Don, New York, bulbs; Horsford's Nurseries, Charlotte, Vt., herbaceous perennials; Standard Pump & Engine Company, Cleveland, Ohio, engines; John C. Moninger Company, Chicago, greenhouse construction; E. H. Krelage & Son, Haarlem, Holland, bulbs; C. C. Pollworth Company, Milwaukee, Wis., palms and ferns; Charles D. Ball, Philadelphia, Pa., palms, etc.; Funk Brothers Seed Company, Bloomington, Ill., seeds; John Lucas & Company, Philadelphia, Pa., paints; The Fraser Nursery, Huntsville, Ala., nursery stock; G. J. Alberts & Company, Boskoop, Holland, nursery stock; R. Schmidhtn, M. D., St. Paul, Minn., orchids; Bobbink & Atkins, Rutherford, N. J., bulbs; Chicago Carnation Company, Joliet, Ill., carnations; A. N. Pierson, Cromwell, Conn., palms and ferns.

OUR PASTIMES.

Announcements of coming Contests or other events of interests to our bowling, shooting and sporting readers are solicited and will be given place in this column.

Address all correspondence for this department to Wm. J. Stewart, 79 Milk St., Boston, Mass.; Robt. Kift, 1725 Chestnut St., Philadelphia, Pa.; or to the American Florist Co., 324 Dearborn St., Chicago, Ill.

At Philadelphia.

The Milwaukee and Asheville teams had another tussel on the alleys last Wednesday night which proved to be a very exciting match and resulted in the defeat of the champions by 23 pins. The rubber is to be bowled off on Wednesday next. The score follows:

ASHEVILLE.

Player.	1	2	3	T'l
Moss	200	192	162	554
Starkey	155	155	137	447
Kift	113	157	135	405
Anderson	104	177	183	464
Watson	173	186	186	517
Robertson	184	147	190	521
Totals	929	986	993	2908

MILWAUKEE.

Player.	1	2	3	T'l
Connor	155	166	165	486
Polites	157	187	137	481
Kift	113	157	135	405
Adelberger	127	164	180	471
Yates	233	234	144	571
Robinson	184	147	190	521
Totals	969	966	951	2885

K.

Base-ball at Madbury, N. H.

On Saturday, August 29, the base ball team of the Exeter Rose Conservatories, at Exeter, N. H., went down to Madbury, where a spirited game was played with N. H. Elliott's men at that place. The score was 14 to 2 in favor of the Exeters.　　　G. W. H.

New Haven Horticulturists' Outing.

The members of the New Haven County Horticultural Society held their annual outing on Thursday, August 27, at Lake Compounce. Upon the arrival of the train at Meriden they were joined by the Hartford Florists' Club, which had arranged to meet them there, and all went by special trolley cars to the lake. A fine dinner was served at 12 o'clock, Theodore Wirth, superintendent of the Hartford public parks, presiding. After dinner speeches were made by a number of the notables present. In the afternoon the members strolled around viewing the different places of interest, shortly after which came the contest for the silver cup between bowling teams, composed of eight men of the Hartford florists and eight men of the New Haven Club. This being the first year that these two societies have met in a bowling contest, the game was a close one and keen interest was displayed throughout, although it is understood that the winning team must win the cup two years out of three before it can be the rightful owner of it. The match resulted as follows:

	1st	2d	3d	T'l
New Haven	710	795	786	2291
Hartford	690	846	614	2150

It Is to Laugh.

HOW THEY DO IT.

"Well," said the New Yorker, tauntingly, "you don't see any grass growing in our streets." "That's so," replied the Philadelphian, "clever scheme of yours." "What's that?" "To keep tearing your streets up so the grass can't grow."—Washington Star.

Buffalo.

Messrs. Palmer, Rebstock and Rapin handled most of the K. P. conclave decorations, which were good. Our leading flower store windows showed K. P. emblems. Sunday saw some handsome funeral designs, American Beauty roses and lily of the valley were used. S. C. Anderson had a large American Beauty decoration and used that new wagon.

Trade is about normal. Funeral work good. Asters are very nearly perfect. Those shipped by Brookins, of Orchard Park, N. Y., and Boettger, of Eggertsville, N. Y., are the best. In fact the three largest wholesale dealers in New York are taking all that can be sent to them.

Arthur Beger has succeeded C. A. Schnell at Palmer's upper store and W. H. Grever, for many years with Adams, has assumed the management of the lower store. C. A. Schnell will locate in Butte, Montana.

We are pleased to learn that our former Buffalonian E. J. Mepstead, has been elected president of the C. H. S. and the society can be congratulated on its choice.

Our Dan. Long's artistic photos received many compliments at Milwaukee.

Visitors: Edward Sceery and wife, of Patterson, N. J.; Alex. Guttman and Chas. Millang, of New York; C. D. Ball and daughter; F. R. Pierson; Max Beattus, of Dayton Paper Company; George Asmus, Chicago.　　　BISON.

ELGIN, ILL.—B. O'Neil has returned after a sojourn of three months in Ireland.

NEWPORT, R. I.—Elsewhere I send you an account of our recent events which I trust may interest your readers in the retail trade. The season closes this week with the horse show. Recent visitors: J. H. Cox with Stump & Walter Company, J. Marshall, with Thorburn & Company, C. Shoepke, with Bobbink & Atkins.　　　P. L. Z.

THE ALLIED TRADES.

Descriptive particulars—with drawings or photographs, if possible—of any new apparatus or device which may prove helpful to the trade are solicited for this department.

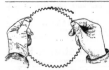

Chessman's Adjustable Pot Hanger.

Chessman's Adjustable Pot Hanger.

We present herewith an illustration showing the important principle of Chessman's new adjustable pot hanger, which renders pot hangers very handy and reasonable in price. Mr. Chessman reports strong demand for his new device.

LOCKLAND, O.—The Lockland Lumber Company is supplying the cypress material for the range of seven houses that S. Alfred Baur, of Erie, Pa., is building, and has nearly ready for shipment besides this a house 27x300 feet for W. W. Woodford, Pittsburg, Pa. Greenhouse building has been very active the past month with this firm.

Very True.

The teaching of horticulture to children seems to have the good results that might be expected. The professional gardener is usually steady, industrious, even tempered, safe and systematic man, and it appears that young students acquire in some degree the same qualities, says the Natick, Mass., Bulletin. They also learn honesty. After a boy knows just how much hard work is needed to produce a crop, he naturally sides with the growers, and stolen fruit loses its sweetness.

Hollow Tile Wall.

ED. AM. FLORIST:—Would you kindly inform me in your next issue as to the practicability of a hollow tile wall for rose and carnation houses. Wishing to put in the same for north wall, also division wall, measuring in height from three to six feet. Would like to know whether this kind of a building could be as easily heated as a board wall. Tile is 8x8x16 inches. J. C. S.

Hollow tile walls would necessarily need to be made very tight jointed for the outside of a greenhouse at any rate, and if I were building walls of such I would put a coat of good Portland cement stucco over the whole surface outside in addition to making the joints absolutely tight, otherwise it is very doubtful if some of the joints would not get loose during the winter and that would mean a lot of cold air finding its way into the house, hence more cost for heating. With these precautions there is no reason why a tile wall of such as J. C. S. describes should not be satisfactory, but the comparative cost can be best figured out by him, one thing he must take into consideration for such walls, is a good solid foundation sufficient to ensure the tiles remaining permanently where set. J. N. MAY.

Washington, D. C.

The Florists' Club met at Hotel Johnson September 2. President Freeman being absent, Vice-President Geo. Field occupied the chair. Wm. F. Gude gave a very interesting and instructive talk on the Milwaukee convention. A vote of thanks was extended to the Chicago, Philadelphia and Milwaukee clubs for their hospitality to our visiting members. A letter was read from David Bisset, thanking the club for its timely aid. The corresponding secretary was directed to send a letter of condolence to Mrs. Esch on the death of her husband. Accepting the views of the executive committee, election of officers will be deferred until March next. Adjournment was made to the bowling alleys.

We are the prize winners of 1904 if an early start will get the plum.　P. G.

HYDE PARK, PA.—Wm. Kern has recently begun business at this place. One greenhouse is already completed and another, measuring 17x80 feet, is in course of construction. Bedding plants will be the principal stock handled.

Minneapolis.

TRADE QUIET OWING TO RAINY WEATHER. —STATE FAIR DOES NOT GREATLY BENEFIT BUSINESS.—CITY ITEMS.

Trade the past week has been quiet, caused by the heavy rainy weather. The state fair has attracted large numbers to the city, but trade has not been largely benefited, as the people were not, generally of the flower loving class. Market is unchanged, asters and tea roses forming the bulk of the stock, although American Beauty roses with good stems and blooms are appearing and meet ready sale. No house grown carnations can yet be secured.

Floral exhibitors at the state fair were E. Nagel & Company, R. J. Mendenhall, John Vasatka and the Minneapolis Floral Company, of this city.

The William Donaldson & Company opening, August 31, was a scene of grandeur and attracted crowds.

L. P. Lord, of Owatonna, was a recent visitor. He makes strong claims for his plant shipping box.   C. F. R.

TERRE HAUTE, IND.—Otto Heinl is building a fern house, measuring 10x100 feet, and is also erecting a new boiler at his West Terre Haute greenhouses.

Toronto.

Nashville, Tenn.

PREPARATIONS FOR FALL AND WINTER IN FULL SWING—COMING HORSE SHOW—NEWS.

All the florists in this city are busy with their preparations for the fall and winter trade and hoping for an early break in the quiet summer monotony that has characterized business for many weeks past. The trade has been kept alive almost exclusively by funeral work, which at times has been heavy. The quality of stock too has been poor and rather scarce. Very few roses have been allowed to bloom and carnations have an out-of-door summer look that detracts very much from their value, but they are still useful in funeral work.

The Joy & Son Company is cutting a few American Beauty roses, but has not permitted the larger houses to come on yet. The growth is fine and the company will be able to meet a large demand this season with first-class stock. The chrysanthemums are in excellent shape and it is thought they will bring in some of the earlier varieties by the last of this month.

Geny Brothers have greatly enlarged their greenhouses and improved their facilities and will have a good and abundant stock for the winter. Their carnations and chrysanthemums are looking fine and their violets will be early on the market.

The florists are all looking forward to and preparing for the horse show, which opens the first week in October and calls for a profusion of flowers, as all swelldom goes there to see and be seen.

M. C. DORRIS.

THE NICKEL PLATE ROAD -

With its eastern connections—the Delaware, Lackawanna & Western and West Shore and Boston & Maine Railroads—is considered by those who have patronized it as a most desirable line between Chicago and New York, Boston and other eastern points, and takes its place among the first-class lines leading eastbound from Chicago. It is operating three through first-class trains, all daily, and equipped with modern improvements, for the convenience and comforts of the traveling public, and has succeeded to a remarkable degree, in pleasing its patrons, growing in popularity every day. One of its attractive features and thoroughly appreciated by the traveling public, is its dining car service, meals being served on American Club Plan, ranging in price from 35c to $1.00; also service à la carte. Colored porters are in charge to look after the comfort of passengers in coaches, and especially to assist ladies traveling with children. All passenger trains arrive at and depart from the La Salle St. Station, Chicago, the only passenger station in Chicago on the Elevated Loop. When going east. try the Nickel Plate Road. City Ticket Office, 111-Adams St., Chicago. 20

MOLLER'S DEUTSCHE

GARTNER ZEITUNG.

The most widely circulated German gardening journal, treating of all departments of horticulture and floriculture. Numerous eminent correspondents in all parts of the world. An advertising medium of the highest class.

Moller's Deutsche Gartner Zeitung is published weekly and richly illustrated. Subscription $3 00 per annum, including postage. Sample copies free.

LUDWIG MOLLER ERFURT, Germany

·PLEASE mention the AMERICAN FLORIST every time you write to an advertiser.

THE Gardeners' Chronicle.

A Weekly Illustrated Journal.

ESTABLISHED 1841.

The GARDENERS' CHRONICLE has been FOR OVER SIXTY YEARS THE LEADING JOURNAL of its class. It has achieved this position because, while specially devoting itself so supplying the daily requirements of gardeners of all classes, the information furnished is of such general and permanent value that the GARDENERS' CHRONICLE is looked up to as the STANDARD AUTHORITY on the subjects of which it treats.

Subscription to the United States, $4 20 per year. Remittances to be made payable to H. G. COVE.

OFFICE:—
41 Wellington St., Covent Garden, London. England.

THE Regan Printing House

Nursery Seed Florists' CATALOGUES

87-91 Plymouth Place, CHICAGO.

BARGAINS
For Greenhousemen.

Boiler Tubes.

In good condition. We have been selling them for many years past to greenhouse men. They are economical and practical, and make a first-class pipe line. We clean and paint them. We furnish without additional charge sleeve or jacket couplings; also oakum and cement to make tight joints. They are in straight, long lengths. Note our prices:

3-inch, per foot	4c
3¼-inch, per foot	5c
3½-inch, "	8c
4-inch, per foot	11c
6-inch, "	21c

Pipes.

Our stock of second-hand pipe, standard black wrought iron, with guaranteed threads and couplings, consists of all sizes from ¾-inch to 12-inch. Write us your wants.

Radiation.

100,000 ft. second-hand, cast iron radiation, per foot.............................18c.
300,000 ft. second-hand, wrought iron radiation. per foot.............................16c.
Also valves, heaters and all necessary apparatus.

Roofing Glass.

¼-inch, thick ribbed roofing glass from the Pan-American Exposition Buildings. Per square foot, 5c.

Valves.

250 iron body, brass trimmed Gate, Check, Globe and Angle valves, ranging in sizes from 3 to 16 inches. They are second-hand, overhauled and in first-class condition. Write us your wants. Also all kinds of fittings.

Boilers.

Over 250 good boilers in stock. Can furnish anything you may require in the line.

Hot Bed Sash.

Several jobs to offer. Write us your wants.

Hose.

All kinds of garden and water-conducting hose for sale at low prices.

WRITE FOR OUR CATALOGUE NO. 47.

We handle building material, plumbing material, hardware and stocks of every kind.

Chicago House Wrecking Co.,
WEST 35th & IRON STS.,
CHICAGO, ILL.

NICKEL PLATE.
The NewYork, Chicago & St. Louis R.R.

NO EXCESS FARE ON ANY TRAIN

Three Express Trains East every day in the year. Pullman Drawing Room Sleeping Cars on all Trains. Trans-Continental Tourist Car's leave Chicago Tri-Weekly on Tuesdays and Saturdays at 2:30 p. m., on Wednesdays at 10:35 a. m. Chicago to Boston without change. Modern Dining Cars serving meals on individual club plan, ranging in price from 35c to $1.00; also service a la carte. Direct line to Fort Wayne, Findlay, Cleveland, Erie, Buffalo, Rochester, Syracuse, Binghamton, Scranton, New York City; Boston and all points East. Rates always the lowest. Colored porters in uniform in attendance on all Coach Passengers. If you contemplate a trip East, call on any convenient Ticket Agent, or address   JOHN Y. CALAHAN, Gen'l Agent,
119 Adams St., Chicago, Ill.

Always mention the.......

·American Florist
when you write to an advertiser.

THE AMERICAN FLORIST

A WEEKLY JOURNAL FOR THE TRADE

America is "the Prow of the Vessel; there may be more comfort Amidships, but we are the first to touch Unknown Seas."

| Vol. XXI. | CHICAGO AND NEW YORK, SEPTEMBER 19, 1903. | No. 798. |

THE AMERICAN FLORIST

NINETEENTH YEAR.

Copyright 1903, by American Florist Company
Entered as Second-Class Mail Matter.

PUBLISHED EVERY SATURDAY BY

AMERICAN FLORIST COMPANY,
324 Dearborn St., Chicago.
Eastern Office: 79 Milk St., Boston.

Subscription, $1.00 a year. To Europe, $2.00.
Subscriptions accepted only from the trade.
Volumes half-yearly from August, 1901.

THIS ISSUE 36 PAGES WITH COVER.

CONTENTS.

The Peony—Rival of the Rose.

[Read by George C. Watson, of Philadelphia,
secretary of the S. A. F. Peony Association, before
the Germantown, Pa., Horticultural Society, September 14, 1903.]

I must preface the few
remarks I have to make
on the subject of Peonies
by stating that I am not
in any sense to be considered an expert in peony
culture. What I don't
know about that would
fill a book. I appear before
you merely as a lover of this fine old-
fashioned flower and in the hope that I
may be able to bring out some new ideas
by starting the discussion.

I do not even know how the name
ought to be spelled. I have a friend who
is the editor of a horticultural journal
and a graduate of Kew who calls me
down every time I spell it peony. He
says it ought to be pæonia, because it
was named after Pæoni, a Greek physician. I looked up the dictionary and I
found that the said Pæoni was mythical,
and if there ever having been any such person.

As for the English—Gerarde has it
peionie and his editor peionee. Shakespeare in "The Tempest" mentions
"—banks with Pionied and Lilied brims,"
while others have it Piney and Pyony.
Among the moderns, Baily's Cyclopedia
of American Horticulture has it Peony,
and Walter Crane sings of

Great Peonies in crimson pride
And budding ones in green that hide.

so it would seem that you can spell it
any old way and still be in good company.

In Shakespeare's time and long before
they grew most of the European species,
including the handsome double red and
double white. Since then our gardens
have been greatly enriched by the addition of the Chinese and Japanese species
and by the labors of the French and English nurserymen—especially the French,
as can be seen by the large preponderance
of French names among the list of varieties now in cultivation in American gardens. Some authorities claim that the
French did not raise all these' varieties
themselves, but only re-named many of
the Chinese and Japanese sorts and it is
feared that some of the English and
American importers have done the same
thing, so that it is likely that among the
thousand or more varieties now in commerce there are many masquerading
under three or four aliases. The S. A. F.

Peony Association has made a start in
trying to bring order out of this confusion and has registered already fifty-four
varieties of the Japanese, publishing the
Japanese name in brackets after the new
name.

I have brought with me to-night the
album containing the colored plates of
these fifty-four varieties and twenty-three
others so that you can have an idea of
what those clever gardeners, the japs,
have done for us in peonies. We are told
that they have been cultivating this
flower in Japan for over 1,500 years, and
as C. Harman Payne says, that is an
impressive fact. Cast yourself in imagination away back to the time when the
tramp of the Roman legions resounded
through the land of our birth, to the
time when our forefathers were clothed
in skins and lived in caves and consider
for a moment that even then the Japanese and Chinese were hybridizing peonies
and chrysanthemums and the big events
in their existence were the Flower Festivals as the Horse Show and the Football
match are with us to-day.

The fifty-four varieties mentioned, one
plant of each, were set out in Fairmount
park last spring by the S. A. F. Peony
Association, under the supervision of
Oglesby Paul, the landscape gardener of
the park, and all can have an opportunity of examining it for themselves.
There can be no better way than this
field test for arriving at an authoritative
conclusion as to which are the best varieties and which are duplicates. They
have to be tested side by side in the field
to make sure. The S. A. F. Peony Association asks every one having a collection of peonies to send a small piece of
each of their varieties with name and
description attached so that they can be
planted out and tested. Those in charge
of this work are doing it free and at some
sacrifice of their own time and means for
the benefit of all and they feel justified in
asking for the hearty co-operation of all
who are interested in the peony.

John T. Morris, who I understand
has been and is a pillar of your society,
has a fine collection of peonies which I
had the honor of examining during their
blooming season. I did not count them
but I should say there were over 200
varieties in this collection and I made a
careful note of the twenty-five choicest
sorts, not only as to size of blossom,
form, substance, color, etc., but considering also their habit of growth, their
foliage, vigor, and other good points.

As this list of twenty-five extra good

ones may be of interest to some of you, I give it here. I also give the three best of his Japanese collection.

THREE BEST JAPANESE.

No. 1. NINE-NO-ICHII, claret and gold. A beautiful variety which I think is the same as Sami-no-ichi now named "Ebony" in the S. A. F. list. Perhaps Mr. Morris can clear that point up by examining his list. It may only be a mistake in writing the label. No. 15 in the album.

No. 2. KASANE-JISHI, pale pink and orange. This is No. 1 in the album and has been christened "Rosalind."

No. 3. KAME-NO-KEGOROMA, light magenta and gold. This is No. 13 in the album and is now named "Flamboyant."

The foregoing three were the choicest of the new Japanese sorts in the collection. An English firm catalogues something like them this year, if one may judge by the descriptions, under the imposing title of "New Imperial Peonies," with the firm's own name tacked on in front and priced at ten shillings six and fifteen shillings each. $2.50 to $4 of our money. If they are the same they can be bought from dealers here at 50 cents each. The twenty-five varieties which follow are all full double flowers and an entirely different type from the three Japs just mentioned.

TWENTY-FIVE CHOICE KINDS.

No.	Name	Description.
1.	AMANDINE MECHIN, bright claret, very high and double, no collar.
2.	AUGUSTINE D'HONNEUR, deep pink, very double.
3.	BELLE CHATELAINE, white, pale pink collar, large and round.
4.	COMTESSE DE MONTALIVET, white shading to blush at outside, large, rather flat.
5.	FESTIVE MAXIME, pure white, carmine dot in centre.
6.	JEANNE D'ARC, white, large flower, wide gaurd petals, center fringy.
7.	LADY ANNA, pink, medium size, round and perfect.
8.	LA COQUETTE, pale pink, medium size, very deep flower, good collar.
9.	MME. BAILLET DESCHAMPS, blush, a large flower, rather ragged, but very good and distinct.
10.	MME. BOULANGER, pale pink, flat, very smooth and perfect.
11.	MME. DE VERNEVILLE, bright claret, large, flat, no collar, a grand flower.
12.	COMTE DE NIEPERG, ruby, medium.
13.	MUSLE DE DESSAISSON, pale pink, shading to deeper at base of petals, medium, ragged, no collar, flat.
14.	MOISSONIER, crimson round, medium fringed center, ragged wide gaurd petals.
15.	MME. EDOUARD ANDRE, resembles Festive maxima but smaller and not as perfect; but must still find a place in the best 25.
16.	M. BOUCHARLET, bright pink, round, perfect shape, very double, well expanded.
17.	M. DUPONT, pure white loose but quite double, medium, no gaurd, fine shape.
18.	M. GAILLARD, magenta, a conical flower with wide collar.
19.	M. LAMOINER, white, a large, loose, conical flower with blush gaurd petals.
20.	PAGANINI, snow white, medium, ragged, good flower.
21.	POLLSI PLENA, claret, large, ragged, good flower.
22.	SOUV. DE AUGUSTE MIELLETZ, pale pink, very double, good.
23.	SOLFATERRE, white, shading to orange at base.
24.	VIRGO MARIA, white, very large, flat, a grand flower.
25.	LIVINGSTONE, pink, round, no collar.

I may state that these were nearly all in bloom on May 31, the date of my visit, and they were therefore not compared with earlier or later blooming varieties. My notes were submitted to and approved by two good judges—Mr. Lonsdale and Mr. Gould, who went over the collection with me at the time. There were some hot arguments as to which should go in, but none were admitted unless a majority agreed.

I will not say anything as to the culture of the peony except to remark that even an amateur like myself, manages to

get some good results out of a small collection which are given precious little attention. I make bold to say, therefore, that those who can devote more time and care to them than myself, will be sure to be well repaid for their trouble. I hope your society will organize a peony exhibition next May and help to inform the people more about this grand old flower, rival of the rose in splendor, fragrant as the carnation, hardy as the oak, disease proof and bug proof, the flower of the past, the present and the future.

The Carnation.

CULTURAL REMINDERS.

Frosty nights will soon be with us again, and with them recollections of wintery scenes, and while we meditate upon the icy grasp that will soon clutch upon the tender verdure outdoors we will naturally think of making our winter's retreat more secure. Leaky roofs should be gone over with a putty bulb and made perfectly drip-tight and all broken panes should be replaced. It is well to put off repairs on the roof until fall, for the hot sun of summer is apt to bake the life out of the putty and separate it from the wood and glass. A good mixture to use with the bulb or machine is made as follows: Ordinary putty seven parts, white lead one part, add enough raw linseed oil to allow stirring with a paddle, stir and mix thoroughly, grinding up all lumps. This mixture should be about as thick as dough. Add enough turpentine to make it run freely through the nozzle of the bulb or machine. Strain through a wire mesh about as fine as mosquito netting. This is laid on the cracks with a steady stroke of the bulb and is thin enough to penetrate into the cracks and spread out sufficiently without the aid of the brush that is supplied with the bulb—a useless adjunct. Within a few hours the turpentine will have evaporated from the putty and a tough skin will have formed upon the surface. After this has lain twenty-four hours no rain will be strong enough to rupture this skin and spread the putty over the glass. There are no doubt some plants in the field that were passed over at planting time as too small to bench. These, if healthy, will make good stock to propagate from. Plant in a cool, light house in good soil, quite close together. After well established they will give a crop of cuttings every few weeks. A few days before lifting remove the leading shoots to encourage the formation of good plump pips. These are taken off with the heel—that is right down to where they connect on to the parent stem—as soon as large enough to be independent of the parent plant. The idea has lately suggested itself to the writer that summer blooming stock might be saved from the first few early pots by building a number of small wood fires around the patch on frosty nights. There is usually a lot of discarded bench lumber around at this time that would serve well for the pur pose. There is nothing new in the idea, for it has been tried with grapes and other plants to protect from late spring frosts with good results. A nice patch of carnations in good bloom is worth saving as long as possible, and it is an inexpensive way in which to do it. The attendance of a night fireman would, of course, be necessary, but as most of us have our regular night fireman on about this time this would not cut any figure. The idea is certainly worth a trial.

The ventilators will require careful adjusting on these cool nights. While in dry, sunny weather it is safe to allow the temperature to drop as low as 45°, damp and cloudy weather presents a different problem, and even if the temperature should not fall below 50° at such times, considerable damage will result from the dampness with which the atmosphere is saturated. The remedy is to keep a line of heating pipes going for a few hours after midnight, and longer in extreme cases. A crack of air should be on the same time and this will require adjusting according to the temperature. If there is danger of forcing the temperature abnormally high with a line of pipes turned on the ventilator should be raised accordingly. Better have eight or ten inches of air on and a little heat to keep the air moving than a close atmosphere in which the moisture is very near the point of precipitation. Along with this hint will also go advice to use the greatest care in watering and syringing. There will still be a number of hot days upon which it will be necessary to cool off the house once or twice during the day. Do not throw the water into the corners or other places into which the sun does not penetrate, but confine it to those places that receive the full glare of the sun. It will do no good anywhere else.

Syringing after 1:30 p. m. is not advisable from now on, no matter how hot it may be. Take advantage of every bright day to syringe with a fine cutting spray for red spiders. After about October 1 we will not have such a good chance to fight this pest. A light fumigating with strong tobacco stems or dust will be in order once a week from now on. With well established plants we smoke throughout the winter, believing that the smoke of tobacco has a greater effect upon thrips than it has applied in any other form. The object should be to use the strongest stems and keep the plants always free from any suspicion of insects. In this way heavy smoking, with its attending evils, will never be necessary.

Tying should not be delayed once the shoots begin to run up. A last stirring and a thorough cleaning up of all dead leaves and weeds should be given just before placing the supports. With plants that have made a considerable growth care should be had not to scratch deep enough to destroy the young roots that are by this time ramifying very near the surface.

There is usually a good demand for flowers from now on, and all strong shoots should be allowed to mature, except with late planted stock, which will still require every encouragement to form a good root system. It is no great trick to lift a plant set with a crop of buds about ready to open and get a good flower on almost every shoot, but it is a trick to get a good crop of flowers around Christmas from plants so treated.

A very light mulch of rotted cow manure and some bone meal, if the soil is rather poor, will do no harm at that time. A 6-inch pot full of finely ground bone, or bone and blood, to two bushels of mulching material will be about the right strength. One part of good soil to two parts of manure will be better than to use the manure alone, and it is well to use the mixture through a sieve or grinder. One-quarter of an inch thick will be sufficient, in fact, a heavy mulch is not desirable in fall, for it is apt to foster stem-rot. Just a little to keep the surface open is all that is permissible.

J.

VIEW IN PHALÆNOPSIS HOUSE OF DR. R. SCHIFFMANN, ST. PAUL.

Florists' Plant Notes.

Vincas.—These plants should be lifted as soon as possible. and potted into 4-inch or 5-inch pots and placed along the edge of a high bench, allowing their long vines to hang over the edge. Use rich soil in which to pot them and water them copiously, as the pots will soon be filled with a mass of roots. Many of the vines will be found to have roots at some of the eyes; these vines can be cut off and removed into 3-inch pots, which is a desirable size for hanging baskets. It is also a good time now to propagate vincas for next year's stock. Take some of the good vincas and cut them up into eye cuttings, leaving an eye at the base, and insert them into the sand. The cuttings should be taken before the first frost strikes them, for while the plants can stand a slight frost, and the roots can even stand a mild winter out of doors, the cuttings made from frosted vines do not root very well. Keep the plants moderately moist in the sand; they root rather slowly but surely, and should be given 2½-inch pots when rooted.

Hydrangeas.—As soon as the wood of Hydrangea Otaksa has been properly ripened by the touch of a few light frosts the plants should be lifted, potted into pots of appropriate size and stored in a cellar or under a cool greenhouse bench until the first of the year. Do not crowd the roots into under sized pots, for when forcing time commences they will soon exhaust the soil. They must never be permitted to come in contact with a heavy frost, or the ends of the flowering shoots are liable to be nipped, thus ruining the undeveloped buds. While they are resting under the bench, do not water them too heavily, but rather withhold water to such an extent as will permit the old leaves to drop, and leave the plants in a state of semi-dormancy. Drain the pots well, using rich and rather heavy soil in which to grow them. The question of different soils and their effect upon the color of the flowers has been quite extensively discussed. Some still hold to the opinion that iron filings or charcoal added to the soil will cause the flowers to come blue. There is no doubt in the writer's mind that the chemical state of the soil has some effect upon the color of the flowers, for we have had batches of hydrangeas in which the majority were pink with a very small percentage of blue among them, and we have had the proportion reversed the following year on stock propagated from the same plants. At the same time we have observed cases in which some of the flowers were a clear pink and some of a bluish tint on the same plants, which to some extent disproves the soil theory. It is a matter with which the florist may well experiment with profit.

Making Room.—This is one of the seasons of the year when every available foot of bench room must be pressed into service. Tuberous begonias and gloxinias, which are now past their blooming season, should be dried off, the soil shaken from the roots, and the bulbs placed in boxes of dry sand under a moderately warm bench for their winter's rest.

Old plants of fuchsias, that are not needed for stock, should be thrown out on the dump heap to make room for more profitable stock, unless it is desired to grow a few on to specimen plants.

Lilium auratum and speciosum, which are now through blooming can be cut off and the bulbs planted into the herbaceous border, for with a light protection they are quite hardy.

Dracæna indivisa brought in from out-of-doors, can have its long leaves tied up loosely and placed along the edge of a wide walk for a month or two until the pressure for room is relieved with the passing of the chrysanthemum, holding the dracænas slightly on the dry side while in this position.

Plants of anthuricum and of the more common begonias used for the spring trade, such as Alba picta, metallica and others, can be placed under a high bench, where light and warmth are not totally excluded, for a few months, partially withholding water the while. Here they can remain until February 1, when the old soil is partially shaken out and the plants started into growth again. G.

Herbaceous Plant Notes.

Where fall planting of perennials is contemplated, the work should be performed during the month of September. Later in the season many, if not all of the plants may not have time enough to form new rootlets and establish themselves in their new quarters; frost is likely to stop all growth above and below the ground. Success depends largely on what we term early planting, both in spring and fall; most perennials start into growth very early in spring and should be permitted to perfect the whole of a season's growth undisturbed in their respective beds; by September this growth is about finished and ripened, although even so the plants are still showing buds or blooms in abundance and it will not damage them very seriously at this time to be cut down and be transplanted.

In September the earth still retains its summer warmth and under these conditions root action will commence at once after replanting. The new fibres will feed and prevent the shriveling of the crowns or tops of the plants, thus carrying them safe and sound through the winter, while at a later date, when the soil is more or less cooled off by frosty nights or cold rains, the plants are much slower to form new roots and therefore more liable to decay or other injury. As a rule, young vigorous stock, even if small, is preferable for planting, because it has an abundance of small fibrous roots, while larger and older clumps of most species must start new fibers, often from hard and wiry old roots, which naturally is a much slower process and with them success is more doubtful than it would be with the younger plants.

All the spring and early summer flowering stock should invariably be planted in or before fall to insure a fair show of bloom for the coming season. If we defer planting until spring we can not reasonably expect to see this class of perennials in perfection during their first season, except when plants have been specially prepared for the purpose of removal and are then taken up carefully with a ball of earth clinging to the roots. This method, however, although recommendable, is not practiced very often.

With late summer and fall blooming plants fair success generally follows a spring planting, because they have several months of growing weather before their blooming time is expected, but the the spring flowering species should be firmly established in their quarters before frost and the month of September is late enough for such plantings. Prepare the beds or borders by digging deeply and mix a liberal quantity of good old decayed manure into the soil; remember that the plants are to remain here for some years.

J. B. K.

Chicago Through Eastern Eyes.

II.

Vaughan's Greenhouses:—Arriving at Vaughan's Greenhouses at Western Springs, after a pleasant ride of twenty miles through the suburbs, we were delighted with the sight of an immense table, the full length of the packing shed, surrounded by a merry party who were doing justice to the good things provided by the host, who personally was the busiest of the many helpers and never rested until he was satisfied that all had been fully served.

Everything here was in apple pie order and a great credit to Jas. S. Wilson, the manager.

The houses of Boston ferns, palms and other decorative plants were in fine condition and had the ranges not been so hot would have received better consideration at our hands. The surrounding grounds were planted with great blocks of cannas, geraniums, dahlias, carnations and large quantities of herbaceous stock. The collection of hardy phloxes is the largest in the country, to which is added all the meritorious varieties as they come out. The geranium beds were a veritable blaze of bloom.

Bassett & Washburn's:—After a somewhat strenuous ride in a hay wagon this Bassett & Washburn establishment hove in sight; 750,000 feet of glass, with all the stock found to be in most excellent condition. Not a few of the Eastern rose growers, whose little 75,000 to 150,000-foot places had been left so contentedly a week previous and who had expected to find large but very rough houses and more and less crude methods of culture, now began to open their eyes in astonishment, for here they found American Beauty and other roses with a growth and state of health that they could hardly duplicate.

In every house all over the place all the stock, either on high or low benches, was planted on tiles running crossways of the tables, the openings all showing below the side boards that held in the soil. Much of all the stock was in its second and some in its third year. The soil is changed each season; the plants are first dried off, then lifted, most of the soil shook off and, after the beds are refilled, planted at once without being removed from the house. They are then started and take hold of the new soil immediately.

Better stock was being cut than could then have been obtained in the eastern markets, the American Beauty and Kaiserin roses being particularly noticeable.

The storage room or ice box is underneath an ice house, which requires but one filling each season. A temperature below 50° can be kept without trouble. The product of this large place is sent twice a day to the city store in the wholesale district. From seventy-five to ninety per cent is shipped out of town, the balance going to local consumers.

The stock for the city store is graded; twenty-five roses are placed in a package, wrapped in newspaper and then packed in the boxes. Mr. Bassett who has charge of the wholesale department says they find this most satisfactory as they carry without bruising and are more easily handled. When finally shipped they are packed in the regular way in layers, which is the best for long distances.   ROBERT KIFT.

Dahlias at Philadelphia.

The Dahlia exhibition at the monthly meeting of the Pennsylvania Horticultural Society was a great success, both in point of blooms shown and the attendance, which crowded the hall uncomfortably. The principle exhibitors were W. P. Peacock, of Atco, N. J.; R. Vincent, Jr., & Son, White Marsh, Md.; H. F. Bart, Taunton, Mass.; and Henry A. Dreer, of this city.

The entire table space of the lower hall was filled with choice ferns, and quite a few vases were crowded with flowers and placed too close together to show them off to the best advantage.

The Dreer collection was displayed on banks of spagnum, carpeted with fronds of Nephrolepsis Personii, which made a very pretty background. The flowers were staged flat and made a very fine display, as each specimen was brought out to its largest size. The same firm had a large table, the width of the hall, filled with flowers of herbaceous stock, which attracted much attention. In the center of the exhibit was a large basket filled with fine spikes of Tritoma Pfitzeri, whose high plumes were very striking.

R. Vincent & Son made a large exhibit of seventy-five vases, many of them containing over fifty blooms. They were arranged across one end of the hall on a raised staging and were greatly admired. Over forty crates were used in packing this exhibit, and the Messrs. Vincent deserve great credit for their enterprise.

H. F. Burt, of Taunton, Mass., also staged an exceedingly choice lot of flowers and entered in nearly all the classes. Some of his flowers were exceptionally fine. His A. E. Johnson, a very large and finely formed decorative flower, a lilac pink in color, was one of the best things in the hall.

W. P. Peacock, of Atco, made his usual large entry and it seemed his flowers had been given extra care in the selection, they were so uniformly good. His large vases of long stemmed Twentieth Century and Clifford Bruton were just a trifle in advance of anything yet seen in this line. Another fine flower, a trifle darker shade of pink than the old favorite sympllea, was also seen in the Peacock collection; it is called Madam Van den Stahl or Madam Van den Dael. It is the finest thing seen here in pink decoration dahlia to date and should have a great sale. Mrs. Roosevelt, a new one, is a fine pink, it might be called a pink Grand Duke Alexis, so closely does it resemble this famous variety.

L. K. Peacock gives the following as the best in their classes for florists' use, they excelling in color, stem and keeping qualities.

DECORATIVE.—Clifford Bruton, pink; Mad. Van der Stahl, pink; Lyndhurst, scarlet; Henry Patrick, and Perle De Or, white; Eureka, rose pink; Clarible, reddish purple.

SHOW.—Queen of Belgians, light pink; Emily, lavender; Storm King, white; Client, red; Sport, lavender pink; Sir Chas. Mills, deep golden yellow.

CACTUS. — Sindolt, light pink; Mary Service, progenitor; Volker, yellow; Sigfried and Winsome, white.

SINGLE.— Twentieth Century, rosy crimson, white tips; Avemore, white; Wildfire, red; Lawrence Kramer, pink; Gold Standard, yellow; Mrs. Bowman, purple.

There was no entrance fee and as a consequence the hall was crowded. It will be a good advertisement for the society and will no doubt help the fall show.   K.

Minneapolis.

The market has been cleaned up daily of what there was to be secured and the trade has experienced a good design business, which has used up the short new cut stock in roses to quite an extent. Asters, especially white, are in demand and the cut is decreasing daily on account of rainy cold weather. American Beauty roses are numerous and find ready sale.

A committee appointed by court to investigate the enlargement of Lakewood Cemetery reported favorably. This means quite a controversy regarding value of property to be bought, and the owners should realize a good price for their lands. R. Wessling is one.

The trains from the east Saturday were delayed by a heavy storm. Shipments due in the early morning arrived late in the afternoon. Many buyers were affected.

Otto Will is again on the sick list.

C. F. R.

PALMS AT VAUGHAN'S GREENHOUSES, WESTERN SPRINGS, ILL.

The Retail Trade.

BED many tulips outside. They will make profitable, cut blooms and be a good advertisement besides.

ARE some of the store plants rusty and defective? Get them away to the hospital. Display perfect ones only.

Josh Billings said: "I luv a rooster for few things—one is the krow that is in him, and the other is the spurs that air on him to bak up his krow with."

DON'T send good enough flowers to your best customers. Send the very best or tell them plainly you can't fill the order. It often pays in the long run.

SOME CUSTOMERS seem to think that flowers just grow and are not merchandise with good intrinsic value. Make a business like office of your salesroom and show people you are a merchant.

NEVER display a plant for sale in a dirty pot. Speaking about cleanliness, A. Newell has his store floor scrubbed white and clean every morning. That's pretty good for a Missouri river town.

A Floral Horseshoe.

In the accompanying illustration may be seen a floral horseshoe, which was presented to President Roosevelt by the National Association of Letter Carriers on September 7, who held their annual convention at Syracuse, N. Y. The horseshoe is six feet high. The calks were made of Liberty roses and the body of Kaiserin Augusta Victoria roses, Japan lilies, asparagus vine and fronds of the Boston fern. It was the work of W. S. Wheadon. A. J. B.

Anchor on Base.

While it is necessary for the florist to cater to the whims of the public whom it is his business to serve, he need not let go of the duty he owes his profession in emphasizing the beauty of the flowers he uses, particularly the individual beauty of the finer specimens at his command. Unfortunately the color tints of this arrangement did not lend themselves well to photography. The outlines of

ANCHOR ON BASE

the anchor in reality did not require labeling, although the sentiment which prompted the use of the emblem did not protrude itself over the nature of the flowers in their own beauty. Thus sentiment came in as an addition to beauty rather than having beauty entirely consumed at the expense of beauty. The mahonia with its cluster of blooms in the center of its whirl of evergreen leaves, the long, drooping leaves of the royal palm (oreodoxa) and the dracæna are useful in this sort of work, so are the long sprays of jasmine, Asparagus Sprengeri and Stevia. C. B. W.

Louisville.

Wm. Mann grows a general stock of plants and cut flowers and has a beautiful stock of Boston ferns and palms and keeps the neatest place about Louisville. Whenever there is a competition for prizes in floral designs Mr. Mann is always at the front, and is generally a prize winner, on floral arrangements as well.

Henry Lichtenfelt has charge of the planting and care of the grounds of Mrs. K. W. Smith, and for beauty of arrangement, contrast of colors and true examples of the gardener's art his work can not be excelled. He despises shams of any kind and is an enthusiastic member of the Kentucky Society of Florists.

A Floral Horseshoe.

Mrs. Lang, for twelve years in charge of the cut flower department of Jacob Schulz, will take a position with F. Walker & Company after September 15.

Asters have been plentiful in Louisville and of excellent quality, and have sold better than anything else, showing that people like a change once in a while.

Anders Rassmussen is building a residence and completing a large greenhouse 25x150 feet. He uses an iron ventilator of his own invention.

Mrs. C. B. Thompson has completed a beautiful conservatory in the rear of her store; both greenhouse and store will be steam heated.

Chas. Rayner, the rose specialist, is shipping fine stock of Brides, Bridesmaids and Golden Gate. He grows mostly on solid beds.

Geo. Thompson has purchased five acres of beautiful blue grass land near the city and will build in the near future.

John G. Bettman & Sons are completing a greenhouse 20x100 feet at their New Albany establishment.

William Walker and bride are abroad visiting relatives in Scotland. H. G. W.

GEORGE SOUSTER, of Elgin has gone to Hot Springs, Ark., for his health.

Palms and Ferns.

SUGGESTIONS FOR EARLY AUTUMN.

In the late summer and early autumn space in the palm houses is likely to be scanty, from the fact that the stock is only beginning to be in demand, while the plants are making most rapid growth and should be given room enough for their best development.

The wholesale dealer usually begins to dispose of his stock in August, but the retail demand does not increase to any great extent until the consumers of this class of plants return from their summer outings, a period that seems to become later in arriving from year to year. But as the stock begins to move, every advantage should be taken during the few weeks of good growing weather that remain and no empty bench space should be permitted, for the prompt utilization of benches is required to enable any fair remuneration to be secured in our business, the rapidity with which a crop can be turned out having much to do with the question of profits.

Some of the early sown palm seeds may now be in a fit condition for potting off, the first of these to be ready being usually seedlings of Latania Borbonica, the seeds of this palm coming into the market quite early in the year and being also among the most rapid in germination.

Areca lutescens generally follows the latanias in earliness of germination, though this season most of the areca seeds were late in landing in this country, and in consequence many growers may be a little behind time in potting off the seedlings of this useful palm. It is a good rule to observe, in potting seedlings of palms in general, that the seedlings are ready for potting as soon as the second leaf begins to push up in the center of the plant, though it is advisable to pot just as soon as the first leaf is fully expanded, this being the more necessary when the seed has been sown very thickly.

When palm seedlings are allowed to remain in the seed pots or seed bed too long they naturally become too crowded for the welfare of the plants, and not only do the tops draw up long and spindly, but the roots become so long that there is difficulty in getting them into a small pot, and in consequence many of the roots are broken and a much greater percentage of the young plants are liable to rot off.

As is well known, the greater number of Areca lutescens that are sold nowadays are in the form of compound plants, several young plants being bunched together in the effort to produce very bushy specimens. In the effort to save time in this process many growers adopted the plan of potting off several seedlings together into a 3-inch pot instead of potting them singly into 2-inch pots, this being done with a view to saving the labor of at least one shift. This practice is still in vogue to some extent, but after a series of experiments covering several years the writer is of the opinion that little if any gain is secured by this method, the pots with several seedlings in them taking longer in making a given size than do the plants from the same lot of seed that were potted off singly, probably owing to the fact that the single plants receive more light and air than the compound plants of small size. We therefore find it better practice to pot off the areca seedlings singly into 2-inch pots, afterward shift them on into 3-inch pots, and when sufficiently grown in the latter size to bunch them together in a 6-inch pot, feeling confident that good salable plants in 6-inch pots may be grown in less time by this plan than they are when bunched together from the seed bed.

These may seem to be minor details to the men of abundant experience, but it is by close attention to these details that one is enabled to produce plants successfully.

Latania Borbonica only reaches its full beauty when potted singly, given a liberal amount of bench room and kept clean and thrifty, from which it will be readily understood that there can be no sufficient margin of profit if one attempts to send out plants in 6-inch pots properly

grown for much under 75 cents each at wholesale. Seedling palms are much more tender than the mature plant of the same species, and it is well to keep this fact in mind when potting them, for when too many seedlings are exposed on the potting bench at one time, some of them are bound to suffer from the exposure, and after potting them there should be no delay in giving the young plants a good watering, at the same time avoiding any protracted exposure to full sunshine.

Deep pots, such as are frequently used for young roses, are the most convenient to use for seedling palms, the extra depth of a 2x3-inch pot being a decided advantage in disposing of the long and stiff roots with which most young palms are supplied.

There is also work that should be done in the fern house at this season, for early seedlings of strong growing species may now be quite ready to be shifted into 3-inch or 4-inch pots, according to the needs of the species in question. Where there are many fern pans to be filled, one naturally desires to have the ferns in as small pots as possible, for the space in the average fern pan does not allow for much soil, but there is also some demand for ferns of a larger size, a demand that will doubtless increase in the future.

It has been remarked in a former paper that the growers of the best Boston ferns usually grow them in pots altogether, those soft and sappy plants that have been grown on a bench like chrysanthemums being frequently very unsatisfactory to the purchaser, owing to their unestablished condition. Many of the Boston ferns that are intended for early sales will have been given their final repotting before this article shall appear in print, but there is still time to shift on plants that are intended for Christmas sales, though I should prefer to have it done not later than early October, so that the plants have time to fill out nicely before the dark weather arrives.

The new Pierson fern will be given a fair test for public favor this season in competition with its parent, there having been an immense stock distributed among the growers of the country, and while this fern sometimes shows some disposition to revert to the original type, yet it is very beautiful, just as free in growth and reproduction as the original and will probably become more fixed in character when its needs are fully understood.

Young plants of Adiantum Farleyense may still be repotted, there being sufficient time for them to become well rooted before winter, this fern enjoying a rich soil much more than was thought possible a few years ago.

As soon as the nights continue cool it is by far the best practice to have enough fire made in the boilers to circulate the water and to drive out the super-abundant moisture that the low temperature would otherwise condense upon the plants, for while too much fire heat may be injurious to plants of this character, yet an overplus of moisture may soon injure some plants beyond repair. But with the fire heat continue the ventilation at night, strong tough foliage being a prime object for the grower of foliage plants to strive for.   W. H. TAPLIN.

Fruit Column at St. Louis.

DULUTH, MINN.—The South Superior Floral Club held its second annual flower show here September 9 and 10. The prize list covered a wide scope from children to janitors and from cut flowers to shrubs and yards.

Chicago.

MARKET IMPROVES.—EXPERIENCE MEETING OF ENTERTAINMENT COMMITTEE.—A PLEDGE OF MORE SHOULDERS TO THE WHEEL.—ABOUT TOWN.—VISITORS.

Some twenty representative men in the trade gathered at the Union restaurant Thursday night for a final report on committee work on the occasion of the recent visit of the S. A. F. Treasurer Rudd presented his report and the same was accepted and ordered printed and distributed. A refund of approximately thirty· per cent of the subscriptions goes with it. After closing this matter the subject of what to do for horticulture in Chicago was brought up, and an expression asked for and given by nearly every member present. Two hours' conference simmered down to a call for a special meeting of the Florists' Club and a pledge by a unanimous rising vote to attend the club meetings and bring another member alongs. A committee of nine was appointed to offer suggestions for prompt future work. The opinion seemed to prevail that much good should result from the discussion.

The cold weather, which has prevailed during the past few days has stimulated business to some extent and a marked improvement is shown in the rose stock. It is said, however, that trade is not up to last year's mark. The rain that fell the earlier part of the week has practically spoiled the aster crop and the end is no doubt in sight for this flower, as it is very hard to fill orders satisfactorily. American Beauty roses are becoming fine in quality, Brides and Bridesmaids also improving. Kaiserins are about off crop and what remain bring good figures. Carnations are looking a great deal better and coming in in just about the right quantities. A demand for orchids has been noticed around the market. Auratum and longiflorum lilies are in good supply.

A "round robin" to Michael Barker of the AMERICAN FLORIST was signed at the Thursday night meeting and mailed to him at his vacation resort in the Colorado rockies.

H. F. Halle, returned from a trip to North Europe, finds park work in Denmark quite up to date. In flower stores, however, Copenhagen does not rival Hamburg.

Walter Kreitling celebrated this week the twentieth anniversary of his business career, and yet Walter is no older, in fact there is a suspicion that he is younger.

Geo. B. Kessler, landscape architect, St. Louis Fair, called last Friday. Mr. Kessier will visit Milwaukee and next week Kansas City.

J. F. Klimmer, of Oak Park, will shortly give up his sales store for the winter, doing his business at the greenhouses.

Phyllis, W. N. Rudd's handsome pink carnation, decorated the table Thursday night and received three cheers.

A Dietsch & Company have incorporated with a capital of $30,000. There is no change in the management.

J. B. Deamud is handling some superb specimens of dahlias. Violets have appeared on the tables.

Peter Reihberg and John Muno will go to Sleepy Eye, Minn., next Tuesday on a hunting trip.

Max Ringier, of Amling's, has a new addition to his household, a baby girl.

A. C. Kohlbrand, with E. C. Amling, is on deck again after a slight illness.

In town: T. L. Metcalfe, of Hopkinsville, Ky.; L. Wasserman, Muskegon, Mich.; E. Bernsee, Berkeley, Cal.

Boston.

MARKET IN USUAL CONDITION FOR SEASON.—FRUIT DISPLAY.—VISITORS.

Following so close upon the death of Mrs. Dawson, the announcement of the death on September 15, of Charles J., son of Jackson Dawson, will arouse deepest sympathy for this much bereaved family wherever the honored superintendent of the Arnold Arboretum is known. After a long illness with pneumonia, Mr. Dawson was convalescent as announced in our Boston Notes last week, but a relapse brought a fatal termination on Tuesday. Mr. Dawson's age was 31 years, 11 months and 1 day. As a young man he served a several years' course of study in the greenhouses of the Bussey institution, after which he filled a position of responsibility in the management of the Essex County park, N. J., resigning to take charge of the nursery business of the Eastern Nurseries, established by his sister and himself. He was a young man of exemplary character and with promise of a useful and honored career.

The cut flower market is in its customary condition for the season, but in some respects is even less satisfactory, as a result of the very torrid weather prevailing at present. Roses suffer more than anything else in this respect. Carnations are so scarce that they are not to be considered as a factor. The general supply is very heavy, especially in the line of asters, gladioli, etc., and prices are low.

The display of fruit at the biennial exhibition of the American Pomological Society last week was very fine. An outcome of the meeting was the organization of a society for horticultural science, of which Prof. L. H. Bailey has been elected president and Prof. S. A. Beach, secretary.

Welch Brothers establishment is undergoing a great overhauling and remodelling. The ice-chests are being renovated and are to have asphalt floors instead of sheet iron as heretofore. Messrs. Welch are in hopes to have everything finished by the end of this week.

The annual auction sale of choice stalls at the co-operative market, which was held last Saturday, was exceedingly satisfactory, every stall being disposed of and the aggregate premiums paid amounting to $6,200.

Messrs. Leuthy, Fellows and Sutermeister have all returned from their season and report having had a fine time. E. N. Peirce has also returned from Bermuda.

Recent visitors: Wesley Greene, secretary Iowa, State Horticultural Society; A. T. Erwin, Agricultural Experiment Station, Ames, Ia.; F. W. Taylor, World's Fair, St. Louis; Chas. Schneider, of Central Floral Co., Chicago; Carl Jurgens, Newport.

Orchids at St. Paul.

We illustrate in this issue a view in a Phalænopsis house of Dr. R. Schiffman, St. Paul. Its equal will probably not be found in the United States, if in the world, outside of the native habitat of these flowers and as the Doctor says should show Orchid growers that the "wild and wooly west" is fairly up to the times. The picture shows one end of the house only and the other parts of the house contain as many more plants of all sizes. The mass of roots prove conclusively that the plants have had the proper care. Close inspection of the photograph will show plenty of flower spikes and the house when they are in bloom will be a sight worth seeing.

New York.

MARKET FLAT—MINOR NEWS ITEMS.

Condition of the flower market is worse; there are no values; it is a case of get what you can. The heat of the past few days, with the dull trade, has lowered prices even on stock such as American Beauty roses and carnations, which up to Monday had held up to a fair figure. Violets of course are away off as no one seems to want them.

Cards are out announcing the wedding of Phil. Pitzenberger to Miss Marguerite C. Meyerholz to be held at St. John's Evangelical church, Eighty-fourth street and Sixteenth avenue, Brooklyn, Wednesday evening, September 30. Reception at Karn's dramatic hall, 708 Third avenue, Brooklyn.

George Saltford has more than doubled the size of his store by removing the partition in the rear. He has now one of the best appointed stores on Twenty-ninth street.

John Young is receiving quantities of very choice orchids now, and his window is resplendent with fine lælias and other fine things suitable for high class decorative work.

Wm. Elliott & Son held their first auction sale of plants for this season on Tuesday, September 15. Sales will continue every Tuesday and Friday.

A fire broke out in the building occupied by Frank C. Mitten, No. 509 DeKalb avenue, Brooklyn. Damage to building and stock amounted to $175.

Painting and papering is still the order of the day among the wholesalers. John Young and Traendly & Schenck have just finished their places.

L. Jenke has opened a retail store at 420 Fourth avenue, between Twenty-eighth and Twenty-ninth streets.

The storm of Wednesday made havoc with Broadway windows; Fleischman, Brower and others lost glass.

Herman Steinhoff is in the market with cut blooms of longiflorum.

Alfred Dimmock is expected September 19.

Visitors in town: A. M. Murdoch, Pittsburg, Pa.; L. M. Noe, Madison, N. J.; B. Dorrance, Dorrancetown, Pa.; Harry Payne, Dover, N. J.

"Fruit Column" at St. Louis.

The accompanying illustration shows a column constructed of fruit, recently prepared and placed on exhibition by Chas. Beyer at the annual picnic of the St. Louis Schwaben Verein at Lemps park. The column is forty feet high, eleven feet in circumference at the base and nine feet at the top. Damask pluma, red and yellow tomatoes, white onions, red and black radishes, corn, apples, pumpkins, etc., were utilized in the work. The top was crowned with sheaves of rye, oats and wheat.

To illustrate the great amount of labor necessary in p epa ing such a column, Mr. Beyer said that it occupied the attention of his entire force two weeks in simply getting ready, i. e., in cleaning and sorting the material to be used. B.

BOOKKEEPING and account forms for same by R. F. Tesson, as read at the Milwaukee convention will be printed in pamphlet form by the AMERICAN FLORIST and mailed FREE on request to any florist and extra copies to employers wishing the same to distribute among their employes. The address is of much permanent value and well worth studying by our young men.

THE AMERICAN FLORIST

NINETEENTH YEAR.

Subscription, $1.00 a year. To Europe, $2.00.
Subscriptions accepted only from those
in the trade.
Advertisements, on all except cover pages,
10 Cents a Line, Agate; $1 00 per inch.
Cash with Order.

No Special Position Guaranteed.

Discounts are allowed only on consecutive insertions, as follows:—6 times, 5 per cent; 13 times,
10 per cent; 26 times, 20 per cent;
52 times, 30 per cent.

Cover space sold only on yearly contract at
$1.00 per inch, net, in the case of the two
front pages, regular discounts applying only to the back pages.

The Advertising Department of the AMERICAN
FLORIST is for florists, seedsmen and nurserymen
and dealers in wares pertaining to those lines only.

Orders for less than one-half inch space not accepted.

Advertisements must reach us by Wednesday to
secure insertion in the issue for the following
Saturday. Address

AMERICAN FLORIST CO., Chicago.

THERE are many qualities which we
need alike in private citizen and in public
man, but there above all—three for the
lack of which no brilliancy and no genius
can atone—and these three are courage,
honesty and common sense.—*President
Roosevelt at Antietam.*

FROST any night.

LESSEN the shade.

CLOSE the houses earlier cool afternoons and save firing.

FRAME, earliest blooming perennials
such as Phlox divaricata, Primula veris,
etc., to lift in bloom for Easter pot sales.

SEND your wagon to the woods and
bring back a load of autumn leaves, bittersweet, pine cones, etc., for effective
and seasonable store decoration.

IF you have a small place and must
decide between the growing of cut flowers and bedding plants be careful how
you decide against the former; it is growing four times as fast as the latter and
furnishes some income nearly all the
time.

"THE FRONT: RIVAL OF THE ROSE IN
SPLENDOR; FRAGRANT AS THE CARNATION;
HARDY AS THE OAK; DISEASE PROOF AND
HOW PROOF; THE FLOWER OF THE PAST,
THE PRESENT AND THE FUTURE."

JOIN the S. A. F. and get in the S. A. P.
Peony association. Fee, $5 the first
year; $3 per annum thereafter. Secretary's address, W. J. Stewart, 79 Milk
street, Boston, Mass.   W.

American Carnation Society.

Jerome A. Suydam, Flatbush, N. Y.,
registers carnation as follows: "Amaze,"
an A No. 1 commercial scarlet, will
stand the heat of the sun without loosing its brightness; of good size and has
an excellent stem. One of the best
bloomers we have ever grown and we
have failed to see a brusted calyx.
         ALBERT M. HERR.

Portland Cement Chimney.

ED. AM. FLORIST:—Can any of your
readers, who have ever built or had
experience with a greenhouse chimney,
constructed of Portland cement and concrete, inform me whether or not such a
chimney is desirable?   L. C. L.

I have never used cement for this purpose and doubt if it will be satisfactory
for the entire chimney, although it would
answer well for the base. If used at all
it should be put up so as to form distinct
blocks twelve to eighteen inches deep.
         L. R. TAFT.

Fair Price for Carnations.

ED. AM. FLORIST:—What would be a
fair price to pay for carnation blooms on
a season contract, entire cut being taken
and the varieties being Queen Louise,
Estelle, Prosperity, Enchantress, Lawson, Norway, Lorna and Dorothy?
         VIRGINIA.

The writer is not familiar with costs,
except at Chicago. Coal there may be
had for $3 to $3.50 per ton delivered, and
we fire nearly eight months. Queen
Louise, Estelle, Lawson, Norway, Lorna
and Dorothy could be grown of good
quality for 2½ cents, with profit.
Enchantress being new and expensive,
should bring a cent more, and Prosperity
should bring double. I take it for granted
the varieties are in about equal quantity.
         W. N. RUDD.

Working Force For Retail Place.

ED. AM. FLORIST:—I have 15,000 feet
of glass and grow roses, chrysanthemums, carnations, some violets, potted
plants and some palms and ferns for
retail. How much help should be
required on such a place, the proprietor
waiting on customers, and lending a
hand?   WESTERNER.

Much depends upon the amount of
outside work that will be done in the
way of decorating, etc., as well as on the
convenience of the arrangement. To
keep the houses in good condition two
men beside the proprietor will be required,
with some additional help at busy periods if a retail business is done.
         L. R. TAFT.

Chrysanthemums Diseased.

ED. AM. FLORIST:—Enclosed please find
some chrysanthemum leaves. I wish you
would inform me through your paper of
the proper name of the disease affecting
the plants and of the best remedies.
         W. L. T.

The trouble seems to be a form of
œdema or dropsy. This physiological
disturbance is not unusual among various plants. Tomatoes grown under
glass are perhaps most susceptible to it.
Pelargoniums likewise are similarly
troubled. The reason for this unhealthy
condition is to be found in the circumstances under which the plants are
grown, and a wet warm soil is a leading
factor in this dropsical condition. Insufficient light is another element and on this
account œdema is more abundant in
midwinter than when the days are long
and the light is strong. Therefore, provide abundant light and see to it that
the chrysanthemums have a cool soil not
saturated with water.
         BYRON D. HALSTED.

Training Smilax.

ED. AM. FLORIST:—In training smilax,
what is to be done with the side branches
the plants throw out, which become
tangled in adjoining vines.   L. C. L.

The vines usually send out side branches
when the top has been broken off. The
best thing to do is to train the side
branches into the main string, but in
case they become unmanageable it might
be better to carefully cut them out. Be
careful in training the smilax not to
break off the ends of the main vines, for
this is usually the cause of the trouble.
         G.

Rose Pests.

ED. AM. FLORIST:—We send you sample of Rose Branches and worm which
has affected our house for the last three
weeks very badly. We do not know the
worm and do not know how to get rid
of same. We have been picking the pests
off every morning but they are getting
so numerous now, we have to find some
other remedy. Please advise us. W. S.

ED. AM. FLORIST:—Our rose houses are
infested with slugs or rose worms, of
which I enclose sample. Kindly give the
proper name of the worm, also some
way of destroying the pest as hand-picking does not prove very effective.
         GREENHORN.

The sample of caterpillars enclosed with
the leaves from Greenhorn were simply
dried up crushed matter when they
reached here so it is simply impossible to
recognize to what variety they belong,
but presume they belong to one of the
small yellow butterfly family.

To destroy them make a strong solution of soap water by paring very thinly
a large cake of soap, either Ivory or any
good grade. Dissolve in boiling water
by continually stirring until all is thoroughly dissolved, then add water enough
to make the whole six gallons. To this
add four ounces of pyrethrum (Persian
insect powder) of good quality, keeping
the mixture well stirred while sprinkling
the whole of the foliage with it. Early
morning is the best time to apply this
solution and if one dose does not kill
them all repeat in three or four days. It
would not be advisable to use the flowers that get dosed with this solution,
that is, those which have the petals partially opened.

A preventative of this pest is much
safer than a remedy. It can be prevented
by killing the butterflies when they first
appear in the house, or in case of moths,
which often do not show themselves during the day but come out from their hiding places in the evening; as soon as it
gets dark catch them. A good lamp or
lantern is necessary and nimble fingers
and it should be remembered also that
each one killed will prevent hundreds of
the caterpillars from coming later.
         J. N. MAY.

Crops For Dark House.

ED. AM. FLORIST:—I have a greenhouse
20x50 feet which I want to make good
use of this winter. I am rather in doubt,
however, as to what would thrive in it,
and give good profit, either in vegetables
or decorative plants. I have the advantage of a good market for anything I can
raise, so the main point to determine is
what will thrive best in winter under the
following circumstances. The house is a
three-quarter span, built entirely of wood
except on one slope of roof, which faces
east. The sashbars are sixteen inches
apart and made of 2¼x6-inch lumber, so
you will understand that no direct rays
of the sun enter the house after 9 or 10
a. m. throughout the winter. On the
other hand, there is an abundance of heat
if required. What do you advise me to
do for profit in such a house?
South Dakota.   PROFIT.

There are few flowering plants that
will thrive in a house like that described
above. Violets will do fairly well, and it
can be used for the starting of bulbs.
Large palms and similar decorative
plants can be stored. The darker portion of the house can be used for onions,
rhubarb and mushrooms. L. R. TAFT.

Philadelphia.

BRIGHTER BUSINESS PROSPECTS.—ROSES ARE BECOMING PLENTIFUL. — CARNATIONS SCARCE AND POOR.—NOTES OF THE TOWN.

Things are brightening up a bit and all the stores seem to feel the gentle breeze that is stirring. Some have early fall weddings, some have store openings and others report a run of funeral work. Flowers are more plentiful, that is roses at least, as every few days another grower's name is added to the list of those who thinks his stock is good enough to send in and who commences shipping for the season. Prices range about the same as last week. Carnations are scarce and not very good. Asters will last a little longer but the quality is getting poor. The dahlias are looming up and will cut quite a figure until Jack Frost lays them low, which seems, now with the thermometer near the nineties every day, a long way off.

The Wm. Graham Company opened its new store on Monday, September 14. It is elaborately furnished with everything the most modern. There are no counters, a handsome mahogany table in the center of the store taking the place of these. All work will be made up in the rear. Valuable rugs adorn the floor. Large Welsbach gas fixtures in the latest globes give an abundance of light. Handsome vases are seen on pedestals and in the cases and altogether the store presents a very unique and up-to-date appearance.

Leo Niessen has captured Jos. Beavis & Son's roses the coming winter. Mr. Beavis has always sold his stock to the retailers direct, but in keeping with the sentiment that is rapidly growing in this city, he will attend to their production and leave the selling to the men who make it their business. The Messrs. Bevis were credited with having the finest Brides and Bridesmaids that came to town last season, and as their stock is looking better than ever some great specials can be looked for.

William Reynolds, Ernst Bernheimer's, hustler, has opened a store at No. 1736 South Second street. Mrs. Reynolds, who is to have charge has had a long experience in her brother's store, and will no doubt build up a good trade, as the location is a good one.

Ed Reids' convention shooting prizes arrived a day or two ago. Edward is a great shot and is now on his home ward journey from Dakota where he has spent the weeks since the convention and where he has had abundant opportunity to bring down big game.

Julius Wolff, Jr., of North Nineteenth street, is quite busy with decorations. Together with his large retail business he caters to other retailers in the matter of decorative plants.

S. S. Pennock is reported home on September 29. In his recent letters he has failed to speak of the European consignment secured.

Joseph Heacock is busy with his palms as florists out of town are stocking up while there is no danger of frost during transit.

W. K. Harris is busy with shipping orders in Boston ferns. His stock is fine, being short and bushy.

Robt. Craig & Son are still cutting longiflorum lilies.

K.

KINGSTON, N. Y.—C. Lawritzen was married on August 11 to Miss Margaret Condon.

Buffalo.

With the thermometer registering a range of heat we should have had in July and August, good trade has not resulted. Asters and gladioli are still good. Some good dahlias are coming in. The best roses are American Beauty and Meteor. Carnations are very good for this date.

Our Mr. Peek, superintendent for J. H. Rebstock, was presented with a little Peck of about ten pounds. A person calling now can see three Pecks and all happy.

Recent visitors: E. J. Fancourt, Philadelphia; W. N. Rudd, 'P. J. Hauswirth, wife and daughter, with Miss Anna Kreitling, of Chicago.

E. C. Brucker, with W. F. Kasting, has just returned from Hamburg on the Lake, where he took a well-earned vacation.

Coming store openings promise a good lot of palms and greens. Nearly all the stores have some of that work.

Mrs. R. E. Boettger, of Eggertsville, is in Detroit for a few weeks. Wm. Scott was one of the judges at Toronto this year. John C. Pickleman, an old time florist, died September 3.

Mr. and Mrs. Sanderson were in Olean, N. Y., last week. BISON.

BERKELEY, CAL.—E. Bernsec, employe of J. Young, has gone to Germany. His partners, Rudolph Scheffler and Fred Fischer, surprised him with a parting reception recently.

Eine absolute Nothwendigkeit!

Hiermit $1.00 für mein Abonnement. Es ist die Pflicht eines Jeden prompt für den "American Florist" zu begahlen, weil dieser eine absolute Nothwendigkeit für jeden Blumenzüchter ist.

Carl Roegner, Alabama.

SITUATIONS, WANTS, FOR SALE.

One Cent Per Word.

Cash with the Adv.

Plant Advs. NOT admitted under this head.

Every paid subscriber to the AMERICAN FLORIST for the year 1903 is entitled to a five-line WANT ADV. (situations only) free, to be used at any time during the year.

Situation Wanted—By a florist, age 27, single. 10 years' experience in commercial places. FRANK WILHELM, care A. Klokner. Milwaukee.

Situation Wanted—In an up-to-date place as working foreman by practical young man. Single, age 24. Rose grower, grafter and propagator of American Beauties. Well posted in forcing plants and ferns. LAWRIN NIELSEN. 8128 Sherman Ave., Chicago.

Help Wanted—A night fireman. Steam heat. $12.00 a week. MORTON GROVE GREENHOUSES, Morton Grove, Ill.

Help Wanted—A general all-around man for retail greenhouse. Address J. F. KIDWELL & BRO., 160 43rd St., Chicago.

Help Wanted—An all-around, steady florist. Western man preferred. State wages wanted and send references. BYRON H. IVES. Albuquerque, N. M.

Help Wanted—At once: a sober, reliable, all-around man for commercial place. Single and German preferred. BOEHRINGER BROS., Bay City, Mich.

Help Wanted—Florist; competent to take charge of 6,000 feet of glass, grow cut flowers and general stock. State wages with reference, etc. J. C. STEINHAUSER, Pittsburg, Kansas.

Help Wanted—2 young men with some experience in the retail florist business. Address stating salary expected C. A. SAMUELSON, 2129 Michigan Ave., Chicago.

Cincinnati.

FLOWER EXHIBITIONS AT CINCINNATI FALL FESTIVAL.—PRIZE WINNERS.—BUSINESS IMPROVES.

W. K. Partridge's display consisted of lilies, cannas, asters, gladioli, marigolds, lilies of the valley, heliotrope and a large assortment of roses of all kinds. The George & Allan display, which took second prize, consisted of vincas, salvias, snap dragons and all kinds of roses and palms. In the display was the new adiantum fern, for which George & Allan were awarded a silver medal from S. A. F. J. H. Rodgers, who received third prize for the general display, had a very neat showing, as did Charles McCrea, winner of the fourth prize. J. W. Rodgers had an especially fine display of carnations for this time of the year. The Cushman Gladiolus Company had an elaborate showing of gladioli. The judge was Theo. Bock, of Hamilton, O., and everybody seemed well pleased with the decisions.

The premiums were awarded as follows: For best general display, first prize, W. K. Patridge, $150; second, George & Allan, $100; third, J. W. Rodgers, $75; fourth, Charles McCrea, $50. Best vase or display of roses: George & Allan, $15; Charles McCrea, $10. Best vase or display of carnations: J. W. Rodgers, $12; Charles McCrea, $8; R. A. Betz, $5. Best display of asters: George & Allan, $15; T. W. Hardesty, $10; A. H. Konzelman, $5. Best display or vase of lilies: George & Allan, $15; T. W. Hardesty & Company, $10; A. H. Konzelman, $5. Best vase or display of dahlias: R. V. Price, Home City, $15; Wagner Park Conservatories, Sidney, O., $10; Cushman gladiolus Company, $5.

Business is a little better than last week, there being less stock around, which is playing out and it won't be long before they are a thing of the past.

Thursday, September 10 was flower day at the Cincinnati fall festival, which was held at Music hall and Washington park, September 7 to 19. Over 26,000 people attended this exhibition.

The second exhibition was held on September 16, at which T. W. Hardesty took first prize; Julius Baer, second and Chas. Gardner third.   ALEX.

FORT COLLINS, COLO.—B. J. Clippinger succeeds E. B. Davis.

HOBOKEN, N. J.—Kogge Brothers, who have one of the neatest stores, have refitted it with new counters and cases for fall trade.

Wholesale Flower Markets

MILWAUKEE, Sept. 17.
Roses, Beauty, med. per doz.	1.50
" short "	.75@1.00
" Liberty	4.00@ 6.00
" Bride, Bridesmaid	4.00@ 6.00
" Meteor, Golden Gate	4.00@ 6.00
" Perle	4.00@ 6.00
Carnations	1.00
Smilax	10.0@12.50
Asparagus	50.00
Gladioli	2.00@ 3.00
Asters	1.00@ 2.00

PITTSBURG, Sept. 17.
Roses, Beauty, specials, per doz.	2.50@3.50
" " extras	1.00@2.00
" " No. 1	.75@1.00
" " No. 2	2.00@ 5.00
" Bride, Bridesmaid	1.00@ 6.00
" Meteor	2.00@ 6.00
" Kaiserin, Liberties	2.00@ 6.00
Carnations	.75@ 1.00
Lily of the Valley	3.00@ 4.00
Smilax	10.00@12.50
Adiantum	.75@ 1.00
Asparagus, strings	30.00@50.00
" Sprengeri	1.00@ 4.00
Gladioli	1.00@ 3.00
Asters	.25@ 1.00

CINCINNATI, Sept. 17.
Roses, Beauty	10.00@35.00
" Bride, Bridesmaid	2.00@ 6.00
" Liberty	2.00@ 6.00
" Meteor, Golden Gate	2.00@ 6.00
Carnations	1.00@ 2.00
Lily of the valley	3.00@ 4.00
Asparagus	12.50@15.00
Adiantum	1.00@ 1.50
Gladioli	1.00
Asters	.75@ 2.00

ST. LOUIS Sept. 17.
Roses, Beauty, long stem	2.00
" Beauty, medium stem	12.50
" Beauty, short stem	4.00@ 6.00
" Lib-ity	2.00@ 6.00
" Bride, Bridesmaid	2.00@ 4.00
" Golden Gate	2.00@ 4.00
Carnations	1.00@ 1.50
Smilax	12.50
Asparagus Sprengeri	1.00@ 1.50
" Plumosus	14.00@25.00
Ferns	per 1000 1.50
China Asters	1.00@ 2.00
Tube-r s-s	5.00@ 8.00

WM. MURPHY,

Grower and Commission Dealer in

Cut Flowers ᴬᴺᴰ Florists' Supplies,

130 East Third Street,
'Phone Main 980.   CINCINNATI, O.

E. H. Hunt,

WHOLESALE

Cut Flowers

"THE OLD RELIABLE."

76 Wabash Ave., ...CHICAGO.

RICE BROTHERS

128 N. 6th St.,   MINNEAPOLIS, MINN.

Wholesale Cut Flowers and Supplies.

Wild Smilax | Flowers billed at Market Prices.

Shippers of choice Cut Flowers and Greens of all kinds. Try us.

H. G. BERNING

Wholesale Florist

1322 Pine St.,   ST. LOUIS, MO.

FOR SOUTHERN WILD SMILAX

(Where Quality is First Consideration.)
Write, Wire or Phone the introducers,

Caldwell The Woodsman Co., Evergreen, Ala.
or their agents: L. J. Kreshover, New York; J. B. Deamud, Chicago; H. Bayersdorfer & Co., Philadelphia; W. F. Kasting, Buffalo; J. M. McCullough's Sons. Cincinnati, Ohio; H. G. Berning, St. Louis. Mo.

HEADQUARTERS IN MICHIGAN FOR FANCY CUT FERNS.

Michigan Cut Flower Exchange.

FANCY FERNS, $1.50 per 1000. Discount on large orders. Give us a trial for Ferns the year around. GALAX, Green and Bronze, $1.00 per 1000.

28 Miami Ave.,   DETROIT, MICH.

GEORGE SALTFORD,

WHOLESALE FLORIST.

46 W. 29th Street,   NEW YORK.

TEL. 3393 MADISON SQUARE.
Specialties: VIOLETS AND CARNATIONS.
Consignments of any good flowers solicited.

Always   mention the American Florist when you order stock.

INTERNATIONAL FLOWER DELIVERY.

PASSENGER STEAMSHIP MOVEMENTS.

The tabl s herewith give the scheduled time of depa ture of ocean steamships carrying first-class p ssengers from the principal American and foreign ports covering the space of two weeks from date of this issue of the AMERICAN FLORIST. Much disappointment often resu lts from attempts to forward flowers for steamer delivery by express to the care of the ships steward or otherwise. The carriers of these packages are not infrequently refused admission on board and even those delivered on board are not always certain to reach the parties for whom they were intended. Hence florists in interior cities having orders for the delivery of flowers to passengers on out-going steamers are advised to intrust the filling of such orders to some reliable florist in the port of departure, who understands the necessary details and formalities and has the facilities for attending to it properly. For the addresses of such firms we refer our readers to the advertisements on this page:

FROM	TO	STEAMER	*LINE	DAY	DUE ABOUT
New York	Liverpool	Umbria	1	Sat. Sept. 26, 9:00 a. m.	Oct. 2
New York	"	Lucania	1	Sat. Oct. 3, 2:00 p. m.	Oct. 9
New York	Glasgow	Numidian	2	Thur. Oct. 1, Noon.	Oct. 12
New York	Hamburg	Auguste Victoria	3	Thur. Sept. 24, 10:00 a. m	
New York	"	Moltke	3	Thur. Oct. 1, 1:00 p. m.	Oct. 8
New York	"	Pennsylvania	3	Sat. Oct. 3, 3:00 p. m.	Oct. 13
New York	Coppnhagen	Hellig Olav	4	Wed. Sept. 30.	
New York	Glasgow	Astoria	4	Sat. Sept. 26, Noon.	
New York	"	Ethiopia	5	Sat. Oct. 3, Noon.	
New York	Southampton	Ma-quette	6	Fri. Se t. 25, 8:00 a. m.	
New York	"	St. Louis	6	Wed. Sept. 30, 10:00 a. m.	
New York	"	Philadelphia	6	Wed. Sept. 23, 10:00 a. m.	
New York	Antwerp	Kroonland	6	Sat. Sept. 26, 10:00 a. m.	Oct. 5
New York	"	Zeeland	6	Sat. Oct. 3, 10:00 a. m.	Oct. 13
New York	London	Minneapolis	6	Sat. Sept. 26, 9:00 a. m.	Oct. 5
New York	"	Minnehaha	6	Sat. Oct. 3, 3:00 p. m.	Oct. 13
New York	Liverpool	Oceanic	7	Wed. Sept. 23, 7:00 a. m.	Sept. 30
New York	"	Cymbric	7	Fri. Sept 25, 8:00 a. m.	Oct. 3
New York	"	Teutonic	7	Wed. Sept. 30, Noon.	Oct. 7
N w York	"	Arabic	7	Fri. Oct. 2, 8:30 p. m.	Oct. 10
New York	Havre	La Bretagne	10	Thur. Sept. 24, 10:00 a. m	Oct. 2
New York	"	La Lorraine	10	Thur. Oct. 1, 10:00 a. m.	
New York	Rotterdam	Ryndam	11	Wed. Sept. 23, 10:00 a. m.	Oct. 2
New York	"	Noordam	11	Wed. Sept. 30, 10:00 a. m.	
New York	Genoa	Lombardia	12	Tues. Sept 29, 11:00 a. m.	
New York	"	Lahn	13	Sat. Se t. 26, 11:00 a. m.	Oct. 5
New York	Bremen	Kaiser Wilh. II	13	Tues. Sept. 29, 9:30 a. m.	Sept. 29
New York	"	Koenig Albert	13	Thur. Sept. 24, Noon	Oct. 4
New York	"	K. Wil. Der Grosse	13	Tues. Sept. 29, 10:00 a. m.	Oct. 6
New York	"	Bremen	13	Thur. Oct. 1, Noon.	Oct. 11
Boston	Liverpool	Commonwealth	15	Thur. Sept 24, Noon.	Oct. 1
Boston	"	New England	15	Thur. Oct. 1, 2:00 p. m.	Oct. 8
Boston	"	Saxonia	15	Tues. Sept. 29, 10:30 a. m.	Sept. 30
Boston	"	DeVonian	16	Sat. Sept. 26, 1.30 p. m.	
Boston	"	Winifredian	16	Sat. Oct. 3, 7:30 a. m.	
Montreal	"	Canada	15	Sat. Se t. 26, Daylight.	
Montreal	"	Kensington	15	Sat. Oct. 3, Daylight.	
San Francisco	Hotgkong	Chita	17	Tues. Sept. 29, 1:0 p. m.	Oct. 28
San Fra cisco	Honolulu	Alameda	18	Sat. Sept. 26, Noon.	Oct. 2
Vancouver	Hotgkong	Athenian	20	Mon. Sept. 21,	Oct. 19
Vancouver	"	Empress of India	20	Mon. Oct. 5,	
Seattle	"	Aki Maru	22	Sat. Oct. 3, a. m.	Nov. 9

*1 Cunard; 2 Allen-State; 3 Hamburg-American; 4 Scandinavian-American; 5 Anchor Line; 6 Atlantic Transport; 7 White Star; 8 American; 9 Red Star; 10 French; 11 Holland-American; 13 Italian Royal Mail; 13 North German Lloyd; 15 Dominion; 16 Leyland; 17 Occidental and Oriental; 18 Oceanic; 19 Allan; 20 Can. Pacific Ry.; 21 N. Pacific Ry.; 22 Hongkong-Seattle.

INTERNATIONAL FLOWER DELIVERY.

STEAMSHIPS LEAVE FOREIGN PORTS.

FROM	TO	STEAMER	*LINE	DAY	DUE ABOUT
Liverpool	New York	Etruria	1	Sat. Sept. 26,	Oct. 1
Liverpool	"	Campania	1	Sat. Oct. 3,	Oct. 9
Liverpool	"	Germanic	7	Wed. Sept. 23, 5:00 p. m.	Sept. 31
Liverpool	"	Cedric	7	Fri. Sept. 25, 5:00 p. m.	
Liverpool	"	Majestic	7	Wed. Sept. 30, 5:00 p. m.	
Liverpool	"	Celtic	7	Fri. Oct. 2, 5:00 p. m.	
Liverpool	Boston	Ivernia	1	Tues. Sept. 22,	Sept. 30
Liverpool	"	Bohemian	16	Fri. Sept. 25,	
Liverpool	"	Canadian	16	Fri. Oct. 2,	Oct. 11
Liverpool	Montreal	Dominion	15	Wed. Sept. 23,	
Liverpool	"	Southwalk	15	Wed. Sept. 30,	
Glasgow	New York	Anchoria	6	Thur. Sept. 26,	Oct. 3
Glasgow	"	Columbia	5	Sat. Oct. 3,	
Glasgow	"	Laurentian	6	Sat. Oct. 3,	Oct. 13
Genoa	"	Sardegna	12	Mon. Sept. 21,	
Genoa	"	Citta di Napoli	12	Mon. Sept. 28,	Oct. 15
Genoa	"	Liguria	12	Mon. Oct. 5,	
Southampton	"	New York	3	Sat. Sept. 26, Noon.	Oct. 3
Southampton	"	Philadelphia	3	Sat. Oct. 3, Noon.	
Antwerp	"	Finland	9	Sat. Sept. 26, 2:00 p. m.	Oct. 5
Antwerp	"	Vaderland	9	Sat. Oct. 3, 11:00 a. m.	Oct. 13
Southampton	"	Manitou	8	Wed. Sept. 26,	
London	"	Messba	8	Sat. Sept. 26,	
London	"	Minnetonka	8	Sat. Oct. 3,	
Hamburg	"	Furst Bismarck	5	Thur. Sept. 24,	Oct. 2
Hamburg	"	Deutschland	5	Tues. Sept. 29,	
Hamburg	"	Bluecher	5	Thur. Oct. 1,	Oct. 8
Hamburg	"	Pretoria	5	Sat. Oct. 3,	
Havre	"	La Touraine	10	Sat. Sept. 26,	Oct. 3
Havre	"	La Savoie	10	Sat. Oct. 3,	
Copenhagen	"	Oscar II	4	Wed. Sept. 23,	
Rotterdam	"	Potsdam	11	Sat. Sept. 26,	Oct. 5
Rotterdam	"	Statendam	11	Sat. Oct. 3,	
Genoa	"	Prinzess Irene	13	Thur. Oct. 1,	Oct. 14
Bremen	"	Kronprinz Wilh.	13	Tues. Sept. 22,	Sept. 29
Bremen	"	Barbarossa	13	Sat. Sept. 26,	Oct. 6
Sydney	SanFrancisco	Sierra	18	Mon. Sept. 28,	Oct. 13
Sydney	Vancouver	Aorangi	20	Mon. Oct. 5,	Oct. 22
Hongkong	"	Empress of Japan	20	Wed. Sept. 23,	Oct. 14
Hongkong	SanFrancisco	Coptic	17	Sat. Sept. 26,	Oct. 16
Hongkong	"	America Maru	17	Sat. Oct. 3,	Oct. 31
Hongkong	Seattle	Tosa Maru	22	Tues. Sept. 22, p. m.	Oct. 22

* See steamship list on opposite page.

Albert Fuchs,
PALMS, FERNS, FICUS.
Established 1884. CHICAGO, 2045-59 Clarendon Ave.

HONORABLE MENTION AT MILWAUKEE FOR OUR HOME-GROWN PALMS.

[advertisement text]

PRIMROSES. | ASPARAGUS.

JOS. H. CUNNINGHAM, Delaware, O.

The F. R. WILLIAMS CO.
Wholesale Florists,
CLEVELAND, - OHIO.

SUCCESSFUL SELLERS
are the successful growers who advertise in THE AMERICAN FLORIST.

THE SEED TRADE.

AMERICAN SEED TRADE ASSOCIATION.
S. F. Willard, Pres.; J. Charles McCullough, First Vice-Pres.; C. E. Kendel, Cleveland, O., Sec'y and Treas.
Twenty-second annual convention St. Louis, Mo., June, 1904.

The maple's bright, tri-colored leaves
The signal wave that summer's done;
And Ceres gives her bursting sheaves
To deck the earth for Harvest Home.

C. CROPP and family arrived at New York September 15.

VALLEY, NEB., Sept. 16. — A fairly heavy frost occurred here last night.

ROCKY FORD, COLO., September 18.—A killing frost last night finished the canteloupe crop.

SOUTHPORT Globe onions, red and white, are reported as short with some of the California growers.

ST. PAUL.—J. B. Coment, representing Carter, Dunnett & Beale, of London, England, passed through here a week ago on his annual tour.

THE Wisconsin Bouquet Green district has been flooded by heavy rains and picking will not be easy, especially on the lower grounds where the best quality is often gathered.

LATEST bean crop reports are unfavorable and only three fourths of a crop predicted. The Michigan pea crops have been damaged by late rains and extra picking will be required.

VISITED CHICAGO.—J. Dwight Funk, of Funk Bros.' Seed Company, Bloomington, Ill.; M. M. Miese, Lancaster, O.; Arthur B. Clark, of E. B. Clark & Son; L. L. Olds, Clinton, Wis.

THE bean outlook is far from favorable at present, and unless corn weather prevails again soon the crop may be seriously affected. Shrewd judges of the prospects are looking around for bargain lots of '02 crop.

GERMAN wholesale houses are advertising French Roman hyacinths 12 to 15 ctm. at $24. Considering the prices quoted by the American importers and keeping in mind the twenty-five per cent duty and extra freight, the American houses are taking less profit than the German dealers.

FRENCH BULBS.—This seems to be another bad season for those American importers who speculated on the market by making lower prices than the French outlook warranted. To fail to fill their accepted orders may not entirely satisfy their customers, and to fill complete may mean a loss. There is no reason to think cut blooms of Roman hyacinths will not bring a fair price the coming winter.

WATERLOO, NEB., September 17—The freeze of Wednesday night, September 15, was hard enough to make a slight coating of ice over standing water in shallow places and seriously scorched the tender vines. The recent weather has tended more to the growth of corn than ripening it. If this cold snap is not followed by drying weather our worst fears for the corn crop are likely to be realized. The outlook for musk-melons is probably poorer than for any other of the vine seeds.

BIRMINGHAM. PA.—Thomas Sharpless will complete his new mushroom house by October 1.

Joyville's County Fair.

Through the days o' parchin' sunshine,
through the days o' drenchin' rain,
We have wrastled with the meadow grass, the garden truck an' grain.
An' at last we're on the journey fer to claim our rightful share ;
O' the glory for the farmer at the Joyville county fair.

You that come from out the city for to see the bosses race
Needn't think you know the pleasures o' our country meetin' place,
For it's no one but us farmers has the kind of eyes to see
What's the real inside good time o' the Joyville jubilee.

Mother brings some canned tomatoes an' they stand upon a shelf
With her name in printed letters; an' the county judge hisself
Tries a spoonful, tries another, smiles an' says he'd like to state
Them's the tastin'est tomattusses he ever, ever ate.

In the art hall, where the ladies go to learn the latest stitch,
Sister's fancy work exhibit, 'broidered table cloths an' sich.
Draws a monstrous crowd o' people, an' they praise it loud an' free
Till its all in all the greatest day in sister's history.

Down 'among the pens an' stables an' the heaps o 'fodder corn,
Daddy's got a speckled heifer with a ribbon on her horn.
Bud has took the silver medal in the water melon line.
An' the loudest rooster crowin' in the poultry house is mine.

You may shout about St. Louis an' your Pan-Americans.
With their lakes and lordly buildin's an' their camel caravans.
But I'll bet my crowin' rooster 'gainst your shoe lace, if you dare,
That They ain't a little circumstance to Joyville's county fair.
—Newark News.

Cucumber Blight.

ED. AM. FLORIST:—Your inquiry concerning cucumber blight no doubt has reference to the downy mildew fungus, Plasmopara Cubensis, which was so destructive to musk melons and very injurious to cucumbers in Connecticut and other eastern states last year. Blight is a name very commonly used for any fungus trouble of these plants but should be restricted to the bacterial trouble that wilts down the green vines by clogging up the ducts of the bundles through which the water is carried and thus cuts off this supply to the parts beyond.

Curious as it may seem, I have not so far this season, found a single leaf of either the melon or cucumber that has been attacked by the downy mildew. In consequence the spraying experiments on cucumbers and melons against this fungus yield no special results. However, another fungus, not before reported from Connecticut, has done considerable damage to some melon patches. This is the scab fungus or Cladosposium cucumerinum, which in past years has been reported a number of times as injurious to cucumbers. The sprayed melons so far have not been injured by this fungus, while it is doing considerable damage in the check plot. Scab is not a very good name for the fungus. It occurs on the stems, or more commonly on the fruit, and produces prominent sunken areas which are usually covered with the olive green fruiting stage of the fungus.
The fact that the downy mildew has not been found here this year, after being so common last year, and that I have been unable to find any sign of a winter spore stage inclines me to the belief that this fungus is carried north from southern regions each season, that it appears and is injurious during those seasons especially adapted to its early appearance and vigorous development in the north.
　　　　　　　　　G. P. CLINTON.

Good News if True.

The United States Cut Flower Company, of New York City, is to build a greenhouse upon a sixty-two acre site near Elmira, with an area of one million square feet of glass to cost not less than $350,000. The Elmira board of trade will pay for one-half the cost of the site, or about $5,375. The greenhouse will do exclusively a wholesale business. It guarantees to employ not less than 300 male hands, with a pay-roll of not less than $1,800 a week. The site will probably be where the old Halfway House stood, on the road to Horseheads. It is said that this will be the largest greenhouse in the world. — Corning N. Y. Journal.

KENOSHA, WIS.—The Kenosha Greenhouses are doing a good business and adding to their glass.

MARIETTA, OHIO.—J. W. Dudley & Son, of Parkersburg, W. Va., have reopened their branch store here on Putnam street, September 5.

THE NURSERY TRADE.

AM. ASSOCIATION OF NURSERYMEN.
N. W. HALE, Knoxville, Tenn. Pres.; FRANK
A. WEBER, St. Louis, Mo., Vice-Pres.; GEORGE C.
SEAGER, Rochester, N. Y., Sec'y.
Twenty-ninth annual convention, Atlanta, Ga.,
June, 1904.

WESTERN SPRINGS, ILL. — Vaughan's
Seed Store is tiling thirty acres of its new
nursery ground.

ASHLAND, O.—The Forest Nursery &
Lumber Company has been incorporated with $100,000 capital.

WAUPACA, WIS.—A. D. Appletree Barnes
has taken a large planting contract at
Chain o' Lakes. He judged fruits at
Wausau last week.

THE Hawks Nursery Company, a New
York corporation, filed articles to oper-
ate in Wisconsin. T. J. Ferguson, of
Wauwatosa, is vice president.

MINNEAPOLIS, MINN.—Wyman Elliott
and T. E. Perkins attended the Boston
meeting of the American Pomological
Society as representatives of the Horticultural Society of this state, taking with
them some of the finest fruits shown at
our state fair.

WASHINGTON, D. C.—Under the direction of Elliot Woods, superintendent
of the Capitol building and grounds, all
the rare trees and shrubs in the grounds
of the Capitol are being plainly marked
to show their common and botanical
names. Within these grounds there are
several hundred rare trees and shrubs
from all parts of the world. The work
of marking the trees and shrubs is being
done by Wm. C. Cogan, the gardener.
The Capitol grounds were laid out by
the elder Olmstead twenty-five years ago.

German Growers.

J. C. Schmidt Berlin.—This old and
important establishment is one of the
sights in our line of trade at this grand
city. The manager entertained the writer
on the occasion of his visit there this
summer. There are fifty acres devoted
entirely to cut flowers and plants supplemented by about 100,000 feet of glass,
half of which is devoted to roses and
carnations and the other half to forcing
bulbs, lilacs, flowering shrubbery, ferns
and palms. Five acres of roses are grown
out of doors for summer bloom. Three
acres are devoted to asters and about the
same to dahlias. I counted from forty
to fifty blooms on a single plant of the
latter. Some two acres of fancy grasses
are cultivated, the use of this stock in
floral pieces being extensive in Germany.
Aquatic plants are produced in a pond
covering about two acres. The firm produces its own lilacs, and I have never
seen better. They force about 5,000 of
these each winter. In chrysanthemums
they grow about 10,000 single stems
and bush plants and about the same
number of cyclamen. Plants in 6-inch and
7-inch pots measured eighteen inches
across. Primulas and poinsettias are
grown in deep hotbeds under glass
during the summer. Some fine plants of
Begonia Gloire de Lorraine were also a
feature. In forcing bulbs, some 15,000
dutch hyacinths, 100,000 tulips, 10,000
Lilium auratum, rubrum and longiflorum,
5,000 callas and 400,000 lily of the
valley, about half of these for summer
and half for cold storage, will indicate

something of the business done. They
have 5,000 plants of asparagus, about
half plumosus and half Sprengeri.
A large building 30x300 feet, without
glass, except a skylight, is used for
storage of shrubs, from which building
they are brought into forcing houses as
needed. The whole plant is heated by
hot water. A fine house 24x200 was
devoted to adiantums in 4-inch and 5-inch
pots. The whole growing establishment
is cared for by one foreman, sixteen
florists and ten laborers. Everything is
kept as clean as a parlor. The store is
on one of the best streets of Berlin, connected with a conservatory, on their own
property. Five florist decorators, fifteen
young ladies, two men in the office, in
addition to the manager, Mr. Swoboda,
comprise the store force. The floral
designs are excellent and the window
display the most artistic that I have
ever seen. Nearly every morning during
my visit could be seen displayed from
ten to fifteen designs in wreaths and
baskets, some five to six feet high with
combination designs of palms, ferns, crotons, etc. The firm will add a large
range of glass next year to accommodate
40,000 carnations and 20,000 roses.
O. Beroth, Marienfeld, near Berlin.—A
famous orchid grower having eleven
greenhouses with about 75,000 plants,
comprising nearly all known varieties.
The houses are constructed like our own
in America and he uses the Belgium
system of shading and covering glass in
case of hail. Under the benches are tanks
of water for moisture. Seventeen men
are employed and his production is
famous all over Europe. His shipments
are made in wholesale only. I saw one
order being packed, comprising about 600
cattleyas to go to Dresden at 25 cents
each. He ships them also to St. Petersburg, Austrian points, and even to Paris.
His employes are paid by the hour, about
eleven cents in American money.
J. J. H.

Colorado Springs.

THE HORTICULTURAL SOCIETY'S ANNUAL
FLOWER SHOW A SUCCESS.—TRADE CON-
DITIONS IMPROVED SINCE LAST REPORT.
—NOTES.

The annual flower show of the El Paso
County Horticultural Society held in
North Park, this city, August '19 to 21
inclusive, was a magnificent success, surpassing financially and otherwise all
efforts of previous years. Flowers, of
course were the leading attraction, but
the fruit and vegetable exhibits added
much to the educational value of the
show. A special attempt will be made
to enlarge the fruit exhibits of future
exhibitions. Three large tents sheltered
the space occupied, the area being practically enclosed by one huge tent. A
special feature of this show, not appearing on previous occasions, was a tent
assigned to the use of the ladies for giving afternoon teas and for the sale of ice
cream, cake and cut flowers, the proceeds
going to the Colorado Springs Day
Nursery. Mrs. W. K. Jewett and Mrs.
F. W. Goddard, two well known society
ladies, had charge of this throughout
the three days and by their personality
did much to aid the success of the whole
affair. A collection of pressed flowers,
showing wonderful skill in mounting and
preserving, was loaned by Mrs. Walker
for the occasion. Over 200 varieties of
Colorado flowers appeared in this collection. Another notable set of Colorado
pressed flowers was shown by Miss A.
M. Hertlein. This collection is the

amateur work of an invalid from Indiana,
who did the work as a pastime. Sweet
peas and dahlias, as on previous occasions, elicited the liveliest competition
from the school children. There were
thousands of vases shown, displaying
much care in cultivation and an enthusiastic interest on the part of those making the exhibits. Space will permit of the
enumeration of only the leading prizes in
the professional line, and the following is
a list of first prizes: Wm. Clark, best collection of decorative plants, best collection of foliage plants, not less than eight
varieties, best mantel decoration, best
flower basket; best collection of cut flowers, best single flower of cactus dahlia,
best twelve spikes of cannas, one variety.
Colorado Springs Floral Company, best
collection of geranium plants, best vase
of white carnations, thirty-six blooms,
best vase of mixed carnations, fifty
blooms, best table decoration, best bridal
bouquet, best vase of cannas, six spikes.
F. F. Crump, best floral design. W. W.
Wilmore, of Denver, carried off most of
the dahlia prizes, as usual. Two mounds
of ferns, one of Boston ferns and the
other of adiantum, were much admired.
These were entered by Wm. Clark and
were not for competition. It was proposed to award a special prize to Mr.
Clark for a fine vase of gladioli, the
exhibit being disqualified because of one
spike appearing over the number called
for. The Colorado Springs Floral Company's vase was also disqualified for the
same reason.
Trade has greatly improved since last
report, several large weddings and funerals having helped things along very
materially. There is no surplus of stock,
except such common flowers as gladioli,
rudbeckias, etc., and white roses and
carnations are very scarce. Young roses
have not yet come into a crop to any
extent and what roses are being cut are
not of high quality. Carnations have
been practically all planted and growers
are obliged to fall back on outdoor
grown flowers of this staple. The cool
weather and abundance of rain have
helped outdoor stock along wonderfully.
Stem-rot is remarkably scarce this season throughout this section. Dahlias
are very fine.
Clarke & Burnette, of Colorado City,
have dissolved partnership. Stephen
Clark continues the business.
The Colorado Springs Floral Company
is cutting a few good carnation blooms
from early planted stock.
Wm. Clark has some excellent outside
carnations in bearing.   S. S.

Cleveland.

While the days are often very warm
now, the nights are extremely cold, which
makes stock very backward in developing properly. The color of both roses
and carnations is good and the stems are
fairly long, but the flowers are small.
Some nice crotons are shown, also double
sunflowers are seen in the florists' windows in basket decorations, etc., and it
is surprising what a pretty showing they
make. Outside stock looks fine, and
arranged beds of cannas, salvias, geraniums, etc, never looked better.
Messrs. Herman Hart and Peter Pro-
beck have arrived home from Europe.
At the regular meeting of the Florist
Club, September 23 was decided on as
the date of its picnic.   O. G.

NEWARK, N. J.—George Peneck has
opened a new store at 615 Broad street.

OUR PASTIMES.

Announcements of coming contests or other events of interest to our bowling, shooting and sporting readers are solicited and will be given place in this column.

Address all correspondence for this department to Wm. J. Stewart, 79 Milk St., Boston, Mass.; Robt. Kift, 1725 Chestnut St., Philadelphia, Pa.; or to the American Florist Co., 334 Dearborn St., Chicago, Ill.

At Philadelphia.

The last game of the series or rubber between the Milwaukee and Asheville teams, each having won one, was played on the home alleys last Wednesday evening. It was a close and exciting contest all the way through, the first game going to the Milwaukee team by 27 pins. In the second Geo. Moss made 247, a great score, and the Asheville won by 55 pins, putting them 28 pins to the good. Milwaukee made this up in the third game and won out by close margin in the total of 3 pins. The score follows:

MILWAUKEE.

Player.	1	2	3	T'l
Kift	129	161	149	439
Connor	103	186	149	418
Yates	149	380	171	440
Adelberger	199	150	167	509
Polites	151	145	181	477
Robinson	148	185	186	470
Totals	918	907	918	2868

ASHEVILLE.

Player.	1	2	3	T'l
Moss	174	247	193	614
Anderson	156	173	148	477
Robertson	148	186	186	470
Watson	149	158	140	439
Craig	145	137	156	426
Kift	128	161	149	438
Totals	891	1013	922	2865
				K.

St. Louis.

ST. LOUIS FLORISTS' CLUB MEETS AT EDWARDSVILLE. — ENTERTAINMENT BY FRED. AMMANN.—NOTES.

The meeting of the St. Louis Florist Club at Fred Ammann's on last Thursday, September 10, was one of the most successful and enthusiastic meetings that the club has had in many a day. We arrived in Edwardsville after a delightful ride of twenty-two miles and found Mr. Ammann on hand to meet us and act as escort to his home. Upon reaching the house we proceeded to make a tour of inspection through the carnation and rose range. There are seven houses in all, each 18x165 feet. The Dietch system with Wolfe ventilators is used throughout. Five are planted to roses, and two to carnations. The plants were in a condition to well warrant the praise given them. A house of American Beauties and a bunch of Ivory roses being especially attractive. After reviewing the houses Vice-President Windler, in the temporary absence of the president, requested everyone to move to the north end of the potting shed where arrangements had been made for holding the meeting. Twenty-eight members and two visitors were present. After the usual form of opening Mr. Ammann, by request, read the invitation, which was presented to the S. A. F., inviting that body to hold its convention for 1904 in St. Louis. All those who were in attendance at Milwaukee were given a rousing vote of thanks for the good work they had done. F. K. Balthis was then elected to membership in the club, after which installation of officers was in order. President Beneke, before assuming the chair, spoke enthusiastically of the coming convention and said that if every member put his shoulder to the wheel all would be well and St. Louis would have the most successful meeting in the history of the association. Convention talks were then in order and everyone seemed to feel that he must take his share of the individual responsibility necessary to make the convention a success. On opening the question box the question "Is stem-rot prevalent in St. Louis?" brought out lively discussion, Dr. Halstead, Fillmore, Fehr, Guy and Herzog, taking an active part. As usual no one was qualified to enlighten us as to who "St. Patrick is"—must be Irish otherwise. What's in a name.—The question box has become an important adjunct at the meetings. The announcement was made that the October meeting would be held at the down-town club rooms and on motion by Mohr adjournment was in order. We had been treated royally up to this time, but Mr. Ammann had a surprise in store for us in the shape of a big "spread" out under the trees. After everyone had satisfied the inner man President Beneke, acting as toast master, called upon Hunford, Koenig, Dr. Halstead, Guy and Ammann for a few remarks. Each gentleman responded with a word about the St. Louis meet in 1904. The lateness of the hour brought the visit to a sudden termination and we departed for home filled with the kindliest thoughts towards Edwardsville, of Mr. Ammann's generous hospitality, and that the club was returning home a much stronger organization than when it left in the morning.

The Michel Plant and Bulb Company has secured the collection for housing and caring for the collection of orchids recently brought over from Manilla by J. L. Irwin, secretary of the Philippine commission. About 50 per cent of the plants survived the journey. The collection is now at Michel's place in Old Orchard, Mo.

There is practically no demand for stock. Roses are plentiful as well as everything else. American Beauty is in demand and sells rapidly. Prices are about as last week.

Dr. Halstead, of Bellville, is planning to erect five new rose houses. He will grow Kaiserin, Carnot, La France and American Beauties for summer flowering.

R. J. Mohr went on a collecting trip for the World's Fair this week. He is increasing the collection of native plants in the horticultural department.   B.

BOWLING GREEN, KY.—Burdell Floral Company, of Warren county, has incorporated, with $2,500 capital. R. W., C. J. and Florence Burdell are incorporators.

KANSAS CITY, MO.—Carl Phillips, a florist recently employed by Edward Humfeld, was sentenced September 12 to one year in the county jail for disposing of flowers taken from his employer.

Pittsburg.

BUSINESS STILL QUIET.—WEATHER WARM.
—FALL OUTLOOK GOOD.—NOTES.

Nothing remarkable has happened to disturb the quietude of business. The present hot weather is similar to that which usually comes in july. There will be numerous weddings this fall and the outlook for a good season is bright. Roses are beginning to improve, home-grown American Beauty making fine headway on the benches. Bridesmaids are still tired looking and need color badly. Bride and Liberty roses are fairly good. Good carnations are beginning to come, the stems being quite short, but a few weeks will eliminate this defect. Asters are very good. Gladioli as a whole did not come up to the standard this year and some growers blame it on the great rainfall during the season, as some say this season's rain was peculiar in action, seldom penetrating the soil to any considerable extent. Lilies of the valley are fine but not in demand. Cosmos and anemones are seen in the windows.

Henry Blind entertained the entire party from this vicinity who attended the recent convention at Milwaukee, to a corn roast and other delightful refreshments. The party met at G. & J. W. Ludwig's establishment, Tuesday afternoon and proceeded to Mr. Blind's in a body.

E. L. McGrath, wife and son will spend two weeks at Saxonburg.   E. L. M.

Newport, R. I.

The dahlia show September 22 and 23 promises to be a grand affair. A great many varieties of cactus dahlias have been grown in this city. They are used a great deal for center pieces at dinners, etc. F. J. Butt, formerly gardener with H. W. Marrion of Newton, N. J., for the last eighteen years, has taken charge of Col. L. C. Ledyardes place.

Mrs. M. Vaniceck, wife of Mr. V. A. Vaniceck, the nurseryman, died of apoplexy September 8, suddenly.

The Caswell greenhouses have cut the first lot of carnations September 10. They are good flowers.   F. L. Z.

Columbus, O.

Aside from funeral work there is not much doing in the cut flower line. Asters are more plentiful than they were but quality is not up to standard. Some good gladioli are displayed but there is not much sale for them. A few roses are cut from the newly planted stock but mostly with short stems. Some improvement is noticed in the carnations since they were housed.

Harry Night, formerly with the Livingston Seed Company, has taken the position of manager for the S. W. Smith Floral Company.

E. J. Bolans, from Akron, was a visitor last week and explained the simplicity of his newly invented hinge. W. Sabransky, of Kenton, O., was also a recent visitor.　　　CARL.

SPRINGFIELD, MASS.—Business at the stores still continues quiet. About all that keeps moving is a little funeral work and there is none too much of that. The storemen are getting ready for business, stocking up the store with necessary supplies, etc. Asters in this vicinity have not done their best, thousands of them having been injured by the heavy rains and hail storms we have had lately, and it is hard to get perfect flowers from the field. Chrysanthemums are looking good at the different growers', and I think there is considerably more grown around here than in former years.　　　A. B.

WEST CHESTER, PA.—Isaac Passmore, of near Strode's Mill, has nearly completed his new carnation house and has begun moving in the plants. The new house is much larger than his others.

Boston Fern

Extra fine bench grown stock. $25.00, $35.00 and $50.00 per 100.

ASPARAGUS SPRENGERI.
2½-inch strong, $3.00 per 100; $25.00 per 1000.

ASPARAGUS PLUMOSUS NANUS.
3-inch, per 100 ....$6.00

ARAUCARIA EXCELSA.
Each ....75c. $1.00 and $1.50

SEEDLING FERNS IN FLATS.
Assorted Varieties, per flat $2.00

Ozone Park Nurseries,
OZONE PARK, L. I., N. Y.
Please mention the American Florist when writing.

BOSTON FERNS.

Extra fine, 2¼-inch, ready for 4-inch, only $4.00 per 100. 5-inch to 6-inch, ready for 7 and 8-inch, 40c to 50c. Bench stock October delivery, $3.00 to $4.00 per 100. Orders booked now.

A. J. Baldwin, NEWARK, OHIO.

Geo. Wittbold Co.,
1657 Buckingham Pl., CHICAGO, ILL.
Send for Price List on call

Palms and Ferns

Christmas Trees.

Gents write me for price list on Christmas Trees before placing your order elsewhere. We have a nice lot of them.

H. ALLEN, Harshaw, Wis.
Please mention the American Florist when writing.

CANANDAIGUA, N. Y.—The Florists' and Gardeners' Association is already making arrangements for its annual fall exhibition of flowers, which will probably be held the fore part of November. At a meeting September 9 Duncan Rhind, president, read a paper on the cultivation of chrysanthemums and Robert B. Ballantyne is to read a paper on roses at the next meeting.

Syracuse, N. Y.

The floral exhibit under the superintendency of H. C. Bard was the finest in the history of the State fair. P. R. Quinlan & Co. were the largest local exhibitors, carrying off thirty-one prizes. Hugh Mcneilly secured twenty-one prizes; John W. Mcneilly, twenty-two; David Mcneilly, twenty-eight; Joseph Hullar, forty; Mrs. Carrie Wittman, ten; John T. Roberts, one. W. S. Wheadon, took the first prize for floral designs, among which was the yacht "Reliance." Arthur Cowee exhibited several fans of gladioli, showing the possibility of indoor and outdoor decorations with these flowers. Mr. Cowee also exhibited a quantity of gladioli spikes of Groff's hybrids. Of the designs one fan was eight feet across. The other designs were a star and a maltese cross. James F. Barclay exhibited Nephrolepsis · Piersoni. Chas. Bechstadt of Oswego took first prize for a flower harp. Furness Brothers of Auburn made a fine exhibit of dahlias. School children showed a floral model of a building 4x9 feet. P. R. Quinlan & Co. supplied the floral blanket used on the trotting horse Major Delmar. This was designed by W. S. Wheadon and made of Liberty and Meteor roses, with asparagus and appropriately lettered.   A. J. B.

Detroit.

LOCAL CLUB HOLDS LIVELY SESSION.—
DONATION FOR HENRY SCHWEITZER.—A
NEW FLOWER STORE.—VISITORS.

A cold rainy night, such as last Wednesday evening was, did not deter over thirty members of the club from attending the regular meeting. The session was a lively one and embraced many matters for consideration. Another applicant was admitted to membership and two more applications received. Another donation of $25 was given to Henry Schweitzer, Mendota, Ill., whose letter of grateful acknowledgement of the previous remittance, was read. The attention of the club was called to the practice of some dealers selling palms and ferns on the market in violation of the city ordinance, which requires all persons selling such stock to be the actual growers of the same. A committee was appointed to bring the matter to the notice of the proper authorities. President Rackham, of the American Carnation Society, announced the offer of the Foley Manufacturing Company, Chicago, to give three $25 vases as prizes for the carnation exhibition. the class to be designated by the president. President Flowerday announced the entertainment committee for the season to consist of E. H. Beard. John Dunn, Walter Taepke, Eugene Oestreicher, Hugo Schroeter and Norman Sullivan. The congratulations of the club were extended to Fred Miesel, Jr., who that night was absent from the meeting attending his own marriage to Miss Amelia Kullmann, a popular East Side lady. At the next meeting of the club, October 7, the subject of soils will be discussed. The secretary will open the discussion by reading extracts from "King's Book on Soils."

Mrs. N. M. Nettleton has opened a neat little floral store at 126 Miami avenue. The equipment of the place indicates success for the popular owner who has the assistance in her enterprise of Miss K. Gentleman, a Toronto lady of extensive experience.

Visitors: Miss Eischen. Duluth. Minn.; Mrs. Gamble, Chas. W. Lewis, Mr. Smith, of Smith & Fetters, Cleveland.
J. F. S.

District of Columbia Notes.

Alexander B. Garden has just housed a lot of fine carnation plants and has other good ones yet in the field. He has a good showing of the new varieties, notwithstanding that there has been complaint in this vicinity of losses in field stock this year. James Quinn, formerly of Philadelphia, but more recently of Hagerstown, Md., is now fireman for A. B. Garden.

The ornamental bedding in the parks of Washington look well at this time. Cannas entered largely into the bedding this year, and some of the beds, notably in Lafayette park, are very fine.

Philip Gauges, of the botanical gardens is suffering from a muscular trouble, and walks with crutches. It is hoped that he may soon be again restored to health.

While there is a fair trade at times, the weather is yet too warm to expect business to be brisk.

A. Gude & Brother, at their Anacostia range, are preparing for a big winter business.

Fred. H. Kramer is pushing things for coming business.
S. E.

CHATHAM, N. J.—J. J. Foley had a notable wedding decoration September 9.

THE AMERICAN FLORIST

A WEEKLY JOURNAL FOR THE TRADE

America is "the Prow of the Vessel; there may be more comfort Amidships, but we are the first to touch Unknown Seas."

Vol. XXI.	CHICAGO AND NEW YORK, SEPTEMBER 26, 1903.	No. 799.

THE AMERICAN FLORIST

NINETEENTH YEAR.

Copyright 1903, by American Florist Company
Entered as Second-Class Mail Matter.

PUBLISHED EVERY SATURDAY BY

AMERICAN FLORIST COMPANY,

324 Dearborn St., Chicago.

Eastern Office: 79 Milk St., Boston.

Subscription, $1.00 a year. To Europe, $2.00.
Subscriptions accepted only from the trade.
Volumes half-yearly from August, 1901.

SOCIETY OF AMERICAN FLORISTS AND ORNAMENTAL HORTICULTURISTS.

OFFICERS—JOHN BURTON, Philadelphia, Pa., president; C. C. POLLWORTH, Milwaukee, Wis., vice-president; WM. J. STEWART, 79 Milk Street, Boston, Mass., secretary; H. B. BEATTY, Oil City, Pa., treasurer.

OFFICERS-ELECT—PHILIP BREITMEYER, president; J. J. BENEKE, vice-president; secretary and treasurer as before. Twentieth annual meeting at St. Louis, Mo., August, 1904.

THE AMERICAN CARNATION SOCIETY.

Annual convention at Detroit, Mich., March 3, 1904. ALBERT M. HERR, Lancaster, Pa., secretary.

AMERICAN ROSE SOCIETY.

Annual meeting and exhibition, Philadelphia, March, 1904. LEONARD BARRON, 136 Liberty St., New York, secretary.

CHRYSANTHEMUM SOCIETY OF AMERICA.

Annual convention and exhibition, New York, November 10-13, 1903. FRED H. LEMON, Richmond, Ind., secretary.

THIS ISSUE 40 PAGES WITH COVER.

The Canadians are Coming.

U. S. CUT FLOWER COMPANY AT ELMIRA.

[We give herewith additional particulars regarding the proposed cut flower growing establishment noted in our issue of September 19; these details appearing in the Elmira *Advertiser* of Sept. 11.—ED.]

Plans have been practically consummated for the establishment here of the largest greenhouse in the world. The enterprise will be backed by a capital of $600,000, and it will require an outlay of nearly $400,000 to get the buildings on a running basis. The parties at the head of the concern now have a large establishment at Brampton, Canada. President H. C. Mandeville, of the board of trade and William R. Compton will go to Canada to look over that plant.

The Board of trade announces that a contract has been made with the United States Cut Flower Company of New York, having a capital stock of $600,000, by which this company contracts to establish near this city a greenhouse plant with an area of 1,000,000 square feet of glass to cost in the neighborhood of $400,000 and not less than $350,000; the whole plant to be completed as soon as possible after the ground is broken.

The company agrees to employ not less than 300 male hands in its operation with a pay roll not less than $1,800 per week. This plant guarantees to operate for at least five years.

The United States Cut Flower Company will pay one-half of the costs of the location provided the city raises the other half. The total cost of the site will be $10,750 and must be raised within one month.

The president of this company is William Algie, who is one of the executors of the Dale estate, having now in operation at Brampton, Canada, a greenhouse plant with an area of 350,000 feet of glass. With his co-executor Mr. Algie has managed this plant for the past five years, during which time it has tripled in size. The vice-president is A. H. Mattox, of New York city. Robert O. King is the constructing engineer. He is a constructor of greenhouses and a member of one of the firms who erected and designed the Brampton plant. The treasurer of the company is G. C. St.

John, president of the New York Steam Company. The New York office of the company is No. 13 Astor place.

The company is ready to commence operations and at the request of Mr. Algie, William R. Compton and the president of the Board of Trade will at once investigate the Canada plant and upon their return a meeting of the Board of Trade will be called at which their report will be made; and means taken to raise the necessary money on the part of the city. So far as the company is concerned it is bound by contract to perform all the above statements provided the city performs its part.

The plan of accounting for the expense of production in each house is also as elaborate and complete as the book-keeping system of a big department store. Mr. Algie and his associates have long had their eye on the American market, as they could not compete from Canada, as this government charges a twenty-five per cent duty on all cut flowers sent into the country from with out. "In Canada," said Mr. Algie, "there are but 4,500,000 people, 2,000,000 of whom never spend a cent, but within a radius of 350 miles from this city there are 35,000,000 people, all of whom are good spenders." Though a million feet of glass should be used in the Elmira plant, that would furnish but two per cent of the cut flowers used in the city of New York alone, so that the field is practically unlimited. After careful looking over the ground in the various places he returned to Elmira. The great trunk lines running through Elmira attracted him here, as well as the many other facilities afforded in the Chemung valley. The business here would in no way interfere with local greenhouses, as flowers will only be sold to the trade. No retail store will be opened.

[September 19, it is reported that the United States Cut Flower Company will not ask a contribution from the city to apply on the cost of the land required for the plant, they being so well pleased that they purchased the site outright on their own account.—ED.]

The Evodias.

The natural order rutaceæ, although containing over eighty genera, has given comparatively few plants to the gardener to try his skill upon. Perhaps the best known genera are choisya, dictamnus, ptelea, citrus, skimmia, boronia, eriostemon and correa, and representatives of these have been grown for many years in gardens. To these may now be added another genus called evodia which has sprung into prominence within the past few years, chiefly owing to the introduction of a new species, E. elegans, from New Guinea. This plant has been put into commerce by Sander & Sons, of St. Albans, England, and may be regarded as a distinct and elegant addition to our stove plants. It has woody stems and in cultivation reaches a height of two to three feet in a 5-inch or 6-inch pot. In appearance Evodia elegans reminds one somewhat of a fine-leaved aralia—A. elegantissima, for instance—but the foliage is of a beautiful bright and fresh-looking green. The habit of the plant is also more compact and gracefully furnished with slender branches. Each leaf is divided into three long, narrow, strongly undulating leaflets, the edges of which are deeply and irregularly crenate, so that the whole plant also resembles some of the narrow-leaved and wavy crotons in character. As the lower leaves advance in age they gradually droop and thus effectively hide the pot in which the plant is growing.

The cultivation of this plant seems to be quite simple. Being a native of New Guinea it naturally requires plenty of heat and moisture, and must therefore be given stove treatment. A compost of good turfy loam, with a sprinkling of leaf mould and a dash of silver sand will suit it admirably, the drainage, of course, likewise being perfect. This species may be propagated in two ways, namely, by seeds and by cuttings. The plants flower freely, but the individual blossoms are by no means showy, being greenish in color and insignificant in size. They possess an odor, however, in common with many other rutaceous plants and this peculiarity has apparently been responsible for the generic name of evodia. Seeds are freely produced after the blossoms. They germinate readily and from them numerous examples may be produced. Cuttings of the half-ripened side shoots, with a heel of the old wood attached if possible, make nice plants if inserted in sandy soil, and kept in a warm and moist case for a short time until well rooted. From a commercial point of view Evodia elegans must be looked at as chiefly valuable for conservatory decoration, and there is no doubt that if hardened off somewhat it would also be a great acquisition as an ornamental table plant.

Another very ornamental evodia is E. triphylla. It is more sturdy in habit than E. elegans, and the leaves have much broader and more deeply lobed segments, which, however, are remarkable for their fresh and bright green appearance, and resemble some of the panaxes. The cultural treatment is precisely the same as for E. elegans, and I am not quite sure if E. triphylla would not make the handsomer plant of the two when well grown.

A species called E. hortensis has oblong simple leaves, with a somewhat wrinkled surface, but it has no particular claims to beauty. E. micrococca and E. fraxinifolia have been cultivated in botanic gardens, but are otherwise scarcely known.   W.

Exhibitions.

PART I.

[This article, while written originally for the private gardener, contains so much of general good sense that we believe the trade may profit by it.—ED.]

The time of the year has now arrived when we can with some degree of certainty fix the approximate output of our season's labor and forethought. There is no other time of the year fraught with such interest to the rural classes, nor do they at any other time feel so disposed to sociability and good fellowship; as proof of this mark the many country fairs, flower shows, and other exhibitions throughout the country. These exhibitions serve many purposes. The highest political dignitaries are there ascribing the success of the season to their righteous guardianship, or to the brand of seed that the government distributed free at their instigation. The fakir is there with old tricks and borrowed jokes ready to amuse everybody at his expense, and there is also present the careful student of men and crops. His interest is centered around the exhibits, he has come there to learn what others have been doing during the spring and summer. He forms his own mental picture and draws a comparison with his own products. There is also present the exhibitor himself and he is the man who above all others is likely to receive the most benefit. He may not receive a premium, he may not even get an honorable mention, nevertheless he has brought his best with him, he wants to know how he compares with the others. In comparison it is like a plumb or level in the hands of a good mechanic, or like putting the ten commandments up against our daily morals. Exhibitions are not at all times infallible. There are many things found on a show table that should not be found anywhere else; this, however, is the exception, not the rule. The fact that one exhibits proves an awakened interest, and it is also a fact that the average exhibitor does not receive many blue ribbons upon his first appearance. This is no discouragement, or ought not to be, to the beginner. It is the old hand who has seen many successful frays who takes defeat hard, while the beginner is spurred on by renewed success. The fact that any one is producing vegetables up to exhibition standard proves that he has his garden in the best possible condition up to the standard of intensive cultivation. This is when crops pay it shows the awakened interest and the desire to keep abreast of the times. It shows the man alive to the fitness of things and clearly demonstrates his knowledge of when a thing is at perfection. I could name many suc-

EVODIA ELEGANS.

Barge of the City of Ghent.   Decorated Steam Yacht.
WATER FLOWER CORSO IN GHENT.

cessful exhibitors to-day who commenced a few years ago by exhibiting a quart of onions, or half a dozen leeks; perhaps six heads of celery, or several ears of corn. The desire like that of putting money in the savings bank has grown, and like the same only needs a beginning. There is at most exhibitions much unseemly wrangling, and this is much to be deplored. Human nature is selfishly biased. Burns very properly says, "If it were a gift that God would give us, to see ourselves as others see us, it would from many an evil free us, and foolish notion." While we do not claim that all judges are perfect, we do assert that very few of them are dishonest. They are selected for their experience and integrity, and their decisions if rendered according to the schedule should be accepted in good faith. When exhibiting every exhibitor should make him or herself thoroughly conversant with the rules regulating the exhibition.

· JAS. T. SCOTT.

Floral Water Festival At Ghent.

The Society L'Avenir Horticole organized and directed a flower water festival under the auspices of the municipal authorities here. The festival took place along the canals and their banks and was very largely attended locally and by other visitors. The fire department very fittingly decorated its fire boat. A superb group of palms and plants was placed in front, while sixteen dolphins showing through the foliage cast jets of water from their conch shells. The eight-oared ▸kull of the Nautical Club excited much admiration. A steam yacht completely transformed into a floral garden of bluebells was another feature.

This action taken by the municipal authorities to develop the æsthetic sentiments, so seldom characteristic of these popular fetes, is certainly commendable and praiseworthy. Such an event is a lasting tribute to the reputation of Ghent, the city of flowers.—*Revue L' Horticole.*

Phalænopsis Amabilis Rimestadiana.

The genus phalænopsis is unquestionably among the finest orchids yet introduced, and although nearly all varieties are beautiful, the subject of our illustration is considered decidedly the best.

Phalænopsis Grandiflora Rimestadiana was imported from Java, where it is found growing at a higher elevation than any other species of phalænopsis, consequently it can be successfully grown in the cattleya house, as it does not

require the heat of other varieties. Its free growing habit and the freedom with which it produces its large flowers make it quite an acquisition to our orchid houses. This variety has been quite extensively distributed throughout England and the continent of Europe during

the past year. It is easily distinguished from the Bornean variety by its light green foliage and dark green flower spike, whereas in the Bornean variety the stem is yellow. The plant has just flowered in the collection of Dr. R. Schiffmann, St. Paul, Minn.

PHALÆNOPSIS AMABILIS RIMESTADIANA.

With the Growers.

W. K. HARRIS, PHILADELPHIA.

To spend an hour or two going about the Harris greenhouses is a great treat. One is here presented with the result of years of experience, coupled with intelligent effort, which together have produced beautiful and at the same time popular lines of stock, and all done in such an economical manner as to show a comfortable balance on the right side of the ledger at the end of each season.

Mr. Harris has long been a grower of specialties; his early winters were heliotropes and geraniums in pots in which he was an acknowledged leader in the early seventies. He imported and took hold of new varieties when they were very dear and when their survival of the ocean voyage was an uncertainty. New Life, Madam Lemoine and later Marie Lemoine were first imported by him and important American dealers were supplied from his stock. After that came the rose General Jacqueminot and then chrysanthemums, with which flower, in this country, at least, his name will always be associated. Pandanus Vietchii was another winner. Mr. Harris being the first grower to produce it in quantity and sell at a popular price. He then took up Ficus elastica, and his stock was easily much the largest and finest in this country for many years. Genista racemosa has been a favorite with him and is seldom seen as well done as here. Otaheite oranges were also made a leading specialty, and beautiful specimens produced in quantity.

The great virtue of the lily that bears his name was discovered by him and many thousands were sold at the time of its introduction. He also had the honor to find out and bring to the notice of the trade the good qualities of Bougainvillea Sanderiana, and his large specimens of this beautiful plant were truly a revelation to the flower buying public.

At present one of his leading specialties is the Boston fern, of which he has an immense stock, all in the very best condition, ranging in size from 6-inch pots up to 12 and 14-inch pans, the largest sizes all being finished on iron plant stands, an invention of his own, and are used in large quantities by all growers of choice

plants. He was not one of the early enthusiasts of this popular plant, but took it up when he saw the demand for well grown plants was not being filled. His stock in the various sizes is exceptionally well grown, it getting the necessary room and care.

Mr. Mills, Mr. Harris' foreman, says the Boston is a great decorative plant, and is bound to become even more popular in the future. "It is one of the best and one of the worst plants introduced of late years, good on account of its many virtues, and bad because it has driven out or cut down the production of what has been popular stock. However as we can take more money out of a house in a given space of time with the Boston than with the old favorites, we will let some one else supply them and go on working up the Boston." A new form of this fern has developed here, the feature being a crimping of the pinnate, which gives it quite a distinct appearance. It has the same robust and graceful flowing fronds and will, we think, be selected in preference to the original form when the two are placed side by side on the greenhouse floor.

Arecas are well done here. Mr. Mills likes to get good, strong plants in fives when making up larger plants, as when put together they grow more evenly, and their breaks at the bottom soon thicken up and fill up the base of the plant.

A house of Sago stumps, with nice heads, had been grown to give a little variety. Three houses had been given to rubbers the past few years, but this season the space has been cut down to two, owing to its wavering popularity or the competition of the Boston fern. A large lot of tree rubbers had just been brought in from outside, where they had been planted out for the summer. Mr. Mills said outside rubbers are apt to drop their leaves in early winter if not given a shift and a little new growth inside.

The house for extra large palms was devoid of such specimens, as above a certain size they are not found profitable. When they have to hunt a market Mr. Mills says they have to take a buyer's price, and this does not pay, so they are dropped for a while.

Several houses of chrysanthemums are coming on nicely, nearly all Mr. Harris' seedlings, good kinds which he has never sent out, preferring to have a monopoly of the flowers.

A house is devoted to a new or rather rare primrose, a yellow variety of the cowslip type which he hopes to have to at Christmas. From Mr. Mills' description it should prove a ready seller.

A house is given up to gardenias, the plants being all young, about twelve to

fifteen inches high, planted out on tables and looking to be in a very satisfactory condition, at least so says Mr. Mills.

The genista house is full of closely trimmed specimens. These are grown inside all the year round. A house of Pandanus Vietchii, with the Harris finish, and another filled with Dracena Ferminalis were both in splendid condition.

The Otaheite oranges will be showy plants when they ripen, being loaded with fruit. Outside a large block of ponderosa lemons were making a great growth and will soon be housed. The Bougainvilleas, of which there was a large number of thrifty plants, will be lifted and taken inside before danger of frost.

Large beds of hydrangeas plunged in hope and manure, had made a good summer growth and appeared to be ideal stock for forcing.

A long section of lath shading covered large plants of Deutzia gracilis that had been lifted from the open ground and potted and were being established anew preparatory to their winter rest. They ripen their wood and force much better than when lifted later in the season.

Long rows of the best pepper and solanum plants we have ever seen were soon to be lifted and gotten ready for the holiday season. Mr. Mills said there would be no difficulty with either the fruit or foliage when properly handled.

A large invoice of forcing bulbs had just arrived, principally jonquils and narcissus. Last season as many as 50,000 Von Sions were in flower at once and were all sold. A large supply has kept up all through the season, and this year the number forced will be largely increased. Large invoices of azaleas are also on the way, as this is also one of Mr. Harris' specialties.

Insects are kept well in hand by the liberal use of boiled tobacco dust and flower of sulphur thrown on with a Peerless blower. This is considered a very efficient remedy for green fly and red spider.

The executive force of the establishment is Mr. Harris, who spends here the early half of the day; his son, William K., Jr., a very careful and diligent young man, and Mary Mills, the foreman, who is as stock full of energy as a steam engine, and a salesman that tells one what he needs and who feels it his duty to see that he gets it. ROBERT KIFT.

PANDANUS VEITCHII is still a standard plant and we cannot get along without it. One advantage, however, that P. Sanderi has is that in large specimens it always retains its variegation clear to the bottom of the plant, whereas Veitchii becomes green.

ESTABLISHMENT OF MRS. R. MAUFF, DENVER, COL.

The Carnation. ✓

DISBUDDING.

No other work is more pleasant than disbudding carnations and the men most fitted for the work are glad to take their turn at it. The nimble fingers of the practiced hand glide swiftly from bud to bud, and a bench is gone over in a short space of time, with little mental or muscular effort spent on the work; that is, if it is done under proper conditions. It should not be necessary to lean painfully over wide benches or reach away above the line of vision, nor to stoop very low to disbud plants on solid beds. All these inconveniences can be done away with by having benches of a proper width— no more than five feet for middle benches —and having them of a proper height from the ground. Even in solid beds, where such are found to pay better than benches can at small expense be raised eighteen inches or more from the path and thus bring the buds into convenient reach. Side benches should be no more than three feet wide, or the back row of plants is apt to be neglected or attended to at the expense of the front row. The supports should be well down in the body of the plants, so as to have no useless tying material in the way, which is no small item when we consider that the plants are gone over at least once a week.

The disbudder should have a bag or box with him, for it is not well to drop even the smallest buds on the bench, and the walk is no place for them either. A little practice will teach him how to do the work with the greatest ease and dispatch. Care should be taken not to injure the leaves and stems. A carnation flower with half the leaves gone from the stem, or mutilated, is a sorry sight. If the stem is injured up near the bud it is apt to twist around and throw the flower into an awkward position. The laterals should be allowed to remain until they can be removed without injuring the remaining parts, but not until they have handles on them, so to speak.

Most varieties produce from four to six short-stemmed lateral buds on each leading shoot and from one to five growths below that are usually taken off for cuttings. It takes some experience to tell just when the one kind stops and the other begins, and it is well to learn to distinguish between a growth that will make a good plant and one that will root but produce nothing but buds. In case the pips near the base are not wanted for cuttings they should be removed in disbudding and all the strength thrown into the terminal buds. Cuttings taken from the flowering stems are not always ready before the flowers are cut, but on varieties on which they mature early they should by all means be taken off as soon as ready.

The length of stems produced will depend somewhat upon the judgment used in disbudding and in the removal of the cuttings. Some varieties produce a number of strong side growths well up the main stems, while the base is apt to remain bare. Especially is this the case when the plants are set too close together. It is well to remove the laterals as low down as possible, leaving only a few strong growths to depend on for future flowers. This will give greater length to the stems and keep the body of the plants low. A large cluster of side growths left on each main stem will result in overcrowding and an inferior grade of flowers later on.

There can be little doubt that disbudding properly performed tends greatly

to conserve the strength of the plants at a time when nature is very inactive. During the winter months most plants are more inclined to produce leaves than flowers, and forcing them to bloom at that season must be very exhausting. If we allowed every bud to develop, the plants would probably be greatly weakened, but allowing as little energy as possible to be spent in the production of bloom tissue should work a benefit of untold value to the plants.

As to whether or not it pays to disbud there is no longer any question. The grower who does not disbud is simply not in it with his competitors and must place his flowers into a grade all by themselves, for there is no grade recognized in the modern market so low as to comprehend stock of this character.

No matter what season of the year may be considered, the main fact remains the same—the man who supplies the highest grade of flowers gets the trade every time, other things being equal. There are those who believe in keeping up quality to the highest notch at seasons when the demand is brisk and prices soar up into the higher altitudes, but who, when the rush of flowers begins to swamp even the greatest demand slacken up on their efforts to keep up quality, utterly failing to see that at such times quality is needed more than ever in order to catch the eye and patronage of the best trade. It pays better to allow houses to stand idle than to produce flowers that will not pay for handling and other incidental expenses. When there is no profit in the best, the chance of making a profit out of the lower grades diminishes in direct ratio with the amount of drop down the scale of quality. The line of the mediocre, which is the boundry line between success and failure, will always be far removed from the man whose watchword is "quality."

.J.

The Decoration of Home Grounds.

No. 4.—Lonesome they are, but sometimes a single individual like this will awaken the dormant emotions of a person, after which companions are added and a healthy arrangement of characters is developed from the trivial beginning.

No. 5.—This picture shows how to protect and beautify without covering your house. Be careful and not destroy any point of utility.

No. 4. THE DECORATION OF HOME GROUNDS.

Establishment of Mrs. R. Mauff, Denver.

Our illustration shows a range of four houses recently erected by Mrs. R. Mauff, of Denver, Col. The houses are 100 feet long and sixteen and one-half feet wide. One side of the block is closed by a permanent outside wall. The other side and one end are arranged for future extension. The gutters are of cast iron, five inches wide, and the truss work enables the supporting points to be twelve and one-half feet apart. As the purlin is also supported by small trusses that go from the ridge to the gutter, and as ridge posts are avoided by the use of tie rods there are remarkably few posts in the structure. The leakage from the glass and the condensation gathers in small V gutters under the edge of the iron gutter. These small V gutters discharge into the arches or the post tops. From there the discharge is carried down the inside of the supporting posts to drains under the walks. The center valley gutter of the block is carried on arches whose legs span the walk, and the valley gutters on either side are carried on single posts.

The houses were built according to the patented system of the King Construction Company.

American Institute Show, N. Y.

I give you herewith briefly the features of the fall exhibition, held September 23-25. The vegetable section undoubtedly suffered because of the great storm of last week.

Decorative plants from Siebrecht & Son; orchids from Julius Roehrs and Lager & Harrell; fancy-leaved caladiums, a grand collection, from John Lewis Childs; native grapes from N. Corbury, of Montclair, N. J.; apples and pears from Elwanger & Barry.

The strawberry-raspberry was shown by L. A. Martin, gardener to H. H. S. Wood, and got as much appreciation as it deserved. In my opinion it ought never to have been shown as a "new fruit."

X.

MARY MORTON KEHEW, South Beacon street, Boston, secretary of the Civic League of Massachusetts, appeals for donations for the aid of school gardens, which may be given up for lack of some $400.

No. 5. THE DECORATION OF HOME GROUNDS.

Florists' Plant Notes.

DAHLIAS.

After the frost has destroyed the dahlias outside they should have the tops cut off and the clumps lifted and placed under a carnation bench. Keep them perfectly dry, but if a quantity of sand is thrown over the bulbs it will prevent them from shriveling. Be particular about keeping the varieties separate with board partitions, marking each sort with a large label. Cannas and caladiums should also be lifted and placed under the bench for the winter. A good plan is to place them on boards to keep them from growing before the proper time.

SWEET PEAS.

If any early sweet peas are wanted it is time now to sow a few of the leading varieties. Sown now they will come into bloom about the first of February. Blanche Ferry, Emily Henderson and Lady Penzance, are some of the best varieties to force. Sow them in 4-inch pots in rather heavy soil, and when about three inches high plant them out on a low bench with plenty of head room. Plant them eight inches apart in the row, with a two-foot space between the rows. They require rich, heavy soil and plenty of water and syringing. For support, use chicken wire stretched along each row. We sometimes plant them along the iron posts at the edge of a carnation bench, but this is hardly doing justice to the carnations, and the other plan will be found to be more satisfactory.

BULBS.

The Dutch bulbs, tulips, hyacinths and narcissus should be planted as soon as possible after they are received Tulips, Von Sion and Paper Whites, we plant in boxes of a convenient size for one man to handle. Any ordinary soil will grow them, sandy soil being preferred. Place them in a cold frame, and after a thorough watering cover them with a thin layer of sand before putting on the covering of soil. Four inches of soil covering is sufficient. It is a serious mistake to cover them with any material that has hard lumps of any kind in it, for as the bulbs grow they must have easy passage through the covering or they are liable to grow crooked. Dutch hyacinths of the first size we plant in pots, either singly in 4-inch pots, or three or four in 6-inch and 7-inch low azalea pots.

Miniature hyacinths are planted either in pans or boxes and handled precisely as the Romans are handled. It is also a good plan to plant a few tulips in small pans, but these must not be allowed to freeze too hard or the pans will crack. Before extremely cold weather sets in cover the bulbs with four or five inches of stable manure in addition to the soil to prevent them from freezing too hard, for while the bulbs can stand any amount of hard freezing, it is easier on the man that brings them inside to force if they are not frozen too solid. Do not attempt to force any Dutch bulbs before the first of the year, excepting Tulip Duc van Thol, which can be had for Christmas if brought into heat about the first of December. Paper White narcissus, also, can be forced as soon as they form roots; they can be had for Thanksgiving or before, but these bulbs must never be allowed to freeze for they cannot stand the slightest frost.   G.

Fall Work—Lawn, Shrubs, Trees.

At this time we are still able to distinguish the dead branches in the trees and shrubs from the live ones, and if we delay longer the leaves will have fallen, when it will require the eye of an expert to tell a dead branch from a live one, therefore take out the dead wood now.

Do not put away the lawn-mower yet. Another cutting will give you a chance to find the bare spots in your lawn, where a little seed sown now will make an even sward next June.

The spring is always such a busy season for the landscape man, and any work he can do now puts him just so much ahead then.

Soon after the hard frosts cut off the dead stalks of the herbaceous plants, such as boltonias, asters, helianthus, etc., and burn the rubbish; this will save work in the spring and during the winter the beds will have an orderly appearance, and besides you can apply mulching or fertilizer with more care should you wish to use any, as of course you will, for one cannot expect hardy plants to grow on from year to year without some stimulant. To be successful with these, as with annuals, they must have attention.

Tulip bulbs may be planted as late as the frosts will allow. Preferably, however, get them in before November 1. They need a little time to make roots. It

is not necessary to cover the tulip beds immediately after planting. The ground should first be frozen a couple of inches deep before any covering is put on, then when it is on the bulbs will remain at a somewhat even temperature and will not be injured by the sudden changes of heat and cold during the winter.

If contemplating planting groups of trees or shrubbery this is an excellent time to prepare the ground, and later on when the planting time arrives there will be no delay. Spade the ground where you intend to make the plantation; if the soil is poor add manure or commercial fertilizer. Many do not like fall planting believing that the plants are injured by the winter winds and heaved up by action of frosts and rains. This is partly true, but where one has much planting to do we must take advantage of every day that we can plant, because the spring planting season is very short indeed. A month in the fall and one in the spring is about all we can really depend upon. The writer believes that fall planting is equally as safe as spring, only that fall planted stock requires more attention; they must be properly mulched and the larger trees must be anchored against the action of wind and frost. With planting we must exercise more care, and see that the roots are down well and that the ground is well pounded down around them. Where the soil is very wet and the drainage poor better defer planting until the spring, for such conditions no fall planted tree or shrub can withstand.
    KAN.

New England Notes.

A movement is on foot in Hartford, Conn., for the better enforcement of the law against wild carrots and Canada thistles. The statute, which has been on the books since 1881, is as follows:

Every owner or possessor of lands shall cut down all wild carrots and Canada thistles growing thereon, or in the highway adjoining, so often as to prevent their going to seed: and upon failure to do so, any person aggrieved, or any citizen of the town wherein the lands are situated, may complain to any grand juror of said town, who shall thereupon forthwith notify such owner or possessor of such complaint; and said grand juror shall be paid for such service from the treasury of the town 10 cents for each mile of travel in giving such notice. If said owner or possessor shall still neglect to comply with the provisions of this section, he shall be fined not more than $5, for each and every day of such neglect after said notice; and the expense of the grand juror who served the notice shall be included in the cost of the prosecution.

The Retail Trade.

THE variegated pine apple has no equal in its class as specimen plant.

AMONG recent introductions for decorative work, Dracæna Goldeana is one of the most useful of plants because of its great durability.

CUT FLOWERS are in a broad sense a luxury. In the sale and delivery of them handsome boxes may be used as effectively and profitably as in the sale of confectionery.

EARLY CHRYSANTHEMUMS do not always bring in the money that the late ones do. People are not all back from the country in September, and then there are the asters. At Thanksgiving is the time to sell chrysanthemums.　　S.

A Model Village Establishment.

Hanover, Mass., in a town of some 2,000 inhabitants. In the directory it appears that George F. Sylvester is the only florist in town. One possible reason for Mr. Sylvester's monopoly appears, we think, in the view of his establishment herewith presented. Does it not stand to reason that, while provided with such a tasteful little place, flower buyers would never care to go elsewhere? Compared with many of the country greenhouses, unadorned, weather-beaten and slovenly, it is a gem, indeed.

A Model Village Establishment.

In these houses Mr. Sylvester grows a good variety of the plants and flowers most generally called for in local trade. When a larger supply is needed for special occasions he has access to the Boston wholesale markets. He is much interested in and does a good business in the planting of trees, shrubs and hardy perennials, which he supplies from a nursery connected with his establishment. He finds an increasing demand and growing satisfaction generally in the old-fashioned hardy plants, such as phloxes, hollyhocks, canterbury bells, columbines, sweet williams, larkspurs, foxgloves, etc., which give so much brilliancy and variety all the season through and are prized by favorites with people of refined taste and cultivated mind. Another specialty which Mr. Sylvester believes should be more generally encouraged is the chrysanthemum in the hardy garden varieties.

The Art of Decoration.

The florist, when called upon to execute a piece of decorative work, frequently finds himself confronted with a customer with decided opinions, which may or may not be commendable, as to what is required and how the work is to be done. Sometimes a little diplomatic persuasion may be used to good effect, but where evidences of insistence on the part of the customer are apparent it is usually the wisest course to submit and carry out the work as ordered, otherwise a good customer may be lost, and at best nothing gained, as it is too much to expect a buyer to be pleased with work done contrary to his or her preferences. Unfortunately the element of imitation often enters much too strongly into the consideration of a prospective decoration; local rivalries and a desire to have something more pretentious than something previously seen elsewhere frequently interferes disastrously with a proper handling of the affair. There are other considerations which may, at times tend to thwart the decorator's conceptions of what would be appropriate, such as limitations regarding the cost, the transportation of material in very cold weather, etc., but when given a reasonable freedom as to the material and the method of its use, the only remaining essential to success in a majority of cases is an artistic perception combined with a liberal measure of common sense on the part of the decorator.

Fashion and "prevailing styles" count for nothing except in a very general way, and hard and fast rules for floral decorative work are impracticable. Styles of expression may and do change with the ever-varying fashions in architecture or dress; periods of plain alternate with periods of ornate; dark and massive with light and graceful, but, as in architecture so in floral adornment, true art is never out of fashion; its principles cannot change.　　W. J. S.

Pansies.

The colors exhibited by pansies are most extraordinary. Some are as near black as flowers can be. The richest purples are common, with clear, yellow, intense violets, lavenders, tender dove-colors, rich maroons and browns. On the lower petal, which in the violets is hollowed behind into a nectar bearing spur, they can be usually seen, when the ground tint is not too dark to obscure them, the so-called "guiding lines" to which old Sprengel first called attention. He claimed for them a significance which science has of late re-affirmed, maintaining that they serve as so many clues or lines of direction to assist insects in finding the nectar.—*Dr. W. Whitman Bailey in American Botanist.*

Lespedeza Bicolor.

Herbaceous Plant Notes.

Purple asters, pale baltonias and tall and stately veronicas with immense, broadly branched heads, all the Japanese anemones are out in full bloom. The Gaillardias seem to be at their very best. Anthemis tinctoria and Coreopsis monstrosa are still a compact mass of yellow, the blue dense spikes of Lobelia syphilitica and the gorgeous colored hybrids of L. cardinalis with their taller spikes and larger flowers are grand in the month of September. A number of the sedums, among them S spectabile, S. anacampseros and S. Sieboldii, the deep pink Silene Schaftæ, the ever blooming, large flowered Geranium Manescavii, the pretty cobalt blue Plumbago larpentæ, the free profuse blooming blue Eupatorium cœlestinum the golden Rudbeckia speciosa and the larger Zinnia-like, lasting R. purpurata, Campanula rotundifolia, Lychnis Flos-cuculi semperflorens, Tricyrtis hirta, Lespedeza bicolor, Clematis paniculata and Polygonum cuspidatum are all September flowers, and yet we often hear the complaint that there is a lack of variety in color of fall blooming perennials.

Clematis Paniculata.

Most all of the above mentioned will continue in good shape until severe frost sets in, and the list could easily be enlarged by adding plants which are now in bud ready to open out later in the season. There should be no difficulty in finding fall bloomers of effective colors in perennials for every possible situation in a garden. The trouble seems to be that there are too many to select from and the right things are overlooked.　　J. B. K.

The American Pomological Society.

The American Pomological Society held its twenty-eighth biennial convention in Horticultural Hall, Boston, on September 11, 12 and 13. The exhibition in connection therewith was very comprehensive and interesting, some two thousand plates of fruit from all parts of the continent being shown. Ellwanger & Barry, of Rochester, N. Y., were the largest exhibitors. The sessions were busy ones, the number of addresses and discussions being probably greater than the Society of American Florists has listened to in five consecutive years. Some of the papers read were: "The San Jose Scale in the Orient," by Dr. C. L. Marlatt; "The Attitude of the Schools to Country Life," Prof. L. H. Bailey; "Fruit Gardens, What They Are and What They Are For," J. Horace McFarland; "Relation of Cold Storage to Commercial Orcharding," G. H. Powell; "Progress of Pomology in America," Prof. John Craig; "Grading and Packing Fruits for Long Shipment," J. H. Hale; "Fruit Inspection and the Export Trade," Hon. W. A. McKinnon; "Pure Food Legislation and Its Relation to the Fruit Grower," Dr. W. D. Bigelow; "Pomology at the St. Louis World's Fair," F. W. Taylor; "Fruit Culture in the Pacific Northwest," Prof. S. W. Fletcher; "Judging Fruits by Scale of Points," Prof. A. Waugh, and "Ideals in Pomology," the latter subject being divided into some twenty sub-heads, assigned to as many different speakers.

Officers were elected as follows: President, J. H. Hale, South Glastonbury, Conn.; secretary, Prof. John Craig, of Cornell University; first vice-president, C. W. Garfield, Grand Rapids, Mich.; treasurer, L. R. Taft, Michigan Agricultural College.

The visitors were given a ride in the Boston parks by courtesy of the Park Department.

Resolutions expressing thanks for the efficient, devoted and untiring services of the retiring officers, President Charles L. Watrous and Secretary William A. Taylor, and thanking the Massachusetts Horticultural Society for its hospitality and its aid in making the convention a notable success were passed. Another resolution, approving the enactment of a federal law to regulate commerce in foods between the United States and foreign countries, and between the various states, to the end that consumers shall be protected against imitation fruit products under false labels, was passed, and a resolution, authorizing the appointment of a committee to formulate and publish scales of points for the judging of fruits with special reference to their use at the Louisiana purchase exposition in 1904, was approved and passed.

Greenhouse Building.

Gloversville, N. Y.—Thomas Barson, one house.

Baldwinsville, Mass.—C. C. Streeter, cucumber house 24x108.

Norfolk, Conn.—The Misses Eldridge, one house.

Whitinsville, Mass.—G. M. Whitin, conservatory.

Greenland, N. H.—E. G. Clough, range of houses.

Whitenton, Mass.—Albert Field, range of houses.

Clinton, Mass.—F. P. Sawyer, carnation house 22x122.

Westfield, Mass.—S. E. Barton, one.

Philadelphia.

FLOWERS SCARCE, BUT HOPES ARE HIGH.
—NO VIOLETS.—DAHLIAS PLENTY AND
GREENS PLUS.—STEM ROT IN CARNATION
BELT.—LOCAL.

There is quite a bunch of buyers at the market every morning and all interested are much pleased with the outlook. Sampman, of Myers & Sampman, says: "You can say what you like, but I tell you this market is going to be the American Beauty center this season, as we have three of the largest growers who are sending nearly all their stock here, and the boxes wont be opened until they get here for anybody. There will be no opening up at the depot as last year. We have all made an agreement and the buyers must come to the market if they want the goods."

From the general appearance of the stock it looks as if the coming season's flowers will exceed that of last year both in quality as well as quality, the commission men saying, almost without exception, that their stocks will be larger this winter. The extra supply of the commission houses is due partly to new out of town shippers, and their list of consignors also comprizes quite a few of the local growers, who have gotten tired of lugging their boxes every morning over the route of the stores.

Dahlias are now about their height, but the quality is not quite as good as last year. This is probably due to the late storm, which knocked them about at a great rate. Word comes from the Acto dahlia farm, however, that the plants have straightened up and that good flowers may be expected.

Single violets are offered every day, but they are disappointing, as all they have is fragrance; the color is bad, and they are very small and hardly last the day out. Fred Ehret was first in with doubles last Tuesday, but the fact that they were the first was about the only point in their favor. Specials in all the classes move lively at good prices, in fact, there does not seem to be enough to go around. The quality is improving, although not any too fast, as the discriminating customers are putting in an appearance, and any old thing will no longer do.

Eugene Bernheimer, who visited the carnation growers of Chester and Lancaster counties, says some complain of the loss of 50 per cent of their plants from stem rot and rather than buy more plants some are filling in with tomatoes.

The H. A. Dreer Company are reunpacking this season's importation of azaleas. There are 52,000 of them all told, about enough to fill a good-sized ship. They arrived in excellent condition.

There is a good demand for carnations, which is not being filled. S. S. Pennock is handling a few fine white and something extra in pink in Floriana, an extra choice flower for the season of the year. Asters are about done, and there will be a scarcity of small flowers until carnations increase and the small chrysanthemums make their appearance. None of any kind have reached this market as yet.

Robert Crawford, of Eleventh and Locust streets, underwent an operation at the hospital last Tuesday to release the muscles of his right hand, which had contracted.

Leo Niessen says there is no longer any doubt about it, the wholesale cut-flower center of the city is below Thirteenth street.

There is fair amount of business doing,

although one would suppose from the scarcity that the demand was much greater.

Green is the long suit of all the dealers at this time, but in spite of all they can do it seems to accumulate.

Visitors: John N. May, Philip Hauswirth and family. K.

Boston.

MARKET LANGUISHES.—ROSES ARE POOR.—CHOICE VALLEY AND ASTILBE JAPONICA.—LOCAL.

Business suffering from general debility just now brought on by a variety of causes. Roses extremely poor in quality, particularly American Beauties, which look as though a blight had struck the bud and stopped both color and growth. Asters are plentiful and good. The first chrysanthemums are in market and bring $1 to $1.50 a dozen, while the asters with flowers equally as good bring the same figure for a hundred as the chrysanthemums fetch for a dozen. Why is it?

The Massachusetts Horticultural Society's annual exhibition opened Thursday afternoon and closes Sunday night. The show contained much of interest. The usual superb display of stove and greenhouse plants from large private establishments has been brought out, and excels in some respects any recent exhibition. That crotons especially is far ahead of anything ever seen here.

Yamanaka, the Japanese importer, was awarded a silver gilt medal for a group of Japanese p a and H. A. Dreer honorable mention for a new ornamental grass and new asparagus. Lager & Hurrell made a fine display of orchids including some lælias. In the cut flower section dahlias unique predominated, and in variety and quality excelled all past exhibitions. The cactus varieties were especially striking. The choicest flower in evidence at present is lily of the valley of excellent quality and the oddest thing for the season is Astilbe japonica, which Carl Jurgens is sending from Newport to Welch Brothers. Nobody seems to want it, but it suggests vividly the possibilities of cold storage.

Capt. D. W. Simpson entertained a happy delegation of the Horticultural Club on a harbor excursion, September 19. It was one of the memorable events of the season.

Edward L. Hallowell, 42 years old, was found dead in the office of the Shady Hill Nursery, of which he was treasurer, on the morning of September 19.

A. Jackson Norton, late with H. P. Kelsey, is now reported with W. A. Manda on the road with much success.

Ed. Hatch has arrived home from his European trip in fine order.

Visitors: J. F. Huss and Theo. Wirth, ford, Conn.; J. A. Evans, Richmond, Ind.; Lawrence Cotter, Danville, Pa.

DENVER, COLO., September 25.—Telegram.—A. B. Seaman, secretary of the Park Floral Company, died this morning very suddenly.

ITHACA, N. Y.—John E. Foote, florist, is reported to have disappeared about September 3. Attachment notice was posted on the door of his greenhouse. Foote had been located here several years.

JOLIET, ILL.—Joliet Improvement Association, James K. Ferriss, secretary, is out with the preliminary premium list of their second annual show which occurs November 4-7. Write for entry blanks.

Chicago.

TRADE ACTIVE.—WHITE STOCK IN DEMAND.
—CENTENNIAL FESTIVAL BEGINS.—THE
ENTERTAINMENT COMMITTEE ROOMING
HORTICULTURE.—PIESER CLAIMS PRICES
NOT ADVANCED WITH ADDED COST TO
PRODUCE.—LOCAL.

Trade has been quite active all week with a brisk demand for good roses. Carnations are much improved in quality, but the demand for these, particularly colored, has not been lively. Whites, however, have found a fairly good market. Asters, particularly white, are still in good demand, but this week will probably wind up the best of them.

Manny Pieser, of Kennicott Bros. Company, reports a good shipping trade up to the latter part of the week. Since it has been dull, although business is about on a par as compared to this time last year. He states that some growers complain that the price of flowers has not advanced in proportion to the increase in price of coal and other supplies, and they hope for a good demand throughout the fall and winter season so they can have something left in the stocking after settling up with the coal, glass and the many other trusts.

Bassett & Washburn are cutting the first Easter lilies of the season and they are in good demand at a $1.50 to $2.00 per dozen. They are produced from Longiflorum giganteum (cold storage), and Mr. Washburn states that while not as free blooming as Harrisii or other varieties of Japan longiflorum, they are practically free from disease.

E. F. Winterson Company are receiving some very choice single violets and Higinbotham carnations, both of which find a ready sale. The fall catalogue of the firm is now going out. Ed says "There's nothing to it" when asked about the report of losing his voice.

E. C. Amling has the pipes laid for some special lines of desirable stock which he will uncover a little later.

E. H. Hunt is busy with French and Dutch bulbs and reports a good demand for both hyacinths and tulips.

· Gladiolus and tuberoses are holding their own. A few auratums are still to be had.

Deamud is handling some good dahlias from Cushman Gladiolus Company.

Frank Garland is receiving some good Perles and Sunsets.

At the final meeting of the entertainment committee of florists, seedsmen and allied trades Monday night it was thought wise to try to canvass some of the existing esprit der corps and turn it for the good of horticulture in the Garden City. To that end a committee consisting of Messrs. Rudd, Wienhoeber, Dickenson, Bentley, Foley, Reardon, Bruns, Hanswirth, Winterson, Kill and Vaughan was appointed to suggest ways and means to that end and be prepared to report Friday night.

The centennial festival begins to-day. State street is gay with bunting and huge typical canvases on store fronts, not omitting O'Leary's cow. Night signs will blaze. A big influx of visitors is certain. Much persuasion is not needed to bring excursionists to Chicago in September. The George Wittbold Company have big jobs on hand in this connection, and an advance visitor has already bumped himself in falling over logs the Wittbolds are using for the historic block-house of Fort Dearborn.

At the monthly meeting September 22 of the special park commission of the city of Chicago, Architect D. H. Perkins, chairman of the committee on rural

parks, was selected to prepare a report on a metropolitan park system for the city. Mr. J. Jensen, who is a member of the commission, is to prepare that part of the report applying to dendrology and geology.

The good old times have come again when the hustlers in the wholesale shops will chase the depots for the night trains with a big box in each hand and under each arm, as the union express drivers will not pound on the doors after six o'clock.

The Schiller estate has entirely remodeled its store and conservatory at 897-899 West Madison street and is putting in a new steel front in the Jackson boulevard store.

Three lookout committees are searching for a possible location for the fall flower show. Vacant buildings, new or old, near or far, are being considered.

"Gentleman Joe" Curran at Fleishmann's has been busy with Standard club and other work consequent on the Jewish holidays.

A special meeting of the Florist Club is called for Friday evening at the Sherman House and a big attendance is expected.

The next regular meeting of the Florist Club will occur October 14. Election of officers will be the order of business.

Phil Hauswirth has returned from his Eastern trip, having visited Philadelphia, New York and Billy Kasting.

Capt. A. I. Simmons, 342 West Sixty-third street, is installing a new heating system in his show house.

The Peterson nursery is busy with peonies. Other stock is ripening up well and can be dug early.

The horse show is carded for October 26-31. It cannot fail to benefit the retailers.

J. F. Kidwell has left for northern Wisconsin on a hunting trip, to be gone two weeks.

The funeral of ex-Senator C. B. Farwell drained the market of white stock Friday.

S. Nelson & Sons have added glass 16 by 28 feet to their Indiana street place.

Visitors: J. D. Eisele, with H. A. Dreer.

St. Louis.

STOCKS LIGHT.—DEMAND SLOW.—WORLD'S
FAIR DEPARTMENT ACTIVE.—ANNUAL
FAIR AT HAND.

The propagating department at the World's Fair grounds is a busy place just now. Henry Stocke, formerly propagator at Forest Park, is in charge. Two hundred thousand plants are already on hand, with thirty men making cuttings. It is estimated that four million plants will be used in the landscape department. About one million pansies and bellis will be used in the early spring. The range of hot beds is being piped for steam heating.

Alex. Johnson, of Wellston, is hustling to get his new 20x125 house finished before frost. He is doing the constructing work himself, and as he expressed it, "it takes more work than one imagines." The carnations are not as good as they might be, but they are coming on. Other stock is doing nicely.

There is not much in the way of trade in St. Louis. Stock has been coming in in limited quantities though of much better quality. The weather has been so unfavorable that there is practically no demand. Prices change but little.

The Missouri Botanical Garden received four big tree ferns from the Hawaiian Islands last Monday, the 21st. The plants are thirteen to sixteen feet in

height and came in fine condition. They are quite an addition to the fern dome, where they may be found.

The meeting of the St. Louis Florist Club will not be held on Thursday, October 8, as formerly announced, but will be on Thursday, October 15. The 8th is the big day at the St. Louis Fair and many of the florists have exhibits to attend to.

Visitors: J. P. Brown, editor of Arboroculture; J. D. Eisele and Geo. D. Clark, of H. A. Dreer Company.

Geo. Waldbart has recently filled his show houses with a fine lot of palms.

New York.

The cut flower market took an upward turn last Saturday and has continued to advance steadily, all good material finding a satisfactory sale. All kinds of fancy material is scarce owing partly to the demands of the Jewish holidays.

Another small greenhouse is to be added to the nursery range at the Botanical Garden and two large aquatic tents are to be constructed.

William Sampson has given up his wholesale business at the New York Cut Flower Company to take a position with Thomas Young, Jr.

The greenhouses of Cassidy & Sons were damaged by fire to the amount of $5,000 on the morning of September 12.

Albany, N. Y.

The fall season is opening with every prospect that business will be up to expectations. Society people have already announced a number of debutantes. The Hebrew holidays this week caused a demand for considerable high grade stock most of which was used for gifts.

H. G. Eyres has decorators at work in his store on North Pearl street, making some notable improvements, among which are green burlap covered sidewalls with gilt panels, an installation of mirrors, and a new system of electric lamps. Mr. Eyres will build a new forcing house for Easter stock 18x100 feet. Lord & Burnham will do the work.

Visitor: Walter Mott, who reports business good. R. D.

WINCHESTER, MASS.—Mr. and Mrs. S. W. Twombly celebrated the sixtieth anniversary of their marriage on September 14. Mr. Twombly is 81 years of age and still very sprightly.

NEWTOWN, PA.—H. W. Wieland is much pleased with the season's outlook. A new soil tried has brought great results and he says his stock never looked finer at this season.

CANANDAIGUA, N. Y.—McKerr & Hawley have succeeded R. H. McKerr, florist, here, Fred. C. Hawley having purchased an interest. The new firm will build one greenhouse 30x85 feet.

DURHAM, N. H.—Progress on the New Hampshire College greenhouses is very slow. The appropriation for them by the state was $7,000.

REMSEN, N. Y.—Edward S. Pirnie has commenced business with two carnation houses, one 20x100 and one 12x30 feet.

TACOMA, WASH.—Mary Hayden has opened a flower store at 912 Pacific avenue.

DANBURY, CONN.—T. H. Judd has moved his flower store to 197 Main street.

MILWAUKEE, WIS.—Kapsalis & Lam bros succeeded Kapsalis & Company.

THE AMERICAN FLORIST

NINETEENTH YEAR.

Subscription, $1.00 a year. To Europe, $2.00.
Subscriptions accepted only from those
in the trade.

Advertisements on all except cover pages,
10 Cents a Line Agate: $1 00 per inch.
Cash with Order.

No Special Position Guaranteed.

Discounts are allowed only on consecutive insertions, as follows—6 times, 5 per cent; 13 times,
10 per cent; 26 times. 20 per cent;
52 times, 30 per cent.

Cover space sold only on yearly contract at
$1.00 per inch. net, in the case of the two
front pages, regular discounts applying only to the back pages.

The Advertising Department of the AMERICAN
FLORIST is for florists, seedsmen and nurserymen
and dealers in wares pertaining to those lines only.

Orders for less than one-half inch space not accepted.

Advertisements must reach us by Wednesday to
secure insertion in the issue for the following
Saturday.   Address

AMERICAN FLORIST CO., Chicago.

THE days are at hand when on the
banks of the Wabash "the scarlet maple
leaves are reflected on the dark and silent
stream," as Robert Craig said at the
Horticultural Congress of 1893.

WILL Subscriber, Manayunk, Pa.,
kindly give us his name, also the address
of the makers of the boiler referred to.

THE old wide petaled form of decorative dahlias have almost disappeared from
English shows, according to *Garden.*

THE Canadian Florist deplores the fact
that it must depend on its American
friends for so much of its local news. So
sorry.

PLAN now regarding shipments of
plants, shrubs, bulbs or other perishable
stock by freight, not to be on the road
after November 10.

THE advertisements of palms, ferns and
decorative plants in this issue are timely.
Careful buyers should ship this stock by
freight during October.

WITH the cooler weather comes exemption from the necessity of cutting rose
buds so close. The market will now
stand a more mature flower.

THE Co-Operative Produce Company,
hailing from 111 Nassau street, New
York, are out with a "Talk on Mushrooms" which savors of ginseng literature. It says, among other things, "Success is ever now knocking at your door."

CROTONS should be left out in the open
air as late as possible in order to get fine
color on the foliage. The high-colored
tops may be easily made into beautiful
low-foliaged specimens by mossing the
stems. After the roots have begun to
appear cut the stems and plunge the tops
in a hotbed for about two weeks.

THE PRESENT is a critical time in rose
growing. They must be held up to the
mark yet not carried beyond it in the
matter of temperature, ventilation,
watering and feeding. A little firing is
needed on the damp, dewy nights now
prevailing, even if the ventilators must
be left open to restrict the temperature.

MANY of the wholesale growers about
New York are using the folding corrugated pasteboard boxes instead of
wooden cases in which to ship their
flowers on account of the heavy express
charges on return empties. The pasteboard boxes are held at the wholesalers
until there is a large number on hand
which when packed flat make a small,
compact package.

BOOKKEEPING and account forms for
same by R. F. Tesson, as read at the
Milwaukee convention has been printed
in pamphlet form by the AMERICAN
FLORIST and will be mailed FREE on
request to any florist. Employers may
have extra copies to distribute among
their employes. The address is of much
permanent value and well worth the
study of our young men.

THIS season has been a very profitable
one for indoor cucumber growing. The
crop has now been all marketed and
spinach and lettuce will fill the houses
until late winter when it is again time to
put in cucumbers. Sterilization of soil is
generally followed by the large growers
The past season has been the most
unfavorable for many years in New
England for the out-door cucumber
growers.

Florists' Hail Association.

Since August 1, 1903, the Florists'
Hail Association has adjusted and paid
53 losses, amounting to about $7,100.
Insurance has been taken upon nearly
half a million square feet of glass since
the above date in addition to that
already insured.

JOHN. G. ESLER, Sec'y.

Shippers' Responsibility.

Although the law as interpreted by
certain courts and in certain states may
tend to put responsibility for loss or
delay in transit on to the buyer, we believe
shippers should take concerted action in
such matters. They should make it
unprofitable for the express companies
to ignore any demand made by their
customers or themselves to compensate
for careless service. If not we will pat-
ronize markets which are nearer home
than Chicago. There are times when
delay is almost fatal to the retailer. He
is depending upon an order, it may be a
large one, for a funeral or wedding,
which if not received on time will be a
dead loss to him, besides, in the case of a
funeral, the loss of many customers, for
it will be too late for either florist or
customers to send elsewhere. Further,
it seems to us that the wholesale dealer
is in a much more favorable position for
dealing with the express companies.
Unless shipper and retailer work together
it will result in the western trade making
itself independent of the eastern markets,
by increasing its growing capacity.

RETAIL FLORIST.

Nebraska City, Neb.

BLACK SPOT REMEDY.

ED. AM. FLORIST:—I enclose some diseased rose leaves and wish to know
whether the trouble is black spot. Please
give remedy.   H.

The leaves received were certainly
affected with black spot, with regard to
which one of our most successful rose
growers prescribes as follows: "Two
ounces of carbonate of copper to one
quart of 26° ammonia water. Use one
gill of the mixture to about two gallons
of water. This is a preventive rather
than a cure. We spray with the solution
two or three times a week, syringing well
under the leaves. It does no harm whatever to the plants."

Invaluable.

Your paper is invaluable to me.
Owatonna, Minn.   L. P. LORD.

Greenhouse Sash.

ED. AM. FLORIST:—I am about to
build two houses, each measuring 11x74
feet, one side of each house to be of movable sash. On which side of the house
would you think it advisable to place the
sash? High winds are generally from the
west, southwest or northwest, the cold
waves and snow, usually from the east
and northeast. There is some protection
from trees on the north side. The sash
is the regular 3½x16 feet with 8x10 glass.
The heating is to be hot water with
pipes under benches. I enclose sketch.
S. K.

So far as the winds are concerned there
appears to be little choice whether the
movable sash are on the south or the
north sides. As a rule I would have
them on the sides least exposed to wind.
As the hot-bed sash will obstruct more
light than sash-bars it will be well to
have the sash on the north side of the
houses.   L. R. TAFT.

Glazing Greenhouse.

ED. AM. FLORIST:—In glazing a greenhouse with liquid or rubber putty is it
necessary to bed the glass in putty or
should it just be covered, glass to be
lapped.   A. J. S.

In using liquid putty it is only necessary
to apply sufficient to give the wood on
which the glass rests a free coating and
fill the indentations if any exist.

Apprenticeship of a German Gardener.

First of all, it is required of an aspirant
to have a fair school education; if possible,
language (Latin especially) and geography,
which help him considerably and save a lot
of study in after days. If the young man
has found a place to enter as an appren-
tice, the majority of establishments charge
a certain sum per annum. Germany generally from 100 to 150 marks ($25 to $37.50);
France and Belgium about the same. Then
he must enter a contract to serve a time,
generally three years. In rare cases he
will be allowed a small compensation at the
last year of his time.

There are some places which take apprentices without pay, but then he must generally serve a time of four years.

This time will never be forgotten by any
young man who has passed through it. It is a
time of hard work and not only long days
of hard work—in many places it is compulsory to pass through evening school to
collect knowledge in landscape drawing,
geometry and surveying. This goes through
to sometimes three years during winter.
Then besides at home it is not only practical work, which occupies the young man,
but also theoretical. There are the names
of all the plants to be learned, their nature, native country, under what conditions
they grow best, what soil is best for them;
books have to be bought and studied; many
employers require their apprentices to keep
a day book in which all work done during
the day has to be entered. Not only super-
ficial, but to the minutest detail. After
twenty-six years the writer recalls many
instances of apparent negligence and the
rather strong reprimands he received. In
this way the time passes for the appren-
tice under constant work with few and
long between pleasures. After the expiration of his time he is called an assistant
and leaves his certificate, of which every
young gardener is as proud of as any
young girl of a new Easter hat.

Then his time comes to travel. Of every
young gardener it is expected that he sees
other establishments, if possible, other
countries, and widen his knowledge. We
all, who passed through the mill, know how
proud we felt and thought we knew it all;
but no matter how hard we worked and
studied, after getting to a new place he finds
out how little he really does know. Wherever he goes there are different methods,
other plants, always something new; so it
keeps him hustling to keep up to date.
It is a constant learning as long as he is
in the profession. But that is a gardener.
In a future issue we will go more into
details regarding the different branches as
above mentioned.—*H. W. Unger, in Union
Gardener.*

Cincinnati.

CARNATIONS AND ROSES ARE BACKWARD.—GREENS PLENTY.—FLORAL DISPLAY AT FESTIVAL A SUCCESS.—LOCALS.

The floral display Thursday at the fall festival was a grand success. The show was under the auspices of the Cincinnati Florists' Society; but one thing the writer regrets very much is that not one of the exhibitors was a member of the society. It is surprising that not one of the local storemen, with the exception of George & Allan, is a member of the society. As stated last week, Hardesty & Company received first prize with table of American Beauties and lily of the valley; Julius Baer second, with Kaiserin and Bride roses, Farleyense and lily of the valley; Chas. Gardner third, with center piece built of crotons, Adiantum Farleyense and rune-atum, Pandanus Veitchii and Cocos Weddeliana. This table was arranged by Robt. Betz and Miss Edith Kyatt and attracted much attention. R. A. Kelly Company had a table of American Beauties, lily of the valley and cattleyas. J. T. Conger, of Hartwell, O., had a neat table of American Beauties. A. Wiegand, of Indianapolis, a visitor, was very enthusiastic, believing it the first exhibit of table decorations ever shown in this country.

Trade for this time of the year is excellent, with not enough stock for demand. Good carnations are very scarce, also roses. A nice lot of asters are being shipped into the city, which help out considerably. No lily of the valley at present, while smilax, adiantum and asparagus is plentiful. George Corbett, of College Hill, has his place looking in excellent shape and unless all signs fail will have a nice cut the coming winter. Two things worthy of mention are his house of Lawson carnations and two houses of violets.

Mrs. Schlachter, wife of the Winton Place florist, had the misfortune to lose a pocket book containing $125 last Monday.

Albert McCullough left Thursday for Chicago and the north.

Louis Kyrk is on the sick list.

A. O.

Wholesale Flower Markets

MILWAUKEE, Sept. 24.	
Roses, Beauty, med. per doz.	1.50
" short "	.75@1.00
" Liberty	4.00@ 6.00
" Bride, Bridesmaid	4.00@ 6.00
" Meteor, Golden Gate	4.00@ 6.00
" Perle	4.00@ 6.00
Carnations	1.00
Smilax	10.00@12.50
Asparagus	50.00
Gladioli	2.00@ 3.00
Asters	1.50@ 2.00

PITTSBURG, Sept. 24.	
Roses, Beauty, specials, per doz.	2.50@5.50
" " extras	1.00@3.00
" " No. 1	75@1.00
" " No. 2	3.00@ 5
" Bride, Bridesmaid	1.00@ 6
" Meteor	3.00@ 4
" Kaiserin, Liberties	3.00@ 6
Carnations	1.00@ 2
Lily of the valley	3.00@ 4
Smilax	12.50@15
Adiantum	1
Asparagus, strings	30.00@50
" Sprengeri	2.00@ 4
Gladioli	3.00@ 4.00
Asters	.75@ 2.00

CINCINNATI, Sept. 24.	
Roses, Beauty	10.00@35
" Bride, Bridesmaid	3.00@ 6
" Liberty	3.00@ 6
" Meteor, Golden Gate	3.00@ 6
Carnations	1.00@ 2
Lily of the valley	3.00@ 4
Asparagus	50.
Smilax	12.00@15.
Adiantum	1.00@ 1.
Gladioli	3.00
Asters	.75@ 2

ST. LOUIS, Sep'. 24.	
Roses, Beauty, long stem	2.50
" Beauty, medium stem	12.50
" Beauty, short stem	4.00@ 6.00
" Liberty	3.00@ 6.00
" Bride, Bridesmaid	2.00@ 4.00
" Golden Gate	2.00@ 4.00
Carnations	1.00@ 1.50
Smilax	12.50@15.
Asparagus Sprengeri	1.00@ 1.50
" Plumosus	15.00@50.00
Ferns	per 1000 1.5)
China Asters	1.0@ 2.00
Tuberose	4.00@ 5.00

INTERNATIONAL FLOWER DELIVERY.

INTERNATIONAL FLOWER DELIVERY.

STEAMSHIPS LEAVE FOREIGN PORTS.

FROM	TO	STEAMER	*LINE	DAY	DUE ABOUT
Liverpool	New York	Etruria	1	Sat. Sept. 26,	Oct. 1
Liverpool	"	Campania	1	Sat. Oct. 8,	Oct. 8
Liverpool	"	Germanic	7	Wed. Sept. 28, 8:00 p. m.	Sept. 81
Liverpool	"	Cedric	7	Fri. Sept. 25, 8:00 p. m.	
Liverpool	"	Majestic	7	Wed. Sept. 30, 8:00 p. m.	
Liverpool	"	Celtic	1	Fri. Oct. 2, 8:00 p. m.	
Liverpool	Boston	Ivernia	1	Tues. Sept. 28,	Sept. 28
Liverpool	"	Bohemian	16	Fri. Sept. 25,	
Liverpool	"	Canadian	16	Fri. Oct. 2,	Oct. 11
Liverpool	Montreal	Dominion	16	Wed. Sept. 23,	
Liverpool	"	Southwalk	16	Wed. Sept. 30,	
Glasgow	New York	Anchoria	6	Thur. Sept. 24,	Oct. 6
Glasgow	"	Columbia	6	Sat. Oct. 3,	
Glasgow	"	Laurentian	2	Sat. Oct. 8,	Oct. 13
Genoa	"	Sardegna	12	Mon. Sept. 21,	
Genoa	"	Citta di Napoli	12	Mon. Sept. 28,	Oct. 15
Genoa	"	Liguria	12	Mon. Oct. 5,	
Southampton	"	New York	3	Sat. Sept. 26, Noon.	Oct. 3
Southampton	"	Philadelphia	3	Sat. Oct. 3, Noon.	
Antwerp	"	Finland	9	Sat. Sept. 26, 2:00 p. m.	Oct. 6
Antwerp	"	Vaderland	9	Sat. Oct. 3, 11:00 a. m.	Oct. 12
Southampton	"	Manitou	6	Wed. Sept. 23,	
London	"	Mesaba	6	Sat. Sept. 28,	
London	"	Minnetonka	6	Sat. Oct. 3,	
Hamburg	"	Furst Bismarck	8	Thur. Sept. 24,	Oct. 2
Hamburg	"	Deutschland	8	Tues. Sept. 29,	
Hamburg	"	Bluecher	8	Thur. Oct. 1,	Oct. 8
Hamburg	"	Pretoria	8	Sat. Oct. 3,	
Havre	"	La Touraine	10	Sat. Sept. 26,	Oct. 3
Havre	"	La Savoie	10	Sat. Oct. 3,	
Copenhagen	"	Oscar II	4	Wed. Sept. 23,	
Rotterdam	"	Potsdam	11	Sat. Sept. 26,	Oct. 6
Rotterdam	"	Statendam	11	Sat. Oct. 3,	
Genoa	"	Prinzess Irene	13	Thur. Oct. 1,	Oct. 14
Bremen	"	Kronprinz Wilh.	13	Tues. Sept. 22,	Sept. 29
Bremen	"	Barbarossa	13	Sat. Sept. 26,	Oct. 6
Sydney	SanFrancisco	Sierra	18	Mon. Sept. 21,	Oct. 19
Sydney	Vancouver	Aorangi	20	Mon. Oct. 5,	Oct. 29
Hongkong	"	Empress of Japan	20	Wed. Sept. 23,	Oct. 14
Hongkong	SanFrancisco	Coptic	17	Sat. Sept. 26,	Oct. 33
Hongkong	"	America Maru	17	Sat. Oct. 3,	Oct. 31
Hongkong	Seattle	Tosa Maru	22	Tues. Sept. 22, p. m.	Oct. 22

* See steamship list on opposite page.

The F. R. WILLIAMS CO.
Wholesale Florists,
CLEVELAND, - OHIO.

Please mention the American Florist when writing.

G. A. HOLDER
HOOKER, N. C.
WHOLESALE DEALER IN
Galax Leaves.
Give me an order. I will please you. Large orders solicited.

Please mention the American Florist when writing.

GALAX...
Bronze or green. 75c per 1000, in 2,000 ots orf more. Leucothoe Sprays, green, 90c per 100. Southern Smilax, fresh stock, per 50-lb. case, $6.00; per 25-lb. case, $3.50. Green Sheet Moss, choice stock, $2.50 per barrel sack. Spagnum Moss, $1.75 per large bale.

FLORIST' SUPPLIES of Every DESCRIPTION.

Tel. 597 Madison L. J. KRESHOVER,
Square. 110-112 W. 27th St., New York.

Please mention the American Florist when writing.

HARDY CUT FERNS.
Write for Prices.

FANCY DAGGER
L. B. BRAGUE, Hinsdale, Mass.
Oldest, largest and most reliable dealer in U. S. Mr. Brague will have an exhibit at the Convention Hall.

Please mention the American Florist when writing.

THE SEED TRADE.

AMERICAN SEED TRADE ASSOCIATION.
S. F. Willard, Pres't J. Charles McCullough; First Vice-Pres.; C. E. Kendel, Cleveland, O., Sec'y and Treas. Twenty-second annual convention St. Louis, Mo., June, 1904.

F. W. Barteldes.

A. BLANC is a stamp specialist.

VISITORS: Geo. D. Clark, with H. A. Dreer; J. C. Robinson; Geo. Tilton, Cleveland; E. M. Haven.

PROVIDENCE, R. I.—The Providence Seed Company exhibited 260 varieties of dahlias at its store recently.

SWEET PEAS, common mixed, which have been a drug on the market for three years or so, is now a scarce article.

PHILADELPHIA.—Mrs. Leopold Landreth, who has been ill at the German hospital, is now on the way to recovery.

POTATOES in the best Minnesota growing districts have been hurt some on low ground by standing water from recent rains.

WILLIAM HENRY MAULE is telling the farmers how to broadcast their wheat, through the columns of the Practical Farmer.

PUEBLO, COLO.—Produce shippers estimate a $300,000 loss in the tomato crop along the Arkansas valley by frost September 17.

IN musk melon seed of 1903 crop the shortages will be irregular. Some varieties like Netted Gem will be filled in full, while others will be very scarce.

WATERLOO, NEB., September 21, 1903. —We have fine growing corn weather with some sunlight and south wind. The damage by frosts here amounted to but little.

PARIS, September 15.—Notwithstanding the present cold weather, seed crops are coming in about as usual. Some warmer, dry weather would, however, encourage the growers.

ONION set prices at Chicago are opening lower than last year. Yellows sold this week at 85 cents to 95 cents for October shipment. Reds 10 cents higher. Whites scarce at $1.20 to $1.25.

WATERLOO, NEB., September 23.— Weather cooler. Corn is ripening fast and is almost out of the way of frost, showing good, hard ears. We expect a pretty fair crop of corn here.

HARRISBURG, PA.—Holmes Seed Company held a dahlia exhibition this week in their store rooms. They staged sixty-one varieties of fifty flowers each. The public attendance was good.

THE Western Seedsmen's Association met at the Sherman House, Chicago,

September 24. Among those present were Mel. L. Webster, J. E. Northrup, H. A. Johns and J. T. Buckbee. The local seedsmen also attended the meeting.

SOUTH HAVEN, MICH.—E. M. Haven, president of the Haven Seed Company, has gone to Central California, where in future the headquarters of the company will be located, although retaining their grounds and interests here.—Messenger.

PROVIDENCE, R. I.—John Barclay, formerly traveler for John Gardiner & Company, Philadelphia, Wm. Elliott & Sons, and Vaughan's Seed Store, died in this city September 18. He had no relatives in this country. His wife lived in Edinburg, Scotland, and one son residing in Jamaica, W. I.

ST. PAUL.—Corn was not hurt by frost here. With the continuance of the present weather an average crop should mature. The first shipments of new crop peas have arrived and show considerable shrinkage in cleaning. L. L. May is visiting Chicago and Ohio points. W. Utterman has returned from California.

Are Seeds Insured at Cost or Market Value.

An interesting matter of adjustment has arisen in connection with the burning of the seed warehouse of H. W. Buckbee, at Rockford, June 4. The insurance on the property amounted to $80,500. The position taken by the representatives of some of the companies is that they are liable to the assured for the cost of the seeds destroyed instead of the market value at the time of the fire, and the companies, represented by W. M. Bament of the Western Adjustment Company. George R. Herrick, of the Royal, and H. B. Heaford, of the Phoenix, of Hartford, have demanded an appraisal. The American, of Newark, and the Security, of Rockford, through their manager, Charles E. Sheldon, have just paid the face of their policies on the ground that the companies are liable for the market value of the seeds at the time of the fire. The appraisers selected have not yet agreed upon an umpire.—Record-Herald.

An Appeal from Customs Valuations.

New York, September 15.—Judge Waite, of the Board of United States General Appraisers, gave a hearing to-day on representatives of the D. M. Ferry Seed Company, of Detroit, at which testimony was submitted purporting to show the values upon which duties should be estimated by the customs authorities. The Ferry Company imports large quantities of seeds, and the collector at Detroit levied duties on the basis of the contract price on seeds shipped from France, though the market price dropped before the time of shipment.

The questions at issue are of much interest to the seed-importing trade, and the outcome of the controversy is being watched by importers. Judge Waite took considerable testimony in the case last spring and with the additional testimony made soon. It is reported that the Ferry protest involves customs duties aggregating $850,000.

STURGEON BAY, WIS.—The John H. Allan Seed Company's warehouse burned September 22 in the early morning. Six thousand bushels of seed peas were destroyed. The loss on the stock is $15,000, and the building $4,000, and on the machinery $2,000, a total of $21,000, all covered by insurance.— Special to Inter-Ocean.

THE Wholesale Seedsmen's League convened at the Auditorium Hotel, Friday, September 25. Among the directors and other representatives present were: B. Landreth, F. W. Brugerhoff; W. Atlee Burpee, Jno. Hunt, of J. B. Rice & Company; J. B. Rice, Jr., S. F. Willard, L. L. May, Albert McCullough, F. W. Barteldes, Carl Cropp, of Vaughan's seed store. A general discussion of seed-crop conditions and prospects was had.

Bloomington, Ill.

The outlook for a good season is promising. Roses and carnations are in excellent condition with a fair prospect for violets. There is but little doing in the cut flower trade, and excepting for funeral work sales would not be worth recording. Asters have come and gone—with the aster disease, and damages by the aster bug and from rains, the crop has been unsatisfactory. The crop of gladioli has been excellent and the flowers good, but the sale for them is quite limited. Chrysanthemums are in excellent condition.

W. T. Hempsted has nearly completed the three greenhouses built new this season. They are planted mostly with carnations, which are looking well. A. R, Kunoles has extended his plant and grows principally carnations and violets, which are looking very promising.. F. A. Baller has removed and rebuilt his greenhouses in a more desirable location and will sell off the grounds of his former plant for building lots, for which there is an increasing demand. A. Washburn & Sons have built the past summer three new houses about 5,000 feet each, which are planted to roses. They have also purchased the lot at 318 N. Main street and will next year build on it a modern three-story building to accommodate their increasing trade. Max.

WACO, TEXAS.—It is hoped to make this year's flower show a record breaker.

, THE NURSERY TRADE.

AM. ASSOCIATION OF NURSERYMEN.
N. W. HALE, Knoxville, Tenn.- Pres.; FRANK A. WEBER, St. Louis, Mo., Vice-Pres.; GEORGE C. SEAGER, Rochester, N. Y., Sec'y. Twenty-ninth annual convention, Atlanta, Ga., June, 1904.

THE new rose Philadelphia Rambler is well thought of, an improvement on the original Crimson Rambler.

NURSERY stock is reported as ripening well and is expected to be in condition to dig and ship early next month.

"Let us plant fruit trees for shade trees all along our streets," says Mrs. Gordon, of Milwaukee, "so the boys can have the fruit and fun."

PRINCIPLES OF AMERICAN FORESTRY.— A volume of 334 pages with seventy-three illustrations, mostly halftones, has just been issued by John Wiley & Sons, New York. The author is Samuel B. Green, of the University of Minnesota. The work is exceptionally practical and readily adapted to the beginner, and valuable as well to him who has already made extensive plantings. Cost $1.50.

THE American Grape Acid Association has deposited securities with Daniel Meyer, Esq., banker, San Francisco, for the payment of $25,000 to any person who devises a process or formula for the utilization of California grapes containing over twenty per cent of saccharine, worth $10 per ton, to produce tartaric acid, (perhaps by transforming the sugar in the grape into acid) at a price which would permit exportation without loss. The decision in awarding the amount to rest with three out of five of a jury who have been appointed to determine the matter, whose verdict would be final; the offer to close December 1st, 1904, American Grape Acid Association, 318 Front street, San Francisco.

The Elberta.

Last summer when we parted, sweet
Elberta,
You looked quite fair enough to eat,
Elberta!
Yet this for absence may atone.
Since last we met you've fairer grown;
Yes, though you have a heart of stone,
Elberta, you're a peach!

Your cheeks reflect the sunset glow,
Elberta!
Your rounded outlines lure me so,
Elberta!
Your breath is sweet as summer dew;
Your life-blood richly flowing through
Imparts a matchless charm to you.
Elberta, you're a peach!

You've caused me many an aching pain,
Elberta!
I swore you never would again.
Elberta!
Your ripening beauty tempts like wine,
Yet though your charms were all divine;
Touch not your downy cheek to mine;
Elberta, you're a peach!

I would not mar your bloom so fresh,
Elberta!
Nor bruise the fairness of your flesh,
Elberta!
I promised my right worthy mate
That I would be most temperate.
And gaze on you with thought sedate;
Elberta, you're a peach!

I would devour you with my eyes,
Elberta!
But gazing never satisfies,
Elberta!
Soon in your flesh so rosy bright
I'll set my teeth most sharp and white,
For when you're peeled you're out of sight;
Elberta, you're a peach!
—Mabel Swarts Withoft.

Park Management.

In connection with some newspaper criticisms of lack of economy in the expenditure of public funds in the Baltimore parks, Charles L. Siebold, superintendent of Patterson park, writes as follows in the Sun of September 21:

"I was very much impressed with the German system of economic park management. Special appropriations are made for all new improvements, no matter how small, and the work is done after mature consideration by the landscape architect and head gardeners. Everything done must harmonize with existing conditions, be they natural or ornamental.

"I noticed in European parks a very perceptible distinction between gardeners, skilled laborers and ordinary laborers.

"In Baltimore conditions are different, and men experienced in park work are very scarce. Our city is known as one offering small chances for experienced gardeners. Gardeners, as a rule, are very poor politicians and have little chance to advance themselves. The first requisites on most private places are that a gardener must be able to milk cows, attend to stable work and the furnace, etc.

"In my own experience and travels I found that successful park management can be obtained only by having a well-organized force of experienced men. We should have a more equal distribution of park districts and examine into the amount of work to be done in each district in order to give the Park Commissioners and Board of Estimates an opportunity to judiciously regulate the apportionment of funds to maintain them. Then, again, a large emergency fund should be had each year for storm repairs, etc. This season has been no extraordinary one for heavy rainstorms, and the roadways in all the large parks have been severely damaged. Good gardeners and skilled laborers should be permanently employed and equally distributed in the districts.

all ordinary labor to be employed only when needed and from time to time. "All superintendents of city parks in Europe are men of technical training and many years of practical experience in all branches of gardening."

OUR PASTIMES.

Announcements of coming contests or other events of interests to our bowling, shooting and sporting readers are solicited and will be given place in this column.
Address all correspondence for this department to Wm. J. Stewart. 79 Milk St., Boston, Mass.; Robt. Kift, 1725 Chestnut St., Philadelphia, Pa.; or to the American Florist Co., Chicago, Ill.

Baltimore.

The bowlers of the Gardeners' Club are anxious to hear from their Philadelphia friends, in order to arrange for the inter-city cup games between Washington, Philadelphia and Baltimore.

Base-ball at Madbury, N. H.

The return game between the Exeter Rose Conservatories' team and the Rose Farm team of Madbury, N. H., was played September 7 at Exeter. The score at the end of the sixth inning, when the game was called on account of an accident to a player, was 15 to 5 in favor of Rose Farm.

Philadelphia Veterans Meet Again.

The second challenge match between the Anderson and Harris two men teams took place on the Central alleys September 21, resulting in another victory for the former. The scores were as follows:

HARRIS TEAM.

Player	1st	2d	3d	T'l
Harris	126	148	148	422
Eimerman	163	148	151	462
Total	289	296	299	884

ANDERSON TEAM.

Player	1st	2d	3d	T'l
Anderson	172	172	134	478
Watson	159	117	142	418
Total	331	289	276	896

The stakes were all expenses for the evening and supper for the losers and their friends. Harris is a wonder at his age but seemed to do best on the Home alleys. G. A. seems to have carried his point about the "Home alley bowlers" for the time being. Nevertheless W. K. H. has the record for convention with 240 made at St. Louis, so he was more than a "home alley bowler once" and is willing to tackle any man of his age anywhere for any stake. G. C. W.

DOVER, N. J.—Harry Payne, Sunnyside Greenhouses, has a nice range of glass devoted to the growing of carnations, smilax and bedding plants for local trade only. He supplied bedding plants at all D. L. & W. R. R. stations between Boonton, N. J., and Binghamton, N. Y, this year, which was his first, very satisfactory.

MUSHROOM SPAWN.

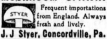

Frequent importations from England. Always fresh and lively.

J. J Styer, Concordville, Pa.

CLUCAS & BODDINGTON CO.
Importers and Exporters of

Seeds, Bulbs and Plants

612-814 Greenwich Street,
..............NEW YORK CITY.
Send for quotations on all Florists' Bulb Stock.
Please mention the American Florist when writing.

CARNATIONS.

FIRM, HEALTHY, FIELD-GROWN PLANTS.

	Per 100	1000		Per 100	1000
F. Hill	$6.00	$45.00	Guardian Angel (sport)	4.00	35.00
White Cloud	5.00	40.00	America	4.00	30.00
Norway	5.00	40.00	Chicago (Red Bradt)	5.00	
Queen Louise	5.00	45.00	Lawson	7.00	65.00
Her Majesty	7.00	60.00	Marquis	4.00	35.00
Prosperity	7.00	60.00			

WIETOR BROS.,
51-53 Wabash Ave.   CHICAGO.

Strong, Field Grown Plants.

	Per 100	1000
Harlowarden, crimson	$12.00	$100.00
Roosevelt	6.00	
Norway, white	5.00	40.00
Her Majesty, white	10.00	80.00
Gaiety, variegated	5.00	40.00
Higinbotham, light pink	5.00	40.00
Mrs. Potter Palmer	5.00	40.00

Roses.

2,000 Bridesmaids strong,
3-inch...................... 4.00   35.00

Chicago Carnation Co.,
JOLIET, ILL.

Fairmont, W. Va., Aug. 31, 1903.
Chicago Carnation Co.
Sirs:—Enclosed find check for $50.00 for the carnation plants. They were very fine plants and I am well pleased with them. They were packed so nice and came in good condition.
Yours, (signed) H. GLENN FLEMING.

BOOKS FOR FLORISTS.

The time is coming along when these are needed and opportunity at hand for reading them. Every one of the following should be in your library.
Send prices quoted and we send the books.

HOW TO GROW CUT FLOWERS (Hunt). —The only book on the subject. It is a thoroughly reliable work by an eminently successful practical florist. Illustrated. $2.00.

STEAM HEATING FOR BUILDINGS (Baldwin).—Contains valuable data and hints for steam fitters and those who employ this method of heating. The 350 pages are fully illustrated. $2 50.

HOW TO MAKE MONEY GROWING VIOLETS (Saltford).—This is by a practical grower who has made a success of the business. No grower of violets can afford to be without it. Price 25 cents.

GREENHOUSE CONSTRUCTION (Taft).—It tells the whole story about how to build, and heat a greenhouse, be it large or small, and that too in a plain, easily understood, practical way. It has 118 illustrations. $1.50.

THE NEW RHUBARB CULTURE (J. E. Morse & G. B. Fiske)—A complete, practical, scientific and up-to-date treatise on the latest method of cultivating rhubarb. 130 pages. 50 cents.

125,000 Field-Grown CARNATION PLANTS.

	Per 100	Per 1000
Flora Hill	5.00	40.00
White Cloud	5.00	40.00
Queen Louise	5.00	40.00
Norway	4.00	35.00
Guardian Angel	4.00	35.00
Joost	3.00	25.00
Marquis	3.00	25.00
Genevieve Lord	3.00	25.00
Triumph	4.00	35.00

The large Surplus of Plants which we have left enables us to select the very best stock there is to be had.

Order at once and get first choice.

GEO. REINBERG,
51 Wabash Ave., ...CHICAGO.

CARNATION PLANTS.

1,200 SERVIA, a good white: 300 MRS. JOOST, $5.00 per 100; $35.00 per 1000. Good plants and all right.

A. BATLEY & SON, Maynard, Mass.

THE AMERICAN CARNATION (C. W. Ward).—A complete treatment of all the most modern methods of cultivating this most important flower. Illustrated. $3.50.

THE ROSE—Its cultivation, varieties, etc. (H. B. Ellwanger.)—A complete guide of the cultivation of the rose, together with a classification of all the leading varieties. $1.25.

PRACTICAL FLORICULTURE (Peter Henderson).—A guide to the successful propagation and cultivation of florists' plants. Illustrated. 325 pages. $1.50.

THE AMERICAN GARDENERS' ASSISTANT (Thomas Bridgeman).—Complete guide for the cultivation of vegetables, fruit trees, grape vine and flowers. Illustrated. 522 pages. $1.00.

AMERICAN FLORIST CO.,
324 Dearborn Street,   CHICAGO.

It is good business policy to mention
The....
AMERICAN FLORIST
When you write to an advertiser.

Denver.

A heavy frost or two the past week, has put the finishing touches on outdoor stuff, leaving the market in rather a slim condition. Carnations, though coming in in small lots, are as yet hardly up to a good salable condition. In roses the market is in better condition; some very good teas are seen, while American Beauty roses, though scarce, promise to be in ample supply shortly. Trade is very good, a steady call keeping the limited supply well cleaned up. A look around the different growing establishments shows stock in first-class shape for the coming season. Little evidence is noticed of the late hail storm.

Chrysanthemums are well along and looking good. American Beauty roses at Mauff's are as usual doing well and at present a good cut is on. At the Park Floral Company's greenhouses Bridesmaids, Brides and Liberties are doing well and the quality of the cut just now could not be much better in November, also at this place I noticed a grand house of cyclamen. A lot of poinsettias at the Colfax Floral Company are in pretty fine shape, both in small stuff for pans and single stems; their place in general looks good. At the Daniels & Fisher place at Mud Lake, American Beauty roses are doing well; they also are well up on poinsettias, cyclamen and begonias.

It is a little late, perhaps, to thank Milwaukee and Chicago boys for fine times and also the many press notices for those big hats. We did have a good time and would go again next year even if the convention was held at Boston. Michael Barker, of the AMERICAN FLORIST, is now prepared to write "before and after" testimonials on our glorious climate, having gained fourteen pounds during twenty-one days vacation.

St. Paul.

, Clouds and coldness ·have given place to warmth and sunshine. The sunshine has brought stock with a rush until there is now a surplus, especially of roses on the market. Carnations are coming in slowly but still short of demand. The storms cut down nearly all of the outside flowers. Frost has done but little damage. The parks are as green as early spring, while the flower beds retain all their myriad hues of beauty.

Christ. Hansen's carnations are extra good. His Enchantress are very promising. Guardian Angel is exceedingly productive with him and always a good seller. Mr. Hansen certainly knows how to grow Liberty roses. The well developed flowers with good stems which he cuts always bring the highest market price. His Piersoni ferns are looking well.

The Warrendale greenhouses, under management of Carlsen and Lauritsen, are in first-class shape and ought to give a good financial account of themselves the coming winter. Own root roses are preferred by them to the grafted stock.

Chas. Vogt met with a bad accident in the tug of war at the Florists' annual picnic in August and is just now able to be about. In some manner he severely sprained or lacerated his leg muscles

A. N. Kinsman & Son, of Austin, were callers during fair week. Despite reverses and bad luck in several ways during the past few years Mr. K. wears a happy smile and is prospering.

Bulbs are arriving very slowly. Dutch stock is nearly all here, but French stock is still in transit. Those who depend on Romans for early flowers will be discommoded this season.

Mayor & Company are bringing in some very nice American Beauty roses. Their Fitzwygram chrysanthemums will be ready in a few days.

Richard Alston, of Winnipeg, was a recent visitor. He reports business good in that hustling Canadian city. FELIX.

MENOMINEE, MICH.—E. L. Parmenter has had a good year and will enlarge his nursery.

FORT SMITH, ARK.—A flower show will be given here November 5, 6 and 7 under the auspices of the Fort Smith Charity Hospital. Shipments of cut blooms from professional florists are solicited and every facility will be given for display of advertising.

500,000 PANSIES.

Giants, mixed; also yellow and white, $3.00 per 1000

Asparagus Sprengeri, 2-inch, strong, 2 cents each.

Primula Obconica Grandiflora, A-B4, ROSEA,

Also BABY (Forbesii), fine stock, 2c for 2-inch.

DAISIES: Double Longfellow, Giant, Snowball, $3.00 per 1000.

FORGET-ME-NOTS: Victoria, blue, white, pink, $3.00 per $.00.

SWEET WILLIAMS: Double and single, $3.00 per 100.

HOLLYHOCK: Double, separate colors, $1.00 per 100. Single, mixed, 90c per 100.

ENGLISH IVY: Field-grown, 5c.

RUBBERS: Top cuttings, 4 and 5-inch pots, every plant perfect and cheap at price. 20c and 35c. 100 3½-inch side cuttings, 5c.

Boston Ferns.

Bench plants, fine for 5- and 7-inch pots, 15 and 25c. Customer of St. Louis says: "Well pleased with ferns which arrived in fine shape." Cash.

BYER BROS., Chambersburg, Pa.

Louisville.

Mr. and Mrs. C. H. Kunzman left September 18, for Baltimore for a two weeks' visit with relatives. Mr. Kunzman has built a large potting and packing shed two stories high at an expense of $1,000. Mr. Kunzman, although a cigar maker by trade, has become one of the most capable carnation growers in the state.

Mr. Chas. Rayner is building a new chimney eighty feet high. He suffered a very painful accident caused by a rock falling on his hand while excavating for the subway under his greenhouses.

Mrs. Reimers has had several large decorations the past week.

Our first frost occurred September 18. Business is picking up. H. G. W.

New Bedford, Mass.

We are having a few days of very warm weather, although last week there was a slight frost on low ground. It is still very quiet in a business way. The stores are mostly filled with asters and gladioli, with a few roses. No carnations in market at present. The carnation growers have their houses nearly filled, but had to send out of town for plants, not having enough of their own.

S. S. Peckham has succeeded in getting water enough for his greenhouse by pumping it from a spring, a distance of 1,500 feet.

The exhibition of the New Bedford Horticultural Society was held Thursday and Friday, September 16 and 17.

Arthur Ashley is building a house 18x140 for carnations.

Richard Noftz has returned from a trip to Europe.

New Bedford, Mass.—There was a good attendance at the flower show here on September 17, despite the rainstorm. All the sections were well filled, but the display of dahlias was unprecedentedly grand. Mrs. J. K. M. L. Farquhar and W. C. Winter acted as judges and had their hands full.

Salem, Mass.—W. T. Walke has just completed a new boiler house.

Please mention the American Florist to advertisers.

Worcester, Mass.

A visit to Herbert A. Cook's large establishment at Shrewsbury found the proprietor busy planting his last house of carnations. Carnations are grown exclusively at this place with the exception of about 3,000 violets, which were looking strong and thrifty. Mr. Cook has housed about 20,000 plants this season, including Enchantress, Queen, Boston Market and a white seedling of his own which he thinks highly of. Solid beds are used entirely and the same soil is used year after year with great success. No manure is used and chemicals, etc., mixed after his own formula, are depended on entirely for fertilizers, both for field and inside culture. The entire cut is shipped to Boston. Mr. Cook has made many improvements and is just finishing a commodious residence on a commanding site near his peach orchard.

Trade has run along without any especial feature, funeral work still being the greatest factor. Flowers are plentiful in all seasonable lines.

The floral exhibition at the Worcester County Agricultural Society's fair held September 7-9 was far ahead of last year and some fine displays of summer flowers were shown.

The last two exhibitions of the Horticultural Society brought out exceptionally fine displays of gloxinias and dahlias.

Lowell, Mass.

The first half of September has been the hottest of the season. Clear weather now prevails, which, with the return of the vacationists, starts business along in good shape. Early fall openings have stimulated the retail trade, with the usual line of funeral work. All in all, the month has been good, and the prospects are bright for a busy October when we hear of wedding decorations to come. Storms and cold nights have seriously damaged outdoor stock. Indoor flowers are gaining day by day. Some growers are inclined to leave their old plants on the benches until after Christmas, they showing a mass of bud and bloom with plants in perfect condition and flowers selling at $6.00 per hundred. The Boston fern has not lost its old-time popularity, judging by the shop windows. Our local commercial florists ignored the annual fair.

Down in Tewksbury at Patten & Co. they have a new seedling that can't be beat. A little girl arrived there last week, and great rejoicing. Mother and baby getting along nicely.

Collins & Gallagher will open a flower store opposite the postoffice September 26. Good luck to C. and G.

William Whittet and wife have returned from the Maine coast.

A. Roper, of Tewksbury, is visiting his parents in New Jersey.　　　A. M.

Clinton, Mass.

At the fair held September 16—18, the flower display was better than usual. E. W. Breed made the only commercial exhibit. From the greenhouses of amateurs were shown: Orchids from E. V. R. Thayer; alamandas from Col. J. E. Thayer; aquatics from Bayard Thayer; W. G. Winsor, of Brockton, and Ross Brothers, of Worcester, exhibited dahlias; F. A. Blake, of Rochdale, showed cut flowers in variety. Messrs. Orpet, Meredith, Clark and Anderson, gardeners to the Thayer estates, are deserving of much credit for their interest in making this part of the fair a success.

ELDORA, IA.—John Poland has nearly completed his greenhouse. It is the first here and badly needed.

Pueblo, Colo.

At the State Fair held here September 14–19, the Colorado Society of Floriculture held their first flower show. The classes were well filled and a very creditable show was put up. The amateurs came out strong and did very much to make the show a success. Many visiting florists attended and took a lively interest in the show, which should do much to help the trade throughout the state.

George Fleisher, of Pueblo, shone prominently in the design and decorative work, much to the pleasure of his friends, for George is popular, his reference in Pueblo being "any business man in town." His elation over one first and three seconds in four entries did not cease at the show grounds, but visiting florists spent the evening with him at the bowling alley.

The largest exhibitors from out of town were The Park Floral Company of Denver, the Wm. Clark Company of Colorado Springs and the Crump Floral Company of Colorado Springs. In the professional classes good premiums were offered which brought out strong competition and gave the local florist judges plenty to do.

The following exhibitors were prominent in the classes named and all won premiums:

Palms and ferns, roses, begonias, geraniums, perennials and window box, Park Floral Company; carnations and pansies, Colorado Springs Floral Company; table decorations, Wm. Clark Company; mantel decorations, flower basket and fuchsias, Crump Floral Company.

W. W. Wilmore, of Denver, made a very fine show of dahlias and carried home most of the premiums on them. B.

CHAMPAIGN, ILL.—Thomas Franks is building two houses on East University avenue, using material from his old houses on Randolph street. He will change from hot water to steam and has installed a new boiler. Mr. F. has taken a new and firm grip on the floral scythe snath and proposes to cut a big and wide swath for the next few years.

PARKERSBURG, W. VA.—Dudley's Market street store, as repainted and remodeled, with handsome French plate mirrors, will probably be the finest in this state.

HOPKINSVILLE, KY.—I desire the address of Geo. P. Mayhood, who was here until recently. T. L. METCALFE.

THE AMERICAN FLORIST

America is "the Prow of the Vessel; there may be more comfort Amidships, but we are the first to touch Unknown Seas."

| Vol. XXI. | CHICAGO AND NEW YORK, OCTOBER 3, 1903. | No. 800. |

THE AMERICAN FLORIST

NINETEENTH YEAR.

Copyright 1903, by American Florist Company
Entered as Second-Class Mail Matter.

PUBLISHED EVERY SATURDAY BY

AMERICAN FLORIST COMPANY,
324 Dearborn St., Chicago.
Eastern Office: 79 Milk St., Boston.

Subscription, $1.00 a year. To Europe, $2.00.
Subscriptions accepted only from the trade.
Volumes half-yearly from August, 1901.

SOCIETY OF AMERICAN FLORISTS AND
ORNAMENTAL HORTICULTURISTS.

OFFICERS—JOHN BURTON, Philadelphia, Pa.,
president; C. C. POLLWORTH, Milwaukee, Wis.,
vice-president; WM. J. STEWART, 79 Milk Street,
Boston, Mass., secretary; H. B. BEATTY, Oil City,
Pa., treasurer.

OFFICERS-ELECT—PHILIP BREITMEYER, president; J. J. BENEKE, vice-president; secretary and
treasurer as before. Twentieth annual meeting
at St. Louis, Mo., August, 1904.

THE AMERICAN CARNATION SOCIETY.

Annual convention at Detroit, Mich., March 3,
1904. ALBERT M. HERR, Lancaster, Pa., secretary.

AMERICAN ROSE SOCIETY.

Annual meeting and exhibition, Philadelphia,
March, 1904. LEONARD BARRON, 136 Liberty St.,
New York, secretary.

CHRYSANTHEMUM SOCIETY OF AMERICA

Annual convention and exhibition, New York,
November 10-13, 1903. FRED H. LEMON, Richmond,
Ind., secretary.

THIS ISSUE 40 PAGES WITH COVER.

CACTUS DAHLIAS EXHIBITED BY PEACOCK AT PHILADELPHIA.

Increasing Popularity of Dahlias.

The first exhibition of the New Bedford
Horticultural Society, New Bedford,
Mass., was held last week and was a
decided success. There were some very
fine groups of decorative plants, a few
asters, sweet peas, gladioli, etc., but it
was practically a dahlia show. The
people had eyes for nothing but dahlias.
Several dahlia specialists from out of
town brought in a grand collection, especially fine in the cactus section, which
opened the eyes of some of the flower
growers here. Our florists have not paid

much attention to growing dahlias, considering them coarse, common flowers
not worth bothering with. But after
seeing such noble flowers and delicate
colors as were shown here this year, and
after finding that there are hundreds of
flower cranks looking for the new and
choice varieties and willing to pay good
prices for them, some converts have been
made, and the importance of the dahlia
felt.

There promises to be a dahlia craze
throughout the country. Somebody is
going to make money originating new

varieties. The people are always wanting something new. When things get common they lose their interest in them. Time was when everybody was crazy over chrysanthemums. But they do not buy the plants now to any extent. Is there not a fine chance for any number of intelligent and enterprising florists to exercise their brains and skill in originating new varieties in all kinds of plants that the people can grow?

The lesson then to be learned from this first show of the New Bedford Horticultural Society is to cultivate dahlias and also cultivate flower cranks. N. B. H.

The Return of the Dahlia.

This is the subject of an editorial in the N. Y. Mail and Express. It says:

We are not greatly surprised to hear that the Newport cottage people are swarming to the Horticultural Society's autumnal exhibition to see the dahlias. They seem to think that they need an excuse for a "dahlia fad," and the excuse is that this show, having for local reasons been given much earlier than usual, could not be a

chrysanthemum exhibition. As it came exactly at the height of the season of dahlias, why not make it a dahlia show?

Why not, indeed? The dahlia is laughed at because it is so absurdly like an artificial flower; and yet, it may well enough be said of it that it is exactly the excellent thing that Nature has brought forth in an effort to prove that she can make a much more beautiful artificial flower than man can. The perfect frankness of the dahlia's formal, almost mechanical, arrangement of its ray-florets really makes one forgive the artificiality of its appearance. And the gladness, the cheriness, the superb responsiveness of the flower make it a real delight to simple-hearted people. It produces colors that are a wonder of wealth and brilliancy.

Born on the radiant mountains of Mexico, the dahlia plant retains, either expressed or latent in its spontaneous and productive body, so much of the wealth and splendor of the tropics that it has added an exotic delight to tens of thousands of northern gardens. Uncritical children, who perhaps after all have the best title to say whether a flower is beautiful or not, think it the finest flower in the world. They watch its unfolding with pure and expectant delight, and are deliriously rejoiced by the gift of a rich and perfect dahlia.

As the child triumphantly survives in

the person of every normal adult, and as the rich can do no better than to return at times to the esthetic delights of the poor, it is rather pleasant than otherwise to see the Newport society people take up the "dahlia fad."

Exhibitions.

[This article, while written originally for the private gardener, contains so much of general good sense that we believe the trade may profit by it.—ED.]

PART II.

If the schedule calls for a certain quantity let that and no more be in your collection. We have seen many an otherwise excellent collection disqualified on that ground. If the schedule calls for size only the selection is very simple, but if it is the best for table use then much discrimination is needed, freshness, form, uniformity and size must all be considered. The appearance and make-up of the collection has also much to do in rendering a decision. If the different subjects be not uniform much is detracted from the appearance of the whole. For instance, two or three large parsnips, or carrots and several smaller ones does much to detract from the appearance of a collection, and moreover it looks as if the exhibitor had only a limited quantity to pick from. The rating of different vegetables also influences many a close decision. A dish of nice green peas at the present time would outrival a large pumpkin or squash, and so on. Healthy green foliage adds much to the fresh appearance when staged; for instance, carrots, parsnips, beets or turnips should not be denuded of their leaves right down to the crown. Such an appearance gives them a cold storage look. The up-to-date vegetable peddler recognizes this, and the housewife in quest of something fresh will invariably choose the bunch with a quantity of leaves on it in preference to the one with the cold storage look, even though the one may be superior to the other. In staging a collection one is sometimes tempted to use a certain thing which may have a flaw in it, being careful of course to hide this by placing it in a position where the flaw will not be readily seen, just because it may possess other desirable attributes. This is very often a stumbling block. If a close decision has to be rendered every point counts, and each subject is examined individually. Blemishes must be avoided and all scratching or scraping. Use a knife as little as possible, but have everything washed clean and looking as natural as possible. In most cases nowadays horticultural and other societies provide all dishes and receptacles for staging purposes, but where this is not so, and each exhibitor has to provide his own, let them be of uniform size and color. Nothing looks worse than a miscellaneous lot of wooden, earthenware and semi-color dishes. Nothing looks better than white earthenware, and it need not be expensive. The use of white plates is universal for the smaller subjects, but when a collection is staged they may be dispensed with. Sheets of clean white paper make an effective setting and on the whole looks more natural. Parsley is often used as a ground work, and where the collection is not limited there may be no objection, but if the schedule calls for twelve or more varieties its use is sometimes misconstrued. When it is to be used as one of the number it is safer to lift two or three plants, roots and all and stage them as you would the others. In staging commence at the back of the table with the larger

DAHLIA 20TH CENTURY, PHOTOGRAPHED IN AUGUST.

DAHLIA 20TH CENTURY, PHOTOGRAPHED IN OCTOBER.

subjects such as cabbage, leek, squash, etc., and taper off towards the front with the smaller ones so that the whole may be seen at a glance. Do not have your cabbage and cauliflowers stripped of every leaf as if they were ready to be put in the pot. Leave every respectable leaf on them, and a considerable portion of stem, and have them put up to look as natural as possible. See that everything is p o e y and neatly named, have uniform cards with the names printed or written, much of the good that results from such exhibitions is often lost by the public having to guess at what they are looking at. If you win a prize do not berate your neighbor's futile attempt, it may be his turn next. Neither be discouraged by a failure: "Rome was not built in one day." Whatever you stage, let it be your own production, and if you win you will have the satisfaction of knowing that you are not strutting in borrowed feathers. If you lose you can also feel that the attempt was no disgrace.   JAS. T. SCOTT.

Propagating Poinsettia Pulcherrima.

A method of propagating Poinsettia pulcherrima, says the Gardeners' Chronicle of July 4, which prevents the large loss of sap caused by the usual way of propagation of this plant when cuttings are made. The cut should be made only half way through the stalk. After a weak callous has formed where the cut was made and the cutting is then taken off completely. This method is said to insure a quicker and surer rooting of the cuttings.

ADIANTUM CROWEANUM seems to have a great future before it.

Chicago Through Eastern Eyes.

Wholesale Trade:—The wholesale flower business of Chicago is ideal from one point of view; all the houses are practically within one block. There is no running about from one part of the city to another to find what is in the market, as it is all there, spread out before the buyer, who can see almost at a glance the kind of flowers he wants.

This open competition regulates prices to a nicety so that the painstaking grower is sure of the best market price for his stock.

They are an independent lot. these wholesalers, or rather the system is different from those in the east. They have no wagons or errand boys to deliver orders; the greatest volume of business, from seventy-five to ninety per cent, is shipped out of the city. There is no peddling about town as is the custom in Philadelphia. The city storekeeper must be on the spot or have his order in and take it away with him. The shipping boxes are all called for by the express companies who have their regular hours to meet the various trains.

Retail Trade:—There are a number of fine retail stores. The Fleischman Floral Company, P. J. Hauswirth, Chas. A. Samuelson, Wm. J. Smythe and the Ernst Weinhober Floral Company all have fine establishments and there are a number of other stores which do a nice business. Mr. Samuelson has a stable of six horses and as many fancy wagons which take more horses, when all out at once. These should move considerable stock in a day.

There is no street peddling in Chicago. When this law went into effect it was a great blow to the wholesalers, as the curbstone gentlemen sold large quanti-

ties of cheap stock, but it all goes somewhere, although they have much difficulty in moving it now when a glut sets in.

Altogether we were much pleased with our western trip and particularly with the hospitable reception everywhere received, we only regret that we could not spare the time to visit more of the large places that are so interesting to the smaller growers of the east.
                                          ROBERT KIFT.

Hedysarum Multijugum.

Hedysarum multijugum is one of our prettiest of hardy flowering shrubs. It was introduced from China about 1880, is perfectly hardy, and blooms in June. The flowers are borne in clusters and are of a very bright carmine red. They are borne well above the foliage and can therefore be seen a long ways off. The bushes are round and dense and the branches as well as the under side of the foliage white with silvery gray hair.

Pentas Carnea.

One of the plants which should be revivified is Pentas carnea, according to *Die Gardenvelt:* It belongs to the Rubiaceæ and comes from tropical Africa. It is a free bloomer. Not in the summer only in a cool house or sheltered spot in the garden does it develop its magnificent, rosy lilac, upright clusters of flowers, but in the fall and winter also it is perpetually in bloom. It is easily raised from seeds or cuttings and thrives best in a rich sandy soil.

PENNISETUM MACROPHYLLUM ATROSANGUINEUM the new grass for which H. A. Dreer received honorable mention at the late exhibition in Boston is of a dark bronzy red, a rare color in grasses.

Rhinebeck and Its Violet Growers.

PART I.

Away up in fertile Dutchess county, its rolling hills mantled with oaks and superb rock maples and affording a glorious outlook over the broad Hudson to Kingston on the other shore and the distant Catskills beyond, lies Rhinebeck, the Arcadia of the violet grower, whose fragrant product has figured in many a romance of high life and low life, turned the scale in favor of many an ardent wooer and often incited the nightmare and the flibbertigibbet to cut up most uncanny antics in the nocturnal visions of the bewildered commission man.

From Rhinecliff on the Hudson the nearest railroad station, Rhinebeck, is reached by a two-and-a-half-mile ride over a beautiful country road in a conveyance, the driver of which has attained an intimate personal acquaintance with every New York wholesaler having any ambition to dabble in the violet market, and who is expected to know, and generally does know, by heart the name of every violet grower in the district, the number of new houses he has erected, whether he has "commenced to pick" and the name of the commission man honored with his kind shipments for the time being.

At this season of the year one meets a continuous procession of apple-laden wagons bound for market—fruit that commands a fancy price wherever it goes, but whose luster as a leading crop of Dutchess county is already dimmed by the wonderful development of the new craze over the fragrant greenhouse product, a handful of which equals in value a whole barrel of pippins.

The Rhinebeck hotel, to which gravitates and from which radiates most of the business and social activities of the town, is quaint, old-fashioned and extremely comfortable, built of brick, with a three-decked veranda fronting on a maple and elm-shaded lawn, just now going through a siege of tussock moths, but otherwise well-kept and bright with geranium beds and clumps of old-fashioned cannas. Its presiding genius, a green parrot of uncertain age, extends a voluble welcome, inquires with much kindly concern whether you have had your breakfast, informs you that it is a "p-r-r-r-et-ty burd," calls the cat, mocks the rooster and bids you good.bye, all in one breath. This particular parrot is not addicted to profanity, as most parrots are reputed to be, although he has abundant opportunity to learn the real thing, for the typical, untitled native frequenter of Rhinebeck center is a reprobate with a never-failing vocabulary and can and does "swear like a trooper." And here the party of the first part and the party of the second part comfortably ensconced in the easy chairs on the broad piazza, the silent stars blinking at them through the autumn foliage, is where many a pledge of life-long devotion has

been recorded between the artless violet grower and his beloved friend the commission man.

It is only a few years since the number of violet growers in Rhinebeck could be counted on the fingers of one hand. The latest census places the number at seventy-three, and there are more a'coming. Within the present season the following new men have gone into the business, each with one house, except as otherwise mentioned: John Barringer, F. Curnan three houses, W. Cramer, J. C. Hamlin, J. W. Kipp, F. D, Lown, G. Lang, Milroy Brothers, W. E. Pultz, Walter Pells, John Schwartz, F. R. Snyder, Jas. Snyder, George Turner, C. Van Wagner, Jan Van Steenburg, F. Veily, L. Van Vredenburg, John Kissaur. At Red Hook, an outlying district, W. F. Fuller, F. Nelson, W. Steinburg. At Rock City F. G. Schaffer, two houses. At Enterprise, V. Demorest and at Bull's Head De Witt Hestler. Additions have been made to old establishments as follows: Ackert & Brown, Stephen Burns, Q. Van der Linden, W. Traver, Jas. Newman, Harvey Stewart, each one house, Wm. Burger and S. Rockefeller, each two houses. At Barrytown Mr. Henion, one house and one carnation house. These new houses are usually about 19½x150 feet. As a rule they have all been erected by a local builder on a uniform plan, each alternate sash being hinged below the ventilator so as to raise from the sill to facilitate the moving of soil in and out of the houses and admit, when needed, a free circulation of air. Some of the more recent houses have been constructed with stationary roofs, and most of these have side ventilation in the walls, and where this is not provided it is customary to remove a couple of lights from each alternate sash when moving soil, a temporary wooden frame being used to protect the glass from breakage. Of the buildings erected this year a few have been provided with a special soil sash, but these have developed a serious defect in the way of leakage and are already giving trouble. These local-built houses

have one very desirable feature in the shape of an iron band under each rafter applied so as to form a truss and prevent any sagging.

One iron house—the first of the kind in this section—has been erected this season for Milroy Brothers by the Lord & Burnham Company, and is likely to be followed by others equally up-to-date in type and equipment. Milroy Brothers are experimenting with a wash of cement instead or paint for the hot-water pipes, hoping it may prove cheaper and also more durable.

The walks in these violet houses are all very narrow, and when the beds are built high a 200-pound man can only get through by performing a sort of diagonal chasser.

H. H. Rogers Estate at Fairhaven, Mass.

Fairhaven, New Bedford's beautiful suburb, is best known as the home of the Standard Oil magnate, H. H. Rogers. The town is beautiful, partly because nature so made it and partly because of what public-spirited Mr. Rogers has done in the way of fine public edifices. Mr. Rogers' summer home, of which a number of views are herewith shown occupies a sightly position, the mansion surrounded by gardens, spacious lawns and stretches of woodland, all scrupulously cared for and affording a delightful view seaward in one direction and across the Acushnet river to New Bedford in the other. The estate comprises now twenty-five acres under the care of James Garthley who has had its supervision ever since the time its improvement was begun fifteen years ago, when it was but two acres in extent. The lawns are the most conspicuous feature of the estate. They are skirted by a wavy border of shrubs and hardy perennials accentuated by masses of salvias, geraniums, cannas and other

RESIDENCE OF H. H. ROGERS, FAIRHAVEN, MASS.

brilliant flowering plants. In one direction the lawn merges into a picturesque out-cropping of rock clothed with sturdy firs and cedars, beyond which stretches the woodland to the shore. On the lawn are some fine elms, purple beeches and nyssas, the latter being among the most beautiful of trees for brilliant fall coloring. The purple beeches, trees about sixty years old, and with trunk circumference of four feet, were successfully moved by Mr. Garthley seven years ago. He attributes his success in this operation to the extreme care exercised in preserving all the roots entire no matter how far they reached. In a bed of cannas the most effective variety is Pandora, a cross between Crozy and Springer, having rich, dark foliage in rare combination with very large bright orange flowers. The flower gardens in the rear are extensive and brilliant. Here are cosmoses eight feet tall, veritable trees, also an endless variety of Drummond's phlox, snapdragons, etc., useful for cutting, and especially noticeable is a large bed of pentstemons, such as well deserve a place in every garden. Unfortunately these handsome flowers will not survive the winters here without protection. Mr. Garthley raised them from seed sown in March and then keeps the plants in cold frame during the winter, making cuttings from them in spring. Plants from cuttings produce better flowers and more of them than those direct from seed.

NYSSA VILLOSA ON GROUNDS OF H. H. ROGERS, FAIRHAVEN, MASS.

Portecochere of H. H. Rogers, Fairhaven, Mass.

The soil of Fairhaven is light and sandy with ledge underneath. Sod is hard to procure and salt spray storms are frequent. With these drawbacks, the perfection to which everything is grown is all the more to Mr. Garthly's credit. He has been the recipient of many high awards for his exhibits at Horticultural Hall in Boston. There is a range of greenhouses recently built well supplied with the usual material. One of our views shows the formal parterre adjacent to the mansion.

The garden committee of the Massachusetts Horticultural Society recently visited the estate, which is entered in competition for the Hunnewell triennial premium and were sumptuously entertained.

AMONG the New England contracts recently taken by Hitchings & Company are the following: For the Soldiers' Home at Togus, Me., iron frame greenhouse and workroom. J. B. Craig, Weston, Mass., three houses and work-room. C. R. Curtis, Swampscott, Mass., one house. Union Hill, Cemetery, Woonsocket, R. I., one house.

With the Growers.

JOY & SON, NASHVILLE, TENN.

Your correspondent had the pleasure of a visit to the splendid establishment of the Joy & Son Company. It was well worth a visit, showing enterprise and very great promise of an abundant supply of floral beauties for the local flower lover. The company is composed of T. S. Joy, president; T. C. Joy, vice-president and manager of the growing department; Messrs. C B. Harrison, Paul Sloan and F. H. Hoen. T. S. Joy, the senior member of the firm, superintends the floral store and salesroom. Mr. T. C. Joy spends his entire time at the greenhouses, and takes great pleasure in showing his well managed, thrifty range of houses. He is an experienced grower and produces blossoms that would rival any grown anywhere.

The first plants observed were the palms, which by skillful handling, care and attention have overcome the jaded and worn look which palms, like society belles, acquire after a particularly brilliant season. A great variety of large, handsome palms belong to the collection.

The company has abandoned the idea of replanting the rose beds every year, but finds they can get better results by holding them over at least two successive seasons. There is one rose house 400 feet long planted to Brides, Bridesmaids and Kaiserin, but the house has not been allowed to come into bloom yet. The American Beauty houses, of which there are several, show thrifty, vigorous plants that will produce a fine quality of roses all through the season. Mr. Joy does not replant his Beauty houses, but cuts back the plant and grows it on into another season. Liberty roses were treated in the same way, and the yield is generally most excellent.

They are equally as successful with car-

nations as with roses. They grow White Cloud, Marquis, America, Lawson, Prosperity and others.

The chrysanthemums are looking fine. Mr. Joy is growing most of the leading varieties, graded so as to give successive flowering from early in October until December.

The violet beds next attracted our attention. This company has had great success with violets. They have numerous beds already under glass, but the novelty was a field-grown bed, which, when it gets colder, Mr. Joy proposes to divide into small beds, put frames around each section and cover with sash. This bed was some seventy-five feet square and should yield an immense crop. This bed is made up mostly of the variety California.

The greenery, smilax, Asparagus Sprengeri, Maiden hair and a large variety of ferns have whole houses devoted to their growth and promise a prolific supply. There are 10,000 square feet in the entire plant, and one-fourth of this is devoted to the culture of carnations alone, all the finer varieties in white, pink and red being grown, all of which look thrifty and well.

Miss Kitty Sharpless is designer and saleswoman for the company, having been with them for many years. She is not only a most affable and tactful sales woman, but has rare artistic taste in the arrangement of flowers.   M. C. D.

A Bedding Plant of Merit.

Eupatorium riparium var. from its character of growth it is more desirable than Piqueria trinervia var., better known as Stevia serrata compacta var. It being more spreading and not so brittle as the stevia, only one drawback, and that is the variegation will run out or one side of the branch will come all green and the other all white. But that can be easily avoided by only selecting the well marked pieces for cuttings. In the miscellaneous border it makes an interesting object with the different markings; color rich green, irregularly marked and splashed with creamy white, the young growth shaded pink.

Substitutes for Coal.

PART I.

BY W. R. BEATTIE, WASHINGTON, D. C.

[We give below such extracts from the valuable paper read at the Milwaukee convention as time and space, as our crowded columns will admit.—ED.]

Coal.—Coal is the principal source of the production of artificial heat, and so long as it remains the principal source we will naturally adopt it as the standard by which to measure all other fuels. In order, then, that we may determine the relative value of the various substitutes for coal it will be necessary, first, that we understand something of the heating power of the various grades of coal and the methods of determining this efficiency.

In all our calculations we use the B. T. U. (British Thermal Unit) as our unit for measuring the heat given off by the combustion of any fuel. This unit is the amount of heat required to raise one pound of water one degree at and from 32 degrees Farenheit. Reference is also made to the number of pounds of water evaporated from and at 212 degrees per pound of fuel and per pound of actual combustible. The value of any fuel is measured by the number of heat units that its combustion will generate. Carbon and hydrogen represent the combustible portion of a fuel, and its heating value depends upon the proportion in which these elements are present. All solid fuels contain some moisture and more or less incombustible matter, either sulphur or ash. The anthracite coals contain a moderate percentage of moisture, are low in hydrogen, high in carbon and moderately high in ash. These produce very little flame. Ordinary wood, on the other hand, is high in moisture, comparatively high in hydrogen and low in carbon and ash.

The following table shows the comparative heating value of the various classes of coals:

Kind of coal.	Carbon.	Volatile matter.	H. T. U. per lb. of coal.	Water evap'd per lb. coal.
Anthracite	86.00	3.86	13,230	13.66
Semi-bituminous	73.84	18.86	14,780	14.08
Bituminous	55.00	35.00	12,000	13.50
Lignites	38.78	40.19	9,670	10.00

No. 6. THE DECORATION OF HOME GROUNDS.

It will be observed that as we pass from anthracite to the softer grades of coal, as the carbon decreases the volatile matter increases and the heating value decreases, except in certain of the semi-bituminous coals found in Pennsylvania, Maryland and West Virginia, which contain a higher number of heat units and are capable of evaporating more water per pound than are the anthracite coals. The highest of these being that known

as Broad Top, Pa., containing 14,820 heat units per pound of coal.

By reference to the above table of heating values of the various classes of coals we can ascertain the comparative cost per thousand heat units at the prices of coal delivered. Assuming the price per ton for the various coals to be that given in the following table we have:

Kind of coal.	Price per ton of 2240 lbs.	Price per lb.	Cost per 1000 H.T.U.
Anthracite	$6.50	$0.290	$0.021936
Semi-bituminous	4.50	.200	.013578
Bituminous	3.50	.156	.012018
Average			$0.015844

These figures, however, would not be comparable with actual results accomplished by burning coal under the ordinary boiler, for they are based upon the theoretical heating efficiency of the coal according to chemical analysis. The results obtained in burning coal, as reported by the United States Naval Fuel Board, were as an average for seventeen tests about eight pounds of water evaporated per pound of coal burned. Upon this basis the foregoing table should be corrected to read as follows:

Kind of coal.	Price per ton.	Price per lb.	Cost of evap. 1 lb. water.
Anthracite	$6.50	$0.290	$0.036
Semi-bituminous	4.50	.200	.025
Bituminous	3.50	.156	.0195
Average			$0.0268

It should be stated, however, that the above included the raising of the water from about 130 degrees F. and evaporating it under a pressure of 380 pounds. This would require a greater expenditure of energy and would in a measure compensate for the losses that are common when using coal under ordinary conditions.

Substitutes for Coal.—Among the solid fuels that might be named under this head are wood, peat, charcoal, coke, sawdust, spent tanbark, wheat or rye straw, bagasse or crushed cane, corn fodder, corncobs and cotton stems. Of the gaseous fuels, natural gas, blast furnace gas, water gas and coal or illuminating gas. In the line of liquid fuels there are two, petroleum in its various forms and alcohol.

Wood.—Where plenty of wood is available it is perhaps the best and in the end the cheapest substitute for coal, princi-

pally because no special appliances are required for using it. Perfectly dry hardwood contains almost as many heat units per pound as does coal, and two cords of ordinary fire wood are generally considered to be equal to one ton of bituminous coal, so far as heating efficiency is concerned.

Peat.—In some parts of the country there are large beds of peat that might be used as fuel, especially if put up in

the form of briquettes. It is about equivalent to good wood as a heat producer.

Charcoal.—If charcoal be burned in ovens, the by-products of its manufacture make the process profitable, but owing to the limited quantity of charcoal produced it can scarcely be considered as a regular fuel. There can be no advantage connected with the use of charcoal for heat production, as it contains as a rule only about 60 per cent of the original heating value of the wood, and it is more economical to burn the wood itself. Charcoal has about the same heating efficiency as coke and anthracite coal.

Coke.—Coke is prepared by the distillation of bituminous coal in ovens or retorts. Unfortunately the same conditions that govern the output of coal also control the production and shipment of coke, and it cannot be depended upon for use as a substitute for coal. Coke has about the same heating value per pound as anthracite coal and burns more freely, but does not last so long in the furnace.

Sawdust.—Sawdust can be utilized for fuel, but to get the best results it should be first dried, then burned in a specially constructed furnace.

Straw.—Either wheat or rye straw have an application as a fuel wherever it is very plentiful, three and one-half pounds being equal to one pound of coal.

The Decoration of Home Grounds.

No. 6.—The illustration shows a difference in two elm trees due to the difference in character of two owners. The vegetation about a house indicates the character of the occupants. A beautiful home grows beautiful as it develops under the influence of good people. A gardener may plan, lay out and establish a home decoration, but as soon as the plants begin to grow they adapt themselves to influences for which the occupants are chiefly responsible.

Aralia Chinensis Variegata.

Under the name of Dimorphanthus Mandschuricus variegatus, this graceful Chinese shrub has been attracting much attention in England. It grows six to twelve feet high and has large spreading leaves, pinnately divided into many ovate acute leaflets. In the common form these are green, and do not particularly attract the attention. But in the variegated variety the leaflets are irregularly bordered with a creamy white band that gives the foliage a unique and distinct appearance, as shown in the illustration. As the leaves become older they assume a beautiful and conspicuous flush of soft magenta purple and are then more decidedly ornamental than ever. The flowers individually small and creamy white, are borne on the young shoots in large divided clusters. When protected in a cold greenhouse they appear in June, but later on in the open air. In mild localities, this plant flourishes in the open air in England. It likes a rich and rather moist, loamy soil, and if two or three plants are placed in a group by themselves in a sheltered nook on the grass or shrubbery border they are very attractive.

Commercially speaking this is a plant that pays to propagate. In fact enough of it cannot be produced. Quite recently I know a specimen about five feet high for which six guineas had been offered but was refused. Quite small plants easily fetch a guinea apiece. They are easily raised by grafting on stocks of the green variety, either lower down near the root or on the top of the spiny stem. A nice warm greenhouse is necessary to have the operation quickly performed.

W.

Palms and Ferns.

THE PHŒNIX—ABOUT SEEDS—PALM DISHES

Speaking in a general way spiney palms are not popular either among the decorators or the general public, this being one of the objections urged against the phœnix, a group of palms that are highly decorative and also of a very enduring character.

The most graceful of the phœnixes, and also the least objectionable on account of spines is P. rupicola, but even of this fine palm but few are grown, comparatively speaking, for the growers find but little profit in handling it.

There is no difficulty in germinating phœnix seeds, though sometimes occupying several months in the process, but the young plants are very slow indeed in arriving at a useful size, the interval between 2-inch and 6-inch pots being entirely too long to suit most growers, and a phœnix does not show much character before reaching the 6-inch size, the only exception to this rule that is known to the writer being .that very dwarf species known as P. Rœbelenii. The phœnix that is most in use among our decorators at the present time is P. Canariensis, this being probably the quickest in making a useful size, and one that grows in beauty as it gains in years, an example of which may be seen in the magnificent specimen of this palm that is growing in the large palm house at Lincoln park, Chicago.

Within the past five or six years great numbers of P. Canariensis have been imported from Europe in all sizes from 5-inch or 6-inch pots up to large specimens in tubs, there having been such great quantities of this palm grown by some of the continental growers that comparatively low prices have been quoted on them.

Many of these plants are of good quality when shipped from the other side, but they frequently suffer to some extent while in transit, and are therefore somewhat of an unknown quantity until they are re-established. These phœnixes are doubtless useful to those having much decorating to do, their tough foliage enduring much exposure without injury, provided they are kept moist, and to do this requires frequent and thorough waterings for they are thirsty subjects. The plants of this palm that are imported in the spring seem to travel best, possibly because the growth is harder and more mature at that season, and in any event the early arrival of such plants gives one time to get them in shape for the fall work. When newly imported plants are received they should be unpacked promptly and stood upright upon a bench, giving them a good syringing or watering overhead in order to refresh the foliage, the place in which the plants are stood being sheltered from draughts and also from sunshine.

Then repot promptly, removing as much of the loose earth from the upper portion of the balls as possible without serious disturbance to the roots, and potting the plants firmly in as small sized pots as the roots will allow.

If any of the plants are found to be dry they should be given a good soaking in a bucket or tub of water before being potted if there is any water about to get the old ball wetted through if it should be repotted while dry.

The plants should then be placed in a shaded house and kept rather close for two or three weeks, syringing them overhead two or three times a day if the weather is warm and dry; but at the same time being careful not to get the soil sodden with water before the plants have a chance to make some roots. In the course of a week or two some of the lower leaves may be lost as a result of the long journey, and occasionally an entire plant may go off, but some troubles of this character are sure to arise in the experience of every importer of plants and allowance for such possible injury should be taken into consideration when making import orders, the prices at which the stock is first offered being only about two-thirds of the final cost. It will be readily understood that it is sometimes necessary to import palms in order to secure certain sizes of stock of which the home market may have been depleted, but it must also be remembered that there are risks to be taken in such business, and that if one can secure home-grown stock there is more likely to be more satisfaction from it in the long run.

The business of palm growing fluctuates to some degree from the fact that the supplies of seed have been offered rather irregularly, some years there having been difficulty in getting enough good seed to go around, while in other seasons there may have been an over-supply of some kinds and in consequence some bargain lots offered that induce a number of growers to take a "flyer" in such stock as a side line. The natural result is that an over-supply of small stock may appear in the course of a year or two, and those growers who have not secured a regular outlet for such stock are quite likely to make some bitter offers in order to get rid of their surplus, a perfectly proper business method, though one that usually tends to disarrange values for a time at least. We have before noted the popularity of Cocos Weddelliana in small sizes for uses among ferns in fern dishes, and in very many cases there is nothing prettier than this graceful palm for such a use, but if one dwarf palm may be made up in compound plants in 4-inch or 5-inch pots that often prove good sellers, such a plant when standing in a silver filagree pot or in a neat china jardiniere being a decided adornment. to a table.

It is best to make up these compound cocoses in the early summer if one can manage it at that time, thus giving the advantage of the warm weather in which to establish them, but even now the plants could be put together, though such late plants may not wear so well as those that have had more time in which to root.

A well established cocos bears the conditions of exposure in a dwelling to dry air and dust much better than do some much stronger looking palms, and where properly cared for they have been known to keep in good condition for three or four years.

ARALIA CHINENSIS VARIEGATA.

Small plants of Kentia Belmoreana in 2½-inch or 3-inch pots are also found very useful for fern pans, but in order to have such short and shapely plants as are demanded for this use one should give the young plants sufficient space and light for their perfect development.

A careful selection from among a lot of seedling Kentia Belmoreana would pro. duce a nice lot of small plants suitable for this particular use, for it should be remembered that all palm seedlings of a given species are by no means alike in all their characteristics, and that a more careful selection would develop a superior stock.

There may yet come a time when this principle of selection in plant growing will be considered much more important than it now is, and when thin and anæmic seedling palms will be at once condemned, instead of allowing them to occupy valuable space on the benches as is so often done now.   W. H. TAPLIN.

A California Decoration.

The house was beautiful with decorations of a type suggestive of the out-of. door life of Belvedere. The masses of greens and flowers were arranged with artistic effect. The windows and doors connecting the rooms in the house with the gallery were thrown open, so on every side a beautiful scene met the eye.

In the room in which Miss Laughton was married only greens and American Beauties were blended. A great Indian basket filled with the graceful long-stemmed roses formed a bower under which the young couple stood. In the window, against a background of charm. ing landscape, hung a jar filled with the same deep pink blossoms.—*San Francisco Chronicle, September 16, 1903.*

The Retail Trade.

THE new patterns of Porto Rico mattings are very attractive. Your supply dealer has them.

WHITE PIGEONS for florists' uses are scarce. The supply houses are unable to secure anything except inferior stock.

OUTDOOR flowers are now working under special permit from Jack Frost, subject to cancellation without notice.

W. K. HARRIS allows that three blooms to a chrysanthemum plant at 12 cents to 15 cents each is better than one flower to a plant at 25 cents.

THE importation of dried cycas leaves has reached fabulous proportions. But a few years ago an importation of 10,000 leaves was regarded as a stupendous transaction. Now millions upon millions are brought over without exciting surprise.

The Art of Decorating.

It is a very exasperating circumstance when a florist, employed to execute a piece of decorating, is compelled to discard a wealth of beautiful and appropriate material that he may have at hand and could make use of with profit as well as credit, and to ransack the market for something less appropriate just because the madam has set her mind upon it, but this is an experience that every florist must repeatedly undergo, for crotchety and arbitrary people are found everywhere, and especially among the oppulent classes, with whom a florist's services are most in demand. On the other hand we have occasionally the customer who comes with implicit confidence in our ability to serve him well, and who unhesitatingly places the hall or suite of apartments at our disposal with full liberty to go ahead and make a nice job of it. In such a case it is a fortunate responsibility that devolves upon the florist, and he should be able to fulfill his commission in such a manner that it shall leave no opportunity for criticism on the part of people of refined taste. These are the occasions which mean the upbuilding or the downfall of a florist's prestige. If he does not rise to the occasion and is not capable of taking full advantage of his opportunity or is negligent in it then he proves himself unfit for the position he assumes and he need feel no surprise when he sees a competitor outstripping him in his own territory. The character of the apartments to be adorned, the known tastes of the hosts or their guests, the nature of the occasion, all are important factors influencing the decorator in the choice of the material used and the manner of its application. Yet, with all these and other minor limitations, it remains true that the man who understands his business can adapt himself to the times and circumstances as to the material at hand and make prominent use of that most easily available and still score a pronounced success in his work, for consistency and harmony, not the material used, are the potential characteristics of the work of the true artist. Given the same room, under identical conditions, two or more independent decorators might, and probably would, carry out the work according to different designs and in a very different manner, and one or the other might best please the fancy of different persons, so that the question of merit might be variously decided, yet

BASKET OF DAHLIA LEONE.

each might be equally correct from an artistic standpoint. Then, conceding equal artistic merit to each, keeping qualities being also equal, he is the best master of his art who has achieved the result with the least expenditure.

W. J. S.

New York.

MARKET CLEANS UP WELL.—'MUMS HERE. —LOCAL NEWS.

All stock is cleaning out well for this time of year; market at this writing is not over-supplied, and although carnations are coming in more plentifully they are cleaned out daily at a fair figure. Roses dropped slightly Friday and Saturday, but Tuesday, weather becoming cooler, prices stiffened again to the prices of the early part of last week. American Beauties are holding their own, namely, good ones, there are quantities coming in which do not deserve the name, and, as a rule, these are cleaned out to the Greeks at a ridiculously low figure, which certainly cannot pay the grower. Violets are more plentiful, but quality still leaves much to be desired. Not many go over the fifty cent mark, but many go away below. Chrysanthemums are coming along now. Moore, Hentz & Nash received a fine lot of yellows this week, but most of those coming now are very poor in quality. Steinhoff's longiflorum lilies are very fine; they readily bring 10

and 12 cents per flower. Lily of the valley is about the same as last week, not very much of it around, but demand is light. Smilax and all green goods find slow sale. Gladioli have been scarce since the storm; those coming in are very poor. Dahlias also have suffered, but there are still quantities coming in at the early markets. Asters are about finished up, even those from the upper part of the state showing the effect of the late season.

In response to Park Commissioner Young's request for $802,454 for parks and parkways in Brooklyn and Queens the Board of Estimate and Apportionment has appropriated $50,000 and decided that this sum would have to suffice for the year.

Dr. N. L. Britton, director of the Botanical Garden, has just returned from a second exploration trip in Cuba, bringing a large number of botanical specimens.

J. Suydam is shipping excellent carnations to Slinn & Hughes, the new firm with the New Jersey Cut Flower Company.

S. Geller has opened, at 158—160 W. 27th street, a capacious store room for fall goods.

Langjahr expects to open his new place on 28th street in early October. John Young had some very fine white orchids this week.

Chicago.

CENTENNIAL CELEBRATION MAKES LITTLE IMPROVEMENT IN TRADE. — SHIPPING BUSINESS ACTIVE.—STOCK PLENTIFUL IN MOST LINES.—UNION GARDENERS SUBMIT SCALE AND REQUEST ACTION.—NOTES.

Notwithstanding that there has been during the week hundreds of thousands of visitors to the city, local retailers say that the centennial celebration has created little extra demand. A few of the down town members of the craft have had some good business in connection with entertainments to Sir Thomas Lipton and other prominent men who are here helping to celebrate the 100th birthday of the city. Shipping trade has been active the past week and the supply of good roses, especially Bridesmaids and Brides is hardly equal to the demand. Beauties, which are of very fair quality, can now be had in good supply. Carnations are much improved in quality but there is not a stiff demand for them, and there has been during the past three days a glut of seconds. Outdoor stock is about off but there are still a few gladioli, tuberoses and asters of fair quality coming in. Yonkeepor (day of atonement), the Jewish holiday, occurred Thursday and made considerable improvement in the local demand.

Frank Fischer, for the last five years foreman for the Chicago Carnation Company, has severed his connections with that concern. He has rented, with Carl Poppe, the grounds and greenhouses of the Art Floral Company, at Blue Island, for five years. His late employer and fellow employes gave him a banquet and presented him with a handsome silver smoking set as a token of their esteem. Carl Poppe, his associate, has had charge of some of the palm houses at Humboldt park for the last five years.

Several hundred Indians have been camped in Lincoln park the past week in connection with the centennial celebration, many of them having come from the bouquet green districts of Wisconsin. One of these fellows, whose ancestors were "old Chicagoans," stated to our representative that Chicago was a "heap much" green town but he would not like to locate here permanently as everybody seemed to be "heap quick."

While Harry Berkowitz, of H. Bayersdorfer & Company, was on the coast he received a telegram from his 22-year-old son stating that he had graduated from the Philadelphia law school. The genial Harry hardly seems to be over 22 himself. He is on his way back to Philadelphia and reports a good business.

The representatives of the Gardeners' and Florists' Union have requested C. L. Washburn to take up the matter of wages with other growers and he has consented to do so. Mr. Washburn fears, however, that little progress can be made while so many hands in other lines are out of employment.

Schiller, the florist, had a special palm sale this week and George Asmus, manager of this concern, says it was a howling success. They distributed a neat circular 'to their trade in which it was stated not more than two plants would be sold to one customer at the prices they were offered at.

Charles Reardon, who has charge of the large private estate of E. M. Barton, at Hinsdale, anticipates building three greenhouses the coming fall for roses, carnations, show plants, etc., the output of which will be used by Mr. Barton for his personal benefit.

There was an attendance of twenty-three at the special meeting of the Florists'

Club held at the Sherman House September 25. A number of committees were appointed and life membership and the flower show were discussed.

The types last week made us locate Joe Curran with Fleischman, when everybody knows Joe is and long has been body known Joe is and long has been with Friedman. Our local reporter must improve his handwriting.

E. C. Amling has received some fine samples of Monrovia chrysanthemum blooms, this week, from Gunnar Tellmann, Marion, Ind. The blooms brought $3 to $4 per dozen.

Fleischman had a float in the centennial parade which was a credit to the trade. Hustling Joe Beaver had this in charge.

Dora Niles has opened a flower stand in the Sherman House. Open all night and Sundays, reads the card.

Louis Gresenz, of Bassett & Washburn's, who has been on the sick list a week, is again at business.

Brant & Noe have taken three stands, eighty square feet, at the Flower Growers' Market.

The E. F. Winterson Company is handling large quantities of kentias for one of their growers.

Mrs. W. Ellison, of St. Louis, was a visitor, this week, buying stock for her new store.

Kennicott Brothers are receiving some fine outdoor single violets.

Visitors: Court Dallwig, F. H. Holton and B. G. Lambros, Milwaukee; F. T. Manahan, Beloit, Wis.; E. C. Keck, Washington, Ia.; J. Groves, Atchison, Kans.; Mr. and Mrs. Gesler, of Gesler & Drury, Galesburg, Ill.; Miss Violet Moreno, Pensacola, Fla.; John Wilins, Danville; W. L. Morris, Des Moines; Hugo Schroeter, Detroit; Michael Stauch, Council Bluffs, enroute to Terre Haute, Ind.

Philadelphia.

FAIR DEMAND FOR ALL KINDS OF STOCK.— HAIL HITS JOSEPH KIFT.—MEEHAN HORTICULTURAL SOCIETY BANQUET.—A BIG TRADE SALE.

Business is about up to the standard for the season. There is a fair demand for all kinds of stock, with Beauties and white leading in rose demand. Carnations are more plentiful, although they bring a good price and all seem to be sold. Dahlias are now at their best, and if they escape the frosty nights we are now experiencing will last two weeks longer. Last year a heavy frost on October 15 retired them for the season. Cosmos is coming in slowly, but is furnishing most of the stock. Violets are a trifle better but are nothing much to speak of as yet. Chrysanthemums are here, the first local blooms coming in on Monday. Glory of the Pacific was the variety. Orchids are becoming more plentiful with the price a shade lower, but they still command a high figure.

The first anniversary and banquet of the Thomas Meehan Horticultural Society was held at Harkinson's cafe, Germantown, last Tuesday evening. The annual election of officers resulted in Ernst Hemming being chosen president and Warren Chandler secretary and treasurer. The society, which consists of some forty members, is composed of the employes of the Thomas Meehan Nursery Company. Meetings are held once a week which matters pertaining to horticulture only are discussed. The banquet was a most enjoyable affair. Edwin Lonsdale was an invited guest.

A public sale, being almost the first of

its kind in this city, is to be held next Wednesday and Thursday, October 6-7, at Robert Craig & Son's, Forty-ninth and Market streets. In addition to a large catalogue list of their well grown stock Wm. K. Harris will send a large block of assorted plants. J. P. Cleary will have charge of the sale, and in his hands there will be no delay. The sale is absolute and the stock will be open for inspection on Monday and Tuesday. Messrs. Harris and Craig & Son have a reputation second to none for well grown commercial plants.

The next meeting of the Florists' Club, Tuesday, October 6, will be very interesting. Walter Whetstone is to read a paper on "Vacuum Heating" and Edward Reid will state his experience in the far west. · K.

Boston.

SLOW MARKET AND ABUNDANT STOCK.— FROSTS STRIKE HARD.—AUCTION SALES.

Still a slow market with overstock on most lines. Frosts have been prevalent throughout the state this week, and, while the immediate vicinity of Boston has escaped, it is to be assumed that the receipts of outdoor flowers, such as asters, dahlias, etc., will now rapidly diminish and thus help the market to brace up. Districts within twenty-five miles of the city have been struck hard by the early frosts and dahlias are completely ruined to the ground. So long as asters are so abundant as of late not much improvement may be looked for in the carnation business. The latter are improving generally in quality, but there is a sufficiency of the cheap grades in evidence still. Roses in all classes are going very slowly. Bride and Bridesmaid have improved in quality during the past few days, but the demand is light and the sale drags. American Beauty shows up better than when last reported, but there is plenty of room for improvement yet. Very few violets are seen in this market so far, and they are now in moderate demand. Those being received are mainly of the single sorts.

On Sunday evening, the closing night of the Horticultural exhibition, during a thunder storm, the electric lights were extinguished by the burning out of a connection During the ten minutes of darkness that ensued the fruit display was materially diminished.

The auction sales at McCarthy's have begun and the first disclosure is that good carnation plants are scarce. The few offered found active bidders and there is a ready sale for more than are in evidence. Other fall specialties still satisfactory.

Visitors: Axel Bjorn, Stockholm, Sweden; Jas. Begbie, representing Clucas & Boddington Company, New York; W. Taat, representing Van Waveren & Herzog, Wessenfels, Saale, Germany; Alex. Fraser and E. N. Anthony, Newport, R. I.

DAVENPORT, Ia.—Charles Dannacher, who retired a few years ago on account of his health, will again resume business at 110 E. Third street, October 1. Mrs. Dannacher will have charge of the store, which will be fitted up with all the latest improvements. Third street is rapidly becoming one of the important streets of the city in a retail way.

AUBURN, MAINE.—Geo. M. Roak's new daughter Edith arrived September 29. A welcome guest.

THE AMERICAN FLORIST

NINETEENTH YEAR.

Subscription, $1.00 a year. To Europe, $2.00.
Subscriptions accepted only from those
in the trade.

Advertisements, on all except cover pages,
10 Cents a Line, Agate: $1.00 per inch.
Cash with Order.

No Special Position Guaranteed.

Discounts are allowed only on consecutive insertions, as follows:—6 times, 5 per cent; 13 times,
10 per cent; 26 times, 20 per cent;
52 times, 30 per cent.

Cover space, sold only on yearly contract at
$1.00 per inch. net, in the case of the two
front pages, regular discounts applying only to the back pages.

The Advertising Department of the AMERICAN
FLORIST is for florists, seedsmen and nurserymen
and dealers in wares pertaining to those lines only.

Orders for less than one-half inch space not accepted.

Advertisements must reach us by Wednesday to
secure insertion in the issue for the following
Saturday.   Address

AMERICAN FLORIST CO., Chicago.

THE dahlia next.

JACOB BECKER's new rose Ideal is well
liked in Philadelphia. It seems to hold
its head up better than La France.

ARDISIAS in fruit should be kept at a
temperature of not above 60° now as
too much heat is liable to induce young
growth.

Now comes the growing season for
Gloire de Lorraine begonia. They move
along very rapidly in September and
October if given a chance.

CROTONS show highest color when pot-
bound and exposure to the cool nights of
October will accentuate it and make
them all right for Christmas trade. As
a rule anything that checks growth
heightens color.

CYCLAMENS that have been in shaded
frames all summer should now have an
opportunity to get the full sun. House
them early in October. If the buds have
been carefully pulled off through August
the plants will bloom all the better.

THERE are said to be two varieties of
Ardisia crenulata. The European variety
is much superior as a commercial plant
to the Japanese variety which has smaller
foliage which also droops and partially
hides the fruit.

THE announcement in this issue of the
grand combination sale of W. K. Harris
and Robt. Craig & Son, to be held at
Craig's Market street place, Philadelphia, will be of interest to the whole
trade and should attract a record breaking attendance.

CANNA plants may be scorched by the
frost before lifting, but should be taken
up before a freeze hard enough
to kill the stalks more than half way
down; otherwise the sour and frozen sap
returning down the stalks into the roots
may poison them so they will decay
during early winter.

Ginseng Information Needed.

ED. AM. FLORIST:—I have noticed
recently very extensive advertisements
calling the attention of the public to
the enormous (?) profits to be obtained
in the cultivation of ginseng, also a brief
editorial note in the last issue that—
"savored of ginseng culture literature."
Now I desire to ask has the experiment
of growing ginseng been tried commercially? Are the profits to be obtained by
the advertiser who sells the seeds? Can
you give me further information? I have
read the advertisement, and doubtless
other of your subscribers have, and if

you can answer these questions, either
through your columns or otherwise, it
would be appreciated by me and doubtless by others. I know the AMERICAN
FLORIST is always disposed to sift these
doubtful questions.   B. S. C.
P. S.—Is it a quicker way to get rich
than extracting gold from sea water?

"See How Wee Apples Swim."

ED. AM. FLORIST:—An individual sign-
ing himself "J. J. B." makes it his special
business to criticise the personnel and
management of the St. Louis parks.
Some time ago this self appointed
censor stated that A. Meyer, Jr., was
appointed as superintendent of the
St. Louis parks and that he was a
very young man only 23 years old, and
had a big undertaking on his hands.
This was a falsehood as "J. J. B." knew
that he was quite a bit older, that he
was 28. Five years' study of the arts
of the plantsman, the grower, the gardener and the florist might make even
"J. J. B." capable of judging in such matters.

In a later article, having in the meantime (to the amazement of many who
know him) secured an election to a high
office in the S. A. F., he gives vent to the
following: "The City Hall square is in a
very bad condition. It's up to the park
commissioner and his superintendent,"
etc.

Now, that City Hall park or square
looks comparatively well now, and did
also at the time of his writing, and as the
new superintendent had then been in office
only two months he could not claim the
credit or the blame, if there had been
any for the spring and early summer
work of his predecessor.

The last item reads, "William Lamar is
still keeper of Forest park and it looks as
if he will remain. Mr. Lamar is a republican working under a democratic administration and is perhaps too good a man
to dispense with, and is kept to help
those who know very little about running a big park like Forest."

Our present administration, though
democratic, was elected on a platform of
honest business principles, and had the
support of very many republicans left in
office and they are retained for their
ability and the valuable services they are
rendering in their respective positions.
So it should be, for the benefit of the citizens and taxpayers; and it is to be hoped
that the park officials will continue in
their present course unmindful of the
barking of the "J. J. B.'s".
    FAIR PLAY.
[We fear our correspondent takes
"J. J. B." too seriously.—ED.]

The American Carnation Society.

In addition to the regular line of
premiums and specials heretofore noted
in the trade papers, the following are
offered:

By The Foley Manufacturing Company
of Chicago, Ill., three silver cups valued
at $25 each.

One for the best vase of Michigan seedlings not yet disseminated.

One for the best 100 yellow, any variety
and open to all.

One for the best vase of 150 blooms
not less than three nor more than five
varieties, any variety permissable and
the vase to be arranged for harmony and
effect.   ALBERT M. HERR, Sec'y.
Lancaster, Pa.

Chrysanthemum Society of America.

President Herrington has announced
the committees to examine chrysanthemum seedlings and sports on dates as
follows: October 10, 17, 24 and 31, and
November 7, 14, 21, 28, 1903.

Boston, Mass.—E. A. Wood, chairman,
Boston Flower Market, care of John
Walsh; Wm. Nicholson and James
Wheeler.

New York, N. Y.—Eugene Dailledouze,
chairman, care of New York Cut Flower
Company, Twenty-sixth street and
Sixth avenue; Wm. H. Duckham and
Wm. Plumb.

Philadelphia, Pa.—A. B. Cartledge,
chairman, 1514 Chestnut street; William
K. Harris and John Westcott.

Chicago, Ill.—James S. Wilson, chairman, care of J. B. Deamud, 51 Wabash
avenue; Edwin A. Kaust and B. Wienhoeber.

Cincinnati, O.—Richard Witterstaetter,
chairman, to Jabez Elliott Flower Market, care of janitor; James B. Allan and
Wm. Jackson.

Exhibits to receive attention from the
committees must in all cases be prepaid
to destination, and the entry fee of $2
should be forwarded to the secretary not
later than Tuesday of the week preceding
examination.

Attention of the exhibitors is called to
the action taken at the last meeting of
the C. S. A., requiring all sports to be
exhibited before at least three committees
before becoming eligible to receive certificate.   FRED. H. LEMON, Sec'y.
Richmond, Ind.

Greenhouse Heating.

ED. AM. FLORIST:—I am building a
house 25x65 feet, 14 feet high, east to
west. Office and potting shed on the
west side and about two feet fall from
east end to potting shed. Intend to heat
with hot water. How many feet of pipe
will it take to heat this house 60° in zero
weather? Would like to run one main
overhead and balance of pipes along the
sides, as there are no benches to put
pipes under. How many feet of different
size pipe will it take and what size boiler
is best suited to heat the same? How
should these pipes be arranged, if different sizes are to be used?   C. W. B.

It will be well to use two 2½-inch
flows either on the purlin or center posts
and seven 2-inch returns on each of the
side walls. The return coils should
extend for about ten feet from the corners
on the exposed end of the house.
    L. R. TAFT.

Greenhouse Building.

Dobbs Ferry, N. Y.—Isaac Stern, one
house.

Upton, Mass.—Oak Grove Nurseries,
house 47x50.

Westfield, Mass.—Henry Barton, house
25x100.

Dalton, Mass.—F. B. B. Sears, violet
house.

Waltham, Mass.—E. N. Peirce & Sons,
carnation house 30x300; forcing house
20x300.

Baker City, Ore.—Ira B. Sturges, one
house 20x60.

Marlboro, Mass.—George Bemis, one
house.

Gloucester, Mass.—A, B. Tuck, house
15x50.

Stoughton, Mass.—Davis & Jones, one
house 22x150.

New Bedford, Mass.—Arthur Ashley,
one carnation house 18x140.

Massachusetts Horticultural Society.

In the annual exhibition of the Massachusetts Horticultural Society which has just closed, the most notable features were the crotons in the plant section and the dahlias in the cut flower section. The crotons were of the character popularized in Philadelphia in recent years by Robert Craig and others—young, quick-grown specimens from eighteen inches to two and a-half or three feet in height, beautifully colored and far excelling anything in this line heretofore shown here. E. J. Mitton, J. S. Bailey and E. S. Converse were the contributors. Mr. Mitton's group of twenty-five took first prize, but Mr. Bailey's was a very close second. The winning group excelled in the broad leaf varieties. Thompsonii, Dayspring, Mortii, Reedii, Dolina and Czar Alexander III were splendid. In the second group Flambeau, Johannus, Hanburyanum superba, Hawkeri and Sunshine excelled. From J. W. Tuft's came some large specimens, big, massive plants of Fasciatum, Heroicus and Evansianum, seven to eight feet high.

The display of dahlias was a revelation and the interest shown in the varieties and their names was a convincing evidence of the great public interest awakened in the dahlia since the appearance of the cactus and loose flowered decorative varieties. There were many thousands of blooms, show, decorative, fancy, cactus, single and pompon being all well represented but the cactus predominating and the quality was ahead of any previously shown here. The number of exhibitors was large, many being commercial men. "Master Carl" was adjudged the best single bloom of any variety introduced since 1901.

A group of large-foliaged coleuses from W. B. Roberts made an exceedingly brilliant effect and was suggestive of the wealth of bold color available in these easily grown subjects. Their adaptability for effective exhibition use at this season of the year cannot be overdrawn.

From the Harvard Botanic Garden came the largest and most comprehensive group in the hall, including stove plants and medicinal and economic plants from all over the world but the group was placed, with questionable judgment, so as to obstruct the best view of the hall. The groups of stove and greenhouse decorative-foliaged plants from various large private estates were as usual very fine and the ferns from the same exhibitors were fully up to the standard. The Pierson fern in J. S. Bailey's group came in for great admiration. Some of the massive fronds measured over a foot across from tip to tip of the pinnæ. Other specially admired things were Dreer's Asparagus myriocladus, the "lace plants" in tubs of water illuminated from below, a well-bloomed specimen of Dipladenia rosacæa from J. S. Bailey, the Anna Foster fern and the displays of Groff's hybrid gladioli. A border of Saintpaulia ionantha along the front of Mrs. J. L. Gardner's group made an admirable finish line.

There were extensive collections of hardy herbaceous flowers in the small hall, contributed by Carl Blomberg and Blue Hill Nursery. Cattleya labiata, var. Cooksonii was the rarest plant in Lager & Hurrell's orchid group.

The musicians were screened from view by a big group of bays, palms and ferns illumined with lilies and gladioli from R. & J. Farquhar. Mrs. M. L. Atwood was given a bronze medal for home cultivation of achimenes. The plants grown in an ordinary dwelling house window were very fine.

J. E. Rothwell's collection of orchids comprised many rare hybrid cypripediums. A feature of all Mr. Rothwell's exhibits is the legible and attractive manner in which each flower is labelled. D. F. Roy, as usual, did himself credit with a nice group of Begonia Rex. The displays of fancy caladiums once so prominent in these fall shows were missed. Dracænas also were seen in limited number.

On the third day of the exhibition, M. H. Walsh brought in some handsome specimen blooms of his rose Urania, also some sprays of flowers from his seedling rambler Debutante, the latter being especially interesting from the fact that they were the second crop of bloom from the plant this season.

The October fruit show was combined this year with the plant and flower show. Apples were not up to the standard.

SITUATIONS, WANTS, FOR SALE.

One Cent Per Word.

Cash with the Adv.

Plant Advs. NOT admitted under this head.

Every paid subscriber to the AMERICAN FLORIST for the year 1903 is entitled to a five-line WANT ADV. (situations only) free, to be used at any time during the year.

Situation Wanted—As all-around grower. Cut flower place preferred. Address
J. F., care American Florist.

Situation Wanted—By florist and gardener in private place. Best of references. Age 35.
F F., care American Florist.

Situation Wanted—By November 1, or after, by a young man. German. For general greenhouse work.
H A., care American Florist.

Situation Wanted—By a sober, reliable and experienced man; position as rose grower in a first-class place. Address
B B., care American Florist.

Situation Wanted—As manager; first-class grower, designer and decorator; 25 years' experience. Address
MANAGER,
care Welch Bros., Boston, Mass.

Situation Wanted—By an expert grower of pot plants; 30 years' experience; as working foreman or manager of any nice place. German, married.
E M., care American Florist.

Situation Wanted—By young man of 19; either in store or greenhouse, where retail business is conducted. Present employer as reference whose business is wholesale only. Address
WILLIFRED EMMONS, Washington, Ia.

Situation Wanted—By expert grower of roses, carnations, 'mums and all kinds of pot plants, understands grafting also decorating. 24 years of age, single. State wages and particulars.
JNO. G. FLEUTI, care A. Osterwalder, 768 N. Halsted St., Chicago.

Help Wanted—A first-class rose grower. Call or address L. B. CODDINGTON, Murray Hill, N. J.

Help Wanted—At once, a sober, reliable, experienced man for commercial place. Steady work.
GUSTAV NOACK, Batavia, N. Y.

Help Wanted—Four good rose growers. Good positions with liberal wages for the right men.
ROSE GROWER, care American Florist.

Help Wanted—Man who has had experience in the bulb business. Address
CAMBRIDGE TILE MFG. CO., Covington, Ky.

Help Wanted—Two experienced carnation growers. Liberal wages will be paid for good men. CARNATION, care American Florist.

Help Wanted—Two laborers for private park work; married men preferred. For particulars address K. L. KELLER, Redstone, Colo.

Help Wanted—A good all-around florist as assistant. Send references and state wages wanted. Address CHRIS. HANSEN, St. Paul, Minn.

Help Wanted—At once; a sober, reliable, all-around man for commercial place. Single and German preferred. Reference required.
BOEHRINGER BROS., Bay City, Mich.

INTERNATIONAL FLOWER DELIVERY.

PASSENGER STEAMSHIP MOVEMENTS.

FROM	TO	STEAMER	*LINE	DAY	DUE ABOUT
New York	Liverpool	Etruria	1	Sat. Oct. 10, 8:00 a. m.	Oct. 16
New York	"	Campania	1	Sat. Oct. 17, 8:00 p. m.	Oct. 23
New York	Glasgow	Mongolian	2	Thur. Oct. 8, 11:00 a. m.	Oct. 17
New York	"	Anchoria	2	Sat. Oct. 10, Noon.	Oct. 21
New York	"	Columbia	3	Sat. Oct. 17, 3:00 p. m.	
New York	Hamburg	Furst Bismarck	3	Thur. Oct. 8, 10:00 a. m.	Oct. 16
New York	"	Patricia	3	Sat. Oct. 10, 7:00 a. m.	Oct. 22
New York	"	Deutschland	3	Tues. Oct. 13, 10:00 a. m.	
New York	"	Bluecher	3	Thur. Oct. 14, Noon.	Oct. 10
New York	Copenhagen	Oscar II	4	Sat. Oct. 16.	
New York	London	Mesaba	6	Sat. Oct. 10, 9:00 a. m.	
New York	"	Minnetonka	6	Sat. Oct. 17, 1:30 p. m.	
New York	Southampton	Manitou	6	Fri. Oct. 9, 9:30 a. m.	
New York	"	New York	6	Wed. Oct. 7, 10:00 a. m.	Oct. 14
New York	"	Philadelphia	6	Wed. Oct. 14, 10:00 a. m.	
New York	Antwerp	Finland	9	Sat. Oct. 10, 10:00 a. m.	Oct. 19
New York	"	Vaderland	9	Sat. Oct. 17, 10:00 a. m.	Oct. 26
New York	Liverpool	Germanic	7	Wed. Oct. 7, Noon.	Oct. 15
New York	"	Cedric	7	Fri. Oct. 9, 7:00 a. m.	
New York	"	Majestic	7	Wed. Oct. 14, Noon.	
New York	"	Celtic	7	Fri. Oct. 16, 1:30 p. m.	
New York	Havre	La Touraine	10	Thur. Oct. 8, 10:00 a. m.	Oct. 15
New York	"	La Savoie	10	Thur. Oct. 15, 10:00 a. m.	
New York	Rotterdam	Rotterdam	11	Wed. Oct. 7, 10:00 a. m.	
New York	"	Potsdam	11	Wed. Oct. 14, 10:00 a. m.	Oct. 23
New York	Genoa	Nord America	12	Tues. Oct. 6, 11:00 a. m.	
New York	"	Sardegna	12	Tues. Oct. 13, 11:00 a. m.	
New York	"	Hohenzollern	*12	Sat. Oct. 10, 11:00 a. m.	Oct. 23
New York	Bremen	Kronprinz Wilh.	13	Tues. Oct. 6, 4:00 p. m.	Oct. 13
New York	"	Prdk. Der Grosse	13	Thur. Oct. 8, 11:00 a. m.	Oct. 15
New York	"	Barbarossa	13	Thur. Oct. 15, Noon.	Oct. 26
New York	Naples	Germania	14	Tues. Oct. 6.	Oct. 15
Boston	Genoa	Vancouver	15	Sat. Oct. 10, 12:30 p. m.	
Boston	Liverpool	Bohemian	16	Sat. Oct. 10, Noon.	
Boston	"	Canadian	16	Sat. Oct. 17, 6:30 a. m.	Oct. 26
Boston	"	Ivernia	1	Tues. Oct. 6, 9:30 p. m.	Oct. 13
Montreal	"	Dominion	16	Sat. Oct. 10, Daylight.	
Montreal	"	Southwark	16	Sat. Oct. 17, Daylight.	
San Francisco	Hongkong	Doric	17	Wed. Oct. 7, 1:00 p. m.	Nov. 5
San Francisco	"	Nippon Maru	17	Thur. Oct. 15, 1:00 p. m.	Nov. 14
San Francisco	Sydney	Ventura	18	Thur. Oct. 8, 2:00 p. m.	Oct. 30
San Francisco	Honolulu	Alameda	18	Sat. Oct. 17, 11:00 a. m.	Oct. 23
Vancouver	Hongkong	Empress of India	20	Mon. Oct. 6.	Oct. 27
Vancouver	Sydney	Miowera	20	Fri. Oct. 16.	Nov. 10

INTERNATIONAL FLOWER DELIVERY.

STEAMSHIPS LEAVE FOREIGN PORTS.

FROM	TO	STEAMER	*LINE	DAY	DUE ABOUT
Liverpool........	New York	Umbria	1	Sat. Oct. 10,	Oct. 16
Liverpool........	"	Oceanic	7	Wed. Oct. 7,	Oct. 14
Liverpool........	"	Cymbric	7	Fri. Oct. 9,	Oct. 17
Liverpool........	"	Teutonic	7	Wed. Oct. 14,	Oct. 21
Liverpool........	"	Arabic	7	Fri. Oct. 16,	Oct. 24
Liverpool........	Boston	Saxonia	1	Tues. Oct. 6,	Oct. 12
Liverpool........	"	Cestrian	16	Fri. Oct. 9,	
Liverpool........	"	Devonian	16	Fri. Oct. 16,	
Liverpool........	Montreal	Canada	15	Wed. Oct. 14,	
Glasgow..........	New York	Furnessia	5	Thur. Oct. 8,	
Glasgow..........	"	Astoria	5	Thur. Oct. 15,	
Glasgow..........	"	Numidian	3	Sat. Oct. 17,	Oct. 26
Genoa............	"	Liguria	12	Mon. Oct. 5,	
Genoa............	"	Citta di Milano	12	Mon. Oct. 12,	
Southampton.....	"	St. Louis	8	Sat. Oct. 10, Noon.	
Southampton.....	"	New York	8	Sat. Oct. 17, Noon.	Oct .24
Southampton.....	"	Menominee	6	Wed. Oct. 7,	Oct. 17
London...........	"	Minneapolis	6	Sat. Oct. 10,	Oct. 19
London...........	"	Minnehaha	6	Sat. Oct. 17,	Oct. 27
Antwerp..........	"	Kroonland	9	Sat. Oct. 10, 1:03 p. m.	Oct. 19
Antwerp..........	"	Zeeland	9	Sat. Oct. 17,10:00 a. m.	Oct. 26
Hamburg.........	"	Auguste Victoria	3	Thur. Oct. 8,	
Hamburg.........	"	Graf Waldersee	3	Sat. Oct. 10,	Oct. 23
Havre............	"	La Bretagne	10	Sat. Oct. 10,	Oct. 18
Havre............	"	La Lorra ne	10	Sat. Oct. 17,	
Rotterdam........	"	Ryndam	11	Sat. Oct. 10,	Oct. 19
Rotterdam........	"	Noordam	11	Sat. Oct. 17,	
Genoa............	"	Lahn	12	Thur. Oct. 15,	Oct. 27
Bremen...........	"	Neckar	13	Sat. Oct. 10,	Oct. 20
Bremen...........	"	K. Wil. Der Grosse	13	Tues. Oct. 13,	Oct. 20
Bremen...........	"	Bremen	13	Sat. Oct. 17,	Oct. 26
Naples...........	"	Roma	14	Wed. Oct. 7,	Oct. 19
Sydney...........	SanFrancisco	Sonoma	18	Mon. Oct. 19,	Nov. 9
Sydney...........	Vancouver	Aorangi	20	Mon. Oct. 12,	Oct. 9
Hongkong........	"	Tartar	20	Wed. Oct. 7,	Oct. 1
Hongkong........	SanFrancisco	Korea	17	Tues. Oct. 13,	Nov. 10
Hongkong........	Seattle	Kaga Maru	22	Tues Oct. 6, p. m.	Nov. 5
Tahiti...........	SanFrancisco	Mariposa	18	Tues. Oct. 6.	Oct. 16

* See steamship list on opposite page.

The F. R. WILLIAMS CO.
Wholesale Florists,
CLEVELAND, - OHIO.
Please mention the American Florist when writing.

Albert Fuchs,
PALMS, FERNS, FICUS.
Established 1884. CHICAGO, 2045-59 Clarendon Ave.

HONORABLE MENTION AT MILWAUKEE FOR OUR HOME-GROWN PALMS.

50,000 Kentias, in finest condition, strong seedlings, $9 per 100; $80 per 1000. 3-in. 8c. 3-in. 12½c. 4-in. 25c-40c, 5-in. 50c-70c, 6-in. $1.00-$1.25, 7-in. $3-$3. 8-in. $3-$5.

Latania Borbonica. strong seedlings, $3 per 100; $25 per 1000. Strong 4-in. 25c, 5-in. 40c, 6-in. 75c, 7-in. $1.00.

Areca Lutescens, 5-in., three in a pot, 50c.

Pandanus Utilis, 5-in., fine color, 50c; Veitchii, $1-$3 each.

Pteris Magnifica, Cristata and Wymsetti, elegant hard stock for dishes, $3 per 100.

We offer 3000 strong, 5-in. **Kentia Belmoreana,** 4-5 leaves, 75c size, not perfect, at $40 per 100; $300 per 1000; fine for growing on, especially for outdoor.

5% discount in dozen lots and 10% in hundred lots where prices are quoted per piece, besides 3% for cash discount. We sell for cash but allow you to inspect our goods before you pay for them.

Craig—Harris
GREAT SALE, PAGE 271.

Northern Ohio CUT FLOWERS
ARE the BEST   THE J. M. GASSER CO., Wholesale Growers. CLEVELAND.

Some Madison Rose Growers.

The new-style rose houses erected by the Pierson-Selton Company this season for Righter & Barton will be watched with interest by local growers. In so far as they are an experiment they certainly have the advantage of being in good hands, for Mr. Barton is ever vigilant, seldom leaving the place before 10 p. m. each day, and Louis Thebault, the foreman, is an acknowledged expert in rose culture. There are few establishments where the many small details, attention to which is so essential in turning out a first-class product, are so thoroughly cared for. The natural consequence is seen in a well-established reputation for fine roses, and the contents of the houses present a pleasing picture of perfect health.

The approach to these greenhouses is through a winding avenue bordered by tasteful plantations of evergreens, beyond which spreads a velvety, flower-bordered lawn with a fine distant landscape outlook. There are two of the new curvilinear houses, each 27x142, connected by a corridor of similar construction. A substantial addition has been put on the old office and work-room in which has been installed a refrigerator having a capacity of one and one-half tons of ice. Here, as elsewhere, extreme neatness prevails, and the visitor must pass the scrutiny of a sad-eyed bull dog with an abnormally developed bump of espionage and capacious jaws that suggest possibilities of embarrassing complications for any unwelcome caller.

The houses are built with walls and sills of cement blocks and all the iron structural work is galvanized. Each contains four benches with walks next the walls. The grade of the houses rises from front to back sufficient to give the back an advantage of thirteen inches in height, and as each bench is about three inches higher than the one in front of it an average raise of about seven inches is secured for each bench and the plan of the house carries the back sufficiently high to give five feet ten inches headroom over the rear bench.

In these houses, as well as in the older range, nothing but American Beauty, Bride and Bridesmaid roses are grown. It has been the custom hitherto to plant Beauty in two or three benches and teas in the remainder of each house. While this plan has always given satisfaction Mr. Barton will make a partial trial this year of the separate-house system, an undoubtedly better arrangement, which is likely to so demonstrate its superiority that it will eventually be followed in all the houses.

From the earliest planted houses a crop of very fine cherry-colored Beauties are now finding their way to John I. Raynor's mart in New York City and in all the houses "specials" are stretching upward their long willowy necks. Grafted stock has never been planted here and no liquid manure is used at any time.

Another place where American Beauty is clinching its hold as the money-making crop of Madison is Marmaduke Tilden's, where there are six houses in which are grown Beauty, Ivory, Bride and Bridesmaid. Since the departure of the former foreman, Mr. Miller, Mr. Gilbert, hitherto outside foreman, has been in charge and his watchfulness and industry are being rewarded with an exceedingly promising

crop of sturdy Beauties of very aspiring habit.

A close neighbor of the Tilden place is the Villa Lorraine greenhouses, enjoying the most sightly and desirable location for the purpose in the district. The houses have been thoroughly overhauled during the summer and the contents, Beauty, Bride and Bridesmaid, are looking good and already giving some nice blooms under the care of Michael Noonan.

It is but a short distance from the above to the neighboring town of Chatham, renowned as well as a rose-growing center. Here the establishment of Samuel Lum has just been enlarged by the addition of four 150-foot houses, a propagating house, boiler house and work rooms, built by the Lord & Burnham Company. Hugh Lee, famous as the discoverer of the Bridesmaid rose while he was employed at F. L. Moore's, presides here over the range of sixteen houses. In addition to the varieties above mentioned, Meteor and Mrs. Morgan are specialties here. All plants are on their own roots and several houses are in their second year. One house of last year Meteors was cut down in August and the other tied down. The latter is now producing, but the cut back house looks promising and it will be interesting to follow the two throughout the season and compare results.

W. J. STEWART.

Nolens Volens.

AMERICAN FLORIST CO.:—I like your paper best of all. I subscribed for the paper — because they persisted in sending me free sample copies, though I never wrote them in my life.

Salem, Ind. O. P. FORDYCE, Florist.

GREEN SILKALINE.

Do not be put off with cheap substitutes.

John C. Meyer & Co.,

80 Kingston St., BOSTON, MASS

Please mention the American Florist when writing.

RIBBONS...

FOR YOUR TRADE AT

SIMON RODH,

40 W. 28th St.,   NEW YORK.

Chiffons, all Widths and Colors.

Please mention the American Florist when writing.

Boston Florist Letter Co.

MANUFACTURERS OF

FLORISTS' LETTERS.

This wooden box nicely stained and varnished, 18x30x12 made in two sections, one for each size letter, given away with first order of 500 letters.

Block Letters, 1¼ or 2-inch size, per 100, $2.00.
Script Letters $4. Fastener with each letter or word.

Used by leading florists everywhere and for sale by all wholesale florists and supply dealers.

N. F. McCARTHY, Treas. and Manager,
84 Hawley St., BOSTON, MASS.

Please mention the American Florist when writing.

THE SEED TRADE.

AUGUST RHOTERT returned from Europe September 22.

PORTLAND, ORE.—The Mann Seed Company has incorporated.

ALFALFA seed is expected to be a good sample this season but scarce.

BOSTON VISITORS: ·J.Comont, London; A. Emerich and Count d'Estienne, of Paris.

ROCHESTER, MICH.—D. M. Ferry Seed Company are adding to their seed farm buildings here.

SEATTLE, WASH.—E. J. Bowen reports, September 19, seed trade improving and the future bright.

GINSENG companies are as plenty as huckleberries and spending much money for newspaper advertisements.

DUTCH stock on the scarce list—mixed hyacinths, double Tournesol and Murillo tulips. Price on French bulbs also is firmer at present.

NEW YORK.—Six hundred and seventy-five cases of bulbs were sold at auction by order of the collector of customs at this port, September 28.

WINTER squash in and about Chicago has ripened poorly and is not keeping well. This vegetable will probably bring a high price next winter.

THE value of agricultural implements exported from the United States has increased during the past ten years from four million to twenty million dollars.

THE Scientific American supplement, Number 1443, August 29, gives a fine illustrated account of the seed farms of C. C. Morse & Company, Santa Clara, Cal.

CHICAGO VISITORS.—W. F. Kendal, Cleveland, on his vacation trip to Nebraska; George H. Dicks, of Cooper, Taber & Company; M. Mitchell, of Iowa Seed Company.

NEW YORK.—The steamship Gallia, carrying bulbs from southern France, arrived at Halifax, Nova Scotia, with a broken shaft September 28. The cargo will therefore be a week late in reaching New York.

ROCKY FORD, COL. — Rocky Ford cantaloupes of good quality sold, September 26, at $1400 per car. This is a record price. Recent visitors: W. Utterman; C. P. Coy, E. L. Coulter and J. B. Rice's representative.

· BOSTON.—The steamship Gallia, which was towed into Halifax, N. S., with a broken shaft last week, carried the main shipment of French bulbs, due in New York on Sunday, September 27. The delayed shipments include almost the entire supply for Boston houses.

UTICA, N. Y.—The Batchelor seed store on Liberty street, which has been a landmark here for thirty-five years, has been purchased by Ross E. Langdon, a prominent young man who will continue the business. Charles Soder, for fourteen years connected with the establishment, will continue the business.

Cleveland.

The annual picnic of the Florists' Club, Wednesday, was very enjoyable, with perfect weather until early evening, when a threatening storm turned the gathering homeward. The ladies' bowling contest was a feature. Mesdames Utzinger, Mollinkopf, A. Schmidt and A. Brown were prize winners. Adam Graham made the presentation speeches in his usual felicitous way.

The annual election occurred at the Monday evening meeting of the Florists' Club, resulting as follows:

A. Schmidt, president; J. Kelley, first vice-president; C. Bartells, second vice-president; Isaac Kennedy, secretary; A. L. Brown, assistant secretary; H. Hart, treasurer; Chas. Grabasse, Wm. Stade, Arthur Doeble, M. Bloy and Ogden Gaul, executive committee.

The J. M. Gasser Company made a very large casket pall for the Mrs. F. F. Prentiss funeral, consisting of 1,500 American Beauties. The casket will be sent away in a private car also suitably decorated.

Funeral work has been good. The supply of flowers is well cleaned up every day. The general tone of the market is improving with the quality of the stock. Roses and carnations are coming in fairly well for this date.

John Daubach, of Pittsburg, and F. Parker elected to membership in the club. After adjournment some fair bowling scores were made.

Fred Ponting is building five new houses, each 18x64 feet.

Visitor: S. S. Skidelsky. · O. G.

Baltimore.

Fine roses are beginning to come in but are not yet produced in quantities. American Beauties are still very scarce in this market.

The dahlia show held September 28 was a great success. Several thousand visitors attended. Messrs. R. Vincent & Sons deserve great credit, their exhibit alone containing 15,000 blooms. Messrs. Berger, Anderson, Burger and Halliday Brothers all aided to make this free dahlia show one of the best ever held in America. Over one hundred varieties were shown and the wonderful development of the dahlia illustrated by the rare specimens produced by Maryland gardeners. The flowers were arranged with a background of specimen palms supplied by Halliday Brothers. One must admit that the weather has been particularly favorable for dahlias. Your readers may be interested in a few notes on the varieties most admired: Austin Cannell, a rich magenta; Countess of. Lonsdale, flame-colored; Gloriosa, scarlet; Strohlen Krone, brilliant crimson tipped with purple; Harry Stedwick, garnet; Hohensollern, a beautiful yellow; Earl of Pembroke, rich plum color; Mrs. Bennett, soft scarlet; King of Cactus, Majesty, Henry Patrick, H. F. Michell, Grand Duke Alexis, Edna Hauline, a charming golden bronze sport from C. W. Bruton.

Horticulture in Germany.

(FROM ITS TRADE PAPERS.)

New Heliotrope. — Oberbürgermeister Köhler is the name of a new heliotrope which, according to all reports from Germany, is a most desirable novelty in the line of pot and bedding plants. Its habit is described as short-jointed, bushy and very compact; its height, when fully developed, from 8 to 12 inches; foliage, deep green, broad and hearty, surmounted by immense trusses of rich, dark blue flowers with large white centers. It propagates easy, is a rapid grower and the most willing bloomer of all heliotropes. It is unexcelled as a pot plant, and its even growth, great fragrance and constant flowering make it a splendid border-plant. Such an improved form of heliotrope is much needed. Our old run of varieties, as seen everywhere, make but indifferent pot plants or bedding material. It is especially their unshapely habit which renders them undesirable, and but for their odor they would be poor sellers. This new variety, however, it would seem shows none of those defects in the growth; there is nothing long and straggling about it—nothing but its name.

Remarkable Fuchsia.—A private citizen of Berlin, Germany, owners a fuchsia seventy-five years old. The plant grows in a large tub and is still hale and hearty, having produced and hanging on its branches at one time this summer over six thousand blooms. At least the gardener, who made an attempt to count the flowers, got tired and give up the laborious task when he got to that number—so says a Berlin paper.

New Palm.—Novelties in palms are few and far between, and any new addition of real merit to our short list of useful commercial varieties is hailed with pleasure. At an exhibition of pot plants recently held at Wandsbeck, near Hamburg, F. Goepel, of that city, showed Corypha macrophilla, which, unlike the old corypha australis, was of deep, rich green and perfectly developed foliage, the fans or fronds not showing any dried tips at their ends, as is invariably the case in the old variety. Freed of this fault, the coryphas would certainly be far superior to the Latanias for decorative material and as house plants, being much hardier of constitution and also easier to grow.

Fern Culture increasing.—Many of the German growers, including some of the larger firms, have begin in the last two or three years to devote all their time and space to the growing of ferns, dropping all other cultures. They grow them by the tens of thousands, selling and exhibiting them in all sizes from those still in flats up to those grand show specimens the Germans know how to grow so well. On the other hand, the growing of small palms has almost entirely ceased in Germany, everybody, so it seems, perfectly willing to let Belgium have that end of the rope.

Mossbacks.—A contributor to a German horticultural paper asks: Why do so many commercial florists and gardeners continue from year to year to grow their old, out of date and comparatively worthless varieties of pot plants and bedding stuff, when it is certain money-gain in their pockets to start in with the newer and better kinds, which are just as easy to raise, take up no more room, sell better and bring a better price? Why, indeed!

La France.—This is considered the finest and most profitable rose for outdoor summer culture by all German growers.

SAN FRANCISCO.—The Pacific Coast Horticultural Society held its complimentary dahlia exhibition at Maple Hall, September 19. Many private gardeners exhibited and the show was noteworthy in the variety, size, form and color of flowers shown. J. A. Carbone, of West Berkeley, was a trade exhibitor and was awarded certificate of merit for chrysanthemums and carnation Enchantress.

ALBANY, N. Y.—Local seedsmen report that the market gardeners here had a prosperous season. Owing to their methods of cultivation they had stock to sell when the farmers, on account of the backward season, had none. Indian

corn is a failure here, but the celery crop is excellent.

Farm with Greenhouses

For Sale or To Let.

Two modern Greenhouses for market growing. 24 acres with fruit orchards. Commodious house and barns. One mile from Brockport, N. Y. Fine country place near Normal School. Perfect climate. Apply

Thos. V. Pierson,
BROCKPORT, N. Y., R. F. D.

Please mention the American Florist when writing.

THE NURSERY TRADE.

AM. ASSOCIATION OF NURSERYMEN.
N. W. HALE, Knoxville, Tenn., Pres.; FRANK
A. WEBER, St. Louis, Mo., Vice-Pres.; GEORGE C.
SEAGER, Rochester, N. Y., Sec'y.
Twenty-ninth annual convention, Atlanta, Ga.,
June, 1904.

THERE is practically no crop of Colorado fir seeds this year.

LOUISIANA, Mo.—Stark Brothers' Nurseries and Orchard Company, incorporated September 22, under Illinois law; capital stock, $500,000, capital in Illinois, $2,500.

GENEVA, N. Y.—Wm. Smith, the well known nurseryman, will endow Wm. Smith college for women. It will be located on a site of thirty acres in one of the most beautiful sections in the outskirts of Geneva, and will cost $150,000. Mr. Smith maintains the Smith Observatory here.

ORANGE, N. J.—The laws passed by the New Jersey legislature at its last session regarding the San Jose scale, permitting the entrance upon private property and the destruction of affected trees by anyone after due notice had been given received both approval and disapproval at horticultural society meeting.

POMFRET, CONN.—Miss E. Jackson exhibited grapes at the Massachusetts Horticultural Society September exhibition in Boston last week. One of the bunches measured fourteen inches long from the top to the bottom, and weighed six and a half pounds. This lady also sent large specimens of Muscat Alexandria grapes.

Buffalo.

The Buffalo Florists' Club should be reminded by the appearance of chrysanthemums that some good work is in line for the autumn show if the club is to secure that much to be desired location on Easy street.

The opening night of Maxine Elliott's new play at the Star Theatre brought out some artistic bunch arrangements of American Beauties, violets and lily of the valley.

The frost is in the air and is expected nightly. We have said goodby to the asters. The retail stores have had a good and busy week.

S. A. Anderson had a big church wedding with an elaborate decoration at the house, using a large amount of stock.

J. H. Rebstock is among us again, though with crutches or behind a very quiet horse.

Reichert Brothers had several store openings and keep a supply of palms for this purpose.

W. J. Palmer was first in the market with some very good white chrysanthemums.

W. F. Kasting is attending to fall trade with a little politics on the side.

L. H. Newbeck is making good progress with his new place.

Byrne & Slattery and J. C. Pickleman report good business.

Numerous October weddings hold out hope to the retailers.

Wm. Scott is making his headquarters at Corfu.

Professor Cowell is busy with piping affairs.

S. C. Anderson has a fine lot of primroses.　　　　BISON.

Troy, N. Y.

Considerable progress is being made in the work of transforming the site of Prospect park into an ideal place of recreation. Work is nearing completion on an artificial lake for which 17,000 cubic yards of earth must be excavated. The lake will be about 600 feet long and from 90 to 150 feet in width. A thoroughfare to be known as Prospect avenue is being laid out, and when completed will afford the lovers of the park splendid views of the foot-hills of the Adirondacks and the distant Catskills. The old Warren mansion on the property is being converted into a refectory with toilet rooms and lavatories. The water works department employes are engaged in laying mains for the water supply to the lake, a large fountain and the several buildings.　　　　R. D.

PARTIAL VIEW OF JOSEPH KIFT'S GREENHOUSES, WEST CHESTER, PA., AFTER THREE MINUTES OF HAIL.

Destructive Hail Storm.

A very heavy hail storm passed over West Chester, Pa., Sunday afternoon, September 27. It came up very suddenly about 3:45, and the actual fall of hail did not last probably over three minutes, a very heavy rain following. The stones were very large, averaging about the size of horse chestnuts, although some were found as large as eggs. Many of them had the appearance of being composed of a number of small stones frozen together. The result of this bombardment was very destructive. Joseph Kift lost practically all his glass, a careful estimate showing but ten per cent intact. So violent was the storm here that a tin roof was pierced in a number of places where there were spaces in the boards beneath. The plants inside the houses were badly beaten down and probably twenty-five per cent are worthless. The loss is estimated at $2,000. No hail insurance. This is Mr. Kift's second experience in fifty-two years, the first about thirty-five years ago.

Hoopes Brothers & Thomas and Geo. Achelis, nurserymen, also lost practically all their glass. Chas. Dumey, vegetables and grapes, was most unfortunate, as he had just finished glazing two houses which suffered from a similar storm about three months ago. These are now a total wreck, all the glass being destroyed. K.

Springfield, Mass.

Business has started up nicely although the weather has been warm with no frost to hurt outside flowers. Asters are about done. Chrysanthemums are coming along nicely and with cooler weather will find ready sale. Roses and carnations are not over plentiful but are of fair quality and in demand. The plant trade is picking up, Boston ferns go quickly, palms and rubbers move slowly. Dutch bulbs are in and of good quality and satisfactory. The dahlia craze has struck this city. The amateur growers have fine collections. A. B.

SPRINGFIELD, O.—A. R. Aldrich had the misfortune, September 21, to slip down the steep bank cut in the street at his Belmont avenue greenhouses and broke his leg at the ankle. The city is probably liable.

English Lavender.

ED. AM. FLORIST:—Could we winter English lavender in a cold frame or would it be better to keep the plants in a greenhouse.   D. SANSUM. .
Baraboo, Wis.

I have never grown the lavender, but experience with other plants English and what I know of lavender by hearsay, I have no doubt it will winter successfully in a cold frame in Baraboo, provided the soil is well drained and covered.
C. B. WHITNALL.

Wood Burner For Greenhouse.

ED. AM. FLORIST:—Can you tell me what kind of wood stove I should procure to heat a greenhouse 10x40 feet, 6-inch stove pipe to be used?   C. W. S.

A cast-iron box stove that will take 30-inch wood gives as good results as any. If a temperature above 40° is required, where the mercury drops below zero, there should be two stoves with a line of pipe on each side of the house. By building a brick arch that will burn 4-foot wood with an 8x12-inch brick flue, better results can be obtained. If preferred 12-inch sewer pipe can be used for the half of the house nearest the chimney.   L. R. TAFT.

Cincinnati.

TRADE GOOD.—WHITE STOCK MOST IN DEMAND.—GROWERS' PROSPECTS BRIGHT. —LOCAL EVENTS.

Trade the past week has been very good. Several large orders for white roses, carnations and valley had to be turned down owing to scarcity of stock. White flowers of all kinds are in good demand. There is a surplus of colored stuff such as roses, carnations and asters. Some fine American Beauties are to be seen, but they are all shipped into the city as none of the growers hereabout are cutting any quantity of them as yet. Gus. Meier, of Hyde Park, is sending in some fine Liberty and Duchess of Albany which bring top market prices. Henry Benziger, of Covington, is cutting a fine crop of a pink carnation, the best coming in at present. It is a seedling and looks to be a comer.

A trip to Murphysville found all hands busy putting the finishing touches on planting their last batch of carnations. The growers here have been contending with much dry weather and some of them had the unpleasant task of hauling water. Their plants have been troubled with stem rot in the field, losing a good many plants and Murphy's White seems to be badly infected.

Dick Witterstaetter has his place in elegant shape and from present indications he will be right in it again the coming winter with those fine cut blooms for which his place is noted. It is a little too early as yet to describe Dick's new seedlings, but later on we are promised for the FLORIST full details regarding them.

Will Murphy returned Saturday night from a month's vacation spent up in the northern part of Michigan and his thrilling experiences with bears and mountain cats will produce cold chills and goose flesh.

Mrs. R. J. Murphy has made extensive improvements on her place the past summer and has everything in fine condition, and can expect a good cut the coming winter.

Al. Gray was in a runaway accident last Monday and came very near being fatally injured. He is thankful that he is able to be about again.   A. O.

Milwaukee.

The kindness of Jack Frost has kept field-grown carnation flowers in the market and of fairly good quality. Greenhouse flowers are coming slowly and are pretty short yet. Roses are in supply about equal to the demand. Some Chatenay are coming in and sell on sight. Holton & Hunkel are showing some of the finest American Beauties ever offered in the west at this time of year. Single violets are coming in now from Loeffler Brothers. First chrysanthemums came in last week.

The Florists' Club meets October 6, the first since election. Final convention matter reports will be heard. The bowlers who have been champing under restraint lately will organize for the winter under Captain Kennedy.

Currie Brothers have torn things wide open at their Wisconsin street retail store and are putting in a big plate glass projecting front, so passersby can hardly lose them.

A wedding decoration by Kapsaulis & Lambros, September 24. They used a four-leaf clover canopy which was much admired for its novelty and effectiveness.

The Citizens' Trust Company, whose vaults on Tracy street are in charge of C. B. Whitnall, were handsomely decorated at their opening September 22.

August Kellner has built 24x100 feet for decorative plants at 1184 Humboldt avenue, on leased ground. He will do a decorating business.

McKenna & Company had two large weddings September 24 and cleaned up the stock of flowers about town to the last bud.

Blaumeuser & Howard, big vegetable growers on Howell avenue, will devote their glass mostly to carnations this winter.

Heitmann & Baerman have completed their three new houses and have them stocked with fancy carnations, looking well.

Mrs. Florence Ennis has enlarged her place in the Plankinton house.

Nic. Zweifel is bringing in fine blooms of Crane and Lord.   H.

Orange, N. J.

The regular monthly meeting and exhibition of the New Jersey Floricultural Society took place on Friday evening, September 4, at their rooms in Orange. The change of day from the first Wednesday to the first Friday of each month has proved rather an advantage, though done to accommodate the Elks society, of whom the society are tenants, and the attendance and exhibits were good.

What with dahlias and Japan lilies the room presented even more than its accustomed brilliancy. The exhibit of fruit and vegetables was well filled, as also plants in pots, one adiantum attracting particular attention for its perfect symmetry. President George Smith, in his exhibit of fruit, showed some Brighton grapes displayed upon their foliage. The display of named varieties of dahlias by J. C. Williams was not entered for competition for the four silver cups, but the exhibition committee acknowledged their excellence by a certificate of merit, John Hayes had a vase of Lawson carnations of merit, and Peter Duff-Lilium rubrum.

Professor Apgar, of Newark, made some remarks upon the habits of plants, notably the desmodium and nymphæa. The first for the peculiar movement of the flower in bright sunshine and the last of a peculiar phase in its history

where it disappeared from Egypt for four hundred years and then appeared again.

The sentiment of the society was asked by one of the judges of the evening as to whether the cash value of a plant should influence the number of points in judging. It was decided that merit only as regards its cultivation should decide this at the society's shows.

Mention was made of the particular destructiveness this season of birds and squirrels to fruit. Notice was made as to the probable appearance of Mr. Gardiner, of Jobstown, at the next monthly meeting and the announcement that Prof. Britton would visit the society probably in November was also received with marked pleasure.   J. B. D.

New England Notes.

George Milne has sold his place at Concord Junction and located in Winchester, Mass., where he has purchased a promising establishment, rebuilding two greenhouses and getting ready for winter business.

A new florist firm under the name of Davis & Jones has started business at North Stoughton, Mass. They have two houses, each 21x75 feet, and contemplate erecting a new one 22x150.

THREE students sent out by Harvard University last June on a trip to Venezuela have returned with over 4,500 botanical specimens from the island of Margarita.

Guinivan & McFarland have formed a partnership for the business of mushroom growing in Beverly, Mass. A large mushroom cellar is in process of construction.

W. A. Dawson, an employe of the J. A. Budlong & Sons Company, of Auburn, R. I., was married to Miss Annie D. Storer, at Leicester, Mass., on September 8.

George Milne has moved from Concord Junction to Winchester, Mass., where he has rebuilt two greenhouses and will soon be ready for active business.

August Gaedeke & Company were the winners of all the first premiums for floral designs and greenhouse plants at the Nashua, N. H., fair last week.

Mrs. Elizabeth Thornton, mother of the Thornton Brothers, of Lawrence, Mass., celebrated her seventy-fifth birthday on September 1.

Fire did a slight damage to the greenhouses of E. D. Kaulback & Son at Malden, Mass., on the night of September 4.

NEW HAVEN, CONN.—Mrs. Alfred T. Osterman, formerly with J. N. Champion, has opened a new store on Church street.

LANCASTER, MASS., is proud of the fact that Luther Burbank, the great California hybridizér, was born there.

M. B. Kingman, of Amherst, Mass., has leased a new and centrally located store for his business.

Alexander Dallas opened his new store in Waterbury, Conn., on September 9.

AMHERST, MASS.—Professor Geo. O. Green, of the Kansas Agricultural College, has been appointed assistant instructor in horticulture here. M. B. Kingman, florist, has opened a new salesroom in connection with his business.

GIANT Cyclamen

Well set with buds, 2½-in. $4, 3-in. $7 per 100

PRIMROSES, strong 3-inch, $5.00 per 100.

OBCONICAS. They are well-grown, strong plants, 4-inch, $12.00, 5-inch, $20.00 per 100, ready for 6-inch and 7-inch pots.

CARNATIONS, field-grown, now in 4-inch pots, for late planting, Joost, Glory, Lawson, $8.00 per 100.

ASPARAGUS SPRENGERI, 2-inch, $1.50 per 100; $12.00 per 1000.

☞ The above is all well-grown stock. Satisfaction guaranteed.

C. WINTERICH, Defiance, O.

SPECIAL OFFER.

CYCLAMEN PERSICUM SPLENDENS GIGANTEUM.

Finest strain in the world in four true colors, a splendid lot of plants, well budded from 3, 3½, 4-inch pots at $7.00, $10.00, $12.00 per 100.

CHINESE PRIMROSES.

No finer strain on the market, all colors, well grown plants, from 2½, 3, 3½-inch pots, at $3.00 $5.00, $7.00 per 100. SATISFACTION GUARANTEED.

PAUL MADER. East Stroudsburg, Pa.

75,000 Geranium Cuttings.

Our cuttings this fall are perfection. Order now and secure the best stock of the ONLY varieties to grow for profit which are: Jean Viaud (pink); S. A. Nutt (crimson); Alphonse Riccard (scarlet); Mme. Buchner (white); Beaute Poitevine and Mrs. E. G. Hill (salmons). All semi-double, strong rooted cuttings, $1.25 per 100; $12.00 per 1000. FIELD PLANTS of the above varieties, 25 plants for $1.00; $3.00 per 100.

Petunias. Double Fringed, 12 novelties from Henderson's and Dreer's latest sets, strong rooted cuttings, $1.00 per 100; $9.00 per 1000.

Smilax. Strong 2-inch plants ready for planting, $1.00 per 100; $8.00 per 1000.

Salvia. The two best, St. Louis and Bonfire, rooted cuttings, $1.00 per 100; $8.00 per 1000. Samples gladly sent,

The W. T. BUCKLEY PLANT CO., SPRINGFIELD, ILL.

Always mention the.......
American Florist
when you write to an advertiser.

PRIMROSES.

	Per 100
Chinese, Obconica, Alba and Rosea..........	$2.00
Asparagus Sprengeri, 2¼-inch pots	2.00
Asparagus Plumosus, 2¼-inch pots	2.50
P. W. Narcissus Bulbs, 13 cent. and up...	1.00
Pansy Plants..................per 1000, $3.00	.50

—CASH—

Jos. H. Cunningham, Delaware, O.

Geraniums

ROOTED CUTTINGS NOW READY.

	Per 100	1000
S. A. Nutt, Perkins and Buchner......	$1.50	$10.00
Poitevine, Riccard, Viaud and Castellaine..........	2.00	15.50
Le Soliel and L Francais..............	2.50	20.00
Trego..................................	5.00	40.00

Not less than 25 of one variety will be sent. 250 can be figured at thousand rates.

Send for list of po grown geraniums at $2.00 per 100; $15.00 per 1000.

PANSIES.

An exceptionally fine strain, small plants from seed beds at 75c per 100; $4.00 per 1000.

ALBERT M. HERR, Lancaster, Pa.

3,000 FINE SURPLUS STOCK

Of 2½-inch 'Mums, including Wedding, Reiman, Chadwick, Estelle, Morel, Appleton and many others, $20.00 per 1000.

2,000 extra nice, 3½-inch Maids, $40.00 per 1000.

Liger and Richardson, the two new Pinks, fine 2½-inch stock, $15.00 per 100.

Poehlmann Bros. Co., Morton Grove, Ill.

THE SERVICE OF THE NICKEL PLATE ROAD

To New York City and Boston, is unsurpassed. Three fast express trains, in each direction, daily. These trains are composed of modern first-class day coaches, elegant vestibuled sleeping cars between Chicago, New York and Boston and other eastern points; superior dining-car service, meals being served on American Club Plan, ranging in price from 35c to $1.00; also service a la carte. Passengers can travel comfortably, and economically via the Nickel Plate. See that your ticket reads that way. Chicago City Office, 111 Adams St. Depot, La Salle St. and Van Buren St., on the elevated loop. 21

HELLER BROS. South Park Floral Co., NEW CASTLE, IND.

All grades and kinds of

...ROSES...

cheap, medium or high-grade

carefully packed and promptly shipped to all points. New customers that commence now will get best service when roses are scarce.

New England Notes.

DOVER, N. H.—Since the addition of his new range of houses, C. L. Howe has probably the largest place for local business purposes in the state. He has about 20,000 feet of glass devoted to roses, 15,000 to carnations and the balance to a general line of violets, lilies, etc. Mr. Howe has adopted the scheme of employing a builder by the year and expects to keep him busy getting out material and building and repairing right along.

The Newport, R. I., Horticultural Society is arranging to give one of the most extensive exhibitions ever given in that city. The show will be held at Masonic Hall on September 22, to 24. The prize schedule amounts to upwards of $1,000, there being seventy-seven classes. The table decorations, which will be a feature of the second day, are to be judged by ladies.

On Tuesday, Wednesday and Thursday, October 27, 28 and 29, the third annual exhibition of the Lenox Horticultural Society will be held at the town hall, Lenox, Mass. The prospects are for a show larger even than the phenomenal one of last year. Lenox is the home of a large number of the most expert gardeners in America, and their exhibitions have always been of a high grade. Schedules are ready and may be had on application to Fred. Hermans, secretary of the society.

Asparagus.

SPRENGERI. Now is the right time to bench for a good winter's supply of green. Field-grown stock is far superior to pot plants for this purpose, being heavily rooted and well set with eyes. When benched they immediately start into active growth, throwing up numerous growths, which come to perfection much earlier than those from pot plants.

Field-plants, $4.00, $6.00 and $8.00 per 100, according to size. Well established plants **from 2½-inch pots,** ready for 4-inch pots, $4.00 per 100.

PLUMOSUS NANUS. Our plants are exceptionally fine this season. Buy now for fall and holiday sales. From 2½-inch pots, $5.00 per 100; 4-inch pots, $12.00 per 100.

CORMORENSIS. Extra strong 3-in. pot plants, now throwing heavy growths, $10.00 per 100.

NEPHROLEPIS PIERSONI. Have a large stock in excellent condition. From 2¼-inch pots, 30c each; $25.00 per 100.

SMILAX. Large, well rooted, field-grown clumps, $3.00 per 100.

VIOLET, CALIFORNIA. Healthy field clumps, $4.00 per 100.

Send for fall trade list of other seasonable stock.

NATHAN SMITH & SON, ADRIAN, MICH.

Please mention the American Florist when writing.

A FEW GOOD THINGS YOU WANT.

Special low prices on palms to close out. Fine clean stock, cool grown and well shaped plants, none better.

ARECA LUTESCENS, 3 plants to pot, 4, 5 and 6-inch, $25, $40 and $100 per 100.

KENTIA Belmoreana and Forsteriana, 3, 4, 5 and 6-inch, $12, $25, $40, $100 per 100.

REX BEGONIA, 2 and 3-inch, $4 and $6 per 100.

DRACAENA INDIVISA, 3-inch, $5.00 per 100; 4-inch, $10 per 100

ENGLISH IVY, 2 and 3-inch, $3 and $6 per 100.

BOSTON FERNS, 5-inch, $30 per 100. From beds, for 2, 3 and 4-inch pots, $4.00, $6.00, $15.00 per 100.

ASPARAGUS PLUMOSUS, 3-inch, $8.00 per 100.
" **SPRENGERI,** 2-inch, $3.00 per 100.

CHINESE PRIMROSES, Fringed, 3-inch, $4.00 per 100.

CYCLAMEN GIGANTEUM, 3-inch, $6.00 per 100.

Place orders now for Rooted Geranium Cuttings.

CASH OR C. O. D.

GEO. M. EMMANS, NEWTON, N. J.

Please mention the American Florist when writing.

PALMS, FERNS, ETC.

We offer good values; saving in express and freight to buyers west of Ohio.

BOSTON FERNS. Nephrolepis Exaltata Bostoniensis.

We have the finest stock in the West. All our plants are pot-grown, bushy stock, well furnished with fronds from the pot up, and cannot be compared with the cheap, long-drawn-up, lifted stock from the bench. A sample shipment will convince you of our superior stock.

	Each	Per doz.	Per 100
2½ inch pot plants	$	$ .60	$ 5.00
3 " " "		1.50	10.00
4 " " "		2.50	20.00
5 " " "	.50	5.00	40.00
6 " pan "	.75	8.00	60.00
7 " " "	1.00	10.00	75.00
8 " " "	1.50	15.00	
9 " " "	$2.00 to 2.50		
10 " " "	3.00 to 3.50		

PIERSONI FERN.

Well-grown, bushy stock.

2½-inch pots	$25.00 per 100; $200.00 per 1000
4-inch	$ .75 each
5-inch pots	1.00 each
6-inch pots	1.50 each
7-inch pots	2.50 each
8-inch pots	3.00 each

ANNA FOSTER FERN.

Elegant stock.

2½-inch pots	$ 8.00 per 100
3 inch pots	15.00 per 100
4-inch pots	25.00 per 100
5-inch pots	50 00 per 100
6-inch pots	$ 9.00 per dozen
7-inch pots	12.00 per dozen
8 inch pots	18 00 per dozen

Cycas Revoluta.

With fine crowns, pots full of roots. Plants in all sizes from 25c to $3.00 each, at 5c per leaf

Asparagus Plumosus Nanus We are Headquarters.

2½-inch pots	per doz., 75c; per 100, $5.00
3-inch pots	per doz., $1.00; per 100, 8.00

Send for our Special Price List of Palms, Ferns, Araucarias and Rubbers.

If you are a buyer of Palms, Ferns, etc., a personal visit of inspection to our Greenhouses at Western Springs, Ill., (one-half hour's ride from Chicago), will pay you. Long Distance Telephone No. 221 Western Springs, Ill.

CHICAGO. Vaughan's Greenhouses, WESTERN SPRINGS, ILL.

Palms and Asparagus.

	Pots.	Leaves.	In high.	12	100
Latania Borbonica,	3-in.	4-5	8 10	$.75	$ 5.00
"	5-in.	3-5 chr.	12-15	2.00	15.00
"	5-in.	3-5 "	15-18	2.50	18.00
Kentia Belmoreana,	2½"	3-4 "	8-10	1.50	10.00
"	3-in.	3-5 "	10-15	1.75	13.00
Asparagus Sprengeri, 2-inch pots					1.50
Asparagus Plumosus, 2-inch pots					3 00
Begonias, 3-inch pots					5 00

We grow a large assortment of Hardy Shrubs and evergreens. Prices made on application.

SHERMAN NURSERY CO.
CHARLES CITY, IOWA.

For Sale

Twenty-two large and beautiful

Palms.

Must be sold at once. Write for list and description. No reasonable offer refused.

H. L. CONDE,
Oswego, N. Y.

JOSEPH HEACOCK,

WYNCOTE, PA.

GROWER OF **Areca Lutescens Kentia Belmoreana Kentia Forsteriana**

For prices see page 345, Sept. 26th issue.

FERNS for SALE.

20,000 Ferns, 2 and 2½-inch pots, $3.00 per 100; $25.00 per 1000.

BOSTON FERNS, 5 and 6-inch pots; prices upon application.

P. R. QUINLAN & CO., Syracuse, N. Y.

STUDER OFFERS,

FERNS Fine Healthy Plants.

	Per Doz.
ALSOPHILA AUSTRALIS, Specimen in 11-in. pots, 5 feet size ....$4.00 each;	$45.00
DAVALLIOIDES FURCANS and BOSTONS,	
From 5-inch pots	4.00
From 6 inch pots	6.00
LOMARIA GIBBA and COMPACTA CORDATA,	
From 5-inch pots	3.50
From 6-inch pots	4.50
PLANTS FOR FERN DISHES, 2½-inch pots	.40
ROSES, Field-Grown, 2 and 3-year old, best varieties of Hybrids, Teas, Moss and Climbers	1.20

5 per cent discount for cash with order.

N. STUDER, Anacostia, D. C.

Please Mention The American Florist When Writing.

Alexandria, Va.

J. Louis Loose has roses, carnations and chrysanthemums in fine shape for the season. A number of improvements have been made during the summer and a new boiler is now being installed. From a small beginning twelve years ago Mr. Loose has enlarged and improved until he now has a large and well equipped range of houses.

C. A. Shaffer, who has hitherto confined his efforts to carnations, chrysanthemums and bedding stock, has planted roses this year.

Kreamer & Son have made some improvements on their place and are doing a good retail business.

Grilbertzer Brothers have their new houses finished and planted with carnations. VIRGINIAN.

Columbus, O.

A few of the early chrysanthemums are beginning to show color and will be ready to cut in about ten days. This will afford great relief, since there is practically nothing in this locality fit to cut for ground work in designs.

The Underwood Brothers are giving their place quite an overhauling in the way of repairs for winter, while the Fifth Avenue Floral Company, J. R. Hellenthal and Gus Drobisch have their new additions under cover and ready for use.

Friend Hellenthal, who never gets left on coal in zero weather, again has the black diamonds stacked mountain high on his premises ready for use.

Davey & Son have devoted their entire attention to chrysanthemums this season and contracted the crop to C. A. Roth.

There was a light frost in this vicinity last week, but was not hard enough to even affect cannas or coleus.   CARL.

Little Rock, Ark.

Good flowers have been in demand. In fact, we have had a fair trade all summer. Roses and dahlias are doing best service this month. The clear weather of the past two weeks has brought out inquiring customers who are looking over the palms for fall and winter decorations.

G. L. Tipton has added a new house 19x80 which is used for chrysanthemums. Tipton & Hurst have rebuilt one of their rose houses.

Mr. and Mrs. D. M. Tipton lost their little boy, two years old, August 28.

    C. T. L.

Louisville, Ky.

Mrs. C. W. Reimer made an effective store decoration consisting of broad arches reaching from side to side of the building and nearly to the ceiling. The arches were covered with wild smilax, golden rod and autumn leaves. Doves hovered suspended over the arches, carrying ribbons.

C. H. Kunzman's foreman reports carnations looking fine and no stem rot except in some Enchantress. His opinion is that such is caused by weakened vitality from over propagation or from improper treatment.

Miss Thompson made an effective store front decoration with long strings of asparagus plumosus, with pendant pink rose buds in great profusion.

C. Haupt, until recently with his brother, will open in market street and his ability in our line will insure success.

Verbenas have suffered from the dry weather and few cuttings can be made. The horse show opens September 28 and will help business.

Fall openings by all the leading stores have benefited our trade.   H. G. W.

WACO, TEXAS.—A floral parade will be held in connection with the fall show, some thirty floats are promised.

Syracuse, N. Y.

P. R. Quinlan & Company are making rapid progress on the building of their new plant at Onondaga Valley. Their retail store windows contains a bulb display. Boston ferns seem more popular than ever and begonias are selling well. Carnations are hard to get, bringing 75 cents a dozen. Manager W. S. Wheadon recently made a novel pall for a funeral. It was composed of Asparagus plumosus and strands of English ivy with the leaves polished. The pall was fringed with white roses and there were clusters of white roses scattered over the surface.

With the advent of cool weather and frost, outdoor stock is on its last legs. The summer has been better than usual for this side of the florists' business. Stock for future flowers is looking well. There has been considerable funeral work. Carnations are still scarce and bring 75 cents a dozen. Asters are nearly gone. The season has been only fair and not as good as some years. All the florists are now displaying bulbs in their windows and the sale has started briskly.

L. M. Marquisee has in the neighborhood of 16,000 plants of Carnation Flamingo housed and all are looking fine, the feature being that the entire growth is of flowering shoots. Besides the Flamingo, Mr. Marquisee is growing the new Albatros and Sunbird. Mr. Marquisee reports the sale of cut flowers excellent.

Henry Morris will commence business in his new store October 1. Mr. Morris moves from 216 East Genesee street to number 210 in the same block. He is very centrally located and has large show windows on both Genessee and East Washington streets. The store is 50x18 feet with good cellar.

A. J. B.

DAVENPORT, IA.—Otto Klingbiel has done record breaking work in building operations on his new land. He closed a deal for four acres on Rockingham Road near Fairmount Cemetery, August 29 and September 25, when the writer visited the place the houses were up, all under glass, 5,000 feet, and 2,000 plants of fine carnations were already benched. A.

Indianapolis.

The horse show sentiment being in the air, both artists competing for the premium for show designs chose to represent that noble animal. Both these steeds were endowed with Albino colorings, white with pink eyes. One represented the head of a western bronco, with its bump of vice well developed. The other suggested a pacing horse of the light harness class, but badly windpuffed, while his mane suggested the presence of a skin disease of some kind.

The floral exhibit at the Indiana State Fair this year was larger and better than for several years past, although only about half the prizes were entered for. The following well known members of the trade received premiums: E. A. Nelson, Baur & Smith, John Rieman, W. W. Coles.

Messrs. Hartje, Hill, H. W. Rieman and Baur met with the officers of the association to complete the premium list by adding a few more premiums.

Boiler insurance companies are making a strong effort to secure boiler insurance. As the policy does not cover stock most florists decline.

Bertermann Brothers Company were among those who received premiums for window display during horse show week. The Indiana Floral Festival and Chrysanthemum Show has rented an office, No. 412 Majestic building.

Besides a very creditable display of design work, John Rieman showed a fine collection of cut dahlias.

W. W. Coles has taken the first prize for roses for twelve consecutive years at the Indiana State Fair.

Irvin Bertermann is well pleased with the liberal subscriptions he has secured from the city florists.

E. A. Nelson's vases were the finest seen at the State Fair for a long time.

Recent visitors: Herbert Heller, E. G. Hill, Fred. Dorner, Jr.

Everybody is getting bulbs these days —discount for cash.

Baur & Smith are good on specimen Boston ferns.   J.

PORTSMOUTH, N. H.—R. E. Hanford has opened a handsome new store in the Hotel Kearsage block.

LACONIA, N. H.—The Laconia Florist Company opened a new place of business on September 21.

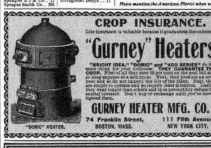

THE AMERICAN FLORIST

A WEEKLY JOURNAL FOR THE TRADE

America is "the Prow of the Vessel; there may be more comfort Amidships, but we are the first to touch Unknown Seas."

Vol. XXI.   CHICAGO AND NEW YORK, OCTOBER 10, 1903.   **No. 801.**

THE AMERICAN FLORIST

NINETEENTH YEAR.

Copyright 1903, by American Florist Company
Entered as Second-Class Mail Matter.

PUBLISHED EVERY SATURDAY BY

AMERICAN FLORIST COMPANY,

324 Dearborn St., Chicago.

Eastern Office: 79 Milk St., Boston.

Subscription, $1.00 a year. To Europe, $2.00.
Subscriptions accepted only from the trade.
Volumes half-yearly from August, 1901.

SOCIETY OF AMERICAN FLORISTS AND
ORNAMENTAL HORTICULTURISTS.

Officers—John Burton, Philadelphia, Pa.,
president; C. C. Pollworth, Milwaukee, Wis.,
vice-president; Wm. J. Stewart, 79 Milk Street,
Boston, Mass., secretary; H. B. Beatty, Oil City,
Pa., treasurer.

Officers-elect—Philip Breitmeyer, president; J. J. Beneke, vice-president; secretary and
treasurer as before. Twentieth annual meeting
at St. Louis, Mo., August, 1904.

THE AMERICAN CARNATION SOCIETY.

Annual convention at Detroit, Mich., March 2,
1904. Albert M. Herr, Lancaster, Pa., secretary.

AMERICAN ROSE SOCIETY.

Annual meeting and exhibition, Philadelphia,
March, 1904. Leonard Barron, 136 Liberty St.,
New York, secretary.

CHRYSANTHEMUM SOCIETY OF AMERICA

Annual convention and exhibition, New York,
November 10-13, 1903. Fred H. Lemon, Richmond,
Ind., secretary.

THIS ISSUE 36 PAGES WITH COVER.

CONTENTS.

The Rose.

SEASONABLE NOTES.

The ventilation of the rose houses will need careful attention now that we are experiencing changeable fall weather. It will be an easy matter to encourage a case of mildew or black spot, both of which will be attended with bad results unless care is exercised in this matter. The stock should be hardened off as soon as it is possible to do so without giving the plants a check, but avoid too much air on a day when there is a strong wind. It will be better to allow the temperature to go a few degrees too high than permit the plants to wilt.

The young stock which was planted early will have sent the roots too near the surface to allow anymore cultivation of the soil, but the beds should be kept free from weeds and leaves. The cool weather will induce a more sturdy, hard growth and a light feeding will be of great benefit. Do not be too anxious to start cutting on the young stock, but wait until the plants have attained considerable size. It is especially dangerous to American Beauty to cut from the young plants. Golden Gate and Ivory will in all probability have made a great deal of blind wood, which should be trimmed out sufficiently to allow a liberal amount of sunshine to the plants and soil.

The rose houses will all need night fires from now on, whether we have warm spells or not, as it is unsafe to risk the chance of sudden changes during the night. At this season of the year a great deal of harm may be done by careless watering and it will take close watching to keep the beds in their proper condition. Whenever the beds become crusted, or in such condition that the water flows to low places, they should be attended to so that the watering can be done properly. A good way to remedy this evil is to spread a light mulch, which has been worked up quite fine over the soil. This will help to hold the water where it is needed. R. I.

Pruning Roses.

Ed. Am. Florist:—I have some Lamarque and Chromatella climbing roses, which are growing very fast at present. When is the proper time to trim the above varieties to induce blooming during the Christmas season? Should they be cut back severely? L. C. L.

To induce these to bloom for the holidays, start at once and withold water from their roots as much as pos, sible to give them a slight check from now till November 1, then go over them and carefully remove any small spray wood or old blooming wood that can be spared, leaving all the strong, vigorous shoots unpruned. These should be spread out as much as possible, giving each shoot light and air if possible, then look each over carefully to find where the eyes are fairly prominent. At the last of these from the base up give the shoots a twist once around, then bend the top down low, or loosely tie it back under the base of the same shoots. This will give a moderate check and prevent the top growing any more, or practically do so, at the same time it will cause all the prominent eyes back of the twist to break readily, and if properly manipulated by this means each eye that bursts will produce a flowering shoot. On the other hand, if these same soft tops of the shoots are cut away at once the chances are that nearly every shoot will start another vigorous growth from near the cut and no bloom of any amount. After the flower buds are well set, and beginning to swell, the shoots which have been bent back in the original operation can be cut away altogether. That will divert a little more vigor in the flowers from that time till the flowers are all cut, and liberal treatment can be given the plants to induce the flowers to mature in the best possible condition. As soon as the crop of flowers is cut away pruning, thinning, etc., that may be necessary should be done. This is the time to do the main pruning of the plants, then allow them to make good strong leading shoots again and when these are sufficiently advanced repeat the twisting, tying back, etc., to produce another crop of bloom. By this method the varieties quoted, also Marechal Niel, etc., can be depended on to produce three good crops each year, as the spring and summer growths are much more rapid than at this season.

John N. May.

Manetti for Grafting.

Ed. Am. Florist:—I have 400 fine bushy plants of Manetti growing in the field. Shall I take cuttings from same and from these cuttings graft my rose plants next January? J. C. P. C.

Manetti stocks for grafting must have good working roots to be any way successful. "J. C. F. C." would, I think, have difficulty in getting grafts to take by the method he proposes, unless he could get the cuttings well rooted and established in small pots before grafting them, which would mean hard forcing of the cuttings from now on, weakening the stock so much that it is very doubtful if the plants would be any good, but as it would not cost much to make the experiment, he could try two or three hundred cuttings. If he wishes to graft some roses my advice would be to get some good stocks which have been grown in the open ground the past summer. As soon as they are well rested, pot these up into 2½-inch pots, place in a moderately cool house to make active roots before the eyes break, then as soon as they are in good condition graft in the usual way with whatever varieties he wishes to put on them.

JOHN N. MAY.

With the Growers.

BREITMEYER'S SONS, DETROIT, MICH.

A visit to Breitmeyers' Mount Clemens establishment of 175,000 square feet of glass is always full of interest, and especially so since they came into possession of their new rose, which is as yet unnamed. Fred. Breitmeyer is manager of this vast place, and he is most ably assisted by his brother William, who, together with their brother Philip, compose the firm of John Breitmeyer's Sons. The first houses of this branch of their business were built here eighteen years ago. Prior to this time the producing of their stock was carried on at their Mack avenue place, which is still in operation but mostly devoted to palms, ferns, lilies and other pot plants, although the present year about 20,000 chrysanthemums are being grown there for cut blooms.

In the spring of 1885 the necessity for enlarging their growing facilities became very apparent, due to their rapidly increasing retail trade, and Mount Clemens was selected for the future development of their glass area, which is now the largest in the state. At present they are about to build another house 36x250 feet. It will be modern in all respects and equal in size to the last three built two years ago, which are also modern, and placed some distance away from the original plant, and where, hereafter, all additional houses will be built. They will at once install in this new division a new 150 horse-power boiler, and with this increased steam capacity will undertake to heat the old plant, conveying the steam under ground by a main pipe a distance of 800 feet to the

connecting point of the older plant. The condensation will be returned by the use of a steam engine. The water supply for the whole place is taken from the Clinton river close by, and under direct pressure by steam pump until recently, when a gasoline engine was installed for the purpose.

Some of the first houses built here were devoted to forcing hybrids, the varieties General Jacqueminot, Magna Charta, Paul Neyron, Anna de Diesbach and Ulrich Brunner. These were under the personal care of the late John Breitmeyer, who took especial pride in them and was rewarded with continued success in their culture year after year until his death, which occurred over three years ago. During their earlier years on this place when they had new houses, new and suitable soil and other favorable conditions, their success with roses was amazing to the local trade, but in more recent years, even with increasing efforts, they met with only ordinary results with this flower, the present year being no exception.

In carnations this firm has always succeeded well and devoted a large part of their place to them. Some years ago considerable attention was given to raising seedlings, and they gave to the trade several varieties which were considered good in their day. Governor Pingrée, a distinct yellow variety, was the last one disseminated by them. Several good varieties originating with them were not offered to the trade but grown for their own use exclusively. At present they have growing 25,000 plants, embracing such varieties as J. H. Manley, a red one, early cropper, and although small is considered by them valuable because of its extraordinary productiveness. Dorothy with them does well, especially so they say until the end of February. Bon Homme Richard, Crested, Cerise Queen, Lawson and Morning Glory are grown extensively. They have a thousand Enchantress, some Governor Wolcott and some new varieties in lesser numbers are being tried. All of their plants are at present looking well, with no appearance of stem rot, which is so prevalent in these parts this season.

About 20,000 chrysanthemums are being grown. Some single stem calculated for specimen blooms and others with two and three shoots to the plant, the latter method being most generally used here. They are all in splendid shape and indicate a gorgeous sight by the time of the visit of the Florists' Club, which takes place annually to this and other Mount Clemens' growers about November 1. By far the larger portion of the place has always been devoted to the and hybrid tea roses, the popular forcing

varieties being grown in the greatest numbers, and added to them were the newer varieties, as they appeared from time to time, fairly testing these novelties. When one was found even fairly productive it was retained for the purpose deemed important by them, of adding and maintaining variety in the flowers offered to their retail trade, and to that end even old Bon Silene and Isabella Sprunt are still grown. At present all the varieties planted in the new houses, including American Beauty, Liberty, Mme. Hoste, Mrs. Morgan, Mme. Cusin and Bridesmaid are doing exceptionally well, while those in the older houses are fairly good, including one house of Meteor and three houses of Kaiserin, the latter having yielded heavy crops through the summer.

The great center of attraction on this place now, however, is their new rose. This variety originated with Hopp & Lempke, Grand Rapids, Mich., about five years ago and was acquired by this firm last spring. In the early part of last March Fred Breitmeyer visited, for the second time, the home of the rose and by its appearance at that time, and unaided by its excellent record with the originators, felt convinced of its productive merits as a forcing variety. The attractiveness of its bloom was no longer a question with them as they had followed closely the impressions it had made in retail circles of Grand Rapids and also with the trade of a prominent Chicago retailer who had disposed of all the blooms sent to that market.

The first impression it gives to the observer is the apparent extraordinary vigor and its tendency to make long and strong shoots. This trait is manifested even in the smaller stock, and large as the blooms are the growth would seem to indicate still larger ones. It is a seedling of Bridesmaid and Mme. Testout. It does not resemble, in either foliage or flower, the former variety, but the Testout type is easily seen in it, particularly the foliage, showing in the latter a decided improvement. The leaves are a dark, glossy green of extra heavy substance, while the color of the flower resembles Testout somewhat. It has many more petals than that variety while, perhaps, not quite so heavy. The form is cup-shaped and the fragrance good. It is in its decidedly striking color, which seems to defy accurate description, they base their strongest claims for it.

Speaking of the character of the plants, Fred Breitmeyer said that it was very sturdy and always indicated most rampant growth, and to substantiate his claim pointed with pride to the stock, consisting of 11,000 plants in various sizes and stages of growth. He showed a photograph, taken August 20 last, of

ESTABLISHMENT OF BREITMEYER'S SONS, MT. CLEMENS, MICH.

a table planted June 15 with stock of which the cuttings were put into the sand March 17 previous. It showed a forest of strong shoots, by actual measurement forty to forty-four inches high, with fast developing buds, and at the time of our visit, exactly one month later, many strong breaks were being made from the same shoots after the crop of buds shown in the picture had been cut off.

Bearing in mind the susceptibility of roses of the Testout type to black spot, we asked Mr. Breitmeyer for the result of his experience and observation with it in that respect. He stated that no black spot had yet appeared on it with them, although a table of American Beauty in the same house, and close to it, was affected. George Hopp, the originator of the rose, who was present, frankly stated that the rose was not invulnerable to the attacks of black spot, but he had never seen it affected except under conditions most favorable to that disease, and even then to no great extent.

Mr. Breitmeyer also stated that the heavy texture of the foliage enabled it to resist mildew under circumstances where other varieties would suffer, and pointed to such a case on their own place at the time. He said that it was the easiest rose to grow he ever handled and good results were possible without extraordinary care. A night temperature of 56° to 58° appears to be most agreeable to it. He also claimed for it the entire absence of blind wood, as every shoot terminated with a bud, and the present condition of the rose throughout the place bears out his statement. He said that it was very easy to propagate and gave assurance of their ability to grow young, healthy stock with unimpaired vitality to supply the trade without weakening the stock by over propagation, as they have now 17,000 plants growing on the benches, 2,000 of them being with their eastern representative, E. Asmus, of West Hoboken, N. J., 4,000 yet with the originators and the balance here under their personal attention. The new house now being built will be used exclusively for growing young plants and no plant will be sent out before April 1 next, although many orders are now being booked for delivery at that time.

Philip Breitmeyer, speaking of his experience with the cut blooms in their store, said that it receives the most flattering comments of the most critical and exacting customers, and never fails to excite interest and expressions of approval and delight. Referring to its keeping qualities, he said that a vase of them kept in a living room during the warm weather of June for ten days, were at the end of that time still attractive, although somewhat faded in color, and holding well together. He describes the flower as large, double and cup-shaped, the prevailing color a beautiful shell pink shading in the center to a soft rose pink. The reverse of the outer petals is of a creamy flesh tint, shading to silvery toward the base. The full open flower discloses a vivid richness of coloring rare and fascinating in the extreme, while the substance and formation of its petals, aided by the dark, glossy foliage, bears a striking similarity to some of the grandest hybrid perpetuals, with an exquisite fragrance to complete its merits as a forcing variety.

It is believed that this variety will also prove valuable as an outdoor bedder, and to test its hardiness and habits as such plantations will be made in different parts of the country and the results

closely watched. This firm, believing that the rose is entitled to a name commensurate with its value, is making extraordinary efforts to secure it, and to that end an advertisement will appear in the *Ladies' Home Journal* for November offering $100 for one suitable and descriptive.   J. F. S.

Palms and Ferns.

PALM NOVELTIES—FERN NOTES.

Novelties in the palm line do not attract so much attention among the trade as some notable flowering plant may do, the commercial grower well knowing that it may be a number of years before he will be able to get up a sufficient stock of a new palm to make

Breitmeyer's New Rose.

The illustration shows the rose exploited by Frederick Breitmeyer, Jr. Master Breitmeyer is 6 years old and four feet high.

much of a display. In addition to this the high price at which such a plant must be sold usually puts it out of the reach of the general public, and it is doubtless "the plant for the million" that proves most profitable to the grower. These conditions restrict the choice of species very greatly among the growers, but nevertheless it is interesting to the plantsman to take note of some of the newer plants and also some of the rarer species among those that have been long under cultivation.

Among the novelties may be counted Kentia Sanderii, a compact growing palm with dark green pinnate leaves, the foliage being divided into quite narrow leaflets with blunt tips. No very large leaflets of this palm are being offered as yet, in this country at least, so it would be premature to offer a judgement upon its merits at this time, but the young plants that are being offered show decided evidence of throwing several shoots or suckers from the base of the parent stem,

an indication that compact and bushy plants may be had without much effort. The foliage of Kentia Sanderii seems to be tough in texture, but the plant has not been sufficiently tested to enable one to say much concerning its enduring qualities. Regarding the culture of this palm it would seem best to grow it under the same conditions as Areca lutescens, namely, a night temperature of 65°, plenty of water and a well enriched loamy soil, shading from the sun fairly well during the summer months in order to keep the color in the foliage.

Kentia Wendlandii is also a handsome palm and one that has been under cultivation much longer than the preceding, this species usually showing a lighter shade of green in its foliage, while the leaves have a less number of leaflets and the latter are much broader, of good substance, and also blunt at the tips. K. Wendlandii is a strong growing palm, though rather slow in growth in its early years, and though it may sucker to some extent when grown to a good size, yet this characteristic is not nearly so marked as in the former species. This kentia is frequently grown under the same conditions as the ordinary kentias of commerce, but I am inclined to the opinion that a little more heat will not hurt it, especially while the plants are small.

Among the varities in trade collections, though exceedingly beautiful as specimens, are Oncosperma Van Houtteana and Stevensonia grandifolia, both warm house species such as enjoy a night temperature of 70° and abundant moisture. The oncosperma is a pinnate leaved palm, the leaves being divided into a large number of narrow leaflets of drooping habit, and the stems ornamented with a strong array of long black spines, the latter being a characteristic that would operate against its popularity even were it possible to raise a stock at popular prices.

Stevensonia grandifolia is the so-called "thief" palm, formerly known under the awkward title of Phenicophorium Seychellarum, also a spiney stemmed species, but one of the most distinct palms in cultivation. The leaves of this palm are simply bifid until the plant gets to a considerable size, when several broad divisions will appear, and the pinnate character of the species becomes manifest. The leaf stems of Stevensonia and also the ribs of the leaves are tinted with orange, and the leaves themselves not infrequently show spots of coloring that may be mistaken for disease by one unfamiliar with this peculiarity, and the contrast between the light stems and the dark spines is very noticeable. Both these palms are warm house species and require not only plenty of water at the root, but also a moist atmosphere and abundant syringing, an attack of thrips or red spiders soon destroying the beauty of the foliage.

Hyophorbe (Areca) Verschaffelti is more often seen than the foregoing, though by no means common among growers in general, this palm forming an admirable specimen in a 10-inch or 12-inch pot, but having the objection to a commercial grower of being slow in growth while young. H. Verschaffelti is a strong grower, its pinnate leaves standing up well on stiff stems of triangular outline, the stems of the leaves being marked with a dull orange or brownish stripe, and the midribs of the leaflets being whitish. The leaflets are rather narrow, those of a vigorous plant in a 10-inch pot being about one inch wide, and the plant is entirely without spines. H. Verschaffelti shows no indication of producing suckers around the base so far as I have been able to observe it, but the plant holds its foliage well when properly treated. Seeds of this palm are offered by dealers most

Soil Carrying Machine.

The illustrations herewith show a new soil conveying machine for emptying and refilling rose and carnation houses as used this season by the Lake View Rose Gardens. The Engineering & Power Company, of Jamestown, N. Y., are the

SOIL CARRYING MACHINE. Fig. 1.

seasons, and should be sown in a light compost and placed in a warm house to germinate, a process that may take three months. The seedlings are rather tender and should be kept in a temperature of 70° at night, given a good allowance of moisture and shaded from the full sun, it being a well-known fact that many plants require more or less shading when grown under glass, even though they may endure full sunshine when growing in the open air.

The ferns that have been brought in from outdoor frames require plenty of light and air, for when they are placed in too close and dark a house they will soon grow long and drawn, and thus become useless for filling table ferneries. The adiantums in particular require lots of ventilation at this season to avoid damping of the foliage, and if these useful though tender ferns are grown in a rather stiff clay soil the foliage will be shorter and more sturdy than that of plants that are potted in a light compost. Young adiantums may still be shifted on from thumbs to 3-inch pots, or from 3-inch to 4-inch pots as may be necessary, and should be in nice condition by the beginning of the year.

Very few of the many forms of Adiantum Capillus-Veneris, or common Maidenhair, are of any value to the florist, from the fact that this fern is liable to get more or less rusty in foliage during the winter, and owing to the creeping rootstocks the plants may soon grow out of shape, thus becoming much less satisfactory for most purposes than A. cuneatum. A. rhodophyllum forms a very pretty close growing small plant, its large primules reminding one of A. Farleyense, and like the latter this species may only be propagated freely by division, a process that is more satisfactory when performed during the spring and summer months than it is at this late season.   W. H. TAPLIN.

designers and builders and the machine has the endorsement of the Lake View Rose Gardens as a success for the purposes for which it was intended.

As the pictures show, the soil is carried in on an endless belt twelve inches wide, the machine being operated by an electric motor although gasoline or steam engine power will answer the purpose

SOIL CARRYING MACHINE. Fig. 2.

just as well. The machine is portable throughout and built in sections of ten feet so that two men can handle and carry them easily. It is adapted to fit any length or width of house, having side conveyors for wide houses and will drop the soil just where it is wanted.

Picture No. 1 shows the tripper, which is moveable and runs on a railroad of 1-inch square iron. As will be seen, one man operates and moves along rapidly as the desired amount of soil is deposited in the beds. Notice the belt full of soil as it goes up to the tripper, also the pile of soil on the bed as it is emptied from the chute.

Picture No. 2 shows the men emptying a house and shoveling the soil into the hopper and depositing on belt which is carried very rapidly out and into the wagons. The hopper also runs on the railroad and is moved along as desired. It is twelve feet long and five men are used on each side, taking the entire house as they go. Houses 33x300 feet, with five 5-foot beds can be emptied with this force in three and one-half hours and again filled in four and one-half hours. It formerly took a day and a half for each operation, with a much larger force of men; besides, the machine empties directly into the wagons as shown in in picture No. 3—a decided advantage in handling.

One of the many good points of this machine is its hopper fitted with grinder and mixer as used when filling the houses. This is a roller four feet long, cast solid, with heavy dull teeth. Ordinary stones do not affect it; they are broken and ground up and if a big stone gets in, the sides of the hopper are fitted with springs that readily release it. The soil can be had in any desired way, fine or coarse, by setting springs on each side of hopper. It is then carried into the buckets up the elevator and dumped down the chute on belt, which carries it to the tripper.

Another good point is the reversible elevator which both fills and empties the houses and can be reversed in ten minutes. Pictures No. 4 and No. 3 show this in both positions and it is quite important, for after the machine is set up in a house it is never changed until the house is finished, and the quickness in changing the elevator from emptying to refilling keeps your teams busy all the time. As soon as the last load of soil is out of the house, they commence bringing the new soil back so that not a minute's time is lost. Picture No. 5 shows how the new machine works.

The machine is a decided advantage over wheelbarrows or any other contrivance in the florist world today, both in economy and as a time saver, besides the advantages gained in early planting. It is a twentieth century idea and will save its cost in one year.

The Lake View Rose Gardens have no interest in this machine. Our experience is given simply as a help to some of our suffering brethren. C. H. RONBY.

Florists' Plant Notes.

LILIES.

A close watch must be kept up for aphis on the lilies that are being forced for Thanksgiving and Christmas. Fumigate them regularly, but not too heavily, or the tips of the leaves will burn. The aphides get down into the crown of the plants, whence they are difficult to dislodge. Rose leaf extract of tobacco diluted one hundred to one, or water soaked in strong tobacco stems over night, applied with a syringe or hand sprinkler is an effective remedy. As soon as the buds begin to show, applications of manure water should be given once a week. Frequent syringing is necessary if a high temperature is being maintained and the plants should each have a stake when about a foot in height. Those for Easter, which are still in the frames, can remain there until about November 1. They must be covered well with sash at night to keep out frost, but require abundant ventilation on warm days. Of course the covering of sand or stable litter should have been removed as soon as the tops begin to grow, otherwise an unsightly, leafless stem for several inches above the pot will be the result. The bulbs of Lilium candidum can be planted out now in the open ground; these will be found useful for Memorial day.

HARDY PERENNIALS.

This is a good time to transplant the herbaceous plants in the garden or border.

SOIL CARRYING MACHINE. Fig. 4.

plant the roots several inches below the surface or the winter will raise them out of the soil. A light covering of stable manure during the winter will be found beneficial. Several hundred varieties might be mentioned all of which are more or less useful to the florist, but manure and work it well into the soil;

for practical purposes to cover the range both of color and season the following small list of perennials is quite sufficient: For early spring Aquiligia cœrulea, irises (both German and Japanese) and Doronicum excelsum. Early summer, peonies, aquilegias (in variety), gaillardias, Coreopsis lanceolata, Dielytra spectabilis and the Oriental poppy. Late summer and

SOIL CARRYING MACHINE. Fig. 3.

The average florist requires a good collection of these plants both for cutting and to supply his customers' demands. With a judicious selection of the different species flowers can be had in the border from early spring until late in the fall. In preparing the ground add plenty of

fall, Monarda didyma, Heleanthus multidorus flore pleno, achillea The Pearl, Anemone Japonica alba, Phlox (in variety), Rudbeckia Golden Glow, Shasta daisy, hardy asters and delphiniums..

STOCK PLANTS.

Clumps of Snowcrest and Longfellow

daises should be lifted and either planted in cold frames or in a cool corner of the violet house for division in the spring. They may be divided now if so desired, and about the first of March can be divided again. Echeviras for carpet bedding should be taken up and boxed in sandy soil. Separate the small shoots from the parent plants and plant them a couple of inches apart in flats of sandy soil, and keep them only moderately moist during the winter in a temperature of about 50°. The old plants require but little water and will stand a lower temperature. Small plants of English ivy planted out in spring should now be lifted and given 4-inch pots. Place them along the edge of a bench and allow the vines to hang over the edge, or give each plant a good stake and grow them upright. These plants will be found most useful in spring for veranda boxes, and for supplying retail demand for a hardy vine, one warranted not to drop its leaves in the winter time. Cuttings of the Japanese honeysuckle and the common feverfew should be made now. Eye cuttings of the honeysuckle root readily in the sand now. The small plants are very useful in spring for vases and hanging baskets. G.

The Carnation.

SPECIAL TREATMENT OF VARIETIES.

In this and one or two subsequent articles it will be my purpose to give a few short hints as to the best treatment of the leading standard varieties. While the treatment outlined here may not give the best results under all conditions, when followed by us the results are most gratifying. It is not always possible to ascertain in one or two seasons' experience with a variety just what treatment will suit it best and often after a year's successful work another season under seemingly the same conditions may produce results entirely the opposite. However, success with a variety is the surest indication as to what treatment is best to adopt the season following and all knowledge founded upon such experience is a valuable asset in subsequent work. It is always safest to follow your own personal experience rather than be guided by the directions of one who may be working under very different conditions and with different soil, and these notes are not penned with the purpose of leading anyone to abandon a course of treatment which has given good results, no matter how radically it may differ from the treatment recommended here. To show how good growers may differ I will cite the case of Dorothy. In the catalogue of a reputable firm I find the following: "Soil must be heavy and well manured; 48° to 50°. Now, last year we had this variety planted in a rather heavy soil and the result was a very scanty yield. We concluded that the soil was too heavy, and acting upon that theory made the soil very light this year, and the way the plants are coming into bud certainly proves that our theory was correct. We also find that with us a temperature at least 5° higher is required to produce the best results.

White Cloud.—Heavy soil. Will stand lots of feeding after heavy crop of buds is well formed, say after January 1. Temperature 50°. Does its best work between January 1 and May 15. No good after this crop is off. The weighty flowers necessitate a high support.

Lorna.—Similar to White Cloud, requiring the same soil and temperature. More continuous in bloom, though not actually much freer. After well established and active growth has commenced light feeding steadily kept up suits this variety best.

Glacier. — Temperature 48° to 50°.

against overfeeding or it will produce a luxuriant growth at expense of bloom.

Queen Louise.—An easily grown variety and very adaptable, free, early and continuous. Light feeding regularly kept up and a temperature of 52° will encourage all its good qualities. In soil strike a fair average.

Governor Wolcott.—Our first year with this variety and we are growing it in the same house with Queen Louise. From present indications it seems to require about the same treatment.

Bon Homme Richard.—Blooms early and produces long stems from the beginning. Continues in heavy crop until about March 1. Heavy soil and temperature of 50°. Feed liberally while crop is developing.

Her Majesty.—The following is the originator's advice: "Soil liberally rich. Plant August 1. Temperature, night 46° to 48°; day 56°. Allow flowers to develop before picking, then the touch of pink will have faded away.

Mrs. Lawson.—This variety holds without dispute the title of queen of all carnations and as such has received the great measure of attention to which it is entitled. It has a very strong constitution and will stand more abuse than most varieties, but to insure proper development of the blooms and secure its richest color, watering and other points must be carefully handled. A temperature of 55° will in most cases be found essential to prevent splitting. It will stand heavy feeding after the soil is

GOOD WEATHER BRINGS STOCK IN WITH RUSH.—QUALITY DOES NOT COMMAND HIGH PRICES. — THE SHIPPING TRADE IMPROVES.—TRADE LOOKS FOR "JACK FROST'S" COMING.

Borrowing the Irishman's remark, the market the last week has "neither been up nor down but very much in the middle." Good weather has caused stock to come in with a rush, especially carnations, and the quality of a large part of the supply is not such as induces high prices. Some very fair chrysanthemums are coming in, and while they are bringing reasonably good prices there is no active city call for them as yet, which is due no doubt to the sluggish condition of the retail trade. Shipping trade continues to improve with a rather stiff demand for American Beauties and first-class roses. American Beauties, by the way, are showing up in grand style, nearly all the growers hereabouts shipping in good wares. Outside orders for these have kept the market fairly well cleaned up. The trade is anxiously awaiting a visit from "Jack Frost," when it is expected there will be a boom that will place the market in a more healthy condition. Greens, greens, you see them everywhere. The quality is good, and with store openings, weddings, etc., there should soon be a large call for them.

A local supply house was offered last week by a Chicago representative of Indiana factories a large lot of greenhouse glass in various sizes, said to be first quality and at prices very much below the market. But after tendering orders within two days after the quotation was made this firm was informed that the stock was exhausted. Evidently "the agent" had been away on a fishing trip and was not posted on the market.

T. J. Corbrey has gone to the Pacific coast again and is succeeded at Oak Park by Albert A. Sawyer. The place has been in Mr. Sawyer's hands since July and he makes a specialty of pansies, of which he has 100,000 in fine shape. Mr. Sawyer was formerly with the firm of Willis & Frankstein, real estate men.

John Degnan, of the E. F. Winterson Company spent a few days of last week visiting the Milwaukee craft and while there attended a meeting of the Florists' Club Wednesday night. They have a live membership and with a big surplus in the treasury are laying plans to have a mammoth Flower Show next fall.

Leonard O. Starett, the 17-year-old son of John Starett, with Weiland & Risch, was found dead on the C. & N. W. tracks Friday morning, evidently having fallen from the train. The little fellow was well known in the downtown market and the sympathy of the trade is extended to his father and family.

C. S. Ford has just returned from a six weeks, successful western trip. He reports that florists throughout the western flood section are recovering from the knockout blow received last spring. Indications are for good corn crops, and a generally healthy condition of trade for the coming fall and winter.

W. N. Rudd has been elected president of the Illinois Association of Cemeteries, organised at Springfield last week. The first meeting of the new association will be held in Chicago next year, in connection with the annual convention of the Association of Cemetery Superintendents.

The last meeting of the Florist Club, held October 7, was undoubtedly one of the best in its history. C. M. Dickinson was quite aggressive in pushing the good

SOIL CARRYING MACHINE. Fig. 5.

Heavy soil. Stems are too short to be a fancy variety, but pays well where second grade flowers are in demand. A very pure white.

Flora Hill.—Still a valuable variety for fall and spring work. Wants to be housed very early to enhance the value of the early crop. Whatever early feeding is done should be confined as much as possible to fertilizers rich in potash, of which wood ashes are the standard. to strengthen the stems. A medium light soil suits it best and a temperature of 54° is necessary to reduce its inclination to burst. Wants light treatment all the way through.

Norway.—Requires extra careful handling at transplanting. Wants a light soil and a temperature of 55°. Guard

somewhat exhausted. Soil medium heavy, its tendency to burn under clear glass in spring necessitates shading early and a very light shade should be applied to the glass about February 1; increasing the strength as the season advances.

Ethel Crocker.—One of the best pink carnations in cultivation, though not profitable with every grower. It is rather a shy bloomer under ordinary treatment and requires a high temperature to produce blooms in paying quantity. Flowers sometimes come out sleepy, which is probably due to extremes of dryness or overfeeding. Grown at a temperature of 56°, on a good sunny bench and kept rather hungry in dark weather, this variety will hold its own as a payer with the best.　　　J.

work along. J. A. McDowell, of Mexico, was a welcome guest. There were twenty-six members in attendance.

The George Wittbold Company should have been given credit last week for the float in the centennial parade, which was a credit to the trade, instead of Fleischman, who only decorated his regular delivery wagon for the occasion.

Vaughan's Seed Store employes have been busy this week with the first consignment of azaleas. The plants have come through this season in excellent condition.

Captain Schuenemann has sailed on his annual trip to Michigan and expects to be at the same location, Clark street bridge, in about six weeks.

John Sterrett, for a number of years with the E. F. Winterson Company, is now with Wieland & Risch.

Large quantities of cosmos are coming in but some of it does not show up well, owing to poor packing.

Edgar Sanders, dean of American horticulture, is seventy-six years of age to-day.

Willowbrook is the best early white chrysanthemum in this market now.

J. F. Kidwell & Brother have a fine stock of Boston ferns in all sizes.

Oscar J. Friedman is the happy papa of a bouncing baby girl.

Visitors: John Bertermann, Indianapolis; Miss Lillian Anderson, Des Moines, Ia.; Joseph Cole and wife, Peoria, Ill.; John A. Evans, Richmond, Ind.

New York.

QUIET OF EARLY FALL PREVAILS IN TRADE.—
GREENHOUSE PRODUCTS IMPROVED.—
MANY VARIETIES OF CHRYSANTHEMUMS OFFERED.

The customary quiet of early October, perhaps a little more pronounced than usual, prevails in this section. Sometimes the market takes a sudden spurt in a special line and the upward tendency is hailed with satisfaction for a few hours or a day only to be followed by a quick return to former conditions. The quality of most products of greenhouse origin shows a marked improvement. Cattleya labiata is coming in in great abundance and anyone wishing to make a record orchid decoration can do it just now, at an astonishingly small cost. Dahlias are still a favorite material in window adornment, the use of contrasting colors in large masses being very effective, especially with a setting of autumn-tinted oak foliage. Chrysanthemums are marching on. The list of varieties now offered includes Bergmann, Polly Rose, Glory of the Pacific, Lager, Meadowbrook and White Monarch. The full effect of all this material is augmented by large quantities of cosmos bloom which several dealers are receiving.

A. H. Langjahr has opened his new wholesale place at 55 West Twenty-eighth street and is now in a position to hustle for the share of the growers' gracious favors.

American Gardening, under its new management, is receiving numerous favorable comments on its improved appearance and seasonable contents.

C. Costos has opened a new retail store at the corner of Columbus avenue and One Hundred and Fourth street.

Samuel Henshaw, the ever youthful, was in town Wednesday attending his brother-in-law's golden wedding.

Messrs. H. A. Siebrecht, Sr., has been very sick for some months but is now recovering slowly.

W. P. Sears returned last week from

his summer cottage at Spring Lake, N. J. Ernst Asmus, who was recovering from a painful illness, is down again.

Cornelius Van Brunt, the botanist, died on October 1, aged 76 years.

Visitors: Ed. McMulkin, Boston; W. P. Craig, Philadelphia; J. Breitenstein, Pittsburg, Pa.

Pittsburg.

COLD WEATHER BRINGS BOOM IN TRADE.
—CHRYSANTHEMUMS PROMISE WELL.—
ROSES DEVELOPING RAPIDLY—ALL STOCK IS IN GOOD DEMAND.

The chilly blasts and rainy weather are now having their inning and with them comes the reawakening of business. While we have passed through a dull summer all indications point to a prosperous winter trade. Rose growers seem to be in a happy mood over the condition of their young stock. The same may be said of chrysanthemums, of which there is a much greater supply than last fall. Roses are much improved and rapidly developing into good stock. American Beauties, Kaiserins and Meteors are of a very high standard. All grades are to be had and they are good values for the price. In carnations Enchantress seems to be the most pleasing, while Lawsons and Florianas are coming in well and selling rapidly. Violets are not very satisfactory as yet, but they are selling just the same. Some white, yellow and pink chrysanthemums are seen in the store windows. Gladiolus and cosmos are about done. All stock is moving nicely with practically no surplus in any line.

The Pittsburg Florists' and Gardeners' Club held a very successful and enthusiastic meeting October 6. Many fine specimens of the dahlia were on display. A feature of the meeting was the serving of ice cream at the expense of the president, Mr. Faulkner.

The Pittsburg Florist Exchange is the name of the new wholesale house on Diamond street. Mr. Peter J. Deunas is the manager. He has the utmost confidence in the success of his new venture.

David Geddes and Henry Blind will open their new store on Fifth street near Penn avenue during the early part of next month. Both gentlemen have had long experience.

Howard Carney, late of the Pittsburg Cut Flower Company, has accepted a position with the Pittsburg Floral Exchange as bookkeeper.

Thos. Ulum & Company are having their store painted and rearranged and the electric lights in their window changed.

Shipments of roses from the east do not show any improvement over the local stock at the present time.

The Oakwood Rose Garden, of Oil City, continues to ship great quantities of good roses to this market.

A. W. Smith is receiving some fine single and double dahlias from Jarvis Smith's farm in Ohio.

Theo. Beckert is cutting some fine chrysanthemums. E. L. M.

Washington.

WEATHER FAVORS GROWERS AND TRADE IMPROVES.—VIOLETS MAKE AN EARLY APPEARANCE.—SOCIAL SEASON EXPECTED TO BOOM BUSINESS.

There is a noticeable improvement in trade, and as the clear and warm weather of the past two weeks has been favorable to growers, stock is fairly plentiful and good. American Beauties sell "for

all we can get for them," one of the leading retailers remarked recently, but $6 and $7 a dozen for the best, is about the limit. Brides, Bridesmaids and Mme. Carnots range from $1 to $1.50 a dozen. There are plenty of carnations to supply the demand, at 25 cents to 50 cents a dozen. Violets are about two weeks earlier than last year, of fair quality, and largely Virginia grown, selling freely at 50 cents a bunch. Dahlias are plentiful and cheap.

The center market is a busy place especially on Saturday nights. There the perfumes of the rose and limberger cheese mingle and commingle, and the carnation and cabbage are good neighbors. Flowers are also sold in the Riggs market. It has been suggested that the district authorities provide a suitable building to be used exclusively as a flower market, but no definite steps have yet been taken to that end.

The early convening of congress gives promise of brisk trade next month. There are indications that the coming social season will be of unusual brilliancy, consequently good business is expected.

J. H. Ley has a fine stock of his fern, Adiantum hybridum. He is also growing successfully, the Piersoni fern.

George C. Shafer is handling some good Bridesmaids and Mme. Carnots, grown by C. Schellhorn.

Z. D. Blackstone offers well grown American Beauties, also fine orchids, grown by Field.

J. Louis Loose is cutting good American Beauties, as also are A. Gude & Brother.
S. E.

St. Louis.

The unsettled weather conditions of the past week have prevented any marked improvement in trade. There are too many plants outside in private gardens to enable the growers to increase their trade to any great extent. Prices remain the same except for American Beauty roses which are advancing.

The meeting of the St. Louis Florists' Club will be held October 15, at 2 p. m., at the hall in the Odd Fellows' building. Important matters pertaining to the S. A. F. convention are to be acted upon.

Geo. Waldbart has had a busy week. A wedding or two served to liven up his trade considerably. He supplied a large number of American Beauty and Bridesmaid roses for the Veiled Prophet's ball. The judging of the plant exhibits at the St. Louis Fair was postponed from Monday until Thursday. Wm. Schray & Sons and C. Young & Sons had exhibits.

The Veiled Prophet's ball marked the opening of the social season in St. Louis, so the retailers look for an immediate increase in demand for stock.

Visitors: J. F. Craig, Chicago; Mr. Scott, with Vaughan & Company, Chicago. F. K. B.

EUREKA, CAL.—At the wedding of Guy L. Roberts and Miss Camille Lombard, a prominent social affair of September 25, Florist Henry Meide supplied elaborate decorations of evergreens and flowers, of which the predominating feature was the cactus dahlia.

NEPHROLEPIS PIERSONI was given a full page in colors in the Chicago Sunday *Tribune*, October 4, and described thereon as the "most beautiful fern in America."

PLEASANT, HILL, MO.—Billy Bastin, foreman for Geo. M. Kellogg, is rejoicing in the arrival of a 10-pound boy.

THE AMERICAN FLORIST

NINETEENTH YEAR.

Subscription, $1.00 a year. To Europe, $2.00. Subscriptions accepted only from those in the trade.

Advertisements, on all except cover pages, 10 Cents a Line, Agate; $1.00 per inch. Cash with Order.

No Special Position Guaranteed.

Discounts are allowed only on consecutive insertions, as follows:—6 times, 5 per cent; 13 times, 10 per cent; 26 times, 20 per cent; 52 times, 30 per cent.

Cover space sold only on yearly contract at $1.00 per inch, net, in the case of the two front pages, regular discounts applying only to the back pages.

The Advertising Department of the AMERICAN FLORIST is for florists, seedsmen and nurserymen and dealers in wares pertaining to those lines only.

Orders for less than one-half inch space not accepted.

Advertisements must reach us by Wednesday to secure insertion in the issue for the following Saturday. Address

AMERICAN FLORIST CO., Chicago.

BUYERS of flowers in New Mexico and thereabouts, like the crimson shade of the Roosevelt carnation.

THE astor fly, or flies (descriptions indicate more than one), has been very destructive in the west this season.

WE are receiving inquiries daily from employers who are anxious to secure competent greenhouse and store men.

IT is an encouraging sign that the growth of demand for set designs in cut flower work does not keep pace with that for loose flowers and artistic arrangements.

The Boston Fern.

The Boston fern, either in the old form or the new types, rests its reputation on its ability to withstand the trying conditions of the living room, hall or parlor. To attain this character it should be grown in full sunlight. It is better without shade at any time of the year. Another essential rule which applies to this fern as well as to all palms and decorative material sold to retail customers is never to send out newly potted plants. It is better business in the long run to refuse an order than to fill it with fresh-potted plants which are sure to decline and thus breed dissatisfaction.

A Dangerous Practice.

The daily papers say that Vanderbilt will abandon Biltmore, and the reason given is because he is disgusted with the peculations of his employes, many of whom he has been forced to discharge. The trade will note this with much regret. The question may well be asked if representative horticulturists can afford to continue to overlook the apparently growing disposition among gardening assistants in certain lines to demand and accept a commission on transactions which would ordinarily be considered in their plain line of duty and paid for by their regular salaries? Is there not danger that the men of wealth, of whom Vanderbilt is a type, and who, because of their great wealth, we are so much in need of, may lose interest in our art?

CHARLESTON, S. C.—The Carolina Floral Company has been incorporated with $2,000 capital stock. The officers are J. Henry Stuhr, president; Henry Viohl, vice-president and George L. Metz, secretary and treasurer.

The American Institute Show.

The horticultural fair of the American Institute, held in the Institute building, East Forty-fourth street, New York, September 22, 23 and 24, showed very markedly the effect of the backward season in the east. Vegetables were not nearly up to the standard of former years, with only one exception—cauliflower. This was well represented in quantity and the heads were excellent. Several brands of Snowball cauliflower were shown, but the peer of all was undoubtedly Thorburn's Guiltedge. The staging in most cases was very faulty. As already stated in these notes, the visitor had to guess at nearly every exhibit he looked at, there being no names to denote varieties. Better identification really ought to be insisted on. No prize should be given to a collection or single class that has not the name of the variety attached to each specimen in plain writing. Again, in only one instance were the beets and carrots shown with leaves attached. This exception was the exhibit of the children from the De Witt Clinton Park Farm School, Fifty-third street and Eleventh avenue, New York. Their exhibit was very interesting and well staged. Great credit must be given to those who are pioneering this project. Other prominent exhibitors were Martin Bell, Sparkhill, N. Y.; L. Clifford Bell, Sparkhill, N. Y., and T. J. Young and Howard Nicol, of Yonkers.

JAS. T. SCOTT.

Passing Events In Denmark.

The weather being of such great importance to horticulture I start with an account of the climatic pranks of the year so far. The winter was very mild, unusually so, but in the latter part of April a reaction set in, with the climax of a heavy snowstorm in Copenhagen and its vicinity. The storm did considerable damage to most of the establishments of the city, in some cases entirely wrecking greenhouses. Many fine specimens of evergreens were badly damaged. This snow left the ground in poor shape and all planting was delayed. The next couple of months were dry enough, hardly a decent shower relieving the drought; but since then the weather committee has been handling the hose almost incessantly, to make up for lost time. The truckers don't mind it much, as the crops are growing well, although the weeds are growing better, hoeing being almost impossible. The florists are praying for a little ray of sunshine being sick and tired of the monotonous accompaniment of the rain on the glass to their work. The seedsmen, having harvested turnips and kohlrabi in fine shape, are waiting for a change to ripen cauliflower, cabbage, mangels and other late crops. The nurserymen have been pleased with the rain so far, but now they join the rest in asking for good weather to ripen the late growth of their stock.

As to prices, the year commenced good for the florists, but of late the flower market has been quite demoralized. The truckers have fared exactly the opposite. The early season was poor, but all summer they had things their own way and their smiles almost reach their ears. The berry crop was large and prices good, but otherwise the outlook for the fruit growers is not bright, only plums being in abundance. All vegetarians and fruitarians are looking wistfully to America to come to the rescue with those large red apples.

The spring trade show was a success

with plenty of visitors, plenty of sales, plenty of money for all parties interested and consequently good will all around. The best things of the show were the cinerarias and melons from L. Dachnfeldt, Odense, and the tuberous begonias from D. T. Poulsen, Copenhagen. We have just had a flower festival for the benefit of a home for aged gardeners. The festival was under the auspices of the popular Princess Maria. There was a flower parade through the streets and a three days' fete in the "Tivoli," with a patronage unequaled in the annals of this popular establishment, and that means a great deal. The hoseman up above must have had compassion on the old gardeners for, strange to say, he held his thumb over the nozzle all three days. A large share of the success must be credited to the weather. The committee is busy yet counting the surplus and I may soon have the pleasure to report the laying of the cornerstone of the home.

H. HANSEN.

Mexico.

G. N. Pringle, noted herbarium collector, and Prof. Rose, of Washington, are traveling in this country collecting botanical specimens. Prof. Starr, of the University of Chicago, is also here in the interest of anthropology.

J. A. McDowell will leave this week for St. Louis to select the horticultural space for Mexico, and at the same time to plant some cycads and tree ferns. He expects to carry four car loads of plants in spring.

Prof. Cowell's idea of identification as expressed in the AMERICAN FLORIST of September 12 should be put in practice at St. Louis. Many new florists will probably attend that meeting.

The demand for large Resurrection plants is quite lively, heavy exports having recently been made. Amaryllis formosissima in large size is becoming quite scarce.

BETHLEHEM, PA.—Fall business has started in. Roses and carnations are still scarce. Horn Brothers, Rittersville, have finished their new carnation house, 30x305 feet. J. E. Haines is growing seedling carnations and the three are 'ooking fine. These are a fancy red, a large yellow and a very fine pink, which he will show the coming winter. He has also a fine bench of cyclamen in 6-inch and 8-inch pots, and one bench of primula obconica, I. Fries and Chas. Vorkeller both received a goodly number of prizes for design work and plant collections at the state fair here.

HANS.

JOLIET, ILL.—The chrysanthemum show will be held the first week in November. F. S. Allen and J. F. Ferriss are confident it will be a success, and if energetic efforts on their part count for anything, the exhibition will be one of the best ever held in this part of the country.

COUNCIL BLUFFS, Iowa.—J. F. Wilcox has completed a $25,000 residence this summer. Mr. Wilcox is adding to his gardens and has secured most of the land that joins him.

CLARKSBURG, W. VA.—Charles Dudley, a florist of Parkersburg, W. Va., has leased a room in the Waldo hotel for an up-to-date horticultural store.

COOL, damp nights and soft growth are the parents of black spot in the American Beauty house.

Philadelphia.

WEATHER WARMER.—ROSES PLENTIFUL AND IN GOOD DEMAND.—CHRYSANTHEMUMS MADE THEIR APPEARANCE.—BRISK TRADE KEEPS PRICES UP.

The debutante season has arrived and there have been a number of teas, principally at country mansions, for which the demand for bouqets has been good and which shows that this feature is still to be in vogue the coming season, and for many more let us hope. The October meeting of the Florist's Club was very well attended. There were two speakers, Walter Whetstone, in "Vacuum Heating," and Ed Reid on his experiences at the convention and in the far west. Mr. Whetstone uses Allen air valves, which are attached to the pipes in greenhouses, as are other automatic valves. These release the air when the steam is up, but do not open when it goes down. A vacuum is thus formed when the steam goes down and if the pipes are tight can be held for ten to twelve hours. This releases the natural atmospheric pressure on the water in the boiler and it will then boil and make steam at a heat varying from 160° to 212°, depending on the strength of the vacuum maintained. If a vacuum is held in a single coil the moment the valves opened after the steam is turned on it fills the entire coil instantly, as the suction is so strong that the steam is instantly carried to every inch of space. Mr. Whetstone states that this is by far the most economic method of handling steam, taking the place of the pumps which are kept continuously going in some systems to keep up the circulation. The system appeared to be entirely new to the Philadelphia growers and all were willing to try it, but seemed to doubt its practicability in greenhouse work, as it was thought possible to keep up a sufficient vacuum with the piping now in use.

We seem to be going backwards as to the weather, as for the last week each succeeding day has appeared to be warmer than the last. Wednesday the glass registered 76° in the shade. Roses are being brought on in quantity by the warm spell. There has been no change in prices, as the October weddings are now on and there is quite a demand for good stock. Commission men also report a good shipping trade, which helps keep down the surplus. Chrysanthemums are now coming in such quantity as to be depended on. White, pink, yellow, Polly Rose, Mme. Bergman, Glory of the Pacific, Merry Monarch, Monrovia, Marion Henderson and Willowbrook are the varieties. Carnations are more plentiful, but with the exception of a few white are not up to the standard as yet, although some lots received from out of town are the exception and bring almost double the price of the home grown. Violets are getting better. The Market Company have some choice singles, and Moore, Niessen & Pennock carry a stock of pretty fair doubles. Dahlias are much in evidence these days. The stock is large and varied and they appear to move lively.

A new rose was exhibited by John A. Shellem which promises to be a winner. It is a cross between Golden Gate and Mme. Testout. In color, as some call it gaslight, it is much the same as President Carnot, which it also resembles in form. It has a fine, stout stem without any sign of weakness at the neck, such as the Mme. Testout and is well clothed with foliage well up to the flower. The leaves are vigorous and green.

Horace Dumont says the Philadelphia Carnation Company have suffered badly from stem rot in their plants. One lot of 1000 Joosts received from the west have all died or had to be thrown out, and from reports of other growers of Chester and Deleware counties he finds the disease is making great ravages among the stocks. The Market Company report business moving lively. They now have nine employes on the roll.

The combined sale of W. K. Harris and Robert Craig & Son was a great success. There were 200 buyers present, half of them from out of town, and the bidding was lively. While some stock sold at bargain figures all desirable stock brought good trade prices and some of it even more.

Mr. and Mrs. S. S. Pennock have returned from a European tour.

Doan & Co. are handling some choice chrysanthemums. R. K.

SITUATIONS, WANTS, FOR SALE.

One Cent Per Word.

Cash with the Adv.

Plant Adva. NOT admitted under this head.

Every paid subscriber to the AMERICAN FLORIST for the year 1903 is entitled to a five-line WANT ADV. (situations only) free, to be used at any time during the year.

INTERNATIONAL FLOWER DELIVERY.

PASSENGER STEAMSHIP MOVEMENTS.

The table s herewith give the scheduled time of departure of ocean steamships carrying first-class passengers from the principal American and foreign ports, covering the space of two weeks from date of this issue of the AMERICAN FLORIST. Much disappointment often results from attempts to forward flowers for steamer delivery by express, to the care of the ship's steward or otherwise. The carriers of these packages are not infrequently refused admission on board and even those delivered on board are not always certain to reach the parties for whom they were intended. Hence florists in interior cities having orders for the delivery of flowers to passengers on out-going steamers are advised to intrust the filling of such orders to some reliable florist in the port of departure, who understands the necessary details and formalities and has the facilities for attending to it properly. For the addresses of such firms we refer our readers to the advertisements on this page:

FROM	TO	STEAMER	*LINE	DAY	DUE ABOUT
New York	Liverpool	Campania	1	Sat. Oct. 17, 2:00 p. m.	Oct. 23
New York	"	Umbria	1	Sat. Oct. 24, 9:00 a. m.	Oct. 30
Boston	"	Saxonia	1	Sat. Oct. 24, 12:30 p. m.	Oct. 31
Boston	"	Columbus	15	Thur. Oct. 22,	
Boston	"	Commonwealth	15	Thur. Oct. 22,	
New York	Glasgow	Columbia	5	Sat. Oct. 17, 3:00 p. m.	
New York	"	Furnessia	5	Sat. Oct. 24,	
New York	"	Laurentian	5	Thur. Oct. 22, 11:00 a. m.	
New York	Hamburg	Deutschland	3	Sat. Oct. 13, 10:00 a. m.	
New York	"	Bluecher	3	Thur. Oct. 15, Noon.	
New York	"	Auguste Victoria	3	Thur. Oct. 22, 10:00 a. m.	
New York	Copenhagen	Oscar II	4	Wed. Oct. 14,	
New York	London	Minnetonka	6	Sat. Oct. 17, 1:30 p. m.	
New York	"	Minneapolis	6	Sat. Oct. 24, 9:00 a. m.	Nov. 2
New York	Southampton	Majomtiuc	6	Fri. Oct. 23, 9:00 a. m.	Nov.
New York	"	Philadelphia	8	Wed. Oct. 14, 10:00 a. m.	
New York	"	St. Louis	8	Wed. Oct. 21, 10:00 a. m.	
New York	Antwerp	Vaderland	9	Sat. Oct. 17, 10:00 a. m.	Oct. 26
New York	"	Kroonland	9	Sat. Oct. 24, 10:00 a. m.	Nov. 2
New York	Liverpool	Majestic	7	Wed. Oct. 14, Noon.	
New York	"	Celtic	7	Fri. Oct. 16, 1:30 p. m.	
New York	"	Oceanic	7	Wed. Oct. 21, 6:00 a. m.	Oct. 28
New York	"	Cymbric	7	Fri. Oct. 23, 7:00 a. m.	Oct. 31
New York	Havre	La Savoie	10	Thur. Oct. 15, 10:00 a. m.	Oct. 22
New York	"	La Gascogne	10	Sat. Oct. 17, 10:00 a. m.	Oct. 25
New York	"	La Bretagne	10	Thur. Oct. 22, 10:00 a. m.	Oct. 30
New York	Rotterdam	Potsdam	11	Wed. Oct. 14, 10:00 a. m.	Oct. 22
New York	"	Staatendam	11	Wed. Oct. 21, 10:00 a. m.	Oct. 28
New York	Genoa	Sardegna	12	Sat. Oct. 13, 1:00 p. m.	
New York	"	Citta di Napoli	12	Tues. Oct. 20, 11:00 a. m.	Nov. 6
New York	Bremen	Kaiser Wilh. II	13	Tues. Oct. 20, 10:00 a. m.	Oct. 31
New York	"	Grosser Kurfuerst	13	Thur. Oct. 22, 11:00 a. m.	
New York	Genoa	Prinzess Irene	13	Thur. Oct. 24,	Nov. 6
Boston	Liverpool	Canadian	16	Sat. Oct. 17, 6:30 a. m.	
Boston	"	Cestrian	16	Sat. Oct. 24, 12:30 a. m.	
Montreal	"	Kensington	16	Sat. Oct. 17, Daylight.	
San Francisco	Hongkong	Nippon Maru	17	Thur. Oct. 15, 1:00 p. m.	Nov. 14
San Francisco	"	Siberia	17	Sat. Oct. 24, 1:00 p. m.	Nov. 22
San Francisco	Honolulu	Alameda	18	Sat. Oct. 17, 11:00 a. m.	Nov. 22
Vancouver	Sydney	Miowera	20	Fri. Oct. 16,	Nov. 10
Seattle	Hongkong	Shinano Maru	22	Tues. Oct. 20,	Nov. 22

*1 Cunard; 2 Allen-State; 3 Hamburg-American; 4 Scandinavian-American; 5 Anchor Line; 6 Atlantic Transport; 7 White Star; 8 American; 9 Red Star; 10 French; 11 Holland-American; 12 Italian Royal Mail; 13 North German Lloyd; 14 Fabre; 16 Dominion; 16 Leyland; 17 Occidental and Oriental; 18 Oceanic; 19 Allan; 20 Can. Pacific Ry.; 21 N. Pacific Ry.; 22 Hongkong-Seattle.

INTERNATIONAL FLOWER DELIVERY.

STEAMSHIPS LEAVE FOREIGN PORTS.

FROM	TO	STEAMER	*LINE	DAY	DUE ABOUT
Liverpool......	New York	Teutonic	7	Wed. Oct. 14, 5:00 p. m.	Oct. 21
Liverpool......	"	Arabic	7	Fri. Oct. 16, 5:00 p. m.	Oct. 24
Liverpool......	"	Germanic	7	Wed. Oct. 21, 3:30 p. m.	Oct. 29
Liverpool......	"	Cedric	7	Fri Oct. 23, 3:30 p. m.	
Liverpool......	Boston	Devonian	16	Fri. Oct. 16	
Liverpool......	"	Winifredian	16	Fri. Oct. 23,	Oct .28
Liverpool......	"	Ivernia	1	Tues. Oct. 20,	
Liverpool......	Montreal	Canada	15	Wed. Oct. 14,	
Glasgow........	New York	Astoria	5	Thur. Oct. 15,	
Glasgow........	"	Ethiopia	5	Thur. Oct. 22,	Oct. 26
Glasgow........	"	Numidian	5	Sat. Oct. 17,	
Glasgow........	"	Mongolian	5	Sat. Oct. 24,	
Hamourg........	"	Moltke	3	Sat. Oct. 24,	
Genoa........	"	Citta di Milano	12	Mon. Oct. 12,	Oct. 29
Southampton...	"	New York	8	Sat. Oct. 17, Noon.	Oct. 24
Southampton...	"	Philadelphia	8	Sat. Oct. 24, Noon.	
London........	"	Minnehaha	6	Sat. Oct. 17,	Oct. 27
London	"	Mesaba	6	Sat. Oct. 24,	Nov. 3
Southampton...	"	Marquette	6	Wed. Oct. 21,	
Antwerp........	"	Zeeland	3	Sat. Oct. 17, 10:00 a. m.	Oct. 26
Havre........	"	La Lorraine	10	Sat. Oct. 17,	Oct. 24
Havre........	"	La Touraine	10	Sat. Oct. 24,	Oct. 31
Rotterdam	"	Noordam	11	Sat. Oct. 17,	
Rotterdam	"	Rotterdam	11	Sat. Oct. 24,	
Genoa........	"	Lahn	12	Thur. Oct. 15,	Oct. 27
Bremen........	"	K. Wil. Der Grosse	13	Tues. Oct. 13,	Oct. 20
Bremen........	"	Bremen	13	Sat. Oct. 17,	Oct. 26
Bremen........	"	Kronprinz Wilh.	13	Tues. Oct. 20,	Oct. 27
Bremen........	"	Frdr. Der Grosse	13	Sat. Oct. 24,	Nov. 3
Sydney........	SanFrancisco	Sonoma	13	Mon. Oct. 19,	Nov. 9
Sydney........	Vancouver	Aorangi	20	Mon. Oct. 12,	Oct. 29
Liverpool......	Montreal	Canada	15	Wed. Oct. 14,	
Liverpool......	"	Kensington	15	Wed. Oct. 21,	
Hongkong......	SanFrancisco	Korea	17	Tues. Oct. 13,	Nov. 10
Hongkong......	"	Gaelic	17	Tues. Oct. 20,	Nov. 17
Hongkong......	Vancouver	Empress of China	20	Wed. Oct. 21,	Nov. 11
Hongkong......	Seattle	Riojun Maru	22	Tues. Oct. 20,	Nov. 30

* See steamship list on opposite page.

Wild Smilax ALWAYS On Hand.

Also PLUMOSUS, SPRENGERI, ADIANTUMS,
GALAX AND LEUCOTHOES.

We are Growers of HIGH-GRADE **Cut Flowers.** All orders promptly filled. Consignments solicited.

FRANK GARLAND, 55-57 Wabash Ave., Chicago.

The F. R. WILLIAMS CO.

Wholesale Florists,

CLEVELAND, - OHIO.

Please mention the American Florist when writing.

We Have Removed to No. 11 Province St.

ORDER DIRECT FROM HEADQUARTERS.

We carry the largest, most complete line of Florists' Hardy Supplies, Dagger and Fancy Ferns, best quality. $1.00 per 1000. Discounts on larger orders. Bronze and Green Galax, best quality, $1.00 per 1000. Laurel Festooning, best quality, 8c and 6c per yd.. Green Moss. $1.00 per bbl.; 75c per bag. Sphagnum Moss, $1.00 per bbl.; 50c per bag. We can fill your orders at a moments notice. Orders by mail, telegraph and telephone, will receive our prompt, personal attention.

HENRY W. ROBINSON, No. 11 Province St., BOSTON, MASS.

Please mention the American Florist when writing

Albert Fuchs,

PALMS, FERNS, FICUS.
Established 1884. CHICAGO, 2045-59 Clarendon Ave.

IF YOU HAVE STOCK TO SELL.....

The best way to make that fact known to the trade is by regular advertising in the

The American Florist.

THE SEED TRADE.

AMERICAN SEED TRADE ASSOCIATION.
S. F. Willard, Pres.; J. Charles McCullough,
First Vice-Pres.; C. E. Kendel, Cleveland, O.,
Sec'y and Treas.
Twenty-second annual convention St. Louis,
Mo., June, 1904.

HINSDALE, ILL., October 7.—E. G. Gray
& Company's mushroom houses burned
last night. Loss total.

CHICAGO VISITORS: W. A. Gilbraith,
with J. M. McCullough's Sons, Cincinnati;
G. H. Dicks, of Cooper, Taber County,
London, Eng.

BIRMINGHAM, ALA.—The Amzi Godden
Company has added a bone meal plant
to its business and will make a specialty
of high grade fertilizers.

CHICAGO.—Barnard & Company have
located their onion set storage house on
the Belt Line R. R. and will receive sets
there in bulk and then reclean and ship.

WE are in receipt of the twenty-first
annual report of the American Seed Trade
Association, containing the proceedings
at the Atlantic City meeting, June 23-25.

BIRMINGHAM, ALA.—The Amzi Godden
Company has sold its greenhouse stock
and business to John L. Parker, the
increased business in the seed department requiring all its attention.

COPENHAGEN, DENMARK.—Cauliflower
Early Dwarf Erfurt and Snowball are
looking well, but of Large Danish the
crop will be short and high prices are
asked for this last variety. Cabbage
Ball Head is promising well.

THE Jerome B. Rice Seed Company
makes the following comment on this
season's onion crop: "There seems to be
a less tendency on the part of the growers to store onions this year than formerly, and also a more ready market for
good stock than was experienced at this
time last season. Reports from several
of the larger producing districts, notably
Ohio, shows a large portion of the crop
has already passed into dealers' hands.

THE United States General Appraisers
at New York, September 18, 1903, decide
that Winter Vetch (Vicia villosa) and
Giant Spurry (Spergula maxima) are
neither of them grass seeds, either in a
botanical or a commercial sense, and
that Spergula maxima is not identical
with Spergula arvensis; which is a species of clover. They find that Phalaris
arundinacea is a grass seed and is exempt
from duty, while the other two are dutiable at thirty per cent.

Denver, Col.

Frank E. Smith, formerly with the
Sioux City Seed and Nursery Company
of Sioux City, Ia., is making strong
efforts to put the business of the late
A. L. Mitchell on a new basis. The new
style of the concern is the Denver Seed
and Floral Company.

Adrien Traverse has charge of the seed
department of the L. A. Watkins Company, and says the business has improved
very much during the past year or two.

Congress Will Probe Seed Contract Scandal.

WASHINGTON, October 5.—The Seed contract
scandal, through which it is alleged the Agricultural Department permitting inferior seeds
and less quantity than were required to be applied
is to be investigated by Congress.

The department has for some time been taking
testimony in this case for the purpose of meeting
a suit for moneys claimed to be due by Arthur C.
Nellis, of New York. No evidence is to be
taken in the case in Boston this week. In Philadelphia last week several prominent seedmen

made affidavits that the seed packages sent out
were short in weight and contained inferior
grades.

Members of Congress all over the country have
suffered from this fraud. The testimony taken
so far shows that the department had been
warned of the fraud, but permitted it to continue.
—*New York Journal, October 6.*

European Seed Report.

September, the principal harvest month for
vegetable and flower seeds, in the center of
Germany began with excellent conditions of
weather, so that all the field fruits being cut
and spread out dried quickly and could be brought
in in good condition. The heat on September 4,
5 and 6 reached 33° Celsius (91° Fahrenheit) in
the shade, which is far beyond the normal, and
it seems that all middle and western Europe had
at the same time an equal heat, for we hear of
several cases of sunstroke happening in Paris.
Chiefly the asters profited by this tropical temperature, developing the flowers splendidly, which
were considerably behind in comparison with
former years. Indeed a good crop of aster seed is
needed, the stock at disposal being small, and
certain much sought after varieties are cleared
out entirely. All other flowers like tagetes, zinnia,
phlox, verbena, helichrysum, etc., which are not
picked yet will benefit also by these sunny days.
And it is to be hoped that they may last for some
time, though this appears doubtful as the sky has
again become clouded and they seem a disposition to rain. The crop of early summer flowers
has been good both in quality and quantity,
especially pansy and myosotis seeds gave good
results.

The vegetable seeds are gathered out for the
greater part, but large quantities are lying still in
the fields in order to dry, and for this reason some
weeks of constant warm weather would be very
acceptable. The meteorological conditions seem
to have changed recently, and it is likely that the
last third of September may bring a period of
rainy days, which would probably spoil a good deal
of the crops still out in the fields, such as beans,
carrots, fodder and sugar beets and beet seeds.
The state of these beets has been rather weak and
a great part of the plantations dried even before
maturity, thus producing very small seeds which
are lost in cleaning and so reduce the quantity.
Beans will be under the medium, as well as
most of the cabbage varieties; the Savoy sorts are
better.

Red carrots without being abundant will produce sufficient quantities. White carrots, on the
contrary, are scarce and will probably cost money
this year.

Parsley, leek and onions are not out yet; they
still need dry weather and their present condition
justifies the expectation of a good average crop.

Peas this year had rather a slow sale, only
varieties like William Hurst, Telephone, American Wonder and some others went away quickly
at good prices.

Radish and spinach give good crops.

Lettuce has suffered a little, but the crop in
general may be satisfactory, a good part of the
later varieties not in yet.

Cucumbers have turned out a failure altogether;
the article will be very scarce this season, and so
much the more as there are no stocks in existence.

In France the general crop will be normal,
excepting some articles like white carrots.
Egyptian beets, kohlrabi, which were partly
spoiled by drought.

Cabbage is cut and partly cleaned, and furnishes
normal quantities. Sufficient plantations have
been made for next year.

Carrots will probably be under the normal, and
fodder carrots still worse, but there remains stocks
of these from last year.

Cucumbers promise an average crop.

Onions and leek will give in general a very good
crop both in quantity and quality.

Beans stand well, but will perhaps not yield the
usual quantities.

Parsley is good and there are great plantations
for next year.

Peas yielded sufficient quantities almost everywhere and are sold at low prices.

Radish has given a good crop.

Beets did not reach the expected quantities,
especially in Anjou; they are far below the average,
and chiefly the red beets turn out very badly.

Tomatoes are in a satisfactory state.

Italy is suffering under a long spell of heat, for
several months hardly any rain has fallen, so that
certain cultures are lost entirely.

Detroit.

The chief feature of the club meeting Wednesday evening, October 7, was the presentation to ex-President E. H. Beard of a gold ring set with diamonds. The presentation address was made by Philip Breitmeyer, president-elect of the S. A. F., who reviewed the splendid work of the club during Mr. Beard's term as presiding officer. The subject for the evening's discussion was "Soils." General discussion was postponed to the next meeting, October 21. Two more applicants were admitted to membership. On Friday, October 16, the club will visit the greenhouse establishments of all the East Side florists and later in the month will visit the Mt. Clemens establishments.

W. J. Pearce, the Pontiac, Mich., florist who disappeared August 17 last, was discovered at Elgin, Ill., a few days ago and returned home last Thursday. Although at present seeming perfectly rational, he is unable to account for any of his actions or whereabouts during his absence.

Geo. A. Rackham visited the establishment of W. J. & M. S. Vesey, Fort Wayne, Ind., last Sunday. He reported their stock as being in very fine condition, particularly the chrysanthemums, of which they have an immense supply, much of it being grown for exhibition purposes.

B. Schroeter is completing an orchid house 18x100 feet. His decorations for the opening of the largest dry goods store here last week were very extensive and called for the use of several thousand roses and carnations. Daintily filled and trimmed baskets were a prominent feature.

The Jefferson Avenue Flower Shop is the name of a new retail store opened last week at 376 Jefferson avenue by two eastern ladies, Miss Ruth Jenkins of New York and Miss Julia Wells of Philadelphia. They will make a specialty of decorations for social functions.

The advent of cooler weather and the opening of the chrysanthemum season are giving quite an impetus to trade, which is much relished by both growers and retailers, the stores of the latter being ablaze with the splendor of the gorgeous flowers.

Fred Pautke has finished his house, 30x230 feet, and has planted with carnations and violets. He will add another house of similar size in the early spring.

J. Pinckert, 932 Baldwin avenue, has joined partnership with A. Devriese and opened a floral store at 568 Gratiot avenue.

Hugo Schroeter made a business trip to Chicago last week and William Dilger went to Buffalo.

Visitor: H. D. Byers, Dayton, Ohio.

J. F. S.

ROWAYTON, CONN.—Five men engaged in sorting roses at George H. Traendly's greenhouses on the evening of September 27 were rudely interrupted by a lightning bolt which fortunately did trifling damage to the greenhouses. All felt the shock more or less severely.

PITTSBURG, PA.—J. McNamara is preparing the new grounds of the Pittsburg Country Club, fourteen acres in extent, for fall planting of trees and shrubs. It is the intention to add a range of greenhouses later.

AMHERST, MASS.—M. B. Kingman has opened a new store in Amity block.

Farm with Greenhouses

For Sale or To Let.

Two modern Greenhouses for market growing. 24 acres with fruit orchards. Commodious house and barns. One mile from Brockport. N. Y. Fine country place near Normal School. Perfect climate. Apply

Thos. V. Pierson,

BROCKPORT, N. Y., R. F. D.

Mention the American Florist when writing to advertisers on this page.

THE NURSERY TRADE.

AM. ASSOCIATION OF NURSERYMEN.
N. W. HALE, Knoxville, Tenn., Pres.; FRANK A. WEBER, St. Louis, Mo., Vice-Pres.; GEORGE C. SEAGER, Rochester, N. Y., Sec'y.
Twenty-ninth annual convention, Atlanta, Ga., June, 1904.

READING, MASS.—George E. Burnham has sold his floral establishment comprising twelve acres of land to Mrs. Almund Banelle, of Cincinnati, O., who has taken possession.

DANSVILLE, N. Y.—Frank Hartman, long engaged in the nursery business here, was married to Miss Hortense Pauline Armstrong at the home of the bride's parents in Allenhurst, N. J., October 1.

Thomas Meehan Horticultural Society.

Just about one year ago a bright idea struck some one of the members of the firm of Thomas Meehan & Sons (inc.) and the Thomas Meehan Horticultural Society was organized. The membership is composed nearly if not entirely of the members of the firm and the heads of the various departments and others connected therewith. The meetings are held weekly in a part of the office building of the firm and generally speaking are well attended. Horticultural subjects of special and general interest are discussed, and the admonition laid down by J. Franklin Meehan, president of the incorporated firm, at the initial meeting of the horticultural society a year ago not to argue subjects but to discuss them, has been strictly adhered to.

At the first annual meeting, held last week, Ernest Hemming was elected president, R. Hebler, vice-president, and Warren J. Chandler, re-elected secretary-treasurer. After the business meeting was over an adjournment was made to Harkinson's cafe, Germantown, and the first annual banquet was on in earnest, and a right jolly affair it was. While at the business meetings only serious subjects are considered, and those in a thoroughly intelligent manner, all restraint was thrown to the winds on this occasion, and wit and humor with but few exceptions were the order of the evening.

J. Franklin Meehan was appointed by the retiring president, Robert B. Cridland, toastmaster, but before entering upon his duties as such he gave some wholesome advice as to the future of the society. Mr. Cridland was called upon to answer to the toast of "Women and Flowers," which he did very effectively, and adroitly referred to President-elect Hemming's successful botanizing trips on the battlefield of Gettysburg. S. Mendelson Meehan (Vice-President of Thomas Meehan & Sons) was called upon to reply to the toast of "Fruits," which he did most acceptably, with a commingling of humor and sound sense. Harry Brown's reply to the "Seasons" was all too brief. As was expected G. Russell Wright was at home on the "Tulips" subject, for it could not have fallen into better hands or rather more appreciative lips; the way he pouted and puckered was a treat to behold. Frank Suter on "Misuse of Botany" bristled all over with wit and wisdom. Charles W. Kesser, who has charge of the advertising for the firm, assumed a very dignified attitude when called upon to descant on the "Standing of a Nurseryman in Society," eventually rousing into celestial bliss. Ernest Hemming answered the toast of "Hybrids" in a very learned manner, delving deeply into history and mythology to illustrate his various points, perorating in masterly pathetic style upon A. Mule. James Berry talked entertainingly on "Shamrock," nor could he resist the opportunity of predicting the lifting of a certain cup with a four-leaved shamrock. Samuel Newman Baxter talked and talked about "Wall Flowers," winding up with the sensible remark not to try to get something for nothing, but to faithfully work for it. Vernon Cassel, whose musical proclivities have never yet been assailed, gave a very edifying dissertation on the "Elevating Influences of a Nursery Spade." The toast "American Beauties" was handled with keen appreciation by Enos Drakely. William Lamb climbed all over himself in extolling the value of "Weeds," and Stanley V. Wilcox quoted from Bailey to prove that a "Bud" was a cabbage head, or was it that a cabbage head was merely a bud? Fortunately there were no debutantes present. Warren J. Chandler handled what would naturally appear to most people a time-worn and wordy subject, namely "Chestnuts," in quite an original way and Mr. Hebler had "Corn" to respond to, which he repeatedly and invariably referred to in the plural.

Unfortunately Thomas B. Meehan, the secretary and treasurer of the company, and John F. Burn, who was to have been discoursed on "Sports" were unavoidably among the absentees. Out of

a membership of nearly forty there were twenty-five present. Organizations of this character could with profit and pleasure to all concerned be connected with other firms where the employes and others interested were in sufficient numbers to make such a society possible. E. L.

Who Will Be Try It On?

The women of the United States will probably be interested to learn that Uncle Sam is cultivating a beauty plant in the experimental farm at Washington. The women of Algeria eat the seeds of this plant to make them beautiful, and the government experts are trying to determine what grounds they have for the faith that is in them.—Newport (R. I.) News.

GALAX LEAVES, ETC.,
Fresh New Crop.

Green Galax Leaves, per 1000	$ .60
Cut Fancy Ferns, per 1000	1.00
Cut Dagger Ferns, per 1000	1.00
Leucothoe Sprays, per 1000	3.00
Rhododendron Sprays, per 1000	8.00

Orders filled on short notice. Largest dealer in the U. S. Send cash with first order. Ask for prices on Native Shrubbery.
J. N. PRITCHARD, Elk Park, N. C.
Please mention the American Florist when writing.

PÆONIAS.

In 10 distinct, named kinds, selected for florists' use. Earliest to latest, all colors. $1.50 per dozen: $10.00 per 100. Hybrid Perpetual Roses, 2-year, and Clematis. Write for prices.

F. BALLER, Bloomington, Ill.
Please mention the American Florist when writing.

800,000 CAL. PRIVET.

1, 2, 3 and 4 YEARS OLD.
1, 2, 3 and 4 FEET.
1, 2, 3 and 4 DOLLARS PER 100.

Write for 1000 Rates and Trade List. State Entomologist certificate with each package.

J. H. O'HAGAN,
River View Nurseries, LITTLE SILVER, N. J.
Please mention the American Florist when writing.

500,000 Choice California Privet

Well branched, 3 to 4 feet, $4.00 per 100; 3½ to 3 feet, $3.35 per 100; 2 to 3½ feet, $2 75 per 100; 18 to 24 inches, 3-year old, $2.00 per 100. Packing free. Terms: Cash with order.

ATLANTIC COAST NURSERIES,
Office, 806 4th Ave., ASBURY PARK, N. J.
Please mention the American Florist when writing.

Send to **THE MOON Company**
For Your Trees, Shrubs, Vines and Small Fruits.
Descriptive Illustrated Catalogue Free.
THE WM. H. MOON CO.
Morrisville, Pa.

Orange, N. J.

A large audience gathered at the monthly meeting of the New Jersey Floriticultural Society to listen to Arthur Herrington, of Madison, on "The Hardy Perennial." The speaker dwelt on gardeners' neglect of herbaceous perennials for hardy borders by which brilliant effects could be secured with but little labor and no outlay beyond the first cost. He advised a close study of nature in the fields and woods where a succession of bloom was to be met from the first hepatica and violet till, as we see it today, the goldenrod and aster close the last note of color." The introduction of bulbs he said would brighten a border. In the flower display the Cypripedium Ashburtonii shown by D. Kindsgrab, received seventy-five points. A specimen of Begonia Gloire de Lorraine was shown by Malcolm MacRorie and a vase of Grand Duke Alexis dahlia by Peter Duff. There was the usual array of fruits and vegetables.

At the close of the talk a special invitation was extended by Mr. Herrington to the New York show of the Chrysanthemum Society of America. He urged a loyal support. It was decided to include at the November meeting a special chrysanthemum exhibit.

A press committee was appointed, consisting of President George Smith, Isaac Vance and J. B. Davis.

Visitor: William Duckham, of Madison.
J. B. D.

Springfield, Ill.

The florists of Springfield made a very creditable display of plants, cut blooms and decorations at the state fair. In the exhibition of plants Louis Unverzagt won eight firsts, George Brinkerhoff three firsts, and A. C. Brown three firsts. In the show of cut flowers and designs Messrs. Unverzagt, Brown, Brinkerhoff and Albert T. Hey divided honors.

Miss Belle Miller has done considerable rebuilding and added one new house. She has given up the growing of pot plants, with the exception of a few ferns, and is devoting her entire place to roses, carnations, chrysanthemums and bulbous stock.

Carl Rauth has added to his place this season and is growing very fine carnations. He is trying most of the new varieties.

David Wirth has just completed a range of three houses, two 24x130 and one 10x130, to be used for carnations and ferns. C. W. S.

Boston.

Market conditions here remain stationary as to demand and values. Asters are steadily diminishing, gladioli are about ended, dahlias begin to show the wear and tear of the season and carnations and roses show general improvement in quality. Of chrysanthemums a regularly increasing supply appear daily. Violets are thus far limited principally to the single kinds.

The reception given to the Honorable Artillery Company, of London, made a welcome inroad on the local market Monday. The decorations of the tables and Symphony hall, where the banquet took place were by Thos. F. Galvin.

George Melvin, gardener to Col. Chas. Pfaff, showed a finely flowered miltonia which received a certificate of merit.

Visitors: Charles Thorley, New York, whose daughter is very sick here and A. Dimmock, of St. Albans, Eng.

OUR PASTIMES.

Announcements of coming contests or other events of interests to our bowling, shooting and sporting readers are solicited and will be given place in this column.
Address all correspondence for this department to Wm. J. Stewart, 79 Milk St., Boston, Mass.; Robt. Kift, 1725 Chestnut St., Philadelphia, Pa.; or to the American Florist Co., Chicago, Ill.

Philadelphia Growers Win.

There was a warm game in the club alleys last Friday night between the growers and dealers which resulted in the growers winning by 80 pins. W. K. Harris is now in great shape and last Tuesday put up 623 in three games, within one po n of 208 to a game. The dealers' and growers' scores follow:

GROWERS.	1st	2d	3d	
Player	194	186	138	
Yates	143	148	182	
Anderson	145	160	167	
Elmerman	163	149	188	
Adelberger	147	181	190	
Westcott	138	145	189	
Harris				
. Total	922	918	964	2844

DEALERS.	1st	2d	3d	
Player	163	204	148	
Kift	133	106	111	
Gibson	164	186	175	
Dunbam	147	150	178	
Falck	133	164	181	
Hanna	176	174	196	
Moss				
Total	905	995	864	2764

HORTICULTURAL visitors at the St. Louis World's Fair are complaining of the distance from the central buildings to the location of the horticultural and agricultural departments.

San Francisco.

BUSINESS COMMENCING TO IMPROVE.—ROSES AND CARNATIONS ARE SCARCE.—A COMPLIMENTARY DAHLIA SHOW.—VARIOUS JOTTINGS.

The annual dahlia show given by the Pacific Coast Horticultural Society took place, September 19, in the maple room, Palace Hotel, and was in every way a success. The show was held from noon until 10 p. m. The fine exhibits staged elicited general admiration from the large and appreciative attendance. During the evening an excellent programme of vocal and instrumental music added to the attractions of the show. The following are the awards made: George A. Pope, Wm. Kittlewell, gardener, best general collection of dahlias, first prize, best twelve of cactus, show, decorative and pompon, each first prize. Best collection of single dahlias. R. Lichtenberg, silver medal; best seedling of cactus, show, fancy and decorative, each a certificate of merit. Golden Gate Park staged a very fine collection of dahlias, receiving honorary mention. Crocker Estate, collection of dahlias, honorary mention; seedling gladiolus, certificate of merit. W. H. Crocker, Burlingame, dahlias and flowering shrubs, honorable mention. F. Tillman, E. Bengel, gardener, seedling cannas, certificate of merit. J. M. Halsted, cactus dahlias, honorable mention. J. A. Carbone, chrysanthemums, honorable mention. J. H. Sievers & Company, decorative plants, honorable mention. H. Maier, lilies, honorable mention.

Trade conditions have shown a marked improvement of late, the return of the flower buying people from the mountain and seaside resorts and the reopening of the social season will undoubtedly keep the florists busy from now on. Considerable difficulty is occasionally experienced in obtaining stock of the better grade. Roses are poor, carnations short stemmed and quite scarce yet. A few chrysanthemums and violets have made their appearance.

The large glass area of P. C. Meyer at Burlingame is almost completed. It consists of ten houses each 25x150 feet and one house for propagating 10x150 feet. Two houses are planted to carnations of standard varieties, two houses are planted with chrysanthemums and one with roses. Steam will be the heating medium and a 100-horse-power boiler has been installed.

To supply a constantly increasing demand for ferns H. Plath has completed another house 25x125. A new forty horse-power steam boiler has also been added. Mr. Plath has a seedling Adiantum of which he thinks a great deal, he considers it to be a cross between A. Roenbeckii and A. gracillimum.

A. Mann, Jr., has admitted his brother as partner, and the firm will now be Mann Brothers.

C. Baker has started a flower store at Twenty-second and Mission streets.

Visitor: George P. Struck, representing Lager & Hurrell.   ROMNEYA.

SAN FRANCISCO, CAL.—John Horn, for some time with the Cox Company, has joined the staff of the Germain Seed Company, Los Angeles, Cal.

FAIRMONT, NEB.—The Emerson Seed Company, of Waterloo, has purchased a strip of ground south of the railroad tracks, and will erect a building at a cost of $6,000. The firm will establish headquarters here next spring.

BOOKS FOR FLORISTS.

The time is coming along when these are needed and opportunity at hand for reading them. Every one of the following should be in your library.

Send prices quoted and we send the books.

HOW TO GROW CUT FLOWERS (Hunt).—The only book on the subject. It is a thoroughly reliable work by an eminently successful practical florist. Illustrated. $2.00.

STEAM HEATING FOR BUILDINGS (Baldwin).—Contains valuable data and hints for steam fitters and those who employ this method of heating. The 350 pages are fully illustrated. $2.50.

HOW TO MAKE MONEY GROWING VIOLETS (Saltford).—This is by a practical grower who has made a success of the business. No grower of violets can afford to be without it. Price 25 cents.

GREENHOUSE CONSTRUCTION (Taft).—It tells the whole story about how to build, and heat a greenhouse, be it large or small, and that too in a plain, easily understood, practical way. It has 118 illustrations. $1.50.

THE NEW RHUBARB CULTURE (J. E. Morse & G. B. Fiske).—A complete, practical, scientific and up-to-date treatise on the latest method of cultivating rhubarb. 130 pages. 50 cents.

THE AMERICAN CARNATION (C. W. Ward).—A complete treatment of all the most modern methods of cultivating this most important flower. Illustrated. $3.50.

THE ROSE—Its cultivation, varieties, etc. (H. B. Ellwanger).—A complete guide of the cultivation of the rose, together with a classification of all the leading varieties. $1.25.

PRACTICAL FLORICULTURE (Peter Henderson).—A guide to the successful propagation and cultivation of florists' plants. Illustrated. 325 pages. $1.50.

THE HORTICULTURISTS' RULE-BOOK (L. H. Bailey).—Contains information valuable to all those engaged in any branch of horticulture. Illustrated. 312 pages. 75 cents.

THE AMERICAN GARDENERS' ASSISTANT (Thomas Bridgeman).—Complete guide for the cultivation of vegetables, fruit trees, grape vine and flowers. Illustrated. 522 pages. $1.00.

AMERICAN FLORIST CO.,
324 Dearborn Street,   CHICAGO.

It is good business policy to mention
The....
AMERICAN FLORIST
When you write to an advertiser.

Dallas.

Business is picking up and prospects are for a good fall trade. The late rains have made a decided improvement in outside flowers.

Otto Lang has contracts for decorations at the Idlewild ball and several large weddings which will keep him busy for the next two weeks.

Ernst Nitche recently had a narrow escape for his life while driving across the tracks of the T. P. R. R. His wagon was struck by a train, which smashed it to kindling wood and killed his horse. The only thing that saved his life was his ability as a long jumper.

Mrs. Holtcamp and daughter are busy with funeral work and report a fine trade in cut flowers.

At the Haskel Avenue Floral Company's outside roses are making a rapid growth and are blooming profusely. Hundreds visit the grounds daily to view the beautiful display. Carnations also give promise of a fine crop.

The State Fair is now on and thousands of strangers are visiting the city. Nowhere can such a display of flowers be found in a fair grounds as here. The buildings are covered with vines and innumerable bedding plants are to be seen.

Visitors: H. O. Hannah, of Sherman, Will. B. Munson, of Denison, James Wolf and daughter, of Waco. LONE STAR.

Asparagus.

SPRENGERI. Now is the right time to bench for a good winter's supply of green. Field-grown stock is far superior to pot plants for this purpose, being heavily rooted and well set with eyes. When benched they immediately start into active growth, throwing up numerous growths, which come to perfection much earlier than those from pot plants.

Field-plants, $4.00, $6.00 and $8.00 per 100, according to size. Well established plants from 2¼-inch pots, ready for 4-inch pots, $4.00 per 100.

PLUMOSUS NANUS. Our plants are exceptionally fine this season. Buy now for fall and holiday sales. From 2½-inch pots, $5.00 per 100; 4-inch pots, $12.00 per 100.

CORMORENSIS. Extra strong 3-in. pot plants, now throwing heavy growths, $10.00 per 100.

NEPHROLEPIS PIERSONI. Have a large stock in excellent condition. From 3½-inch pots, 50c each; $35 00 per 100.

SMILAX. Large, well rooted, field-grown c'umps, $3.00 per 100.

VIOLET, CALIFORNIA. Healthy field clumps, $4.00 per 100.

Send for fall trade list of other seasonable stock.

NATHAN SMITH & SON, ADRIAN, MICH.

Please mention the American Florist when writing.

A FEW GOOD THINGS YOU WANT.

Special low prices on palms to close out. Fine clean stock, cool grown and well shaped plants, none better.

ARECA LUTESCENS, 5 plants to pot, 4, 5 and 6-inch, $25, $40 and $100 per 100.

KENTIA Belmoreana and Forsteriana, 3, 4, 5 and 6-inch, $12, $25, $40, $100 per 100.

REX BEGONIA, 2 and 3-inch, $4 and $6 per 100.

DRACAENA INDIVISA, 3-inch, $5.00 per 100; 4-inch, $10 per 100.

ENGLISH IVY, 2 and 3-inch, $3 and $6 per 100.

BOSTON FERNS, 5-inch, $30 per 100. From beds, for 2, 3 and 4-inch pots, $4.00, $8.00, $15.00 per 100.

ASPARAGUS PLUMOSUS, 2-inch, $6.00 per 100.

" SPRENGERI, 2-inch, $3.00 per 100.

CHINESE PRIMROSES, Fringed, 2-inch, $4.00 per 100.

CYCLAMEN GIGANTEUM, 3-inch, $5.00 per 100.

Place orders now for Rooted Geranium Cuttings.

CASH OR C. O. D.

GEO. M. EMMANS, NEWTON, N. J.

Please mention the American Florist when writing.

PALMS, FERNS, ETC.

We offer good.values; saving in express and freight to buyers west of Ohio.

BOSTON FERNS. Nephrolepis Exaltata Bostoniensis.

We have the finest stock in the West. All our plants are pot-grown, bushy stock, well furnished with fronds from the pot up, and cannot be compared with the cheap, long-drawn-up, lifted stock from the bench. A sample shipment will convince you of our superior stock.

		Each	Per doz.	Per 100
2½ inch pot plants	$	$ .60	$ 5.00
3 " " "			1.50	10.00
4 " " "			2.50	20.00
5 " " "		.50	5.00	40.00
6 " pan "		.75	8.00	60.00
7 " " "		1.00	10.00	75.00
8 " " "		1.50	15.00	
9 " " "		$2.00 to 2.50		
10 " " "		3.00 to 3.50		

PIERSONI FERN.

Well-grown, bushy stock.

2½-inch pots	$25.00 per 100; $200.00 per 1000
4-inch	$ .75 each
5-inch pots	1.00 each
6-inch pots	1.50 each
7-inch pots	2.5* each
8-inch pots	4.00 each

ANNA FOSTER FERN.

Elegant stock.

2½-inch pots	$ 8.00 per 100
3-inch pots	15.00 per 100
4-inch pots	25.00 per 100
5-inch pots	50 00 per 100
6-inch pots	$ 9.00 per dozen
7-inch pots	12.00 per dozen
8-inch pots	18 00 per dozen

Cycas Revoluta.

With fine crowns, pots full of roots. Plants in all sizes from 25c to $3.00 each, at 5c per leaf.

Asparagus Plumosus Nanus We are Headquarters.

2½-inch pots	per doz., 75c; per 100, $5.00
3-inch pots	per doz., $1.00; per 100, 8.00

Send for our Special Price List of Palms, Ferns, Araucarias and Rubbers.

If you are a buyer of Palms, Ferns, etc., a personal visit of inspection to our Greenhouses at Western Springs, Ill., tone-half hour's ride from Chicago, will pay you. Long Distance Telephone No. 221 Western Springs, Ill.

CHICAGO. Vaughan's Greenhouses, WESTERN SPRINGS. ILL.

Palms and Asparagus.

	Pots.	Leaves.	In high.	10	100
Latania Borbonica,	3-in.	4-5	2	10 $.75	$ 8.00
"	5-in.	3-5 obt.	12-15	2.00	15.00
Kentia Belmoreana,	3½ "	3-4	15-18	2.50	18.00
"	3-in.	3-5	8-10	1.60	10.00
	3-in.	3-5	10-15	1.75	13.00
Asparagus Sprengeri, 2-inch pots					1.50
Asparagus Plumosus, 2-inch pots					3 00
Begonias, 3-inch pots					5 00

We grow a large assortment of Hardy Shrubs and evergreens. Prices made on application.

SHERMAN NURSERY CO.

CHARLES CITY, IOWA.

For Sale

Twenty-two large and beautiful

Palms.

Must be sold at once. Write for list and description. No reasonable offer refused.

H. L. CONDE,

Oswego, N. Y.

GIANT Cyclamen

Well set with buds, 2½-in. $4, 3-in. $7 per 100

PRIMROSES, strong 3-inch, $5.00 per 100.

OBCONICAS. They are well-grown, strong plants, 4-inch, $12.00, 6-inch, $20.00 per 100, ready for 4-inch and 7-inch pots.

CARNATIONS, field-grown, now in 4-inch pots, for late planting, Joost, Glory, Lawson, $6.00 per 100.

ASPARAGUS SPRENGERI, 3-inch, $1.50 per 100; $12.00 per 1000.

☞ The above is all well-grown stock. Satisfaction guaranteed.

C. WINTERICH, Defiance, 0.

STUDER OFFERS.

FERNS Fine Healthy Plants.

	Per Doz.
ALSOPHILA AUSTRALIS, Specimen in 11-in. pots, 6 feet size	$4.00 each; $45.00
DAVALLIOIDES FURCANS and BOSTONS, 6-inch pots	4.00
From 5-inch pots	6.00
LOMARIA GIBBA and COMPACTA CORDATA, From 8-inch pots	3.50
From 6-inch pots	.60
PLANTS FOR FERN DISHES, 2½-inch pots	
ROSES, Field-Grown, 2 and 3 year old, best Varieties of Hybrids, Teas, Moss and Climbers	1.20

5 per cent discount for cash with order.

N. STUDER, Anacostia, D. C.

Please Mention The American Florist When Writing.

Propagation of Violets.

The Colorado Springs Floral Company does not propagate violets from runners early in the season, as is the common practice, but during winter select plants with regard to their good qualities and when the flowering season is over these are lifted with a good lump and placed close together outside within reach of the hose. No protection is given. About July 1, when the spring work is over, the strongest and best rooted divisions are detached from these clumps and planted directly on the benches. All old crowns are discarded. This is certainly an inexpensive way of starting the young plants and the quality of the stock at this time speaks well for the method.

Pentas Albas.

Noting an article in the last issue of the AMERICAN FLORIST on Pentas carnea, I would suggest that the white form be not ignored. It is equally as good a bloomer as P. carnea but the flowers are larger and better for cutting. I only know it as Pentas alba.   P. G.

HAVING attained so many other good points in the cactus dahlia, the enthusiasts should now emulate the carnation raisers and devote their attention assiduously to producing varieties with stems strong enough to hold the flowers up.

Boston Fern

We have a large stock of this desirable plant. Our plants are compact and well furnished.

6-inch pots or pans............$25.00 per 100
7-inch pots or pans............ 35.00 per 100
8-inch pots or pans............ 50.00 per 100

ASPARAGUS PLUMOSUS NANUS.

4-inch..............................$10.00 per 100

ASPARAGUS SPRENGERI.

3½-inch........................... $2.50 per 100

Ozone Park Nurseries,
OZONE PARK, L. I., N. Y.

The Most Popular Fern

The Anna Foster.

At $35.00 per 100, for 6-inch pots from bench. Pot Plants, 50c, 75c, $1.00, $2.00, $3.00, $4.00 and $5.00 each; very fine.

BOSTON FERNS.

Large plants, from bench, $50.00 per 100.

Very fine KENTIA PALMS, at 50c to $3.00 each. Asparagus Plumosus Nanus, 3-inch, $8.00 per 100. Asparagus Sprengeri, 3-inch, $4.00 per 100.

L. H. FOSTER,
45 King Street,   DORCHESTER, MASS.

FERNS.

Boston Ferns.	Piersoni Ferns.
3½-inch...$ 5.00 per 100	2½-inch...... $ .35 each
3-inch..... 10.00 per 100	50 at...... .30 each
4-inch..... 15.00 per 100	3-inch...... .25 each
5-inch..... 25.00 per 100	4-inch...... .50 each
6-inch..... 40.00 per 100	5-inch...... .75 each
7-inch..... 60.00 per 100	6-inch...... 1.00 each
8-inch $1 to $1.50 each	6-inch...... 1.50 each
10-inch, 2 to 2.50 each	7-inch...... 2.50 each
	8-inch...... 3.00 each

Order 2-in. Cinerarias, Chinese Primula and Obconica. Cut Roses and Carnations.

See last week's papers for list of Field-Grown Carnations. Write

GEO. A. KUHL, Pekin, Ill.

World's Fair Notes.

Commissioner H. Fukauba, master of ceremonies of the imperial court of Japan, who will have charge of laying out the Japanese gardens surrounding the castle of Shinshinden—a reproduction of the original—arrived in St. Louis early in the week. Work on the gardens will commence as soon as the necessary arrangements can be made.

The Mexican plant exhibit will be of great interest. Geo. Macdowell, the commissioner in charge, says a large assortment of dracaenas, fancy-leaved caladiums and kindred plants will reach the grounds soon. They will be housed in one of the conservatories during the winter. Several car loads of succulents will follow in the early spring. The succulent exhibit at Buffalo was very fine, but the Mexican government will surpass it at St. Louis.

Plans are being laid for introducing a typical English garden at the British building. T. W. Brown, who laid out several places for the English government, and later superintended the laying out of the grounds surrounding the palace of the sultan of Morocco, will have charge of the work. R. J. Mahr, of St. Louis, is assistant in charge. A sunken garden 126x240 feet will be made immediately in front of the building. In the rear a bowling green will be laid out. Surrounding the grounds a mixed border of shrubs and herbaceous plants will be planted. A fine display of bulbous stock will be used for early spring flowering. Grading will commence at once.

Nothing is being left undone toward beautifying the grounds in the Horticultural section. J. H. Hadkinson, superintendent of outdoor planting for the department, has made tremendous strides in the work. What was once a barren clay field is rapidly becoming a place of beauty. Thousands of roses have been planted and are making luxuriant growth. It is a matter of record that the Paul Neyron had growths of four feet this season. The grass seed which was sown the latter part of September is already casting its shade of green over the great terrace in front of the Palace of Agriculture. Many of the seedsmen throughout the country are busy seeding down their sections. The Plant Seed Company, of St. Louis, is practically through. The aquatic section just south of the terrace is ready for the exhibitors. H. A. Dreer will install a large collection of all varieties of these beautiful plants.

The Palace of Horticulture is rapidly assuming shape. It consists of a main central room 400 feet square, with wings extending on either side each 204x230 feet, the whole building covering six acres. No exhibition will be located on any but the main floor. The center of the building will be devoted to a large collection of palms and decorative plants. Surrounding this is a 200-foot area for low table exhibits. No exhibits of plants more than thirty inches in height will be installed.

The Pomological department, in charge of Mr. Stiltson, is doing a great work. Thousands of cases of fruit of high quality are being preserved in formulin. A continual exhibition of fruit from cold storage will be made during the exposition. Canada and all other countries will exhibit their produce in this way. Every day fruit is arriving from the different states to be placed in cold storage.

Minneapolis.

Trade conditions have been much improved by heavy funeral orders the last week. Although there has been a heavy supply the demand has equaled it. Flowers are improving in quality and the supply promises to be not so large the coming week. Violets are making their appearance.

W. T. Atlee has resigned his position with R. J. Mendenhall and will take charge of the decorating for Wm. Donaldson & Company.

Rice Brothers have closed a contract for the entire output of one grower, including tea roses and American Beauty. Importations of bulbs are arriving daily. The quality seems good. A shortage in Romans is reported.

E. Nagel is doing his best to get the growers together for a chrysanthemum show this fall.

Mrs. S. P. Lord, of Owatonna, was in the city securing flowers for a large order.

The stock has all been housed successfully and firing has commenced.

There will be no meeting of the Florists' Club this month.   C. F. R.

BATAVIA, ILL.—The Bellevue Place Company has rebuilt and enlarged twenty of its houses.

New Orleans.

At the last meeting of the Gardeners' Club, Messrs. F. Valdejo and P. A. Chopin, who attended the S. A. F. convention, gave full details of their trip and reception. New Orleans florists are considering a plan for bringing the convention two years from now to the far south. It is believed New Orleans could offer good inducements to the northern florists to make the long journey.

Otto Abel, of Abel Brothers, gave to his florist friends a party to celebrate the birth of his first baby. Abel Brothers' big stock of palms, ferns and general foliage plants has not been housed yet, awaiting the completion of a new greenhouse.

The long hot weather season is nearing its end and better business is looked for every day. The weather has been favorable for chrysanthemums, which will be ready by November 1. More every year are grown under glass. M. M. L.

DENVER, COL.—C. R. Root, of Barteldes & Company, has returned from the east, but Mrs. Root is still at Chicago.

NEW ORLEANS.—Superintendent Anseman, of the city park, has asked the board of commissioners for a hothouse.

SEATTLE, WASH.—The market on seeds is not very active largely due to the many rainstorms that prevailed throughout September and which retarded the farmers in their winter sowing.

Cincinnati.

Trade during the past week has been very good. Roses are selling well but the demand is not equal to the supply. The street fakirs are now in their glory, selling roses at 10 and 15 cents a dozen. American Beauties are very good in quality but are in poor demand. Carnations are very short .in stem with enough to fill all orders. A few asters are yet to be seen, but they are poor in quality.

A trip to Thomas Windrum's place at Cold Springs, Ky., found everything in excellent shape. Mr. Windrum has added four new houses to his range during the past summer and is devoting all his space to carnations. A house each of Lawson and Estelle are worthy of mention. He is also growing White Cloud, Murphy's White and Glacier for white and Joost for pink, which are looking especially fine.

T. W. Hardesty & Company had the table decoration for Governor Nash's luncheon at the St. Nicolas Hotel last Saturday. American Beauties and lilies of the valley were used.

J. M. McCullough's Sons received the first consignment of chrysanthemums October 5, and they found a ready sale at from $1 to $2 per dozen.

Visitor: L. A. Thomas, of Troy.

A. O.

Colorado Springs, Col.

A general scarcity of flowers is the leading feature in trade circles. Two heavy frosts have cut down almost everything outdoors and indoor stock has not yet come into good bearing. The demand for good roses and carnations is brisk and if the necessary flowers were obtainable business would be altogether satisfactory. Long-stemmed flowers sell quickly and funeral work cleans up everything. Cupid also has been unusually busy.

At Tuesday night's meeting of the El Paso County Horticultural Society the following officers were nominated: President, W. W. Williamson; vice-presidents, Wm. Clark B. F. St. John, W. H. Evans, F. F. Crump and Dr. H. E. Gates; secretary, E. T. Reed; treasurer, J. B. Braidwood. These nominations will be passed upon the second Tuesday in October.

The fall trade has already made a considerable draft on pot plants. The outlook for a good supply of carnations is very good, while roses are still a doubtful quantity. Violets and chrysanthemums appear in good form. Of the latter the first will be cut about October 7, with Bergman and Pacific the earliest.

Outdoor asters this summer were spoiled by a small white fly which was proof to all the standard insecticides. The Pierson fern is shown in good shape at William Clark's.

The Colorado Springs Floral Company show a promising lot of chrysanthemums and violets.   S. S.

Pueblo, Col.

G. Fleischer makes a fine display at his new store, 621 North Main street. The place is well stocked with up-to-date material in all lines and S. R. Lundy, formerly with The Park Floral Company, Denver, is in charge.

Miss Fannie Hudson, formerly with Pleischer, is the manager of a neat new store at 214 North Main street. The Flower Store is the name of the concern and Miss Carrie Bathe is the proprietor.

Victor Johnson is now superintendent of the grounds of the Colorado Fuel and Iron Company.

Denver.

FUNERAL · MAKES HEAVY DEMAND FOR STOCK.—MUCH HUSTLING TO ·SECURE ENOUGH ON TIME.—SET DESIGNS ALMOST ENTIRELY ABSENT.—NOTES.

The funeral last week of A. B. Seaman, secretary of the Park Floral Company, made great demand for flowers in this section and there was very little stock to meet it. Everything in sight was used up clean and it was found necessary to import a good deal of the material required. The offerings generally were in the form of bunches or wreathes. Nothing in the shape of a broken column, lyre or things of that sort, was to be noticed. The only set design to be seen was a large open book sent by the directors of the city library. This was made appropriate, perhaps, but not in keeping with the other flowers at the funeral. I noticed some pretty and also large bunches of American Beauty, a couple of fine bunches of Chatenay, a half dozen of Bridesmaid that were really good and about as many bunches of Bride. Wreathes were numerous, one of the prettiest being a large crescent shaped or empire wreath of white roses, lily of the valley and violets. The employes of the company sent an empire wreath of laurel leaves tied with purple ribbon, which was hung just under Mr. Seaman's picture. The casket was covered with an ivy blanket in the center of which was arranged a crescent shaped wreath of Liberty roses. The grave was decorated with autumn foliage and grain just harvested. ···

Arthur H. Bush, manager for Daniels & Fisher, has been very busy this week with store decorations for the fall opening of that concern. American Beauty roses, supplied by Wietor Brothers, of Chicago, were used very extensively.

Thomas Chapman has put up a new chimney and now has his heating apparatus in good shape for the winter. He is about to start for Wisconsin on a hunting trip and incidentally to look into the green situation.

The Park Floral Company's new store and showhouse is rapidly nearing completion. The firm will move in about November 1, but expects to do some business at its Sixteenth street place till January 1.

President Beer, of the Colfax Avenue Floral Company wishes the trade to know of the prompt settlement of its loss by the Florists' Hail Association. Payment in full was made in five days.

Bessie Hortop & Company are now pretty well settled in their new location at 622 Fifteenth street and Miss Hortop says she is kept busy from morning till night.

Albert E. Mauff is cutting some fine American Beauty roses at the new range of his firm. These new houses are devoted exclusively to this variety.

N. A. Benson has added a new house 21x100 feet. The carnations and American Beauty roses at this establishment are looking extremely well.

The Curtis Park Floral Company finds wire netting covering for their greenhouses a profitable investment hail storm time.

Lyle C. Waterbury, the new wholesale florist and commission dealer, reports excellent business.

Ben Bolt has made marked improvement in the Daniels & Fisher greenhouses and stock.

Maler & Dankworth are sending in some nice violets.

THE AMERICAN FLORIST

A WEEKLY JOURNAL FOR THE TRADE

America is "the Prow of the Vessel; there may be more comfort Amidships, but we are the first to touch Unknown Seas."

| Vol. XXI. | CHICAGO AND NEW YORK, OCTOBER 17, 1903. | No. 802. |

THE AMERICAN FLORIST

NINETEENTH YEAR.

Copyright 1903, by American Florist Company
Entered as Second-Class Mail Matter.

PUBLISHED EVERY SATURDAY BY

AMERICAN FLORIST COMPANY,

324 Dearborn St., Chicago.

Eastern Office: 79 Milk St., Boston.

Subscription, $1.00 a year. To Europe, $2.00.
Subscriptions accepted only from the trade.

Volumes half-yearly from August, 1901.

THIS ISSUE 40 PAGES WITH COVER.

CONTENTS

...CHRYSANTHEMUMS...
In Decorative Work.

BY ROBERT KIFT, PHILADELPHIA, PA.

[Presented to the Chrysanthemum Society of America at the Chicago meeting, November, 1903.]

There is perhaps no other flower that is so decorative or with which such grand effects can be produced as the gorgeous chrysanthemum. Years ago, before the importation of the new varieties from Japan which gave such impetus to its cultivation and consequent popularity, there was absolutely nothing to relieve the somberness of the banks of green used in decorative work, except perhaps a few dahlias. The horticultural exhibitions were but park conservatories on a large scale containing little from door to door but tables of palms, ferns and foliage plants.

The introduction of the new types of flowers and their rapid increase by careful fertilization soon brought a welcome change; new varieties, improving with each recurring season, created the greatest enthusiasm and the popularity of the flower has grown until it overshadows all others in its season. There is scarcely any kind of floral work in which the chrysanthemum cannot be used to advantage, while for large decorations where masses of color are desired it has the field almost to itself.

For golden wedding anniversaries the yellow blooms are especially appropriate; in fact one of the most popular varieties has been given this name and frequently large quantities of it are used on these occasions.

How chaste and pure are the flowers of the white varieties, suitable according to their size for all purposes for which white flowers are used. Clusters of choice blossoms, artistically arranged, are carried by the bridal party, and again to celebrate the silver anniversary they are, with their silvery whiteness, a fitting symbol.

In the arrangement of design work they play a large part, and immense quantities of medium sized flowers are used for this purpose. In church or large hall decorations, where the long stem of the flower can be given full scope, they probably show to the best advantage. Here the natural grace of the flower is brought out and if properly arranged in tall vases

each specimen stands forth showing its beautiful form and color and yet producing a harmonious effect as a whole that compels admiration.

In the house a vase of these lovely flowers gives a life to any room, and when their lasting qualities are considered they are especially desirable. Then when occasion arises and the various rooms are to be decorated fine effects can be produced with this or that variety or shade of color according to the furnishings of the apartment. Over doorways, around mirrors, on mantels, on the newell post, in fact almost everywhere, they can be used to turn the house into a very bower of beauty.

For the dinner table they are also very acceptable, some really very beautiful flowers in tall vases which carry the flowers above the line of vision, or used in low bowls and on the cloth, so low as not to obstruct the view. For this work the smaller pompon varieties with their miniature blossoms borne on graceful sprays can be used very effectively. These small sprays are often used to give a touch to a cluster of fine specimens just where the contrast in size (if there is one) is tied, the contrast in size being very pronounced. Autumn leaves are a great addition where chrysanthemums are arranged for effect; in fact, where even two or three flowers are gathered together a spray or branch of autumn leaves with their glow, ing tints seems to blend with the color of the flowers and adds greatly to the finish of the cluster. Chrysanthemums are also used for personal adornment, but their value here is not so pronounced.

Introducers of new varieties should strive for strong stems if large flowers are desired, and avoid if possible a solid formation, as in the variety Timothy Eaton. The varieties Philadelphia and Pennsylvania are ideal in shape and form in their class and the weight of the flowers never carries it down, as is the case of many of the massive solid kinds, of which the first few flowers are grand but which soon develop such weight that the stems cannot support the flower, and then become useless for almost any purpose.

One of the missions of the chrysanthemum; has been educational, and we will venture to say that it has done more to increase the love for flowers in the past decade than almost any other agency. The exhibitions that have been held all over the country and which have become annual events would not have been possible without the wealth of bloom of

Begonia Helene Von Seutter.
(From Moller's Gartner-Zeitung.)

this "queen of autumn." And while in some places there seems to be a falling off or lack of interest, we believe it is not the general public that shows this apathy as much as the promotors of the show who do not keep up their enthusiasm and so lower the tone or quality of the displays. Some cities are noted as better flower centers than others, and we believe it to be due in a large degree to the florists themselves, who keep their business to the fore, using every opportunity by means of exhibitions and special displays to bring their products to the notice of the people and create a love for them.

CARE OF EARLY VARIETIES—NOVELTIES.

The early varieties of chrysanthemums are fast expanding now and the second earlies are well along in color, and when they arrive at this stage extra care must be taken to keep the beds a little more on on the dry side than they have been while in active growth. Also particular attention must be given to the temperature and atmosphere of the house so as to prevent dampness settling on the blooms. To do this it is necessary that ventilation be given them on all favorable days but not so that the wind has full sweep of the beds so as to dry them out too much and cause the plants to wilt, which would mean a stunted bloom. Also have a little ventilation all night, maintaining a night temperature as nearly as possible 48° to 50°. It will be necessary very soon to use a little steam heat to keep this temperature, still leaving the ventilators open at the same time, which will go a long way towards preventing the blooms from spot.

Should a warm rainy spell set in for a day or two put on a little steam for a short while to dry up the dampness. The feeding of liquid manures should be stopped on varieties that are showing color and see to it that the plants are properly staked and head-room enough from the glass given for the blooms

to develop. After strictly attending to these items we can watch with pleasure the fruition of another season's work and we shall soon know whether our expectations will be realized in the novelties and seedlings on trial, and where we shall suffer disappointment.

Among the novelties some of which are well along in color we find Mrs. Alexander McKinley of a very taking shade of light bronze promising a large flower and fi e foliage attaining a height of four feet.

Mrs. J. W. Pockett is well advanced with second crown buds of a light yellow which open up somewhat like those of Golden Wedding. It is a strong grower, the height attained being six feet.

Mlle. Marie Liger is a fine grower, three and one-half feet high, with fine large buds just showing color and very promising.

Mme. Rogers is red and old gold, a good grower and will make a fine large flower but is a little long in the neck on early buds.

C. J. Salter, the best growing of any of the new foreign varieties, has strong, stiff stems clothed with handsome foliage and second crown buds just showing the color, promising a fine commercial yellow.

The other novelties are not far enough advanced in color yet to tell much about them. Most of the American

Begonia Dr. Hermann Von Lingg.
(From Moller's Gartner-Zeitung.)

novelties are rather late, none of them showing very large buds as yet. Glory of Pacific is nearly done but the Pink and White Ivory are getting there rapidly and in a short time several others will be in their glory.   C. W. JOHNSON.

New Fancy-Leaved Begonias.

These are the result of a cross between Begonia discolor and B. diadema. They are valuable on account of their beautiful leaves and are suitable for cutting purposes as well as for decorative uses. These begonias must be kept in a cool house while they are young, otherwise they are too tender and when large plants will shed their leaves at the slightest change of temperature. The new varieties illustrated herewith were figured in Moller's Deutsche Gartner-Zeitung, January 3, 1903.

Dr. Hermann von Lingg grows tall and the leaf is deeply cut, dark green with silvery white markings.

Heinrich Lingg is somewhat lower than the above, has very attractive growth and compact foliage, is silvery white, deeply cut, with green veins in the center and irregular green markings around the edges of the leaves. This is particularly suited to cut flower work.

Helene von Seutter is a tall growing sort, splendidly marked. The leaf is silvery white, threaded with olive green, which runs along the veins. This is a very distinct variety and will attract attention everywhere.

Florists' Plant Notes.

AZALEAS.

The new stock of Azalea Indica. will soon arrive from the old country and should be potted as soon as received. Reduce the size of the ball with a knife so as to fit a 7 or 8-inch pot and soak the roots for a minute or two in a tub of water before potting. Drain the pots with several pieces of potsherds and use light leaf mould soil in which to grow them. Keep them shaded for several days after unpacking, but after that the shading should be removed and the plants exposed to the full light. Those intended for Christmas flowering should be selected and placed in a mild heat, say 60°. In a week or ten days the heat may be increased to 65° or 70° at night, but a higher temperature is not safe. Syringe these plants several times every day as long as they are exposed to a high temperature, but as soon as the buds begin to swell and the flowers to open, overhead syringing must cease. Plenty of water is required at the root and if the water is heated to the forcing temperature it will drive them along all the faster. Give the plants plenty of room so as to allow them to develop perfectly all around. The best varieties for forcing are Deutsche Perle, Vervæneana, Simon Mardner, Mme. Van der Cruyssen and Apollo. Mme. Van der Cruyssen requires about a week longer to force into flower than the others, so due allowance must be made. From seven to eight weeks is sufficient time in which to force the other varieties named. The later sorts, Niobe, Emperor of Brazil, Empress of India and others, should be placed in a cool house and kept at a temperature of 40° throughout the winter. The old plants which were summered over, require the same treatment as the fresh imported ones, excepting that from three to four

Begonia Heinrich Lingg.
(From Moller's Gartner-Zeitung.)

LUNCHEON DECORATIONS BY THE KREITLING COMPANY, CHICAGO.
(Lunch tendered Ex-President Cleveland by James H. Eckels, October 15, 1903.)

weeks in a good heat is sufficient to force them.

METROSIDEROS.

Metrosideros robusta or bottle brush plant, of which a limited number find ready sale, usually arrive with the azaleas and should be potted at once after soaking the ball well. These must not be forced too early in the season, or they will shed their flowers, and no attempt should be made to get them into flower for Christmas. They require a cool house until the first of the year, after which the heat can be gradually increased until a maximum temperature of 65° is reached, which will bring them into bloom nicely for Easter.

DEUTZIAS.

Deutzia gracilis and Lemoinei, will also arrive about the same time, and although a perfectly hardy shrub must not be subjected to a hard freeze after the plants are unpacked. The branches are set with buds to the tip, hence no pruning should be done. Keep them in the coolest house on the place or in a cold frame until the forcing time commences. It requires about seven weeks in a temperature of 55° to bring them into flower properly.

FUCHSIAS.

The old stock plants of fuchsias should now be shortened back to firm wood and placed in a temperature of about 60°; in about a week or ten days shake out and repot in the same size pot in fresh soil. Add plenty of old hot bed manure or leaf mould to the soil. In a few weeks a batch of cuttings can be taken and inserted in the sand. They will root

readily from now on throughout the winter in a mild bottom heat.

LILACS.

Imported lilacs can be forced into flower in about six or seven weeks in a temperature of 60°. Keep them cool until forcing commences. They can be had in bloom for Christmas but must not be given too high a temperature.

RHODODENDRONS.

Rhododendrons should be placed in a temperature of 40°-until about twelve weeks from the time they are wanted in flower, when the temperature can be increased ten or fifteen degrees. G.

World's Fair Notes.

A visit to the range of hot houses at the Fair Grounds reveals much activity. The range is located about 400 feet southwest of the administration building. It consists of six houses, each 300 feet long. Thirty-one men are employed at present, but the number will be increased as necessity requires. Thousands of seedlings of verbascum, digitalis, linum, etc., are being transplanted into flats. One bench contains 20,000 California Privet in 3-inch pots. Two long frames outside are packed with telanthera or alternanthera. Forty-three thousand nine hundred named varieties of tulips have arrived from C. Keur & Sons, of Hillegom, Holland. The bulbs are part of the company's exhibit and will be planted in the beds on the terrace in front of the agricultural building. The Michel Plant & Bulb Company of St. Louis will have charge of the work.

Ten car loads of decorative plants were received early in the week from Siebrecht & Son, of New Rochelle, N. Y. The shipments consisted of palms, pines, hibiscus, buxus and other plants in variety valued at $6,000. They are to be used in the landscape department.

Work has already begun on the new conservatory, which will be 40 feet wide, 90 feet long and 30 feet high. It is a much needed improvement, as at present there is no place in which to store the larger plants.

The Philippine section is attracting a great many visitors. Work has commenced on the grounds. There are forty acres in the tract, which is located just west of the agricultural building and includes Arrowhead Lake. The planting will be quite extensive, as hundreds of banana, betelnut, pineapple, rice, bamboo, cocoanut, sago plants, figs, crinum, latana, agave and pandanus plants will be utilized. A large number of aquatics will also be used. Several thousand wild plants from the vicinity of St. Louis are being collected and heeled in for future use. The Michel plant & Bulb Company has been awarded the contract for the work.

Swain Nelson, of Chicago, was on the grounds this week attending to exhibit matters.

A Bedding Plant of Merit.

Alternanthera rubra nana (a sport from A. rosea nana) coloring to a fine rich crimson, making a more decided contrast with A. aurea nana than A. rosea nana. It is dwarf like its parent.
. . . . P. G.

Rhinebeck and Its Violet Growers.

II.

According to the gazetteers, Rhinebeck had a population, fifty years ago, of 2,938. At the present time it is credited with but 1,600. It is safe to say, however, that the 1,600 make quite as much of a stir in the world as did their more numerous ancestors, especially since the discovery of the rich violet mines in their midst. The pioneers in the violet industry, George Saltford, J. C. Rockefeller, Stanton Rockefeller, John Hermance, Pascal Tremper, Alvah Bishop, W. T. Rynders, Alvin Coon and Judson Traver, have seen their neighbors—painters, blacksmiths, farmers and so on—follow suit, one after the other, until now all the hills and meadows are flecked with broad patches of white glass and the violet business has grown to be the leading industry of the town, furnishing an easy living, either as an exclusive avocation or as a side-issue for a goodly percentage of the inhabitants.

Rhinebeck, although mature in years, is still young, and as frisky as a colt. At present base-ball and the Hiawatha ditty are rampant. When a base-ball game is scheduled it is the absorbing topic of the town and for days in advance old and young find a fruitful theme in the subject of curves and hot liners. On the day of the game they flock to the field from all directions on foot, in gigs and on bicycles and the visitor who would look to find a violet-grower at his greenhouses on such an occasion doesn't understand Rhinebeck.

Very few of the violet men have had any previous horticultural experience. They are recruited from any and all trades and occupations and it must be confessed that one sees mighty little difference between the stock of the novice and that of the old gardener. With a piece of Rhinebeck's enchanted ground, a house like his neighbor's and an aptness in imitation combined with a little industry, the novice "gets there" at the first attempt and not infrequently is in a position shortly to give his older compeer good advice.

Much speculation is indulged in this fall as to the effect of the large increase of growing establishments upon the violet market and the winter prices. It is generally conceded that the outlook is uncertain and that with the enormous crop in sight the commission man's ability to equal the returns of past years is doubtful, and much shifting around from one wholesale house to another, as a result of disaffection, is predicted. The average number of flowers produced per plant for the season is about seventy. The average number of plants to a 150-ot house being about 4,400 would ⸱ake the total yield per house upwards of 300,000 flowers, and a conservative estimate of the aggregate crop for the entire Rhinebeck district would be 40,000,000 flowers, or upwards of

200,000 per day for the coming season, most of which finds its outlet through the commission men of New York city.

Outdoor Lily of the Valley.

ED. AM. FLORIST:—Please give brief directions for the best treatment of lily of the valley grown outdoors in southern New England.   R. B. K.

Lily of the valley pips for outdoor blooming are usually planted in rows nine inches apart in beds of convenient width. The ground should be well enriched and then, with an occasional application of manure, nothing remains necessary for several years except to keep the beds free of weeds. When the plants become over-crowded they can be thinned out or taken up and replanted.

"R. B. K.'s" query is understood as referring simply to lily of the valley grown for flowering purposes only. Where the intention is to raise pips for future forcing use, special handling is, of course, necessary, the three-year-old pips being sorted out every year and the younger ones replanted.

The experience of growers who have essayed to produce outdoor lily of the valley in quantity for market purposes has not been particularly encouraging. In the event of rain or fog at the blooming season the flowers proceed to rot at once and its only under exceptional conditions that they reach the market in presentable condition. At best the flowers are coarse in texture, lacking the clear whiteness of the indoor product. Even with the protection of frames the purity so much to be desired is quickly dissipated when the full air is admitted. From the fact that it makes so little show when used in floral work lily of the valley must always rely for its main sale upon the people who choose it because of its choiceness and delicacy. The outdoor crop lacks these qualifications and even when the outdoor flowers are heaped up in the wholesale markets awaiting a customer at a few cents a hundred, the green house product from cold storage pips is but little affected either as to demand or price.

Lily of the valley is now a regular daily stock in the flower market the year round. The quality averages much better and more uniform than formerly. The cold storage of lily of the valley pips

in America probably dates from the year 1872, when Carl Jurgens, of Newport, R. I., packed a quantity of roots away in the ice house and astonished the trade by bringing in the flowers in mid-summer. In the early years of the industry the buyer found it necessary to go over to Germany and collect the pips in lots of varying quality from different sources. Through the rapid development of the export trade the production of the pips is now in commercial hands in Germany and has become a business of considerable magnitude so that, whereas a few years ago the securing of a lot of 200,000 was a puzzle, an order of several million pips can now be placed with a reasonable certainty that the buyer will receive it in full and of a reliable and even grade throughout.

Retarded Lily of the Valley.

A correspondent of an English trade paper has the following with reference to retarded lily of the valley: "It is only too clearly remembered what futile attempts have been made with home-grown and purchased roots with the view of forcing them into early growth, in past times. These so grown, too, were bereft of the natural foil which their own foliage supply and lily of the valley is not much without foliage. The forcing of these flowers now becomes a very simple matter. A warm greenhouse will in the space of from two to three weeks afford a display of flowers in number and effect consistent with the extent of purchase. That they are more expensive to purchase is a fact that justifies the thought, for the cost and maintenance of the retarding plant must be borne by those for whom it is provided. The certainty of result, however, together with such finely developed leaves and flower spikes, makes the cost appear much less, and except for late spring use I should not adopt nor advise the purchase of any but retarded roots. The crowns are so well selected that rarely does there appear a flowerless growth. The investment, therefore, combines a profitable as well as pleasurable aspect that can not long remain unrealised and untried by every class of cultivator."

PLACE orders for perishable freight shipments before the cold weather sets in.

NEW ENGLAND PARK SUPERINTENDENTS AT THE GRAVE OF A. J. DOWNING, NEWBURG, N. Y., JUNE 25, 1903.
(See issue of July 18, 1903, page 917.)

Standing Cross.   Casket Spray.

WHITNALL'S FLORAL DESIGNS.

The Retail Trade.

THE Shasta daisy is a good plant if one gets the right stock and grows it well.

CHIRONIA LINOIDES, a soft-rooted greenhouse plant of easy culture, with pink flowers, is used in England for table decorations. It is said to be excellent for that purpose.

AN EUROPEAN decorator recommends Zea Japonica and other varieties of corn for bold effects. The stem should be cut close to the soil and immediately placed in water to prevent wilting.

BRANCHES of bamboo, firs and smilax as a background for bouquets and hanging baskets of La France roses were used in striking decorations at the wedding of Miss Florence Williams and Edward Nicolaus in Sacremento, Cal., September 31.

ONE great essential, if not the greatest essential in connection with decorative work, says a recent writer, is that it must possess elements of boldness if it is to achieve more than passing notice. The huge trumpet-shaped vases often used in entrance halls and large rooms, are capable of contributing the necessary boldness, provided they are well arranged with suitable material; but they are too often dressed with a total disregard to proportion, and few things look more incongruous than to see a big vase supporting an arrangement of flowers and foliage, so insignificant in size and devoid of striking effect as to make the vase appear far more prominent than the decorations.

THE ART OF DECORATING.

Church decorations are sometimes a disappointment because the florist in charge has failed to fully comprehend the extent of the space to be filled or to consider the great distance at which the decorations will be seen by the company. It is remarkable how a group of plants, impressively large while in the greenhouse, and giants while in the wagon, shrinks into an inadequate little bunch when viewed from the pews of a big church. Height is the factor and generally faulty and the larger the edifice the more apt the novice to get tripped up in this respect. There are now offered by supply houses generally, neat and serviceable iron plant stands of adjustable height, of which every florist should have a supply as part of his necessary equipment. Without some such accessories the best results with plant groups are impracticable.

He is a fortunate florist who secures a church decoration during dahlia time. Even the chrysanthemum at its best does not compare with the dahlia in serviceable decorative characteristics. Its wide range of color, its strong effect when arranged in solid colors, and especially its cheapness, are among its special qualifications. Displayed in ample masses against a background of palms, the cactus dahlias in light colors are admirably adapted for chancel decoration and they look equally well in strong light or semi-obscurity.

Dahlias have been used very extensively this fall in the decoration of stores for fall openings. Large branches are cut, from eighteen inches to three feet tall, with foliage and buds, and arranged in

jars and high vases, umbrella stands being sometimes utilized for the tallest. It should be borne in mind that dahlias require a background to show them off to greatest advantrge and that in their arrangement stiffness should be carefully avoided. The common practice followed by dahlia growers of cutting flower and short stem without foliage destroys the value of the material for good work and florists depending upon the wholesale market for their supply should insist upon a reform in this respect. As with the chrysanthemum so with the dahlia, oak and other autumn foliage makes a harmonious and pleasing combination, particularly with the yellows and dark reds.

Those who have tried the new white canna, Mont Blanc, have found it very satisfactory in chancel work. The spikes should be cut to the ground and held over night plunged deep in water. The buds will open nicely and the effect in large vases is exceedingly good.

W. J. S.

WHITNALL'S FLORAL DESIGNS.

The casket spray was built on a stem of the royal palm, oredoxa regina weigela, begonias, papyrus, asparagus and grass. It was, of course, made in the season when outdoor weigela was in bloom. The standing cross is beautiful and artistic and has additional interest in the introduction of the Spanish iris, which is rapidly gaining popularity with growers and decorators.

THE Chicago & Northwestern railroad makes free use of Teas' weeping mulberry on its many improved depot grounds.

The Carnation.

LESSONS LEARNED THIS YEAR.

From April 15 to the middle of October this year, carnations suffered more from unfavorable weather conditions than in any one season before in my experience with them. That nothing can happen but what is productive of some good is evidenced by the fact that some of us growers who thought we knew something about carnation culture have had the conceit knocked out of us, and had to do some pretty hard thinking and careful manipulating of plants that our carnations might not be a total failure. Starting at the beginning, I, for one, shall harden my young plants in the spring sufficiently to enable them to stand a few degrees of frost and then shall plant out early enough to make sure of catching the spring rains. If we get a May drought, which has seemed to be a pretty common occurence the last five years, the plants will then be in condition to benefit rather than suffer by it. This season the drought started the middle of April and next season will find my plants in the field the first week in April if the weather will permit.

I shall continue to plant on elevated ridges with the rows far enough apart to work with a horse cultivator, principally because with all the extreme wet weather we have had through July and August there was not a single plant lost in the field by stem rot, and, better yet, we have had no stem rot in the houses. Every grower that I have heard of and every grower that I know of who planted his carnations close and worked with a hand cultivator, has had trouble with stem rot in the field and has it now to a much greater extent in his houses, the most of them enough to curtail seriously their profits for the winter. There are, of course, growers innumerable whom I know nothing about, but the case is as stated and carries with it a lesson for those who care to learn it.

It has always been my opinion that the great proportion of stem rot comes from the cutting bench in the shape of fungus and I have had no reason as yet to change that opinion; but thorough cultivation, an abundance of light and air (such as can not be obtained by close planting and hand cultivation) and a start without check in the spring will, in a great measure, restore a cutting to normal health and a cutting that may have had a slight attack from fungus in the cutting bench will make a good healthy plant, and unless it is that some special condition arises to induce fungus growth again, will live until the end of the season.

A condition to induce this fungus growth, in fact to create it in a perfectly healthy plant, is often seen when carnations are first housed. With our early planting, July and August, we are compelled to water heavily and keep the soil well filled with water for about ten days if we want our plants to start with the least possible check; very often before the expiration of the starting period we have a spell of hot, sultry weather day and night. This, with our wet soil and the slow root action of the newly transplanted plant, makes a perfect combination for the development of stem rot fungus. With a good healthy plant, such as is produced by liberal cultivation, the danger, from stem rot during these ten days is minimized and as soon as the plants are nicely started the bench or bed can be brought back to a more normal condition of moisture and the danger

season is passed. If, however, the soil has gotten into such a condition as to actually breed or create the fungus, then there is nothing better than a good liberal application of air slaked lime and the soil stirred to the depth of one or two inches every week until the disease is brought into check.

We started to plant in the houses the second week of August and finished the first week in September with rain every few days during the whole period, giving us soft plants full of moisture when they were brought in and troublesome in get-

Roses at the World's Fair.—Fig. 1.

ting started properly. As a result of this we have on some of the varieties hardest to start a number of dry leaves around the bottom of the plant. It would have been impossible to select a dry spell of weather in which to bring in our plants this season, but when the opportunity presents we shall certainly use dry weather for planting the houses in preference to wet. These dry leaves are something of an eyesore, but are better left on the plants than taken off, for no matter how carefully it is done there will be considerable injury to the plant. This I demonstrated to my complete satisfaction with a bed of Triumph some years ago that was certainly a sight, as plants had more dead and dry leaves on them than good ones. One half the bed was cleaned up perfectly, the other left without any attention being paid to the dead leaves, except to keep the ground clean and sweet, and there was quite a difference in results in favor of the plants that were left to work out their own salvation. This experiment was made across the

bed, half of each to a side so there could be no difference in the growing conditions, and while not so cleanly as the practice of removing these dry leaves, the difference in results will not warrant the time spent, as the latter is quite an item aside from the injury to the plants.

A. M. H.

The Rose.

CARE NEEDED IN SHIPPING.

After all that has been said concerning the proper treatment of roses to produce good stock, one is apt to lose sight of the fact that great care must be exercised in handling the blooms from the time they are cut until they are shipped, for when competition is as strong as it is at present, every little thing which will tend to improve the condition of stock when marketed should be looked after.

The first important thing to watch is the cutting. A bud should not be cut too soon, neither should it be allowed to remain after it is time to cut it. There can be no definite way of advising the proper time to cut a bud. Each establishment must determine this from experience. Much of the profit will be wasted if the blooms are cut before they are developed or if they are allowed to open too far. When cutting it is important that a sharp knife be used, making a clean incision. If the stem is bruised it will not absorb water as it should when being kept. Also watch carefully each time and cut at the proper eye, securing as much stem as it is possible without robbing the plant.

After the buds are cut they should be assorted and placed in water as soon as possible. Grade them according to the size and color of bud as well as the length of stem, making three grades at least—firsts, seconds, thirds—and when extra good buds are being cut they may be classified as extras, fancies and specials. The room where the cut is kept should be dry and cool, as near to 50° as possible and without draughts of air. It is a safe plan to keep the store room at the same as the night temperature of the houses. By giving careful attention to all the details the stock should be in good condition when marketed and the returns proportionately increased.

R. I.

GRUB WORMS IN ROSE BENCH.

ED. AM. FLORIST:—Would be glad to know how to exterminate grub worms that infest one of my rose benches. Every day or so a plant or two will wilt and on removing it a grub will be found curled up in the roots.

A SUBSCRIBER.

The habit of white grubs of passing the greater part of their existence underground and at a considerable depth renders it a matter of difficulty to reach them with insecticides. Against some forms bisulphide of carbon, kerosene emulsion and poisoned baits have been used with some success. For use in greenhouses the best remedy, everything considered, is the poisoned baits. Of these one of the best is the bran-arsenic mash, which is prepared by combining one part by weight of white arsenic, one of sugar or a like quantity of molasses, with six of bran and enough water to form a mash. This is spread about the plants to be protected. In addition to the use of this mash, it is always advisable to pursue the cleanest of cultural methods, which includes the avoidance of fresh soil which might contain these creatures, the keeping down of all grasses in the immediate vicinity of greenhouses, and particularly in the soil of the greenhouse itself. The use of fertilizers is also advisable, as it enables plants to resist insect attack at the roots.

Sterilizing the soil by means of heat or steam is also of value. As manures are frequently infested by white grubs, and some of these are at times troublesome, it is well to exclude such forms as experience has shown contain an excess of

ROSES AT THE WORLD'S FAIR.—Fig. 2.

these creatures—as, for example, horse manure. They can be identified readily by disintegrating the material, and chickens and other fowls could be utilized in destroying them before the manure is used in the greenhouses.

ROSES AT THE WORLD'S FAIR.

The accompanying views (Nos. 1 and 2) show a section of the rose gardens and roses of the World's Fair planted by the department of horticulture as exhibits. In the foreground are beds of Paul Neyron, planted May 14 and 15, 1903, from which the stems of Paul Neyron were cut which appear at the right of one of the small pictures and measure four feet and one-half in length. The other rose stems were cut from bed to the extreme right and at the back and measure over six feet in length. In the background to the right is a large bed of Clio almost as tall and of uniform growth. The terrace directly back of the roses is being prepared for seeding with grass. Beds for autumn planting of bulbs, to be followed by bedding plants in spring, are on this terrace also. In the background is a small section of the east elevation of the agriculture building, along which, on the east side, the rose section extends.

The other illustration (No. 3) shows lengthwise view of the rose plantations situated east of the agriculture building and, north of east wing of the horticulture building; this wing is the conservatory reserved for inside floriculture exhibits. In the foreground of the picture is a bed of Althæas and close behind are beds of roses extending as far back as 1,000 feet north. These were planted between the dates of April 22 and May 27, 1903, and up to the time of writing having have made a growth as high as six feet, Paul Neyron averaging four feet. These exhibits are from various growers.

LYNN, MASS.—James M. Teel, city forester for nearly forty years, died on October 8, aged 84 years.

Some Good Phloxes.

I had the pleasure of looking over the Vaughan collection of phloxes during the after-convention visit of the delegates to Western Springs. This is one of the largest and most select collections of these now favorite flowers that I have seen. The plants were in full bloom with the exception of some extra early and some of the later sorts, and a good opportunity was had to secure some field notes. I give below a memorandum of those which appeared to me to be the finest in the collection.

Sunshine.—Bright pink.

Pantheon.—Bright pink, a smaller flower than Sunshine, but a very compact and showy variety.

Wilson's New Seedling.—This variety varies from pink to white, some plants being one color, some the other. It is a good free grower and free flowerer, with large trusses.

Montagnard.—This variety I consider one of the very best on the grounds. It is a deep bright magenta-scarlet and shines and shows up brilliantly at a long distance.

Marquise St. Paul.—Pink.

Lothair.—Also pink, but a little darker in shade than Marquise St. Paul.

Mme. Pape Carpenter.—This variety is of the purest white and should be included in all collections where a good white is desired,

Beranger.—Pale pink; same shade as Daybreak carnation.

Aquillon.—Pink with a darker eye; very large flowers.

Semiramis.—Dark pink, lighter eye, very free flowering.

Liliput.—Pink to lavander.

Eugene Langervillier.—Pale lilac.

Champes Elysee.—Brilliant ruby very free, varies a little and not as dark as Montagnard, also sports to white stripes.

Japonais.—Fine dwarf compact grower, pale pink; this variety produces large trusses of flowers, compact and fine. Large flowers.

Earliest Seedling No. 4.—This one I believe is to be called Alice Pearson. It is a salmon pink, compact head, deeper in center. Large compact trusses and a strong compact grower; very free flowering.

Best Whites.—In addition to Mme. Pape Carpenter I should name Berenice, Jeanne D'Arc and Pearl. Mme. Carpenter is the dwarfest of the four.

J. T. Temple.—Bright pink, free flowering and dwarf.

Snowdown.—Pure white, belongs to the suffruticosa section.

Lady Masgrove.—At a distance this looks like a fine brilliant lilac flower, but on examining closely it is found to be beautifully and regularly striped pink and pale lilac.

Cross of Honor.—Same as preceding but lighter shade.

Seedling No. 1.—White with beautifully dotted pink eye. This has a fringe of dots around the pink eye, which gives it a very charming effect.

Suffruticosa Circle.—White with pink eye.

Mme. Fournier.—Smaller flower and a little lighter eye than Suffruticosa Circle.

J. A. German.—Peach blossom pink, with darker eye.

Seedling No. 1 A.—White shaded lilac, deep pink eye, large florets and large truss.

Prof. Schlieman.—Salmon rose, deeper eye, fine pyramidal head, small florets.

Boule de Feu.—Scarlet with crimson eye. This is a beautiful variety, but it is

said to be very hard to propagate.

Auguste Revere.—Brighter and purer color, but otherwise identical with Boule de Feu.

Amor.—Pink lighter center, fine dwarf grower with compact flower, very free, somewhat resembles Japonais.

ROSES AT THE WORLD'S FAIR.—Fig. 3.

Cameron—Pink, with large crimson center. Large florets and large compact trusses.

Coquelicot.—Orange scarlet with crimson eye, large heads, dwarf grower, very free. Said to be hard to propagate.

Eclaireur.—Dark crimson, rosy center, surrounded with a dotted circle of rosy white. This is a fine, tall grower, very vigorous and free, good propagator.

Esclarmond.—Rosy lilac shaded white, purple center with white. Very large flowers. Tall grower, 2½ to 3 feet.

The phlox department at Vaughan's is under the management of Nels Pearson, who is an enthusiast on this flower and glad to impart to visitors every information in regard to his favorite work. I was very much surprised to see so much progress in the west. The phlox is only just coming into its birthright as a brilliant midsummer and fall subject. The people in the west are certainly as much alive to this as those in the east. I can well remember the splendid pot and tub grown plants produced by the old country gardeners at the flower show twenty-five years ago, and now we are drawing from the European collections for enlarging our own assortment of this fine old American plant.　　G. C. WATSON.

Chicago.

CHRYSANTHEMUM SHOW OCTOBER 24.—FLORIST'S CLUB WILL HAVE ENTIRE CONTROL.—FINE DECORATIONS IN HONOR OF CLEVELAND.—NOTES OF THE TRADE.

The first monthly exhibition of the Chicago Florists' Club will be held October 24, being devoted to cut chrysanthemums and carnations, prizes to be awarded for the best collection of each. Those having seedling chrysanthemums to be judged can have it done at this show, as the judges are the ones selected by the Chrysanthemum Society of America, and exhibitors will be entitled to registration by paying the necessary fees. Blooms intended for exhibition should be sent to E. F. Winterson, 45-49 Wabash avenue, Chicago, charges prepaid, not later than 1 p. m. October 24. Mr. Winterson will see to the staging of the same. Arrangements are under way for a supper at one of the down town hotels to be held the same evening.

There were a number of epicurean events during the week owing to the visit of ex-President Cleveland. Phil Hauswirth had the work for the dinner given by the Commercial Club in the banquet hall of the Auditorium, October 14. The materials used were white and yellow chrysanthemums, asparagus and autumn foliage. The Walter Kreitling Company had two luncheons at the Chicago Club, the most elaborate being that given by James H. Eckels, where yellow dahlias and asparagus were employed. The latter is illustrated on page 423.

There has been an oversupply of carnations and lower grade roses the past week. While trade has been fair the demand has not been sufficient to clean out the market. Outdoor stock, such as dahlias, gladioli, fewview, coreopsis, etc., is still to be had. Violets are improving but they have not as yet struck their gait. Shipping trade conditions seem to improve.

A large quantity of work was ordered for the funeral of the late Wm. G. Hibbard, early in the week, but the family did not want flowers at the funeral and all that could be properly used were sent to the hospitals. A large quantity of the material was disposed of in this way, but where it could not be used the orders were countermanded.

Chicago public school grounds are to be beautified with flower beds, trees and shrubberies until they are the finest in the United States. Various Chicago women's clubs have promised to co-operate with the Outdoor Art Association in this work and the board of education will lend its assistance.

The Ernst Wienhoeber Company has mailed customers a very attractive blank book for the entry of engagements. It is much the same as that of last year, differing in the color of the cover. A good business note, type-written on fine stationery, accompanies the book.

The executive and membership committees of the Florists' Club met at the Union Restaurant Monday night with a fair attendance. Recommendations were adopted for the next club meeting and plans of the membership committee were furthered.

The South Park board has accepted the offer of a $5,000 premium for $2,000,000 worth of 4 per cent bonds issued to carry out the extensive south side improvements.

Some very fine white and yellow chrysanthemums are coming in from Vaughan's Greenhouses. Deamud is handling them.

Some fair choice cosmos is now being received from R. E. Kennicott, Carbondale, Ill. It goes to most of the commission houses.

S. Garland has taken two stands in the Flower Growers' Market which he will occupy from October 19.

P. L. Howard is at the German Hospital undergoing an operation for stomach trouble.

The west park board has refused the request of the gardeners for increased wages.

John Degnan, with the E. F. Winterson Company, was in Indianapolis this week.

New York.

ENTHUSIASTIC CLUB MEETING.—BUSINESS UNSTEADY.—GOOD VIOLETS PLENTIFUL.—DEATH OF THORLEY'S DAUGHTER.—NOTES.

The October meeting of the New York Florists' Club brought out a large and enthusiastic attendance last Monday evening. There were over forty members in the club room. Very interesting talks on the recent S. A. F. convention were given by Messrs. O'Mara, Wallace, Du Rie and Shaw. A. Herrington made a stirring address on the coming exhibition of the Chrysanthemum Society of America, indicating confidence in a fine display, assurances and practical support having been freely given by many clubs and societies all over the country. The labor question came up and was thrashed out by Messrs. O'Mara. Lenker, Scott, Kelsey and Wallace. The outing committee reported through its chairman a creditable balance from the summer picnic.

Business still remains unsteady. The dark weather has left its impress on the roses and pink varieties are bleached and soft generally. American Beauty has suffered with the rest, but there are, however, some good special blooms in the market. Of these none too many and the price is well maintained. Chrysanthemums are more plentiful and prices have fallen somewhat as compared with last week, and many of those received indicate that the long rainstorm did them no good. Carnations are in lighter supply and a better price prevails. The violet cut is very heavy and the stock mostly good. It remains difficult to advance the price in line with

past seasons in the face of so heavy a cut. Orchids are elegant and abundant. Cattleyas lead and Dendrobium formosum is of fine quality. Oncidiums are now seen in all the prominent windows. Vanda cærulea is in good demand but scarce. The market is full of chrysanthemum plants at 50 cents.

We are sorry to have to record the death of Charles Thorley's daughter, Miss Lulu before marriage. The funeral was on Sunday afternoon from Mr. Thorley's residence, Riverside drive.

Mrs. J. W. Scallen's new store in the Imperial Hotel is nearing completion and will be a beauty.

A good delegation of New Yorkers attended the Craig-Harris' sale at Philadelphia.

John Young is handling a quantity of fine chrysanthemum plants in handy sizes.

The wedding of young Mr. Wadley at Newport was a very happy affair.

Boston.

INTERESTING CLUB MEETING.—CHARLES SANDER ON BEGONIAS.—IMPROVED MARKET CONDITIONS.—NOTES.

The Gardeners' and Florists' Club held its initial meeting for the season on Tuesday evening, October 13, President Pettigrew in the chair. The meeting was the best in point of attendance and interest which the club has had for years and was an encouraging augury for the coming winter series. Charles Sander entertained the members with an excellent paper on begonias, a subject which that gentleman is well qualified to handle. He said that since the appearance of the first begonia (B. nitida) in England in 1777 over 350 species have been described. The earliest one in his own affections was Weltoniensis, a hybrid raised in England by Col. Clarke from Dregel and Sutherlandi, and be considered this still worthy of a place, being a fine pot plant and a good bedder in semi-shady situations. Up to the memorable introduction of Vesuvius, the herald of the great tuberous rooted section, by the Messrs. Veitch, his acquaintance had been limited to semperflorens, fuchsioides, glaucophylla scandens, Verschafelti, manicata, sanguinea in flowering kinds and Rex and Marshalli in fancy-leaved. He spoke appreciatively of Richard Pearce, a traveler for Messrs. Veitch, to whom we are indebted for the discovery of Boliviensis Pearcii and Veitchii, the progenitors of the splendid race of tuberous begonias which has now assumed large commercial proportions, many millions of tubers being produced annually for the trade.

Mr. Sander enumerated a large number of species that had come under his observation, such as diversifolia, a fine fall bloomer, Evansiana a good bedder, rubra valuable to train on a pillar, rosea gigantea, a veritable rosy plant; Metallica and its dark foliaged progeny Credneri and Thurstonii. Speaking of the bedding varieties he expressed the opinion that Begonia Vernon was a rechristened atrosanguinea. The true type of semperflorens, Vernon ranks among the most valuable bedding plants, ever-blooming and doing well either in sun or shade, also making an excellent pot plant. Erfordii he characterized as fully equal to Vernon, but from its variable habit and its freedom in intercrossing he recommended that where uniformity of growth and color are desired, it should be propagated from seed only. Among the best "to have and to hold" he mentioned Vesuvius, a hybrid sent out by Lemoine and unequaled as a brilliant blooming bedder.

Reverting to the winter blooming species he spoke approvingly of socotrana and its rare characteristic of holding its flowers for a long time—a plant to which we are indebted through the agency of that great hybridizer, Lemoine, for the finest flowering plant ever given the gardening world, Begonia Gloire de Lorraine. The first plant of Lorraine ever imported to America was grown and flowered by the late F. L. Harris, of Wellesley, Mass.

Referring to his own experiments in raising seedlings he said that one of his earliest successes had been a seedling from incarnata which is now quite widely grown in the neighborhood of Boston under the name of Improved Incarnata. He had achieved abundant success with the tuberous-rooted sorts, but when it came to hybridizing these with other species he found the work almost insurmountable. Between diversifolia and the tuberous rooted varieties he had got good seed and got characteristic progeny but the seedlings proved to be mules and the tubers were sickly and valueless the second year. Using the much-heralded Froebeli as a parent he found the results equally discouraging. He has been for some time industriously working to secure a hybrid between socotrana and incarnata, thus far without satisfactory results, but will continue experimenting, hoping to strike it sometime.

In hybridizing, some begonias will fertilize readily, others not at all, or producing seed so sparingly and of such low germinating power as to be of no value. Varieties of hybrid origin especially, have not shown the slightest tendency to set seed after having been fertilized with their own or other pollen. I have never been able to get seed of rosea gigantea, Verschaffeltiana, Paul Bruant, President Carnot, nitida and a few others. I have confined myself mostly to insignis and socotrana for pollen.

Mr. Sander closed by expressing the hope than eventually we might get a race of summer-blooming varieties endowed with the qualities of Gloire de Lorraine and in great variety of colors.

J. K. M. L. Farquhar followed Mr. Sander with some interesting reminiscences of a visit to Mr. Lemoine. He expressed the opinion that most of the varied forms of Lorraine stock were from Lemoine's stock, it having been found necessary to use seedlings to fill out the overwhelming orders received for Lorraine when originally disseminated, and stated that nana compacta came to light in this manner. Mr. Farquhar spoke in approval of the dwarf type of tuberous begonias of which Duc de Zeppelin is an example, these being better bedders than those of large straggly growth. He had seen Lorraine used successfully in England as a summer bedder. Jackson Dawson said that he had recently received some unidentified begonia seed from South Africa, of which a number had already germinated satisfactorily. Mr. Pettigrew said that Weltoniensis had been used successfully by him as a summer bedder in the Chicago parks.

Mr. Sander in conclusion, replying to several queries said that Dregii and Sutherlandi were the parents of Weltoniensis and Dregii and socotrana the parents of Lorraine. He would select as the best greenhouse kinds Lorraine, incarnata, rubra and the Erfordii type. He expressed the view that to obtain uniform stock of Vernon, propagations should be from cuttings because of cross-fertilization by

bees producing varying colors and irregular habit. This J. H. Morton was not inclined to endorse, having had better results by relying entirely upon seedlings.

Up to within a few days the cut flower trade was in a bad shape owing to over-production, but the spell of bad weather recently experienced cut off the larger part of the supply and gave an opportunity of unloading. It also had a bad effect on roses, for a good proportion of those coming in are covered with mildew. Carnations are short-stemmed and generally poor as yet and violets are of very inferior quality. Buyers are finding fault with them on all sides. They need cooler weather.

At a meeting called on October 15 for an informal expression of opinion regarding the nomination of officers of the Massachusetts Horticultural Society for the coming year the matter was referred to the same committee which reported the new constitution last spring. The election of officers will be held on November 14.

Mrs. Mary S. Ames, of North Easton, has donated six large specimen palms and A. F. Estabrook, of Clifton, has given two enormous ferns to the Massachusetts Horticultural Society to be used as permanent attractions in Horticultural Hall.

Mrs. H. L. T. Wolcott, a useful member of the Massachusetts Horticultural Society for many years and a leader in the philanthropic and educational life of Boston, died at her home in Dedham on October 8.

Fred Dawson returned last Thursday from his European trip. As the voyage had been taken on account of his health the news of his brother's death was not communicated to him until his return.

The chrysanthemum exhibition will be held at Horticultural Hall on November 5-8.

Philadelphia.

CHRYSANTHEMUMS BRIGHTEN THE STORE WINDOWS—BUSINESS IS LIVELY AT THE MARKET—NEW SEEDLING ROSE PROMISING—NOTES OF THE TRADE.

Chrysanthemums are now in, and fine white, pink and yellow now enliven the stores. These with autumn leaves make a great combination, and many beautiful effects are to be seen. Polly Rose seems to be the best early white, with Glory of the Pacific for pink. Yellow has been scarce, but a day or two more will see them in quantity. Roses are getting better, but the cloudy weather of last week took the color out of the Maids. Jacob Becker's new rose, Ideal, is coming in from Craig's and some nice flowers are to be seen. The next growth will produce fine stock. Carnations are improving, and all kinds are as good and some better than generally seen at this season. They seem to move fairly well. Violets are true form, although the doubles are not yet much to look at. Dahlias are still in their glory and with cosmos, which is now to be had in quantity, monopolize the attention of those who want a good deal for their money.

At Robert Craig's most of the stock disposed of at the time of the sale has been delivered, and while some $7,000 worth was handled one would hardly judge so to look through the houses, as nothing is missed save a few large specimens. The rest of the stock when spread out has only the needed room. At this sale both buyers and seller seem to have

been satisfied, which speaks well for the future.

We had a look at John A. Shellem's new seedling rose spoken of last week. It is a strong and healthy grower and appears to be a very free bloomer. The stems support the large flower perfectly erect and are well clothed with foliage. It will certainly be heard from in the near future. Mr. Shellem has also a few choice seedling carnations, a large scarlet giving promise of being equal to anything now in cultivation.

At the market things are moving lively. There is a good assortment to select from if one gets there on time. After the growers are cleared out, Manager Meehan takes customers in charge and the capacious ice box is explored, generally with good results. The stock of Beauties here seems to hold out well throughout the day, due mainly to the good telephone service.

A new putty roller with which the laying on of putty in glazing is greatly facilitated has been invented by Wm. McClenahan. Wm. Stevens, of John Burton's establishment, has an interest in the roller, and in his hands it certainly looks a wonder. With a little practice any one can manipulate it. The selling price is 50 cents.

S. S. Pennock is receiving some choice Floriana, Lawson's and Lillian Pond from Reuter at Westerly, R. I. Mr. Pennock looked over the Reuter place last week, and says he never saw such perfection in carnations at this season of the year.

Leo Niessen has southern smilax in stock in half and quarter cases, which will be a great convenience for small decorators where a full case is not required. Leo says he is much pleased with the outlook.

George M. Moss, the Seventeenth street commission merchant, will open up again on October 20 with a stock of the best flowers. George Farrell, the Jenkintown hustler, will be first assistant.

The Wm. Graham company has some large store decorations on hand at the present time.

The Floral Exchange is sending Eugene Bersheimer some fine Beauties and Edgelys.

Craig & Son's Enchantress are fine, as is also President McKinley.   K.

Cleveland.

There is considerable decoration work and making of designs in flowers and dried stuff for the Knights Templar Conclave here this week. The city has a festive appearance with its gay banners and flags. The weather is fine. Gray's armory, where the banquet will be held, is decorated inside with colored bunting, southern smilax and large crosses of cape flowers.

Dahlias are coming in plentifully and are selling freely with a large demand for the better sorts. Carnations and roses are looking good and all the growers have some to sell.

Harry Piggott, of South Brooklyn, has started a store on Clark avenue near Pearl street. The store scheme is gold and white and many mirrors help to set off the place.

Robt. Huchins is rapidly recovering from his injuries and will soon be out of the hospital.

James Wilson's carnations are exceptionally fine.   O. G.

HOLYOKE, MASS.—The Horticultural Society will hold its next annual meeting on November 4.

THE AMERICAN FLORIST

NINETEENTH YEAR.

Subscription, $1.00 a year. To Europe, $2.00.
Subscriptions accepted only from those
in the trade.

Advertisements, on all except cover pages,
10 Cents a Line, Agate; $1.00 per inch.
Cash with Order.

No Special Position Guaranteed.

Discounts are allowed only on consecutive insertions, as follows:—6 times, 5 per cent; 13 times,
10 per cent; 26 times, 20 per cent;
52 times, 30 per cent.

Cover space sold only on yearly contract at
$1.00 per inch, net, in the case of the two
front pages, regular discounts applying only to the back pages.

The Advertising Department of the AMERICAN
FLORIST is for florists, seedsmen and nurserymen
and dealers in wares pertaining to those lines only.
Orders for less than one-half inch space not accepted.
Advertisements must reach us by Wednesday to
secure insertion in the issue for the following
Saturday. Address

AMERICAN FLORIST CO., Chicago.

CHICAGO CHRYSANTHEMUM SHOW next week. See page 428 for particulars.

DIG the cannas now.

THIS is good weather to get the coal in and housed.

POT the bulbs soon; there is nothing gained by allowing them to lie around and dry out.

A GOOD article of sphagnum moss is said to be scarce in the Wisconsin district where it is gathered.

DRACÆNA TERMINALIS is being got into line in a large way for Christmas in several enterprising Philadelphia establishments.

WE are in receipt of the fourteenth annual report of the Missouri Botanic Garden. In addition to the usual matter, it contains a synopsis of the genus lonicera, by Alfred Rheder, with twenty plates.

SOME criticism regarding a tendency in the Pierson fern to revert to the type brings out the assertion on the part of observant growers that this takes place only when the plant is grown too hot in winter.

OUR captious, but always esteemed, New York contemporary, alias Job, varies its characteristic comments in a recent issue by bestowing a lavish compliment upon the humor it has detected in our Rhinebeck correspondence. We gladly return the compliment as we contemplate that artless morsel of "accentuated humor" on their opposite page, in which our friends, the violet raisers of Rhinebeck, are accused of making ten thousand dollars a year of late.

Annual Production of Pelargoniums.

ED. AM. FLORIST:—Perhaps some reader can oblige by stating how many zonale pelargoniums there are grown in the United States and Canada annually.
A. P.

Premium Lists Received.

We are in receipt of the premium lists of the Indiana floral festival and chrysanthemum show to be held at Indianapolis, November 10–14, and the flower show to be held at Buffalo, N. Y., November 11–14. Copies of the former may be had on application to Irwin Bertermann, 241 Massachusetts avenue, Indianapolis, Ind., and of the latter on application to Chas. Keitsch, 460–70 Main street, Buffalo, N. Y.

The chrysanthemum and orchid exhibition premium list of the Woman's Auxiliary to the Northwestern Manufacturers' Association, St. Paul, Minn., has been issued. Mrs. A. P. Moss, 295 Nelson avenue, St. Paul, Minn., is the secretary.

Reed's Views of the West.

We have been favored with a copy of Edward Reed's paper on the Milwaukee convention and the west, read before the Florists' Club of Philadelphia, October 6, and extend our best thanks. It would be sophistry, if not worse, to state that Mr. Reed's views regarding the possibilities are overdrawn. The prospects of the great western section of this country are indisputably phenomenal, especially so since the government has taken the question of irrigation in hand. Let human kind do what it will, the smoke of the west goes up the chimney. No conflict of labor and capital can bar its progress. The supremacy of the west, due in a large measure to its natural resources and the energy and perseverance of its inhabitants, is as inevitable as the destiny of mankind.

Mr. Reed, following in the wake of President Burton, is pessimistic in the matter of our large areas of glass. Long before Mr. Burton gave expression to his views, a more conservative course was recommended in these columns. In later days we have almost come to the conclusion that our fears were in a measure unwarranted, but even to-day we are not wholly optimistic. Any prolonged period of depression would write ruin for many extensive growers, ruin in their finances and ruin in their establishments, as would similar conditions in any other line of trade. There is no necessity at this time to be apprehensive, but the future is entirely unreadable and the tendency in our lines of business is toward development at many points rather than few.

But let us like ourselves to the source of inspiration. It was a Quaker City poet of the trade, whole-souled and absolutely destitute of the rhymster's tinsel, who led us on. Perhaps he is forgotten as such, but we shall remember always his magic words of nearly twenty years ago:

There is a crowd of jolly men that live about
this town;
Some have more and some have less, but all
possess renown.
They're fond of hearty living, and they're
bound to have it too.
So once a year they come down here and say,
"How do you do?"

There's Harris and George Anderson, John
Dick and Coldfoon Bill,
There's Kent, and Davy Lutzie, and Bob
out on the hill.
All working hard as beavers and piling up
the cash,
But every season down it comes and all
goes into hash.

For many years after that time no flowers worthy of mention, roses, carnations, etc., were grown in the west. The stock was grown eastward and sold here by such expert salesmen at Patrick Welch, of Boston. We mention Mr. Welch merely as a type because we were familiar with his work. There were others like him, who hailed from New York and Philadelphia, but they were not numerous.

Brother Reed's reference to hospitality compels us to forego the otherwise keen pleasure of reproducing his essay. This is an art we have not yet acquired; we haven't the time. To paraphrase another bard:

We were but as the wind passing heedlessly over,
And all the wild music we waked was thine
own.

Society of American Florists.

DEPARTMENT OF PLANT REGISTRATION.

The Conard & Jones Company ask to withdraw the name Leo XIII as applied to a new rose registered by them on July 30, 1903, and to substitute therefor that of Sir Thomas Lipton, it having been ascertained that a rose under the name of Leo XIII was already in existence at the time of registering. Any one knowing of any reason against the registration, as now applied for, under the name of Sir Thomas Lipton will please notify promptly. WM. J. STEWART, Sec'y.

American Carnation Society.

DEPARTMENT OF REGISTRATION.

The following new varieties of carnations have been registered:

By John E. Haines, Bethlehem, Pa., "John E. Haines," deep scarlet, size 3½ inches, free and early bloomer, good, strong growth, never bursting calyx and long stiff stems. "Star of Bethlehem," pure yellow, very free continuous bloomer, a strong grower with long, stiff stems and flowers 3 to 3½-inches with never bursting calyx. No. 77, a pure pink with 3½-inch flower, a never bursting calyx, long, stiff stems and very fragrant; free, continual bloomer and very free grower, good for twelve months of the year.

ALBERT M. HERR, SEC'Y.

Chrysanthemum Society of America.

ADDITIONAL PREMIUMS.—The attention of prospective exhibitors is called to the following prizes which have been recently added to the already fine schedule for the Exhibition of the Chrysanthemum Society of America, in New York, November 10.

Offered by the Pennsylvania Horticultural Society. Open to all—for the best vase of 40 blooms of chrysanthemums of one or several varieties, correctly named, stems not less than 24 inches long, two prizes—$30 and $20.

Offered by Lawrence Cedarhurst Horticultural Society of Long Island, 25 blooms in 25 varieties, $10, $7; 12 blooms in 12 varieties, $5 and $3. To be competed for by members of this society only.

FRED H. LEMON, Sec'y.

San Francisco.

BUSINESS RATHER QUIET.—CHRYSANTHEMUMS ARE GETTING PLENTIFUL.—GOOD ROSES AND CARNATIONS SCARCE YET.— PACIFIC COAST HORSICULTURAL SOCIETY'S ANNUAL ELECTION OF OFFICERS.

Trade during the past week has been somewhat quieter, with most of the florists. Stock is commencing to arrive in more liberal quantities but in regard to quality much is yet to be desired, with the exception of chrysanthemums, of which lots of excellent blooms may be seen in all the stores. White and yellow Queen, Bonnaffon and Mrs. Hunt predominating and bringing $1 to $2 a dozen. Roses and carnations, although in fair supply, are as yet very poor, roses being teas from 50 cents to 75 cents a dozen. Carnations are short and from 20 cents to 50 cents is the average price, a few Spreckels, Enchantress and Hobart bringing from 75 cents to $1. Violets are coming in more freely but are yet off color and bring from 75 cents to $1 a dozen bunches. Some fine Cattleya labiata sell for 50 cents.

The Pacific Coast Horticultural Society's annual election of officers took place October 3 and resulted as follows: President, H. Plath; vice-president, Thos. H. Munroe; financial secretary, M. Borkheim; recording secretary, N. Peterson; treasurer. F. Cleis; trustees, W. H. Krabbenhoft, J. Atkinson, W. J. Bagge; librarian, A. Tymchiow; ushers, Messrs. Niedemuller and Martin.

Mann Brothers suffered considerable damage recently by fire in their dwelling the basement of which was used as a storeroom for florists supplies, moss, baskets and boxes worth over $500 being ruined, with no insurance.

F. Pelicano & Company are remodeling and preparing their place for the coming busy season. Marble counters and six large plate glass mirrors will considerably enhance the attractiveness of the store.

Visitors: Sidney Clack, of Menlo Park, and Mr. Forbes, of Martin & Forbes, Portland, O.   ROMNEYA.

Cincinnati.

GOOD DEMAND FOR CARNATIONS AND CHRYSANTHEMUMS.—MANY EXHIBITIONS PLANNED.—SUNDAY OPENING OF EDEN PARK.

Chrysanthemums, such varieties as Estelle, Willowbrook and Glory of the Pacific, are now arriving in quantities, and they have found a good market to date. Carnations are more plentiful; we do not get enough white, but enough pink and red for all orders. Will Murphy, our leading carnation man, informs me that he has the cut from forty-eight houses at Murphyville, and declares that very few find their way to the barrel. There are just about enough American Beauties to go around and the pleasant thing is that we do not see the street fakirs with their stands full of them. Some very good cosmos is to be had and lily of the valley is fine. Brides and Bridesmaids from Gus Meier's place are the best around town and easily bring $5 per hundred. Smilax, adiantum and asparagus, both Sprengeri and plumosus, are plentifull. All the commission man needs is time to have it cut, and there are no orders too large at present for green goods.

At the meeting of the Florists' Society Saturday night the schedule committee recommended that the schedule of premiums used by the society for their monthly exhibitions last winter be adopted for the shows the coming winter. The only thing needed now is enough money for the premiums, and we trust the committee will have no trouble in raising the necessary funds to carry on these shows. A free lunch was served.

The nine greenhouses at Eden Park will present a beautiful sight in the next few weeks and they will be thrown open to the public until 5 p. m. There is a fine lot of chrysanthemums, begonias and orchids in bloom; crotons, palms and ferns also on exhibition.   ALEX.

Cleveland.

We have had two quite severe frosts in the last week, but the outside plants and flowers all stand as well as if no frosts had touched them. Florists had been wishing for a good frost, and now that it has come it has not benefited them. Market gardeners are tired of bringing tomatoes in at ten cents a half bushel. Florists who order bulbs from

foreign agents find much difficulty getting the goods shipped on time. There is always a vexatious delay at the foreign ports and again at the custom house, which crowd the work when the bulbs arrive. Narcissus Paper White, Romans and freesia should have been planted by August 1 and some of them are still on the way.

There is no abating of the funeral work. Flowers are bought up rapidly, and lots of outside flowers are used, even the homely yellow dahlia being drafted into service. Some early chrysanthemums are shown, but they are not up to the standard.

Henry F. Piggott, who has large greenhouses in South Brooklyn, has established a store on Clark avenue near Pearl street. The color scheme is white and gold, and many mirrors help to make the place attractive.

Smith & Son, on Wade Park avenue have three new delivery wagons.   O. G.

INTERNATIONAL FLOWER DELIVERY.

INTERNATIONAL FLOWER DELIVERY.

STEAMSHIPS LEAVE FOREIGN PORTS.

FROM	TO	STEAMER	*LINE	DAY	DUE ABOUT
Liverpool	New York	Germanic	7	Wed. Oct. 21, 3:30 p. m.	Oct. 29
Liverpool	"	Cedric	7	Fri Oct. 23, 3:30 p. m.	Oct. 31
Liverpool	"	Majestic	7	Wed. Oct. 28, 3:30 p. m.	Nov. 5
Liverpool	"	Celtic	7	Fri. Oct. 30, 3:30 p. m.	Nov. 7
Liverpool	Boston	Winifredian	16	Fri. Oct. 23,	Nov. 1
Liverpool	"	Bohemian	16	Fri. Oct. 30,	Nov. 8
Liverpool	"	Ivernia	1	Tues. Oct. 20,	O.t. 28
Liverpool	"	Mayflower	15	Thur. Oct. 22,	Oct. 29
Liverpool	"	Columbus	15	Thur. Oct. 29,	Nov. 5
Glasgow	New York	Ethiopia	5	Wed. Oct. 22,	
Glasgow	"	Columbia	5	Thur. Oct. 29,	
Glasgow	"	Mongolian	8	Sat. Oct. 24,	Nov. 2
Hamburg	"	Moltke	8	Sat. Oct. 24,	Oct. 31
Hamburg	"	Pennsylvania	8	Sat. Oct. 31,	
Hamburg	"	Deutschland	8	Sun. Nov. 1,	
London	"	Menaba	6	Sat. Oct. 24,	Nov. 3
London	"	Minnetonka	6	Sat. Oct. 31,	
Southampton	"	Philadelphia	8	Sat. Oct. 24, Noon.	
Southampton	"	St. Louis	8	Sat. Oct. 31,	Nov. 6
Southampton	"	Marquette	9	Wed. Oct. 21,	
Rotterdam	"	Rotterdam	11	Sat. Oct. 24,	
Rotterdam	"	Potsdam	11	Sat. Oct. 31,	Nov. 8
Havre	"	La Touraine	10	Sat. Oct. 24,	Oct. 31
Havre	"	La Savoie	10	Sat. Oct. 31,	
Genoa	"	Hohenzollern	13	Thur. Oct. 22,	Nov. 11
Genoa	"	Lombardia	13	Mon. Oct. 26,	
Bremen	"	Kronprinz Wilh.	13	Tues. Oct. 20,	Oct. 27
Bremen	"	Frdk. Der Grosse	13	Sat. Oct. 24,	Nov. 3
Sydney	San Francisco	Sonoma	18	Mon. Oct. 19,	Nov. 9
Hongkong	Vancouver	Empress of China	20	Wed. Oct. 21,	Nov. 6
Hongkong	Seattle	Riojun Maru	22	Tues Oct. 20,	Nov. 30

* See steamship list on opposite page.

Wild Smilax ALWAYS On Hand.

Also PLUMOSUS, SPRENGERI, ADIANTUMS, GALAX AND LEUCOTHOES.

We are Growers of **HIGH-GRADE Cut Flowers.** All orders promptly filled. Consignments solicited.

FRANK GARLAND, 55-57 Wabash Ave., Chicago.

Please mention the American Florist when writing

The F. R. WILLIAMS CO.

Wholesale Florists,

CLEVELAND, - OHIO.

Please mention the American Florist when writing

WILD SMILAX. ORDER DIRECT FROM HEADQUARTERS.

We carry the finest and most complete stock of Florists' Hardy Supplies. Dagger and Fancy Ferns, $1.00 per 1000 A No. 1 quality. Bronze and Green Galax, $1.00 per 1000 A No. 1 quality. Southern Wild Smilax, 50 pound case, $7.00. 25 pound case, $3.50 per case. Laurel Festooning, good and full, 5c and 6c per yard. Leucothoe Sprays, $1.00 per 100. Green Moss, $1.00 per bbl.; 75c per bag. Sphagnum Moss, $1.00 per bbl., 50c per bag. Order by mail, telegraph or telephone will reach our personal and prompt attention. Long Dist. 'Phone 2618 Main.

HENRY W. ROBINSON, No. 11 Province St., BOSTON, MASS.

Please mention the American Florist when writing.

Albert Fuchs,

PALMS, FERNS, FICUS.

Established 1884. CHICAGO. 2045-59 Clarendon Ave.

Please mention the American Florist when writing.

LONDON.

COMMISSIONS CARRIED OUT IN LONDON

or any part of Great Britain.

Messrs. WILLS & SEGAR will attend to any commission from American florists for the supply of Cut Flowers, birthday Flowers, Bouquets, High Class Floral Designs, etc. to their clients who may be travelling in England.

WILLS & SEGAR, Court Florists to his Majesty, The King.

ROYAL EXOTIC NURSERY.

TELEGRAMS, Onslow Crescent, South Kensington. FLOSCULO, LONDON. LONDON, ENGLAND.

DENVER.

FLORAL DESIGNS AND FLOWERS.

Best Quality on Shortest Notice.

DANIELS & FISHER, DENVER, COLO.

Order by mail, telephone, telegraph or cable. Cable address: "Daniels Denver."

GALAX...

Bronze or green, 75c per 1000, in 3,000 cts or more. **Leucothoe Sprays,** green, 90c per 100. **Southern Smilax,** fresh stock, per 50-lb. case, $6.00; per 25-lb case, $3.50. **Green Sheet Moss,** choice stock, $3.50 per barrel sack. **Spagnum Moss,** $1.75 per large bale.

FLORIST' SUPPLIES of Every DESCRIPTION.

Tel. 597 Madison **L. J. KRESHOVER,** Square. 110-112 W. 27th St., New York.

..WILD SMILAX..

The Celebrated

"Superior Quality" Brand.

Greens of all Kinds

Always on hand and at the right prices.

E. F. WINTERSON CO.,

45-47-49 Wabash Ave., CHICAGO.

Catalogue Free.

HARDY CUT FERNS.

Write for Prices.

FANCY   DAGGER

L. B. BRAGUE, Hinsdale, Mass.

Oldest, largest and most reliable dealer in U. S. Mr. Brague will have an exhibit at the Convention Hall.

Please mention the American Florist when writing.

IF YOU HAVE STOCK TO SELL.....

The best way to make that fact known to the trade is by regular advertising in the

The American Florist.

THE SEED TRADE.

AMERICAN SEED TRADE ASSOCIATION.
S. F. Willard, Pres.; J. Charles McCullough, First Vice-Pres.; C. E. Kendel, Cleveland, O., Sec'y and Treas.
Twenty-second annual convention St. Louis, Mo., June, 1904.

ONION SET set stocks stored at Chicago have suffered some by inclement weather.

NEW YORK.—H. M. Wall, the seedsmen's lithographer, is making a western trip.

SHIOCTON, WIS.—It is estimated that 100,000 bushels of onions were grown here this season.

PROFESSOR HENRY, of Wisconsin, states that the corn crop in that state is better than last year.

SEED POTATO prices in the west are opening at 10 to 15 cents per bushel higher than in 1902.

BOUQUET GREEN picking has begun in a moderate way in the Wisconsin districts. Weather good, almost too good.

VISITED BOSTON: F. Hamilton, secretary of J. A. Everitt, Indianapolis, and Albert McCullough, Cincinnati.

MILWAUKEE, WIS.—Currie Brothers have been appointed to collect Wisconsin seeds for the St. Louis World's Fair.

THE Department of Agriculture has had 160 tests of cucumbers made this season by E. L. Coy in Northern New York.

GROWERS of orchard grass in Clark county, Ind., failed to maintain an attempted combine on prices. This seed goes mainly to Germany.

THE new warehouse of the Emerson Seed Company, to which reference was made in our last issue, should have been located at Fremont, Neb., not Fairmont.

THE cold, wet August weather was disastrous to cucumber seed crops. The fruit could not set. Such a condition has not been experienced for the last thirty years.

NEW YORK.—A petition in bankruptcy has been filed against the Cape Vincent Seed Company, wholesale dealers in peas and beans, at 260 West Broadway, with plant at Cape Vincent, N. Y.

VISITED CHICAGO: Count d'Estienne and A. Emerich, of Paris; Henry Dunkley, Burmuda; E. L. Coy, Melrose, Mass; L. L. Olds, Clinton, Wis.; S. Y. Haines, Tompkins, Mich.; Theo. Payne, Los Angeles, Cal., the latter returning from Europe.

NEW YORK.—Judge Holt has appointed Howard Payson Wilds receiver in bankruptcy of the assets of the Cape Vincent Seed Company, of 260 West Broaday and Cape Vincent, N. Y., and he is empowered to carry on the business for ten days. The liabilities are $75,000 and the assets will not exceed $25,000.

WASHINGTON, D. C., Oct. 15.—Prof. W. W. Tracey arrived home today from his California trip, visiting the Rocky Ford, Col., and Waterloo, Neb., seed growing districts enroute. The Rocky Ford melon seed crop will be much better in quality than last year owing to September frosts, which rendered fruit worthless for shipping but valuable for seed purposes.

Waterloo, Neb.

C. P. Coy & Son are moving their two warehouses into town and will locate one each side of a track at the station and build a connecting roof, thus insuring loading under shelter.

The Western Seed & Irrigation Company has sold its warehouse here, to J. C. Robinson.

Prof. W. W. Tracy, Sr., made us a visit October 12.

Field corn crops are looking fine.

French Bulb Growers.

In Ollioules, where the greater part of the French bulbs are cultivated, the growers raise potatoes, carnations, roses and other cut flowers for the Paris, Berlin, St. Petersburg and London markets. Some of the ground used is worth 40,000 francs ($8,000) per acre and the tenants must pay rent on such valuation. The potato crop is often a profitable one, as in favorable seasons they bring as high as $8 per hundred weight. When the potato prices are low the growers rely to some extent on the bulb crop for their revenue, but they are by no means dependent upon it and can usually afford to wait until market conditions suit them.

The average grower produces about 40,000 bulbs per annum and the largest grower about 100,000. The number, scattered condition, and independence of the growers thus render it difficult to secure accurate information as to the extent of the crop in any given year. In addition, these men usually handle their other products through commission dealers and are quite familiar with the methods of business men.

St. Louis.

CHRYSANTHEMUM SHOW TO BE HELD AT SHAW'S GARDENS.—TRADE CONDITIONS SHOW IMPROVEMENT.—NOTES.

A chrysanthemum show will be held in the conservatories at Shaw's Garden this month. The plants in two houses are to be removed to make room for the exhibits. About three hundred varieties, including the oldest and newest introductions of early and late varieties, pompons, anemone-flowered, and reflexed and incurred sorts will be on exhibition. No show of such magnitude has ever before been held at the garden. The collection is under the direct care of G. E. McClure.

Trade conditions show a slight improvement over last week. There is a sufficient supply of stock to meet the immediate demand. There is no sale for cosmos, dahlias or any out-of-door stuff. But few fancy blooms are sent in as climatic conditions continue unfavor-

able. Carnations and roses are of good quality. Chrysanthemums are not extra, Glory of Pacific being almost white. Violets move slowly. Tuberoses are again on the market in limited quantities. Lily of the valley is good, although cut rather close.

The Ellison Floral Company is displaying rustic baskets and vases made of light wood and covered with cork.

Sam Trelease, second son of Professor Trelease of the Botanical Garden, is slowly recovering from a serious attack of appendicitis.

The big sewerage system is practically finished through Tower Grove Park. But few trees were destroyed during the work, although the newly planted maze was missed by a few yards only.

Wm. Schray & Sons captured all the first prizes but two in the plant exhibit at the St. Louis fair. R. Frow won first for the best specimen plant of Cycas revoluta.   F. K. B.

Uncle Sam :- "Waal, I guess we must give the Old Country best in some Things."

U.S.A.

BRITAIN

W. W. JOHNSON & SON, Ltd., Boston, England.

GROWERS AND EXPORTERS TO ALL PARTS. Invite correspondence from the Seed Trade of the United States.

Please mention the American Florist when writing.

Farm with Greenhouses

For Sale or To Let.

Two modern Greenhouses for market growing. 24 acres with fruit orchards. Commodious house and barns. One mile from Brockport, N. Y. Fine country place near Normal School. Perfect climate. Apply

Thos. V. Pierson,

BROCKPORT, N. Y., R. F. D.

Please mention the American Florist when writing.

DAHLIAS Pot Roots

Largest and most up-to-date collection in the world.
Cactus vars. of 1902.................................$1.00
  "   "   1901.................................. .50
  "   "   1900.................................. .40
    best of older vars ....35c to .35
Pompon vars ....35c; newest.............. .50
All per 100 in 25 or more sorts. Special price for 1000, 10,0 0 or 50 000 lots. Carefully packed f. o. b., Liverpool. Cash with order.

The Horticultural Company

CHEADLE-HULME. England.

Please mention the American Florist when writing.

Eine absolute Nothwendigkeit!
Hiermit $1.00 für mein Abonnement. Es ist die Pflicht eines Jeden prompt für den „American Florist" zu bezahlen, weil dieser eine absolute Nothwendigkeit für jeden Blumenzüchter ist.

Carl Roegner, Alabama.

FLOWER SEEDS

For Present Sowing.

10 Per Cent Special Cash Discount, on Orders over $2.00 for Flower Seeds if the Cash is enclosed.

BROWALLIA SPECIOSA MAJOR. The plants grow only about a foot high, form dense little bushes, which are covered the entire year with an abundance of the most delightful sky-blue flowers. T ade pk. (250 seeds), 25c.
ASPARAGUS PLUMOSUS NANUS,100 seeds, $1.00; 250 seeds, $2.00 100 seeds, $7.5 .
SPRENGERI, 100 seeds, 50c; 1000 seeds, 75c: 5000 seeds, $2.25.
DECUMBENS, produce vines, 3 feet long, clothed with bluish green leaves. Cultivate like A. Sprengeri. 100 seeds 65c; 1000 seeds, $5. 0.
SCANDENS DEFLEXUS, suitable for hanging baskets and to cut. 100 seeds, $1.50.
CANDYTUFT, Giant Hyacinth-Flowered. This strain is superior to Empress. Sow now out-doors. Lb., $2.50; pkt., 10c; oz., 30c.
Empress. Our strain of this is extra fine, lb., $1.60; pkt., 10c; oz., 20c.
VAUGHAN'S GIANT FLOWERED CYCLAMEN. Our seed has been grown for us by a specialist in Europe. Shape and size of flowers, foliage and stems are points on which seed plants are selected. Pure White, (Mont Blanc), Dark Crimson, Rosa von Marienthal, "DeYufvak" Pink, White with Red Carmine Eye, 100 seeds, 60c; 1000 seeds, $5.00; 250 seeds at the 1000 rate.
GIANT-FLOWERED CYCLAMEN. Extra Choice Mixed. This mixture is made up fr m the above separate colors. 100 seeds, 50c; 250 seeds $1.15; 1000 seeds, $4.50, 5000 seeds, $20 00.
NEW GIANT ORCHID-FLOWERED CYCLAMEN. We have the following separate colors. (*red-r by number). No. C 100. Lilac Colored, 10 seed , 30c; 100 seeds, $2.50. No. C 101. Dark Red fringed. No. C 102. Pink, fringed. No. C 103. Pure White. No. C 104. Red Eye. Each 10 seeds, 30c; 100 seeds, $2.50. No. C 105. White with Red Eye, fringed. No. C 106. Giant Orchid-Flowered Cyclamen in choicest mixture; all the above and others. 25 seeds, 40c; 100 seeds, $1.50.
GIANT ORCHID-FLOWERED CYCLAMEN in mixture; 25 seeds, 25c; 100 seeds, 75c.
DRACAENA INDIVISA T ade pkt. 10 ; 0c; lb , $2.55.
SWEET PEAS: Extra Early Blanche Ferry, pink and white, ¼-lb., 10; lb. 3'c. Earliest of All, pink and white, ¼-lb., 10c; lb. 30 . Countess of Radnor, lavender ¼-lb., 10c; lb. 35c. Emily Henderson, white, ¼-lb., 10c; lb. 35c. Josephine White, white, ¼-lb., 10c; lb. 50c. Mont Blanc, white, ¼-lb., 15c; lb 75c. Lady Grisel Hamilton, lavender, ¼-lb., 15c; lb., 50c. Prima Donna, soft pink, ¼-lb., 15c; lb., 35c. For other sorts see our book for Florists.

ASPARAGUS PLUMOSUS NANUS.

Vaughan's Seed Store,

Chicago. New York.

Please mention the American Florist to advertisers.

THE NURSERY TRADE.

AM. ASSOCIATION OF NURSERYMEN.
N. W. Hale, Knoxville, Tenn., Pres.; Frank A. Weber, St. Louis, Mo., Vice-Pres.; George C. Seager, Rochester, N. Y., Sec'y.
Twenty-ninth annual convention, Atlanta, Ga., June, 1904.

LEAVENWORTH, KAS.—Dr. Joseph Stayman, a noted horticulturist, originator of the Stayman apple and the Stayman strawberry, died October 5, at his home here, aged 86 years. In 1860 he took half a million fruit grafts to Kansas from Illinois. He was the first man to start the apple industry in Kansas.

Planting Trees and Shrubs.

PREPARATION OF THE GROUND.

The preparation of ground for the planting of trees or shrubbery is as much a matter for consideration as the question of when to plant or what to plant. Due importance is frequently not given to this fact. Trees and shrubs are often crowded into holes that are not large enough to permit even their roots being extended. Such planting generally is accompanied by a lack of subsequent cultivation, and the result is failure.

A proper preparation of the ground (when intended for mass planting) entails plowing and subsoil plowing, continued in cross directions until the ground is thoroughly broken up and reduced to a mellow condition. Should humus, or organic matter, be deficient in the soil, this should be corrected by a dressing of stable manure, peat or other organic matter. This treatment will insure a condition of the soil which will make it hold moisture and assimilate fertilizers. In dry, sandy or gravelly soils too much importance can not be given to the value of surface mulching, or constant cultivation, after planting.

For single specimen trees, or for widely spaced trees, holes for planting should be prepared of not less than fifteen feet square, and three and a half feet deep. If the soil is good a simple loosening up, with an admixture of stable manure or peat, will be sufficient; if of sand or sterile gravel, and the best results are desired, it would be better to excavate the whole and substitute loam. "A silk purse can not be made from a sow's ear," neither can a tree be grown to fine proportions unless the proper conditions are given.—J. A. Pettigrew in Bulletin New England Park Superintendents.

To Save Porto Rico Fruits.

NEW YORK, October 8.—Leading fruit growers in Porto Rico held a meeting a few days ago, and arranged for the appointment of a commission to inspect all fruit buds, all cuttings, seeds and other means of propagating fruits. As things are now the fruit trees and vines are remarkably free from disease. The oranges have the old form of scale, which is common wherever oranges grow, but there is no San Jose scale and the white fly is unknown.

The commission which has been appointed in response to the requests of the fruit growers, will rigidly inspect all importations for propagating fruits, subjecting them to such curative treatment as may be required. In this way they hope to control all diseases of fruit plants, if they cannot entirely prevent them.

The fruit interests of the island are a unit in seeking to establish this preventive system and have agreed that no cuttings, pads or seeds will be used which do not bear the inspectors' declaration that they are free from the dangerous diseases common to fruit plants elsewhere.—*Special, New York Commercial.*

CAMBRIDGE CITY, IND.—The chrysanthemum fair will be held the second week in November.

Washington.

FASHIONABLE WEDDINGS CREATE DEMAND FOR STOCK.—DECORATIONS AT BRITISH AMBASSADOR'S FUNERAL.—NOTES.

Quite a number of weddings have taken place and the florists have had a chance to use up some of their stock, which is plentiful and fine. The decorations at St. John's church for the commemorative services in honor of Sir Michael Herbert, late British ambassador to the United States, were exceedingly simple. A long, wide strip of black was hung about the sanctuary, while an enormous wreath on the left was sent as a tribute from the Mexican ambassador. Some palms and other foliage plants were used; on the altar were small white bouquets. The pew of Sir Michael Herbert was draped in royal purple.

George H. Cooke furnished the decorations for the marriage of Miss Elizabeth Wright Young, daughter of Gen. S. B. M. Young, to Capt. J. R.-R. Hannay. The bride wore a wreath of orange blossoms and carried a shower bouquet of Bride roses and lilies of the valley. The house decorations were of white chrysanthemums.

The engineer in charge of public buildings and grounds has given notice that all requests for the loan of plants from the public gardens for use at churches, fairs and festivals must be refused, as to grant them would be in violation of the law. G.

Catalogues Received.

Albert Fuchs, Chicago, palms, ferns, etc.; N. L. Willet Drug Company, Augusta, Ga., seeds; Expansive Tree Protector Company, Toronto, Ontario, tree protector; Williams & Sons Company, Batavia, Ill., labels; Woods Floral Com, pany, Wilmington, Cal., bulbs; A. Dessert, Indre-et-Loire, France, peonies; M. Crawford Company, Cuyahoga Falls, Ohio, strawberries; B. W. Dirken, Oudenbosch, Holland, nursery stock; Elbridge E. Wheeler, Bridgeport, Conn., bulbs; W. E. Beaudry, Chicago, nursery stock; Elm City Nursery Company, New Haven, Conn., nursery stock; D. H. B. Hooper, Biddeford, Maine, tree guard; H. C. & F. M. Hatten, New Carlisle, Ohio, nursery stock; Dillon Greenhouse Manufacturing Company, Bloomsburg, Pa., greenhouse construction; E. Hippard, Youngstown, Ohio, steam trap; Paducah Pottery Company, Paducah, Ky., pots; W. J. Cowee, Berlin, N. Y., toothpicks; Engineering and Power Company, Jamestown, N. Y., soil conveyor; Franz Birnstiel, Coburg, Germany, vases, etc.; Hasslach & Roumanille, St. Remy-De-Provence, France, vegetable seeds; Sluis & Groot, Enkhuizen, Holland, seeds; Eugene Bricon, Trousebe, par Ussy (Calvados) France, nursery stock; C. E. Finley, Joliet, Ill., pot washer; Cordley & Hayes, New York, indurated florists' vases; Leopold Koropp, Chicago, greenhouse hanger; Louis Paillet, Vallee de Chatenay, Chatenay (Seine) near Paris, France, peonies; H. C. Chessman, Richmond, Ind., pot hanger; Clare & Scharrath, Chicago, prepared greens, etc.; Vilmorin-Andrieux Company, Paris, France, seeds; Michler Brothers, Lexington, Ky., seeds; Benjamin Hammond, Fiskill-on-Hudson, N. Y., circular; W. S. Powell & Company, Baltimore, Md., fertilizers; Clovena Nurseries, New York, seeds; Newell & Ames, Comstock, Texas, cacti.

OSHKOSH, WIS.—Carl Flugleburg, is making a Texas trip.

OUR PASTIMES.

Announcements of coming contests or other events of interests to our bowling, shooting and sporting readers are solicited and will be given place in this column.

Address all correspondence for this department to Wm. J. Stewart, 79 Milk St., Boston, Mass.; Robt. Kift, 1725 Chestnut St., Philadelphia, Pa.; or to the American Florist Co., Chicago, Ill.

CHICAGO bowlers are the guests of W. N. Rudd this (Saturday) evening.

At Denver.

The Denver florists have organized a bowling club, taking in about fifteen members. Phil. Scott is president, and John Berry secretary and treasurer. The club is organized for the purpose of sending a good team to St. Louis, and also to get others interested and try to get a good crowd to go along. Each member is assessed a like amount each week, which the treasurer shall keep in trust until convention time, and any member failing to go to the convention forfeits what he contributes, and the fund is at the disposal of those who do go.

B.

Notes of a European Tour.

Thurgan, Switzerland.—A few days ago I visited a carnation grower and was surprised to find such a nice place with 30,000 feet of glass mostly devoted to carnations, such varieties as Lawson, Hill, Scott, Lizzie McGowan, Alphonse Karr, etc. Carnot is a very dark red and very double, good stem, and the best I have seen. R. Groh, the proprietor, showed me all over his place and the way they grow carnations, and after all the method is much the same as in America. Mr. Groh grows 12,000 plants, and about 1,500 in pots, for which he has a special house. He says he could sell 10,000 per season in pots if he had the room for them. The construction of his houses is the same as ours, the glass is ⅛-inch thick and the panes 26x36 inches. Heating is by hot water. All his carnations are sold in the surrounding cities and bring now $2.40 per 100. I bought carnations in Zurich and had to pay 8 cents apiece for them. They have a fine climate here for carnations as the day temperature never rises above 80°, night 55° to 60°. I have not seen any good roses grown under glass on account of the cold nights, for the growers would have to fire all summer nights to keep down the rust and mildew. They have some very good and salable garden roses, such as La France, Carnot, Captain Christy, Paul Neyron, etc. Crimson Rambler one sees everywhere in Switzerland, in fact I never saw such beautiful gardens in all my life as are found here, or so well kept. Geneva is a paradise for flowers and there are some very fine florists' stores there, as good as in Paris. I watched the market very close in all the cities and found the florists everywhere have stands in the market and sell all kinds of potted plants and bouquets at good prices. The florists would like to secure the American varieties of carnations but it seems the government is very strict on plant importations on account of their liability to convey plant diseases and noxious insect pests. The removal of this barrier in all European countries would, no doubt, render them much better markets for American specialties than they are at present.

Zurich, Switzerland.—When I visited Zurich I called on O. Frobel. He has an attractive store on one of the best streets and makes up fine work. Frobel's establishment is one of the oldest concerns in Switzerland and is right in the heart of the best residence district. It comprises five acres and the store is connected with a palm house. He has two houses devoted to orchids of the very finest varieties and they are in good condition. His foreman, Mr. Schweizer, showed me all he has, including a fine lot of palms and tropical plants and a large collection, in fact the best in Europe, of Alpine plants. It looks more like a botanical garden than a commercial place. He has a fine house full of cyclamens planted on benches, to be potted up this fall, and gloxinias, etc. The cyclamens seem to thrive much better under this treatment. He does not grow any roses and carnations worth speaking of. Water lilies are grown there to perfection and the flowers are sold in the store. He has plenty of good dahlias, asters, daisies and all kinds of outdoor flowers, also a nice variety of grasses (fancy) for floral work. Mr. Frobel also carries on a nursery of ornamental trees and shrubbery on the outskirts of Zurich and he does good landscape gardening. The place all around looks clean and is a model in every respect. He buys his carnations from a grower in Turtlingen Germany, and roses from the south of France in the winter time. There is the best opening possible for a carnation and rose grower at his place, in fact everywhere one may go out there. All the florists' stores are kept clean and inviting and they pay more attention to window display than the average than we do. Their work is good and artistic.

Wuerttemberg, Germany.—On my trip through southern Germany I visited W. Rall's nursery at Elmingen, Wuerttemberg. It is one of the cleanest nurseries I have ever seen. He has 120 acres of fruit and ornamental trees, shrubs, conifers and hardy roses, and does an extensive business, wholesale only, employing eighty men. He also handles seeds and has an extra large building for that department. One son takes care of the office force and the two other sons have charge of the outdoor work. When I was there the outdoor roses were in full bloom and it was a grand sight to see ten acres of them in bloom. W. Rall started this place some thirty years ago with one acre of ground and has built it up to the present extent, and had to pay $100 to $400 per acre for the ground. This shows a wide-awake man and hard worker can make money wherever he may be.

J. J. HESS.

Substitutes for Coal.

PART II.

Gaseous Fuels.—Through certain sections of the United States there is to be found an abundance of natural gas. Where it occurs in great quantities it is even cheaper than coal. It is usually supplied on the basis of the cost of doing the same work with coal, and as it requires very little attention it makes a very desirable fuel. Very little is known regarding the thermal efficiency of natural gas, and it varies greatly in different localities and betwen different wells in the same locality. It is estimated, however, that 30,000 cubic feet are required to equal one ton of the best coal. With coal at $4.50 per ton natural gas would have to sell at 15 cents per thousand cubic feet to be on an equality with coal. However the price would be comparable at 20 cents per thousand since no fireman is required, at least not for full time, and there are no ashes to handle.

Coal or Illuminating Gas.—This gas is produced by heating bituminous coal in air tight retorts. Coal gas contains only about 20 per cent of the heating value of coal, and could not profitably be used except in an extreme emergency.

Blast Furnace Gas.—Blast furnace gas is that which is given off by the partial burning of coal in a blast furnace. This gas usually represents about 60 per cent of the heating value of the coal. Its composition, however, is irregular and its use practically limited to the firing of boilers connected with the blast furnace establishment.

Water Gas.—Water gas is produced by passing water vapor or steam over hot coal. This process produces a gas containing about 58 per cent of the heating value of the coal.

By comparing the data already given it will readily be seen that aside from wood and natural gas, where it can be obtained, there is very little among the solid and gaseous fuels that can be depended upon as substitutes for coal. We now turn our attention to the liquid fuels, of which there are but two that are worthy of consideration. These are petroleum, either as it comes from the well or some of its products, and alcohol. The present supply and the methods of the manufacture of alcohol would not warrant its extensive use as a fuel, but the time may not be far distant when it may be produced in great quantities from plants, perhaps ten to fifteen tons from an acre of ground. The thermal efficiency of alcohol is not exceptionally high, being about 12,600 units per pound, or 2,000 units less than the best semi-bituminous coal. Alcohol is exceptionally efficient as a fuel, owing to the fact that most of the heat is available and very little is lost in the process of combustion.

Petroleum.—We now come to the consideration of the most important of all the substitutes for coal; in fact, the only substitute aside from the wood that reaches any degree of comparison. During the scarcity of coal last year there were many attempts made to replace coal with oil, some few of which were rather satisfactory. There is no longer any doubt regarding the mechanical part of oil burning, but the expense connected therewith is so much greater than with the use of coal as to make it impracticable under most circumstances.

At the wells, if the oil is worth, say, 2 cents per gallon, the cost is equivalent to $3.80 per ton for coal at the same place, while, say, at 3 cents per gallon, the lowest price at which it can be delivered in the vicinity of New York, it costs the same as coal at $5.70 per ton. The Standard Oil Company estimates that 173 gallons are equal to a gross ton of coal, allowing for incidental savings, as in grate bars, carting ashes, attendance, etc."

The use of crude oil is, however, attended with several difficulties. It kills animals that take it inwardly and plants with which it comes in contact. Crude oil contains all the more volatile elements, including the naphtha, and is highly explosive, and care must be taken in handling it. When burning it in an enclosed furnace explosions are liable to occur should the flow of oil become temporarily interrupted. Upon the oils resuming its flow the furnace becomes filled with gas, which, upon igniting, produces an explosion. Where artificial gas is available it is desirable to maintain a small jet within the furnace and near the burner to serve as a lighter should the oil gas become extinguished. Broken fire brick, which become white hot, will serve to relight the gases.

In burning oil it is necessary to either transform it into a gas and mix with the required amount of air before it is burned or to spray or atomize it as it is fed into the furnace. The object of a burner in the use of oil as fuel is to get the oil into a finely divided state and to get the particles in direct contact with the oxygen of the air. The atomizing may be accomplished either by means of steam or compressed air, the steam being the simpler where the burner is used in connection with a steam boiler. In a large heating plant, where low pressure steam is the method used, it would be necessary to install a small auxiliary boiler to furnish high pressure steam with which to feed the oil burners used under the low pressure boilers. Where electric power is available a motor-driven air compressor could be used to furnish the supply of air for atomizing the oil. The higher the temperature of the steam or air used for atomizing the oil the greater will be the efficiency of the burner.

Conclusions.—That coal is the cheapest and best fuel that the market affords, one pound under ordinary conditions evaporating about seven and one-half pounds of water at 212 degrees Fahrenheit.

That the provision for a liberal reserve supply of coal is under most circumstances the safest method of providing for an emergency. This supply need not be stored near the boilers, and should only be used when coal cannot be secured from the regular sources. The interest on the money invested in such reserve supply of coal will be wisely expended.

That a pound of dry wood will evaporate about four pounds of water at 212 degrees Fahrenheit. That wood is in many cases the most efficient substitute for coal during a short period.

That where crude oil can be secured at a reasonable price it is the best and most reliable substitute for coal, and where it can be purchased as low as $1 per barrel it is preferable to coal at $3.50 and upwards per ton. That one pound of crude oil will evaporate 13.3 pounds of water at 212 degrees Fahrenheit, and that one pound of oil has a heating efficiency equal to that of about 1.6 pounds of coal. Also that the use of oil is clean and economical so far as the fire room work is concerned, and if properly burned no smoke is produced.

That the mechanical part of oil burning has passed the first experimental stage and has proved successful. That there are a number of good burners upon the market, especially of the sprayer class, using compressed air or steam for volatilizing the oil.

That a cheap and efficient burner can be made from comparatively inexpensive materials.

That oil can be burned in an even and effective manner, especially under steam boilers of the watertube class.

That petroleum will probably never replace coal for general use.

HAMPTON, IA.—The Curtis Floral Company has made improvements and enlargements until the greenhouses consist of 10,000 feet of glass. The greenhouses are well filled with plants and flowers, among which are 1,700 roses, 2,200 carnations and 600 chrysanthemums.

Meetings of Florists' Clubs.

BALTIMORE, MD.—Gardeners' Club of Baltimore, Royal Arcanum building, 18 W. Saratoga street. Second and fourth Monday of each month, at 8 p. m. John J. Perry, Sec'y, Gay and Eager streets.

BOSTON, MASS.—Gardeners' and Florists' Club of Boston, Horticultural Hall. Meets second Tuesday of each month. October to March inclusive. W. E. Fischer, Sec'y, 18 Union Terrace, Jamaica Plain, Mass.

BROCTON, MASS.—Brocton Gardeners' and Florists' Club, store of W. W. Hathaway, Times Building. First and third Tuesday of each month, at 8 p. m. W. W. Hathaway, Sec'y, Brockton, Mass.

BUFFALO, N. Y.—Buffalo, Florists' Club, 481 Washington street. Second Wednesday of each month, at 8 p m. Wm. Legg, Sec'y, 1440 Delaware avenue, Buffalo.

BUTTE, MONT.—Montana Florists' Club, 45 W. Broadway. First Saturday in each month. D. E. Law, Sec'y.

CHICAGO, ILL.—Chicago Florists' Club, Handel Hall, 40 Randolph street. Second and fourth Wednesday of each month, at 8 p. m. George Wienhoeber, Sec'y, 413 Elm street, Chicago.

CINCINNATI, O.—Cincinnati Florists' Society, Jabez Elliott Flower Market. Second Saturday of each month, at 8 p. m. Geo. Murphy, Sec'y, Sta. F., Cincinnati, O.

CLEVELAND, O.—Cleveland Florists' Club, Progress Hall, 344 Detroit street. Second and fourth Monday of each month, at 8 p. m. Isaac Kennedy, Sec'y, Westpark, O.

DENVER, COLO.—Denver Floral Club, 312 Charles Block. Second and fourth Friday of each month, at 8 p. m. Adam Balmer, Sec'y.

DETROIT, MICH.—Detroit Florists' Club, Cowie Building, Farran and Gratiot avenue. First and third Wednesday of each month, at 8 p. m. J. F. Sullivan, Sec'y, 214 Woodward avenue.

GRAND RAPIDS, MICH.—Grand Rapids Florists' Club, Board of Trade rooms, Pearl street. Fourth Monday of each month. N. B. Stover, Sec'y, Grandville, Mich.

HAMILTON, ONT.—Hamilton Gardeners' and Florists' Club, 126½ James street, North. First and third Tuesday of each month at 8 p. m. Chas. M. Webster, Sec'y.

HARTFORD, CONN.—Hartford Florists' Club. Second and fourth Thursday of each month at 8 p. m. J F Coombs Sec'y.

INDIANAPOLIS, IND.—State Florists' Association of Indiana. Commercial Club rooms, Indianapolis. First Tuesday of each month, at 8 p. m. H. Junge, Sec'y, 456 E. Washington street, Indianapolis.

MILWAUKEE, WIS.—Milwaukee Florists' Club. Meets first Tuesday of each month at St. Charles Hotel club rooms. H. V. Hunkel, Sec'y.

MINNEAPOLIS, MINN.—Minneapolis Florists' Club, West Hotel. First Thursday of each month, at— p. m. C F. Rice, Sec'y, 1441 N. Sixth street.

MONTREAL, QUE.—Montreal Gardeners' and Florists' Club, Alexandria rooms, 2204 St. Catherine street. First and third Monday of each month. W. H. Horobin, Sec'y, 23 Closse street.

NEW LONDON, CONN.—Gardeners' and Florists' Club, first and third Tuesday of each month at greenhouses of secretary. R. H. Appledorn, Sec'y.

NEW YORK, N. Y.—New York Florists' Club, Grand Opera House Bldg., 8th avenue and 23d St Second Monday of each month, at 7:30 p. m. John Young, Sec'y, 51 West Twenty-eighth street, New York.

OMAHA, NEB.—Nebraska Florists' Society, Y. M. C. A. Hall. Second Thursday in each month at 3 p m. Louis Henderson, Sec'y, 1519 Farnam street, Omaha.

PHILADELPHIA, PA.—Florists' Club of Philadelphia, Horticultural Hall, Broad street above Spruce. First Tuesday of each month, at 8 p. m. Edwin Lonsdale, sec'y Wyndmoor, Philadelphia.

PITTSBURG, PA.—Pittsburg and Allegheny Florists' and Gardeners' Club, at Gerson Benedickt Bldg., 6th and Cherry avenue. Second Thursday of each month, at 8 p. m. H. P. Joslin, Sec'y, Ben Avon. Pa.

PROVIDENCE, R. I.—Florists' and Gardeners' Club of Rhode Island, 96 Westminster street, Providence. Second Thursday of each month at 8 p. m. Alexander Rennie, Sec'y, 41 Washington street, Providence.

RICHMOND, IND.—Richmond Florists' Club, at the greenhouses of members. Third Monday of each month. H. O. Cheasman, Sec'y.

SALT LAKE CITY, UTAH.—Salt Lake Florists' Society, office of Huddart Floral Company, 214 E. Second South street. Second and fourth Friday of each month. P. T. Huddart, Sec'y.

SAN FRANCISCO, CAL.—Pacific Coast Horticultural Society. First and third Thursdays of each month. Thos. H. Minroe, Sec'y.

SEATTLE, WASH.—Seattle Commercial Horticultural Club. First and third Tuesdays. First Wednesday of each month. Wm. Hopkins, Sec'y, 623 First avenue.

ST. LOUIS, Mo.—St. Louis Florists' Club. Odd Fellows Hall No 3. Ninth and Olive streets. Second Thursday of each month, at 8 p. m. Emil Schray, Sec'y, 4101 Pennsylvania avenue, St. Louis.

TORONTO, ONT.—Toronto Gardeners' and Florists' Association, St. George's Hall, Elm street. Third Tuesday of each month, at 8 p. m. E. F. Collins, Sec'y, 2 Hurst place, Toronto.

UTICA, N. Y.—Utica Florists' Club, 168 Genesee street. First Thursday of each month at 8 p. m. J. C. Spencer, Sec'y.

WASHINGTON, D. C. — Washington Florists' Club. Meets first Wednesday in each month. Wm. F. Gude, Sec'y.

Coming Exhibitions.

[Secretaries are requested to supply any omissions from this list.]

BOSTON, MASS., November 6-8, 1903.—Chrysanthemum exhibition Massachusetts Horticultural Society. W. P. Rich. Sec'y, Horticultural Hall, 300 Massachusetts avenue, Boston.

BUFFALO, N. Y., November 11-14, 1903.—H. A. Meldrum Co.'s flower show; direction, Buffalo Florists' Club. Wm, Legg, Sec'y, 1440 Delaware avenue, Buffalo.

INDIANAPOLIS, IND., November 10-14, 1903.—Indiana Floral Festival and Chrysanthemum exhibition State Florists' Association of Indiana. Irwin Bertermann, Sec'y, 241 Massachusetts avenue, Indianapolis.

LENOX, MASS., October 27-29 1903.—Fall exhibition Lenox Horticultural Society. Fred. Heckmann, Sec'y, Lenox. Mass.

MADISON, N. J., November 5-6, 1903.—Annual exhibition Morris County Gardeners' and Florists' Society. S. Redstone Sec'y, Madison, N. J.

NEW YORK, November 10-12, 1903.—Chrysanthemum exhibition Chrysanthemum Society of America. Fred H. Lemon, Sec'y, Richmond, Ind.

PHILADELPHIA, PA., November 10-14, 19 3.—Annual exhibition Pennsylvania Horticultural Society. David Rust, Sec'y, Horticultural Hall, Philadelphia, Pa.

MONTREAL, QUE.—November 11-12, 1903.—Chrysanthemum exhibition Montreal Gardeners' and Florists' Club. W. H. Horobin, Sec'y, 23 Closse street, Montreal.

PROVIDENCE, R. I., November 12-13, 1903.—Chrysanthemum exhibition Rhode Island Horticultural Society. C. W. Smith, Secretary, 27-29 Exchange street. Providence.

ST. PAUL, MINN., Second week in November. 1903.—Chrysanthemum and orchid exhibition Ladies Auxiliary of Northwestern Manufacturers' Association. Mrs. M. Helen Moss, Sec'y, St. Paul.

TARRYTOWN, N. Y., November 4-6. 1903.— Fifth annual exhibition Tarrytown Horticultural Society. Edw. W. Neubrand, Sec'y, Tarrytown. N Y.

OCALA, FLA.—O. M. Goodrich has sold his interest in the Ocala Greenhouse Company to Chas. F. Schneider, P. W. Spellman having sold his interest some time ago to Mr. Hines. Messrs. Hines and Schneider, who will conduct the business hereafter, are florists and landscape gardeners of many years' standing.

Denver.

Trade is fair. It would be better perhaps, and the quality of stock also if the warm spell would let up. Carnations are coming in now in very good lots and of almost any color and grade. N. A. Benson's stock is improving as the season advances. Enchantress from this place is coming up very fast. The variety is proving very popular with the public. Violets do not seem to mind the heat and are improving each day. There is a good supply of teas but owing to weather conditions they are rather soft and hard to handle. Beauties are getting plentiful but meet with very good demand. Chrysanthemums are coming on fast now, Mrs. Robinson being in good supply and meeting with a good sale. Of the yellows Robert Halliday is the best so far. B.

Salt Lake City.

The nurseries and florist establishments of Salt Lake City were described at length in the Salt Lake City *News* of October 2. The Salt Lake Huddart Floral Company is declared to have the largest and most up-to-date greenhouse business west of the Missouri river. "The greenhouses where all the cut flowers and young plants are grown, cover over three acres with glass and three acres more is devoted to the raising of all kinds of choice hardy shrubs, roses, bulb plants, etc. This firm has just put in a new 100 horse-power steam boiler, engine, additions, and other improvements at a cost of over $10,000, and has also many more improvements mapped out for next spring," says the article. The Salt Lake Floral Company was originally organised by Mr. Clark, of Butte, about two years ago, and was bought by J. S. Bransford, who consolidated the business with the Huddart Floral Company.

Schwars & Heinecke, florists and seedsmen, who began business in Salt Lake City in February, 1903, are said to have built up a large wholesale and retail trade, shipping their flowers, plants, seeds and bulbs to all adjacent centers. They make a specialty of floral decorations at public functions.

The Davis County Nurseries, Utah Nursery Company and Pioneer Nurseries Company are credited with doing much to encourage the development of orchards and woodlands in the region. All the firms have many patrons, the first named sending traveling men from California to Illinois.

The B. C. Morris Floral Company is complimented on the excellence of floral decorations furnished for public functions, of which the firm makes a specialty. Two stores are maintained and extensive greenhouses.

The Florists' Society held its first annual banquet October 8 at the Commercial club. The dining hall was profusely decorated in roses, carnations, palm greens, and the general effect was very pleasing. Twenty-five members of the society and invited guests were present, among the guests being Hon. Fisher Harris, C. A. Erickson, A. J. Davis and John Reading. P. T. Huddart was toastmaster.

SELL YOUR FREIGHT STOCK BEFORE FROSTS.

Syracuse, N. Y.

FIRST CHRYSANTHEMUMS ARE SHOWN.—COLD WEATHER MAKES BUSINESS PICK UP.—FLOWER SHOW IS DROPPED AS TOO COSTLY.

The first chrysanthemums of the season were exhibited Saturday and all the windows of the florists are ablaze with yellow. They are of splendid quality and sell for from $2 to $5 a dozen. Business in general is picking up owing to the cold weather. At the greenhouses florists are busy putting in bulbs for winter use and preparing their soil before winter weather sets in. Carnations are still scarce and poor in quality. An improvement is noticed in roses, which are better than they have been in some time.

S. T. Betts, president of the Central New York Horticultural Society, says there will be no flower show this year. The reason is that the show blossoms cost so much to raise that florists will not spend the time and money simply for the sake of putting them on exhibition. In 1895 and 1896 famous shows were held here, attracting people from all over the country. The society will meet this fall and endeavor to awaken an interest in flowers.

The contest of the will of Henry Burt, the aged florist who recently died in this city, has been adjourned until November 9. At a recent hearing Mr. Burt's dress, which used to cause much comment on the streets, was described by a witness. "It wasn't what the fashion papers would call up-to-date," said he, "he usually wore a blue frock and dressed like a farmer." Mr. Burt was about 80 years old when he died.

Francis M. French, who formerly was a florist at 1208 East Genesee street, took the state medical examination at the Syracuse College of Medicine a few days ago. The decision of Mr. French to become a physician is remarkable on account of his advanced age, 64 years.

Henry Morris is settled in his new store. He has just received a big shipment of bay trees which are prominently displayed. Mr. Morris says the prospect for violets is excellent.　　　A. J. B.

Providence.

Trade is not at all busy, but will improve shortly. Hazard & Macnair had some beautiful work at the Samuels Bros' opening recently. Carnations are selling at $1 to $2 a hundred, with white at a premium. Roses are entirely off crop with everyone and chrysanthemums have a fair sale at $2 to $2.50 a dozen retail. Violets move well at 50 cents a hundred wholesale. The weather is stormy, but greenhouse property is reported safe thus far.

The monthly meeting of the Florist Club witnessed a good attendance and an interesting discussion of ferns.　　　M. M.

BROOKLYN, N. Y.—We are indebted to John Orb for a large colored poster advertising the horticultural and agricultural exhibition at Ridgewood Park, L. L., September 6–13. This is certainly an excellent way to attract the public.

ORANGE, N. J.—James Hayes, a prominent florist and expert designer of Topeka, Kansas, has been visiting his brother at the "Terraces," Llewellyn Park, en route for a two months' vacation in Europe, where he will visit the scenes of his early training in his profession in England, and of his birth, near Belfast, Ireland.

Hartford, Conn.

In a paper read before the Hartford Florists' Club, October 6, C. S. Mason, of Farmington, Conn., described his experience as a gardener in Hartford before the civil war. In 1850 there were but two commercial greenhouses in Hartford. The varieties of roses grown for sale were very few. Of hardy roses there were Queen of the Prairies, Baltimore Belle, Crimson Boursalt, Pink Boursalt, Princess Adelaide, Moss, Centifolia and Baron Brevort. Of tender roses there were Cloth of Gold, Lamarque, Louis Phillipe, Hermosa, Agrippina and Safrano. The coming of Col. Samuel Colt to Hartford gave an impetus to all matters pertaining to horticulture.

Richmond, Ind.

The controversy over the proposed sale of a portion of Glen Miller park to E. G. Hill in order that he might enlarge his floral plant, came to a sudden termination, October 5, at the meeting of the city council. City Attorney John F. Robbins, gave his opinion of the legality of the proposed proceedings and made further consideration useless. He says the property in question cannot be sold without special action by the legislature.

Nephrolepis Ferns.

NEPHROLEPIS BOSTONIENSIS. A large lot in fine condition, bushy and of a beautiful deep green color. From 5-inch pots, 30c each; 6-inch pots, 40c each.

NEPHROLEPIS CORDATA COMPACTA. Clean, bushy plants from 5-inch pans, 30c each; 6-inch pans, 40c each.

NEPHROLEPIS DAVALLIOIDES FURCANS. Nice sturdy plants, well established in 2½-inch pots, with 8 to 10 leaves, $8.00 per 100.

NEPHROLEPIS PLUMOSUS. From 2½-inch pots, and just as well shaped as above, $8.00 per 100. From 2¼-inch pots, $6.00 per 100.

NEPHROLEPIS EXALTATA. Strong, 2½-inch pot plants, $5.00 per 100.

NEPHROLEPIS PIERSONI. Having purchased a large stock in the spring, and being short of room, we are now compelled to offer at reduced prices. None better for the money. All sizes offered are well established. From 2¼-pots, $3.00 per dozen; $22.50 per 100; $200.00 per 1000. Large plants from 4-inch pots, 75c each; 5-inch pans, $1.00 each; 6-inch pans, $1.50 each; 7-inch pans, $2.00 each; 8-inch pans, $2.50 each.

NATHAN SMITH & SON, ADRIAN, MICH.

Please mention the American Florist when writing.

A FEW GOOD THINGS YOU WANT.

Special low prices on palms to close out. Fine clean stock, cool grown and well shaped plants, none better.

ARECA LUTESCENS, 3 plants to pot, 4, 5 and 6-inch, $25, $40 and $100 per 100.
KENTIA BELMOREANA and **FORSTERIANA**, 3, 4, 5 and 6-inch, $12, $25, $40, $100 per 100.
REX BEGONIA, 2 and 3-inch, $4 and $6 per 100.
DRACAENA INDIVISA, 3-inch, $5 per 100; 4-inch, $10 per 100.
ENGLISH IVY, 2 and 3-inch, $3 and $6 per 100.
BOSTON FERNS, 5-inch, $30 per 100. From beds, for 2, 3 and 4-inch pots, $4, $8, $15 per 100
ASPARAGUS PLUMOSUS, 3-inch, $8.00 per 100.
" **SPRENGERI**, 2-inch, $3.00 per 100.
CHINESE PRIMROSES, Fringed, 3-inch, $4.00 per 100.
CYCLAMEN GIGANTEUM, 4-inch, $10.00 per 100.
CARNATIONS, Queen Louise, 2-in., $2.00 per 100.
" Lawson, 2-inch, $2.50 per 100.
GERANIUMS, rooted cuttings. Double and single Grant, Bonnot, S. A. Nutt, $1.00 per 100. Perkins, LaFavorite, John Doyle, $1.25 per 100. Poitevine, Viaud, Castellane, Riccard, Mrs. E. G. Hill, $1.50 per 100.

CASH OR C. O. D.

GEO. M. EMMANS, NEWTON, N. J.

Please mention the American Florist when writing.

PALMS, FERNS, ETC.

We offer good values; saving in express and freight to buyers west of Ohio.

BOSTON FERNS. Nephrolepis Exaltata Bostoniensis.

We have the finest stock in the West. All our plants are pot-grown, bushy stock, well furnished with fronds from the pot up, and cannot be compared with the cheap, long-drawn-up, lifted stock from the bench. A sample shipment will convince you of our superior stock.

	Each	Per doz.	Per 100
2½ inch pot plants	$	$ .60	$ 5.00
3 " " "		1.50	10.00
4 " " "		2.50	20.00
5 " " "	.50	5.00	40.00
6 " pan "	.75	8.00	60.00
7 " " "	1.00	10.00	75.00
8 " " "	1.50	15.00	
9 " " "	$2.00 to 2.50		
10 " " "	3.00 to 3.50		

PIERSONI FERN.

Well-grown, bushy stock.

2½-inch pots	$25.00 per 100; $200.00 per 1000
4-inch	$ .75 each
5-inch pots	1.00 each
6-inch pots	1.50 each
7-inch pots	2.5? each
8-inch pots	3.00 each

ANNA FOSTER FERN.

Elegant stock.

2½-inch pots	$ 8.00 per 100
3-inch pots	15.00 per 100
4-inch pots	25.00 per 100
5-inch pots	50 00 per 100
6-inch pots	$ 9.00 per dozen
7-inch pots	12.00 per dozen
8 inch pots	18.00 per dozen

Cycas Revoluta.

With fine crowns, pots full of roots. Plants in all sizes from 25c to $3.00 each, at 5c per leaf

Asparagus Plumosus Nanus We are Headquarters.

2½-inch pots...per doz., 75c; per 100, $5.00
3-inch pots...per doz., $1.00; per 100, 8.00

Send for our Special Price List of Palms, Ferns, Araucarias and Rubbers.

If you are a buyer of Palms, Ferns, etc., a personal visit of inspection to our Greenhouses at Western Springs, Ill., (one-half hour's ride from Chicago), will pay you. Long Distance Telephone No. 221 Western Springs, Ill.

CHICAGO. **Vaughan's Greenhouses,** WESTERN SPRINGS, ILL.

Palms and Asparagus.

	Pots.	Leaves.	In high.	12	100
Latania Borbonica,	3-in.	4-5	8 10	$.75	$ 5.00
"	5-in.	3-5 chr.	12-15	2.00	15.00
"	5-in.	3-5 "	15-18	2.50	18.00
Kentia Belmoreana,	2½"	3-4 "	8-10	1.50	10.00
"	3-in.	3-5 "	10-15	1.75	13 00
Asparagus Sprengeri, 2-inch pots					1.50
Asparagus Plumosus, 2-inch pots					3 00
Begonias, 3-inch pots					5 00

We grow a large assortment of Hardy Shrubs and evergreens. Prices made on application.

SHERMAN NURSERY CO.
CHARLES CITY, IOWA.

The Most Popular Fern

The Anna Foster.

At $35.00 per 100, for 6-inch pots from bench. **Pot Plants**, 50c, 75c, $1.00, $2.00, $3.00, $4.00 and $5.00 each; very fine.

BOSTON FERNS.

Large plants, from bench, $50.00 per 100.

Very fine **KENTIA PALMS**, at 50c to $3.00 each. **Asparagus Plumosus Nanus**, 3-inch, $8.00 per 100. **Asparagus Sprengeri**, 3-inch, $4.00 per 100.

L. H. FOSTER,
45 King Street, DORCHESTER, MASS.

For Sale

Twenty-two large and beautiful

Palms.

Must be sold at once. Write for list and description. No reasonable offer refused.

H. L. CONDE,
Oswego, N. Y.

FERNS.

Boston Ferns.

2½-inch	$ 5.00 per 100
3-inch	10.00 per 100
4-inch	15.00 per 100
5-inch	25.00 per 100
6-inch	40.00 per 100
7-inch	60.00 per 100
8-inch, $1 to	$1.50 each
10-inch, 2 to	2.50 each

Piersoni Ferns.

2¼-inch	$ .35 each
50 at	.30 each
100 at	.25 each
3-inch	.50 each
4-inch	.75 each
5-inch	1.00 each
6-inch	1.50 each
7-inch	2.50 each
8-inch	3.00 each

Order 2-in. Cinerarias. Chinese Primula and Obconica. Cut Roses and Carnations.

See last week's papers for list of Field-Grown Carnations. Write

GEO. A. KUHL. Pekln, Ill.

Please Mention The American Florist When Writing.

Nashville.

HORSE SHOW WEEK WITH MANY GAYETIES BRINGS TRADE FOR THE FLORISTS.

Horse show week has come and gone, bringing with it a brilliant series of gayeties and trade for everybody. The florist was largely in it, and as the lady patronesses and chairmen appointed for each night gave handsome entertainments at their homes the call for flowers was large. Nor was this all; these same lady patronesses sat at the show in boxes embowered in American Beauty roses and southern smilax. Each also carried a huge bouquet of elegant specimens of Beauties, with long stems and very handsome flowers.

The rose season has opened up and they are coming in nicely, not so abundantly as they will later, but sufficient for the present demand. American Beauty, Kaiserin, Brides and Bridesmaids are good in quality.

The prolonged pleasant weather has enabled the growers in this section to get everything housed and in good shape for the cold weather.

Since the rain the fall flowers are coming in beautifully. Cosmos and dahlias form quite a display in the florists' windows.

The Joy & Son Company has had the honor of showing the first chrysanthemums.

The funeral of J. B. Hancock called for a lot of beautiful funeral emblems.
M. C. D.

Montreal.

We had a large attendance at the last meeting of the Florist Club. The membership roll is still increasing. C. Wells, of Maisonneuve was elected a member. The chairman named Jos. Bennett and G. Robinson to report upon the exhibition of Opah sent by Nathan Smith & Son, Adrian, Mich. Opah was favorably commented upon. The Express canna was too bruised and withered to judge it according to its merit. A well known grower spoke in favor of retaining the duty upon azaleas as it stands, but it was pointed out that the national society of Canada had already passed a motion to ask the government to drop it and this was favored by a unanimous vote.

The storemen report fairly good business, but the fine autumn weather we are having just now does not bring improvement as there are yet many outdoor flowers. We have had some early frosts but not enough to injure anything outside. The chrysanthemums offered now on the market are Bergman, Midge, Monrovia, Willowbrook and Opah. Roses are improving and some good flowers are cut. Carnations with rather short stems are good and sell well.

P. McKenna & Son are having trouble in getting water for their houses. They cut some good Monrovia lately.

Jos. Bennett has a good collection of new crysanthemums and carnations which promise well.

Hall & Robinson cut their first Opah chrysanthemums on September 25.
G. V.

TONAWANDA, N. Y.—Julius Schultz, a florist, cut the artery in his right wrist with a piece of glass while trying to repair a broken pane in a greenhouse and almost bled to death. He fell, too weak to call for assistance, and his limp form was found by a member of his family who summoned aid. The flow of blood was stopped and the injured man will recover.

Columbus, O.

Great quantities of chrysanthemums, in which the varieties Glory of the Pacific and Polly Rose lead, are now brought to the market, but as far as the general public is concerned a real interest in them has not been awakened. The first week of the season, however, hardly ever brings a very great demand for them. Private grounds about here are aglow with a fine crop of cosmos, and it is quite evident that this flower is growing in popularity. We are having a fine spell of weather, which is helping the carnations and roses under glass, of which the greater portion are in fine growing condition.

Gravitt & Sons, of Lancaster, O., are cutting a fine lot of roses, but owing to the drought their carnation crop will be a trifle later than in former years. CARL.

Huntington, N. Y.

The recently organized Huntington Agricultural and Horticultural Society made a rousing success of its first exhibition at the Opera House on October 7, and put up a show which was a revelation to the two or three thousand people who thronged the hall, of the capabilities of Long Island soil in the production of garden flowers, fruits and vegetables. The local florists, H. T. & A. H. Funnell and Wm. O'Hara joined hands with the gardeners on the numerous private estates in this section and the display of greenhouse favorites was extensive and of the highest order of merit. Altogether the affair exceeded the highest anticipations of its promoters.

KINGSTON, JAMAICA.—Dr. N. S. Britton, director of the Bronx Park Botanical Garden, has arranged to leave here for the Chuncona Botanical Station, in the Blue Mountain range, for the purpose of establishing a laboratory and concluding researches among tropical flora. He will occupy the building formerly used by the Jamaica Government for similar work.

LAKE GENEVA, WIS.—Riemer & Radmer, of Milwaukee, have secured the contract for the heating of the private conservatory of H. C. Lytton. Furman boilers are to be used.

ONION Sets

Write for samples and prices.

Seed Potatoes, Red River stock...

VAUGHAN'S SEED STORE, Chicago.

Lowell, Mass.

OCTOBER AND FROST START BUSINESS AT GOOD RATE.—COLD RAINS HINDER PROGRESS OF INDOOR STOCK.—PRICES HIGH.

With the coming of October business seems to have been well started. In the last week everyone has been on the jump. Some have been extremely busy handling plants and decorations for the openings of the department stores, but the bulk of work has been in getting out funeral orders, which at times has been a hard task, owing to the outdoor supply of flowers being laid low by frost. For a week past we have had cold dreary rains of long duration. The conditions have retarded and at the same taxed the indoor supply of flowers heavily, so much so that the prices asked for carnations are much above those asked a year ago. But this will soon be remedied when the chrysanthemums get in good shape. Already they are appearing. So far Polly Rose and Bergmann are the early varieties, but in a few days the queen of autumn will be ready.

Last year only two growers were growing the ever popular Fairmaid extensively and were raking in the shekels at a good rate. This year every grower around here is growing it largely. The parks, under the supervision of Chas. W. Whittet have been kept in excellent shape the last summer. George W. Patten, who has been away for the past two months, has returned very much improved in health. James J. McMannon is a candidate for congressman from the twenty-fifth district.   A. M.

Albany, N. Y.

UNUSUALLY LARGE WEDDING AND FUNERAL ORDERS KEEP THE FLORISTS BUSY.

The last week was notable for the number of funerals and wedding decoration orders that the local trade secured. On Tuesday H. G. Eyres, tor the funeral of S. G. Merrill, supplied a 24-inch wreath of cattleyas, one of Liberty roses, another of Bridesmaids and lily of the valley, a five-foot cross of Bride roses, six casket bunches of from two to three dozen each of American Beauties, and one of five dozen Glory of the Pacific chrysanthemums. The order filled three wagons. On the same day Eyres supplied a twenty-four-inch wreath of violets for the funeral of Mrs. M. A. Glassford.

On Wednesday the local trade had a rush of wedding orders which kept all hands busy for days beforehand. Whittle Brothers sent men down to Hudson early in the week to do the decorations for the Conover-Cady wedding, which took place in Christ church in that city. The rood screen was decorated with smilax, as were also the pews. Palms ten feet high stood on either side of the altar and also in the chancel. White and yellow chrysanthemums were used to complete the decorations. The firm also furnished the decorations in white and yellow chrysanthemums in the house of Judge Cady, the father of the bride. On the same day F. A. Danker filled an order for the decorations at the Curtis-Bacon wedding in Northville, Fulton county.

The firm of Lord & Burnham is making good progress with the new forcing house under construction for H. G. Eyres. It is expected that the house will be ready for occupancy November 10.   R. D.

JOLIET, ILL.—The second annual flower show will be held November 4–7. James H. Ferriss is the secretary.

Piping For Frames.

ED. AM. FLORIST:—I have twelve frames, each 150 feet long; which I will use this coming winter for herbaceous and bedding stock. I intend to run a 1-inch pipe through each of these frames, about one foot underground, to keep the stock in action and prevent any freezing. The frames run east and west with a slope of about one foot. Will a 2½-inch main feed all the 1-inch pipe? Is a 1½-inch return sufficient? I have an automatic valve in the return system. Is one foot below the ground the right depth? Have a boiler pressure of seventy-five pounds with enough boiler capacity to heat twice the glass on my place.   W. M.

The question seems to be, "Will one 2½-inch main supply twelve 1-inch pipes 150 feet long?" and to that the answer is "Yes." A 1½-inch return is sufficient for this radiation. For bottom heat twelve inches is a good depth for the class of plants mentioned, but eighteen inches is better where the plants are growing in the soil. If the plants are to be kept dormant I would prefer to have the pipes above ground on the sides of the frames. The question does not tell what climate must be planned for, but where the mercury drops below zero an additional run of pipe will certainly be necessary. For wintering plants my plan would be to use a 1-inch pipe on each side of the frames, and for starting plants in the spring two 1-inch pipe at a depth of fifteen to eighteen inches.   L. R. TAFT.

Piping for Greenhouse.

ED. AM. FLORIST:—How many runs of 1-inch pipe will be required for a small greenhouse, 24x50 feet, using steam heat, temperature 45° in zero weather? The house is double, running east and west. The north wall is 6 feet high and the south wall 4½ feet. The benches on north side are raised, the two houses being all in one. How many return pipes should be used (same size) and how much higher should they be than the top of water in boiler?   I. N. G.

Use about eleven 1-inch pipes, placing three on each side wall and the others under the benches and on the center posts. A 1½-inch pipe will suffice as a common return for all of the coils. This should be two feet above the water level in the boiler.   L. R. TAFT.

New Bedford, Mass.

After the summer vacation, for the first time, the Florists' Club met September 30, with twenty members present. A short business session was held and two new members elected. The club then adjourned to enjoy the first annual clam-bake and entertainment, which closed with a dance. It was comical to see the antics of our fat man.

John Driscol, one of our oldest and most esteemed private gardeners, died suddenly at his home. He had been gardener for Wm. J. Rotch for the past thirty-five years.

Carnations are now getting quite plentiful. What we want now is some good freezing weather to kill all the outdoor flowers and then business will start up.

Business is still very quiet. Chrysanthemums have made their appearance. We are having some very good Polly Rose, Estelle and Merry Monarch.

Mr. Mosher has built a house, 16x60 feet, for carnations.   A. B. H.

Springfield, Mass.

The weather up to the end of last week has been ideal for getting outside work completed although a little warm for chrysanthemums, violets, etc. Business is improving some and a few good wedding orders have been placed. Chrysanthemums, white, pink and yellow, are to be seen but not in any great quantity; but unless we get a change of weather there will be a glut of roses and carnations. Lily of the valley is plentiful and fair in quality. A few violets, single and double, are to be seen but are off color and small. What is needed is cooler weather, with a few good frosts thrown in, to start business. There are too many outside flowers. Dahlias are as good now as at any time this season.   A. B.

Newport.

Albert William Wadley, of Wadley & Smythe, was married to Miss Mary Gorton, of Newport, October 12, at the Central Baptist church. The church was beautifully decorated with palms, white chrysanthemums and white roses. The bride carried a bouquet of orchids and lily of the valley.   F. L. Z.

LA ROSE, ILL.—The annual chrysanthemum show will occur November 18–20.

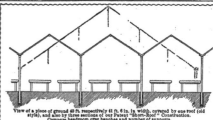

Please mention the American Florist when writing.

THE AMERICAN FLORIST

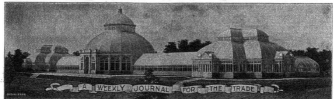

A WEEKLY JOURNAL FOR THE TRADE

America is "the Prow of the Vessel; there may be more comfort Amidships, but we are the first to touch Unknown Seas."

Vol. XXI.　　　CHICAGO AND NEW YORK, OCTOBER 24, 1903.　　　No. 803.

THE AMERICAN FLORIST

NINETEENTH YEAR.

Copyright 1903, by American Florist Company
Entered as Second-Class Mail Matter.

PUBLISHED EVERY SATURDAY BY

AMERICAN FLORIST COMPANY,
324 Dearborn St., Chicago.
Eastern Office: 79 Milk St., Boston.

Subscription, $1.00 a year.　To Europe, $2.00.
Subscriptions accepted only from the trade.
Volumes half-yearly from August, 1901.

SOCIETY OF AMERICAN FLORISTS AND
ORNAMENTAL HORTICULTURISTS.
OFFICERS—JOHN BURTON, Philadelphia, Pa.,
president; C. C. POLLWORTH, Milwaukee, Wis.,
vice-president; WM. J. STEWART, 79 Milk Street,
Boston, Mass., secretary; H. B. BEATTY, Oil City,
Pa., treasurer.
OFFICERS-ELECT—PHILIP BREITMEYER, president; J. J. BENEKE, vice-president; secretary and
treasurer as before.　Twentieth annual meeting
at St. Louis, Mo., August, 1904.

THE AMERICAN CARNATION SOCIETY.
Annual convention at Detroit, Mich., March 2,
1904.　ALBERT M. HERR, Lancaster, Pa., secretary.

AMERICAN ROSE SOCIETY.
Annual meeting and exhibition, Philadelphia,
March, 1904.　LEONARD BARRON, 136 Liberty St.,
New York, secretary.

CHRYSANTHEMUM SOCIETY OF AMERICA
Annual convention and exhibition, New York,
November 10-12, 1903.　FRED H. LEMON, Richmond,
Ind., secretary.

THIS ISSUE 40 PAGES WITH COVER.

Fair Prices for Carnations.

The following question and answer, which appeared in a recent issue of the AMERICAN FLORIST, were submitted to a number of experienced growers in different parts of the country with a request for comment, and their replies, which are given, are instructive and interesting:

ED. AM. FLORIST:—What would be a fair price to pay for carnation blooms on a season contract, entire cut being taken and the varieties being Queen Louise, Estelle, Prosperity, Enchantress, Lawson, Norway, Lorna and Dorothy.
VIRGINIA.

The writer is not familiar with costs, except at Chicago. Coal there may be had for $3 to $3.50 per ton delivered, and we fire nearly eight months. Queen Louise, Estelle, Lawson, Norway, Lorna and Dorothy could be grown of good quality for 2½ cents, with profit. Enchantress being new and expensive, should bring a cent more, and Prosperity should bring double. I take it for granted the varieties are in about equal quantity.
W. N. RUDD.

I have been out of the carnation business for several years, but I should not care to grow good carnations of the varieties named at an average price of 2½ cents.　PAUL M. PIERSON.
Scarborough-on-Hudson.

As to a season contract price on Queen Louise, Estelle, Norway, Lorna. Dorothy and Lawson, they could be grown at Cincinnati at the present price of fuel for $2 per 100, counting five months in the season. I cannot say about Enchantress and Prosperity as this is our first season with them.　WM. MURPHY.
Cincinnati, O.

Regarding season contract prices for carnations, it is difficult to make a definite statement. The chief factors in determining the price are quality and market. Price here would average, perhaps, 3 cents for first-class stock. The writer would suggest that Virginia had better send a fair sample of his stock to several reputable dealers and ask what they would pay for it.　L. E. MARQUISEE.
Syracuse, N. Y.

So much depends on the ability of the grower that it is difficult to give an opinion as to carnation prices, but with ordinary growers I would judge that 2 cents would be a fair price on a season contract. In giving my opinion on this I take it for granted that the season would be from October 1 to July 1 and that about equal quantities of each variety would be grown.
London, Ont.　W. W. GAMMAGE.

We have never contracted for a season, but know of growers that have contracted to sell carnations from September to December at 2 cents, April at 3 cents, and April to July at 1½ cents. We would not sell ours at that rate. There is a very wide range of prices as well as the quality of stock. We sold last season at from 50 cents to $20 per 100. Carnations are selling to-day at from 50 cents to $4 per 100.
WM. NICHOLSON.
Framingham, Mass. ·

Under modern requirements as to size, stem and other qualities, 2½ cents is not too high for Queen Louise, Lawson, Dorothy and similar varieties. Prosperity to be profitable as compared with other carnations should, in the opinion of the writer, be classified as the American Beauty is among roses. Enchantress is still too little known to talk intelligently as to price. On the quality of the blooms it should bring relatively a high price. As a general proposition, the average grower gets nothing that he does not earn. Your inquirer asks questions which can only be answered intelligently through a thorough knowledge of local conditions. In handling perishable products he will have at times to take what he can get and be thankful. The rest of the time he will have to get all he can. The average season's price depends upon the relation of the above two factors.
Cleveland, O.　ADAM GRAHAM.

Commenting on the query of "Virginia" as to a fair price for the entire cut the season through of Queen Louise, Estelle, Prosperity, Enchantress, Lawson, Lorna and Dorothy carnations, I should consider Mr. Rudd's figures as very just, though I have myself recently contracted in a similar way to buy Adonis and Prosperity at 6 cents, Enchantress at 4 cents and Her Majesty, Nelson and Apollo at 3 cents. Last year I contracted Crane from the same grower at 3 cents, and that was cheaper than we could produce it on our own place. Much depends however on the grower and his reputation for quality, and still more on his disposition to be fair in his dealings. I would not like to contract at all, and I certainly would not pay this price to a grower who could not be trusted or be of high grade. If the expression "entire cut" is meant to include all blooms without regard to quality I would consider that the figures named by Mr. Rudd are too high. Because Mr. Rudd seems to place emphasis on the price of coal I am led to remark that I believe most growers are deceived in the relation which their coal bill bears to their total expense. On our place the last year our fuel account was only eight per cent of the total which we charged to greenhouse expense.

Denver, Col.   J. A. VALENTINE.

I am of the opinion the grower is not getting the price for the goods in our part of the country that he should. Eastern quotations are higher at almost any time and the quality and variety about the same. Owing to circumstances connected with the growing of carnations they should bring the highest market price obtainable, and when the season is ripe they do bring it if the grower or the commission man bears in mind the cost of production. Of course it may all hinge on supply and demand. Now for the question. What constitutes a season? If September would open and June 1 close it then 2½ cents ought to be a good return, for the average plant will produce twenty to thirty blooms. We all know that labor varies. While a gentleman's place with high priced labor would cost a certain per cent for production the man who labors himself and has an assistant will greatly lessen the cost of production comparatively. No doubt many minds will center on this subject, and it ought to do good to get some discussion. I know some cases where the grower is selling choice carnations at 1½ cents to-day when if he insisted he would get 3 cents easily. The retailer is getting the lion's share and has no chances to run whatever. In conclusion I would say Mr. Rudd is about right with a tendency of an increase.

Detroit, Mich.   PHILIP BREITMEYER.

Gaillardias.

The original old Gaillardia aristata can hardly be found now in any of the gardens. It has been slowly but gradually improved in size as well as in coloring of the flowers. The ray florets are broader and longer in the improved varieties. Some of them show the quilled florets of G. fistulosa, others the characteristics of G. lanceolata and what we call to-day G. grandiflora and grandiflora major, is surely a mixture of the three species, though there is no record of hybridizing these species as far as I know. We have now flowers of superior size, some of them measuring four to five inches across, while the old G. aristata had a diameter of less than two inches. The coloring, too, is brighter and more varied. The dull red near the disk has been transformed to a soft carmine and vivid crimson, colors never seen in the older forms. Its growth and habit are more compact; it rarely

exceeds one and one-half to two feet in height and the flowering time has been lengthened. It begins to bloom earlier and holds out longer in the season, often lasting well into November.

Planted in large compact masses, the gaillardias show off to best advantage. Such beds bear an uninterrupted, continuous succession of bloom from June to November and their gorgeous colors are effective wherever introduced. The individual flowers are very durable, even in the height of summer, with very hot weather, they last in perfection for at least a full week and correspondingly longer in the coolness of autumn. Their lasting qualities as cut flowers are well known and duly appreciated by growers. The plants are easily grown in ordinary garden soil, but in stiff and rather moist ground they are apt to succumb. A covering does not prevent their dying out. It seems to be the moisture that is hurtful. Seedlings will flower the first year, but not as profusely as the older plants. Cuttings taken early in the season root readily and make better stock than seed-

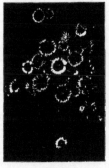

Gaillardias.

lings and where any special variety is to be propagated, green cuttings or root cuttings in the spring months are the only means we can resort to for increasing the variety, as we can hardly expect them to come true from the seed.

   J. B. K.

Forcing Spanish Irises.

ED. AM. FLORIST: Will some of your correspondents please give us their experience in forcing Spanish irises?   K.

We have never been able to force Spanish irises successfully. For the past few winters we have tried to force a few hundred bulbs, experimenting in different ways, but our efforts have been in vain—the bulbs, with the exception of a few, simply do not flower. One batch we handled just as we do Dutch bulbs—that is, we planted them in boxes and allowed them to remain outside in a frame until February, and then subjected them to a temperature of 50°; another batch we kept indoors in a cool house of 45° all through the winter; a third batch we

placed in a temperature of 60° after the bulbs were nicely started; in all three cases, however, the bulbs failed to flower finally come to the conclusion that they cannot be forced successfully. If any florist has had success in forcing them, we should all be pleased to hear of his method.   G

Palms and Ferns.

DINING CAR DECORATIONS.

The modern decorator finds room for his art in many ways that were not thought of until a few years ago, and must practice that art under varying and trying conditions. The decoration of dining cars on the leading railroads of this country furnishes an outlet for some of the stock of our growers, and owing to the trying conditions existing on such cars these decorations have to be renewed quite frequently, with the result that many thousands of small palms and ferns and also some other foliage plants in considerable quantities are used up every year.

The limited space available for plants in the average dining car makes it necessary that the stock used be in small sizes, the plants well furnished and grown in small pots, for the receptacles for these plants are usually in the form of narrow bracket ferneries attached to the sides of the cars, the root space being naturally very limited under such conditions. The best palms for this purpose are nice young plants of Cocos Weddelliana and Kentia Belmoreana from 2½ or 3-inch pots, the latter being about the limit in size of pot for the majority of these car ferneries. The cocos may be made-up plants if one has such stock, these filling up to better advantage than single plants of this species, and the same method is applicable to some of the stock of kentias to be used for this purpose, but made-up kentias that are to be used in this way ought to be grown together from the seed bed, selecting short and stocky plants and giving them space enough while growing to keep them from drawing up. A few plants of Livistona rotundifolia may also be found useful, but this plant does not endure the hardships of travel quite as well as those referred to above, and consequently does not pay to use in great quantity, there being a limit in cost of material that must be observed in all such work.

Ferns that are to be used in such decorations must be those having the most enduring foliage, and the maidenhairs are thus of little value, their fronds being much too tender for such an exposure. Some of the aspidiums are especially adapted for this work, among the best being A. Capense, A. Tsussimense, A. aristata var., and A. opaca. Polystichium setosum, Cyrtomium falcatum, Davallia stricta and Scolopendrium vulgare are also good, while some few of the great family of pteris may be added for the sake of variety, the latter being ferns that are easy to obtain, growing rapidly and enduring exposure to adverse conditions fairly well, among the best of the pteris for our present purpose being P. adiantoides, P. cretica Mayii and P. cretica magnifica. The fern list could readily be extended, but those mentioned are among those that are usually to be had in quantity and at a moderate cost, and may also be considered a first choice for filling table ferneries. Mention having been made of other foliage plants in this connection, it may be proper to add that three of the most useful for car decoration

Dicentra Formosa.   Golden Sun Ma·guerite.

TWO MERITORIOUS NOVELTIES.

are the following: Asparagus plumosus, Dracæna Sanderiana and Dracæna Godseffiana, none of which are difficult to get, while all are of good constitution and stand the abuses of railroading fairly well.

As already noted, small pots are one of the essentials in the preparation of stock for the purpose under consideration, and another is to have the plants well rooted and grown in a light and well ventilated house, thus producing hardy foliage and well furnished stock. The use of cheap and ill-prepared plants for work of this character may seem more profitable at first, but even the patience of a wealthy corporation has been known to give out, and lasting success is usually built upon fair and liberal dealing in our profession as in others.   W. H. Taplin.

Two Meritorious Novelties.

DICENTRA FORMOSA.

Dicentra formosa, illustrated herewith, comes from the high sierras of California where it grows at an altitude of from 5,000 to 9,000 feet. About five years ago a very graceful plant of the white variety was discovered in Modoc county. It will of course therefore be hardy about everywhere in the United States. This new white perennial has qualities for the florist as well as the amateur. The large, graceful pinnate leaves are light green, glaucous and finely divided, almost like some of the finest ferns. The freely produced clusters of pure white flowers droop gracefully from the summit of an upright naked scape a foot or more in height. It has thick, creeping under-

ground rootstalks, and is easily grown, hardy and multiplies rapidly in sun or shade, in the house, or in open borders or under field culture. LUTHER BURBANK.

MARGUERITE GOLDEN SUN.

The new yellow marguerite, Golden Sun, herewith illustrated, has been introduced by Walshaw & Son, of Scarborough, Eng., where the variety has been well received. The plant is as compact and bushy and as large or larger in the flower as the white variety. The blooms are of a good shade and thrown well above the foliage, a characteristic which renders it very suitable for cutting. It is said to be a continuous bloomer and to make attractive pot plants for spring sales.

Florists' Plant Notes.

BULBS.

It is too early at this time to force Dutch bulbs successfully excepting Paper White narcissus, which, if brought in now from the frames, can be forced into flower nicely for Thanksgiving day. Roman hyacinths, too, can be had in flower by that time if brought in now, provided, of course, that they are well rooted. For the first week or so they can be placed under a bench if no other space can be had, but after that they must have a good light place on a bench or they will grow too soft. Paper Whites must not be forced too hard or the buds will blast. A mild temperature of 50° or 60° will bring both Romans and Paper Whites into flower nicely for Thanksgiving. In order to have a supply of

these bulbs constantly on hand a few should be brought into the greenhouse every week, but of course until the chrysanthemums are gone no great demand for bulbous stock of any kind will be had. It must always be remembered that Paper Whites cannot stand any frost, hence they must be carefully protected with sash or straw after they commence to peep through the soil covering. We usually have them all forced by the middle of January, for after that date other bulbs can usually be had in quantity, forcing the Paper White to the rear. Freesias should be given a light place in a temperature of about 60° to have them in flower for the holidays. Give each pot of bulbs three or four match sticks, with a piece of string passed from one to the other around the plants, so as to grow them straight.

BEGONIAS.

Begonia Gloire de Lorraine, without which no assortment of Christmas plants is complete, makes most of its growth in the fall, and by this time should be fine plants in 6-inch pans. These plants require a rose house temperature, and should have the full light at this time of the year. As with cyclamens, it is a good plan to stand them on inverted 6-inch pots, for when the plants are covered with their profusion of bloom they must have plenty of room between the pots to permit of careful watering. No overhead watering should be done, but the end of the hose should be carefully passed between the plants with only a little water turned on, each plant to be watered as it needs it. Keep fresh tobacco stems scattered between the pots or the greenfly is sure to get a foothold, but do not fumigate them with tobacco for it fades the flowers. Each branch should be tied separately with raffia to a neat little match stick so as to form a shapely plant.

PRIMULAS.

With the advent of the Lorraine begonia the primula has to a large degree lost its importance as a Christmas plant, but a limited quantity is still grown every year to supply the demand for cheap flowering plants. If any are still in the cold frames they should be brought in at once. They ought to be strong, well formed plants by this time, and will soon send up their trusses of flowers. It is a custom with some growers to pick off the first flower stem so as to encourage the side trusses to develop more quickly, but this is not a good plan for it destroys the symmetry of the plant. Give them a cool house, 45° at night is about right, and be careful with the watering not to over-do it; neither should any water ever touch the flowers. Fumigation, while it does no harm, is unnecessary for the plants are rarely troubled with insects of any kind.

CYCLAMENS.

Cyclamens ought to be well established by this time in their flowering pots. They must have plenty of room to allow their handsome foliage to develop perfectly. A good plan is to stand them on inverted 6-inch pots; this will bring them nearer the glass and will give a better circulation of air around the plants. Until the flowers are developed it is safe to fumigate lightly, but after that no more fumigating should be done, for tobacco smoke ruins the flowers. A better way to hold aphis in check is to scatter stems between the pots. Overhead watering must also be discontinued after the flower buds commence to open.

POINSETTIAS.

Now that the bracts are forming on the poinsettias their roots must not be disturbed any more by shifting into larger pots or in any other way. Give each plant a neat stake and tie with raffia. The plants should have plenty of room and all the light possible. Feeding them with weak liquid manure once a week until the bracts are fully developed will increase their size and darken the foliage. Above all never allow the temperature to fall below 60° at night, for to chill the

plants in the slightest will cause them to drop their leaves. Syringe them daily as a preventive of red spider, and fumigate lightly once a week.   G.

The Carnation.

NEW DISEASE—BACTERIAL SPOT.

We have recently received for examination from Pennsylvania and the District of Columbia a number of carnation plants suffering from a spot disease of the leaves and stems that appears to be distinct from anything hitherto described. In its earlier stages the disease looks something like stigmonose, or puncture disease, but the small spots are usually surrounded by a narrow water-soaked area or ring, while the center of the spot is usually slightly brown. As the spots grow larger they resemble more the ordinary carnation spot caused by Septoria dianthi. The water-soaked marginal area, however, makes it easy to distinguish from this latter disease. The spots increase in size more rapidly in soft-leaved varieties and soon collapse and dry, leaving a brown sunken area. Badly diseased leaves soon wither. Microscopical examination shows that the spots in all stages are filled with bacteria, which, in the early and middle stages of the disease, are usually in poor cultures. These bacteria grow readily in beef broth and nutrient agar (acidity plus 15 of Fuller's scale) and on ten per cent nutrient gelatine of the same acidity, but where malic acid is added to the nutrient gelatine at the rate of one-half gramme per one hundred cubic centimeters, the growth is extremely slow. The germ also grows well upon steamed potatoes. The colonies are round and unbranched, pearly white, wet, shining, and do not spread rapidly over the culture medium. After a few days the central portions of the colonies break up into zoolloca. The complete cultural characters for various media have not yet been determined, but are being investigated. It is evident that the organism causing this disease is quite distinct from the orange-colored one, Bacterium dianthi, described by Arthur and Bolley as the cause of bacteriosis of carnations. Inoculation experiments have been tried, both from a maceration of young diseased spots in distilled water and from pure cultures in beef bullion. Bacteria from both sources, when applied

to the surface of leaves, old or young, where there was the slightest abrasion of the epidermis, produced by a fine needle, give characteristic spots filled with bacteria in from forty-eight to seventy-two hours. Characteristic spots have also been secured by simply brushing or spraying the bacteria on the uninjured leaves. Under natural conditions the bacteria appear to gain entrance to the leaves and stems from the slight injuries produced by the red spider and by other causes. Slugs have been observed eating diseased spots, and infection from slug bites was observed. It is also evident that the organism has other ways of gaining entrance to the tissues possibly through the stomata.

We have found the disease so far on the varieties Mrs. McKinley, Mrs. Nelson, Lawson and Crane, and it will doubtless be found on numerous other varieties. In some cases observed nearly every leaf and many of the stems were so badly spotted that it would be practically impossible to save the plants. When the disease has not progressed so far, however, it can be checked by thoroughly cleaning the plants of all diseased leaves and stems and burning what is removed. Then syringe the plants with a solution of commercial formaldehyde, one part to five hundred parts of water. This should be done in the forenoon so that the plants may dry before night. Syringe occasionally with water under pressure to keep down the red spider. Give the plants as much light and air as possible, and keep the foliage as dry as practicable. Give the plants a second thorough cleaning after the new growth is well started and follow with a second light syringing with formaldehyde solution.

It is probable these recommendations may be modified after further investigation. The procedure outlined is the best we can suggest at the present time. Every grower who observes what he thinks may be the disease is urged to send specimens to the Plant Pathologist, United States Department of Agriculture, Washington, accompanied by letter giving the necessary data, address of sender, etc. A report on the material submitted will be promptly returned in each case. A careful study of the disease and the organism causing it will be completed as soon as possible. Messrs. Lloyd Tenny and J. B. Korer, assistants in pathology, are actively aiding in the investigation.
A. F. WOODS.

A California House of Tuberous Begonias.

The accompanying illustrations show a house of giant flowering tuberous begonias grown by John H. Sievers & Company, San Francisco, Cal. The tubers were started in the early part of May (rather late), in light, rich soil, watered very sparingly until active growth had commenced, when a liberal supply of water was necessary. The plants were placed in a slightly shaded house and given plenty of air, in fact the ventilators were wide open both day and night. Staking, tying and disbudding having been given attention, they made a grand showing during August and September. The strain of begonias, originated by the above firm comprises some forty-five varieties, whose large and showy flowers of nearly every shade of color are carried particularly upright on strong, stiff stems. This flowers are much in demand for table and other decorations, where only a temporary effect is desired, as their keeping qualities after being cut are of rather limited duration.
N. PETERSON.

HOUSE OF TUBEROUS BEGONIAS AT SAN FRANCISCO, CAL.

NEW EARLY CHRYSANTHEMUMS.

Left—1. Etienne Bonnefond; 2. Baron Chiseuli; 3. Ethel Fitzroy; 4. Mrs. A. McKinley; 5. Neveu Rene. Right—1. Mlle. Martha More; 2. Early Chadwick; 3. Miss Olive Miller; 4. Salome; 5. M. Paul Sahut.

Chrysanthemums.

WE are in receipt of a copy of the new supplement to the official catalogue of the National Chrysanthemum Society of England, and this reminds us that it is about time we had a supplement to the catalogue of the Chrysanthemum Society of America.

EARLY VARIETIES OF THIS YEAR.

The fall of 1902 brought some delightful revelations in new chrysanthemums, but the present season promises to surpass the former in interest, judging by the blooms developed on October 15 and the other buds rapidly expanding in the most wonderful collection we have ever had the pleasure of trying. Among the earlies Carrie (Wells) is a beautiful September yellow of fine color; Goacher's Crimson is a nice, formal red for early October; this variety is having quite a run in England. On October 15 we photographed ten varieties, all of them large enough for exhibition.

Ethel Fitzroy has the rich coloring of Source d'Or or Kate Broomhead, it has broad incurving petals and builds up a fine, long stemmed flower.

Miss Olive Miller is probably the best for the date in the pink or lavender section. The color is very pleasing, and it is a fine, large, reflexing flower, with incurved center.

Mrs. A. McKinley is a very pleasing shade of buff and orange and light red. The form is very fine, a full incurved, or, from a second bud, incurving at the center with reflexing outer petals.

Among the French sorts Etienne Bonnefond stands pre-eminent for size and build, a grand incurved, 8½ inches straight through, and of good buff color. Mlle. Marthe Morel is a lively pearl pink, very broad and of V. Morel style, fine for this date and very beautiful.

Neveu Rene is an exhibition color, bright magenta reflexing with a "tourie" of silver.

Salome is a golden yellow with horizontal petals, large and substantial. (Raised by Charmet.)

Baron Chiseuli is red and chamois color, finely built and large.

Mme. Paul Sahut (Calvat) is a pure commercial variety, at the present writing large in size, round and "fluffy" and of yellow and pink, which disappear as the bloom expands.

There is not a poor grower nor a bad habit in the lot; they are really an exhibition set fully done by October 15.

Among the varieties of which we got a glimpse last year and which are now perfectly enormous buds are:

S. T. Wright, red and gold; the king and the whole chrysanthemum family.

W. Duckham, a beautiful, giant incurving pink.

Mrs. Emmerton, yellow, long drooping florets.

Mrs. Thirkell, yellow, of enormous size, which is evidently going to fulfill its last year's promise to the letter.

Mrs. Trantor, an enormous white incurved variety, with very long drooping outer petals which will certainly jostle all the older whites.

And even with all the stunning yellow new-comers, and many of them are gorgeous in the extreme, it still does one good to look down the ranks of the Yellow Eaton; stem, foliage, height, docility, all make this a standard of measurement among commercial varieties.

S. A. HILL.

Chrysanthemum Society of America.

JUDGING COMMITTEES.

President Herrington has announced the committees to examine chrysanthe-

mum seedlings and sports on dates as follows: October 10, 17, 24 and 31, and November 7, 14, 21, 28, 1903.

Boston, Mass.—E. A. Wood, chairman, Boston Flower Market, care of John Walsh; Wm. Nicholson and James Wheeler.

New York, N. Y.—Eugene Dailledouze, chairman, care of New York Cut Flower avenue; Wm. H. Duckham and Wm. Plumb.

Philadelphia, Pa.—A. B. Cartledge, chairman, 1514 Chestnut street; William K. Harris and John Westcott.

Chicago, Ill.—James S. Wilson, chairman, care of J. B. Deamud, 51 Wabash avenue; Edwin A. Kanst and E. Wienhoeber.

Cincinnati, O.—Richard Witterstaetter, chairman, to Jabez-Elliott Flower Market, care of janitor; James B. Allan and Wm. Jackson.

Exhibits to receive attention from the committees must in all cases be prepaid to destination, and the entry fee of $2 should be forwarded to the secretary not later than Tuesday of the week preceding examination.

Attention of the exhibitors is called to the action taken at the last meeting of the C. S. A., requiring all sports to be exhibited before at least three committees before becoming eligible to receive certificate. : FRED. H. LEMON, Sec'y.

SAVANNAH, GA.—Within a short while this city will establish a tree nursery. The nursery will be for the benefit of the county as well. The move means that the city will eventually pass ordinances that will forbid citizens planting trees in front of their property at will. All trees will be planted by the city, without cost to property owners, and in this way only one variety of tree need be planted on one street.

With the Growers.

R. T. M'GORUM, NATICK, MASS.

Robert McGorum, like a good many other capable rose growers in his section, is a past pupil of Alexander Montgomery. His establishment at Natick, Mass., comprises eight houses, four of which are 212 feet long each, the rest somewhat smaller. The range is heated by steam, three boilers of seventy-five, thirty and eighteen horse-power respectively, being available. The heating system is well arranged for uniform service. There are two lines of pipe in each house, both ends of each line. The two 2½-inch return pipes from each house are carried separately back close to the boiler where they all join a short 3-inch section, a check valve being provided in each to keep the water down. The exhaust warm water is utilized to temper the manure water which is distributed by a small pump throughout the houses by a system similar to that employed at Waban Conservatories and the exhaust steam goes to warm the dwelling house close by. A further demonstration of prudent economy is the use of a blower operated by a two horse-power engine whereby thorough combustion of everything that goes into the heater is secured and a considerable saving of fuel effected. The smoke also is consumed and thus frequent cleaning of the boilers is avoided. A complete outfit of tools enables all pipe fitting and threading to be done on the place. In line with other intelligent improvements Mr. McGorum has been substituting iron pipe supports for the heavy chestnut posts in the sides of the houses. These are set in a foundation wall composed of five parts coal ashes and one part cement.

Two of the smaller houses are now filled with an early crop of mignonette. Two others contain Kaiserin Augusta Victoria and Pres. Carnot roses which have been yielding a profitable summer crop and will be kept going until Thanksgiving, when they will be allowed to freeze up and remain so until about the middle of March. In the four large houses the only varieties grown are grafted Bride and Bridesmaid with a few Morgans, all on solid beds. Liberty has been tried in the past, successfully when grafted, disastrously when not.

Mr. McGorum is evidently a believer in the old advice, "not to venture all his eggs in one basket," for his stock is fairly divided between one, two and three year-old plants, and thus the advantage of a good distribution of crops is assured. It is his opinion that three years is the limit to which roses may profitably be left undisturbed in a bed. Not only does the soil become impoverished, despite generous mulchings but after three years' occupancy the roots have reached such a depth that they are out of reach of stimulants or other control.

Last May when throwing out and replanting, being short of young stock, Mr. McGorum undertook an experiment which has thus far given good satisfaction and will no doubt be of general interest. He took the plants, five feet high, from a two-year-old bed of Brides and removed them, with as large a ball of earth as possible, to the field where they were given one good watering and then allowed to ripen their wood. After three weeks they were pruned back to about twelve inches, the soil shaken off, and put into 3½-inch and 4-inch pots, all the roots possible being crowded in, particularly the ends of the roots so as to encourage a flow of sap, then taken into the house and syringed freely. Perhaps larger pots would have been better, but they were not at hand at that time.

In about three weeks' time there were abundant strong breaks from the base of the plants and they were then planted in a new bed in the rose house. At the present time, after three months' growth, these roses are in very fine condition, throwing up numbers of those strong, vigorous stems from the base of the plants which rose growers delight to see. Compared with two rows in the same bed which were simply transplanted in the ordinary manner these plants appear stronger, lower and bushier in habit, and the young growths getting better access to light and air than is the case with plants pruned in the usual way.

G. H. TAEPKE, DETROIT, MICH.

This place, which is now completed, is located on McClellan avenue, four miles from the city hall and two miles from Mr. Taepke's Elmwood avenue place. There are three houses, each 30x175 feet and four tables in each house, two of them six feet wide and two five feet wide. There are no division walls between the houses and the gutters are six feet above ground, supported by red cedar posts 10 feet long, to insure a good depth in the ground. The ventilators are opened at the top by the Foley machine, which is giving good satisfaction. The glass used is 16x16, single strength. The place is heated with steam from a ninety-six horse-power boiler, depressed about four feet below the ground level, on a con-

crete floor. The condensation is returned to the boiler by a Morehead steam trap. The work shed, which includes the coal bins, is of ample size, and extends entirely across the ends of the houses. The entire place is neat and complete in every detail. The improvement includes a neat dwelling house for the foreman.

Here only cut flowers will be grown and at present the entire place is planted with carnations, over 25,000 in number and embracing in large quantities, Lawson, Joost, Wm. Scott, Marquis, Hill, Glacier, Crane, Cerise Queen and Guardian Angel. In lesser quantities: Enchantress, Fair Maid, White Bradt, Lillian Pond, Adonis and Fragrance are grown. It would be difficult to find as many plants on any place so uniformly clean and vigorous, and it reflects much credit on the foreman, Otto Blatt, Mr. Taepke's brother-in-law.   J. F. S.

Encourage the Amateur.

At this season of the year we read much regarding the little exhibitions, festivals and reunions of the amateur gardening societies, children's garden clubs, etc., but are apt to pass them by as too trivial and devoid of any interest to the professional, and in our trade journals mention is rarely made of such matters.

Perhaps we undervalue these things. The children of to-day are the men and women of tomorrow upon whose patronage our business in the coming days must depend, and apart from the interest we should feel, as patriotic citizens, in the assembling of the young people in healthy rivalry in the most healthful of all pursuits, there are good reasons from a business standpoint for recognizing and encouraging a universal taste for flowers and their cultivation. Once acquired, the fondness for floral surroundings continues through life, and the more we can do to bring the children to feel that life without the accompaniment of plants and flowers is not worth living the more we are accomplishing for the future prosperity of our calling. Every suburban florist should use his influence to promote the existence of these local associations in his neighborhood. The additional interest in the care of home surroundings will be a good thing for his business.

SAN FRANCISCO, CAL.—Serveau Brothers have moved to their new store at 2114 Fillmore street, combining in the commodious quarters there the stores heretofore maintained at Fillmore and Sacramento streets and 2328 California street.

ROBERT McGORUM'S PLANT, NATICK, MASS.

The Retail Trade.

The maple in the swamp begins
To flaunt in gold and red.
And in the elm the fire-bird's nest
Swings empty o'erhead.

AUTUMN foliage, smilax and white and
pink chrysanthemums were used to
decorate the house at the wedding of
Miss Grace Anna Cosgrove and Charles
Albert Gale, of Chicago, at the bride's
home, Le Cleur, Minn., October 7. The
bride carried a bouquet of white chrysanthemums.

AUGUST KELLNER, of Milwaukee, Wis.,
has been doing some very good work
lately. A wedding at the Phœnix club
was praiseworthy particularly on
account of the clever and tasteful
arrangement of the large dining room
with autumn foliage in which the witch
hazel was prominent with the oak, also
two apple trees, some sweet corn in
flower and grapes grown over the tree
branches and covering the large chandeliers.

AUTUMN FOLIAGE AND FLOWERS.

We have recently received many inquiries
regarding the highly colored autumn
foliage seen betimes in the florists'
windows of New York. We have here
two or three Frenchmen who make a
specialty of dealing in wild flowers. They
are very alert and travel through the
woods for many miles around the city.
These dealers generally supply the florists
with the beautiful foliage often seen in
the stores and at a much less cost than
it could be procured by the storemen
themselves. Many of the growers and
wholesalers now, however, are selling or
giving bundles of it to their customers.
We would appeal to every florist who
anticipates having designs or decorative
work to do in the near or far future to go
out and study the grand models and
lessons to be seen in the woodlands to-day.
You will not see the green of the pin oak leading a charm to the yellow and scarlet of
the maple, the claret red of the sumach.
There is no jar in the great galaxy of
colors. There is perfect harmony, even
in the widest range. You may see many
beautiful combinations that it would be
well to allow to sink deep into your
memory, for there can be no better ideals.
Foolish is he, no matter how exalted,
who permits his egotism to tell him that
even his best work can compare with
that to be seen in some isolated nook
where Nature hides and laughs.
Many of you will no doubt have more
or less elaborate decorations to arrange
in the next few weeks where autumn
foliage can be used to special advantage,
but it is well to know that many are
averse to having it used in their wedding
decorations merely because of its senti-
mentality. Some people see sadness
blended with the colors in the trees, and
that is to be diligently avoided until
Cupid ties the fatal knot, but even in
such extreme cases the main hallway in
almost all cases should be embellished
with a profuse use of autumn tints. You
will find that the more different shades
you use the more beauties can be displayed in your work, dark green, light
green, yellow, orange, scarlet, a little
yellow, then a dash of light green, then
the claret color, the bronze, and so on.
A surfeit of one color is like a single idea
in design. It becomes at once monotonous and lacks the inventive ability necessary to please.
There are, of course, different degrees
of decorative work, which can be likened
to the many schools in painting. It is

easier to use a large brush than a cameo
point—requires less ability to cover a
wall than design a tracery, yet both can
be made to excel. A laborer may do the
ground work. It requires an artist to
apply the finishing touches. And some
very beautiful work can be done where
there is a disregard for rigid formal lines,
as in the case of covering a wall or beams
there should be some impression created
besides the too frequent apparent one
that the thing had to be hid and is
covered at all hazards.
It is not necessary to use up a great lot
of fine material in order to produce
pretty effects. In most cases a large
quantity of poor material can be used

for the background or corners, reserving
the best for the most prominent place,
and do not forget the immense virtue and
beauty of simplicity. An overhanging
vine or naturally arranged spray of any
foliage is far more pleasing than the flat
and wired one. Care should be taken to
have the bright side of your work, like
the bright side of yourself, most prominent to the eye. In these days time
economy is essential to success, and the
question is how to best use either what
you may have on hand or can easily
procure.
Chrysanthemums abound everywhere,
and there can be no mistaking the fact
that they are very valuable flowers. Very
likely on account of the great supply
most wholesalers, growers and many
retailers look upon them as a great evil.
Nevertheless it is a growing evil and not
without its good features. It enables a
poorer class of people to enjoy the pleasure of handling the flowers and insures
the wealthy a more imposing display for
a small outlay. The flowers lend themselves more to the large and spectacular
rather than the small and dainty forms
of decorative work, and the old style of
dotting single flowers trellis fashion over
a particular site is no longer considered
proper. Styles advance with wealth, and
art necessarily goes with education.
There is a wonderful difference in the
methods employed in decoration to-day
to those of a few years ago, and even the
humblest florist in a country town may
unconsciously give pointers to the city
autocrat. Yes, the worst of us and the
best of us can learn from one another
with tolerance smiles.
But to return to the material. Suppose
we have a big house, hall or church to
decorate. Well, we could make use of
those left-over bay trees splendidly, be
they standards or pyramids and if we do
not like their foliage, why we can soon
change their whole appearance by stick-
ing in them branches of highly colored
autumn leaves, and then we go all around

them and arrange at regular distances
our poorest chrysanthemum blooms so
as they will stick out from six to nine
inches. Then come our best blooms.
Some of these may need extra support.
We can wire them to sprays of such plants
as Prunus Pissardi or maple, and arrange
them so that they will be six to twelve
inches above the others in the bay trees.
By a little care you can manufacture
most excellent looking chrysanthemum
plants out of a few blooms. A little foliage
and a bay tree and concentrating the
flowers in one given point or design will
attract more attention and praise than
scattering them merely to display their
meagerness. We have no space here to

NEW ESTABLISHMENT OF G. H. TAEPKE, DETROIT, MICH.

dwell upon the innumerable ways in
which these great, showy flowers can be
shown to special advantage. Try to give
them a background of green foliage.
Intersperse them with bright sprays.
Berberis Thunbergii, although thorny, is
fine for this work, but proper selection
make many others equally as effective.
You may have noticed that the old flower
trusses of Hydrangea paniculata grandiflora have now assumed an old rosy tint.
Well, they are excellent when arranged
in masses for balcony or high decorative
effects. Then, too, how beautiful the
cosmos. How pretty it looks in great
light clusters. These clusters show up
best surrounded with green.   D.

Chicago.

FLORISTS' CLUB NAMES OFFICERS.—ATTEN-
DANCE BREAKS RECORDS.—CHRYSANTHE-
MUM SHOW TO-DAY.—BUSINESS SUFFERS
A SLUMP.—NOTES.

The regular meeting of the Florists'
Club, held October 21, was a record
breaker in many respects. There was an
attendance of forty-five, and twelve new
members were admitted. A letter was
received from the New York Florists'
Club thanking the local trade for the
courtesies of convention time. Edgar
Sanders, the worthy treasurer of the
club, tendered his resignation, which was
not accepted. Mr. Sanders, however,
was made an honorary member. C. M.
Dickinson, chairman of the programme
committee, announced that arrangements
were well advanced for the monthly exhibitions of seasonable stock to be held
throughout the season. As told elsewhere in these notes, the first exhibition
will be held this (Saturday) afternoon
and the second, to cover carnations and
the later varieties of chrysanthemums,
about the middle of November. The following officers were elected for the ensuing year: W. N. Rudd, president; P. J.
Foley, vice-president; George W. Wienhoeber; secretary; Edgar Sanders, treas-

urer; Alexander Henderson, financial secretary; George Woodward, Leonard Kill, John Reardon, F. F. Benthey and Robert Johnstone, trustees. The effort to change the name of the club was defeated.

Secretary Springer, of the Gardeners' and Florists' Union, writes as follows October 20: "The florists of the various wholesale cut flower greenhouses which are unionized have had their conditions bettered, with an increase of ten to fifteen per-cent in wages, and are now working ten hours a day, which puts practically all the large places on an equal basis in regard to working hours and wages, some of the places having increased their men ten to fifteen per cent two months ago. Mr. Washburn, of the firm of Bassett & Washburn, in an interview with Business Agent Richard Warner and President Neiman, said 'the union is a good thing, and after it is a little stronger we can look to your organization for good men, and will be a benefit to both parties.' "

Business started out well the first part of the week, everything selling out fine. Towards the latter end it slumped off and customers and orders were at a premium. Roses and carnations have not been as plentiful as last week. The supply, however, is sufficient for the demand. Dahlias and gladioli, while still coming to market, are beginning to be of poorer quality. The retailers are complaining of poor business.

The Florists' and Gardeners' Union has adopted resolutions requesting Mayor Harrison to remove E. F. Rolland, a stock broker at 226 La Salle street, from the board of education. The grievance against Mr. Rolland is that "he was responsible for the discharge of Terence Rogers, 225 South Desplaines street."

A. C. Wasson, some time at Lincoln park and formerly of Cleveland, Ohio, died recently at the County hospital, having been stricken a short time previously with an affection of the kidneys. He was buried at the Elmwood cemetery, October 17, the funeral being in charge of Lake View Tent No. 28, Knights of the Maccabees.

The Florists' Club chrysanthemum and carnation exhibition will open this (Saturday) afternoon at 4 p. m. in the blue parlor, third floor, Handel hall. Premiums for exhibits of merit have been donated by the Foley Manufacturing Company.

Frank Lockyear is again at work after a short illness.

Visitors: Henry Smith, Mrs. James Schols and Eli Cross, of Grand Rapids, Mich.; Miss Pfunder, of Portland, Ore., returning from vacation in New York; J. A. Peterson, Cincinnati, O.; Henry Smith, of Grand Rapids, Mich.

Philadelphia.

TRADE SHOW.—DAHLIAS CONTINUE FINE BEYOND USUAL TIME.—ABOUT PALMS.— A CORRECTION.—MUSHROOMS TO THE RESCUE.

Business has not been as lively as could be desired during the past few days, and there has been an accumulation of stock. Chrysanthemums have grown to be a factor, and as each day brings in one or more new kinds to add to the variety they form a large portion of the store-keepers' stock. Dahlias are very fine and Peacock is shipping thousands of blooms every day. S. S. Pennock receives a large express wagon load twice each day and finds good sale for them. Last season Jack Frost cut them out October 15, but

he is a full week behind and not yet in sight. Carnations are improving and are much better now than a week ago. From the looks of the stock and the quantity coming in it would seem as if there will be enough for the season's demands in spite of the great loss by stem rot. Violets are abundant, in fact with the exception of good doubles there are more than can be sold with profit to the grower. Mignonette has made its appearance and is a welcome addition. A few sweet peas are also to be had, quite nice flowers for the season. American Beauty is now to be had with stems any length and of very good quality. Bridesmaid appears the slowest in getting into form and but little really good stock has been seen as yet. There is great demand for lily of the valley, the many weddings

President W. N. Rudd.
(Chicago Florists' Club. Elected October 21.)

using it in quantity. All the commission men appear now to have shippers of this stock.

A. Leuthe, of Boston, was a visitor last week. He says his stock is not complete without Philadelphia palms, ferns, pradanusus, etc., and he bought largely of these plants while here. He says that small and medium sized kentias cannot be imported from Belgium to compete with the stock of the size as sold here, and as he has just returned from a visit to that famous palm land he ought to know.

In thinking of Westerly, R. I., S. J. Reuter's name seems to come up naturally, and we made a mistake in this column last week when we said that he was shipping to S. S. Pennock. Mr. Pennock's flowers came from W. W. Foster, of the Riverside greenhouses at Westerly. All of Mr. Reuter's products are handled exclusively by Welch Brothers, of Boston.

The Philadelphia Carnation Company has just completed filling a large mushroom house. This fungus is getting to be a sort of sheet anchor among carnationists of Chester county, where more than half the growers have special houses or cellars or grow them under the tables in their houses.

S. S. Pennock shipped 500 long chrysanthemums, 2,000 lily of the valley, 100 cattleyas, 200 long American Beauty roses, 2,000 Lawson carnations and

some other items to one party one day last week. Quite a nice order for the season.

C. B. Herr has fine Enchantress and Lawson carnations. Lawson promises to cut quite a figure in the market the coming season as it has been planted largely by most of the growers in this section.

H. Marchant, at Ivy Hill, met with quite a loss during the heavy rains of two weeks ago, which caused the sides of a new boiler pit to cave in. It will take $200 to repair the damage.

Leo Niessen's special delivery service is about the best organized force we have yet seen. It seems to be a ball bearing, rubber-tired affair and is always on time to the minute.

Eugene Bernheimer is first to get sweet peas, and fine flowers they are. His special Appleton, Childs and Simpson chrysanthemums are exhibition blooms.

The Market Company is handling some choice double violets. Lily of the valley here is also fine, Stokes sending a shipment every day.

P. M. DeWitt, of Croyden, is sending some fine Robinson chrysanthemums to S. S. Pennock.   K.

Boston.

STOCK MOVES SLOWLY.—AT EDGAR'S.— HATCH RECEPTION.—RAILROAD GARDENING.—NOTES.

We have now the poorest week of the fall for business. The condition of the market is very unsatisfactory from the flower dealers' point of view, and stock received is disposed of with difficulty. The chrysanthemum comes on apace and will soon reach its height, although the fine exhibition varieties have not yet put in an appearance. Prices are low as compared with former seasons on same grade of material. Carnations are more plentiful and show a considerable improvement. The leading varieties at present are The Queen, Fairmaid, Lillian Pond and Enchantress. Lawson is producing good flowers, but the stems are still short. A large number of Joost and varieties of similar grade are in the market, but do not bring the prices attained by the sorts above enumerated and at best they are selling low. American Beauty shows marked improvement in quality, gaining steadily for the past three or four weeks with longer stems, fairer faliage and more perfect flowers. Queen of Edgely shipments from Philadelphia indicate that this flower will soon be in good shape and has a promising season before it. Violets are scarce and of poor quality.

W. W. Edgar is feasting his eyes these days with affectionate tenderness on a long bench of Simpkins chrysanthemums grown with the special object in view of tempting the coin out of the pockets of the Harvard "rooters" at the time of the annual football games. Thinking ahead is one of Mr. Edgar's cardinal principles.

The Springdale Greenhouses at Canton, owned by Patrick Welch, have been leased for a term of years to Dennis J. Murphy, recently of Springfield, who will grow Bride and Bridesmaid roses exclusively.

The "Old Guard" broke loose again on Tuesday evening, October 20, and gave a rousing reception and dinner at Young's hotel to Edward Hatch, in recognition of his safe return from Europe.

The Boston and Maine railroad has made its annual distribution of prizes for gardening about the station grounds, Arlington, Mass., securing first prize of $50.

The Horticultural Club met at the Quincy house on Thursday evening,October 22, Wm. F. Anderson presiding. A. Cowee, of Berlin, N. Y., was in town Tuesday.

Washington.

ELABORATE DECORATIONS USED AT UNVEILING OF SHERMAN STATUE.—HEAVY RAIN IS FOLLOWED BY FROST, BUT OUTSIDE FLOWERS STILL THRIVE.

The unveiling of the Sherman statue October 15, with the attending banquets and receptions by the four great army societies assembled in the city to participate in the ceremony, was the occasion of an exhibit of striking and effective decorations. There were.four shields, each 6x9 feet, made of red, white and blue immortelles, bordered with green galax leaves, leucothoe sprays and a large cluster of palm leaves tied with red, white and blue ribbon at the base. Each shield bore the inscription of the army society.which it represented; the letters being made of white immortelles. The shield bearing the inscription, "Society of the Army of the Tennessee," was on the north; the "Ohio" on the south; the "Potomac" on the east, and the "Cumberland" on the west. The four smaller statues, one on each corner of the pedestal, representing the artillery, the cavalry, the engineers and the infantry, were each encircled by an 8-foot wreath of green galax leaves and leucothoe sprays, tied with the national colors. Five hundred feet of 12-inch roping was used in draping the pedestal and joining together the wreaths and the insignia of the four great armies.

The effect was appropriate and creditable to A. Gude & Brother, the floral decorators. At the conclusion of the ceremonies the decorations were taken down and rearranged at Raucher's Hall, where a reception and banquet were given by the four army societies. At the farewell banquet at the Arlington hotel, the night of October 16, the decorations were by J. H. Small & Sons.

There has been heavy rain followed by a sharp frost, but the outside flowers seem to have withstood it, as they are still coming in. Early chrysanthemums have appeared in the stores, and most of the growers have promise of a good stock in a week or two. Gen. Appleton is being largely grown this year.

While we are proud of our bowlers, it is but fair to mention that several of the boys have other diversions. Fred. Hill plays the clarionet in the Y. M. C. A. orchestra.

The tendency among the larger growers seems to be toward more pot plants, such as azaleas, poinsettias, Boston ferns and adiantums.

Of the new varieties of carnations, it is too early in the season to make predictions. At present, Enchantress looks promising.   S. E.

San Francisco.

UNUSUALLY HOT WEATHER HAS A WEAKING EFFECT ON THE MARKET.—OVERABENDANCE OF SECOND GRADE STOCK.—NOTES.—VISITORS.

In the early part of last week climatic conditions were very unsatisfactory for business, with mercury climbing between 80 ° and 90 °, for the time of the year an unprecedented high temperature, the depressing influence of which was generally felt by most of the storekeepers. The greatly increased receipts of

cut flowers, which with the exception of chrysanthemums, are hardly up the standard, coupled with a very limited demand, occasioned a good many flowers going to waste in the stores. This state of affairs, however, abated with the more normal weather conditions prevailing during the closing part of the week. Good stock is scarce but second grade more than plentiful and moves slowly. There seems to be a dearth of really first-class cut flowers. Many growers seem predisposed to quantity at the expense of quality. Also a stricter adherence to proper grading would not be amiss. The glass area has been considerably augmented in San Francisco and vicinity this season, upwards of seventy-five houses of varying size and modern construction, being built.

P. J. Thorsted, Fruitvale, has his carnation houses in first class condition. The plants are all healthy and thrifty. Mr. Thorsted has recently purchased 1¼ acres near his present. location and intends in the spring to erect two 200-foot carnation house thereon.

A. Galloway also at Fruitvale, has finished the building of one carnation house 25x135 feet, the benches of which were erected and carnations planted in the early part of the season. The plants are in fine condition and give promise of good returns later on.

W. H. Krabbenhoft, gardener to Claus Spreckles, has returned from a three months' visit to Germany and Switzerland. Mr. Krabbenhoft was very much impressed with the many improvements he saw over there along the lines of horticulture, particularly in the public park systems.

H. Foukouba, director of the imperial park Tokio, Japan, and expert in chief for the Japanese Garden at the St. Louis World's Fair, was a recent visitor in this city.

Mann Bros. are out with an elegant new delivery wagon.   ROMNEYA.

St. Louis.

COMMITTEES ON CONVENTION ARRANGEMENTS APPOINTED.—LIST OF CHAIRMEN.—FLORISTS' CLUB TO HOLD A CHRYSANTHEMUM SHOW..

The regular monthly meeting of the St. Louis Florists' Club was held on Thursday, October 15. Thirty-one members and two visitors were present. Applications for membership in the club were presented by Max Potter, Walter Hummel and N. Silverstone. Wm. Busche was elected a member. F. J. Fillmore suggested that the club raise a collection for H. Schweitzer, of Mendota, Ill., who suffered a severe loss in a recent wind storm. The suggestion was favored and $21.50 forwarded to Mr. Schweitzer. On opening the discussion of convention matters for 1904 President Beneke said he had appointed the members of the different committees, the following to be chairmen:

Reception—J. F. Ammann, Edwardsville, Ill.
President's Reception—J. J. Beneke.
Ladies' Reception—F. C. Weber.
Souvenir Publications of St. Louis Florists' Club—R. F. Tesson.
Press—A. S. Halsted, Belleville, Ill.
Advertising and Printing—F. H. Meinhardt.
Hotel—Edward Brechel.
Finance—Otto G. Koenig.
Entertainment and Sports—C. Beyer.
Hall and Decoration—Henry Ostertag.
Superintendent of Trade's Display—C. A Kuehn.

Discussion followed as to how the chairmen were to reach the members of their committees, and it was decided that each chairman is to notify the members of his committee what work they are to do and when and where to meet, so that no matter on what committee a man is placed he will be notified of the fact and brought in constant communication with his committee's chairman.

It was decided to hold an exhibition of chrysanthemums at the next meeting of the club. Prizes will be given for the best twelve blooms of any variety. Stock must be grown by members of the club. First prize is $5, second $3, third $2. Winning blooms become the property of the club, to dispose of at auction. After adjournment luncheon was served.

Messrs. J. H. Hadkinson, of the horticultural department of the World's Fair, and Berdan were visitors. Mr. Hadkinson said he was glad to be present and would like to see the members of the club at the Fair grounds.

Cincinnati.

TRADE IS GOOD.—STOCK IS PLENTIFUL.—FROST .HAS NOT YET COME.—ALBERT SUNDERBRUCH WEDDING A SURPRISE.

Trade last week was all that could be expected. True there was a surplus of good roses, but chrysanthemums and carnations were sold out every day. Some very good American Beauty are being shipped from out-of-town growers and at present there are no orders being turned down. There is quite a demand for good violets and those received are readily disposed of at 50 cents and 75 cents per hundred. At this writing chrysanthemums are coming in more abundantly and it will not be long before we have a surplus of them. Carnations, however, especially the white ones, are still a little scarce and from present indications it will be some time before the supply will equal the demand. Not having had a killing frost as yet, some very good cosmos, fine dahlias and other outdoor flowers are still on the market. Smilax and other green goods are plentiful.

Albert Sunderbruch stole a march on his friends, October 21, and was quietly married to Miss Lucia Genert, of Covington, Ky., by Rev. Gervaise Roughton at Wesley chapel. The bride is a handsome and accomplished young lady vocalist of much ability, being one of the most promising pupils of Prof. Burgott. We extend the happy couple our best wishes.

C. C. Murphy last Thursday gave about forty of his friends and neighbors a grand fish fry. Christ. does this annually and after partaking of the good things the company have a good time, singing, dancing and telling stories. The fish used for this affair are caught in Mr. Murphy's own pond on his place.

The Rosebank Company, with Wm. McFadden as president, occupying quarters at 140 East Fourth street, has purchased the Queen City Flower Company, 138 East Fourth street, from N. Fry and will conduct business in the future at that place.

Miss Edith P. Kyrk, formerly manager of the Queen City Flower Company, will open a retail flower store in Avondale in the near future.   ALEX.

DUQUOIN, ILL.—The Horticultural Society of southern Illinois will hold its annual meeting at Salem November 24 and 25.

THE AMERICAN FLORIST

NINETEENTH YEAR.

Subscription, $1.00 a year. To Europe, $2.00.
Subscriptions accepted only from those
in the trade.
Advertisements, on all except cover pages,
10 Cents a Line, Agate; $1.00 per inch.
Cash with Order.

No Special Position Guaranteed.

Discounts are allowed only on consecutive insertions, as follows—6 times, 5 per cent; 13 times,
10 per cent; 26 times, 20 per cent;
52 times, 30 per cent.

Cover space sold only on yearly contract at
$1.00 per inch, net, in the case of the two
front pages, regular discounts applying only to the back pages.

The Advertising Department of the AMERICAN
FLORIST is for florists, seedsmen and nurserymen
and dealers in wares pertaining to those lines only.

Orders for less than one-half inch space not accepted.

Advertisements must reach us by Wednesday to
secure insertion in the issue for the following
Saturday. Address

AMERICAN FLORIST CO., Chicago.

THE cold weather will come soon
enough. Are you ready for it?

SWEET peas and dahlias, where they
can be cultivated in the Rocky mountain
region, thrive better and give more satisfaction than most other outdoor flowers.

EREMURUS HIMROB is the name of a new
hybrid of E. Himalaicus and E. robustus,
offered by Van Tubergen, Haarlem, Holland. The foliage resembles that of E.
Himalaicus and is said to be hardier than
that of E. robustus. The flowers are
like those of E. Elwesianus but clearer.

JAMES VEITCH & SONS, of Chelsea, London, Eng., have a new smilax called S.
sagittæfolia which is described as a free
growing climber with tough, shining
green leaves that are broadly arrow-
shaped, but have both apex and basal
lobes rounded. The stems are spiny, as
also is the midrib of the leaves.

A Correction.

We regret to find that the prices as
printed in the dahlia advertisement of
the Horticultural Company, Cheadle-
Hulme, Cheshire, Eng., are erroneous.
The correct prices appear in this issue.

Lilac Salvia.

Replying to "A. L.", we beg to state
that we do not know of any lilac variety
of Salvia splendens, but the flowers of
S. leucantha may be described as lilac or
lavender.

Lignite Coal Ashes.

Charles Mauff, a grower of Denver,
Col., says lignite coal ashes are positively dangerous as bench material on
account of the alkali they contain. It
would be interesting to hear from other
growers in this matter.

Finds It an Aid.

ED. AM. FLORIST:—I much prefer your
paper to others. I have just started
growing cut flowers for the New York
market, and find your paper very valuable. WM. SIMMONDS.
Staten Island, N. Y.

Indiana Floral Festival.

The following change has been made
in the official premium list for the Indiana
Floral Festival and Chrysanthemum
Show: Section 3, No. 13, which now
reads "twenty-five single stem plants,

assorted colors," should read "twenty-
five plants, any other color, one variety,"
as stated in the preliminary premium list.
IRWIN BERTERMANN.

Check Valves On Return Pipes.

ED. AM. FLORIST—Is it necessary to
have check valves on the return pipes on
a low pressure boiler? I came near an
accident when I forgot to close a return
pipe valve, the water backing into it,
leaving the boiler empty, causing the top
packing to dry out and allowing water
to run into the fire chamber. How long
should a Monitor boiler last if kept in
a good condition?
SUBSCRIBER.

Check valves are not necessary when
everything is in proper working order.
As I understand the conditions, the difficulty described could have occurred with
or without a check valve.
L. R. TAFT.

From Steam to Hot Water.

ED. AMERICAN FLORIST.—I have a low
pressure steam boiler which does not
make steam enough for my houses. I
have been told it would make more hot
water than steam. Would it be practical
to put hot water under pressure? I have
a windmill standing over the boiler room
tank, elevated 20 feet, with a capacity of
1,500 gallons and a pressure of about
twelve pounds. Would this help circulate the water faster? The piping is 3-
inch, 6 feet from boiler, then a 4½-inch
main overhead running 48 feet, full length
of boiler room and dropping down with
2-inch pipes to the front end of the houses,
which are 68 feet long. Then they drop
down under the benches to manifold,
returning with 3 1¼-inch pipes under the
benches. I have three houses, one with
two runs of 2-inch pipe at the ridge at
the front end of the house returning with
four 1¼-inch pipes under the benches on
each side of the house. The other two
are connected with a Jennings gutter and
open houses. They have four 2-inch overhead pipes and twelve 1¼-inch returns.
I want a temperature of 60° at night.
Have I got enough pipe for hot water?
Where would it connect with the tank?
I have two returns, one at each side of
the boiler, for the condensed water to
return at the bottom of the boiler.
J. L. N.

Nothing is said regarding the size of
the houses, and the only way to determine whether the radiation is sufficient
for heating them with hot water from
the data given is to compare the relative
efficiency of hot water and steam
radiation. First it may be said
that ordinarily if a boiler is not
large enough to give the required
temperature with steam, it will fail with
hot water also. When hot water is carried under a high pressure it will give a
temperature even higher than that of
steam at the pressure generally carried.
However, this is not an economical
method of heating, and can only be used
with anything like satisfaction where
there is a fireman on duty at all times.
It will generally give best results when
50 to 100 per cent more radiation is used
for hot water than for steam.
For hot water circulation the size of
the return should equal that of the flows.
If the flow pipe rises from the boiler and
then runs down-hill it will suffice if the
expansion pipe is connected at the highest
point, and the safety valve removed
unless it will hold water under pressure.
If the houses are 100 feet or more in

length it will be best to use 2-inch pipe
for the return, although 1½-inch will
answer for water under pressure. A
2-inch flow pipe should not be used for
more than 200 square feet of radiation,
including what it supplies itself.
L. R. TAFT.

Pittsburg.

BUSINESS CHANGES FOR THE BETTER.—
WHITE AND YELLOW CHRYSANTHEMUMS
PLENTIFUL.—ROSE CROP IS PROMISING.—
NOTES OF THE TRADE.

Great interest attended the monthly
meeting of the Pittsburg and Allegheny
Florists and Gardeners' Club at the German Beneficial Union hall, October 6,
the special feature being a number of
extensive exhibits of rare specimens of
dahlias and cannas by florists of other
states. The president of the club, William Falconer, delivered an address on
"Cannas, Dahlias and Hardy Flowers."
Robert R. Vincent, of White Marsh, Md.,
brought a large collection of dahlias.
Among other out-of-town exhibits were
blooms of hardy perennials by Henry A.
Dreer, Philadelphia; cactus and show
dahlias by F. R. Pierson, Tarrytown, N.
Y.; fancy dahlias by W. P. Peacock, Atco,
N. J., and of specialties in cannas by
Conard & Jones, West Grove, Pa.

There was a slight change for the better in this week's business. Chrysanthemums are in evidence everywhere and
some exceptionally fine white and yellow
blooms are to be had. Pink chrysanthemums lack good color, which is detrimental to their sale. Roses continue to
improve and all kinds are plentiful and it
seems as though the outdoor stock would
never cease coming in. It has a tendency
to interfere with the sale of the more
important staples. Carnations are good
but not too plentiful. Valley, sweet peas
and violets meet with good sale.

The outlook for a great American
Beauty crop this year is very promising.
With a reasonable amount of clear
weather it will be assured. The chrysanthemums in the houses are reported to
be in perfect shape and many odd and
new varieties will be seen at the annual
display, which will soon be announced.

M. M. Bunting, of Cheswick, Pa., a
fugitive from justice, had a large consignment of bulbs sent to his former
place at Cheswick. During Mr. Bunting's absence it will be useless for firms
to fill his previous orders.

A. W. Smith filled an order last
Thursday for ten crane travelers and
ten standing wreaths one of each being
sent to the family of each victim of the
Wabash bridge disaster of last Monday,
October 19.

The Pittsburgh Rose and Carnation
Company will soon be connected with
the city by telephone. They will have to
put up thirty-six poles before this connection can be made.

John L. Wyland, of De Haven, Pa., is
sending in his rose and carnation stock,
equal to the best now coming into this
market.

Randolph & McClements are making
extensive preparations for the growing
of great quantities of ferns.

Benjamin Elliott contemplates erecting
a new American Beauty house which will
be about 30x100 feet.

Fred Burki will move his family this
week to Bakerstown, where they will
permanently reside.

Charles L. Siebert appears much
improved in health and comes down to
the city frequently.

J. B. Murdoch & Company have received a large consignment of carnation plants.

The chrysanthemum show at Phipps' conservatory will be open to the public next week. E. L. M.

Indianapolis.

ELABORATE ARRANGEMENTS FOR CHRYSANTHEMUM SHOW.—PRIZE LIST A LONG ONE.—EXHIBITORS TO BE ENTERTAINED.

Irwin Bertermann, secretary of the Indiana Floral Festival-Association, is well pleased with the prospects for the chrysanthemum show. Subscriptions came in in a most satisfactory way, enabling the promoters to add more premiums to their list, which is already a very liberal one. The show has been advertised extensively through the middle west. Mr. McPhetridge, a newspaper man well known among the trade, is enlightening the general public on the mysteries of flower "forcing." Emil Buettner, of Chicago, and Theodore Bock, of Hamilton, will be judges at the show. Some prominent exhibitors will be John N. May, the E. G. Hill Company, M. S. & W. J. Vesey, Gunnar Teilmann, Nathan Smith & Son, Bassett & Washburn and many of the local dealers. Exhibitors are requested to make entries early.

At the October meeting of the State Florists' Association of Indiana it was decided to award the national society's medals for 1903 at the chrysanthemum show, the awarding to be done by a committee of the S. F. A. I. The association also arranged to entertain visiting florists Thursday evening of the show week. Messrs. Huckriede, Alley, Heidemeich, Smith and Judge were appointed as entertainment committee.

Sidney Smith during his recent trip through Texas and the southwest took great interest in the cotton growing of that region, of which he gave the members a very interesting account.

The chrysanthemum show management is out with a fine poster announcing the exhibition for November 10–14.

Fred Huckriede, John Grande and E. A. Nelson visited Anderson and Marion last Sunday. H. J.

Dallas, Texas.

At Fort Worth the dealers are all busy and report business good. Baker Brothers report an unusual demand for funeral flowers. The Drumm Seed Company is finishing two new greenhouses and making extentions to its packing shed. W. L. McCart, the superintendent of parks, has added three fine new houses to his plant.

There has been no frost as yet, plenty of rain has put outside flowers up to the limit in bloom and the flowers are now the best of the season, especially roses. Every dooryard is a bower of roses. Cosmos is grown largely here. It blooms profusely with flowers of immense size. Albert Brandenberger, with the Haskell Avenue Floral Company is wearing an unusually broad smile. Its a girl—just what he wanted—and the cigars are being passed around. LONE STAR.

New England Notes.

L. A. MARTIN, gardener to W. H. S. Wood, Greenwich, Conn., in a communication to the editor regarding the report of the American Institute Show of our issue of September 26, in which the statement was made that he should never

have exhibited the strawberry-raspberry as a new fruit, says his exhibit was not entered as a new plant or fruit but merely as a special exhibit.

HYDE PARK, MASS.—Leslie Fellows has recently returned from an extensive tour in Europe during which he made an exhaustive study of the European methods of floriculture and market gardening, with a special view to improving the local method of mushroom growing.

GLASTONBURY, CONN.—J. H. Hale, the nurseryman, complains that deer are feeding off the tops of his young apple trees and as the deer are protected by the state he will ask for damages.

EASTHAMPTON, MASS., has a village improvement society which has been so successful that it is proposed to further extend its usefulness by organizing a horticultural society.

PITTSFIELD, MASS.—Mrs. Drake, wife of F. I. Drake was assaulted and robbed of her purse while on her way home ward on the evening of October 13.

NEWPORT, N. H.—The ninth annual exhibition of the New Hampshire Horticultural Society will be held at the town hall on October 21–23.

MANCHESTER, MASS.—E. S. Knight was buncoed out of ten dollars one day last week by a voluble stranger who subsequently disappeared.

NORTH BEVERLY, MASS.—C. O. Caldwell is erecting a huge water tank of several thousand gallons capacity at his greenhouses.

WALLINGFORD, CONN.—Geo. H. Rowden had a sumptuous celebration of his sixty-third birthday anniversary on October 10.

SITUATIONS, WANTS, FOR SALE.

One Cent Per Word.

Cash with the Adv.

Plant Advs. NOT admitted under this head.

Every paid subscriber to the AMERICAN FLORIST for the year 1903 is entitled to a five-line want ADV. (situations only) free, to be used at any time during the year.

Situation Wanted—By an all-around florist and gardener. Best of references. Alone.
103 N. Clark St., Chicago.

Situation Wanted—As foreman or manager; eighteen years' practical experience. Thoroughly conversant with all branches of the business.
G P. care American Florist.

Situation Wanted—As medium-sized place, as grower of roses and carnations; 11 years' experience. Address
C A L. 309 S. Laurel St., Richmond, Va.

Situation Wanted—By experienced gardener as foreman in good establishment, where good wages are paid; married. Address S P.
227 E. Sharpnack St., Germantown, Phila.

Situation Wanted—Propagator of roses and clematis by grafting: 25 years' practical experience in Europe and America. Address
FLORIST, 609 East Second St., Los Angeles, Cal.

Situation Wanted—By first-class rose and carnation grower by first of May in or near Chicago. Experienced in decorating and designing. Best references. T P. care American Florist.

Situation Wanted—By a single, middle aged German. Life experience in cut flowers, pot plants; at present employed in a large Chicago concern. Please state wages. Address
C B, care American Florist.

New England Notes.—By first-class man: 21 years' experience in greenhouse plants, fruit and vegetables, also landscape gardening, have diploma. Address
E L, care American Florist.

Situation Wanted—As foreman or to take full charge of a place, by expert grower of pot plants; well posted in forcing, grafting and propagating; 20 years' experience, German, married. Address
F E. care American Florist.

INTERNATIONAL FLOWER DELIVERY.

PASSENGER STEAMSHIP MOVEMENTS.

The tables herewith give the scheduled time of departure of ocean steamships carrying first-class passengers from the principal American and foreign ports, covering the space of two weeks from date of this issue of the AMERICAN FLORIST. Much disappointment often results from attempts to forward flowers for steamer delivery by express, to the care of the ship's steward or otherwise. The carriers of these packages are not infrequently refused admission on board and even those delivered on board are not always certain to reach the parties for whom they were intended. Hence florists in interior cities having orders for the delivery of flowers to passengers on out-going steamers are advised to intrust the filling of such orders to some reliable florist in the port of departure, who understands the necessary details and formalities and has the facilities for attending to it properly. For the addresses of such firms we refer our readers to the advertisements on this page:

FROM	TO	STEAMER	*LINE	DAY	DUE ABOUT
New York......	Liverpool	Lucania	1	Sat. Oct. 31, Noon.	Nov. 6
New York......	"	Etruria	1	Sat. Nov. 7, 7:00 a. m.	Nov. 13
New York......	"	Teutonic	7	Wed. Oct. 28, Noon.	Nov. 4
New York......	"	Arabic	7	Fri. Oct. 30, 12:30 p. m.	Nov. 7
New York......	"	Germanic	7	Wed. Nov. 4, Noon.	Nov. 12
New York......	"	Cedric	7	Fri. Nov. 6, 6:00 a. m.	
Boston	"	Cambroman	15	Thur. Oct. 29,	
Boston	"	New England	15	Thur. Oct. 29, 4:00 p. m.	Nov. 5
Boston	"	Mayflower	15	Thur. Nov. 5, 10:00 a. m.	Nov. 12
Boston..........	"	Ivernia	1	Sat. Nov. 7, 11:00 a. m.	Nov. 15.
Boston..........	"	Devonian	16	Sat. Oct. 31, 6:00 a. m.	
Boston..........	"	Winifredian	16	Sat. Nov. 7, 11:00 a. m.	
New York......	Glasgow	Astoria	5	Sat. Oct. 31, 3:00 p. m.	
New York......	"	Ethiopia	5	Sat. Nov. 7, Noon.	
New York......	"	Numidian	9	Thur. Nov. 5, 11:00 a. m.	Nov. 10
New York......	Naples	Roma	14	Tues. Oct. 27,	Nov. 8
New York......	Hamburg	Graf Waldersee	3	Sat. Oct. 31, 1:00 p. m.	Nov. 13
New York......	Antwerp	Zeeland	8	Sat. Oct. 31, 10:00 a. m.	Nov. 9
New York......	"	Finland	8	Sat. Nov. 7, 10:00 a. m.	Nov. 16
New York......	London	Minnehaha	6	Sat. Oct. 31, 1:30 p. m.	Nov. 10
New York......	"	Mesaba	6	Sat. Nov. 7, 9:00 a. m.	
New York......	Southampton	Marquette	6	Fri. Nov. 6, 9:00 a. m.	
New York......	"	New York	8	Wed. Oct. 28, 10:00 a. m.	Nov. 5
New York......	"	Philadelphia	8	Wed. Nov. 4, 10:00 a. m.	
New York......	Havre	La Lorraine	10	Thur. Oct. 29,	Nov. 5
New York......	"	La Touraine	10	Thur. Nov. 5,	Nov. 12
New York......	Rotterdam	Ryndam	11	Sat. Oct. 28, 10:00 a. m.	Nov. 6
New York......	"	Noordam	11	Wed. Nov. 4, 10:00 a. m.	
New York......	Genoa	Lahn	13	Sat. Nov. 7, 11:00 a. m.	Nov. 19.
New York......	"	Liguria	12	Tues. Oct. 27,	
New York......	"	Citta di Milano	12	Tues. Nov. 3,	
New York......	Bremen	K. Wil. Der Grosse	13	Tues. Oct. 27, 11:00 a. m.	Nov. 4
New York......	"	Neckar	13	Thur. Oct. 29, 11:00 a. m.	Nov. 10
New York......	"	Kronprinz Wilh.	13	Tues. Nov. 3, 9:00 p. m.	Nov. 10
New York......	"	Rhein	13	Thur. Nov. 5, 10:00 a. m.	Nov. 16

*1 Cunard; 2 Allen-State; 3 Hamburg-American; 4 Scandinavian-American; 5 Anchor Line; 6 Atlantic Transport; 7 White Star; 8 American; 9 Red Star; 10 French; 11 Holland-American; 12 Italian Royal Mail; 13 North German Lloyd; 14 Fabre; 15 Dominion; 16 Leyland; 17 Occidental and Oriental; 18 Oceanic; 19 Allan; 20 Can. Pacific Ry.; 21 N. Pacific Ry.; 22 Hongkong-Seattle.

INTERNATIONAL FLOWER DELIVERY.

STEAMSHIPS LEAVE FOREIGN PORTS.

FROM	TO	STEAMER	*LINE	DAY	DUE ABOUT
Liverpool........	New York	Majestic	7	Wed. Oct. 28, 3:30 p. m.	
Liverpool........	"	Celtic	7	Fri. Oct. 30, 3:30 p. m.	
Liverpool........	"	Oceanic	7	Wed. Nov. 4, 3:30 p. m.	Nov 11
Liverpool........	"	Cymbric	7	Fri. Nov. 6, 3:30 p. m.	Nov. 16
Liverpool........	Boston	Bohemian	16	Fri. Oct. 30, 3:30 a. m.	
Liverpool........	"	Canadian	16	Fri. Nov. 6, 11:00 a. m.	Nov. 15
Liverpool........	"	Columbus	16	Thur. Oct. 29,	Nov. 5
Liverpool........	"	Commonwealth	15	Tues. Nov. 5,	Nov. 12
Hamburg........	New York	Pennsylvania	3	Sat. Oct. 31,	Nov. 9
Hamburg........	"	Deutschland	3	Sun. Nov. 1,	Nov. 9
Hamburg........	"	Auguste Victoria	3	Thur. Nov. 5,	
Southampton...	"	St. Louis	8	Sat. Oct. 31, Noon.	
Southampton...	"	New York	8	Sat. Nov. 7, Noon.	Nov. 14
Antwerp........	"	Vaderland	8	Sat. Oct. 31, 9:00 a. m.	
Antwerp........	"	Kensington	8	Sat. Nov. 7, Noon.	
London.........	"	Minnetonka	6	Sat. Oct. 31, 1:30 p. m.	
London.........	"	Minneapolis	6	Sat. Nov. 7, 7:00 a. m.	Nov. 16
Naples.........	"	Germania	14	Wed. Oct. 28,	Nov. 6
Rotterdam.....	"	Potsdam	11	Sat. Oct. 31,	Nov. 9
Rotterdam.....	"	Statendam	11	Sat. Nov. 7,	
Havre..........	"	La Savoie	10	Sat. Oct. 31,	
Havre..........	"	La Bretagne	10	Sat. Nov. 7,	Nov. 15
Genoa..........	"	Hohenzollern	13	Thur. Oct. 29,	Nov. 11
Genoa..........	"	Lombardia	12	Mon. Oct. 26,	
Genoa..........	"	Nord America	12	Mon. Nov. 2,	
Genoa..........	"	Sardegna	12	Mon. Nov. 9,	
Bremen.........	"	Main	13	Sat. Oct. 31,	Nov. 9
Bremen.........	"	Kaiser Wilh. II	13	Tues. Nov. 3,	Nov. 10
Glasgow........	"	Columbia	5	Sat. Oct. 31,	Nov. 16
Liverpool	"	Campania	1	Sat. Oct. 31,	Nov. 6
Liverpool	"	Umbria	1	Sat. Nov. 7,	Nov. 13
Liverpool.......	Boston	Ivernia	1	Tues. Oct. 30,	Oct. 27

* See steamship list on opposite page.

Wild Smilax ALWAYS On Hand.

Also PLUMOSUS, SPRENGERI, ADIANTUMS, GALAX AND LEUCOTHOES.

We are Growers of HIGH-GRADE **Cut Flowers.** All orders promptly filled. Consignments solicited.

FRANK GARLAND, 55-57 Wabash Ave., Chicago.

Please mention the American Florist when writing

The F. R. WILLIAMS CO.

Wholesale Florists,

CLEVELAND, - OHIO.

Please mention the American Florist when writing.

WILD SMILAX. ORDER DIRECT FROM HEADQUARTERS.

We carry the finest and most complete stock of Florists' Hardy Supplies, Dagger and Fancy Ferns, $1.00 per 1000. A No. 1 quality. Bronze and Green Galax, $1.00 per 1000 A No. 1 quality. Southern Wild Smilax, 50 pound case, $7.00. 25 pound case $3.50 per case. Laurel Festooning, good and full, 5c and 6c per yard. Leucothoe Sprays, $1.00 per 100. Green Moss, $1.00 per bbl.; 75c per bag. Sphagnum Moss, $1.00 per bbl., 50c per bag. Order by mail, telegraph or telephone will receive our prompt attention. Long Dist. 'Phone 2618 Main.

HENRY W. ROBINSON, No. 11 Province St., BOSTON, MASS.

Please mention the American Florist when writing.

Albert Fuchs,

PALMS, FERNS, FICUS.

Established 1884.   **CHICAGO.**   2045-59 Clarendon Ave.

Please mention the American Florist when writing.

IF YOU HAVE STOCK TO SELL.....

The best way to make that fact known to the trade is by regular advertising in the   The American Florist.

THE SEED TRADE.

AMERICAN SEED TRADE ASSOCIATION.
S. F. Willard, Pres.; J. Charles McCullough, First Vice-Pres.; C. E. Kendel, Cleveland, O., Sec'y and Treas.
Twenty-second annual convention St. Louis, Mo., June, 1904.

PEA prices on canners' varieties are weak but in some cases stocks are also of doubtful quality.

OMAHA, NEB. — The Nebraska Seed Company is making alterations at its Jones street place to cost $1,000.

NEWPORT, R. I.—M. B. Faxon was married on October 19 to Miss Elizabeth A. O'Brien, at St. Cecelia's church.

THE Department of Commerce and Labor has issued a useful report on foreign markets for agricultural implements and vehicles.

P. C. HEINEMANN, Erfurt, Germany, among other novelties is offering two attractive schizanthuses of dwarf habit and two new torenias.

COLUMBUS, O.—Eleven thousand dollars' worth of imported bulbs passed the custom house in this city in September. They were shipped to Springfield.

VISITED CHICAGO: Wm. F. A. Kendal, of Cleveland, returning from a hunting trip in Colorado; B. F. Brown, of the Brown Bag Filling Machine Company, Fitchburg, Mass.

FREDERICK ROEMER, Quedlinburg, Germany, is offering two new pansies, a red cineraria, fringed primula and Begonia Golden King, a yellow variegated form of semperflorens.

VISITED BOSTON: M. B. Faxon, representing G. A. Weaver Company, Newport, R. I.; John H. Cox, representing Stumpp & Walter Company, August Rhotert, Leonard Barron and J. A. Blanchard, New York; E. B. Holt, of Whitney-Eckstein Seed Company, Buffalo, N. Y.; A. C. Johnson, re-presenting the Albert Dickinson Company. Chicago; J. McHutchinson, New York.

Pollination of Sweet Peas.

Sweet peas are never pollinated by bees. There are rarely any bees found among sweet peas excepting bumble bees, and they only take to full grown blossoms. Sweet peas are usually pollinated when quite young in the bud, and to cross them artificially it is necessary to take a very young bud. If the sweet peas were allowed to go to seed before any blossoms were gathered the seed would be all right, but the seed is rarely good when the first blossoms are gathered and only the last and inferior blossoms allowed to go to seed.   L. L. MORSE.

Detroit.

SOILS DISCUSSED BY CLUB.—INTERESTING EXHIBITS.—UNUSUAL DEPRESSION IN BUSINESS.—CLUB OUTINGS.

The club meeting, Wednesday evening last, brought out a good attendance. "Soils" was the subject discussed, and much valuable information was brought out. A report by the treasurer showed the finances to be in good condition. The Cushman Gladiolus Co., Sylvania, Ohio, sent a collection of cut dahlias for exhibition. One of the varieties sent was a beautiful shade of pink, of seemingly extraordinary merit, and it was very

favorably commented upon. Nathan Smith & Son, Adrian, Mich., sent some specimen blooms of cannas and chrysanthemums. The variety of the former was The Express, one of their own production. It is a bright crimson, trusses large and compact, and much like Philadelphia. The chrysanthemums included Cremo, the yellow sport from Glory of Pacific, and Amorita, a large incurved flower, bright, clear pink with strong stem and heavy foliage. The latter was especially fine and most favorably commented upon by all.

The general activity in local circles the first part of the month was of short duration. The very mild weather of the present time and past two weeks is evidently responsible for a depression in business not at all usual at this season of the year, and it is doubtful if we ever before had such an abundance of flowers in excess of the ordinary demands. A glut is apparent in every direction of roses, carnations and chrysanthemums. The early varieties of the latter are fast maturing by the untimely warm weather that we are having. Some violets are being picked but they are yet small, light colored and meet with slow demand. Growers and retailers alike, are complaining, and cold weather is looked to for relief. No killing frosts have yet appeared, and all outdoor flowers are still uninjured.

The twenty-five members of the Club visited, in a body, the East side florists, including the establishments of B.Schroeter, H. Flammer, Chas. Plumb, Geo. Rackham and the Breitmeyers' Mack avenue place, October 16. Everywhere a kindly reception was given the visitors. The pleasures of the day were ended with a few games on the alleys at Pfeiffer's. The west side florists will be visited in like manner October 23, and the annual outing of the club to Mt. Clemens will take place October 30, leaving the City Hall by special car at 10 a. m.

The Belle Isle Horticultural building is now about completed and open to the public. It cost $60,000 and was under construction the past year.

Beard Brothers have found a sport from a Boston fern on their place. It is identical in every respect with Nephrolepis Piersoni.

Andrew Ferguson, Collins street, is building a new chimney and making many other improvements.

Philip Breitmeyer and J. F. Sullivan visited the growers of Grand Rapids Thursday, 22nd.

A. Woodward's 5 and 10 cent store has put in a flower department to operate on Saturdays only.
Fred Breitmeyer started for New York, October 21, in the interest of his new rose.
Visitors: W. H. Watson, Lapeer, Mich.; Dan'l B. Long, Buffalo, N. Y.; H. D. Byers, Dayton, Ohio.   J. F. S.

Columbus, O.

The Livingston Seed Company is erecting three new houses, 16x100, but using the Hippard duplex gutter. It is the intention of the company to build all further houses with iron gutters and flat tile tables. The company is growing 10,000 chrysanthemums for the retail trade and is now cutting some fine Bassetts and Robinsons. It has just finished cutting a table of fine Estelles.

RUTHERFORD, N. J.—Thomas Knight is now with Julius Roehrs.

Uncle Sam :- "Waal. I guess we must give the Old Country best in some Things."

U.S.A.   BRITAIN

W. W. JOHNSON & SON, Ltd., Boston, England,

Growers and Exporters to All Parts.   Invite correspondence from the Seed Trade of the United States,

Farm with Greenhouses

For Sale or To Let.

Two modern Greenhouses for market growing. 24 acres with fruit orchards. Commodious house and barns. One mile from Brockport, N. Y. Fine country place near Normal School. Perfect climate. Apply

Thos. V. Pierson,

BROCKPORT, N. Y., R. F. D.

Please mention the American Florist when writing.

DAHLIAS Pot Roots

Largest and most up-to-date collection in the world.
Cactus vars. of 1902 ....$12.00
   "   "   1901 .... 6.00
   "   "   1900 .... 5.00
   "   best of older vars ....$3.00 to 4.00
Pompon vars ....$4.00; newest 6.00
All per 100 in 25 or more sorts. Special price for 1000, 10,000 or 20,000 lots. Carefully packed f. o. b., Liverpool. Cash with order.

The Horticultural Company

CHEADLE-HULME, England.

Please mention the American Florist when writing.

Eine absolute Nothwendigkeit!

Hiermit $1.00 für mein Abonnement. Es ist die Pflicht eines Jeden prompt für den „American Florist" zu bezahlen, weil dieser eine absolute Nothwendigkeit für jeden Blumenzüchter ist.

Carl Roegner, Alabama.

FLOWER SEEDS

For Present Sowing.

10 Per Cent Special Cash Discount, on Orders over $2.00 for Flower Seeds if the Cash is enclosed.

BROWALLIA SPECIOSA MAJOR. The plants grow only about a foot high, form dense little bushes, which are covered the entire year with an abundance of the most delightful sky-blue flowers. Trade pkt. (250 seeds), 25c.

ASPARAGUS PLUMOSUS NANUS, 100 seeds, $1.00; 250 seeds, $2.00; 1000 seeds, $7.50.

SPRENGERI, 100 seeds, 30c; 1000 seeds, 75c; 5000 seeds, $3.25.

DECUMBENS, produce vines, 3 feet long, clothed with bluish green leaves. Cultivate like A. Sprengeri. 100 seeds, 65c; 1000 seeds, $5.10.

SCANDENS DEFLEXUS, suitable for hanging baskets and to cut. 100 seeds, $1.50.

CANDYTUFT, Giant Hyacinth-Flowered. This strain is superior to 'Empress. Sow now out-doors. Lb., $2.50; pkt., 10c; oz., 30c.

Empress. Our strain of this is extra fine, lb., $1.60; pkt., 10c; oz., 20c.

VAUGHAN'S GIANT FLOWERED CYCLAMEN. Our seed has been grown for us by a specialist in Europe. Shape and size of flowers, foliage and stems, are points on which seed plants are selected. Pure White, (Mont Blanc), Dark Crimson, Rosa von Marienthal, "Daybreak" Pink. White with Carmine Eye, 100 seeds, 65c; 1000 seeds, $6.00; 250 seeds at the 1000 rate.

GIANT-FLOWERED CYCLAMEN. Extra Choice Mixed. This mixture is made up from the above separate colors. 100 seeds, 50c; 250 seeds, $1.15; 1000 seeds, $4.50; 5000 seeds, $20.00.

NEW GIANT ORCHID-FLOWERED CYCLAMEN. We have the following separate colors. (Order by number). No. C 100. Lilac Colored, 10 seeds, 30c; 100 seeds, $2.50. No. C Eye. Each, 10 seeds, 35c; 100 seeds, $3.00. No. C 105. White with Red 101. Pure White. No. C 105. Giant Orchid-Flowered Cyclamen in choicest mixture; all the above and others. 25 seeds, 40c. 100 seeds, $1.50.

ASPARAGUS PLUMOSUS NANUS.

101. Dark Red, fringed. No. C 102. Pink, fringed. No. C 103.

GIANT ORCHID-FLOWERED CYCLAMEN in mixture; 35 seeds, 85c; 100 seeds, 75c.

DRACENA INDIVISA. Trade pkt, 10c; oz., 30c; lb., $2.50.

SWEET PEAS: Extra Early Blanche Ferry, pink and white, ¼-lb., 10; lb., 3'c. Earliest of All, Pink and white, ¼-lb., 10c; lb., 30c. Countess of Radnor, lavender. ¼-lb., 10c; lb., 25c. Emily Henderson, white, ¼-lb., 10c; lb., 35c. Josephine White, white, ¼-lb., 15c; lb., 50c. Mont Blanc, white, ¼-lb., 15c; lb., 50c. Lady Grisel Hamilton, lavender, ¼-lb., 15c. lb., 50c. Prima Donna, soft pink, ¼-lb., 15c; lb., 50c. For other sorts see our book for Florists.

Vaughan's Seed Store,

Chicago.   New York.

Please mention the American Florist to advertisers.

Los Angeles.

LACK OF RAIN KEEPS VIOLETS BACK.— LARGE CARNATION FIELDS OF THE REDONDO NURSERY COMPANY.—NOTES OF THE TRADE.

Henry Feder, president of the Redondo Nursery Company has 50,000 carnation plants in his field divided almost equally between Los Angeles, white; J. J. Corbet; pink; and Dr. Choate and Alegatiere, scarlet. He intends cutting about 3,000 good flowers daily during the season. He also has 25,000 violet plants and expects to pick 200 bunches of sixty each daily. On a contract selling the carnations at $1 per hundred and the violets at 85 cents per dozen bunches, it may be readily seen that a good income is assured. The only enemy to be feared is Jack Frost.

Violets are coming in but are so small that they do not command a ready sale. It requires rain to make nice violets in this country. Irrigation will not do it.

Independent growers of plants and general bedding stock are waking up and a generally superior grade of goods is being put on the market. They not only command a better price when true to name but confidence is gained and larger sales result. The trade generally looks forward to doing far more business than last year.

The old trouble in getting competent men is still experienced here. F. Edward Gray of the Ingleside Floral Company became discouraged, let his man go and is managing his own gardens.

The Central Park Floral Company is already receiving hot house carnations from the Grace Hill nurseries. They are not quite up to what they will be a little later but are very fair.

Mrs. M. B. Hariston has opened a floral store and built a greenhouse at Silver City, New Mexico. She will purchase most of her cut flowers in Los Angeles.

P. G. Murray, of Fresno, who purchased the "Up To Date" Floral Company on South Broadway some months ago has sold out and returned to Fresno.

Chrysanthemums are beginning to come. They seem to be of better quality than for several years past and retail from $2 to $3 per dozen.

The Woods Floral Company has moved from South Broadway to Fourth and Spring streets and has a much better location.

The Elite Floral Company has moved from West Fourth street near Hill street to Main street near Fourth. POPPY.

Albany, N. Y.

A late caller was Harry Bunyard, with the Clucas & Boddington Company, New York. Harry made a very optimistic report on the state of trade in his line and the popularity of the AMERICAN FLORIST.

Trade during the last week has been largely confined to funeral work and minor orders.

H. G. Eyres went to New York early in the week to purchase stock.

JOLIET, ILL.—The McCray Refrigerator Company, of Kendalville, Ind., is installing for the Chicago Carnation Company a fine new tile lined refrigerator.

LENOX, MASS.—It is expected that the annual fall exhibition of the Lenox Horticultural Society, to be held Oct. 27-29, will this year be the finest ever given in western Massachusetts.

OUR PASTIMES.

Announcements of coming contests or other events of interests to our bowling, shooting and sporting readers are solicited and will be given place in this column.

Address all correspondence for this department to Wm. J. Stewart, 79 Milk St., Boston, Mass.; Robt. Kift, 1725 Chestnut St., Philadelphia, Pa.; or to the American Florist Co., Chicago, Ill.

At Colorado Springs.

At the last meeting of the Florists' Club the Colorado Springs Florists' Bowling Club was organized, with W. H. Evans president, J. B. Braidwood vice-president and Wm. Dunman secretary-treasurer.

            S. S.

At Chicago.

At the meeting of the bowling club, October 21, arrangements were made to hold the annual meeting next Thursday evening, October 29, at Phil. Hauswirth's store, Auditorium annex. All florists and persons in the allied trades are invited to attend and join the club if not already members.

A number of the members of the club were entertained by W. N. Rudd, October 27.

The Decoration of Home Grounds.

No. 10.—A brick walk, made with the ordinary rigid lines, but has since become a beautiful path by being let alone. The habits of the owner are not destructive of anything that is kind enough to develop beauty where he may gaze upon it.

Catalogues Received.

Samuel C. Moon, Morrisville, Pa., nursery stock; M. Rice & Company, Philadelphia, Pa., florists' supplies; Wm. Paul & Sons, Waltham Cross, Herats, Eng., nursery stock; Thos. Meehan & Sons, Philadelphia, Pa., hardy plants; Harlan P. Kelsey, Boston, Mass., rhododendrons; John Lewis Childs, Floral Park, N. Y., bulbs and plants; Bay State Nurseries, North Abington, Mass., nursery stock; P. James & Sons, Ussy, France, nursery stock; W. W. Thomas, Anna, Ill., strawberry plants; Wm. Elliott & Sons, New York, bulbs; Peter Henderson & Company, New York, agricultural seeds and bulbs; Paul Swanson, Chicago, mushroom spawn; The H. S. Taylor Nursery Company, Rochester, N. Y., nursery stock; Sackett Brothers, Lebanon Springs, N. Y., nursery stock; Frederick H. Horsford, Charlotte, Vt., nursery plants; Glen Saint Mary Nurseries, Glen Saint Mary Fla., nursery stock; H. P. Kelsey, Boston, Mass., hardy plants and nursery stock; Weiland & Risch, Chicago, cut flowers; Reasoner Brothers, Oneco, Fla., nursery stock; Thaddeus N. Yates & Co., Philadelphia, Pa., nursery stock; Barr & Sons, London, Eng., bulbs; Clucas & Boddington, New York, bulbs, seeds, etc.; Cherry Hill Nurseries, West Newbury, Mass., phlox, nursery stock; J. Lambert & Son, Trier, Germany, hydrangea; Jas. B. Wild & Brother, Sarcoxie, Mo., nursery stock; Schlegel & Fottler Company, Boston, Mass., bulbs, plants, etc; Sanders & Sons, plants; W. E. Caldwell Company, Louisville, Ky., tanks. etc.; W. B. Rowe & Son, Worcester, Eng., new apple; Wilhelm Pfitzer, Stuttgart, Germany, plants, bulbs, etc; Hardy Plant Farm, London, N. Eng., bulbs; V. Lemoine & Sons, Nancy, France, bulbs; Robert Holmes, Tuckswood Farm, Norwich, Eng., daisy; Victor Detriche, Angers (Maine-et-Loire) France, plants, bulbs, etc.; Max Kornacker, Wehrden, a. d. Weser, Germany, bulbs.

Cleveland.

C. W. Fuller was appointed receiver of the Grant-Wilson Floral Company, October 7, by Judge Neff. Mrs. Elia G. Wilson filed a petition asking for a dissolution of the corporation.

M. A. Wilhelmy, for years a south side florist, attempted suicide, October 13, but will recover it is thought.

Baltimore.

Maj. Venable, president of the park board, estimates that $2,000,000 will be sufficient to carry out the plan for a chain of parks connected by parkways or boulevards. The legislature will be asked to pass an enabling act for the city to issue bonds for the work.

German Perfume Making.

United States Consul-general Guenther, stationed at Frankfort, Germany, writes to the State Department under date of September 5, 1903, as follows:

The city of Grasse, the most important industrial place of the Riviera, is widely known on account of its perfume manufacture. At present thirty-five concerns making essences of flowers are in operation there. The average consumption of roses for that purpose is about 3,650,000 pounds and that of orange flowers about 660,000 pounds per year. The annual sale of these essences amount to $1,000,000. Vallauris has nine such factories.

The most important product of this industry is oil of neroli, made from the flowers of the bitter orange. A kilogram (2.3 pounds) of this oil is worth $60. From the peel of the bitter orange oil of orange is made. The peel of the sweet orange is seldom used for making oil. The manufacture of essence of roses is also very extensive. The so-called oil of roses is manufactured from the grass Andropogon Schoenanthus.

The flowers of the large-flowered jasmine yield the oil of jasmine. A hectare (2.471 acres) planted with jasmine is said to yield a yearly product worth $3 000, but requires a great deal of work. Field violets formerly brought from $1 to $3 per kilogram (2.2 pounds); at present, however, they bring only 50 cents. A kilogram of essence of violets is worth from $4.50 to $5.

Oil of geranium is produced from the flowers of Pelargonium capitatum. The flowers of the tuberose, of the jonquil, and of a species of narcissus are manufactured into essences; also the leaves of the citronella plant, the root of the Iris Florentina (Violet root), the patchouli and sandalwood, etc. Fortunately for many places in the Riviera, the consumption of these essences has not decreased in late years.

Although some of these perfumes are bad for the nervous system, others are recognized as antiseptics. It is claimed that the typhus bacillus is killed in twelve minutes by essence of cinnamon, in thirty-five minutes by essence of thyme, and in eighty minutes by essence of patchouli.

No. 10. THE DECORATION OF HOME GROUNDS.

St. Paul.

LONG RAINS CEASE AND FROSTS MAKE TRADE IMPROVE. — CHRYSANTHEMUMS PLENTINUL.—NEW VARIETIES OF CARNATIONS ARE DISPLAYED.

After several weeks of rain and darkness the weather is again settled. By a peculiar circumstance trade was at its height during the worst weather, but frost has now cut off outside' stock and trade is improving each week and shows an increase over a year ago. Chrysanthemums are coming in quite freely. Roses have improved in quality. Ivory, which is being grown here for the first time, shows a decided improvement over its parent, Golden Gate. Liberty is much better than ever before. American Beauties have been coming in freely but sell readily. Carnations have scarcely commenced blooming in the proper manner, though some very good specimens have been seen on the market. Enchantress appears to lead all others here in size of bloom, length of stem and vigor of plant. A few sample blooms of Nelson Fisher and Mrs. M. A. Patten were received a few days ago. Fisher is best described as an improved Lawson. The blooms are as large or larger, the stems strong and erect and the color a decided improvement on Lawson. Patten is a large, bold bloom, pure white, lightly streaked with pink. It is a variety that sells at eight. Violets of fair quality are coming in now. They sell readily.

Aug. S. Swanson has sold his Minneapolis business to his brother, who managed it, and who will continue at the the same place. Mr. Swanson will shortly open a store on East Sixth street in this city. He will retain his present store in the Endicott Arcade.

J. D. Thompson, of Joliet carnation fame was a visitor during the week. H. V. Hunkle and W. G. Schricht, of Milwaukee, were also callers.

E. F. Lemke and Christ. Hansen are both on the sick list. FELIX.

Colorado Springs, Col.

Trade is in a very healthy condition, responding to the stimulus of the cool weather and increased social activity. Flowers are becoming more plentiful and of better quality, but there is still a scarcity of high grade roses and carnations. Violets of fine quality are coming in and are used as fast as available. Chrysanthemums have made their appearance and are rapidly increasing in numbers. There are very few poorly grown ones to be seen, and there seems to be no likelihood of an oversupply.

At Tuesday night's meeting of the Horticultural Society the chief business transacted was the election of officers. W. W. Williamson was unanimously chosen president; Wm. Clark, first vice-president; W. H. Evans, second vice-president; A. T. Reed, secretary, and J. B. Braidwood treasurer. The committee on schedules and awards will meet soon to begin the work of preparing next year's flower show programme. Arrangements were made for the annual drawing contest. The society each year secures the design for the cover of its flower show program from the pupils of the public schools through a prize contest. About $13 will be offered, the prizes to number about eight, from $5 down.
S. S.

SAN FRANCISCO, CAL.—The State Floral Society has promised to render all aid possible in making the new park at Telegraph Hill one of beauty.

Kansas City, Mo.

CARNIVAL WEEK PROFITS STOREMEN.—STOCK IS AMPLE.—ABANDONMENT OF FLOWER SHOW A DISAPPOINTMENT.

Social affairs have begun and storemen wear smiles. Stock, locally, is ample to supply the demand and of fair quality. Chrysanthemums are beginning to show up fairly well. A nice lot of yellow Monrovia will come in very conveniently or horse show week. Quite a number of fancy chrysanthemums were grown hereabouts this season under the impression that there would be a flower show this fall. Outdoor violets are coming in very well and command a ready sale. The prevailing wholesale prices of roses and carnations are about the same as Chicago prices. This has been an unexceptionally good season for fall flowers such as cosmos and dahlias, the latter, such as Gloriosa and Goliath, in crimson, and Livoni, in pink, make a gorgeous display and find a ready sale.

Carnival week brought its usual number of out of town visitors and the storemen who handle small plants profited thereby, for the trade that week runs to small purchases by country people and lots of bargaining is required to complete sales. There were no notable decorations. Convention Hall was prettily adorned, but principally with lights and bunting, no greens being used except palms.

Geo. Kellogg has remodeled his Grand avenue store and with Mr. Ellsworth in charge something ought to be doing up on the hill.

Mr. Helje, of the Rock Flower Company, is passing out good cigars in honor of the arrival of an eight-pound boy.

Recent visitors: Paul Berkowitz, of Philadelphia, and Mr. Ford, representing Hermann's, of New York.   W.

Tewkesbury Center, Mass.

The town of Tewkesbury has not been known many years in the floral world, but with the invasion of M. A. Patten & Company, A. Roper, A C. Kingley and others it has become prominent as a carnation center, in fact the largest I believe in the eastern part of Massachusetts. M. A. Patten & Company's place is now a veritable sea of glass. A new 33x300 foot house was built last summer. By its side are nine others, although not all 300-footers. Here one can see all the up-to-date varieties of carnations growing, including Enchantress, Fairmaid, Mrs. Patten (named after the owner's wife), Lawson, Her Majesty, Harlowarden, Goddard Yellow, Queen, Boston Market, Dorothy Whitney, Harry Fenn and Manley. One house is planted with mignonette, a sport from Allen's Defiance, which looks very promising. Another is devoted to A. Sprengeri and the new fern, Personi.

At A. C. Tingley's place there is a very fine stock of chrysanthemums, carnations, violets, callas, etc. A. Roper, like M. A. Patten, grows nothing but carnations, but grows only plants that were born here. This is the home of Fairmaid and here you can see it in all its glory. Another variety is Edwin Sheppard.

Lew Smith is picking some violet blooms of excellent quality, both single and double varieties. Lewis Small is growing carnations. Fairmaid predominates, other varieties being Enchantress, Lawson and Boston Market. George Foster's carnations are of good quality.   A. M.

Heavy Rooted Carnations Now Ready

California Carnation Co., Lock Box, 103, LOOMIS, CAL.

Denver.

The Curtis Park Floral Company held its annual meeting October 8, at which some decided changes were made. The following officers were elected: Oliver Wheatley, president; A. E. Gregory, vice-president; Benton Gregory, secretary; John Satterthwaite, treasurer. Thus one of the oldest firms in the west is again in possession of new blood.

Mrs. Mauff's Fifth avenue place has perhaps the record of the season as far as improvements are concerned. The new 90-foot brick stack is now completed and the four new American Beauty houses are as perfect as experience and money can build.

Interest in bowling is growing and Denver must certainly be heard from next year at the convention.   LYLE.

Providence.

Outdoor flowers suffered a relapse during the cold nights late in September, but the following warm weather brought another good cut of asters and tided over an apparent shortage of funeral flowers. By this time the dealers are falling back on greenhouse stock and readily obtained pink and white carnations at $1 to $1.50 per hundred. Roses are in supply at from 2 cents to 6 cents and violets can be had at 50 cents per hundred. Business is satisfactory generally. A few chrysanthemums sell at $2.50 to $3 per dozen, but two weeks must elapse before there is any hope of a steady call. The demand for house plants is poor and one is prompted to believe the department stores have "queered" this branch of florists' trade.   M.

FAIRMONT, W. VA.—H. Glenn Fleming has just completed one of the largest flower growing houses in this part of the country. This is his second plant, the first being at his residence where there was no ground room. The building covers 75x120 feet of ground, exclusive of the furnaces, offices and packing house.

Elmira, N. Y.

At a meeting of the directors of the United States Cut Flower Company, held at New York, October 13, it was definitely and finally decided that the plant of the company would be located on the site already selected on the Horseheads road where the old Halfway house was formerly located. The flower company will purchase this site outright. R. O. King, one of the directors of the company, and the consulting engineer, will arrive in Elmira soon to survey the site.

It is the intention of the company to put a gang of men at work at once grading the land and cutting the sod. This sod will be cut and piled so that it can decompose and make rich dirt for use in the plant next year The greenhouses, which it is expected will have an area of a million square feet of glass, will be made in the factories this winter. These houses are so far made that they can be quickly put together and erected. The houses will be erected in the spring.

The orders have already been given for the propagation of the carnations, roses, violets, chrysanthemums, etc., that will be raised in the Elmira plant and by a year from now it is expected the company will be ready to fill orders.

Nephrolepis Ferns.

NEPHROLEPIS BOSTONIENSIS. A large lot in fine condition, bushy and of a beautiful deep green color. From 5-inch pots, 30c each; 6-inch pots, 40c each.

NEPHROLEPIS CORDATA COMPACTA. Clean, bushy plants from 5-inch pans, 30c each; 6-inch pans, 40c each.

NEPHROLEPIS DAVALLIOIDES FURCANS. Nice sturdy plants, well established in 2¼-inch pots, with 8 to 10 leaves, $8.00 per 100.

NEPHROLEPIS PLUMOSUS. From 2½-inch pots, and just as well shaped as above, $8.00 per 100. From 2¼-inch pots, $6.00 per 100.

NEPHROLEPIS EXALTATA. Strong, 2½-inch pot plants, $5.00 per 100.

NEPHROLEPIS PIERSONI. Having purchased a large stock in the spring, and being short of room, we are now compelled to offer at reduced prices. None better for the money. All sizes offered are well established. From 2¼-pots, $3.00 per dozen; $22.50 per 100; $200.00 per 1000. Large plants from 4-inch pots, 75c each; 5-inch pans, $1.00 each; 6-inch pans, $1.50 each; 7-inch pans, $2.00 each; 8-inch pans, $2.50 each.

NATHAN SMITH & SON, ADRIAN, MICH.

Boston Ferns

	Per 100
2½-inch	$ 4.00
3-inch	8.00
4-inch	15.00
5-inch	25.00
6-inch	40.00
7-inch	60.00
8-inch	$75.00

PIERSON FERNS.

2½-inch	$20.00
4-inch, Each,	.50
5-inch, Each	.75

Our ferns are of the finest quality, short, bushy and of beautiful color, Cash must accompany order.

DAVIS BROS., Geneva, Ill.

A Choice Lot of
BOSTON FERNS

in 5-inch and 6-inch pots,
25 cents each.

WAGNER PARK CONSERTATORIES, Sidney, O.

PLEASE mention the AMERICAN FLORIST every time you write to an advertiser.

PALMS, FERNS, ETC.

We offer good values; saving in express and freight to buyers west of Ohio.

BOSTON FERNS. Nephrolepis Exaltata Bostoniensis.

We have the finest stock in the West. All our plants are pot-grown, bushy stock, well furnished with fronds from the pot up, and cannot be compared with the cheap, long-drawn-up, lifted stock from the bench. A sample shipment will convince you of our superior stock.

	Each	Per doz.	Per 100
2½ inch pot plants	$	$ .60	$ 5.00
3 " " "		1.50	10.00
5 " " "	.50	5.00	40.00
6 " pan "	.75	8.00	60.00
7 " " "	1.00	10.00	75.00
8 " " "	1.50	15.00	
9 " " "	$2.00 to 2.50		
10 " " "	3.00 to 3.50		

PIERSONI FERN.
Well-grown, bushy stock.

2½-inch pots	$25.00 per 100; $200.00 per 1000
4-inch	$ .75 each
5-inch pots	1.00 each
6-inch pots	1.50 each
7-inch pots	2.50 each
8-inch pots	3.00 each

ANNA FOSTER FERN.
Elegant stock.

2½-inch pots	$ 8.00 per 100
3-inch pots	15.00 per 100
4-inch pots	25.00 per 100
5-inch pots	50 00 per 100
6-inch pots	$ 9.00 per dozen
7-inch pots	12.00 per dozen
8 inch pots	18.00 per dozen

RUBBER PLANTS. (Ficus Elastica)

Very fine well-grown perfect plants.

5-inch pots, 18 to 20-inches high..........per dozen, $4.50; per 100, $35.00
6-inch pots, 22 to 24-inches high..........per dozen, 6.00; per 100, 45.00

Latania Borbonica.

Extra strong stock.

4-inch..........per dozen, $2.50; per 100, $20.00
5-inch..........per dozen, 4.00; per 100, 38.00

Cycas Revoluta.

With fine crowns, pots full of roots. Plants in all sizes from 25c to $3.00 each, at 5c per leaf.

Asparagus Plumosus Nanus. We are Headquarters.

2½-inch pots..........per doz., 75c; per 100, $5.00
3-inch pots..........per doz., $1.00; per 100, 8.00

Send for our Special Price List of Palms, Ferns, Araucarias and Rubbers.

If you are a buyer of Palms, Ferns, etc., a personal visit of inspection to our Greenhouses at Western Springs, Ill., (one-half hour's ride from Chicago), will pay you. Long Distance Telephone No. 221 Western Springs, Ill.

CHICAGO. Vaughan's Greenhouses, WESTERN SPRINGS, ILL.

Palms and Asparagus.

	Pots.	Leaves.	In high.	12	100
Latania Borbonica,	3-in.	4-5	8 10	$.75	$ 5.00
"	5-in.	3-5 chr.	12-15	2.00	15.00
"	5-in.	3-5 "	15-18	2.50	18.00
Kentia Belmoreana,	2½"	2-4 "	8-10	1.50	10.00
"	3-in.	3-5 "	10-15	1.75	13.00
Asparagus Sprengeri, 2-inch pots					1.50
Asparagus Plumosus, 2-inch pots					3 00
Begonias, 3-inch pots					5 00

We grow a large assortment of Hardy Shrubs and evergreens. Prices made on application.

SHERMAN NURSERY CO.
CHARLES CITY, IOWA.

Piersoni and Anna Foster Ferns

Piersoni,	2½-inch pots	$22.00 per 100
"	7-inch pots	2.00 each
"	8-inch pots	2.50 each
Foster,	2½-inch pots	7.00 per 100
"	6-inch pots	10.00 per doz.

Extra fine stock. Write us.

GEO. M. BRINKERHOFF, Springfield, Ill.

The Most Popular Fern
The Anna Foster.

At $35.00 per 100, for 6-inch pots from bench. Pot Plants, 50c, 75c, $1.00, $2 00, $3.00, $4.00 and $5.00 each; very fine.

BOSTON FERNS.

Large plants, from bench, $50.00 per 100.

Very fine **KENTIA PALMS**, at 50c to $3.00 each.
Asparagus Plumosus Nanus, 3-inch, $8.00 per 100.
Asparagus Sprengeri, 3-inch, $4 00 per 100.

L. H. FOSTER,
45 King Street, DORCHESTER, MASS.

Finest lot of Pot-Grown
BOSTONS
in the West. All sizes.

Write **GEO. A. KUHL, Pekin, Ill.**

Successful Growers are Wanted

To know that they can dispose of all their surplus stock by advertising in the American Florist. TRY IT NOW.

Buffalo.

ARRANGEMENTS FOR CHRYSANTHEMUM SHOW NEARLY COMPLETED.—PRIMULA OBCONICA SELLS WELL.

J. H. Rebstock and S. A. Anderson are having a warm dispute over their cyclamen plants as to which are the largest and most perfect. They are going to put them before judges when in bloom. The exhibit will probably take place at one of the Florists' Club meetings.

Trade is about as good as can be expected. The weather is moderate but a cooler spell for the rest of the month would be very acceptable. The Buffalo Florists' Club Flower Show is booming. Chrysanthemums are plentiful but not of many varieties. Violets are fine. One of our leading dry goods stores is celebrating an anniversary and G. D. Hale had an elaborate decoration.

J. H. Rebstock had a large wedding last week, the second one in the same family within a few months. Joe can stand them right along if the daughters hold out.

The funeral of ex-Postmaster General Bissell created a demand for a few very choice bunches, but no elaborate designs, simplicity being the wish of the family.

Collins & Forbach, who succeeded L. H. Rapin, of Pine Hill, have every prospect of a fine stock this winter.

Byrne & Slattery are running a flower stand at the Mardi Gras, which is being held at Convention hall.

W. J. Palmer & Son have had several out-of-town weddings within a radius of fifty miles of Buffalo.

J. C. Pickelman, of Chippewa street, had a big run of funeral work last Saturday and Sunday.

W. F. Kasting is making a spirited run for county treasurer and will certainly poll a big vote.

L. H. Neubeck is nearly ready to move into his new store and greenhouse.

Wm. Scott is cutting a fine lot of chrysanthemums at Corfu.   BISON.

Visitors: Chas. H. Ford, Philadelphia, Pa.; W. C. Stroh, Attica, N. Y.; Jerry Brookin, Orchard Park, N. Y.

Minneapolis.

Trade conditions have been at a low tide the last few days. There seems to be more than enough stock to supply all orders. White carnations are the only flowers in demand. Chrysanthemums of early variety are appearing, and will daily increase from now on. Roses and carnations will probably witness a decided lull in demand until after the chrysanthemum season is over.

The Minneapolis Floral Company has rented space in Northrup, King & Co.'s store on Nicollet avenue, where they will retail the surplus of their production. Some choice Mme. Chatenay were displayed in their window.

Oscar Swanson has purchased the Minneapolis store of August Swanson and will carry on the business. Heretofore he was manager for his brother.

Wm. Donaldson & Co. have had large decoration orders the last week, receiving a greater share of the trade the social functions have called for.

The flower department of Powers' Mercantile Company under the management of C. Johnson is commanding an extensive trade.

E. Nagel & Co. report trade of a good average. They are cutting some good sized carnations and also choice chrysanthemums.

Ted Nagel was on the sick list for a few days last week.   C. F. R.

Milwaukee.

BUSINESS IS GOOD AND STOCK IS PLENTI-
FUL.—FLORISTS' CLUB'S NEW QUARTERS.
—TRADE NOTES.

Business has been very good during
the past week with plenty of stock to fill
all orders. Carnations are improving in
quality daily and will be in good condition in a few weeks. Mme. Chatenay
roses are in excellent demand. Sunrise is
also taking well here. American Beauties are coming in in good shape, especially those grown by Adam Zender.
Plenty of chrysanthemums to fill all
orders are available, but the quality is
not of the best. Violets are very fine and
are to be had in quantity.

The Milwaukee Florists' Club has
secured quarters in the Empire building
and will hereafter have a nice room. The
club is prosperous and is now making
arrangements for a big chrysanthemum
show to be held next year. It was impossible to have a show this season owing
to the work of the S. A. F. convention.

Ferdinand Knorr is now running the
greenhouses on the Schandien place for
commercial purposes. This was the finest
private place in the city.

The entire force at the greenhouses of
the Holton & Hunkel Company is busy
packing plants, the business in this direction increasing rapidly.

F. P. Dilger has completed his new
house and is now busy planting his
Dutch bulbs of which he grows several
hundred thousand.

Ben Gregory had the misfortune
recently to fall and break his hip but he
expects to be out in a short time.

W. Freytag has turned his attention to
building dwelling houses on some of his
land.

McKenney & Company have been busy
with funeral work the past week.

The Boston store has opened a plant
and flower department.

Wm. Edlefsen spent a week in St. Louis
visiting relatives.

C. B. Whitnall has been appointed on
the school board. H.

QUINCY, ILL.—The house of F. W.
Heckenkamp, florist, was wrecked in a
cyclone here October 6. A large chimney
was blown down, tearing through the
roof and splintering the rafters. Trees
and shrubs throughout the southern
end of the city were ruined.

Lowell, Mass.

REIGN OF CHRYSANTHEMUMS BEGINS.—
MRS. ROBINSON OFFERED.—ALL VARIETIES
EARLIER.

Once more the queen of autumn has started her splendid reign of two months. The early varieties are fast disappearing to make way for the crack-a-jacks which are showing up daily. Mrs. Robinson is already on deck in all its glory. The way these blooms are coming in would indicate that they are earlier than last season. Business has been brisk the last week. Several wedding decorations have used up some good stock. The largest decoration so far this month was the Chalifoux-Ellsworth nuptials, the material used mostly being autumn foliage and white chrysanthemums. The florists here received somewhat of a jar when the job was let to a bunting decorator. Patten furnished the flowers for the table, which consisted of white chrysanthemums standing 3 feet high. McManmon furnished the plants and chrysanthemums for the decorator. One of the swellest affairs of the season will be the Pollard-Sheppard wedding the night before Thanksgiving.

The last three days of last week were busy ones at the Highland Conservatories. They were having their eighth annual opening. The crowds that attended were larger than ever before. The ten houses under the supervision of William Hodge were all arranged to look very pretty especially at night, when they were flooded with electric light from vari-colored incandescent lamps. Saturday was children's day. Each child visitor was presented with a Paper White narcissus bulb.

McManmon has embellished the front of his shop by putting out a couple of bay trees.

Some of the finest chrysanthemums being sent in are coming from Peter Healy.

George W. Patten has had his store front painted. A. M.

AUBURN, ME.—It was a son-in-law and not a daughter that George M. Roak added to his family, as stated in our issue of October 3.

Meetings of Florists' Clubs.

BALTIMORE. MD.—Gardeners' Club of Baltimore. Royal Arcanum buildi g, 18 W. Saratoga street. Second and fourth M nday of each mo th, at 8 p. m. John J. Perry, Sec'y; Gay and Eager streets.

BOSTON, MASS —Gardeners' and Florists' Club of Bos on, Horticultural Hall. Meets second Tuesday of each month. Oc ober in Mer h inclusive. W. K. Fiacher, Sec'y, 18 Union Terrace, Jamaica Plain, Mass.

BROCTON. MASS. — Brocton Gardeners' ard Florists' Club. state of W. W. Hathaw-y, Times Buil ding. First an l third Tuesday of ea-h mon h at 8 p. m. W. W. Hathaway, Sec'y. Brockton, Mass.

BUFFALO. N. Y.—Buffalo Florists' Club, 481 Washington street. Second Wednesday of each month, at 8 p. m. Wm. Legg, Sec'y, 1440 Delaware avenue B ffalo.

BU-TE. MONT —Mon ana Flori ts' Club, 44 W. B oadway. First Saturday in each month. D. E. Law, Sec'y.

CHICAGO. ILL —Chicago Florists' Club. Handel Hall. 40 Randolph street. S cond and fourth W-dnesday of each month. at 8 p m. George Wienhoeber Sec'y, 413 Elm street, Chicago.

CINCINNATI O.—Cincinnati Florists' Society. Jabo: E liott Flower Market. Second Saturday of each month a 8 p m. Geo. Murphy, Sec'y Sta. F., incinna i, O.

CLEVELAND, O —Cleveland Florists' Club Progress Hall 344 Detr it street. second and fourth Monday of each month, at 8 p. m. Isaac Kennedy, Sec'y, Westpark 'l.

DENVER COL.—Denv r Floral Club, 313 Charles Block. Second an l fourth Fr day of e ch month, at 8 p. m. Adam Balmer, Sec'y.

DETROIT, MICH.—De roit Florists' Club. Cowie Buildi g, Farran and Gratiot avenue. First and third Wednesday of each month at 8 p m. J. F. Sullivan. Sec'y. 314 wood ward avenue

GRAND RAPIDS, MICH.—Grand (a) ids Florists' Club, B ard of Trade rooms. Pe-rl s reet Fourth Monday of each month. N. B siever, sec'y Grandville, Mich.

HAMILTON, ONT.—Hamilton Gardeners' and Florists Club 12061 James street. North. First and third Tuesday of each month at 8 p m. Chas. M. Webster, Sec'y.

HARTFORD, CONN.—Hartford Florists' Club. Second and ourth Tuesday of each month at 8 p. m. J F Coombs Sec'y.

INDIANAPOLIS. IND.—State Florists' Association of In iana. Commercial Club rooms. Indianapolis. First Tuesday of each month. at 8 p m. H. Junge. Sec'y, 456 E. Washington street, Indianapolis.

MILWAUKEE, WIS.—Milwaukee Florists' Club. Meets first Tuesday of each month at St. Charles Hotel clubrooms. H. V. Hunkel, Sec'y.

MINNEAPOLIS, MINN. — Minneapolis Florists' Club. West Hotel. First Thursday of each month. at —p. m. C F. Rice. Sec'y, 11- N. Sixth street.

MONTREAL QUE —Mon real ardeners' and Florists' Club leased-in rooms, 2204 St Catherine street F r-t and third Monday of each month. W H Hor-bin S c'y 23 Cl-sse street.

NEW LONDON, CONN.—Gardeners' and Florists' Club, first and third Tuesday of each month at greenhouses of each iety. H. B. Appeldorn. Sec'y.

NEW YORK. N. Y.—New York orists' ociet. aut. Grand Op'r-Hou-e Bldg.. 8th avenue and 23d St Second Monday of each month, at 7:30 p. m. John Young, Sec'y, 51 West Twenty-eighth street. New York

OMAHA NEB.—Nebraska Florists' Society. City Hall. Second Thursday in each month at 8 p. m. Louis Henderson, Sec'y, 1519 Farnam street, Omaha.

PHILADELPHIA, PA—Florists' Club of Philadelphia. Horticultural Hall. Broad street above B ruce. First Tuesday of each month at 8 p. m Edwin Lonsdale, sec'y W ndsmoor Philadelphia.

PITTSBURG. PA.—Pittsburg and Allegheny Florists' an- Garde ers' C ub, at Gorman Ben-ficial Bldg., 6th and Cherry avenue. Seco d Thursday of each month. at 8 p. m. H. P. Joslin. Sec'y. Bet veen Pa.

PROVIDENCE R. I.—Florists' and Gardeners' Clu of Rh de Isl and. Swarts, 88 Westmins er street. Providence Second Thur day of each month at 8 p. m. Alexander Reonie, Sec'y, 41 W ashington street, Providence.

RICHMOND, IND.—Richmond Florists' Club at the ore shouses of members. Th id Monday of each month. H. l. Cheasman, Sec'y.

SALT LAKE CITY, UTAH.—salt Lake Florists' Society. office of Hudd rth Floral Company, 214 E Second South str-et. Second and fourth Fri ay o' eac h mo-th. P. T. Huddart, Sec'y.

SAN FRANCISCO. CAL.—Pacific Coast Horticultural society. First Saturday and third Monday of ea-h mo-th. Wm. H. Munroe. Sec'y.

SEATTLE WASH.—S attle Commercial Horticultural Club First and Cherry a-enue. First Wednes lay of each month. Wm. Hopkins. Sec'y, 502 First avenue.

ST. LOUIS, MO.—St. Louis Florists' Club. Odd Fellows Hall No 2. Ninth and Olive stre-te, Second Thursday of each m onth. at 8 p m. Emil Schray. Sec'y, 4101 Pennsylvania avenue. St. Louis.

TORONTO, ONT.—Toronto Gardeners' and Florists' Association. St. George's Hall. Elm street Third Tuesday of each month, at 8 p. m. E F.

Coll'ns, S o'y, 2 Hurst place. Toronto.
UTICA, N. Y.—Utica Florists' Club, 183 Genesee street F rst Thursday or each month at 8 p m J. C. Spencer, S o'y.
WASHI GTON. D. C. — Washington Florists' Club. Meets first Wednesday in each month. Wm. F. Gude, Sec'y.

Coming Exhibitions.

[Secretaries are requested to supply any omissions from this list.]

BOSTON. MASS. November 5-8. 1903.—Chrysanthemum exhibit in Massachusetts Horticultural Society. W. P. Rich Sec'y, Horticultural Hall, 300 Ma-sachusetts avenue, Boston.

B FFALO, N. Y., November 11-14, 1903.—H. A. Me-drum Co.'s flower show: direction, Buffalo Florists' Club. Wm Legg Sec'y, 1440 Delaware avenue, Buffalo.

INDIANAPO IS, IND., November 10-14, 1903.—Indiana Flo al Festival and Chrys nthemum exhibition State Florists' Association of Indiana. Irwin Bettermann. Sec'y, 211 Massachusetts avenue, In ianapolis.

LENOX, MASS., O tober 27-29 1903—Fall exhibition Lenox Horticultural Society. Fred. Hardens. Se-'y, Lenox. Mass.

MADISON. N. J., November 5-6, 1903.—Annual exhibit ion Morris County Gardeners' and Florists' Society. S. Redstone, Sen'y Madison. N. J.

NEW YORK. November 10-12, 1903.—Chrysanthemum exhibition Chrysanthemum Society of America. Fred H. Lemon. Sec'y Richmond. Ind.

PHILADELPHIA, PA. November 1-14, 19 3.—Annual exhibition Penns lvania Horticultural Society. David Rust. Sec y, Horticultural Hall, Philad-lphia. Pa.

MONTREAL QUE. November 11-12, 1903.—Chrys-anthemum exhi tion Montreal Gardeners' and Florists Club W H. Horobin. Sec'y, 23 Closse street. Montreal.

PROVIDENCE, R. I., November 12-13, 1903.—Chrysanthemum exhibition Rhode I land Horticultural Society. C. W. Smith. Secretary, 27-29 exchange street Providence.

ST. PAUL. MINN., November 10 to 12, 1903.—Chrysanthemum and orchid exhibition Ladies Auxiliary of Northwestern Manufacturers' Association. Mrs. M. Helen Moss, Sec'y, St. Paul.

TARRYTOWN, N. Y., November 4-6. 1903.—Fifth annual exhibition Tarrytown Horticultural Socie y. Edw. W. Neubrand, Sec'y, Tarrytown. N. Y.

MOLLER'S DEUTSCHE

GARTNER ZEITUNG

The most widely circulated German gardening journal treating of all departments of horticulture and floriculture. Numerous eminent correspondents in all parts of the world. An advertising medium of the highest class.

Moller's Deutsche Gartner Zeitung is published weekly and richly illustrated. Subscription $8 00 per annum, including postage. Sample copies free.

LUDWIG MOLLER ERFURT, Germany

Greenhouse Building.

Pittsburg, Pa.—Pittsburg Country Club, range of greenhouses.
Fairbury, Ill.—Kring Brothers, one carnation house 30x300.
New Orleans.—Abel Brothers, one house.
Springfield, Ill.—David Wirth, two houses each 24x130, one house 10x130, for carnations and ferns. Carl Rauth, addition to house. Miss Belle Miller, one house.
Ann Arbor, Mich.—F. Worden, house.
Dudleyville, W. Va.—Dudley & Son, one house.
Hartford, Conn.—Drake & Carlson, one house.
Wakefield, Mass.—C. A. Gardner, one house.
Adams, Mass.—A. J. Boothman, two houses.
Rutherford, N. J.—Julius Roehrs, house 25x150; two houses each 15x120. Large range of palm houses rebuilt.
Detroit, Mich.—Fred . Pautke, house 30x23, for violets and carnations.
New Bedford, Mass.—Mr. Mosher, one house 16x60.
Pittsburg, Pa.—Benj. Elliott, American Beauty house 30x100.
Elizabeth, N. J.—Mrs. C. M. Hutchinson, one house 36x100.
Baltimore, Md.—House of Refuge, carnation house 25x125.
Sterling, Mass.—Ole Nelson, two houses each-10x51.
Chatham, N. J.—C. L. Trowbridge, house 100 feet long.
Stonington, Conn.—Dr. Maine, conservatory.
Lenox, Mass.—John E. Alexander, range of conservatories.
West Gloucester, Mass.—S. T. Haskell, one house.
Gardner, Mass.—J. R. Davis, cucumber house.
Hanover, Mass.—Mrs. E. Q. Sylvester, one house.
Norway, Me.—F. H. Cummings, one house.
Silver City, N. M.—Mrs. M. B. Hariston, one house.
Hartford, Mich.—W. H. Blashfield, one house 15x40.
Cromwell, Conn.—A. N. Pierson, one house.
Mercer, Pa.—James Clelland, house 28x200.
East Greenwich, R. I. — Pierce & Hawkes, two cucumber houses each 175 feet in length.
Elwood, Ind.—Albert Duebendorfer, two carnation houses 18x50.
Swansea, Mass.—Traynor Bros., cucumber house 18x275.
North Beverly, Mass.—C. E. Streamberg, conservatory.
Keene, N. H.—Ellis Bros., violet house ninety feet long.
Essex, Conn.—F. Scholes, one house.
Columbus, O.—Livingston Seed Company, three houses each 16x100.
Carlstadt, N. J.—Jacob Hullman, two houses 11x100 feet.

GRAND RAPIDS, MICH.—Miss Harriet Cross, sister of Eli Cross and J. C. Schipman were married October 14.

LONG ISLAND CITY, L. I.—The Jamaica board has accepted a plot of land at Ingleside offered the city for a public park valued at $40,000.

COLUMBIA, MO.—The forty-ninth annual meeting of the Missouri Horticultural Society will be held here December 8-10, and promises to be the greatest meeting the society ever held.

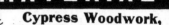

THE AMERICAN FLORIST

A WEEKLY JOURNAL FOR THE TRADE

America is "the Prow of the Vessel; there may be more comfort Amidships, but we are the first to touch Unknown Seas."

Vol. XXI.　　　　**CHICAGO AND NEW YORK, OCTOBER 31, 1903.**　　　　**No. 804.**

THE AMERICAN FLORIST

NINETEENTH YEAR.

Copyright 1903, by American Florist Company
Entered as Second-Class Mail Matter.

PUBLISHED EVERY SATURDAY BY

AMERICAN FLORIST COMPANY,
324 Dearborn St., Chicago.
Eastern Office: 79 Milk St., Boston.

Subscription, $1.00 a Year.　To Europe, $2.00.
Subscriptions accepted only from the trade.
Volumes half-yearly from August, 1901.

SOCIETY OF AMERICAN FLORISTS AND ORNAMENTAL HORTICULTURISTS.
Officers—John Burton, Philadelphia, Pa., president; C. C. Pollworth, Milwaukee, Wis., vice-president; Wm. J. Stewart, 79 Milk Street, Boston, Mass., secretary; H. B. Beatty, Oil City, Pa., treasurer.
Officers-elect—Philip Breitmeyer, president; J. J. Beneke, vice-president; secretary and treasurer as before. Twentieth annual meeting at St. Louis, Mo., August, 1904.

THE AMERICAN CARNATION SOCIETY.
Annual Convention at Detroit, Mich., March 2, 1904. Albert M. Herr, Lancaster, Pa., secretary.

AMERICAN ROSE SOCIETY.
Annual meeting and exhibition, Philadelphia, March, 1904. Leonard Barron, 136 Liberty St., New York, secretary.

CHRYSANTHEMUM SOCIETY OF AMERICA.
Annual Convention and exhibition, New York, November 10-12, 1903. Fred H. Lemon, Richmond, Ind., secretary.

THIS ISSUE 40 PAGES WITH COVER.

CHRYSANTHEMUM COMMENTS.

N looking over the early varieties we find we are still deficient in extra early pure white, pink and yellow. Of the Glory of Pacific type, Crane, a yellow sport, is an acquisition; and those who are successful with this class need have no hesitancy in growing the yellow form. Estelle, the white sport, sent out last season, so far as we can see, is identical with Polly Rose. We had both varieties planted side by side upon the same bench and grown under the same conditions.

It seems strange that varieties of American origin possess so much more commercial value than those originated in foreign countries. If we scan the list of varieties which have been imported during the past fifteen years, we find there very few that have stood the test from a commercial standpoint. Probably W. H. Lincoln of 1889, V. Morel of '91, and Golden wedding of '93, are the most prominent and are to-day grown to a considerable extent.

Among the new comers of foreign origin, there are several which are unquestionably acquisitions. The first one of mention is Etienne Bonnefond, Calvat, 1903. In color it is a golden bronze, resembling Boule d'Or in this as well as in form, but more vigorous and much more easily handled. An incurved Japanese with large diameter and great depth, it will be a welcome addition to the bronze section, and to use the pugilistic term, it will be a hard hitter.

Mme. Henry Douillet is another of great promise. It is a bright rose with a slight violet tinge and a silvery reverse. The form is very much like the old variety Mrs. C. Harman Payne, extremely double, with every appearance of being a good variety for exhibition purposes.

Henry II. is another variety which possesses the dwarf habit so much desired in this country for commercial varieties, but the color is bronzy red. It will be very acceptable as an exhibition flower, being fully double.

Mlle. Martha Morel possesses great diameter, and if it can be grown strong enough to secure an early bud, may be an acquisition, but from late buds it is too single for commercial value. The color is beautiful, a light Daybreak pink.

Mme. A. Duhamel is not fully developed, but promises well, and from present indications I believe it is going to be a splendid white.

M. Paul Labbe is a very beautiful bright amaranth with a decided purplish reverse; a flat flower but of great diameter, about eight inches.

All of the foregoing are of Calvat's origin for the present year, and are of dwarf, sturdy growth.

Among other newer kinds we notice a resemblance between Sensation, an English variety, and Mrs. Harry Emmerton, of Australian origin. It is difficult to separate the two.

The King, a new incurved variety of English origin, promises to be of unusual English origin, promises to be of unusual size and to be sought for by those interested in exhibitions. Its color is too dull for commercial purposes.

In the crimson section there are many additions that are very interesting, both those of crimson and old gold and those of a purplish crimson hue. We might mention such varieties as Louis Leveque, Mrs. C. J. Salter, Millicent Richardson, Quo Vadis, T. Humphreys, Lord Hope, toun, Chas. Longley and Henry Barnes. Our flowers are not sufficiently advanced to allow us to write intelligently upon their real value. It will require some ten days before this will be fully determined, but from the appearance of the buds it is safe to predict some marked improvements in these colors.

In the yellow varieties there are also a number that appear very fine at this writing, such as C. J. Salter, Mrs. H. Emmerton, F. S. Vallis, Calvat's Sun and Mrs. Thos. W. Pockett.

In the foreign varieties there is a great dearth of pink. Most of the importations are inclined to be yellow, bronzy yellow or crimson. The Australians, however, have furnished us several that are, quite prominent, such as Daisy Moore, Lucy Evans and Silver Queen, which have every appearance of being first-class. Among the whites, Guy Hamilton, a large loose, tubular petaled variety, from present indications will outrank all others in diameter. Mrs. J. C. Neville promises well, has fine buds and will eventually develop a wonderful bloom.

The variety disseminated last year as Mrs. J. F. Tranter we find by referring to English authority, should be Mrs. J. R. Trantor. This is a wonderful flower in many respects, having extremely long tubular petals which are nearly or quite white from crown buds. From late buds they are splashed with pink. The ends

Chrysanthemum Wm. Duckham.

of the petals hook up, making a very graceful appearing bloom and one of the largest size.   ELMER D. SMITH.

W. DUCKHAM AND CHELTONI.

We waited long and expectantly for a pink chrysanthemum that should be on an equality with the good white and yellow ones. The outcry has been, too much white and yellow, give us pink, and in the endeavor to supply the cut flower market with pink the fickle and uncertain Viviand-Morel has been the grower's mainstay, but with more vexation than profit. We need no longer deplore the paucity of pink, however, for an early pink variety, Mrs. Coombes, improves with age and is here to stay, and succeeding it Marie Liger has strengthened the good impression it created last year. In W. Duckham, however, we have the advent of a peerless beauty of surpassing merit, vigorous in growth, stout in stem, well clothed with heavy foliage and crowned with a flower that may be termed perfection alike in form, finish and color. Our English contemporaries gave it great praise when it won the silver medal at Edinburgh last year, but some of their greatest acquisitions have refused to adapt themselves to American conditions. Here we have one that asserts itself at once, attains the zenith of chrysanthemum beauty in its first season, and apparently deserves the highest meed of unqualified praise. Chrysanthemum W. Duckham was raised in England from Australian seed, and probably herein lies the secret of its ready adaptability, since

the Australian varieties have already shown a facility of response more marked than those entirely of European origin. The flower photographed is from a bud taken early in August. Those from later buds differ from it only in showing a greater breadth of petal. A photograph at hand of the same flower, shows a portion of the stem. The short neck is no detriment, in fact rather enhances the beauty of the flower by giving it a slight elevation above its mantle of luxurious foliage, so that the eye can better appreciate its bold yet graceful contour. The color is a clear, uniform, light pink.

Cheltoni is a sport from Nellie Pockett. It is in every respect a counterpart of its parent in a really good shade of yellow, altogether brighter than is usually seen in a yellow sport from a white variety. There appears to be a slight variation in form, the petals more closely infolding, giving more solidity to the flower. Should this prove a constant characteristic it will make Cheltoni much more amenable to commercial needs, while the private grower for home use will find it a gem.   A. H.

WORK OF THE C. S. A. COMMITTEES.

There were six varieties before the Chicago committee Saturday, October 24. The results of the committee's examination follow:

Mrs. H. W. Buckbee, exhibited by H. W. Buckbee, Rockford, Ill.; pure white, center incurved, outer petals reflex, Japanese; scored, commercial scale, 91 points.

Rockford, by the same exhibitor, yellow, Japanese incurved; scored, commercial scale, 88 points.

Cinna, exhibited by the E. G. Hill Company, Richmond, Ind.; deep yellow, Chinese type; scored, commercial scale, 85 points.

Lord Hopetoun, by the same exhibitors; color of Geo. W. Childs, Japanese; scored, commercial scale, 87 points.

Ethel Fitzroy, by the same exhibitor; bronze and gold, Japanese; scored, exhibition scale, 86 points.

Mme. J. H. Perraud, by the same exhibitor; cream colored, Japanese; scored, commercial scale, 80 points.
          FRED. H. LEMON, Sec'y.
Richmond, Ind.

Colors in Foliage and Flowers.

All who are accustomed to observe vegetation must have been struck with the great variety of shades of green which the foliage of different plants presents, writes a correspondent of the Journal of Horticulture. It may also be noticed that the same description of plant will exhibit very characteristic differences, not only at different stages of growth, but at the same stage, in different conditions of luxuriance, as affected by the external conditions of soil, season and manuring, but especially under the influence of different conditions of manuring.

From some researches made at the Rothamsted Experimental Station on this subject, it was found that the green chlorophyll formation in plants has a close connection with the amount of nitrogen assimilated, but that the carbon assimilated is not in proportion to the chlorophyll formed. Further, it has been found that the presence in the soil of certain mineral or ash constituents of plants, and especially of potash, is essential for the assimilation of carbon, no starch being formed in the grains of chlorophyll without the aid of the element potash.

In regard to the colors of flowers, it

has been found by Dr. Hansen that there are three distinct pigments which make up the different tints, in addition to chlorophyll, which forms the green coloring matter in the stems and foliage of all plants. These colors are yellows, reds and blues. The yellows are mostly in combination with the plasmic sap, while the others exist chiefly in solution in the cell sap. The yellow pigment forms an insoluble compound with fatty matters, and is termed lipochrome. Orange is formed by a denser deposit of yellow, and the color in the rind of an orange is identical with that found in many flowers. The red in flowers is a single pigment, soluble in water and decolorised by alcohol, but capable of being restored by the addition of acids.

Lipochrome, combined with this red pigment, produces the scarlets and reds of poppies, and the heps of roses and hawthorns. But the varying intensity of reds in roses, carnations and peonies and other flowers, depends on the presence of a greater or lesser quantity of acids in the soil or in the manure employed. This may be one of the reasons why superphosphate of lime, which is always more or less acid, forms such an excellent manure in the growth of most flowering plants. The blue and violet colors are also decolorised by alcohol, but are reddened by acid solutions. Florists have already succeeded in producing many unusual colors in flowers, and there seem to be very good grounds for believing that it is possible so to manipulate nature by means of chemical manurial agents that she will produce blossoms of every conceivable tint and hue.

Nolens Volens.

AMERICAN FLORIST CO.:—I like your paper best of all. I subscribed for the — because they persisted in sending me free sample copies, though I never wrote them in my life.
          Salem, Ind. O. P. FORDYCE. Florist.

Chrysanthemum Cheltoni.

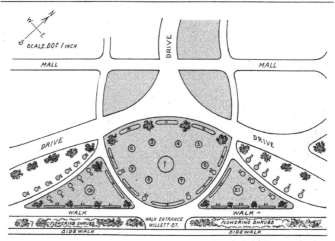

GROUND PLAN OF WILLETT STREET FLOWER GARDEN, ALBANY, N. Y.

Washington Park, Albany, N. Y.

The park system of Albany comprises Washington park, area ninety acres, Beaver park, seventy-eight acres, and a number of lesser reservations aggregating about eighty-five acres. Washington park was laid out w. s. egerton. thirty-three years ago and has the distinction of being one of the oldest in the long list of city parks now existing. Although of moderate extent as compared with many other metropolitan reservations it presents in a noteworthy degree every desirable feature of a popular recreation ground and is so cleverly laid out and planted that to the visitor it appears to be of much greater area than it actually is. Of the ninety acres, sixty-five are in lawn and six in water. There are six miles of walks and three miles of driveway, and points of interest are well distributed over the entire territory.

Although there are several buildings of considerable architectural beauty and two notable monuments—one being the famous Claverly statue of Robert Burns and the other a fountain surmounted by a figure of "Moses Striking the Rock"—yet the chief charm of Washington park lies in its simplicity, its restful landscape effects, its aquatic and tropical gardens—impressive, yet unobtrusive—and especially in the extreme neatness everywhere prevalent.

There are two sections of moderate extent reserved for flower gardens, one known as the Willett-street garden and the other as the Fountain garden. A view in the first of these is herewith

given. Of all the examples of park bedding which the writer has seen the Willett street garden pleases best. The grouping is in good taste as to form and colors, well adapted to cater to the popular love for flowers and massed colors, yet without strained effects, and when seen at its best in the July and August days goes far to remove the prejudice born of distaste at the incongruous constructions and discordant mixtures one finds so often in grounds of this character.

A good view of the gardens can be obtained from several slight eminences and the city constructions are entirely concealed by the border plantings. The skyline in any direction is particularly effective, and at early morning or sunset the garden has great charm. The beds about the fountain are composed of verbenas and heliotropes planted in mass. We think, however, that the fountain would look much better if these formal features in its immediate neighborhood were omitted, but the designer appears to have been the original offender in placing a regular stone curb around such a work.

To give a better idea of the contents of the various flower beds than is afforded by the accompanying illustration we present a simple tracing of the ground plan of the Willett street garden and a complete index to the same as planted for 1903. Beds No. 1, 19 and 21 are combination sub-tropical foliage and flower beds for high center effect. The contents of the central bed (No. 1) enumerated from the center outward to the edge were Ricinus Borboniensis, Canna robusta, Canna Austria, Canna Crozy, Caladium esculentum, Salvia splendens, Ageratum Blue Perfection and

golden alternanthera. This bed is thirty-five feet in diameter and the central plants fifteen feet in height. Bed No. 19 was composed of Ricinus arborea, Canna Austria, Canna Alphonse Bouvier, Canna Pres. McKinley, Achyranthes Emersoni and golden alternanthera. Bed No. 21 was planted with Ricinus arborea, Ricinus Gibsoni, Canna Queen Charlotte, Canna Pres. McKinley, Achyranthes acuminata and golden alternanthera. Bed No. 2, Canna Mlle. Berat bordered with ageratum; No. 3 Canna Egandale with Cineraria maritima; No. 4, Canna Eldorado with red alternanthera; No. 5, Canna Manda's Ideal with variegated alyssum; No. 6 Canna Mme. Crozy with Achyranthes Emersoni; No. 7, Canna Alphonse Bouvier, with golden alternanthera; No. 8, Canna Queen Charlotte with Achyranthes acuminata; No. 9, Canna J. D. Cabos with Cineraria maritima; Nos. 10 and 12, Geranium Wm. Park (a dark red seedling) with Geranium Mme. Salleroi; No. 11, Geranium Streak of Luck with bronze alternanthera; No. 13, heliotrope with red alternanthera; No. 14 and 16, mixed geraniums with golden alternanthera; No. 15, Begonia Vernon and hybrids with bronze alternanthera; No. 17, heliotrope with bronze alternanthera; Nos. 18 and 20, tuberous begonias, single and double, bordered with bronze alternanthera; Nos. 22, 23, 24, 25, crotons in variety with Dracæna indivisa; Nos. 26 to 47, selected annuals changed several times during the season; Nos. 49 and 52, green-house plants plunged in pots; Nos. 50 and 53 ferns plunged in pots; No. 51, fancy-leaved caladiums; No, 54, coleuses in variety. At the corners of the walks, in the shade, the smaller palms and exotics were grouped. The illustration shows one of the beds of tuberous begonias, No. 18 in the diagram. This and the corresponding bed (No. 20) were among the most beautiful in the garden. The somewhat heavy effect of the large flowered varieties was overcome by a liberal use of such sorts as Duc Zeppelin, Vesuvius and Lafayette. All the beds are planted in the fall with tulips, hyacinths, narcissuses, crocuses, pansies, daisies, etc., for early spring effect.

The mall is a transit walk well shaded and arched over with large elms. This walk is bordered with large palms during the summer. The Willett street interior park walk is shaded on the street side by elms and a twenty-five foot border of flowering shrubs and or the garden side by Norway maples. There is a vista 1,800 feet in length extending through the park on this walk and on the mall The character of the tree growth is well shown in the illustration. The maintenance of the entire garden section is entrusted to one gardener who mows the grass, keeps the beds in order and answers numerous questions and does it all well. The preparation and planting is done by the park force. The details of the next year's planting are planned in advance and the number of plants of each variety to be propagated carefully estimated.

W. S. Egerton, the superintendent of Albany's park system, whose portrait we present herewith, has given the best part of his life to the park interests of the city, having had continuous charge of Washington park since its beginning a generation ago. He takes much pride in his work and is always ready to give full credit to his workmen when they do well. That he has held his position so long without interruption through all administrations is a striking tribute to his fitness and highly creditable to the city he serves.

BOOKKEEPING and account forms for same by R. F. Tesson, as read at the Milwaukee convention has been printed in pamphlet form by the AMERICAN FLORIST and will be mailed FREE on request to any florist. Employers may have extra copies to distribute among their employes. The address is of much permanent value and well worth the study of our young men.

The Rose.

THRIPS ON ROSES.

To kill thrips burn a double handful of insect powder in three pans for a house 20x100 feet. Put some paper under the powder, light it, and let it smoulder like punk.

CULTURAL REMINDERS.

We have now arrived at a season when it would be folly to attempt to do without steady firing in the rose houses. Generally this important matter is put off as late as possible for economy, but it is always well to make sure that economy is practiced and not neglect. At this time of the year very serious results are liable to be caused by neglect in ventilating and firing. On warm, muggy nights the steam should not be shut off, instead run one pipe and ventilate so the air will be dry and clear. When the houses are shut down close all night the air becomes sour and unfit for a strong growth, inducing mildew and black spot. The ventilation should be attended to at night as well as in the day, so as to avoid sudden changes. Remember plants need plenty of fresh air to produce a healthy growth, and at this season it is important the growth should be vigorous and hard.

Avoid any undue forcing. If the plants are late nothing will be gained by forcing them into an unnatural growth, as they will be weakened and the crops of inferior quality. Keep the plants continually tied, thereby allowing plenty of air space around them and also keeping the stems straight and stiff. The beds should be kept clean, allowing no decayed leaves to remain on them. If the sun is not allowed to reach the surface, the soil soon becomes sour and unfit for growth. Feeding the stock is another matter important at this time. On this depends the quality of the buds to be cut. If the plants were started reasonably early by this time they should have well filled the beds with roots and also exhausted what nourishment was in the soil. It is now necessary to supply them with the nutriment needed. Mulching is a very satisfactory method of reaching this end, and with reasonable care in preparing it and also in watering the beds after it has been applied the result should be gratifying. A mulch composed one-fourth of rose soil and three-fourths of rotted cow manure is very good at this time of the year. It should be well

pulverized and put on about two inches thick. It is well to work this over with the hands, occasionally breaking up the larger lumps and also giving a chance for the air to penetrate, thereby keeping it from becoming sour.

After the mulch has been applied it will be necessary to take care the watering is attended to properly, as it will be very easy to allow the lower part of the soil to become wet and sour when the surface appears in good condition. When testing be sure to go deep enough and not be deceived by the condition of the soil only two or three inches below the surface. In cloudy, damp weather air-slaked lime may be used to advantage, especially in the Beauty houses. Sow lightly over the soil and if the walks are wet a light dusting over will tend to sweeten the air in the houses.　　　R. I.

Palms and Ferns.

SUNDRY NOTES.

The outdoor culture of young palms in frames has sometimes been tested by growers, and when the summer proves to be warm through the greater portion of its length, some of the common species of trade palms may be thus grown fairly well, such a practice giving one an opportunity for making needed repairs and repainting the houses or portions of houses that are usually occupied by the small palms. Kentias and latanias may be handled this way as a makeshift, the plants being either plunged in some moisture-retaining material or planted out in a rich and well prepared bed, and being shaded from the sun with muslin or by shading the sashes and raising them on a framework sufficiently above the plants to allow a good circulation of air. Syringing must be attended to regularly in the case of these outdoor grown plants, else the insects will be liable to get ahead, and it is not quite safe to put such plants out of doors before the first or second week of June, the nights being frequently cool up to that time. The plants will be safer indoors after September 15.

If any of these young palms are planted out as suggested it must be taken into consideration that they will need some time in which to become re-established after lifting in the autumn, and on the whole it is doubtful if as much progress will be made by the outdoor plants as those that have been grown indoors for the whole summer, this method being rather a makeshift than an actual advantage when the changeable weather of our latitude is taken into consideration. One may control the conditions to a great extent when growing plants in a well arranged greenhouse, but there is a large volume of uncertainty in outdoor operations.

The fall sowing of fern spores should now be showing up nicely, and will need careful attention in the matters of watering and ventilation in order to prevent the seedlings from damping off. It is sometimes very difficult to avoid this fungus among the seedling ferns, the condition of the weather having much to do with it, but an attack is sometimes aggravated by allowing the seed pots to get too dry and then giving them a thorough soaking of water, the tiny seedlings having been weakened by the want of water, thus laying them open to the attack of the fungus. Keeping the seed bed moderately close during the day and ventilating freely at night is the best practice to observe, but even so there is

WILLETT STREET GARDEN, WASHINGTON PARK ALBANY, N. Y.

always a possibility of finding some well defined spots of fungus among the seedlings when making the morning examination.

Sometimes this fungus may be checked to some extent by sprinkling the affected spot with some fine dry sand, or a little air-slaked lime carefully dusted on, but

CANNA PAPA NARDY.
(Height four feet.)

if any seed pot seems to be badly affected it is safer for the welfare of the others to remove it from the frame and throw it away rather than to try doctoring it.

W. H. TAPLIN.

New Cannas at Vaughan's.

The latest improved cannas, not all of them, but the crack-a-jacks, or prize winners, as one might say, are planted out in a prominent place in the Vaughan grounds at Western Springs, Ill., and visitors to the place after the convention had a good chance to examine and pass on the merits of each in comparison with others. I got some field notes on this occasion, which I transcribe for the benefit of those who did not enjoy the privilege of seeing them.

Victory.—This one has been out three years. It has green foliage, is a strong grower and bears immense trusses of large orange flowers, with a small line of gold around the edge.

King Humbert.—This is the second year of this variety. It has dark foliage mixed with brownish green. It is darker in foliage effect than David Harum. The flowers are scarlet and immense in size.

David Harum.—Has brighter scarlet flowers, but they are not so large as King Humbert.

Seedling No. 100:—Second year, green foliage, scarlet flowers, very fine, solid self color of the purest scarlet shade.

Papa Croxy.—Second year, dark foliage, about the same shade as David Harum. Flowers are orange scarlet and of good size.

Papa Nardy.—Second year, green foliage, big trusses of crimson flowers.

Express.—Almost identical in color with 801, but has green foliage and is a much dwarfer grower.

Seedling No. 801.—Second year, dark foliage, strong grower, scarlet, fine large flowers. I consider this a magnificent sort and, taking it all around, one of the very best up-to-date cannas at the present in existence, not forgetting the fine

novelties that have been introduced in the past year or two.

There were other varieties in the collection but these being better known a mention of them is not called for. I think Mr. Vaughan deserves a vote of thanks for having these novelties in such good shape for us to examine and I for one was grateful for the chance to see them.
G. C. WATSON.

The Carnation.

CULTURE TO AVOID STEM ROT.

From the amount of stem rot that is in evidence among carnations this season, I think it would profit growers to make this a special study. Some years ago when it got a start on my place, I read and studied everything available relating to this and kindred diseases in other plants. I am not prepared to prove that my present exemption from

is a variety I had last season. From the originator I had 250 plants. A few were lost from stem rot, or more properly speaking from cutting bench fungus, in the pots, a very few in the field, and when housed the disease progressed rapidly, the plants dying off continually until when thrown out in June there were only twenty good plants left. The latter part of January we took some 500 cuttings from the plants that were in good health at that time. (Quite a number of these died with stem rot before spring.) Some of the plants from the cuttings died from the drouth when planted in the field in the spring, but most of them are in the house to-day, planted in August and up to this day, October 24, there has not been one to die from any show signs of stem rot. As before stated, I do not want to claim that this is entirely due to my method of culture, but some of it may be and a few of the methods here described may be applicable to some grower having trouble with stem rot.

Never plant a cutting that has any sign of cutting bench fungus on it, for it will be almost sure to stem rot at some time in its existence. Plant your plants in the field on slightly elevated ridges with room enough between the rows to cultivate with horse and harrow. All this I have said before a number of times but it is good doctrine and will bear repetition. The field for your next season's planting should have immediate consideration. This matter is too often neglected in the rush of fall work, but is really as important as having the houses in which to force them. Here as everywhere else in nature some variation in treatment is productive of the best results. An ideal field is made by sowing rye or wheat as soon as the carnations are housed. Let this reach a good height in the spring and then turn it down for green manure and sow a quick growing summer grass. Turn this down in the fall and sow again to wheat, to turn down early in the spring when the field is considered ready for another planting of carnations. By giving it a liberal coat of manure just

CANNA EXPRESS.
(Height four and one-half feet.)

this dread disease is due to my system of culture, but I think it is and I base my assumption on the fact that I frequently get stem rot in a new variety and after propagating and growing my own stock it disappears. A notable instance of this

before the grass is sown you will have your soil in better shape than by applying the manure just before planting the carnations. But if your soil is of such a character that manure looses its value quickly then it is best to apply it when the carnations are planted. This gives your field one year for the preparation of the soil and one year for carnation growing, but it is the best paying investment you can possibly make.

Every fifth year, which is a grass year, the grass is turned down as late in the fall as possible just before the ground freezes, first applying a liberal coat of air slacked lime. It is left as 'rough as possible, no-harrowing being done and the plowing being as deep as the plow will run. No matter if the subsoil is turned up; it will be turned down again in the spring. This treatment allows the frost to act better on the soil than if it is left covered, and better than if it is left bare without plowing. The object of the late plowing is to catch any insects that may be in the soil and destroy some of them by the plowing and others by freezing them. The purpose of the whole treatment is to get the soil in good mechanical condition, a condition that is too often overlooked and that has quite as much to do with the health and welfare of your plants as fertilizers, or any other one particular thing. Another point is to see that the weeds are all cut down around the edges of the field and burned, as these weeds make a perfect harbor for thrips over winter and nothing worse can happen to the carnations in the field than to have a bad attack of thrips, unless you are luckier than the writer and know of some good practical remedy.

There is a sort of general opinion among some growers that an ideal carnation field is one that has been in grass for a number of years, but unfortunately these grass fields have been shown to be affected with stem rot to a greater or less extent, and this is my reason for sowing grass annually and plowing it down in the fall, following up with wheat for those years when I want the ground covered over winter. Ground that has been used for tobacco is not desirable for carnations, as tobacco is very susceptible to stem rot, and so are many varieties of our common weeds. Under no consideration should a piece of ground be used that has been allowed to grow up to weeds the previous season. For fertilizers in the field there is nothing the equal of good stable manure and an occasional application of air-slaked lime (occasional meaning, in this instance, every three to five years). Concentrated fertilizers are not necessary, in fact they are very often detrimental and should be used only in the houses where the supply of moisture can be regulated artificially. There are few soils that really need much in the way of a fertilizer to make good plants in a good season, but the liberal addition of manure will be a great help in an unfavorable season, as aside from its manurial benefit it keeps the soil in better mechanical condition, better able to get moisture to the plants by capillary attraction, better able to supply the natural plant foods that may be in the soil. If the soil is in poor mechanical condition it may be full of plant food and yet produce poor plants on account of these foods not being liberated properly and made available for the roots. Practice and science both agree in recommending crop rotation for keeping up the fertility and proper condition of the soil, and for carnations the rotation recommended seems to be as nearly right as it is possible to get.

Just as an object lesson in favor of crop rotation, it has been demonstrated by actual experiments that wheat can be grown on the same field for a period of

fifty consecutive years without any fertilizer being added to the soil in any way, shape or form, the yield decreasing from thirty-five to fifteen bushels per acre. A similar experiment extending over a period of forty years, alternating wheat with grass but without the addition of any fertilizer for either wheat or grass has kept up the yield to an almost equal amount each year (thirty-five bushels). This goes to show that rotation will even keep up the fertility of the soil without fertilizers. The method we employ increases the fertility of the soil (not as much as might be supposed from the amount of manure used) but enough to produce good results; and so long as we are improving and not deteriorating we are on the road to success.
A. M. HERR.

Sterilizing Soil.

The accompanying illustration shows the method of cooking soil with the boiler of an ordinary thrashing engine, employed by Davis Brothers, of Morrison and Geneva, Ill. A bed or bin 6x50 feet is constructed on one side of the soil pile,

Davis Brothers' Soil Sterilizer.

being made of 2-inch planks. Five rows of ordinary 3-inch drain tile are laid the full length of this bin. A box header is laid across the bin at the center with five holes in each side to let the steam out into the tile. The steam is conducted from the engine to this header through a 1-inch pipe. After the bin is filled level full of soil and boards are placed on top, the steam, already under pressure, is turned on and left until the soil is thoroughly cooked, which usually takes about forty-five minutes, with plenty of steam.

After one batch is steamed it is shoveled out, the tile relaid and the bin refilled again as quickly as possible. Soil can be cooked in the benches after the house are filled by the same method, placing the engine at the end of the house. In the sections of houses that are heated by steam the heating boiler is used instead of a traction engine, by turning the steam into the water pipe and connecting from faucet to header by a short hose, but this soon ruins the hose and the gaskets in the faucets.

Although sterilizing soil is considered an unnecessary expense by some growers,

we have taken the trouble for three seasons and think it pays and expect to cook every house another year. It not only kills all worms and insects in the soil but leaves it in nicer shape, soft, moist and thoroughly decomposed. All weed seed being killed, the expense and trouble of weeding is done away with.
D. B.

Espied in Philadelphia.

Robert Craig shows with satisfaction a big lot of cyclamens in 7-inch pots which are remarkable for size and luxuriance. They are but a year old, the seed having been sown in October, 1902. The flower buds have been kept carefully pinched off as they appeared all summer. The first house will be ready for market at Thanksgiving. Messrs. Craig lost 16,000 lights of glass in the late hail storm and it has caused them no little inconvenience. Mr. Craig in speaking of the effect of hail on glass of various sizes relates a little story where the joke is on himself. During the centennial year he bought a greenhouse in which the glass was 28x28. Entirely too large, he concluded, for safety so he had it all cut in halves.

George Anderson, being a profound philosopher, takes a broad view of the glass question and allows that hailstorms are helpful to the glass dealer, hence should be encouraged. It is worthy of remark, however, that he reaches an opposite conclusion when the lumber man's welfare is concerned as he confines his houses to solid beds principally, because benches are prone to rot and necessitate the buying of lumber. Mr. Anderson has just finished building a fine new even-span house and if he isn't proud of its mechanical execution he ought to be. The joints are like cabinet work.

Looking inside the houses we find some two-year-old Bon Silene and Safrano roses the crop from which is sold before it is grown, to Pennock Brothers; a house of American Beauty in which the plants were cut down close in summer as an experiment; several houses of roses carried over two years without any change of soil; some Liberty roses, three years old which look very fine; most of the roses on the place grafted stock; the glass in the new house laid the long way between the bars, but Mr. Anderson expressing lack of confidence in the superiority of this method. Altogether the establishment bears the impress of a man who is a good manager and runs his place economically and at the same time very successfully.

Close to Mr. Anderson's is the place of J. W. Colflesh, another of the old Darby standbys. His loss from the hail visitation was fortunately very slight. Here a house of the old favorite Jacqueminot roses recalls the lines of that tuneful idyl of a dozen years ago:

There's long-legged Willie Colflesh
Who lives upon a hill,
The last remaining friend of "Jacq"
Whose fame is living still.

Mr. Colflesh freezes up the Jacq beds and brings in a crop of bloom in spring in the time honored way. His houses contain a fine lot of palms, chrysanthemums, roses and carnations.

ELWOOD, IND.—Albert Dubendorfer is completing two carnation houses, each 18x50 feet.

INDIANAPOLIS, IND.—The Indianapolis News of October 24 states that the home violet market has been cornered by the Smith & Young Company.

The Retail Trade.

HOUSTONIA CŒRULEA, an American plant commonly known as bluets, has proved very attractive in England, grown as a pot plant.

PHYSALIS FRANCHETI, the Chinese lantern plant, is little heard of now. When first introduced it was found very useful in decorative work during the fall months.

CONIFERS FOR WINDOW BOXES.

This is the time when every effort should be made to encourage a more extensive use of conifers in exterior window boxes and vases. Get as much of this work done now as you possibly can. It is next to madness, nay even barbarous to have this work delayed until the soil is frozen, when shrubs are dug up with pickaxes, roots broken and the soil shaken away, and the work otherwise carelessly done, with the inevitable result that the work must be done over and you possibly lose a customer. A neatly written letter to your customers, explaining the advantage of having the work properly done now, will, in most cases, be considered and acted upon. Ivy seems to have done remarkably well this year. You need not disturb those growing in the vases or boxes, and when you order your conifers insist that the roots be kept moist.

There are tremendous possibilities in every large city for those who will specialize in garden work. A greatly increased quantity of trees, shrubs, bulbs and sodding could be used up profitably if proper methods were employed. As it is, the average florist turns his nose up at garden labor. To him it is negro or messenger boy work, and often where it is compulsory to take an order for such work the most inexperienced kind of help is sent to execute it. There are many thousands of small yards to-day which the owners would have beautified if they knew seeds and bulbs and plants could be purchased and planted properly at little cost. Amateur gardening is greatly on the increase. Modern architecture specially and prominently provides for both exterior and interior plant ornamentation; and the florist should be equal to every occasion.   D.

AN IMPERIAL WREATH.

One of the finest, most tasteful and best executed floral decorations I ever had the pleasure to see was the wreath laid on the sarcophagus of the late Queen Louisa, of Denmark, by Emperor William during his visit to Copenhagen. The wreath came from the establishment of Dina Schuldt, and as the illustration shows, was made of two magnificent cycas leaves with a bunch of smaller ones at the left side, decorated with callas and sprigs of laurel; next to these came Augusta Victoria roses on a body of violets and at the base by the ribbon Cattleva Trianæ on a base of Primula Sieboldi of corresponding color, the whole veiled with Adiantum cuneatum. The ribbons were in the German colors, with the Emperor's initials, W. I. R., in golden letters.

The wreath was about six feet in diameter. As it had to be delivered on very short notice there was no time for securing a photo of the wreath itself. This illustration is taken from the sketch in black and white submitted to the emperor, and is, of course, not as graceful as the wreath. The emperor was highly pleased with it and complimented the firm for being able to deliver so fine a decoration in so short a time.   H.

AN IMPERIAL WREATH.

Chicago Florists' Club's Exhibition.

The exhibition of the Chicago Florists' Club, October 24, was one of the most interesting and instructive ever held in that city. The exhibits being mostly novelties were of far greater importance to growers and dealers alike than a larger array of better known material. Too much praise cannot be bestowed upon the management, which kept so well in view the needs of the trade and only presented those features likely to be of value to those engaged in the business either for pleasure or profit. It is all the more pleasing to be able to make this record since the time for preparation was very limited. It was unfortunate, perhaps, that the day and duration of the show did not permit a larger number of those directly interested to view it. We understand, however, that future exhibitions will be arranged so that the greatest number may be benefited.

Chrysanthemums, of course, were the leading feature, and the comments of C. W. Johnson on these are appended. Car. nations were a strong second. The J. D. Thompson Carnation Company made by far the best display of carnations, staging eleven varieties, fifty of each, as follows: Nelson Fisher, Mrs. M. A. Patten, Enchantress, Adonis, Gov. Wolcott, Estelle, Boston Market, Lawson, Prosperity, Harry Fenn and Apollo. In the scoring, however, the Chicago Carnation Company, was first with Fiancee, which was given 91 points; the Mount Greenwood Cemetery Association was second with Phyllis, 90 points; the Chicago Carnation Company third with Reliance, 89 points. The other scores were as follows: F. Dorner & Sons Company, Lafayette, Ind., Lady Bountiful, white, 87; The Belle, white, 86; No. 193 (1900), pure deep pink, 82; and No. 37, white, striped and splashed, 75. J. D. Thompson Company, Nelson Fisher, cerise pink, 87; Mrs. M. A. Patten, variegated, 85. Chicago Carnation Company, Crusader, red, 85; No. 822 A, red, 85; Gunnar Teilmann, Marion, Ind., Marion Beauty, maroon, 79. B. K. & B. Floral Company, Richmond, Ind., Richmond Gem, scarlet, 75. The E. G. Hill Company exhibited a very fine vase of Adonis, and in the display of the Chicago Carnation Company we noticed John Hartje's Moonlight. Jos. Kohout, with Bassett & Washburn, exhibited ten vases of seedlings and a vase of Hannah Hobart. Several of the seedlings looked very promising.

John Breitmeyer's Sons' new pink rose, a vase of which was exhibited, attracted much attention, but Philip Breitmeyer assured us that the blooms were by no means at their best. The E. G. Hill Company exhibited an attractive yellow seedling rose which is considered an improvement on Perle. Nathan Smith & Son, Adrain, Mich., exhibited a vase of Express cannas; Vaughan's Greenhouses, Nephrolepis Piersoni and Christmas peppers; F. A. Baller, Bloomington, Ill., clematis blooms of very fine quality for this period of the year; and the Geo.

Wittbold Company a general collection of decorative plants.

The prizes offered by the Foley Manufacturing Company were awarded respectively to the E. G. Hill Company, Thompson Carnation Company and H. W. Buckbee. In the evening about forty-five, including guests, sat down to sup. per which proved an enjoyable affair.

The visitors included President Breitmeyer of the S. A. F. and J. F. Sullivan, Detroit, Mich.; Fred. Dorner, Jr., Lafayette, Ind.; Fred. H. Lemon, Richmond, Ind.; Otto Speidel, Oconomowoc, Wis.; Geo. F. Crabb, Grand Rapids, Mich.; B. Juerjens. Peoria, Ill.; Mr. Kring, of Kring Brothers, Fairbury, Ill.; C. W. Johnson, Rockford, Ill. and W. A. Hartman, South Haven, Mich.

CHRYSANTHEMUM EXHIBITS.

The first of the Chicago Florists' Club's new series of monthly exhibitions brought out an extensive array of extra fine blooms of chrysanthemums and carnations. The exhibitors of chrysanthemums were the E. G. Hill Company, Gunnar Teilmann, Nathan Smith & Son, Vaughan's Greenhouses and H. W. Buckbee. The E. G. Hill Company had much the largest display which was awarded the first prize for the best collection, the second prize going to the J. D. Thompson Carnation Company for a magnificent display of carnations, some of which were extra fine for so early in the season. The third premium on collections went to H. W. Buckbee for forty-four varieties of chrysanthemums, sixteen of which were of the curious and feathery type. The latter exhibitor placed before the judging committee two seedlings as follows:

Mrs. H. W. Buckbee.—Niveus × Mrs. Henry Robinson; pale white, slightly incurved, lower petals reflexing; flower of good size with fine stem and foliage; scored 91 points.

Rockford.—Mrs. Henry Robinson × Col. D. Appleton; yellow incurved, fine form; fine stem and foliage; should prove a good commercial variety; might be called a yellow Evangeline, which it resembles very much; scored 88 points.

The E. G. Hill Company exhibited four importations for certificate:

Lord Hopetoun.—Crimson, with old gold reverse, center incurving, while the outer petals reflex showing both colors to advantage; a fine large flower with strong stems and good foliage; scored 87 points.

Ethel Fitzroy.—Bronze, extra large, incurving flower, promising a best sort or exhibition; scored, exhibition scale, 86 points.

Cinna.—Yellow; short, reflexing petals with lots of substance; good stem and foliage, promising a fine commercial variety; scored 85 points.

G. Perraud.—Lemon color; a large flower, but not decided enough in color and apparently somewhat soft in petalage; scored 80 points.

The most prominent blooms in the E. G. Hill Company's collection included:

F. S. Vallis.—Carnot type, long reflexing petals, making an extra large flower; very fine.

Louis Leroux.—Bright amber color, incurving bloom of good size.

Mme. L. Chevrant.—Color a fine salmon pink; stiff petals, large flower; looks promising.

C. J. Salter.—A very fine yellow with handsome foliage.

Miss Olive Miller.—A large, deep pink.

M. P. Sahut.—A fine white.

Miss Alice Byron.—One of the very best

white varieties.

The select blooms in the H. W. Buckbee collection:

Mrs. T. W. Pockett.—A very large reflexing yellow.

Durban's Pride.—Large mauve pink.

Matchless.—A very fine large deep crimson.

T. Humphreys.—Large reflexing red.

C. J. Salter.—Yellow, extra fine.

Mlle. M. Douillet.—Reflexing white.

Mrs. Coombes.—Fine large pink.

Mme. E. Nicoulland.—Incurving white, fine form.

Nathan Smith & Son staged a number of single seedlings after the Mizpah type, also Creino, a light yellow sport from Polly Rose, and Amorita, a fine incurving pink.

Gunnar Teilmann showed big vases of Alice Byron, Mrs. Coombes and Col. D. Appleton, also a collection of varieties. Some of the latter were a little green and under done.

Vaughan's Greenhouses exhibited a vase of Mrs. Robinson.

C. W. JOHNSON.

Chicago.

ROSES AND CARNATIONS SCARCE AT END OF WEEK.—HORSE SHOW BOOMS VIOLETS.—ELABORATE PREPARATIONS FOR NEXT CLUB SHOW, NOVEMBER 17.

Everything was plentiful during the first part of the week, but towards the latter end there was a great scarcity of roses and carnations. Violets have met with ready sale, more on account of the horse show, which has been on this week at the Coliseum. New Orleans has been taking large quantities of flowers for All Saints day. Fall decorations have started and will similar seems to be the principal decorating material.

Chairman Dickinson of the Florists' Club committee advises us that the next exhibition will be held November 17, and preparations are under way to make it quite elaborate and more like our regular fall shows than that of last week. The printed announcements with regard to this exhibition will be ready and mailed early next week, together with the programme for the entire season. Leonard Kill has been appointed manager of this exhibition and John Risch assistant.

The following firms have recently started in business: Chas. Erlman, 1214 N. Halsted street; Chas. Heyme, 5422 S. Halsted street; Lincoln. Floral Company, J. and G. Granakopolos, proprietors, 1643 N. Clark street; J. Polatschek, 83 E. Monroe street.

Crabb & Hunter, of Grand Rapids, Mich., have taken space in the Flower Growers' Market and will make this place their headquarters in disposing of their product.

The John Crerar library is getting together a fine collection of horticultural and floricultural books. H. G. Selfridge is interested in the good work.

N. J. Rupp, of the John C. Moninger Company, reports that his firm has sufficient orders on hand to keep everyone busy till March.

J. P. Foley has had the stork around. It was a girl and that makes seven, but they are not all girls.

Jas. S. Wilson, of Vaughan's Greenhouses, has been at St. Louis this week on a business trip.

Orr & Lockett are building a fine ice box for Schiller's Jackson boulevard store.

Anton Then's son John recently celebrated his twenty-first birthday.

John Degnan, of the E. F. Winterson Company, returned October 30...

Visitors: Alfred Dimmock, representing Sander & Sons, of Bruges, Belgium; F. A. Dean, Esterville, Ia.

New York.

COLD WEATHER IMPROVES MARKET CONDITIONS.—BUSINESS CHANGES HANDS.—RAILROAD SETTLES WITH WADLEY.—ASMUS BOUND SOUTH.

The cut flower trade is just now engaged in a mighty effort to drag itself out of one of the worst slumps on record. Last week was a tough problem for everybody and it was a great relief when the weather came bravely to the rescue on Sunday. The temperature since has been almost wintry, and on Monday afternoon several flurries of snow gladdened the hearts of flower growers and wholesalers. This finishes the dahlia's reign for this season, and leaves the field open for the chrysanthemum to take possession. The worst of the chrysanthemums are already past. The receipts from now on will be mainly of the better grades, and already very handsome specimen blooms are in sight which bring substantial prices. Violets have shown a disposition to wake up under the influences of the bracing atmosphere. For the present, it is to be hoped that the twenty-five cent kind has done the vanishing act. The weather conditions are just right for better flowers and better demand. A prompt and decided improvement in the quality of roses is also now in order. While a general limbering up may reasonably be looked for, yet no one expects anything very remarkable in the way of business until after the shows are over and election day has passed into history. Among the specially nice things in choice cut flowers seen in the wholesale district this week were Cattleya Dowiana, of which John Young is receiving a regular supply, and cape jasmines, which are coming in regularly now to Young & Nugent. The end of the week found business almost at a standstill with the generality of stock very abundant and of best quality, but there was no activity in any line.

The Kurzman-Dacre Company, Inc., has bought out the New Jersey Cut- Flower Company on Twenty-eighth street and will open on Monday, November 2, as a retail and wholesale establishment.

Albert Wadley has settled with the railroad company for the injuries sustained in the tunnel collision, the amount received being $35,000.

Ernst Asmus is about to go south for the winter, on account of his health.

Visitors in town: Carl Jurgens, Jr., Newport, R. I.; Harry Bayersdorfer, Philadelphia, Pa.; Fred Brietmeyer, Detroit, Mich.

Philadelphia.

BUSINESS UP AND DOWN.—GOOD PRICE FOR CARNATIONS.—ABOUT FORCING DAHLIAS.—CUTTING AND SHIPPING FLOWERS.—OUT AND ABOUT.

The chrysanthemum is now queen and holds the boards, having but little trouble with its more or less attractive neighbors. Colonel Appleton and Ivory are two of the leading kinds that have been added to the assortment this week, and there are a number of new ones that it is hard to keep track track of. Weber, of Deer Park, Maryland, is sending some mammoth Eatons to S. S. Pennock that are world beaters. While the many kinds sent in are beautiful about twenty-five per cent are cut too soon and fail to give satisfaction to anyone who handles them. Some growers will persist in cutting and shipping at once. This stock rarely arrives in good condition and is most unsatisfactory. A little more care before shipping will more than pay for the trouble. It is the same with roses, many being cut too soon. They should be allowed to get some size on the plants and not taken as soon as big enough to see, as is often the case. A rose cut too green will open slowly, and by the time, if ever, it is of fit size for sale it is away off color and presents a stale appearance.

Business is quiet, some days bringing a brisk demand and others lagging, yet there appears to be no accumulation of flowers to speak of, all lines cleaning up fairly well at about the same prices as last week. The debutants are fairly started, and their teas and receptions are using much of the cream of the stock. Nothing is too good and the ingenuity of the florist is tried to avoid sameness, when so many bouquets are delivered at once. Carnations continue to improve and the standard is now so high that the best flowers are held at about the same price as good tea roses. Good Enchantress seems to bring 6 cents quite readily, which is about almost the top price for good Bride and Bridesmaid roses. Violets, both single and double, are scarce, the cool spell of the past week apparently holding them back. Dahlias are done; last Monday's frost finished them up. We understand that quite a few rose and carnation growers in this neighborhood sent letters of condolence to Atco which in a measure helped to assuage the grief of Brother Peacock. There is talk of forcing some of the white ones for Easter. Let us hope not; they are essentially outside garden flowers, and we feel sure they would not compare favorably with the flowers of spring.

M. Rice & Company report a fine run on their new screens for decorative purposes. They are six feet high by two wide, are made light and durable, and by fastening two or more together they stand up like the ordinary Japanese article. Used in connection with a few palms and clusters of flowers they add greatly to a decoration, particularly where a doorway is to be screened, and in many other ways they will be found useful. Mr. Rice says the season is a resord breaker.

S. S. Pennock is handling some fine orchids and finds a good demand for Dendrobium formosum, the white variety. He claims to have the largest stock of lily of the valley in the country, and it certainly seems so from the amount always in sight.

Mrs. M. D. Young has succeeded to the business lately conducted by her mother, Mrs. J. Wolf, Sr., at Ridge avenue and Dauphin street. Mrs. Young having had considerable experience in the business with her mother, will no doubt carry it on successfully.

C. A. Dunn & Company are going into florists' supplies in connection with their commission business and will keep a general line of ribbons, letters, wheat sheaves, wire frames, baskets, etc. The adjoining building has been added.

Mr. and Mrs. Brown, of Brown & Mann, Richmond, Va., were in town. Some American Beauty roses shipped from their place were quite the equal of the Philadelphia stock.

John Leach, of Habermede's, has returned to Chicago to Samuelson.

Visitors: H. C. Shauff, of Mrs. Williams' staff, Pittsburg; Charles L. Schmidt,

Harrisburg; W. R. Smith, Washington, D. C.; Francis Canning, Amherst, Mass.   K.

London.

The National Chrysanthemum Society's show held at Crystal Palace, was not quite equal to the exhibit at the Aquarium last year. Many growers complained that the wet season had kept the blooms back, and even those that should have been ready had suffered much from damping. However, there were some very good exhibits. Among the largest blooms I noted were Mme. Paolo Radaelli, Mrs. A. R. Wright, Mrs. T. W. Pockett, Mrs. G. Mileham, Mme. Von Andre, Lady Pearce, Gustave Henry, October Rose and Yellow Prince. A new variety, Renee, gained a first-class certificate. It is a Japanese with long, drooping florets of a peculiar shade of pink, suffused with mauve or lavender. The flowers are of good depth and well finished. It was raised and shown by Mr. Bullimore, of Edgware. I may here mention that the same grower brought up another fine variety to the Royal Horticultural Society's meeting October 13, but he came too late to submit it to the floral committee. It is a Japanese variety named Maud du Cros, a flower of great size, with long drooping florets of soft primrose yellow.

The trade exhibits at the N. C. S. were far from equal to last year. Mr. Davis had some large blooms and took the first gold medal offered by the Crystal Palace company, and Mr. Godfrey was second. Messrs. Cannell had some useful early varieties from the open ground, and Mr. Jones also had a collection which included some promising seedlings. We missed Messrs. Pulling, who have exhibited so well for several years, but their place seems likely to be taken by Messrs. Reed & Sons, who took first prize in the competitive class for a "group" with a very fine lot of plants.

At the Royal Horticultural Society's meeting on the thirteenth this firm again made a very fine exhibit, with plants carrying good foliage and large blooms. Veitch & Sons also staged a splendid group, certainly the best exhibit of chrysanthemums seen this season. Mr. Wells and Mr. Godfrey were also there with some cut blooms. Of other subjects of interest at the R. H. S. dahlias were well shown. Continued advance is being made with the cactus varieties. Hobbies, Ltd., exhibited some very pretty things, Dainty, Effective, Sweet Nell, Dorothy Vernon, Northern Star and Harbor Lights being among the best. Begonia Gloire de Lorraine and the Irvinford Hall variety were shown in fine condition, and Veitch & Sons had several other good varieties, including Agattia compacta, of very bright foliage almost hidden with bloom of a bright coral pink, and Ideala, somewhat after Mrs. J. Heal, but more compact and well flowered, a good flowering variety. The same firm also had some good zonal geraniums. Messrs. Cutbush & Sons made a great display of their Michaelmas daisies, Osprey, King Edward, Duchess of Albany, Triumph, and cordifolius profusus being worthy of note. H. B. May gained a first-class certificate for Nephrolepis Mayi, a rather congested form, with erect fronds, the rather long pinnæ very erect and twisted. As an example of Nephrolepis Piersoni, a very elegant form of N. exaltata, the side pinnules being much elongated and again divided. This will make a valuable fern for decorations.

Bouvardias in great variety were shown, including the new King of Scarlets, Pride of Brooklyn and Bridesmaid. Messrs. Wm. Bull & Sons made a grand show with their new Dracæna Victoria. In D. Lindeni the color is brightest in the young leaves and becomes dull with age, but in Victoria the young leaves have a slight green shade but change with age to a bright golden yellow with just a green band through the centre. Polygonum Molle, shown by A. Perry, should make a useful subject for cutting.

The annual trade auction sales of pot plants brought a large number of provincial nurserymen to London, who reported the season has not been good for trade generally, though, considering the weather, it might have been worse. At the various auctions things went about as usual, but there was very little demand for anything in the way of choice plants, except such as are likely to be of use for general trade. Of ordinary stock roses were most in demand, especially Marechal Niel and other climbing roses. The variegated ivies, ampelopsis and clematis also went well. All ordinary ferns sold well, but there was very little demand for the choicer sorts.

At Covent Garden Market buyers have been able to have their own way pretty much lately, but a spell of frost would alter things and make it better for trade all round. Chrysanthemums in pots are very good and these seem to go fairly well. Good cyclamens are in, also, Gloire de Lorraine, some of the finest we have seen, but it is too early for a good trade for these. Marguerites are always to be had. Some Erica gracilis and its white variety is offered. Ferns are over plentiful. At closing time Tuesday, October 13, some stands were left nearly full. Palms move a little better, but when you see hawkers taking them out in quantities you may be sure the prices do not run high. Hardy shrubs are already coming in. Cut flowers are plentiful. The Messrs. Rochford have a grand lot of lilliums, also lily of the valley. Mr. Dutton, a comparatively new grower, has made a great success with the American carnations, growing them in real American fashion, and those who depreciated them on account of the fringed petals are compelled to admit that they rival our English varieties, on some points at least, the long, stiff stems being a great advantage in our present style of decorating. Barly chrysanthemums have sold well, but the first early sorts are nearly over. Mr. Sawyer's new varieties have done well this season; of those I have seen I should select Miss B. Miller, yellow; Nellie Blake, chestnut red; Murillo, rose pink, and Black Prince, bright crimson, golden reverse.
                A. HEMSLEY.

GHENT, KY.—The local chrysanthemum show will be held November 12-14.

RIEGELSVILLE, PA.—J. S. Bloom, suffered a loss of about $600 in the recent floods.

JOLIET, ILL.—The management of the local flower show has issued an extensive list of additional premiums.

MILWAUKEE, WIS.—A recent issue of the *Milwaukee Sentinel* gives C. C. Pollworth an extensive write-up as a rose grower, with portrait.

JONES CITY, OKLA.—F. A. Beebe, proprietor of the Beebe fruit farm, is arranging to start a nursery and already has the work well under way.

THE AMERICAN FLORIST

NINETEENTH YEAR.

Subscription, $1.00 a year. To Europe, $2.00.
Subscriptions accepted only from those
in the trade.

Advertisements, on all except cover pages,
10 Cents a Line, Agate: $1.00 per inch.
Cash with Order.

No Special Position Guaranteed.

Discounts are allowed only on consecutive insertions, as follows:—6 times, 5 per cent; 13 times,
10 per cent; 26 times, 20 per cent;
52 times, 30 per cent.

Cover space sold only on yearly contract at
$1.00 per inch, net, in the case of the two
front pages, regular discounts applying only to the back pages.

The Advertising Department of the AMERICAN
FLORIST is for florists, seedsmen and nurserymen
and dealers in wares pertaining to those lines only.
Orders for less than one-half inch space not accepted.

Advertisements must reach us by Wednesday to
secure insertion in the issue for the following
Saturday. Address

AMERICAN FLORIST CO., Chicago.

W. N. RUDD says ivory soap is dangerous as an insecticide, if not used with
caution.

THE double Primula obconica which
has appeared this season is quite pretty,
the individual blooms of the darker varieties closely resembling the double violet.

AN international exhibition of art and
horticulture will be held at Dusseldorf,
the garden city of the Rhine, next year,
May 1 to October 23. Full information
may be had on application to Emil Hess,
10 Wilhelmsplatz, Dusseldorf, Germany.

IT is an interesting point, says the
Journal of Horticulture, that the first
experiment in cross-breeding was performed upon the common pink. This
was just two centuries ago. Fairchild
was the experimenter and the result was
a perfect success.

Spraying Melons.

ED. AM. FLORIST:—Mr. Clinton will
oblige by stating through your columns
the solution he has used on melons with
the best results, how and when to use it
and how often.　　　　　C. K.

I would say in the first place that spraying against the diseases of the melon certainly does not give as good results as it
does with the cucumber, which has the
same fungus foes. It is to be remembered
that the musk melon needs warm and
not too moist weather and is not able to
overcome severe backsets. So any injury,
whether from weather, fungus or spray,
counts seriously against it, especially in
that very essential point the flavor of the
fruit. From what I have seen so far of
the results, I am not quite sure whether
spraying will or will not pay. If I were
to spray, however, I should use Bordeaux
mixture. The first application should be
given as soon as the vines begin to run,
and this should be followed with at least
three or four additional treatments at
intervals of seven to twelve days, according to the weather. This makes the last
application come about the middle of
August, or about the time the fruit first
begins to ripen. In some cases even later
applications may be needed. Do the
spraying thoroughly. The sediment that
leaves on the fruit can do no harm, but if
one is afraid this will injure the sale the
last application can be made with potassium sulphide (three ounces dissolved in
ten gallons water). I make Bordeaux by
slaking four pounds fresh lime in water
and then straining into half a barrel of
water. Into this I pour the copper sul-
phate (four pounds) dissolved in about ten

gallons water, stirring the mixture, and
then dilute to make about forty-five
gallons.　　　　G. P. CLINTON.

Poinsettias.

Among the Christmas specialties that
have recently made rapid strides into
the popular favor, low-bloomed poinsettias singly in pots or grouped in pans
hold a leading place. All growers of
holiday plants for the trade are going
more heavily each year into this specialty
which gives in a more showy form than
does any other plant the true universal
Christmas color.

Poinsettias are struck from cuttings in
July and August the latter only being
available for use in the popular pan form
as those made earlier grow much too tall
for this purpose and are better adapted as
single specimens in large pots or for cut
flower uses.

The cuttings are rooted in a bed of
mixed sand and peat in the cold side of
the house and as soon as roots have
formed are transferred to small pots, to
be shifted later into pans or large pots.
A very moderate temperature is essential
to secure the desired dwarf habit and
they should have air both night and day
to hold them back and make them tough.
Watering with the hose is not safe,
especially in the hands of irresponsible
employes, for either overwatering or the
reverse is liable to cause poinsettias to
shed their leaves. A close watch for
mealy bug must be kept up. A sharp
stream of water from a very fine nozzle
is the best weapon to use.

Diseased Begonia.

ED. AM. FLORIST:—Will you please
settle a dispute as to the root affection
of the enclosed Begonia Erfordii? Is it
injurious? Is it curable? Is is contagious?
　　　　　　　　G. O. M.

The roots of the plant are badly infested
with nematodes. These worms force
their way into the young roots, multiply there in enormous quantities, and
often produce characteristic galls or
root knots. The amount of damage
to cultivated crops caused by nematodes is very great. It is not due
to the feeding of the worms upon the
roots, but rather to the fact that the
circulation of the sap is interfered with
by the abnormal development of tissues.
Root galls due to nematodes are found
on a great variety of cultivated plants,
among the more important of which may
be mentioned cowpea, peach, fig, grape,
rose, and on many greenhouse plants,
including violets and carnations. They
are also present on a large number of
wild plants.

In certain cases the disease produced
by nematodes is curable, but it is far easier
to prevent than to cure. When it occurs
on a large number of plants extending
over a large area in the open, there is no
practical method of controlling it. Peach
trees can be made to outgrow the disease
to a certain extent by high manuring.
They can be made somewhat more resistant by the persistent use of potash fertilizers. Applications of lime to the soil
will tend to reduce the number of nematodes.

Success has been attained in the treatment of roses and other shrubs in small
outdoor beds by the use of a one per cent
solution of formaldehyde. The soil must
be wet with this solution to the depth of
three or four inches. For a few days after
the treatment the plants will wilt badly,
but they will soon put out new feeding
roots and resume their normal growth.

If the infected soil in small flower beds,
in which flowers are to be set out in the
spring, is turned up and thoroughly
frozen two or three times during the
winter, the majority of the worms will
be killed.

In combating the disease in the greenhouse the sterilizing of the soil by steam
will be found to be most efficacious. To
do this place rows of perforated iron
pipes one foot apart in the bottom of the
bed or a box specially made for the purpose, and connect with the. A high-
pressure boiler. The pipes should be
connected with each other at the ends in
order to allow a circulation of the steam.
A steam pressure of at least forty or fifty
pounds should be used, so that the soil
will not become soggy. The pipes may
be covered with soil to the depth of one
and one-half to two feet. The heating
should continue for at least one hour,
and while in progress the bed, or box,
should be loosely covered with boards or
hotbed sash to keep in the steam. Before
replacing the soil wash the empty beds,
flats, etc., with a two per cent formaldehyde solution. Always sterilize the sand
in which cuttings are rooted and be careful not to set out in the beds any plant
affected with the root galls. Sterilizing
soil by steam is largely practiced by commercial florists as it kills, in addition to
the nematodes, all parasitic fungous
spores and insect eggs. Moreover, the
plants seem to do better in a sterilized
soil.

This disease is not contagious in the
strict sense of the word, but as it is caused
by living organisms which multiply very
rapidly and are capable of moving from
place to place, the soil becomes so infected
that susceptible varieties of plants can
not be grown upon it.

　　　　　　　B. T. GALLOWAY.

Chrysanthemums at Hartford, Conn.

Fully 3,000 persons visited the greenhouses at Elizabeth park Sunday, October 25, 1850, being actually counted
between half-past one and five o'clock, in
the afternoon. One house, 100 feet long,
is filled to its utmost capacity with chrysanthemums in pots, most of them in full
blossom, with enough buds to prolong
the show for at least two weeks longer.
There are 132 varieties grown here and
to perfection, reflecting credit on those in
charge. Among the new pink varieties
the following are the most noteworthy:

Miss Minnie Bailey has large blooms
and exceptionally fine foliage, improvement on Mrs. Perrin.

Mlle. Marie Liger, is a large, very good
light pink, incurved, stiff stem.

Silver Queen is a good light pink variety with unusually broad incurved petals,
good stem and foliage.

Daisy Moore, an improvement on Viviand-Morel, has loose flowers of good
color and stiff stem.

Durban's Pride, a very loose flower
with long petals, somewhat twisted.

Lucy Evans, bright pink, very fine,
large blooms on good stems.

Among the new yellow varieties grown
here the Yellow Eaton is undoubtedly
the largest. F. J. Taggard is a hairy
bloom on a five-foot stem. Mrs. E. H.
Thirkell is a golden yellow variety, loosely
built, with long reflexed petals. Sephia
is globular, incurved.

In the collection of white blooms the
largest are Convention Hall,
flowers rather flat on a good stem;
Algoma and Mme. Ch. Diederiechs, both
with good stems and fine foliage; Globosa Alba, which may rival Mrs. Robin-

son on the market; Mlle. Marg. Douillet, especially good for single stem, of loose globular form; Guy Hamilton, a dwarf variety.

Among the older and better known kinds are Gold Mine, Colonel D. Appleton, Mrs. Trainor L. Park and Peter Kay in yellow.

The most imposing whites are Merza, loose globular blossoms; Timothy Eaton, Mrs. Weeks, Miss Nellie Pockett, loose reflexed; W. H. Chadwick and the Queen. A gem in the whites is the National Chrysanthemum Jubilee, a beautiful creamy white, not a cream in color but with just a touch of pink relieving the marble white of the blossom and making a creamy effect.

Prominent among the pink blossoms is Ethelyn, a delicate rose pink; R. C. Richardson and Viviand-Morel, still probably the best of the pinks.

In the collection of purple and fancy colored blossoms is Edgar Sanders, crimson with incurved large flowers, golden on the outside; Barrington, silver outside and crimson within; Brutus, of good habit, short and dwarfy with handsome close foliage, crimson outside, a handsome reflexed flower.

Among the dark reds are Carrington, Malcolm Lamond (very dark), Black Hawk, probably the best; John Shrimpton, Cullingfordii and Mrs. Geo. West. The Japanese hairy varieties are among the gems of the exhibit. There is Child of Two Worlds, white incurved; Louis Boehmer, purple; Monarch of Ostrich Plumes, yellow; and Pluma, a creamy color.

In addition to this, here are grown about forty varieties of pompons. They are all very fine and are worth growing. In fact, it is a pity we don't see more of them. What showier and more satisfactory pot plants can be had at this time of the year? A few of the best ones are: White, Miss Ada Williams, Soeur Melanie, Lula, La Purite, White Jardin des Plantes; yellow, Flora, Veuve Clicquot, Canary, Golden Fleece, Mignon, Guinola, Yellow Jardin des Plantes, Mlle. Elise Doran, Baby Pompon; pink, Strathmeath, President; dark red, Aigle d'Or; red and yellow, Nellie Rainsford, Fred. Peele, Tiber, Regulus; white and yellow, l'Ami Couderchet, Pettitane.

R. K.

Flower Culture for Perfumes.

United States Vice-Consul Piatti, stationed at Nice, France, writes to the State Department under date of August 25, 1903, as follows:

A considerable number of inquiries have been received at this consulate during the past few years touching the cultivation of flowers for the purposes of distillation. They indicate that the writers are not at all informed as to this branch of industry, and I have thought that a special report on the subject would be of service.

Culture.—Land having a southern exposure is invariably chosen, and terraces upon hillsides, of which there are very many in this mountainous district, have often given the best results. The ground is well dug and well manured certain products for enriching the soil have as been used only to a limited extent; beyond this no special treatment is used. Cultivation proceeding as with ordinary crops. In exposed places precautions are taken to cover the plants during December and January, when frosts are liable to occur. These are very light and never sufficient to affect the roots of the plant, and the coverings are intended to protect the blossoms, which during the winter season are sold to florists and are kept to the northern cities of Europe. Roses and other perennial plants are cut down, dug around, and manured in September. The winter crop of blossoms, coming from November to February, is sold to florists. The plants rest until about May, when a second crop of blossoms is produced, which is sold for purposes of distillation. A protection against insects and diseases, sulphur,

lime and the Bordeaux mixture for vines are generally the only preventive measures used.

Kinds of Plants.—The popular names of the plants used for the purpose of distillation, together with their botanical names, are as follows:

Popular Name.	Botanical Name.
Parma Violet	Viola odorata.
Acacia	Acacia Farnesiana.
Jonquil	Narcissus Jonquilla.
Mignonette	Reseda odorata.
Roses	(Various, see elsewhere.)
Orange flowers	Citrus Bigaradia.
Jasmine	Jasminum grandiflorum.
Tuberose	Polianthes tuberosa.
Pink or Carnation	Dianthus caryophyllus.

Prices.—The prices paid for the different kinds of blossoms vary naturally with the supply. Very high prices range only when, for some reason or other, any special crop fails. As a general rule, the crops, being of a very perishable nature and requiring to be utilized as soon as practicable after being picked, are sold at prices fixed by the distilleries themselves. The producers are therefore more or less at the mercy of immediate buyers in the district, as the loss through spoiling, freights, and other expenses would be very serious, even if it were practicable to forward the crops for long distances to other markets.

The market of Grasse being the principal one, I give below the prices paid per kilogram (2.2046 pounds) for these blossoms during the past three years. It should be noted that these prices are for the bare blossoms alone, and in the case of roses for the bare loose leaves:

Flower.	1901	1902	1903
Parma violet	$.48	$.48	$.48
Acacia	.81	1.15	1.15
Jonquil	1.02	.48	.76
Mignonette	.24	.24	.19
Roses	.19	.15	.13
Orange flowers	.17	.10	.09
Jasmine	.57	.67	
Tuberose	.43	.48	
Pink or Carnation	.06	.07	.06

All these blossoms are used in the new system of distillation known as the "enfleurage system," or absorption by grease. Some of them—roses, orange flowers, who a limited amount of jasmine—are submitted to the old process of distillation. This year, in the case of orange flowers, the distillery fixed a price of 5 cents per 2.2046 pounds for the crop, and in many sections proprietors and cultivators preferred to lose their crop, as the price did not cover the expenses of picking and sending to market. Referring to the Nice market, only here say that the Rose de Mai is the one used principally for distilling. Of late years, however, a quantity of Bobrinski roses and Paul roses have been used. The quantity of Roses de Mai distilled annually here is about 120,000 pounds. The price per kilogram (2.2046 pounds) has varied for years between 10 and 18 cents—this last price in 1901. This year the price was 13 cents. Regarding Mignonette there is but one distillery there, and the only products distilled are orange leaves and flowers. The average price paid for young leaves is 6 cents per 2.2046 pounds and 10 and 12 cents for the flowers.

Rose Geranium Leaves.—I have preferred to treat this subject separately, as it has come to my knowledge that official inquiries on the subject are being made by representatives of other governments. This crop has attained large proportions in this district and the annual production now reaches not less than 3,300,000 pounds. I have also ascertained that 1 hectare (2.471 acres) will produce 55,000 to 66,000 pounds of leaves, which are sold at from $1.14 to $1.33 per 220 pounds. The product in pure essence of each 2.204 pounds is 2.3 pounds. A small quantity is annually imported into Grasse from Italy, about 66,000 pounds are brought from Africa, and 55,000 pounds from Île de la Reunion, near Mauritius. It should be borne in mind that what is known as "Turkish geranium" is the United States is simply a superior quality of essence of Palmarosa manufactured in British India and is not geranium at all. In point of fact I can not ascertain that any essence of geranium is manufactured in Turkey.

Mint.—Experiments as to the cultivation of mint for distilling are going on and a certain amount of land is being cultivated; but I have not yet sufficient data to report thereon.

SITUATIONS, WANTS, FOR SALE.

One Cent Per Word.

Cash with the Adv.

Plant Advs. NOT admitted under this head.

Every paid subscriber to the AMERICAN FLORIST for the year 1903 is entitled to a five-line want ADV. (situations only!) free, to be used at any time during the year.

Situation Wanted—As assistant propagator of roses in a commercial place. Address
FLORIST, 146 Bowmanville Ave., Chicago.

Situation Wanted—As foreman or manager; eighteen years' practical experience. Thoroughly conversant with all branches of the business.
G P., care American Florist.

Situation Wanted—By a single Hollander, aged 28; for ferns, etc., or as second hand on a private place; state wages. Address
S V., care American Florist.

Situation Wanted—Young man wants position where he can acquire a knowledge of vegetable culture under glass. Address
B H., care American Florist.

Situation Wanted—By single man, able to propagate and graft all kinds of fruit, oranges and grapes, desires tropical position. Address
G P., 50 Tenth St., New Rochelle, N. Y.

Situation Wanted—By experienced gardener as foreman in good establishment, where good wages are paid; married. Address
S T.
227 E. Sharpnack St., Germantown, Phila.

Situation Wanted—By first-class man; 21 years' experience in greenhouse plants, fruit and vegetables, also landscape gardening, have diploma. Address
E L., care American Florist.

Situation Wanted—By an all-around florist and grower. 22 years of commercial experience. Strictly sober and not afraid of work, private or commercial. Address
W. A. HICKEY, Box 587 Naperville, Ill.

Situation Wanted—On private or commercial place by capable and sober young man, married, no children; thoroughly understands all herbaceous and nursery stock, landscaping in all its branches and everything pertaining to out-door gardening; also expert grower of roses, carnations, 'mums, rare and decorative plants. Moderate wages expected. Excellent references. Address with full particulars
GARDENER AND FLORIST,
Irvington-on-Hudson, N. Y.

Help Wanted—An experienced plant salesman.
J. F. KIDWELL & BRO.,
3806 Wentworth Ave., Chicago.

Help Wanted—A good, reliable, young man or woman who will be willing to help and learn the florist business on florist place. Address
C. H. BAGLEY, Abilene, Kans.

Help Wanted—Good florist to take charge of three greenhouses 20x100. Grow cut flowers and general stock. Give reference and wages expected with room. Address
C S, care American Florist.

Help Wanted—A competent and up-to-date florist, not over 40, for retail store in Chicago, to wait on trade, decorate and make-up. Must be sober and reliable. No greenhouse work. References. State salary expected. Address
F C., care American Florist.

Help Wanted—At once, a competent man to take charge of a retail store in a city of about 50,000 inhabitants. Must be steady and reliable; also a good salesman; married man preferred; good wages paid and a steady position; remember only first-class man need answer, also state how long in last position. Address
FIRST-CLASS, care American Florist.

Wanted—To rent a place of from 25 to 40 thousand square feet of glass for wholesale trade only. Must have dwelling, barns; outside ground, etc., all in good condition. Must be within 25 miles of Chicago.
M S, care American Florist.

For Sale—Furman boiler No. 2 in good shape. Price $35.
C. A. PETERS, Huntington, W. Va.

For Sale—A bargain; about 4 acres of land in Rogers Park. Finest location for truck gardening or greenhouses. For particulars inquire at the office of
K. G. SCHMITT & SON,
809 Clybourn Ave., cor. North Ave., Chicago.

INTERNATIONAL FLOWER DELIVERY.

PASSENGER STEAMSHIP MOVEMENTS.

FROM	TO	STEAMER	*LINE	DAY	DUE ABOUT
New York......	Liverpool	Etruria	1	Sat. Nov. 7, 7:00 a. m.	Nov 18
New York......	"	Campania	1	Sat. Nov. 14, Noon.	Nov. 20
Boston.........	"	Ivernia	1	Sat. Nov. 7, 7:00 a. m.	Nov. 16
New York......	Hamburg	Deutschland	2	Thur. Nov. 12, 11:00 a. m.	Nov. 19
New York......	"	Moltke	2	Sat. Nov. 14, 1:00 p. m.	Nov. 21
New York......	Glasgow	Columbia	3	Sat. Nov. 14, 3:00 p. m.	
New York......	London	Menaba	6	Sat. Nov. 7, 9:00 a. m.	
New York......	"	Minnetonka	6	Sat. Nov. 14, 1:30 p. m.	Nov. 23
New York......	Southampton	Marquette	6	Fri. Nov. 6, 9:00 a. m.	
New York......	Liverpool	Germanic	7	Wed. Nov. 4, Noon.	Nov. 13
New York......	"	Cedric	7	Fri. Nov. 6, 6:00 a. m.	Nov. 14
New York......	"	Majestic	7	Wed. Nov. 11, Noon.	Nov. 19
New York......	"	Celtic	7	Fri. Nov. 13, Noon.	Nov. 21
New York......	Southampton	Philadelphia	8	Wed. Nov. 4, 10:00 a. m.	Nov. 11
New York......	"	St. Louis	8	Wed. Nov. 11, 10:00 a. m.	Nov. 18
New York......	Antwerp	Finland	8	Sat. Nov. 7, 10:00 a. m.	Nov. 16
New York......	"	Vaderland	8	Sat. Nov. 14, 10:00 a. m.	Nov. 23
New York......	Havre	La Touraine	10	Thur. Nov. 5, 10:00 a. m.	Nov. 13
New York......	"	La Savoie	10	Thur. Nov. 12, 10:00 a. m.	Nov. 20
New York......	Rotterdam	Noordam	11	Wed. Nov. 4, 10:00 a. m.	Nov. 13
New York......	"	Rotterdam	11	Wed. Nov. 11, 10:00 p. m.	Nov. 20
New York......	Genoa	Citta di Milano	12	Tues. Nov. 3.	Nov. 20
New York......	Bremen	Kronprinz Wilh.	13	Tues. Nov. 3, 3:00 p. m.	Nov. 10
New York......	"	Rhein	13	Thur. Nov. 5, 10:00 a. m.	Nov. 15
New York......	"	Frdk. Der Grosse	13	Thur. Nov. 12, 10:00 a. m.	Nov. 22
New York......	Genoa	Lahn	13	Sat. Nov. 7,	Nov. 19
Boston.........	Liverpool	Mayflower	15	Thur. Nov. 5, 10:00 a. m.	Nov. 12
Boston.........	"	Columbus	15	Thur. Nov. 12, 3:00 p. m.	Nov. 15
Boston.........	"	Winifredian	16	Sat. Nov. 7, 11:00 a. m.	Nov. 16
Boston.........	"	Bohemian	16	Sat. Nov. 14, 5:30 a. m.	Nov. 22

INTERNATIONAL FLOWER DELIVERY.

STEAMSHIPS LEAVE FOREIGN PORTS.

FROM	TO	STEAMER	*LINE	DAY		DUE ABOUT
Liverpool........	New York	Umbria	1	Sat.	Nov. 7,	Nov. 13
Liverpool........	Boston	Saxonia	1	Tues.	Nov. 10,	Nov. 17
Hamburg........	New York	Auguste Victoria	3	Thur.	Nov. 5,	
Hamburg........		Bluecher	3	Sat.	Nov. 14,	
Glasgow.........	"	Furnessia	3	Thur.	Nov. 12,	Nov. 22
London..........	"	Minneapolis	6	Sat.	Nov. 7, 7:00 a. m.	Nov. 17
London..........	"	Minnehaha	6	Sat.	Nov. 14, Noon.	Nov. 24
Southampton....	"	Manitou	6	Wed.	Nov. 4,	
Liverpool........	"	Oceanic	7	Wed.	Nov. 4, 3:30 p. m.	Nov. 11
Liverpool........	"	Cymeric	7	Fri.	Nov. 6, 3:30 p. m.	Nov. 14
Liverpool........	"	Teutonic	7	Wed.	Nov. 11, 3:30 p. m.	Nov. 18
Liverpool........	"	Arabic	7	Fri.	Nov. 13, 3:30 p. m.	Nov. 21
Southampton....	"	New York'	8	Sat.	Nov. 7, Noon.	Nov. 14
Southampton....	"	Philadelphia	8	Sat.	Nov. 14, Noon.	Nov. 21
Antwerp.........	"	Kensington	8	Sat.	Nov. 7, Noon.	Nov. 16
Antwerp.........	"	Kroonland	8	Sat.	Nov. 14, 9:30 a. m.	Nov. 23
Havre...........	"	La Bretagne	10	Sat.	Nov. 7,	Nov. 16
Havre...........	"	La Lorraine	10	Sat.	Nov. 14,	Nov 23
Rotterdam	"	Statendam	11	Sat.	Nov. 7,	Nov. 16
Rotterdam	"	Rhyndam	11	Sat.	Nov. 14,	Nov. 23
Genoa...........	"	Nord America	12	Mon.	Nov. 2,	
Genoa...........	"	Sardegna	12	Mon.	Nov. 9,	
Genoa...........	"	Citta di Napoli	12	Mon.	Nov. 16,	Dec. 2
Bremen..........	"	Kaiser Wilh. II	13	Tues.	Nov. 3,	Nov. 10
Bremen..........	"	K. Wil. Der Grosse	13	Tues.	Nov. 10,	Nov. 17
Genoa...........	"	Prinzess Irene	13	Thur.	Nov. 12,	Nov. 25
Liverpool........	Boston	Commonwealth	15	Thur.	Nov. 12,	Nov. 18
Liverpool........	"	Kensington	15	Thur.	Nov. 12,	Nov. 19
Liverpool........	"	Canadian	16	Fri.	Nov. 6,	Nov. 15
Liverpool........	"	Cestrian	16	Fri.	Nov. 13,	Nov. 22

* See steamship list on opposite page.

Wild Smilax ALWAYS On Hand.

Also PLUMOSUS, SPRENGERI, ADIANTUMS, GALAX AND LEUCOTHOES.

We are Growers of HIGH-GRADE **Cut Flowers.** All orders promptly filled. Consignments solicited.

FRANK GARLAND, 55-57 Wabash Ave., Chicago.

Please mention the American Florist when writing

The F. R. WILLIAMS CO.

Wholesale Florists,

CLEVELAND, - OHIO.

Please mention the American Florist when writing

WILD SMILAX. ORDER DIRECT FROM HEADQUARTERS.

We carry the finest and most complete stock of Florists' Hardy Supplies, Dagger and Fancy Ferns, $1.00 per 1000. A No. 1 quality. Bronze and Green Galax, $1.00 per 1000 A No. 1 quality. Southern Wild Smilax, 50 pound case, $7.00, 25 pound case $3.50 per case, Laurel Festooning, good and full, 5c and 6c per yard. Leucothoe Sprays, $1.00 per 100. Green Moss, $1.00 per bbl.; 75c per bag. Sphagnum Moss, $1.00 per bbl., 50c per bag. Order by mail, telegraph or tele-phone will receive our personal and prompt attention. Long Dist. 'Phone 2618 Main.

HENRY W. ROBINSON, No. 11 Province St., BOSTON, MASS.

Please mention the American Florist when writing.

Albert Fuchs,

PALMS, FERNS, FICUS.

Established 1884. CHICAGO, 2045-59 Clarendon Ave.

Please mention the American Florist when writing.

IF YOU HAVE STOCK TO SELL.....

The best way to make that fact known to the trade is by regular advertising in the

The American Florist.

LONDON. · COMMISSIONS CARRIED OUT IN LONDON

or any part of Great Britain.

Messrs. WILLS & SEGAR will attend to any commission from American florists for the supply of Cut Flowers, birthday Flowers, Bouquets, High Class Floral Designs, etc. to their clients who may be traveling in England.

WILLS & SEGAR, Court Florists to his Majesty, The King.

ROYAL EXOTIC NURSERY.

TELEGRAMS, Onslow Crescent, South Kensington,
FLOSCULO, LONDON. LONDON, ENGLAND.

DENVER.
FLORAL DESIGNS AND FLOWERS.

Best Quality on Shortest Notice.

DANIELS & FISHER, DENVER, COLO.

Order by mail, telephone, telegraph or cable. Cable address: "Daniels Denver."

GALAX...

Bronze or green, 75c per 1000, in 3,000 cts or more, **Leucothoe Sprays,** green, 90c per 100. **Southern Smilax,** fresh stock, per 50-lb case, $6.00; per 25-lb. case, $3.50. **Green Sheet Moss,** choice stock, $2.50 per barrel sack. **Spagnum Moss,** $1.75 per large bale.

FLORIST' SUPPLIES of Every DESCRIPTION.

Tel. 597 Madison Square. **L. J. KRESHOVER,** 110-112 W. 27th St., New York.

HARDY CUT FERNS.

Write for Prices.

FANCY DAGGER

L. B. BRAGUE, Hinsdale, Mass.

Oldest, largest and most reli-ble d-aler in U. S.
Please mention the American Florist when writing.

HARDY CUT FERNS.

Fancy or Dagger, now 75c per 1000. Cash with all orders. Bouquet Green, lo-se, $6.00 per 100 lbs and 8c per yd. Laurel Festooning, 4½c per yd. Fine Sphagnum Moss, 60c per bbl. Christmas Trees by the car load. Spruce or Balsam will be furnished in any quantity required. All orders by mail or dispatch promptly attended to.

THOMAS COLLINS,

Box 241. Hinsdale, Mass.

THE SEED TRADE.

AMERICAN SEED TRADE ASSOCIATION.
S. F. Willard, Pres.; J. Charles McCullough, First Vice-Pres.; C. E. Kendel, Cleveland, O., Sec'y and Treas. Twenty-second annual convention St. Louis, Mo., June, 1904.

WHITE bottom onion sets are poor and likely to be scarce.

VISITED PHILADELPHIA: William M. Alison, representing Peter Lawson & Sons, Ltd., Edinburgh, Scotland.

BOSTON, MASS.—Edwin R. Baldwin, representing Benjamin Hammond, Fishkill, N. J., was a visitor this week.

MONTREAL, QUE.—Dupuy & Ferguson's establishment was flooded with water October 18, due to fire in the building.

THE supply of French Paper White narcissus bulbs has been well cleaned up and the same seems to be true of regular grades of Roman hyacinths.

HOLLAND reports indicate but half a crop of spinach, mustard, beet, carrot, radish and onion because of continual unfavorable weather since August 1.

BOSTON, MASS.—Geo. C. Thomson, of R. & J. Farquhar's, has received news of the death of his mother, Mrs. Geo. Thomson, at her home in Aberdeen, Scotland.

D. V. BURRELL, of Rocky Ford, Col., who was bitten by a dog October 9, has been at the Pasteur Institute, Chicago, for treatment since October 27. He is progressing favorably.

THE market for cucumber seed is unsettled. Prices so far made seem to range from $1 to $2, and a report comes from Boston that $500 has been offered and refused for 200 pounds of the best pickling strain.

MILWAUKEE, WIS.—The John H. Allan Seed Company, E. M. Parmelee president, with a capital stock of $50,000, of which not more than $25,000 is represented in Wisconsin, has filed articles to operate in this state.

REPLYING to "Lambert," we would advise that he write the Department of Agriculture, Washington, D. C., for Scofield's bulletin on the "Description of Wheat Varieties," which contains some useful information on the subject.

LONDON, ENG., October 15.—Pea and bean crops in England are said to be the worst for many years, but the trade there will be helped out by the good yield in Canada. Gradus and kindred sorts are very dear. Everything points to a good season.

ERNST BENARY, of Erfurt, Germany, among other novelties, is offering a promising new winter-flowering stock named Beauty of Nice. It is said to bloom satisfactorily from September to April, and to come sixty to seventy-five per cent double. The flowers are of a flesh pink shade.

ARROYO GRANDE, CAL.—The Routzahn Seed Company, of Arroyo Grande, has filed articles of incorporation for a period of fifty years. Among those prominently identified with the new company are D. D. Barnard, E. W. Clark, L. C. Routzahn and Henry Bahr. The new company has bought up the McClure Seed Company's interests.

THE picking of bouquet green has advanced but slowly during October and the quantity in sight is probably less than one-half the usual amount gathered at this time in the Wisconsin district. If the weather continues fine and picking increases and the season is fairly long, an average amount may yet be secured, but the present outlook is for a lighter crop and higher prices.

Foreign Seeds Have No Wholesale Price.

Judge Waite of the board of United States general appraisers, made a decision at New York, October 23, in the re-appraisal protest cases of D. M. Ferry & Company, and the Lohrman Seed Company, which seems to settle the question of whether there is a wholesale price for foreign garden seeds in the strict sense of the term.

Ferry & Company and the Lohrman Seed Company entered garden seed at Detroit at valuations which Collector Rich thought insufficient, notwithstanding the fact that the appraiser of the port was of the opinion that the seeds were properly entered so far as values were concerned. The collector, it is said, acted on information furnished by the United States special treasury agents. Not being satisfied with the conclusions reached by the local appraiser, he appealed to the board of general appraisers for a review of the appraiser's decision.

Judge Waite took the cases under consideration, and has devoted a great deal of time to taking testimony. The leading importers of seeds in New York and elsewhere have been called for information. The greater part of the evidence placed before Judge Waite appears to have supported the contention that garden seeds are to be classed with those commodities which have what may be termed a personal characteristic, such as belongs to works of art or such articles, dependent for their value upon the reputation of the producer.

Another point established by the testimony was to the effect that practically all the garden seeds under consideration are produced upon contract, the usual quantities being quite large. Judge Waite reaches the conclusion that there are no wholesale prices for garden seeds, and that consequently the American customs authorities will arrive at the invoice price under section II of the custom administrative act by analogy.

Should Collector Rich decide to appeal from Judge Waite's decision, to the full board of re-appraisement, that tribunal's decision will be final.—Detroit Tribune, October 21, 1903.

Hartford, Conn.

At a meeting of the Hartford Florists' Club October 21, a letter of thanks was read from the New Haven Horticultural Society in response to a large photograph of the members of the Hartford and New Haven Clubs taken at Hubbard park at their joint outing to Lake Compounce in August. Another bowling contest with the New Haven society was discussed and may possibly take place in the near future. Hans Schmid was elected a member of the club.

Anton Pauly, late of Murray Hill, N. J., has accepted the position as forester at Keney park. Mr. Pauly will commence his duties November 1.

ROBERT KARLSTROM.

WACO, TEX.—At Franklin and Sixth streets, a temporary building to be used by the Floral society in the exhibition of November 11 to 14 has been erected. The structure is 70x150 feet, frame and of one story.

DENVER, COLO.—We want some cold weather very badly. All cut flowers are to be had in abundance. Outdoor stock is still abundant, including sweet peas and cosmos. This is quite unusual for this section.

Toronto.

TRADE ERRATIC.—GROWERS CUT BACK
ROSES PREPARING FOR CHRISTMAS.—
CHRYSANTHEMUMS GLUT MARKET. —
NOTES OF THE TRADE.

Trade has been erratic. Although there have been a number of weddings and occasional calls for design work, nothing has transpired to make business above a fair average. The fall races and a few other social affairs called for only small orders, and though sometimes there is a scarcity of certain varieties of roses it is because some houses have been cut back to bring them in for Christmas trade. Our local growers show great foresight in arranging their houses this way, especially just at present when there is a glut of chrysanthemums and roses are very little in demand. What there are are very good, especially American Beauty, which is coming in with nice stems and good color and fine foliage. Ivory, Golden Gate, Liberty, Helen Gould and other varieties less extensively grown are seen in very fine shape, while teas are about the average, selling at $5 a 100. Carnations are very plentiful and good for this season of the year. Enchantress, Lawson, Lillian Pond, Prosperity, Gaiety and many other of the newer varieties are exceptionally well grown, though unfortunately there is little demand at this season. Lily of the valley has been scarce for the past few days. Those offered are pale in foliage and the flowers have a forced appearance. Chrysanthemums predominate everywhere and very good varieties are shown. As the chrysanthemum show is not to be held until November 10 many flowers which otherwise would have been held back are coming in and the stores have a very fine appearance. Prices are lower than former years and flowers can be had exceedingly cheap, 10 cents being about the highest for special blooms. Violets are fine with very good stems and big flowers, the best quoted at $1 a 100.

Chas. Grobba has about completed his new residence which is quite modern in every respect. Grobba & Wandrey had quite a number of early chrysanthemums. Their cyclamens are in very fine shape. Poinsettias have made good growth and are about the only ones in this section.

There have been quite a number of orchids displayed. W. Hill, of Yonge street has had some very fine cattleyas on view in his window. They are of his own growing.

R. Fendlay, the violet specialist, was also in town placing his cut for the next two weeks. His flowers are fine. He is going north for the next two weeks, deer hunting.

A recent visitor was R. Jennings, of Brampton. He is growing chrysanthemums extensively and has been cutting since August 20, commencing with Fitzwygram.

The Florists' and Gardeners' Association held a meeting in St. George's hall October 20, but as there were but few present the meeting turned into a social one.

The Canadian Thanksgiving day helped to relieve monotony and relieve the dealers of surplus stock. Many stores were decorated with autumn foliage. J. H. Dunlop's place is in fine condition. Carnations and many of the newer varieties look well. H. G. D.

LOWELL, MASS.—G. W. Patten has returned from Hot Springs, Ark., where he has been for a month.

FLOWER SEEDS

For Present Sowing.

10 Per Cent Special Cash Discount, on Orders over $2.00 for Flower Seeds if the Cash is enclosed. except Asparagus plumosus nanus, where the discount is 3 per cent.

BROWALLIA SPECIOSA MAJOR. The plants grow only about a foot high, form dense little bushes, which are covered with the entire year with an abundance of the most delightful sky-blue flowers. Trade pk. (250 seeds), 25c.
ASPARAGUS PLUMOSUS NANUS, 100 seeds, $1.00; 250 seeds, $2.00; 1000 seeds, $7.50.
SPRENGERI, 100 seeds, 30c; 1000 seeds, 75c; 5000 seeds, $3.25.
DECUMBENS, produce vines, 3 feet long, clothed with bluish green leaves. Cultivate like A. Sprengeri. 100 seeds, 60c; 1000 seeds, $5.00.
SCANDENS DEFLEXUS, suitable for hanging baskets and to cut. 100 seeds, $1.50.
CANDYTUFT, Giant Hyacinth-Flowered. This strain is superior to Empress. Sow now out-doors. Lb., $2.50; pkt., 10c; oz., 30c.
Empress. Our strain of this is extra fine, lb., $1.60; pkt., 10c; oz., 20c.
VAUGHAN'S GIANT FLOWERED CYCLAMEN. Our seed has been grown for us by a specialist in Europe. Shape and size of flowers, foliage and stems, are points on which seed plants are selected. **Pure White,** (Mont Blanc), Dark **Crimson, Ross von Marienthal,** "Daybreak" Pink, **White with Carmine Eye,** 100 seeds, 50c; 1000 seeds, $5.00; 250 seeds at the 1000 rate.
GIANT-FLOWERED CYCLAMEN, Extra Choice Mixed. This mixture is made up from the above separate colors. 100 seeds, 50c; 250 seeds, $1.15; 1000 seeds, $4.50; 5000 seeds, $20.00.
NEW GIANT ORCHID-FLOWERED CYCLAMEN. We have the following separate colors. (Order by number). No. C 100. **Lilac Colored,** 10 seeds, 30c; 100 seeds, $2.50. No. C 101. **Dark Red,** fringed. No. C 102. **Pink,** fringed. No. C 103. **Pure White.** No. C 105. **White with Red Eye.** Each, 10 seeds, 30c; 25 seeds, 50c; 100 seeds, $2.00. No. C 106. **Giant Orchid-Flowered Cyclamen** in choicest mixture, all the above and others. 25 seeds, 40c. 100 seeds, $1.50.
GIANT ORCHID-FLOWERED CYCLAMEN in mixture, 25 seeds, 25c; 100 seeds, 75c.
DRACÆNA INDIVISA. Trade pkt. 10c; oz., 30c; lb., $2.50.
SWEET PEAS: Extra Early Blanche Ferry, pink and white, ¼-lb., 10c; lb., 33c. **Earliest of All,** pink and white, ¼-lb., 10c; lb., 30c. **Countess of Radnor,** lavender, ¼-lb., 10c; lb., 35c. **Emily Henderson,** white, ¼-lb., 10c; lb., 30c. **Josephine White,** white, ¼-lb., 15c; lb., 50c. **Mont Blanc,** white, ¼-lb., 10c; lb., 50c. **Lady Grisel Hamilton,** lavender, ¼-lb., 15c; lb., 50c. **Prima Donna,** soft pink, ¼-lb., 10c; lb., 35c. For other sorts see our book for Florists.

ASPARAGUS PLUMOSUS NANUS.

Vaughan's Seed Store,
Chicago. New York.

Baltimore.

At the last meeting of the Gardeners' Club C. L. Seybold delivered an essay on the requirements of a landscape architect and general superintendent for a city park system, comparison being made between European and American park management. Mr. Vincent gave the members an interesting talk on dahlias.

Business in cut flowers is still dull. Dahlias are yet in their glory. There has been a good supply of carnations and inferior roses. Chrysanthemums are more plentiful and of good quality. Considerable wedding decoration and funeral design work is reported. Violets are in generally good shape.

Begonia Anna Regina, originated by Wm. Pfitzer, Stuttgart, Germany, has been put to a thorough test at Paterson park, and as a flowering bedding plant is excellent.

Newark, N. J.

SUCCESSFUL EXHIBITION.—LEADING FEATURES AND PRIZE WINNERS.

The German Horticultural Society's chrysanthemum exhibition at Birkenhauer & Baumann's hall, October 25-27, was a very pretty and creditable affair and the attendance was excellent. No better adapted or more attractive little hall could be imagined for the purpose. The balconies, proscenium and columns were decorated with oak foliage, making an appropriate setting for the groups of palms and chrysanthemums. C. Weier, who received the special prize offered for the best general exhibit, showed a lot of very evenly grown single bloom plants of Ivory and pink Ivory, some bush plants, a basket of chrysanthemum blooms and some carnations. John L. Pfeuffer was represented by a large display of carnations, chrysanthemums and violets, also pink Ivory in neat plants and well-colored flowers. He had a promising white carnation, a cross between Mrs. Lawson and Mrs. Bradt.

The stage was occupied by Philips Bros. with a group of large palms. This firm also showed a number of elaborate baskets, bouquets and designs and a collection of carnations. Geo. Smith, gardener to S. M. Colgate, won a gold medal with a set of superb chrysanthemum blooms, and a gold medal also went to D. Kindsgrab for a superb group of decorative foliage plants which occupied the center of the hall. C. Daum, gardener to Tongo Savage, had a big group of very large palms effectively placed.

Carl Baumann made a very extensive display of cactus, and from the Llewelyn Japanese Nursery came a large collection of characteristic Japanese dwarfed evergreens and maples and other curios. Peter Butternel showed artificial flowers in profusion, Weismantel had a number of funeral designs and W. G. Muller a collection of good carnations.

St. Joseph, Mo.

L. J. Stuppy will open another store at 822 Frederick avenue about November 26. Frank Stuppy will have charge of both places for the present. The greenhouses are in fine shape and cutting plenty of good stock.

Krumm Brothers are cutting good roses and carnations, and report business good.

D. M. Reichard as usual has plenty of good stock and says business was never better. C. W. S.

OUR PASTIMES.

Announcements of coming contests or other events of interest to our bowling, shooting and sporting readers are solicited and will be given place in this column.
Address all correspondence for this department to Wm. J. Stewart, 79 Milk St., Boston, Mass.; Robt. Kift, 1725 Chestnut St., Philadelphia, Pa.; or to the American Florist Co., Chicago, Ill.

At Chicago.

The meeting of the Chicago Florists' Bowling Club was held at Phil. Hauswirth's store, Auditorium annex, October 29. The programme for the coming season was discussed. George Asmus was elected president and J G. Lambros, 95 Wabash avenue, secretary. A meeting will be held Tuesday evening, Novem-

George Asmus.
(President Chicago Florists' Bowling Club.)

ber 3, to complete plans for the season's campaign. The secretary will notify all interested parties of the hour and place of meeting and it is urgently requested that all attend on this occasion.

At Colorado Springs, Col.

Following are scores made by the Florists' Club bowlers organized to compete at St. Louis next year. We hope to make a better showing as the season advances:

Player	1st	2d	3d
Betz	120	125	116
Harris	136	137	91
Jackson	139	102	
Stocker	81	97	113
Monaghan	87	111	139
Evans	177		
Dunman	136	141	148
Crump	114	103	188
Vinson	136	150	163
Harris	117	147	135
Duff	148	127	135
Baur	107	126	122
Mann	163	154	150
Braidwood		104	142

W. H. D.

TWO RIVERS, WIS.—The large greenhouse which Louis Hartung has been erecting the past summer is now completed. A new residence is also on the premises.

Minneapolis.

BUSINESS SLACK WITH SUPPLY IN SURPLUS.
—CHRYSANTHEMUM SHOW DROPPED.—
GOOD NEW CARNATIONS.

Business the last week has been very quiet, with suplus in nearly all lines of stock, especially in Bridesmaid and Bride roses. Carnations and American Beauty have been in good demand but have not brought the money the quality deserved, as the summer weather we have had for two weeks has made summer prices. Greens of all kinds are scarce. Chrysanthemums are increasing daily, which has the effect of diminishing sales of other flowers.

L. P. Lord, of Owatonna, Minn., has been sending to market some new carnations of his own hybridizing. They embrace a red, a dark pink, a white and a variegated kind. The white especially promises to be exceptional both in size and stem and its keeping qualties are remarkable. It resembles the White Cloud.

Many growers are storing their bulbs in a chemical cold storage plant. Those who have tried this report good results at moderate expense.

The chrysanthemum show, which was expected to take place next month, has been dropped for this year.

Rice Brothers are receiving large quantities of southern smilax and putting it in storage.   C. F. R.

Springfield, Mass.

Business has improved the last two weeks. We have had two good frosts, killing outside stock completely and helping the sale of chrysanthemums, which was a little slow in the earlier varieties. Violets, double and single, are more plentiful and improving in quality. Roses, carnations and valley are good and plentiful enough to supply the demand. All stores are showing good displays of cut chrysanthemums. A fine assortment of palms, ferns, rubbers and a few good orchids are in evidence.

Wholesale growers report business fair and are busy these days getting things in shape for winter trade. Carnations, chrysanthemums, etc., with all are better than in former years.

E. S. Barier has resigned his position with Mark Aiken, taking one with Thorley, of New York.

H. Merrill has gone to Texas to try his luck in the cotton business.   A. B.

Columbus, O.

Local trade was very satisfactory last week there being quite a demand for funeral work and for material suitable for parties and receptions. Chrysanthemums are now. in and there is a brisk demand for good stock, of which there seems to be a good supply. Violets are improving rapidly both in size and color and are now not far from standard.

Some of our local craftsmen are contemplating a trip to visit the chrysanthemum show at Indianapolis November 10 to 14. Columbus florists have not yet forgotten the hospitality shown to them by their Indianapolis brethren at the time of the meeting of the American Carnation Society a year ago last February.   Carl.

BRIDGEWATER, MASS.—Linus W. Snow, well known as an extensive grower of dahlias, died at his home October 20, aged 79 years.

St. Paul.

We have now had several weeks of fine weather and all stock is faring well. Chrysanthemums, which looked as if they were going to come in too late for our show, are looking just right. There is some disappointment among the exhibitors on account of the small hall they will be obliged to show in this year. The armory hall, which it was expected would be ready in time, has not any roof yet, and the ladies' committee having the matter in charge was not able to do any better at this late date.

August S. Swanson opened his new branch store on East Sixth street last Saturday. He had a fine display of salvia, cosmos and chrysanthemums.

Charlie Keiper has been cutting some very fine Appleton. They are some of the best chrysanthemums ever seen here.

Chris. Hansen is up again after his recent illness. He is cutting some very good Lawsons.

Trade has been up to record in most stocks with chrysanthemums selling on sight.

Carnations are very plentiful at present and all are of the best quality.

Hangen & Swanson have been cutting large and fine Kaiserins.

E. F. Lemke is reported nearly well again.

C. W. Scott is calling on the trade this week. O.

Denver.

Chrysanthemums are coming in plentifully and some of very fine quality are offered. The best Robinson, Appleton and Viviand-Morel bring $15 a hundred, while smaller varieties may be had for $8. The quality of stock is hurt somewhat by mild weather. With the arrival of chrysanthemums the market is well filled in all lines, but prices hold firm. Pot chrysanthemums are plentiful in small sizes, but sell only fairly well.

Funeral work has been brisk the past week owing to the death of several prominent people. White chrysanthemums and Beauty were in good demand. Large decorative orders are scarce, though there is a steady call for flowers for small affairs, and in general business is in a healthy state.

The Park Floral Company is the first to offer Begonia Gloire de Lorraine. They are making a good display of these plants at their store and meeting with good sale. This firm also is sending in good cyclamens. B.

New Bedford, Mass.

Business is still slow. We are flooded with chrysanthemums. The stores are prettily decorated with chrysanthemums and autumn leaves.

Many trees and shrubs are being planted in the parks and by private owners. I noticed a lawn covered with evergreens trimmed to represent figures of swans and geese. This work is also popular in our cemeteries. First the evergreens were trimmed in the form of globes and umbrellas and now they have made an attack on the shrubs. There are a good many Deutzia gracilis in one cemetery which have been sheared into little round balls somewhat like overgrown toadstools. A. B. H.

ELIZABETH, N. J.—Mrs. C. M. Hutchinson has added to her plant a new house 36x100 feet.

Heavy Rooted Carnations
Now Ready

WHITE.	Per 100	1000
Queen Louise	$1.20	$11.00
Flora Hill	1.30	11.00
Alba	3.40	30.00
Wolcott	3.40	30.00
Norway	1.30	11.00
White Cloud	1.30	11.00

PINK AND SHADES.		
Lawson	$1.40	$12.50
Marquis	1.30	11.00
Mermaid	1.30	11.00
Success	5.00	45.00

SCARLET.		
G. H. Crane	$1.40	$12.50
America	1.30	11.00

SCARLET.	Per 100	1000
Mrs. P. Palmer	1.50	14.00
Apollo	3.50	30.00
Estelle	1.50	14.00

CRIMSONS.		
Harlowarden	$5.00	$45.00
Gov. Roosevelt	1.30	11.00
Harry Fenn	3.00	25.00

YELLOW.		
Eldorado	$1.30	$11.00

VARIEGATED.		
Stella	$5.00	$25.00
Armazindy	1.30	11.00

25 at 100 rates. $50 at 1000 rates.

Express prepaid to your city at above prices. Spot Cash, no discount.

California Carnation Co., Lock Box, 103, LOOMIS, CAL.

E. T. GRAVE, RICHMOND, IND.
WHOLESALE FLORIST.
CARNATIONS and ROSES.

500,000 VERBENAS
THE CHOICEST VARIETIES IN CULTIVATION.

Fine pot plants, $2.50 per 100; $20 per 1000. Rooted Cuttings, 60c per 100; $5 per 1000; $45 per 10,000.

NO RUST OR MILDEW.

PACKED LIGHT, AND SATISFACTION GUARANTEED. SEND FOR CIRCULAR.

We are the Largest Growers of Verbenas in the country. Our plants cannot be surpassed.

J. L. DILLON, BLOOMSBURG, PA.

FERNS.

Boston Ferns.		Piersoni Ferns.	
2¼-inch	$5.00 per 100	2¼-inch	$.35 each
3-inch	10.00 per 100	50 at	.30 each
4-inch	15.00 per 100	100 at	.25 each
5-inch	20.00 per 100	3-inch	.50 each
6-inch	40.00 per 100	4-inch	.75 each
7-inch	60.00 per 100	5-inch	1.00 each
8-inch	75.00 each	6-inch	1.50 each
10-inch, 3 to	2.50 each	7-inch	2.50 each
		8-inch	3.00 each

ASPARAGUS Plumosus, 2-in. $6. 2½-in. $8 per 100; Sprengeri, 2-in. $3.50, 3-in. $5, 4-in. $10 per 100.

Order 2-in. Cinerarias, Chinese Primula and Obconica. Cut Roses and Carnations.

Only Mrs. Joost and Fisher, field-grown Carnations left. Order at once.

GEO. A. KUHL, Pekin, Ill.

Smilax Plants.

5,000 extra strong Smilax plants, 3-inch at 1.00 per 100.

Asparagus Sprengeri, from February sown seed, 3-inch pots, $3.00 per 100

1000 Norway Carnation Plants, to close out, $3.50 per 100.

JOHN BROD, Chicago, Ill.

Pansy Plants.

50c per 100; $3.00 per 1000. CASH.

JOS. H. CUNNINGHAM. Delaware, O.

GARDENING

This is the paper to recommend to your customers, the leading horticultural journal in America for amateurs ....

$2.00 Per Year. Sample Copies Free.

Liberal terms to florists who take subscriptions.

THE GARDENING CO. Monon Building, Chicago, Ill., U.S.A.

Crimson Ramblers FOR EASTER.

3 to 4 feet, fine, 50 for $9.00; $3.50 per dozen.
2,000 Princess of Wales and Swanley White Violets, clumps $5.00 per 100. Extra 5,000 Forcing Tomato Plants, Lorillard and Mayflower selected stock, 3½-in pot plants, $2.00 per 100; 500 for $9.00. Cash please.

BENJ. CONNELL, West Grove, Pa.

Boston Ferns.

A Choice Stock. Well Grown.

150 in 3-inch pots	$8.00 per 100
75 in 4-inch pots	15.00 "
75 in 5-inch pots	30.00 "
350 Asp. Sprengeri, 3½-inch pots	4.00 "

GELLON & WOLF, DOWNERS GROVE, ILL.

Vinca Variegata Major.

Not less than 5 vines 3 feet. JOOST CARNATION PLANTS strong, field-grown, $3 per 100. HYDRANGEA OTAKSA, large enough for ½ barrel tubs, $1.00 each; $10.00 per doz. COLEUS and ENGLISH IVY, from 3-inch pots, $2.00 per 100.

J. H. DANN & SONS, Westfield, N. Y.

BOSTON FERN RUNNERS

Extra nice, strong runners from bench at $15.00 per 100.

J. W. Bernard,
MARION. IND.

Syracuse, N. Y.

COLD SNAP STARTS HEATING PLANTS GOING. — ALL FLORISTS PREPARED. — LARGE THANKSGIVING TRADE EXPECTED.

The weather the last week has been extremely cold and trade has been picked up. None of the florists was unprepared for the cold snap. All had their heating systems in good order...A large Thanksgiving trade is looked for, although the announcement that turkeys will be 30 cents a pound has caused some to fear there will be no money left for flowers. Chrysanthemums are selling well in the sizes that bring from $1.50 to $3 a dozen. But few of the larger sizes have been on the market. Roses are as good as can be expected, selling for $1.25 to $2.50 a dozen. There continues to be a scarcity of carnations and the quality is not as good as could be desired. Violets have not been offered to any extent. The few that have been sold brought about $2 a hundred.

Carnation experts are more than pleased at the success of L. E. Marquisee's new Flamingo. It has been demonstrated this fall that it will be in full flower for Thanksgiving. It is now full of buds. Its prospects for success are good. It supplies the handsome red flower which has been lacking. Mr. Marquisee's white carnation, Albatross, is notable as one which will flower in the field.

P. R. Quinlan & Company have completed their carnation house at Onondaga Valley and work on their entire plant is being pushed. Manager W. S. Wheadon, of the South Salina street store is in the west on a hunting trip.

George Stuart, well known as an authority on flowers and field culture, died at his home in Skaneateles, October 17. He was born in Scotland in 1828 and had been for thirty-three years gardener at the S. N. Roosevelt place.

Henry Morris, who has finished settling his new store, has had an extra large trade in bulbs, tulips, hyacinths and daffodils being the most in demand.

                   A. J. B.

LINCOLN, ILL.—It is reported that Hans Schonalzi will open a new greenhouse in West Lincoln.

CEDAR RAPIDS, IA.—James G. Crozer will open to the public his new flower store at 327 Second avenue October 24. He will carry a complete stock of cut flowers, foliage and potted plants.

Cincinnati.

FROST TOWARDS WEEK'S END AIDS THE FLORISTS.—GREENHOUSE STOCK SCARCE AND BRINGS GOOD PRICES.

Trade the last week has been very good. All kinds of flowers were plentiful the first of the week. A heavy frost later killed all outdoor flowers and has a tendency to make stock scarce. Bride and Bridesmaid are improving in quality and the best easily bring $6 per 100. The supply of Liberty and Meteor does not equal the demand. American Beauty roses are decreasing in quantity and are bringing better prices. Carnations, especially white, are still very scarce. Violets are selling well at 50 cents and 75 cents per hundred. As to chrysanthemums, yellows seem to have had the call the past few days and quite a number of good orders for this color were turned down. White blooms are plentiful enough to fill all orders. Small white chrysanthemums are scarce and would sell well as there seems to be a call for this kind of flowers. Smilax and other green goods are plentiful.

Mrs. Anna Popp, widow of the late John Popp, of Central Covington, Ky., died Friday, October 23, and was buried at Linden Grove cemetery, Sunday. Many relatives, friends and members of the craft attended the funeral.

Miss Edith F. Kyrk has opened a retail store at 3446 Reading road, Avondale, under the firm name of Edith F. Kyrk & Company.   A. O.

The Missing Potts.

John D. Rockefeller had for some months an expert greenhouse superintendent named Potts who knew a good deal about greenhouse management. A recent visitor at the Rockefeller house missed Potts and inquired for him. Then, according to The Saturday Evening Post, this conversation took place:

"Oh, Potts," said Mr. Rockefeller. "Yes, he knew more about greenhouse plants than any man I ever saw."

"But where is he?"

"Well, he's gone. It was wonderful, his knowledge of plants."

"You must have hated to part with him."

"Yes, I did. But it had to be. You see, he kept coming later and later every day and going home earlier and earlier."

"Well, a man of his ability might have been worth retaining even on short hours."

"Perhaps, perhaps. First he came and stayed eight hours, then six, then four; then he got down to two."

"But two hours of such a man's time was worth having."

"Yes, yes," answered Mr. Rockefeller slowly. "Of course, I hope I appreciated Potts. I didn't object to two hours' service. But he got so he didn't come at all—just sent his card; then I dispensed with him."—Ottawa (Ontario) Press.

MAYVILLE, WIS.—Miss Ella Naber opened to the public her greenhouse on North Main street October 15.

JOLIET, ILL.—The Republican, of this city, complains that the local growers are barred from competing in important classes at the flower show to be held November 4–7.

For Sale

Twenty-two large and beautiful

Palms.

Must be sold at once. Write for list and description. No reasonable offer refused.

H. L. CONDE,
Oswego, N. Y.

Cleveland.

FINE DAYS AND COLD NIGHTS GIVE FLORISTS TROUBLE.—TRADE GOOD AND STOCK PLENTIFUL.—DAHLIAS STILL TO BE SEEN.

At the meeting of the Cleveland Florists' Club Messrs. George and Thomas Ponting were elected to membership. Nathan Smith & Son, of Adrian, Mich., sent over to the club a sample bunch of their new Canna Express. A committee of three was appointed to judge its merits and considered it a very good stock canna.

The usual early varieties of chrysanthemums are in, pink, white and yellow. The ideal weather parodoxically helps add hinders the florist. The sun shines beautifully all day, but the nights are so cold he has to fire up. In the day time he can open the ventilators and let the fire go down. Roses and carnations are plentiful and of good quality. A few belated dahlias can still be seen and cosmos is in its glory, more beautiful than ever and more in demand.

Westman & Getz furnished the decorations at the National Hardware Company's banquet at Chamber of Commerce Hall October 22. The place was festooned with wild smilax, the musicians' platform banked with palms and draped with bunting. Ten small tables were used with a vase of large white chrysanthemums on each table and smilax festooned around it. It was a very striking display.

Mrs. Leisy, on Vega avenue, whose florist is Fred Schneider, has two patriarch palms, a latania and a Seaforthia elegans, each about fifty feet tall and about 25 years old.

Elmer Wilcox, formerly with the J. M. Gasser Company, is now connected with Miss Jane Eadie's flower store.

Messrs. Jones & Russell have returned from Canton, where they had a large decorating order. O. G.

WENATCHEE, WASH.—To prove that crocuses and freesias can be easily grown here a midwinter flower show is to be held, to be participated in solely by children.

WARREN, ILL.—The Stanford University at Palo Alto, Cal., has engaged Francis Murray to supply them with specimens of the various kinds of plants that grow in this region.

KIFT'S ADJUSTABLE VASE HOLDER.

No. 1.—Brass, nickel, 4 feet long. 6 clasps to each rod. Price complete (with green or white tumblers) $3.95. Price complete (with green or white cornucopia vases) $4.50. No. 2.—Heavy 4 ft. rod, brassed and nickeled, with three clasps for 5 to 6-inch pots, each $1.75.
KIFT'S PATENT Rubber Capped FLOWER TUBES, 1¾-inch diameter, per 100, $3.50.
JOSEPH KIFT & SON, 1725 Chestnut St., Phila., Pa.

Wired Toothpicks

10,000, $1.50; 50,000, $6.25. Manufactured by
W. J. COWEE, BERLIN, N. Y.
Sample Free. For sale by dealers.

Please mention the American Florist when writing.

Foley's Floral Fotographs.

Floral Album, size 12x11 containing 24 different funeral designs. By express $7.00 c. o. d.
226-228½ BOWERY, NEW YORK.

Please mention the American Florist when writing.

LISTEN HERE...

It is time to wake up for Fall Business. Our new goods are now in and no wide-awake florist will try to get along without them. They are strictly up-to-date. No other house offers such a variety and none can compete with us on prices. Fall styles in Baskets, Fern Dishes, etc., are novel and beautiful. Try a sample order. It will please you.

ILLUSTRATED CATALOGUE ON APPLICATION.

H. BAYERSDORFER & CO.

IMPORTERS AND MANUFACTURERS OF FLORISTS' SUPPLIES.
50-56 North Fourth St., PHILADELPHIA, PA.

MODEL EXTENSION CARNATION SUPPORT

Made with two or three circles. Endorsed by all the Leading Carnation growers as the best support on the market.

Pat. July 27, '97, May 17, '98

Prompt Shipment Guaranteed.

IGOE BROS.

226 North 9th St., BROOKLYN, N. Y.

Please mention the American Florist when writing.

Boston Florist Letter Co.

MANUFACTURERS OF
FLORISTS' LETTERS.

This wooden box nicely stained and varnished, 18x30x12 made in two sections, one for each size letter, given away with first order of 500 letters.

Block Letters, 1½ or 2-inch size, per 100, $2.00. Script Letters $4. Fastener with each letter or word.

Used by leading florists everywhere and for sale by all wholesale florists and supply dealers.

N. F. McCARTHY, Treas. and Manager,
84 Hawley St., BOSTON, MASS.

Please mention the American Florist when writing.

New Through Sleepers to Los Angeles via the Wabash.

The Wabash has inaugurated a line of standard Pullman sleepers between Chicago and Los Angeles, Cal., leaving Chicago daily at 9:17 p. m. The car runs via the Wabash to St. Louis, Iron Mountain to Texarkana, T. & P. to El Paso and thence Southern Pacific, arriving in Los Angeles at 12:25 noon.

For sleeping car reservations, folders, etc, apply to your nearest ticket agent, or to

F. A. PALMER, A. G. P. A., CHICAGO.

FLOREO

The Only Food Known to Science or Practice for Cut Flowers, Floral Pieces, Foliage, Etc.

Saves completely the ever present struggle against wilt and decay. Tills every sire of the branch and flower with food and lifegiving substance. The flower simply goes on feeding, living and breathing after being separated from the parent stock. Guaranteed to retain form, color and fragrance for longer periods than are possible by any other means. Not affected by heat or cold, it is odorless, harmless and will not stain. Simply put it in the water used in preserving the flowers.

For Sale by All Dealers.

If any there, write us direct and we will see that you are supplied. Send today for circulars, prices, etc. Sent free. Liberal Discount to the Trade.

FLOREO CHEMICAL COMPANY, Dep B, 608 First Nat'l Bank Bldg., CHICAGO.

Sample by mail postpaid 10c.

BEST AND Cheapest ALL-ROUND INSECTICIDE on the Market.

ROSE LEAF EXTRACT OF TOBACCO INSECTICIDE

For Sale by Seedsmen. Write to The Kentucky Tobacco Product Co., Louisville, Ky.

SIGMUND GELLER

Importer and Manufacturer of

FLORISTS' SUPPLIES

All new Fall Goods in now. Ask to see the latest, Embossed and Pleated Crepe Paper,
108 W. 28th Street, NEW YORK.

GREEN SILKALINE.

Do not be put off with cheap substitutes.

John C. Meyer & Co.,
80 Kingston St., BOSTON, MASS

RIBBONS...

FOR YOUR TRADE AT

SIMON RODH,

40 W. 28th St., NEW YORK,
Chiffons, all Widths and Colors.

It is good business policy to mention the

American Florist

When you write to an advertiser.

Milwaukee.

MARKET CONDITIONS IMPROVE.—CHRYSAN-
THEMUM SHOW PROPOSED FOR NEXT
YEAR.—CLUB MEMBERS TO BANQUET.—
NOTES.

There has been a marked improvement the past few days in the condition of the market, this being no doubt due to the cooler weather. There are carnations enough for all orders but the stock is being cleaned out very well. Some very fine chrysanthemums are arriving, a particularly good lot of Bonnaffons being noted. The quality of the violets is improving daily with sufficient supply for all demands. American Beauty is in heavy demand as well as Mme. Chatenay. There is plenty of adiantum and smilax in the market to take care of the demand, which is exceptionally heavy at the present time.

The Florists' Club decided at its last meeting in 1904 and committees are now at work in the preliminary work. The success of the convention exhibition has encouraged the local florists to such an extent that they are confident they can hold a flower show equal to any in the country.

The Florists' Club will hold its next regular meeting at the new quarters in the Empire building. The committee promises a very good banquet. All members are requested to be present.

August Kellner is building two houses of moderate size for the care of decorative plants. He will make a specialty of this in winter months and of landscape work in summer.

Currie Brothers were recently incorporated and will be known as the Currie Brothers' Company. There will be no change in the management.

McKenney & Company have installed a beautiful chandelier, which helps to make their already fine store still more attractive.

The death of some very prominent men lately has boomed the florists' business to a considerable extent.

Kapsalis and Lambros are making excellent use of their chrysanthemums in their window display. "H."

MARSHALL, MO.—The new improvements at D. H. Heskett's are about completed. Additions of carnation and rose houses have been made and their contents are now in bloom. A new office and improvements for watering and heating have been made.

RAFFIA

St. Louis.

EXPRESSMEN'S STRIKE AND RUN ON TRUST COMPANIES HAVE BAD EFFECT ON MARKET.—STOCK IN GOOD SHAPE.

The condition of trade is not as satisfactory as it has been. A strike of expressmen is now on, and is causing a great deal of inconvenience in making deliveries. A threatened run on several of the Trust companies effected the market considerably. There is a greater demand for American Beauty. Carnations move slowly, a few bringing fancy prices. There is no demand for out-of-door stock. A few violets (fancy) bring 40 cents per hundred. Tuberoses are out of the market.

Several carloads of agaves were received at the World's Fair recently. They were purchased from the landscape department of the Notre Dame university, South Bend, Ind. The plants had grown to such a size as to be practically useless to the university.

F. W. Taylor, chief of the agricultural department at the World's Fair, gave a very interesting talk at the meeting of the Engelmann Botanical Club the evening of October 26.

Otto Koenig has had a busy week. He has cut all his early chrysanthemums and commenced on the intermediate varieties.

The Chicago Carnation Company is sending in some good carnations, among them the new varieties, Fiancee and N. Chandler.

In all probability the next meeting of the Florists' Club will be held at Shaws' Garden.

Geo. Waldbart says he has his hands full of funeral work and parties.

F. K. B.

Greenhouse Building.

Bridgewater, Mass.—D. F. Lehan, conservatory.

Newark, N.J.—Frank Dolger, conservatory 45x45.

Newburyport, Mass.—E. W. Pearson, house 200 feet long.

Westerly, R. I.—S. J. Reuter, two houses each 35x500.

Auburn, R. I.—Budlong Company, carnation house 700 feet long.

Cromwell, Conn.—A. N. Pierson, carnation house 40x140.

MARSHALLTOWN, IA.—Kembel's chrysanthemum display is attracting much attention.

Meetings of Florists' Clubs.

BALTIMORE, MD.—Gardeners' Club of Baltimore, Royal Arcanum building, 18 W. Saratoga street. Second and fourth Monday of each month, at 8 p. m. John J. Perry, Sec'y, Gay and Eager streets.

BOSTON, MASS.—Gardeners' and Florists' Club of Boston, Horticultural Hall. Meets second Tuesday of each month, October to March inclusive. W. E. Fischer, Sec'y, 18 Union Terrace, Jamaica Plain, Mass.

BROCKTON, MASS. — Brockton Gardeners' and Florists' Club, store of W. W. Hathaway, Times Building. First and third Tuesday of each month, at 8 p. m. W. W. Hathaway, Sec'y, Brockton, Mass.

BUFFALO, N. Y.—Buffalo Florists' Club, 481 Washington street. Second Wednesday of each month, at 8 p. m. Wm. Legg, Sec'y, 1440 Delaware avenue, Buffalo.

BUTTE, MONT.—Montana Florists' Club, 45 W. Broadway. First Saturday in each month, D. E. Law, Sec'y.

CHICAGO, ILL.—Chicago Florists' Club, Handel Hall, 40 Randolph street. Second and fourth Wednesday of each month, at 8 p. m. George Wienhoeber, Sec'y, 413 Elm street, Chicago.

CINCINNATI, O.—Cincinnati Florists' Society, Jabez Elliott, Flower Market. Second Saturday of each month, at 8 p. m. Geo. Murphy, Sec'y, Sta. F., Cincinnati, O.

CLEVELAND, O.—Cleveland Florists' Club, Progress Hall, 244 Detroit street. Second and fourth Monday of each month, at 8 p. m. Isaac Kennedy, Sec'y, Westpark, O.

DENVER, COLO.—Denver Floral Club, 233 Charles Block. Second and fourth Friday of each month, at 8 p. m. Adam Balmer, Sec'y.

DETROIT, MICH.—Detroit Florists' Club, Cowie Building. Farran and Gratiot avenue. First and third Wednesday of each month at 8 p. m. J. F. Sullivan, Sec'y, 214 Woodward avenue.

GRAND RAPIDS, MICH.—Grand Rapids Florists' Club. Board of Trade rooms, Pearl street. Fourth Monday of each month. N. B. Stover, Sec'y, Grandville, Mich.

HAMILTON, ONT.—Hamilton Gardeners' and Florists' Club, 130½ James street, North. First and third Tuesday of each month at 8 p. m. Chas. M. Webster, Sec'y.

HARTFORD, CONN.—Hartford Florists' Club. Second and fourth Tuesday of each month at 8 p. m. J. F. Coombs, Sec'y.

INDIANAPOLIS, IND.—State Florists' Association of Indiana, Commercial Club rooms, Indianapolis. First Tuesday of each month, at 8 p. m. H. Junge, Sec'y, 456 E. Washington street, Indianapolis.

MILWAUKEE, WIS.—Milwaukee Florists' Club. Meets first Tuesday of each month at St. Charles Hotel club rooms. H. V. Hunkel, Sec'y.

MINNEAPOLIS, MINN.—Minneapolis Florists' Club, West Hotel. First Thursday of each month, at — p. m. O. F. Rice, Sec'y, 124 N. Sixth street.

MONTREAL, QUE.—Montreal Gardeners' and Florists' Club, Alexandra rooms, 2204 St. Catherine street. First and third Monday of each month. W. H. Horobin, Sec'y, 22 Closse street.

NEW LONDON, CONN.—Gardeners' and Florists' Club, first and third Tuesday of each month at greenhouses of secretary. H. B. Appeldorn, Sec'y.

NEW YORK, N. Y.—New York Florists' Club, Grand Opera House Bldg., 8th avenue and 23d St. Second Monday of each month, at 7:30 p. m. John Young, Sec'y, 51 West Twenty-eighth street, New York.

OMAHA, NEB.—Nebraska Florists' Society, City Hall. Second Thursday in each month at 8 p. m. Louis Henderson, Sec'y, 1519 Farnam street, Omaha.

PHILADELPHIA, PA.—Florists' Club of Philadelphia, Horticultural Hall, Broad street above Spruce. First Tuesday of each month, at 8 p. m. Edwin Lonsdale, Sec'y, Wyndmoor, Philadelphia.

PITTSBURG, PA.—Pittsburg and Allegheny Florists' and Gardeners' Club, at Gerana Beneficial Bldg., 6th and Cherry avenue. Second Thursday of each month, at 8 p. m. H. P. Joslin, Sec'y, Ben Avon, Pa.

PROVIDENCE, R. I.—Florists' and Gardeners' Club, of Rhode Island, 96 Westminster street, Providence. Second Thursday of each month, at 8 p. m. Alexander Rennie, Sec'y, 41 Washington street, Providence.

RICHMOND, IND.—Richmond Florists' Club, at the greenhouses of members. Third Monday of each month. H. G. Chessman, Sec'y.

SALT LAKE CITY, UTAH.—Salt Lake Florists' Society, office of Huddart Floral Company, 214 S. Second South street. Second and fourth Friday of each month. H. T. Huddart, Sec'y.

SAN FRANCISCO, CAL.—Pacific Coast Horticultural Society. First saturday and third Monday of each month. Thos H. Munroe, Sec'y.

SEATTLE, WASH.—Seattle Commercial Horticultural Club, First and Cherry streets. First Wednesday of each month. Wm. Hopkins, Sec'y, 622 First avenue.

ST. LOUIS, MO.—St. Louis Florists' Club, Odd Fellows Hall No 3, Ninth and Olive streets. Second Thursday of each month, at 3 p. m. Emil Schray, Sec'y, 4101 Pennsylvania avenue, St. Louis.

TORONTO, ONT.—Toronto Gardeners' and Florists' Association, St. George's Hall, Elm street. Third Tuesday of each month, at 8 p. m. E. F. Collins, Sec'y, 9 Hurst place, Toronto.

UTICA, N. Y.—Utica Florists' Club, 283 Genesee street. First Thursday of each month at 8 p. m. J. C. Spencer, Sec'y.

WASHINGTON, D. C. — Washington Florists' Club. Meets first Wednesday in each month. Wm. F. Gude, Sec'y.

Coming Exhibitions.

[Secretaries are requested to supply any omissions from this list.]

BOSTON, MASS., November 5-8, 1903.—Chrysanthemum exhibition Massachusetts Horticultural Society. W. P. Rich, Sec'y, Horticultural Hall, 300 Massachusetts avenue, Boston.

BUFFALO, N. Y., November 11-14, 1903.—H. A. Meldrum Co.'s flower show; direction. Buffalo Florists' Club. Wm. Legg, Sec'y, 1440 Delaware avenue, Buffalo.

INDIANAPOLIS, IND., November 10-14, 1903.—Indiana Floral Festival and Chrysanthemum exhibition State Florists' Association of Indiana. Irwin Bertermann, Sec'y, 241 Massachusetts avenue, Indianapolis.

JOLIET, ILL., November 4-7, 1903.—Second annual flower show Joliet Improvement Association. Jas. H. Ferriss, Sec'y, Joliet, Ill.

LOUISVILLE, KY., November 11-14, 1903.—Chrysanthemum exhibition florists of Louisville. Nanz & Neuner and E. G. Reimers, Louisville, committee.

MADISON, N. J., November 5-6, 1903.—Annual exhibition Morris County Gardeners' and Florists' Society. S. Redstone, Sec'y, Madison, N. J.

NEW YORK, November 10-12, 1903.—Chrysanthemum exhibition Chrysanthemum Society of America. Fred H. Lemon, Sec'y, Richmond, Ind.

PHILADELPHIA, PA., November 10-14, 1903.—Annual exhibition Pennsylvania Horticultural Society. David Rust, Sec'y, Horticultural Hall, Philadelphia, Pa.

MONTREAL, QUE., November 11-12, 1903.—Chrysanthemum exhi.'tion Montreal Gardeners' and Florists' Club. W. H. Horobin, Sec'y, 22 Closse street, Montreal.

PROVIDENCE, R. I., November 12-13, 1903.—Chrysanthemum exhibition Rhode Island Horticultural Society. C. W. Smith, secretary, 27-29 Exchange street, Providence.

ST. PAUL, MINN., November 10 to 12, 1903.—Chrysanthemum and orchid exhibition Ladies' Auxiliary of Northwestern Manufacturers' Association. Mrs. M. Helen Moss, Sec'y, St. Paul.

TARRYTOWN, N. Y., November 4-6, 1903.—Fifth annual exhibition Tarrytown Horticultural Society. Edw. W. Neubrand, Sec'y, Tarrytown, N. Y.

Please mention the American Florist when writing.

Pittsburg.

SOCIAL ACTIVITY MAKES BUSINESS IMPROVE.
—SNOW VISITS CITY.—FLORISTS ESCAPE
IN BANK FAILURES.

Business continues to improve. The resumption of social activities has helped much. At present we are experiencing the extremes of weather, snows included. Two of our national banks suspended last week, but none of our craft were ·depositors. Stock is moving nicely with the exception of cosmos and gladiolus. Roses of all kinds and grades are plentiful. Carnations are doing nicely, White Cloud, Mrs. Lawson, Enchantress and Floriana being especially fine.

The Pittsburg Cut Flower Company reports business as very satisfactory, the shipping trade especially much improved. This firm sends a shipment of chrysanthemums and carnations to New Orleans, La., three times each week.

Randolph & McClements have received a large shipment of palms from the east, and are also displaying a large assortment of Anna Foster ferns.

The Pittsburg Florists' exchange states that·business up to date has exceeded expectations. An arrangement for more room has been made.

Application has been made for a charter by the Elliott Nursery Company, capitalized at $10,000.

The new Arcade building to be constructed in "Masters' Way" is endeavoring to secure Florists' stands. E. W. S.

Buffalo, N. Y.

The weather was clear and cold last week. The first fall of snow was October 26. It fell again the 27th. Trade has been fair, although there were very few receptions. Everything is politics. W. Scott wrote a letter to the press eulogizing W. F. Kasting.

The greenhouses of Anton Wean on Main street near Humboldt parkway were destroyed by fire. The loss was about $3,000 on greenhouses and stock. Whether he will rebuild is doubtful. He has another place at Black Rock.

Buffalo florists stick to the agreement signed three years ago and do not donate. Everyone is used to it. The trade comes without giving a dozen palms with a $5 smilax and cut flower order.

Jos. Streit, foreman at S. A. Anderson's greenhouse, ran a long wire, such as are ·used on chrysanthemum plants, almost through his arm, which disabled him for several days.

Supt. Keitsch, of the H. A. Neeldrum Company flower show, says the committee has·invited leading florists as judges.

Wm. C. Stroh, of Attica, N. Y., and Wise Brothers, East Aurora, are sending in some fine violets.

D. B. Long has a new design for a letter head, a small, very artistic cluster of roses. BISON.

LOUISVILLE, Ky.—The florists of this city have arranged for a chrysanthemum show, to be held November 11-14.

HARTFORD, MICH.—W. H. Blashfield is preparing to erect a greenhouse 15x40 feet and will engage in the culture of flowers as a business proposition. There is a good opening for a greenhouse in Hartford and Mr. Blashfield has proved himself a successful florist in his private gardens.

ALWAYS mention the AMERICAN FLORIST when writing to advertisers.

The Standard

The lightest running, most rapid and powerful ventilating machinery in the market.

DUPLEX GUTTERS

Made of wrought or cast iron with self-adjusting sash bar clips. The only Drip Proof Metal Gutter offered to the public. Send for my catalogue free.

E. HIPPARD, Youngstown, O.

THE "NEW DEPARTURE" VENTILATING APPLIANCE.

This is a funny looking thing but it will do the work easier and cost less than any other apparatus on earth or any other place. Send for a descriptive circular to

J. D. CARMODY, Evansville, Ind.

NATIONAL FLORISTS
Board of Trade,

Offices: 56 Pine St., NEW YORK.

CREDIT REFERENCE BOOK. A subscription to our Credit List will cost you $10 a year, and it may save you $100 the first month.

SPECIAL REPORTS. We make a specialty of this part of our work, and spare neither trouble nor money to get for our clients the very latest and most reliable information, as to the standing of any person concerning whom inquiries are made.

COLLECTIONS. We collect slow and doubtful accounts. Why not go through your books at once, and send us all the claims that are in arrears?

Call and see us when you are in the city.

"PIERSON" BOILERS

WATER AND STEAM. The Most Complete and Perfect line of Horticultural Boilers

OVER 100 SIZES AND STYLES.

Iron Frame Conservatories, Palm Houses and Greenhouses, Red Gulf Cypress Greenhouse Material, Ventilating Apparatus, Plans, Specifications and Estimates. Prompt Shipments.

THE PIERSON-SEFTON CO.

Designers, Manufacturers and Builders of Horticultural Structures.

West Side Ave., South, Jersey City, N. J.

THE AMERICAN FLORIST

A WEEKLY JOURNAL FOR THE TRADE

America is "the Prow of the Vessel; there may be more comfort Amidships, but we are the first to touch Unknown Seas."

Vol. XXI.   CHICAGO AND NEW YORK, NOVEMBER 7, 1903.   No, 805.

THE AMERICAN FLORIST

NINETEENTH YEAR.

Copyright 1903, by American Florist Company
Entered as Second-Class Mail Matter.

PUBLISHED EVERY SATURDAY BY

AMERICAN FLORIST COMPANY,
324 Dearborn St., Chicago.
Eastern Office: 79 Milk St., Boston.

Subscription, $1.00 a year.   To Europe, $2.00.
Subscriptions accepted only from the trade.
Volumes half-yearly from August, 1901.

SOCIETY OF AMERICAN FLORISTS AND
ORNAMENTAL HORTICULTURISTS.
OFFICERS—JOHN BURTON, Philadelphia, Pa.,
president; C. C. POLLWORTH, Milwaukee, Wis.,
vice-president; WM. J. STEWART, 79 Milk Street,
Boston, Mass., secretary; H. B. BEATTY, Oil City,
Pa., treasurer.
OFFICERS-ELECT—PHILIP BREITMEYER, president; J. J. BENEKE, vice-president; secretary and
treasurer as before. Twentieth annual meeting
at St. Louis, Mo., August, 1904.

THE AMERICAN CARNATION SOCIETY.
Annual convention at Detroit, Mich., March 9,
1904. ALBERT M. HERR, Lancaster, Pa., secretary.

AMERICAN ROSE SOCIETY.
Annual meeting and exhibition, Philadelphia,
March, 1904. LEONARD BARRON, 136 Liberty St.,
New York, secretary.

CHRYSANTHEMUM SOCIETY OF AMERICA
Annual convention and exhibition, New York,
November 10-13, 1903. FRED H. LEMON, Richmond,
Ind., secretary.

THIS ISSUE 40 PAGES WITH COVER.

The Carnation.

J. C. JENSEN says salt water is the best spray for carnations infested with thrips.

A HANDSOME sport from Prosperity carnation has developed with A. N. Pierson at Cromwell, Conn., in which the color is massed toward the center of the flower somewhat in the way of Maud Dean.

FAIR PRICES FOR CARNATIONS.

In our issues of September 19 and October 24 some comments on this subject were published. Additional opinions are now given herewith:

I think the prices given by Mr. Rudd would be as low as good blooms could be sold for, taking the season's cut.

Fall River, Mass.   C. WARBURTON.

We would say that prices for Lawson, Norway and Lorna should average 4 cents and Queen Louise, Dorothy and Estelle 3 cents. We fire nearly nine months. The best grade of soft coal costs, delivered, $3 per ton. Our trade is almost entirely a shipping one, and we have express rates to consider in all our calculations.   H. WEBER & SONS.

Oakland, Md.

We have not been able to produce good Prosperity at less than $6 per 100, and would not care to accept a contract here for Norway, Lawson, Estelle, Dorothy and Queen Louise for less than $4 per 100. These figures are based on our past experience with these varieties and it might be well to add that carnations do not seem to take hold of our soil early in the season, and this increases the cost per bloom, as we do not have as long a season as if they produced flowers earlier.   GEO. M. KELLOGG.

Pleasant Hill, Mo.

Here in Minnesota, where we are obliged to fire from October to June 1 with coal at from $4 to $5 per ton, in my opinion such varieties as Queen Louise, Estelle, Lawson, Norway, Lorna and Dorothy cannot be grown for less than 2½ cents on a season's contract, allowing that the contract would run eleven months of the year and also that the blooms be grown to a good average standard, for it is well known that while such varieties as Lawson, Norway and Lorna, as grown by some growers, are easily worth 3 cents, as grown by others they may not be worth 2 cents on a season's contract. While this is my first year's experience with Enchantress, I should judge that 3½ cents would be a good season's average, while Prosperity should bring from 5 to 6 cents.

Minneapolis, Minn.   OTTO A. WILL.

To contract for a season's cut of carnations I would first figure the expense of growing, allowing for extra heat for certain varieties and their productiveness. Of course the blooms are to be first-class, and it takes more heat to grow Lawson and Estelle, therefore they will have to bring more money. I would rate them as follows:

Queen Louise..)
Dorothy.......) ....2½ cents.
Norway ..)
Lorna...) 3   "
Estelle...)
Lawson ..) ....3½   "
Enchantress........................4   "
Prosperity.........................7   "

Richmond, Ind.   CHAS. KNOPF.

One of the difficult parts of our business is to make prices so that we have a living profit and not a loss at the end of the season. No matter how carefully grown nor how good the grower there will always be some portion of a carnation house that will be run at a dead loss, either owing to misplaced judgment in buying a variety or some mistake in handling one of the older varieties, a mistake that you do not know where to place nor perhaps will ever know. These losses are part and parcel of the business and must be taken into account. Queen Louise, Estelle, Lorna and Dorothy could be grown for $2.50 or $3 per 100; if the latter figure they could be furnished October 1 to June 1; if $2.50, then the price should be doubled the week preceding and including Christmas and Easter. Norway I never grew. Lawson should be $4 per 100, and if no split calyxs are included it should be $5. Enchantress should be $5 and Prosperity $8 or $10. At these prices the flowers should be first class and no seconds put in.

Lancaster, Pa.   A. M. HERR.

The price of carnation blooms for an entire season's cut for all the varieties named, excepting Prosperity and Enchantress, should be 2 cents. It should be double that for Prosperity, with no data by which even to guess at

Enchantress. I believe that, being new and a fine flower, although freely produced it should be at least 3 cents. The price will vary, according to location and expense of growing. The man who can get coal for $1.50 per ton, being near a mine, can grow profitably at a less figure than his competitor who pays $3.50 or more for it. Again, the expense of labor will affect the problem. An adverse growing season with late planting and sunless weather, such as was experienced in the middle west last season would also have a bearing on the production and price. The season for the prices mentioned would be from September 1 to July 1, and only marketable flowers would be included. These figures are for the average florist, having a moderately sized plant, and growing for a wholesale market only; whether these prices would be satisfactory to very large growers I do not know. But I am convinced that from the varying conditions and circumstances surrounding the problem it will be as hard of accurate solution as it is to figure out, how old is Ann?

GEO. F. CRABB.
Grand Rapids, Mich.

It is my opinion that a more satisfactory basis could be concluded by dividing the varieties mentioned into classes and seasons as follows in the case of Queen Louise, Norway, Lorna and Dorothy:

October 15 to December 1	2 cents.
December 1 to February 15	3 "
February 15 to April 15	3½ "
April 15 until close of season	1½ "

The grower would lose a little by this plan on Lorna, which gives out early in the spring, but he would make it up on Queen Louise, which variety is at its best at this time. Dorothy also being very plentiful late in the season, although fading as the weather gets warmer, the seller would be able to make bargain sales and still not be a loser. Then I would class Prosperity, Lawson, Estelle and Enchantress and price them as follows:

October 15 to December 1	2½ cents.
December 1 to February 15	4 "
February 15 to April 1	3 "
April 1 until close of season	2 "

Several points should be taken into consideration when entering into a contract of this kind. On the grower's side

there is a big difference in the productiveness of these varieties, and on the seller's a wide margin in the demand and selling qualities. But if the quantities of the varieties are about the same I believe a satisfactory agreement could be arrived at on the basis I have stated.

Rockford, Ill. C. W. JOHNSON.

I have kept a very careful record for a number of years, and find that while the entire cut from my place will some months average more than 2½ cents, the average for the entire season, including the summer months, is far below this figure. Your querist says the entire cut, which, I take it, means short stem and split flowers included, at least in the winter months, when flowers are scarce. The figures given below are for the entire season every year from September 1 to August 31, and all short-stemmed and split flowers are included, also all that were thrown away in times of glut. That is to say, if 3,000 flowers were sent in and only 2,700 of them sold, the others being poor specimens, the 300 unsold pulled down the average of the 2,700. This, I think, is the only fair way to figure. The customary commission also is deducted:

SEASON 1902-03.

Month	Price per 100.
September	$ .95 1-10
October	.94 5-10
November	1.31 7-10
December	2.16 8-10
January	2.92 7-10
February	3.34 3-10
March	2.42 3-10
April	2.50
May	.79 6-10
June	1.00
July	.60 7-10
August	.58

FIVE SEASON'S AVERAGE.

Season	Price per 100.
1898-99	$1.16 6-10
1899-00	1.48 1-10
1900-01	1.46 9-10
1901-02	1.27
1902-03	1.48 8-10

While we have made money at above figures, considering the present cost of building and maintainance, labor and coal especially, the prices are not what they ought to be. If any one department of the business ought to make the most money, it is the growing end of it. The grower has the most to risk and the most money invested.

Clayton, Mo. J. W. DUNFORD.

CULTURAL REMINDERS.

About the time these notes are printed most of us can look for periodical changes of the fall weather into winter, which, however, cannot be expected to last for any length of time. The alternating weeks of wintry weather, warm days, and cloudy, wet weather are looked on as the natural dispensation of the season. The cultural reminders written some weeks ago will apply with extra force to this time. Daily we are approaching near to the season of short days, when the forces of nature are hardly sufficient to keep the organs of the plants above a semi-dormant state of activity. And in addition to the adverse conditions outside we must take into account the inherited habit of the plants to expect and quickly respond to any influence that has a tendency to encourage rest.

Those of us who are acquainted with the habits of the rose and other tender plants and have observed their custom of remaining for some months under the spell of a check received during the fall can appreciate the fact that the carnation is more or less subject to the same laws, and though to the inexperienced it may be slow to show the effect of adverse surroundings, the results are sure to be seen in their full magnitude later on.

In the case of a bench of roses a soggy soil and a few chilly nights would result in a bad case of mildew or black spot before the change of the moon, while in the case of carnations such a condition would not lessen the quality of the cut for the time being and the plants would retain their bloom of health for some weeks. But in a month or so the actual state of affairs would crop out in various ways. The stems would become weak, the flowers small and dull in color and the plants would take on a feeble appearance. All this would be the result of the check to the root action a few weeks before. Too much care cannot be exercised at this season with respect to watering and ventilating, and especially should we seek during a period of one kind of weather to keep the plants in shape to meet a sudden change. During cloudy spells it should be our aim to maintain as dry an atmosphere as possible and keep the soil a little on the dry side, at the same time giving an abundance of air, so that in the event of a change to sunny, warm weather the plants will not be inclined to wilt from the increased sunlight and a more rapid circulation of air.

Some varieties will be in shape to receive a little extra nourishment. If the stems need stiffening a very light top-dressing of hard wood ashes will help to remedy the defect. Sheep manure is rich in nitrogen and will promote growth. Soot will improve the color of nearly all varieties. Bone meal encourages bud formation. Lime, while in itself a valuable fertilizer, tends to set free unavailable nourishment in the soil and prevent sourness, and is therefore especially valuable at this season. A very light dressing, just enough to whiten the surface of the soil, once a month will counterbalance adverse weather conditions. In no case should any feeding be done before the plants have taken full possession of the soil, or when for any reason they are not in a good growing condition.

From now on the plants will need every bit of light they can possibly get and the glass above them should be free from all foreign matter, inside and outside. In the case of butted glass more or less dirt is apt to find its way through the cracks and adhere to the under surface. To

No. 7. THE DECORATION OF HOME GROUNDS.

remove this choose a bright, sunny day and early in the morning, before there is any air in the house and the glass is still wet, rub the under surface with a rag or brush. The soil, having been soaked in the condensation over night, will come off easily. When several rows have been rubbed direct a strong spray of clear water against the glass to rinse off the dirt. The change will be very marked and even with lapped glass, where the

was adapted to the situation or that harmony of companionship was requisite for the decoration of the house. A beautiful plant, but it has not made the house more beautiful, that is, the house is in no wise incorporated into the beauty created by the planting of the spiræa. No. 9.—This shows the tendency in park culture. The roses and shrubbery are thrifty and pleasing, but they, like us pedestrians, are warned to keep off

The Rose.

LIBERTY rose requires from eight to ten degrees more heat than is usually given to Bride and Bridesmaid. Above all never let it receive any check that will encourage its propensity to go to sleep in cold weather. When it once is allowed to get drowsy that settles it.

SOUVENIR DE PIERRE NOTTING is a new rose which has the approval of several growers who have been trying it. It is a fine grower, free bloomer and bears a large and long-petalled bud of creamy color suffused with rose. The color is not decided enough to make a sensation, however.

FEEDING WITH LIQUID MANURE, '
When a house of roses is in a vigorous state of growth, with the soil in such a condition that nutriment is needed, an application of liquid manure is very beneficial. This form of feeding is rapid in effect and is also easily controlled. When the plants are just starting a new crop with the young breaks four or five inches long it is a good time to start the feeding. Start with the liquid quite weak and gradually increase the strength. An application about twice a week at this time of the year is sufficient. If the plants show any signs of feeble growth the liquid should be withheld until they have returned to their proper state.

No. 8. THE DECORATION OF HOME GROUNDS.

quantity of accumulated soil is very small, the difference is very appreciable.

There is no reason why any good side growths available for cuttings should go to waste from now on. There are a few varieties that will grow overly large if propagated before January 1, but with the great majority we are only too glad to commence early, for the early cuttings are always ahead of the later batches and anything gained in size is appreciated in these days of early housing. The reason why early propagated stock so often falls short of paying for the few months extra given is because about the time it is rooted, and for a month or two thereafter, room is very scarce and the young plants are usually crowded into odd corners, there to remain long after a bench of chrysanthemums has been cleared off and space has become more plentiful.

Now is the time to take advantage of every chance to pile up next year's supply of soil. If space is no object, and it seldom is in winter, have the pile no more than a foot deep, so as to give the elements free access to every particle. I do not like the practice of putting up a lot of soil in the fall with alternating layers of soil and manure. The manure may as well be left out until the first spring turning, and it will have plenty of time to permeate the whole mass in the few months before housing time. J.

Decoration of Home Grounds.

No. 7.—A large Babylonica willow. The seat below it and general care shown is evidence of the owner's appreciation, and causes a stranger to feel that he is within a friendly influence while under the shelter of such a tree.

No. 8.—A beautiful shrub, Spiræa sorbifolia, but there are indications that it came by express and a convenient place for planting selected without regard or knowledge as to whether its individuality

the grass." The dividing line, "Thus far shalt thou go and no farther," is visible and denotes rigid rule in place of harmonious feelings. The stone edged walk, kept bare, trying and painful to look at, is an expense; the man with the hoe is in daily conflict with nature.

BOOKKEEPING and account forms for same by R. F. Tesson, as read at the Milwaukee convention has been printed in pamphlet form by the AMERICAN FLORIST and will be mailed FREE on request to any florist. Employers may have extra copies to distribute among

their employes. The address is of much permanent value and well worth the study of our young men.

Cow manure is best adapted for a liquid food, as it supplies all the elements necessary to the rose, and it does not contain any which are injurious. A good way to arrange the feeding process is to use two tanks one larger than the other. The larger one should be of sufficient capacity to water one house at least. In the smaller tank place the manure, drain from this to the larger one and pump from here into the pipes. It is very important that all straw and refuse be removed before the liquid enters the last tank or the pump will be unable to deliver the stream. A screen of ¼ inch mesh will allow the water to pass through and also retain the refuse. It will be found necessary to stir the manure occasionally

No. 9. THE DECORATION OF HOME GROUNDS.

in the first tank and keep it from packing closely against the screen or the fluid will not filter through.

When feeding liquid manure keep a careful watch on the plants and do not feed too often or too strongly. Study the plants continually, endeavoring at all times to meet their demands. Stock of first quality is what pays and it is only possible to grow the best by watching the smallest points from start to finish.
R. I.

Chrysanthemum Society of America.

Unless all signs fail the exhibition of the Chrysanthemum Society of America and the American Institute to be held in New York November 10-12, will be all that its promoters have striven to make it, the greatest feast of chrysanthemums we have ever seen. The Herald square exhibition hall is certainly the largest and best lighted hall in New York to-day. There is abundant space to display all the exhibits that may be brought there and under perfect daylight their merits can be seen to the best advantage and true color values appreciated. It rests now with those who have the material to bring it to the show. Intending exhibitors who have not already done so will help the management materially by at once sending their entries to Dr. F. M. Hexamer, 52 Lafayette Place, New York City.

The regulations call for exhibits to be in position by noon Tuesday, November 10, and judging will be commenced at 1 p. m. It is the intention to adhere strictly to those regulations so all judging may be completed and the awards made when the show opens to the general public at 3 p. m. Thoroughly competent judges have been selected by the executive committee of the C. S. A. There will be nine judges, working in groups of three so there should be no undue delay in rendering decisions, except where unavoidable through closeness of competition demanding prolonged careful deliberation.

A meeting of members of the C. S. A. will be held on the second day of the show at 3 p. m. Anyone wishing to join the society can do so previous to this meeting by paying one dollar and may participate in the meeting. In addition to the regular business there will be an important paper presented dealing with the diseases of the chrysanthemum, prepared by Prof. A. F. Woods, of Washington, or some other experiment station expert. This should be a fertile theme for discussion and can not fail to be helpful to all growers.　　A. HERRINGTON.

It is later announced that the speaker on "Diseases of Chrysanthemums" will be Prof. George E. Stone, of Hatch Experiment Station, Amherst, Mass., Agricultural College.

WORK OF COMMITTEES.

Andrew Morrison, gardener for Curwen Stoddart, Rydal, Pa., exhibited seedling "A" before the Philadelphia committee. This variety is described as a light rose pink, reflex Japanese; scored, commercial scale, 78 points; exhibition scale, 83 points. In the committee's judgment the flowers sent were past their best.
FRED. H. LEMON, Sec'y.

SPRINGFIELD, O.—John W. Yates has moved his cut flower store from 22 W. Liberty street to 51 S. Fountain avenue.

PASADENA, CAL.—It was decided at a meeting of the Tournament association, October 29 to hold a tournament of roses again this year.

A Successful New Jersey Florist.

The oldest established florist in Paterson, N. J., is Edward Sceery, 182-184 Main street, whose store is shown in the accompanying engraving. Mr. Sceery located here after being burned out on Van Houten street in the great fire of 1902. The store was fitted up at a cost of $4,000. It has a 25-foot front and is 125 feet deep, with counters and show cases of the latest designs and mirrors on each side of the sales room, thirty in all. The ice box has a plate glass front, with mirrors and is tiled inside. The firm's delivery wagon is painted a light green and has rubber tires. It took a prize at the recent business men's carnival.

Mr. Sceery was brought up in the florists' business in New York city and went to Paterson over twenty years ago in the employ of Joseph Towell, with whom he remained as manager until he started in business in partnership with the late Charles Thurston, forming the firm of Thurston & Sceery. In a year Mr. Thurston retired. Mr. Sceery has been a member of the Paterson park board for several years and has just been reappointed for a term of five years more. He is a member of the New York Florists' Club and various social and fraternal organizations. He is also a large owner of real estate. Mr. Sceery has an able corps of assistants in his store. William Thurston, his superintendent, has been with him several years.

Florists' Plant Notes.

GERANIUMS.

Now that the early chrysanthemums are over with, the soil should be taken out at once and the bench prepared for other crops. There is no profit in empty benches. A half inch of sand or finely sifted coal ashes spread over the bench is necessary to provide proper drainage for the pots, and to prevent them from drying out too fast. The small geraniums propagated in September need working over by this time. All the dead leaves should be removed and the plants be given more room between the pots to keep them from drawing up. Keep them a little on the dry side so as to induce a slow, stocky growth, for they will not require shifting into 3-inch pots until the first part of the year. The old stock plants should also be cleaned and given more room. By this time a crop of cuttings can be taken off and potted in sandy soil. These old plants will furnish an abundance of cuttings throughout the winter if kept growing in a temperature of about 55°. Those varieties of which the stock is limited can be planted out on a bench in good soil; in this way they will grow stronger and produce more cuttings.

CRIMSON RAMBLERS.

The two-year-old plants of Crimson Rambler will soon arrive from the nursery and should be potted in heavy clay soil as soon as received. If the canes are six or seven feet long shorten them back to three or four feet. These canes can be twisted and bent into any desired shape; they should never be left straight or the breaks will be uneven. Start them in a cool house, as near to 40° as possible, until about twelve weeks before they are wanted in bloom, when the temperature can be gradually increased each week until 55° at night is reached, which will

bring them into flower nicely for Easter. Success in forcing Ramblers for Easter depends largely upon the way they are handled now. Start them gradually, water sparingly as long as there is little root action, gradually increasing the water supply as the temperature is raised and growth commences.

LILIES.

The Bermuda lilies in the frames should be brought into the greenhouse at once. It is to be hoped that they were well protected up to date, and suffered no frosts. Give them a night temperature of about 55°, which will bring them along slowly until the first of the year, when the temperature can be raised if thought necessary to bring them into bloom for Easter. It is not a good plan to keep them too cool at the present time. Remember that the bulbs are native to warmer zones, and for this reason should never be subjected to a temperature lower than 50° at night. It is far better to give them an average temperature of 55° throughout the winter than to grow them cool at first and later apply extreme heat. We have not suffered much loss so far this year from diseased bulbs. Possibly, however, more will show signs of disease later on, and if so they should be taken out and thrown on the dump heap, for they will never outgrow the disease and if badly infected are entirely worthless.

SOLANUMS.

Solanum capsicastrum (Jerusalem cherry) and Celestial peppers ought to be well berried by this time. The fruit hangs on for a long time and is now assuming its many colored hues. Give the plants plenty of room to keep the foliage a dark green color. They should be well syringed daily, for the scale is liable to infest them and is difficult to dislodge when it once gets a foothold. A temperature of 55° at night and the full light at all times is an essential.

HYDRANGEAS.

Get the hyrangeas from under the benches and give them the benefit of bench room so long as there is plenty to spare. They still require a cool house, 40° or thereabout, for they must not be started into growth until the first of the year. Clean off the dead leaves and hold them on the dry side, and if all the old leaves drop no harm is done as long as the wood is not shriveled.　　　G.

English Market Plants.

Poinsettias.—During the season these are in bloom there is no other flower to vie with them in brightness, but it is remarkable how difficult it is to extend the time of flowering. Perhaps we ought not to grumble, for they come in when they are most welcome. In the ordinary way they only last about six weeks or two months at the outside. The earliest I have seen them has been the third week in November, but they are not offered in any quantity until about the middle of December, and last well over the New Year's festivities, though many growers clear out at Christmas. For late work the double variety, plenissima, is the best. I have seen this in good condition as late as the second week in February. The various growers treat their plants differently. I have always found it of the first importance to look after the stock early. The strong, well ripened plants keep the best and also make the strongest cuttings.

Strong cuttings are the first step towards success. The stock plants are stored by being laid on their sides under a stage where they can be kept quite dry in a warm house. It may be quite close to the pipes. About February or March they are taken up on the benches. Before they begin to start they may be dipped in some strong insecticide to kill any lurking germs of insects. The syringe may be used freely, but little water should be given the roots until well started when a little weak liquid manure may be used.

Although it is advisable to propagate as soon as the first cuttings are ready, it is those propagated in June that make the best pot plants. There is no difficulty in rooting the strongest cuttings it is possible to get and thin, weakly cuttings are of no use whatever. The suggestion of cutting half through and leaving the incision to callus before taking off, is not practical for market growers and is quite unnecessary for them. It is of the first importance to prevent the cuttings from getting withered, and is quite as much as possible. I have rooted a good many thousands, losing very few. My practice has been to have everything ready so they can be put into the close propagating pit with as little delay as possible. Three-inch pots are filled with a light sandy compost and a little extra sand on the surface. A tray with some warm, quite dry sand is at hand, and each cutting as it is taken off is dipped into this. This effectually stops bleeding. Put the cuttings singly into the pots, give a slight sprinkling of warm water and then put them into the pit. If not watered until the next day it gives time for them to dry at the base and the callus is formed quicker. They should be kept shaded and close for a few days and as soon as the leaves begin to lift up less shade and a little air is given, and as soon as rooted they are removed to where they get more light.

They must not be left a day too long in the close pit, for if they start to make long jointed growth they cannot be put back. They should be changed into larger pots as soon as sufficiently rooted. I may add the tops may be taken off the early plants, but if the stem is hollow it must be cut quite close below the leaf or joint. I have heard it said that after the stem is hollow they will not root, and this is quite true unless careful attention

is given to cutting off close to the joint. After the plants are well established they may be grown on during the summer without heat. Some growers put them in pits and take the lights off, but I have always succeeded best with those kept under glass. It may be necessary to give a slight shade in very bright weather, but the less shade the better. Watering requires care, and after the pots are well filled with roots manure is given regularly. In the autumn, as soon as the nights get cold, heat is given. I find poinsettias will stand well in quite a cold house without appearing to suffer in the least, but the mischief is seen as soon as given a little warmth, the leaves all gradually turning yellow and then falling off.

I believe more stock of this useful plant is ruined through not giving warmth early enough in the autumn than from any other cause, but care has to be taken not to over-do it, especially before the bracts are properly set, or the plants will run up tall. I find they develop their bracts and finish off best in a high temperature and kept up as close to the glass as possible. Kept fairly moist, with frequent applications of manure,

they should make heads of bracts from thirteen to fifteen inches across in 5-inch pots. Those grown in larger pots, or planted out, will make larger. There are several slight variations from the type. A rather pale variety makes much larger bracts. The white variety is useful when well grown, but this requires some care. It should be grown on throughout the heat. Plenissima is rather delicate but pays for attention, for when well done it commands good prices. When cutting poinsettias the stems should be dipped in hot water. This sends the sap up and prevents bleeding and they keep much better.   Hortus.

High Priced Plants.

At the exhibition of the Royal Horticultural Society of England, held in London from May 26 to 28, 1903, were shown six of C. Vuylsteke's odontoglossum hybrids, which had already been sold by him for $6,000, two of them having been bought by Sander, one of these two for $2,400. Vuylsteke told his friends that the six there exhibited were by no means his best; that he had a hybrid for which he had refused a cash offer of $5,000. F. Sander & Sons, St. Albans, showed under a glass globe a puny, tender little plant with only two flowers, but these of most wonderfully exquisite beauty. An Odontoglossum crispum called Fred K. Sander, which created a sensation among the orchid lovers present. The price asked by Sander was $10,000 but H. P. Pitt, Stamford Hill, Rosslyn, became the happy owner of it for $8,750. A. Peetere, Brussels, offered $500 for the pollen of one of the flowers but was refused. At the end of the show Sander's man took possession of the two flowers, carefully gathered the pollen into a feather quill and betook himself to St. Albans, while the two plants were taken home by Pitt's gardener. Next day an orchid, ready for fertilization, received the costly pollen, compared to the price of which diamonds are ridiculously cheap. — *Der Deutsche Gartenrath.*

Albuquerque, N. M.—Roswell has a new hot house of 5,000 feet of glass. The cost of same will be approximately $5,000.

INTERIOR OF EDWARD SCEERY'S STORE.

EDWARD SCEERY'S DELIVERY WAGON.

Detroit Florists' Club Outing.

The Florists' Club outing, October 30, was enjoyed by fifty-two members, who journeyed to Mt. Clemens in response to the invitation of John Breitmeyer's Sons and the other Mt. Clemens florists. The party started from the City Hall at 10 a. m. in a special car provided by Philip Breitmeyer. A stop was made on the way at J. F. Sullivan's greenhouses, where, after an inspection of the stock and the enjoyment of refreshments, a photograph was taken of the entire group. Arriving at Mt. Clemens the visitors were met by the local growers, who increased the party to sixty-four.

At noon Breitmeyer's establishment was reached, where a bountiful lunch awaited the visitors. After luncheon an inspection of their stock followed. The greatest interest centered on the new rose. After viewing the beauty of the blooms and most excellent condition of the stock of the novelty, admiration and approval were expressed by all present. A house of American Beauty and one of Perle and Sunrise were particularly fine. a table of a thousand Mme. Hoste were in full crop, making a splendid appearance. The 20,000 chrysanthemums here were a gorgeous sight. They include the best standard commercial varieties in greatest quantities, but over a hundred novelties and exhibition varieties complete the collection. The latter were grown chiefly as a feature for the firm's annual show at their Miami avenue store. Their violets, which have been rather unsatisfactory, are showing much improvement and a good yield is yet expected. The splendid condition of the carnations, numbering over 20,000 plants, bears evidence of the careful treatment they have received.

Robert Klagge's place was next visited, and while he freely confesses to only fair

are planted with violets, which are fine and considered by far the best lot grown by any of the six florists of the town. A house of Lawsons in full crop was particularly fine and highly commended, while his other two houses, planted with Morning Glory, Glazier, Crane and Dorothy, were fully up to the standard.

From here we continued to James Taylor's establishment, about a mile away, where we found his seven houses devoted exclusively to violets and carnations. He who enjoyed the title of "Violet King" for several seasons does not claim it so strongly this year, although most of his plants are promising and daily improving. His carnations are all fine, and include the varieties Morning Glory, Glazier, Joost, White Cloud, Enchantress and Lawson. His success with the latter variety the last three seasons has earned for him considerable local fame.

From here we proceeded to John Carey's, the mention of whose name among local growers suggests his uninterrupted success with Meteor roses. At the time of our visit we found two houses of them in most excellent condition, as well as a house of Beauty, two of Bridesmaid and Bride, two of carnations, one of chrysanthemums and two of violets. His return as a grower of the latter after an interval of five years is meeting with flattering success.

The latest accession to the growers' ranks in Mt. Clemens is August Von Boeselager, whose place just outside the city limits on Gratiot road we visited last. We found four new houses, one containing carnations, one of chrysanthemums, from which an early crop was cut last, which will be succeeded by sweet peas, and two of violets, the latter being very fine and already yielding heavy pickings which find a ready market.

From here the party repaired to a ban-

The photograph from which the accompanying illustration was prepared was taken at J. F. Sullivan's on the way to Mount Clemens, October 30. President Robert Flowerday is in the chair and directly behind him are Philip Breitmeyer, president of the S. A. F. and Geo. A. Rackham, president of the American Carnation Society. J. F. S.

Special Treatment of Carnations.

Mrs. Frances Joost.—Succeeds best in a light soil and a temperature of 54°, with little feeding before spring; must have a good sunny exposure. This variety, as well as Ethel Crocker, is a summer bloomer and should be treated with that fact in mind.

Dorothy.—Light soil, liberally rich; temperature 54°. This variety is a continuous bloomer and will stand plenty of feeding after a heavy crop of buds is set. It is good the year around. The flowers should be allowed to age on the plants if a pleasing shade of pink is desired.

Marquis.—Heavy soil; temperature 50°. Feed liberally from December 1 on and bear in mind that it is a winter bloomer and no good after the heavy spring crop is off. It is a shining mark for thrips and extra care must be taken to keep this pest in subjection.

Mrs. E. A. Nelson.—Wants a heavy soil to harden the growth. It is very subject to rest and should have a very dry and airy situation. Cuttings are difficult to root. Every encouragement should be be given to produce a firm growth and this difficulty will disappear in proportion. It is a good winter bloomer and should be liberally fed while in crop. Temperature 50°.

Mrs. Higinbotham.—Wants a rich, heavy soil and plenty of feeding. It is an early and continuous bloomer. Propagate early and give the young plants every chance to make large plants. Plants are usually small at planting time and to make it pay it must be set closer together than most varieties. It makes very little side growth after housing. Temperature 50°.

Sunbeam.—A very free and early bloomer and one of the best paying daybreak pinks, though not a fancy one. Soil medium light; temperature 52°. The flowers fade easily and it should be shaded early. A good feeder.

Morning Glory.—Medium heavy and rich soil; wants liberal treatment. It blooms well the year round. Temperature 52°.

G. H. Crane.—A light soil and a warm, light situation will bring out its best points. It wants little feeding until towards spring. Soot will brighten the color. Temperature 53°.

Mrs. Potter Palmer.—Must be potted extra early to get an early crop. Have soil medium heavy and liberally rich. A temperature of 54° is necessary to prevent bursting. Feed moderately and use wood ashes liberally to strengthen the stems. Shade early.

Estelle.—A valuable variety for midwinter and spring work. Early crop is apt to come single, so bench extra early. Soil medium heavy and well enriched. Feed well after January 1. Temperature 52°.

Governor Roosevelt.—One of the best dark crimsons previous to last year's introductions. House early and give liberal treatment. Temperature 50°.

Harlowarden.—A mammoth dark crimson and bound to be a winner. Wants a heavy soil and lots of feeding. Temperature 50°. J.

DETROIT FLORISTS' CLUB OUTING.

success with violets this year he points with pride to his carnations, which are surely grand. A thousand plants each of Enchantress and Harlowarden are conspicuous marks of his success. His many other varieties are but little below those named in points of merit. In roses his large house of Kaiserin was particularly fine, and a house of Bridesmaid in full crop was a beautiful sight.

L. Stevens' neat place of six houses was next visited. Three of the houses

quet at the Sherman house, where speeches, songs and an exchange of pleasantries were enjoyed until 10 o'clock, when the return trip was made to Detroit. The very pleasant weather of the day and the great number who participated in the outing contributed to make the event by far the most enjoyable and successful of the kind in the history of the club. Out-of-town visitors for the occasion were Elmer D. Smith, Adrian, Mich., and O. D. Stoll, Oxford, Mich.

The Retail Trade.

DRACÆNA BAPTISTI is one of the most valuable of decorative plants where a big plant is wanted in a short time. Specimens five to six feet can be grown in one year from the cane, which is about three times the result that can be obtained with D. amabile in the same time. One precaution necessary, however, is that the plants be kept constantly growing as, if permitted to come to a standstill, they will never amount to anything as specimens.

PHYSALIS FRANCHETTI.

This, though a hardy plant and easy to grow, well repays the extra culture necessary for pot work, according to an English trade journal. A good soil is required to make the most of this plant for either pot or cutting purposes. When cultivated inside red spider must ever be guarded against. Fire heat is another thing to avoid. Our note is practically the result of seeing from time to time fine specimen plants in 8-inch pots selling at 50 cents each at J. Seabrook's stand in Covent Garden. These well trained plants, with a dozen to fourteen stems, each well loaded with well colored pods and growing foliage, being particularly clean and healthy. The old P. Alkekengi (winter cherry of the south of Europe) is very useful as a border plant, as also for cutting, but the market prefers the newer variety. At times we hear of this as the cape gooseberry, which is not correct, as the P. edulis from South America is the cape gooseberry. Reverting to the subject of our note, Mr. Seabrook informs us he will have handled 1,000 plants by the end of the season, selling up to fifty on a market morning. Both when in pots and when cut the plant with its large bright red pods is used extensively for harvest festivals and other decorative purposes.

RICE AND ROSES.

Brides come and go, and when they go it has been the custom from time immemorial to throw rice after them. The fashion of going away gowns changes from year to year, but the nuptial cereal that finds its way into the creases of these gowns remains ever the same. But at a recent English wedding in high life a deviation was made from this time honored custom and the departing pair were pelted with dried rose leaves. Of course this innovation has its practical and sentimental side. On the practical side it will appeal to those thrifty housewives who have deplored the number of possible puddings that have gone to waste at weddings and have sadly estimated the number of hungry mouths that they might have fed. Of course rose leaves have something of a sentimental suggestion, but the fact that dried rose leaves are used would seem to imply that romance had entered the sere and yellow leaf stage; and then again the question arises, how is it possible to throw a thing of such airiness and unsubstantiality as a rose leaf? Yet no doubt if this custom is permanently adopted in England it will soon find its way to American wedding celebrations. Hereafter it will be the scent of dried rose leaves rather than the presence of rice that will betray bridal couples and, do what these interesting individuals will to hide their identity and newly marriedness, the scent of roses will cling to them still.—*Chicago Tribune.*

DECORATIONS FOR GRAVE.

The accompanying half-tone shows a casket in a grave which is lined with white cloth and freely trimmed with ferns and sweet peas. The various floral designs show for themselves. The whole work was executed by L. P. Lord, of Owatonna, Minn.

Cannot Do Without It.

ED. AM. FLORIST:—Enclosed please find $1 for renewal of subscription. We cannot do without this paper and would consider ourselves back numbers if we did not get it.   J. SYLVESTER.

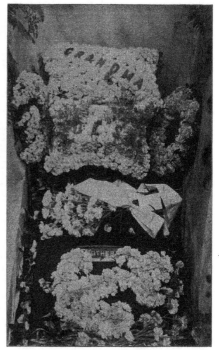

DECORATIONS FOR GRAVE.

Chicago Florists' Club.

The regular meeting of the Chicago Florists' Club, held Wednesday evening, November 4, proved as interesting and instructive as any of the present series of meetings. The attendance was large and everyone manifested a particular interest in the business and discussions of the evening. The new officers were formally installed, Pres. W. N. Rudd wielding the gavel in a veteran like manner. The report of the judges on the recent flower exhibitions, given under the club's auspices, was read. The full report has already been reviewed in these columns.

A vote of thanks and appreciation was extended by the club to the judges for their services and to the Foley Manufacturing Company for the prizes they donated for meritorious exhibits. The most interesting feature of the meeting was the report of the committee having in charge the programme for the coming season. This was submitted by C. M. Dickinson, chairman of the committee. It will be noted by a perusal of this enter-taining schedule of winter and spring events that all will not be "shop." Social pleasantries, receptions, banquets and dramatic entertainments are some of the good things provided. The monthly exhibits promise to surpass any of the club's previous efforts. The programme was unanimously adopted and the committee was empowered to make any minor alterations they might deem necessary. The schedule in detail follows:

Tuesday, November 17—Flower exhibit at room 522 Atlas block, from 2 to 8 p. m. Leonard Kill will have charge of this exhibition and all exhibits should be sent to him prepaid, prior to noon, Tuesday, November 17. The public will be invited by card from 2 to 4 p. m. A 50 cent din-ner will follow the exhibit at Becker &

Jackson's, and among the prominent speakers of the occasion will be Hon. J. J. Freeley, of Chicago.

Wednesday, November 18—Club meeting. The meeting will be devoted to "Diseases and Insect Pests Attacking Greenhouse Plants." H. Hasselbring, of the University of Chicago, will read a paper on "Fungus Attacking Greenhouse Plants," and will illustrate his talk with charts, etc. F. A. Thompson, of Detroit, will read a paper on the same subject and will also talk on "Preventives to be Used and Best Methods of Using Them."

December 2—The regular club meeting will be dispensed with on this date and the club will give its first annual Florists' Club ball. John P. Risch will have the management of this event.

Wednesday, December 16 — Club's exhibit of holiday plants. Judges will be appointed and prizes offered. The exhibition will be followed by a club meeting at 8:30 p. m., and a ten minute paper will be read by a prominent retail florist of Chicago on "Desirable Holiday Plants not Produced by the Chicago Market." This will be followed by a ten minute paper by prominent plant growers. A general discussion regarding holiday plants by members of the club will close the session.

Wednesday, January 6, 1904— Club meeting, at which the holiday business will be reviewed. Prominent members of the trade in the east will read papers regarding the stock marketed during the holidays and what was the best stock that sold during this time.

Wednesday, January 20—First allied trades meeting. Topics to be discussed will be "Pipe," "Fittings," "Glass" and "Paint." Specialists in these lines will read papers regarding these articles.

Wednesday, February 3— The programme committee has decided to leave this date open, but details of an event for this date will be issued at least six weeks prior to this meeting.

Wednesday, February 17 — Guests' night. The club extends an invitation to men out of Chicago, engaged in the florist business, and will call on them for talks on specialties which each represents. A dinner will follow this in the evening.

Wednesday, March 5—Second allied trades' meeting. The evening will be devoted particularly to greenhouse construction. Charts, plans and papers regarding the best methods of construction will be shown and papers read by prominent men in these lines.

Wednesday, March 19 — Retailers' night. The retailers of Chicago and elsewhere will be asked to tell and illustrate what can be done in the line of floral work, including all branches from the handling of loose flowers to elaborate decorations. A general discussion by members will follow and criticisms brought out as to what is to be avoided in floral work. The committee may decide to hold an exhibition of Easter plants on this date, admitting bulbous stock, roses and carnations. If this is done a special programme will be provided, judges appointed and prizes offered.

Wednesday, April 9 — Wholesalers' night. Papers will be read by wholesalers on the general Easter business, what stock sold best and why; advantages and disadvantages of growers holding their stock for holiday demands; trials and tribulations of the wholesaler.

Wednesday, April 16—Bedding plant exhibit open at 4 p. m. Judges and prizes. A club meeting will follow in the evening and papers on the subject of general bedding work will be read.

Wednesday, May 7—General discussion of fertilizers and coal. Papers by men who handle these articles.

Wednesday, May 21—Exhibit of carnations and roses. open at 2 o'clock, admitting the public by card. Judges will be appointed and prizes offered. The show will close at 6 p. m. and will then be followed by an elaborate dinner. At the regular club meeting to follow the members and trade men will talk of the successes and failures of the season. Finis for winter and spring events.

Chicago.

FLORISTS' CLUB ISSUES PROGRAMME FOR SEASON OF 1903-04.—OFFICERS ARE INSTALLED. — MARKET GLUTTED AND STOCK IS MOVING SLOWLY.—WEATHER IMPROVING.

The market has been congested with stock all week and little has been moved. The abnormal November weather is to blame for this condition of affairs. If the cold snap which developed Thursday continues the market may be expected to open up and reach something like standard November business. Of course the chrysanthemum is holding full sway, with the lesser lights claiming little attention. Roses are growing better and violets are rapidly coming up to standard. Fall decorations are now on and this will perceptibly stimulate the demand for ferns, wild smilax and the like.

F. F. Benthy is showing a particularly fine lot of Bridesmaid and Bride roses. Mr. Benthey, in company with W. N. Rudd and Philip Foley, attended the Joliet show Thursday.

The E. F. Winterson company this week secured twenty-five barrels of fancy fern dishes, something new. The Christmas supply of immortelles and capeflowers is also coming in.

E. E. Pieser, of Kennicott's, voices the sentiment of all the florists of the city when he describes the past week as the "most peculiar and remarkable week in trade of the year."

Weiland & Risch this week handled some giant Timothy Eaton chrysanthemums, the largest of which easily hid a dinner plate from view.

J. A. Budlong's chrysanthemum stock is very complete, and includes Timothy Eaton, Chadwick, Golden Wedding, Murdoch and Maudine.

Messrs. Asmus, Lambros, Balluff, Kreitling, Hauswirth, Degnan and the Winterson brothers will visit the Joliet exhibition to-day.

Peter Reinberg is handling some fine Sunrise and Mme. Chatenay roses. A new rose, Uncle John, is also on his counters.

Bassett & Washburn are sending out many fine chrysanthemums which are worthy of special mention.

Peter Manusos Thursday received a cablegram announcing the death of his mother, in Greece.

Vaughan's seed store is advertising a free flower show for November 12-14, day and evening.

A. E. Hunt, of Deamud's, attended the Joliet show this week and reports a grand exhibit.

George Reinberg has been cutting a heavy supply of American Beauty and Liberty roses.

Frank Garland is this week making a specialty of histerns, which are of splendid quality.

The first snow of the season fell Thursday and the local trade is in consequence elated.

Wietor Brothers are cutting splendid chrysanthemums in large quantities.

Amling's smilax and asparagus are as good as any we have seen this year. The parks are making elaborate displays of chrysanthemums.

New York.

BIG SALE OF DECORATIVE PLANTS SCHEDULED FOR NEXT WEEK.—NEW COLLECTOR OF RENTS FOR THE CUT FLOWER EXCHANGE.—DEATH OF FLORISTS' WIFE.—NOTES OF THE TRADE.

Monday morning business was fairly brisk, but plenty of chrysanthemums, carnations and roses were left over. Violets cleaned out well. Tuesday being election day business was at a standstill, the same as in former years, and consequently quite a drop in prices followed. New York is having model Indian summer weather, and if it holds out will bring chrysanthemums along in a hurry. Ivory, Bonnaffon and Appleton are the principal ones at the present time. Mignonette and Paper White narcissi are also coming in, but only in limited quantities. Benjamin Slinn has some very fine sweet peas, something unusual for this time of year.

The Cut Flower Exchange is prospering. Charles Smith has been appointed collector of rents in place of Philip Miller, resigned. Gustave Schrader, proprietor of the Hopedale Greenhouses, of Elmhurst, who makes a specialty of smilax, adiantum and asparagus, brings his goods in his automobile and usually has one of the growers as a passenger on the return trip. The next monthly meeting of the board of directors will be held Saturday, November 7, at 9 a. m., at their office in the Coogan building.

An unprecedented auction sale of palms, decorative plants and orchids is scheduled for Wednesday and Thursday, November 11 and 12, on the premises of Julius Roehrs, at Rutherford, N. J., at which time an enormous quantity of stock will be sold to make room for importations now arriving. The magnificent high quality of Mr. Roehr's products will, no doubt, insure a good attendance. J. P. Cleary will wield the hammer.

The next meeting of the New York Florists' Club will be held Monday evening, November 9. The secretary has complimentary tickets for the exhibition of the Chrysanthemum Society of America, to be distributed, two to each member of the New York Florists' Club present at the meeting. These tickets can be procured only by attendance at the meeting; none will be mailed.

Mr. and Mrs. George M. Stumpp celebrated their silver wedding and Mr. Stumpp's father and mother their golden wedding together on the same day during Mr. Stumpp's recent visit to Germany.

Edward Branch, the wholesale florist of First avenue and Thirty-eighth street, has been seriously ill at his home for the past two weeks. The business is being carried on by his two sons.

The wholesalers are crowded with chrysanthemums. On Monday everyone had a large supply on hand with but little demand for them.

George Matthews, of Great Neck, L. I., is cutting seventy-five dozen Ivory and Bonnaffon daily, and they are of the best quality.

Frank Millang is receiving some choice new varieties of chrysanthemums which promise to become popular market staples.

Wm. Simpson is sending blooms of the new rose, Ideal, to Traendly & Schenck.

It is greatly admired for its soft luminous color.

W. H. Waite, late gardener at Greystone, Yonkers, has leased the greenhouses of Fred Boulon at Sea Cliff.

The Kurzman-Dacre Company opened their new wholesale place Monday, November 2.

Ernest Berger, of Yonkers, has a fine lot of California violets, for which he finds a ready sale.

Fred. Engel, of West Hoboken, mourns the loss of his wife, who died Wednesday, October 30.

Thos. Young, Jr., is receiving some fine gardenias from the Jersey City greenhouses.

Siebrecht & Son expect to open their new store on Fifth avenue November 20.

The first lilac of the fall season has appeared at Langjahr's.

Robert Craig was a visitor in town early in the week.

Boston.

ANNUAL VISIT TO WABAN CONSERVATORIES HELD.—MANY VISITORS ATTEND.—WARM WEATHER SPOILS TRADE.—STOCK IN PLENTY WITHOUT DEMAND.

The annual visit to the Waban rose conservatories took place Wednesday, November 4, seventy-two gentlemen of the craft participating. Coaches carried the party from the station to the greenhouses, where welcome was extended by Mr. Montgomery, and after two hours' interesting and instructive inspection of the magnificent establishment and the finest roses on the continent all were conveyed to Bayley's hotel, where the annual banquet was served. The exercises following the banquet were of a peculiarly spontaneous and happy character. Alex. Montgomery presided and Wm. J. Stewart served as toastmaster. Many affectionate words were said in memory of Edmund M. Wood, as well as cordial words of praise for Mr. Montgomery's matchless skill and appreciation of the good fellowship of these unique annual gatherings. There were many sanguine auguries for the future well-being of New England floriculture. Among the speakers were Peter Crowe. Utica; W. C. Steckel, president of the flower market; Robt. Smithson, Clifton, N. J.; Joseph Tailby; Frank H. Traendly of New York; E. N. Pierce, Warren Bird, John Farquhar and Judge Hoitt.

Weather of the July brand is playing the mischief with the flower trade this week. Stock is coming in by car loads, and the business is utterly incapable of absorbing more than a fraction of it. The wholesalers have not had such a puzzle on their hands for a long time.

There have been many visitors in town, some on business, some to attend the chrysanthemum show at Horticultural hall and others to take part in the annual visit to the Waban conservatories. Among them were F. H. Traendly, Chas. Loechner and Jas. McHutchison, of New York; Peter Crowe, of Utica; Robert Simpson, Clifton, N. J.; E. Leuly, West Hoboken, N. J.; Paul Berkowitz, Philadelphia; Frank Main. Concord, N. H.; Paul Dailledouze, Flatbush; Timothy O'Connor, Providence, K. I.; B. N. Kirk and W. T. Burton, Bar Harbor, Me.; C. W. Warburton and E. Pernley, of Fall River, Mass.

PORTLAND, ME.—J. A. Dirwanger has sold the business he conducted at 719 Congress street for six years. The new firm's name is W. B. Portland Florist Company.

Philadelphia.

ELABORATE DEPARTMENT STORE OPENINGS.—QUAKER CITY MARKET UNSTEADY AND OVERSTOCKED.—NOTES OF CLUB MEETING. — CHRYSANTHEMUM SHOW NEXT WEEK.

The event of the week was the floral decoration and flower show at Gimbel Brothers' large department store. This was arranged by Hugh Graham, and in addition to the satisfaction it must have given the Gimbel Brothers it should be a good advertisement for young Mr. Graham, as it gave him an opportunity to show what he and his force could do. The exhibition was held on the large main, cross aisle, on the second floor. This immense aisle, covering 12,000 square feet, was filled with the exception of about an eight-foot walk on either side for half its length, with a gorgeous display of palms and other foliage and flowering plants and artistic arrangements of cut flowers. On either side of the aisle, about ten feet apart, stood immense arecas, while down the center, on raised mounds of bark, were other fine specimen plants. Between these center plants the floor was laid out as a garden; within each alternate space there was a mirror, 4x6 feet, surrounded by a fine grouping of plants representing a lake in which the foliage and flowers were reflected. One was surrounded by Farley-ease and cattleyas, fine plants full of flowers; another by cypripediums; another was decorated with pots of pink Ivory chrysanthemums. A rustic bridge crossed about midway, near which was a tree; a mound of bark supporting a fine palm vied with orchid plants in full flower, consisting of cattleyas, oncidiums, dendrobiums and other kinds. At either end of this garden a three-tier fountain was playing, adding much to the realism. This center decoration covered a space of nearly two thousand square feet, every inch of which was covered with plants and flowers. The other half of the aisle was flanked on both sides with choice flowers in vases. A space was set aside for chrysanthemums, which were for display and each chrysanthemum displayed here. In the center of this exhibit was an ox hitched to a rustic cart filled with chrysanthemum plants.

There were fine large alcoves like store windows, with printed backgrounds, in which were arranged large vases of American Beauty roses, choice long stemmed blooms, fifty to a vase. Another had the same number of vases filled with specimen chrysanthemums. One of the most beautiful had a mirror lake in the center, on which a flock of china swans were drawing a water chariot filled with cattleyas and valley. There were also many vases of Pennsylvania and Philadelphia chrysanthemums displayed here.

All the pillars that lined this avenue were covered with bark or green burlap. About ten feet from the floor a shelf or platform was filled with plants from which also projected bamboo poles to which were attached small Japanese lanterns. All through the decorations there were numberless miniature electric lights which glowed from among the leaves.

Altogether the variety of good display and introduces a new era in store decorating as nothing could have been finer had the occasion been a select social function. Mr. Graham is to be congratulated on his achievement, the more so, too, when it is known that nearly if not all the plants and flowers used, came from his nurseries at Logan.

The Wm. Graham Company also had a decoration on a similar plan but smaller scale at Snellenberg's department store. Here the ends of all the counters bordering the main cross aisle of the first floor were banked with plants and chrysanthemums. There was also a center display in the middle of the aisle with tables of flowers in vases. A lake of orchids was made with the aid of mirrors, ferns and orchid plants.

At Wanamaker's they had great bunches of autumn leaves at the top of the posts along the main aisle and all around the central dome. It must have taken several car loads to do the work, over which Habermehls had charge.

Business is erratic, one day dull, the next busy. Anyone with a good order should come out well financially as all kinds of flowers are very plentiful and cheap. The quality of the stock is improving, there being no fault to find anywhere, but if the warm weather does not let up there will be more than can be moved and prices will be very unsatisfactory.

The chrysanthemum show, which opens next Tuesday, promises to be a hummer, and the committee will have difficulty in finding room to stage the exhibits. Secretary Rust says the entries now in give promise of the largest show ever held.

At the meeting of the club last Tuesday evening it was decided to have a smoker next Wednesday evening and a large sum was appropriated to oil the machinery and see that everything ran smoothly.

Bernheimer has fine specimen chrysanthemums. His Golden Gates from the Flower Exchange Nurseries are great stock.

Fahrenwold is sending in choice Beauties to Leo Niessen. Andre's Bridesmaids to same house are hard to beat.

W. K. Harris is now president of the company, having been elected at the annual meeting last Monday.

S. S. Pennock says the shipping trade is all O. K., much good stock going out of town.

S. S. Pennock will tell of his European trip at the next meeting.

Jos. Heacock is sending in some choice special Beauties.   K.

Greenhouse Building.

Gloucester, Conn.—H. L. Sayles, one house.

Stonington, Conn.—Dr. C. O. Maine, conservatory.

Asbury Park, N. J.—Daniel O'Day, conservatory.

North Ashburnham, Mass. — H. J. Blanchard, lettuce house 26x36.

Manchester, Mass.—Jas. K. Tappan, one house.

Georgetown, Mass.—Robert Graham, conservatory.

So. Orange, N. J.—W. A. Manda, range of palm houses.

Washington, Pa.—Washington Floral Company, seven houses, each 15x162.

Sharon, Mass. — Adolph Low, one house.

Denton, Tex.—Girls' Industrial College, three houses each 18x32.

Chilean Nitrate.

It has been stated by competent authorities that ten per cent is a reasonable estimate of the average increase for every five years during the next twenty years in the output of Chilean nitrate. At the end of twenty years, when 35,000,000 tons will have been extracted, on this basis, it is predicted that the exhaustion of these nitrate deposits will be near at hand.

THE AMERICAN FLORIST

NINETEENTH YEAR.

Subscription, $1.00 a year. To Europe, $2.00.
Subscriptions accepted only from those
in the trade.

Advertisements, on all except cover pages,
10 Cents a Line, Agate; $1.00 per inch.
Cash with Order.

No Special Position Guaranteed.

Discounts are allowed only on consecutive insertions, as follows—6 times, 5 per cent; 13 times,
10 per cent; 26 times, 20 per cent;
52 times, 30 per cent.

Cover space sold only on yearly contract at
$1.00 per inch, net, in the case of the two
front pages, regular discounts applying only to the back pages.

The Advertising Department of the AMERICAN
FLORIST is for florists, seedsmen and nurserymen
and dealers in wares pertaining to those lines only.

Orders for less than one-half inch space not accepted.

Advertisements must reach us by Wednesday to
secure insertion in the issue for the following
Saturday. Address

AMERICAN FLORIST CO., Chicago.

A NUMBER of detailed reports of exhibitions are unavoidably held over.

THE AUTUMN NUMBER will be issued
November 14. Send your advertisement
now.

FIANCEE, the Chicago Carnation Company's new carnation, was awarded the
gold medal at the Joliet (Ill.) exhibition
this week.

ARDISIAS, in order to insure finely colored berries for the holidays, should now
have plenty of air at night and all possible sunlight in the daytime.

To COLOR dracænas well for Christmas
begin now to keep them rather dry,
rather cool and plenty of air on fine
days.

NOVEMBER 10, says an authority who
has observed the weather closely for
twenty-five. years, is the latest date
when common box cars may be safely
used for the shipment of perishable stock.

THREE POINSETTIAS taken now and
planted in an 8-inch pan make a fine subject for Christmas decoration. Each
year shows an increased demand for
these bright things. A little selaginella
to cover the soil gives a tasty finish.

BEGONIA PERLE DE LORRAINE for which
much has been promised in growing luxuriantly and is being watched with deep
interest for its blooming, which should
come in January. The foliage is of good
size and oddly mottled with irregular
markings of purplish brown.

Vanderbilt's Biltmore Estate.

ED. AM. FLORIST:—The daily papers,
recently quoted by the AMERICAN FLORIST,
seem to have little ground for surmising
that George Vanderbilt will abandon his
home at Biltmore, N. C. While making
notes at the herbarium library on the
estate and sojourning in Biltmore village for some time I heard no rumor of
the kind. Mr. Vanderbilt had recently
come home from Europe to make some
changes in the management of the estate,
as peculations to the amount of $9,000
or more had been discovered. These,
however, were in the bookkeeping
department, and not among the horticultural employes, as your comment
would seem to indicate. Mr. McNamee's
health having failed, he also will go
abroad, and Mr. Harding is now in
charge. I understood that the Vanderbilt family would remain abroad for
some time, and that affairs would not be
conducted on such a lavish scale as heretofore, but there was no hint of abandon-

ing the place. The florist in chief of the
greenhouse department in three months
will retire, but C. D, Beadle still conducts
other horticultural matters, and the students of forestry seem to have no fear
that their work will end prematurely.
     L. GREENLEE.

[We are very pleased to have the facts
in the case, more especially since they
exonerate the horticultural employes.—
ED.]

Society for Horticultural Science.

The constitution and by-laws with the
announcement of the above society have
been issued. The society's first meeting,
with scientific programme, will be held
at St. Louis in connection with the meeting of the American Association for the
Advancement of Science, December 28 to
January 2 next. The date has not yet
been decided on, but that and other
details will be duly announced.

The Strawberry Raspberry.

On page 321 of the AMERICAN FLORIST
for September 26 "X," in speaking of the
strawberry-raspberry, says it got as
much appreciation in his opinion as it
deserved. I should like to ask "X" if he
has ever eaten any of the fruit, and
whether he has seen it growing. Was
the strawberry-raspberry, as shown by
L. A. Martin, the Rubus rosæfolius,
sometimes called the India raspberry. Is
the above berry the same as that shown
by Mrs. A. E. Monblo, of Malden, Mass.?
     H.

Packing Palms and Ferns.

The packing of plants for shipment is a
large item in the expense account of
every grower who does a shipping trade
and an item that the grower cannot
charge up to the buyer of the stock without going contrary to the usual custom.
It is true efforts were made to get the
plant men in line with the nurserymen in
this matter of charging for packing, but
so far there does not seem to have been
any great unanimity of opinion, and in
consequence the bills for lumber, paper,
twine and other packing materials still
continue to pile up without any chance
to share them with the other fellow. The
packing of tender plants may. well be
divided into two sections, namely, winter packing and warm weather packing,
the methods for these two seasons
diverging to a considerable extent, it
being a matter requiring judgment on the
part of the packer to show just when to
quit using warm weather methods and
to start in with full winter protection.
But unless it be an order from the
extreme south it is much safer to expect
frost and to prepare accordingly after
October 15 and to continue to pack
under this rule until April 1, taking all
proper precautions and rushing out
orders in moderate weather. Palms in
general are easy subjects to pack, the
foliage being gathered up from the bottom and drawn together with paper
bands, then covered with several thicknesses of paper from top to bottom. If
shipped in pots the plant should be tied
into the pot with some excelsior over the
soil, this preventing the plant from shaking loose, but both weight and space are
saved to a great extent by turning the
plants out of the pots and balling them
up either in excelsior or in paper. The
boxes should be of sufficient length to
enclose the plants fully when cleated in
the ends of the box, then either being made
tight and then lined with one or more
layers of felt paper such as is used for

sheathing buildings. A complete layer
of excelsior packing is then put in the
bottom and ends of the box to a depth
of about two inches, the box being now
ready to receive the plants. By packing
the plants in double ranks, one row being
in front of the other, much space may be
saved, and whether the plants be packed
in this manner or in single rows there is
one item in particular to bear in mind,
and that is to pack them tightly so they
cannot shake about when. the case is
carelessly handled. Press in the balls
firmly and fill in all interstices with excelsior. The layers of plants having been
firmly cleated in place with a cross strip
of 1x1 or 1x2-inch lumber, according to
the size of the plants, the sides of the box
should be filled in with excelsior, and the
successive layers of plants having been
treated in like manner until the box is
filled, the tops should be covered with a
similar layer of packing and this in turn
covered with the felt paper. With a well
fitted and firmly nailed cover such a box
is reasonably secure from frost unless it
should be exposed to a low temperature
for a considerable period of time.

When packing some of the tender,
broad-leaved palms, such as Stevensonia
grandifolia, Verschaffeltia splendida or
young plants of Ceroxylon niveum a
somewhat different course should be pursued from the fact that the foliage of
palms of this character may easily be
cracked or bruised if drawn up in a close
roll as is commonly done with a kentia
or areca. In the case of one of these
broad-leaved palms it is better first to
put in two stout stakes on opposite sides
of the pot and tie a cross bar between
them to keep the stakes from drawing
together with the ties. Then draw up
the leaves perfectly flat between the two
stakes and bind them in place with strips
of soft paper or broad pieces of raffia,
afterward covering the whole with a
thorough wrapping of large sheets of
paper, the wrapped plant being afterward boxed up. With a view to the saving of weight large plants are sometimes
packed upright in a box, the tops being
crated up to protect them in shipment,
but in winter such a practice is very
risky unless the top is very carefully
packed in paper, excelsior and burlap.
One method of packing palms is a very
different proposition, the main point then
being to protect them from injury in
transit while admitting all the air possible to the foliage, thus preventing heating and bleaching. With this in view,
when making a long distance shipment
in warm weather the foliage should only
be drawn together enough for convenience in packing and tied with a soft
string or a piece of raffia, no paper being
needed. The plants turned out of the
pots should have the roots balled up in
damp excelsior, and are then ready for
boxing. The box should have holes for
ventilation in the sides, top and bottom,
these holes being protected with wire
netting to keep out rats and mice, vermin which are plentiful on board most
steamers and in freight houses. Provided the plants have been first well
watered and then carefully packed after
this plan, they ought to stand a two
weeks' trip with but little injury.

One method of packing small ferns that
has been quite successfully used by the
writer in sharp winter weather is to roll
the plants in double papers, then either
to twist or tie the papers at the top so
as to make a tight package, and to pack
them standing up in a well lined box, the
latter being an inch or two .deeper than
the height of the plants when rolled up.

The plants were packed as close together in the box as possible, and then all spaces around the plants and over the top were filled in with cut hay, which had been run through a feed cutter set to cut about one inch lengths and was shaken down among the plants as much as possible before nailing on the cover of the box. This method gave a reasonably frostproof package and was used satisfactorily many seasons.

In warm weather the ferns demand quite as much ventilation as palms, the most satisfactory plan being to pack them upright in shallow boxes with the foliage exposed to the air as much as possible, the plants being cleated in with narrow strips so that they cannot readily be displaced. The cover of the box should have plenty of air spaces, a cover of narrow boards being safest, allowing freight agents to see which is the right side up; but if the plants are to be shipped a long distance they will be safer with the openings of the cover protected with wire netting. Some of these details may seem trivial, but sometimes the collection of a claim from some careless transportation company depends very much on the observance of them, to say nothing of the felicity of having a complimentary letter from a satisfied customer.

W. H. TAPLIN.

Obituary.

GEORGE RAE.

George Rae, well known as a gardener among the profession about New York City, died at Scarborough on October 12 after an illness extending over a year. He first became known as assistant gardener on the estate of the late Gov. Morgan, at Throggs Neck. He next took charge of J. W. Mason's place at Scarborough, where he remained twenty-three years, retaining the position for six years more after its sale to the late Col. Elliott F. Shepard, after which he held the position of superintendent at Georgian Court, Lakewood, N. J., where he remained for two years. The funeral services were conducted by Westchester Lodge of Masons of Ossining, and he was buried in Sleepy Hollow Cemetery. He leaves a widow, five sons and four daughters.

Horticulture in Germany.

[FROM ITS TRADE PAPERS.]

Cobæa variegata.—This is a form of C. scandens which is considered one of the finest of climbers, especially good for indoor work and conservatories, though it does well outside if started in mid-winter and plants well provided with roots are used at planting time in spring. All the fine qualities as a clean, rapid climber found in the old, well known Cobæa scandens unite in this splendid new variety with the additional charm of its unique color-variegation of foliage and flower. The dark green leaves are bordered by a band of deep golden yellow, becoming almost pure white on the matured foliage. If exposed to the sun this variegation is blended and interlaced with delicate red and violet shades, all this exquisite coloration extending from base to top, enhancing greatly the beauty of the flowers. It is also claimed that this new kind in all its parts is more robust and vigorous than the old sort, yet in its growth and habit more refined and graceful. It would seem that a plant with these attributes would soon be found in every garden and conservatory on the continent. It is feared such will not be the case as it may be many years before plants of Cobæa variegata can be obtained at anything like a reasonable price. It was introduced by J. Veitch & Sons, Chelsea, but as yet is not listed in catalogues of German growers, though found on a few private places. Its scarcity is owing to the fact that this novelty is one of the most difficult to propagate. From seeds, as, in the case with all German propagation resulted in disappointment, both seed-grafting was a total failure and nearly all the cuttings taken in the usual way, rotted. Still the latter method is the only

one resorted to, short, stocky shoots furnishing the largest percentage of callus forming cuttings. About five out of 100 will root.

Cut Flower Trade Poor.—A review of last season's trade, as regards the various branches of commercial floriculture in Germany, published in the form of a detailed report, reveals the fact that the business done in cut flowers was most unsatisfactory, owing partly to the prevailing disagreeable weather all through the season, but chiefly due to large importations of cut material from southern France and Italy during the most important period from late autumn to early spring and equally heavy receipts from Holland at Easter and through all the months of spring and summer. In consequence of this competition, growing in dimensions from year to year, German home-grown flowers were sold, if sold at all, at so low a price that the returns in many instances did not cover the expense of production; a condition which has forced many of the growers to curtail or entirely cut off this branch of their business. However, the report does not fail to state that the season's wet and chilly weather during the summer considerably increased the number of funeral orders. In potted plants business was somewhat better; but not up to that of former years on account of the unseasonable weather. During the winter well grown plants of the better class brought fair prices; inferior stock did not sell. Spring business was good, because the demand for plants for the decoration of summer gardens, house grounds and cemeteries, as well as for the filling of vases, verandas and window boxes increased, although a decided falling off in the demand for material for formal or carpet bedding is noted. Best sellers were roses in pots, ericas, cyclamen and Begonia Gloire de Lorraine.

Valley Growers Alarmed.—Growers of lily of the valley pips in northern Germany are greatly alarmed at the strenuous efforts being made by the vigilant Hollanders to gain a foothold on the market for this most important commodity. They fear a gradual decline in the profits derived from this specialty will be the consequence of this competition. This apprehension, however, was met by measuring words from a correspondent of a trade paper which cannot fail to dispel all such fears. He says: "During a stay in England I frequently had occasion to see Dutch and German lily of the valley grown side by side in places where their forcing was conducted on a large scale as a specialty, and invariably found that those from Holland were very much inferior to the German article, so much so that the English growers, after testing both kinds, will rather pay the higher price for the German pips than invest in those from Dutch sources, although such cheaper. One grower, who tried both kinds, utilizing the cold storage process in holding them over, stated that the German pips came through in fine shape, while the Dutch product proved worthless."

Fuchsia microphylla.—It is with great pleasure that we hail this old, almost forgotten favorite. E. J. Peters, who in an article sounds its praise, is doing it but justice, and every old practitioner in floriculture will agree with him when he says: "Growers of to-day have so little, so room to spare in their overstocked greenhouses, to give a fair and thorough trial to new introductions, and novelty has to make room for another, and that is thrown out to afford room for the next. How then can it be expected that gems of the past like this one and many others far superior to ninety per cent of present day novelties, will find recognition? Their place is our greenhouses is occupied by new plants and yet was there ever a pot plant so thrifty, so floriferous, so beautiful in its mantle of hundreds of purplish red blossoms, its finely cut foliage and so easy to propagate and to grow as Fuchsia microphylla?"

Nicotiana Sanderiana.—This is spoken of as the new plant which, of all novelties exhibited last year in the principal cities of Europe, ranks as the most promising for general use, and which is sure eventually to find its way into every park and garden. It is a cross between Nicotiana affinis and an unnamed plant of the same genus received by Sander & Sons, St. Albans, from one of their collectors. The flowers are of the brightest carmine red, are large and numerous and last fully two weeks. One of the plants shown had twenty-two flower stalks with 234 open flowers. The time of flowering is about three months.

Adiantum cuneatum.—Plants of this fern with yellow and white variegated fronds are not scarce in Germany.

Campanula Mayi.—This is said to be one of the best plants for vases and hanging baskets. Mahænzollern and Japan asters.—These are highly spoken of as most valuable new sorts.

SITUATIONS, WANTS, FOR SALE.

One Cent Per Word.

Cash with the Adv.

Plant Advs. NOT admitted under this head.

Every paid subscriber to the AMERICAN FLORIST for the year 1903 is entitled to a five-line want Adv. (situations only) free, to be used at any time during the year.

Situation Wanted—As assistant propagator of roses in a commercial place. Address FLORIST, 146 Bowmanville Ave., Chicago.

Situation Wanted—By expert lady florist, designer, saleswoman and window dresser. Competent to take entire charge. FLORIST, 138 S. 15th St., Philadelphia.

Situation Wanted—As foreman or manager; eighteen years' practical experience. Thoroughly conversant with all branches of the business. G P, care American Florist.

Situation Wanted—By single man, able to propagate and graft all kinds of fruit, oranges and grapes, desires tropical position. Address G P, N. 50 1st St., New Rochelle, N. Y.

Situation Wanted—By an all-around florist and grower. 28 years of commercial experience. Strictly sober and not afraid of work, private or commercial. M. A. HICKEY, Box 687 Naperville, Ill.

Situation Wanted—On private place; by florist and gardener in vicinity of Boston, Mass., or Providence, R. I.: understands greenhouses, fruits, flowers, etc. A1 references; 16 years in America; Scotch, married. Address J C, care American Florist.

Help Wanted—Competent greenhouse men. Apply to J. M. GASSER CO., ROCKY RIVER, O.

Help Wanted—Salesman who thoroughly understands the seed business, especially the market garden trade. Apply by letter to W. W. RAWSON & CO., Boston, Mass.

Help Wanted—Good man as assistant foreman. Capable of taking full charge when manager is away; American preferred. State wages wanted. Address C H, care American Florist.

Help Wanted—Good florist to take charge of three greenhouses 20x100. Grow cut flowers and general stock. Give reference and wages expected with room. Address C S, care American Florist.

Help Wanted—A competent and up-to-date florist, not over 40, for retail store in Chicago, to wait on trade, decorate and make-up. Must be sober and reliable. No greenhouse work. References. State salary expected. F C, care American Florist.

Wanted—To rent a place of from 25 to 40 thousand square feet of glass for wholesale trade only. Must have dwelling, barns, outside ground, etc., all in good condition. Must be within 35 miles of Chicago. M S, care American Florist.

For Sale—Ballard's Greenhouses, Perry, Iowa. Cause poor health. Address WM. BALLARD, Perry, Iowa.

INTERNATIONAL FLOWER DELIVERY.

PASSENGER STEAMSHIP MOVEMENTS.

The tables herewith give the scheduled time of departure of ocean steamships carrying first-class passengers from the principal American and foreign ports, covering the space of two weeks from date of this issue of the AMERICAN FLORIST. Much disappointment often results from attempts to forward flowers for steamer delivery by express, to the care of the ship's steward or otherwise. The carriers of these packages are not infrequently refused admission on board and even those delivered on board are not always certain to reach the parties for whom they were intended. Hence florists in interior cities having orders for the delivery of flowers to passengers on out-going steamers are advised to intrust the filing of such orders to some reliable florist in the port of departure, who understands the necessary details and formalities and has the facilities for attending to it properly. For the addresses of such firms we refer our readers to the advertisements on this page.

FROM	TO	STEAMER	*LINE	DAY	DUE ABOUT
New York	Liverpool	Campania	1	Sat. Nov. 14, Noon.	Nov 20
New York	"	Umbria	1	Sat. Nov. 21, 7:00 a. m.	Nov. 27
Boston	"	Ivernia	1	Sat. Nov. 7, 11:00 a. m.	Nov. 15
New York	Hamburg	Deutschland	3	Thur. Nov. 12, 11:00 a. m.	Nov. 19
New York	"	Moltke	3	Sat. Nov. 14, 1:00 p. m.	Nov. 23
New York	"	Auguste Victoria	3	Thur. Nov. 19, 10:00 a. m.	Nov. 27
New York	"	Pennsylvania	3	Sat. Dec. 21, 6:00 a. m.	Dec. 1
New York	Glasgow	Columbia	5	Sat. Nov. 14, 3:00 p m.	
New York	London	Minnetonka	6	Sat. Nov. 14, 1:30 p. m.	Nov. 24
New York	"	Minneapolis	6	Sat. Nov. 21, 7:00 a. m.	Dec. 1
New York	Liverpool	Majestic	7	Wed. Nov. 11, Noon.	Nov. 18
New York	"	Celtic	7	Fri. Nov. 13, Noon.	Nov. 21
New York	"	Oceanic	7	Wed. Nov. 18, 6:00 a. m.	Nov. 25
New York	"	Cymeric	7	Fri. Nov. 20, 6:00 a. m.	Nov. 28
New York	Southampton	St. Louis	8	Sat. Nov. 14, 9:30 a. m.	Nov. 21
New York	"	New York	8	Sat. Nov. 21, 9:30 a. m.	Nov. 28
New York	Antwerp	Vaderland	9	Sat. Nov. 14, 10:00 a. m.	
New York	"	Kensington	9	Sat. Nov. 21, 10:00 a. m.	
New York	Havre	La Savoie	10	Thur. Nov. 12, 10:00 a. m.	Nov. 20
New York	"	La Bretagne	10	Thur. Nov. 19, 10:00 a. m.	Nov. 27
New York	Rotterdam	Rotterdam	11	Wed. Nov. 11, 10:00 a. m.	Nov. 20
New York	"	Potsdam	11	Wed. Nov. 18, 10:00 a. m.	Nov. 27
New York	Genoa	Lombardia	12	Sat. Nov. 17, 11:00 a. m.	
New York	"	Hohenzollern	12	Sat. Nov. 21, 11:00 a. m.	Dec. 4
New York	Bremen	Frdk. Der Grosse	13	Thur. Nov. 12, 10:00 a. m.	Nov. 22
New York	"	Kaiser Wilh. II	13	Tues. Nov. 17, 2 00 p. m	Nov. 24
New York	"	Main	13	Thur. Nov. 19, 10:00 a. m.	Nov. 30
New York	Naples	Germania	14	Tues. Nov. 17,	Nov. 25
Boston	Liverpool	Columbus	15	Thur. Nov. 12, 8:00 p. m.	Nov. 19
Boston	"	Commonwealth	15	Thur. Nov. 19, 10 00 a. m.	Nov. 26
Boston	Genoa	Vancouver	15	Sat. Nov. 21, 11:00 a. m.	Dec. 7
Boston	Liverpool	Bohemian	16	Sat. Nov. 14, 5:30 a. m.	Nov. 23
Boston	"	Canadian	16	Sat. Nov. 21, 11:00 a. m.	Nov. 30

*1 Cunard; 2 Allen-State; 3 Hamburg-American; 4 Scandinavian-American; 5 Anchor Line; 6 Atlantic Transport; 7 White Star; 8 American; 9 Red Star; 10 French; 11 Holland-American; 12 Italian Royal Mail; 13 North German Lloyd; 14 Fabre; 15 Dominion; 16 Leyland; 17 Occidental and Oriental; 18 Oceanic; 19 Allan; 20 Can. Pacific Ry.; 21 N. Pacific Ry.; 22 Hongkong-Seattle.

INTERNATIONAL FLOWER DELIVERY.

STEAMSHIPS LEAVE FOREIGN PORTS.

FROM	TO	STEAMER	*LINE	DAY	DUE ABOUT
Liverpool........	New York	Lucania	1	Sat. Nov. 14,	Nov. 20
Liverpool........	"	Etruria	1	Sat. Nov. 21,	Nov. 27
Liverpool........	Boston	Saxonia	1	Tues. Nov. 10,	Nov. 18
Hamburg........	New York	Bluecher	3	Sat. Nov. 14,	
Hamburg........	"	Pretoria	3	Sat. Nov. 21,	
Glasgow........	"	Furnessia	5	Thur. Nov. 12,	
Glasgow........	"	Astoria	5	Thur. Nov. 19,	
London..........	"	Minnehaha	6	Sat. Nov. 14,	Nov. 24
London..........	"	Menominee	6	Thur. Nov. 19,	Nov. 29
Liverpool........	"	Teutonic	7	Wed. Nov. 11, 3:30 p. m.	Nov. 18
Liverpool........	"	Arabic	7	Fri. Nov. 13, 3:30 p. m.	Nov. 21
Liverpool........	"	Germanic	7	Wed. Nov. 18, 3:30 p. m.	Nov. 26
Liverpool........	"	Cedric	7	Fri. Nov. 20, 3:30 p. m.	Nov. 28
Southampton....	"	St. Paul	8	Sat. Nov. 14, Noon.	Nov. 21
Southampton....	"	Philadelphia	8	Sat. Nov. 21, Noon.	Nov. 28
Antwerp........	"	Kroonland	8	Sat. Nov. 14, 9:00 a. m.	Nov. 23
Antwerp........	"	Zeeland	8	Sat. Nov. 21, Noon.	Nov. 30
Havre..........	"	La Lorraine	8	Sat. Nov. 14,	Nov. 22
Havre..........	"	La Champagne	10	Sat. Nov. 21,	Nov. 29
Rotterdam......	"	Rhyndam	10	Sat. Nov. 14,	Nov. 23
Rotterdam......	"	Noordam	11	Sat. Nov. 21,	
Genoa..........	"	Citta di Napoli	11	Mon. Nov. 16,	Dec. 3
Genoa..........	"	Prinzess Irene	12	Thur. Nov. 12,	Nov. 25
Bremen........	"	K. Wil. Der Grosse	12	Tues. Nov. 10,	Nov. 19
Bremen........	"	Kronprinz Wilh.	12	Tues. Nov. 17,	Nov. 27
Naples..........	"	Roma	13	Sat. Nov. 21,	Dec. 3
Liverpool........	Boston	Kensington	15	Tuar. Nov. 12,	Nov. 19
Liverpool........	"	Canada	15	Sat. N v. 19,	Nov. 26
Liverpool........	"	New England	15	Sat. Nov. 28,	Nov. 28
Liverpool........	"	Cestrian	16	Fri. Nov. 13,	Nov. 22
Liverpool........	"	Devonian	16	Fri. Nov. 20,	Nov. 29

* See steamship list on opposite page.

Wild Smilax ALWAYS On Hand.

Also PLUMOSUS, SPRENGERI, ADIANTUMS,
GALAX AND LEUCOTHOES.

We are Growers of **HIGH-GRADE** **Cut Flowers.** All orders promptly filled. Consignments solicited.

FRANK GARLAND, 55-57 Wabash Ave., Chicago.

Please mention the American Florist when writing

The F. R. WILLIAMS CO.

Wholesale Florists,

CLEVELAND, - OHIO.

Please mention the American Florist when writing.

WILD SMILAX. ORDER DIRECT FROM HEADQUARTERS.

We carry the finest and most complete stock of Florists' Hardy Supplies, Dagger and Fancy Ferns, $1.00 per 1000 A No. 1 quality. Bronze and Green Galax. $1.00 per 1000 A No. 1 quality. See here Wild Smilax, 50 pound case, $7.00. 25 pound case, $3.50 per case, Laurel Festooning, good and full, 5c and 6c per yard. Leucothoe sprays, $1.00 per 100. Green Moss, $1.00 per bbl.; 75c per bag. Sphagnum Moss, $1.00 per bbl., 50c per bag. Order by mail, telegraph or telephone will receive our personal and prompt attention. Long Dist. 'Phone 2618 Main.

HENRY W. ROBINSON, No. 11 Province St., BOSTON, MASS.

Please mention the American Florist when writing.

Albert Fuchs,

PALMS, FERNS, FICUS.

Established 1884. CHICAGO. 2045-59 Clarendon Ave.

Please mention the American Florist when writing

IF YOU HAVE STOCK TO SELL.....

The best way to make that fact known to the trade is by regular advertising in the

The American Florist.

THE SEED TRADE.

AMERICAN SEED TRADE ASSOCIATION.
S. F. Willard, Pres.; J. Charles McCullough,
First Vice-Pres.; C. E. Kendel, Cleveland, O.,
Sec'y and Treas.
Twenty-second annual convention St. Louis,
Mo., June, 1904.

LESTER L. MORSE, of C. C. Morse &
Company, is making an eastern trip.

HIBERNIA, N. Y.—O. H. Drew's grist
mill was destroyed by fire last month.

SAN FRANCISCO, CAL.—Wm. A. Cox, of
the Cox Seed Company, left on an eastern
trip, October 30.

CUCUMBER SEED prices are unsettled;
latest advices from growers report seed
light and chaffy and a lesser percentage
of deliveries than expected

A. H. GOODWIN, of the Goodwin, Har-
res Company reports Wisconsin yields of
peas disappointing. Michigan has had
a better harvest, reversing last year's
condition.

LOUISVILLE, KY.—Wood, Stubbs &
Company, according to the Lexington
Herald, have been incorporated with a
capital stock of $75.000, by C. F. Wood
and W. P. Stubbs.

WISCONSIN growers of seed peas who
have raised stocks without pedigree and
with no expert roguing find difficulty in
marketing same and sales are being made
as low as $1.25.

BOUQUET GREEN is not coming in freely
yet in Wisconsin, and while there are
some back counties to hear from the output is likely to be considerably below
that of last year.

VISITED CHICAGO: J. Chas. McCullough,
Cincinnati, Ohio; A. J. Brown, Grand
Rapids. Mich.; C. R. Kimberlin, Santa
Clara, Cal.; Wm. M. Allison, representing
Peter Lawson & Sons, Ltd., Edinburgh,
Scotland.

European Seed Report.

The autumn of 1903 has brought us some splendid days thus making up a little for what the
summer did but afford. Indeed since two weeks
ago, all reports from middle Europe announce
high barometric standing and fine weather, and
it looks as if this would last for some time.
Under these favorable circumstances the crop
could be brought in be usefully, the seeds are in
an excellent state of dryness and appearance.
Chiefly the flowers profited by these magnificent conditions. Asters, for instance, came to
perfect maturity and promise a good crop both in
quality and quantity so that very likely the
prices for all varieties will be considerably lower.
But a large crop is necessary for there are almost
no stocks on hand. Wallflowers, Balsams and
poppies are cleaned and seem to have furnished
good crops so that the prices generally will also
go lower but stocks (mathiola) have suffered
somewhat and will probably rest at about the
same level in price. All other flowers with very
few exceptions seem to satisfy the growers; one
of these exceptions is sweet peas which were
damaged in many districts by insects. Some delicate varieties especially are scarce.

The Vegetable seeds are now for the greater
part stored and seem in general to have furnished
normal crops. Some articles gave even abundant
quantities, like peas, radish and chervil, which in
addition to the big stock at disposal has caused a
considerable falling off in prices. Most of the
other articles, as beets cabbage, carrot, spinach,
parsley, onions, lettuce and turnips, show normal
crops and will therefore be quoted as ordinary;
there are only some cabbage varieties like Brass-
wick and Winningstadt, etc., which are much in
demand. These will go higher, while borecole
sorts are generally cheaper owing to big stocks
and sufficient crop.

My Italian friend writes about the crops as follows: "Our present year finishes for many seed
varieties with a great disappointment for the
season was again quite abnormal. The night of
April 19 brought a late frost which damaged
greatly the early Beans and tomatoes, both crops
of much importance in our southern provinces.
Almost all was destroyed and had to be resown.

which could be done only incompletely for seed
Beans were very scarce on account of bad crops
the previous year. In certain exposed places the
frost damaged the little pods of cauliflower and
kohlrabi. The latter especially, were much
affected, the greater part being found empty
when cleaned.

"For the first time in many years we can
announce a good onion crop. Although the area
cultivated was not important, the quantities harvested pretty well covered the demand and thus
made up a little for the losses of former years.
Certain crops failed entirely and this disaster
finds its explanation in the abnormal summer
with its long period of absolute dryness lasting
until the middle of September. The effects of the
difference between the cool nights and hot days
have caused disease in most districts to the
extent that some varieties of beans did not yield
the quantity sowed. Cucumbers and melons
in particular have suffered greatly.

"Lettuce, for the same reason, also gave a very
bad crop, and as this has been the case for several years the growers will no more fear of that
crop, especially as the prices are not at all
encouraging. Horse Beans also gave only a moderate crop. Peas, which are cultivated on a large
scale for canning purposes, have been satisfactory.
Cabbage, radish and carrots are relatively little
grown. Leeks seem to have given a better crop
For several years large lots of sugar Beets have
been cultivated in the Naples district. The pe as-
ants are satisfied with this crop, new to our
region, and have obtained a good heavy seed.
Pepper and egg plants seem to have given normal
crops. Spinach is not grown much. Clover,
lucerne and other agricultural seeds are not good;
in consequence we expect high prices for these
articles.

"Among flower seeds, many varieties of aster
have suffered by the above mentioned conditions
of weather, also phlox, lavatera and others.
Viola tricolor, reseda, Margaret carnations, our
chief flower crops gave average yields in quantity
and quality. The other summer flowers, being
for the most part grown in irrigated gardens or
in soils possessing natural humidity, developed
nicely and are now cleaned, and the crop will be
generally normal."

In France the situation seems to have changed
somewhat since my last report. It seems that
the low temperature of August, interrupted by
tempests and heavy rains, has been of judic.al
to the ripening of the seeds. The crop will generally be a little under the normal and, as in the
case of several articles there are no stocks on
hand, there is a probability of good prices.
Vegetables being as much in demand as well as
beans and cabbage, the two latter seeds showing
a somewhat bad appearance this year. Cucumbers could not develop and will give a small crop,
as in Germany. Lettuce and red carrots gave a
good crop. White carrots, on the contrary, have
failed altogether. Radish, parsley and turnips,
yielded sufficient quantities. Leek and onions
will furnish an ordinary crop and will probably
be sold at reasonable prices. Celery and spinach
have given good results. Fodder Beets have suffered considerably by insects but could be
brought in under favorable conditions. The crop
may turn out somewhat under the average.

The general seed trade is now commencing and
seems to be brisk, as far as can be judged by the
orders and demands in hand at present.

BIRMINGHAM, ALA.—Hugh Seales opened
a flower store here last week. Mr. Seales
has a large greenhouse and grows his
stock.

Paris Academy of Flowers.

The daily papers announce the founding at Paris of the Academy of Flowers
in the great Paris art colony. The great
palm house in the Parc des Princes, with
thousands of exotics and plants, has been
given by the state for the new institution, besides the magnificent garden of
eighteen acres adjoining, for the study of
the thousands of strange specimens for
artistic purposes.

MANCHESTER, N. H.—The Ray Brook
Garden Company is suing the city for
damages sustained from the overflow of
Ray Brook in 1900.

GENEVA, N. Y.—Prof. F. C. Stewart, of
the New York Experiment Station, will
be in charge of the pathology exhibit of
the experiment stations at the St. Louis
exposition.

Washington, D. C.

GOVERNMENT CHRYSANTHEMUM SHOWS ATTRACT LARGE C**>**OWDS.—NEW VARIE-TIES SHOWN.—MRS. ROOSEVELT HONORS OPENING.—TRADE PROSPERS.

The star of the chrysanthemum is in the ascendancy, while the rose, carnation and violet are in eclipse and the ice box. With two shows in progress under the auspices of the government and thousands of blooms in the florists' and department stores, even the most fastidious football rooter should be pleased. At the propagating gardens, which are under the direction of Col. Symonds, chief of buildings and grounds, the genial landscape gardener Geo. H. Brown, has been showing the past week a collection of good chrysanthemums, including two new ones, Mrs. J. H. Wilson and Hon. Walter Q. Gresham, which have attracted considerable attention. At the Agricultural Department greenhouses under the direction of Prof. Galloway, assisted by Mr. Byrnes, another show is in progress. There are quite a variety of good blooms. Mrs. W. B. Chamberlain, pink; Honesty, white; and Yellow Carnot are worthy of mention. Mr. Appleton is good at both shows, in fact it seems to be the favorite of the season. Both the exhibits have attracted crowds of visitors, Mrs. Roosevelt having honored the opening by her presence, as have also many of the high officials and their families.

Henry Pfister, who for twenty-five years was a florist at the White House conservatories, has leased the Chevy Chase conservatories and will grow a general stock for his Connecticut avenue store.

Alex. B. Garden has just received a large shipment of azaleas from Belgium. James Quinn, rose grower for Mr. Garden, has a good crop of Bride and Bridesmaid coming on.

Trade is quite good and with the prevailing fine weather there is a prospect of the bountiful supply of chrysanthemums and other flowers keeping up for some time.

J. Louis Loose has a good stock of chrysanthemums grown at his Alexandria range, also very good blooms of Enchantress carnation.

J. H. Small & Sons have fine blooms of Eaton chrysanthemum and Prosperity carnation grown by H. Weber & Sons, of Oakland, Md.

F. H. Kramer has opened a store at 916 F street, N. W. Mr. Oehlmer, well known among the florists of Washington, is in charge.

C. Fonnett, of Alexandria, Va., is about to open a store in the new Colorado building, Fourth and G streets, N. W.

Geo. H. Cooke, proprietor of a flower store on Connecticut avenue is an authority on good stock.

S. E.

For Beginners.

Lime water is the best worm exterminator for pots or benches. A 6-inch pot of lime to twelve gallons of water. Let the lime settle before using, and there should be a few days' interval between applications of lime water and liquid manure.

If you experience difficulty in rooting some kinds of stock in sand, try hard coal ashes which have been passed through a half-inch screen.

Katherine Tracy is the best soft pink sweet pea for winter cutting. G.

THE NURSERY TRADE.

AM. ASSOCIATION OF NURSERYMEN.
N. W. HALE, Knoxville, Tenn.. Pres.; FRANK
A. WEBER, St. Louis, Mo., Vice-Pres.; GEORGE C.
SEAGER, Rochester, N. Y., Sec'y.
Twenty-ninth annual convention, Atlanta, Ga.,
June, 1904.

EAU CLAIRE, MICH.—The incorporators
of the Callahan Nurseries are James P.,
James E., Margaret N. and Cornelius L.
Callahan and John McLane of Eau
Claire, and J. W. Loftus, of Dansville,
N. Y.

CLEVELAND, TENN.—The Easterly Nursery Company has been incorporated.
The incorporators are W. A. Easterly, G.
M. Bazemore, J. E. Johnson, W. D. Long
and J. F. Johnson. The capital stock is
fixed at $10,000.

CHATTANOOGA, TENN.—The nurserymen and cotton men of this section are
doing the largest shipping business ever
known. There are six nurseries in this
county, and every one of them has more
orders than it can fill.

GEORGE DASH, a nurseryman of Poca-
tello, Idaho, discharged a small rifle into
the air to frighten a crowd of boys who
were throwing stones through the roof of
his greenhouse on Halloween. One shot
accidentally struck a 14-year-old lad,
inflicting a slight flesh wound.

INDIANAPOLIS, IND.—Secretary Freeman,
of the State Board of Forestry, will spend
this week on the state forest reservation,
superintending seed planting, which
was begun to-day. Seeds for the more
valuable of the forest trees will be planted
including the oak, walnut, hickory and
chestnut.

CARTHAGE, MO.—The Stark Brothers
Nurseries and Orchards Company, of
Louisiana, Mo., filed suit October 19 for
$12,000 damages against Jas. B. Wild
& Brothers, of Sarcoxie, Mo., nurserymen. The plaintiff charges that Jas. B.
Wild & Brothers have been selling apple
trees since July, 1902, under the names of
"Senator," "Champion," "Black Ben
Davis" and "Apple of Commerce," names
which the Stark company says it has
registered both with the Missouri secretary of state and in the U. S. patent
office. The Stark nursery claims that it
originated the varieties so named.

National Nut Growers' Association.

The second annual convention of the
National Nut Growers' Association was
held in New Orleans, La., the last week
in October. Prominent nut growers
were present from all the southern and a
number of the northern states. The
attendance was very encouraging and
the interest manifested was a source of
much gratification to the officers and all
interested in the industry. The programme was carried out as previously
arranged with remarkably few variations or exceptions, as only one of the
twenty-five speakers failed to put in an
appearance.

This meeting was devoted largely to
the discussion of the pecan, the leading
nut in southern territory. The reports
from state vice-presidents showed rapid
increase in planting of this nut for commercial purposes. The matter of relative
value of budded and grafted trees versus
seedlings received prominent attention,
and the sentiment in favor of propagating only the best known varieties by
grafting and budding is very marked.

Probably the most important feature of
the convention was the report of the committee on nomenclature and standards,
which provides for the scientific naming
of varieties in a way which will preclude
the duplicating of names for different
nuts, as well as giving different names
for the same nut, which has given rise to
much confusion. This committee also
submitted a scale for grading pecan nuts,
which promises to be of much value in
determining the relative merits of the
different varieties for commercial purposes. A scale for amateur use is in
anticipation, as well as a plan for determining tree characteristics.

The report of the committee on ethics
shows that the association has been
instrumental to a great extent in preventing the operations of the fraudulent tree
dealer. The ways and means committee
exploited a plan for accumulating funds
for prosecuting the work of the association which promises most for the industry. The next convention will be held at
St Louis, Mo.

The following officers were elected:
G. M. Bacon, De Witt, Ga., president;
Wm. Nelson, New Orleans, La., first vice-
president; B. Curtis, Orange Heights,
Fla., second vice-president; J. F. Wilson,
Poulan, Ga., secretary-treasurer; G. M.
Bacon, De Witt, Ga., Wm. Nelson, New
Orleans, La., J. B. Curtis, Orange Heights,
Fla., J. F. Wilson, Poulan, Ga., H. C.

White, De Witt, Ga., E. W. Kirkpatrick,
McKinney, Texas, E. Mead Wilcox,
Auburn, Ala., Theo. Bechtel, Ocean
Springs, Miss., S. H. James, Mound, La.,
executive committee.

CHATTANOOGA, TENN.—Geo. Bradt, the
former president of the board of park
commissioners, claims title to about
1,200 of the rarest plants in the conservatories at East Lake park, which he
says that he loaned to the city when
connected with that department. In
furtherance of his claims he has filed a
bill in chancery against all the present
commissioners individually.

OUR PASTIMES.

Announcements of coming contests or other events of interests to our bowling, shooting and sporting readers are solicited and will be given place in this column.
Address all correspondence for this department to Wm. J. Stewart, 79 Milk St., Boston, Mass.; Robt. Kift, 1725 Chestnut St., Philadelphia, Pa.; or to the American Florist Co., Chicago, Ill.

At St. Louis.

The bowling club is working steadily in anticipation of a more closely contested match next year. The scores made on Monday evening, November 2 follow:

Player	1st	2d	3d	T'l
Beneke	166	190	173	5 7
Allen	158	203	131	498
Ellis		173	143	485
Young	196	156	194	476
Miller	167	151	137	455
Weber	155	156	137	448
Meinhardt	137	126	142	405

F. K. B.

At Chicago.

The first bowling games of the season were played on the Giroux alleys November 3. The scores were as follows:

Player	1st	2d	3d
Lambros	183	140	139
George	193	203	136
Balluf	164	129	145
Winterson	198	128	145
Newett	87	162	113
Foerester	193	155	187
Asmus	169	164	199
Andrew	136	124	144
Hauswirth		176	
Degnan		148	
Vournakis	123	141	112
Krietling	159	126	135
Charles	108		

At Philadelphia.

To make home bowling more attractive a six team league has been organized composed entirely of active and associate members of the Florists' Club who will contest for the championship, the first series commencing November 6 and ending December 18. Prizes aggregating $75 will be awarded in this tournament and the teams have been selected from the best men having monthly averages on the home alleys. The teams will be known by the names of their captains and the make-up of each follows:
WESTCOTT TEAM. — Westcott, Yates, Adelberger, McLorter, Seaman.
KIFT TEAM — Kift, Mooney, Craig, Holmes, Hanna.
MOSS TEAM. — Moss, Bonsall, Polites, Gibson, Dunlap.
HARRIS TEAM. — Harris, Johnson, Robertson, Graham, Baxter.
DUNHAM TEAM. — Dunham, Moore, Watson, Anderson, Merbitz.
EIMERMAN TEAM. — Eimerman, Falck, Connor, Dungan, Baker.
Mondays, Wednesdays and Fridays will be the match nights, but no team will have to play more than one match a week. The following is the play schedule:

Mon. Nov. 16 Kift	team plays Dunham team
Wed. " 18 Harris	" " Moss "
Fri. " 20 Eimerman	" " Westcott "
Mon. " 23 Harris	" " Dunham "
Wed. " 25 Moss	" " Westcott "
Fri. " 27 Kift	" " Eimerman "
Mon. " 30 Eimerman	" " Dunham "
Wed. Dec. 2 Moss	" " Kift "
Fri. " 4 Westcott	" " Harris "
Mon. " 7 Kift	" " Harris "
Wed. " 9 Dunham	" " Westcott "
Fri. " 11 Moss	" " Eimerman "
Mon. " 14 Dunham	" " Moss "
Wed. " 17 Harris	" " Eimerman "
Fri. " 18 Westcott	" " Kift "

G. C. W.

NORWALK, O. — Mr. and Mrs. John Klink, proprietors of the Woodbine Greenhouse, expect to leave for Cuba soon.

Indianapolis.

PROSPECTS FOR BIG SHOW ARE PROMISING.
—DINNER FOR EXHIBITORS.—NEW CARNATION VARIETIES MANY.

The outlook for the fall show is very promising, and with some respectable weather it is sure to be a success. Entries are made in great numbers and the local florists expect a greater number of visitors than ever before. They will entertain at dinner in the German house Thursday, November 12. After dinner there will be bowling and other amusements.
All members of the state association who give their names to the doorkeeper at the coming exhibition will receive five complimentary tickets each and a badge. The tickets are for members of their families only; this includes nothing further than second cousin twice removed.
Carnation novelties are numerous. Gunnar Teilmann has an excellent and profitable crimson in his Marion Beauty. John Hartje's Moonlight promises to become a standard commercial white. Baur & Smith have several good novelties; Indianapolis is the best.
At last night's meeting, Irvin Bertermann, H. W. Rieman and Charles Wheatcraft were appointed a committee to see the prosecuting attorney concerning the removal of foreign flower peddlers from the streets of this city.
Messrs. Huckriede, Junge and Harritt were appointed a committee to award the S. A. F. O. H. medals for 1903 at the coming exhibition. The awarding is to be done by direction of Messrs. Bock and Buettner, the judges.
We have never seen H. W. Rieman's place in better trim than this fall. He has the finest lot of latanias in this city and a fine pink carnation.
Albin Schneiber attended an oyster supper instead of the meeting; he says he prefers oysters to hash if he can get them.
Fred Huckriede contracted a severe cold while visiting gas belt cities; he is now sufficiently recovered to be about.
Frank Alley, one of the oldest members of the society, is now engaged in the manufacture of wire goods.
J. A. E. Haugh, of Anderson, Mrs. Vesey, of Fort Wayne, and E. G. Hill, of Richmond were visitors.
H. J.

KEOKUK, IA. — In a floral fiesta recently held by the women's club, the Keokuk club, entered a tallyho decked in scarlet poppies, completely hiding the body and gear. An automobile was apparently drawn by a huge yellow and black butterfly, while the car was covered with yellow blooms.

ROSES...

30,000 H. P. and Everblooming or Monthly Roses. Strong, 2-years old, field-grown on own roots. We have all the new ones and some of the good old-timers. Write us for list of varieties and prices.

Ozone Park Nurseries, OZONE PARK, L. N. Y.

Please mention the American Florist when writing.

Boston Ferns.

BRILLIANTISSIMA, THE NEW ALTERNANTHERA, what you want if you want the best. $6 per 100; $50 per 1000.

CANNAS. NICE CLUMPS. F. Vaughan, J. C. Vaughan, Egandale, Chas. Henderson. A. Bouvier, Burbank, Etc., $2.00 per 100; $15.00 per 1000.

A. J. BALDWIN, - - - Newark, Ohio.

Please mention the American Florist when writing.

St. Louis.

HORSE SHOW ON.—TRADE ONLY FAIR.— NEW OFFICERS OF CACTUS ASSOCIATION.

Chrysanthemums are the mainstay of the trade just now. Some excellent blooms are coming in, a few bringing high prices. The horse show, which is in full blast, takes a great many, in fact they are the only blooms in demand. Trade was good generally until the past few days, when the demand fell off considerably. Prices fluctuate greatly and those quoted are for the best stock. Carnations and roses are of good quality, with an increased amount of fancy stock coming in.

On account of the horse show being in progress this week several of the downtown florists decorated their windows with more than ordinary care. H. C. Berning, the wholesaler, used white and green bunting, which are the colors of the Bit and Bridle club, with artistic effect. Teresa Badaracco used a background of ribbons and bunting, showing a fine saddler's outfit. On both sides were large vases of white chrysanthemums, carnations and roses.

The following officers were elected at the monthly meeting of the St. Louis Cactus Association, November 2: Geo. H. Abeel, president; John Nagel, vice-president; F. K. Balthis, secretary and treasurer; R. Holtzwart, librarian.

Owing to the chrysanthemum exhibition, the next meeting of the St. Louis Florists' Club will be held at the usual place, in Odd Fellows building, November 12, at 2 o'clock.

The Michel Plant and Bulb Company has a bench of fine Timothy Eaton chrysanthemums. The blooms are large and of a clear, solid color.

The opening of the St. Louis Women's Club created a demand for many chrysanthemums, roses and carnations.

F. K. B.

Rutherford, N. J.

During the past week Julius Roehrs has rebuilt a portion of his old range and added another cold house 35x100. One new house is 25x150 and there are two 15x120 each. These are of the most substantial modern construction and "built to last." The stock of palms here is in splendid condition, but palm growing, according to Mr. Roehrs is not as profitable as it formerly was. The city florists, who are the best buyers of this kind of material, do not have as many greenhouses as formerly, the numerous growers and the telephone facilities rendering it unnecessary that they should carry stock in any great quantity, hence the orders for palms and similar things are nowadays "hand to mouth" transactions mainly. Large Cocos Weddelliana are scarce, but other sorts are in satisfactory supply.

Mr. Roehrs has a good word to say for the variety of Begonia Lorraine, known as Glory of Wellesley, a more robust but denser grower than the type and with larger flowers. Cattleya Roehrsiana is a splendid flower with a gorgeous lip, of which Mr. Roehrs is justly proud. It is a hybrid (C. Mendelii × C. Hardyana) raised by Sander & Company, St. Albans, England, and named by Mr. Sander in honor of Mr. Roehrs, who has done so much to popularize the cattleya as a commercial flower in America.

CHILLICOTHE, ILL.—A chrysanthemum show will be given here November 5.

Detroit.

VISIT TO TOLEDO PLANNED.—J. D. THOMP-
SON CARNATION CO. EXHIBITS HERE.

The club meeting Wednesday evening brought out a good attendance. Only business of a miscellaneous character was transacted, which included a review of incidents of the club's outing last week. A vote of thanks was given to the Mt. Clemens' florists for the generous treatment accorded the visitors, and to Philip Breitmeyer, who provided the special car for the occasion. The club will visit the Toledo florists in the near future. The trip will be made in a special car on the new electric road when that line is completed. There was on exhibition a display of new carnations from J. D. Thompson Carnation Company, Joliet, Ill. The varieties were: Mrs. M. A. Patten, Gov. Wolcott, Boston Market and Nelson Fisher. The blooms were fine specimens and excited the greatest interest of all present. A vase of pompon chrysanthemums was also sent, by N. Smith & Son, Adrian, Mich., which were much appreciated. Henry Smith of Grosse Point also showed a dozen flowers of extra well grown chrysanthemums, and at the next meeting, November 18, he will read a paper on "Recent Introductions of Chrysanthemums." At the same meeting, H. Knope will give an address on "Cultural Methods of the Best Standard Varieties of Chrysanthemums."

A party consisting of Frank Holznagle, Fred Breitmeyer, James Taylor, John Carey, Frank Beard, Robt. Flowerday and J. F. Sullivan visited the establishment of Nathan Smith & Son, Adrian, Mich., Friday, November 6.

John Breitmeyer's Sons and B. Schroeter are the only local florists making special exhibits of chrysanthemums this fall. Both exhibits are being held this week and include roses and orchids.

Philip Breitmeyer starts for New York Sunday, November 8. He will attend the New York Flower Show, where he will also make an exhibit of their new rose.

Visitors: Thos. Magee and Geo. A. Heinl, Toledo; Elmer D. Smith, Adrian, O. A. Stoll, Oxford, Mich.   J. F. S.

Joliet, Ill.

The second annual flower show opened in this city November 4 and will continue during the week. It has proved a highly successful venture and hereafter will no doubt be ranked among the leading exhibitions of the country. The principal exhibitors included the Chicago Carnation Company and the J. D. Thompson Carnation Company of this city; W. H. Buckbee, Rockford, Ill.; Nathan Smith & Son, Adrian, Mich.; The E. G. Hill Company, Richmond, Ind.; Geo. A. Kuhl, Pekin, Ill., and Vaughan's Greenhouses, Western Springs, Ill. It is expected that there will be a bowling contest this (Saturday) evening. Further details next week.

WHEELING, W. VA.—It is not likely a chrysanthemum show will be held at the Carroll Club this year. There will, however, be many shows in the various florists' stores.

LEXINGTON, KY.—A large building on the place of H. F. Hillenmeyer was burned October 30 entailing a loss of $3,000. The building was 30x80 feet and was used as a nursery room, containing valuable implements and plants.

Carnation Rooted Cuttings NOW READY.

WHITE.	Per 100	1000	5000
Queen Louise	$1.20	$11.00	$ 50.00
Flora Hill	1.20	11.00	50.00
Alba	3.40	30.00	125.00
Wolcott	3.40	30.00	125.00
Los Angeles	3.00	25.00	100.00
Norway	1.20	11.00	50.00
Lillian Pond	6.00	50.00	225.00
White Cloud	1.20	11.00	50.00

PINK.			
Lawson	1.40	12.50	60.00
Marquis	1.20	11.00	50.00
Genevieve Lord	1.20	11.00	50.00
Argyle	1.20	11.00	50.00
Mrs. Joost	1.20	11.00	50.00
Mermaid	1.20	11.00	50.00
Guardian Angel	1.20	11.00	50.00
Mrs. Higinbotham	2.50	20.00	90.00
Cressbrook	2.50	20.00	90.00
Mrs. Roosevelt	6.00	55.00	250.00
Enchantress	6.00	55.00	250.00
Success	5.00	45.00	200.00

SCARLET.			
G. H. Crane	1.40	12.50	60.00

SCARLET.	Per 100	1000	5000
America	1.20	11.00	50.00
Estelle	1.40	14.00	65.00
Mrs. Palmer	1.50	14.00	65.00
Apollo	3.50	30.00	125.00
Adonis	7.00	65.00	300.00

CRIMSON.			
Harlowarden	5.00	45.00	200.00
Gov. Roosevelt	1.20	11.00	50.00
Gen. Maceo	1.20	11.00	50.00
Gen. Gomez	1.20	11.00	50.00
Harry Fenn	3.50	25.00	100.00

YELLOW.			
Golden Beauty	1.75	16.00	75.00
Eldorado	1.21	11.00	50.00
Gold Nugget	1.50	14.00	65.00

VARIEGATED.			
Violinia (4-inch bloom)	12.00	100.00	450.00
Marshall Field	5.00	45.00	200.00
Tiger (Fancy)	5.00	45.00	200.00
Stella	3.00	25.00	100.00
Bradt	1.75	16.00	70.00
Armazindy	1.20	11.00	50.00
Prosperity	1.20	11.00	52.00

Twenty-five at 100 rates; 250 at 1,000 rates; 2,500 at 5,000 rates.

Terms: SPOT CASH. No discount given, no matter how large the order. We prepay express charges at above figures to your city. If on arrival they are not satisfactory return at once, and boxes will be refunded at once; we cannot vary from these terms.

CALIFORNIA CARNATION CO., Look Box 103, LOOMIS, CAL.

E. T. GRAVE, RICHMOND, IND.

WHOLESALE FLORIST.

CARNATIONS and ROSES.

500,000 VERBENAS THE CHOICEST VARIETIES IN CULTIVATION.

Fine pot plants, $2.50 per 100; $20 per 1000. Rooted Cuttings, 60c per 100; $5 per 1000; $45 per 10,000.

NO RUST OR MILDEW.

PACKED LIGHT, AND SATISFACTION GUARANTEED. SEND FOR CIRCULAR.
We are the Largest Growers of Verbenas in the country. Our plants cannot be surpassed.

J. L. DILLON,   BLOOMSBURG, PA.

Boston and Pierson Ferns.

Boston Ferns.	Piersoni Ferns.
2½-inch...$ 5.1-0 per 100	2½-inch....$ .25 each
3-inch......10.00 per 100	3-inch........ .50 each
4-inch......15.00 per 100	4-inch........ .75 each
5-inch......25.00 per 100	5-inch........1.00 each
6-inch......40.00 per 100	6-inch........1.50 each
7-inch......60.00 per 100	8-inch........3.00 each
8-inch, $1 to $1.50 each	8-inch, extra, 3.00 each
10-inch, 2 to 2.50 each	

Best value for your money in the west.

GEO. A. KUHL, Pekin, Ill.

Smilax Plants.

5,000 extra strong Smilax plants, 2-inch at 1.00 per 100.

Asparagus Sprengeri, from February sown seed, 2-inch pots, $2.00 per 100.

1000 Norway Carnation Plants, to close out, $3.50 per 100.

JOHN BROD, Chicago, Ill.

Through Sleepers to Galveston, Texas via the Wabash.

The Wabash Road has inaugurated a line of first-class Pullman sleepers between Chicago and Galveston, leaving Chicago daily at 11:03 a. m. and arriving at Galveston the second morning at 7:30; a convenient leaving and arriving time. The route is Wabash to St. Louis, Iron Mountain to Texarkana, T. & P. to Longview and thence I. & G. N. R. R.

For sleeping car reservations, folders, etc., apply to your nearest ticket agent, or to
F. A. PALMER, A. G. P. A., CHICAGO.

Crimson Ramblers FOR EASTER.

3 to 4 feet, fine, 50 for $9.00; $2.50 per dozen. 2,000 Princess of Wales and Swanley White Violets, clumps $5.00 per 1.0. Extra 5,000 Forcing Tomato Plants, Lorillard and May flower selected stock, 2½-in pot plants, $4.00 per 104; $30 per 90.00. Cash please.

BENJ. CONNELL, West Grove, Pa.

PÆONIAS.

Fragrants $6.00 per 100.
For 1,000 rates or other varieties write.

GILBERT H. WILD, Sarcoxie, Mo.

Vinca Variegata Major.

Not less than 5 vines 2 feet. JOOST CARNATION PLANTS strong, field-grown, $5 per 100. HYDRANGEA OTAKSA, large enough for ¼ barrel tubs, $1.00 each; $10.00 per doz. COLEUS and ENGLISH IVY, from 3-inch pots, $2.00 per 100.

J. H. DANN & SONS, Westfield, N.Y.

BOSTON FERN RUNNERS

Extra nice, strong runners from bench at $15.00 per 1000.

J. W. Bernard,

MARION. IND.

Please mention the American Florist when writing.

Please mention the American Florist to advertisers.

San Francisco.

BUSINESS FAIR, BUT UNABLE TO MOVE THE TOO HEAVY RECEIPTS OF STOCK.— CHRYSANTHEMUMS FINER THAN USUAL. —VARIOUS ITEMS.—VISITORS.

The annual convention of the American Bankers' association took place in this city last week, and was the occasion of considerable extra business, especially with downtown florists. The call was insufficient, however, to clean up the stock brought in. Chrysanthemums, which are very fine this year, possess for the present the favor of the flower-buying public, and nearly everything else is a drug on the market. Fine chrysanthemums sell at retail all the way from 50 cents to $3.50 per dozen. Many of them are grown outdoors, in some instances having a covering of some light material and producing blooms nearly as good as inside grown, and of course at much less cost. Roses and carnations are improving in color and length of stem. The colder weather has also benefited violets. Valley is quite scarce. The demand for decorative plants such as palms and ferns has improved of late.

A recent visit to M. Lynch, of Menlo Park found this establishment in first-class condition, with everything in good shape for the coming season. Six houses are devoted to carnations of the leading varieties, Estelle and Lawson being particularly in favor. Lawson has shown quite a sporting propensity. Two variations, one a light pink and the other a white variegated, are being watched with interest. One house is grown to chrysanthemums and later on will be planted to carnations for summer blooms. Two houses are devoted to roses, mainly Bridesmaid, Bride and Kaiserin. A batch of chrysanthemums numbering nearly 60,000, grown outdoors, appeared in prime condition, producing upwards of 200 dozen blooms a day. There were also 15,000 strings of smilax, also outdoor grown, of uniform length and of that deep glossy foliage so much desired in smilax. The bulk of the output of this place is shipped to Oregon, Colorado and Utah.

The Leedham Bulb Company, Santa Cruz, captured the Dreer silver cup at a recent flower show at Santa Barbara for the best collection of cactus dahlias.

Sievers & Boland are handling some very fine Prosperity carnations from F. Abie, Berkeley.

Visitors: Sidney Clack, Menlo Park and J. Thompson, Santa Cruz.   ROMNEYA.

A FEW GOOD THINGS

YOU WANT.

Special low prices on palms to close out. Fine clean stock, cool grown and well shaped plants, none better.
ARECA LUTESCENS, 3 plants to pot, 4, 5 and 6-inch, $25, $40 and $100 per 100.
KENTIA BELMOREANA and FORSTERIANA, 3, 4, 5 and 6-inch, $12, $25, $40, $100 per 100.
REX BEGONIA, 3 and 3-inch, $4 and $6 per 100.
DRACAENA INDIVISA, 3-inch, $6 per 100; 4-inch, $10 per 100.
ENGLISH IVY, 2 and 3-inch, $3 and $6 per 100.
BOSTON FERNS, 6-inch, $30 per 100. From beds, for 2, 3 and 4-inch pots, $4, $6, $15 per 100.
ASPARAGUS PLUMOSUS, 3-inch, $6.00 per 100.
SPRENGERI, 3-inch, $3.00 per 100.
VINCA VARIEGATA, 3-inch, $2.00 per 100.
CARNATIONS, Queen Louise, 2-in., $2.00 per 100.
Lawson, 3-inch, $2.50 per 100.
CINERARIAS, 2 and 3-inch, $3 and $4 per 100.
GERANIUMS, rooted cuttings. Double and single Grant, Bonnot, S. A. Nutt, $1.00 per 100. Perkins, LaFavorite, John Doyle, $1.25 per 100. Riccard, Mrs. E. G. Hill, $1.50 per 100.
CASH OR C. O. D.

GEO. M. EMMANS, NEWTON, N. J.

ALWAYS mention the AMERICAN FLORIST when writing to advertisers.

St. Paul.

Trade has been very good the last week. Several large receptions with some good funeral work have kept everybody busy. All those intending to exhibit at the show next week are now busy tieing up their chrysanthemum plants and polishing up decorative plants. Quite a feature has been added by the ladies arranging for a floral parade the opening day of the show. Prizes are offered for the best decorated automobile, carriage and pony cart. Visits to the growers show nearly everything in fine shape.

The much famed Pandanus Sanderi has just been received here, and though a little lighter in color than was expected is certainly a fine acquisition for decorative work.

The best chrysanthemums here are the white and yellow Eaton and some fine Viviand-Morel. There is a lot of well grown pot plants.

Frank Gustafson, of L. L. May & Company, has some benches of Bridesmaid and Bride.   O.

Louisville.

Henry Nanz has been given charge of the grounds of the Kentucky exhibit at the St. Louis World's Fair and will attend to ornamenting and planting.

Joseph B. Stuessy & Son have built a house 16x120 feet with side benches of slate and center of concrete at 1536 Haldeman avenue.

C. H. Kunzman has invented and patented a carnation stake or holder and is making arrangements to have them manufactured.

Nanz & Neuner will hold a chrysanthemum show at their conservatory in the rear of their Fourth avenue store.

The Fourteenth annual chrysanthemum show of the Louisville florists takes place November 13 to 14.

F. Haupt won second prize at the horse show for the best delivery wagon and horse.

Miss Hattie Walker has returned from a visit to Colorado Springs and Denver.

The dry weather is seriously affecting the sale of trees, etc., for fall planting.
                                        H. G. W.

HOPEDALE, MASS.—The park system of Hopedale, Mass., is to be extended by the addition of a 1,000-acre tract west of the river which has been purchased recently by Gen. Wm. F. Draper.

The ANNUAL—

Autumn Number

RIGHT FOR THANKSGIVING

What They Say:

TWICE AS GOOD AS OTHERS.
ED. AM. FLORIST:—The adv. in your paper brought more than twice the amount of orders of any other paper.
Greene, N. Y.   THE PAGE SEED CO.

HIS BEST INVESTMENT.
ED. AM. FLORIST:—My first dollar invested in the FLORIST has proved to be the best investment I ever made.
Fremont, Neb.   G. T. G. LOLLICH.

SWAMPED WITH ORDERS.
ED. AM. FLORIST:—Please do not again print our 1-inch advertisement for carnation plants. One insertion sold them all, in fact brought orders for several times our surplus.
Hughsonville, N. Y.   A. LAUB & SONS.

ADVERTISING IN THE AMERICAN FLORIST
NO WASTE; NO FICTICIOUS INQUIRIES.

IT IS BUSINESS that pays the advertiser, and this publication goes to buyers of stock in all lines. The seasonable and permanent value of our Special Numbers for advertising purposes is well known.

OUR SPECIAL NUMBERS ARE READ, PRESERVED AND RE-READ.

Advertisements in body pages will be taken at our ordinary rates, namely, $1.00 per inch, $30.00 per page of thirty inches, with the usual discounts on time contracts. Advertisements on second, third and fourth SPECIAL COVER PAGES, (printed on heavy toned paper) $30.00 per page, net.

MAIL YOUR ADVERTISEMENT TO REACH US NOT LATER THAN NOVEMBER 11th.

TO BE ISSUED
November 14,
1903.

AMERICAN FLORIST CO.

324 Dearborn Street,

——CHICAGO.

Milwaukee.

BUSINESS BOOMED BY STORE OPENING.—PLORISTS' CLUB MEETING AND BANQUET.—AROUND TOWN.

The Milwaukee Florists' Club had a well attended meeting last Tuesday, some important matters being passed, among them being the adoption of a new constitution for the club as well as the appointment of a committee to arrange preliminary prizes for the show which will be held next year. Judging from the interest being taken we ought to have the best show the club has ever held. A banquet followed the meeting which lasted well into the night. W. A. Kennedy presided and some good speeches were made, all advocating a closer relationship among the members of the craft.

Business in this city received a boom last Monday, due to the opening of a large jewelry house, that used up thousands of flowers for souvenirs. Since that time, however, the market has been filled up with flowers, but the cold spell of Wednesday will no doubt help to shorten up stock before the week is over. Chrysanthemums are in full swing at present with more than enough to fill all orders. American Beauty is in good demand.

James Chaconna is making lavish use of chrysanthemums in the decoration of his windows. Some very large funeral designs were lately turned out by him.

G. Kellner had the decoration for the recent opening of Gimbel Brothers. He used large quantities of asparagus and chrysanthemums.

Holton & Hunkel Company has its new house completed and stocked up.

C. C. Pollworth has been spending a week with his out-of-town customers.

Wm. Edlefsen is sending in a very fine grade of chrysanthemums. H.

BAY SHORE, L. I.—The second annual exhibition of the Suffolk County Horticultural Association was held October 28 and 29. Flowers, fruits and vegetables were exhibited, the showrooms being crowded with the best results of the vegetable and flower gardens and conservatories of the Brooklyn and Manhattan colonies hereabout. William K. Vanderbilt sent an assortment of plants and garden truck from his Idle Hour estate. The total value of the prizes offered by the association was $700.

Cincinnati.

MARKET HAS GLUT OF ROSES.—VIOLETS ARE SCARCE.—FLORISTS' SOCIETY STARTS EXHIBITS.—PREMIUMS.

We are having a glut of roses and many good ones are finding their way to the barrel. Chrysanthemums and carnations, however, are none too plentiful, while good violets are scarce and sell for $1 per 100. American Beauty the past few days has arrived in quantities and owing to the warm weather does not last very well in the ice chest. The fakirs' stands are full of them. Lily of the valley is good but not selling very well at present. Green goods are plentiful. There was a good demand for chrysanthemums for All Saints' day, and the stand holders in the Jabez Elliott flower market had their stands well filled with fine plants and cut blooms. Apparently they all did a good business for they all seemed satisfied.

Saturday, November 14, the Cincinnati Florists' Society will hold its first monthly exhibit for the season of 1903-1904 at the Jabez Elliott flower market. The following are subscribers to the exhibition fund: Wm. Schuman, E. G. Gillett, R. Witterstaetter, Cambridge Tile Manufacturing Company, J. H. Rodgers, Heller Brothers, Wm. Speck, Lockland Lumber Company, D. Rusconi, Wm. Murphy, George & Allan, Louis H. Kyrk, W. K. Partridge, C. J. Ohmer, August Sunderbruch. The premiums to be awarded follow:

Best vase of chrysanthemums, Bonnaffon, twenty-five blooms, first, $10; second, $8; third, $6.

Best vase chrysanthemums, white, twelve blooms, first, $6; second $4; third, $3.

Best vase of chrysanthemums, pink, twelve blooms, first, $6; second, $4; third, $3.

Best vase chrysanthemums, yellow, twelve blooms, first, $6; second, $4; third, $3.

Best general display, $10.

ALEX.

Hartford, Conn.

An injunction has been applied for, restraining the owners of the Heublein conservatory from making certain changes in the property involving alleged violations of the restrictions contained in the deed. Some time ago this building was opened as a greenhouse and store by Miss Frey, but the venture was not successful. Recently it was announced that the premises would be leased to a laundryman for a laundry, and the application for an injunction followed. The Heublein conservatory is a beautiful structure, containing a large palm house with curved roof, a florist store with splendid furnishings and a cozy little plant house over the store, also with curved roof. The building was put up by Hitchings last year at a cost of about $14,000.

H. D. Brooks, employed in the greenhouses of John Coombs, has accepted the position as gardener to one of the Cheney families in South Manchester, Conn.

Finds It an Aid.

ED. AM. FLORIST:—I much prefer your paper to others. I have just started growing cut flowers for the New York market, and find your paper very valuable. WM. SIMMONDS.
Staten Island, N. Y.

Meetings of Florists' Clubs.

BALTIMORE, MD.—Gardeners' Club of Baltimore. Royal Arcanum building, 18 W. Saratoga street. Second and fourth Monday of each month, at 8 p. m. John J. Perry, Sec'y, Gay and Eager streets.

BOSTON, MASS.—Gardeners' and Florists' Club of Boston, Horticultural Hall. Meets second Tuesday of each month, October to March inclusive. W. E. Fischer, Sec'y, 18 Union Terrace, Jamaica Plain, Mass.

BROCTON, MASS.— Brocton Gardeners' and Florists' Club, store of W. W. Hathaway, Times Building. First and third Tuesday of each month, at 8 p. m. W. W. Hathaway, Sec'y, Brockton, Mass.

BUFFALO, N. Y.—Buffalo Florists' Club, 481 Washington street. Second Wednesday of each month, at 8 p. m. Wm. Legg, Sec'y, 1440 Delaware avenue, Buffalo.

BUTTE, MONT.—Montana Florists' Club, 45 W. Broadway. First Saturday in each month. D. E. Law, Sec'y.

CHICAGO, ILL.—Chicago Florists' Club, Handel Hall, 40 Randolph street. Second and fourth Wednesday of each month, at 8 p. m. George Wienhoeber, Sec'y, 413 Elm street, Chicago.

CINCINNATI, O.—Cincinnati Florists' Society, Jabez Elliott Flower Market. Second Saturday of each month, at 8 p. m. Geo. Murphy, Sec'y, Sta. F., Cincinnati, O.

CLEVELAND, O.—Cleveland Florists' Club, Progress Hall, 344 Detroit street. Second and fourth Monday of each month, at 8 p. m. Isaac Kennedy, Sec'y, Westpark, O.

DENVER, COLO.—Denver Floral Club, 308 Charles Block. Second and fourth Friday of each month, at 8 p. m. Adam Balmer, Sec'y.

DETROIT, MICH.—Detroit Florists' Club, Cowie Building, Farran and Gratiot avenue. First and third Wednesday of each month, at 8 p. m. J. F. Sullivan, Sec'y, 214 Woodward avenue.

GRAND RAPIDS, MICH.—Grand Rapids Florists' Club, Board of Trade rooms, Pearl street. Fourth Monday of each month. N. B. Stover, Sec'y, Grandville, Mich.

HAMILTON, ONT.—Hamilton Gardeners' and Florists' Club, offices of members. First and third Tuesday of each month at 8 p. m. Chas. M. Webster, Sec'y.

HARTFORD, CONN.—Hartford Florists' Club, Second and fourth Tuesday of each month at 8 p. m. J F Coombs, Sec'y.

INDIANAPOLIS, IND.—State Florists' Association of Indiana, Commercial Club rooms, Indianapolis. First Tuesday of each month, at 8 p. m. Ed. Junge, Sec'y, 456 E. Washington street, Indianapolis.

MILWAUKEE, WIS.—Milwaukee Florists' Club. Meets first Tuesday of each month at St. Charles Hotel club rooms. H. V. Runkel, Sec'y.

MINNEAPOLIS, MINN.— Minneapolis Florists' Club, West Hotel. First Thursday of each month, at — p. m. C. F. Rice, Sec'y, 12x N. Sixth street.

MONTREAL, QUE.—Montreal Gardeners' and Florists' Club, Alexandria rooms, 2204 St. Catherine street. First and third Monday of each month. W. H. Horobin, Sec'y, 23 Closse street.

NEW LONDON, CONN.—Gardeners' and Florists' Club, first and third Tuesday of each month at greenhouses of secretary. H. B. Appeldorn, Sec'y.

NEW YORK, N. Y.—New York Florists' Club. Grand Opera House Bldg., 8th avenue and 23d St. Second Monday of each month, at 7:30 p. m. John Young, Sec'y, 51 West Twenty-eighth street, New York

OMAHA, NEB.—Nebraska Florists' Society, City Hall. Second Thursday in each month at 8 p. m. Louis Henderson. Sec'y, 1519 Farnam street, Omaha.

PHILADELPHIA, PA.—Florists' Club of Philadelphia, Horticultural Hall, Broad street above Spruce. First Tuesday of each month, at 8 p. m. Edwin Lonsdale, Sec'y. Wyndmoor, Philadelphia.

PITTSBURG, PA.—Pittsburg and Allegheny Florists' and Gardeners' Club, at German Beneficial Bldg., 6th and Cherry avenue. Second Thursday of each month, at 8 p. m. H. P. Joslin, Sec'y, Ben Avon, Pa.

PROVIDENCE, R. I.—Florists' and Gardeners' Club of Rhode Island, 96 Westminster street, Providence. Second Thursday of each month, at 8 p. m. Alexander Rennie, Sec'y, 41 Washington street, Providence.

RICHMOND, IND.—Richmond Florists' Club, at the greenhouses of members. Third Monday of each month. H. G. Cheasman, Sec'y.

SALT LAKE CITY, UTAH.—Salt Lake Florists' Society, office of Huddart - Floral Company, 314 E. Second South street. Second and fourth Friday of each month. P. T. Huddart, Sec'y.

SAN FRANCISCO, CAL.—Pacific Coast Horticultural Society. First saturday and third Monday of each month. Thos. H. Munroe, Sec'y.

SEATTLE, WASH.—Seattle Commercial Horticultural Club, First and Cherry streets. First Wednesday of each month. Wm. Hopkins, Sec'y, 622 First avenue.

ST. LOUIS, MO.—St. Louis Florists' Club, Odd Fellows Hall No 3, Ninth and Olive streets. Second Thursday of each month, at 3 p. m. Emil Schray, Sec'y, 4101 Pennsylvania avenue, St. Louis.

TORONTO, ONT.—Toronto Gardeners' and Florists' Association, St. George's Hall, Elm street. Third Tuesday of each month, at 8 p. m. E. F. Collins, Sec'y, 8 Hurst place, Toronto.

UTICA, N. Y.—Utica Florists' Club, 193 Genesee street. First Thursday of each month at 8 p. m. J. C. Spencer, Sec'y.

WASHINGTON, D. C.— Washington Florists' Club. Meets first Wednesday in each month. Wm. F. Gude, Sec'y.

Coming Exhibitions.

[Secretaries are requested to supply any omissions from this list.]

BUFFALO, N. Y., November 11-14, 1903.—H. A. Meldrum Co.'s flower show; direction, Buffalo Florists' Club. Wm. Legg, Sec'y, 1440 Delaware avenue, Buffalo.

INDIANAPOLIS, IND., November 10-14, 1903.—Indiana Floral Festival and Chrysanthemum exhibition State Florists' Association of Indiana. Irwin Bertermann, Sec'y, 241 Massachusetts avenue, Indianapolis.

LOUISVILLE, KY., November 11-14, 1903.—Chrysanthemum exhibition florists of Louisville. Nanz & Neuner and E. G. Reimers, Louisville, committee.

NEW YORK, November 10-13, 1903.—Chrysanthemum exhibition Chrysanthemum Society of America. Fred H. Lemon, Sec'y, Richmond, Ind.

PHILADELPHIA, PA., November 10-14, 1903.—Annual exhibition Pennsylvania Horticultural Society. David Rust, Sec'y, Horticultural Hall, Philadelphia, Pa.

MONTREAL, QUE., November 11-12, 1903.—Chrysanthemum exhibition Montreal Gardeners' and Florists' Club. W H. Horobin, Sec'y, 23 Closse street, Montreal.

PROVIDENCE, R. I., November 12-13, 1903.—Chrysanthemum exhibition Rhode Island Horticultural Society. C. W. Smith, Secretary, 27-29 Exchange street, Providence.

ST. PAUL, MINN., November 10 to 12, 1903.—Chrysanthemum and orchid exhibition Ladies Auxiliary of Northwestern Manufacturers' Association. Mrs. M. Helen Moss, Sec'y, St. Paul.

Headquarters for

APHIS PUNK, NICOTICIDE, NICOTEEN, ROSE LEAF EXTRACT, VAN REYPER'S GLAZING POINTS, MASTICA AND MACHINE. Also LIVE SQUIRRELS AND GOLDFISH. Send for catalogue.

Schmid's Bird Store, 712 12th Street, N.W. WASHINGTON, D. C.

Montreal.

The meeting of the Florists' Club held November 2 had the largest attendance in many years. Two new applicants were presented and elected the same night to permit them to exhibit at our chrysanthemum show November 11. The offer of D. J. Sinclair, of Toronto, to make a display of florists' supplies at our chrysanthemum show was accepted. The committee request all exhibitors to send in plants Tuesday afternoon to permit the judging to be done earlier Wednesday. Mr. Kean's paper on roses was read by Mr. Walker, as the former was ill. Before the adjournment the president named the following gentlemen to act as auditors: Jos. Bennett, J. Walsh and Jas. KcKenna. Arthur Robertson, superintendent of Westmount park, and Ernest Bradbury, of Outremont, were the new members elected.

The Lachine Horticultural Society held its fourth annual meeting the last of October and a good many gardeners of Montreal came to attend the meeting. T. Church, of Lachine was elected president. C. A. Smith was named vice-president. Gabriel Vrengde was chosen as secretary-treasurer.

Dreer's golden pandanus, Pandanus Sanderi, has been received with a good deal of disappointment. The color, quality and size are all claimed.

Hall & Robinson report good business in the store recently opened at Matthew and St. Catherine streets.

Mr. Scrim, of Ottawa, was in town visiting the trade. G. V.

Santa Barbara, Cal.

The annual chrysanthemum show was held here October 20 and 21. The chrysanthemums were very fine, the principal varieties being Mrs. Robinson, Timothy Eaton, Golden Wedding, H. L. Sunderbruch, Chestnut Hill, and of the new pink varieties Columbia, Marie Liger, Durban's Pride, Lady Hopetown and Silver Queen. The latter were excellent. The prizes were good. A silver cup donated by D. Richardson, to be contested for two years in succession, was won by W. Adair. A gold medal donated by Mrs. C. B. Hale on the same conditions was won by W. H. Morse, gardener to Mrs. C. B. Hale. Cameron Rogers donated a silver cup for eighteen blooms. This was won by T. Poole, gardener to Cameron Rogers. Some remarkable Timothy Eaton blooms were shown in this class. Dahlias were well represented. W. F. Dreer donated a silver cup to be contested for two years in succession for cactus varieties. This was won by Mr. Leedham, of Santa Cruz, with a large collection. F. Kables was first with a collection of show varieties. In groups of plants there were some rare and choice specimens.

R. Armstrong, of the Eli Montecito Nursery Company, is covering an area of 10,000 feet with glass.

Mrs. Helmer has purchased some land and intends to grow for her own trade. H. W. M.

RICHMOND, IND.—Fulle Brothers have completed extensive improvements in their greenhouses, which included the tearing down of all their houses and their reconstruction with all the latest improvements. The heating apparatus was reinstalled and made larger. The plant now contains chrysanthemum, rose and carnation houses, besides three others for miscellaneous work.

THE AMERICAN FLORIST

America is "the Prow of the Vessel; there may be more comfort Amidships, but we are the first to touch Unknown Seas."

Vol. XXI.　　　CHICAGO AND NEW YORK, NOVEMBER 14, 1903.　　　No. 806.

THE AMERICAN FLORIST

NINETEENTH YEAR.

Copyright 1903, by American Florist Company
Entered as Second-Class Mail Matter.

PUBLISHED EVERY SATURDAY BY

AMERICAN FLORIST COMPANY,
324 Dearborn St., Chicago.

Eastern Office: 42 W. 28th St., New York.

Subscription, $1.00 a year.　To Europe, $2.00.
Subscriptions accepted only from the trade.

Volumes half-yearly from August, 1901.

SOCIETY OF AMERICAN FLORISTS AND
ORNAMENTAL HORTICULTURISTS.

Officers—John Burton, Philadelphia, Pa.,
president; C. C. Pollworth, Milwaukee, Wis.,
vice-president; Wm. J. Stewart, 79 Milk Street,
Boston, Mass., secretary; H. B. Beatty, Oil City,
Pa., treasurer.
Officers-elect—Philip Breitmeyer, president; J. J. Benneke, vice-president; secretary and
treasurer as before. Twentieth annual meeting
at St. Louis, Mo., August, 1904.

THE AMERICAN CARNATION SOCIETY.

Annual convention at Detroit, Mich., March 2,
1904. Albert M. Herr, Lancaster, Pa., secretary.

AMERICAN ROSE SOCIETY.

Annual meeting and exhibition, Philadelphia,
March, 1904. Leonard Barron, 136 Liberty St.,
New York, secretary.

CHRYSANTHEMUM SOCIETY OF AMERICA.

Annual convention and exhibition, November,
1904. Fred H. Lemon, Richmond, Ind., secretary.

Autumn Vagaries.

The thrifty woodland people, taking heed
Of worn and dulled array,
That slowly drops away
Just at the time when all their clothes they
need,
Have cast about them to renew the sheen
That has departed from their summer green.

And so, by alchemy of autumn sun
And pallid autumn syn.
They've tried it, one by one,
But lately they've found out to their despair
That, though to simply renovate they tried,
Most any one would say that they had dyed.

They now are flaunting in gay crimson gowns,
Unusually bold,
Or clad in shining gold—
The least conspicuous are russet browns;
Their threadbare textures now escape the
sight,
Diverted, dazzled by their colors bright.

The maple—shame upon her; who would dream
Of such a garish change?—
And, what seems very strange,
The oak has tampered with his color scheme
And blushes duskily, as well as he may,
To rouge himself in such a shameful way.

Well, after all, 'twill do them little good;
They'll shed this vesture grand
Ere soon and naked stand.
Gaunt, somber spectacles within the wood
All winter long, till kindly time shall bring
Them new and stylish raiment in the spring.
　　　　　　　—*Chicago Daily News.*

CHRYSANTHEMUM SOCIETY
Of America.

SECOND ANNUAL CONVENTION NEW YORK, NOV. 10-12, 1903.

THE annual meeting of the Chrysanthemum Society of America was held at New York Wednesday afternoon, November 11, with President Herrington in the chair. There was a good attendance of members and after the delivery of the president's able address, interesting and encouraging reports were presented by the secretary and treasurer. Prof. Geo. E. Stone's lecture on the "Diseases of Chrysanthemums" was well received. As a result of the president's recommendations the committee on

revising constitution was instructed to report at the next annual convention. The annual report was ordered printed.

It was announced that Elmer D. Smith, of Adrian, Mich., had made a complete card index of all varieties of chrysanthemums of domestic origin or introduction from foreign sources since the year 1887, together with the name of raiser, disseminator and other descriptive notes. This is a very valuable compilation requiring

much labor and worthy of the highest appreciation by chrysanthemum lovers. This also was ordered printed.

All the present officers were re-elected to serve during the ensuing year. In the evening President Herrington entertained about twenty-five friends at the Herald Square hotel, where an informal but sumptuous dinner was served. Among the guests were President-elect Breitmeyer, of the S. A. F.; President Rackham, of the American Carnation Society; officers of the chrysanthemum society and the chief exhibitors. Judge Vesey, of Fort Wayne, Ind., and Patrick O'Mara, of New York, were the principal speakers.

The Exhibition.

The much-heralded exhibition of the Chrysanthemum Society of America, cooperating with the American Institute of New York city, and materially supported by a large number of horticultural societies throughout the country, which was held in New York city on November 10-12, was a pronounced success and equalled it it did not surpass the expectations of those who have worked so hard in its behalf. President Herrington received many well-merited commendations for the success of his efforts, and Dr. Hexamer, always cordial, was sunshine in motion as he contemplated the animated scene on the evening of the first day.

The hall is a new one and proved excellently adapted for use as a flower exhibition room. Its area is vast—nearly an acre and a half—but the quarter acre comprised under the central dome was sufficient for the occasion and was shut in by a high belt or hedge of evergreens, palms, bays, box trees and oak branches contributed by H. A. Siebrecht & Son, whose decorative work contributed not a little to the fine general effect. The central tables, on which were displayed great vases of long-stemmed blooms, forming one of the most impressive exhibitions of its kind ever staged in this country, were simply raised platforms about ten inches from the floor, thus giving a better view than is possible with the higher tables generally used.

The tables around the sides on which were shown the shorter-stemmed blooms were of ordinary height.

The plan of special prizes contributed by various societies for exclusive competition between members of those societies respectively brought out a more widely-extended list of exhibitors than would otherwise have been the case. Mentioning a few of the most notable exhibits under this head, D. Willis James, Wm. Duckham, gardener, won the Chrysanthemum Society's special for ten blooms of any variety with the new pink favorite Wm. Duckham. Miss E. J. Clark, John Ash, gardener, won the Massachusetts Horticultural Society's prizes and the "open to all" prize contributed by the same society for twenty-five blooms of any one variety was won by H. W. Buckbee, who, it might here be said, was one of the largest, if not the largest, contributor to the show. The variety winning this distinction was Col. Appleton. H. McK. Twombly, A. Herrington, gardener, won first New York Florists' Club prize, Pennsylvania Horticultural Society prize and one of the premiums offered by the Morris County Gardeners' and Florists' Society. D. Willis James got the other Morris county prize, and E. D. Adams, G. H. Hale, gardener, won the Monmouth County and J. C. Brown, Peter Duff, gardener, the New Jersey Horticultural Society's special. The Tarrytown first premiums were secured by Jas. Eastman, Wm. Scott, gardener; the Tuxedo prize by C. B. Alexander, Wm. Hastings, gardener, and the Lawrence-Cedarhurst prizes by Talbot J. Taylor, Z. Piddington, gardener, and G. C. Rand, J. G. McNicoll, gardener, respectively. The E. G. Hill Company offered a prize for ten blooms of any undisseminated variety, either seedling or foreign variety, which was won by Nathan Smith & Son with a fine white named Mrs. Nathan Smith. J. N. May's special was won by E. G. Hill Company.

Another pen will take up the subject of the newer chrysanthemums and their qualities, but it will not be out of place to digress from the general character of this report and refer to the very promising pink variety Dr. Englehardt, shown by F. R. Pierson Company and by W. A. Manda. Also we cannot resist to mention a seedling from W. Meneilly & Sons named Miss Charlotte Land, an incurved Japanese of a rich yellow color unapproached by anything in sight. E. G. Hill's big vase of Percy Plumridge caused a sensation. There were extensive collections of named varieties from the E. G. Hill Company, H. W. Buckbee and F. R. Pierson Company, as representing the commercial establishments, and from D. Willis James, H. McK. Twombly, E. D. Adams, T. J. Taylor, Jos. Eastman, all private estates, winning first premiums in many classes. Other exhibitors of greater or less magnitude, in the cut flower classes, were H. J. Park, Thos. Kelley, gardener; H. W. Poor, R. Frank, gardener; Miss Blanche Potter, Wm. Nye, gardener; Wm. Rockefeller, G. Middlecon, gardener; G. C. Rand, W. J. & M. S. Vesey, Wm. Kleinkeinz, C. B. Alexander, W. Hastings, gardener; Robt. Mallory, W. Smith, gardener; Aug. Hecksher, W. Shaw, gardener; W. M. Johnson, P. Seidelien, gardener; C. Hathaway, H. Hornaker, gardener; C. E. Borden, Wm. Turner, gardener, and Vaughan's Greenhouses.

Pompons were shown in grand shape and remarkable variety by R. Vincent, Jr., who won first prize. Another splendid

collection came from W. H. S. Wood, L. A. Martin, gardener, also from Nathan Smith & Son, F. R. Pierson Company, J. H. Troy and D. F. Roy, Mr. Roy also contributing Chinese incurved and anemones. Of bush plants there were but few. The best were from D. F. Roy. Two good specimens also came from W. C. Roberts. Plants grown to single stem and flower were limited to the exhibits of D. E. Oppenheimer, Jas. Hawarth, gardener, and J. Crosby Brown, but they were excellent examples of their class.

W. Wells & Company, Ltd., Red Hill, Surrey, England, forwarded a set of blooms that arrived in excellent condition, the variety William Duckham being as fresh as though cut on the spot. Golden Chain from Vaughan's Greenhouses, Western Springs, Ill., with minute, fragrant yellow flowers, was much admired.

The number of exhibits outside of chrysanthemums was fairly representative and served to give a pleasing variety. In fact,

Chrysanthemums Mayflower and Mrs. H. Weeks
(Grown by C. W. Neb, gardener to L. H. Biglow.)

the carnation section seemed to give especial pleasure and the ladies flocked around the exhibits with an enthusiasm unequalled in any other part of the hall. C. H. Allan had some good vases, including his white Lawson, which showed up well. Peter Fisher exhibited his specialties in his customary perfect manner and C. W. Ward and Chas. Weber were represented by some excellent vases. J. N. May's new Bride was much admired. L. E. Marquisee, J. T. Williams, H. A. Jahn, C. Barson and J. C. Hayden were among the leading contributors to this section.

In roses there were some very interesting entries. Such were Breitmeyer's nameless beauty, J. N. May's crimson Gen. McArthur and four attractive new productions under number from John Cook. Among the staple varieties were fine Beauties, Bridesmaids, etc., from L. A. Noe, L. M. Noe, Wm. Johnson, J. T. Williams, E. D. Adams, Miss Blanche Potter and J. R. Mitchell.

Besides the extensive decorations above mentioned there were from Siebrecht &

Sons grand tree ferns, big bay trees and a comprehensive group of palms. Julius Roehrs put up a splendid group of decorative foliaged plants interspersed with rich orchids, Lorraine begonias, primulas and other flowering plants. A very large display of palms, begonias, crotons, etc., was staged by J. Lewis Childs and Lager & Hurrell put up a beautiful group of orchids comprising fifty-two varieties, including Cypripedium insigne Sanderæ, Cattleya Percivalliana alba and some superbly bloomed specimens of Cattleya Dowiana. Nephrolepis was represented by some elegant plants of Piersoni and a group of the graceful little Scottii. Frank Weinberg showed a very large collection of cactuses and succulents. F. A. Constable, S. Riddle, gardener, had Begonia Lorraine in large and handsome plants. In violets there were fine bunches from Lyon & Strickland and Geo. T. Schunemann. Bobbink & Atkins had a very effective group of conifers interspersed with variegated-foliaged specimens of hollies, aucubas and euonymus admirably bedded in brown oak foliage.

It is worthy of note in closing that probably more than half the chrysanthemum display came from the west. This is partly accounted for by the large number of local exhibitions held in places in the vicinity of New York.

Among the familiar people seen inspecting the show were: Prof. J. F. Cowell, of Buffalo, who served as a judge; Ed. Lonsdale, of Philadelphia, who did also; J. K. M. L. Farquhar, Boston; Wm. Nicholson, Framingham, Mass.; Peter Fisher, Ellis, Mass.; M. A. Patten, Tewksbury, Mass.; John Cook, Jr., Baltimore; R. Vincent; Jr., and son, White Marsh, Md.; Robt. Bottomly and R. Bottomly, Jr., Biltmore; T. J. Johnson and E. J. Brooke, Providence; T. W. Head, New London; Thos. Roland, Nahant, Mass.; Thos. B. Meehan and Robt. Craig, Philadelphia, Pa.; Judge Vesey, Fort Wayne, Ind.; Fred. Lemon, Richmond, Ind.; Alex. Montgomery, Natick, Mass.; Albert M. Herr, Lancaster, Pa.; Prof. Eison, Boston, Mass.; P. J. Donaghue, Lenox, Mass.; Wm. R. Smith and Peter Bissett, Washington.

WORK OF COMMITTEES.

There were two varieties before the Cincinnati committee November 7. The examination resulted as follows:

Madona, exhibited by H. W. Rieman, Indianapolis, Ind.; light pink, Japanese incurved; scored, commercial scale 86 points.

Golden Age, exhibited by Nathan Smith & Son, Adrian, Mich.; deep yellow, Japanese reflexed; scored, commercial scale, 86 points.

There were two varieties before the Philadelphia committee the examination of which resulted as follows:

Seedling No. 3, exhibited by Richard Rothe, gardener to Clay Kemble, Esq., Laverock, Pa.; white, reflex Japanese; scored, commercial scale, 84 points; exhibition scale, 84 points.

Golden Age, exhibited by Nathan Smith & Son, Adrian, Mich.; rich yellow, reflex Japanese; scored, commercial scale, 86 points; exhibition scale, 82 points.

FRED. H. LEMON, Sec'y.

Chrysanthemum Grande.

A notable peculiarity of this Algerian plant is the absence of ray florets in its large, yellow, densely packed flower heads, according to an European paper. It is perfectly hardy, grows two feet to three feet high, flowers in autumn, and is altogether interesting and striking.

MAIN HALL AT THE PHILADELPHIA SHOW.

Pennsylvania Horticultural Society.

The chrysanthemum show and fall exhibition of the Pennsylvania Horticultural Society opened last Tuesday evening with a good first night attendance, which gave promise of a successful run for the week. The exhibition as a whole is very good, there being fewer poor exhibits than ever before. Particularly is this the case with the pot chrysanthemums, which are a very even lot, and gave the judges much trouble before the question of prizes was settled.

There were many well-grown plants among them. The majority of these were arranged in the larger hall. An interesting lot of nicely grown plants in 8-inch pots were to be seen in the foyer. These were also nicely flowered and were much admired.

The collection of cut blooms is about the finest that has ever been staged in the hall. These were arranged in vases on low tables around the staircase lobby. There were also many vases of extra sized ferns on the steps on both sides of the staircase, where they made a great display. Thos. Meehan's Sons had over seventy-five vases of pompons in the lower hall, and H. Michell also made a nice display of the same class. When one tired of the masses of color of these showy flowers they could rest their eyes on the green of the groups and single specimen foliage plants that banked the walls of the foyer and main hall. This city is fast coming to the front as a center for fine specimen palms, and the number of private places that are collecting and growing fine specimens is annually increasing.

In the foyer there was a magnificent Raphis, nine to ten feet high and eight feet through, exhibited by Jos. Hurley, and in one of the arches in the main hall stood a plant of Nephrolepis Piersoni, exhibited by Thos. Long, that would made Mr. Pierson green with envy could he have seen it. It stood eight feet high and as much through, and was in perfect condition. In the lower foyer there was a great plant of Cibotium Schiedii; it was probably eight feet through, of fine color, and every one of its many leaves perfect. This was exhibited by Samuel Batcher. John Hobson won first prize for group of ornamental plants and they were certainly well grown. It was a case of Hobson's choice with the judges. H. A. Dreer Company decorated the stage with choice palms, among which were interspersed some of the plants of their new Pandanus Sanderi. There were also two magnificent crotons, beautifully colored plants, six feet high and bushy, exhibited. There were many groups of ornamental foliage plants grown in small pots which showed great signs, and in their brilliant coloring was to be seen the results of careful culture, made necessary by the keen competition of late years. Dracænas, marantas, crotons and alocasias were among the prominent plants in these groups. John Hobson, Thos. Long, Joseph Hurley and John Thatcher were prominent exhibitors in these classes.

Joseph Hurley, gardener to James Paul, president of the society, had some rare palms, his Phœnix Roebelinii and Linospadix Petrickiana being very, notable.

In the lower hall there were some collections of choice ornamental foliage plants in 6-inch pots that were perfect miniature specimens of those in the hall above. C. H. Campbell had a table of well-grown Piersoni, small plants, but very perfect. Robert Craig also had some fine specimens of the same fern and a sample dozen of his choice cyclamens in nice flower. There was also a table of Begonia Rex shown by several exhibitors.

The feature of the decorative plants was a group of new Ficus pandarata, exhibited by Robert Craig & Son, who have bought the entire stock from Sanders, the introducer. It is called pandarata from the shape of the leaf, which is fiddle-shaped. The plant is a striking novelty and is a strong grower, with large, glossy leaves, which have a thick, leathery feeling when handled. It can be grown either single stemmed or branched, and from its strong, vigorous look, will likely prove most valuable as a decorative plant. The group on exhibition had just arrived from Europe, but showed none of the marks of transportation.

The prettiest exhibit in the main hall was arranged by the Wm. Graham Company; it was a pagoda of white birch bark pillars, canopied with asparagus and Chinese lanterns. The pillars were studded with choice blooms of chrysanthemums with short stems inserted in glass bulbs. In the center was a pyramid group of choice chrysanthemums in vases and in the top of each pillar was a basket of choice autumn leaves. At the head of the staircase a group of ornamental evergreens by the Wm. H. Moon Company was most attractive. In the lower foyer Mr. Long's specimen Gleichenia rupestris glaucescens, a plant nine feet in diameter, was in a class by itself.

H. Michell exhibited a bed of paper tulips which was the most perfect fac simile of the natural that could be made; he also had a collection of garden requisites. H. Wateus also had a nice table of bulbs, all good stock. H. A. Dreer showed a complete line of tools for the garden, and grass seeds.

K.

Massachusetts Horticultural Society.

Many visitors there are who come every year a long distance to the Boston chrysanthemum exhibition, fully convinced that they are to see the finest show in the country. In so far as trained plants are concerned, no one who knows anything about it will question the correctness of this assumption. For years the expert private gardeners of Massachusetts have set the standard for the country in chrysanthemum plants—a standard which but few care to attempt and which has never been reached outside of this annual Boston show. And it is gratifying to be able to state that, although several names heretofore familiar on the first prize cards are missing, their successors have proved worthy to fill their places and the plants shown are in all respects equal to those that have excited our admiration in the past.

Regarding the cut flower section, however, there is room for a difference of opinion. Time was when nearly everything new in the line of chrysanthemums made its bow to the public at Boston, at least as early as elsewhere. This year's exhibition is noticeably deficient in novelties. Miss E. J. Clark, John Ash, gardener, is to be credited with showing a fair number of the newer sorts, but outside of this one exception the flowers shown are closely limited to the varieties that have attained high repute in past years, and there is little field for the enthusiast with the notebook.

The flowers, familiar though they be, are, however, fully up to the record as to size, that quality being more pronounced, perhaps, than ever before. The explanation of this feature is understood when one runs through the list of varieties shown and realizes that the private gardener, always inclined to scoff at the commercial florist, because of his propensity to limit his horticultural product to a few showy things, has apparently fallen in with the procession which his commercial brother has set up, gorgeous Appletons, huge Eatons, stately Joneses and comely Morels and left the less pretentious sorts to their fate. On these and other well established commercial favorites the majority of the entries base largely their claim for recognition, and were it not for the persistent loyalty of D. F. Roy, gardener to E. S. Converse, the beautiful incurved section, the odd anemones and cherry little pompons would be nowhere. So it is that the cut flower section, replete as it is with marvelously finished blooms, lacks variety, and this condition is accentuated by the absence of the great vases of blooms arranged for effect, which have for years contributed so much to the decorative character of the exhibition but which, for some reason, were cut out of the prize schedule for this year.

But let us take a look at the plant hall. Here the bareness always apparent in our chrysanthemum shows is slightly

relieved by the presence of several splendid palms recently donated to the society and a profuse draping of red, white and blue bunting lends a rather garish suggestion of festivity to the scene. One finds himself pondering on what the picture would be were all the flags out of the way and their place filled with a few wagon loads of hemlock boughs and autumn-bronzed oak foliage. The plants are nicely arranged in open groups and a polite young colored attendant finds plenty to do preventing visitors from brushing in between the plants in their desire to read the names of the different varieties. Why not have the labels inscribed sufficiently large so that they may be read at a reasonable distance?

The groups entered for the various prizes were more closely matched than

Chrys. Timothy Eaton and Col. Appleton.

(Grown by C. W. Neth, gardener to L. H. Biglow.)

usual, plants of some varieties in different exhibits running nearly abreast. All were grand without a single exception. The exhibitors were H. Dumaresq, Wm. Anderson gardener, J. S. Bailey, A. J. Newell gardener, E. S. Converse, D. F. Roy gardener, E. W. Converse, Robert Marshall gardener, and E. A. Clark, Wm. Riggs gardener. Mr. Dumaresq's winning set in the display of eight plants consisted of Mutual Friend, Iora, Arethusa, Pink Ivory, Col. Appleton, The Bard, Lady Hanham and Kate Broomhead. E. S. Converse's set of ten in 9-inch pots were veritable gems. His winning entries for three Japanese incurved were Georgianna Bramhall, Pink Ivory and Louis Boehmer. J. S. Bailey won on three reflexed with Arethusa, Theo and John Shrimpton. On specimen Japanese incurved Mr. Dumaresq won with Peter Kay. On specimen reflexed, E. S. Converse won with Chas. Davis, on specimen anemone the same exhibitor with Garza and on specimen pompon Mr. Dumaresq with Savannah. The Gane memorial prize for specimen of

Mrs. Jerome Jones went to J. S. Bailey and for Marcia Jones to E. S. Converse. The competition in the six classes for groups of plants grown to single stem and flower was limited to E. S. Converse and James Nicol, each winning three firsts and three seconds, and their exhibits were splendid examples in their class. Mrs. J. L. Gardner, Wm. Thatcher gardener, was the only competitor in the class for groups arranged with palms and other foliage plants.

The cut flowers were displayed on long tables in the lecture hall. First on twenty-five blooms was won by Miss E. J. Clark. Among the modern gems in her collection were Violet Lady Beaumont, Wm. Duckham, Henry Barnes, Guy Hamilton, Chas. Longley and J. R. Upton. The same exhibitor won out on six vases of ten blooms each, Queen Alexandra and Guy Hamilton being particularly worthy of mention. Col. Pfaff, George Melvin gardener, won the first Gane prize with Mrs. Jerome Jones and Thos. Howden the second with yellow Mrs. Jerome Jones. In the classes for twelve and six blooms E. S. Converse, Miss E. J. Clark, E. A. Clark, P. B. Moen, A. Abrahams gardener, and Thos. Doliber, Michael Byrne, gardener, were the principal contestants, Mr. Abrahams, a new comer, winning first in all cases where he entered. The winner in the vase of pink class was C. D. Sias, J. Porter gardener, with Viviand-Morel, E. A. Clark vase of red with John Shrimpton, Mrs. R. C. Hooper, Wm. Swan gardener, vase of white with Eaton, Thos. Howden vase of yellow with Col. Appleton and H. Dumaresq vase of any other color with Lady Hanham. Miss E. J. Clark captured the prize for best seedling with a noble white Japanese incurved raised by Nathan Smith & Son under number 49-4-00. W. A. Manda sent up a fine table of the fine pink Dr. Englehardt and got a certificate of merit for it. Miss E. J. Clark's winning set of six introductions of the present year included Wm. Duckham and Chel-toni. The latter proved to be very floppy. Big displays by parties not named above were by Peter B. Robb, F. S. Mosely, Mrs. E. M. Gill and many others, all deserving of fuller description. E. S. Converse got a well deserved silver medal for a very large collection of pompons.

The exhibits other than chrysanthemums were unusually large and varied. Col. Pfaff won a silver gilt medal with a beautiful display of cut orchids. Lager & Hurrell showed a superb collection of orchid plants in bloom and J. S. Bailey a lot of fine cattleyas. R. & J. Farquhar & Company had a table of fifty grand plants of Lorraine compacta begonia, one of which has sported to white. J. E. Rothwell received a silver gilt medal for seedling orchid, Cattleya Bowringiana × Lælio-Cattleya Clive and a certificate for seedling Lælia tenebrosa × Cattleya Gaskelliana and Mrs. J. L. Gardner honorable mention for an unidentified solandra. L. H. Foster showed the Foster fern in splendid shape and from R. & J. Farquhar & Company came a collection of superb canna spikes, the varieties comprised being Crozy's St. Clair and Comte de Sach and Farquhar's Salmon Queen, Golden Leopard, Meteor, Golden Queen, Bridesmaid and Hyde Park. The Breitmeyer rose came from Detroit in good shape and was the recipient of great admiration, receiving a certificate of merit.

The Sears prize brought out a big and altogether glorious display of carnations. Peter Fisher had large vases of Nelson

CHRYSANTHEMUM SHOW SCENES IN LONDON, ENG.

Fisher and Mrs. M. A. Patten, receiving a certificate for the latter. Patten & Company were in with Mrs. M. A. Patten, Lawson, Fair Maid, Adonis, Boston Market, a yellow seedling, S. Goddard, Her Majesty and Enchantress. Miss M. W. Pierce, D. J. Kerrington gardener, had vases of high grade bloom, J. E. Haines several seedlings, John Ash a vase of seedlings and H. A. Stevens a new white variety.

Visitors: W. Boyd, A. Griffin, Ben Anthony, John Urquhart, John Marshall, W. J. Lynch, Wm. Postings, all of Newport, R. I.; Francis Canning, Amherst.; Mr. and Mrs. George Young.

The show closed on Sunday night.

English Chrysanthemum Exhibitions.

We reproduce herewith, from a newspaper some scenes at the fifty-seventh annual show of the National Chrysanthemum Society of England, held last November, at the Royal Aquarium, London. This will be interesting to many growers in this country as showing the different methods pursued by the craft across the ocean. The staging on boards has been seen in a few isolated cases but the dressing of the flowers is practically unknown here. The Royal Aquarium has been famous for the annual displays of this veteran society, but we are informed that the exhibition of last year was the final one in the long series at this place. Growers and exhibitors of all lands, who have visited the shows held there in the past, will sigh with regret as they think they may meet no more on the old field of battle.

YOUNGSTOWN, O.—One of the finest floral displays ever seen in this city is to be found in the store of Walker & McLean in West Federal street. The place was filled with chrysanthemums November 7. The show window was stocked with them, each variety being properly labeled, and the salesroom contained a large assortment. The flowers were grown in the firm's hot houses at Crab Creek.

The Mosquito Plant.

The above has been given to Ocimum viride, a congener of the common basil (O. Basilicum). The newcomer is a native of Northern Nigeria, and a live specimen brought home by Capt. H. T. Larymore has just been accepted by the Kew authorities. Like the common garden basil, the leaves are pleasantly scented, and the captain testifies that, if two or three growing plants in pots are placed in a room and along the windward veranda, the house could be kept clear of the troubling mosquito. He got one of the malaria-giving specimens, and carefully enclosed it in a leaf of the plant, and it lost consciousness in a few seconds. Another interesting point about this plant is that the natives prefer an infusion of the leaves to quinine when attacked by malarial fever. They consider an infusion more efficacious than quinine. The captain also suggests that the plant would prove of undoubted comfort to the soldiers in barrack rooms in India.—*Gardening World.*

New Plants.

LILIUM ELEGANS PETER BARR.

Lilium elegans Peter Barr is described as the largest of the numerous varieties of this species. The flowers measure seven inches across without being spread out. The individual segments are four and a half to five inches long and the inner ones in the finer forms at least two inches across. The flowers vary somewhat from different bulbs in the breadth of the segments. The color is a rich golden apricot, flushed with orange and having a few crimson spots below the middle. Like most of the varieties of this species, according to a European writer, the stems are dwarf and densely covered with dark green glossy leaves. The various forms of L. elegans come into bloom during the month of July and the new variety, judging from its behavior this year, at least, about a fortnight later, thus tending to keep up a succession.

MIGNONETTE WHITE PEARL.

Under the above name the firm of Pape & Bergmann, of Quedlinburg, Germany, introduce a new variety of mignonette which should prove useful if it can be kept true to type. The habit of White Pearl is similar to the Machet class, vigorous, compact and free branching. The flowers are white and borne in clusters of good size on stout stems. This variety is said to force well.

Chicago Carnation Company's Retail Place.

The Chicago Carnation Company on Thursday formally opened its city branch at the corner of Cass and Casseday streets. The store is unique in many respects. The entire exterior of the front is constructed to take a finish of oak bark just as it comes from the tree. A greenhouse fifty feet long forms the east and west wings with a northern extension of 100 feet. A steam heating plant has been installed.

PORTSMOUTH, N. H.—The magnificent conservatories of the late Frank Jones have been closed and the contents disposed of.

NASHUA, N. H.—Frank Chase, who graduated from market gardening into a full fledged carnation grower last season, is sending to Welch Brothers Fair Maid blooms such as have never been seen in Boston heretofore. They give that variety a better standing with critical buyers.

The Rose.

GOLDEN GATE.

This rose has not been received by the florists of the country as it deserves to be. The growers were slow to give to it the proper place and the public has been slow to show it favor. Of course it would be unwise to say that this is altogether unmerited, but the fact that the Golden Gate at the present time is gaining friends proves that it is worth considering. A few reasons why the rose has been treated in this way and the remedies for these defects will be of value.

The most serious fault is the poor form of the flower. The bud is long, and often flabby and deformed. This can be remedied to a certain extent by reducing the day and night temperatures. Although this variety grows rapidly and sends out good stems in a Bridesmaid temperature, where it is possible to grow it in a house by itself the flowers can be improved by reducing the temperature to 55° at night and allowing a day temperature of no higher than 70°, with air on and the sun shining. The first important result shown by this treatment is the size of the flowers. The color is also improved, while the cut is not materially reduced. When grown in this cooler temperature the water will have to be withheld somewhat and careful attention given to its food supply.

The Golden Gate is a rank grower, and it is well to commence when the plants are small to remove the larger part of the blind wood; unless this is done the cut will be lessened and the quality lowered. There has been complaint in regard to keeping qualities, claim being made that the buds wilt too easily. This, no doubt, is a bad habit with the rose, but by careful ventilation, and also careful handling after the buds are cut, the defect may be lessened. On windy days avoid all draughts of air in the house; better allow the temperature to go a few degrees too high than to allow the bud to become wilted. After cutting lose no time in getting them in water and avoid all draughts at this time also.

Although the prices brought by Golden Gate are not quite up to those of Bride and Bridesmaid, the number of blooms cut is in excess of the former varieties, and in many places there is no other rose that will take its place, the color being very fine when properly grown. Another point in its favor is its value for funeral purposes. Where a deep color—such as

that of Bridesmaid—is not wanted, the Golden Gate comes in very handily. It has a truly beautiful effect in set pieces or bunches. What has been said for Golden Gate in regard to habit and treatment may be also applied to Ivory. This rose is identical in growth. Both are also good summer varieties, neither being susceptible to mildew or black spot to any extent. These varieties do very well when tied down a second year, and the canes sent but from the old wood are very fine. One thing to remember in tying them down is to prune very hard and leave only strong canes for the next growth to start from. They should be dried quite severely also to get the best results from two-year-old plants. In conclusion I would say, study its peculiarities and faults and endeavor to remedy them, and you will be amply repaid. It responds readily to kind treatment and thereby increases its value as a forcing rose. The great mistake made in handling this rose is by thinking—because it is a rank grower—that it will grow itself with any kind of treatment.   R. I.

SEABRIGHT AND LITTLE SILVER.

There is probably no rose-growing establishment in the neighborhood of New York where the work is conducted under greater disadvantages and yet the product supplied of such uniformly high grade as is shipped from the greenhouses of Frank McMahon at Seabright, N. J. All the loam used has to be transported from Little Silver, several miles distant, Seabright's sandy soil being useless for the purpose of rose growing.

Mr. McMahon's houses, seventeen in number, are of the most practical type, the limit of economy consistent with the limit of efficiency being kept constantly in mind. The late John Henderson, one of the clearest-headed men who ever grew a rose, always maintained that not a penny should be expended on a house which it could be avoided without injury to the crops or impairing the stability of the house and this phase of the question in building is as important to-day as it was in John Henderson's time. It is well that rose establishments are usually best in the first four or five years of their existence. It is an advantage where houses of moderate cost have been erected, to feel free to abandon an old place for a new one when cultural necessities make this desirable. Mr. McMahon has used rough, unplaned lumber in the construction of his houses. Many may not look

CHICAGO CARNATION COMPANY'S NEW STORE, JOLIET, ILL.

Lilium Peter Barr.

Mignonette White Pearl.

NEW PLANTS.

upon this as wise, but it evidences business sagacity and favors a good dividend on the investment and the man who can do this is a winner every time. An important problem for growers to consider always and more particularly at the present time when profits have been reduced to a very narrow margin, is what kind of houses to build and this little digression on the subject is submitted for what it is worth.

For economical reasons Mr. McMahon prefers solid beds to benches for his roses, for they can be run indefinitely without rebuilding. Here again John Henderson may be quoted as having expressed himself in doubt as to the relative desirability of solid beds or benches but inclined to favor the former. Grafted roses do much better at Seabright than own root stock. Mr. McMahon seldom holds the plants over more than two seasons, his experience with older plants having been that they are doubtful, and regards it as much safer to replant every two years. He does all his own grafting, and now, after three year's experience has got the art down so fine that he can count upon ninety-five per cent to take. He uses English stock exclusively, as being more reliable than the French. One point he emphasizes particularly is that the grafts must for the first few days be kept up to a steady temperature of from 75° to 80°, after which they may be gradually cooled off. The local Long Branch trade has been very poor this season. Wall street is blamed with a part of the responsibility. Everybody has been talking conservatism.

The Dean & Company place at Little Silver, in which Mr. McMahon is also interested, consists of five houses so long that the farther end seems to disappear in the distant horison. Like those of Seabright they are eminently practical and, while always kept in perfect repair and repainted frequently, no money has been spent foolishly on them. Here the plants are all on their own roots and they do excellently in the same soil which, carted to Seabright fails to grow good own root roses. This question has always been regarded by practical and observant growers as one of soil, but how is the difference explained in this instance? The new house built last year has steel purlins; otherwise the structure is of wood. Two new 60-foot brick stacks are going up. Asked regarding his methods of fumigation to keep the plants so absolutely clean as the writer found them, Mr. Dean replied that he smokes the houses twice a week lightly. From the condition the stock is in this would seem to be a most excellent plan.

Herbaceous Plant Notes.

We had a taste of wintry weather at the beginning of November. The thermometer read 22°. The autumn colored foliage fell to the ground and now find a resting place on the ground among the shrubbery stems or flower stalks of the perennials in the woods and meadows, thus providing a natural protection to the roots and crowns of plants, if they can find protection among old stems.

The winds do not allow them to rest thickly on a more or less smooth surface. On undulating grounds moisture loving plants grow naturally in the lower places and the leaves will lodge thickly in the deeper, moister hollows. But few will remain on the dry knolls or hills if these are bare of shrubbery growth.

Nature here gives us a clear advice how, where and what we should protect from winter's sun or cold. Dwarf, compact growing perennials with evergreen foliage would suffer seriously if covered with a layer of leaves. A very light scattering may in a few instances be beneficial to them. Bog and moisture loving plants can always stand a good covering. So can all those with stiff, branchy stems, which in a natural state would offer a lodging place for the falling leaves. But none of these latter should be covered very thickly. Better not cover them at all than to smother them under heavy material. More plants are lost by too much protection than by severe winter's cold, but all young stock or divisions lately planted, should have a light covering of some sort. Any kind of litter, evergreen boughs, leaves or long strawy manure will do.

It is not necessary to cover them on the first approach of cold weather. We may safely wait for a favorable spell of mild weather in December or January. There is enough other pressing work to be performed at present; in fact covering now would mean to destroy the beauties and charms of November in the herbaceous grounds, for although we had severe and so-called killing frosts, Aconitum

Japonicum and A. autumnale are still perfect. The stately Aster Tartaricus and A. grandiflorus have not been seriously injured as yet. The pompos chrysanthemums, Corydalis lutea, tricyrtis, Geranium Manescavei and colchicums do not mind the first hard frosts. Gaillardias, Saponaria Caucasica, Anthemis tinctoria, delphiniums, Coreopsis grandiflora, stokesias, phloxes and quite a number of other things brighten up the grounds still with a few scattered flowers, while violets, the pink and white little daisies, some primulas and the pansies are also blooming profusely. Even the tender plants among the herbaceous, such as the acanthus, may wait for their winter coat until the ground is frozen hard in December or January, we gain nothing by furnishing protection early in the winter and may do more harm than good by so doing, for as long as there remains a certain warmth in the earth plant life is not asleep and needs the benefit of pure air to breathe in. All beds and borders should be looked over and probably cleaned before covering, loose,

The Carnation.

CULTURE TO CURE STEM ROT.

Stem rot in the houses is not so easily corrected as it is avoided by the methods described in former articles, but a few observations may help for future use and it can be partly overcome by methods hereinafter described. Much was expected from the sterilizing of the soil and much, no doubt, will be realised when we learn more about it and know just how to do it effectively. But all the sterilising in the world will not keep a plant from stem-rotting if it has brought fungus with it as part of its inheritance from the cutting bench or from the field. Such a plant may live and thrive, if conditions are favorable, until thrown out the next summer, but the first time conditions are favorable for stem rot, off will go that plant.

It has been practically demonstrated that soil made up from sod is especially liable to produce stem rot; it has also been demonstrated that stable manure often has this fungus as part of its make-

up. If you lay up a pile of sod soil and manure, making alternate layers of each, you have a perfect home for stem rot. Such soil should by all means be sterilized thoroughly. By sterilizing thoroughly I mean to cook the soil for three or four hours and then dry it out with sun heat until it is nearly as dry you can get it (dust dry we call it). It is then ready for the beds or benches, where it should be watered about a week before planting time so it may be in the proper condition for planting.

A good method of preparing soil that will not need sterilizing is to take a piece of ground that has been used for some such crop as corn or wheat without being manured; let it then dry it very heavily in the early spring and plow it down, repeating the plowing every thirty days. This gives you a good rich soil in perfect mechanical condition. Another good method is to prepare the soil the same as above and then throw it up in ridges about two feet high and turn it once or twice during the summer by hand. Where the houses are emptied, say right after Decoration day, soil that has lain bare all winter in the field can be brought into the houses, heavily manured there and the whole thing turned and let lay without any watering through the hot suns of July, with the ventilators closed the two hottest weeks so it becomes dust dry. Put clean plants into soils of this kind and give them the proper attention as to watering and ventilation and you will need no sterilizing apparatus.

If you have had stem rot in a bed or bench to get immunity by sterilizing the soil you will have to take all the lumber out and put in new. It has been proved by actual trials that lumber from a cutting bench that was infected with fungus will hold that fungus for a period of three to five years, and if used again will start the fungus in a fresh batch of sand. In like manner the lumber from a bench that has had stem rot will distribute that stem rot to the soil the following season, no matter what sort of soil you use. I know of a bench that was badly affected with stem rot one season. In the summer it was white-washed with lime and sulphur and allowed to dry out thoroughly and

FLOWER MARKET OF WELCH BROTHERS, BOSTON. MASS.

lately dug ground will allow the water to sink away readily, otherwise the crowns of many a plant may suffer injury from too much moisture near the surface.   J. B. K.

An Enterprising Firm.

Welch Brothers' City Hall Cut Flower Market in Boston, of which we give an illustration, has a record of twenty-six years' steadily growing business, until now the quantity of cut flowers handled by the house daily is enormous, seventeen men being regularly employed. The general management is in the hands of P. Welch, the floor and ice chests are taken care of by E. J. Welch and the bookkeeping department is under the management of David Welch. One of the delivery wagons is illustrated herewith. It is not decorated with dahlias nor festooned with ribbons, but as a business proposition it is a success.

PATERSON, N. J.—Frank Grundman, 64 years old died, in Bellevue hospital on October 26, from the effects of a mental breakdown resulting from the loss of his greenhouses and a flock of valuable pheasants in the recent floods.

DELIVERY WAGON OF WELCH BROTHERS, BOSTON, MASS.

then filled with sterilised soil. For several months after planting there was no loss by stem rot, while there was considerable loss in benches that were filled with the ordinary sod soil, unsterilised, but along in December and January these plants began to go off with stem rot one after another until the bench was pretty nearly empty. A house newly built and filled with sterilised soil had practically no stem rot and the only possible condifusion is that the boards in the first bench held the fungus and gradually distributed it to the soil, killing off all plants that were not strong enough to withstand the disease.

If you have stem rot in the houses and do not want to throw the whole batch out and replant, the proper thing in nine cases out of ten is to apply liberally air slacked lime to the soil. Where it is especially bad hold the plant together with one hand and with the other put a small handful right down along the stem, making a little hill of lime around the base. Keep the soil in just the right condition as regards moisture and also keep it well worked and loosened up right in the middle between the rows for a space three to four inches wide. It will not hurt to go that many inches deep; in fact it is a benefit, as the few roots that you cut are more than counterbalanced by the healthy condition of the roots left on the plant. But to follow up this method

With the Growers.

PETER REINBERG, CHICAGO.

George Collins.

When we are told that the greenhouses of Peter Reinberg represent in round numbers one million square feet of glass, we are already overwhelmed with the extent of this enormous establishment. When we pay an actual visit to the place, and see for ourselves the vast ranges, we are still more deeply impressed. One can not go through the mammoth establishment and see everything at one visit. All you can do is to walk down the center aisle and see on each side a sight which can be appreciated only by the real grower. His plant, and Mr. Reinberg is adding new ranges every year, is considered one of the largest in the world. It is in every sense a modern establishment, equipped throughout with the latest and most approved heating and ventilating systems, and only roses and carnations are grown. The houses a e age about 27x304 feet in dimensions, lightly constructed. Last spring a range of exceptionally high houses was built and all this space is devoted to roses. The highroof idea is yet an experiment and its efficacy can only be ascertained after a

winter has been gone through. The superintendent, George Collins, informs us that at the present time sixty-five men are employed in the greenhouses. Mr. Reinberg with judgment and foresight has already got in the greater part of his winter supply of coal. He has contracted for 250 carloads.

A walk through the houses will give one a fair idea of the immensity of the place and the labor necessary to keep the machine running, from planting and propagating to cutting and marketing the blooms. One hundred houses are devoted to the rose, which Mr. Reinberg makes his specialty. Here are found American Beauty, La France, Sunrise, Bride and Bridesmaid, Ivory, Perle, Chatenay, Liberty, Golden Gate, Kaiserin and Perle von Godesberg. Every plant has a thrifty appearance which reflects great credit on Mr. Collins and his corps of assistants. The Sunrise houses present a remarkably attractive appearance, the beautiful foliage, full of buds and flowers being a sight not easily forgotten. Mr. Reinberg is emphasizing his Chatenay, which appears to be as good commercially as it is beautiful. One of the high roofed houses in the new range is devoted to Golden Gate. The fumigation which is done in the range materially damages the delicate coloring of this rose and hereafter it will probably be grown in a house of its own.

The carnations grown here cover numerous profitable varieties. Five entire houses are devoted to the Lawson, every bench looking thrifty and strong. A few benches of the new Adonis are also doing well. Flora Hill, Murphy's white, and the dainty Queen Louise are all looking nice. The plants are remarkably free from disease. Some new white varieties are being tried, with encouraging success thus far, but none will be heard of them later. White Bradt, however, is not coming up to the expectations of its exploiters. The prospects for the winter season are bright. The houses are equipped with a double heating system, both steam and hot water. Mr. Reinberg has pronounced ideas about heating and ventilation and this is regarded as the most important part of the work.

Here is a table indicating the approximate number of the plants of the leading varieties of both roses and carnations, now being grown, there being numerous other benches of varieties not so well known: Roses—American Beauty,50,000; Chatenay, 28,000; Liberty, 26,000;

AMERICAN BEAUTY ROSES IN NEW RANGE OF PETER REINBERG, CHICAGO.

of deep cultivation you must not allow too many roots to form between the rows or your root pruning will be too severe. If you think the soil is full of roots now and want to try this method, select a cloudy spell of weather for the first time and then follow it up with such a working at least every ten days all through the season, or until you quit cultivating entirely, as it will not do to allow this space between the rows to become filled with roots and then tear them up.

Next to lime water and cultivation comes the proper airing of the houses, and this is quite as important as any of the others. A perfectly tight house should either have automatic ventilation or be heated sufficiently to allow a slight opening (an eighth or quarter inch wide) of the ventilators, for when you have stem rot you do not want to have confined and stagnated air in the house. In fact, such a condition will bring stem rot with it. A. M. HERR.

LAWSON CARNATIONS AT PETER REINBERG'S, CHICAGO, SOON AFTER PLANTING.

Bride, 20,000; Bridesmaid, 20,000; Golden Gate, 20,000; Sunrise, 10,000; Perle, 8,000; Kaiserin, 5,000; La France, 1,000; Godesberg, 1,000; total 189,000. Carnations—Lawson, 40,000; Flora Hill, 20,000; Queen Louise, 16,000;

and grapes are also specialties that find a ready market among critical buyers. James Hart, of New York wholesaler fame, has now a fine place at Madison, where the favorite stand-bys Beauty, Bride and Bridesmaid are grown in large

to two inches across and is seated on a stalk two or three inches long, which allows the flowers to be regularly disposed on all sides, forming a perfect globe. The segments of the flower are lanceolate-linear, acute, and spread out horizontally. The weakest part of the flowers is their color, which may be described as a silky or glossy purple above, and deep purple on the back, with green keel. The stamens are also dark purple, the filaments being sublate, while the ovary in the center is green. Had the flowers been blue or of some bright color the species would have at once formed a desideratum for all gardens, notwithstanding the decided garlic scent which permeates all parts of the plant as it does in others. As a mere garden ornament, however, it certainly has its uses and it would be a most interesting addition to any collection of strange and quaint forms for the herbaceous border.

"The strap-shaped leaves are somewhat grooved above, glaucous, eighteen inches long, and one to two inches wide. The under surface and the edge are thinly covered with white hairs which fact supplies the botanist with the specific name of the plant. This strange and striking allium comes from the mountain range which lies between Transcaspia and Persia, where it was collected by Sintenis in 1901. It found its way to Kew last year and the bulbs produced four leafless stems. These stems were two feet high and that fact, together with the width of the umbels, as mentioned above, will give an idea of the relative size of this new claimant for our attention.

"It may be described as a bold and handsome species in comparison with the onion tribe generally. A very large number of alliums have been described, but of these some of them are used as food in the form of onions, others again as leeks and shallots, while we have chives, garlic, ramsons and others of that nature, variously used in domestic cookery. With the exception of rapsons very few of these have flowers that might be described as ornamental. There are several, however, out of the vast number introduced to cultivation at one time or other that are decidedly ornamental. The species under notice would certainly take front rank as an ornamental allium purely for the sake of

INTERIOR VIEW OF ONE OF L. M. NOE'S ROSE HOUSES, MADISON, N. J.

Estelle, 17,000; Guardian Angel, 16,-000; Peru, 10,000; Nelson, 8,000; Higinbotham, 8,000; Bradt, 6,000; Chicago, 3,000; Leopoldine, 3,000; Adonis, 1,000; White Cloud, 1,000; Joost, 1,000; Norway, 1,000; total 151,000.

AT MADISON, N. J.

Things have undergone many changes in Madison since the time when the old town came bounding to the front as the foremost rose-forcing center on the continent. A good many of the pioneers have disappeared from the list, some dead, others retired. Among the latter is our old friend, P. Connelly, who, having amassed a snug competence, has now leased his greenhouses and become a dapper gentleman of elegant leisure. But, as the old sailor long domiciled in the Snug Harbor is still wont to scan the horizon for a passing sail so at this season of the year we find our old veteran down at the railroad station scrutinizing the arrivals just as in the good old days when the market price of roses was made in the stoke hole and each time a commission man disembarked at Madison meant an advance of a dollar per hundred on the crop.

The largest establishment in Madison and one of the most prosperous is that of L. M. Noe. Mr. Noe was early on the ground when the American Beauty first demonstrated its pre-eminence as a money-maker for the man who could successfully grow it and has ever since given it the leading place in his list of varieties. There are thirty five houses on the place and the cleanliness prevailing throughout easily furnishes one explanation of the high quality of the flowers produced here.

Another establishment which enjoys a wide reputation is that of Florham Farms, under the management of A. Herrington, one of the best growers in the country. Here are produced chrysanthemums of unexcelled quality. Orchids quantities and excellent quality, and for

which a ready outlet is always found at the old commission stand in West Thirtieth street, tenderloin district.

Allium Albopilosum.

The Gardening World recently gave an illustration of a pretty species of allium with bright, sky-blue flowers. In its issue of August 29 that journal reproduced a photograph of Allium albopilosum which flowered at Kew last May and June. It is a new species and remarkable for the immense size of its flower heads or globular umbels, which measure from six to eight inches in diameter and carry from sixty to eighty flowers each. Additional particulars are given as follows:

"Each flower measures one and a half

L. M. NOE'S WEST RANGE AT MADISON, N. J.

its flowers. Others are A. kansuense, A. cæruleum, A. cyaneum, etc. It may be as well to remind our readers that the white-flowered A. Neapolitanum is one of the most popular of white flowers that are forced in early spring and is sold in the florists' shops."

Palms and Ferns.

SUGGESTIONS FOR EARLY NOVEMBER.

The days are rapidly shortening at this season of the year, and as a natural result we find that the growth of palms in general shows much less activity than was seen a month ago. Of course, there is still growth to be seen, but it will be more noticeable among well established plants than in those that have been recently potted, the exception to this rule being found in the kentias, these most useful of the trade species of palms continuing to develop both roots and foliage during the winter season.

It is one of the many singular and interesting facts noted in connection with plant growing that the habits and characteristics of plants are likely to be perpetuated, even though the plant may be growing under artificial conditions, this fact being apparently exemplified in the case of the kentias, whose native home is south of the equator, the habit of growth during what is our winter season being evidently a survival of the habit of the plant in its original home, where a reversal of our seasons is experienced.

The season of rest is quite marked among the members of the livistona family, usually commencing about November 1 and continuing for fully three months, or even longer if the spring should happen to be cold and cloudy. With this in view there is but little to be gained by potting latanias into larger pots after November 1 unless it may be some plants that are badly in need of a shift, for though one may force a latania into growth to some extent during the winter by giving strong heat, yet the growth produced in that way is likely to be thin and weak and more liable to the attacks of insects.

The same rule will apply to Livistona rotundifolia and to Corypha australis, neither of which plants make much progress when potted too late in the autumn. The root action of these plants is too slow at that season to help them along much, the newly potted plants making only a few coarse roots during the winter, while the valuable fibers or feeders are formed too scantily to take up the nourishment from the soil before it becomes sour.

Areca lutesceus continues to grow somewhat later than the various livistonas, and may therefore be repotted somewhat later, but as we have remarked in former papers, it is best that these plants should not be given large shifts in the latter part of the season, it being much easier to control a plant that is somewhat pot-bound than one that has been over-potted.

Cocos Weddelliana also resents much disturbance of its roots at this season, and late potted seedlings seldom make satisfactory plants. It is therefore necessary to get the seeds of this palm planted as early in the spring as they can safely be had, for the growth of seedling cocos is quite a deliberate matter, though helped along to some extent by strong heat and moisture.

Palms are safe without shading now, though even as late as October some

CHRYSANTHEMUM TIMOTHY EATON.
(Grown by Mrs. J. McKerrighan, Toronto, Ont.)

leaves may be scorched by defective glass in the greenhouse roof if the latter is unshaded, and as by February 15 to March 1 we usually find it needful to apply a light shade to the west side of the roofs, the unshaded period is but a short one.

It is at this season of the year that the advantage of having a careful night fireman is felt, it being a nearer approach to the natural conditions to have the temperature of the houses fall gradually during the night until it reaches a minimum of 62° to 65° in the areca houses, the same for the welfare of the cocos, while a minimum of 58° to 60° will keep the kentias, latanias, coryphas, seaforthias and Phoenix Canariensis in good condition.

Phoenix rupicola may be grown in company with the arecas very well, though enduring a dryer atmosphere to greater advantage than the areca. In fact, it would seem the part of wisdom if we should observe the natural conditions that obtain where many of these phoenix are found, plenty of water at the root but a comparatively dry atmosphere being characteristics of the best date growing districts. The artificial methods of high temperature, much moisture, and an over-indulgence in strong fertilisers may have something to do with the frequent appearance of fungus on the foliage of phoenix, a trouble that seems to be spreading to a considerable extent, judging by the frequent inquiries regarding diseased leaves.

This phoenix fungus is by no means a new discovery on the part of the modern plantsman, for the same trouble was noted fully twenty-five years ago and possibly longer, the attention of the writer having been called to it quite that long ago, the infested plants being some Belgium grown phoenix and licualas that were imported at that time. But this disease was not then viewed with nearly as much concern as the great variety and number of scale, thrips and other insects that were imported (duty free) with those early lots of foliage plants from Europe, a condition that is not quite so marked at the present day among imported plants, at least those from reliable growers. Scale insects of various kinds are seldom entirely absent from palm collections, and are always troublesome to dispose of, but red spider and thrips are also liable to appear from time to time, the spread of these pests being encouraged by insufficient or careless syringing.

The nearest approach to a specific for red spider on palms is probably a good sulphur soap in solution, but one application either by dipping or syringing will seldom prove a cure, and the treatment will have to be repeated, while for thrips tobacco extract or nicotine is the surest remedy. But the use of strong tobacco extracts should not be practiced on latanias, or on Livistona rotundifolia, either of these palms being liable to injury from too free an application of tobacco.

The vaporization of nicotine at intervals in the palm houses has given good results in reducing the number of insects very greatly, but this practice may be carried to excess and do some injury to the plants, especially when the vapor pans are attached to the steam pipes of a high pressure system, the high temperature of such a system producing too strong a vapor for general use.

IN THE FERN HOUSES

Adiantum Farleyense grows in favor with those dealers whose trade demands high class plants, and this most beautiful fern is just the plant to satisfy when tastefully used in a decoration. It is frequently remarked that this fern is most attractive when the young fronds show that delicate pink tint upon their partly grown pinnules, but in order to get this color effect the plants must have plenty of light, and from this time forward little or no shading will be required on the glass. Fresh air is needful for the best growth of this or any other fern, but A. Farleyense is quite susceptible to cold draughts, such as exposure being quite enough to cripple the edges of the tender young fronds.

Another very beautiful adiantum, and one that will sell when offered in nice plants, is A. Ghiesbrechtii (or A. scutum), this fern approaching closely to A. Farleyense in beauty, but from the fact that A. Ghiesbrechtii does not usually make so many crowns as the former there may be more difficulty in getting up a stock by division. This fern may be grown well under the same conditions as A. Farleyense and may possibly endure a little more exposure to cold air than the last named.

All watering in the fern houses should be done early in the day at this season, for excessive moisture on the foliage at night will soon leave its mark.

W. H. TAPLIN.

LE ROY, N. Y.—R. & M. Baxter have dissolved partnership in business.

Rhinebeck and Its Violet Growers.

III.

According to the Rhinebeck standard, the ideal violet plant carries its crown high above the soil; the outer leaves are dark green, of heavy texture and carried well out from the crown on stout stems of good length; the centre leaves are not too numerous and are of a lighter green, giving evidence that the plant is in continuous growth, for when the centre foliage is dark and hard it indicates a suspension of growth owing to inaction of the roots because of insufficient water or other check. Concerning side crowns, there appears a little difference in the methods of various Rhinebeck growers as to their removal, some following their plants up closely and keeping side growths well picked off, others taking off little more than the long runners in the early part of the season, arguing that the side crowns have a good value by augmenting the crop of flowers during November and December when the flowers bring their highest price, and that it is too great a sacrifice to pull the side growths off too clean in the early part of the season. All admit, however, the danger in "too much top" and the risk taken in allowing side growths to get so numerous and so strong that their removal all at once is a shock to the plant. Generally speaking, it is customary to go over the plants once a week and remove such growth as is regarded as superfluous. This is done either by plucking or cutting and has to be done with care and judgment, and inexperienced help are apt to make bad work of it.

Young stock is propagated from the side runners. Sometimes when stock is scarce the crown offsets are also used, but plants raised in this manner are not regarded as good, and it is not done when it can be avoided. The cuttings are struck in about three inches of sand, a few growers having a special propagating house but the majority merely using one end of the regular bed, from which enough plants have been pulled out to give them the required room. Growers generally like to have their plants all set out in the beds early in June. One advantage of early planted houses is that in the event of a cold fall and early winter the stock requires no hurrying up, always a dangerous proceeding in violet culture. On the other hand it is true that where, from unavoidable delays, planting has been deferred until July, the difference in an ordinary season is not very marked by the time fall comes around, and there are times. such as a prolonged warm spell in the fall, when it is found to be a decided advantage if plants are not too forward. The soil is renewed to the depth of twelve to fifteen inches in the beds each spring. It is well pulverized by winter exposure and several turnings, and at time of filling in is mixed with a large proportion of finely

chopped manure. Wood ashes, in quantity about six or seven bushels to a 150-foot house, are spread on top and thoroughly raked in.

The number of plants required for a 150-foot house is about 4,400. Beds are of varying width, according to the views of their owners, but some shrewd growers prefer to make the middle bed as wide as possible, reasoning that the side beds are usually the latest in crop and that the best money is made early in the season. At the time of planting, the houses are well-shaded with lime and for the first two weeks the plants require a very great quantity of water. After that, until fall, the care of the houses is a routine of frequent stirrings of the surface of the soil, picking off runners and spotted or dying leaves, ever on the alert for and combatting red spider, green fly, black fly, grub and spot, giving abundant fresh air and watering with care with a view to promoting the steady but moderate growth so much to be desired and, above all, maintaining scrupulous cleanliness in and about the houses. Then comes the commission man from New York.

"A man he seems of cheerful yesterdays
And confident to-morrows,"
who
"Counts his sure gains,
And hurries back for more."

Greenhouse Heating.

ED. AM. FLORIST:—I am building a greenhouse 14x40 feet inside measurement, north wall six feet high, south wall four feet high, and floor two feet below ground level. The roof is a three-quarter span. I have bought an upright boiler 24x48 inches, with a one-inch fire ring and with, I may say, a substantial boiler inside which is 15x21 inches, with a one-inch fire ring. On each side of the house I have one two-inch flow and return pipes, the water flowing from the top of the boiler and returning into the bottom. The heat from the fire box is to be utilized by being conducted through a ten-inch sewer pipe or tiling laid on the greenhouse floor down one side under the bench, across at the opposite end and returning on the opposite side under the bench, entering a brick chimney with a flue 3x14 inches. Will I get enough heat from such a hot water plant for winter bulbs and carnations? SUBSCRIBER.

I am not sure that I fully understand the construction of the boiler, but as near as I can make out it is a double coil boiler. As a rule, those plants arranged to afford a combination of hot water and hot air do not prove satisfactory, and it is more than probable that in the present instance there will be difficulty in securing a good draft unless the flue can be arranged so as to have a good incline. The heater appears to be large enough to heat the house using hot water only, and I would prefer to put in a coil of four two-inch pipes running around the house and leave out the flue altogether.

L. R. TAFT.

Excusable Error.

"Marie, that new breakfast food is an improvement over those you've been buying lately," remarked Quizz.
"What breakfast food, Henry?" asked the lady.
"That stuff you had in the saucer on the sideboard. I poured some cream over it and sprinkled it with sugar and it went down nicely."
"That wasn't a patent health food," gasped Mrs. Quizz.
"What?" exclaimed Quizz, sitting bolt upright in his chair.
"No, it was a dish of hollyhock seed.—Portland Telegram.

The Retail Trade.

THE ART OF DECORATION.

The abundance of cattleyas at this season of the year brings this regal beauty within the reach of everyone. Fine blooms of Cattleya labiata can be bought in the New York wholesale establishments at present at an average price of $25 a hundred. Used with taste and good judgment they will produce more effect in the way of elegance and finish than can possibly be obtained from an equal amount invested in any other flower, and a big debt of gratitude is due the introducers of this splendid acquisition to the trade.

Nothing is gained by huddling cattleya blooms together. The effect where several or many are used should be of a flock or bevy rather than a mass. Each individual bloom should have space to spread and show itself.

The best green for background or to use among cattleyas is asparagus, preferably plumosus, and Adiantum Farleyense. In archways and draped effects economy may in most cases be observed without detracting in the least from the effect, by making the main background of southern smilax and then skimming the surface with asparagus. Half a dozen cattleya plants in bloom may be used at bold points with impressive results. These should be suspended so that the pot is hidden by the drapery. Pretty blooming plants are obtainable at $3 or $4 each at the present time from growers making a specialty of such things. Odontoglossum grande, Dendrobium formosum giganteum, Vanda coerulea and several of the oncidiums are available for similar use and can also now be had at easy prices.

All cattleya blooms should be inserted in slender glass tubes suspended by fine wire among the green. In fact very few decorators, now-a-days, think of using any choice flower without these little appliances for keeping the bloom bright and fresh.

The latest "wrinkle" in church weddings, where the edifice is large or the company limited in number, is to cut off a certain part of the space by the use of palms, etc., placing an arch of white orchids and lily of the valley or similar appropriate material over the main aisle at the point where the reserved portion of the church begins. Supposing white orchids to be scarce—and they generally are—eucharis blooms or white gladioli can be drawn upon to help out. Where not subject to very close inspection individual white gladiolus flowers can be made to do duty among white orchids very nicely, but roses and carnations, being of a totally different character, have no place in such a combination.

THE ROXBURGH-GOELET WEDDING.

This event, which originally was expected to eclipse any previous affair of the kind in New York, was made as unostentaneous as possible owing to a recent bereavement in one of the families. The floral decorations were, however, very rich and beautiful. St. Thomas Church on Fifth avenue, where the ceremony was performed, was decorated by Thorley most elegantly. Owing to the limited company and the vastness of the church the chancel and the immediate center pews were shut in by a forest of palms, ferns and hanging baskets. The reredos back of the altar was banked with masses of longiflorum lilies and on the altar itself were gold vases of Kaiserin

A FUNERAL BUNCH.

Victoria roses. The altar rail of white marble was also adorned with immense vases of Kaiserin roses and longiflorums. The choir stalls were festooned with garlands of asparagus and lilies and the pulpit beautifully draped with asparagus and orchids.

The decorations at the house were by Small. Here also richness and simplicity prevailed. The staircase was adorned with nodding groups of American Beauties inserted in vases enclosed in gilt wall baskets attached to the banisters. Where the couple stood to receive their friends a canopied veil of asparagus, twined with cattleyas and Dendrobium phalænopsis, was arranged, and throughout the house where there was a mantle or place to set a vase effectively American Beauty roses, Kaiserins, lily of the valley, cattleyas, vandas and dendrobiums were profusely massed in Farleyense ferns. No southern smilax or other coarse material was used in either the church or house.

A FUNERAL BUNCH.

The popularity of the funeral bunch has come to us through more than one cause, the chief being the aversion to so-called set pieces. Since the advent of long-stemmed flowers the set arrangement has been repudiated by many of the most tasteful people. However, it sometimes happens that at funerals where the flowers represent an outlay of hundreds of dollars, the most beautiful arrangement is a bunch, while the most unpardonable use of flowers is also in the form of a bunch. The accompanying illustration shows a simple bunch, white, pink and straw color. Azalea mollis, Begonia Gloire de Lorraine, deutzia, foliage of dusty miller, and asparagus and laurel in bloom.

C. B. W.

WEDDING DECORATIONS AT PITTSBURG.

The decorations for the Abbott-Worrall wedding November 3, according to a local paper, were marked by simplicity and quiet dignity. Over the white marble recedes back of the altar was a floral curtain of smilax, while at each side of the altar were tall palms, reaching almost to the ceiling. At each end of the chancel rail and also at the chancel steps were large clusters of white chrysanthemums, and windows were banked with ferns and the palms and over the sidelights were garlands of autumn leaves and smilax. Dividing off the pews reserved for the reception guests were tall white wicker standards of white chrysanthemums tied with white satin ribbon. Equally beautiful were the decorations at the house. American Beauty roses appeared in the drawing room and were the only decoration with the exception of a few palms in the double windows, which formed a background for the receiving party. The roses were placed on the mantel and piano. A screen of green rush concealed the musicians in the hall, the screen being decked with southern smilax. From the archway in the hall hung a rush basket of yellow chrysanthemums. These blossoms were also placed on the chimneypiece and a tall palm stood sentinel-like at the foot of the stairs. Palms appeared on the second landing at the turn of the stairs. An exquisite centerpiece on the bride's table, which was placed in the library, was formed of American Beauty roses and Farleyense ferns. No other flowers were seen in this apartment. In the dining room, where the guests were served, the centerpiece was of yellow chrysanthemums. American Beauties adorned the mantel and sideboard. Throughout the first floor of the house asparagus festooned the chandeliers.

Local Advertising.

The advertisement reproduced herewith shows how Wm. H. Evans, of the Colorado Springs Floral Company, attracts customers by means of local newspapers. This advertisement was originally printed in a double-column space and it was certainly a catchy one. Mr. Evans, however, believes in good advertising. In the Colorado Springs *Gazette* of November 5 he had another advertisement which certainly commands attention. This likewise occupied a double-column space and had a black border one inch in width, the entire advertisement being four and a half inches wide. The white space in the advertisement was black with the exception of six lines in small type in the center calling attention to the business.

A New Saccharine Plant.

The *Technical Review*, of Berlin, states that a plant has recently been found in South America which contains a considerable quantity of saccharine matter, is not fermentable, and possesses an unusually strong saccharine taste. The plant is of the same genus as the German Kunigundenkraut Eupatorium cannabinum, is herbaceous, and is from eight to twelve inches high. The chemist Bertoni considers this plant as of highly important value from an industrial standpoint on account of its natural sugar properties, which are of a high percentage. Its scientific name is Eupatorium rebandinum. According to experiments made by the discoverer, the director of the Agricultural Institute at Asuncion, this interesting plant is said to yield a sugar which is from twenty to thirty times as sweet as ordinary cane or beet sugar.

PADUCAH, KY.—C. L. Brunson & Company held a chrysanthemum exhibit at their store November 6 and 7.

Georgian Court.

We are pleased to be able to present in this issue a number of views showing some of the more distinctive features of the grounds and plantations at the palatial country home of George J. Gould, at Lakewood, in the New Jersey pines.

ALEX. McCONNELL.

One finds it difficult to realize that until four years ago this paradise in the wilderness was but a barren waste, so marvelously has it been transformed under the magic influences, on the one hand, of wealth and liberality on the part of its owner and, on the other hand, of genius and painstaking zeal on the part of those intrusted with the responsibilities of the work.

Georgian Court includes 180 acres of land of which nearly 100 acres are devoted

Roses $1.50 a doz.

The C. S. FLORAL CO.

An effective retail florist's advertisement.

to lawns and polo grounds. We must pass over the mansion, the "court" with its arenas, marble baths and sumptuous apartments, the costly fountains and sculptured works of art, the stables and carriage houses, the kennels of wolfhounds and beagles, the sheepfold and many other notable features on which a vast fortune has been expended and the army of trained employes who care for each department, all of which are very interesting to the visitor, but outside of the scope of this sketch, and confine ourselves to the gardening aspects of the place only.

The native soil being simply yellow sand the splendid lawns and close-sodded polo fields which excite our admiration for their hard level turf, the extensive plantations of conifers and rich greenery everywhere prevailing, have only been made possible by a top-soiling of from eight to twelve inches of fine loam, a Herculean undertaking when carried out over so extensive a tract and especially so from the fact that all this soil was brought from a place some thirty-two miles distant. The walks and drives are surfaced with a crushed blue stone transported a still greater distance, this having been brought up from the Hudson river.

The avenue forming the approach to the great marble gateway is planted with lines of Lombardy poplar, as shown

in one of the illustrations. The grounds are surrounded by a brick wall surmounted by a high iron fence, with marble posts half covered with English ivy. Inside, practically everything is evergreen. Lakewood is a late fall and early spring resort and, with the object in view of modifying the winter aspect and producing as cheery an effect as possible, all deciduous trees were cut out and the pines only allowed to remain and the new plantings have been confined entirely to evergreens. As seen in the illustrations, a broad belt of conifers in variety extends in an undulating line all along the inside of the boundary wall. For this belt, spruces, firs, hemlocks, retinosporas, thuyas and junipers in wide variety have been made use of, the nurseries of this country as well as foreign sources having been drawn upon for large and perfect specimens. On all sides are great groups and fringes of rhododendrons and laurels, and Azalea amœna has been planted in enormous quantities, it having been found to thrive unusually well here. How beautifully the English ivy does is well shown in one of the photographs. It has been extensively planted in available locations.

From the beginning, the planting and turfing has been all under the direction of Alex. McConnell, of New York city, and that gentleman has every reason to feel elated over the success which has attended his work. For the Italian garden which he has just completed this year, 9,000 arbor-vitæs were required in the hedge planting. Pyramidalis was the species preferred, but it was found to be impossible to secure that many in the entire country and so several kinds had, of necessity, to be made use of. The corners of the divisions in the Italian garden are planted with Thuya elegantissima, Retinosporas squarosa, pisifera, filifera, Taxus fastigiata and T. Hibernica, etc., each in separate groups and the general effect is very pleasing.

One of the few beds of summer-flowering plants is shown in the accompanying illustration. It was planted this season with dark-foliaged cannas at the back, scarlet-flowering cannas and salvias, and in the front row, golden coleus, the contrast of these strong colors against the marble balustrade being very striking. There is also a formal flower garden enclosed by a privet hedge, in which are grown heliotropes, geraniums, dahlias, cannas, ageratums and similar things in trim box-edged plats.

The character of the immediate surroundings of the mansion is shown in the illustration of the pine solitude. Here a fine green carpet of grass has been secured through the use of loam repeatedly enriched by the application of sheep manure. Many pines have been lost through the ravages of the borer. The most effective check thus far found is a wash of soft soap and kerosene.

Mr. Gillespie, the present head gardener, is an enthusiast in his profession and everything seems to flourish under his care. A range of conservatories is contemplated for the near future.

DAYTON, OHIO.—H. H. Ritter's greenhouses were destroyed by fire November 8. The loss is total, as Mr. Ritter carried no insurance.

ESCANABA, MICH.—Work was started November 2 on an addition to the greenhouse plant of C. Peterson & Sons, 22x105. Mr. Peterson is putting in a more modern heating apparatus.

Chicago.

TRADE CONDITIONS IMPROVING.—FIRE IN SCHAU'S GREENHOUSE.—OLD FIRM DISSOLVES PARTNERSHIP.—CARNATIONS ARE SHORT.—NOTES.

This week saw an encouraging increase in business, a condition which generally precedes the Thanksgiving season. The week opened with a brisk demand and the stock was not given an opportunity to accumulate with last week's rapidity. Roses of all kinds are beginning to come in in great quantities and are quite ready to supplement the chrysanthemum, whose season is now waning. Carnations are a little timid and fear is expressed than this Thanksgiving staple will be a disappointment this year. Chrysanthemums are still coming in hale, hearty and large. A wide range of prices prevails for them, from $2 to $4 per dozen. The subordinate flowers, violets, valley, etc., are finding a moderate sale. Wholesale quotations on all flowers remain practically the same as last week. Easter lilies are beginning to come in in quantity. Bassett & Washburn expect to have an extremely large stock for Thanksgiving, and they figured on cutting between six and eight thousand fine specimens. The weather has been of a particularly open variety, growing much more brisk, however, toward the end of the week.

A deal was consummated Tuesday by which the greenhouses located at New Castle, Ind., owned by Reinberg & Weiland, pass into the hands of the junior partner, Peter Weiland. The new owner will take possession July 1, 1904. The New Castle houses were built three years ago; there are ten in number, 33x300 feet, and covering 125,000 feet of glass. Growing is confined to roses, asparagus and peonies. The new owner is a son of Mathew Weiland with whom he was in business several years ago.

Fire in Julius Schau's greenhouse last week did $1,000 worth of damage at One Hundred and Fourth street and Curtis avenue. The fire originated in the boiler room from an overheated furnace. After destroying about $300 worth of plants and damaging the building to the amount of $500 it was extinguished. John Nelson owns the building.

The George Wittbold Company is sending out large shipments of ferns for fall decorations. This week they executed the elaborate autumn window decoration of the Marshall Field store. Oak leaves were used in profusion, and old moss-covered tree stumps and branches give the decorations a suggestive Thanksgiving season touch.

The loss by fire at Graceland cemetery November 8 included barn, sheds, tools and some nursery stock. The loss in the last item was not so great as the newspapers stated and the greenhouses were not injured, as they are quite some distance away from the scene of the fire. The total loss was probably in the vicinity of $10,000.

President Rudd, P. J. Foley, Philip Hauswirth and J. D. Thompson were among the Chicago visitors at Indianapolis this week. C. W. Johnson is attending the annual convention of the Chrysanthemum Society of America at New York this week.

To illustrate the universal shortage in the carnation crop this season, it might be noted that where one of the leading growers of Chicago cut 160,000 carnations during October, 1902, the same space this year produced but 90,000.

The annual Lincoln park chrysanthe-

mum show opened last Saturday and continued throughout the week. Hundreds of visitors were attracted by the large collection of exceptionally fine flowers.

The three New Castle, Ind., growers—Benthey & Company, South Park Floral Company and Reinberg & Weiland—are represented at the Indianapolis show this week with extensive exhibits.

We noted some elegant Chadwick and Murdoch chrysanthemums on the tables at J. A. Budlong's this week. The chrysanthemum outlook for Thanksgiving is encouraging.

George Collins, superintendent at Peter Reinberg's, and family are residing in a new house recently built and located on

ENGLISH IVY AT GEORGIAN COURT.

Robey street opposite the greenhouses.

Leonard Kill, of Peter Reinberg's, spent Tuesday at New Castle, Ind., on business connected with the Reinberg establishment there.

A number of local wholesalers are shipping flowers in corrugated paper boxes, using them only for short runs however.

C. M. Dickinson, manager of Hunt's, has been confined to his home the greater part of the week on account of illness.

Kennicott Brothers Company handled an exceptionally high grade lot of violets, single and double, this week.

Albert Fuchs says business continues excellent in his new store.

The bulb shipping season is rapidly closing.

John B. Amphlett, with the Ionia Pottery Company, and Miss A. G. Strickland were married October 26, and will be at home after December 10 at 6302 Jackson Park avenue.

Visitors: Prof. A. C. Beal and Ralph B. Howe, of Urbana, Ill.

BELT OF EVERGREENS AT GEORGIAN COURT.

New York.

BUSINESS AT A STANDSTILL.—STOCK IN PLENTY BUT NO DEMAND.—PRICES ON ROSES AND VIOLETS ESPECIALLY LOW. —ENTHUSIASTIC FLORISTS' CLUB MEETING.—NOTES OF LOCAL INTEREST.

Business is at a standstill with plenty of all kinds of flowers on hand. Wholesalers, retailers and growers are all complaining of dullness, and don't seem to know what the trouble is.. The fine weather we are experiencing no doubt has hurried the flowers along much ahead of their time, especially chrysanthemums, and the daily receipts being far greater than the outlet trouble follows naturally. The collapse came about the middle of last week, since which there have been practically no quotable values on anything. But roses and violets took the greatest tumble, the highest price obtainable for the best type of American Beauty rose being but $10 a hundred, and many that had accumulated going at half that price. The decline in violet values was unexpected by the operators, being something unheard of at this date, and all the more surprising because the growers are picking thus far only about half a crop owing to the warm weather. Some wholesalers were caught with embarrassing obligations as to price on their hands. Wintry weather and the finishing off of the chrysanthemum crop are necessary before normal market conditions can be looked for.

The New York Florists' Club had a grand meeting last Monday evening. Sixty members were present, and the session was prolonged until an unusually late hour. There were present, also, Philip Breitmeyer, of Detroit, president-elect of the Society of American Florists; George A. Rackham, Detroit, president of the American Carnation Society; Elmer D. Smith, Adrian, Mich., and Peter Crowe, Utica, N. Y. These distinguished guests received a most cordial welcome from President Troy and the members. The exhibition table displayed two notable

roses, the beautiful and fragrant Breitmeyer variety for which a sufficiently worthy name has not yet been secured, and J. N. May's General McArthur, a crimson gem of the first grade which promises to become widely popular as soon as disseminated. John Scott showed

his variety of the Boston fern, Nephrolepis Scottii, in several graceful specimens and received for it a certificate of merit.

The principal event of the evening was the reading by Alex. Wallace of extracts from his recently published book on the Scottish heather, to which all listened with deep interest. Mr. O'Mara followed with a line of anecdotes, and John Scott told how, because of extreme bashfulness, he "proposed" with a sprig of white heather. The visitors were all called on, and each responded appreciatively, Mr.

CANNA BORDER AT GEORGIAN COURT.

Breitmeyer urging all to arrange to attend the convention at St. Louis next year. Mr. Rackham followed in the same line on behalf of the coming carnation meeting. Mr. Smith told of his deep

interest in the chrysanthemum exhibition and Mr. Crowe made a very juicy speech, which was replete with cultured eloquence resultant from his recent visit to Boston. The committee for the nomination of officers for the coming year reported, naming three candidates for each office to be voted on at the next meeting. Five new members were admitted, a generous purse was made up for an unfortunate brother florist in the west, whose all was lost in the recent floods, and the meeting adjourned so all might congratulate John Birnie on his birthday anniversary which occurred the previous day.

The Cut Flower Exchange has increased its membership steadily until now it numbers 106. One absent-minded member of the early-rising fraternity recently astonished his friends and dumbfounded himself by tipping 25 cents to the waiter upon the conclusion of a 10-cent breakfast. The waiter has been suffering from shock ever since. On Thursday a surprise party was given to Philip F. Kessler, of the Cut Flower Exchange, in honor of his thirtieth birthday. About twenty-five of his friends were present and all had a pleasant time.

Helmar Duncan, secretary of Parsons & Sons Company, Flushing, was arrested on November 4 on a charge of having robbed the safe of his employers and set fire to the papers. His friends believe his mind is unbalanced by grief over the recent death of a young lady to whom he was engaged.

David Clark's Sons had, November 10, the Welsh wedding, which used up about 2,000 chrysanthemums besides a lot of other flowers. The same firm made, November 11, a casket cover which took about 8,000 violets and lily of the valley.

George Matthews, of Great Neck, L. I., intends installing one of Lord & Burnham's new boilers to heat his dwelling, and Charles Smith, of Woodside, L. I., has replaced two of Hitchings' No. 16 boilers by a larger one from the same firm.

J. Bowne Hyatt, of Winfield, L. I., who has been an invalid for the last six months, is slowly improving.

Edward Branch is around again after two weeks' illness.

LAGOON TERRACE AT GEORGIAN COURT.

Philadelphia.

PROMINENT GROWER'S DAUGHTER MAR-
RIED.—GIMBEL'S SHOW CONTINUES AN-
OTHER WEEK.—QUAKER CITY MARKET
OVERSTOCKED.—TRADE NOTES.

There seems to be a lull in the social
season, and business is consequently slow.
Flowers are booming, however, at a great
rate, and it is taxing the facilities of the
various branches of the business to move
them. Prices are in a very chaotic condition; there is nothing regular, and the
man with a large order can buy practically at his own price. Extra fine
chrysanthemums do not bring half what
inferior flowers of the same kinds did a
week ago. W. K. Harris with his Dear
Friend, a fine yellow and a light pink
sport of Maud Dean, has two extra fine
varieties, quite the equal, if grown to
single stems, of any of the new ones.
Mr. Harris does not put the plants on the
market, preferring to sell only the flowers.
Although they are grown about three
flowers to a plant, the stock is fine and
brings about top market prices. Taking
the chrysanthemum crop as a whole, they
seem to be overdone, for with the
quantity coming in at present and the
prices obtained it is difficult to see how
the growers can get out with any reasonable profit. Roses and carnations are
also plentiful, with prices ruling extremely
low. Violets are about the only scarce
flowers, and all the good stock is moved
quickly. Chrysanthemum plants are now
to be had in variety, but are selling
slowly.

The daughter of William K. Harris,
Miss Elizabeth U. Harris, was married
Tuesday evening, November 10, to Wm.
Armstrong Dill. The ceremony was performed at the bride's home under a
beautiful canopy of roses, lilies of the valley and chrysanthemums. The house
was elaborately decorated with palms,
chrysanthemums and smilax. There was
a room full of costly presents. Over four
hundred guests attended the reception,
which was a brilliant affair. At 10:30
p. m. the happy couple departed on their
honeymoon trip amid showers of rice
and confetti.

At the Harris greenhouses there was a
nuptial feast for all the employes, where
the health of the bride was toasted among
most pleasant surroundings. The party

broke up at a late hour, after having spent
a night long to be remembered.

At the market things are quite snug
since the quarters are more confined.
There is still room for more growers,
however. Manager Meehan says that
things are very satisfactory for the
season.

The decoration at Gimbel's by Hugh
Graham was so satisfactory that it was
continued for another week, all the perishable plants and flowers being renewed.
Wm. Reynolds has left Bernheimer and
is now a broker on his own account,
with no permanent location as yet.

C. Dunn & Company report a satisfactory business in their new supply
department.

B. Eschner, of M. Rice & Company, is
making a western trip.   K.

LEBANON, PA.—D. H. Mish will soon
erect another large greenhouse at Rock-
dale for carnation growing.

St. Louis.

SHAW'S GARDENS VISITED BY DAMAGING
FIRE.—MANY VALUABLE PLANTS DE-
STROYED.—LEGION OF HONOR BANQUET.
—MARKET ACTIVE.

Shaw's garden was visited by a most
destructive fire early Saturday morning,
November 7. The boiler house, which
supplies heat for the orchid range and
several of the growing houses, was completely destroyed. Half the East India
and Mexican houses were a wreck, as
were also portions of the orchid and
succulent propagating houses. From a
monetary standpoint it is estimated that
$1,000 will cover the loss to the build-
ings and $2,500 the loss in plants. The
latter loss is much greater than the
figures indicate, as a large number of
species and varieties, 200 in number, will
require years to replace. This is especially true in the orchid houses, which,
while not destroyed entirely, were subjected to heavy smoke and intense heat.
The collection of selaginella, representing
28 species, was completely destroyed, the
heat being so intense that the heavy zinc
labels were melted down to the soil in
the pots. Among the varieties lost were
a number of staghorn ferns, such as
Platycerium grande and P. Æthiopicum.
Among the palms were single and grand
specimens of Licuala grandis with a
spread of 10 feet; Martinezia caryota-
folia, Licuala Jeananceyi, Dæmonorops
Melanochætes, Chamædorea ne plus
ultra, Hyophorbe Verschaffeltii, and
Linospadix Petrickiana. The nepenthes,
carniverous plants and many of finest
anthuriums, such as A. Veitchii, were
badly damaged. Of the collection of
orchids, which comprised about 600
species and varieties, there were only 75
species uninjured. A remarkably fine specimen of Cattleya Percivaliana; Angrae-
cum sesquipedale, all of the vandas and
perhaps the finest collection of Florida
orchids in the United States are in the
ruins. Cypripedium Wm. Trelease a
cross between C. Rothschildianum and
C. Parishii, was also badly damaged. It
was one of the most beautiful cypripediums in the garden and was highly prized,
as it was named in honor of the director
of the garden.

The market remains about the same as

IN THE QUIET OF THE PINES AT GEORGIAN COURT.

last week, although trade in general is growing better. Stock is all that could be desired, the better grades coming from outside the city. Of course, quite a quantity of fancy blooms are grown by the local growers for their own use, but not enough to supply the market. Chrysanthemum growers are having some trouble with rot, but so far it has done but little damage.

J. J. Beneke furnished a large number of Perle roses for the banquet given by the Legion of Honor at the Odean, Wednesday evening. He is showing some excellent chrysanthemums and carnations in his windows this week. F. K. B.

President Herrington's Address.

[*Delivered at annual meeting of the Chrysanthemum Society of America, New York, November 10-12, 1909*]

A year ago, in Chicago, in first convention assembled, we reviewed the past so far as it pertained to the work of the Chrysanthemum Society of America from its inception, took a careful survey of our position as a national society and, imbued with enthusiasm by the support accorded that meeting, resolved that its annual fixity was thenceforth an assured fact. A desire long cherished in the minds of many had at last been consummated, and the consummation was justified by the results attained, as shown then in the general interest manifested in the society's work, and since by a large addition to its roll of membership. In all undertakings diligence in the advocacy of aim and object is usually a stepping stone to recognition, and a well-directed effort to give a larger national significance to the work of the Chrysanthemum Society has already met with such marked encouragement and responsive support as to justify the belief that there is a bright and useful future assured the society.

The general interest in the chrysanthemum is well sustained, and there is no apparent reason for any abatement thereof in a flower of such inherent variability. If "variety is the spice of life," how richly endowed with this particular trait is the life and history and the unknown future development of the flower for which we stand as sponsors, endeavoring to obtain for it a larger measure of popularity, exceeding even that which it receives today. Coincident with this, in fact a necessity towards its attainments, is the organized effort for which the society exists, and dealing with a subject so comprehensive, so rich in latent charm, it behooves us to rise equal to the exigencies of our day, to pursue our aims diligently and thoroughly, to keep a careful record of what American growers have done in the past, to see that the trend of present efforts is upwardly progressive, and to foster future development along all possible lines so that more and more the chrysanthemum may become the people's flower, a flower for the amateur as well as for the professional florist and the wealthy owner of a finely-equipped estate employing a skilled gardener.

Giving honor to whom honor is due, we must admit, professional men, florists and gardeners have been the pioneer workers in the chrysanthemum field, and that they, too, were the organizers, and are today the main support of the society, as they saw concerted effort materially enhanced progress. It should be the ambition of us all to work for a broader development and our society can only be truly national in its work by taking cognizance of all types of the flower, of all conditions of culture, thus centering in itself, and work, the interest, and commanding the support of chrysanthemum lovers, professional and amateur, of the greenhouse and the open air.

The thoughts herein expressed are perhaps a repetition of those uttered a year ago, and are intentionally repeated in the hope that other minds will deliberate on them, as it must in truth be admitted we cannot ignore any part or aspect of the work to which we are committed. Where we lead others will follow, and a generous co-operation is assured to us. We have ample evidence of this, as demonstrated by the united effort that has culminated in the grand exhibition amassed to celebrate this occasion. When the invitation of the American Institute of New York was

accepted your president, on behalf of the Chrysanthemum Society, visited a number of the local societies and invited them to co-operate. How generous was the response! Is it not cause for congratulation that the substantial provision made by the American Institute has been supplemented by contributory exhibits from ten other separate horticultural societies, all uniting in the common desire to make this exhibition worthy of the occasion, to honor the national society?

Insofar as the organizing of chrysanthemum exhibitions is concerned there is little for us to do; they are amply provided for, but would it not be wise to devise some means to encourage them further with suitable awards, such as a medal or some token that would carry with it the prestige of being a national award? This idea, too, was suggested a year ago. The time for action is here, and now that we are in convention assembled, it would be well, also, that we should give some thought to ways and means toward improving our organization. We should now be in a position to think and act intelligently along these lines, as the constitution and by-laws of the society heretofore only available in the original typewritten copy, were ordered to be printed in the proceedings of our Chicago meeting, and they will be found in that publication, a copy of which has been sent to all members.

A careful perusal of the constitution reveals that we have a reserve of available executive force that has never yet been brought into action. Article IV. entitles us to have district vice-presidents for seven specified districts. Let us call out the reserves and, given men in sympathy with the cause, what a fertile field of missionary work these districts should prove! As a means towards securing a large aggregation of membership probably none better could be devised. Some amendments are needed also to adapt our laws to present conditions of the society's work. One instance only need be cited, that of the committee that for a long time have been doing such admirable work annually in passing judgment on the novelties submitted to them. These irregularities could probably be best rectified by the appointment of a committee to revise the constitution and by-laws and submit its recommendations in accordance with Article IX.

The record of the proceedings of the society, as published, has already been alluded to. It is a valuable compendium of information, containing that remarkably comprehensive series of papers submitted at the Chicago meeting and which, if justly appraised, more than compensates for the cost of membership. It was, by motion, ordered also to incorporate in this publication a record of all new chrysanthemums introduced in America since 1880. Elmer D. Smith having tendered the society the use of his records. No adequate provision, however, was made for the copying of the valuable records that are in Mr. Smith's possession, and which obviously will involve quite some time and labor to classify. Compile and make ready for printing. Action should be taken at this meeting and author-

ity granted providing ways and means for the preparation of this important matter for publication in our next volume. Not alone do we need to have this information available for ready reference; our continental co-workers are also anxious we should publish it.

A subject worthy of thought is how we may enhance the interest and the resultant practical value of our annual publication so as to make it sought after, to make it a means of bringing into and keeping within the fold of membership those members—and there might be hundreds of them—that are prevented or are unable to attend the annual meetings. Could we not enlarge the scope of our publication; make it a chrysanthemum Year Book and therein review the season of the flower, enumerate the new ones as they appear, and describe them in a few terse but readable articles that would tell more, and with better effect, than the conventional catalogue descriptions? Even work of this character is directly in line with our object, and can be better done by our society than by the average individual. We extol the fact that the literature of the chrysanthemum surpasses that of any other flower. Do we not, then, owe it to those who shall come after that the record of our time shall be handed down complete and unimpaired?

It is easy to be critical, to say here and there are vulnerable points of attack. The defensive part is the harder part, and calls for the exercise of a careful discrimination in laying out an aggressive policy. We assemble but once a year, and time is too limited for great accomplishments involving a mass of detail. A way suggests itself, however, in which, if we could agree on the desirability of diligently prosecuting certain lines of work, to create special committees to carry on the work deputed to them between our annual sessions. This would conduce to rapidity of progress and show in our annual reports a larger measure of attained results.

In this city in August, 1900, I for the first time attended a meeting of the faithful few who for a decade had held the society true to active purpose, confident in the belief there was a need for it to be, though general apathy discouraged their efforts. The election of officers brought to me the responsibility of directing its affairs. From that moment one hope was dominant—the hope that ways and means might be found to establish a closer community of interest between the work and the workers; the hope that the society might meet in association with some important exhibition and thus better fulfil its mission. The Horticultural Society of Chicago provided the first opportunity, and its noble effort has been ably seconded by the American Institute of New York, with ten other societies co-operating. In Chicago, contrary to his personal wishes, you saw fit to continue your president in office, one member quoting the old adage as to its being unwise to "swap horses in crossing a stream." Today we have more than crossed the stream; we are assuredly on high, dry ground, for how otherwise could such a fire of enthusiasm be kindled as enlivened the

AFTER THE FIRE AT THE MISSOURI BOTANIC GARDEN.
(See St. Louis notes.)

scene of action today? For your warm encouragement, hearty assistance and patient toleration thanks is tendered, coupled with the wish that you will all unite in upholding others with the same cordial support you have given those in whom past authority and responsibility have been vested, and so individually and collectively ensure for the Chrysanthemum Society of America a lasting and progressive future.

Diseases of Chrysanthemums.

BY PROF. GEORGE E. STONE, AMHERST, MASS.

[Read before the Chrysanthemum Society of America at the New York convention, November 10-12, 1903.]

The diseases to which plants are subject under glass require different methods of prevention than those out of doors, since in greenhouses the crop conditions are largely under control, whereas in outdoor crops they are left to the mercy of the weather and whims of the season. To meet the unforeseen seasonal conditions, to which outdoor crops are subject, it is necessary to resort to methods of prevention each year. Such methods consist in spraying crops or applying other methods of treatment before certain pests have made their appearance. There is, however, very little need of the application of spraying mixtures to greenhouse plants, since the conditions which give rise to diseases can be, and are, controlled to a very large extent by expert gardeners. The recommendations, therefore, for a general system of spraying for indoor crops, such as is expedient at the present time for outdoor crops, would be irrational and would constitute a step in the wrong direction. Every expert grower realizes this, and the more skilled the gardener is, the fewer diseases he has to contend with. The gardener who can turn out a nearly perfect crop as regularly as a manufacturing establishment turns out its products, is qualified for the severest tests of proficiency. The increased production of high grade greenhouse products has been the means of training and developing a large class of men as efficient growers, and with this increased skill and knowledge there has come about a better understanding of the causes of diseases and the methods of controlling them. Were greenhouse men on the same level, as regards knowledge of plant production, with the rather backward and conservative outdoor growers, the number of diseases which they would have to contend with would far exceed those which confront them at present. In this respect there exists a great gulf between the ordinary farmer and the intelligent floriculturist. It is indeed only where absolute care and management of plants falls under the supervision of gardeners that we are likely to see manifested an intimate knowledge of the plant's normal functions and limitations. We have often been amazed at the superior skill and knowledge displayed by the gardeners, and would affirm, without hesitation, that some of them possess a most profound knowledge of facts pertaining to practical plant physiology.

The greater part of our knowledge concerning the control of greenhouse diseases has been derived from the intelligence and skill of the progressive gardeners, whereas, in a case of outdoor crops, the experiment station specialists have been foremost in offering suggestions for their control. The trained agriculturist can consistently give information in regard to the control of specific diseases affecting outdoor crops, in which he is more or less familiar, but in cases of greenhouse crops the methods of treatment are so different and require such an insight into the crop requirements that it is almost necessary that one should be an expert grower, or, at any rate, one must understand something about the normal requirements of the crop before his judgment and advice can be of much value. It is necessary, at least, that he should possess a thorough understanding of the influence on plant growth of the three cardinal factors, heat, light and moisture, and the part which they play in the production of normal crops, together with their relationship to the development of pathogenic or disease producing organisms. Such matters as soil texture and soil fertility also constitute important features which must necessarily be understood. The great attention that must be given to such matters as heat, moisture, light and the circulation of air in greenhouse culture is only appreciated by the trained gardener. Some of the most troublesome and disastrous diseases are entirely controlled by the intelligent utilization of these factors, and others, which are more or less common, could no doubt be controlled or greatly alleviated, if modifications in the methods of growing certain crops were practicable.

The beneficial results which have resulted from spraying outdoor crops have unfortunately been the means of inducing some to believe that this is the only method of treating plant diseases, and where spraying is not recommended as a remedy, their enthusiasm diminishes, because they cannot conceive of any other methods of treatment. We have grown for some years many experimental crops in the greenhouse, and we have seldom had occasion to see the need of applying spraying mixtures to greenhouse crops. In the elimination of diseases from greenhouse crops, the ultimate aim should be to select varieties of plants which will prove immune from disease, as well as to study and devise conditions which will not favor the development of diseases. The most perfect and hardiest plant organism can become diseased in a remarkably short period of time if the conditions that are suitable for its normal requirements are changed. For example, the geranium constitutes one of our most hardy greenhouse plants, nevertheless, if such a rugged plant is placed under a bell glass it becomes sickly in a very short time and in a few days it will succumb to disease, even when subject to light and supplied with all the necessary elements of plant food. Such an experiment is interesting, as it shows how quickly the healthiest organism can fall a prey to disease and become dilapidated. We all have observed, no doubt, how the master craftsman will select his stock and create something worthy of attention; where another, less skillful, will start the same material and his product will be a lot of poor, sickly specimens, adapted only to the confines of the clinic or the show case of some pathological museum. The latter has felt obliged to doctor his plants with the standard mixtures, but would it not have been better if his time had been spent in obtaining a little more knowledge pertaining to the growing of healthy plants, and he had devoted less attention to securing the knowledge of decoctions?

The appearance of some of our most troublesome diseases affecting plants at the present time must therefore be attributed in part to lack of knowledge and lack of skill in handling the crop. Diseases may also be encouraged by extensive modifications of the natural habits of growth, through breeding and cultivation, and to the practice of increased forcing. New parasitic organisms, however, have been introduced from time to time from other countries through traffic. Some of these fungi, however, which have recently proven disastrous, have been with us for some years, if not always, and one of the principal reasons of their becoming more troublesome at the present time may be attributed to the increased production of more succulent, tender plants, brought about by forcing, which enables these parasites to find more favorable conditions under which to thrive. With every modification and innovation in the growing of plants, there are likely to occur new difficulties and obstacles to be overcome. Constitutional weaknesses which develop in some varieties, and are inherited in others, are unfavorable to immunity. Varieties of carnations inclined to succulency, or having two or three per cent more water contents in their leaves, have proven much more susceptible to rust than those containing less water.

There is little doubt but that many diseases could be prevented by modifications in the methods of growing plants, if such could be adopted. The so-called "drop" in lettuce would prove less disastrous if the plants could be elevated from the soil sufficiently to allow air and light to penetrate to the stem. This would result in producing firmer and more resistant tissues. Experiments have shown that a covering of coarse sand about lettuce plants materially reduced rot, simply from the fact that sand retains moisture much less readily than loam, thus offering less favorable opportunities for fungus infection; and no doubt a circulation of air about the stems would prove beneficial. In the same manner, sub-irrigation reduces stem rot by maintaining a smaller amount of moisture in the top layers of soil. The shutting out of light and air by planting too thickly, constitutes a source of danger to disease. Water cress and parsley offer good examples of the effects of overcrowding, due to luxuriant growth. When these crops are allowed to grow high and become thick, they produce weak stems, and develop stem rot, whereas being closely cropped there is little loss from this disease. The exclusion of light and air necessarily arising from an overcrowded condition are responsible for this. In most instances the stem rot of the chrysanthemums have been induced by overcrowding, and undoubtedly the carnation would suffer less if more light and air could reach the stem. Various stem rots could undoubtedly be eliminated, to a large extent, by changing the soil conditions about the plants, such as by the application of coarse sand around the stems. In one case stem rot in parsley was eliminated by setting the plants well up above the soil, thus exposing the stem and crown to light and air, which resulted in the development of more resistant tissues.

The matter of moisture on the foliage plays an important part in infection. The carnation rust has been largely reduced by sub-irrigation methods and also by applying water absorbents, such as lime, to the foliage. In short, many fungus diseases, peculiar to foliage, can be much lessened and in many instances prevented, by regulating the moisture conditions of the air. The cucumber and melon blights which have raised havoc with these crops the last few years in New England, have never troubled our greenhouse crops grown under minimum moisture conditions, notwithstanding the fact that infected crops were abundant out of doors in the immediate vicinity. If it were possible to control the moisture conditions out of doors, the same would hold true there. For example, a cold, wet spring induces peach leaf curl, while a dry, warm spring is not favorable for the development of the fungus which causes curl. Many other cases might be cited where infection is due to weather conditions which cannot be controlled, whereas, in under-glass culture there would be little difficulty in controlling these conditions, and preventing such diseases. The application of moisture absorbents to asparagus plants have in some instances perceptibly reduced the rust, and even the cover of an apple tree is often sufficient to keep the dew off and render the plants free from infection. With this idea in mind, tent cloth crops have been tried with some degree of encouragement, although the expense of tent covers and the results obtained from their use do not at present appear to be such as to warrant their employment in all cases.

Another element which has a great bearing on the health of plants in general is proper feeding. The influence which proper feeding and cultivation has on the susceptibility of crops to disease is quite marked. There is little doubt but that in many cases time and money could be better spent in securing robust crops by cultivating and feeding, than in spraying sickly plants.

Chrysanthemum Disease.—The diseases which chrysanthemums are subject to, are not especially numerous, and, on the whole, the crop must be considered a tolerably clean one to grow. Among those diseases which are more or less common may be mentioned the following:

Powdery Mildew.—Mildew frequently shows itself to a slight extent on the lower and more mature leaves of the chrysanthemum. It is of little consequence, however, to the careful grower. The mildew is similar in appearance to that found on roses, and can no doubt, if necessary, be checked by the same means, namely, the application of sulphur.

Rust.—Most growers are familiar with the chrysanthemum rust, although I have no doubt that some of you have had no personal experience with it. The rust occurs in small blisters, usually on the under side of the leaves. These blisters eventually break open, exposing a brownish powdery mass. This powdery substance constitutes uredo-spores, which are the only spores known to be produced by this fungus in this country. The first appearance of the chrysanthemum rust in America, so far as known, occurred in Massachusetts in the fall of 1896, on which occasion it was discovered doing considerable damage to the plants of George H. Hastings, of Fitchburg, Mass. This outbreak appears to have been the only one recognized that year. The next year, however, the rust became much more widely distributed, and since that time it has spread over a considerable portion of the United States, and some growers have experienced quite a little difficulty with it. It appears to have occurred in England in 1895 and on the continent two years later, where it became rather common. The first two or three years of the outbreak in this country proved the worst, and at present little is heard from the rust in the east, especially from our largest and most efficient growers. Its disappearance appears to be due to two causes, namely, the discovery and application of cultural methods which render rust infection less common and the limitation of the fungus to a single stage (uredo) of existence. Prof. Arthur, of the Indiana station, has pointed out that the latter feature is at least somewhat responsible for its decline. Upon this point Prof. Arthur writes as follows: "Another circumstance much in the cultivator's favor is the propagation of the disease without the formation of the customary teleuto spores, or third stage. Not only does this render the disease far less persistent, but without doubt indicates that it is less vigorous in its attacks. In general, when a rust is confined to the uredo forms for a number of generations, its vitality is much reduced, and also its power of injuring the crop. So long as the teleuto spores do not make an appearance in this country the careful cultivator may feel assured that a moderate amount of timely effort will enable him to rid his establishment of the rust."

That cultural methods have also had a great deal to do with the disappearance of the rust is evident from the fact that our most skillful growers of chrysanthemums have never had it but one or two years, and some not at all; while less skillful and less painstaking growers have been more or less subject to it every year. From the first we have never apprehended any very serious trouble from the rust because we believed that some cultural method could be devised that would render it less troublesome. About four years after the rust had made its appearance in our state we sent out a number of circulars to chrysanthemum growers, requesting information upon various points. The answers given to this circular showed that the rust was more widely distributed and most destructive the second year following its arrival, and from that time it decreased in vigor and abundance. One-third of the growers stated that they never had the rust on their plants, and were familiar with it only as they had seen it on other stock, while others had only experienced a slight infection one year. One florist who cultivates 40,000 plants stated that he has not had the rust since 1898, and at that time he had it only to a very slight extent. The amount of infection which has been prevalent varied from 1 per cent to 50 per cent, the latter figure being exceptionally high, for very few have had even 25 per cent as a maximum amount of infection.

The financial damage is by no means proportional to the amount of infection, and in most instances it amounts to nothing. The worst injury appears to be to the gardener's pride, inasmuch as a large percentage of the plants are grown for competition in shows, and even a slight blemish caused by two or three rust pastules on a single leaf is very annoying to gardeners who take pride in exhibiting their plants. Most gardeners agree that weak stock is the most susceptible to rust; and if weak, infected plants are allowed to remain in close proximity to strong, healthy ones, the latter will subsequently become infected. The method of preventing rust consists in hand-picking the affected leaves, selecting clean, strong stock, discarding susceptible varieties, and inside culture. If these suggestions are carried out, the rust can be practically eliminated. In regard to inside culture during the summer, we find that many excellent growers lay much stress on this practice, and from our observations we consider it very essential in order to obtain plants free from rust. The reason that inside culture results in less infection is probably due to the avoiding of mists and dews on the foliage, hence furnishing less favorable opportunity for rust spores to germinate and cause infection. Care should also be taken to keep all unnecessary water off the foliage in cultivation in the greenhouse. Most growers are unanimous in considering the chrysanthemum rust of little consequence, and others look upon it as a thing of the past. There are a few, however, who have not succeeded in subduing it and who still think it a serious disease. Some have resorted to spraying, with results that amount to little more than partial suppression. It appears from our own observations, as well as from those obtained from the most successful growers of this plant, that the proper remedy lies in the judicious selection of healthy, rust-free stock and inside cultivation. Give the plants plenty of air and keep the soil in good physical condition. If, however, any of the leaves become infected, they should be removed and burned immediately; and if a plant is badly affected it should be destroyed. In whatever manner the plants are cultivated, whether indoor or outdoor, endeavor to keep the dew and moisture off the foliage as much as possible.

Stem Rot.—More or less trouble from stem rot has been experienced by chrysanthemum growers in the last few years, and is considered by some as a serious trouble threatening this important plant. It is characterized by a slow fading and withering of the leaves, beginning towards the bottom and gradually working up the stem. The flower develops poorly or not at all, and the whole plant finally dies prematurely. The cause of the disease is a fungus which grows in the stem and fills up the large ducts or vessels through which the water must pass in coming up from the roots. The fungus giving rise to this trouble is a species of fusarium, similar forms of which cause like diseases in other species, and there can be but little doubt that the plant is first attacked from the soil, whence the fungus spreads into the stem and on up through it to a considerable height. As the pores become more and more clogged with the fungus threads the water supply to the leaves is diminished, and consequently they gradually wither away and die. It is noticeable that this disease appears most commonly as a result of conditions favoring damping off. Where young plants are crowded in flats or beds those in the center are generally the ones to show the trouble. This is likewise true with the other diseases of this class, and such conditions should be avoided. The soil is to be looked upon as the chief source of infection in all such troubles. There is little danger of contagion in well-rooted plants by spores in the air, as with rusts, mildew and similar diseases. Healthy propagating stock, fresh soil, avoidance of overcrowding to prevent damping off and hygienic conditions are the most effectual means of controlling this trouble.

Other fungus diseases of chrysanthemums have been noted, particularly the anthracnose and two-leaf spots, but we have had no experience with them. They are foliage diseases, and in some instances they have been reported as threatening. Where too close planting occurs, causing a deficiency in light and air, there is not infrequently a loss of foliage, especially of the lower leaves, and fungi occasionally found on such leaves will appear to be mostly of secondary importance.

In conclusion, we will state that the combating of diseases characteristic of greenhouse crops should be, as a rule, along cultural lines rather than other methods of treatment, and we have faith enough in the skill and knowledge displayed by our American florists to believe that they will by this means be able to master in time all difficulties which may occur.

Exhibition at Indianapolis.

Tomlinson Hall looked more beautiful this year than ever before. The new arrangements of the balconies gave the decorator, Ed Bertermann, splendid opportunity to display his skill. One of the most beautiful features of the hall was the centerpiece, consisting of a group of orchids, which as usual attracted much attention. Next to the orchids in popularity was the display of individual chrysanthemum blooms, consisting of Australian varieties. In these the E. G. Hill Company took most premiums, closely followed by Nathan Smith & Son. Experts say that the display of single stem pot plants was not as fine as in former years. Fred Huckriede's display (Mrs. Robinson) was probably the best.

The display of cut flowers was very good. Mrs. E. G. Vesey's vase of 100 Appleton; H. W. Rieman's fifty white, his seedling Adelia; Bertermann's vase of fifty Bonnaffon, and last, but not least, E. G. Hill's Lord Hopetoun deserve special mention. Lord Hopetoun is a red Australian variety of striking beauty.

In tha display of specimen plants, which was not as large as in former years, nothing proved more interesting than Vaughan's Golden Chain. The stage was occupied by a large display of American Beauty roses from the South Park Floral Company of New Castle, Ind. Over 600 blooms were used, and Herbert Heller arranged the display.

The show of this year had a larger display of carnations than any previous show, as far as the general public is concerned. Fred Dorner & Sons Company's display of seedlings was the center of interest with its many striking colors.

Breitmeyer's new rose proved very interesting; the florists surrounded it in great numbers, discusing its merits and future. Most of the experts were favorably impressed with it.

Bertermann Brothers Company took all the prizes in sight on decorative and foliage plants.

The awards in detail were as follows:

Specimen plants, chrysanthemums, white—Vaughan's Greenhouses, Western Springs, Ill., first; H. W. Buckbee, Rockford, Ill., second.

Yellow—Vaughan's Greenhouses, first; H. W. Rieman, second; F. A. Conway, third.

Pink—F. A. Conway, first; H. W. Buckbee, second; E. Hukriede & Son, third.

Any other color—Vaughan's Greenhouses, first; H. W. Rieman, second; F. A. Conway, third.

Six plants, three varieties—E. Hukriede & Son, first; H. W. Rieman, second; Gunnar Teilman, Marion, Ind., third.

White—F. A. Conway, first; H. W. Rieman, second; John Hartje, third.

Yellow—John Hartje, first; H. W. Rieman, second.

Pink—John Hartje, first; H. W. Rieman, second.

Six varieties—F. A. Conway, first; H. W. Rieman second; John Hartje, third.

Twenty-five plants, single stems, white—E. Hukriede & Son, first; H. W. Rieman, second.

Yellow—John Hartje, first; Bertermann Bros., second; E. Hukriede & Son, third.

Pink—H. W. Rieman, first; John Hartje, second.

Any other color—John Hartje, first; F. A. Conway, second.

Novelty—Vaughan's Greenhouses, with Golden Chain.

Cut blooms, one hundred, Timothy Eaton—Mrs. E. G. Vesey, Fort Wayne, Ind., third.

One hundred, Col. D. Appleton—Mrs. Vesey, first; E. G. Hill Company, Richmond, Ind., second.

Fifty blooms, pink—Mrs. E. G. Vesey, first; H. W. Rieman, second; E. G. Hill Company, third.

Red—Gunnar Teilman, first.

White—H W. Rieman, first; E. G. Hill Company, second; Gunnar Teilman, third.

Twenty blooms, white—H. W. Rieman, first; G. Teilman, second; Bertermann Bros., third.

Yellow—Bertermann Bros., first; H. W. Rieman, second; E. G. Hill Company, third.

Pink—H. W. Buckbee, first; E. G. Hill Company, second; Mrs. E. G. Vesey, third.

Red—E. G. Hill Company, first; Bertelmann Bros., second; H. W. Buckbee, third.

Bronze—E. G. Hill Company, first; G. Teilman, second; H. W. Rieman, third.

Six blooms, white—G. Teilman, first; Nathan Smith & Son, Adrian, Mich., second; H. W. Rieman, third.

Yellow—E. G. Hill Company, first; G. Teilman, second; Bertermann Bros., third.

Pink—Nathan Smith & Son, first; E. G. Hill Company, second; Mrs. E. G. Vesey, third.

Red—G. R. Gause & Co., Richmond, Ind., first; N. Smith & Son, second; H. W. Buckbee, third.

Bronze—E. G. Hill Company, first; G. R. Gause & Co., second; Nathan Smith & Son, third

Any other color—E. G. Hill Company, first; N. Smith & Son, second; John Hartje, third.

Two blooms, ten varieties, Australian—N. Smith & Son, first; E. G. Hill Company, secoud; H. W. Buckbee, third.

Thirty-six varieties—E. G. Hill Company, first; N. Smith & Son, second; H. W. Buckbee, third.

Twenty-four varieties—E. G. Hill Company, first; N. Smith & Son, second; G. Teilman, third; H. W. Buckbee, fourth.

Twelve varieties—N. Smith & Son, first; E. G. Hill Company, second; Bertermann Bros., third; John Hartje, fourth.

One hundred blooms, pompons, white, light pink and yellow—N. Smith & Son, first.

Three roses, Columbian, Yellow Eaton and R. E. Richardson—Gunnar Teilman, first.

Twelve blooms, Convention Hall—N. Smith & Son, first.

Twelve oddities—N. Smith & Son, first; E. G. Hill Company, second.

Cut roses, one hundred, American Beauty—Benthey & Co., Chicago, first; South Park Floral Company, New Castle, Ind., second;

Reinberg & Weiland, New Castle, Ind., third.

Carnations, fifty variegated—J. D. Thompson Carnation Company, Joliet, Ill., first; Mrs. E. G. Vesey, second.

White—B., K. & B. Floral Company, Richmond, Ind., first; J. D. Thompson Carnation Company, second.

Red—J. D. Thompson Carnation Company, first; E. G. Hill Company, second.

Pink, lighter than Scott—J. D. Thompson Carnation Company, first; B., K. & B. Floral Company, second.

Crimson—B., K. & B. Floral Company, first.

Pink, darker than Scott—E. T. Grove, Richmond, Ind., first; J. D. Thompson Carnation Company, second.

Yellow—Stuart & Haugh, Anderson, Ind., first.

One hundred blooms, one variety—J. D. Thompson Carnation Company, first.

Collection—Mrs. E. G. Vesey, first; W. K. Partridge, Lockland, O., second.

Twelve, undisseminated, pink—Swan Peterson, Gibson City, Ind., first; J. D. Thompson Carnation Company, second.

Red—B., K. & B. Floral Company, first.

White—Fred Dorner Sons & Co., Lafayette, Ind., first.

Any other color—J. D. Thompson Carnation Company, first; F. Dorner Sons & Co., second.

General display, specimen Asparagus Sprengeri—Bertermann Bros., first.

Boston fern—Bertermann Bros., first.

Six special ferns—Bertermann Bros., first.

Ten cyclamens—H. W. Rieman, first; Bertermanu Bros., second.

Ten variegated foliage plants—H. W. Rieman, first.

Six Begonia de Lorraine—Bertermanu Bros., first.

Violets—Smith & Young Company, first; J. Hartje, second.

The following were in attendance or represented: Richard Witterstaetter, Cincinnati; Mrs. Will Dittmann, New Castle; William Walker, Louisville; O. B. Heinl, Jr., West Terre Haute; J. D. Thompson, Joliet; J. W. Schrader, Mattoon; — Elberson, New Britton; H. Dorner, Lafayette; — Bissell, Marion; Ed G. Brown, Shelbyville; Vaughan's Seed Store, Chicago; H. W. Buckbee, Rockford; H. Stein, Richmond; L. H. Reishig, Adrian; Theodore Bock, Hamilton; E. Buettner, Chicago; F. Dorner, Jr., Lafayette; S. S. Skidelsky, Philadelphia; — Leity, Fort Wayne; M. Waldele, Richmond; Mr. and Mrs. G. Tellmann, Marion; F. H. Hensley, Nashville; Ernst Weinhoeber, Chicago; S. Peterson, Gibson City; F. F. Benthey, Chicago; B. Eschner, Philadelphia; — McDonald, Crawfordsville; H. Heller, New Castle; Messrs. Schulz, Louisville; W. K. Partridge, Cincinnati; Edith Kyrk, Cincinnati; Jos. Heinl, Jacksonville; John Leach, Hartford City; J. J. Bailey, Hartford City; Robert Ellis, Anderson; C. C. Clark, Muncie; J. C. Stuart, Anderson; — Weiland, New Castle; W. W. Coles, Kokomo; Charles Barnaby, Columbus; John Breitmeyer, Detroit; J. A. Evans, Charles Knopf, and Messrs. Burdick and Backmeyer, Richmond.

NOTE.—Catalogue sections 40-49, covering some rose exhibits, were not judged in time for this issue.

Exhibition at Joliet, Ill.

The second annual flower show, given under the auspices of the Joliet Improvement Society, held the boards in that city last week, November 4-7. To say that the exhibition was a success is putting it far too mildly. In quality and extent of variety the exhibit compared favorably with similar shows on a larger scale.

The florists of Joliet and the officers of the Joliet Improvement Society who had charge of the exhibition deserve much credit for the success of the venture. Nothing was left undone to make the event one long to be remembered. Rohwedder's orchestra furnished music and a reception committee of twenty ladies was appointed each day to make it pleasant for the visitors. The daily attendance was large, the crowds being augmented considerably by the teachers who attended the annual convention of the Northeastern Illinois Teachers' Association.

The exhibition was brought to a close Saturday night with an elaborate banquet at Hobbs' dining rooms, given by the florists and members of the Joliet Improvement Society.

One of the pleasing and significant features of the show was the interest manifested by private gardeners, amateurs and private institutions, whose exhibits did much to fill the catalogue of entries. Among the principal exhibitors were the J. D. Thompson Carnation Company, the Chicago Carnation Company and Joseph Labo, local florists; W. H. Buckbee, Rockford, Ill.; Vaughan's Greenhouses, Western Springs, Ill.; Nathan Smith & Son, Adrian, Mich.; Geo. A. Kuhl, Pekin, Ill.; The E. G. Hill Company, Richmond, Ind.; Gunnar Tellmann, Marion, Ind.; W. N. Rudd, Mt. Greenwood, Ill.; St. Francis Academy, Woodland & Longfellow Schools, and Western Park, of Joliet, were also represented with creditable displays. The state penitentiary showed a fine group of greenhouse plants. C. E. Carter staged a beautiful collection of plants, including geraniums, hibiscus, orange trees in fruit and flower, ferns, palms, etc.; the George Wittbold Company, Chicago, exhibited Cocos Bonnetti; West Park had an interesting exhibit of cacti. The Lambert collection of stove and decorative plants was very imposing and reflected much credit on the gardener, Charles Shepard. Labo showed good collections of ferns, palms, chrysanthemums, begonias and salvias. Bassett & Washburn sent two large bunches of Lilium giganteum with their compliments. George Kuhl, of Pekin, Ill., sent several hanging baskets of fine Boston ferns and Piersoni. Gunnar Tellmann's chrysanthemum display, Col. Appleton and Marie Liger, a dozen to each vase, took first prize in their respective classes.

The exhibits of the Chicago Carnation Company and the J. D. Thompson Carnation Company were among the most complete, varied and imposing. The carnation competition resolved itself into a brisk fight for honors between these two important Joliet concerns. The former's Fiancee proved to be the queen of the show and carried off the Foley gold medal as the best carnation of any color and the silver medal as the best pink. The Thompson people did well with their varieties. Their white, Gov. Walcott, was awarded the silver medal for the best white; their Estelle (very fine blooms) took the medal for the best red carnation.

Of course the chrysanthemum was given a large share of attention and admiration and the entries were numerous and varied, also showing an exceptional fine quality. There were four exhibitors showing forty named varieties, Nathan Smith & Son, the E. G. Hill Co., H. W. Buckbee and Gunnar Tellmann.

Owing to a mistake made in staging the rose exhibit, but one award was made. The rules called for forty blooms in each exhibit, but only twenty-five were staged. The exhibit was consequently outlawed and declared no contest. The American Beauty competition, which called for but twenty-five blooms, was won by the Chicago Carnation Company. The new unnamed pink rose of John Breitmeyer's Sons was exhibited and attracted considerable attention. The exploiters of this new wonder are offering $100 in cash for the best name suggested for the flower.

John Lambert gardens was awarded first prize for the best display of stove and greenhouse plants.

Vaughan's Greenhouses took first for grafted chrysanthemums and Celestial peppers.

E. A. Kaust, of Chicago, officiated as judge.

Exhibition at Tarrytown, N. Y.

The Tarrytown Horticultural Society opened its fifth annual exhibition November 4 to continue to November 6. As usually seen at this place, some very fine plants and flowers are on exhibition and the opinion of many is that larger blooms of chrysanthemums are seen today than ever before. Thanks to the manager and the committee on attendance, who deserve great credit for the perfect arrangement and preparations made, no delay was experienced in staging the exhibits and the judges were able to start their work at the appointed time, and great satisfaction was felt by all upon their decision. As usual, the F. R. Pierson Co. helped greatly with their various exhibits, principally noticeable among them being some very fine vases of Daheim, Dorothy Whitney, Enchantress, White Lawson, Variegated Lawson, Mrs. M. A. Patten and Fair Maid carnations. The sensation of all was a pure white seedling of immense size and texture, a cross between Lawson and Prosperity. Another bench was filled with new chrysanthemums, with a new yellow seedling that will be heard from later on, also a vase of the new rose from John Breitmeyer's Sons. Favorable comments were passed on this new rose.

New chrysanthemums were greatly in evidence, those following being exhibited by different growers: Mme. Milchan, Yellow Eaton, Lord Salisbury, Chas. Langley, Mrs. Thirkell, C. J. Salter, Mme. Rehout, Mabel Morgan, Mrs. Neville, Millicent Richardson, Queen Alexandra, Mrs. T. W. Pockett (the above were in the winning lot for the Pierson cup), Godfrey's King, King Edward VII, Meib Demay and W. R. Church.

The feature of the show was the special prize offered by F. R. Pierson Co., a silver cup, for thirty-six blooms of chysanthemums, six varieties, three of each, selected from twenty-four varieties of last year's introduction; three entries were received, but unfortunately only one lot was exhibited and the cup won by Wm. Scott, gardener to Joseph Eastman, Tarrytown, N. Y. The prize offered for Nephrolepis Piersoni brought out three very fine specimens of this now well-known fern. Special prize from Cooke & McCord Co. for plants suitable for table decoration, brought out two well-filled tables with some well-grown material. The president's prize for Begonia Gloire de Lorraine brought only one exhibitor, John H. Troy, of New York. Prize for best decorative plant other than fern was awarded to a large Cycas revolutu. For John L. Whyte's prize for specimen Asparagus Sprengeri only one plant competed. C. P. Johnson's prize for hardy pompon chrysanthemum, only one exhibitor, but with forty varieties.

Some fine and larger cut chrysanthemums were exhibited in the different classes calling for distinct varieties and different colors. Principally noticeable were Eaton, Merza, Mrs. R. Weeks, Appleton, Peter Kay, Nellie Pockett, Kate Broomhead. Amongst the winners were George Middleton, gardener to Wm. Rockefeller; Wm. Scott, Wm. Nye, gardener to Miss Blanche Potter; Edw. Parker, gardener to Joseph Milbank; John Wahlquist, gardener to D. Archbold, and Samuel Riddel, gardener to F. A. Constable. The prize for the largest bloom of the show went to Wm. Scott for an immense bloom of Lord Salisbury. Only one group of chrysanthemum plants was exhibited, the prize being won by D. McFarlane, gardener to Mrs. S. Walter Webb. Several lots of specimens, standards and plants in 6-inch pots were also shown.

The carnations were all of excellent quality and competition was very keen in every class. Varieties in evidence were Gov. Walcott, Enchantress, J. H. Manley, Lawson, Prosperity, Gov. Roosevelt, Estelle Harlowarden, etc. Roses, especially American Beauty, were not of the usual standard seen at these exhibitions. There were a few vases of good Liberty, Bride and Bridesmaids, also one of Franz Deegan. Violets were few and the same might be said of the vegetable classes, but the quality was excellent in the last named. Hothouse grapes were fine, also other collections of fruits.

F. R. and P. M. Pierson were awarded a certificate of merit for American Beauty roses.

The F. R. Pierson Co. received a certificate of merit for the new carnation Daheim.

Scattered through the hall were two fine groups of palms, also specimens, and some splendid ferns that helped greatly to give variety and color to the decorations of the hall.

Attendance for the first day of the show was away ahead of previous exhibitions, showing great interest taken by the public.

The judges were M. C. Connellan, Bay Shore, N. Y.; Wm. Turner, Oceanic, N. J.; Patrick O'Mara, New York, N. Y.; H. McNichols, Lawrence, N. Y.; Peter McDonald, Yonkers, N. Y., and D. Harrison, Rhine. Nichols, Cedarhurst, N. Y.; Peter McDonald, Yonkers, N. Y., and D. Harrison, Glen Cove, N. Y.

L. A. M.

Exhibition at Canandaigua, N. Y.

The first annual exhibition of the Canandaigua Florists' and Gardeners' Club, held November 5-6 at the Town Hall, was a thoroughly artistic success. There were over 150 entries in the various classes of cut flowers, potted plants and vegetables. Over 100 pots of chrysanthemums from Mrs. Thompson's Sonnenberg conservatories were shown, as well as palms, ferns and orchids from the same greenhouse and others in town. Among the display were five varieties of Australian chrysanthemums, shown for the first time in America, which were contributed to the display by Charles H. Totty, of Madison, N. J.

THE AMERICAN FLORIST

NINETEENTH YEAR.

Subscription, $1.00 a year. To Europe, $2.00.
   Subscriptions accepted only from those
      in the trade.
Advertisements, on all except cover pages,
   10 Cents a Line, Agate; $1.00 per inch.
      Cash with Order.

No Special Position Guaranteed.

Discounts are allowed only on consecutive inser-
tions, as follows:—6 times, 5 per cent; 13 times,
10 per cent; 26 times, 20 per cent;
      52 times, 30 per cent.
Cover space sold only on yearly contract at
$1.00 per inch, net, in the case of the two
   front pages, regular discounts apply-
      ing only to the back pages.
The Advertising Department of the AMERICAN
FLORIST is for florists, seedsmen and nurserymen
and dealers in wares pertaining to those lines only.
Orders for less than one-half inch space not accepted.
Advertisements must reach us by Wednesday to
secure insertion in the issue for the following
Saturday. Address
   AMERICAN FLORIST CO., Chicago.

THIS ISSUE 76 PAGES WITH COVERS.

CONTENTS.

Papaver Lady Roscoe.

This new poppy, a variety of Papaver
orientale, is said to be quite distinct from
any other variety of the family. The
flowers are of a distinct shade of terra-
cotta or salmon pink. The whole flower
has a striking sheen, good substance and
generally two rows of petals, while the
growth of the plant is strong and vigorous. This new variety will be offered to
the trade by R. C. Notcutt, Woodbridge,
England, next spring.

The Anna Foster fern seems to be
gaining popularity steadily.

Now that much additional heating
apparatus is starting up, guard against
fires.

PLEASE note that our eastern office is
now located at 42 West, Twenty-eighth
street, New York.

WE are indebted to Nathan Smith &
Son, Adrian, Mich., for flowers of the
interesting types of chrysanthemums
shown on our cover design.

J. E. JENSEN writes to state that he
intended to advise salt water as a remedy
for red spider in carnation culture, not
thrips, as given in our last issue.

WE have received a very handsome
colored plate representing several genera
of orchids from Otto Beyrodt, of Marien-
felde, Berlin, Germany.

NUMEROUS friends in the trade will learn
with regret of the death of Henrietta,
wife of Denys Zirngiebel, November 8.
Mrs. Zirngiebel was born in Switzerland
seventy-four years ago. Pneumonia was
the cause of death, at Needham, Mass.

LONICERA HECKROTTI, the red-flowered
ever-blooming honeysuckle, is now, first
week in November, covered with flowers
and young flower buds. It makes a
pretty companion, intertwined with the
white-flowered Halliana.

AZALEAS Vervæneana, Deutsche Perle,
Simon Mardner, Pauline Mardner and
Apollo, which are the best holiday varieties, should now be put into a regular
temperature of 60° at night and will then
come in just right for Christmas.

DAHLIA tubers should be allowed to
remain in the ground as long as possible
after the tops have frozen down in order
that they may get well ripened. Most
of the difficulty in keeping tubers through
winter arises from too early digging.

AT this season the fruit bearing shrubs
are the most attractive ornaments of the
garden and lawn. Rosa multiflora, the
berberises, euonymuses, cratæguses,
celastruses and some of the pyruses
are now all aglow in scarlet and crimson
rivaling the show of the blooming
season.

To assure symmetry and graceful proportions, the Pierson fern should be
grown on raised stands or suspended
from the roof of the greenhouse and the
results will amply repay the grower who
aims to produce fine specimens. This
fern should not be shaded except in the
hottest midsummer days when a slight
wash on the glass may be needed to prevent burning. It is a gross feeder and is
happiest when pot-bound and given
liberal stimulant, with cool culture,
abundant light and plenty of room. If
these hints are followed there will be little or no tendency to "revert to type."

The Glass Situation.

The window glass market is in a disturbed condition, due to different causes
says Dun's Review. The interference in
in building operations by strikes reduced
the demand in window and plate glass,
and two labor organizations with trifling differences affect the trade unfa-
vorably. Efforts are being made to con-
solidate these two organizations and
labor conditions will be improved thereby.
There are now only 500 pots in operation, and a general resumption is not
expected until after December 1. Very
little glass has been made since last

March. Wages are high and prices low,
with considerable cutting. Collections
and money conditions are fair. Buyers
have been supplying only present wants,
and no new busins for 1904 delivery is
reported.

Looking Backward.

On the evening of Nov. 3, 1886, seventeen years ago, at a well attended meeting of florists of Chicago and vicinity, an
organization was formed under the title
of the Chicago Florists' Club. The club
was intended for members of the trade
only, and was primarily meant for a
social organization. At the first meeting
fifty members were enrolled, with the late
J. T. Anthony president.

"The Orchid."

The opening of the new Gaiety
theatre, London, was celebrated by
the performance of a piece under
this name, says the Gardeners'
Chronicle. Aubrey Chesterton—not the
orchid collector by that name—who is
got up to simulate a very well-known
orchid grower and ex-minister, makes a
bet with M. Belcasse that he will produce
a second specimen of a rare orchid, which
the latter thinks unique. Mr. Chesterton
succeeds through the mediation of a
gardener at a ladies' horticultural college and a professional orchid hunter.
We can not enter into all the details, but
chronicle the event as probably the first
occasion in which the orchid and orchid
growers have been brought before the
public in this way.

Piping for Rose Houses.

ED. AM. FLORIST:—I am going to put
up two rose houses 22x100 feet in the
vicinity of Philadelphia, where you know
we do not have very severe winter
weather. The houses will have plates
elevated six feet from the ground and
will be on the ridge and furrow plan with
no partitions between. What would be
the best method of piping and how much
piping ought there to be? Also what
size hot water boiler should I get?
                                          W. J. R.

If there is glass in the outside walls it
will be best to have a boiler rated for
2,000 square feet of hot water radiation.
The number and arrangement of the
heating pipes will depend a good deal on
the number and arrangement of the
benches. Three 2½-inch flows with nine
2-inch returns will give good results, or
four flows and eight returns may be used
in each house. If only 2-inch pipe is used
thirteen will be needed, and it should be
arranged so that there will be no more
than two returns for a flow.
                                          L. R. TAFT.

To Force Hydrangeas.

ED. AM. FLORIST:—Please state the best
method of treating hydrangeas, that have
been potted in the spring and plunged
outside, to bring them in for Easter.
Should they be dried for awhile or potted
at once?   M. S.

At the present time and until the first
of the year hydrangeas should be kept
on the dry side (not too dry, however,
so as not to shrivel the wood). Give
them a temperature of 40° for the next
two months. The object is to hold them
dormant until the first of the year, and if
all the old leaves fall no harm is done.
Three months before Easter they should
be placed in a temperature of 60° and
started into growth by watering more

freely. As soon as growth commences, if the plants are pot-bound, they should then be shifted into a size larger pot in good rich soil. To shift them at the present time, when the plants should be dormant, would do more harm than good. They require an abundance of water throughout the forcing season and to heighten the color of the flowers and darken the foliage, applications of liquid manure should be given twice a week after the buds are set. They must have the full light and plenty of room to keep the plants from drawing up. G.

A Disease of Phoenix.

ED. AM. FLORIST:—The enclosed phoenix leaves are infested with something which is not affected; in the least by whale-oil soap. "My larger phoenix, latania, kentia. and areca plants are not affected by the trouble. If there is anything that will clean them, I would like to know it. .

A SOUTHERN SUBSCRIBER.

The injured phoenix leaflets submitted with this query were evidently suffering from a severe attack of the phoenix fungus, Peronospora phoenixæ, a trouble that not infrequently appears among plants of this genus. This fungus is often found upon P. Canariensis, and also P. dactylifera, and may spread to any of the species. From the fact that the fungus develops within the tissues of the leaf and only completes its growth and fruition on the surface of the same, it becomes a difficult matter to treat it with fungicides. If the plants are all affected as much as the specimens forwarded I should be tempted to burn them rather than to attempt a cure, but there may be a possibility of checking the trouble with applications of Bordeaux mixture of moderate strength. A warm and moist atmosphere favors the growth of this fungus, and it would therefore be wise to try a night temperature of 50° and a moderately dry atmosphere while treating with the fungicide.

W. H. TAPLIN.

Obituary.

M. A. WILHELMY.

Mathias A. Wilhelmy, retired, formerly one of the most prominent nurserymen, seedsmen and florists of Cleveland, Ohio, died at his home November 11. He had been ill for some time. He had been in business in Cleveland for nearly thirty-five years, and during that time drew about himself a large circle of friends. Within the last year he lost by death his wife, his father and a son and daughter. Mr. Wilhemy was born in Germany fifty-two years ago, and came to this country and to Cleveland when ten years of age. He became interested in the nursery business when still a boy, and when still a young man established one of the most successful houses in this city. About four years ago he retired and the charge of the establishment was assumed by his sons. He was prominently identified with the Fraternal Order of Eagles, the Harigaria and the Independent Order of Foresters. He was long interested in the civic improvement and growth of Cleveland. The family surviving consists of six children, four sons and two daughters. The funeral services will be held at the residence Saturday afternoon, November 14, at 2 o'clock; burial at Riverside cemetery, where short private services will be held.

HERBERT CHARLES.

Herbert Charles, Marion, Ind., owner of the Marion Floral Company, died November 3, at his home after several weeks' illness from typhoid fever. He leaves a wife and two children. Mr. Charles was formerly principal of the high school at Cambridge City, Ind., but came to Marion in 1898 to take a place in the Marion high school as algebra teacher. He remained in the high school for nearly five years, when he was forced to resign on account of ill health. After leaving the high school he purchased a greenhouse on the Sand pike, where he had since resided.

SITUATIONS, WANTS, FOR SALE.

One Cent Per Word.
Cash with the Adv.
Plant Advs. NOT admitted under this head.

Every paid subscriber to the AMERICAN FLORIST for the year 1903 is entitled to a five-line WANT ADV. (situations only) free, to be used at any time during the year.

Situation Wanted—By young lady, thoroughly experienced desires position in store.
B B. care American Florist.

Situation Wanted—As assistant propagator of roses in a commercial place. Address
FLORIST, 146 Bowmanville Ave., Chicago.

Situation Wanted—By first-class grower and propagator of cut flowers and plants. Single, German, middle-aged. Address
H. care American Florist.

Situation Wanted—As foreman or manager; eighteen years' practical experience. Thoroughly conversant with all branches of the business.
G P. care American Florist.

Situation Wanted—By good all-around florist. 30 years' experience in all branches of the business. First-class reference; single. State wages.
ALPHA, care American Florist.

Situation Wanted—By young man as practical gardener in carnation grower and all around man, in up-to-date establishment where things are done right and standard wages paid. State wages.
ILLINOIS, care Am. Florist.

Situation Wanted—By young man with fair knowledge of plants and not afraid of work. In good establishment to thoroughly learn the florist business. Good references.
T. J. LAMISON, Le Roy, Kas.

Situation Wanted—As foreman; by middle-aged married man, where a first-class grower is wanted for all-kinds of greenhouse stock. Good decorator and designer.
P. O. BOX 171, Canton Corner, Mass.

Situation Wanted—By sober, industrious, single florist, German. 15 years' experience in floral and pot plant culture. Wages not less than $30.00 per month and board. Private or commercial place.
Ross, care American Florist

Help Wanted—Competent greenhouse men. Apply to J. M. GASSER CO., Rocky River, O.

Help Wanted—Young man competent to manage flower store wanted by November 15.
W. care American Florist.

Help Wanted—Good man as assistant foreman, capable of taking full charge when manager is away; American preferred. State wages wanted.
O. H. FREY, Lincoln, Neb.

Help Wanted—Salesman who thoroughly understands the seed business, especially the market garden trade. Apply by letter to
W. W. RAWSON & Co., Boston, Mass.

Help Wanted—Good florist to take charge of three greenhouses 20x100. Grow cut flowers and general stock. Give reference and wages expected with room. Address
C S. care American Florist.

Help Wanted—Young man for general greenhouse work. One who is willing to learn, making up funeral work and decorating preferred. State wages. Address
FRED RENTSCHLER, Madison, Wis.

Help Wanted—A young man as helper in greenhouses. One who is willing to work. State wages wanted with or without board in first letter and send copy of reference.
P. O. BOX 273, Huntington, L. I., N. Y.

Help Wanted—A first-class rose-grower on commercial place. One who thoroughly understands his business. Must be steady and sober. State wages. Address
T O, care American Florist.

Help Wanted—Rose grower in modern up-to-date establishment to take charge of section of houses. Give names of former employers and state wages expected. No novice need apply.
F J A, care American Florist.

Help Wanted—A competent young man, fully experienced, thoroughly reliable and steady, to take charge of city store or large establishment in Chicago. Must be a good make-up man and know how to handle large stock. Good permanent position to the right man. References.
X Y, care American Florist.

Help Wanted—Bright, energetic young man of good address for a Chicago retail store. Must be thoroughly up-to-date as a decorator and designer and a first-class salesman. Address with references as to character and ability, stating wages expected. Address
C R S, care American Florist.

Wanted—Some reliable retailer to take surplus stock of out flowers.
FRANK SAHAN, Red Oak, Ia.

For Sale—To rent a place of from 25 to 40 thousand square feet of glass for wholesale trade only. Must have dwelling. barns, outside ground, etc. all in good condition. Must be within 25 miles of Chicago. M S, care American Florist.

For Sale—Ballard's Greenhouse. Perry, Iowa. Cause poor health. Address
WM. BALLARD, Perry, Iowa.

For Sale—Wishing to retire from business I will sell the fixtures and rent my store. It is an old established business. Address
MRS. J. WIRNBONER, 370 Center St., Chicago.

For Sale—Greenhouses. Good location for local and shipping business. Well stocked; winter coal laid in. Will sell cheap if sold at once. Selling on account of failing health.
JAS. RICHARDSON, London, O.

For Sale—Entire business of Rheder Bros. Florists. Formerly owned by Mrs. Rheder. Reason for selling the recent death of a member of the firm. A splendid paying business in good condition. Fine climate. Write for particulars.
RHEDER BROS., Wilmington, N. C.

Wanted...

A first-class nursery foreman in the east. Salary limited by ability only.

Address FOREMAN, care American Florist.

NOTICE.

ALWAYS mention the AMERICAN FLORIST when writing to advertisers.

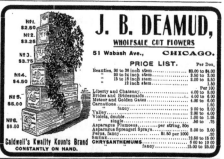

INTERNATIONAL FLOWER DELIVERY.

PASSENGER STEAMSHIP MOVEMENTS.

FROM	TO	STEAMER	*LINE	DAY	DUE ABOUT
New York......	Liverpool	Umbria	1	Sat. Nov. 21, 7:00 a. m.	Nov. 27
New York......	"	Lucania	1	Sat. Nov. 28, 11:00 a. m.	Dec. 4
Boston........	"	Saxonia	1	Sat. Nov. 28, 3:30 p. m.	Dec. 4
New York......	Hamburg	Auguste Victoria	8	Thur. Nov. 19, 10:00 a. m.	Nov 29
New York......	"	Pennsylvania	8	Sat. Nov. 21, 8:00 a. m.	Dec. 1
New York......	"	Patricia	8	Sat. Nov. 28, 11:00 a. m.	Dec. 10
New York......	Glasgow	Furnesia	8	Sat. Nov. 28, Noon.	Dec. 8
New York......	London	Minneapolis	6	Sat. Nov. 21, 7:00 a. m.	Nov. 3
New York......	"	Minnehaha	6	Sat. Nov. 28, Noon.	Dec. 8
New York......	Liverpool	Oceanic	7	Wed. Nov. 18, 4:00 a. m.	Nov. 25
New York......	"	Cymeric	7	Fri. Nov. 20, 6:00 a. m.	Nov. 88
New York......	"	Teutonic	7	Wed. Nov. 25, Noon.	Dec. 2
New York......	"	Arabic	7	Fri. Nov. 27, 11:00 a. m.	Dec. 5
New York......	Antwerp	Kensington	8	Sat. Nov. 21, 10:00 a. m.	Nov. 80
New York......	"	Kroonland	8	Sat. Nov. 28, 10:00 a. m.	Dec. 7
New York......	Southampton	New York	8	Sat. Nov. 21, 10:00 a. m.	Nov. 88
New York......	"	St. Paul	8	Sat. Nov. 28, 10:00 a. m.	Dec. 5
New York......	Havre	La Savoie	10	Thur. Nov. 19, 10:00 a. m.	Nov. 27
New York......	"	La Bretagne	10	Thur. Nov. 26, 10:00 a. m.	Dec. 4
New York......	Rotterdam	Potsdam	11	Wed. Nov. 18, 10:00 a. m.	Nov. 27
New York......	"	Statendam	11	Wed. Nov. 25, 10:00 a. m.	Dec. 4
New York......	Genoa	Nord America	12	Tues. Nov. 24, 11:00 a. m.	Dec. 7
New York......	"	Hohenzollern	12	Sat. Nov. 21, 11:00 a. m.	Dec. 4
New York......	Bremen	Kaiser Wilh. II	12	Tues. Nov. 17, 2.50 p. m.	Nov. 24
New York......	"	Main	12	Tues. Nov. 19, 10:00 a. m.	Dec. 1
New York......	"	K. Wil. Der Grosse	12	Tues. Nov. 26, 10:00 a. m.	Dec. 1
New York......	"	Grosser Kurfuerst	12	Thur. Nov. 26, 10:00 a. m.	Dec. 6
New York......	Naples	Germania	14	Tues. Nov. 17,	Nov. 27
Boston........	Liverpool	Commonwealth	15	Thur. Nov. 19, 10:00 a. m.	Nov. 25
Boston........	"	Kensington	8	Sat. Nov. 28, 3:80 p. m.	Dec. 5
Boston........	"	Canadian	16	Wed. Nov. 25, 2:20 p. m.	Dec. 4

INTERNATIONAL FLOWER DELIVERY.

STEAMSHIPS LEAVE FOREIGN PORTS.

FROM	TO	STEAMER	*LINE	DAY	DUE ABOUT
Liverpool.......	New York	Etruria	1	Sat. Nov. 21,	Nov. 27
Liverpool.......	"	Campania	1	Sat. Nov. 28,	Dec. 4
Liverpool.......	Boston	Ivernia	1	Tues. Nov. 24,	Dec. 1
Hamburg.......	New York	Pretoria	3	Sat. Nov. 21,	Dec. 4
Hamburg.......	"	Graf Waldersee	3	Sat. Nov. 28,	Dec. 11
Glasgow.......	"	Astoria	5	Thur. Nov. 19,	Nov. 29
Glasgow.......	"	Columbia	5	Sat. Nov. 28,	Dec. 8
London.......	"	Menominee	6	Thur. Nov. 19,	Nov. 29
London.......	"	Minnetonka	6	Sat. Nov. 28,	Dec. 8
Liverpool.......	"	Germanic	7	Wed. Nov. 18, 3:30 p. m.	Nov. 26
Liverpool.......	"	Cedric	7	Fri. Nov. 20, 3:30 p. m.	Nov. 28
Liverpool.......	"	Majestic	7	Wed. Nov. 25, 3:30 p. m.	Dec. 2
Liverpool.......	"	Celtic	7	Fri. Nov. 27, 3:30 p. m.	Dec. 4
Antwerp.......	"	Zeeland	8	Sat. Nov. 21, Noon.	Nov. 30
Antwerp.......	"	Finland	8	Sat. Nov. 28, 7:30 a. m.	Dec. 7
Southampton...	"	St. Louis	8	Sat. Nov. 21, 5:00 p. m.	Nov. 28
Southampton...	"	New York	8	Sat. Nov. 28, 5:00 p. m.	Dec. 5
Havre.......	"	La Champagne	10	Sat. Nov. 21,	Nov. 29
Havre.......	"	La Touraine	10	Sat. Nov. 28,	Dec. 5
Rotterdam	"	Noordam	11	Sat. Nov. 21,	Nov. 30
Rotterdam	"	Rotterdam	11	Sat. Nov. 28,	Dec. 7
Bremen.......	"	Citta di Napoli	12	Mon. Nov. 16,	Dec. 8
Genoa.......	"	Liguria	12	Mon. Nov. 23,	Dec. 10
Genoa.......	"	Lahn	12	Tues. Nov. 24,	Dec. 6
Genoa.......	"	Kronprinz Wilh.	12	Tues. Nov. 17,	Nov. 24
Naples.......	"	Roma	14	Sat. Nov. 21,	Dec. 8
Liverpool.......	Boston	Canada	15	Thur. Nov. 19,	Nov. 26
Liverpool.......	"	New England	15	Sat. Nov. 21,	Nov. 28
Liverpool.......	"	Mayflower	15	Thur. Nov. 19,	Dec. 1
Liverpool.......	"	Devonian	16	Sat. Nov. 21,	Nov. 30
Liverpool.......	"	Winifredian	16	Sat. Nov. 28,	Dec. 7

* See steamship list on opposite page.

RUTHERFORD, N. J.—The fire at the
greenhouses of Bobbink & Atkins November 6 did not cause any great amount of
harm.

MANCHESTER, O.—George R. McNeil
sold his stock of plants to Wilber V.
Cooley, his only competitor in the town,
November 1.

THE SEED TRADE.

AMERICAN SEED TRADE ASSOCIATION.
S. F. Willard, Pres.; J. Charles McCullough, First Vice-Pres.; C. E. Kendel, Cleveland, O., Sec'y and Treas.
Twenty-second annual convention St. Louis, Mo., June, 1904.

SNOW is reported in the Wisconsin green district.

IT is estimated that southern California will ship 1,500 car loads of celery this season.

SOME varieties of onion bulbs for next season's planting in California are reported scarce.

VISITED CHICAGO: Lester L. Morse and W. J. Fosgate, Santa Clara, Cal.; D. L. Sloan, Palo Alto, Cal.

M. A. WILHELMY, of Cleveland, Ohio, died November 11. Obituary notice appears elsewhere in this issue.

VISITED CLEVELAND:—Howard M. Earl, with W. Atlee Burpee & Co., Philadelphia; W. S. Woodruff, of S. D. Woodruff & Sons, Orange, Conn.

SWEET CORN growers (farmers) in Connecticut are asking from $4.50 per bushel up for late sorts, some asking double that and loath to sell.

SAN JOSE, CAL.—Charles P. Braslan has fully recovered from the injuries sustained in an automobile upset and started for the east November 12.

FROSTY weather has come in the tuberose district and the bulbs of these and caladiums that were not promptly housed will suffer from freezing.

NEW YORK.—Ralph M. Ward has withdrawn from the firm of Wm. Hagemann & Company and formed the new firm of Ralph M. Ward & Company, 17 Battery place.

THE wholesale dealers in Europe who do business in Cuba allow the Cuban merchants almost unlimited time to meet their accounts, which consideration the merchants seem to think more of than any discount for a cash or shorter payment.

M. HERB, of Naples, Italy, will introduce next spring Coleus salicifolius nanus, the undulated and willow-like leaves of which are richly colored, and Helianthus Apollo, a compact variety which grows about two feet high. The flowers of the latter are single, golden yellow with black center.

LOUISVILLE, KY.—The Southern Seed Company filed articles of incorporation, with a capital stock of $50,000, divided into 500 shares of $100 each. The incorporators are James G. Tinsley, Richmond, Va.; T. G. Tinsley, Nashville, Tenn.; A. D. Ledoux, New York; J. S. Merimee, T. H. Merimee and Edwin C. Foltz. The last three stockholders are citizens of Louisville.

San Francisco.

NOVEMBER 7.—The weather is lovely but we need rain. This time last year we had had three inches, but up to the present date we have had less than one-third of an inch.
The Cox Seed Company shipped six carloads of beans for eastern points during the present week.

Receiver Appointed for D. Landreth & Sons.

In the United States district court November 6 creditors filed a petition to have Burnett Landreth and Leopold Landreth, trading as D. Landreth & Sons, seed merchants, of 1217 Market street, Philadelphia, adjudged involuntary bankrupts. In conjunction with the seed store in this city the concern owns large farms in Pennsylvania, New Jersey and Virginia, on which they raised their seeds and sent them to this city for sale.

The firm for some time past, it is understood, has been financially embarrassed, and on July 24 last a committee of creditors inventoried the concern in a going capacity at $134,197.08 and at a forced sale $53,545.98. A meeting was held by the creditors to try to effect a compromise, which they were unable to do.

In a letter to Julius C. Levi, attorney for sundry creditors, the firm admits its insolvency. The letter is as follows:

PHILADELPHIA, October 30, 1903.
Julius C. Levi, Esq.:
My Dear Sir—As a member of the committee of creditors of D. Landreth & Sons and representative of sundry banks to whom we are indebted, we beg to advise you that we have been unable to effect the compromise offered, owing to the refusal of a number of banks and other creditors to accept terms of the settlement offered. As the firm of D. Landreth & Sons, and each of us individually, are insolvent and unable to pay our debts, there can be no other recourse than by proceedings in bankruptcy, and we are willing to be adjudged bankrupts on these grounds.
Yours truly,
B. LANDRETH & SONS.
BURNETT LANDRETH.
LEOPOLD LANDRETH.

Mr. Levi on behalf of the creditors filed a petition in the court for a receiver to be appointed for the concern. He averred that it was necessary for the business to continue, owing to the fact, peculiar to the seed business, that seeds are marketable only in season; that in order to protect assets of the estate it will be necessary to harvest the crops and operate the farms in order that all the products will not be lost to the creditors.

Judge McPherson, upon consideration of the petition, appointed former State Senator Bayard Henry as receiver with authority to operate the concern until further notice from the court. Security was fixed at $25,000.

Uncle Sam Versus the Seed Trade.

STILL TRYING FOR A KNOCKOUT BLOW.

WASHINGTON, D. C., Nov. 3.—Distribution of garden seed in the aggregate amount of 1,000 tons is in progress in every State and territory in the union by the department of agriculture to-day. The value of the packages will exhaust the appropriation of $270,000 voted by the last congress, and the packages will number 48,000,000. Every senator, representative and delegate in congress will have 19,500 packages to distribute among his constituents, while the department will itself send out 700,000 packages to correspondents and 300,000 to state grange organizations, and several hundred thousand more to weather bureaus and government experiment stations. It is the largest distribution ever made by the government.
The distribution this year is several months in advance of that of last year and is being sent into six districts, into which the country has been divided. Congressmen having city constituencies will receive a large supply of packages for window boxes, lots and dooryards, and may trade in their vegetable seeds for more flower seeds if they desire.
Cotton and tobacco seeds also will be distributed in large quantities to districts where they are available.—Chicago Daily News.

WASHINGTON, PA.— The Washington Floral Company formally opened a retail flower store November 5 in the Swan building.

OSHKOSH, WIS.— The Algoma Horticultural Society held a chrysanthemum fair at the city hall, Oshkosh, November 11 and 12.

Washington.

OPENING OF CONGRESS ATTENDED BY ELABORATE FLORAL DISPLAYS—UNIQUE DESIGNS FOR SENATORS—BUSINESS IS BOOMED BY EVENT—WEATHER FINE AND STOCK GOOD—NOTES.

The opening of the extra session of the Fifty-eighth Congress was marked by floral displays on the desks of senators and members of the house of representatives. Old residents of the capital aver that seldom has there been such an exhibit of rare and costly blooms. The friends and constituents of the most prominent members sent bouquets, baskets and set pieces in such profusion that their desks would not hold them, and they were deposited for the time being in the aisles. One prominent senator received a shield 3½x4½ feet. On the shield, which was of blue immortelles, a design of the American eagle was worked in grasses, ribbons, and red, white and blue immortelles. Over the shield was a cluster of American Beauty roses. Another member received a floral automobile and another a miniature railroad. American Beauty was so much in evidence as to cause wonder where the bloom all came from. Orchids, chrysanthemums and carnations had their innings, the result being that available stock was pretty well cleaned out. All this made busy times for the florists, but as one man they rose up to the emergency and "caved in the emergency's head."

At the greenhouses of the bureau of plant industry, Agricultural Department, may be seen a fine collection of carnation plants, and if the southern hereabouts can produce finer ones let them now be heard. Especially worthy of mention are: Mrs. Theo. Roosevelt, Her Majesty, Harlowarden, Enchantress, Boston Market, Lillian Pond, Murphy's White and Lawson. A white sport from Bradt looks promising. The bureau's chrysanthemum show closed November 8, having been well attended throughout. Wm. J. Bryan, white; A. J. Balfour, pink, and Edgar Sanders, bronze, were good ones not previously mentioned. Karnishiki, its name proclaims its nationality, was a real novelty.

The weather is beautiful for this season of the year and the grower is unfortunate that cannot bring on roses and carnations. The Center market florists, who "catch 'em both comin' an' goin'" with a wholesale and retail trade, are now getting busy and expect to keep at it till after Easter. Chrysanthemums have been plentiful in the market for the last week, and Harry Robey, C. Schellhorn and George Comley have disposed of a lot of them at good prices.

J. H. Small & Sons have chrysanthemum blooms of Edgar Sanders, bronze, and Mlle. Marie Liger, pink, that are extra fine. Mrs. President McKinley is a good yellow.

P. H. Meehan, a Bloomington, Ill., boy, now attends to the blooming-o'-the-rose at F. K. Kramer's range; he has also fine specimens of Nephrolepis Piersoni and the adiantums.

John Robertson is doing a good business at his Connecticut avenue store and laying plans to increase it; there is nothing wrong with John's thinking apparatus.

Grillbortzer Brothers, of Alexandria, Va., are sending to the Washington stores good blooms of Lawson, Guardian Angel and Morning Glory carnations.
　　　　　　　　　　　　　S. E.

CHAS. P. BRASLAN

of the

Braslan Seed Growers Company,

SAN JOSE, CAL.,

Started on his Annual Eastern Trip
November 12.

THE NURSERY TRADE.

AM. ASSOCIATION OF NURSERYMEN.
N. W. HALE, Knoxville, Tenn.- Pres.; FRANK
A. WEBER, St. Louis, Mo., Vice-Pres.; GEORGE C.
SEAGER, Rochester, N. Y., Sec'y.
Twenty-ninth annual convention, Atlanta, Ga.,
June, 1904.

KEYSER, W. VA.—A certificate of incorporation has been granted the Sleepy Creek Orchard Company, of Sleepy Creek, Berkeley county, to engage in the fruit growing and nursery business; capital $25,000. Incorporators, W. M. Scott, S. H. Fulton, M. P. Scott, L. R. Fulton, Washington, D. C.; A. H. Apperson, Atlanta, Ga.

Cutting Trees by Electricity.

It is reported in the German press that successful experiments have been made in various forests of France in cutting trees by means of electricity. A platinum wire is heated to a white heat by an electric current and used like a saw. In this manner the tree is felled much easier and quicker than in the old way; no sawdust is produced, and the slight carbonization caused by the hot wire acts as preservative of the wood. The new method is said to require only one-eighth of the time consumed by the old sawing process.

Toronto.

MILD WEATHER KEEPS BUSINESS DOWN.—AMERICAN BEAUTY SCARCE.—THE BEST CHRYSANTHEMUMS HELD FOR SHOW.—TRADE NOTES.

Business is only fairly good, the weather continuing too mild for social functions of any importance. There is also a noticeable falling off in funeral work, about the only trade being the ordinary counter sales. Chrysanthemums of course predominate at present and are in evidence in all the stores, making each place a show in itself. The finest blooms are not plentiful as most of them are being held back for the Horticultural show next week. Consequently the demand for the good blooms is above the average. Medium or small stock is plentiful and moving rather slowly with prices low. Several new seedlings of merit have made their appearance, though it will be hard to surpass Western King, Bonnaffon and other standard varieties. Even with the large supply of chrysanthemums find a ready sale, the excellent quality of American Beauty making the supply much less than the demand. Meteor, Bride and Bridesmaid are very good and some very good Morgan are offered. Carnations are more plentiful at present than they have been for years at this season and with the exception of very select blooms are hard to dispose of, the choice stock bringing $3 per hundred. Smaller stock can be had at almost any price. Violets have been much in demand and at present are scarce, which is unusual for this section. We are having many inquiries for double violets. In other seasons they have been hard to dispose of, but it seems that they will now become popular. Smilax and asparagus are plentiful and good. Good cyclamen plants are coming in from Grobba & Wandrey's place. Although they have not as many plants as in former years they are in much better shape. Chrysanthemums have done very well with them and another year will see an increased space devoted to their growing.

Several orchid decorations used up all the cattleyas which could be procured in this city. The local growers are loathe to part with their blooms as they are looking forward to the first prize at the show.

The many entries for the Horticultural exhibit which will be held in St. George's hall next week, foretell a successful show in point of blooms. Every foot of space will be occupied.

Some very good pansy blooms are sent from P. Fogarty's place. He says his plants are in fine shape and no doubt his special strain will prove as valuable as other years.

Manton Brothers are the first to cut Paper White narcissi. They are also cutting some very good oncidiums and Nephrolepis Piersoni.

Louis I. Vair, of Barrie, has been sending in some fine pink and white Ivory chrysanthemums. His Princess violets are also very good.

Arthur Frost is the first in this market with calla lilies, which find ready sale.
                                                H. G. D.

Syracuse, N. Y.

The quantity and quality of stock now on the market has not been equalled for a long time. Chrysanthemums have the lead and the sale of roses would be very much lessened were it not that several large funerals in the last week have made a good market for them. The feature of the fall trade is the demand for bulbous stock for outdoor planting. In speaking of this feature Henry Morris said: "I expect before many years to see in this country, as is the case abroad, yards all blooming with tulips, hyacinths and daffodils in the spring." There is every prospect of a good Thanksgiving trade. While money is not as plentiful as it has been, a fair share will be spent with the florists. Social events have not been well started as yet.

The Florists' and Gardeners' Society of Canandaigua is holding its first annual exhibition at the town hall. There are over 150 entries of flowers, potted plants, fruit and vegetables. Charles H. Tolly, of Madison, N. Y., a former florist of Sonnenberg, N. Y., is exhibiting five varieties of Australian chrysanthemums.

P. R. Quinlan & Company have a beautiful window of orchids, the blooms of which are selling at $6 a dozen. The firm is picking a large quantity of carnations from its new greenhouse at Onondaga Valley. Fine American Beauty may be seen here. They have 6-foot stems and bring from $5 to $10 a dozen.

Manager W. S. Wheadon, of P. R. Quinlan & Company's place, has returned from a three weeks' western trip, two weeks of which were spent hunting quail and partridge and one week in Chicago.

P. A. Bennett, the Watertown florist, is exhibiting a new carnation which he has been cultivating for three years. The blossoms measure four inches in diameter and are of a brilliant scarlet color.
                                                A. J. B.

DAHLIAS Pot Roots

Largest and most up-to-date collection in the world.
Cactus vars. of 1902 .... $12.00
    "   "   1901 .... 6.00
    "   "   1900 .... 5.00
    "   best of older vars .... 88.00 to 4.00
Pompon vars .... $4.00; newest 4.00
All per 100 in 25 or more sorts. Special price for 1000, 10,000 or 2000 lots. Carefully packed, f. o. b., Liverpool. Cash with order.

The Horticultural Company
CHEADLE-HULME, England.

THE PIERSON FERN

NEPHROLEPIS PIERSONI

The Most Valuable Novelty Introduced in Years

Awarded 6 Gold Medals

The Society of American Florists. The only gold medal ever awarded by the National Society.

The Massachusetts Horticultural Society. A rare distinction, having been awarded only a very few times in the history of the Society.

The Horticultural Society of New York. For 'the best horticultural novelty.

The Pennsylvania Horticultural Society. Pronounced "the star of the show."

The Great Kansas City Flower Show. For the best new plant of sterling merit.

The Rhode Island Horticultural Society.

Chicago Horticultural Society. The judges recommended that it be given the highest award possible in the gift of the Society.

Exceptional Awards

The highest honors that can be bestowed on any horticultural novelty in America, and an endorsement never before received by any other new plant.

Send for full Description and Price List.

Novelties in Chrysanthemums

Our introductions this season have been conceded to be wonderful improvements over previous introductions, but next year we shall offer

THE GRANDEST LOT OF NOVELTIES EVER SENT OUT

We desire to call particular attention to the

NEW PINK CHRYSANTHEMUM, DR. ENGLEHART

the finest commercial pink chrysanthemum ever introduced. This is going to be in pink chrysanthemums what Col. D. Appleton has been in yellow or Timothy Eaton in white—a phenomenal variety in every respect. Our exhibit of this variety won first prize for the best pink novelty in chrysanthemums at the New York Show.

We shall also have to offer the following varieties, which will be seen on the exhibition tables for the first time this year—WILLIAM DUCKHAM, MAYNELL, DONALD McLEOD, BEN WELLS, HENRY BARNES, CHELTONI, HARRISON DICK, MILDRED WARE, LADY ROBERTS, LEILA FILKINS, MARY INGLIS, F. A. COBBOLD, S. T. WRIGHT, and others, for which see Novelty List.

Novelties in Carnations

These are great improvements over existing varieties, and are exceedingly valuable introductions. Let us book your orders at once and secure early delivery.

WHITE LAWSON, DAHEIM, FLAMINGO, MRS. M. A. PATTEN, ALBATROSS, NELSON FISHER and SUNBIRD. Send for full description and prices.

F. R. PIERSON COMPANY
Tarrytown-on-Hudson, New York.

598   THE AMERICAN FLORIST.   Nov. 14,

OUR PASTIMES.

·Announcements of coming contests or other
events of interest to our bowling, shooting and
sporting readers are solicited and will be given
place in this column.
Address all correspondence for this department
to Wm. J. Stewart, 42 W. 28th St., New York.
Robt. Kift, 1725 Chestnut St., Philadelphia, Pa.;
or to the American Florist Co., Chicago, Ill.

At St. Louis.

·Following are the scores of the recent
bowling match. C. A. Kuehn carried off
the honors, both in individual high score
and totals:

Player.	1st	2d	3d	T'l
Kuehn	170	211	129	510
Baehie	173	155	171	499
Miller	159	153	102	364
Weber	162	180	141	479
Young	137	137	130	394
Weber	148	100		348

F. K. B.

At Colorado Springs, Col.

The Florists' Club bowlers, who are
preparing for the St. Louis convention
games, made the following scores last
week:

Player	1st	2d	3d	4th
Monaghan	140	141	77	
Braidwood	115	113	145	114
Vinson	155	107	119	105
Hayden	143	114	101	
Ruhl	148	100	146	162
Dunman	151	103	105	171
Johnson	107	182	161	179
Cramp	105	113	146	122
Harris	139	165	118	135
Baur	148	138	131	
Duff	151	145	128	
Harris	145	115	133	161

W. H. D.

At Chicago.

The bowlers crossed lances Tuesday
evening at the Giroux alleys in a set of
three games. The team captained by J.
G. Lambros won two of three games
rolled, Messrs. Lambros, E. F. Winterson
and Asmus rolling over the 200 mark.
The bowlers have not yet been organized
into regular teams and are now "picked"
from those who attend the sessions. Following are the scores in the last contest:

Player.	1st	2d	3d
Lambros	202	140	133
Concobos	177	166	120
E. F. Winterson	133	201	169
Ballard	172	176	131
Andrew	164	120	116
Foerester	192	183	180
	1040	1015	844
Stephens	149	163	172
Asmus	217	179	136
Hauswirth	153	164	146
Degnat	131	113	166
L. Winterson	109	101	121
Kreitling	128	195	190
	987	874	900

At Joliet.

One of the most pleasant features of
the Joliet show last week was that which
closed the three days' festivities Saturday
night, the banquet tendered the visitors
by the Joliet florists and members of the
Improvement Society. P. J. Hauswirth,
George Asmus, E. F. Winterson, Alex.
Newett, John Lambros, Joseph Foerester,
A. I. Simmons, August Lang, W. H. Kidwell and J. B. Deamud formed a party of
Chicago florists who were royally entertained by the hosts. They were met at
the depot by James Hartshorne and other
Joliet florists and escorted to a bowling
alley which had been previously arranged
for by the Joliet people. Here the Chicago
bowlers found themselves up against a
team which had been secured for the
occasion by Mr. Hartshorne. The Windy
City aggregation was defeated by the

tune of two games out of three. After
the regular match an individual encounter
was witnessed between J. Foerester and
George Asmus on the Chicago side and
Sheick and Hoffman on the other. This
time the Joliet colors were trailed in the
dust by the narrow margin of seven pins.
From the alleys the party was escorted
to the Elks' hall, where the tables groaned
under a sumptuous repast. The mayor
of the city acted as toastmaster and a
number of Chicago men responded. At
1:30 a. m. a fire alarm was turned in and
several companies and the chief responded
returning the call in the phenomenal
time of forty seconds. Later a patrol
wagon was called and the party was
given a free ride to the St. Nicholas hotel.
The scores in all the contests were as
as follows:

JOLIET.

Player.	1st	2d	3d
Fritz	·	159	145	188
Sehiok	156	158	171
Lindero	145	148	131
Olson	115	148	180
Perris	148	117	144
Hoffman	156	159	153
Totals	884	875	937

CHICAGO.

Player.	1st	2d	3d
Hauswirth	142	177	108
Lambros	146	140	197
Balluff	142	145	169
Asmus	162	183	195
Winterson	89	125	112
Foerester	156	149	160
Totals	837	919	807
Joliet Sheick	165	} 310
Hoffman	145	
Chicago Foerester	145	} 317
Asmus	172	

Chicago Bowling League.

To pick the men who will represent the
Chicago Florists' Club at the St. Louis convention games, Secretary Lambros of the
bowling club has divided the players into
four teams, as follows:

FIRST TEAM.	THIRD TEAM.
ASMUS.	BALLUFF.
E. WINTERSON.	CONCOBOS.
VOGNRAKIS.	DEGNAN.
PRIEBE.	L. WINTERSON.
SECOND TEAM.	FOURTH TEAM.
HAUSWITH.	LAMBROS.
STEPHENS.	MUNO.
W. KREITLING.	J. HUBBNER.
ANDREW.	FOERESTER.

On Tuesday evening next, November 17,
names will be given to the various teams.
A series of games will be played throughout the coming winter and spring to decide
who will represent Chicago at St. Louis.
It is also proposed to put up prizes as the
season goes on.

Philadelphia Bowling League.

The following are the rules governing the
bowling tournament of the Philadelphia
Florists' Club league, the makeup and
code of which were given in our last
issue:

1. The league shall consist of six five-
men teams, each member thereof to be an
active or associate member of the Florists'
Club of Philadelphia in good standing.
2. The teams shall be as nearly as possible of an equal strength and the basis of
such strength shall be the yearly average
of each member, counting from the twelve
months immediately preceding the date of
this contest. The selecting of the men for
each team shall be done by the committee.
3. Each team shall roll one game with
every other team in this league until the
series is complete, the total games won
to decide the winner at end of tourney.
Each game won is to count one point.
Ties at end of tournament to be rolled
off on date selected by committee. Best
two games in three to decide.
4. All games to be rolled on the home
alleys, one game each week, play commencing on Monday, November 16, and ending
Friday, December 18, 1903. Captain of
each team must notify his men of date of
contest.
5. The matches to be confined to Mondays,
Wednesdays and Fridays of each week, so
as to leave the other nights open for such
members of the club as are not participating
in this tournament.

6. In the absence of a member or two
members of any team on play night the
team shall be allowed to count the
yearly average computed by the committee
of such absent member or two members.
But if any member be absent more than
one night in succession when his team
is to play his place may, at the discretion
of the committee, be declared vacant and
another member appointed. No substitutes
allowed.
7. Players not on hand at finish of the
fifth frame of game being played shall
be given their average and must wait until commencement of next game to bowl.
8. Games to be called at 8 p. m. and
must be started at or before 8:30 p. m.
Should either team fail to produce a majority of its men by that time the captain
of the opposing team may claim the game;
provided the opposing team has a majority.
But if both teams are short of a majority
the game shall be void and shall be rolled
off on a subsequent date to be specified
by the committee.
9. Should there be a tie in the tenth
frame play shall continue on the same
alley until a majority of the points upon an
equal number of frames shall be attained—
the same manner of scoring to prevail in
rolling off ties as in the tenth frame.
10. A player in delivering his ball must
not step on or over the line nor allow
any part of his body to touch on or beyond
the line, nor any portion of his foot while
at rest to project over the line until after
the ball has reached the pins. Any ball
so delivered shall be deemed a foul and
the pins shall be respotted. Should any
ball leave the alley before reaching the
pins or any ball rebound from the back
cushions the pins must be respotted. All
such balls to count as balls rolled. Pins
knocked down by pin or pins rebounding
from the side or back to count as pins
down.
11. An official umpire and an official
scorer shall be agreed on by the captains
of opposing teams before commencing play.
A record shall be made of strikes, spares
and split spares, such record to be handed
to committee within twenty-four hours.
12. All disputed points to be referred to
committee for adjustment, their decision
to be final.
13. There shall be no entry money
charged in this contest, but all games to
be paid for at the usual price.
Team Prizes—First prize, to team winning greatest number of games in series,
to consist of a valuable trophy for each
man of the winning team; second prize, to
next highest; third prize, to next highest.
Individual Prizes—First prize for greatest number of strikes made in tournament;
second prize for greatest number of spares
made in tournament; third prize for greatest number of split spares made in tournament; fourth prize for greatest total aggregate in the tournament. (Note—A split
spare counts both as a spare and a split
spare.)
GEORGE C. WATSON,
GEORGE M. MOSS,
JOHN W. DURHAM,
Committee.

New Orleans.

Weather and business were good for
All Saints' Day. A few weeks ago it
looked like our chrysanthemum crop
would be short, but the quantity planted
was large and made up for a few failures
at some places. Everybody seems to be
satisfied, reporting an increase on last
year. We have been learning that it is
the quality which we must try to
improve. It is no use to plant so much
if you are not prepared to protect your
flowers at the right time and in the
proper way. Chrysanthemum growing
under glass in New Orleans will not be
done on a large scale for a long time, but
with good temporary structure of either
glass or canvas we can make a good
flower which will suit the larger part of
our trade.
Artificial designs sell very poorly.
Natural designs are not so much in
demand as bunches of assorted flowers.
M. M. L.

HARTFORD, MICH.—W. H. Blashfield
has a greenhouse nearly completed. He
will not grow any plants before spring.

Cincinnati.

REMARKABLE DEMAND FOR CHRYSANTHE-
MUMS AND CARNATIONS.—ROSES A GLUT
ON THE MARKET.—LOCAL ITEMS.

Chrysanthemums at the present are holding full sway and the remarkable thing is that very few of them are consigned to the barrel; in fact, for the last week everything in the shape of a chrysanthemum was sold. Carnations are coming in more plentifully and Will Murphy remarked that Tuesday was the first day this fall that he had a bunch of carnations on his counter after 10 o'clock in the morning. Bride and Bridesmaid are a glut, it being impossible to sell out half the amount received. The sale of valley has dropped off considerably the last week, but James Allan says the demand from out of town is good.

George Corbett is sending in fine chrysanthemums, violets and carnations to J. M. McCullough's Sons, his Princess of Wales violets being especially worthy of mention. Some very good Marie Louise violets are being shipped into the city and find a ready sale at top market prices. The demand for green goods has been up to the market and nearly everything received meets with fair sales.

Phil. Popp has a fine lot of Mrs. Henry Robinson carnations on his stand in the flower market. G. Bruffner's Sons have a fine lot of Appleton and Richard Witterstactter's carnations are the best displayed and meet with ready sale at good prices.

The news has just reached here that the greenhouses of Herman Ritter, at Dayton, O., were destroyed by fire Monday and the loss was very heavy. Mr. Ritter certainly has the sympathy of the craft in this city.

The chrysanthemum exhibition in the club rooms Saturday, November 14, promises to be successful.

Frank Benson is all smiles. It is a girl.

ALEX.

Cleveland.

C. Miles, greenhouse builder, has completed a fine private conservatory for L. E. Holden. Mr. Holden gave his gardener, Wm. Stade, the privilege of inviting all the members of the Florists' Club to inspect his place Saturday evening, November 7. They found a banquet spread for them with dancing afterwards.

H. Kuns has nearly finished planting violets. He says he would rather have women help than men, as they accomplish a great deal more.

At the last meeting of the Cleveland Florists' Club a stag social for the first Monday in December was arranged.

Fred Ponting has nearly completed his new range of houses.

O. G.

S. S. SKIDELSKY,

708 No. 16th Street,

Philadelphia, Pa.

Correspondence Solicited.

Please mention the American Florist when writing.

Carnation Cuttings

We are now booking orders for rooted cuttings. List of varieties and prices sent on application.

The Cottage Gardens, Queens, L. I.

Pittsburg.

STOCK MOVING WELL.—FLORISTS LAUGH AT HARD TIMES.—CLUB'S EXHIBIT GREAT SUCCESS. — CHRYSANTHEMUM SHOWS ATTRACT VISITORS.

A most enthusiastic meeting was held by the Pittsburg and Allegheny Florists' and Gardners' Club November 3. President Falconer deserves great credit for the many fine exhibits and the arrangements that made the meeting so successful. Chrysanthemums of many colors and kinds filled the room. The firms exhibiting were the E. G. Hill Company, Richmond, Ind.; F. R. Pierson, Tarrytown, N. Y.; R. Vincent, Jr., & Sons, White Marsh, Ind.; J. Galey, Beaver, Pa.; Blind Brothers, West View, Pittsburg; Pittsburg Cut Flower Company; Goodwin & Sons, Bridgeville, Pa., and the Phipps Conservatories, Pittsburg. Mr. Faulkner discoursed on the various qualities of each variety and brought forth much information of value and interest.

Stock is moving nicely, with no surplus accumulating. Chrysanthemums have proved a financial success in every respect this season. Orchids, both cattleyas and oncidiums, are short in supply. Lily of the valley and violets, too, move rapidly. American Beauty, Carnot, Bride and Bridesmaid roses are fine and not too plentiful. Greens are in plenty. Business has brightened up wonderfully, and the talk of the coming of hard times seems to depress no one.

Mrs. E. A. Williams will decorate the Duquesne garden for the Masonic ball on November 13.

P. S. Randolph is inspecting various locations near to Pittsburg with a view of building a big range of houses. Gas, water, good soil and good coal delivery are the points given most consideration.

Both wholesale houses report business good, especially the shipping trade, which is gaining in value each day.

At present, thousands of specimens of chrysanthemums are on display in Pittsburg and Allegheny. The most important displays are at the Phipps Conservatory in Schenly Park, the Phipps Conservatory in West Park, Allegheny, and at H. C. Frick's private houses, which are now open to the public.

The art exhibit and chrysanthemum shows cause all the railroads to grant special reduced rates to Pittsburg each Sunday, and thousands of visitors come.

Messrs. Keppner, Fitzsimons and Weaver, employes of Randolph & McClements, are suffering with various ailments and are off duty this week.

Graves and Reisch, of Beloit, O., have completed a new carnation house 20x50.

Geddes & Blind Brothers have opened their store on Fifth street. It is very complete and effectively decorated.

W. B. Ague has opened a store on the corner of Pennsylvania and Negley avenues, East End.   E. L. M.

Elkhart, Ind.

Henry Schenck's greenhouse, situated just north of the city limits, burned to the ground November 6. This is the second loss that has been inflicted upon Mr. Schenck by fire within a year, his house having burned last spring. Mr. Schenck is unable to explain the cause of the fire, as he had left the greenhouse and gone to his home just a few minutes before. The fire department was called, but was unable to reach the fire.

CHICAGO, OHIO.—John Klink has sold his business to Geo. A. Meyers and will leave for Cuba at once.

Just Arrived, Special Importation

AZALEAS

AZALEA INDICA.

All in the best condition.   All the very best sorts, such as

Simon Mardner,   Mme. Van der Cruyssen,
Vervaeneana,   Empress of India.
Prof. Walters,   Bernard Andrea A ba,
            Apollo, and many others.

Prices for assorted varieties; 25 per cent of any of the above sorts included in any assortment.

	Per Doz.	Per 100
10-inch crowns	$ 5.00	$35.00
12-inch crowns	6.00	45.00
12-inch crowns	7.50	55.00
16-inch crowns	9.00	65.00
18-inch crowns	12.00	
22-inch crowns	24.00	

ARAUCARIA EXCELSA.

4-inch pots,	8 to 10 inches high,	3 whorls	$ .60 each
5-inch pots,	12 inches high,	3 to 4 whorls	.75 each
6-inch pots,	20 inches high,	4 whorls	1.25 each
6-inch pots,	24 inches high,	4 to 5 whorls	1.50 each

ARAUCARIA COMPACTA.

5-inch pots,	12 inches high,	3 whorls	$1.50 each
6-inch pots,	14 inches high,	3 whorls	1.75 each
6-inch pots,	16 inches high,	3 whorls	2.00 each
7-inch pots,	19 inches high,	4 whorls	3.00 each

ARAUCARIA GLAUCA.

6-inch pots,	12 inches high,	3 whorls	$1.00 each
6-inch pots,	15 inches high,	3 whorls	1.50 each
7-inch pots,	18 inches high,	4 whorls	2.00 each
8-inch pots,	26 inches high,	4 whorls	4.00 each

Xmas or Celestial Pepper.

The plants are covered with bright colored, cone-shaped fruit and ready for sale over the counter. For immediate delivery.

5-inch pots		per dozen, $2.00;	per 100, $15.00
6-inch pots		per dozen, 3.00;	per 100, 20.00

Vaughan's Seed Store,

14 Barclay St., NEW YORK.   84-86 Randolph St., CHICAGO.
GREENHOUSES, WESTERN SPRINGS, ILL.

Please mention the American Florist when writing.

BOOKKEEPING and account forms for same by R. F. Tesson, as read at the Milwaukee convention has been printed in pamphlet form by the AMERICAN FLORIST and will be mailed FREE on request to any florist. Employers may have extra copies to distribute among their employes. The address is of much permanent value and well worth the study of our young men.

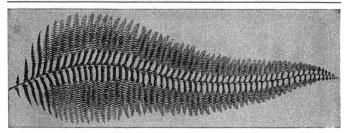

Lowell, Mass.

In the last two weeks we have been having summer weather, which has had telling effects in the way of producing blooms, especially bringing out chrysanthemums. These flowers are to be had at present in any size and quality. Growers who usually have plenty for Thanksgiving will lack them this year, if the warm weather continues. So far some excellent blooms have been sent in, blooms that ought to bring 50 cents each, but $3 and $4 a dozen are the top figures. With so many chrysanthemums on hand other stock has suffered, roses and violets especially. Roses of good quality are to be had for a song. With chrysanthemums at the same figure as roses, the former have the preference and roses will have to keep in the background for some time to come.

Every Saturday so far this fall one of the large department stores has been handling flowers and selling them at prices lower than the storemen could buy for. Of course quality was lacking.

A few wedding orders were executed last week, the largest being at the Putman-Lyman nuptials, but the decoration of the season has been booked by Patten to come Thanksgiving eve.

The Exeter Rose Conservatories, Exeter, N. H., are sending to town some excellent roses. Their Golden Gate and Mme. Chatenay just now are superb as are also their Kaiserin.

John J. McManmon was elected by a handsome majority to represent the Twenty-fifth district in the House of Representatives the coming year.

Business is humming along nicely. Funeral orders have been numerous. As the month advances trade is steadily on the gain.

Charles Mills, who is now in charge of the Ayer estate, is cutting some very fine Marechal Niel roses which are eagerly sought for.

Tom Waterworth is surprising everybody with his chrysanthemums from his two small houses in the cemetery.

Timothy Eatons, from Bourdy & Healy, on the boulevard, is making a hit with the public in Patten's window.   A. M.

Colorado Springs, Colo.

Flowers are coming in more plentifully, but the supply of roses and carnations is still limited. Chrysanthemums are being cut in large quantities and the quality is very fair. There are just about enough to keep pace with the good demand for both in and out of town. Prices range from $1 to $5 per dozen. Dwarf single-stem bench-grown plants, grouped in pots to order when in full bloom, are selling well, and make a far richer appearance than plants grown in pots, which are sold cheap and net a very small profit to the grower. Violets are appearing in increasing numbers, but are small as yet. Settled cool weather, with frosty nights and plenty of sunshine, has created greater activity in the trade. Weddings and funerals cut a considerable figure in the amount of work turned out and there are the usual receptions and and other social functions for the season. The summer tourist season has come to a close, but while transient visitors are disappearing permanent residents are returning home.

C. S. Davis has resigned his position as rose grower at William Clark's and taken a position in the horticultural department of the St. Louis World's Fair.
    S. S.

Greenwich, Conn.

Louis A. Martin, gardener at Malvern, W. H. S. Wood's beautiful estate, is an enthusiast on dahlias, particularly the cactus varieties, of which he has a very large collection including the most promising of the new sorts, under cultivation. Among the varieties most highly prized by Mr. Martin after trial and comparison during the past season, he enumerates Perle de la Tete d'Or, white, Stralenkrone, red, Stella, salmon-rose, Cornet, light salmon, Richard Wallace, bronzed yellow, Alfred Vasay, salmon, very dwarf, Standard Bearer, deep scarlet, Starfish, bright vermilion, Viscountess of Sherbrook, magenta, King of Siam, crimson magenta, Mrs. Charles Turner, yellow, John Bennett, salmon-vermilion, Papa Charmet, dark crimson, and Gloire de Paris, deep claret, all the above-named being cactus-flowered with the exception of the last which is in the decorative class.

A great many trees and shrubs of questionable or unproven hardiness are to be seen in Mr. Wood's grounds and in seemingly thrifty condition. One of the most sensational of these is the Citrus trifoliata which Mr. Martin tells us has withstood several winters successfully and is now well laden with its conspicuous golden fruit. A large bed of Abelia rupestris, another subject generally regarded as doubtful in this latitude, looks the picture of contentment and at November 1 is still flowering profusely. These abelias are planted where they are snugly protected from the morning sun and Mr. Martin advances the belief that such a location and the protection of a few leaves in cold weather is all that is necessary to success.

SOUTH ORANGE, N. J.—W. A. Manda has added another range of glass to his large plant here. The output of the Castlewood houses, owned by Geo. Atkinson, has been 40,000 this year, only a small portion of which is used by local trade, almost the whole going to New York commission houses.

$2.50 Per 1000

GIANT PANSIES, show varieties, strong, stocky plants, plenty of yellow and white.
DOUBLE DAISIES, Snowball. Giant, Longfellow.
SWEET WILLIAMS, double and single.
FORGET-ME-NOTS, blue, white and pink.
All the above are strong plants. We have ¼-acre in seed beds. 5,000 for $11.00.
HOLLYHOCK, single, mixed, 90c per 100. Double 4 colors, $1.00 per 100.
RUBBERS, 5-inch, 30 to 36-inches high, 30c.
ENGLISH IVY, field-grown, 2 to 3 feet, 8c.
CALIFORNIA PRIVET, 15 to 18-inch, branched, $8.00 per 1000.
ALYSSUM, double, 2-inch, strong, 2c.

Asparagus Sprengeri, 2-inch, strong, 8 cents each.
Primula Obconica Grandiflora, ALBA, ROSEA. $1.75 per 100; 300 for $5.00.

Boston Ferns.

Bench plants, fine for 5-inch pots, 10c. Runners $1.00 per 100. CASH.

BYER BROS., Chambersburg, Pa.

Chrysanthemums, for stock plants with strong, healthy stock of following varieties: Estelle, (early white); Appleton, (Yellow); Rieman, and Quito, (pink), at $3.00 per 100; Liger, (white), Yellow Chadwick and Yellow Eaton at $10.00 per 100. Asparagus Sprengeri, in 2¼-in. pots at $2.00 per 100. Grevillea Robusta, in 2¼-in. pots, at $2.50 per 100. Also a fine lot of Ferns, Araucarias and Rubbers. Prices on application.
RIDGE LAWN GREENHOUSES, Pine Ridge, Buffalo, N. Y.

Carnation Rooted Cuttings NOW READY.

WHITE.	Per 100	1000		SCARLET.	Per 100	1000	5000
Queen Louise	$1.30	$11.00	$50.	America	1.30	11.00	50.00
Flora Hill	1.30	11.00	50.	Estelle	1.80	14.00	65.00
Alba	3.40	30.00	125.	Mrs. Palmer	1.50	14.00	65.00
Wolcott	3.40	30.00	125.	Apollo	3.50	30.00	125.00
Los Angeles	3.00	25.00	100.	Adonis	7.00	65.00	300.00
Norway	1.80	11.00	50.	CRIMSON.			
Lillian Pond	6.00	50.00	250.00	Harlowarden	5.00	45.00	200.00
White Cloud	1.30	11.00	50.00	Gov. Roosevelt	1.30	11.00	50.00
PINK.				Gen. Maceo	1.30	11.00	50.00
Lawson	1.40	12.50	60.	Gen. Gomez	1.30	11.00	50.00
Marquis	1.30	11.00	50.	Harry Fenn	3.00	25.00	100.00
Genevieve Lord	1.30	11.00	50.	YELLOW.			
Argyle	1.30	11.00	50.	Golden Beauty	1.75	16.00	75.00
Mrs. Joost	1.30	11.00	50.	Eldorado	1.30	11.00	50.00
Mermaid	1.30	11.00	50	Gold Nugget	1.50	14.00	65.00
Guardian Angel	1.30	11.00	50.	VARIEGATED.			
Mrs. Higinbotham	2.50	20.00	90.	Violania (4-inch bloom)	12.00	100.00	450.00
Cressbrook	3.50	30.00	90	Marshall Field	5.00	45.00	200.00
Mrs. Roosevelt	6.00	55.00	225.	Tiger (Fancy)	5.00	45.00	200.00
Enchantress	5.00	55.00	250.00	Stella	3.00	25.00	100.00
Success	5.00	45.00	200.00	Bradt	1.75	16.00	70.00
SCARLET.				Armazindy	1.30	11.00	50.00
G. H. Crane	1.40	12.50	60.00	Prosperity	1.30	11.00	50.00

Twenty-five at 100 rates; 250 at 1,000 rates; 2,500 at 5,000 rates.

Terms: SPOT CASH. No discount given. no matter how large the order. We prepay express charges at above figures to your city. If on arrival they are not satisfactory return at once, and money will be refunded at once; we cannot vary from these terms.

CALIFORNIA CARNATION CO., Lock Box 103, LOOMIS, CAL.

CARNATIONS.

A fine lot of Rooted Cuttings Ready Now.

ENCHANTRESS.	LILLIAN POND.
$6.00 per 100; $50.00 per 1000.	$5.00 per 100; $40.00 per 1000.

Let us book your order for **The Queen** $5.00 per 100 $40.00 per 1000.

Ready December 1st.

PROSPERITY, $3.00 per 100; $25.00 per 1000. LAWSON, $3.00 per 100; $25.00 per 1000.

LARCHMONT NURSERIES, Larchmont, N. Y.

Adiantum Farleyense.

6,000 strong 4-in. plants, $20 per 100
3,000 strong 3-in. plants, $12 per 100

W. A. HAMMOND,
RICHMOND, VA.

CHRYSANTHEMUM Stock Plants.

Halliday, Coombes, Adrian, Robinson, Cadbury, Chadwick, Yanariva, K. C. Star, 30c.
Alice Byron, Mrs. F. J. Trotter, splendid new whites, F. J. Taggart, new hairy yellow, Gold. Mine, 15c.
50 to 75 varieties in smaller quantities. Prices on application. No order filled for less than $2.

W. A. CHALFANT,
Springfield, MO.

'MUM STOCK PLANTS.

Strong plants carefully packed. Omega, finest early yellow and Geo. S. Kalb the choicest early white. $5.00 per 100. 75c per doz. The following standard sorts at $4.00 per 100; 60c per doz.: Ivonne, White Bonnaffon, Robinson, Modesto, Childs, Glory of Pacific, Polly Rose, Ivory, pink and white. Montmort, Wanamaker, Appleton, and Mrs. A. Parr. About 1,000 3-inch SPRENGER left, ready for 3-inch pots, at $2.00 per 100. We are headquarters for Carnation, Chrysanthemum and Stevia Cuttings in season.

JOHN BROD, Wholesale Florist, NILES-CENTER, ILL.

SurplusStock CHEAP.

Asparagus Sprengeri, 3-inch pots	$ 4.00
Asparagus Plumosus, 2¼-inch pots	.3.00
Kentia Forsteriana, 3-inch pots	15.00
Kentia Forsteriana, 4-inch pots	30.00
Latania Borbonica, 5-inch pots	40.00
Adiantum Cuneatum, 4-inch pots	15.00
Nephrolepis Wittboldi, 3-inch pots	8.00
Dracæna Indivisa, from flats	1.50

Stock Chrysanthemums.

Yellow Eaton; Columbia, Mrs. R. Smith, $20.00 per 100.
R. E. Richardson, Marie Liger, $12.00 per 100.
Philadelphia, Timothy Eaton, Golden Wedding, Gold Mine, Silver Wedding, Thorndon, $10.00 per 100.
Geo. W. Childs, Viviand-Morel, Col. Appleton, Mutual Friend, Autumn Glow, Fitzwygram, Robinson, Yellow Robinson, Gladys Vanderbilt, Polly Rose, Robt. Halliday, Mrs. Perrin, Jerome Jones, Yellow J. Jones, Maud Dean, Bonnaffon, White Bonnaffon, Riverside, Mrs. Whildin, Ivory, Bergmann, Glory of Pacific, $5.00 per 100.

WALKER & McLEAN,
YOUNGSTOWN, O.

Please mention the American Florist when writing.

Buffalo.

WEATHER NOT COLD ENOUGH.—CHRYS-
ANTHEMUM SHOW OPENS.—STOCK IN
GOOD SHAPE.—TRADE NOTES.

Chrysanthemums, American Beauty
and violets are in good shape, also Bride
and Bridesmaid. Timothy Eaton and
Yellow Eaton are with us in profusion.
Timothy Eaton is a large exhibition
flower, but when grown smaller sells
more readily. Window displays are
principally of chrysanthemums.

In Palmer's uptown store everything
Arthur Beyer puts in, no matter how
small, is a decoration, as the window and
surroundings are such as make a bunch
of American Beauty, orchids or chrysanthemums arranged in his usual artistic
manner an attractive show.

W. J. Palmer & Son have had a pretty
wedding and several receptions of fair
proportion in Buffalo the past two
weeks. A large and expensive wedding
order was booked by a Main street florist
last week, the ceremony in the near
future.

The weather has been favorable,
although not quite cold enough. Trade
has been normal, the election making last
week quiet. The chrysanthemum show
opened November 11. Nearly all the
florists are exhibiting.

We hear that Geo. E. Fancourt, Kingston, Pa., is going to visit us and be a
judge. It will be a treat to see him.

Chas. Newman, formerly at Anderson's
greenhouse, is now managing J. H. Rebstock's place in Lancaster.

We are all looking forward to L. H.
Neubeck's opening at his neat and modern
place.

S. J. Rebstock has left Buffalo and is
going to locate in Waynesville, N. C.

Recent visitors: Harry Bunyard, N. Y.;
H. Dillemuth manager for J. H. Dunlop,
Toronto. BISON.

Nashville.

Chrysanthemum plants are in great
demand here and local dealers report a
fine trade. All kinds of plants, those
with many and those with few blossoms,
are sold. The trade in cut flowers also
has been fine. Appleton, Timothy Eaton
and Chadwick are the most popular
varieties.

To meet the increased demand for flowers both Geny Brothers and the Joy &
Son Company have added extensively to
their plants. Geny Brothers added six
new houses, four of them 25x115 and
two 25x140. They also built a palm
house and a propagating house.

A recent addition to the Geny family
was an infant daughter, born to Leon
Geny, the manager of the up-town store,
whose face glowed with pleasure as he
announced the arrival of the little
stranger, the first to make its advent in
his home.

Violets are not coming in very bounti-
fully as yet, and are for the most part
small. Roses are being held back until
the trade in chrysanthemums is over, but
there is a good demand for most that are
brought in. M. C. D.

ELMIRA, N. Y.—William Algie, president
of the United States Cut Flower Company, threw out the first shovelful of
earth preparatory to the erection of the
gigantic conservatories near Elmira
Heights, October 28. "The houses will
be filled with growing plants by the last
of June," asserted Mr. Algie.

THE GLENWOOD NURSERIES

EVERGREENS.
The largest and most complete assortment of SPECIMENS sheared and of natural form. All root pruned and carefully grown.
EVERGREEN TREES, EVERGREEN SHRUBS and VINES for Window Boxes and winter Decorations.

DECIDUOUS TREES.
20,000 Oriental Plane Trees, 5 to 14 feet.
25,000 Oaks, in variety, 6 to 14 feet.
100,000 Maples, in variety, 8 to 18 feet.
Beech, Birch, Ash, Elms, Ginkgo, Poplars, and other leading varieties.

HEDGE PLANTS.
200,000 California Privet, 1 to 4 feet. She finest growth.
Osage Orange, Berberis Thunbergii, Althaeas, etc.

FLOWERING SHRUBS.
15,000 Hydrangea Paniculata Grandiflora, 1 to 4 feet.
5,000 Deutzias (Gracilis and Lemoinei), for forcing.
A complete assortment of Shrubs of all sizes, including quantities of large shrubs for immediate effect plantings, as well as smaller grades.

CLIMBING VINES.
English and Irish Ivies, Wistarias and other vines.
Crimson Rambler, Wichuraiana and other climbing and running roses.
5,000 Ampelopsis Veitchii, 1 and 2 years.
30,000 Hall's Japan Honeysuckle.
20,000 Clematis Paniculata.

SPECIAL QUOTATIONS TO LARGE BUYERS.   NEW TRADE LIST NOW READY.
DESCRIPTIVE ILLUSTRATED CATALOGUE ON APPLICATION.

THE WM. H. MOON CO., Morrisville, Pa.
60 MILES FROM NEW YORK.   30 MILES FROM PHILADELPHIA.

NOW IS THE TIME TO ORDER

	Per 100
Exochorda Grfl., 18 to 24-inch, bushy....	$ 6.00
Lonicera, ½ Belgica and Heckrotti, 3 to 4 feet, bushy....	8.00
Ampelopsis Japonica, 2¼-inch pots....	4.00
Cedrus Deodara, 15 to 18-inch....	25.00
Cedrus Deodara, 20 to 24-inch....	30.00
Oranges, best sorts, grafted, bearing size 12-inch, bushy, 4-inch pots....	30.00
Ligustrum Amurense, true, 2 to 3-feet branched....	

	Per 100
Oranges, 15 to 18-inch, 5-inch pots......	$0.00
Lemons, grafted, 18 to 24-inch, 5-inch pots....	
Kentia Belmoreana, 13 to 15-inch, 5 leaves	18.00
Latania, 18-inch, 3 to 4 ch. leaves......	20.00
Phoenix Canariensis, 15 to 18-inch, 5 to 8 leaves, showing character........	18.00
Not less than 50 of a kind at above prices.....per 1000, $20.00

Write for Wholesale and Descriptive Catalogue.

P. J. BERCKMANS CO., (Inc.)
FRUITLAND NURSERIES,
Established 1856.   AUGUSTA, GA.

Geraniums.
Rooted cuttings of Jean Viaud, Riccard, Nutt, Perkins, LaFavorite and Mme. Bruant, $1.00 per 100; $10.00 per 1000.
Unrooted Cuttings of above varieties 70c per 100; $6.50 per 1000. Will prepay express on above for 15c per 100; $1.00 per 1000, carefully packed in damp moss.
SMARTA DAISIES from seed bed sown thin, strong, healthy plants, 60c for 50; $1.00 per 100, express prepaid. Cash with order.

DES MOINES PLANT CO.,
Thirty-eighth Street, DES MOINES, IOWA.

Chinese Primrose International Strain, 4-inch, $1.50 per doz.
$10.00 per 100; 3-in., $5.00; 3½-in., $2.50 per 100.
PRIMULA OBCONICA GRANDIFLORA, extra, fine Stock 4-in. extra heavy, $12.00 per 100. Choice 4-in. $10.00 per 100; 3, 3½ and 3-in. at $8.00, $2.50 and $2.00 per 100. CYCLAMEN GIGANTEUM, mixed colors, well grown, and well budded, extra heavy 5-in. $3.00 per doz., 4-in. extra large, $12.00 per 100; 4-in. choice, $10.00 per 100. Also choice Cut Carnations and Mums. Rex Begonia, 2-in. $4.00 per 100, fine varieties.

H. G. CASWELL, Delavan, Ill.

Ferns and Geraniums 10,000 Boston Ferns in 2, 3, 4, 5, 6 and 7-inch pots at $3.00, $15, $25, $40 and $80 per 100. Cut from bench $2, $6, $12, $20, $30 and $50 per 100. Allstrong, fine plants. 100,000 Geraniums, Nutt, Hetheranthe, LaFavorite, Buckner, Perkins, Double Grant, A. Riccard, single Scarlet and Mme. Salleroi, R. C. $10.00 per 100; 2-inch, $2.00 per 100. Other 20 varieties, including M. Castellane, Jean Viaud, Mme. Jaulin, R. C. $1.50; 2-inch $2.50 per 100.

L: Mosbaek, 85th St., near S. Chicago Ave., Chicago.

PLEASE mention the AMERICAN FLORIST every time you write to an advertiser.

Clematis, Hardy Shrubs, Roses, Etc.
Buy now and get first choice of stock. Prices will be higher and stock not so select in the Spring. If not planted now, these hardy plants keep well heeled in the open ground and will be ready in Spring when wanted.
Clematis, finest large-flowered sorts, purple, white, lavender, red, etc., 2-year, 18c; 1-yr., 8c.
Clematis Paniculata, extra, 10c.; 2-Year, 6c; second size, 4c.
Ampelopsis Veitchii, 2-yr., fine, 10c; second size, 6c.
American Ivy, 2-year, fine, 8c. Japanese Ivy, 8c.
Roses assorted, H. P. varieties, Coquette des Alps, Jules Margottin, Gen'l Jacqueminot, etc.; also Crimson and Yellow Rambler and the newer trailing roses, 2-year, first size, 15c; second size, 7c.
Clothilde Soupert, finest pot rose grown, first size, 10c. Second size, 7c.
Crimson Rambler XXX, selected long canes for forcing, 30c.
Hydrangea Pan. Grand., finest hardy shrub, bushy plants, 10c; fine three-shaped specimens, very handsome, 25c.
Golden Glow, most popular perennial, 5c.
Hardy Phlox, choicest varieties, 10c.
Peonies, in fine assortment, 10c.
Deutzias, including LeMoine and Gracilis, Althaeas, Weigelias, Honeysuckles, Spiraeas, Japan Quinces, etc., best sorts and three, 10c.
California Privet Evergreens for pots and boxes, Fruit and Ornamental Trees, etc.
Careful attention to large or small orders, with expert packing free and as light as consistent with safety. Cash, please.

W. H. SALTER, Rochester, N. Y.

A FINE LOT OF

FERNS.
Assorted varieties, in 3½ and 3-inch pots at $3.00 per 100.

WAGNER PARK CONSERVATORIES,
SIDNEY, OHIO.

Exhibition at Monmouth County, N. J.

The sixth annual exhibit of the Monmouth County Horticultural Society was held in the town hall at Red Bank. N. J., November 3, and 4. Some wonderful blooms were shown. George Hale, manager of E. D. Adams' place, had some White Carnot blooms 2½ feet in circumference. In the event for six white blooms Mr. Hale won first with Merza. William Turner, manager of the M. C. D. Borden estate, was second with Nellie Pockett. In the six yellows class N. Butterbach, gardener for C. N. Bliss was first with Mrs. E. Thirkell, a grand yellow over 9 inches in diameter. William Turner got second with Lord Salisbury, also a new variety and a beautifully built bloom. Appleton was shown in several classes and in the best shape, but could not compete with the newer varieties.

In the class for crimsons George Hale won first with H. J. Jones, and Mr. Tierney. gardener for Mr. Hartshorn, was second with N R Church. In the class for pink Mr. Hale won first with Balfour. In any other color Mr. Hale was first with Brutus. In the twelve specimen blooms event Mr. Hale won first with Charles Longley. Mrs. T. W. Pockett, Merza. Appleton. John Pockett. T. Carrington. G. J. Warren. White Cargot. Brutus. Peter Kay and Dagier. William Turner got second in this class. For thirty-six blooms in six varieties William Turner got first with Mabel Morgan. H. J. Jones, Merza. T. Carrington. Nellie Pockett and Peter Kay. George Hale got second. There was much excitement and betting among the exhibitors as to which of the two would win in this event and the judges had a long and careful deliberation. Mr. Turner was victorious by two points. Mr. Hale's White Carnot could not hold upright a bloom ten inches in diameter without support.

There were four entries of vases of twenty-five blooms for effect. George Hale won first and N. Butterbach second. For chrysanthemums in pots in a group of seventy-five square feet N. Butterbach won an easy first, with A. J. Williams, gardener for Telmar Hess, second. In roses George Hale got first for American Beauty and W. W. Kennedy. gardener for M. A. Friedman. Red Bank. was second. For Bride roses Mr. Tierney got first and N. Butterbach second. For Bridesmaid Mr. Tierney got first and Mr. Hale second. In any other Varieties George Hale got first for Morgana. In carnations. pink. Mr. Turner was first. Mr. Kennedy second. For white. Mr. Turner was first with Queen and Mr. Tierney second with Flora Hill. In red Mr. Turner was first with Harlowarden and Tierney second with Maceo. In yellow and any other color Mr. Turner won. Enchantress was shown by Mr. Turner for exhibition only. The blooms measured 3½ inches in diameter. Two big vases of Bride and Bridesmaid roses not for exhibition were shown by Frank McMahon. of Seabright.

For greenhouse grapes. Geo. Hale got first for two fine bunches of Lady Downie's seedling. There were a few entries in violets. but they were not of much account. For foliage plants in a group of 100 square feet. H. A. Kettel, gardener for James Loeb, and James Dowlen. gardener for General Terrell, had a very close competition and after a critical examination Mr. Dowling got first and H. A. Kettel second. For specimen palms N. Butterbach got first and Geo. Hale second. For any other foliage plants Geo. Hale got first and N. Butterbach second. For six specimen ferns J. Dowlen got first. For one specimen fern A. G. Williams got first. For six table plants J. Dowlen got first and A. G. Williams second.

The vegetable classes were well filled. In the collection of twelve varieties Comba & Downing. Madison. N. J., had an excellent exhibit. but were disqualified on account of too many varieties. The committee decided to give them a special prize. H. A. Kettel received special mention for other prize winners in vegetables and fruits were W. W. Kennedy. H. A. Kettel. J. Dowlen. Geo. Kuhn. Wm. Turner and Hugh McCarron, gardener to W. F. Havemeyer. who was also a prize winner with three specimen plants. W. W. Kennedy and Frank Hodges. of Red Bank, had over a hundred fancy pigeons on exhibition in the outer hall, which were a great attraction.
B.

CLINTON, MASS.—F. P. Sawyer, while doing some repairs in his greenhouse, had his face badly cut by a piece of falling glass one afternoon last week.

Denver.

TWO HIGHLY SUCCESSFUL FLOWER SHOWS ARE THE EVENTS OF THE WEEK.—CITY PARK CHRYSANTHEMUMS ATTRACTING LARGE CROWDS.—OTHER NOTES.

The Daniels & Fisher Company's chrysanthemum show, held on Wednesday and Thursday of last week, was a very satisfactory affair. The show was well advertised and the attendance for the two days was very large. The jam on Thursday afternoon was such that one could with difficulty elbow through. The exhibits were arranged along the middle aisle, down the center of which were arranged pyramidal groups of plants. The crowds walked down the right of these groups and came back on the other side, so as to facilitate the movement and avoid congestion. On both sides of the main aisle, the cut chrysanthemums were placed among the pyramidal groups. Some pretty arrangements were seen, one of Mrs. Robinson, a group of araucarias and one of yellow being very fine. In among these groups were staged four specimen plants, sent by Vaughan's Greenhouses, which were highly admired. One was a large standard plant of Yanariva, another a beautiful specimen of the old variety, Louis Boehmer, and two large standards of grafted variety.

At the entrance stood an arrangement of tiers, in which stood Sprengeri plants and Bridesmaid roses. In the center of this arrangement stood a fountain, lending a pretty effect to the scene. Of the home grown exhibits, specimen plants of Mrs. Weeks were the best. The best vase of cut flowers shown was one of twenty fine Timothy Eaton chrysanthemums. The next best was a vase of Philadelphia. Several good vases of Weeks were shown. But this variety, though grand, will not do; it soon went down and on the second day when others stood up this variety was badly wilted. Some of the other varieties shown were Col. D. Appleton, Bloodgood, Viviand Morel, a very good vase of Golden Wedding; also one of Silver Wedding, Lavender Queen, (this variety looks good) Xeno, O. P. Bassett, Robinson and several others. E. G. Hill sent a collection, as did Nathan Smith & Son; each set contained some grand blooms. In roses they showed a fine vase of Bridesmaids, Brides and Chatenays, while the vase of Liberties would be hard to beat. The vase of Beauty was exceptionally good. They also showed a decorated table and mantel, which were altered each day. The balcony over the aisle where the show was given was decorated with southern smilax. At one end of the balcony, hidden by palms, a quartette played. The exhibition was under the charge of Mr. Bush, flower store manager of the company, assisted by Benjamin Boldt, whose handiwork in decorating did much to make the show a success.

At the greenhouses of the City park, the show of chrysanthemums has never been so fair as this year. Frank Rushmore, the foreman, and Adam Kohanke, the grower, justly feel proud. Enormous crowds have taken advantage of the free show which does much to help the trade in general. While the quality of stock grown at this place is perhaps much better than that grown for commercial purposes, the price would be in relative proportions and the flower buying public like what they can pay for, and only look at these giant specimens. Several new varieties are grown here but I will give you a general list of the good things as I saw them, Mr. Kohanke says that the

best was an exhibit of Colonel Appleton and most admired, and they certainly looked it. Of the others there were Carrington, W. J. Bryan, Higinbotham, Frank Hardy, Pennsylvania (very fine), Niveus, Golden Wedding, Nogaya, Bloodgood, Eaton, Jerome Jones, Georgiana Pitcher, Lavender Queen, Iora, Constance, Sunstone, L. D. Black, E. M. Bigelow, Yanariva, Viviand-Morel, Robinson, O. P. Bassett and Mrs. Weeks.

In pot plants a few good specimens of G. Pitcher are grown, mostly as standards. Pot chrysanthemums in general are good. B.

The Park Floral Company has announced that it will soon open the new store on Broadway and after about January 1 will abandon the present location. There has been a good deal of discussion as to how much of its trade the firm will be able to carry up town to the new location. Numerous rumors of new stores to take advantage of the opening have been current, and one of these was to the effect that a store would be opened by Philip Scott, who is now in charge for the Park Floral Company. In response to inquiry he has said to Mr. Valentine that he wished to leave on the first of the year when the present store is vacated and that he had secured the services of Mr. Reynolds, his present assistant. This, of course, complicates the situation for the Park Floral Company, and it will be interesting to watch developments.

Milwaukee.

BUSINESS GOOD BUT HEAVY RECEIPTS MAKE A SURPLUS.—CARNATIONS SELL SLOWLY.—PINK CHRYSANTHEMUMS ARE SCARCE.

Although business has been good the last week the market has been filled with stock and it has been next to impossible to clean out. The present cold weather may shorten the supply but possibly hardly enough to counterbalance the rush of chrysanthemums which is now at its highest point. A peculiar condition in regard to chrysanthemums is the scarcity of pink ones and the exceptionally heavy receipts of yellows. Carnations are arriving in large quantities with slow sale at present, except for the best stock. There are altogether too many Evanston blooms on the market at present. Roses had a slow sale with the the exception of Chatenay, which is in good demand.

Heitman & Baerman are sending in fine carnations and are also busy with cuttings, of which they will send out a considerable quantity.

Ben Gregory, who has been laid up for some weeks, is able to be about again with the aid of crutches.

Miss Emma Timm, a sister-in-law of R. Preuss, died November 7, after a short illness.

Chas. Burmeister intends to build an addition to his large plant.

Fred Schmeling is marketing good Eatons. H.

Exhibition at Lenox, Mass.

The third annual exhibition of the Lenox Horticultural Society was held October 27, 28 and 29. The display of cut flowers was better than ever, the hall being crowded with exhibits. The groups were also very fine. The winning varieties in chrysanthemum classes were Mrs. Robinson, Merza, Mrs. Coombes, Mrs. G. Mileham, T. Carrington, Peter Kay, Col. Appleton and H. J. Jones. A large number of the newer introductions were shown in the classes calling for distinct varieties. John Pockett, Mrs. E. Thirkell, Edward VII, Baden-Powell, Loveliness, C. J. Salter, Yellow Eaton, Mrs. J. C. Neville and a number of others being included. The carnation exhibit was larger than usual. Lawson, Harry Fenn, G. H. Crane and Enchantress being the leading varieties. The vegetables were very good. The exhibits were made principally by cottagers. The credit for the fine appearance of the plants belongs to the gardeners of the exhibitors.

John Dallas, gardener for George H. Morgan, won two second prizes for crysanthemum plants, one first and two third prizes for cut chrysanthemums; one first, two second and one third prize for cut carnations; one first and one second for violets, and one first and one third prize for ferns.

George Thompson, gardener for H. H. Cook, won one first, four second and two third prizes for cut chrysanthemums; three second prizes for roses; one first, one second and one third prize for cut carnations, and one second prize for ferns.

R. A. Smith, gardener for G. G. Haven, won two first prizes for chrysanthemum plants; one first, three second and three third prizes for cut chrysanthemums; three first and one third prize for cut carnations, and one second prize for ferns.

A. H. Wingett, gardener for Charles Lanier, won one third prize for a plant group; one second prize for chrysanthemum plants; three first prizes for cut chrysanthemums; one second and one fourth prize for cut chrysanthemums; two first prizes for violets; one first and two third prizes for ferns, and one first prize for orchids.

S. Carlquist, gardener for Mrs. Robert Winthrop, won one first prize for chrysanthemum plants; two first prizes for cut chrysanthemums; two first prizes for roses; one third prize for violets, and one first and two second prizes for carnations.

R. Jenkins, gardener for Girard Foster, won one first prize for a plant group; two first and one third prize for chrysanthemum plants; two first and two third prizes for cut chrysanthemums; five first and one third prize for roses; two second prizes for violets, and one first prize for ferns.

F. Heermans, gardener for W. D. Sloan, won one second prize for a group of plants; two first and two second prizes for roses; three first, one second and one third prize for carnations; one first prize for orchids; and one second prize for ferns.

A. J. Loveless, gardener for John Sloan, won one first, three seconds and one third prize for cut chrysanthemums; one second and one first prize for cut carnations, and one second prize for orchids.

Exhibition at Tuxedo, N. Y.

The second annual flower exhibition of the Tuxedo Horticultural Society, given under the auspices of the Tuxedo Club, opened November 6 at the club house. There was a fine display of all kinds of chrysanthemums, terns, potted plants, carnations, roses and violets.

The horticultural society, which was organised a little over two years ago, has as members a large number of the Tuxedo society leaders, including Pierre Lorillard, George Griswold, Richard Delafield, Richard Mortimer, George P. Baker, Price Collier, William Kent, Henry W. Poor, Charles M. Alexander, John Murray Mitchell, T., Suffern Tailer and, in fact, nearly all of the owners of cottages in Tuxedo Park.

The judges were I. J. Powell, of Millbrook, gardener to Mr. Samuel Thorn; William Turner, of Oceanic, gardener to Mr. Borden, and William Scott, of Tarrytown. Special prizes were offered for special exhibits of chrysanthemums, bush plants, foliage plants and vegetables by Charles Alexander, Henry W. Poor, Theodore Frelinghuysen and A. D. Juilliard.

C. R. Alexander's special prize of $25 for best twelve blooms of chrysanthemums was won by William Hastings, and the special prize for a table of Rex begonias was won by Carl D. Schaefer.

New Jersey Floricultural Society.

The ninth show in the contest for the four silver cups of the New Jersey Floricultural Society took place November 6 at the society's rooms in Orange, N. J. This series was inaugurated by President George Smith last March; was maintained through the summer months without any falling off of interest, and will terminate next month, when the cups will be given to those securing the highest number of points. The last meeting drew out the full strength of the society and the display, besides the usual merit in point of cultivation, was marked by tasteful arrangement and variety of bloom. President George Smith, gardener for Sydney Colgate, staged his own big chrysanthemum and rose blooms, set off by crotons and greenhouse foliage plants against a solid back of palms. His carnations were mingled, which made them particularly effective—more so than by placing each individual kind by itself and without losing any interest to the generality of observers. His fruit was at one side. Screens of Begonia Gloire de Lorraine in 6-inch pots grown by Detrick Kindsgrab, gardener for Wm. Runkle, and masses of alamada from John Hayes, gardener for O. D. Munn, concealed the office of the treasurer. A pyramidal group of chrysanthemums and palms with a mingling of dracena, having Balfour for a center, surrounded by Garza, was exhibited by Wm. Bennett, gardener for A. C. Van Gasbeck, and was effective at a long distance. Peter Duff, gardener for John Crosby Brown, had just returned from Madison, where he carried off ten firsts, but had reserved some fine blooms for this show, which filled most of one side. His vegetables in another part of the room were excellent.

Chas. Ashmead, gardener for Mrs. Wm. Pierson, exhibited single blooms grouped and bordered by pompons unrelieved, an arrangement simple and effective. His display of fruit and vegetables was large. Malcolm Macrorie brought his specimen ferns from the Mandeville estate. Max Schneider, gardener for Mr. Merck, of Llewellyn Park, brought violets. Geo. Von Qualen, gardener for A. B. Jenkins, exhibited a vase of seedling carnations. John N. May's new rose, General McArthur, was supported on either side by a group of his new chrysanthemums. W. A. Manda had his new pink chrysanthemum, Dr. Englehardt, which attracted attention throughout the evening.

Nor were orchids forgotten. Masses of dendrobium and cattleya from the houses of John Crosby Brown and Mrs. Mandeville adorned the sides of the entrance or marked the division between the exhibits against a back of kentias. The attendance was large, though only a paragraph in the evening papers had noticed the event. It included all the patrons who donated the silver cups and the general public, with a good representation of members and their friends, who look forward to the December meeting, the final one of the contest, when the awards will be given according to the number of points for the entire series.
J. B. D.

LAWRENCE, N. Y.—It has been decided by the Lawrence-Cedarhurst Horticultural Society that there will be no chrysanthemum show here this year.

Columbus.

Carnations are quite plentiful now in this section and the quality is very good. Nelson is one of the best varieties we have of its color. Our soil seems to be just what it prefers. Enchantress is also making an excellent showing. Roses are reported as doing exceptionally well this season with good prospects for a fine holiday cut. Bridesmaid and Golden Gate are the only varieties grown. American Beauty and Liberty, being left for growers more successful with them than Columbus growers have been.

Underwood Brothers claim to have a new variety of red rose which they have named the Morton Scarlet. CARL.

Kramer's Pot Hangers

THE neatest, simplest, most convenient and only practical device for converting ordinary flower pots into hanging baskets. They fit all standard made pots from 2 to 10 inches in diameter. The illustration shows how they are attached. Just the thing for hanging up ferns, begonias, etc. You can make room and money by their use. Try them. For Sale by

Vaughan's Seed Store, Chicago and New York.
E. F. Winterson Co., Chicago.
C. C. Pollworth Co., Milwaukee, Wis.

Price with wire chain as shown in cut, $1.00 per dozen by express. Sample dozen by mail, $1.25.

I. N. KRAMER & SON, Cedar Rapids, Iowa.

UNIQUE AND USEFUL TO U

Send at once for our New Catalogue of

PREPARED PALMS, Fibre Moss, Grasses, Cork Bark, Birch Bark, etc.

Palm Supplies Co. 83 Washington St., CHICAGO.

Standard Flower... POTS

If your greenhouses are within 500 miles of the Capitol, write us, we can save you money.....

W. H. ERNEST, 28th and M Streets, WASHINGTON, D. C.

American Flower and Tree Tub Made from Everlasting Cypress. Various sizes, green or natural finish. Casting black. Feet and bolts packed inside tub for shipment. We also have the neatest Plant Stand on the market. Send for catalogue B 905.

American Wooden Ware Mfg. Co., Toledo, O.

PLEASE mention the AMERICAN FLORIST every time you write to an advertiser.

STANDARD FLOWER POTS!

Packed in small crates, easy to handle.

Price per crate		Price per crate	
1500 2-in., in crate, $4.88	120 7-in., in crate, $4.20
1500 2¼ " 5.25	60 8 " 3.00
1500 2½ " 6.00	HAND MADE.
1000 3 " 5.00	48 9-in., in crate, $3.60
800 3½ " 5.80	48 10 " 4.80
500 4 " 4.50	24 11 " 3.60
320 5 " 4.51	24 12 " 4.80
144 6 " 3.16	12 14 " 4.80
	6 16 " 4.50

Seed pans, same price as pots. Send for price list of Cylinders for Cut Flowers, Hanging Baskets, Lawn Vases, etc. Ten per cent off for cash with order. Address.

HILFINGER BROS. POTTERY, Fort Edward, N. Y.
Or AUGUST ROLKER & SONS, New York Agents, 31 Barclay Street, New York City.

GEO. KELLER & SON,

MANUFACTURERS OF

FLOWER POTS.

Before buying write for prices.
361-363 Herndon Street, near Wrightwood Ave., CHICAGO, ILL.

RED POTS

SAMPLE POT AND PRICE LIST ON APPLICATION.

C. C. POLLWORTH CO., MILWAUKEE, WIS.

WRITE

A. F. KOHR, 1521-23 N. LEAVITT ST., CHICAGO, ILL.

FOR PRICES OF

Standard Pots

which for strength and porosity combined are the best on the market.

FLOWER POTS

ALL KINDS.

STANDARD POTS SPECIALTY

List and SAMPLES FREE.

SWAHN'S POTTERY MF'G CO.,
P. O. Box 78. MINNEAPOLIS, MINN.

THOSE RED POTS

"STANDARDS"
FULL SIZE AND WIDE BOTTOMS.
BULB PANS AND AZALEA POTS.

DETROIT FLOWER POT M'F'Y,
HARRY BALSLEY, DETROIT, MICH., Rep. 490 Howard St.

Please mention the American Florist when writing.

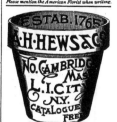

SULPHO-TOBACCO SOAP

COMBINES THE STRONGEST

TOBACCO EXTRACT
with Sulphur and Alkali. Never fails to

KILL BUGS AND INSECTS

GREENHOUSE STOCK
kept healthy by using this popular Insecticide. Satisfaction guaranteed. Prices low. Write for sample cake.

Larkin Soap Co. BUFFALO, N.Y.

Please mention the American Florist when writing.

Standard Flower Pots

The WHILLDIN POTTERY COMPANY,

PHILADELPHIA, PA. JERSEY CITY, N. J. LONG ISLAND CITY, N. Y.
Travelling Representative, U. CUTLER RYERSON, 108 Third Ave. Newark, N. J.

LIGHTNING FLOWER POT WASHER

Washes all sizes of pots, clean as new, about as fast as you can handle them. **Strong Plants are only grown in Clean Pots.** Send for description. Sold direct $15.00 net F. O. B. Joliet.

C. E. FINLEY, Joliet, Illinois.

Heating Apparatus Problems.

ED. AM. FLORIST:—I am not getting satisfaction from my heating apparatus and would like to know what is the trouble. There are two connecting houses each 25x75 feet, with two feet of glass in one side of each. One house is used for roses and carnations and has eight rows of 2-inch pipe under each side bench, with cast iron headers in one piece and one 3-inch flow carried overhead for each side. The other has six rows of 2-inch pipe on the wall under the gutter, and six horizontal rows under the bench on the outside, with one 3-inch flow for each side. The two lower pipes in the wall coil never heat and the third one barely gets warm. It has a fall of eleven inches in the length of the house and a further fall of eighteen inches to the boiler. The other coil has a fall of eight or nine inches with a further fall (gradual) of twelve or fifteen inches to the boiler. The pipes in the carnation house have a fall of nine inches to the main return and about two feet from that to the boiler. The main flows and returns are 4-inch branching to 3-inch in the houses. The flows are highest right over the boiler and gradually fall to the far end of the houses, where they drop from four to six feet to the coils. The tank is about fifteen feet above the boiler. There is an air valve on the highest part of each run, also a 1¼-inch pipe from the highest point of flow to the tank. I have never found any sign of air in any part of the piping. The boiler is a ten-section Carmody. The combustion is perfect. Have I too much piping in the houses? One flow in each house drops a few inches where it is taken off the main, using an angle valve instead of an elbow. The drop in the flow is just enough to clear. I don't find any difference in the heat of the different coils.   W. C.

The complaint seems to be that the lower pipes in the vertical coils do not circulate, and from the statement that the coils are heating equally it would appear that there is a similar trouble with the horizontal coils. The trouble seems to be that the coils are too low or the boiler on too high a level. The 4-inch main flow and return to each house and the 3-inch supply pipes to each coil are sufficiently large, but owing to the coils being on so nearly the level of the boiler the water circulates in the higher pipes only, as these are able to carry all the water that passes through the feed pipes. Of course the best way to correct the difficulty will be to raise the coils or lower the boiler. The circulation, however, can be equalized by placing either valves or reducers in the pipes that do circulate, thus holding back a part of the water and giving the others a chance to circulate.   L. R. TAFT.

Menlo Park, Cal.

J. B. Coryell is erecting a range of houses 155 feet long for roses, carnations, etc. Andrew McDonald is his gardener. S. E. Slade has let a contract to John McBain to add a house to his already extensive range for forcing. George Nunn is his gardener.

CANANDAIGUA, N. Y.—The Canandaigua Florists' and Gardeners' Society held a chrysanthemum and floral show in the town hall on Thursday and Friday November 5 and 6.

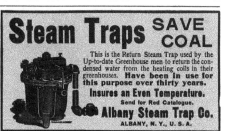

THE AMERICAN FLORIST

A WEEKLY JOURNAL FOR THE TRADE

America is "the Prow of the Vessel; there may be more comfort Amidships, but we are the first to touch Unknown Seas."

Vol. XXI.   CHICAGO AND NEW YORK, NOVEMBER 21, 1903.   No. 807.

THE AMERICAN FLORIST

NINETEENTH YEAR.

Copyright 1903, by American Florist Company
Entered as Second-Class Mail Matter.

PUBLISHED EVERY SATURDAY BY

AMERICAN FLORIST COMPANY,
324 Dearborn St., Chicago.
Eastern Office: 42 W. 28th St., New York.

Subscription, $1.00 a year.   To Europe, $2.00.
Subscriptions accepted only from the trade.
Volumes half-yearly from August, 1901.

SOCIETY OF AMERICAN FLORISTS AND
ORNAMENTAL HORTICULTURISTS.

OFFICERS—JOHN BURTON, Philadelphia, Pa.,
president; C. C. POLLWORTH, Milwaukee, Wis.,
Vice-president; WM. J. STEWART, 79 Milk Street,
Boston, Mass., secretary; H. B. BEATTY, Oil City,
Pa., treasurer.
OFFICERS-ELECT—PHILIP BREITMEYER, president; J. J. BENEKE, vice-president; secretary and
treasurer as before. Twentieth annual meeting
at St. Louis, Mo., August, 1904.

THE AMERICAN CARNATION SOCIETY.

Annual convention at Detroit, Mich., March 2,
1904. ALBERT M. HERR, Lancaster, Pa.; secretary.

AMERICAN ROSE SOCIETY.

Annual meeting-and-exhibition, Philadelphia,
March, 1904. LEONARD BARRON, 136 Liberty St.,
New York, secretary.

CHRYSANTHEMUM SOCIETY OF AMERICA.

Annual convention and exhibition, November,
1904. FRED H. LEMON, Richmond, Ind., secretary.

THIS ISSUE 40 PAGES WITH COVER.

CONTENTS

Chrysanthemums.

NEW VARIETIES AT NEW YORK.

It is not saying a word to belittle the other fine things both in seedlings and new importations at the New York show when I claim that without a doubt the variety Wm. Duckham, sent to this country by Wm. Wells & Company, Red Hill, England, is, all things considered, both from a commercial and exhibition standpoint, the biggest acquisition for the chrysanthemum growers of America, since Col. D. Appleton was sent out. One great thing about it is that when grown as a medium or commercial flower it is, I think, more refined and of better color than when grown to the extreme for exhibition. Having grown it, and therefore being able to speak of its habit, I unhesitatingly say you can make no mistake here. This variety was shown in grand form by Wm. Duckham, the E. G. Hill Company, Nathan Smith & Son and H. W. Buckbee, also in several collections for the local horticultural societies' special prizes.

Another fine commercial pink of great promise is Dr. Englehart, shown by the F. R. Pierson Company. N. Smith & Son showed the following seedlings:

Mrs. Nathan Smith.—Incurved, white, pure in color, fine stem, large size; good beauty.

Seedling No. 1-2-01.—Deep yellow, reflexed, good stem and foliage; quite promising.

Seedling 29-4-03.—Similar in many respects to Timothy Eaton, but with a more refined flower.

Golden Age.—Intense golden yellow; has fine stem and foliage; looks well commercially.

The F. R. Pierson Company showed a very pretty white, closely incurved, forming a perfect flower which, if it can be grown to larger size, will be an excellent variety.

The B. G. Hill Company staged a fine vase of Percy Plumeridge, a light yellow incurved with very broad petals, good form, fine stem and foliage; it is a beauty though perhaps a little light in color.

Harry Plumeridge, shown by the same firm, is a grand white flower somewhat irregular but of the largest size and carried on a good stem with fine foliage.

Lord Hopetoun, an old-gold and red, with a fine, large flower was shown, also Lord Alverstone, a very fine red, a

striking bloom for collections; Duchess of Sutherland, a bright golden yellow with magnificent bloom and Chelton, the golden yellow sport of Nellie Pockett, which will prove good for all purposes.

In Nathan Smith & Son's collection the most striking new things were:
Guy Hamilton, a very fine white variety.
Meredith, a magnificent light bronze for exhibition.
Mme. Von Andre, light yellow sport of Mutual Friend.
Gen. Hutton, a good bronze.
F. S. Vallis, a very large reflexing yellow of Mme. Carnot type.

In Wm. Duckham's collections was a magnificent array of blooms brought up to the highest state of perfection, the most striking new ones besides Wm. Duckham being:
F. Cobbold, a fine reflexing deep pink with foliage right up to the petals.
Florence Molyneux, a grand white.
Miss Neville and Ben Wells, two other grand whites.
Maynell and Harry Barnes, fine reds.
May Inglis, a grand bronze.
Mr. Duckham had also the new yellow variety, Mrs. E. Thirkell, in grand shape, but personally I think his greatest success was in the magnificent blooms of the variety W. R. Church he exhibited.

A. Herrington had in his collection grand blooms of W. R. Church, an "any other color" variety; Mrs. E. Thirkell, a grand reflexing yellow, and Yellow Eaton, unusually fine. He had also some wonderful blooms in the big vases of older varieties, such as Timothy Eaton, Col. D. Appleton, T. Carrington and Mrs. Barclay.

John Ash, of Pomfret, Conn., showed new importations as follows:
W. A. Etherington, a light pink of great size; very fine.
Violet Lady Beaumont, an incurving red; also grand.
Calvat's 1899, white, slightly tinted with lavender; a most beautiful bloom.
La Fusion, a grand white.
Mermaid, a fine incurving light pink.
Guy Hamilton, white; a beauty.
Wells & Company, Red Hill, Surrey, England, showed a collection of fine blooms, their last year's novelties, together with the following new ones:
Merstham, yellow, on the order of Mrs. Thirkell.
Mrs. Pollock, a silvery reflexed pink.
Mrs. Stewart, a very deep rose pink, rather an odd color.
Mrs. Wm. Duckham, yellow with bronze tracing.

Vaughan's Seed Store exhibited a fine

vase of its last year's novelty, Yellow Chadwick.

Walter Meneilly & Son, Syracuse, N. Y., showed a very deep colored yellow incurved named Miss Charlotte Land, but the flowers were much too small.

The number of new carnations was not very great according to western eyes, but I noted that Flamingo, shown by the F. R. Pierson Company, is a very fine red, particularly for so early in the season. The same firm also had a vase of the white sport of Lawson.

J. N. May exhibited a fine vase of The Bride, a promising pure white variety of good size.

James Sackawich, New Hyde Park, N. Y., staged a vase of a dozen blooms of a new red seedling which promises well, the color being very lively and the flower of good size.

There were five vases of seedling roses on exhibition, three from Jas. Cook, Baltimore, Md.:

No. 138.—Pink, style of Mme. Testout.
No. 115,—White after Kaiserin Augusta Victoria.
No. 15.—Somewhat like Souvenir de Wootton.

From John N. May there was one named Gen. McArthur, a deep red and very fragrant. Breitmeyer's Sons, Detroit, showed their new pink variety.

C. W. Johnson.

Florists' Plant Notes.

FOR FOURTH WEEK IN NOVEMBER.

Mignonette.—The mignonette sown last August in the bed should be coming into a good crop for the holidays. If grown sufficiently cool, say in a temperature of 45° to 50°, the plants will not require staking, but if needed they must have it at once or the branches will grow crooked. One stake will be sufficient to support several branches. Keep the laterals pinched from the main flower shoots, allowing about four branches to a plant. Give them full light and abundant ventilation whenever practicable, for this is

necessary to induce a sturdy and vigorous growth. Tobacco smoke does not harm them, unless it is made too heavy, but we have never had occasion to fumigate them, for the plants are rarely troubled with insects of any kind during the winter.

Seeds.—Although it is too early to sow the seeds of most of the annuals usually raised for the spring trade, yet some varieties, if sown now, will make better plants than those sown later in the season. Centaurea candidissima, invaluable for bedding purposes should be sown now, for it grows slowly and does not make sufficiently large plants if sown later on. Lobelia and verbena may also be sown now and will make better and stronger plants than later sown ones if they are kept growing in a rather cool house. Sow these seeds in light and rather sandy soil in flats, and keep moderately moist in a temperature of about 50°. Candytuft may also be sown now that most of the chrysanthemums are gone, making room for other crops. Sow the seed in drills in the same soil in which the chrysanthemums were growing, after leveling it off nicely, leaving a foot of space between the drills. Another sowing may be made about the first of the year, which will furnish a good supply of flowers throughout April and May.

Bulbs.—Roman hyacinths and Paper White narcissi should be brought into heat four weeks before Christmas. In a temperature of 60° four weeks will bring them into flower nicely. They do not require any shade to lengthen out the stem; in fact they should not have a shady place at all or they will grow soft and spindly. Early tulips also require about four weeks in a warm temperature to bring them in on time. Duc van Tholl is the only one we know of that can be forced successfully for Christmas. Proserpine, La Reine and Keizerskroon can also be had in flower, but the stems will be so short as to render them practically useless. It is better to wait three weeks longer before attempting to force these varieties and save the bulbs from being

ruined. Duc van Tholl, however, can be had in bloom with a fair-sized stem if they are handled properly. Under a warm bench, with a piece of canvas tacked in front to keep out the light, is as good a place as any for the first two weeks. Darkness is absolutely necessary in order to get long stems. A temperature of 75° or even 80° is not too high, but plenty of warm water should be given while this temperature is being maintained. At the end of two weeks, more light can be gradually given until the flowers are developed, when they can stand the full light. Do not neglect the Paper White narcissi out in the frames; they are by this time peeping through their covering. Cover them with a few inches of straw and sash to protect them from the frost.
G.

Pennsylvania Horticultural Society.

Last week's exhibition from a financial standpoint was equal if not superior to any yet held. The general excellence of all the exhibits was freely commented on, there being nothing that did not have some feature to commend it. The exhibition of cut flowers, roses and carnations, while not large, was of good quality. Myers & Samtman's American Beauty and Edward Towill's Liberty roses were grand blooms and they easily carried off the prizes.

The Floral Exchange also won with fine blooms of Bride and Meteor and Golden Gate. Becker's Ideal and John Shellem's new seedling rose were both much admired. The chief attraction in this department, however, was the new Breitmeyer, a fine vase of which was staged by Ernst Asmus. It is beautiful in itself, but the card attached offering $100 for a name kept the visitors busy trying to get a winner. Wm. Robertson won twenty-seven prizes in all, which is certainly a very creditable showing when one considers the great competition.

The orchid dinner table of the Wm. Graham Company was much admired.

NEW YORK CHRYSANTHEMUM SHOW, NOVEMBER 10-13.

The orchids were arranged in cork bark logs, crossed over a hollow center in a round table. The center was filled with pot ferns whose foliage rose nearly to a level with the table. The china and other necessaries were included, and there were corsages of lily of the valley and violets. Robert Craig & Son's new Ficus Pandurata was the great plant novelty of the show, and it looks as if every private gardener in the land will have to have one. K.

Chicago Florists' Club.

Leonard Kill.

The second exhibition of the Chicago Florists' Club was held in the Atlas building, Randolph street, November 17. In point of general attendance it was most successful and the duration of the event was much too brief to satisfy the hundreds of visitors. The exhibition was specially notable for the superlative quality of cut blooms, the only disappointing feature being the comparative lack of chrysanthemum displays. Leonard Kill, on whose shoulders rested the burden of the management of the exhibition, is deserving of honorable mention for the success attending his efforts. The public was admitted by card from 2 to 4 p. m., when the trade only was admitted. The hall was a blaze of flowers under a ceiling festooned with long garlands of Asparagus plumosus, which were furnished by Peter Reinberg, who purchased them from Bassett & Washburn.

The principal exhibitors were the Chicago Carnation Company and the J. D. Thompson Carnation Company, Joliet, Ill.; Vaughan's Greenhouses, Western Springs, Ill.; Peter Reinberg, Wietor Bros., J. A. Budlong, George Wittbold Company, Anton Then, Frank Garland, Bassett & Washburn, Weiland & Risch and J. F. Kidwell & Brother, Chicago; W. N. Rudd, Mt. Greenwood; F. Dorner & Sons, La Fayette, Ind., Baur & Smith and John Hartje, Indianapolis, Ind.; Leonard J. Stankowicz, Niles, Ill., and John Reardon.

Carnations were made the leading feature of the exhibition, the Chicago Carnation Company and the J. D. Thompson Carnation Company being the prime competitors. The former's most attractive exhibit was a vase of the new Fiancee, the prize winner at the recent Joliet show. There were also vases of fine Enchantress, Lawson, Reliance, Moonlight, Prosperity, Mrs. E. A. Nelson and President McKinley in the exhibit. The Crusader, a deep red, was especially good, as was Dorothy Whitney, a dazzling yellow. There were also Harlowarden, Mrs. Higinbotham, Sybil and others.

The J. D. Thompson Carnation Company's exhibit was devoted to carnations only. Their tables carried fine vases of Enchantress, fifty to a vase, and Gov. Wolcott, the latter being exceptionally good, with long strong stems. There were also the well known Mrs. M. A. Patten, Estelle, Nelson Fisher and Mrs. E. A Nelson.

Baur & Smith showed their Indianapolis, said to be a very continuous bloomer. Joost & Armazindy were also in this exhibit.

Leonard J. Stankowicz sent three vases of new carnations. One was a white sport of Argyle, one a cross between Flora Hill and Mrs. Ine and the last a white cross between Argyle and Flora Hill.

F. Dorner & Sons Company displayed some choice seedling carnations, including vases of The Belle and Lady Bountiful, also a vase of mixed varieties. There must have been a dozen varieties, among which were noticed some of novel shades and variation. Hubert Hanson showed a vase of choice Mrs. Higiubotham.

Anton Then had several vases of fine carnations, including four white seedlings. Number 304, a deep pink was given much favorable comment. There were also vases of Gov. Wolcott, White Cloud, Sybil, White Crane and Her Majesty, all fine blooms. A collection of cyclamen was also in Mr. Then's display.

W. N. Rudd, of the Mt. Greenwood Cemetery Association showed a vase of splendid Phyllis and one of an exceptionally fine red seedling which was labeled 2001 A.

The rose exhibits were of high quality. Peter Reinberg's display was the most extensive and included vases of rich American Beauty, Perle, Liberty, Bride, Bridesmaid, Ivory, La France, Kaiserin and Uncle John. The last named is a promising new rose, darker than and considered an improvement over Golden Gate. Some fine Sunrise and Chatenay

were also noted. The Chicago Carnation Company had vases of unusually good Golden Gate.

Wietor Brothers showed many perfect blooms of Golden Gate, Bride, Bridesmaid, Liberty, American Beauty, La France, Ivory and Meteor roses. J. A. Budlong's roses were highly creditable and included American Beauty, Bride, Bridesmaid and Golden Gate.

While the chrysanthemum exhibits were few, those few were of rare quality. Vaughan's Greenhouses showed a pot of extra large Golden Chadwick. J. A. Budlong sent three varieties of his good commercial chrysanthemums, Maud Dean, Timothy Eaton and Murdoch. John Reardon, gardener to M. A. Ryerson, sent two fine chrysanthemum plants, Sunstone being most attractive and carrying over a hundred blooms.

The Timothy Eaton blooms staged by Weiland & Risch were the most gigantic in size seen here for some time and they excited much favorable comment. Bassett & Washburn had two fine jars, one each of immense Viviand-Morel and President W. R. Smith. John Hartje sent a bunch of Moonlight carnations which had passed their best before arrival. The George Wittbold Company con-

ASMUS EXHIBIT OF THE BREITMEYER ROSE AT PHILADELPHIA.

tributed largely to the success of the show, by sending an extensive exhibit of decorative plants, ferns and palms. Nearly one entire side of the hall was taken up by numerous fine specimen plants of Cocos Bonnetti, Boston and Piersoni ferns, bay trees, Asparagus plumosus, etc. Schismatoglottis, a variegated foliage plant was also very attractive, as were the Australian tree fern, Alsophila australis; two fine specimens of Dracæna terminalis; Kentia, Forsteriana, Ficus elastica; also the favorite Cibotium Schiedii. A pretty date palm was also noted.

Vaughan's exhibit had many varieties of ferns, including Adiantum Farleyense, the Boston, Piersoni and Anna Foster. The new Pandanus Sanderi also was shown and Asparagus plumosus, Cibotium Schiedii, Celestial peppers, etc.

J. F. Kidwell & Brother displayed some good palms and ferns and two vases of fine narcissi were sent by Frank Garland. Benthey & Company sent several vases of fine American Beauty and Bride roses, which arrived too late, however, to be staged.

George L. Stiles representing the Oklahoma Floral Company of Oklahoma City, had a corner of the hall and showed samples of heavily berried mistletoe which he was placing for the holiday trade.

The judges made the following awards: Peter Reinberg, $5 for new rose Uncle John; Wietor Brothers, $5 for Liberty roses; Chicago Carnation Company, $5 for Bridesmaid roses and $5 for Fiancee carnations; F. Dorner & Sons Company, $5 for seedling carnations; J. D. Thompson Carnation Company, $5 for Gov.

Wolcott carnations; Weiland & Risch, $10 for Timothy Eaton chrysanthemums; Anton Then, $5 for cyclamens; J. A. Budlong, $5 for roses and chrysanthemums. The dinner in the evening was a great success and well attended.

At the regular meeting held November 18 there was a fair attendance. Three new names were proposed for membership—Adam Zender, Albert Woodward and F. S. Allen. A committee composed of H. Hasselbring, James Hartshorne and E. A. Kanst was appointed to formulate regulations for the guidance of exhibitors and judges at future shows. It was unanimously voted that the club request the American Carnation Society to hold the convention of 1905 in this city. Phil Hauswirth was appointed a committee on transportation to the Detroit convention of that society next February.

Among the trade visitors who were in attendance were A. F. J. Baur, Indianapolis; F. Dorner, Jr., Lafayette, Ind.; Geo. L. Stiles, Oklahoma City.

Chrysanthemum Society of America.

WORK OF COMMITTEES.

Before the New York committee, November 11, four varieties were shown, and the examination resulted as follows:

Sunburst, shown by Nathan Smith & Son, Adrian, Mich.; yellow, Japanese incurved; scored 85 points commercial scale.

Mrs. Nathan Smith, exhibited by the same firm; pure white; scored 89 commercial scale.

Seedling, 29-4-03, by the same firm; creamy white, Japanese incurved; 80 points commercial scale.

Golden Age, also by Nathan Smith & Son; bright orange yellow, Japanese reflexed; scored 81 points commercial scale.

Before the same committee November 14, F. R. Pierson Company, Tarrytown, N. Y., exhibited Dr. Englehart; rose pink, silvery reverse; scored 87 points commercial scale.

Before the Chicago committee, on November 7 and 14 respectively, two varieties were shown as follows:

Madonna, shown by H. Rieman, Indianapolis, Ind.; pink, type of Bonnaffon; scored 85 points commercial scale.

Adelia, shown by H. W. Rieman; white, ball shaped; scored 84 points commercial scale.

Before the Cincinnati committee, on November 14, the following varieties were shown:

Dr. Englehart, shown by Nathan Smith & Son; bright pink, Japanese incurved; scored 95 points commercial scale.

Sunburst, by the same firm; deep yellow, Japanese incurved; 84 commercial scale.

Adelia, shown by H. W. Rieman; white, incurved; scored 87 points commercial scale. FRED H. LEMON, Sec'y.

WATERTOWN, N. Y.—The newly fitted up store of George H. Underhill in the Marble block on Washington street, Watertown, is effulgent in bright hues and fragrant odors. The high reputation which was earned by the firm of Greene & Underhill has every promise of being enhanced since Mr. Underhill has taken it over.

FLOWER SHOW AT DANIELS & FISHER'S, DENVER, COL.

GENERAL VIEW OF THE INDIANAPOLIS EXHIBITION.

World's Fair Notes.

The Japanese dedicated their exhibition site with all due formality Tuesday, November 3. As soon as the buildings are completed the landscape gardener will begin work. A most complete system of Japanese gardening will be exhibited, including a real tea garden. Hundreds of dwarfed cedars will be utilized. The site is just west of the cascades. The landscape department has a large force of men planting shrubbery around the main buildings. Heavy mass planting of evergreens and hardy shrubs is being done along the approaches to the cascades. The lawns are in good condition. A gang of men will be kept busy pruning all winter, as many of the trees are badly in need of attention.

J. H. Hadkinson will have charge of the cut flower display in the conservatories. He is doing wonders with the horticultural grounds. Seeding is almost finished and the beds are ready for the bulbous stock which is expected to arrive at any time. On the west side of the agricultural building a garden for wild plants is to be laid out. Every variety of herbaceous plant indigenous to this section will be utilized in the work. Several thousand plants representing many species have already been collected. Collectors are out each day. The scheme is to display the native flora to such an advantage that the visitor will see

what may be done with plants he is wont to call weeds.

John Clark, of Dreer's was here working over the aquatic section. The ponds are practically ready for planting, the boxes for the lilies being already in position, and the shrubbery along the borders is being planted. Sodding has also commenced. The narrow passageway which connects two of the ponds will be crossed by a large rustic bridge on which work will begin as soon as possible.

John H. Brown, representing Peter Brown, of Lancaster, Pa., was also here superintending the planting of a collection of pansies, the first pansy exhibit to be installed. The collection was planted in a large circular bed directly in front of the main entrance to the agricultural building. At present the plants are blooming profusely and represent a large and varied range of color.

Several new ponds are to be added to the series which were not originally planned. Two small ones, for exhibitors' use, are to be made just south of the horticultural building. Inside the conservatories will be six more for tender varieties. In the east wing a pond 40x50 will be used for growing the Victoria regia or royal water lily.

M. Vachrot, the chief gardener of the city of Paris, has arrived. He comes here to superintend the laying out of seven acres of ground allotted to France, which

surrounds the French National building, and has brought four assistants with him. He says he will return to France the latter part of December, when the plants to be used will be shipped.

The floral clock, which was to have been a feature of the landscape department has been abandoned. The Ceylon commission required more space than was at first planned, with the result that the room allotted for the floral clock was encroached upon. A bed of choice cannas will take its place.

The landscape department received a large shipment of miscellaneous stock from Vaughan's Seed Store, Chicago, consisting of thirty-three barrels of iris, canna, funkia, helianthus, hibiscus, etc.

Elwanger & Barry, of Rochester, N. Y., will have a big display of hydrangeas. A lot recently received included five hundred H. paniculata. They are planted in a solid mass between the horticultural and agricultural buildings.

The cold storage plant under the wing of the agricultural building is completed and ready for use.

T. W. Brown, of the English commission, has returned from Chicago, where he went on a business trip. F. K. B.

SPRINGFIELD, Mass.—Alfred J. Buckleton has filed a petition in bankruptcy. Liabilities $8,538 with $6,600 secured; the assets are nominal.

Society of American Florists.

DEPARTMENT OF PLANT REGISTRATION.

C. D. Beadle, of the Biltmore Nursery, N. C., registers seedling chrysanthemums as follows: Miss Birnie-Philip (Mrs. H. Robinson × Advance). Flowers ten to twelve inches in diameter, of the Japanese incurved type, borne on strong, stiff stems six to seven feet tall; color white, with delicate shading of rose-pink at the base of the very numerous rays, the longest of which are five to six inches long, and mostly tubular from one to two-thirds of their length; the upper or ligulate portion one-quarter to one-half inch wide, mostly plaited and sometimes cleft or toothed; foliage gradually diminishing in size from far down the stem; leaves large, lively rich green, produced to within a few inches of the flower.

Caiffer (Mrs. H. Robinson × Advance). Flowers eight to ten inches in diameter, of the Japanese reflexed type, borne on stout, stiff stems about four feet tall; color white with creamy tint, the longest of the numerous rays four or five inches long, rarely five-eighths of an inch wide, furrow-veined, plaited or troughed, their bases sometimes obversely channeled, presenting a decided whorled or whirling effect, especially before complete maturity; foliage gradually diminishing in size upwards; leaves of medium size, deep green, produced to within three or four inches of the flower.

Mrs. Swope (Mrs. Higinbotham × Mrs. H. Robinson). Flowers ten to twelve inches in diameter, of the Japanese incurved type, produced on very stout, stiff and straight stems, five to six feet tall; color creamy white with slight flush of rose; rays numerous; all but the spreading lower ones, incurved, the inner series short-tubular, the outer often with the tubular portion extending to or near the apex; they are channeled or furrow-veined, the longest five to six inches long and with the ligulate portion one-half to five-eighths of an inch wide, foliage produced almost to the flower; leaves large, deep green, almost hiding the stem.

Peter Stuyvesant (Mrs. Higinbotham × Mrs. H. Robinson). Flowers seven to nine inches in diameter, of the pure incurved type, borne on very stout, stiff and straight stems four to five feet tall; color rich canary yellow; the longest of the numerous, strongly incurved and symmetrically arranged rays four to five inches long, some of the outermost of which are occasionally tubular to the apex, but usually with the channeled ligulate portion one-half to three-quarters of an inch wide; they are furrow-veined and marked (only on the inner or ventral surface and unnoticeable except on close examination) by lines or dashes of rose-purple; foliage produced almost to the flower; leaves large, deep green, almost hiding the stem.

Rose Sir Thomas Lipton, presented by the Conard & Jones Company, West Grove, Pa., on October 17, 1903, has been duly registered.

WM. J. STEWART, Sec'y.

Cutting Back Crane Carnations.

ED. AM. FLORIST.—My Crane carnation plants are small, so I want to keep a crop of cuttings about December 1. When shall I stop pinching out to have a good Christmas crop? WESTERN.

It takes about six weeks in a night temperature of 52° to 54° at this time of the year for a carnation bud to open after it is set, that is, just about at that stage at which the laterals begin to show on the stem below. If no flowers are wanted much before Christmas, remove the shoot as fast as the buds are set, up to about seven weeks before Christmas. Top cuttings must not be taken as late as December 1, with the hope of getting any flowers from the resulting breaks, during the best four months of the year, as it would take about four months for the crop to develop. Side shoots make ideal cuttings and it would be advisable to wait a little longer and take the laterals from the blooming stems for this purpose. Be careful, however, to take only those laterals that have a good foundation, which are found well down the stem on Crane, and avoid the thin growths found higher up. The latter will root, but will produce nothing but buds. J.

Special Treatment of Carnations.

Prosperity.—Strictly a fancy variety and will pay only in the best markets where a good price can be obtained. Soil medium light and quite rich. Temperature 54°. Starve until buds are set.

Marshall Field.—A good white variegated of last year's introduction. Rich heavy soil; temperature 48°. Allow flowers to develop fully before cutting.

Chicot.—Rich heavy soil. Will pass either for a variegated or for a white. A free bloomer but not extra early. Temperature 52°.

Mrs. Geo. M. Bradt.—Planted close together it pays well where a good variegated variety is in demand. It wants a heavy soil and plenty of feeding and cuttings should be made early. It is good in midwinter and a poor hot weather variety. The flowers are very heavy and the supports should come well up to take the strain off the stems. J.

Greenhouse Building.

Revere, Mass.—G. W. Marshall, house 24x150.

Lebanon, Pa.—D. Hammond Mish, carnation house.

Philadelphia, Pa.—Karl Muller, house 18x60.

Cambridge, Mass.—A. M. Houghton, conservatory.

Escanaba, Mich.—C. Peterson & Sons, house 22x105.

Rosewell, N. M.—Mrs. J. P. Church, one house.

Hartford, Mich.—W. H. Blashfield, one house.

Gloucester, Mass.—S. F. Haskell, one house.

Chelsea, Mass.—A. E. Jones, conservatory.

Baltimore, Md.—Chas. Siegwart, conservatory 20x75.

Southbridge, Mass.—S. O. Simmons, cucumber-house.

Le Roy, N. Y.—R. V. Baxter, two houses.

HOLM & OLSON'S DISPLAY AT THE ST. PAUL EXHIBITION.

CHURCH DECORATION BY THORLEY, NEW YORK, FOR ROXBURGH-GOELET WEDDING.
(See issue of November 14, page 577.)

The Retail Trade.

THE ARTIST.

Debutante season is once more with us to make the busy ones more busy. We all look forward to this season with expectation and we all hope to be busier than ever. Orders have already started to come in, and a few suggestions may not be amiss.

A very beautiful bouquet may be made with Cypripedium insigne and lily of the valley. The lily of the valley should be mixed through or arranged in spray form on one side or through the middle. A fringe of Adiantum cuneatum should surround the whole, and a Farleyense would add to the richness. An apple-green ribbon tied with long streamers will complete a very effective bouquet.

Liberty roses, dark red carnations and many other flowers combine very well with cypripediums or other "green orchids" as they are often called by our customers. Violets are not often used for these occasions but can be made very effective in combination with red roses, cattleyas or any bright flowers that will harmonize. The ribbons should be violet.

Pink is, of course, the favored color for the "fair debutante," Bridesmaid roses being especially appropriate. These are most effective when the stems are long. They should be tied in a loose bunch made high at the back and graduating towards the front, a few of the weaker-stemmed roses being allowed to hang over the ribbon, which should also be pink and of a lighter shade than the roses. These may also be combined with

lily of the valley, white hyacinths or any of the smaller white flowers.

Carnations are also extensively used for this purpose. Prosperity, Mrs. Thos. W. Lawson, Enchantress and all the finer sorts make very acceptable bouquets. I prefer to use Asparagus plumosus with carnations; the rich green brings out the color.

Handle bouquets should be avoided as much as possible, as the natural stems are more effective and make up more handsomely. Wire should also be left out except, of course, in the cheaper grade of bouquets, where it is sometimes necessary.

A very pretty idea is to pin the card of the sender to the ribbon, with a flower and small piece of green of the variety used in the bouquet.

FIREPLACE DECORATIONS.

The decoration of fireplaces with flowering and fine foliage plants during the summer months has so much to recommend it as to deserve the fullest encouragement at public exhibitions. Yet it is a rare occurrence for this form of decoration to obtain recognition in the schedules of horticultural societies, says the Gardeners' Magazine. The committee of the Carshalton Horticultural Society, which holds very advanced views with regard to the importance of introducing new features from time to time at the society's annual exhibitions, provided a class this season for the most tastefully decorated mantel and fireplace, and the results were eminently satisfactory. There were six or seven competitors, and, as the whole of the arrangements were

characterized by much taste, they constituted a most interesting and attractive feature, as proved by the attention the decorations received from the general body of visitors. The fireplaces and mantels were provided by the society, and it was a point of some interest that the exhibitors were on the whole more successful in decorating the fireplaces than the mantels.

Chicago.

TRADE PICKING UP.—ROSES NOT GOING WELL.—CAR STRIKE AFFECTS SOUTH SIDE BUSINESS.—GENERAL NOTES.

The week saw the entrance of the cold season, which came in with a rush. While its sudden advent Tuesday had the momentary effect of considerably dulling business for the day, the conditions grew better as the week advanced. The supply was shortened up and prices are necessarily ruling higher. There are still plenty of flowers on the market, and it will be some time before the trade is satisfied. The Thanksgiving outlook continues encouraging and all of the dealers say they will have a choice lot of stock on hand to select from. Carnations are quite plentiful, but they are not selling with the rapidity which the incoming supply would accommodate. The sales in roses this week have been low, but chrysanthemums were kept well cleaned up, at good prices, too. Smilax, ferns, etc., are going moderately. Violets and valley are not coming in in great quantity and they are being sold down closely. The general ruling quotations are slightly higher this week in all flowers. A further improvement is looked for next week.

The Wednesday evening meeting of the Chicago Florists' Club was the last which will be held until December 16. The regular meeting of December 2 will be dispensed with and the club will give its first winter ball. John P. Risch will have the management of this event. The Masonic Temple drill hall has been secured and it is expected that a large crowd will attend.

South side florists are complaining that the street car strike now in force is working a damaging effect on their business. Retailers who are not possessed of delivery wagons are experiencing difficulty in getting their flowers to their customers.

Without doubt the largest chrysanthemums seen in the local market this season were the Timothy Eaton cut by Weiland & Risch this week and displayed at the club flower show. The lot was disposed of at a very fancy price.

The next exhibition given by the Florists' Club will occur sometime in the third week in December. Holiday plants will be shown and a program will be carried out by the club after the exhibit.

C. M. Dickinson, manager of Hunt's, is again at his desk regularly, having entirely recovered from his recent illness.

Randall this week handled an extra choice lot of chrysanthemums, and his stock was kept cleaned to the tables.

W. N. Campbell, of Vaughan's Seed

Store, has been suddenly called home by the illness of his mother in New Jersey.

J. B. Deamud made a flying business trip to Desplaines, Ill., Wednesday.

Visitors: C. M. Wagner, Cleveland; C. F. Rohr, Naperville, Ill.; F. A. Friedley, Joliet.

Philadelphia.

TRADE IMPROVING SLOWLY.—MARKET YET OVERSTOCKED AND LOW PRICES PREVAIL.—TWO NEW STORES OPEN.—FIRE IN CLUB GREENHOUSES.

Business is a shade better than last week, but there is still much room for improvement. Every dealer in flowers is stocked to the doors and in anything like a clean up the lot demand, prices are away down. Very fine chrysanthemums are seen on the streets at 10 cents each or twelve for $1. What must be the returns with the commission off? The varieties now most in evidence are Maud Dean, White Bonnaffon, Yellow Bonnaffon, Golden Wedding, Timothy Eaton and Small Ivory. Beauties and all other classes of roses are very plentiful, with the quality improving. Carnations are now looming up and will become a factor with the departure of the chrysanthemum, the first of December. (Should there not be a law passed that any chrysanthemum found growing after this date should be immediately destroyed?) Lawson is much in evidence and bids fair to have a large take the coming season. The McKinley sells well and

appears to be a great keeper. The market is overstocked with valley which sells slowly. Violets are about the only flower that appears to clean up, all good stock being readily taken at fair prices, in fact the doubles have moved up twenty-five per cent the past week.

Charles Fox opened his new store at the corner of Broad and Sansom streets last Saturday. While not fully completed, enough has been done to show that he will have an up-to-date place. The store proper is about 15x30 feet and finished in green oak; there is a greenhouse immediately in the rear and a rustic stairway leads up to a large dome house on the second floor of an adjoining building. These greenhouses were at one time filled with fine plants, and in one of these a tank containing a Victoria regia was a special feature. When finished Mr. Fox will have a very inviting place and the most central in the city.

John Gracey has opened his new store at Twenty-first street and Columbia avenue, a few doors west of his old location. It is large and roomy with two fine bulk windows. The fixtures are of green oak. In the rear a large greenhouse opens with practically no partition between. There are ample tanks and ponds for gold fish in which Mr. Gracey does quite a large business. He is to be congratulated on his beautiful store, which should give a great impetus to his business.

Fire partially destroyed the large greenhouses of the Philadelphia Country Club, at Bala, November 15. Several hundred valuable plants were destroyed and the damage to the house and contents is estimated at $5,000. John Crawford, the gardener, had his feet badly cut with broken glass while fighting the flames.

Leo Niessen is getting in some extra fine Bridesmaid, Liberty and Beauty roses. He says the stock was never better for the season. He had Manager Meehan of the market out to dinner with him one day this week as a compliment to Mr. Meehan's judgment.

Bernheimer is handling some fine stock from the Edgely nurseries. His sweet pea consignments have commenced and the stock is good.

S. S. Pennock's market is a busy place these mornings. His special double violets are hard to beat.

Fred. Ehret, of Fairmount avenue, reports trade good for the season but prices a little lower.

Colflesh is sending in some fine Golden Wedding chrysanthemums.   K.

Abutilon Pink Beauty.

This new abutilon has been highly recommended for growing into pot specimens for Easter sales. The variety was imported from England some years ago by the proprietor of a private place in Massachusetts, where it was noticed by C. B. Knickman, manager of the Ozone Park Nurseries, Ozone Park, N. Y. Mr. Knickman at once saw its merits and has since made a specialty of it. It is a very compact grower and profuse bloomer. The flower is large and the color a soft shell pink. The plant is alike useful for pots and bedding.

LE ROY, N. Y.—The firm of R. & M. Baxter has been dissolved, Miss Mary having withdrawn. R. V. Baxter will run the business under the style of the Old Homestead Florist.

ABUTILON PINK BEAUTY.

New York.

DULL MARKET IN METROPOLIS.—STOCK PLENTIFUL AND PRICES LOW.—GEORGE NASH RETURNS FROM ABROAD.

The general opinion among the growers and wholesalers is that this fall is one of the worst on record. Prices are the same as last week. Violets have been a slump on the market, and fifty cents is about the average price for good quality. American Beauty roses are shortening in crop, but with no increase in price, and the same can be said of all other flowers. Chrysanthemums are plentiful, and are of very good quality. Stevia, Roman hyacinths and Paper White narcissi are now coming into the market.

George V. Nash, head gardener at the Botanical Garden, and his assistant, Harry Baker, returned last week from a collecting expedition to Hayti, bringing over a thousand specimens.

John B. Nugent has leased a large building on Twenty-eight street, formerly occupied by a music publishing house, and is having it newly papered and decorated.

The directors of the New York Cut Flower Company had their monthly meeting on November 17. Important business was transacted.

Hermann Dreyer, of Woodside, L. I., has a fine lot of azaleas in bloom for Thanksgiving.

George T. N. Cottam is at St. John's hospital critically ill.

Boston.

BUSINESS IN A BAD WAY.—TOO MUCH STOCK.—ANNUAL MEETING HORTICULTURAL SOCIETY.—REQUISITION OF FLORISTS' CLUB.

The cut flower market during the past week has been in a condition of unprecedented stagnation. To the roll of a congestion during the height of the chrysanthemum season is nothing unusual and everybody expects it as a matter of course, but its severity and the utter annihilation of values on this occasion is a staggerer for growers and dealers alike. The great accumulation of unsold high grade material is an object lesson in the effect of the big rose and carnation factories which have come into existence within the past year or two and the small growers who have held the control of this market hitherto have good cause for alarm. The process is identical with that which has already taken place in at least two of the large centers in this country where the small grower has been overwhelmed and his influence extinguished. If he be wise he will abandon the staples to those big establishments are devoted and fix upon some small specialty of sterling merit and if he be a good gardener and circumspect business man this will not be difficult of accomplishment. With the chrysanthemum season on the wane, Thanksgiving but a few days off, cold weather well due and the plants depleted of their crop by the continued warm spell, there is every reason to hope that we have passed the worst of the trouble and that a healthy activity and normal values will soon be with us for a prolonged stay. At present writing violets are fairly on their feet and carnations begin to show evidences of revival.

The annual meeting of the Massachusetts Horticultural Society was held on Saturday, November 14. The election of officers for 1904 resulted as follows: President, Henry P. Walcott; vice-president (for two years), Walter Hunnewell; vice-president (for one year), Warren W.

Rawson; treasurer, Charles E. Richardson; secretary, William P. Rich; trustees (for three years), William N. Craig, John K. L. M. Farquhar, Arthur D. Hill, Charles S. Sargent; for two years, Oakes Ames, Arthur H. Fewkes, Charles W. Parker, William H. Spooner; for one year, Arthur F. Estabrook, Robert T. Jackson, John A Pettigrew, Michael Sullivan. Nominating committee, Walter C. Bayles, William H. Elliott, Nathaniel T. Kidder, Richard M. Saltonstall, C. Minot Weld. This was the ticket proposed by the original compromise committee and there was no opposition. Dr. Wolcott was president of the society once before, from 1886 to 1889. Julius Heurlin was appointed to fill the place as chairman of the flower committee, resigned by Kenneth Finlayson.

A widespread movement for the rehabilitation of the Gardeners' and Florists' Club is in progress. This once influential institution has been in a state of "innocuous desuetude" for some years, simply maintaining an existence. Mr. Pettigrew the present presiding officer, is a man of the right material to win the friendly support and advocacy of all classes in the horticultural community and the revival now setting in has the true ring to it.

St. Louis.

MONTHLY CLUB MEETING AND EXHIBITION. —CEMETERY IMPROVEMENTS IN PROGRESS. — EXHIBIT FLOWERS SOLD AT AUCTION.

The monthly meeting and chrysanthemum exhibition of the St. Louis Florists' Club was fairly well attended, twenty-four members and two visitors being present. Three new names, W. H. Hummel, Vincent C. Garley and Max Raetter, were added to the roll. John L. Koenig made application for membership. The finance committee reported that they deemed it advisable for the club to invite all of its members to the banquet to be held in March in honor of the executive committee of the S. A. F., which will then be in session. Each member desiring to attend is to contribute $5 toward the expenses. Any florist in the city, whether a member of the club or not, may attend on payment of the necessary contribution. Several vases of chrysanthemums were on hand for the exhibition. T. O. Klackenkemper won first prize with a vase of twelve mammoth Timothy Eaton; Wm. Schray & Sons won second with a dozen blooms of Liberty, and A. G. Benson third with twelve mixed varieties. E. G. Hill, of Richmond, Ind., exhibited two vases of new varieties which received favorable comment. Wm. Duckham, a large, clear, light pink, was highly praised. Other varieties shown were Lucy Evans, Wm. Duckham, Henry II, Sidonia, S. L. Wright, etc. Baur & Smith, of Indianapolis, sent a bunch of their new carnation Indianapolis, a deep pink. The blooms were of good size and color. Stems were rather soft but will no doubt grow stiffer when cooler weather sets in. Dr. Halstead showed his new seedling carnation, Number 14, a cross between the St. Clair Floral Company's seedling, Number 10 and Alaska. The flowers are a pure white. F. J. Fillmore was appointed club auctioneer for the coming year. All exhibits taking prizes become the property of the club and are disposed of at auction, hence the need of an auctioneer. John Evans, the ventilator man, of Richmond, Ind., made a few opportune

remarks. He said he came around to see how convention matters were progressing.

Con Winthers, gardener at Bellefontaine cemetery, says that he is adding several new beds to the series this fall. Six are being planted with hardy roses and two borders are being filled with rhododendrons, Catawbiense and R. maximum. The last lot of 14,000 tulips are also being planted. The association is extending its water system throughout the grounds.

A. G. Fehr, of Bellville, Ill., reports that trade in his locality is good. He is showing some fine potted chrysanthemums.

Visitors: John Evans, Richmond, Ind.

F. K. B.

Kansas City, Mo.

IDEAL WEATHER HELPS CHRYSANTHEMUMS.—BUSINESS WITH SOME DEALERS BREAKS RECORDS.—PRICES GOOD.—FIRM GIVES FLOWER SHOW.—VISITORS.

Ideal weather has prevailed the last two weeks, an essential element to the development of good show chrysanthemums. Fall trade has been a disappointment to some of the retailers, complaint coming from many that chrysanthemums have moved slower than usual. With two or three of the larger stores the volume of trade has been greater than ever before in the last two weeks in November. No very large decorations but numerous small ones have made up the greater part of the increased business. The present market prices are: American Beauty, $1 to $3, $4 for extras; Bride, Bridesmaid and Liberty, 4 to 6 cents; Perle and Golden Gate, 4 to 5 cents; carnations, 2 cents, fancy, 3 to 4 cents; violets, 75 cents for single, $1 for double; chrysanthemums, $1 to $3, the latter moving slowly.

The Wm. L. Rock Flower Company gave its annual chrysanthemum display last week on Thursday, Friday and Saturday. Nearly 5,000 visitors admired the display. Among the specimen bush and standard plants grown for show purposes was Brutus, a beautiful bronze. Mr. Rock thinks a show the best advertisement possible in the florist business. Some fine roses are coming in from Geo. M. Kellogg's.

Recent visitors: Mr. Scott, with Vaughan's Seed Store; Mr. Riogier, of Barnard's; Mr. Vaughan, of Hunt's; J. W. Furrows, from Guthrie, Ok.; Geo. W. Stiles, of Oklahoma City, who, by the way, is showing some of the finest mistletoe ever brought out of the territory; Mr. Creighton, of Dreer's; Miss Windmiller, of Mankato, Minn., brought down a car of vegetables for this market which netted her good returns; E. G. Bunyar, of Independence, Mo., reports several good wedding orders for his town.

W.

St. Paul.

Last week there were four large receptions, one large wedding and several elaborate dinner decorations, lots of funeral work, and add to this the show and nobody could wish for any more to do.

Violets are scarce here now, but it does not seem to make any difference with some of the stores, as we hear of them being retailed at 25 and 35 cents per bunch.

August S. Swanson reports trade very good in his new store.

Recent callers were Mr. Creighton, for H. A. Dreer, and L. Bauman, Chicago.

O.

THE AMERICAN FLORIST

NINETEENTH YEAR.

Subscription, $1.00 a year. To Europe, $2.00.
Subscriptions accepted only from those
in the trade.

Advertisements, on all except cover pages,
10 Cents a Line, Agate; $1.00 per inch.
Cash with Order.

No Special Position Guaranteed.

Discounts are allowed only on consecutive insertions, as follows—6 times,5 per cent; 13 times,
10 per cent; 26 times, 20 per cent;
52 times, 30 per cent.

Cover space sold only on yearly contract at
$1.00 per inch, net, in the case of the two
front pages, regular discounts applying only to the back pages.

The Advertising Department of the AMERICAN
FLORIST is for florists, seedsmen and nurserymen
and dealers in wares pertaining to those lines only.

Orders for less than one-half inch space not accepted.

Advertisements must reach us by Wednesday to
secure insertion in the issue for the following
Saturday. Address

AMERICAN FLORIST CO., Chicago.

BEDDING plant growers assert that S.
A. Nutt, John Thorpe's introduction, has
never been equalled in its class.

THE smaller growers throughout the
country will find some valuable suggestions in our Boston letter this week,
page 641.

THE Louisville Courier-Journal, of
November 8, devoted a page in colors
to the new calla called Mrs. Theodore
Roosevelt, of which Jos. Tailby, of Wellesley, Mass., possesses the stock.

PANDANUS SANDERI is not showing its
best color yet. Those who feel disappointed in it in this respect are advised
to exercise patience until Christmas by
which time they will be rewarded by a
brighter color.

THE MARQUIS carnation has been
receiving more or less criticism from
growers who have had poor success with
it. Perhaps in the case of this as well as
other carnations it is not all the fault of
the variety. An observant grower
advises us that it requires a decidedly
cool temperature and that surprisingly
good results will be obtained by keeping
this fact in mind. On the Pacific coast
where very little artificial heat is used
Marquis is a beauty.

Nephrolepis Scottii.

ED. AM. FLORIST:—In your report of
the New York show you designate the
exhibit of my new fern, Nephrolepis
Scottii as "the graceful little Scottii."
This may do very well as a term of endear-
ment bestowed upon the fern by your
correspondent, but it is somewhat mis-
leading. N. Scottii grows beyond the
"little" stage, in fact the original plant
of it was shown in New York last year in
a 14-inch pan and measured seven feet in
diameter, being even more graceful than
in a small pot.　　　JOHN SCOTT.

Illinois Horticultural Meetings.

Meetings of the leading horticultural
societies of Illinois will be held as follows:
Horticultural Society of Central Illinois,
Bloomington, November 19–20, F. S.
Phoenix, secretary, Bloomington; Horti-
cultural Society of Southern Illinois,
Salem, November 24–25, E. C. Menden-
hall, secretary, Kinmundy; Horticultural
Society of Northern Illinois, Rockford,
December 9–10, Jacob Friend, secretary,
Nikoma; Illinois State Horticultural
Society, Champaign, December 16–18,
L. R. Bryant, secretary, Princeton.

Cincinnati.

TRADE GOOD AND PROMISES TO BE BETTER.
—CLUB HOLDS CHRYSANTHEMUM SHOW.
—BIG GROWERS MAKE IT A SUCCESS.—
ALECK OSTENDORF A BENEDICT.

The chrysanthemum show at the club
rooms last Saturday was very interesting and choice blooms were on exhibition.
H. W. Rieman, of Indianapolis, Ind.; the
E. G. Hill Company, of Richmond, Ind.;
Gunnar Teilmann, Marion, Ind., and N.
Smith & Son, Aldrian, Mich., were the
out-of-town exhibitors. Richard Witterstaetter and J. W. Rodgers were the local
exhibitors and contributed their share to
make the exhibition a success. George &
Allan sent a very fine vase of Mrs. Weeks,
but as soon as they were staged Mr.
George received a very flattering offer for
them and as he and Louis Pfeiffer were
selected as judges and he did not want to
judge his own flowers, he accepted the
offer. The E. G. Hill Company received
first for the best white with Timothy
Eaton; Gunnar Teilmann was second
with same variety, and Henry Rieman
third with Majestic. In pink the E. G.
Hill Company was first with Marie
Newell, J. W. Rodgers second and third
with Perrin. In yellow Dick Witterstaetter was first with Appleton, the E.
G. Hill Company second with Yellow
Eaton, and Gunnar Teilmann third with
the same variety. For the best twenty-
five Major Bonnaffon Witterstaetter was
first and J. W. Rodgers second and third.
The prize for best general display was
captured by the E. G. Hill Company, and
this firm certainly had a very fine collection of cut blooms. Henry Rieman's
Majestic blooms were fine and his Adelia
and Madonna are particularly worthy of
mention. Gunnar Teilmann's Goldmine
were the largest blooms ever seen in the
clubrooms, and it is regretted that the
stems were so weak or the first prize for
yellow might have been captured by him.
In the seedling line Nathan Smith had Dr.
Engelhart, pink, and Imported and Sunburst, yellow. Henry Rieman sent Adelia,
a very pretty white which looks to be an
addition.

Trade the last week was all that could
be expected. There was an abundance
of roses and a good many found their
way into the barrel, but these were of
inferior quality. The good stock sold at
fair prices. This week the business started
off in a very brisk manner, and if the
present demand keeps up it will be a
record breaker for this time of the year,
as there are many receptions and other
events on the social calendar. Carnations are improving in quality and the
best are bringing $4 per 100. Chrysan-
themums are holding their own at good
prices and at times it is a difficult matter
to get just what you want to fill orders
with. Some excellent violets are coming
in, both single and double, the top price
being $1 per 100. There is enough valley
and green goods for all orders with the
exception of Asparagus plumosus and A.
Sprengeri, the supply of which is decreasing to some extent.

Aleck Ostendorf, of McCullough's, was
married last Monday evening by Rev.
Dr. Gervaise Roughton at the parsonage
of Wesley chapel to Miss Loraine Bole-
son. The happy young couple have the
best wishes and heartiest congratulations
from a large circle of friends. J. M. Mc-
Cullough's Sons and their employees presented the young couple with a beautiful
china closet and full set of dishes.

Messrs. George and Allan had an exciting experience last Saturday just as they
were about to leave the flower market.

The driver was loading the plants, and
went into the market house to get the
cut flowers that remained, when two
men jumped on the wagon and drove
away full speed. However, the thieves
were captured and Judge Lueders says he
will attend to their case.　　　D.

Pittsburg.

BUSINESS, WEATHER AND STOCK ALL GOOD.
— DEALERS ARE ENCOURAGED. — DEBU-
TANTES GET FLORAL OFFERINGS. —
FUNERAL WORK.—TRADE NOTES.

As a result of good stock of sufficient
quantity, some fine weather and a well
proportioned demand last week all the
stores report business good. American
Beauty piled up surprisingly at first, but
relief came at the right time. Bride and
Bridesmaid are fine in bloom and color.
Liberty, Carnot and Bon Silene are of
fine quality and plentiful. Chrysanthemums of every kind and color are to be
had. The finest and most salable varieties are Maud Dean, Golden Wedding and
Timothy Eaton. Carnations are plentiful and excellent values may be had.
Prosperity, Lawson, Enchantress and
White Cloud are the best. Violets and
gardenias are now an absolute staple
and the demand for them increases daily.
Orchids meet with liberal sale and some
very fine ones reach this market. The
introduction of debutantes is almost a
daily occurrence. They are recipients of
many flowers and the custom is so firmly
established that we can rely on much
trade from it. It is said the popularity
of the debutante is judged by the number
of bunches, baskets and bouquets she
receives. Another laudable feature of
this custom is that after the tea most all
the flowers are sent to the hospitals.
Ulam & Company's errand boy went
on a strike a few days ago. They tried
to have an agreement ratified whereby
they would not have to carry packages.
The matter was adjusted by Mr. Ulam,
who fired the crowd.

The passing away of two members of
Pittsburg's council created a demand
for funeral work, for which Tom Ulam &
Company's place seemed the headquarters.

The Pittsburg Florists' Exchange is
receiving some exceptional double violets.
Business is reported very good. P. J.
Demas, of the exchange, is on the sick
list.

The Pittsburg Rose and Carnation
Company is cutting some fine Enchantress and Prosperity carnations, also
some excellent American Beauty.

L. I. Neff has put a new front in his
Braddock store, which adds greatly to
its appearance. His new delivery wagon
is also very attractive.

John Baldinger is improving slowly
from his injuries. It will be about three
weeks before he is able to give attention
to business.

James Dill, Pittsburg's veteran florist,
reports business sky high at Neff's
Lawrenceville store.

Lowe & Rohrig have completed their
arrangements for Christmas greens and
novelties.

John Orth, of McKeesport, reports
business steady and satisfactory.

Randolph & McClements are long on
Cibotium Schiedei ferns.

Both Pierson and Boston ferns are meeting with excellent sale.　　　E. L. M.

NEENAH, WIS.—A new retail store has
been opened here by Louis Otto. Besides
cut flowers, potted plants, funeral
designs, etc., will be handled.

New Bedford, Mass.

The supply of flowers of all kinds is greater than the demand. It looks as though we were going to have an ample supply of everything for the Thanksgiving trade. R. N. Woodhouse has a large stock of chrysanthemums that he is keeping cold and shaded for the Thanksgiving trade. In violets the call is mostly for single. The sale of bulbs has been pretty good, but the department stores have taken it up and are selling tulips for 69 cents per hundred. We have been having two weeks of lovely Indian summer weather.

The New Bedford Horticultural Society meets the second Tuesday in each month. At the meeting last week it was announced that Mr. Farquhar, of Boston, would give a lecture in the near future. The New Bedford Florists' Club meets the second Thursday in each month. The club met last week at the office of Wm. Brown with fourteen members present. There was the usual lively time with a discussion of chrysanthemums. At the close refreshments were served by Mr. Brown.

At Arthur Ashley's new greenhouse, the first night of starting a fire the boiler burst.

A. B. H.

Cleveland.

CITY NURSERY FOR PARK TREES AND SHRUBS NOW BUSY.—EXPERT GROWER AT ITS HEAD.—FINE WEATHER AIDS DEALERS.—NOTES.

For the propagation of trees and shrubs for use in the city parks Cleveland has a nursery of eighteen acres in charge of M. H. Horvath, an expert horticulturist, botanist and forester. His force consists of many men. The nursery proper is on a knoll, where Gordon and Rockefeller parks come together. There are smaller grounds on Shaker heights and between Superior and St. Clair streets, where trees that do not require much care are grown. The nursery was nursed into existence about eight years ago by the old Park board. The parks were just being developed then, and were much in need of shrubs and trees, and to-day we have a park system which is unequaled anywhere.

Work at the nursery this fall consists of propagating a supply of flowers and shrubs for the parks next year. The nursery employes are putting in tulips in the various grounds this fall, including the public square, Lincoln square, Franklyn circle, Fairview park and Edgewater park. Mr. Horvath got his training in a horticultural school at Budapest, and then took a post-graduate course in Vienna. His ideas as to what a city park should be are interesting. He doesn't believe in scattering flowers, as the temptation of children and others to steal them is strong. The flowers should all be crowded into one park, which should be easy of access for the people to visit; then those who love flowers would know where to go and see them.

There is a movement afoot to assist one of our local florists, Robert Hughes, who met with a disastrous accident some months ago. Any one wishing to contribute may see the secretary of the Florists' Club, Isaac Kennedy.

Mr. Carlton, of Willoughby, is sending in fine, large violets. They will actually cover a silver dollar each.

The prolongation of this really ideal weather here has lessened the expenses of the growers considerably.

Wholesale florists report an increase in their sales on chrysanthemums, roses and carnations.

C. M. Merkle & Son. of Mentor, Ohio, are sending in some very fine chrysanthemums.

J. C. Robinson & Son, nurserymen, are well satisfied with this fall's trade.

John Leuschner has two houses, 20x100, just completed.   O. G.

Lowell, Mass.

The warm weather we had the last month seems to be a thing of the past, for now we are experiencing a sample of winter, just a reminder of what is in store for us. This sudden change has filled the growers' hearts with joy, especially those who have houses filled with blooms for Thanksgiving. It will indeed be a Thanksgiving for them. Business continues to hold up well and promises to keep good till the end of month. Last Saturday was a busy day here. Every-one was kept bustling getting up floral tributes for the funeral of W. H. White, the well known leather manufacturer. As early as this the farmers are in with their samples of green goods for Christmas. The storemen that handle bulbs report an increase over last year, especially in single tulips.

M. A. Patten, of Tewksbury, has returned home from the exhibitions at New York and Philadelphia, where he exhibited the Mrs. Patten carnation. He returns much pleased and reports having had a fine time.

Superintendent Whittet, of the parks and commons, has just finished planting his grounds with bulbs. Many thousands have been used.

We had our first snowstorm here November 16.   A. M.

Atmospheric Nitrogen

The gradual but ultimately inevitable exhaustion of the known nitrate deposits of South America lends a growing interest to the methods which have been devised for obtaining a supply of nitrogen for fertilizing purposes from the inexhaustible storehouse of the air. That this can be done on a scientific process has long been known. The first method was by passing a current of air over red-heated copper, whereby the oxygen combined with the metal to form oxide of copper, leaving the nitrogen free. At first the nitrogen thus produced was fixed by combination with calcium carbide to form nitrate of lime (Kalkstickstoff) or calcium cyanide, a combination of calcium cyanide and nitrogen, which had all the essential properties of a nitrate fertilizer. But as the use of calcium carbide rendered the product unduly expensive, a method was sought which would employ a substitute for that material, and this was found by Dr. Erlwein, who brought the nitrogen into a combination with a mixture of powdered charcoal and lime in an electric furnace. The product of this combination is a black substance containing, besides the lime and carbon, 10 to 15 per cent of nitrogen, in perfect condition to be used as a fertilizer. From the experiments that far made with this new artificial nitrate—which is known in commerce as calcium cyanide—it appears that its nitrogen acts upon plants quite as effectively as that contained in a proportionate quantity of nitrate of potassium or sodium nitrate (Chile saltpeter). The scientific problem of obtaining nitrogen for fertilizing purposes from the atmosphere would seem therefore to be satisfactorily solved. Whether it can be done on a very large scale and at a cost which will make it economically available for general agricultural purposes remains to be demonstrated by practical experience.

KEWANEE, ILL.—A chrysanthemum show at Hamilton & Plumer's green-houses last week attracted large crowds November 12, 13 and 14.

Memphis, Tenn.

The social season is on in full blast. All the florists are happy. Chrysanthemums are at their best and naturally are the favorites, with a steady demand for roses and carnations. Violets are getting good, and as this is the "City of Violets" the sale is always satisfactory.

An artistic arch made from asparagus, southern smilax and chrysanthemums, studded with small electric lights, was constructed by the Idlewild Greenhouses for the Mallory-Willnis wedding, which took place this week. A great deal of evergreen wreathing around the massive pillars of Calvary church, together with palms and ferns, made one of the most elaborate decorations executed here recently.

Out of town trade is picking up and all report good sales of bulbs and cut flowers, especially for funeral work. The weather here is perfect at present.　W. W.

BRIDGEPORT, CONN.—Miss Mamie Reck, daughter of John Reck, is seriously ill, and little hopes are entertained for her recovery.

Wholesale Flower Markets

MILWAUKEE, Nov. 19.

Roses, Beauty, med. per doz.	1.50	
" short "	.75@1.00	
" Bride, Bridesmaids	4.00@	6.00
" Meteor, Golden Gate	4.00@	6.00
" Perle		4.00
Carnations	1.00@	2.00
Smilax	10.00@12.50	
Asparagus		50.00
Chrysanthemums, fancy, per doz.	2.00	
" ordinary "	1.00	
Violets	.50@1.00	

PITTSBURG, Nov. 19.

Roses, Beauty, specials, per doz.	2.50@3.00	
" extras "	1.50@2.00	
" No. 1 "	.75@1.00	
" No. 2 "	3.00@	5.00
" Bride, Bridesmaid	1.00@	6.00
" Meteor	2.00@	4.00
" Kaiserin, Liberties	1.00@	6.00
Carnation	.75@	2.50
Lily of the Valley	3.00@	4.00
Smilax	10.00@15.00	
Adiantum		1.00
Asparagus, strings	30.00@60.00	
Asparagus Sprengeri	3.00@	3.00
Chrysanthemum	8.00@15.00	
Sweet Peas	.75@	1.00
Violets	.25@	1.00
Lilies	8.00@12.00	
Mignonette	1.00@	3.00

CINCINNATI, Nov. 19.

Roses, Beauty	5.00@50.00	
" Bride, Bridesmaid	3.00@	6.00
" Liberty	3.00@	6.00
" Meteor, Golden Gate	3.00@	6.00
Carnations	3.00@	4.00
Lily of the valley	3.00@	4.00
Asparagus		50.00
Smilax	13.50@15.00	
Adiantum	1.00@	1.50
Chrysanthemums	6.00@25.00	
Violets	.75@	1.00

ST. LOUIS, Nov. 19.

Roses, Beauty, medium stem	4.00	
" Beauty, short stem		12.50
Liberty	4.00@	6.00
" Bride, Bridesmaid	2.00@	4.00
" Golden Gate	2.00@	4.00
Carnations	1.00@	2.00
Smilax		12.50
Asparagus Sprengeri	1.00@	1.50
" Plumosus	15.00@50.00	
Ferns......... per 1000,	1.50	
Chrysanthemum	6.00@12.50	
Violets, single	.25@	.60
Valley	3.00@	4.00

DENVER, Nov. 19.

Roses, Beauty, long		20.00
" medium		15.00
" short		8.00
" Liberty	4.00@	8.00
" Chatenay	4.00@	7.00
" Bride, Bridesmaid	4.00@	6.00
Carnations	3.00@	4.00
Smilax		20.00
Common ferns		.30
Chrysanthemums, per doz.	1.00@1.50	

INTERNATIONAL FLOWER DELIVERY.

PASSENGER STEAMSHIP MOVEMENTS.

The tables herewith give the scheduled time of departure of ocean steamships carrying first-class passengers from the principal American and foreign ports, covering the space of two weeks from date of this issue of the AMERICAN FLORIST. Much disappointment often results from attempts to forward flowers for steamer delivery by express, to the care of the ship's steward or otherwise. The carriers of these packages are not infrequently refused admission on board and even those delivered on board are not always certain to reach the parties for whom they were intended. Hence florists in interior cities having orders for the delivery of flowers to passengers on out-going steamers are advised to intrust the filling of such orders to some reliable florist in the port of departure, who understands the necessary details and formalities and has the facilities for attending to it properly. For the addresses of such firms we refer our readers to the advertisements on this page:

FROM	TO	STEAMER	*LINE	DAY	DUE ABOUT
New York	Liverpool	Lucania	1	Sat. Nov. 28,	Dec. 4
New York	"	Etruria	1	Sat. Dec. 6,	Dec. 11
Boston	"	Saxonia	1	Sat. Nov. 29,	Dec. 4
New York	Glasgow	Laurentian	2	Thur. Nov. 26, 11:00 a. m.	Dec. 6
New York	Hamburg	Patricia	3	Sat. Nov. 28, 11:00 a. m.	Dec. 10
New York	"	Bluecher	3	Sat. Dec. 5, 4:00 p. m.	Dec. 17
New York	Glasgow	Furnessia	2	Sat. Nov. 28, Noon	Dec. 8
New York	"	Astoria	5	Sat. Dec. 5, 10:00 a. m.	Dec. 15
New York	London	Minnehaha	6	Sat. Nov. 28, Noon.	Dec. 8
New York	"	Menominee	6	Sat. Dec. 5, 9:00 a. m.	Dec. 15
New York	Liverpool	Teutonic	7	Wed. Nov. 25, Noon.	Dec. 2
New York	"	Arabic	7	Fri. Nov. 27, 11:00 a. m.	Dec. 5
New York	"	Germanic	7	Wed. Dec. 2, Noon.	Dec. 10
New York	"	Cedric	7	Fri. Dec. 4, 3:00 a. m.	Dec. 12
New York	Southampton	St. Paul	8	Sat. Nov. 28, 9:30 a. m.	Dec. 5
New York	"	Philadelphia	8	Sat. Dec. 5, 9:30 a. m.	Dec. 12
New York	Antwerp	Zeeland	9	Sat. Nov. 28, 10:30 a. m.	Dec. 7
New York	"	Finland	9	Sat. Dec. 5, 10:30 a. m.	Dec. 14
New York	Havre	La Bretagne	10	Thur. Nov. 26, 10:00 a. m.	Dec. 4
New York	"	La Touraine	10	Thur. Dec. 3, 10:00 a. m.	Dec. 11
New York	Rotterdam	Statendam	11	Sat. Nov. 25, 10:00 a. m.	Dec. 4
New York	"	Rhyndam	11	Wed. Dec. 5, 10:00 a. m.	Dec. 15
New York	Genoa	Nord America	12	Tues. Nov. 24, 11:00 a. m.	Dec. 7
New York	"	Sardegna	12	Tues. Dec. 1, 11:00 a. m.	Dec. 13
New York	"	Prinzess Irene	13	Tues. Dec. 1, 11:00 a. m.	Dec. 14
New York	Bremen	K. Wil. Der Grosse	13	Tues. Nov. 24, 10:00 a. m.	Dec. 1
New York	"	Grosser Kurfuerst	13	Thur. Nov. 26, 10:00 a. m.	Dec. 6
New York	"	Neckar	13	Thur. Dec. 3, 10:00 a. m.	Dec. 13
Boston	Liverpool	Kensington	15	Sat. Nov. 28, 3:30 p. m.	Dec. 4
Boston	"	Canada	15	Sat. Dec. 5, 11:00 a. m.	Dec. 12
Boston	Genoa	New England	15	Sat. Dec. 5, 11:00 a. m.	Dec. 12
Boston	Liverpool	Canadian	16	Wed. Nov. 25, 3:30 p. m.	Dec. 4
Boston	"	Cestrian	16	Wed. Dec. 2, 7:30 a. m.	Dec. 10

*1 Cunard; 2 Allen-State; 3 Hamburg-American; 4 Scandinavian-American; 5 Anchor Line; 6 Atlantic Transport; 7 White Star; 8 American; 9 Red Star; 10 French; 11 Holland-American; 12 Italian Royal Mail; 13 North German Lloyd; 14 Fabre; 15 Dominion; 16 Leyland; 17 Occidental and Oriental; 18 Oceanic; 19 Allan; 20 Can. Pacific Ry.; 21 N. Pacific Ry.; 22 Hongkong-Seattle.

INTERNATIONAL FLOWER DELIVERY.

STEAMSHIPS LEAVE FOREIGN PORTS.

FROM	TO	STEAMER	*LINE	DAY	DUE ABOUT
Liverpool........	New York	Campania	1	Sat. Nov. 28,	Dec. 4
Liverpool........	"	Umbria	1	Sat. Dec. 6,	Dec. 11
Liverpool........	Boston	Ivernia	1	Tues. Nov. 24,	Dec. 1
Glasgow........	New York	Corinthian	3	Sat. Dec. 5,	Dec. 15
Hamburg........	"	Graf Waldersee	3	Sat. Nov. 25,	Dec. 11
Hamburg........	"	Moltke	3	Sat. Dec. 5,	Dec. 17
Glasgow........	"	Columbia	5	Sat. Nov. 28,	Dec. 6
London........	"	Minnetonka	6	Sat. Nov. 28,	Dec. 8
London........	"	Mesaba	6	Thur. Dec. 3,	Dec. 13
Liverpool.......	"	Majestic	7	Wed. Nov. 25, 3:30 p. m.	Dec. 2
Liverpool.......	"	Celtic	7	Fri. Nov. 27, 3:30 p. m.	Dec. 4
Liverpool.......	"	Oceanic	7	Wed. Dec. 2, 3:30 p. m.	Dec. 10
Liverpool.......	"	Cymeric	7	Fri. Dec. 4, 3:30 p. m.	Dec. 13
Southampton...	"	St. Louis	8	Sat. Nov. 28, Noon.	Dec. 5
Southampton...	"	New York	8	Sat. Dec. 5, Noon.	Dec. 12
Antwerp........	"	Vaderland	9	Sat. Nov. 28, 7:30 a. m.	Dec. 7
Antwerp........	"	Kroonland	9	Sat. Dec. 5, Noon.	Dec. 14
Havre........	"	La Champagne	10	Sat. Nov. 28,	Dec. 6
Havre........	"	La Savoie	10	Sat. Dec. 5,	Dec. 13
Rotterdam ...	"	Rotterdam	11	Sat. Nov. 28,	Dec. 7
Rotterdam ...	"	Potsdam	11	Sat. Dec. 5,	Dec. 14
Genoa........	"	Citta di Milano	12	Mon. Nov. 30,	Dec. 17
Genoa........	"	Lahn	12	Tues. Nov. 24,	Dec. 6
Bremen........	"	Kaiser Wilh. II	13	Tues. Dec. 1,	Dec. 8
Liverpool.......	Boston	Mayflower	15	Thur. Nov. 26,	Dec. 8
Liverpool.......	"	Southwark	15	Thur. Dec. 3,	Dec. 11
Liverpool.......	"	Winifredian	16	Sat. Nov. 28,	Dec. 7
Liverpool.......	"	Bohemian	16	Sat. Dec. 5,	Dec. 15

* See steamship list on opposite page.

THE SEED TRADE.

AMERICAN SEED TRADE ASSOCIATION.
S. F. Willard, Pres.; J. Charles McCullough,
First Vice-Pres.; C. E. Kendel, Cleveland, O.,
Sec'y and Treas.
Twenty-second annual convention St. Louis,
Mo., June, 1904.

REPRESENTATIVES of the leading pickle houses were at Chicago this week attending the annual convention.

CUCUMBER prices seem to be settling around $1.50 to $2 per pound, the latter price for fancy pickling strains.

HOLLY is reported of good quality in the Delaware woods. Maryland and Virginia districts will also be cut. Tennessee and Kentucky report poor crops.

A GOOD authority gives it as his opinion that high prices now asked for Stowell's Evergreen sweet corn will not be maintained later; others look for $7 and $8 sweet corn.

VISITED BOSTON: Winfried Rolker, of Aug. Rolker & Sons; Wm. Hagemann, New York; J. W. Jefferson, secretary of the National Seed Company. Louisville, Ky.

GINSENG operators are evidently reaping quite a harvest in the sale of ginseng roots and seeds, quite a few amateurs dabbling in small plantings in their gardens. Some of the circulars come very near fake lines.

HAAGE & SCHMIDT, Erfurt Germany, offer the following novelties: Ageratum Mexicanum, Little Blue Star, Aquilegia ecalcarata, Aster Sinensis fl. pl., Ray-Aster "Fairy", Begonia Schmidtii rosea, Lobelia Cavanillesi lutea, Phlox Drummondi nana compacta Apricot, Silene Asterias grandiflora and Tropæolum Lobbianum Black Prince.

Catalogue Order Blanks.

The post office regulations with regard to catalogue order blanks have been practically a dead letter, but we are informed that they will be rigidly enforced hereafter. Under date of November 5 some rulings with regard to these order blanks were issued substantially as follows:

Printed catalogues containing more than one order blank upon which the blank space exceeds the printing, regardless of the manner in which order blanks may be enclosed, are subject when sent in the mails unsealed to postage at the fourth-class rate, one cent an ounce or fraction thereof.

Order blanks upon which the printing exceeds the blank space are third-class matter and do not subject the catalogues when sent in the mails unsealed, to a higher than third-class rate of postage, one cent for each two ounces or fraction thereof.

In order to guard against any possible misunderstanding, business houses should submit samples of proposed order blanks before the use of same is commenced.

British Dealers and Dutch Bulb Growers.

The following correspondence, which appeared in the *Horticultural Advertiser* (English) of November 4, will no doubt prove interesting to our readers at this time:

TO THE EDITORS OF THE HORTICULTURAL
ADVERTISER.

Dear Sirs: We think it is high time that the British trade should consider how it can best protect its interests against unfair trading of the foreign grower, and we refer more especially to the Dutch bulb grower and dealer.

It is the custom of many firms in Holland to send a representative to this country in May, to solicit orders for bulbs to be delivered about September.

The English houses purchase with a view of disposing of the same during the autumn months, but they find as the season advances that they have as competitors in their retail trade some of those Dutch "wholesale" firms, from whom they had purchased earlier in the season.

A case has just come before our notice and we give you a copy of a letter which we have addressed to the President of the Dutch Bulb Association of Holland, with a view of putting an end to such practices if in any way possible.

We consider the only course open is for the English trade to compel the Dutch grower or dealer that they purchase from to sign an undertaking to the effect that he does not supply retail customers in England.

Surely with the great competition that we have to contend with, added to it, auction sales of bulbs and the unfair mode of business of many Dutch firms, it is time we considered what means should be adopted to protect our interests.

We trust you will see your way to give the whole matter publicity in your valuable and much appreciated paper.

(Signed)   WM. CUTBUSH & SON.

TO THE PRESIDENT OF THE DUTCH BULB ASSOCIATION.

Dear Sir: As president of the Bulb Association of Holland, we feel that you are interested in the welfare of the Dutch bulb trade, and we therefore take the liberty of bringing before your notice a matter which, to our minds, is likely to prove a serious one to all those connected with the production and export to this country of Dutch bulbs.

A few weeks ago a customer of the English houses, the municipal borough council of Hampstead, invited tenders for the supply of bulbs required this season for its cemetery, and in accordance with the custom of many years past, several London firms, including Carter & Co., R. B. Williams & Son and ourselves, sent in tenders. To our surprise and astonishment, we find that the wholesale Dutch firm of M. Veldhuyzen van Zanten & Zonen, of Lisse, had also entered into competition with us, and the tender of this firm being the lowest, was eventually accepted by the Hampstead council.

Messrs. Veldhuyzen van Zanten send a representative to this country in May each year, to solicit orders from the English trade for bulbs for autumn delivery. Having secured orders and supplied goods, they then endeavor to obtain those orders upon which the English houses had relied in placing their orders earlier in the season, and quoting lower prices than those at which they had supplied the trade, are enabled to secure the orders for which the English trade had already purchased with a view of supplying.

We trust you will agree with us that this is far from being a legitimate mode of carrying on business, and apart from the interests of the English bulb dealer, whom we have always found the more respectable Dutch houses anxious to consider, we believe that such practice must necessarily affect the bulb trade of Holland to a considerable extent.

The English dealers finding the demand for Dutch bulbs (which they in no small measure have assisted to create) considerably diminished by the competition of certain Dutch firms, will be compelled to curtail their purchases early in the season, made on the chances of disposing of them during the autumn months, and it will create a tendency on their part to place their orders as far as possible and especially in the case of such bulbs as narcissus, crocus, etc., with growers of others countries who adopt a more legitimate system of trading. We trust your association will express its stern disapproval of the practice we complain of, with its far reaching results, detrimental to all interests concerned, and use every means in its power to restore that confidence which is being impaired, a confidence which to our minds is not only desirable but necessary, if the substantial business connections of the Dutch bulb grower with the English customer is to be maintained and strengthened.

We should also like to touch upon another matter in which the English trader is placed at a decided disadvantage.

Last season your association, with a view of encouraging interest in the culture of Dutch bulbs amongst the English trade, was good enough to offer prizes for hyacinths and tulips, at the Royal Horticultural Society's exhibition.

When the exhibition took place we were greatly astonished to find that a Dutch firm was competing, thus defeating the object you had in offering the prizes.

May we suggest that if you offer such prizes again, a clause should be inserted that "Dutch growers are not allowed to compete."

We have been supporters of the Dutch bulb trade for upwards of seventy-five years and this is our reason for addressing you upon the subject.

(Signed)   WM. CUTBUSH & SON.

Advice to Exporters to the Philippines.

The following article, taken from the *Manila Daily Bulletin* of recent date, may be of interest to United States exporters:

Catalogues should be in Spanish, and should always give the telegraphic addresses and codes employed. Prices should be given. Confidential discount sheets should give the prices current; the importer then can judge prices from his own commercial journals. Weights and dimensions of articles are of great value in a catalogue. The reputation of a house often depends upon the manner of packing as much as on the merchandise itself. Goods for Manila should be packed with special care. The port is unprotected and the sea is often very rough, making unloading at such times impossible. Transfer is made by natives from boats from a point two miles distant. These boats are tossed about by the slightest agitation of the water.

Documents ought to accompany the merchandise. Firms should choose for their representatives persons of great experience. The customs officials of Manila are guided by fixed laws, inform which they do not deviate. The Philippine tariff laws in regard to the different classifications should be carefully studied and persons should draw up their documents in accordance therewith. Manufacturers should not place small samples in their shipments unless they mention them as such in their invoices, otherwise they will be compelled to pay duty thereon, and, perhaps, an additional amount. Every package should bear the name of its destination and its particular marks, and should also show gross and net weight in pounds and kilograms. Invoices should be prepared in regular form. Some important rules of the Philippine customs service follow:

1. Each package should be specified in the invoice, with marks and numbers.
2. The contents of each package should be indicated in detail, in regard to price and destination.
3. Packages containing goods of different classification should be so entered.
4. The weight declared should include the wrapper, since the wrapper pays the same duty as its contents.
5. As the wrapper is destroyed, the invoice should show net and gross weight.
6. Invoices should always be made in triplicate, two for the customs and the third for consignee.

If bills of lading are not payable at sight, a second but nonnegotiable bill should follow, in order to give the consignee information as to freight. It is preferable to insure in companies having legal representatives in Manila.

HILLSDALE, MICH.—Wellington Hughes has just finished a new house for carnations and pot plants, 16x106 feet, corner of Garden and Hillsdale streets.

RIVERSIDE, CAL.—F. P. Hasp has several acres of carnations which are looking thrifty. He is building a small glass house for propagating.   R. H. A.

ROCKFORD, ILL.—S. H. Crowell has disposed of his greenhouses on Rural Route No. 2 to his son, L. H. Crowell, Jr., who will continue the business.

DENTON, TEX.—Work on the greenhouse at the Girls' Industrial college is progressing. The size of the workroom is 54x100 feet and the greenhouse consists of three rooms, each 18x32 feet.

MOLINE, ILL.—The chrysanthemum show at the greenhouse in Central park opened November 1 and continued until the tenth. There were large crowds of visitors continually.

THE NURSERY TRADE.

AM. ASSOCIATION OF NURSERYMEN.
N. W. HALE, Knoxville, Tenn., Pres.; FRANK
A. WEBER, St. Louis, Mo., Vice-Pres.; GEORGE C.
SEAGER, Rochester, N. Y., Sec'y.
Twenty-ninth annual convention, Atlanta, Ga.,
June, 1904.

Best Spray for Trees.

The results obtained in this inquiry
indicate that the best spray to use is
the lime, salt and sulphur. This material
has given the greatest satisfaction in
actual practice in previous years. It is a
cheap mixture. In laboratory experiments it compares favorably with all
the other remedies tried. It is one of the
quickest to kill that we have used, and
its penetrating power is good. It is as
valuable as the Bordeaux mixture for the
control of curl leaf; it is likewise the
most available remedy for the destruction of the San Jose scale, if this be present.
Finally, its general good effect on the
tree, resulting in a more healthy condition of the bark, is well known. The
good qualities of this material more than
counterbalance the unpleasant features
attendant upon its making and application.

How Made.—The generally accepted formula and directions for making the lime,
salt and sulphur are as follows: Lime
(unslacked), forty pounds; sulphur,
twenty pounds; salt, fifteen pounds;
water, sixty gallons. Take ten pounds
of lime and twenty pounds of sulphur
and boil in ten gallons of water from one
or one and a half to two hours, or until
the sulphur is completely dissolved. This
will be shown by the liquid assuming a
clear amber color. Slack the balance of
the lime and to it add the salt. When
this is all dissolved add to the lime and
sulphur solution. Boil from thirty to
forty-five minutes more. Finally add
enough hot water to make the full sixty
gallons and apply to the tree hot. The
efficiency of the lime and salt mixture
depends upon the union of the lime and
sulphur, and this result can only be
obtained by thorough boiling. A simple
mixture of these materials is useless, as
such a mixture has neither penetrating
nor killing power.

How and When Applied.—A mistake commonly made is neglect in spraying the
upper and outer part of the tree. It is
most important that the new wood
should be sprayed. No part of the tree
should be neglected, and least of all the
part where the new growth is found. As
has been previously noted, the worm
generally chooses the new wood crotches
for its hibernating cell, and a neglect to
apply this spray here means the escape
of the worm. The spray should cover
the whole tree. The evidence at hand
seems to indicate that it would be useless
to apply spray before the buds show
signs of swelling. That spraying should
be done after this swelling is evident, but
it should not be delayed until too late,
because of possible injury to the blossoms.
The foregoing was furnished by Geo. E.
Freeman, who had several years' experience with the San Jose scale in California,
and, though now residing in the vicinity
of Boston, still owns large orchards in
California, and this remedy is now being
successfully used by his manager.—Bulletin New England Association of Park
Superintendents.

ALTON, ILL.—The local Horticultural
Society celebrated its fiftieth anniversary
Thursday, November 12. But one charter
member is living, Hon. H. G. McPike.

MAGNOLIA, MASS.—An Italian garden is
to be added to the attractions of Miss
F. M. Stearn's summer home.

GLASTONBURY, CONN.—The Green Park
association will have a larger fund than
ever next year for the purpose of caring
for and improving the park.

SAN DIEGO, CAL.—Miss Kate O. Sessions
is moving her nursery from its present
location in the City park to a place near
the standpipe towards Old Town. As a
consequence a "removal sale" is in progress.　　　R. H. A.

OUR PASTIMES.

Announcements of coming contests or other events of interest to our bowling, shooting and sporting readers are solicited and will be given place in this column.
Address all correspondence for this department to Wm. J. Stewart, 42 W. 28th St., New York. Robt. Kift, 1725 Chestnut St., Philadelphia, Pa.; or to the American Florist Co., Chicago, Ill.

At Chicago.

The meeting of the Florists' Bowling Club was this week postponed from Tuesday to Thursday evening, owing to the show which was held Tuesday. On account of the postponement many of the members could not attend, but the officers hope to start in next week with a full quota. A special meeting will be held next Tuesday evening to elect a captain. Following are the scores of the last games:

Player.	1st	2d	3d
Lambros	188	160	164
Asmus	145	135	138
Conomos	115	143	108
Ed. Winterson	114	141	103
Andrew	150	116	127
Stephens	148	184	164
Huesner	134	143	174
Hauswirth	149	110	146
Geo. Scott	150	138	133
Foerster	221	194	173

At Philadelphia.

The first of the bowling matches between the club members in the home alley tournament was played last Monday night between the teams captained by Dunham and Kift. Goebel of Kift's team, being absent his average score of 155 was counted in, according to the rules. Although the Kift team made the highest total in the three games they made only one point, as they lost the first and last games. Each game won counts a point. The score follows:

Player.	1st	2d	3d
Dunham	158	147	164
Moore	158	149	189
Watson	173	145	142
Anderson	168	133	163
Werlitz	133	132	129
Totals	780	715	786
Player.	1st	2d	3d
Kift	150	184	143
Craig	189	153	149
Holms	123	168	156
Goebel	155	155	155
Allen	168	170	191
Totals	784	830	773

K.

Ashtabula, O.

Herbert Tong, who the last twenty years has had charge of the Scott estate's Massassuga garden and greenhouses at Erie, Pa., has at last severed his connection with that establishment and will in future make his home in this city and take care of his own interests. Mr. Tong has added a rose house 16x165 to his establishment here and now has 20,000 square feet of glass well stocked with smilax and asparagus. Of the latter he makes a specialty, one large house being filled with fine strings of A. plumosus, while many thousands of plants of plumosus and Sprengeri are being grown on benches for sprays, for which there is always a good demand.
At the present cannas and chrysanthemums out of doors are in full bloom which, with the continued warm weather we are having, does not tend to improve trade. No flowers are going to waste, but prices might be better. H.

CAIRO, ILL.—Wm. Davidson has moved to the Lambert building on Eighth street.

Exhibition at Buffalo.

The second chrysanthemum show of the H. A. Meldrun Company, given under the auspices of the Buffalo Florists' Club, was a pronounced success. The flowers were good, the prices were enough to make almost any one willing to compete for them and there were large crowds. The weather was all that could be desired and the only regret was that it was not held by the Buffalo Florists' Club as an independent affair. The club was unfortunate in the selection of judges, as nearly all had engagements elsewhere, but George Fancouth of Wilkesbarre, Pa., was with us for the first two days and then we were honored by having Philip Breitmeyer and George Rackham of Detroit, take up the work of Mr. Fancouth after he had been called home. On Wednesday and Thursday Mr. Fancouth was assisted by Jas. Braik, assistant superintendent of the Buffalo parks, and C. T. Guenther, of Hamburg, N. Y., and their excellent judgment, in plants, cut blooms and bowers was highly satisfactory. Friday Mr. Breitmeyer and Mr. Rackham were the judges on what proved to be the drawing card of the exhibition, the set dinner table decoration of chrysanthemums. Another year the premium for dinner table decorations will be one of the largest, as it certainly was a successful ladies' day event.
The H. A. Meldrun Company next year fully expects to give more space, a larger premium list and increased facilities for getting the crowds up to the show. Maicu's, Buffalo's leading orchestra, was there from noon until 6 p. m. daily, which was another attraction.
C. Sandiford had on exhibition two plants of Garza chrysanthemum, of the pompon class, that were certainly grand, both as to the way they were grown and the flower itself. Another pretty cut flower was a large vase of the new yellow chrysanthemum, Golden Age, exhibited by Nathan Smith & Son, Adrian, Mich. L. E. Marquise, of Syracuse, N. Y., sent a fair lot of his new red carnation, Flamingo, which is a very fine flower and from all appearances a good keeper.
On Friday evening a social dinner was given by the Buffalo Florists' Club for the pleasure of our honored guest, President Breitmeyer, of the Society of American Florists. It was a plain and pleasant affair and while another engagement prevented President Breitmeyer remaining all evening, we were glad to have him and listen to his remarks about what the society would do in St. Louis and the American Carnation Society in Detroit, and extended a hearty welcome to the Buffalo Florists' Club to both places. Addresses were made by J. C. Siler, who represented the E. A. Meldrun Company, and by Supt. Keltsch, of the exhibition. Informal remarks were also made by nearly every one there. We were entertained by Chas. Hess, of the H. A. Meldrun Company, in Jewish character and sleight of hand work. About twenty-five of the florists of Buffalo were there and all had a good time.

In conclusion I wish to say that Supt. C. H. Keltsch, in behalf of the Buffalo Florists' Club, did his work most satisfactorily, and J. C. Siler, advertising manager of the H. A. Meldrun Company, in the same manner.
Among the visitors who were present were G. B. Fancouth, Wilkesbarre, Pa.; President Breitmeyer, Detroit; George Rockham, Detroit; Wm. Mansfield, Lockport, N. Y.; S. A. Bauer, Erie, Pa.; E. G. Hill, Richmond, Ind.
The awards in detail were as follows:
Specimen plants, chrysanthemums, white—C. Sandiford, first.
Yellow—Mrs. G. H. Lewis, Monroe, Mich., first.
Pink—Mrs. G. H. Lewis, first.
Red—C. Sandiford, first.
Any shape or variety—C. Sandiford, first; Mrs. G. H. Lewis, second.
Specimen chrysanthemum blooms, fifty white—C. F. Christensen, first; E. G. Hill Company, Richmond, Ind., second; Wm. Ehmann, Corfu, N. Y., third.
Yellow—Nathan Smith & Son, Adrian, Mich., first; E. G. Hill Company, second; Wm. Ehmann, third.
Pink—C. F. Christensen, first; E. G. Hill Company, second; Wm. Scott, third.
Any other color—Wm. Ehmann, first; W. F. Kasting, second; E. G. Hill Company, third.
Chrysanthemum blooms, twenty-five white—Nathan Smith & Son, first; E. G. Hill Company, second; Wm. Ehmann, third.
Yellow—Nathan Smith & Son, first; E. G. Hill Company, second; Wm. Ehmann, third.
Pink—Nathan Smith & Son, first; E. G. Hill Company, second; Wm. Belsey, third.
Any other color—C. Sandiford, first; Wm. Ehmann, second; E. G. Hill Company, third.
One hundred blooms, more than twenty-five varieties—E. G. Hill Company, first; C. Sandiford, second; Nathan Smith & Son, third.
Fifty blooms introduced in 1903—E. G. Hill Company, first; Nathan Smith & Son, second.
One hundred blooms arranged for effect—W. F. Kasting, first; Wm. Scott, second; S. A. Anderson, third.
Handle basket arrangement—C. Sandiford, first; Wm. Scott, second; C. D. Zimmerman, third.
Table chrysanthemum decoration—Palmer & Son, first; Wm. Scott, second; S. A. Anderson, third.
Roses, 100 American Beauties—S. A. Anderson, first; W. F. Kasting, second; South Park Floral Company, third.
White—T. Guenther, Hamburg, N. Y., first; S. A. Anderson, second; W. F. Kasting, third.
Pink—W. F. Kasting, first; South Park Floral Company, second; S. A. Anderson, third.
Red—W. F. Kasting, first; South Park Floral Company, second. BISON.

KEWANEE, ILL.—Hamilton & Plummer's flower show was a decided success.

Exhibition at Waco, Texas.

The State chrysanthemum show opened in Waco, November 11, and was a decided success in point of attendance and interest. It was held in a large building especially designed for the purpose, called the Chrysanthemum Temple. It was decorated with ornamental foliage and tinted fabrics with trailing moss draping from the ceilings and posts that lent a beautiful tropical effect to the large exhibition hall. Plumage and song birds, ornamental fish in costly aquariums, music and art exhibits reinforced the flowers in lending attraction. The door receipts are said to have been the largest of any floral exhibition ever given in Texas.

Seven states were represented in the exhibits and great credit is due to Mrs. Louis. Crow, the president, for the excellent manner in which she and her assistants managed all the details. While the exhibits of the home growers were fully as good as on former occasions, there was quite a noticeable lack in the display of prominent growers from abroad. This is possibly accounted for by the falling off in the cash premiums offered as compared with the previous lists, as well as the fact that the competitions were strung out to extend for four days, the entire time of the show, and a grower from a distance could not have his blooms in good condition for each day without separate and expensive shipments and would show up badly beside the local grower that had his best in reserve for each consecutive day of competition.

Walter Reese, a local grower, got the lion's share of the premiums. While but an amateur he has for long been the terror of many professional growers. Florists Jas. Wolf and Chas. Mayer divided honors in the number of premiums taken. Mrs. C. J. Costier had a number of blue ribbons to her credit. The surrounding towns all sent large delegations. H. F. Good, of Springfield, O., was the judge.   M.

Exhibition at Pembroke, Ky.

A chrysanthemum fair and floral exhibition was given in Pembroke, Ky., November 11 to 13. It was held under the auspices of the library association of the Pembroke graded schools. R. W. Downer, a prominent citizen and local enthusiast in chrysanthemum culture, was the superintendent. C. E. Dudley, principal of the public school system, was one of the chief directors.

The exposition was held in a spacious warehouse cleared and profusely decorated for the purpose. Entire cedar trees were cut from the woods and the walls inside were completely hidden by foliage and growing plants. Part of the hall was partitioned off where a stage and seats for over 1,000 people were provided. An entertaining programme of music and other features was given twice daily during the three days of the show. A large dining room was also spaced off, where good things to eat were served. Everybody in Pembroke went to the show and every family had its visitors from a distance. The railroads gave a reduced rate and dozens of handsome turnouts could be seen where visitors in many cases had driven over thirty miles to see the show. All the good things that Kentucky is famous for were everywhere to be seen and enjoyed.

There were no classes for florists. J. W. Cross had the finest general display in the exhibition as well as a number of prize-winning plants in many of the other classes. R. W. Downer had a fine display of well-grown plants, though not quite as extensive as that of J. W. Cross. He took first premium for single stems. The Misses Garnett, Mrs. R. Y. Pendleton and Mrs. C. E. Dudley won most of the other premiums offered. Jas. Morton, of Clarksville, Tenn.; Chas. Morgan, of the Metcalf Greenhouses, of Hopkinsville, and Mrs. Annie Wilson, of the Savage Floral Company, Hopkinsville, were the judges.   M.

MANCHESTER, MASS.—The North Shore Horticultural Society's annual chrysanthemum show, on November 11, was acknowledged to be the best in the society's history. A silver medal was awarded to Philip Dexter for display of twenty plants and to Mrs. R. C. Hooper for display of cut blooms. Mrs. Hooper also had a table of fine orchids and one of roses. Most of the "summer colony" were contributors to a greater or less extent, many of the collections being superb.

Exhibition at Baltimore.

The Gardeners' Club of Baltimore held its annual chrysanthemum show at the Royal Arcanum building, November 9. The committee in charge consisted of J. W. Boone, Chas. L. Seybold, F. G. Burger and John Cook. Among the exhibitors were Halliday Brothers, John Cook, R. Vincent, Lehr Brothers, G. Burger, I. H. Moss, E. A. Seidewitz, G. A. Lotze, Mr. Weber and the Buxton Floral Company. The best exhibit from a private place was made by Chas. Wagner, gardener to Chas. R. Diffenderfer. He received several first prizes. An immense white seedling flower which he exhibited was given a special premium. He will name it Cassia. One bloom measured ten and one-half inches in diameter.

Robert Graham exhibited a large basket of American Beauty and lily of the valley. Foliage plants shown by Halliday Brothers and I. H. Moss received first premiums and good roses and violets were exhibited. A few days ago the first heavy frost cleaned up all outdoor flowering stock and it is hoped trade in cut flowers will improve from now on. Up to this time there has been a large stock on the market at extremely low prices. Good roses are not so plentiful.

W. H. Witte, gardener at the House of Refuge, has invented a movable greenhouse bench. He had a model set on exhibition which received honorable mention. The Messrs. Vincent went to the New York show with sixty-five varieties of pompon chrysanthemums.

Premiums were awarded at the show as follows:

Richard Vincent, Jr., first for sixty-five varieties of pompon.

Henry Fisher, special for mixed collection of chrysanthemums, also special for seedling carnations.

Gustav Lotze, first for pink chrysanthemums; second for yellow chrysanthemums and special for seedling chrysanthemums.

H. Weber & Sons, of Oakland, first for Prosperity carnations, first for Enchantress and Adonis carnations, second for vase chrysanthemums.

Frederick Burger, first for basket and wreath of chrysanthemums and Bride roses.

Robert L. Graham, first for basket of American Beauty roses and lily of the valley.

H. Rhinehart, second for white chrysanthemums.

William Madsen, second for Bride roses; second for Bridesmaid roses; first for Golden Gate roses.

Buxton Floral Company, second for pink chrysanthemums.

Halliday Brothers, first for decorative plants.

John McCormick, special for seedling carnations.

F. C. Bauer, first for violets.

I. H. Moss, second for decorative plants; special for vase carnations.

James A. Gary, first for collection of Bridesmaid. Bride, Golden Gate and American Beauty roses; first for pink chrysanthemums; first for yellow vase chrysanthemums; first for Eston chrysanthemums; first for collection of mixed chrysanthemums.

Lehr Brothers, first for yellow chrysanthemums; second for pink chrysanthemums; second for collection of mixed chrysanthemums.

Charles R. Diffenderfer, first for collection of thirty-five varieties of chrysanthemums; second for Colonel Appleton; first for vase of bronze chrysanthemums; special for white seedlings; first for standard and single-stem chrysanthemums; first for bush plants.

Stevenson Brothers, first for Lawson carnations; first for Bride and Bridesmaid roses; first for Perle roses.   C. L. S.

Exhibition at Tyler, Texas.

The first annual chrysanthemum show was held here November 11 and 12 and was well attended. The people in this section have the chrysanthemum fever bad. Many good premiums were offered to competitors not outside of Smith county. Another season it is proposed to offer a premium for professional growers. A fine lot of cut blooms from Morton's Evergreen Lodge Clarksville, Tenn., was on exhibition for display only and was highly admired. The show was given under the auspices of the guild of Christ's church and a neat sum was realized. S. J. Mitchell, of Houston, was judge of the flowers.   M.

Please mention the American Florist to advertisers.

Dutchess County, N. Y., Exhibition.

The eighth annual exhibition of the Dutchess County Horticultural Society opened at Poughkeepsie, N. Y., in the state armory, November 11. It can be safely stated that this year's exhibition was the finest ever seen along the Hudson river and will go down in the history of the society as a very important event. Every square foot of available space was utilized. The hall was decorated with flags, bunting and evergreens of various kinds. Myriads of electric lights were strung, all over the hall from the big steel girders and evergreen trees at the sides were studded with vari-colored lights. In the center of the hall was G. Saltford's big booth decorated in a very handsome manner with evergreens, where were shown fancy florists' supplies. The grange exhibit by Oak Grove, No. 873, Patrons, of Husbandry, was a feature. It was constructed to represent the entrance to the Pantheon. The columns supporting the roof were covered with pretty autumn leaves, all varnished. Instead of steps leading to the Pantheon there was an incline and on this were neatly arranged the products of the grange, including fruits, vegetables, pastry, canned goods, candies, jellies and grains. Another newcomer at this year's show was the handsome exhibit of Town & Son, coopers, with a handsome line of flower tubs and jardiniers. Thursday table decorations were the feature of the day.

But few specimen plants of chrysanthemums were shown, but those few were very good.—W. C. Russell, gardener to Chas. A. Dieterich, Millbrook, took first prize for white and yellow with plants of Miss Alice Byron and W. H. Lincoln. Groups of foliage plants were exhibited in sufficient numbers to relieve the effect of too much color and monotony of form.

First prize for best group of ornaments and flowering plants went to Winthrop Sargent, Fishkill-on-Hudson, F. E. Whitney, gardener; first for group of foliage plants to F. R. Newbold, Thos. Bell, gardener; for table of foliage plants first to Archibald Rogers. Mr. Conners, gardener; for specimen foliage plant, first to F. R. Newbold.

For six foliage plants first went to Winthrop Sargent; for best six ferns of distinct varieties first to F. R. Newbold, with well-grown specimens of Adiantum bulbiferum, Adiantum Wiegandii, Davallia Mooreana, Cyrtomium falcatum. Adiantum cuneatum and the new Adiantum Croweanum. The latter appears to be a decided acquisition to the list of useful ferns.

The display of cut chrysanthemums was larger and better than ever. The prizes were distributed as follows:

Best vase of twenty-five white.—Second to G. Saltford for Silver Wedding.

Twenty-five yellow.—First to W. C. Russell, with Col. D. Appleton, a beautiful vase.

Thirty-six blooms in six varieties.—W. C. Russell first, with Mrs. H. Weeks. Col. D. Appleton, Mrs. E. Thirkell, Merza, T. Carrington and Mrs. Barkley.

Twelve white.—First to Archibald Rogers.

Twelve yellow.—First to Archibald Rogers.

Twelve pink.—First to W. C. Russell, with Mrs. Geo. Mileham.

Twelve any other color.—First to W. C. Russell, with T. Carrington.

Vase of twenty-five blooms arranged for effect.—First to W. G. Saltford.

Twenty-four blooms in twenty-four varieties.—W. C. Russell, first; F. E. Whitney, second.

Twelve blooms, twelve varieties.—Girard Foster, Lenox, Mass., first; Samuel Thorne, Millbrook, I. T. Powell, gardener, second.

Special prize for twenty-four blooms, four varieties.—W. C. Russell.

The rose classes were all well filled and competition was keen. The quality was of the best and some of the exhibits would have done credit to the large rose growing establishments.

The silver cup offered by the American Rose Society for best collection was won by W. D. Sloane, Lenox, Mass., F. Heermaps, gardener. Other awards were:

Twenty American Beauty.—First to Archibald Rogers, Mr. Conners, gardener.

Collection, four varieties, two blooms of each.—First to Girard Foster, gardener.

Twelve Bridesmaid.—First to Col. D. S. Lamout. M. Brophy, gardener; second to Samuel Thorne, W. J. Sealey, Jr., foreman.

Twelve Bride.—First to Col. D. S. Lamont; second to Samuel Thorne.

Twelve of any other variety.—First to Girard Foster, with twelve magnificent blooms of Pres. Carnot; second to W. D. Sloane, with Queen of Edgely.

Carnations were also well shown and competition was good.—W. D. Sloane won first prize for two collections of thirty-six blooms, three varieties twelve of each, staging Enchantress, Lawson and Prosperity.

Other awards were:

Fifty pink.—First to Levi P. Morton, Thomas Talbot, gardener, with Lawson.

Fifty red.—First to W. G. Saltford, with G. H. Crane.

Fifty variegated.—W. G. Saltford first, with Prosperity.

Fifty white.—W. D. Sloane first, with Gov. Wolcott.

For seedling carnation a certificate of merit was awarded Chas. F. Deiterich for Daheim, a fine crimson.

Poughkeepsie being in the heart of the violet growing district of the Hudson valley, a magnificent display is always looked for here and the blooms that were exhibited were all that could be desired. The number of exhibitors was very small in comparison with former years. Mayor Elmer prize for 200 double in two bunches was won by Lyon & Strickland, of Milton, N. Y. The Chas. Mitchell prize for 100 double in two bunches was won by Stanton Rockefeller, Rhinebeck, N. Y. The Dutchess County Horticultural Society prize for 100 double went to Stanton Rockefeller, second to W. B. Willig.

Prizes for fruit were won by Col. D. S. Lamont and Levi P. Morton.

While all the flower exhibits were good "add" a credit to the gentlemen who supplied the means and the gardeners who grew them, some few deserve special mention.

Mrs. H. Weeks when grown as exhibited here is without a peer for magnificent grace and beauty. Merza also was good but lacks stem. Appleton is rich and massive.

Mrs. E. Thirkell was shown in grand size and form. Viviand-Morel seems to have been almost entirely superseded here. A. J. Balfour and Mrs. Geo. Mileham with Mrs. Barkley taking its place as pinks. Armorica was also shown in good form. Of the newer varieties of roses Sunrise and Franz Deegen were shown. The former should find a place in popular favor. The latter as shown here was disappointing. The color is not decided and the neck was weak, although the stems were of good length and size. Enchantress, Lawson, Prosperity, Crane and Gov. Wolcott were the leaders in their respective colors among carnations.

W. G. Sealey, Jr.

GERANIUMS

Well Rooted Cuttings, true to name. Jean Viaud, S. A. Nutt, Mme. Buchner. $1.95 per 100; $10.00 per 1000. Le Soleil, Ricard, Poitevine, Mme. Landry, Perkins. De Harcourt, $1.60 per 100; $12.00 per 1000. Cash with order.

WILLIAMSVILLE GREENHOUSES, Williamsville, N.Y.

Ferns and Geraniums
10,000 Boston Ferns in 2, 3, 4, 5, 6 and 7-inch pots at $3, $6, $15, $25, $40 and $60 per 100. 6'-in. inch bench $2, $5, $12, $25, $30 and $50 per 100. All strong, fine plants. 100,000 Geraniums, Nutt, Hetteranthe, LaFavorite, Buckner, Perkins. Double Grant. A. Ricard, single scarlet and Mme. Salleroi, R. C., $10.00 per 100; 3-inch, $2.00 per 100. Other 20 varieties, including M. Castellane, Jean Viaud, Mme. Jaulin, R. C., $1.50; 2-inch, $2.50 per 100.

L. Mosbaek, 85th St., near S. Chicago Ave., Chicago.

Boston Ferns.

2½-in., $4.00 per 100; $35.00 per 1000.

Pierson Ferns.

2½-inch, $25.00 per 100.

The Conard & Jones Co., WEST GROVE, PA.

A FINE LOT OF

FERNS.

Assorted Varieties, in 2½ and 3-inch pots at $2.00 per 100..........

WAGNER PARK CONSERVATORIES, SIDNEY, OHIO.

Stanley, Ashton & Co.,
Southgate, England.

The live British Orchid importers and growers supply plants singly or by thousands with equal pleasure. Write for quotations and American testimonials. Brazilian Species in bulk shipped direct from Brazilian port.

BOSTON FERNS

2½-in., $4.00; 3-in., $8.00; 4-in., $15.00; 5-in., $25.00 6-in., $40.00; 7-in., $50.00; 8-in., $75.00 per 100.

PIERSON FERNS, young plants from bench. $5.00 per 100; 2½-in., $20.00 per 100; 4-in., $50 each; 5-in., 75c each. Also bench-grown BOSTONS in all sizes. All stock extra fine. Cash with order

DAVIS BROS., Geneva, Ill.

Geo. Wittbold Co.,
1657 Buckingham Pl., CHICAGO, ILL.

Send for Price List on all

Palms and Ferns

Crimson Ramblers FOR EASTER.

3 to 4 feet, fine, 50 for $5.00; $3.50 per dozen. 2,000 Princess of Wales and Swanley White Violets. clumps $3.00 per 100, Extra 5,000 Forcing Tomato Plants, Lorillard and Mayflower selected stock. 2½-in. pot plants, $4.00 per 100; 500 for $9.00. Cash please.

BENJ. CONNELL, West Grove, Pa.

Piersoni and Anna Foster Ferns

Piersoni, 2½-inch pots .... $22.00 per 100
    7-inch pots .... 2.00   each
    6-inch pots .... 1.50   each
Foster, 2½-inch pots .... 7.00 per 100
    6-inch pots .... 10.00 per doz.

Extra fine stock. Write us.

GEO. M. BRINKERHOFF,   Springfield, Ill.

New Chrysanthemums

STOCK PLANTS. Yellow: H. Sinclair, Mrs. J. J. Mitchell, Sephis, H. W. Buckbee, F. J. Taggart. White: Convention Hall, Globosa Alba, Mrs. R. W. Smith. Pink: Minnie Bailey, Algoma, Ethelyn, Columbia, R. E. Richardson, Amorita, Majestic, Uwsara. The above 25c each. $2.50 per dozen. Cresco, Iolantha, Lady Harriet, Bentley, Brunck, Robert Halliday, 15c each; $1.50 per doz.; $10.00 per 100. Bonnaffon, Pink Ivory, Pacific, Mrs. J. Jones, Ivory, Willow Brook, Polly Rose, 10c each; $1.00 per dozen, $6.00 per 100. 15 plants of one variety at 100 rate.

H. WEBER & SONS, Oakland, Md.

Mention the American Florist when writing to advertisers on this page.

500,000 VERBENAS
THE CHOICEST VARIETIES IN CULTIVATION.

Fine pot plants, $2.50 per 100; $20 per 1000. Rooted Cuttings, 60c per 100; $5 per 1000; $45 per 10,000.

NO RUST OR MILDEW.

PACKED LIGHT, AND SATISFACTION GUARANTEED. SEND FOR CIRCULAR.

We are the Largest Growers of Verbenas in the country. Our plants cannot be surpassed.

J. L. DILLON,   BLOOMSBURG, PA.

Please mention the American Florist when writing.

Exhibition at Fort Smith, Ark.

The chrysanthemum show under the auspices of the Belle Point hospital association was held November 6 and 7 in the rooms of A. G. Lee & Bros.' seed store, and was well patronized. The halls were decorated with southern smilax and California peppers in addition to a large amount of autumn foliage deftly worked in. A nice display of palms, ferns and tropical plants was made by Reasoner Brothers, of Oneco, Fla. The F. R. Pierson Company had a fine display of their new fern Nephrolepis Piersoni. Bassett & Washburn, of Chicago, showed Lilium Harrisii and other choice flowers. Herman Krone and A. A. Pantet & Company had the best display of the local exhibitors. Thursday was chrysanthemum day and the display was fine. The liberal premiums offered brought competitors from all over the country.

The first prize on the list for professional growers, $25 for the best twenty-five blooms in five different varieties, was won by Nathan Smith & Son. There being no second prize, honorable mention was made of the other competitors in this class as follows: The E. G. Hill Company, Richmond, Ind.; Morton's Evergreen Lodge, Clarksville, Tenn.; Vaughn's Seed Store, Chicago, and H. W. Buckbee, Rockford, Ill.

The premium of $15 for the best fifteen white was won by Morton's Evergreen Lodge, of Clarksville, Tenn., with fifteen superb blooms of Mrs. Henry Robinson. Honorable mention in this class was made of the exhibit of H. W. Buckbee, Rockford, Ill.

The premium for the best twelve yellow was won by H. W. Buckbee, with honorable mention to Morton's Evergreen Lodge.

In the best twelve new varieties class H. W. Buckbee won, with honorable mention to Morton's Evergreen Lodge.

In the class for the best exhibit of plants in pots with many flowers, not less than three plants, Samuel Murray, of Kansas City, and Morton's Evergreen Lodge were the only competitors. As no particular style of growth was called for, Morton had four handsome standards and Murray had good bush plants. The judges in this case were unable to decide between the standards and the bush plants and gave each exhibitor a first premium.

For the best exhibit of chrysanthemums raised in pots to a single stem and single bloom, pots not to exceed six inches in diameter, the first premium was awarded to Morton's Evergreen Lodge.

For the best twenty-five American Beauty roses the premium was divided between Morton's Evergreen Lodge and the Idlewild Floral Company, of Memphis, Tenn., the judges not being able to reach a decision.

For the best fifteen Kaiserin the first premium was won by the Idlewild Floral Company.

The premium for the best twenty-five carnations of any color was won by J. D. Thompson Carnation Company, of Joliet, Ill.

For the best fifteen carnation novelties first premium was won by Morton's Evergreen Lodge, with honorable mention to the J. D. Thompson Carnation Company and the Idlewild Floral Company.

Class Z, a special class for the best twelve pink chrysanthemum blooms, was won by the E. G. Hill Company, of Richmond, Ind.

Among the amateur growers B. D. Crane and H. B. Salis carried off the largest amount of premiums. D. B. Crane, W. B. Pape and Mrs. R. E. Clarkson were judges in the professional classes.   M.

Exhibition at Macon, Ga.

A chrysanthemum show was given under the direction of the Vineville King's Daughters on November 6 and 7 in the handsomely decorated rooms on Cotton avenue. The show was a success and created much interest. The only premium for florists, $10 for the best collection of chrysanthemums, was won by the E. G. Hill Company, Richmond, Ind., with the Westview Floral Company, of Atlanta, Ga., a good second.

The many prizes in the amateur classes were hotly contested for. Mrs. J. T. Garland, of Hillsboro, took more premiums than any of the local growers. Her exhibit attracted much attention, as there were over 500 well-grown blooms in her collection, representing about 150 different varieties. The show will be held on a larger scale another season. A small admission fee was charged that will be applied to a local charitable cause.   M.

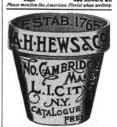

THE ALLIED TRADES

Descriptive part culars—with drawings or photographs, if possible—of any new apparatus or device which may prove helpful to the trade are solicited for this department.

CLARK'S heaters for wagons and carriages are neat, inexpensive and do the work. ......

LEHMAN'S wagon heater has in the past proved very serviceable to the many florists who have made use of it.

SOUTHWORTH'S thermostat is the invention of a practical greenhouse man and should fill a place that has long needed filling in every greenhouse establishment.

Greenhouse Economy.

ED. AM. FLORIST:—Which is the most economical in building and heating, a solid glass greenhouse or a sash greenhouse, and why? W. B.

When a small house is to be constructed and one has the sash on hand they can be used on the roof with good results, in case the house is to be used for the growing of lettuce, violets, bedding plants and many other crops. If one has to buy the sash it will be very poor economy, as it will cost more than to build the roof with sash bars only, and it will be in every way less satisfactory. One objection to sash houses is that the glass is comparatively small and the sash obstruct a great deal of light, as the sides of the sash are three to four inches wide and the two together will cover a space six to eight inches in width, while an ordinary sashbar, even for glass twenty inches wide, has a width of but 1¼ to 1½ inches. This will be a serious objection in houses used for growing nearly all of the ordinary florist's crops. So far as economy of heating is concerned there will be but little difference if the houses are equally tight. Having less glass in the roof the sash houses will probably require less heat at night, but during the day being darker they will require more ventilation, and hence the cost of heating will be more than for the sash bar houses it the same temperature is to be maintained in both, to say nothing of the increased amount of heat that will be furnished by the sun in the sash bar houses owing to the smaller amount of woodwork in the roof. L. R. TAFT.

NATICK, MASS.—John Barr, who has been for seventeen years head gardener at the Cheney estate, has resigned his position and will devote his entire time to the Little South Floral Company business. The employes who had worked under him presented him with a handsome gold watch and chain on the day of his departure.

ATLANTIC CITY, N. J.—John Abercrombie, formerly connected with the Hotel Chelsea, is building a new greenhouse on North Morris avenue. It will be heated with hot water throughout and will be one of the most modern plants in South Jersey.

THE AMERICAN FLORIST

A WEEKLY JOURNAL FOR THE TRADE

America is "the Prow of the Vessel; there may be more comfort Amidships, but we are the first to touch Unknown Seas."

Vol. XXI.   CHICAGO AND NEW YORK, NOVEMBER 28, 1903.   No. 808.

THE AMERICAN FLORIST

NINETEENTH YEAR.

Copyright 1903, by American Florist Company
Entered as Second-Class Mail Matter.

PUBLISHED EVERY SATURDAY BY

AMERICAN FLORIST COMPANY,
324 Dearborn St., Chicago.
Eastern Office: 42 W. 28th St., New York.

Subscription, $1.00 a year.   To Europe, $2 00.
Subscriptions accepted only from the trade.
Volumes half-yearly from August, 1901.

SOCIETY OF AMERICAN FLORISTS AND
ORNAMENTAL HORTICULTURISTS.
OFFICERS—JOHN BURTON, Philadelphia, Pa.,
president; C. C. POLLWORTH, Milwaukee, Wis.,
vice-president; WM. J. STEWART, 79 Milk Street,
Boston, Mass., secretary; H. B. BEATTY, Oil City,
Pa., treasurer.
OFFICERS-ELECT—PHILIP BREITMEYER, president; J. J. BENEKE, vice-president; secretary and
treasurer as before. Twentieth annual meeting
at St. Louis, Mo., August, 1904.

THE AMERICAN CARNATION SOCIETY.
Annual Convention at Detroit, Mich., March 3,
1904. ALBERT M. HERR, Lancaster, Pa., secretary.

AMERICAN ROSE SOCIETY.
Annual meeting and exhibition, Philadelphia,
March, 1904. LEONARD BARRON, 136 Liberty St.,
New York, secretary.

CHRYSANTHEMUM SOCIETY OF AMERICA.
Annual convention and exhibition, November,
1904. FRED H. LEMON, Richmond, Ind., secretary.

THIS ISSUE 40 PAGES WITH COVER.

Hardy Bulbous Plants.

[Digest of paper read before the Boston Gardeners' and Florists' Club by W. N. Craig, North
Easton, Mass. November 19, 1903.]

Hardy bulbous flowering plants are,
and always will be, very popular with
all flower lovers. There is a peculiar
charm and interest attached to the growing of them. Their pretty flowers, many
of which have a fine fragrance, their endless variety, ease of culture, the fact that
usually after blooming they hide themselves away and that their extreme
hardiness makes them indispensable for
the decoration of lawns, shrubberies and
gardens, will all tend to strengthen the
popularity they have already attained.
  Where anything like a proper assortment is grown flowers will be produced
from early March to October. Early
spring is ushered in by chionodoxas,
snowdrops, crocus and scillas; then comes
April and early May and the gorgeous
narcissi, hyacinths and bedding tulips.
In late May and early June the tulip
species, poeticus type of narcissi and
stately eremuri are in season, by which
time some of the earlier liliums are also
open. The Spanish and English irises
flower later in June; early in June the
beautiful Madonna lily opens its fragrant
flowers to be succeeded by many others
of the same family. Montbretias and
other subjects help to prolong the season
until autumnal frosts arrive.
  Most of our remarks will apply to true
bulbous plants as popularly known to
members of the craft, but as the term
"bulbous plant" is applied to practically
all roots which can be dug, collected and
dried, as are certain vegetable crops, we
will refer to a few which may not happen
to come under the category of bulbs.
  All bulbous plants delight in a soil rich
in vegetable mould of good depth and
well drained. Fresh manure at the roots
is undesirable, especially for liliums.
Annual top-dressings of well rotted
manure, where the bulbs are undisturbed,
is very beneficial. The plan of cutting off
green foliage from narcissi and other
sorts can not be too strongly condemned.
The foliage should be allowed to open
naturally, or the plant will suffer severely.
  Hyacinths are accorded the most prominent place in bulb catalogues and while
they are useful for public parks and massing purposes they are far less popular
than tulips and narcissi for general
effects, and their use as outdoor bulbs
will not increase in any such ratio as the
other bulbs named.
  Tulips are undoubtedly the most popular of all hardy bulbous plants in America;

they last well a much longer season than
hyacinths, are less expensive and if lifted
and cared for can be depended upon to
do service over a year. Our selection of
a dozen varieties of bedding tulips would
be scarlet, white and yellow Pottebak-
ker, Prince of Austria, Queen of the
Netherlands, Chrysolora, Cottage Maid,
Proserpine, Keizerskroon, white Joost
Van Vondel and Royal Standard. There
are many other fine varieties, but the
foregoing list contains no poor ones.
Double varieties, while they flower later
than the single ones, are less desirable,
but will always be in some demand.
  The late tulips contain many beautiful
species and too little attention is paid to
this group by gardeners and florists.
The bizarres, byblœmens, roses, breeders and Darwins contain some odd
colors, but many lovely shades, and are
flowering when all bedding tulips are
gone. Parrot tulips are pretty but their
weak stems are a drawback. Cannot
our Dutch or Irish friends develop a
stiffer-stemmed race?
  In what are commonly called the tulip
species are many very beautiful things.
Some are high priced and this is against
their more extended culture. As a rule
the bulbs last from year to year if lifted
and cared for. Some of the varieties are
of special value to florists, flowering in
rainy seasons about Memorial day, if
grown in partially shaded borders.
Excellent varieties of these are Gesne-
riana major, Bouton d'Or, Picotee, Florentina odorata (also called Sylvestris)
retroflexa, viridiflora, Gold Crown,
Greigi, Kaufmanniana (the earliest flowering of all tulips) Oculis-solis præcox,
vitellina (very beautiful). Other interesting and pretty varieties are Korol-
kowi, Lownei, Clusiava, Didieri and
Kolpakowskiana. Many of these lovely
old-fashioned tulips have been preserved
from extinction in the cottage gardens of
humble flower lovers.
  Narcissi are now pushing tulips hard
for supremacy and will eventually pass
them in popularity. The universal
advances being made by such hybridizers
as the Rev. Geo. Engleheart, Barr & Son,
Miss Wilmott and others, and the addition of such grand sorts as Mme. de
Graaf, Weardale Perfection, Glory of
Leyden, Snowflake and other magnificent varieties, have made narcissi easily
the most popular of bulbous plants in
England and very fancy prices are
readily paid for choice novelties. At
present many of the beautiful sorts are
too expensive to retail in America, but a
few years will cheapen them and then

narcissi will usurp the place now occupied by tulips here in the popular estimation.

The large trumpet section includes the most showy and popular narcissi. The most majestic sorts are Horsfieldii and Emperor. Other excellent sorts are Henry Irving (very early), Victoria, Princeps, single Von Sion. spurius, obvallaris, rugilobus, Dean Herbert, Empress and Golden Spur. The white Spanish trumpet daffodil N. moschatus is very pretty. Sir Watkin, the giant Welsh daffodil, towers above all of the incomparabilis section. Barrii conspicuus is very fine and blooms late. Incomparabilis Stella, Cynosure, Queen Bess, C. J. Backhouse and Princess May are all good.

N. poeticus ornatus is the finest of the poets narcissi section. Poeticus itself will always be immensely popular, for no narcissus naturalizes more readily and thrives with less care. N. poeticus poetarum and grandiflorus are good varieties. N. biflorus is useful as being the latest flowering of all narcissi. It carries two flowers on a stem

The Humei type is not considered reliably hardy. We have found Backhousei, Wm. Wilks and C. Wolley Dod perfectly so and their primrose perianths and deep yellow trumpets make them distinct and handsome.

A class deserving of more extended culture is the Leedsi section. Duchess of Brabant is one of the best. Other good forms are Duchess of Westminster, Mrs. Langtry and Minnie Hume. The Leedsi class naturalizes as beautifully in grass land as do the poeticus type.

Double narcissi are less attractive than the single ones. Silver Phoenix is probably the best. Other sorts worth growing are Orange Phoenix, alba plena odorata, and the well known Von Sion. Nearly all the narcissi are suitable for naturalising in the wild garden or in grass land, but the poeticus and Leedsi classes are the best.

Jonquillas simplex, rugilobus and Campernelle are hardy but do not succeed so well from year to year as the narcissi. All daffodils in beds or borders succeed best if replanted once in three or four years.

Crocuses and snowdrops are good bulbs for naturalising, the former in grass land and the latter in the wild garden. Scillas are indispensable. S. Siberica is the best. Good late varieties are S. nutans,

the English wild hyacinth and S. campanulata. Of chionodoxas, perhaps, C. Lucile is the most effective. C. Sardensis and C. gigantea are distinct and well worth growing. Eranthis hyemalis (winter aconite) is the earliest of all bulbs and a patch is worth growing on that account. Allium Neapolatum and Leucojum vernum and L. aestivum are both reliable, either for natural gardening in masses or on margins of shrubberies. Galtonia candicans is a beautiful flowering bulb. Planted in big masses it is most effective and needs very little protection.

Too little attention is paid to Iris Hispanica both by private and trade growers. Some people seem to have an idea that it is not hardy, but it will stand 15° below zero with impunity. No flowers are easier of culture or finer for cut flower purposes. Our American growers seem afraid to handle these bulbs, but over in Europe they are grown by the. million for Covent Garden and other large markets. For forcing purposes they are unexcelled. Of course they will not stand forcing like narcissi or tulips, but for cutting in April or May nothing could be finer. Either at Easter or Decoration day a large quantity would be particularly useful and they could be timed to come in for either occasion. Excellent varieties are Louise, pale blue, Blanche Fleur, pure white, Comte de Nassau, dark blue and Chrysolora, yellow. A covering of leaves or light strawy manure should be placed over outdoor grown stock.

Iris Anglica follow the Spanish iris outdoors. Good varieties are Cleopatra, pale lavender, La Grandesse, pure white and Prince Imperial, dark blue. English irises are excellent for cutting, though hardly as graceful as the Spanish varieties. Other useful and interesting irises include I. Pavonia (Peacock iris), histrioides, Persica, Susiana and tuberosa.

Montbretias are very desirable hardy bulbous plants. By planting thinly in rows two feet apart, in October, and saving some over in a cold frame to plant out in April, a continuous succession of bloom may be had from July to October. Good varieties are Pottsii, Etoile de Feu, Germania Rayon d'Or and Transcendant.

Bremuri are probably the most stately of all bulbous plants, succeeding well in

a bed facing southwest, planted between shrubs in a compost of swamp muck, leaf mould and sand. Good drainage is necessary. Flower spikes range from five to eight feet high, the blooming season being the end of May. Great care is necessary in replanting as the roots are extremely brittle. As growth commences very early in spring, a protection of light leaves and spruce branches is necessary until danger of sharp frost is over. Varieties succeeding well are Bremurus robustus, E. Himalaicus (the best), E. Elwesii and E. Bungei.

Lilies are the most beautiful and ornamental of all hardy bulbous plants. With a reasonable amount of care and forethought and a careful selection of varieties these pre-eminently graceful flowers can be had in bloom over a period of several months. The majority of lilies prefer a rich soil in humus, while some varieties like candidum, Henryi and speciosum succeed in full sunshine. The bulk of the family prefer a shaded location, such as is to be had on the edge of shrubberies, but where they are not planted so close to shrubs that the roots of these will rob them of nutriment and moisture. Two feet of loam well mixed with sand is suitable. Leaf mould is also good.

Varieties like auratum, Henryi, speciosum, testaceum and tigrinum should be planted ten inches deep; small bulbed sorts five to six inches deep; L. candidum four inches deep. Fall we consider the best time to plant, for the bulbs would fritter away much of their strength in winter, even if carefully packed. A good layer of sand below and above the bulbs is advisable. Some sorts seem to like a bed of sphagnum to rest in. Mulching with spent mushroom bed material or some other manure helps to keep the roots cool and moist in summer. Soakings of liquid manure water are very helpful during the growing season.

Disease or blight is the greatest discouragement to extended lily culture. Replanting at least every third season into new ground and not allowing disease to appear before spraying with Bordeaux mixture are the best methods of fighting the disease. Packing bulbs of L. candidum in flowers of sulphur seems to check the disease in that variety and it may be worth a trial on other sorts.

L. auratum is the most gorgeous of the whole family, but owing to pre-

NEW YORK CHRYSANTHEMUM SHOW, NOVEMBER 16-18.

NEW YORK CHRYSANTHEMUM SHOW, NOVEMBER 10-12.

mature digging of the bulbs many shoots have come diseased, and this fine variety must be renewed every second year as it soon runs out. The pretty L. Krameri is fine in its season. L. Leichtlini and L. Humboldtii are not successes. L. Henryi, a comparatively new sort, has never shown any disease. This species increases marvelously under cultivation and will be immensely popular when cheaper. Stems five feet high, carrying thirty of its beautiful orange yellow flowers, were produced last season. L. Henryi has flowered in two years from seed in England.

L. speciosum and its varieties album, roseum, Melpomene and Krœtzeri are very reliable and excellent for cutting. L. Batmanniæ and L. excelsum are two good sorts, with beautiful apricot or buff colored flowers, worth a place in every collection. L. sulphureum (Wallichianum) is a magnificent variety, succeeding well. L. Canadense for naturalizing is good as is L. Philadelphicum. L. tigrinum splendens is a grand variety, often seen on the roadside or in cottage gardens better than where more care was lavished on it. Japanese bulbs of L. longiflorum succeed well for two seasons and then filter away into small bulbs. L. croceum is a very satisfactory kind, as is L. Davuricum umbellatum. Where low growing varieties are liked L. elegans atrosanguineum and auranticium are good. L. giganteum we have not yet grown. L. Chalcedonicum, however, is a good garden lily. We have never seen any disease on L. Brownii. Its beautiful, large flowers, pure white within and purplish outside are among the gems of the whole family. L. tenuifolium is a pretty miniature variety which keeps clean. L. Hansoni we have classed as a reliable sort. L. Grayi is a fine, very early, orange red sort, succeeding well. L. superbum does well in rich loam, growing quite tall.

No lilium is finer than L. candidum when well grown, and none is more

uncertain. For some years we have had no disease on pot-grown plants, but find it very troublesome outdoors. Persistent spraying does not seem to check it, but we hope by means of the sulphur remedy and use of new ground to master it. Our selection of lilies would be L. Henryi, L. Brownii, L. splendens, L. excelsum, L. candidum and L. speciosum in variety.

Time will not permit us to speak of other bulbous plants but would say in closing that members of our craft, whether studying beauty or utility in bulbs—not really discordant flowers—should strive to move along the broad path of intelligence, despising naught because it is new and still less because it is odd; and striving rather to learn from others all he can and from himself the whole of it. Surely no class of plants in the world better invite and reward an observant interest than hardy flowering bulbs.

Florists' Plant Notes.

PROPAGATING.

It is not too early to begin propagating some varieties of spring plants. It is too early yet for coleus, ageratum, German ivy and other quick growing plants, but such plants as Abutilon Savitzii, fuchsias, verbenas and heliotrope, can be propagated at any time now, and the sooner the better. Keep the propagating bench filled from now on; and, if possible use fresh sand for every batch of cuttings; however, if the sand is kept clean and no fungus was present in the preceding batch, no harm will result from using the same sand for two or even three successive lots. Stretch a piece of canvas or other material along the edge of the bench allowing it to reach the ground, so as to provide a gentle bottom heat. A temperature of 50° or 55° at night with the sand 5° warmer is about right for most cuttings. Keep the sand well watered, sprinkle the cuttings

every day, and shade them with newspaper or cheese cloth during the sunny hours of the day.

LILY OF THE VALLEY.

Lily of the valley pips will soon arrive from Germany, and should be taken care of at once. Prepare a place outside in a frame or on the north side of a building where the pips can be stored for the winter. We pack them standing upright with a layer of sand below and between the rows of bundles of pips, then covering them all with a couple of inches of sand. The roots should be dipped a few moments in a bucket of water before storing. They can stand any amount of freezing, but they should be covered with boards, not for protection from the cold, but to prevent them from starting into premature growth, as the spring draws near.

If it is desired to place some in cold storage, this operation can either be done at once or else can be deferred until about the first of February. After soaking the roots thoroughly, pack them into boxes of a convenient size holding the exact number for forcing each week. Select the best pips for this purpose, pack them standing upright in damp sphagnum moss, and nail up the boxes. If you have your own private ice house in which to store them, so much the better; otherwise, it is best to get on friendly terms with the iceman, and get him to take care of a few boxes through the winter and spring. Packed one on top of the other, the boxes take up very little room. Be sure, however, to see that the temperature is always kept as nearly as possible at 28°.

Of course it is useless to try to force these newly imported pips for Christmas. They can be had in flower for that occasion, to be sure, but they will be without foliage. Better wait, therefore, until the first of the year before attempting to force them. Cold storage pips must be depended on for Christmas.

Allow them three weeks time, for they will require it to develop them properly, although in a pinch they may be forced out in a few days less time. Cold storage pips do not require such extreme heat as the others; on the contrary, a milder heat will be conducive to better results. Sixty-five degrees is ample in which to force them out. Place the pips in a rather dark place for the first twelve days, and then gradually inure them to the light. When the flowers and foliage are fully developed, place them in a temperature about 15° lower than the one to which they were subjected in growing, so as to harden them off. Water must be kept away from the flowers, being careful in watering to pass the end of the hose or the nose of the can between the rows and watering only the sand in which they are growing.   G.

Chicago.

THANKSGIVING WEEK DOES NOT CREATE UNUSUAL ACTIVITY.—CARNATIONS ARE SHORT AND CHRYSANTHEMUMS ARE GOING.—NEW FIRM INCORPORATED

Thanksgiving has come and gone, and in the opinion of most of the local wholesalers, commission men and retailers the current week fell far short of the same week of last year. Of course the big holiday had the effect of stimulating things on the market for a short time and Wednesday's business was not so bad, but at no time during the week has the stock been inadequate for the demand. Prices stiffened up perceptibly all along the line, following the slow but sure shortening of the chrysanthemum stock, and the comparative scarcity of carnations. This latter is the only staple now really short. While wholesalers are putting out prices from 2 to 3 cents, yet there are few sold at less than $3 per 100. In roses, Beauty is not overabundant and is holding a stiff price. Neither has there been a surfeit of violets, which ruled at $2 all week. Roman hyacinths and Paper White narcissi are coming in in increased quantity and improved quality, and are finding but a slow call. All week ferns, palms and decorative material of all kinds found a ready market, the Thanksgiving day table being responsible for the run. In the earlier days of the week some heavy shipments were made, but the foreign demand was far less brisk than last year preceding the holiday. The small dealers throughout the Chicago trade belt were apparently timid on the strength of the general tame business so far this season. Green is not appearing in quantities which would indicate a flourishing supply for the winter season. Taking it all in all, the Thanksgiving day business was quite satisfactory, but it did not necessitate the addition of extra clerks in the retail stores.

The date of the third grand annual ball of the Florists' Club draws near and preparations for that event are progressing rapidly. The ball will take place on the evening of Wednesday, December 2, in the large drill room of the Masonic Temple. The committee has secured a room adjoining the ball room in which those not wishing to dance may entertain themselves with cards. The room will be thrown open at 9 p. m, one hour after the main hall is open. An admission fee of $1 has been fixed, admitting gentleman and lady.

A. L. Randall, wholesale commission man, this week sold out three-fourths of the interest in his business, retaining the residue. The new partners are Carl Thomas, formerly with Mr. Randall, Emil Buettner, Park Ridge, and Herman Bauske, Chicago. The new corporation was licensed with a capital of $10,000, and will be known as the A. L. Randall Company. Business will be continued at the old location on Randolph street.

A small shipment of extra choice orchids was seen at Amling's this week. There were only a few, but they were rich, and brought $7.50 per dozen.

Deamud disposed of a choice lot of violets this week. They have now reached the $2 mark and are selling easy at that.

Holly from commission houses was seen about the streets, in poor shape, evidently cut too early.

Carl Hirsch, of Hillsdale, returned this week from a three weeks' hunting trip in Upper Michigan.

W. W. Barnard & Co. have sixty employes at work on evergreen wreathing.

Vaughan's Seed Store handled two carloads of bouquet green this week.

Visitors: B. Eschner, of M. Rose Company, Phiadelphia; Swan Peterson, Gibson City, Ill.; A. Siegel, St. Louis; James Chaconas, Milwaukee, Wis.; Fred Foster, St. Louis.; N. B. Stover, Grand Rapids, Mich.

PAWTUCKET, R. I.—Mrs. James Nesbit died suddenly on Monday, November 16.

New York.

CONDITIONS IMPROVING.—ROSES SELLING AT A HIGH FIGURE.—NEW HOUSES AT GREENWOOD.

On Tuesday morning Beauty brought as high as $5 per dozen, the best Bridesmaid and Bride as high as $10 per 100, carnation novelties such as Enchantress and Prosperity $6. Red and white varieties are very scarce. Some very fine Swanisona is being shipped to B. Shim from Courtney, of Sparkhill, N. Y.; it is three feet long and sells readily.

Market conditions the past week have been very satisfactory. Prices are generally good, particularly for Beauty, Bride, Bridesmaid and carnations. Carnations are very scarce, but chrysanthemums are plentiful. Violets seem to sell very well and there are plenty of them for Thanksgiving.

Alfred Dimmock has removed from Liberty street to 31 Barclay street, where he will make headquarters with Suzuki.

John Daly, of Greenwood Cemetery, has torn down his old greenhouse and built three large new ones.

Fred Smith has fitted out a house at Woodside, L. I.. "Coming events cast their shadows before."

John Young has a fine display of Begonia Gloire de Lorraine in his window.

NEPHROLEPIS PIERSONI AT THE PHILADELPHIA EXHIBITION.

Holly is seen in most of the stores and is of very good quality.

Philadelphia.

SPLENDID HOLIDAY TRADE IN FORCE.— GOOD PRICES ALL ALONG THE LINE.— ROSES A BIT OFF IN STOCK.—NOTES OF THE TRADE.

A change has come over the situation, the demand for everything, except probably chrysanthemums, being greater than the supply. It looked like old times to see the buyers flocking in and out of the commission houses, looking up stock for the Thanksgiving day trade. Prices jumped, of course, and in some instances almost doubled. Beauties, which had to be packed to move at $3 per dozen last week, brought as high as $6, and no specials were offered below $5, and were scarce even at that. Carnations were in good demand and all the choice stock was sold at sight. Many of the rose growers appear to have their houses off crop at present, and this, coupled with a cool spell which shortened the crop as well, cut the usual supply almost in half. There were plenty of chrysanthemums, however, and they were moved at fairly good prices, although a trifle lower than last year. In the case of some fine Chadwicks and Eatons, which brought $3 last year, the best price was $2. Both varieties are now very fine, as is also Maud Dean and Golden Wedding. Violets are in good demand, all the best stock being ordered in advance. The chrysanthemum plants were in good demand and many wagon loads were disposed of.

Pennock Brothers had a handsome Thanksgiving decoration in their windows the past week. Wheat and corn, as it came from the field, formed a background, with vases of fine chrysanthemums in front. Two football games played on Thursday gave them a chance to use the college ribbons. The whole was very effective, and was a great credit to their artist, Baxter.

S. S. Pennock is handling boxes of assorted orchids sold just as they come from the growers in the original package. His stock of fine chrysanthemums was great this week. He sold over 2,000 specials last Tuesday.

Robert Craig & Son had quite a run on their cyclamens for Thanksgiving day. Their stock is now fine and will be in splendid shape for Christmas.

Leo Niessen had a great week; his special Bridemaid and Liberty are certainly fine. He is especially strong on Beauty.

Bernheimer is handling some fine carnations; his special chrysanthemums and Queen of Edgely roses are good stock.

At the market they report a great trade. Everything save a few chrysanthemums sold out clean every day.

Fred Ehret is handling some fine Mrs. Chadwick and Maud Dean chrysanthemums.

Reid shipped an order of 500 chrysanthemums, specials, last Tuesday.   K.

Boston.

UNPRECEDENTED THANKSGIVING TRADE.— PRICES GO UP AND OUTLOOK FOR FUTURE BRIGET.—NEW GREENHOUSE AT MONTROSE.

The Thanksgiving day demand has accomplished wonders for the flower trade here during the past few days. The unprecedented stagnation which had been bringing discouragement daily to so many has been raised, for the

PRIZE GROUP OF PALMS AT THE PHILADELPHIA SHOW.
(Exhibited by Jos. Hurley, gardener to James W. Paul.)

present at least, and the vast accumulations of unsold flowers have at last been moved, while the fresh stock coming in has found a market at fair values. Whether these conditions can be maintained after Thanksgiving cannot be predicted. The revival, if permanent, must have an enormous capacity, for the quantity of material that may be looked for this season far exceeds anything in our previous history and most of it must be used at home, as the shipping trade to any great distance has fallen off greatly. The finish of the chrysanthemums, when it comes, will naturally help the general situation considerably, but notwithstanding hopeful predictions to the contrary based upon the late warm weather then, chrysanthemums give evidence of an intention to prolong their visit for some time yet. Every succeeding year sees Thanksgiving business assuming larger proportions. At this writing the full results of the present occasion are not yet known but enough has been seen to give the assurance that in amount of business done it has a big lead over any previous Thanksgiving day record. The advance in values has met with the customary protest from the retailers, but the prices are high only in comparison with the slaughter prices which have been prevailing for the past few weeks and consequently, as our old friend, Dan Maginnis, used to sing in the "Arkansaw Traveller":

"Says the rag man
To the bag man.
It will do them no harm."

We had the pleasure recently to visit the new enterprise at Montrose, the property owned by N. F. McCarthy and conducted by Eber Holmes. It consists, up to date, of one rose house, 32x500 feet, of Lord & Burnham steel construction. It is proposed to add to this outfit until at least two acres are covered with glass. The location is an ancient farm with a depth of rich soil rarely found in Massachusetts, with an abundance of

fine water, and the vast accumulations track close by and good communication with Boston, ten miles distant. Steam boiler capacity and other adjuncts have been provided in sufficient extent for all future needs. The chimney and boiler room are striking features in the landscape, being constructed of boulders laid in red mortar, and it is intended to add to their attractiveness by covering them with ivy and other vines. This house is filled with grafted Bride, Bridesmaid and Ivory, second year, transplanted and tied down after having had a six weeks' rest. They have that well-fed, luxuriant appearance which always makes one feel like doffing his hat to the grower, and the color developed in the Bridesmaid is of a depth very rarely seen. The estate comprises 100 acres. There is a comfortable old farm house which Mr. McCarthy occupies as his home during summer, enjoying a well earned rest amidst surroundings of most picturesque character.

H. P. Kelsey and Irving T. Guild have formed a partnership as landscape architects.

Among the passengers from Europe per steamer Commonwealth was P. L. Carbone.

FALL RIVER, MASS.—A fire November 20 in the greenhouses belonging to Michael Conroy was caused by the fumigating machine. Several hundred dollars' worth of greenery and foliage plants were destroyed by the smoke.

ALBANY, N. Y.—Park Superintendent Egerton is justly proud of his public chrysanthemum show this year, which comprises eight hundred plants in three hundred and fifty varieties, all named.

LAKE CITY, FLA.—The new greenhouse of the horticultural department of Florida University is well under way and will be a valuable addition. It is located on the site of the old one.

St. Louis.

SUCCESSFUL CHRYSANTHEMUM SHOW.—WESTERN GROWERS ARE ACTIVE.—HETHERINGTON IN CHARGE OF PHILIPPINE GARDENS AT WORLD'S FAIR.

The chrysanthemum exhibition held this week in the conservatories at the Missouri Botanical Garden proved a success in every way surpassing anything of the kind ever seen in St. Louis. Hundreds of visitors took advantage of the opportunity to visit the garden. Three houses were utilized, the benches being first removed to allow sufficient space for staging. In two houses the plants, standards, bush plants and single stemmers, were arranged in a solid bank, which, with the great care exercised in harmonizing colors, made a very beautiful effect. Some two hundred and fifty varieties, including many of the newer sorts, were shown. The beautiful Waban, Godfrey's Pride, Portia, Edgar Sanders, etc., were tried as standards, but on account of lack of space their individual beauty could not be appreciated. By placing some of the pompons, such as Lulu, Diana, Viola and Acto, alongside of Convention Hall, Good Gracious, Adrian, etc., a pleasing contrast was effected. Golden Shower, the new Japanese type, attracted much attention. The exhibition will no doubt become an annual event at the garden, at least preparations are being made for a big show next season.

At Sanders & Sons everything was quiet, no one being in sight, but just enough liberty was taken to walk through the houses. The chrysanthemum benches were about cleaned out. A nice lot of cyclamens are coming on in

good shape. He has Cyperus alternifolius (umbrella plant) planted in a few pans of poinsettias which have dropped the lower leaves. The cyperus makes a good screen for the naked stems. A large amount of stock is heeled in just outside the houses.

A visit through several of the growers' establishments reveals the fact that they are not idle or unprogressive. Since Wm. Kalisch & Sons have renovated their houses and added the show room, sales have increased. one hundred per cent. They intend to sell only the best the market affords, which includes orchids. All the stock is clean, healthy and well grown.

John Hetherington, formerly with the Michel Plant & Bulb Company, has been put in charge of the landscape, horticulture and bedding work on the Philippine reservation at the World's Fair. Mr. Hetherington was connected with the floricultural department at the Pan-American Exposition.

The Missouri Botanical Garden will hold its fourteenth annual banquet to the gardeners of the institution and invited florists, nurserymen and market gardeners at the Mercantile club, Friday, December 11.

J. T. Windt's place is not numbered among the largest in the city, but his stock of miscellaneous plants is in good condition. The nursery stock is excellent.
F. K. B.

CAMDEN, N. J.—John Guthridge died suddenly at his home, 814 Linden street, Camden, aged 75 years. He was one of the oldest florists in Camden and served several terms as a member of the Board of Freeholders from the sixth ward.

San Francisco.

TEAS, DEBUTS AND OTHER SOCIAL FUNCTIONS IN PLENTY.—BRISK BUSINESS CLEANS UP STOCK.—SCARCITY IN ALL LINES.—NOTES.

Although rainy and disagreeable weather was the rule the past week it seemed to have no bad effect on business which certainly was on the boom. Teas, debuts and other social affairs coupled with a great deal of funeral work kept the florists busy, especially in the closing part of the week. The stock which prior to that time was very plentiful was cleaned out entirely. I noticed several stores last evening where the supply of roses and carnations was completely exhausted. The rainy weather has greatly reduced receipts, the chrysanthemum season being practically over. Outdoor blooms were spoiled and greenhouse grown chrysanthemums are scarce. Receipts of roses and carnations are also slim. Violets are yet scarce, but will undoubtedly be plenty and fine as soon as the weather clears. Paper White narcissi have made their appearance in the market. Valley is conspicuous by its absence. Orchids are considerably in demand with the supply short. Here are some quotations for the past week: Roses—Teas 50 cents to $1 per dozen; Beauties $2.50 to $3 50 per dozen; carnations 50 cents to $1 per dozen; chrysanthemums $1 to $2.50 per dozen; Narcissus Paper White 75 cents per hundred. A higher quotation on all lines of cut flowers will undoubtedly be in force in the first part of the coming week.

There has been considerable discussion lately in the florists' and horticultural societies here regarding the alleged mismanagement of the Yosemite Valley park. It is said that the splendid oak trees are ruthlessly being cut down for firewood and to make clearings on which to produce hay to sell to campers, doing incalculable damage. These giant oaks, centuries old, act in a great measure as retainers of moisture, being the means of preventing the too rapid melting of the snow in the spring; besides, their own individual beauty as grand specimens could not be replaced in hundreds of years. It is to be hoped that the movement to check this alleged spoliation of the park, will, as it should, receive the active support of everyone having the preservation of one of nature's most wonderful creations at heart.

J. B. Coryell, of Menlo Park, has under construction one greenhouse 24x150 feet, divided into four compartments for the growing of cut blooms and miscellaneous decorative plants. A. McDonald, the head gardener, was a recent visitor to this city selecting stock for this house, principally ferns, of which he makes a specialty. He purchased a large lot of rhododendrons for garden culture.

The board of public works has under consideration the raising of the grade on Chestnut and Polk streets twenty-five feet. This, if carried through, it is said, will practically ruin the business of John H. Sievers & Company's nursery. Mr. Sievers is claiming damages to the amount of $45,000.

The California State Floral Society will hold a tulip and bulbous flower show in the spring. The exhibition will be an innovation in floral displays.

The Pacific Coast Horticultural Society at its last meeting decided to hold an entertainment and dance the second Saturday in January.

David Mann, of Mann Brothers, left a few days ago for Southern California to solicit orders for his firm.

CROTON SUPERBUS AT THE PHILADELPHIA EXHIBITION.

Miss Kate O'Sessions, who conducts a florist and nursery business in San Diego, was a caller last week.

J. H. Sievers, who has been laid up for quite a while with a severe cold, is rapidly recovering.

John F. Culligan, with Geo. B. Jones, has gone to San Jose on a prolonged vacation. ROMNEYA.

Washington, D. C.

BOOM FOLLOWING CONGRESS' OPENING SUBSIDES.—SOCIAL FUNCTIONS SLOW, BUT BUSINESS IS FAIR.—DEALERS TIRED OF CHRYSANTHEMUMS.—NOTES.

The flurry in trade caused by the opening of congress has subsided, and as no society functions of any importance have yet been given there is no boom. All the stores are doing a fair business, however, and looking ahead. Chrysanthemums are still very much in evidence, and some of the dealers will feel relieved when they are well out of the way. The handling of chrysanthemums for a month or six weeks seems to give a florist that "thirty quails in thirty days" feeling. Roses are reasonably plentiful and good, though considering the excellent weather it is doubtful if they are any better or even as good as at this time a year ago. First class carnations are scarce. There are, however, plenty of the 25 cents a dozen kind. Violets are in good supply, but several of the local growers complain that they are getting but few blooms. There are prospects of a good violet crop when the weather grows cooler.

Some of the best Bridesmaid and Golden Gate roses that are being cut in this vicinity are at N. Studer's. It may give give some rose growers a jolt to say that the beds (solid beds) have not been dried off for five years. All that has been done aside from feeding has been to prune out old wood. There are straight stems of new wood of Golden Gate that measure five and five and a half feet from the tie to the bud.

A. C. Shaffer, of Langdon, D. C., has in addition to his Langdon greenhouse another place at Lowell. Md. He grows for the wholesale trade and has just disposed of a good cut of chrysanthemums. The Shaffers take naturally to flowers, A. C. Shaffer being a grower at Alexandria, Va.

C. Ponnet & Company have opened their store at 711 Fourteenth street, N. W., with Chas. W. Wolf as designer and decorator. This recalls the fact that the florists are "flocking" in the northwest and that particular section of it between F and I and from Ninth to Fourteenth streets.

A. Gude & Brother are cutting good roses and chrysanthemums. This firm got a good share of the bouquet orders for congress and all hands were on the jump filling them. Geo. C. Shaffer, 7. D. Blackistone and J. L. Loose were also in the swim.

O. A. C. Oehmler, leading man at Fred. Kramer's F street store, is a hustler for trade. Business is so good that he has taken on another assistant.

J. R. Freeman has erected two new houses at his Brightwood avenue range, and is going into cut flowers more extensively than ever before.

James McMahon, at one time a grower for Freeman, has taken a position as sexton at Holyrood cemetery.

Mr. Thompson, late of Chicago, is now grower for Studer. S. E.

NEWARK, ILL.—The chrysanthemum show here has been given up.

Pittsburg.

SMOKY CITY FLORISTS ENJOYING GOOD BUSINESS —STOCK NOT UP TO STANDARD. —BANQUETS AND DEDICATIONS CREATE ACTIVITY IN TRADE.—NOTES.

Winter is here in reality and the temperature hovers around the 20° mark. Heavy shipments from the east and west and a very satisfactory report from the wholesale houses certainly indicate that the craft in this section is "up and doing." Teas, dinners, suppers and numerous kinds of decorations keep us

Patrick Maier, of Millvale, is cutting Roman hyacinths, also Harrisii, and all his bulbous stock shows a most satisfactory condition.

Henry Eichholz, of Waynesboro, Pa., continues to cut fine chrysanthemums of which Jerome Jones is the best.

The Pittsburg Cut Flower Company is doing a big shipping business these days in addition to its general trade.

Langham & Company, of Wheeling, W. Va., have been heavy buyers in Pittsburg the last two weeks. E. L. M.

THE GRAHAM COMPANY'S TABLE DECORATION AT PHILADELPHIA SHOW.

busy. Stock in general seems to have taken a turn for the worse. Roses are far below the standard. In Brides and Bridesmaids the colors are bad and most all stock seems soft and sickly. American Beauties are fine and have made a sharp advance upward. In spite of the condition of rose stock they are moving out in very satisfactory order.

Chrysanthemums are almost out of the race, yet some very fine Jerome Jones, Maud Dean and Bonnaffon are coming in and are still in demand. Carnations are nearing the perfection point. They too have advanced in price and the cheaper grades are very scarce. Lily of the valley, gardenias, orchids, violets, Roman hyacinths and Paper White narcissi are all splendid in quality and meeting with a good sale.

Randolph & McClements decorated the large banquet hall and tables for the banquet given by the Pittsburg Chamber of Commerce, Tuesday, November 24. Many celebrities of state and national importance were present.

The chrysanthemum displays in both Pittsburg and Allegheny are at an end for the season. The superintendents of both the Phipps conservatories are greatly pleased with their shows this season.

John Boder, E. C. Ludwig and G. and J. Ludwig decorated the new Elks' Temple in Allegheny City, of which they are members. The Temple was dedicated on November 23.

The Florists' and Gardeners' Club will meet December 1. A display of Christmas novelties and plants will be made and Christmas topics in general will be discussed.

Indianapolis.

SHOW A FINANCIAL SUCCESS.—SURPLUS IN TREASURY PROBABLE.—RIEMAN SELLS CHRYSANTHEMUM SEEDLINGS.—NOTES.

The Chrysanthemum Show association will have no deficit and probably a surplus, which means that the show has been a financial success. Another pleasing feature has been the great number of visiting florists it brought to town, which is a great thing for business as well as pleasure. Seventy-two were present at the dinner given by the association. E. A. Nelson welcomed the guests in behalf of the State Florists' Association of Indiana, and after paying tribute to John Berterman, the able manager of the show, he named Mr. Hill as toastmaster, who called on the foremost lights of the craft, among them Mrs. Vesey and Messrs. Winehuebuer, Carmody, Rudd and Foley. Mr. Foley's recitation, concerning the Italian baseball player, was a treat.

A. Baur, of Baur & Smith, went to Chicago to make a good impression for Indianapolis with his carnation exhibit. He forgot, however, to take Smith & Young's violets along.

Fred Huckriede tried to smoke one of Mr. Elvison's corrugated stogies of the true Pittsburg type, and has been under the care of a doctor ever since.

John Hartje and George Breitmeyer worked over-time booking orders, the former for his carnation Moonlight, the latter for his new variety.

H. Junge, secretary of the association, wishes it to be known that he is still a candidate for re-election. He says two terms are enough.

H. W. Rieman sold his stock of chrysanthemum seedlings—Majestic, Madonna and Adelia—to Breitmeyer's Sons, Detroit.

Irvin Berterman wears the smile that won't come off these days. The show was a success, don't you know.

Smith & Young's pedigree stock of Marie Louise caused a mild sensation among violet men.

The jolliest crowds always hail from Louisville and Chicago.

·Every one congratulates Fred Dorner to his son.
J.

Detroit.

HIGH PRICES PREVAIL FOR THANKSGIVING STOCK.—CHRYSANTHEMUMS GO BEGGING. — LITTLE DEMAND FOR DECORATIVE MATERIAL.

While Thanksgiving day business was an improvement over the same event a year ago, many in the trade think much of it was due to the favorable conditions of the weather, which was, this year, clear, bright and cool enough to be seasonable and far different from the wet, disagreeable weather of the same day a year ago. A notable feature of the trade was the small demand for ferns, palms or plants of any kind, though most dealers were well prepared for this class of trade. Roses, chrysanthemums, violets and carnations all sold well, the stock of the latter being well used up. While violets were held back by the growers the first two days of the week, they were later supplied in sufficient quantity to meet the demand, which was, however, in some cases, disappointingly meager. In roses, good stock of all varieties was available and fully equal to the demand, but there was a surplus only in the poorer grades. Contrary to expectations many chrysanthemums were to be seen. The white ones and clear shades of pink and yellow met with much favor and the stock soon disappeared while all other colors remained unsold and stood as a mute warning to the growers for another season. In prices, except with violets, Beauty roses and the best grades of carnations no advance was noted. Violets brought $3, $3.50 and some especially fine ones $4 per hundred. A wide range of prices prevailed with Beauties, from $3 to $10 per dozen. Carnations were uniformly 75 cents and $1 per dozen; the latter price was only obtained for extra fine stock. The best grade of chrysanthemums sold for $3 to $5 per dozen, most of the stock being disposed of at the former figure.
J. F. S.

Alabany.

MANY WEDDINGS AND SOCIETY FUNCTIONS STIMULATE BUSINESS.—WORK ON PROSPECT PARK ABANDONED.

Monday evening the Catholic Union gave a reception in honor of Archbishop Falconio, the Apostolic delegate to this country from Rome. The decorations for the event were executed by Danker, who used salvias, kentias and other foliage plants for his purpose. On Tuesday the same florist had the decorations for the Pinkerton-Arthur wedding at St. Peter's church. The bride is a daughter of the late President Chester A. Arthur. The altar was banked with white Timothy Eaton chrysanthemums and plants of the same were grouped in the chancel. Chrysanthemums were used to decorate the pews, forming an aisle to the altar. The wedding was a notable event in local society and was attended by many from near and far.

The firm of Whittle Brothers on Tuesday had a very neat decoration at the Adelphi Club for a wedding which took place there. Bridesmaid roses, the Ada Spaulding chrysanthemum, maiden hair fern and Asparagus plumosus were the principal materials used in the decorations. Twenty small tables located in an adjacent room which were used after the ceremony for a wedding breakfast, were prettily decorated with Asparagus plumosus and Bridesmaid roses.

The firm of W. C. King & Company on Wednesday had a pretty church decoration for the Neemes-Hailes wedding. A pleasing novelty was the introduction of a neat bridal basket in which the attendants upon the bride carried their bouquets instead of in their hands as is the usual custom.

The present week was notable for the number of decorations at the various social functions that took place. Practically all the members of the craft benefited by this little wave of prosperity that came among us and all are quite happy.

The employes of the new Prospect Park, were laid off for the season last Saturday, as the appropriation for this year has been expended. The common council will later vote an appropriation to continue the work next year.

The firm of Lord & Burnham is rushing to completion the new forcing house for H. G. Eyres.
R. D.

Minneapolis.

TRADE IMPROVING.—ROSES ARE IN LIGHT DEMAND.—CARNATION SUPPLY LIMITED. —NOTES.

Trade conditions are improving and the past week shows increased sales in both wholesale and retail lines. Stock is shortening up, this being especially noticeable in American Beauty roses, which are far lower in supply than demand calls for. Some choice stock in Bridesmaid and Bride is now being brought in. Golden Gate, Liberty, Sunrise and Perle are appearing equally well. The Perle is enjoying more popularity here than has been noticed for a long time. This variety commands the same price as the other teas at present. Very few Meteors are observed in this city, Liberty alone taking its place. Carnations are limited in supply, but quality cannot be equaled. Prosperity, Crane, Lawson, Enchantress and Wolcott are showing in the lead. Chrysanthemums are moving slowly and football occasions cause any demand. Violets are in great demand and dealers are kept cutting close daily.

The monthly meeting of the Florists Club was held Thursday evening, November 6. It was well attended. After adjournment a social smoker and a bowling contest were indulged in.

The chrysanthemum show at St. Paul was attended by a large body of the trade here, and a pleasant time was enjoyed. The show was a success in every particular.

The Minneapolis Floral Company is cutting large numbers of tea roses, also chrysanthemums of the highest quality.

Rice Brothers' receipts of roses are of fancy quality. They are handling the product of two growers.

R. Will & Son are marketing some choice carnations.
C. F. R.

Springfield, Mass.

Business has been good the last two weeks, there being quite a demand for funeral work and decorations. Chrysanthemums have been hard to get rid of with some growers in this vicinity. They were too early and there was little demand owing to fine weather. A few good frosts the last week have put more life into trade. Roses and carnations are plentiful, the latter selling better than former years in chrysanthemum season. Pot plants for the holiday trade, such as azaleas, cyclamens and primulas, are going in fine shape.

Adams & Son have two houses of carnations which they say are hard to beat. They were grown inside part of the summer, which they say is the secret.

L. Morgan, of Longmeadow, has stock which is in fine shape, as has also Mr. Beals, of Eastern avenue.
A. B.

CANTON, ILL.—A successful chrysanthemum show was held November 16 by the ladies of the Methodist church.

AKRON, O.—H. Heepe's Sons have opened a new floral store at 26 Main street. They now operate two stores, the other at 328 West Market street, adjoining their greenhouse.

E. F. LEMKE'S EXHIBIT AT THE ST. PAUL SHOW.

Toronto.

ACTIVITY GENERAL AND MARKET SETTLES DOWN. — CHRYSANTHEMUM SUPPLY IS SHORTENING.—ROSES SCARCE, BUT OF EXCELLENT QUALITY.—NEWS OF THE DEALERS.

There has been a scarcity of pink chrysanthemums this season, and with the exception of pink Ivory and Viviand-Morel we are lacking in this color. Several dark days have reduced the supply of roses just at the time when chrysanthemums are going off and business coming on; the few flowers that are now cut, however, are mostly of fine quality and are bringing good prices. American Beauty is in fine shape and better ones will be hard to find. Meteor, Bridesmaid and Bride are all looking well. Carnations are in very fine shape but as plentiful as a week ago. Enchantress, Gaiety, Lillian Pond and Lawson are among the very select blooms offered. Our violet growers seem to be troubled with a scarcity; what are coming in are in fine shape but the supply is only about half what is required.

Activity is again general and the market seems to be settling down to more steady business. The last week was a decided improvement and a large quantity of stock was used. Chrysanthemums still predominate, though they are shortening up considerably and medium sized blooms are scarce. Especially is this so in whites. Golden Wedding is conspicuous in most stores, the rich color of this variety and the large well-shaped blooms making it the most desirable of any of the yellows.

Wm. Gammage & Son, of London, sent in samples of their new seedling chrysanthemum. The color is a good, deep pink and the flowers look strong with plenty of substance and nice foliage right up to the neck of the bloom. The growth is very vigorous and five good medium sized blooms were cut from one stem. The flower is naturally a very good keeper.

Our two large department stores, Eaton's and Simpson's, both held chrysanthemum shows last week. They showed some very fine blooms and some very good arrangements; the decorations in both places were creditable.

Thos. Plumb, of Yonge street, has been handling some very fine yellow and white Eaton chrysanthemums. His window is filled entirely with these, and he is showing the different cups and prizes which this variety has won.

Some good Bridesmaid and Bride are coming from the North Toronto Floral Company. Unfortunately an overdose of red pepper has practically ruined the plants in one of their houses.

W. J. Lawrence is sending in some very choice pans of pteris. His stock in general looks very promising.

Ed. Sinclair has returned from the northwest and will again engage in the florist business. H. G. D.

Omaha.

The Nebraska Florists' Club held its annual meeting November 12 and elected the following officers: S. Faulkner, president; E. Ellsworth, vice-president; G. Swoboda, treasurer; J. H. Bath, secretary. The meeting was successful and well attended. Paul Floth showed some very fine Enchantress and Prosperity carnations, of which he has a house full of each.

Chrysanthemums sold well this year, especially the early varieties, as we had a good many weddings and parties in October. American Beauty roses and violets were more in demand than ever before, in fact all flowers sold well this season and none were left in any store.

In King's park they have erected one greenhouse 22x80, heated by a Burnham boiler (hot water). They plan to build one more house next year. King's park, consisting of fifteen acres, is one of the best parks west of Chicago.

Herbert Slocum, the violet grower, brings in some very fine blooms, especially the large single California variety, of which he has 80,000 plants. He says they pay him better than any other variety.

The Forest Lawn Cemetery association has erected a few greenhouses heated by hot water. J. G. Craig, the superintendent, says the heating system in their new houses works like a charm.

G. Sorenson, of Florence, has a seedling carnation he claims is as good as Enchantress. It is somewhat fuller, with a good color and stem.

H. Peterson, of Florence, Neb., has opened a store on Thirteenth street. He reports a good business.

E. Hooge has opened a flower stand in the city market house and says he is doing very nicely.

Mr. Henderson has his two new houses finished, each 22x150, and the roses in them look fine.

A. Donaghue, Jr., will open a store at Sixteenth and Farnam streets.

Cold weather struck us November 17, 10 above zero. GRIPPE.

Redondo, Cal.

BIG GROWING BUSINESS ON TWO BIG FLORAL FARMS.—CARNATIONS THRIVE OUTDOORS. VIOLETS BRING GOOD PRICES.

There are now but two flower-growing firms here, W. Wolfskill having moved to Los Angeles. The Redondo Floral Company is one of the firms, the Beach, Hotel and the Floral companies being practically the same. A. F. Borden is general manager of the Floral company and has charge of the store, 246 South Spring street, Los Angeles. P. K. Lacey is superintendent of the gardens at Redondo. Mr. Lacey is considered one of the most successful carnation growers in southern California. One large glass house is planted to carnations of the varieties Lawson, Roosevelt, Manley and Estelle, with smaller numbers of Golden Beauty, Mrs. Joost and others. The best scarlet for indoors is Manley, with Estelle next. Golden Yellow is the best of its color. Joost does fairly well. Norway, a white, does well under glass. Outdoors the leaders are Allegra, Los Angeles, Corbett and Anna. These are all Redondo varieties, the last named is a dark crimson and a free bloomer. There are about six acres of young plants in splendid condition and as many or more older plants which I did not see, making twelve or fourteen acres in all. In addition to this, five acres more are being prepared for immediate planting. One hundred and fifty to two hundred thousand plants are propagated in a year, of which nearly 70,000 are used at home. At present the cut of blooms is from four to five thousand per day. The cut for the holidays is estimated at from ten to fourteen thousand, Jack Frost permitting. In May the output will exceed these figures a good many times over.

Rose growing under glass has not been a great success. Perhaps Mr. Lacy will do better with a house partly filled with American Beauty over which he was laboring when I called. Paris green had been used too freely by his predecessors and many of the plants had been ruined. A house of 800 adiantums looked well. In the lath-houses—covering about half an acre all told—is a large assortment of ornamentals, smilax and asparagus. The smilax was in fine shape for cutting, the estimated number of strings nearly 20,000. A lath house 75x225 was filled with Asparagus plumosus with two or three thousand strings ready for market, besides sprays. They have five thousand Asparagus Sprengeri and are planting a couple of thousand Boston ferns. Distillate is used for heating the rose, carnation and propagating houses.

The gardens of the Redondo Carnation Company are situated in North Redondo about half a mile from the Redondo station on the Santa Fe. Henry Theder and J. B. Mullen are the proprietors and they have ten acres more or less of which is under cultivation. Mr. Theder was present so that I was obliged to make an estimate myself of the area devoted to flowers. About four acres were in carnations, Corbett, Los Angeles and Allegra. The cut at present is about 1,500 per day, most of which go to the Ingleside Carnation Company. Wholesale prices of out door carnations run from 50 cents to $1 per hundred according to the season. About three acres are in violets which have been blooming for a month. The pick for October was about 1,600 bunches. Some sweet peas were grown last year and were profitable; prices averaged about $1.50 per thousand. A house of smilax was noticed and also an assortment of ornamentals. R. H. A.

Worcester, Mass.

The annual meeting of the Worcester County Horticultural Society was held November 4, and the following officers re-elected:

President, A. B. Hadwen; secretary and librarian, A. A. Hixon; treasurer, Nathaniel Paine. The affairs of the society were reported in good condition and appropriations were made for the exhibitions of next year. The last exhibition this year, November 12, brought out the finest show of chrysanthemums ever held in the county. P. W. Moen exhibited a magnificent lot. His vases of Eaton and Appleton were certainly grand and finished to the minute. Moen was awarded six firsts for six entries. Other prominent exhibitors were Mrs. John C. Whitin, Geo. N. Knowlton, H. F. A. Lange, H. F. Littlefield, F. A. Blake, E. W. Breed and M. J. Whittall, who showed a well grown table of Begonia Gloire de Lorraine. The hall was tastefully arranged with groups of palms, ferns and foliage plants, and the vases of long-stemmed flowers placed on tables below the line of vision.

Trade has been satisfactory and plenty of good material is being sent in. Chrysanthemums of course are the mainstay and we are getting very fine roses, carnations and violets. Though rather early to make predictions Enchantress looks like a winner and the same can be said of Queen.

The Worcester Conservatories have commenced cutting roses and have a stall at the Boston Flower Exchange, where they will market the bulk of their stock. A. H. L.

DEFIANCE, O. — Karl Scharfenberger held his sixteenth annual chrysanthemum display November 15.

THE AMERICAN FLORIST.

NINETEENTH YEAR.

Subscription, $1.00 a year. To Europe, $2.00.
Subscriptions accepted only from those
in the trade.

Advertisements on all except cover pages,
10 Cents a Line, Agate; $1.00 per inch.
Cash with Order.

No Special Position Guaranteed.

Discounts are allowed only on consecutive insertions, as follows—6 times, 5 per cent; 13 times,
10 per cent; 26 times, 20 per cent;
52 times, 30 per cent.

Cover space sold only on yearly contract at
$1.00 per inch, net, in the case of the two
front pages, regular discounts applying only to the back pages.

The Advertising Department of the AMERICAN
FLORIST is for florists, seedsmen and nurserymen
and dealers in wares pertaining to those lines only.

Orders for less than one-half inch space not accepted.

Advertisements must reach us by Wednesday to
secure insertion in the issue for the following
Saturday. Address

AMERICAN FLORIST CO., Chicago.

KEEP Liberty roses on the move. If
they stop to think it is winter it will be
"good day to you."

OUR eastern contemporary has not
roasted the peony committee for two or
three weeks. Why?

EASTER comes on April 3, just eighteen
weeks hence. Lilies should now be
reminded of that fact.

SEEDLING PALMS should also be potted
off as soon as possible so that they may
get roots started for winter growth.

BOSTON FERNS, cyclamens and many
other holiday plants grow as well, look
prettier and are more desirable for the
counter trade when planted in the shallow pots or pans.

WHATEVER you grow keep your plants
and their environs clean. Rubbish of any
kind in a greenhouse is an evidence of a
shiftless grower and is always an expensive luxury in the long run.

CARNATIONS will now require continuous fire heat but the wise grower will
keep them on the cool side and get them
in sturdy condition to withstand trying
circumstances later on. Unless plants
have been growing very rank and thus
absorbing the food in the soil rapidly,
stimulants would best be withheld for
some time yet.

London.

EXHIBITION OF THE ROYAL HORTICULT-
URAL SOCIETY.—CHRYSANTHEMUMS ARE
CHIEF FEATURE.—NEW NEPHROLEPIS.

At the Royal Horticultural Society's
meeting, October 27, chrysanthemums
were shown by the leading growers. Mr.
Davis took first honors with a grand
display of cut blooms, which included
extra fine specimens of Mildred Ware.
We shall expect to see this variety in all
prize winning exhibits this season. Mr.
Davis continues to grow immense blooms
of Mme. Carnot, also the sulphur yellow
sport Mrs. W. Mease. Beauty of Leigh,
a deep golden yellow, with long florets
drooping but turned up at the points is a
promising new variety for distribution
next spring. Lady Pearce, a new
creamy white, looked worth a trial. In
Messrs. Wells & Co's group which
consisted mainly of pot plants there were
some grand blooms. This group was
placed second. A feature was the great
plenty of color, good crimson being very
prominent. Maynell was one of the best,
a deep crimson with bronze reverse.
Lord Alverstone and S. T. Wright, both
deep crimson, are particularly welcome

for it often happens that the finest blooms
are confined to whites and yellows.
Mary Inglis, a bronze terra cotta with
very large flowers, and Princess Henry, a
hairy variety with long drooping florets
of a pleasing shade of pink were also
shown.

Messrs. Cannell & Sons showed an
interesting collection of single varieties.
Of these White Duchess and Marguerite,
another pure white with narrow pointed
petals, were worthy of note. Progress, a
bronze brown with yellow center, and
Sunbeam, a clear yellow, should prove useful. Melowbrook, a medium single pure
white, will make a useful October variety,
of the large flowered Japanese type. Alfris-
ton, crimson, Geo. Lawrence, golden
bronze, Beauty of Sussex, deep rose pink,
and Camden, pink, were noted as good.
Mr. Bullimore secured an award of merit
for his new yellow, Maud du Cross. This
also received a first-class certificate from
the N. C. S. on Monday.

H. J. Jones showed some good cut
blooms of large flowered varieties and a
collection from the open ground. In the
large blooms there were Mildred Ware,
Henry Perkins, Lady Acland, and Lady
Conyers, a very fine pink. In Mr. Godfrey's collection many of the best varieties of his own raising were shown,
including Exmouth Rival, a very fine
crimson, Mrs. J. P. Bryce, a new incurved
white of great merit and a fine yellow
incurved, Devonshire Hero. Blooms of
F. S. Vallis were shown and received the
award of merit. Mafeking Hero was
very fine. Miss E. Halding, a deep pink
incurved variety, also gained an award
of merit.

Of other exhibits the Messrs. Sander
showed two beautiful varieties of Begonia Rex, or rather hybrids of that section
—Our Queen and His Majesty. Both
received awards from the floral committee. Begonia Gloire de Lorraine and the
white variety were seen in better condition than ever. Messrs. Veitch & Sons
had their winter varieties in grand condition, also a fine lot of zonal pelargoniums in pots the best I noted being Dr. E.
Rawson, crimson, Chaucer, rose, Mrs.
Brown Potter, pink, Lady Roscoe, flesh
pink, E. Bidwell, scarlet, Mrs. Cadbury,
salmon, and M. Anatole Rosaleur, semi-
double pink.

Messrs. Cannell & Sons had a splendid
collection of cut blooms of single zonals,
including the Sirdar, scarlet, Mrs. C.
Pearson, salmon rose, Mrs. Williams,
pink, Prince of Orange, orange, Duke of
Norfolk, deep crimson, Lord Curzon, deep
crimson with a shading of blue, and
many other good sorts. Mrs. H. B.
May had a fine collection of colored chra-
cenas. Of these Mayi, Ruby, Charmer,
Prince George and Prince of Wales were
worthy of note. Messrs. Cutbush had a
useful lot of foliage plants suitable for
table decorations, also a fine collection
of herbaceous and alpine plants.

Messrs. B. Ladhams had an interesting collection of lobelias of the cardinalis
type varying in colors from white to
deep purple blue. J. Russel had a good
collection of hardy berried and variegated
plants.

Orchids were extensively shown by
most of the leading growers, and silver
gilt floral medals (the highest award
usually made at these meetings) were
awarded to about half a dozen exhibits
and silver floral medals to several others.
A new fern, Nephrolepis Westoni gained
an award of merit. This was a good
crested variety of N. acuta (or exaltolia).
It will make a good market fern. Another
good market plant which gained the

same award was Erica gracilis nivalis, a
pure white variety. Dahlias are not yet
quite over. Messrs. S. S. Ware staged a
good collection. The single cactus varieties were very attractive. Alice Lee,
pink, Queen Mary, blush and Pirate,
crimson, were all very distinct. Of the
cactus varieties Ajax, amber, and Kriem-
hilda, pink with cream center, were specially good. Some very good carnations
came from Messrs. H. Low & Company,
also from Messrs. Cutbush & Sons.
Messrs. W. Bull & Sons had some good
foliage plants, including some varieties
of Begonia Rex and a fine plant of David-
sonia pruriens, a noble plant with large
pinnate leaves.

Providence.

The chrysanthemum show has come
and gone and the pathetic monotony of
it is more apparent each year. Not that
the quality of blooms is unsatisfactory;
simply that the management does not
put lethargy enterprise into the affair
nor seek good quarters where the public
may be easily coaxed to view the won-
drous display of these charming flowers.
The result is that no great merit is
attached to a first premium from a
grower's point of view, and as far as the
people are concerned, there had better be
no exhibit at all, for the hall is poorly
patronized at even 25 cents admission.
This year the chrysanthemums and other
flowers were handsomely staged in a fine
room on a side street, upstairs, and the
points of contest were between the two
Macraes. Their exhibit needed no apolo-
gies. The Eatons were even better than
in 1902, but the Appleton showed a
falling off in quality. E. J. Johnston and
Howard Almy showed some meritorious
stock, and Mr. Hill made his customary
arrangement of palm and stove plants
which always relieve the barrenness of
exhibition places.

Business is poor and all share alike.
Henry Patrie has agreed to help out J.
F. Wood during the holidays. T. E.
Keller now has a lady assistant in the
store.

Macnair celebrated his tenth anniversary on Saturday. Chrysanthemums
are still in decided surplus.

M. M.

Syracuse, N. Y.

For some unknown reason the market
has not been as good as usual. The
weather has been cold and stormy and
this probably had its effect. Chrysanthemums are not selling as well as in previous years. White and yellow are the
popular colors. The local florists get just
as good prices but are not selling their
usual quantity of cut flowers. Were it
not for an unusual number of large
funerals business would be extremely
quiet. On account of the chrysanthemum season being at its height the
demand for roses is small. But few violets have been sold and those at low
prices. American Beauty is rather scarce.
There will be no contest of the will of
Henry Burt, the aged Syracuse florist
who died a few months ago. Neither of
the sons, Albert and Alfred, were mentioned in the will, although the estate is
said to amount to about $40,000. The reason
for dropping the contest given in court
was that Albert Burt, of Buffalo, was ill
and unable to come here and get wit-
nesses. A contest at some future time is
possible. Mr. Burt left his property to
his daughter and his widow who are

now running the greenhouses and the East Genesee street store.

Henry Morris has a spendid window display of chrysanthemums and he expects the Thanksgiving trade will be up to the average.

The charity ball Wednesday evening proved to be a good thing for the florists both in the matter of decoration and in individual sales. A. J. B.

Utica, N. Y.

In connection with a special meeting at Maennerchor hall the evening of November 10, the Utica Florists' Club held a flower show. There were fifty florists present, among the visitors being Joseph Trandt, of Canajoharie, N. Y., and W. H. Graham, of Little Falls. N. Y. The meeting was successful from both a trade and social standpoint, a banquet concluding the evening.

Their new rose was shown by Breitmeyer's Sons, Detroit. A vase of the new pink carnation Indianapolis was shown by Baur & Smith, and a vase of chrysanthemums exhibited by Nathan Smith & Son. The latter included Yanariva, which attracted much attention. The Yates Flower Company, of Canajoharie, displayed a good specimen of the Begonia Glorie de Lorraine, a plant that is hard to grow, and also a vase of Bridesmaid and Bride roses. William Mathews, of this city, had a fine vase of variously colored chrysanthemums. Charles Cramer, of the Forest Hill Conservatory, displayed a fine vase of Queen chrysanthemums. Peter Crowe showed a fine plant of Pandanus Sanderi. Robert Boyce exhibited a new seedling chrysanthemum, pink in color, and of the incurve variety, which gives much promise.

Colorado, Springs, Colo.

Real winter has set in at last. On the night of the 16th there was a heavy snow storm and the mercury dropped suddenly to 8° below zero. Since then the cold has become tempered somewhat and at the present time it is just cold enough to keep things moving. There is also enough sunshine to keep things growing at a proper rate. Roses are arriving in just about sufficient quantity to keep the local trade going. There are more carnations than the local trade requires and standing orders from out of town take the balance. Chrysanthemums are on the wane. This has been a very successful season for the latter; the quality was good all around and the demand could not have been better. There is no record of a single bloom going to waste. The shipping trade kept them cut close all the time. There are a few Paper White narcissi, also violets in increasing quantity. The labor troubles in this state have somewhat diminished the amount of money in circulation and consequently cash sales have fallen off considerably. Prices are normal for the time of year. The coal strike has not yet caused a scarcity of fuel, although prices have been materially advanced on all grades. S. S.

RICHMOND, IND.—The South Side Improvement Association had a meeting November 12 and decided to make an effort to have the E. G. Hill Company remove its plant to the south end of the city. The company has been cramped for room for some time past, and as is generally known the attempt to get city property adjoining that owned by the company failed.

Obituary.

ANTOINE CROZY.

Antoine Crozy, the world-renowned canna hybridizer, passed away at Lyons, France, October 25, at the age of 72 years. For the past eight years Mr. Crozy lived at Hyeres, on the Mediterranean coast, where he devoted himself to the pastime of canna hybridization and, in company with his son and son-in-law,

The late Antoine Crozy.

carried on the culture of palms. In the past Mr. Crozy had by no means confined his efforts to the hybridizing of cannas but had taken deep interest in such subjects as Pyrethrum roseum, dahlias, delphiniums, Dianthus plumarius, tritonias, phloxes, papaver, etc., as is well known to horticulturists who visited his former home at Lyons. In his declining years, with the desire to find a more equable climate, he moved to Hyeres, and after that time he devoted himself to cannas exclusively. With his hybridizing will be pursued any further by the firm, as his son is more deeply interested in palm growing. It is also a question if the end of the possibilities in the Crozy strain has not been reached. Mr. Crozy's latest ambition was to obtain a pure white canna of good qualities and he had attained better results in this direction than anything accomplished elsewhere, so far as we have seen. Some of his latest red and salmon colored sorts also show improvement over anything seen elsewhere. Mr. Crozy had the honor to be an Officer du Merite Agricole. Personally he was a most genial gentleman, rather reserved and unassuming. He lived for his family and his plants.

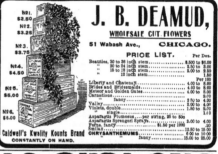

INTERNATIONAL FLOWER DELIVERY.

PASSENGER STEAMSHIP MOVEMENTS.

The table herewith give the scheduled time of departure of ocean steamships carrying first-class passengers from the principal American and foreign ports, covering the space of two weeks from date of this issue of the AMERICAN FLORIST. Much disappointment often results from attempts to forward flowers for steamer delivery by express, to the care of the ship's steward or otherwise. The carriers of these packages are not infrequently refused admission on board and even those delivered on board are not always certain to reach the parties for whom they were intended. Hence florists in interior cities having orders for the delivery of flowers to passengers on out-going steamers are advised to intrust the filling of such orders to some reliable florist in the port of departure, who understands the necessary details and formalities and has the facilities for attending to it properly. For the addresses of such firms we refer our readers to the advertisements on this page:

FROM	TO	STEAMER	*LINE	DAY	DUE ABOUT
New York	Liverpool	Etruria	1	Sat. Dec. 5, 6:00 a. m.	Dec. 11
New York	"	Campania	1	Sat. Dec. 12, 11:00 a. m.	Dec. 18
Boston	"	Ivernia	1	Tues. Dec. 3, 12:30 p. m.	Dec. 15
New York	Fiume	Aurania	1	Tues. Dec. 8, 11:00 a. m.	
New York	Glasgow	Siberian	2	Thur. Dec. 10, 11:00 a. m.	Dec. 20
Boston	"	Pomeranian	2	Wed. Dec. 9,	Dec. 19
New York	Hamburg	Bluecher	3	Sat. Dec. 5, 4:00 p. m.	Dec. 17
New York	"	Pretoria	3	Sat. Dec. 12, Noon	Dec. 22
New York	Glasgow	Astoria	5	Sat. Dec. 5, 10:45 a. m.	Dec. 15
New York	"	Columbia	5	Sat. Dec. 12, 3:00 p. m.	Dec. 22
New York	London	Menominee	6	Sat. Dec. 5, 9:00 a. m.	Dec. 15
New York	"	Minnetonka	6	Sat. Dec. 12, Noon	Dec. 22
New York	Liverpool	Germanic	7	Wed. Dec. 3, Noon	Dec. 10
New York	"	Cedric	7	Fri. Dec. 4, 3:00 a. m.	Dec. 12
New York	"	Majestic	7	Wed. Dec. 9, Noon.	Dec. 17
New York	"	Celtic	7	Fri. Dec. 11, 11:00 a. m.	Dec. 19
New York	Southampton	Philadelphia	8	Sat. Dec. 5, 9:30 a. m.	Dec. 12
New York	"	St. Louis	8	Sat. Dec. 12, 9:30 a. m.	Dec. 19
New York	Antwerp	Finland	9	Sat. Dec. 5, 10:30 a. m.	Dec. 14
New York	"	Vaderland	9	Sat. Dec. 12, 10:30 a. m.	Dec. 21
New York	Havre	La Touraine	10	Thur. Dec. 3, 10:00 a. m.	Dec. 11
New York	"	La Champagne	10	Thur. Dec. 10, 10:00 a. m.	Dec. 19
New York	Rotterdam	Rhyndam	11	Wed. Dec. 3, 10:00 a. m.	Dec. 11
New York	"	Noordam	11	Wed. Dec. 9, 10:00 a. m.	Dec. 18
New York	Genoa	Sardegna	12	Tues. Dec. 1, 11:00 a. m.	Dec. 19
New York	"	Citta di Napoli	12	Sat. Dec. 5, 11:00 a. m.	Dec. 24
New York	"	Prinzess Irene	12	Sat. Dec. 12, 11:00 a. m.	Dec. 22
New York	"	Lahn	12	Thur. Dec. 10, 11:00 a. m.	Dec. 22
New York	Bremen	Kronprinz Wilh.	13	Tues. Dec. 1, 1:00 p. m.	Dec. 8
New York	"	Neckar	13	Thur. Dec. 3, 10:00 a. m.	Dec. 15
New York	"	Rhein	13	Tues. Dec. 10, 10,30 a. m.	Dec. 21
New York	Naples	Roma	14	Thur. Dec. 10,	Dec. 20
Boston	Liverpool	Canada	15	Sat. Dec. 5, 11:00 a. m.	Dec. 12
Boston	"	Mayflower	15	Thur. Dec. 10, 3:00 p. m.	Dec. 18
Boston	Genoa	New England	15	Sat. Dec. 5, 11:00 a. m.	Dec. 19
Boston	"	Cambreman	15	Sat. Dec. 12, 3:00 p. m.	Dec. 23
Boston	Liverpool	Cestrian	16	Wed. Dec. 2, 7:30 a. m.	Dec. 18
Boston	"	Devonian	16	Wed. Dec. 9, 1:30 p. m.	Dec. 19

*1 Cunard; 2 Allan-State; 3 Hamburg-American; 4 Scandinavian-American; 5 Anchor Line; 6 Atlantic Transport; 7 White Star; 8 American; 9 Red Star; 10 French; 11 Holland-American; 12 Italian Royal Mail; 13 North German Lloyd; 14 Fabre; 15 Dominion; 16 Leyland; 17 Occidental and Oriental; 18 Oceanic; 19 Allan; 20 Can. Pacific Ry.; 21 N. Pacific Ry.; 22 Hongkong-Seattle.

American Florist Ads. always do business,
Every day in the week, all over the country,
At Home and Abroad.

INTERNATIONAL FLOWER DELIVERY.

STEAMSHIPS LEAVE FOREIGN PORTS.

THE SEED TRADE.

AMERICAN SEED TRADE ASSOCIATION.
S. F. Willard, Pres.; J. Charles McCullough,
First Vice-Pres.; C. E. Kendel, Cleveland, O.,
Sec'y and Treas.
Twenty-second annual convention St. Louis,
Mo., June, 1904.

THE receiver of the Vail Seed Company has disposed of the firm's business.

VISITED CHICAGO: William A. Cox and James B. Kidd, of San Francisco, Cal.; L. R. Shumway, Rockford, Ill.

VISITED BOSTON: W. H. Small, Evansville, Ind.; J. Cornout, representing Carter, Dunnett & Beale, London, Eng.

CALIFORNIA growers state that Redondo bush lima beans are a complete failure this year on account of the rains.

ROCKFORD, ILL.—R. H. Shumway, Jr., is seriously ill with kidney trouble, which developed from a bad cold contracted on a hunting trip.

THE business of the Vail Seed Company, Indianapolis, Ind., will be carried on under the old firm name, the receiver having turned it over to practical seedsmen.

WATERLOO, NEB.—The Leonard Seed Co. has been a liberal buyer of sweet corn, Stowell's Evergreen and some other varieties, from the farmers here the last week. Evergreen at the sheller at $3.75 to $4.00 per bushel.

THE bouquet green situation in the west has been seriously affected by continued and increasing cold weather and additional snow. Evidently picking is about over for this year and the season closes with a very short output in sight. Bulk green in sight not contracted is limited and florists and dealers who have their supply secured should be able to dispose of what they have to advantage.

Bouquet Green.

November 21.—The bouquet green supply has been further shortened, as indicated possible in our former notes, by freezing weather for the past two weeks which prevented the soft snow which fell November 10 from melting away in the woods. Practically no picking has been done since that date. Even if the weather moderates a good deal it is too late now to expect a full supply. Higher prices will prevail.

The Annual Free Seed Humbug.

That amusing humbug, the gratuitous distribution of field and garden seeds by the federal government, is about to be carried on again, on even a larger scale than usual.

The extent to which the practice has grown is shown by the statement that the aggregate weight of the seeds sent out is more than a thousand tons, while the expense to the government is about $270,000. Over forty million packages have been put up, and each member of congress is entitled to 12,500 of these for the ostensible benefit of his constituents.

As about one-third of the congressmen represent purely urban districts, where people procure their "garden seas" from the markets and have neither the facilities nor the desire to raise it themselves, and as the real farmers and market gardeners certainly do not rely on government seeds, the farcical nature of the whole scheme is evident.

There might be some justification for sending out seed to the various agricultural stations throughout the country, but the policy of franking them all over the United States to persons who neither want nor need them is a petty abuse which should have been dropped long ago. It is as squarely opposed to sound American principles as it would be for the government to distribute boots and shoes or penknives; but these articles would at any rate be of some practical use.—*Philadelphia Bulletin.*

Pasadena, Cal.

NURSERYMEN IN GOOD SPIRITS WITH LARGE STOCKS FOR THE COMING SEASON.—REAL ESTATE SALES BOOM BUSINESS.—NEWS OF THE BIG FIRMS.

The Pasadena nurserymen are in good spirits with stock for the coming season in fine shape. Thomas Chisholm has a splendid lot of asparagus deflexus. Mr. Hansen, the foreman, says this asparagus is one of the most satisfactory of decorative plants, the sprays also being especially effective when used in flower work. The Boston fern is used in large quantities and Asparagus Sprengeri still sells well. A small houseful of adiantum looked happy and thrifty, as also did a block of 2,000 poinsettias in pots. Mr. Chisholm does a good deal of outside work, landscaping, setting lawns, etc. At present he employs eighteen or twenty men. Among the jobs on hand is the planting of a small park at Long Beach for a company which is preparing to place its property on the market. It is getting to be quite thing for owners of new residence tracts to grade and sidewalk the streets and to plant out border trees before offering their lots for sale.

At the Enterprise Nursery, Silas Toms, proprietor, the most notable thing was a lot of 500 young live oaks in the pink of condition. This oak, Quercus agrifolia, a native, is without doubt the finest shade and ornamental tree grown in California. Mr. Toms grows a good many poinsettias as well as hibiscus, using several thousand plants of the latter in a season. He experienced trouble with the damping off his seedling camphoras last spring. The camphora is a good tree, but has a strong rival in the sterculia. The sterculia has much of the general appearance of the camphora, is easier to manage and is becoming very popular.

J. W. Ross, for seventeen years with the Park Nursery Company, is still in charge, although he is branching out for himself as a grower of rose plants with J. R. Vore for partner. They will grow for the coast trade only for the present. Mr. Rust, the president of the company, has also other interests, having a nursery in South Pasadena and a sales yard and houses in Los Angeles. The poinsettia seems to be a favorite in Pasadena, for here we find another large batch of the plant, some 2,000, all in pots. These poinsettias go into the ground when sold and are not grown as potted plants. Outdoors they go and grow and blow, and a gorgeous sight they are at about Christmas time. Hanging baskets are a specialty; something like 1,000 is the number the Park company expects to dispose of this season. Prices run from $1.25 or $1.50 apiece up. Boston ferns, Asparagus Sprengeri and Begonia Arabella are used almost exclusively. This begonia looks well, and, according to Mr. Ross, wears well, standing several degrees of frost without injury. A lot of thirty baskets planted with B. Arabella were sent out to Hollywood last fall and they came through the winter with flying colors. Pteris tremula has been in good demand. Mr. Ross figures on an increase of fifty per cent in the sales of house plants this fall over last. Most of the business in this class is done before New Year. After that the call is largely for outdoor plants. Nephrolepis Piersoni has proved a novelty of real merit—"simply must have a lot of it for next year," said Mr. Ross. In palms Phœnix Canariensis heads the list. Not only is it the most satisfactory for lawn or street, but it is one of the best for the house. Cocos australis is growing in favor for outdoor planting around Pasadena. The demand for Cycas revoluta has fallen off considerably the past season or two yet the Park people have 250 ready for sale. Two hundred Japanese fern balls will be started soon and they sell well.

One or two new flower stores are in prospect for Pasadena—indeed one has already been started, but full announcement will not be made for a few days at the request of the proprietor. Smith Brothers, at the old stand, state that the retail flower trade—present and prospective—is about the same as last year. The firm owns acreage property near Los Angeles, where many of their flowers are grown under the supervision of L. H. Smith, one of the brothers. In carnations the old Redondo varieties, Los Angeles (white) and Corbett (cerise), are the favorites. Dr. Choate is considered to be the best dark crimson. Roosevelt and Empress have not come up to the mark as income bringers. Chrysanthemums have been selling well. Among the newer varieties Timothy Eaton (white) is the favorite, while Appleton is a very good yellow.

While not in the strict sense a commercial place, yet the Raymond Nurseries should not be passed without some mention. This place is owned by the proprietor of the big Raymond Hotel, and most of the stuff grown is used in the hotel or on the grounds. The management of this department of the hotel's domestic economy falls upon the shoulders of Robert Lathede, whom I did not see, but "Billy" did very nicely in his stead. There are a number of houses here, one of which is devoted to carnations—mostly Estelle, Fair Maid and Palmer, with smaller numbers of Lawson, Enchantress, Mermaid and Lillian Pond. Lawson is a failure in southern California as an outdoor variety, the stems being too short, but is fairly good under glass. Inside carnations are a new thing about Los Angeles. Everything has been grown in the open ground until lately. Several houses are devoted to roses. In one house a bench of American Beauty looked fine. Two houses planted in solid beds were set to Bridesmaid and Kaiserin respectively, all in good shape. "Billy" said Kaiserin is the rose, outdoor or in—"best white, free bloomer, equal to Papa Goutier for returns." Naturally a good many bedding and house plants are grown. In pansies the International Mixture has given satisfaction. This year the new Masterpiece is being tested. Fifty plants of Asparagus deflexus have done so well that the stock is to be greatly increased Nephrolepis Piersoni has also given great satisfaction. Anna Foster reverts badly, perhaps half the fronds going back to the old form. Perhaps the especial strain was at fault. N. Bostoniensis is used very extensively for hanging baskets and tubs. "Billy" said they had 15,000 or more plants and use them all for decorative purposes around the hotel. A hundred or so tubs were put in last season—a fifteen or twenty plants in each tub. The temperature in the hotel is so high that the ferns stay in condition but three or four weeks, when they are replaced by a fresh lot.

　　　　　　　　R. H. A.

THE NURSERY TRADE.

Albion, Ia.—J. B. Cripps, the veteran nurseryman, is in a critical condition owing to his failing health, and his family and friends are greatly worried over the possible outcome.

"Pruning" is the title of Farmers' Bulletin No. 181, an instructive illustrated pamphlet of nearly forty pages, prepared by L. C. Corbett for the United States Department of Agriculture, which is now ready for free distribution.

Seizes Nursery Shipment.

Republic, Wash.—George S. Morley, horticultural inspector of Stevens county, sent here November 8 by the state horticultural commissioner at Tacoma, as deputy for Ferry county to act in the case of three different invoices of nursery stock consigned to parties in Ferry and Okanogan counties by the Rochester Nursery company, of Rochester, N. Y., has seized the consignments and holds them subject to the advice of Ferry county's attorney, W. C. Brown. It is alleged that the Rochester company violated the law to protect planters in this state, by reason of failure to take out a license and procure the required bond of $2,000, without which no nursery stock can be imported into or sold in this state.—*Spokane Chronicle, November 11, 1903.*

Catalogues Received.

L. Boehmer & Company, Yokohama, Japan, Japanese plants, bulbs and seeds; Richard Smith & Company, Worcester, Eng., nursery stock; The J. W. Sefton Manufacturing Company, Anderson, Ind., flower boxes; The Lindgren Chemical Company, Grand Rapids, Mich., thistleine; I. N. Kramer & Son, Cedar Rapids, Ia., greenhouse construction; Frank Banning, Kinsman, Ohio, gladioli; Frederick Roemer, Quedlinburg, Germany, seeds; F. C. Heinemann, Erfurt, Germany, seeds; Hardy Plant Farm, London, Eng., hardy plants; Sluis & Groot, Enkhuizen, Holland, vegetable and flower seeds; Ernst Benary, Erfurt, Germany, seeds; Peter Lambert, Trier, Germany, roses; Victor Detriche, Angers, France, plants; seeds, etc.; Ottolander & Hooftman, Boskoop, Holland, plants, seeds, etc.; John Lucas Company, Philadelphia, Pa., paints; Hammond's Slug Shot Works, Fishkill-on-Hudson, N. Y., insecticides; H. Thaden, Atlanta, Ga., wire tendril; John Breitmeyer's Sons, Detroit, Mich., new rose; Letellier, Son & Company, Caen, France, nursery stock; J. M. Thorburn & Company, New York, seeds, Roustan Servan & Company, Saint-Reny-De-Province, France, seeds; Ant. Van Velsen & Company, Haarlem, Holland, bulbs; Soupert & Notting, Luxembourg, Germany, roses, novelties; Jerome B. Rice Seed Company, Cambridge, N. Y., onion seed; C. C. Morse & Company, Santa Clara, Cal., seeds.; J. C. Schmidt, Erfurt, Germany, seeds; Dammann & Co., Naples, Italy, seeds.

Cairo, Ill.—The State Horticultural Society will hold its annual convention at Champaign from December 16 to 18 inclusive.

Prepare plans now for next season.

OUR PASTIMES.

Announcements of coming contests or other events of interest to our bowling, shooting and sporting readers are solicited and will be given place in this column.
Address all correspondence for this department to Wm. J. Stewart, 49 W. 28th St., New York. Robt. Kift, 1725 Chestnut St., Philadelphia, Pa.; or to the American Florist Co., Chicago, Ill.

At St. Louis.

The bowling club rolled four games at the Blue Ribbon alleys Monday night. Kuehn was first by a good margin. The score was:

Player	1st	2d	3d	4th	T'l
Kuehn	119	194	185	194	792
Miller	117	181	178	170	646
Beneke	156	167	167	152	627
Beyer	161	148	150	158	597
Ellis	143	168	156	138	597
Meinhart	89	130	137	130	486

F. K. B.

At Colorado Springs.

The result of the last series rolled by the florists of Colorado Springs follows. W. H. Dunman's score of 189 proved to be the best of the match:

Player	1st	2d	3d	4th
Vipond	143	134	154	180
Johnson	107	119		
No aghan	113	118	102	
Baur	107	146	111	
Braidwood	133	118	143	
Crump	113	119	190	118
Betz	100	147	98	147
Duff	108	144	194	166
Rush	113	147	176	
Harris	141	144		
Pierce	118	115		
Dunman	108	189	189	152

W. H. D.

At Chicago.

The wholesalers and retailers rolled a series of three games Tuesday evening on the Giroux alleys. The former emerged the victors by winning two out of the three games. The last was a four figure game, all of the wholesalers being in fine fettle. The next meeting will be held at Mussey's alleys Tuesday evening, December 1. Regular teams will then be selected and a schedule for the winter prepared. The following are the scores of the last encounter:

WHOLESALERS.

Player	1st	2d	3d
E. Winterson	163	135	156
Scott	197	163	155
Degnan	160	171	197
Lambros	174	142	166
Foster	173	170	184
Essa		116	167
Total	797	896	1007

RETAILERS.

Player	1st	2d	3d
Hauswirth		183	143
Stephens	179	178	171
Cononas	94	143	163
Huebner	173	159	174
Asmus	143	179	186
Kreitling		148	117
☐ Total	767	989	954

At Philadelphia.

The club tournament is becoming very warm and interesting; two more matches were played on November 20 between the Eimerman and Westcott teams, which resulted in the Eimermans winning three straight.

On November 22 the Harris and Dunham teams had a go. Captain Dunham was not able to be present, being confined to the house with a bad cold. His team, however, took two games out of the three, and made 887, the highest single game of the tournament so far. The scores follow:

Player	1st	2d	3d
Eimerman	138	145	165
Dunman	131	197	143
Polok	156	176	142
Baker	124	153	180
Connor	147	153	154
Total	697	756	814
Players	1st	2d	3d
Westcott	98	190	150
Webster	150	16+	136
Seaman	86	114	132
Yates	970	186	143
Adelberger	121	116	130
Total		681	689
Players	1st	2d	3d
Harris	177	159	145
Johnson	158	155	169
Graham	169	146	176
Baxter		198	161
Robertson		198	171	201
Total	738	749	858
Players	1st	2d	3d
Anderson	184	188	190
Wright	136	196	147
Moore	1.0	170	144
Watson	198	183	173
Dunham	172	173	179
Total	781	887	845

Small Rose Blooms.

Ed. Am. Florist:—Please tell us what to do for our Bride and Bridesmaid roses. The plants are in a thrifty condition, the stems and foliage all that one could wish, but the flowers are small and not fully double. Golden Gate and Perle in the same house are giving first class blooms.
N. J. F.

N. J. F. does not say at what temperature he is running his house of Bride, and judging from his description of the kind of buds he is getting it would indicate that the temperature is a little too high to produce large, full buds. Perle, with a little higher temperature than is required for Bride, will develop fine buds. With the cooler weather we are now getting in all probability the Bride plants will begin to produce better quality flowers if the temperature is kept down to an average of 56° at night with a liberal amount of ventilation in all favorable weather by day. In conjunction with other suitable treatment such as water at the roots as required, etc., they certainly should produce good qual-

ity flowers. If the above is not the cause of the trouble then in all probability it arises from the soil not being rich enough in some component element requisite for the full development of perfect flowers, but from N. J. F.'s description of the other varieties growing in the same house and under the same conditions of soil, etc, it would appear that these requisites are not wanting. The very warm weather which has continued so late in the fall has made it very difficult to keep the night temperature down to the desired degree, hence the probable cause of the small, poor quality buds such as have prevailed nearly all the fall. It is better to leave a little air on the top ventilation at night with just enough fire heat to prevent the accumulation of moisture on the foliage as this latter condition is very detrimental to the health of the plants and certainly should be avoided under all conditions. John N. May.

Injured Foliage.

Ed. Am. Florist:—Please tell me what is the matter with the plant foliage of which I enclose samples. For four days we had a heavy fog. One day the fog was very thick with smoke and soot. The plants most affected were in the cool houses where the ventilators were open and included chrysanthemums and primulas. The flowers were not affected but the foliage looks as if it had been burned or scalded by the fog or sewer gas though I did not detect the latter. J. M.

The injury to the leaves was possibly caused by some poisonous substance such as "sulphurous acid" or other injurious fumes or gas carried in by the fog. Careful microscopic examination shows that there is no fungus parasite at work in the leaves. A. R. W.

Louisville, Ky.—Richard T. Lewis, of Huber, formerly a florist in this city, died here of peritonitis November 18, Mr. Lewis was 33 years old. Until four years ago he conducted a floral establishment on Fourth avenue, near Chestnut, but for some time previous to his death had not been engaged in any business.

Hartford.

FOOTBALL GAME STIMULATES TRADE.—FLORISTS' CLUB MEETING.—FINE CARNATION EXHIBIT.

Albert Whitney's greenhouse establishment in West Hartford, consisting of twenty-three houses, containing 10,000 square feet of glass, is well worth a word of comment just now. Two houses have been rebuilt this summer and one new one put up. Mr. Whitney does all this work with his own men, under the direction of his foreman, Charles Peterson. There are just now 10,000 chrysanthemums in full crop and fine condition. They will last up to Christmas and good sales for them are reported. Here are also grown 3,500 grafted roses, Bride and Ivory. They are yielding a fine crop. Twenty thousand carnations of all the latest varieties in healthy condition and there are two houses of violets from which picking has already commenced. In the spring Mr. Whitney has a fine line of Easter stock and later on thousands of bedding plants which, with everything produced here, find ready sale at home. Mr. Whitney is now about 80 years old. He started in the nursery business when a young man and later took up the florist business. He will always be found in his greenhouses, and it is a real pleasure to drop in once in a while and have a chat with the hale and hearty old man.

Messrs. Karlstrom, Zager and Norberg, told of what they saw and did at the New Haven show. Messrs. Wirth and Hass also told some very good stories from the recent New York show. Mr. Zager, of Elisabeth park, exhibited twenty-four varieties of pot-grown carnations, which were exceedingly fine. The varieties were as follows: Prosperity, Mrs. Lawson, Cressbrook, Enchantress, Gov. Roosevelt, Gen. Gomez, Harry Toms, Gen. Maceo, Alba, Queen Louise, Norway, Mrs. Potter Palmer, J. H. Manley, Chicago, Estelle, Wm. Scott, Eldorado, Golden Beauty, Genevieve Lord, Elm City. This collection was given a certificate of merit.

The Hartford Florists' Club met on Tuesday evening, November 17, the regular meeting having been postponed because of the show in New Haven on that day. Resolutions on the death of Thomas McClunie, an honorary member of the club were adopted and ordered sent to the family of the deceased. Application for membership was received from A. Reithenbach, of New Britain. The treasurer read his semi-annual report, and it was assured that the club is in a very good financial standing.

Business had been slow for some time until the Yale-Princeton football game livened matters up a little. Practically all the violets available went to New Haven on that day. On November 18 Mrs. Chas. Chaise, of Prospect avenue, gave a reception to the new vice-president of the Hartford Fire Insurance Company. Seven hundred invitations were sent out. This cleaned out the glut of carnations and roses and the retailers were very busy for a while.

A. G. Gully, of the Connecticut agricultural committee for the St. Louis exposition reports to Secretary Vail that 100 barrels of fruit, consisting of appels, pears and cranberries, have been collected for exhibition at the fair and are now being preserved in cold storage by P. Berry & Sons, of this city.

R. K.

BRIDGEPORT, CONN.—A steam heating plant is to be placed in the new hothouse just completed for G. H. Smith, Fairfield.

Exhibition at Providence, R. I.

The autumn exhibition of chrysanthemums given by the Providence Horticultural Society opened in Frances Willard hall, November 12 and attracted general interest, large numbers being in attendance last evening and throughout today. The exhibition of chrysanthemums was excellent, the display by John A. and Farquhar Macrae being a most extensive and beautiful one. William Hill of Prospect street was awarded the first prize of $15 for his display of potted plants, while Eugene Appleton was awarded the second prize for the most artistically arranged group of potted plants.

The list of premiums awarded were, Chrysanthemums, six plants—William Hill.

A. J. Balfour, twenty-five blooms—First, Farquhar Macrae; second, John A. Macrae.

Jerome Jones, twenty-five blooms—First, E. J. Johnson; second, Farquhar Macrae.

Timothy Eaton—First, John A. Macrae; second, Farquhar Macrae.

Any varieties, fifty blooms—First, John A. Macrae; second, Farquhar Macrae.

Distinct varieties, twelve cut blooms—John A. Macrae.

Distinct varieties, six cut blooms—John A. Macrae.

Best single flower, white—First, John A. Macrae; second, Farquhar Macrae.

Best single flower, pink—First, Farquhar Macrae; second, John A. Macrae.

Best single flower, yellow—First, Farquhar Macrae; second, John A. Macrae.

Best single flower of any variety—First, John A. Macrae; second, Farquhar Macrae.

Six vases of ten blooms each—First, John A. Macrae; second, John A. Macrae; third, Farquhar Macrae.

Prize for best vase of ten blooms, never before exhibited—John A. Macrae.

Carnations; Any crimson variety, twenty-five blooms—John A. Macrae.

Dark pink—First, Farquhar Macrae; second, A. E. Covell.

Any light pink variety, twenty-five blooms—First, Farquhar Macrae; second, John A. Macrae.

Scarlet variety, twenty-five blooms—First, John A. Macrae; second, Farquhar Macrae.

Any white variety, twenty-five blooms—First, Farquhar Macrae; second, John A. Macrae.

Any yellow variety, twenty-five blooms—Farquhar Macrae.

Any other color, twenty-five blooms—Farquhar Macrae.

Best single orchid—William Hill. Most artistically arranged group—First, William Hill; second, Eugene Appleton.

Begonia: Best collection of Glorie de Lorraine—John A. Macrae.

Ornamental basket, Miss A. E. Holland.

Vase of roses, William Hill.

Hardy chrysanthemums, Miss L. Mullin.

Sweet peas, A. E. Covell.

Violets, John A. Macrae.

Two vases of roses, E. Macrae.

Basket of flowers, Lillias A. Bloomer.

Vase of carnations, Miss Bloomer.

Columbus.

There is still a large stock of chrysanthemums on hand, as most of the growers held over for Thanksgiving trade. The demand for this popular flower was greater this season than ever before.

John Hellenthal has a fine lot of Rambler roses potted off and trimmed in shape for early forcing.

Fine weather is causing hundreds of people to visit Greenlawn cemetery, giving Sherman Stephens an opportunity to run off his large stock of chrysanthemums. Mr. Stephens has a fine lot of these, among which are quite a number of promising new varieties.

The Livingstone Seed Company made a special effort the past week in displaying some of its own grown stock of chrysanthemums at its down town store. In the display were a fine lot of specimens in pots.　　C.

WESTPORT, CONN.—Samuel Banks lost all his chrysanthemums by fire November 8. An oil stove used for heating became overheated and set fire to the wood work.

Exhibition at St. Paul.

The second annual flower show is over and with it closed one of the busiest weeks ever experienced here. The show was a great success, both financially and otherwise, the only fault to find was that there was not room enough for display and for the people that came to see it. The show was in charge of the Ladies' Auxiliary of the Northwestern Manufacturers' Association, who comprise about three hundred of the leading society ladies of the city, and that is one reason that it was such a success. It was made quite a social event, with punch and tea being served in the parlors by the ladies. The first night being Colonial night, brought the people out in wigs, powdered hair and colonial dress. The second night was given over to the Germans and they packed the hall and tearooms all day. The third evening was Scandinavian night and this also brought out a big attendance. The young ladies serving refreshments were dressed in the various Scandinavian costumes which were much admired. The last night was Japanese night and all the decorations were very elegant. Chinese lanterns and parasols were displayed to best advantage and the young ladies were dressed in quaint Japanese costumes of rich kimonas of the finest silks. It was worth any one's time to go and see this feature alone, as was attested by the crowded galleries and boxes.

Some very fine flowers were shown, but few novelties. Holm & Olson showed some very fine specimen plants of The Bard, May Foster, Georgiana Pitcher, Mrs. Chamberlain and Golden Chain. These with the large cut blooms of Timothy Eaton, Viviand-Morel and Col. Appleton were the biggest attraction. August S. Swanson had a pretty arrangement of a table cover with a centerpiece of Chateney roses, the cover part being made of Bride roses and Enchantress carnations, with Liberty roses in the border. Mr. Swanson displayed a fine arrangement of orchids in a basket.

Some of the prize-winning roses came from A. N. Kinsman, of Austin, Minn.

Following is a list of the prizes and winners:

Collection of twelve chrysanthemum plants—L. L. May & Co., first; Holm & Olson, second.

Three plants, white—L. L. May & Co., first; Holm & Olson, second.

Yellow—L. L. May & Co., first; Holm & Olson, second.

Any other color—L. L. May & Co., first; Holm & Olson, second.

Specimen white—Holm & Olson, first (May Foster); L. L. May & Co., second.

Yellow—Holm & Olson, first (Georgiana Pitcher); L. L. May & Co., second.

Pink—Holm & Olson, first (Mrs. Chamberlain); L. L. May & Co., second.

Any other color—Holm & Olson, first (The Bard); L. L. May & Co., second.

Collection, twenty-five single chrysanthemums—Holm & Olson, first; L. L. May & Co., second.

Twelve blooms, white—E. F. Lemke, first (Timothy Eaton); Holm & Olson, second.

Yellow—Holm & Olson, first (Col. Appleton); A. S. Swanson, second.

Pink—A. S. Swanson, first (Viviand-Morel); L. L. May & Co., second.

Six blooms, white—A. S. Swanson, first (Quito); Vogt Bros., second.

Yellow—Holm & Olson, first (Col. Appleton); L. L. May & Co., second.

Pink—A. S. Swanson, first (Viviand-Morel); L. L. May & Co., second.

Any other color—L. L. May & Co., first (Intensity); Holm & Olson, second.

Fifty blooms, any color—A. S. Swanson, first (Viviand-Morel); Holm & Olson, second.

Basket of chrysanthemums—A. S. Swanson, first; E. F. Lemke, second.

Roses, twenty-five American Beauty—A. S. Swanson, first; Holm & Olson, second.

Queen of Edgely—Holm & Olson, second; Vogt Bros., second.

Bride—Holm & Olson, first; L. L. May & Co., second.

Bridesmaid—Holm & Olson, first; L. L. May & Co., second.

Kaiserin—Holm & Olson, first; Vogt Bros., second.

Golden Gate—Holm & Olson, first; L. L. May & Co., second.

Mme. Chatenay—Holm & Olson, first; E. F. Lemke, second.

Carnot—Vogt Bros., first; Holm & Olson, second.

Any other variety—Holm & Olson, first (Ivory); E. F. Lemke, second.

Arranged for effect—A. S. Swanson, first (American Beauty); E. F. Lemke, second.

Carnations, fifty white—Holm & Olson, first (Norway); L. L. May & Co., second.

Red—Holm & Olson, first (Estelle); L. L. May & Co., second.

Dark pink—Holm & Olson, first (Nelson Fisher); E. F. Lemke, second.

Light pink—L. L. May & Co., first (Enchantress); Holm & Olson, second.

Any other color—L. L. May & Co., first (Mrs. Patten); Holm & Olson, second.

Twelve white—L. L. May & Co., first (White Cloud); Holm & Olson, second.

Red—Vogt Bros., first (Adonis); Holm & Olson, second.

Dark pink—L. L. May & Co., first (Nelson Fisher); Vogt Bros., second.

Light pink—Holm & Olson, first (Enchantress); L. L. May & Co., second.

Any other color—Holm & Olson, first (Harry Fenn); Vogt Bros, second.

Arranged for effect—Holm & Olson, first; L. L. May & Co., second.

Violets, 200 double—E. F. Lemke, first.

One hundred double—E. F. Lemke, first.

Two hundred single—E. F. Lemke, second.

A. S. Swanson, second.

One hundred single—Vogt Bros., first; E. F. Lemke, second.

Palms and decorative plants, group—A. S. Swanson, first; Holm & Olson, second.

Specimen palm—L. L. May & Co., first; A. S. Swanson, second.

Specimen fern—Holm & Olson, first (Nephrolepis Piersoni); L. L. May & Co., second.

Best design, chrysanthemum—Holm & Olson, first; A. S. Swanson, second.

Best design, any flower—A. S. Swanson, first; Holm & Olson, second.   O.

Flushing,' N. Y.

A. L. Thorne's carnation houses are in excellent trim this season, the only flaw being the extreme prevalence of stem rot in some varieties which has necessitated considerable replanting. Mr. Thorne's seedling, White Layde, holds its good character of last year. It is a splendid high-centered flower. Enchantress, as seen here, is a veritable giantess, with stem in proportion. Adonis is better than in many other places, the plants being good but somewhat slow to get started. Viola Allen is credited with being the best money-maker on the place. Prosperity is as good as ever. Lorna is fair but always desirable for its good length of stem early in the season. There were 1,000 of Gov. Wolcott, which starts off promisingly. Sir Thomas Lipton is a seedling, bright cerise, in which Mr. Thorne has great faith for the future. One 300-foot house is planted half with Mrs. Lawson and half with Genevieve Lord, and a finer house doesn't exist anywhere. These two varieties seem particularly at home in Flushing soil and Flushing aspect.

Exceptional Values in Kentia Forsteriana.

NEVER have we been in position to give as good values in Kentia Forsteriana as just now. All of the sizes offered below will be found of exceptional value either for retailing or for decorative work. For the latter purpose we especially direct attention to the plants offered at $5.00, $6.00, $7.50, $10.00 and $12.50 each; they will be found a good investment. All are clean, thrifty stock of good color and quality.

Pots.	Leaves.	Inches high	Each	Pots.	Leaves.	Inches high	Each
5-inch	6	28 to 30	$1.00	8-inch	6 to 7	4½ feet	5.00
6-inch	6	30 to 32	1.25	9-inch	6 to 7	5 to 5 feet	6.00
6-inch	6	32 to 36	1.50	10-inch	6 to 7	5½ to 6 feet	7.50
7-inch	6 to 7	36 to 40	2.00	10-inch	6 to 7	5½ to 6 feet	10.00
7-inch	6 to 7	40 to 42	2.50	10-inch	6 to 7	6 to 6½ feet	12.50
8-inch	6 to 7	42 to 45	3.00	12-inch	6 to 7	6 to 7 feet	20.00
8-inch	6 to 7	4 feet	4.00				

COCOS WEDDELLIANA,

is always scarce about the holidays and will be scarcer than common this season. We still hold a fine lot of 3-inch pot plants 10 to 12 inches high, at $2.00 per dozen; $15.00 per 100.

ARAUCARIA EXCELSA.

You will require some of this stock for your holiday trade. We can give you perfect plants now which is not always the case late in December and we will send you stock that we know you will be pleased with, and that you can realize a good profit on.

Pots.	Ins. high.	Tiers.	Each	Pots.	Ins. high.	Tiers.	Each
4-inch	10 to 12	2	$.50	6-inch.	18 to 20	4 to 5	$1.25
5-inch.	14 to 16	3 to 4	.75	7-inch.	22 to 24	5	1.50
5-inch.	14 to 16	4 to 5	1.00				

For a full and complete line of DECORATIVE PLANTS as well as all other seasonable stock see our current wholesale list.

HENRY A. DREER, Philadelphia, Pa.

Please mention the American Florist to advertisers.

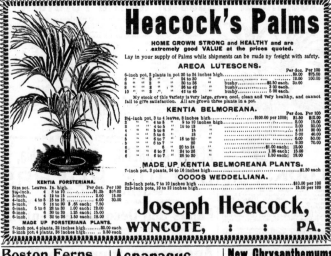

Exhibition at Chestnut Hill, Pa.

At the Chestnut Hill show were some of the best grown plants of Begonia Gloire de Lorraine the writer has ever seen. There were no plants of this popular begonia at either New York or Philadelphia to be compared with them. These were exhibited by William Boyce, gardener to Randal Morgan, Wyndmoor, Chestnut Hill, Pa. The same exhibitor also had some finely grown cut blooms of chrysanthemums. All of Mr. Morgan's exhibits were for exhibition only.

Charles A. Knapp also made some meritorious exhibits for exhibition only. A vase of Timothy Eaton chrysanthemums would have been creditable in any exhibition anywhere.

James Bell, gardener to Louis C. Vanuxem, Chestnut Hill, had the honor of taking the greatest number of prizes. William Vandervoer, gardener to Wm. J. Latta, Wirratuckon Heights, had the honor of carrying off the two best firsts, that for a group of foliage plants and for twelve crotons. The latter were exceedingly well done, the varieties being of the best and well assorted, and they were well furnished with foliage.

The show was held in Christian Hall, the free library building at Chestnut Hill, and was free to the public. The judges were Robert G. Carey, John F. Sibson and Edwin Lonsdale. E. L.

Andover, Mass.

Geo. D. Millet installed a Lord & Burnham hot water heater this season. J. H. Playdon put in a thirty horse-power tubular boiler and intends erecting a new house in the spring, 14x110. Warren Johnson has erected a greenhouse, 25x50. George Piddington and Mrs. C. A. Shattuck have retired from business.
J. H. P.

RAFFIA

We carry a large assortment of COLORED RAFFIA GRASS on hand for immediate delivery. Every strand is dyed its entire length.

SAMPLES FREE.

R. H. COMEY CO.
Dyers, Camden, N. J.

Please Mention The American Florist When Writing.

Greenhouse Building.

Albany, N. Y.—E. L. Menard, house 30x200 feet.

Greenland, N. H.—Edward Clough, one house.

Manchester, Mass.—Jas. K. Tappan, one house.

Lincoln, Mass.—Flint Brothers, range of cucumber houses.

Manchester, Vt.—W. H. Graham, one house.

Cleveland, O.—Fred. Ponting, range of houses.

JOLIET, ILL.—At a meeting of the Joliet Improvement Society held last week Secretary Ferris reported that the receipts of the recent flower show amounted to $800. It was decided to increase the prizes for the principal exhibits next year and a number of minor classes were dispensed with. It was also decided to distinguish between house collections of plants and greenhouse collections, and a new class was established to be called "cottage collections," as distinguished from "stove and greenhouse" collections.

FRESNO, CAL.—John Isaac, secretary of the State Horticultural commission, is arranging for the state convention of fruit growers December 5. Mr. Isaac says interest is general over the state. Papers on viticultural subjects will be read by Percy T. Morgan, president of the California Wine Association; President Robert Boot, Vice-President T. E. White and Treasurer D. D. Allison of the Raisin Growers' Association, and M. Theo. Kearney. Newton B. Pierce, an expert pathologist and authority on the anaheim disease, will have a paper on "California Vine Diseases."

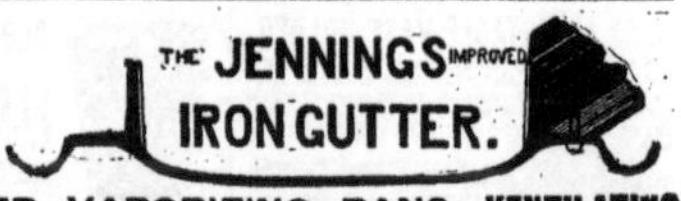

Taunton, Mass.

The demand for chrysanthemums this season has far exceeded that of any previous year. One of our largest growers who usually ships most of his stock, this year sold his entire cut at home.

At the Taunton greenhouses they are busy putting up a fine stock of Boston ferns for the holidays.

E. F. Rose, the Main street florist, advertises green trading stamps given on floral work, flowers and plants. The town is stamp crazy.　　　W.

Grand Island, Neb.

RAINS HURT CARNATIONS.—PLANTS SMALL AND STEM ROT PREVALENT.—A TRIP TO COLORADO POINTS.

Winter is just setting in after a pleasant autumn. Carnations suffered from excessive rains. The plants were small when housed, besides being affected with stem rot. Brewster & Williams planted 2,000 chrysanthemums to single stem and they find ready sale. Otherwise trade is quiet. Ellsworth Brothers have moved their houses and are now in shape for winter.

The writer took a trip to his old home at Denver this fall and found quite a change had taken place in ten years' absence. His first call was at the Gallup Floral and Seed Company. Messrs. Lewis, Schults and Emerick were busy getting ready for a good winter's run. At the Colfax Avenue Floral Company Mr. Bird was on deck and the boys busy replacing glass after a destructive hail storm. At the Park Floral Company John Berry took him in tow and he had the pleasure of seeing a model establishment. Adam Kobinkie was found busy at the City park. They had some fine ornamental beds which would be hard to beat. At Emil Glauber's, Montclair, he saw a fine house of Mme. Chatenay. At Colorado Springs he called on Ed. Johnson, foreman for Mr. Evans. Ernest Flohr, at F. F. Crump's, showed some pot chrysanthemums that couldn't be beat. At Wm. Clark's they were busy getting things in shape for their winter run. The next stop was Pueblo. Mr. Fleischer had just moved into his new store with Sam Lundy behind the counter with his 2x4 smile. E.

Milwaukee.

There is an improvement in business over that of last week, yet it is nothing to be proud of, as considerable improvement can easily be accommodated with the stock which is arriving. Supplies have shortened up considerably the last few days, owing to the cold snap which we are having. Chrysanthemums are not arriving in such large quantities as last week, and the indications are that they will be well cleaned up with the Thanksgiving trade. The supply of roses and carnations is ample for all calls, this being also true of all other flowers. Stevia has made its appearance, as well as some fine mignonette. There is plenty of smilax and adiantum on the market. The Milwaukee Florists' Club is having some difficulty in collecting its convention accounts and has decided to use more urgent means to collect the same. Future convention cities should make note of this fact and sell space only to reliable parties.

Holton & Hunkel Company is receiving some fine smilax and adiantum.

Loeffler Brothers are sending in some fine violets, both single and double.

Adam Zender's long American Beauty roses are extra fine.

A new store was recently opened on the south side by Miss Meyer, who has been with M. Moore for a long time.

Visitors: E. J. McCormick, Green Bay; Tom Hinchliffe, John Bourgaise and Mr. Olson, of Racine. H.

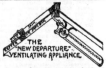

The **Standard**

The lightest running, most rapid and powerful ventilating machinery in the market.

DUPLEX GUTTERS

Made of wrought or cast iron with self-adjusting sash bar clips. The only Drip Proof Metal Gutter offered to the public. Send for my catalogue free.

E. HIPPARD, Youngstown, O.

THE "NEW DEPARTURE" VENTILATING APPLIANCE.

This is a **funny** looking thing but it will do the work easier and cost less than any other apparatus on earth or any other place.
Send for a descriptive circular to

J. D. CARMODY, Evansville, Ind.

Bayside, N. Y.

John H. Taylor's rose houses are his special pride this season. Never before have they produced such fine blooms. A house of grafted plants started last June looks like a section cut right out of the Wahan Conservatories. Tom Williams, the foreman, is particularly impressed, however, by a house of three-year-old Bridesmaid, ungrafted, transplanted to beds from last year's benches. In these plants the flowers are particularly long-petalled. Another house of three-year-olds, rested and tied down, is in superb condition.

THE AMERICAN FLORIST

A WEEKLY JOURNAL FOR THE TRADE

America is "the Prow of the Vessel; there may be more comfort Amidships, but we are the first to touch Unknown Seas."

Vol. XXI.　　　CHICAGO AND NEW YORK, DECEMBER 5, 1903.　　　No. 809.

THE AMERICAN FLORIST

NINETEENTH YEAR.

Copyright 1903, by American Florist Company
Entered as Second-Class Mail Matter.

PUBLISHED EVERY SATURDAY BY

AMERICAN FLORIST COMPANY,
324 Dearborn St., Chicago.
Eastern Office: 42 W. 28th St., New York.

Subscription, $1.00 a year. To Europe, $2.00.
Subscriptions accepted only from the trade.
Volumes half-yearly from August, 1901.

SOCIETY OF AMERICAN FLORISTS AND
ORNAMENTAL HORTICULTURISTS.

OFFICERS—JOHN BURTON, Philadelphia, Pa.,
president; C. C. POLLWORTH, Milwaukee, Wis.,
vice-president; WM. J. STEWART, 79 Milk Street,
Boston, Mass., secretary; H. B. BEATTY, Oil City,
Pa., treasurer.
OFFICERS-ELECT—PHILIP BREITMEYER, president; J. J. BENEKE, vice-president; secretary and
treasurer as before. Twentieth annual meeting
at St. Louis, Mo., August, 1904.

THE AMERICAN CARNATION SOCIETY.

Annual convention at Detroit, Mich., March 2,
1904. ALBERT M. HERR, Lancaster, Pa., secretary.

AMERICAN ROSE SOCIETY.

Annual meeting and exhibition, Philadelphia,
March, 1904. LEONARD BARRON, 136 Liberty St.,
New York, secretary.

CHRYSANTHEMUM SOCIETY OF AMERICA.

Annual convention and exhibition, November,
1904. FRED H. LEMON, Richmond, Ind., secretary.

THIS ISSUE 44 PAGES WITH COVER.

CONTENTS.

The Rose.

METEOR.

This rose is one which must be given special culture to make it a success. It can hardly be said its handling is as easy as is that of some of our other roses but the Meteor has much to recommend it in spite of its faults. The color is very rich and when properly grown the stem and bud are very fine. The principal fact against the Meteor is the necessity for a high temperature, making it impossible to grow it with other roses such as Bride, Bridesmaid or Golden Gate. The night temperature should be from 68° to 70°, and on bright days when the ventilators can be opened the temperature may be allowed to go to 82°. This high temperature at once reminds you that the water must be administered in a more generous supply. Also great care must be taken that the red spider does not gain a foothold. Syringe on all bright days, and be sure to direct the spray from underneath to keep the pest from the lower side of the leaves. Black spot is another source of trouble and when it is necessary that so much syringing be done great care must be exercised in the ventilation. Give plenty of fresh air at all times and keep the plants free from decayed and black-spot foliage. Keep them tied up well, thereby insuring a free circulation of air and also straight stems.

When in proper condition it is a strong feeder, but care must be taken to keep it healthy or the liberal feed will soon show itself in the deformed buds. When cutting the blooms cut well back to the last one or two eyes, which will encourage heavy breaks. Air-slaked lime may be often used to an advantage, especially in dark and cloudy weather. This being a great purifier, its use is conducive of good results and a great aid in checking black spot.　　　R. L.

AT NATICK, MASS.

Having been favored with an invitation to attend the annual rose and chrysanthemum show at Natick, November 4, I, with a few others from New York, gladly accepted and joining the contingent from Boston at the terminal station soon discovered it was to be an affair of considerable magnitude as far as numbers were concerned. At Wellesley we were met by coaches, and though we had to pack pretty close, the ride through the beautiful country was enjoyed by all. To rose growers a trip to Natick is

always something to look forward to with a great deal of pleasure; and I may say that looking back the recollection of such a trip is equally pleasing. The cleanliness, neatness, and perfect order prevailing always strike the visitor to Natick as much perhaps as the luxuriance of the plant growth and superb product of the establishment; in both these particulars the usual standard of excellence has not only been maintained, but surpassed, we think, this season.

If the crops of roses had been arranged to suit the visit, and it had been possible to omit the cutting and marketing of the blooms for several days prior thereto, there could hardly have been a greater showing of bloom through the houses. The beds of two and three year-old Bridesmaid, Bride, Golden Gate and Morgan were superb; looking down a 700-foot house over the top of one of those beds little but white or pink buds could be seen, and these of good size, with fine stems and foliage. To my mind these long houses of roses presented a finer appearance as regards quantity of bloom than any I had ever seen previously, though I have seen larger and better colored blooms frequently in midwinter. Mr. Montgomery's plan with all tea roses is to grow them the first year on benches, give them a little rest in July and lift and transfer to the solid beds where they are good for one or two years more and certainly his two and three year-old plants give promise of larger returns than any young stock could possibly show.

The most recent addition to the establishment is a house 700 feet long, forty feet wide and twenty-four feet high; the sash bars in this house are twenty-four inches apart and the eaves are six feet from the ground on both sides, giving an abundance of head room for the plants, and about as light a house as can be built. The entire house is filled with American Beauty and although they were planted in July and August they have made fine growth and are producing flowers with long stems of good shape and color and plenty of substance. The foliage in this house is very large and leathery in texture and it speaks well for the man in charge, the superintendent and the builders. Solid beds have been adopted for this house and it will be interesting to know how the Beauty behaves during January and February. Some growers find that solid beds for Beauty are at a disadvantage during those months.

The heating of this house interested me very much; the end farthest from the boilers is distant more than 1,000 feet, yet Mr. Montgomery says the circulation through the house is perfect with three or four pounds of steam at the boilers. This is accomplished by providing a large steam main and a proper arrangement of the heating pipes. Steam is taken from the main pipe at four different points through the house, making the average length of circulation about 175 feet. This method solves the problem of expansion and contraction and provides a uniform temperatures at all times and at all points.

Owing to the difficulties most growers have met in handling the rose I was especially interested in the houses of Liberty at Natick, and in learning Mr. Montgomery's method of growing this tricky variety. His preference is evidently for plants more than one year old as he is still growing those purchased when the rose was first introduced. His plan with Liberty is to rest a little during summer, or fall then prune back hard as with a hybrid and start them into growth just the same as, if he were growing hybrid roses. One house so treated had produced a fine crop of long stemmed blooms that were almost ready to cut; another house pruned later will come in during December. If the second and successive crops show the same strength and vigor as the first one then Natick has evidently put Liberty on a paying basis.

The exhibit of chrysanthemum was very fine but not being exactly in our line will leave a description of it to a more able pen and take our place in the coach for the return trip at the end of which our host invites his guests to partake of a feast of good things and satisfy the cravings of an appetite that the air of Natick and Wellesley gives in such wonderful measure.

We all, I think, did full justice to the dinner and enjoyed the wit and repartee of the after dinner speeches, but to me the greatest treat of the day and the one that will linger longest in my memory, I trust, was the stroll through those splendid houses of roses in company with the genial but modest Alexander Montgomery and Alexander, Jr. It is a pleasure to see the son so ably seconding the work of the father and I am glad to accord him his share of credit for the splendid success they together have achieved.

ROBERT SIMPSON.

The Foster Fern.

L. H. Foster is highly pleased with the manner in which the Foster fern has been advancing in the estimation of the trade, judging by the increasing demand for it from every section. Starting out, as it did, with the big handicap of the Pierson fern, which at first was taken to be a rival, it has won its way steadily as the fact became known that the two sports have little in common as to character and that each has a place of its own. It is worthy of note that these two ferns have each, since their introduction, been becoming more pronounced in their special characteristics, thus widening the divergence between them, the Pierson fern becoming more luxuriantly massive, the Foster fern growing more airy and daintily feathered. Mr. Foster gets the best results with it by growing it in the bench and potting it up as required, keeping it from four to six weeks in the pot before sending it out. To remedy its somewhat sparse habit when in the younger stages he puts several small runners together when planting in the bench and thus secures plants of better body than where single growths are used.

Mr. Foster leases the old Meade houses in addition to his own establishment thus acquiring sixteen houses altogether for his fern stock. Mr. Foster's father, J. W. Foster, was the first man, so far as known, to force roses commercially on their own roots for cut flowers in this country, and for many years the establishment held a leading position in rose production. Later violets became the specialty and these in turn were followed by the "green goods," of which the Foster fern is the outcome. This sequence recalls the old school day rhyme:

The rose is red
The violet blue
The grass is green
And so—is the fern.

Chrysanthemum Society of America.

WORK OF THE COMMITTEES.

By the New York committee, November 21, the following were judged:

American Beauty.—Japanese incurved, majenta with silvery reverse, shown by H. Molatsch, Brooklyn, N. Y.; scored, commercial scale, 86 points.

A variety said to be a sport of Viviand-Morel, was shown by F. Backofen, Paterson, N. J. The committee believed the variety to be Eda Prass.

At Chicago, November 21, was shown: Dr. Englehardt.—Type of Col. Appleton, pink, shown by F. R. Pierson Company, scale, 86 points.

Miss Helen Frick.—Pink, shown by Nathan Smith & Son, Adrian, Mich.; scored 87 commercial points.

At Philadelphia, November 21:

Dr. Englehardt.—Pink, Japanese incurved, shown by F. R. Pierson Company, Tarrytown, N. Y.; scored, commercial scale, 86 points; exhibition scale, 86 points.

FRED. H. LEMON, Sec'y.

New Chrysanthemum Successes.

A few of the newer chrysanthemums which growers can safely tie to for next year for commercial cut flower purposes are as follows:

Mrs. Coombes, a second-early pink, in the style of Viviand-Morel; it is easily done and comes in just after Glory of the Pacific.

Alice Byron, a snow-white of easiest culture; finely finished and grand in every respect; medium early; reminds of a mammoth Ivory.

Dr. Englehardt, an English variety, looked upon as the best commercial introduction of the present year; a pink companion for Appleton and Eaton.

W. R. Church, a fine dwarf crimson.

Charles Longley, a crimson incurved.

Millicent Richardson, a crimson Japanese.

Fair Maid, a silvery incurved pink; a long keeper.

Mabel Morgan, a heavy-bloomed reflexed lemon yellow.

There is no better mid-season pink than A. J. Balfour in the commercial class; it resembles a big tree peony.

New Chrysanthemums Illustrated.

Dr Englehardt.—This pink promises to fill, in its color, the place Appleton fills in yellow and Eaton in white; vase shown was exhibited by the F. R. Pierson Company at New York Exhibition and won first prize in its class; attracted admiration for size, build, bright pink color and above all for its solidity and fine keeping qualities.

Mrs. H. W. Buckbee.—Niveus × Mrs. Henry Robinson; pure white, slightly incurved, lower petals reflexing, growth somewhat like Niveus but not so tall; height attained from June planting, four feet; flower of good size with fine stem and foliage, at its best the last of October; a fine commercial variety; scored 91 points before the Chicago committee October 24.

NEW CHRYSANTHEMUM DR. ENGLEHARDT.

Mrs. H. W. Buckbee. Rockford.

TWO OF H. W. BUCKBEE'S NEW CHRYSANTHEMUMS.

Rockford.—Mrs. Henry Robinson × Col. D. Appleton; yellow, incurved, fine form with lots of substance, grand stem and foliage; at its best October 20; will make a fine commercial variety, every flower coming good; is an easy grower and grows to about three and one-half feet from June planting; scored 88 points before Chicago committee.

The Carnation.

- - CARNATION FLAMINGO.

J. D. Thompson, of Joliet, Ill., writes from Syracuse, under date of December 1, as follows: "I arrived here this morning to see Flamingo growing and found it in excellent condition, being in full bloom. The flowers measure three inches in diameter and are borne on stiff stems two feet long. I think it is the best scarlet to date and all that Mr. Marquisee claims for it. It is also a very free bloomer.·

CULTURAL REMINDERS.

The Christmas crop always comes in for some extra attention. The extra demand and high prices obtaining at that time are a great stimulus to extra endeavor and there are few of us who do not, in some way, try to increase both the quantity and quality of the cut. Forcing by the application of extra heat and fertilizers must be attended with extreme caution; for careless manipulation of the temperature and injudicious feeding may defeat the immediate object in view or soften the plants to such an extent that the cut for the subsequent months will suffer far in excess of any immediate gain. To make it at all worth while there should be a good crop of buds on and the plants must be in the very best of health. Much depends upon the treatment the plants receive before the forcing period commences and it should be our aim at this time to do everything in our power to promote a

firm, crisp growth. Keeping the soil slightly on the dry side will encourage the formation of a vigorous and well expanded root system, without which it is useless to expect the plants to respond to an extra draft made upon their resources. A weekly application of weak liquid manure from now on will be a benefit to plants that have somewhat exhausted the soil. In the absence of liquid manure a light top-dressing of sheep manure will answer the same purpose. Overfeeding should always be guarded against. Poor root action and a general enfeeblement of the whole plant is always the result of this. Do not begin to raise the temperature until about December 15, and then raise only a degree or two each night until the desired temperature is reached. This will depend upon the variety and the amount of forcing that prudence will allow in each particular case. A raise of from 4° to 10° is allowable, but no more. In no case should the night temperature be higher than 60°. If the weather is cloudy the raise in the temperature should be correspondingly less. From about the 24th or 25th the temperature should again be reduced to normal by slow stages, not by a sudden drop.

With the advent of steady hard firing red spiders will put in an appearance if syringing is not regularly attended to. A fine cutting spray is what is wanted, not a slow drizzle that saturates the foliage and keeps the plants wet over night. The force of the spray is what does the work, not the drops that hang on after syringing. · If properly done the plants will be comparatively dry after the operation. A good syringing about once a week, from now on until the days lengthen out again, will be sufficient, provided we have a clean start. In extra bright weather two syringings a week will do no harm. A bright day should, of course, be chosen for the operation. In continued cloudy weather it will do

no harm to omit a week if the right opportunity does not present itself.

Cuttings in the sand should be boxed off or potted as soon as well rooted. A good airy and light bench, free from drip, is the right place for them. Soil that was left over from filling the houses is the best material in which to plant them. The flats should be well supplied with cracks in the bottom, not only to allow the free passage of surplus water but also to allow a free circulation of air through the soil. We prefer to use flats to pots at this time of the year, as it saves room and there is less handling. Two inches apart each, will give them plenty of room until about the middle of February, and two inches of soil is sufficient. It is well at this time to do a little extra fumigating, so as to have the plants perfectly clean just before the holidays, when the flowers are usually left on the plants a little longer. Light smoking, while it has very little effect on partly matured flowers, has a very appreciable effect upon the color of well matured blooms. If we can leave off smoking for a week or so around that time we will be so much better off.

A careful watch will need to be kept during hard firing for dry places, especially where the heating pipes come near the bottom of the bench, and on the ends, where the circulation of air is quicker.

About this time each year there is always more or less trouble with mice. They climb up the stem of the flower and eat out the seed, scattering the petals over the soil. We have tried all kinds of schemes to get rid of them, until we adopted our present method, which never fails to clean them out in one or two nights. A half pint of oatmeal and ten cents' worth of strychnine; mix thoroughly (dry); put a small quantity of this on little pieces of boards or broken pots and set around here and there on the soil among the plants. Not much of this mixture will be eaten nor is it likely that many dead mice will be seen as a result of it; but they will disappear just the same; probably because mice are very wise creatures and will not stay where some of their number have died a mysterious death.　　　　　J.

CARNATION GROWING IN TEWKESBURY.

M. A. Patten.

Patten & Company's place at Tewkesbury is one of the best examples of a well managed carnation-growing establishment in the vicinity of Boston and in the orderly neatness and marked cultural sagacity which characterize the place one can readily detect the reason for the pre-eminence of the flowers grown here, in the market and the horticultural exhibitions.

In common with all intelligent carnation growers, Mr. Patten realizes that his specialty is entitled to the advantages of the best modern houses and will repay accordingly. A handsome house, 33x300 feet, has just been added to the range and is a good example of what a carnation house should be if one would keep in the van as to crops and quality. It is an even-span house with double ventilation at the top and also in both side walls. There are five benches, each four feet in width, built quite low and supported by iron pipe. In the center bench and the two outside ones the pipe supports are made to carry the water, and faucets are placed at convenient distances in each path so that not over twenty-five feet of hose is required to reach any spot and the awkward and destructive dragging of hose up and down the walks is wholly avoided.

The entire range is heated by steam from two eighty-five horse-power boilers. A 5-inch main runs the entire length of a transverse corridor, branching overhead by 3-inch pipes to the houses right and left. Through this same corridor has been constructed a 4-foot ditch or subway 300 feet in length through which all the return pipes are laid, every part being quickly accessible by raising a section of the slatted walk. Each house is provided with four pipes on each side and two independent pipes under each bench so that any number from two to twenty pipes may be in operation at once as required.

Thirty thousand plants are grown. The varieties selected for this year are as follows: White, Boston Market; light pink, Enchantress and Fair Maid; dark pink, Lawson and Floriana; scarlet, J. H. Manley; crimson, Harry Fenn; variegated, Mrs. M. A. Patten; yellow, Dorothy Whitney. A few other sorts are under observation in small batches and there is the usual lot of seedlings of greater or less promise. The summer has been a hard one on all carnations in the field here as the soil is light and sandy and there have been long dry spells. The plants last taken in show evidences of the attacks of red spider, a pest which has ravaged all outdoor growth terribly this season. As to the qualities of the various varieties under cultivation, Mr. Patten says that Fair Maid has proved an excellent variety for summer. In winter it is loose-petaled and thin, but with the spring weather it begins to thicken up and makes a good flower the rest of the season. Boston Market he finds to be decidedly the best all around profitable white up to date. He has discarded all other variegated varieties, cleaving only to Mrs. M. A.

Patten in business as well as in domestic life and to the impartial observer he has done wisely, for Mrs. Patten is the handsomest and healthiest plant on the place and is known to be a splendid keeper. Dorothy Whitney grew small this year but will be all right later. Adonis is making a brave struggle to get on its feet.

For supports Mr. Patten uses the individual wires only for a short time after planting. As soon as the plants are established in the benches these are all removed and wires running lengthwise of the bed with strings looped across are substituted. The wires are fastened to pipe frames, at the ends of each bed, constructed with the Jennings clamps which are easily adjustable to any desired height.

The only serious troubles experienced so far this season are the red spider and the cabbage worm. The red spider is combatted with frequent syringings with salt water supplied from a tank in the cellar and driven through the hose by a hand force-pump. The green grub of the cabbage butterfly has been very destructive, cutting stems industriously. It has also been very troublesome on the mignonette but after a dose or two of Paris green peace reigns. Hand picking is the only resort in the carnation houses for obvious reasons.

Mr. Patten is growing the mignonette as a side crop in the house where he grows his young carnation stock. The variety grown hitherto is known as Fottler's Eclipse, an improved form of Allen's Defiance. This year an improved Eclipse, originated on the place, is being grown. It appears to be of a higher color and stronger constitution.

BEHAVIOR OF VARIETIES.

While it is yet too early to expect every variety to be showing up at its best, still there are a number of varieties that we depend upon for early work, and if we have been successful in handling these, so that a substantial crop extends over the period from October 1 to January 1, we can congratulate ourselves upon having

demand at all seasons for design work, while dark pink, red, variegated and yellow must always suffer because their field of usefulness is necessarily monopolized by the chrysanthemum.

Among the light pink varieties, probably the best for early work is Sunbeam. It is too small to be a fancy variety, but it is wonderfully free, continuing in heavy crop during the four months preceding February 1. It covers the early demand for a good all-round light pink carnation, fully, and is in fine form for the holidays. The variety is up to its usual standard with us this year and we expect to cut an increasing number of flowers until past the holidays. Mrs. Higinbotham is a fine midwinter variety, but also produces good flowers during the fall months and is in excellent form by Christmas. Morning Glory takes some time to become thoroughly established and what flowers are cut before December 1 are usually of indifferent quality. After the first of the year it increases in quality and quantity with the advance of the season until settled hot weather sets in. Enchantress is a truly fancy variety and an early and continuous bloomer. It is the best light pink for showy work.

In white, Flora Hill has not yet been supplanted for early work. It covers the fall season well and is usually in good form yet around the holidays, but that is about as far as it can be carried; there is a gap of about three months before it comes in good crop again. Lorna has been blooming steadily for the last two months and is increasing right along. It is a good all-season variety and makes good stems and flowers from the very beginning. Bon Homme Richard we consider indispensable. It covers the same season as Sunbeam and the stems begin to lengthen out as soon as benched. Queen Louise, however, Governor Wolcott and White Cloud we prefer to handle for mid-winter, and later catching the holidays and a good part of December. Her Majesty will probably prove to be in the same class.

Lawson planted very early or grown

CARNATION HOUSE OF PATTEN & CO., TEWKESBURY, MASS.

sailed smoothly through a very difficult season of the year to supply with flowers. Up to December 1 the demand for cut flowers of carnations is somewhat limited on account of the popularity and comparative cheapness of chrysanthemums, but the writer has yet to experience the first glut of really good carnations during chrysanthemum time. We always aim to have a good quantity of white and light pink at this season and a limited quantity of dark pink and red. After December 1 the bright colors find a readier sale. Light pink is an especially useful color on account of its adaptability to different kinds of work. White is in

indoors all summer produces a good fall crop and by the latter method keeps up all winter with little interruption. Planted from the field, the fall crop is apt to be rather short stemmed and there is almost sure to be an off crop for about six weeks from January 1 on. Mrs. E. A. Nelson comes in well about December 1 and continues in a tremendous crop until well on in spring. Dorothy comes in about November 1 and is seldom out of bloom from then on. It is remarkably free and continuous. The light soil which we gave it this year seems to suit it to a dot. Joost comes in quite early with a few good flowers, but waits until the days lengthen before it shows up at its best. The same may be said of Crocker. A few plants of Indianapolis sent us by the originator for trial, are doing exceedingly well. It comes in crop early. The color is a very rich dark pink. The flowers are much above the average in size and are borne on long, wiry stems. It makes no surplus grass and seems to confine its energies to producing a good supply of well balanced blooms. Just now there is a fine lot of buds and flowers on with a good lot of shoots running up.

For red, Crane grown indoors all summer, covers the fall season thoroughly with fine flowers on long stems, and it keeps up throughout the winter. Estelle is also early, but does its best work after the season is well advanced. Mrs. Potter Palmer also waits until well on in the season, covering December with a good crop which continues until hot weather. In dark red, or crimson, Roosevelt has until this year been our best. It comes in early and continues throughout the winter. Harlowarden has thus far come fully up to Roosevelt and outpoints it in size. The color is a few shades darker, which is an advantage, or a drawback, according to the taste of the customer.

We have no steady demand for yellow and consequently do not grow any. Variegated varieties have also been dropped for the same reason. Chicot is the nearest thing we have to variegated. The markings are so light that it passes for a white in ordinary work. It produces a well shaped, large flower on a good stem and is free enough to justify its continued cultivation.   J.

Cattleya Labiata.

The illustration herewith shows a very fine plant of this useful orchid. The specimen bore ninety-five finely developed flowers at one time and was grown by Thos. C. Lynas, recently gardener to Chas. M. Schwab, of Pittsburg, Pa.

The Retail Trade.

THE ARTIST.

A "bridal outfit" is a term well known to florists and calls to mind many a "hurry and scurry" to get finished on a busy day. The term includes all flowers destined for the bridal party, bouquets for the bride and her attendants or bridesmaids, one for the maid of honor, and boutonnieres for the groom, best man and ushers. The most popular bouquet for the bride is lily of the valley, made with a shower effect. It is sometimes made in sections to correspond with the number of bridesmaids, so that it may be easily taken apart and presented to them at the end of the ceremony, but is more often made in one piece. A cluster or spray of white orchids gives a very choice effect. Gardenias may be used in the same way. I avoid mixing flowers all through as the effect is usually too heavy. If roses are to be used a cluster of lily of the valley will add grace to the bouquet. A fringe of Adiantum cuneatum or Adiantum Farleyense is better than mixing it through the bouquet. The shower consists of about thirty or forty yards of No. 2 white silk ribbon, or white silk gauze, the latter giving a light and graceful effect. This is pulled through the flowers and allowed to hang in lengths ranging from two to three feet. Loose knots should then be tied eight to ten inches apart, in each of which a spray of lily of the valley and a small piece of adiantum is inserted and the knot then

CATTLEYA LABIATA.

pulled tight to hold it. A small bow can be tied instead of the knot if preferred. The shower is usually made with the same variety of flowers as the body of the bouquet. A broad sash of No. 60 white ribbon is then attached to the handle, finishing the bouquet.

The bridesmaids' bouquets are usually made to match the dress when possible, and are made all alike, sometimes with a shower but more often without. At this time of the year chrysanthemums are very much used. These are tied into loose bunches, the stems being left very long, and tied in the center with a broad sash of ribbon of appropriate color. Floral muffs are also very fashionable. These are made like the large flat muffs now in vogue. They are silk lined to match the flowers, which are sewed or pinned on the exposed side of the muff only, so that the flowers will not crush against the dress of the wearer.

A very pretty effect is obtained with silk parasols the exact shade of the dress, with a loose bunch of roses or other flowers tied to the handle with a broad sash of ribbon. We have used this idea occasionally for debutantes. The groom's boutonniere should match the bride's bouquet and is usually made with lily of the valley. The best man's can be made the same as the groom's, or of gardenias. The ushers' are made mostly of white carnations and should be of a good generous size.

VELVET RIBBON FOR VIOLET CORSAGES.

A prominent New York florist writes as follows on this subject:

"Personally I have always considered ribbons incongruous with flowers of any kind with the exception, perhaps, of bridal bouquets. I doubt very much if the bow of black would be considered good taste for a lady to wear with her violets. It reminds me of Miles O'Reilly's poem at the unveiling of the monument to the memory of fallen heroes of the 69th regiment in the civil war:

'In mournful guise our banners raise,
Black clouds above the sunbeams burst,' etc.

"I have been conversing with a lady of taste who resides on Fifth avenue and who is of the same opinion as myself, considering the bow of black ribbon on the violets as a mourning badge and not in good taste for that purpose. I understand there was an attempt made sometime ago by a certain New York florist to introduce this black velvet for violets but it did not take very well. I am not in favor of it and will never attempt to introduce it; but if it becomes a fad, of course we will have to follow, adapting ourselves to the old adage, 'When in Rome do as the Romans do.'"

HARDY EVERGREEN FOR VASES.

The use of evergreens in tubs and vases for winter decorative effect on porches, in halls and like places in and about public and private buildings is now quite general and the custom—a most commendable one—is rapidly on the increase.

The more compact forms of retinisporas and arbor-vitaes are most commonly employed for this purpose, one specimen of appropriate size to a vase or in the case of larger vases a tall central specimen with a number of smaller ones about it.

To obtain satisfactory results with such subjects the young evergreens should be specially prepared by frequent transplanting in the nursery, thus securing a close compact ball of fibrous roots. They should be planted in the vases as early in the fall as possible and kept well watered so that the roots may take hold and get the plant well filled with good healthy sap before it freezes up. If possible, set the plant with the same aspect as it has been accustomed to during the preceding season, turning the side which has been facing the sun so that it will again do so.

The conifers best adapted for this work are the retinisporas, such as R. filifera, R. plumosa and plumosa aurea, R. pisifera and pisifera aurea and R. squarrosa; the thuyas, such as T. pyramidalis, T. Standishii, Hovey's Golden, globosa, Wareana and Verveneana; Juniperus Chinensis argenteo-variegata and J. Virginiana glauca and the boxes such as Buxus myrtifolia and B. latifolia. Nicely grown dwarf Austrian pines also make fine tub plants and certain of the spruces and firs may be sometimes used to advantage although as a rule these are too stiff in character to look well. Retinispora (or chamæcyparis), ericoides is excellently adapted in its compact conical form for vase work but it bronzes up with the first touch of cold weather and may be objectionable to some on this account but in some situations, especially in companionship with bright foliaged varieties, it has a distinctive beauty. The hemlocks are very pretty and graceful but are liable to shed their foliage in a short time. Where the exposure is not too severe Euonymus Japonica makes an ideal tub plant. The effect is much improved by planting a fringe of English ivy or Euonymus radicans around the edge to droop in festoons over the vase. There are many lovely conifers that would be admirable for vase work were it not that they are entirely too expensive. The taxuses or yews are as a rule too costly, as are also many of the neat little slow-growing retinisporas and thuyas so effectively used in ornamental garden planting, for, when spring time comes the vase plants are all dead plants.

Chicago.

FLORISTS' CLUB GRAND BALL.—NEW COMPANY INCORPORATED.—PARK PLAN MAY BE DROPPED.—NEWS OF GARDENERS' AND FLORISTS' UNION.—NOTES OF TRADE.

Chicago is just now experiencing a touch of the real brand of winter, but while the trade has been praying for this kind of weather there is no noticeable improvement in market conditions. Trade this week has been very irregular, some days bringing activity while others were practically dead. The week opened with an almost unprecedented demand for colored carnations. Everything in this line was well cleaned up at good prices, while white carnations practically went begging for takers. Sunday one large grower was able to fill an order for 1,000 colored only with the greatest difficulty. All roses, possibly with the exception of Liberty, the shortage of which seems general this season, are more than plentiful. Violets during the latter part of last week and the beginning of the current week, came in in large quantities. Although the stock was superfine and better than has been seen for a long time, yet few could be disposed of at a respectable figure. The situation eased up however toward the end of the week. There are still some chrysanthemums, but the quality of the blooms is steadily diminishing and the queen of autumn appears to be preparing to say au revoir for the season. The bouquet green buyers are beginning to busy themselves and dealers will have an embarrasing problem to face to fill all orders with the limited supply which is promised. Paper White narcissus is selling three bunches for $1, and the limited supply is kept on the move. The wholesalers say that their local business is about nil, but there is adequate compensation in the prevailing brisk shipping trade.

The Florists' Club's third grand annual ball took place Wednesday evening in the drill hall of the Masonic Temple. The affair, which was under the direct management of John P. Risch, proved to be a grand success. Fully 175 responded to the invitations and all mingled in passing

an evening of unalloyed enjoyment. For those not wishing to trip the light fantastic toe the adjoining parlors of the drill room were provided as retreats. Here cards were played and other social pleasantries enjoyed. Christensen's orchestra furnished music for the occasion. The grand march was led by Mr. and Mrs. Walter Kreitling. All the dances were well filled and it was not until a late hour that the party broke up. Refreshments were served and there were many other features which contributed to the success of the affair. Among the ladies who were present were Mmes. John Poehlmann, James Hartshorne, Howard Hollis, George Asmus, Charles Balluff, Walter Kreitling, P. J. Hauswirth, J. P. Risch, E. F. Winterson, A. Spencer, Chas. Samuelson, Anton Then and the Misses Evert, Hills, Wolf, Tonner and Enders. The club and the management are to be congratulated on the success of this annual event.

H. J. Sprenger has resigned the secretaryship of the Chicago Gardeners' and Florists' Union. He recently secured the appointment as superintendent of a cemetery out of the city. At the last meeting of the union A. Vanderpool was elected as his successor. We are informed that the organization will celebrate its first anniversary on the evening of December 9. A consolidation was recently effected between the German

Ten minute papers will be read by prominent growers and retail men.

Captain H. Schuenemann has returned from his annual trip to northern Michigan. His schooner, George L. Wrenn, is at its usual place, at the foot of the Clark street bridge. He has a large supply of Christmas trees and greens.

Peter Reinberg will register his new rose, Uncle John, in the near future. It was named at the Kansas City exhibition last year after the renowned floriculturist "Uncle John" Thorpe.

Some extraordinary white carnations, Flora Hill and White Cloud, were seen at Weiland & Risch's this week. Some of the stems measured two feet long.

Frank Garland's chrysanthemum stock is of the superlative order. In spite of the advanced season he is showing some splendid blooms.

Sinner Brothers' roses and carnations are coming in with a good crop for Christmas, also a nice lot of Paper White narcissi.

Bassett & Washburn are handling an exceptionally choice lot of Easter lilies. Their Liberty roses also are of the superfine order.

Hunt is enjoying a fine shipping business these days and he has the best of stock to fill his orders with.

E. F. Winterson is suffering from a slight attack of erysipelas. He is able to be about however.

AUGUST S. SWANSON'S GROUP AT THE ST. PAUL EXHIBITION.

Gardeners' Union and the Allgemeine Gaertner Verein.

It is probable that the plans for Greater Grant Park, on the lake front, which contemplated the expenditure $1,500,000 and making the park the finest in the country, will be abandoned. The daily papers quote the above sentiment as expressed by President H. G. Foreman, of the Park Board. Opposition of certain property owners on Michigan avenue is the cause.

L. Baumann & Company, capital $20,000, was licensed to incorporate last week. The incorporators named are F. H. Gelderman, Ludolph Baumann and G. A. Malmgran. Manufacturing and dealing in florists' and milliners' supplies will be engaged in.

The Florists' Club will hold its next exhibit Wednesday, December 16. It will be an exhibit of holiday plants. A club meeting will follow at 8:30 p. m.

The eight-year old daughter of W. J. Lynch, of Hunt's, is ill with an attack of pneumonia.

Mrs. Thomas Rogers is confined to her home with pneumonia. Her condition is improving.

Ernst Wienhoeber will spend the winter in the south.

Visitors: Mr. and Mrs. Charles L. Dole, Lockport, N. Y.; Eli Cross, Grand Rapids, Mich.; W. T. League, Hannibal, Mo.

FORT WAYNE, IND.—Geo. Doswell & Son have added three new carnation houses this season, 30x220 feet, and have some very fine stock. This addition gives them a total of six houses.

PERU, ILL.—At a chrysanthemum show at St. Bede's College, November 15, five specimens were shown and a large attendance recorded.

New York.

FLOWERS SCARCE AND EXPECTED TO CONTINUE SO.—PRICES GOOD.—CHRYSANTHEMUMS NEARLY OVER. — FLORIST WEIR LOSES DECORATIONS IN BIG BROOKLYN FIRE.

Flowers have been very scarce since Thanksgiving and from all accounts will be so for some time. Roses are of good quality generally and bring good prices; the same can also be said of carnations. Lilies are bringing about 6 to 8 cents. Violets are coming in more abundantly and bring from 50 cents to $1.50 per 100; all other stock is about the same as last quoted. Chrysanthemums are selling good and many of the growers are out. Bonnaffon and Mrs. Jerome Jones are the principal ones coming in at the present time. Roman hyacinths will not be so plentiful this year, the growers complaining about the high price of the bulbs. Paper Whites are coming in very plentifully; $1 50 to $2 per 100 is about the prevailing price.

John R. Weir had a serious loss last Monday. He had the decorating of the Academy of Music in Brooklyn and had men working for a whole day hanging up wild smilax, about thirty cases in all, when the building caught fire and was burnt to the ground. Mr. Weir's son, James Weir, Jr., had a narrow escape with his men. They lost their coats in escaping from the flames. The occasion was the dinner given to the Democratic leader of Brooklyn. The event was finally held in St. George's Hotel and Weir had to hustle to get things in shape for that evening.

Herman Dreyer, of Woodside, L. I., has sold his property at Woodside to the Pennsylvania Railroad Company for $126,000. Mr. Dreyer intends building again in the near future. Mr. Dreyer has the privilege of the place until next October; he also can take everything away except the dwelling house and the barn.

A. Dimmock, representing Sander & Sons, St. Albans, England, and Bruges, Belgium, will make his headquarters while in this country at 31 Barclay street, New York, instead of 136 Liberty street.

The firm of Miller & Both, of Yonkers, have dissolved partnership. Mr. Both will continue the business. Mr. Miller has accepted a position with Alex. Gofferje, the seedsman of East Thirty-fourth street.

George T. N. Cottam, a well known landscape gardener of this city, died on Sunday last after a long illness. The funeral services on Tuesday evening were attended by many members of the craft.

John Dutcher, of Nyack, also of the New York Cut Flower Company, is seriously ill at his home in Nyack with pneumonia. We hope for his speedy recovery.

C. W. Ward has been sending a few blooms of a superb scarlet seedling carnation of extraordinary size and fullness. Thorley takes the flowers at $6 a dozen.

Bradshaw & Hartman have hired the new store at 48 West Twenty-eighth street for a holiday branch.

Visitors in town: Lawrence Cotter, Danville, Pa.; Carl Jurgens, Jr., Newport, R. I.

Philadelphia.

BUSINESS MOVING QUIETLY. — STOCK IS IMPROVING.—INTERESTING CLUB MEETING.—NOTES OF THE DAY.

Business is moving along quietly, there being no great amount doing and yet on account of the dull and stormy weather the crops are short and it is difficult to

get enough good stock for the work on hand. There is considerable work for the debutantes and the next two weeks will be crowded with these bright affairs which mean so much to the trade. If this custom were to die out it would certainly be hard to handle the stock in the fall season. Roses are getting better in quality each week, with the price raising as well. The best American Beauty have sold as high as $6 per dozen, with teas

ranging up to $12 per 100. Carnations are in good demand and are now getting into their winter form. The Lawson leads in popularity and it looks as if it will have a great sale the coming season. High price so far is $5.

The December meeting of the Florists' Club was well attended. The principal topic was peonies, and there was considerable matter relative to this popular flower given forth by Secretary Lonsdale, who had peony articles from lovers of this flower from all over the country. Dues of the club are now to be paid annually, which will be a great convenience to all concerned and considerably lighten the duties of the secretary.

John Ziegenthaler, of Bokins street, Frankford, has a fine lot of poinsettias; they are just right for the holidays. There are 10,000 of them all told.

The Westerly greenhouses are furnishing some fine Lawson carnations to S. S. Pennock; they are the best seen in this market at this time of the season.

Boston.

THANKSGIVING BOOM SUBSIDES LEAVING DULLNESS IN WAKE.—SUPPLY IS FORTUNATELY NOT LARGE.—ECONOMY ON PART OF PATRONS SHOWN.

After the Thanksgiving hustle business has dropped back into moderate quietude with no prospect of any excitement until the Christmas rush begins. The receipts of flowers are generally light which is fortunate, as any great crop at present would mean demoralization again. If the demand was what it should be to average well with past years all the material in sight would be needed but there is every evidence of a disposition to economize on the part of the patrons most necessary to make the flower business prosperous. A dull season is predicted by sagacious observers. It may

be the tendency to frugality may have an exhilerating influence on the sales of holly and the less expensive plants. The Gardeners' and Florists' Club will meet at Horticultural hall Tuesday evening, December 8, at 8 p. m. A strenuous effort is being made to awaken interest in the meetings and with sufficient success to guarantee to all who attend next Tuesday a full recompense in pleasure for the trouble of coming out. There may

STORE OF C. B. THOMPSON, LOUISVILLE, KY.

be something interesting in the way of exhibits.

The annual exhibition of children's herbariums was held at Horticultural hall last week. More than one thousand sheets of neatly mounted specimens were displayed, presenting a comprehensive illustration of the native flora of New England. The Hunnewell Triennial prize has been awarded to the H. H. Rogers estate, an illustrated description of which was given in a recent issue of the AMERICAN FLORIST. E. S. Converse won both first prizes of the Lowell fund for houses of chrysanthemums. The Hatch prize for fruit house went to Miss E. J. Clark, the prize for house of foreign grapes to the same, those for dahlia gardens to W. P. Lothrop and Mrs. J. B. Lawrence, and silver medals were given to D. F. Roy for superior chrysanthemum culture and Mrs. J. C. Whitin for superior care of estate.

St. Louis.

TRADE FOR THANKSGIVING AND AFTER BREAKS RECORDS OF YEARS. — FIRM SHIPS BIG FUNERAL ORDER, VALUED AT $1,600.

On the occasion of the funeral of Judge Bross, of Cairo, Ill., the Eggeling Floral Company filled and shipped, on short notice, an order valued at $1,600, one of the largest orders ever sent out of St. Louis by a single firm. Nearly half an express car was needed to hold the pieces, many being of immense size. Among others was a beautiful "gates ajar," 6x8 feet, made up almost entirely of Timothy Eaton chrysanthemums and Chatenay roses; and a column four feet high of white carnations and Bridesmaid roses, with a base made up of Sunrise roses. American Beauty roses and Asparagus Sprengeri were made into a large panel. Thanksgiving trade was an improvement over last year. Stock was everywhere in demand. Prices were up and will no doubt remain so. Wholesalers say trade was never better at this season. A number of consignors sent in shipments that did not arrive until Thanksgiving afternoon, which was too late for immediate disposal. White carnations are scarce and always in demand. The chrysanthemums are all cleaned out, except possibly a few late varieties, which are not quoted. Stock generally is excellent. Palms move very slowly.

The St. Louis Cactus association held its monthly meeting on November 29. A paper entitled, "A Few Notes on the Evolution of Cacti," by F. K. Luke, was read and discussed.

Some local representatives of the trade press have evidently forgotten that criticisms of our public parks would help materially to fill out a column.

The Eggeling Floral Company suffered a loss of $150 in palms and ferns last week. A smoke-stack fell over and caused the trouble.

Otto Brueing, H. G. Berning's right-hand man, has been quite ill since Thanksgiving.   F. K. B.

Buffalo.

THANKSGIVING CREATES GOOD TRADE.—KASTING RENTS NEW QUARTERS.—RETAIL TRADE ENJOYING PROSPERITY.—GENERAL NOTES.

J. D. Thompson of Joliet, Ill., who grows those famous carnations, called on the trade last week while on his way east. He says his crop of carnations, especially Lawson, Enchantress and Gov. Wolcott are very fine. He was on his way to Syracuse to see Marquisee's Flamingo as grown by the originator.

J. H. Rebstock found his sale of chrysanthemums and Gloire de Lorraine very large. Palmer's best sale was chrysanthemums and violets as was Anderson's, who also had a fine lot of Gloire de Lorraine. J. H. Rebstock and S. A. Anderson both have fine windows of that most beautiful of all begonias.

Thanksgiving trade was equal to the expectations of all the florists, Palmer, Anderson, J. H. and R. M. Rebstock, Neubeck, Pirkelmah and Zimmerman all reporting a good trade. The real busy part did not start as early as previous years, but the week ended well.

We expect at the next Florists' Club meeting to see the plants of cyclamen of J. H. Rebstock and S. A. Anderson on exhibition. I understand William Scott and L. H. Neubeck are to be the judges and they certainly are equal to the occasion.

Byrne & Slattery on Upper Main street feel very much encouraged with their trade so far this fall. William Peek, formerly with J. H. Rebstock, has not determined what he will do as yet. We hope he will decide to remain in Buffalo.

W. F. Kasting has rented the large four story building on Ellicott street near Genessee, known as Turn Hall, and expects to occupy it on May 1, 1904, as a wholesale house.

While the hustling florists on Williams, Broadway and Elk streets had their usual run, William Scott at Cold Spring was very busy with his uptown trade.

S. A. Anderson had a very pretty church wedding on Wednesday which called for a large quantity of palms and chrysanthemums.

Martin Reukauf, representing H. Bayersdorfer & Company, Philadelphia, called on the trade for the Christmas orders.

R. M. Rebstock has a large order, for funeral work for a prominent family in Batavia, N. Y., this week.

From all reports holly will be good and red bells of all qualities will be in profusion in all the stores.

The market florists do not think that Thanksgiving trade was quite as good as last year.

From all reports S. A. Anderson is going to have a fine lot of poinsettias for Christmas.   BISON.

Pittsburg.

Thanksgiving business was of a stimulating order. Transient sales were very steady, and all kinds of stock moved out surprisingly well. Business is a good deal to the bad this week. Money seems to be getting light. The staple roses are not much improved, excepting American Beauty and Liberty. Chrysanthemums are passing out and carnations are very fine. Valley is good. Violets are a little off and too high in prices. Roman hyacinths and Paper White narcissi are good, also gardenias. Orchids are slow.

A fire broke out Thanksgiving day in the stands outside the Pittsburg market house. Will Lowe had a quantity of immortelles and a boxes of doves stored in one of the stands. He recovered most of his immortelles, but lost the doves. Mr. Lowe was slightly injured in the fire. His loss is about $50.

On the anniversary of the death of the late John Herron, who was assistant superintendent of the Phipps Conservatories, in Allegheny, a number of former fellow-workmen visited his grave and laid flowers on it. Mr. Herron's memory is richly deserving of these expressions of love.

The Botanical society met in the Carnegie Institute Thursday night. Christmas flowers from the Phipps Conservatory were exhibited.

Greens and Christmas trees in great quantities are arriving daily. Mistletoe, for a change, is evidently going to be plentiful.

Frank Schoen, of Murdoch's, has the sincere sympathy of the craft in the loss of his wife, who passed away November 25.

GEO. A. KUHL'S ESTABLISHMENT, PEKIN, ILL., LOOKING SOUTH.

The meeting of the Florists' and Gardeners' Club, December 1, was a success in every way.   E. L. M.

St. Paul.

Trade for Thanksgiving was very good. Most of the stores report an increase over last year. Roses are scarce, those grown locally being off crop. The dark cold weather of the last two weeks has kept them back a good deal. The last week nearly wound up the chrysanthemum season here. Few are to be had here now. Though the chrysanthemums here this season were hardly as fine as in the past they brought better prices than ever and a good many more were sold. Poinsettias have made their appearance and will help much to brighten the show windows.

L. P. Lord, of Owatonna, Minn., was a recent caller. showing and arranging for the sale of his patent plant shipping case.

Nearly all the exhibitors at the recent flower show had some of their plants damaged by frost in taking them home. Holm & Olson sent out their new delivery wagon Thanksgiving morning. It is one of the finest in the city.

Mr. McHutchison was also a caller the latter part of the week booking import orders for palms.   O.

Louisville.

Thanksgiving trade was the best we have ever known. Chrysanthemums sold like hot cakes. American Beauty sold well and there was a great demand for violets, although there were few to be had.

Jacob Schulz held a chrysanthemum show at his store last week, which attracted considerable attention. He had some very fine specimens and advertised extensively in the local papers.

H. G. Walker came near losing his nearly completed residence by fire, but the fire department got out in time to save the building and only one side of the house was damaged.

The school children of Louisville have selected the chrysanthemum for the state flower by a large majority. The daisy was second and the pansy third.

Mr. Rayner is cutting extra nice Bride, Bridesmaid and Golden Gate, and thinks his prospect for Christmas flowers very flattering.

F. Walker & Company had a lot of plants in one of the stores of the Masonic Building, which was destroyed by fire.

J. W. Knadler, the nurseryman, recently met with a severe accident, getting one foot caught in a mowing machine.

Anders Rasmussen, of New Albany, held a chrysanthemum exhibit and made a creditable display. H. G. W.

Baltimore.

TRADE IMPROVING.—MANY BULBS FOR CITY PARKS.—GENERAL PARK SUPERINTENDENT APPOINTED.

Trade conditions have improved somewhat during the past two weeks. A number of society events, some of considerable magnitude, helped to keep things moving.

What has become of the inter-city bowling match between Philadelphia, Baltimore and Washington for the supremacy and possession of the fine silver trophy donated for this purpose by Washington? We are still waiting for Philadelphia, but they have as yet not materialized. Quakers, wake up!

The new park board of Baltimore has decided to depart from the regular order of things and has appointed a road engineer as general superintendent of parks; a great many protests are heard from both the public and the gardeners. The public squares of Baltimore are well supplied with spring flowering bulbs and over 200 flower beds are filled with tulips and hyacinths; $3,000 has been expended for bulbs, which should make a good spring display.

Detroit.

The club meeting Wednesday evening brought out a good attendance. Herman Knope's paper on "Chrysanthemum Culture," which was on the programme for the meeting, was postponed until the meeting of January 6. The bursting of the carnation calyx took up much of the evening session, and though much valuable information was brought out by the experience of different growers, it was decided to take up the question again at the coming carnation meeting. Philip Breitmeyer announced that the formal christening of their new rose would take place at Hotel Cadillac Saturday afternoon, December 5, with much ceremony. The ten thousand names already submitted for consideration will be reviewed and the final selection made by a committee composed of the officers of the Detroit Florists' Club, the local representatives of the trade papers and prominent visiting florists, including Wm J. Stewart, secretary of the Society of American Florists. After the adjournment of the meeting the entire party visited Breitmeyer's store to view an extraordinary exhibit of the new seedling rose.

Visitors: B. Eschner, Philadelphia; Harry D. Byers, Dayton, Ohio.
J. F. S.

Albany, N. Y.

The present week was notable for the number of society functions that took place. In character they varied from a simple assembly to the formal presentation of several debutantes. On Thursday afternoon Mrs. Anthony N. Brady and Mrs. D. Cady Herrick introduced their younger daughters to society. For the reception at the home of Mrs. Brady, Eyres used pink and white roses, chrysanthemums and Farleyense ferns for the mantles; for the function at the home of Mrs. Herrick the same florist used roses, palms and Asparagus Sprengeri.

E. W. Hitchings and C. Armitage, president and vice-president, respectively, of Hitchings & Company, New York, were in the city on Tuesday to inspect the new greenhouse erected by Louis Menand the past summer at his place, Cemetery Station. The visit was for the purpose of securing photographs of the structure and its appliances for use as cuts in a new catalogue that the company will issue. Mr. Menand's greenhouse embodies a number of features which are entirely new in greenhouse construction, hence the desire to secure the photographs. R. D.

Columbus, O.

Thanksgiving trade was all that could be expected. Business as generally reported, was ahead of former years, with stock, especially good chrysanthemums, quite plentiful. The demand for violets was great, with stock in fine shape. Carnations were also fine in quality with a stiff wholesale price attached to them. Prices ranged about as follows: Roses, $1.25 to $2; Beauty, $3 to $6; carnations, 75 cents to $1 per dozen; violets, $3 per hundred.

The thermometer has been registering from 10° to 20° above zero during the last week, which for this section is considered below normal for this time of year. CARL.

Providence, R. I.

Thanksgiving trade was as good as could be expected. Chrysanthemums were plentiful and sold on the retail market at from 10 to 20 cents for medium blooms. Timothy Eaton brought from 25 to 30 cents. Carnations retailed at 50 cents per dozen and 35 cents was paid for a bunch of violets. Roses of medium stem brought $1 per dozen and fancies $2. Chrysanthemums are still plenty at low rates, but business is not good enough to move them quickly. Carnations and roses have firmed up in price since Thanksgiving and should find a ready market till Christmas. A peculiar dullness exists in the flower trade which

is hard to explain but will probably wear off soon.

New Bedford, Mass.

Winter seems to have set in in earnest. A week of cold, dark, cloudy weather has shortened up the local supply of flowers considerably. Thanksgiving day trade was good, but with the most of the dealers not so good as last year. There was no scarcity of flowers except violets and no rise in prices.

R. H. Woodhouse had a large stock of late chrysanthemums which sold extremely well and much funeral work has helped out in the dullness. Thanksgiving balls and dinners and numerous weddings have used up a large quantity of flowers. A prosperous winter trade is expected. The Florists' Club meets next week at the greenhouses of L. L. Peckham, Fairhaven. A. B. H.

Corning, N. Y.

A. H. Woeppel completed the erection of five greenhouses covering two lots on Mill street opposite Hope cemetery. The greenhouses contain 10,000 square feet of glass. The walls are of concrete and the sills of the various buildings are of iron, so that they will last indefinitely. This is believed to be the largest greenhouse plant in Steuben county. At the rear of the p a t Mr. Woeppel has four acres of land which he can use for growing purposes. Mr. Woeppel will continue to conduct his old greenhouse at 34 West Fourth street, and his residence will be at that number. The Mill street greenhouses are fine looking buildings and are a credit to the enterprise of the proprietor. They will be formally opened tomorrow.

Elmira, N. Y.

The United States Cut Flower Company has made application to close up a highway which would cut through one of the greenhouses the company proposes to build. The company is willing to give an equal amount of land on either the northern or southern line of the property. Judge McCann has appointed a commission to look into the matter.

EUREKA, CAL.— Extensive hothouses established by J. G. Loveren have been leased by Mrs. William Brown.

PANDANUSES AT VAUGHAN'S GREENHOUSES, WESTERN SPRINGS, ILL.

With the Growers.

WM. CLARK, COLORADO SPRINGS, COL.

In the gradual emancipation of the west from its dependence on eastern markets for its supply of cut flowers and plants many extensive greenhouse establishments have sprung up to claim their share of the trade. Among these the plant of Wm. Clark holds a prominent position. Besides the 100,000 feet of glass at the old place in the heart of the city, he has extensive nurseries at Broadmoor, five miles away, and at Rosswell, at the north end of the town.

At the latter place the firm has begun the erection of a modern range of houses, comprising at present about 25,000 square feet of glass. The short roof system of construction is used in part of this range, with a ridge pole running north and south. A block of three houses, 30x150 each, with high gutters and no partition walls, is devoted to asparagus, smilax and roses. Some of the latter are in their second year and the cut is of excellent quality. The short roof section is devoted exclusively to carnations. A house of G. H. Crane, grown indoors all summer, is just coming into its first crop and a fine sight it is. Harlowarden and Prosperity are shown in fine form as are also some of the leading standard varieties solid beds were extensively tried in these houses last winter, but the firm concluded that benches would pay better, so this year the beds have been entirely done away with.

At the down town place, from which the retail business is conducted, are found all the great variety of plants needed for such work. The Boston fern is the leading foliage plant for pot sales and many thousands in sizes ranging from 4-inch to 8-inch are handled annually. Good prices are obtained for these and no other one plant is more prominent in the trade of this place than the Boston fern. A great future is anticipated for the Pierson fern and with that in view a bench was planted early in the summer for propagating purposes. The variety promises to be no less prolific in the production of runners than its parent. Anna Foster is also being tried on a smaller scale and it seems to be a fit companion for Piersoni. Several houses of palms in the leading varieties have made a fine growth during the summer. The plants are very free from insects and reflect excellent care. Since the advent of the Boston fern, the increasing taste for flowering plants and the insatiable demand for cut flowers, the space devoted to palms has been gradually contracted and this policy is now being carried to a still greater extent.

Cyclamens are grown in large quantity, as are also primulas, cinerarias and poinsettias, all of which are in excellent shape. A house of Adiantum gracillimum and cuneatum is in full holiday dress and is seldom seen out of crop. Until recently Maidenhair ferns had been a failure on account of the high altitude, alkiline soil and the dry climate, so, it was said. Frequent shaking out of the loose soil among the crowns and topdressing with a mixture composed chiefly of sand, leaf mould and old hotbed manure, with very little of the "dobe" soil, is considered chiefly responsible for the good results by the grower in charge. The soil question is a very difficult one and requires fine powers of discrimination in the growing

of tender plants. A batch of soil containing too large a quantity of alkali has been responsible for many a failure.

In carnations all the leading varieties are grown. Some coming into heavy crop and others holding back their energies for the holiday and midwinter cut. A continual supply of cut flowers is the result aimed at and with this in view some four or five varieties of each color are grown. Lawson is the best paying variety, closely followed by Sunbeam and Bon Homme Richard. Much space is devoted to chrysanthemums both for cut blooms and pot plants.

The firm has long outgrown the local trade and draws its patronage from the whole Rocky mountain territory and a considerable radius east and south. Wm. Clark is the pioneer florist of Colorado, starting in a small way in this city in 1873, long before the vast wealth of the surrounding country was dreamed of. A shrewd financier once said, "Pioneering does not pay," but a good trade founded on fair dealing with confiding customers working under the unfamiliar conditions found in a new country has often been the reward of those who braved the hardships of the frontier, and not the least valuable feature of this reward is the high esteem in which the old warrior is held by the younger generation.

Mr. Clark devotes a large part of his time to the upbuilding of his new place at Rosswell, leaving the duties of general manager to his son-in-law J. B. Braidwood, with G. H. Baur foreman of the downtown place. A large force of contented workmen and expert growers complete the working force.   S. S.

A BEAUTIFUL NURSERY.

The retail nurseryman, in common with his wholesale brother, gives scant thought to the matter of beauty in the layout of his domain. The beauty of health and the beauty of the individual or the variety doubtless do appeal to him, but decorative effect in his plantation counts for but little more with the average nurseryman than with the

farmer in his potato field and to the visitor the typical nursery is a monotonous and strictly practical affair where the buyer is apt to find the task of choosing stock a fatiguing plod through long reaches of rough and often muddy byways.

In the F. R. Pierson nursery at Scarborough, N. Y., we meet with a rare and very pleasing departure from commonly followed methods. Here, instead of the familiar parallel rows, one finds irregular and picturesque groupings of stock so

planted as to set forth the full character of each subject in decorative effect, the taller material in the background and the low in front, skirting well-built, winding driveways from which customers may inspect the stock under best conditions and, if they so choose, make personal selections without leaving their carriages: For a nursery catering to a cultured community this method impresses one as eminently sagacious and practical and we are assured by Mr. Pierson that it pays in every way, the massed plantings being cared for at even-less expense than when laid out on the usual parallel row plan.

The Scarborough property comprises about thirty acres. It was acquired and a range of rose houses erected about ten years ago. The nursery idea came later. The character of the communities occupying the eligible territory all along the eastern shore of the Hudson river gives assurance of an extensive and profitable demand for the choicer grades of ornamental material and this is the kind of stock carried. Rhododendrons, boxes, kalmias and such broad-leaved evergreens, conifers in wide variety, Japan maples, azaleas and other ornamental foliaged and flowering trees and shrubs and hardy garden perennials constitute the leading specialties. The nursery has a frontage of one-third of a mile on the main road and the entire length is planted with a wide belt of all classes of hardy ornamentals, their effectiveness being accentuated by masses of gay cannas, dahlias, etc., interspersed. The outlook over the Hudson river is grand, the view taking in Nyack, Haverstraw and the Old Man of the Mountain on the distant west shore.

The original range of greenhouses is now used principally for chrysanthemums, followed by lilies and for propagating purposes. A later-built range of 300-foot houses is devoted exclusively to roses. Another house, 66x300, of the new Pierson-Sefton type, has been erected during the past season and is to be followed by the addition of several more of

WM. CLARK'S NEW PLACE, COLORADO SPRINGS, COL.

the same pattern. This house is filled with tall palms and ornamental-foliaged plants and over one thousand Pierson ferns suspended from the roof, in 8-inch and 10-inch pans are a striking feature. Mr. Pierson asserts that in no way can the full character of this fern be brought out. so well as by keeping it pot-bound, suspended in abundant light and air and well-fed.

The American Beauty roses furnish unsurpassed examples of what this rose, under favorable circumstances, is capable of doing. The long-pointed, sleek, even-colored buds excite admiring comment on the absence of any trace of the Beauty's greatest pest—thrips. Asked for a reason, Mr. Pierson states his belief that clean culture is the secret of success and repeats that "an ounce of prevention is worth a pound of cure." The houses are cleared of soil and all else every summer and thoroughly whitewashed, fresh lime liberally spread under the benches

hang in great handsome clusters, perfect in color, size and flavor.

The place has been under cultivation some fifty years, being an ideal spot with a water foreground and natural beauty galore. The greenhouse department is kept in excellent shape, everything clean, orderly and interesting, all the more so in view of the relatively small force at work. The chrysanthemums are of all the newest sorts and in good

other potted plants. The fine cut blooms occupied the center of the room and were shown on large tables.

Flowers were offered for sale by the ladies of the church, but the money realized from them did not go to the club.

MUSCATINE, IA.—J. E. Kranz held a chrysanthemum show at his greenhouse the last week of November.

FRANKFORT, KY.—Fire at 3 a. m., November 27, destroyed Congleton Brothers' greenhouse. The loss is complete.

ROSWELL, N. M.—Mrs. J. P. Church's greenhouse is now completed. There are 5,000 feet of glass in the roof of the house 17x100.

LANCASTER, O. — The thirty-seventh annual meeting of the Ohio State Horticultural Society will be held at Delaware, December 9, 10 and 11.

HASTINGS, MICH.—John N. Burroughs has leased his greenhouses to his son, A. P. Burroughs and grandson, who will carry on the business under the old title of Hastings City Greenhouses.

BOSTON, MASS.—Harlan P. Kelsey and Irving T. Guild announce that they have entered into partnership for the practice of landscape architecture, under the style of Kelsey & Guild, at 6 Beacon street, this city.

MOBILE, ALA.—Wm. S. Maull, who for many years has been a wholesale grower for the Philadelphia market, has accepted the position as superintendent of Chatogue Greenhouses which were built here by F. P. Davis the past spring.

WILMINGTON, N. C.—Fire in the extensive greenhouses of Rehder Brothers, Ninth and Red Cross streets, at 3:30 o'clock Thanksgiving morning is estimated to have caused a property loss exceeding $2,000 in buildings and plants. The fire originated in the boiler room.

PHŒNIX, ARIZ.—The board of trade has received from the minister to Ecuador, a quantity of tropical and semi-tropical seed, which he says ought to grow in the Salt River valley. Among the seeds were chirimoya, a splendid fruit; aguacate, fine for salad; Grenada papaya, a luscious fruit, and auclatus.

WHEELING, W. VA.—A greenhouse is to be erected at Bethany for Carl Oglebay. The building is to be one of the finest of its kind in this section of the country and will be fitted up with the latest and most modern appliances. Contractor Seibert has the contract for the masonry and the contract for the other work will be let very shortly.

SHORT ROOF SECTION AT WM. CLARK'S, COLORADO SPRINGS, COL.

and then every second year the houses are painted throughout.

The chrysanthemum houses have been of more than passing interest this season for, in addition to a very full representation of the year's introductions a large number of seedlings have been under test and of these there are several that are candidates beyond any question for next year's first class. A new crimson carnation with flower as large as Lawson is to be sent out next season under the name of Daheim.

Ames Estate, North Easton, Mass.

For an exquisite bit of landscape under the very best care, with all the eye could wish or the heart desire, commend me to the Gov. Ames estate in beautiful North Easton. Situated about midway between Providence and Boston, it is reached by trolly from Mansfield, some seven miles being traversed before the fine stretch of rolling land is reached, with its array of many tree varieties, each botanically described by inscriptions painted on nearby rocks. The grounds comprise about 600 acres with 125 of them under direct cultivation. The working force numbers twelve to twenty, according to the season, and is under the supervision of the head gardener, W. N. Craig, a gentleman of ability and courteous to the last degree. He has full charge of the orchid houses with their wealth of tropical beauties, rare and magnificent. Over 3,000 of these plants are exhibited, including 800 to 1,000 separate varieties, some with flower spikes of exceptional fullness. It would be a lengthy task to tabulate precise descriptions of the different denrobiums, odontoglossums and cypripediums one sees in an afternoon's visit, but it suffices to mention the impressive effect gained by a close inspection of the wonderfully fine colorings. In addition to the regular florist work there is maintained a forced fruit department where are grown peaches, Japanese plums, choice melons, figs and special kinds of grapes, also tomatoes and cucumbers. The grapes

shape for an early cut. Nothing is marketed, all stock going direct to the mansion or the residence in Boston.

The palm house is a revelation in larger sizes, some of the kentias standing twenty-five feet from the ground and the latanias with a spread of fifteen feet and an age of fifty years. Two years ago this collection was sent as an exhibit to Horticultural Hall, Boston. Mr. Craig is a good man in a good place.

MACNAIR.

Richmond, Ind., Exhibition.

The Richmond Floral Club opened its flower show at the Friend's church, November 21, with an exhibition of potted and cut flowers that rivaled anything ever shown in the city. The display contained a brilliant outlay of chrysanthemums, roses and carnations, many of which carried off prizes in the flower show that was held in Indianapolis. The club got up the local show on short notice and mainly for the purpose of giving the local people a chance to see some of the products of the local flower industry.

The corners of the room were banked with fine displays of palms and ferns and

BRIDE AND BRIDESMAID ROSES AT WM. CLARK'S, COLORADO SPRINGS, COL.

THE AMERICAN FLORIST
NINETEENTH YEAR.
Subscription, $1.00 a year. To Europe, $2.00.
Subscriptions accepted only from those
in the trade.
Advertisements, on all except cover pages,
10 Cents a Line. Agate; $1.00 per inch.
Cash with Order.
No Special Position Guaranteed.
Discounts are allowed only on consecutive inser-
tions, as follows—6 times, 5 per cent; 13 times,
10 per cent; 26 times, 20 per cent;
52 times, 30 per cent.
Cover space sold only on yearly contract at
$1.00 per inch, net, in the case of the two
front pages, regular discounts apply-
ing only to the back pages.
The Advertising Department of the AMERICAN
FLORIST is for florists, seedsmen and nurserymen
and dealers in wares pertaining to those lines only.
Orders for less than one-half inch space not accepted.
Advertisements must reach us by Wednesday to
secure insertion in the issue for the following
Saturday. Address
AMERICAN FLORIST CO., Chicago.

THE event of the week is the christening of Breitmeyer's new rose at the Cadil.
lac hotel, Detroit, Mich., this afternoon.

AN international industrial exhibition
will be held at Cape Town, South Africa,
November and December, 1904, and January, 1905.

THE season has arrived when sudden
blizzards and zero weather are imminent.
See to it that nothing inflammable is
within reach of boiler or pipes.

AZALEAS being forced for Christmas
should have frequent lively syringings,
otherwise an unwelcome visitor in the
shape of red spider is very liable to put
in an appearance.

A Correction,

The statement that Robert Hughes
was to receive pecuniary assistance from
Cleveland florists, which appeared in
the AMERICAN FLORIST of November 21,
was erroneous. The mistake was on the
part of the undersigned and the funds
collected were for an entirely different
purpose.   O. G.

Proposed Peony Show.

The members of the Florists' Club of
Philadelphia were talking about peonies
and how long they may be kept in satis
factory condition at its regular monthly
meeting, held December 1, and from
information gathered there it would be a
very easy matter to hold an exhibition
of that very important flower that could
be made a world beater in its line. A
committee was appointed to look into
the matter with the view of holding
such an exhibition and it is to be hoped
that it may report favorably. Philadelphia would be an excellent place for such
an exhibition.

Registration of Peonies.

The following letter was received by
the undersigned October 19, 1903:
                          BOSTON, October 17, 1903.
MR. GEO. C. WATSON.
  DEAR SIR:—I enclose a copy of the registration
announcement made through the AMERICAN
FLORIST, March 7, 1903 of peonies submitted by
MESSRS. SUZUKI & IIDA, of New York. Acceptance
of the registration by the S. A. F. has been
deferred until after an investigation as to the
right of these varieties to registration under the
rules of the society and by vote at the convention
in Milwaukee, August 20, 1903, the list is referred
to the peony committee for decision on this point.
I may add that the list was originally sent to all
the trade papers, as customary, but the AMERICAN
FLORIST was the only one willing to give it room
in its columns. Yours very truly,
                          WM. J. STEWART, Sec'y.

This letter was read and considered at

the meeting of the peony committee of
the S. A. F., held in Philadelphia November 11, 1903. After a full and free discussion it was moved by J. K. M. L.
Farquhar, of Boston, and seconded by
W. R. Smith, of Washington, as follows:
  Believing that it is in the interests of good
nomenclature to admit to registration the English
names of the Japanese peonies given by Suzuki
& Iida, and which are suggestive of the Japanese
descriptive names, the peony committee invites
any interested party to communicate to the secretary their views before January 1, 1904, for the
committee's consideration.

The resolution was carried unanimously
and anyone knowing specifically of previous dissemination in America of any of
the varieties enumerated in the publication stated, March 7, 1903, under American names other than those there given,
or making any claims of priority in connection therewith, will please communicate with the undersigned on or before
the date mentioned in the resolution.
                          GEO. C. WATSON, Sec'y.
Juniper and Locust streets; Philadelphia,
Pa.

Peter Lambert.

Peter Lambert was born at Treves,
on the Mosel, June 1, 1859. His
father, Johann Lambert, had succeeded
his father, Nicolas Lambert, in
1853, and after considerably enlarging the florist establishment had
taken in his brother Nicolas and T.
Reiter in 1860, founding the important
nursery firm of Lambert & Reiter. Johann
Lambert died in 1897, 66 years old, leaving 13 children. The oldest son, Peter,
after attending the high school at Treves
until his seventeenth year, remained
another two years in the above nursery,
paying particular attention to the culture of roses.
  He then went to the Royal garden
school at Wildpark in Potsdam and graduated in 1881, when he joined the army
and served his time of one year as a volunteer. After this he went to France,
where he worked with V. Lemoine in
Nancy, Croux & Fils in Sceaux, H.
Defresne in Vitry, Louis Leroy in Angers,
and then visited all the important nurseries in France. Jean Sisley gave him
special instructions on the fertilization of
roses. In 1884-5 Peter Lambert went to
England, where he worked for Fisher &
Holmes for some time. In England he
also visited many of the most important
nurseries and exhibitions held at that
time. In the summer of 1885 he passed
the examination for Royal head gardener
in Potsdam.
  From the fall of 1885 to 1891 Peter
Lambert managed the rose nurseries of
the firm of Lambert & Reiter and executed many landscape jobs. In 1891 he
was made manager of the club of German
florists and was given the editorship of
the Rosen Zeitung. In the nurseries of
Lambert & Reiter he obtained the first
good German roses, for instance, the
Kaiserin Augusta Victoria. In 1891 he
established his own business in Treves.
He combined an important garden technical business with his rose and nursery
establishment. His catalogue was the
first in which the different varieties of
roses were listed according to the Crepin
system. He continued the artificial
fecundation of roses and has been very
successful.

Here is a list of his introductions:
Aschenbrodel (1902).
Balduin (1898).
Domkapitular D. Lager (1903).
Edu Meyer (1904).
Eugenie Lamesch (1900).

Frau Cecilie Walter (1904).
Frau Geheimrat von Boch (1898).
Frau Lilla Rautenstrauch (1903).
Frau Karl Druschki (1901).
Frau Syndica Roeloffs (1900).
Freiherr von Marschall (1903).
Goldquelle (1899).
Grossherzogin Viktoria Melitta (1898).
Gruss an Zabern (1904).
Gustav Grunerwald (1903).
Helene (1898).
Herzogin Marie v. Ratibor (1898).
Hofgartendirektor Graebener (1899).
Kaiserin Auguste Viktoria (1891).
Katharine Zeimet (1901).
Leonie Lamesch (1900).
Mme. Jean Dupuy (1901).
Morgenrot (1902).
Oberhofgartner Singer (1904).
Oskar Cordel (1898).
Papa Lambert (1899).
Reichsgraf E. von Kesselstatt (1898).
Schneekopf (1902)
Schneewittchen (1901).
Thalia-Remontant (1902).
Unermudliche (1904).

Obituary.

MRS. G. R. SCHLURAFF.

The death of Mrs. Geo. R. Schluraff,
wife of the senior member of the Schluraff
Floral Company, Erie, Pa., which
occurred the night of November 17, has
taken from her family a wife and mother
devoted and beloved and from the social
circle a friend esteemed for sincerity and
unfailing kindness. Mrs. Schluraff was
born at West Millcreek, Erie County, Pa.,
in 1855. She was married in 1875. She
was gifted with more than the average
ability. Her husband has always credited her with a substantial share in laying foundations, and aiding in the
upbuilding of his large business, in which
her artistic taste along the line of designing was an invaluable help. Two children, Miss Iva and Vern L. Schluraff,
survive, the latter being a member of the
Schluraff Floral Company.

GEORGE A. KRUSE.

The funeral of Geo. A. Kruse, who died
November 29 at his residence, 326 Ocean
avenue, Jersey City, N. J., took place
November 30 in the presence of a large
number of mourners. The death of Mr.
Kruse came as a shock to his large circle
of friends and acquaintances. He was
one of the best known citizens of Greenville, and had long been prominent in the
business and social life of the community.
His associates esteemed him as a man of
the highest integrity. For many years
he had been in charge of the floral decorations of the New York Bay Cemetery.
He was for many years president of the
Schwaben Verein, once a prominent social
organization, and was taking an active
part in its proposed reorganization. For
a number of years he attended to the
flower beds in the City Hall plaza, and
in this behalf received much praise. Mr.
Kruse was 63 years old. He leaves two
daughters, Miss Kruse and Mrs. William
Entenmann, and a son. His wife died
only a few months ago.
  We trust he will produce many more
equally meritorious.

GRIFFIN, GA.—A disastrous fire was
narrowly averted at the Georgia Experiment Station November 21. The greenhouse caught fire near the engine room
and was making rapid progress toward
destruction when discovered.

Exhibition at New Haven, Conn.

The third annual flower show given by New Haven County Horticultural Society, was opened November 10 at 2 p. m., in the Music Hall, New Haven, and continued for three days. The whole show was a decided success and in every respect much better than the one given last year. There was evident a decided improvement in size and quality of the flowers shown. The hall was prettily decorated with evergreen trees and mountain laurel boughs, and the arrangement of groups and tables was good. Congratulations are certainly due the New Haven County Horticultural Society in general and the exhibition managers in particular, for getting up such a very creditable exhibition. Chas. Keith, of Bridgeport, Conn., L. F. Atkins, of Rutherford, N. J., and Geo. Thomson, of Lenox, Mass., were judges. Prizes were awarded as follows:

Group fifty foliage and flowering plants.—First to Robert Patton, gardener to Mrs. T. G. Bennett, New Haven; second to Wm. Gardner, gardener to Prof. H. W. Farnam, New Haven.

Best specimen palm.—David Kydd, gardener to Francis Wayland, New Haven, first.

Best specimen adiantum.—Wm. Gardner, first.

Best three foliage greenhouse plants.—David Kydd first.

Best three chrysanthemums in pots not to exceed twelve inches.—John Murray, Yale botanical gardens, first.

Best specimen chrysanthemum, not to exceed twelve inches.—J. F. Hass, Hartford, Conn., first.

Best six chrysanthemums, one flower to each plant.—John Murray, first.

Twenty-four chrysanthemums, one flower to the plant in six-inch pots.—John Murray, first.

Begonia Gloire de Lorraine.—Robert Patton, first.

Best group of specimen plants, not to occupy less than 200 square feet of space.—Robert Patton, first; David Kydd, second.

Best arrangement of potted plants not to occupy over 100 square feet.—David Kydd, first.

Best group of foliage and flowering plants, not to occupy over seventy-five square feet.—Wm. Gardner, first.

Six special geraniums in pots, not less than three varieties—Yale botanical gardens, first; A. J. Thompson, second; West Haven, second.

Three Boston ferns, 8-inch pots.—John N. Champion, florist, New Haven, first; Ernest Carroll, gardener to N. W. Kendall, second.

Specimen asparagus.—Frank E. Duffy, New Haven, first.

Specimen Boston fern.—Yale botanical gardens, first.

Specimen cycads.—J. F. Hass, first.

Three chrysanthemums, distinct varieties, in pots not over twelve inches.—John Murray, first.

Twelve chrysanthemums, six varieties, one bloom to the plant, in 6-inch pots.—John Murray, first.

Best twenty-five chrysanthemums, six varieties, six or more flowers to the plant in 7-inch pots.—Max E. Krause, florist, New Haven, first.

Six begonias, three varieties.—Ernest Carroll, New Haven, first.

Six ferns, six varieties, 12-inch pots.—Ernest Carroll, first.

Nephrolepis Piersoni.—Ernest Carroll, first; A. G. Thompson, second.

Best collection non-deciduous nursery stock.—Elm City Nursery Company, New Haven, first.

Classes open to amateurs:

Specimen palm.—Mrs. C. B. Wirtz, New Haven, first.

Specimen fern.—David Ferguson, first; Edw. Allison, second.

Specimen rubber plant.—John J. Oed, New Haven, first; W. H. Symons, second.

Specimen chrysanthemum.—W. H. Symons, first; David Ferguson, second.

Three geraniums.—W. H. Symons, first; Mrs. Sicwens, New Haven, second.

Three begonias.—W. H. Symons, first; Mrs. W. H. Symons, second.

One foliage plant.—Frank E. Duffy, New Haven, first; Adolph Klaeber, certificate of merit.

One flowering plant.—Mrs. Whitney, New Haven, first.

Three chrysanthemums, single stems, 6-inch pot.—W. H. Symons, first; Edw. Allison, second.

Best exhibit of potted plants.—Frank E. Duffy, first; Edw. Allison, certificate of merit; Wm. C. Pfeffer, certificate of merit; W. H. Symons, certificate of merit.

Classes open to ladies only:

Best basket of chrysanthemums and autumn foliage.—Mrs. Wm. Gardner, New Haven, first.

Classes for cut blooms, open to private gardeners and amateurs:

Twenty-five carnations, four or more varieties.—G. F. Sorensen, Stamford, Conn., first; Henry Cliffe, Fairfield, Conn., second.

Twelve chrysanthemums, not less than four varieties.—Henry Cliffe, first; J. L. Hass, second; Walter Angus, Chapinville, Conn., third.

Bunch of fifty double violets.—Henry Cliffe, first.

Classes for cut blooms, open to all:

Best twenty-five chrysanthemum blooms in fifteen varieties.—John Murray, first; Walter Angus, second.

Vase eighteen pink chrysanthemums.—Walter Angus, first.

Vase of twelve white chrysanthemums, one variety.—Henry Cliffe, first; Wm. A. Long, florist, New Haven, second.

Twelve yellow chrysanthemums.—Henry Cliffe, first; Robert Angus, second.

Vase of twelve any other color.—Henry Cliffe, first; Robert Angus, second.

Twelve chrysanthemums, twelve varieties.—Henry Cliffe, first.

Twelve bride roses.—J. A. Sokel, Bridgeport, Conn., first.

Twelve Bridesmaid.—J. A. Sokel, first; Wm. A. Long, second.

Twelve of any other variety roses.—J. A. Sokel, first.

Six American Beauty.—Henry Cliffe, first.

Twelve Golden Gate.—J. A. Sokel, first.

Twenty red carnations.—Robert Patton, first.

Twenty white carnations.—Robert Angus, first.

Twenty pink carnations.—Robert Angus, first.

Twenty-five carnations, four varieties.—Henry Cliffe, first.

Vase of seedling carnation not yet disseminated.—Henry Cliffe, first.

Bunch of 100 double violets.—John Slocumbe, New Haven, first; A. J. Thompson, second.

Best incurved chrysanthemum bloom in the show.—Henry Cliffe, won.

Best reflexed chrysanthemum in the show.—Yale botanical gardens won.

Best chrysanthemum in the show.—Henry Cliffe won.

Best bunch of fragrant roses.—Henry Cliffe won.

Classes for fruits, open to all:

Best three bunches of black grapes.—J. P. Sorensen, Stamford, first; Walter Angus, second.

Best collection of berries on branches of trees, shrubs and vines, native or imported.—Charles Kerne, landscape gardener of City Park, New Haven, first.

Best collection of vegetables.—A. N. Farnam, first.

Best twelve species of vegetables.—A. N. Farnam, first; Ernest Carroll, second.

Best six species.—Walter Angus, first.

One head of lettuce.—Henry Cliffe, first.

Adam Zeigler, New Haven, was awarded a certificate of merit for horseradish and celery.

John Doughty, of New Haven, John B. Champion and Chas. Munro were given certificates of merit for group for exhibition but not for competition.   R. K.

Exhibition at Wills Point, Texas.

The ladies of the women's club gave a chrysanthemum show November 11 to 13. It was the first chrysanthemum show ever given here, but beautiful specimens of plants and blooms were on exhibition.   M.

ALLIANCE, O.—The eleventh monthly meeting of the Stark County Horticultural Society for 1903 was held November 18. Over 100 members were present.

SITUATIONS, WANTS, FOR SALE.

One Cent Per Word.

Cash with the Adv.

Plant Advs. NOT admitted under this head.

Every paid subscriber to the AMERICAN FLORIST for the year 1903 is entitled to a five-line WANT ADV. (situations only) free, to be used at any time during the year.

Situation Wanted—By first-class decorator, in or around Chicago. Address
    W R, care American Florist.

Situation Wanted—By a Hollander, 27, single, experienced. Ferns, palms and bulbs. Address
    A T, care American Florist.

Situation Wanted—By experienced grower, roses, carnations and general stock. Address
    H C. YEAGER, 17 Cushing St., Cambridge, Mass.

Situation Wanted—As foreman or manager, 18 years' practical experience in wholesale and retail. Apply stating wages, size of place, etc.
    FLORIST, Box 373, Trinidad, Col.

Situation Wanted—By young man of 24, with 8 years' experience in florist's work. Besides other gardening experience. In or near Chicago preferred.
    I L, care American Florist.

Situation Wanted—As decorator or salesman in first-class flower store by young man, eight years experience. Not afraid of work. Best of references.
    K D, care American Florist.

Situation Wanted—By good all-around florist, 30 years' experience in all branches of the business. Good propagator. Best of references. Single. State wages. Address
    ALPHA, care American Florist.

Situation Wanted—By young man age 21, single, with 15 years' experience in growing roses and carnations to perfection. Capable of taking entire charge. State wages you are willing to pay.
    ROSE GROWER, care American Florist.

Situation Wanted—No. 1 grower of roses, carnations, mums, violets, and general line of pot and wedding stuff, with 20 years' experience, wants situation where good stuff is wanted. Capable of taking full charge. Address
    GROWER, care American Florist.

Help Wanted—Propagator, thoroughly competent, on roses and carnations principally. Must have experience. Good wages paid right man. No novice wanted. Apply
    LAKEVIEW ROSE GARDENS, Jamestown, N. Y.

Help Wanted—Bright, energetic young man of good address for a first-class retail store. Must be thoroughly up-to-date as a decorator and designer and a first-class salesman, situation with references as to character and ability, stating wages expected. Address
    C R S, care American Florist.

For Sale—Ballard's Greenhouse, Perry, Iowa. Cause poor health. Address
    WM. BALLARD, Perry, Iowa.

For Sale—Greenhouse property, about 4,000 feet glass. Doing a fine business, 8 room dwelling, if wanted. Established in good repair. Good reason for selling.
    TAGGARTS, St. Clairsville, Ohio.

For Sale—Greenhouses. Good location for local and shipping business. Well stocked; winter coal laid in. Will sell cheap if sold at once. Selling on account of failing health.
    JAS. RICHARDSON, London, O.

For Sale or Lease—Five greenhouse establishment of 10,000 feet of glass, in good condition and well stocked, with or without dwelling. Fine opening for a single man. Stock reasonable.
    A X Z, care American Florist.

For Sale—Established greenhouses, floral business and property, nursery, two dwelling houses, 1500 square feet of greenhouses. No other in south-eastern Idaho. Also supplies northern Utah and western Wyoming. Unexcelled shipping facilities. S X Hood of railroads diverting into rapidly growing towns and country. Its a bargain and the business should be continued. Must be sold on account of death. Address
    THE CHURCH & WHITE CO., Pocatello, Idaho.

Gardeners' and Florists' Union No. 10,615.

Next meeting Wednesday, December 9, 1903, at 106 E. Randolph St., Chicago. Celebration of the First Anniversary of the Union and nomination of officers for the coming year. Wednesday, December 23, 1903, election of officers. All members are earnestly requested to attend both meetings.

Come Out for a Good Time.

Omaha.

Thanksgiving trade was not as good as last year. Chrysanthemums in pots did not sell as well as expected, although the quality of the plants was good. Very few choice cut chrysanthemums could be had, but some good medium-sized blooms were displayed at the florists' stores. Beauty roses sold at $8 per dozen; the best teas, $1 to $1.50; carnations, $1 to $1.50 per dozen. Violets sold at most any price, as they were very scarce. Narcissi are coming in and will be a welcome flower. Poinsettias and azaleas are displayed at some of the stores, which reminds one that Christmas is near. G.

INTERNATIONAL FLOWER DELIVERY.

INTERNATIONAL FLOWER DELIVERY.

STEAMSHIPS LEAVE FOREIGN PORTS.

FROM	TO	STEAMER	*LINE	DAY	DUE ABOUT
Liverpool......	New York	Lucania	1	Sat. Dec. 12,	Dec. 18
Liverpool......	"	Etruria	1	Sat. Dec. 19,	Dec. 25
Liverpool......	Boston	Saxonia	1	Tues. Dec. 15,	Dec. 22
Fiume	New York	Carpathia	1	Fri. Dec. 18,	Dec.
Glasgow.......	Boston	Hungarian	2	Sat. Dec. 12,	Dec. 23
Hamburg.......	New York	Pennsylvania	3	Sat. Dec. 14,	Dec. 22
Hamburg.......	"	Deutschland	3	Sat. Dec. 12,	Dec. 20
Hamburg.......	"	Patricia	3	Sat. Dec. 10,	Dec. 31
London........	"	Minneapolis	6	Thur. Dec. 10,	Dec. 20
London........	"	Minnehaha	6	Thur. Dec. 17,	Dec. 27
Liverpool......	"	Teutonic	7	Wed. Dec. 9, 3:30 p. m.	Dec. 16
Liverpool......	"	Arabic	7	Fri. Dec. 11, 3:30 p. m.	Dec. 19
Liverpool......	"	Germanic	7	Wed. Dec. 16, 3:30 p. m.	Dec. 24
Liverpool......	"	Cedric	7	Fri. Dec. 18, 3:30 p. m.	Dec. 25
Southampton...	"	St. Paul	7	Sat. Dec. 12, Noon.	Dec. 18
Southampton...	"	Philadelphia	8	Sat. Dec. 19, Noon.	Dec. 26
Antwerp.......	"	Zeeland	9	Sat. Dec. 12, 7:30 a. m.	Dec. 21
Antwerp.......	"	Finland	9	Sat. Dec. 19, Noon	Dec. 28
Havre.........	"	La Bretagne	10	Sat. Dec. 12,	Dec. 20
Havre.........	"	La Touraine	10	Sat. Dec. 19,	Dec. 27
Rotterdam......	"	Staatendam	11	Sat. Dec. 12,	Dec. 21
Rotterdam......	"	Rhyndam	11	Sat. Dec. 19,	Dec. 28
Genoa	"	Lombardia	12	Mon. Dec. 7,	
Genoa	"	Nord America	12	Mon. Dec. 14,	
Genoa	"	Hohenzollern	12	Tues. Dec. 8, 7:00 a. m.	Dec. 21
Bremen........	"	Main	13	Tues. Dec. 8, 7:00 a. m.	Dec. 21
Bremen........	"	Koeln	13	Sat. Dec. 12, 7:00 a. m.	Dec. 25
Bremen........	"	Brandenburg	13	Sat. Dec. 19, 7:00 a. m.	Dec. 31
Marseilles.....	"	Patria	14	Fri. Dec. 11,	
Liverpool......	Boston	Dominion	16	Thur. Dec. 10,	Dec. 17
Liverpool......	"	Columbus	16	Thur. Dec. 17,	Dec. 24
Liverpool......	"	Canadian	16	Sat. Dec. 12,	Dec. 20

* See steamship list on opposite page.

THE SEED TRADE.

VISITED BOSTON: S. F. Willard, of Comstock, Ferre & Company.

F. W. BARTELDES celebrated his fifty-first birthday last month.

EX-PRESIDENT STOKES, in his communication on this page, is on the right track.

NASTURTIUMS will be among the short items this season. Contract orders for mixed will not be filled over forty per cent.

VISITED CHICAGO: C. R. Root, Denver, Col.; P. Miller, with the Steele, Briggs Company, Toronto, Ont.; D. L. Sloan, Palo Alto, Cal.; J. B. Agnew, of Agnew, Cal.

APPRAISERS' DECISION 24,800.—G. A. 5,486, November 20,1903, sustains protest of importer and fixes natural millet seed unhulled and not cleaned as grass seed and free of duty.

TORONTO, ONT.—E. Crossland, of the Winnepeg branch of the Steele, Briggs Company, will return here and P. Miller take his place. The trade will be sorry to know that Mr. Briggs is still ill.

SEED growers at Waterloo, Neb., are much exercised over the fact that outside houses have come into their market and bid up prices among contract growers. The farmers are declining to make deliveries on their contracts, and seed growers' see trouble ahead in possible lawsuits necessary to get the crops bargained for.

THERE is a brisk demand for sweet peas, as California has developed practically no surpluses, and with the short crops of many of the staple sorts the present is the most promising season for this article we have known for years. There is quite a lively demand from Europe for the Cupid sorts in particular.

THIS is probably the hardest year the vine seed growers ever experienced. They not only had a bad season, but now comes the hardest struggle when they have to ship and bill cucumber seed at contract prices when the market price is materially higher. The percentage of deliveries of this and other short items should be borne in mind when new contracts are given out by seedsmen for 1904.

PHILADELPHIA, PA.—In the matter of D. Landreth & Son, in bankruptcy, the receiver has a bid from Burnet Landreth, Jr., and S. Philip Landreth of $13,563.97 for certain assets of the estate, which bid must be accepted on or before December 12. Bayard Henry, receiver, has petitioned the United States Supreme Court for privilege to sell the property for the said sum, and will ask for a decree shortly unless cause is shown to the contrary or a larger bid be received for said property.

Bouquet Green and Holly.

The price of bouquet green at Chicago remains firm at $7.50 to $9 per 100-pound crate. Some green has been dug out of cold storage, and this, with the old stock carried over and dyed, is piecing out to some extent the market demands. Holly is now arriving in limited quantities and quality fair.

Dummy Price Lists.

ED. AM. FLORIST:—This is the season when the seedsman who wants to know the price at which his neighbors are purposing to catalogue seeds is sending out his dummy lists. The past week we have received two in familiar handwriting, one purporting to come from Samuel Allen, Lansing, Mich., and the other from H. A. Merrill, Saginaw, Mich. Both of these parties are expecting to go largely into trucking the coming season and they are hoping to sell some seeds to their neighboring truckers. They apologize for wanting prices so early, but they do not want to be delayed in their spring planting. They promise orders by the last of November. Following this is a list of nearly everything in the catalogue, ranging in quantity from quarter pound to three pounds. Allen signs himself, "Answer quickly, yours for business." Merrill signs himself, "Now if you want my order, hurry and quote me low prices quick and maybe I can give you the order. Yours for great big crops," etc.

We are making some little inquiry to find out what seedsmen these parties are clerks of, and when we get the information we will write you again.

　　　　　JOHNSON & STOKES.

South Dakota Corn Palace.

The illustration herewith shows this year's corn palace at Mitchell, S. D., in the decoration of which a large quantity

South Dakota Corn Palace.

of corn in various colors was used. The building was designed chiefly for an exhibition of the horticultural and agricultural products of the state. E. C. Newbury, of Mitchell, was an extensive exhibitor of greenhouse and nursery stock.

Secretary Wilson On Free Seeds.

In his annual report, just issued, Secretary Wilson, of the Department of Agriculture has the following with regard to free seed distribution:

With regard to the securing and distributing o miscellaneous garden and flower seed, the fac remains that this work does not accomplish th ends for which the law was originally framed. There are collected, put up, and distributed now, on Congressional orders, nearly 40,000,000 packets of miscellaneous vegetable and flower seeds each year. These seeds are the best that can be obtained in the market, but from the fact that large numbers of packets are wanted, the seed obtained can be of standard sorts only, such as are to be found everywhere for sale in the open market. As there is no practical object to be gained in distributing this kind of seed, it seems very desirable that some change be made. To this end, it would seem wise to limit our work entirely to the securing and distributing of seeds, plants, etc., of new and rare sorts. There is still much to be done in the way of securing seeds, plants, etc., of this kind from abroad, but still more to be accomplished in careful investigations of our own possibilities in this direction. There are many valuable plants scattered all over this country which are till little known outside of their respective localities. These should be collected, tested, and distributed. There are also great possibilities of improving agricultural industries by distributing specially bred seeds and plants.

Milwaukee.

TRADE HAS GOOD THANKSGIVING BUSINESS. —PREPARATIONS FOR MONTHLY FLOWER SHOW.—THE FLORISTS' CLUB ELECTS OFFICERS.

Trade for Thanksgiving was very satisfactory. Of course the usual amount of pickled stock was on the market, but fortunately for the buyers, and unfortunately for the growers, there was plenty of good stock and the pickled stock went into the dump. On Monday preceding Thanksgiving stock was very scarce and appearances pointed to a short supply for the rest of the week, but on Tuesday and Wednesday stock arrived in larger quantities than the demand called for. Roses sold well all week, as did carnations, but poor stock was hard to move except at very low prices. Violets were in good demand with sufficient to go around. I think that there were more chrysanthemums on the market than I have ever seen at Thanksgiving. This week trade is rather dull, but just about enough to take up the supply which has materially shortened up. With normal demand stock would be difficult to get in quantity. Smilax is plentiful.

The Milwaukee Florists' Club held its regular monthly meeting last Tuesday. The members are enthusiastic about the flower show for next fall, and in consequence a premium list aggregating $1,600 was voted. This ought to assure a good show. The annual election of officers took place and resulted as follows: W. A. Kennedy, president; F. H. Holton, vice-president; H. V. Hunkel, secretary; C. Dallwig, treasurer; J. C. Heitman, T. P. Dilger and R. Zepnick, trustees. The indications are that we will have monthly flower shows hereafter.

Heitman & Baerman had an excellent crop of Estelles for Thanksgiving.　H.

CHAMPAIGN, ILL.—Fred. Atkinson, head gardener at the university grounds, has bought land and will build greenhouses the coming spring.

HARTFORD, CONN.—H. D. Hemenway, director of the School of Horticulture, was married to Miss Myrtle L. Hawley, at Amherst, Mass., November 25.

HINGHAM, MASS.—The annual chrysanthemum show of the Hingham Horticultural Society was held November 12. A. H. Kirkland talked on "Insect Pests and their Remedies."

OAKLAND, CAL.—That the residence of Julius Seulberger, the well known florist, was not destroyed by fire November 18 is due to the presence of mind and quick action of Fred Seulberger, his son.

THE NURSERY TRADE.

AM. ASSOCIATION OF NURSERYMEN.
N. W. HALE, Knoxville, Tenn.. Pres.; FRANK A. WEBER, St. Louis, Mo., Vice-Pres.; GEORGE C. SEAGER, Rochester, N. Y., Sec'y.
Twenty-ninth annual convention, Atlanta, Ga., June, 1905.

REEDLEY, CAL.—The San Dimas Nurseries have an order for two carloads of orange trees for shipment to Johannesburg, South Africa.

ATLANTA, GA.—W. P. Robinson, for years in the nursery business here, died at his home. 303 Grant street, November 23 at the age of 81 years.

DOGWOOD, N. J.—The Dogwood Hardy gardens have been incorporated here with a capital of $25,000 by H. F. Smith, C. Perley Walker and F. E. Williamson.

NEW YORK.—Twenty-two cases of buxus and eight of aucuba, consigned by a Holland firm to a New York house were sold at auction by the collector of customs November 20. Fair prices were paid, but there will be little left for the shipper.

Charles G. Carpenter.

MILWAUKEE'S PARK SUPERINTENDENT. Charles G. Carpenter, of Omaha, Neb., was elected park superintendent of Milwaukee, Wis., last month. Mr. Carpenter, who is a former resident of Milwaukee and a graduate of the University of Wisconsin, will assume his duties January 1. Up to his election to the new

Charles G. Carpenter.

position he was superintendent of parks in Omaha, in which city he has been located for the past twenty years, doing a large amount of good landscape gardening, both public and private. He was born in Madison, Wis., in 1857, and graduated from the local university as civil engineer in 1882. The services of W. H. Manning, Boston, Mass., who has been for some time engaged in park work in Milwaukee, will end when Mr. Carpenter assumes his new office.

The Calaveras big tree committee of the Outdoor Art League of California is making laudable efforts to save the big trees. Interested parties should communicate with the chairman, Mrs. Lovell White, 1616 Clay street, San Francisco, Cal.

MUSKOGEE, I. T.—The Muskogee Nursery Company, of this city, has been incorporated with a capital stock of $20,000. The new officers of the company are: J. L. Knisley, president; Benj. Martin, Jr., vice-president; S. E. Gidney, secretary and James T. Perkins, treasurer.

LOS ANGELES, CAL.—The Los Angeles *Times* says it has gathered information on the citrus fruit crop for the season just beginning which warrants the statement that the yield of Southern California citrus orchards for the season of 1903–4 will be from twenty-five to fifty per cent larger than last year when 22,390 carloads were marketed.

Denton, Tex.

The Girls' Industrial College, of Texas, which was opened to students September 23, is going to make a special feature of horticulture and floriculture. Three new greenhouses 18x40 have just been completed and will be gradually stocked with an assortment of bedding and decorative plants. A small nursery has also been established and a course of instruction in growing, grafting, budding, etc., will be afforded those of the students that desire such instruction. The campus of the institution embraces about seventy acres, a large part of which will be devoted to forestry and landscape gardening. Well made drives, beautiful stretches of green lawn and an artificial lake are some of the leading features now and the entire grounds will be developed gradually. This work is in charge of A. J. Seiders, landscape gardener, of Austin, Tex., formerly head gardener at the State Lunatic Asylum, Austin, and Landa's Park, near San Antonio, Tex.

Carthage, Mo.

Business the past season has been very good for this part of the country. Flowers are not used here as freely as in the north and east. Stephen Hide is adding a new house 20x40 for vegetables only.

Perry Finn has added one new house 30x200 for vegetables. Mr. Finn now has 27,000 square feet of glass all devoted to flowers except the last built house.
F.

Our Pastimes.

Announcements of coming contests or other events of interest to our bowling, shooting and sporting readers are solicited and will be given place in this column.

Address all correspondence for this department to Wm. J. Stewart, 48 W. 29th St., New York; Robt. Kift, 1725 Chestnut St., Philadelphia, Pa.; or to the American Florist Co., Chicago, Ill.

At St. Louis.

The bowling club held an interesting evening November 30. Kuehn won the highest number of points. The score follows:

Player	1st	2d	3d	4th	T'l
Kuehn	231	218	169	174	780
C. Beneke	176	174	187	177	714
J. J. Beneke	186	181	148	179	694
Miller	126	171	160	158	616
Meinhardt	118	129	184	172	558
Ellis	166	151	113	118	548
Fred. Weber	..	99	97	131	101	428

F. K. B.

At Chicago.

The Florists' Bowling Club met Tuesday evening at Benzinger's alleys on Randolph street. Two teams were picked from the ranks of the wholesalers and retailers present and a series of three games was rolled. The Lambros followers held their opponents well in hand until the last game. Foerester distinguished himself by making the high score of the evening, 203. Another meeting will take place December 6, when further plans and details for the season will be discussed. The scores of the last games follow:

Player	1st	2d	3d
Lambros	172	189	199
Foester	203	181	156
Scott	159	152	126
Kreiling	139	144	121
Total	673	616	532

Player	1st	2d	3d
Hauswirth	144	148	187
Stevens	192	184	138
Conomos	132	109	141
Essa	134	129	134
Total	593	586	561

At Philadelphia.

The bowling tournament on the club alleys goes merrily on and there is much interest and good natured rivalry between the various contestants. There are some good scores with close and exciting finishes.

On November 25 the Moss team won two games from the Westcotts; on the 27th the Kifts took three straight from the Eimermans and on November 30 the Dunhams won two from the Eimermans. December 2 saw an exciting contest with close finishes between the Kift and Moss teams which the Kifts won two out of the three. The scores:

Player	1st	2d	3d
Kift	162	147	186
Craig	131	167	143
Holmes	134	138	147
Goebel	156	187	196
Allen	187	162	2 5
Total	75	831	767

Player	1st	2d	3d
Moss	176	177	147
Gibson	149	144	118
Dunlop	129	144	182
Polites	180	155	193
Bonsall	168	177	112
Total	774	815	769

Player	1st	2d	3d
Anderson	142	1•9	143
Merlily	1	114	118
Moore	199	148	167
Dunham	173	173	173
Watson	144	180	149
Total	688	774	769

Player	1st	2d	3d
Eimerman	139	144	146
Dunphan	133	134	164
Fa ck	167	149	123
Baker	130	1 0	118
Connor	182	152	152
Total	711	679	7. 3

Player	1st	2d	3d
Westcott	159	167	162
McLoster	145	140	168
Adelbergt	117	142	138
Seaman	131	164	167
Yates	2 3	164	161
Total	754	776	785

Player	1st	2d	3d
Moss	188	169	167
Gibson	8 6	189	164
Dunlop	169	118	166
Bonsall	186	148	3•0
Polites	15	150	159
Total	821	744	817

Player	1st	2d	3d
Kift	149	169	154
Craig	128	180	166
Holmes	136	161	166
Goebel	148	128	169
Allen	132	168	149
Total	681	741	8..6

Player	1st	2d	3d
Eimerman	143	179	1.8
Dungan	159	119	156
Faick	172	191	169
Baker	115	136	163
Connor	139	173	144
Total	679	728	734

K.

Exhibition at Montreal.

For the first time the gardeners and florists exhibiting at our chrysanthemum show experienced no fear of frost for their exhibits, the weather being ideal. According to the unanimous remarks the exhibition surpassed in quality and quantity the former show. However, the competition in cut blooms was very close. We had many outside exhibitors. Nathan Smith & Son, Adrian, Mich., were well represented with a table of undisseminated chrysanthemums. The H. Dale Estate, of Brampton, Ont., gave us a splendid exhibit of roses and carnations. J. H. Dunlop had a good trade of carnations; J. Gammage, one exhibit of unnamed chrysanthemums. Whittaker Bros., of Cornwall, were quite successful with their first exhibit in Montreal.

Among the visitors were H. Dale, Jr., Brampton, Ont.; B. Mepstead, Pres. C. H. A., of Ottawa; D. C. Nixon, of Toronto, and Whittaker Bros., of Cornwall.

Following is a list of the principal winners:

Group chrysanthemum and foliage plants—F. C. Smith, first; A. Pinsteau, second; W. Alcock, third.

Group chrysanthemum only—C. Pinstress, first; A. Pinsteau, second; R. W. Whiting, third; John Pidduck, third.

Six specimens chrysanthemum plants—W. G. Pascoe, first; Hall & Robinson, second; C. A. Smith, third.

Three plants—W. G. Pascoe, first; Hall & Robinson, second.

Twelve plants in 6-in. pots—Hall & Robinson, first.

Six plants in 6-in. pots—Hall & Robinson, first; C. A. Smith, second.

One hundred mixed ferns—J. Eddy & Sons, first; Hall & Robinson, second.

Twenty-five mixed ferns—F. C. Smith, first.

Three ferns—W. J. Wilshire, first; John Walsh, second; F. C. Smith, third.

Tree fern—W. J. Wilshire, first; F. C. Smith, second.

Fern in hanging basket—F. C. Smith, first; W. H. Horsbin, second.

One specimen palm—F. C. Smith, first.

Six orchids—F. C. Smith, first; W. J. Wilshire, second.

Three orchids—W. J. Wilshire, first.

One orchid—W. J. Wilshire, first; F. C. Smith, second; R. W. Whiting, third.

Six primulas—C. A. Smith, first; Alcock, second; W. J. Wilshire, third.

Six solanums—J. Pidduck, first; Alcock, second.

Two specimens calla—P. McKenna & Son, first; Hall & Robinson, second.

Asparagus Sprengeri—W. Alcock, first.

Begonia Gloire de Lorraine—C. W. McHugh, first; W. J. Wilshire, second.

Six geraniums—R. W. Whiting, first.

Three geraniums—W. Alcock, first; R. W. Whiting, second.

Three cyclamens—W. J. Wilshire, first; W. G. Pascoe, second.

Three flowering begonias—C. A. Smith, first; Hall & Robinson, second.

Chrysanthemum blooms, 24—W. J. Wilshire, first; F. C. Smith, second.

Twelve blooms—C. McHugh, first; C. A. Smith, second.

Six blooms—T. McHugh, first; W. G. Pascoe, second.

Three white—T. McHugh, and W. J. Wilshire divide first.

Three pink—T. Gorman, first; W. J. Wilshire, second; W. G. Pascoe, third.

Three yellow—T. McHugh, first; W. J. Wilshire, second; W. G. Pascoe, third.

Three crimson—W. J. Wilshire, first; Dale Estate, second.

Twelve white, one variety—T. Gorman, first; Hall & Robinson, second.

Twelve pink—No first; Hall & Robinson, second.

Twelve yellow—T. Gorman, first; Hall & Robinson, second.

Roses, 12 Bride—H. Dale Estate, first; T. Gorman, second.

Bridesmaid—H. Dale Estate, first; T. Gorman, second.

Liberty—H. Dale Estate, first.

Perle—H. Dale Estate, first.

Ivory—Hall & Robinson, first.

Meteor—H. Dale Estate, first.

American Beauty—H. Dale Estate, first.

Roses in vase, ½ 50—H. Dale Estate, first; T. Gorman, second.

Twenty-five blooming carnations, white.—first; Hall & Robinson, second.

Twenty-five blooms, carnations, red—H. Dale Estate, first; P. McKenna & Son, second.

Twenty-five blooms, carnations, pink—H. Dale Estate, first; Whittaker Bros., second.

Twenty-five blooms, carnations, pink, dark—H. Dale Estate, first.

Twenty-five blooms. Mrs. T. W. Lawson—H. Dale Estate, first; Whittaker Bros., second.

Twenty-five blooms, yellow—H. Dale Estate, first.

Twenty-five blooms, crimson—H. Dale Estate, first.

Twenty-five blooms, any variety—H. Dale Estate, first; Whittaker Bros., second.

One hundred carnations—H. Dale Estate, first; P. McKenna & Son, second.

Mantel decorations—Jas. Bennett, first; Wilshire Bros., second; Hall & Robinson, third; P. McKenna & Son, fourth.

Vase of chrysanthemums arranged for effect—Hall & Robinson, first; W. H. Noeobin, second; Wilshire Bros., third.

Basket of foliage plants—P. McKenna & Son, first; Jas. Bennett, second; Hall & Robinson, third; John Eddy & Son, fourth.

Basket of chrysanthemums—Hall & Robinson, first.

Basket of flowers—P. McKenna & Son, first; Wilshire Bros., second.

Funeral design—Wilshire Bros., first; John Eddy & Sons, second; Hall & Robinson, third.

Wreath of chrysanthemums—Hall & Robinson, first.

In the classes, G and H, of fruits and vegetables, Geo. Trussel won fourteen prizes; W. Alcock six prizes; C. H. Smith three prizes; P. McKenna & Son, three prizes.

Special exhibits were: Collection of pompons from Nathan Smith & Son, Adrian, Mich.

Collection of chrysanthemums from the same firm.

Roses, Mrs. P. Morgan, H. Dale Estate.

Collection of carnations, J. H. Dunlop, Toronto.

Unnamed chrysanthemums, pink, J. Gammage, London, Ont.

Special report upon Nathan Smith & Son's exhibits: Vera, white flushed pink; Klondike, a good yellow; Acto, a good pink; Julia, a light bronze fringed; all worthy of mention.

New varieties—Sunstone, yellow, color and form good; Lord Alverstone, good crimson, makes a good exhibition bloom; Souvenir de Calvat Fue, silver pink, of good substance and form; Mrs. Nathan Smith, good white substance and form good, apparently a good shipper; Rustique Bronze, yellow globular form; A. J. Balfour, deep pink; Hero of Mafeking, fine flower for exhibitions too loose for trade; Mrs. E. Thirkill, a fine exhibition flower; Yesavive, light pink, of pleasing shade, should be a good commercial flower.

J. Gammage's unnamed pink carnation is recommended for a certificate as a good commercial flower.   G. V.

Toronto.

NOVEMBER A RECORD-BREAKER IN TRADE.
—CHRYSANTHEMUM SHOW IS BIG SUC-
CESS.—WEDDINGS AS NUMEROUS AS IN
JUNE.—TRADE NOTES.

The chrysanthemum show, held in St.
George's hall by the Toronto Horticultural Society, was indeed very creditable as
the blooms displayed and the general
arrangements were satisfactory. Unfortunately the hall was not as large as
desired, but the many flowers only helped
to make it look more attractive. The
orchid display was nicely arranged. In
chrysanthemums, Miller & Sons, of Brac-
ondale, took all the firsts; their yellow
and white Eatons were especially fine,
and the largest flowers ever exhibited in
this city. Wm. Jay & Son won three seconds, the Steele-Briggs Company two
seconds, R. Jennings one second. The
Dale estate, of Brampton, was the only
exhibitor in roses. The very heavy business has shortened the stock and kept
others from exhibiting. Dale's had a
well-filled table of choice Canadian Queen,
Beauty, Bride and Bridesmaid. In orchids
the Exhibition Park took two firsts with
a very choice collection and some very
fine specimens. Wm. Hill won a second
and the Allan Gardens won a second. In
carnations there was much more competition and some very fine blooms were
staged, the flowers being for this season
unusually large, with fine stems. Dun-
lops took four firsts, the Dale Estate
four firsts and the seconds were well distributed among the above two growers
and Wm. Fendley, of Brampton; Chas.
Turpe, Manton Brothers and Miller &
Sons.

November has been a record breaker
from a business standpoint. Business
kept steadily increasing and last week
was an exceptionally busy one. It was
remarkable the amount of weddings there
were. In this section this month seems
to be a rival for June in this respect. Several dark days have shortened the supply
of stock of all lines of roses and carnations are scarce. We are pleased to welcome poinsettias. Mignonette and stevia are being cut and will be plentiful.
Violets are even scarcer than two weeks
ago, and to get them from a grower it is
almost necessary to steal them.

Ford, the Florist, is the name of the
new establishment at 17 King street,
West, which is causing considerable comment. The firm is practically inexperienced, and should it be able to pay
large rental and carry on business satisfactorily will certainly be deserving of
great credit.

Miss Clara Brown, who has been managing the College Flower Shop, was married last Wednesday. She was always
well liked and is certainly deserving of
a good husband.

Chrysanthemums are about out, though
R. Jennings, of Brampton, and Louis I.
Vair, of Barrie, are still sending in some
good ones.

The many wedding decorations have
been using quantities of southern smilax,
which is getting to be very popular with
us.

There are already some Christmas
goods in town. From present indications
this is going to be a record season.

J. H. Dunlop was married November
20, at Nashua, N. H. He has the hearty
congratulations of the local craft.

H. G. D.

YONKERS, N. Y.—We have been advised
that Geo. T. N. Cottam died at this
place November 28.

Lowell, Mass.

The supply of flowers the last two weeks has not been enough at times to meet the heavy demands, especially at Thanksgiving, when there was a large business. Warm weather the first part of the month had a telling effect in the way of producing blooms for Thanksgiving. Business seems to be growing year by year. Prices are good and everything has been cleaned up. Previous to Thanksgiving there was considerable business with the society set. Weddings and receptions used up considerable stock.

The decoration of the season was the Sheppard-Pollard wedding, which went to Patten. The entire house, except the dining room, was decorated lavishly with big Timothy Eaton chrysanthemums and ferns. The dining room was ablaze with Beauties. A feature of the wedding was the bride being showered with rose petals instead of rice. Chrysanthemums are now beginning to look tired and will soon go into retirement for another season, although some Eatons are coming in of extra good size. Frank Slader brought in some that measured nearly a foot in diameter.

The demand for violets for Thanksgiving was more than heavy with not enough to go around. For the football game the week previous the plants had been picked bare. Violets brought $1 a bunch of fifty blooms.

M. A. Patten & Company are cutting some blooms of Enchantress and Mrs. Patten that are worth going a long ways to see. A. M.

Troy, N. Y.

John Pickering, proprietor of the Willow Bank greenhouses at Sycaway, suffered a severe loss by fire on Tuesday morning. The fire was discovered about 3 o'clock over the potting shed through the roof of which extended the chimney of a new boiler that was recently installed. The blaze spread rapidly along a connecting structure to the greenhouses and only by strenuous efforts could the men save anything; as it was four out of seven houses were destroyed and the stock in all of them lost. Mr. Pickering has estimated his loss at about $5,000 while the insurance is in the neighborhood of $600. The loss is a severe one and practically places him out of business for the rest of the season.

A. D. Carpenter, of Cohoes, has lately completed two new houses 40x200 feet, for carnations. The houses were completed too late to be stocked this season and will be used about the middle of the winter for bedding plants. The material for the houses was supplied by Lord & Burnham and put together by local mechanics.

James Moore, a violet grower of Watervliet, suffered the loss of his boiler house and one-half his greenhouse through a fire that occurred over a week ago. Mr. Moore is now trying to adjust his loss with the insurance company.

The firm of Mulholland & Smith has opened a retail store on River street. Mr. Smith was a member of the firm of Boardman & Smith, recently dissolved.

Sambrook & Sons have improved their store on Fulton street materially by renovating the interior. The improvements include green burlap wall covering set off with narrow gilt moulding panels, a white enameled stamped steel ceiling, and an abundance of light.   R. D.

Washington, Pa.

The Washington Floral Company, which was organized in April last and whose capacious greenhouses are located on the company's own property east of town, formerly the McBurney farm, will formally open its retail store to-morrow, Thursday. The company has secured the room in the Swan building formerly occupied by the Real Estate Trust Company, which has been altered to meet the requirements and which will be found a very bright and attractive store. It will be stocked with a profusion of roses, carnations, chrysanthemums and potted plants of all kinds, all grown in the company's own greenhouses. Miss Stella Myers has been placed in charge of the store.

Wilmington, Cal.

Chas. Brazee is somewhat upset as the result of the raise of real estate values. The block which he has been occupying has passed into new hands and lot stakes now dispute possession with carnations and violets. He expects to move to near Los Angeles, where he will put out 40,000 carnations, and will go in extensively for ornamental plants. He is having three acres of fresias planted at Long Beach. He has just begun picking violets, of which he has always made a specialty. His carnations are looking well. Mr. Brazee lately installed a two and a half horse-power gasoline engine and pump to get a better water supply.

House rents have gone upward and D. R. Woods is building two tent houses out beside his violets. Soon he and his wife and daughters will be in their new camp home. Mr. Woods has 12,000 violets in full bearing. Princess of Wales is the only variety grown to any extent in Southern California. Wholesale prices have been set at $1 per dozen bunches the season through. Two acres are in carnations, mostly Los Angeles and Corbett. He grew half a million fresias last season. R. H. A.

Worcester, Mass.

Thanksgiving day trade was very satisfactory and kept everyone hustling to get orders out on time. The weather was cold, necessitating extra wrapping to prevent freezing. With the exception of red roses the supply of flowers was equal to the demand. Chrysanthemums were of fine quality and as popular as ever; carnations were also in good supply and cleaned up well at good prices. Roses were a little off crop, but enough were obtainable to fill orders. Cut flowers made up the bulk of the trade, very few pot plants being sold.

Trade in general has been good, several teas, debuts, etc., helping to keep the ball rolling. The weather is cold and trade is showing a winter briskness.
A. H. L.

OWATONNA, MINN.—L. P. Lord has received a patent on his new frost-proof shipping case.

THE AMERICAN FLORIST

America is "the Prow of the Vessel; there may be more comfort Amidships, but we are the first to touch Unknown Seas."

Vol. XXI.   CHICAGO AND NEW YORK, DECEMBER 12, 1903.   No, 810.

THE AMERICAN FLORIST

NINETEENTH YEAR.

Copyright 1903, by American Florist Company
Entered as Second-Class Mail Matter.

PUBLISHED EVERY SATURDAY BY

AMERICAN FLORIST COMPANY,

324 Dearborn St., Chicago.

Eastern Office: 42 W. 28th St., New York.

Subscription, $1.00 a year.   To Europe, $2.00.
Subscriptions accepted only from the trade.
Volumes half-yearly from August, 1901.

SOCIETY OF AMERICAN FLORISTS AND
ORNAMENTAL HORTICULTURISTS.
OFFICERS—JOHN BURTON, Philadelphia, Pa.,
president; C. C. POLLWORTH, Milwaukee, Wis.,
vice-president; WM. J. STEWART, 79 Milk Street,
Boston, Mass., secretary; H. B. BEATTY, Oil City,
Pa., treasurer.
OFFICERS-ELECT—PHILIP BREITMEYER, president; J. J. BENEKE, vice-president; secretary and
treasurer as before. Twentieth annual meeting
at St. Louis, Mo., August, 1904.

THE AMERICAN CARNATION SOCIETY.
Annual convention at Detroit, Mich., March 9,
1904. ALBERT M. HERR, Lancaster, Pa., secretary.

AMERICAN ROSE SOCIETY.
Annual meeting and exhibition, Philadelphia,
March, 1904. LEONARD BARRON, 136 Liberty St.,
New York, secretary.

CHRYSANTHEMUM SOCIETY OF AMERICA.
Annual convention and exhibition, November,
1904. FRED H. LEMON, Richmond, Ind., secretary.

THIS ISSUE 48 PAGES WITH COVER.

CONTENTS

The Rose Growers.

The New Rose, La Detroit.

BREITMEYERS' CHRISTENING CEREMONY.

The christening of Breitmeyers' new rose took place at the Hotel Cadillac, Detroit, Mich., Saturday afternoon, December 5. The event was attended with many unique features which added much importance to the occasion. The parlors where the ceremony took place were prettily decorated with palms, Asparagus plumosus and great number of cut blooms of the rose, La Detroit. The latter were fastened among the heavy strands of asparagus that were festooned from the corners of the large double parlors to chandeliers and around the large mirrors, which beautifully reflected several large vases filled with specimen blooms of the beautiful pink rose about to receive a name in such extraordinary environment. There were present officers of the Detroit Florists' Club, local representatives of the trade papers, many visiting florists and a large number of society ladies. At the beginning of the ceremonies proper Wm. J. Stewart, secretary of the Society of American Florists, stepped forward and said:

"When we would introduce to the world a new creation, be it a child, a ship or a flower, the selection of a pleasing and appropriate name for the stranger becomes a matter of more than ordinary interest. With what paternal pride we canvass the lists to select a name to which we fondly hope our baby shall bring a lasting luster in the days when he shall have grown to manhood. We launch the beautiful yacht under a name symbolic of our patriotism; we break the bottle on the prow of our noble cruiser, and send her afloat confident that under the name we have given her she will carry our flag triumphantly to glorious victory when the call to fierce battle comes. And so, too, the possessor of a new flower feels an almost fatherly love as he watches his treasure grow and develop from day to day and tries to think of a name which shall typify it's virtues and help to carry it victoriously into the hearts of the flower-loving people.

"It is a most appropriate and auspicious occasion which has brought us together here to-day—this christening of a new rose, the fair and lovely queen of all the flowers, to whom we all pay willing homage, whose charms have been the theme for poets from remotest antiquity, the brightest star in Flora's diadem, the symbol of hope and love, whose radiant, perfumed chalice has so often borne the message of affection from heart to heart, illumined the bridal, cheered the sick room and spoken in mute yet eloquent language the word of consolation and comfort in the house where grief has entered.

> No wooing zephyr ever strayed
> To whisper love or steal a kiss.
> Or dancing sunbeam ever played
> Upon a sweeter flower than this.
>
> The pink may burst its varied hue.
> The violet its azure blue,
> The lily claims the snow its own,
> Yet still thou reign'st, undimmed, alone.

"The advent of a new rose, one that promises to be a rose for blooming continuously throughout the year, and because of its abundance and cheapness within the reach of the poor as well as the rich, thus adding one more to the very limited list of available commercial florists' varieties, is, I think all will agree, an event of sufficient importance to justify our good friend Mr. Breitmeyer in the somewhat extraordinary effort he has made to secure for his floral offspring a help rather than a hindrance in the perilous voyage on the sea of popular favor and in inviting us to come here and assist him at this pretty ceremony of christening the rose. As the next step in the programme I now have the honor to present a gentleman who needs no introduction here, the chief executive of the great city of Detroit, his honor Mayor Maybury."

The mayor in his response congratulated the Breitmeyer firm in the possession of such a treasure and hoped its dissemination would carry cheer to many hearts throughout the country. He then introduced Katherine, the little 7-year-old daughter of Mr. and Mrs. Philip Breitmeyer, who, standing on a pedestal, formally christened the rose by the sprinkling of champagne on a vase of specimen blooms and reciting the following:

One star is the type of the glory of heaven:
A shell from the beach whispers still of
　the sea.
To a rose all the sweetness of summer is
　given.

What with roses can compare,
For you may break, you may shatter the
　vase if you will,
But the scent of the roses will cling 'round
　it still.

Slowly each flower face lifted here to-day,
Each dainty rosebud bursting in many a
　floral spray,
With mist of crystal dewdrops,
I christen here to-day,
The most beautiful pink rose—
　　　　LA DETROIT.

Philip Breitmeyer then, in a few appropriate remarks, thanked the many friends who by their presence showed their interest in the rose and their appreciation of the importance of the event so auspiciously carried out. At the conclusion of his address the orchestra in attendance rendered the intermezzo "Hearts and Flowers."

The ceremony was followed by a banquet held in the Flemish room of the hotel, at which were present Mayor Maybury, Police Commissioner Geo. W. Fowle, the officers of the Detroit Florists' Club, representatives of the press and visiting florists, including Wm. J. Stewart, Geo. A. Heinl, Toledo, O.; Geo. Hopp, Grand Rapids, Mich.; James McHutchinson, New York; J. B. O'Neil, Chicago. Songs, speeches and an exchange of pleasantries were indulged in until a late hour. The large banquet table with its rich silverware and candelabra was strewn with many specimen blooms of the new rose which were the recipients of many compliments during the evening. J. F. Sullivan acted as toastmaster.

The committee appointed to select the name reviewed over 10,000 names submitted. The winner of the $100 in gold was Mrs. Ezra Miller, Landisville, Pa. The Breitmeyers will send a colored lithograph of La Detroit to every person who suggested a name for the new rose.

A handsome illustration of La Detroit, from a photograph, appears in the AMERICAN FLORIST of November 21, page 635.

TRIBUTE TO WM. R. SMITH, WASHINGTON.

At the banquet following the christening of the rose, Mayor Maybury paid the tribute herewith to Wm. R. Smith, ex-president of the Society of American Florists:

"Now, my friends, while in this environment I could not help the constant turning of my thoughts to some old as well as new friends, and I have been importuning Mr. Stewart to know something of a former president of the S. A. F., William R. Smith, of Washington, D. C., who is now approaching his eightieth year, and whom I had the pleasure of meeting some twenty odd years ago. I value him among particular friends whom I cherish beyond price. He is one of those rare souls who took genuine pleasure in living close to the heart of nature, and if there is an environment in this world which is blessed it must be that of living so close to the heart of nature. There are the indications here, all over the world, and especially in that flower. And this venerable friend was so completely possessed with that thought that he could not walk with any pleasure and stamp his foot upon even a pansy at his feet, because it is so simple and so numerous, he would hesitate to step upon it as he would upon the foot of a child. He talked to the trees. They were like children to him. I never saw him angry except when he came across a tree that had been poorly

trimmed or merely butchered, or some bush had been rudely brushed against. So all through every step of his beautiful life was that tenderness of the things of nature and the things of God, and I learned to love him: I learned to love him living, and I shall love him when he becomes a memory. And hence this occasion has been added delight to me when it calls back to my memory such a dear old friend."　　.　　J. F. S.

AMERICAN BEAUTY.

This rose is one which needs a great amount of care if success is expected. Although it responds readily to kind treatment, a little carelessness may often bring it into such a condition that it is impossible for it to make complete recovery; At no time will American Beauty stand any improper handling.

The Late Thos. W. Weathered.
(See obituary page 757.)

From the moment the cuttings are placed in the sand until the last buds are cut, it is necessary to use good judgment. A mistake in the handling of the cuttings will often be found to affect the plants during their entire life.

In order to make a success of American Beauty the cuttings should be struck early from selected wood. Do not propagate from a sickly plant and avoid any soft wood. After placing the cuttings in the sand attend carefully to the watering, being careful that they are not allowed to wilt. They should be protected from the sun at first and gradually hardened as they make roots. The ventilation should also be watched carefully, giving them fresh air whenever possible. Do not allow the cuttings to remain in the sand after they are rooted, but pot at once in 2½ inch pots, using a rather light soil. After potting they should be placed in a light, well ventilated house and watered thoroughly. These young plants should be shaded during the brightest portion of the day at first, but as soon as it is possible to do without shade they should be given the full light.

As the first potting is done in light soil they should not stay long in these pots. As soon as the roots are well through the soil they should be shifted into 3-inch pots with a heavier and richer soil. From this time on it will be necessary to use every precaution against red spider,

green fly and black spot. Repot before the plants become pot-bound, making only small shifts and using plenty of drainage to prevent the soil from becoming sour. As the plants develop the buds should be pinched out, inducing the lower breaks to appear. From now on care will be necessary to form a good plant. As a general rule the American Beauty makes very little wood while in pots which is not needed on the plant, but occasionally a plant will have a bunch of short jointed brush in the center which would be better cut out, providing there are two or more breaks of good wood to carry on the making of the plant. When the leaves become bunched together so that they do not dry off quickly after syringing, trouble is liable to result from black spot.

When setting the pots on the bench they should be allowed sufficient space to insure a free circulation of air. Unless the sun and air is allowed to reach the foliage the breaks will not be strong and vigorous, but spindling and drawn instead. It is also a good plan to reset the pots occasionally, picking off all dead black spot and decayed foliage. Before setting the pots sprinkle the ashes with air slacked lime, this being an excellent preventive of black spot.

To get the best results from this rose it should be planted in the benches as early in May as possible. The treatment from that time on will be discussed in a succeeding article.　　　R. I.

UNDEVELOPED METEOR BUDS.

ED. AM. FLORIST:—Under a separate cover I am sending you a few Meteor rose buds such as we have grown here for over a year. They refuse absolutely to open in any kind of weather and we have tried various temperatures, high and low, with the same result. The plants grow very luxuriantly, could not be better and make numerous buds of this kind. Last season we used sod loam from pasture with cow manure. This season we have the same sod but no manure. We tried replanting some of the old stock but they are of the same good growth and bud. Nothing we do seems to make any difference with the opening of the buds. There is no disease that we can discover. What light can you throw on the subject?　　　W. L. M.

Evidently there is something deficient in the soil for the full development of Meteor flowers. With many growers of this vicinity an occasional bud will come the same way, usually the top or leading bud on the strong shoots, and by picking this bud out as soon as set and then allowing two or three young shoots to break from the top good flowers will develop satisfactorily. If "W. L. M." will try this plan and at the same time hold the beds or benches slightly on the dry side, with an average temperature of 65° at night, I think his flowers will open all right. The wood and foliage sent certainly look healthy enough to produce flowers of good quality. Possibly a little stimulant applied to the plants would help them to develop their flowers much quicker, as the buds sent are too heavy and full of petals to open properly under any treatment.　　　J. N. MAY.

NEWPORT, R. I.—The Horticultural Society held its annual meeting December 2. Officers were elected as follows: President, James Sullivan; vice-presidents, Alex. McLellan and Bruce Butterton; recording secretary, D. McIntosh; financial secretary, Joseph Gibson.

CHRYSANTHEMUM SHOW OF THE NATIONAL HORTICULTURAL SOCIETY OF FRANCE, NOVEMBER 4, 1903.

European Chrysanthemum Shows.

LONDON CHRYSANTHEMUM EXHIBITION.

The National Chrysanthemum Society's show was held November 10 to 12. The large trade exhibitors came out in their usual good form. Norman Davis put up a magnificent group, taking the most valuable prize offered for groups, viz.: First in the open class on a space of 300 square feet. H. J. Jones put up a most imposing exhibit of cut chrysanthemum blooms, chiefly in large vases. In the center of the exhibit was a large vase of Mrs. J. Dunn, a new white variety which may be described as a white form of F. S. Vallis, which is now recognized as one of the finest yellows we have. A first-class certificate was awarded for Mrs. J. Dunn and Mr. Jones secured the society's large gold medal for his exhibit.

The "great vase class," twelve vases, five blooms, one variety in each vase, which is the most important class in the show, fell considerably short of previous exhibitions, there being only two entries, which considering the values of the prize, £10 and the memorial gold medal, was rather surprising. The first prize went to Chas. Beckett, with the following varieties: Mrs. J. Bryant, Mrs. F. S. Vallis, Mrs. Barkley, F. S. Vallis, Mrs. Mease, Gen. Hutton, Mrs. A. K. Wright, W. R. Church, J. R. Upton, Mme. C. Naglemackers, G. Penford and Mme. Paolo Radaelli, all fine examples of good culture. In the second prize collection Lord Ludlow, Bessie Godfrey, T. Carrington, Kimberley and Duchess of Sutherland were very good. In the class for six vases of incurved blooms Mr. Higgs sustained his reputation as the best cultivator of this type, taking first prize with beautifully finished blooms of Lady

Isobel, Hanwell Glory, C. H. Curtis, Duchess of Fife, Nellie Southam and Mrs. Barnard Hankey, a new variety, bright bronzy red with rather a dull reverse. A first class certificate was awarded for this variety. Another important class was that for forty-eight distinct Japanese varieties, and in this Mr. Mease, an old exhibitor, came out a good first with a grand lot of blooms, among which were F. S. Vallis, Capt. Percy Scott, Geo. Lawrence, Lady M. Conyers, Mildred Ware, Lord Ludlow, Godfrey's King, Countess of Arran, Mme. Paolo Radaelli, Mrs. G. Mileham, Lord Salisbury, Sir H. Kitchener and Mrs. F. S. Vallis.

In other classes for incurved blooms C. H. Curtis was very prominent with Mrs. F. Judson, Nellie Southam, Mrs. H. J. Jones, Duchess of Fife, Mme. Ferlat. Hanwell Glory, Frank Hammond, Lady Isobel and Topaz Orientale. The pompons and anemone-flowered seem somewhat neglected, but we are getting a much improved type of single varieties. In the class for six varieties, six blooms of each in vases, that made a great show, the varieties taking first prize were Elsie Neville, Annie Farrant, Admiral Sir T. Symonds, Earlswood Beauty, Crown Jewel and Edith.

In the miscellaneous exhibits were some grand displays. T. Rochford put up a fine bank of lilliums, lily of the valley and azaleas from retarded stock.   H.

FLOWER SHOW AT PARIS.

On November 4 a fine show of chrysanthemums, fruit and vegetables was held by the National Horticultural Society of France in the large greenhouses on the Couer la Reine, forming part of the International Exhibition of 1900. Seed-

lings were shown in great numbers by Calvat, Nonin, Vilmorin-Andrieux & Company, Chantrier, le Marquis de Paris and others. In the groups and exhibits of cut blooms we noticed the following American varieties in good form: Eda Prass, Col. W. B. Smith, W. Tricker, Major Bonnaffon, Hairy Wonder, G. W. Childs, Lillian Bird, Modesto and Waban, the latter of which we recognized under the curious variation of Vaban.

Among the recent novelties of the past year or two, excluding 1903 varieties not yet distributed, those specially good under the sunny sky of France were: F. S. Vallis, a magnificent, long-petaled and yellow Japanese; Jean Calvat, Mme. Paolo Radaelli; Lieut. Col. Ducroisit, one of the finest and best of the new yellow Japanese; Calvat's Sun; Mme. L. Deux, yellow; Mrs. Greenfield, Mrs. Barkley and W. R. Church.

For decorative work, that is to say freely flowered moderate-sized plants to form nice showy little bushes for groups there was a goodly array including Francois Vilon, Princess Alice de Monaco, Duchess d'Orleans, Rajah, Gloire de Feu, Baronne de Vinals, a charming rosy amaranth Japanese, Electra and M. Nicolas Balu.

In new seedlings Calvat's best were: Marguerite de Moris, a large pale blush.

Gab. Martin, deep canary yellow.

Mme. M. Oberthur, creamy white.

Alliance, a big golden yellow Japanese.

Mme. Emile Rosette, pale lilac mauve, very large, Japanese.

Countess de Grailly; another big one, white passing to pale blush.

Mme. Anna Debono, also very big, pure white.

Souvenir de Victorine Calvat, very fine, soft, pinkish flesh.

Others were shown but the colors were not pleasing to our taste. M. Alfred Chantrier showed some Lac d' Estera, a fine yellow being the best.

EXHIBITION OF FRENCH NATIONAL CHRYSANTHEMUM SOCIETY AT LILLE, NOV. 6, 1903

M. le Marquis de Paris, a new grower, showed a lot of seedlings, some very promising. Poupoule, rosy amaranth, is good. Souvenir de Montbrun, ochre yellow, tinted chestnut, is another. Mme. de Castelbajac and Mme. Plaque were also marked.

Auguste Nonin has raised some good seedlings and was awarded six first-class certificates. He, like Calvat, has a very good idea of a show flower and his catalogue contains some tiptoppers. He is one of the most genial and best liked men in the chrysanthemum world. He staged some fine groups of pot plants.

M. Leon Caveon showed standards, many of them grafted, curious to the general public, but of no great value from a cultural point of view. A Japanese gardener, W. Hata, showed trained plants of European varieties in big wooden boxes. He was awarded a gold medal for a composition of wire, wooden lattice work, foliage and flowers. These were pyramids in form, but it is doubtful if they were up to the best Japanese quality, like that described in the AMERICAN FLORIST of fourteen years ago as being done in the gardens of the Emperor of Japan.				P.

CHRYSANTHEMUMS AT LILLE, FRANCE.

The members of the French Chrysanthemum Society, although having their headquarters at Lyons, hold a show every year in some other town of France. They are jolly fellows and always make guests happy and at home. The writer knows them nearly all, has fraternized with them under various circumstances, and in divers places, so could not resist the temptation of going this year to their show at Lille, which opened November 6. A deputation of the English society went. The Palais Rameau is a capital building for the purpose of a show, and it was filled with a lot of very choice exhibits. Calvat and Nonin both showed seedlings. The former had some good ones

that were not at Paris. L. Liban, a fine yellow, was one, Vercingetorix, a deep golden yellow flushed reddish chestnut, another. Then we made a special note of Chrysanthemiste Remy, deep reddish carmine with golden reverse; Marquise

Visconti Venosta, immense in size, pure white; Maurice Rivoire, another big one, pale, rosy chestnut with gold reverse; Femina, a big lilac mauve; and Blondinette, deep primrose yellow, another of the big brigade.

Nonin's seedlings were also pretty good. M. Antonin Marmonbel, Prof. Gilliet, Leclaire Mulnard, Aug. Henri and Amateur Marchaud are the writer's selection for a possible place on the English show boards. Vases and floral compositions were pretty and effective. Drawing and dining room decorations were also taken well in hand by several local exhibitors.

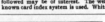

A conference was held on various subjects relating to insects and diseases, the rust, etc., at which there was a good attendance. Mr. Viger presided, as he also did at the banquet in the evening. This was a joyful occasion, English, Belgian and Dutch visitors being present.

The secretary, P. Rivoire, presented to Harman Payne, foreign secretary of the National Chrysanthemum Society of England, a silver gilt medal as a souvenir of the visit to Lille by the English deputation. The medal is of an artistic design quite new this year and is mounted on a crimson velvet stand with an inscription on a small tablet attached.			P.

EXHIBITION PLANNED AT PIEDMONT.

The Royal Horto-Agricultural Society of Piedmont, Italy, will celebrate the fiftieth year of its foundation in May, 1904. A grand international exposition is being organized to take place in Turin, Italy. The Dowager Queen of Italy is patroness and the Duke of Aosta honory president of the committee of honor. The schedule and prize list is an important one and comprises nearly 300 classes. The secretary is Mr. Palestrino. Entries close on March 30, 1904, and must be addressed to the executive committee, Rue Stampalori 4, Turin, Italy.		P.

Chrysanthemum Society of America.

VALUABLE RECORDS.

Several notes appeared in the trade papers shortly after the New York chrysanthemum show referring to the gift of Elmer D. Smith, of Adrian, Mich., to the Chrysanthemum Society of America, consisting of a list of all the varieties of chrysanthemums introduced in America since the early eighties. These records have now become the property of the C. S. A. and are in the hands of the secretary. The care with which the records have been compiled, the earnest and painstaking effort which has been made to cover the ground thoroughly, and the eminently practical and convenient manner in which the records are kept, call for the highest commendation from all lovers of the chrysanthemum throughout America. A brief explanation of the system followed may be of interest. The well known card index system is used. White

EXHIBITION OF FRENCH NATIONAL CHRYSANTHEMUM SOCIETY AT LILLE, NOV. 6, 1903

Flamingo. Albatross.

MARQUISEE'S TWO NEW CARNATIONS.

cards designate varieties raised in America, blue cards imported varieties and synonyms are placed on yellow cards. The name of the variety is given followed by the name of the introducer and the raiser when possible. The year it was sent out in the United States and the description complete the card. Each year the secretary of the society will add cards covering all the introductions of the twelve months, thus keeping the records up to date. When the report of the convention held in New York, November 10, is published a copy of this list will be included and will become the property of each member of the C. S. A.

FRED. H. LEMON, Sec'y.

WORK OF COMMITTEES.

At Boston, November 28, the following was shown:

Seedling No. 3-3-01: Light pink, shown by Nathan Smith & Son, Adrian, Mich.; scored 73 points, exhibition scale.

At Cincinnati, November 28, the following was shown:

No. 2—16—01., Bright deep pink, incurved Japanese, shown by Nathan Smith & Son, Adrian, Mich.; scored 83 points, commercial scale.

FRED. H. LEMON, Sec'y.

BOOKKEEPING and account forms for same by R. F. Tesson, as read at the Milwaukee convention has been printed in pamphlet form by the AMERICAN FLORIST and will be mailed FREE on request to any florist. Employers may have extra copies to distribute among their employes. The address is of much permanent value and well worth the study of our young men.

The Carnation.

L. E. MARQUISEE says that sales of Flamingo amounted to 200,000 November 24.

DORNER'S NOVELTIES.

The F. Dorner & Sons Company, of Lafayette, Ind., offers two highly meritorious novelties this season, namely, Lady Bountiful, an illustration of which appears in this issue, and The Belle. Both are white and have been highly spoken of as commercial varieties, the former having earned especially favorable comment.

A COMING SCARLET.

Amaze, the dazzling scarlet seedling, which Jerome Suydam of Flatbush, N. Y., will disseminate the coming season, gives good promise of being a remunerative Christmas carnation. It is well-known that a scarlet variety must do most of its work previous to January 1, as after that date the color finds but little demand. Mr. Suydam's houses at present are fairly ablaze. The flower is of medium size, but all the other characteristics required in a carnation to-day appear to be present and it is growing equally well on shallow bench and solid bed. Mr. Suydam states that it requires no shade. The variety is now in its fourth year.

Mr. Suydam has several more seedlings that are likely to be heard from in the future. One of these, a superb white was greatly admired at the Brooklyn exhibition last spring and is being grown in quantity now for the New York market. It was stated at the time that it was the progeny of Flora Hill × White Cloud.

Mr. Suydam desires to correct this now and states that the parentage was Flora Hill × Daybreak. In size of flower and stem it compares favorably with Lawson and the texture of the bloom is very heavy.

Mr. Suydam drifted into carnation growing from vegetable forcing some years ago, his first reputation being attained with Lizzie McGowan, a variety which he produced in such perfection as to make a decided sensation in the New York market. His soil is lighter than the typical Flatbush loam which is usually a heavy retentive clay and seems well suited to most carnations. One of the few sorts that do poorly with him is Lawson, a variety that has been more generally successful elsewhere than any carnation of recent years. Genevieve Lord, Wm. Scott and Queen Louise all do satisfactorily. Admiral Cervera is remarkably fine and has the reputation with Mr. Suydam of being the best money maker on the list. A brilliant crimson seedling, a cross between Pres. Roosevelt and Amaze, holds out good promise for the future.

PROPAGATING.

Settled cold weather with steady firing properly opens up the propagating season for carnations. The steady, cool temperature required to produce uniform success with this work is then at our command and for about three months we are reasonably free from some of the harrowing details that attend a fluctuating temperature and changing atmosphere. Those who have solved the problem of rooting carnation cuttings by years of experience consider it a very ordinary thing to root from ninety-five per cent to

HOUSE OF CYCLAMENS GROWN BY E. HAASCH, MILWAUKEE, WIS.

one hundred per cent of nearly every batch put in, where conditions are well under control, while to beginners the most vexatious problems present themselves, and a good strike is often the exception rather than the rule. It is for the benefit of the latter that I wish to point out some of the most essential points in handling a batch of cuttings.

A cool, moderately dry atmosphere is a primary necessity and there should be little fluctuation in the temperature. These conditions are probably best obtained in a north side lean-to house. But comparatively few of us have a regular propagating house and we are forced to employ space in our regular carnation houses for this work. In that case the north bench of an even span house is the best place. To obtain a mild bottom heat the heating pipes should be partially or wholly shut in by nailing up the front and back with boards. When it is desired to shut off the heat only partially a strip of muslin tacked on either edge and dropped down to within a few inches of the ground answers very well. To afford an ideal shade another strip of muslin is hung vertically from the roof, flush with the front edge of the bench. This shuts off the cutting space from the rest of the house, yet admits a constant change of air, and the slanting rays of the sun are excluded. Towards spring, when the sun rises above the shading material, it is necessary to supplement it with paper laid directly on the cuttings for part of the day. There should be no heating pipes near the cuttings overhead or along the sides of the bench and whatever pipes are beneath the bench should be far enough away to allow the heat from them to become diffused so as not to heat up one part of the bench more than another. During extra hard firing it is well to keep the walk sprinkled to charge the air with a moderate degree of moisture. There should be no drip from overhead and the bench should be well drained. Standing water is as injurious to a cutting as it is to a growing plant. The sand should be rather sharp, composed of grains that do not lie too compactly together. Such a sand drains freely and if the bottom of the bench does not act as a stop to the water there will

be little danger of over-watering for the first two weeks. Slate or brick, being good conductors of heat, probably makes the best bottom for a propagating bench, but we have always had very good success with the ordinary board bottom. The boards, wherever the sand or cuttings came in contact with them, should be thoroughly whitewashed with hot lime wash to which a quart of salt to the pailful has been added. Leave the cracks open until the wash is thoroughly dry, then plug them up with sphagnum moss, but leave the moss loose enough to allow the water to pass through freely. The sand, which should be perfectly clean and free from all clods and stones, goes on top of this to the depth of from two to four inches, is levelled off, well firmed and thoroughly watered.

An experienced man with a good eye and sound judgment should take the cuttings from the plants and see that they are properly labeled. Only well devel-

oped growths should be taken. The rest of the work until the cuttings are in the sand is comparatively simple. The side growths taken from the flowering stems need very little trimming. They are best taken off clean down to the base or heel of the lateral by grasping firmly between the thumb and first two fingers and giving a steady upward and sideways pull, steadying the plant with the other hand. In this way that objectionable "tail" at at the base of the cutting is avoided. If the leaves are overly long it is well to cut them back about one third their length. Any straggly leaves at the base should be cut away with a sharp knife. During all this work the cuttings should be kept sprinkled to prevent wilting and to keep the wound at the base from searing over. When the sand has been well firmed and thoroughly watered you are ready to insert the cuttings. An old table knife is the only tool necessary, if you can draw a straight line without a ruler. A slit is drawn straight across the bench, deep enough to admit the cuttings to a sufficient depth to hold them upright after they are thoroughly watered. When one row is full press the sand firmly against each cutting with the fingers and proceed with the next row. It is best not to have the cuttings so close together that the roots of one cutting will get tangled with those of its neighbor. Three-quarters of an inch in the row is close enough and with this extra allowance of room in the row the rows can be put closer together, the distance depending upon the size of the cuttings. To allow a free circulation of air around each cutting it is necessary to give them enough space so that the greater part of the sand will be visible. When eight or ten rows have been finished water thoroughly. This first watering is of great importance and cannot be overdone if the bench is well drained. After that it is only necessary to give a light watering early in the morning for the first two weeks to refresh the sand and a sprinkling with a fine spray two or three times a day. Always see that the cuttings have time to dry off by nightfall.

With the sand at a temperature of 60° to 65° and the top about 50° the cuttings will take about thirty days to root. After the first two weeks the most crit-

PALMS AT THE GEORGE WITTBOLD COMPANY'S, CHICAGO.

ical time is over and it will be safe to reduce the watering and sprinkling gradually, until the beginning of the last week, when very little water will be needed, either overhead or in the sand. It is well to give the full sun during this week. This hardens the cuttings up somewhat and prepares them for the transfer to the soil. The cuttings should be thoroughly rooted before the transplanting. After transplanting shade from the bright sunshine for the first week.

Cleanliness is a vital point to watch and no decaying vegetable matter should ever find its way near the cuttings. The freer the sand is from litter of any kind and the nearer it comes to being composed entirely of fine grains of stone the smaller will be the danger of infection from the myriads of germs floating in the air. The cuttings themselves should be clean in every respect and perfectly healthy. A bruised leaf is an ideal starting point for rot or fungus. Attention has often been called in these notes to the importance of selecting cuttings only from healthy plants. Plants showing undesirable qualities, such as weak stems, a large proportion of split calyxes, poorly developed flowers, or a tendency to run to grass rather than bloom must be avoided as well, in order to keep the stock up to a high standard.   J.

Florists' Plant Notes.

AZALEAS.

As soon as the azaleas have opened about a dozen flowers to the plant they should be removed to a cooler house for a week or two before being offered for sale. A temperature of 55° is about right in which to harden them off. To be sure, a plant with most of its flowers developed will make a better show for a time, but it is questionable if it will give the same satisfaction to the customer as one with about half the flowers developed and the other half buds. The backward ones can stand extreme forcing to bring them into flower on time; 75° or even 80° at night is not too high, if this extreme heat is necessary. Warm water given daily will also hurry them along, but overhead syringing must cease as soon as the buds commence to open. A few days before Christmas, before they are offered for sale over the counter, the pots should be dressed neatly with crepe paper and ribbon, which will add greatly to their appearance and incidentally to the price.

GLOIRE DE LORRAINE.

This marvelous begonia is by far the leading favorite as a Christmas plant. A well grown plant in a 6-inch pan, with its mass of pink flowers, is a sight to behold. Stand them on inverted 6-inch pots, so as to keep the overhanging flowers from becoming soiled, and also to allow the circulation of air around the plants. Do not let tobacco smoke get near them, for it fades the flowers, but keep fresh stems scattered between the pots. Water carefully with the can or with the hose, with a small stream of water turned on so as not to wet the flowers. A temperature of 56° to 58° at night is about right. Grown under proper conditions this plant adapts itself quite well to the dwelling room, where its flowers will hang on for a long time. For festival occasions, however, it is chiefly valuable, for a good plant will make as good an appearance as a nice vase of roses, and will last a great deal longer.

DORNER'S NEW CARNATION LADY BOUNTIFUL.

POINSETTIAS.

These plants should have their bracts well formed by this time. For decorating purposes, both as plants and cut flowers, they are invaluable. They must never be subjected to the slightest chill, or the leaves and bracts will droop and turn yellow. For selling over the counter we find made-up pans chiefly in demand. Those grown to single stems in six-inch pots are usually too tall to use for any thing excepting decorating. These pans can be made up at once, and the sooner the better. Three nice stocky plants from 4-inch pots will nicely fill an 8-inch pan and leave a little room for several small ferns along the edge to add to its appearance. Single plants in 4 or 5-inch pots are also in great demand. In transplanting them into pans, the roots must not be disturbed or the leaves are liable to drop. These plants can safely be recommended to any customer, for they

will always give good value for the money. The foliage soon drops in a living room, but the fiery bracts hang on for many weeks.

CYCLAMENS.

There are few plants that make more desirable Christmas gifts than the ever popular cyclamen. A well grown plant in a 7-inch pot, dressed with crepe paper and ribbon, with its handsome foliage and mass of bloom, combined with its great durability as a house plant, make it a universal favorite. These plants should be placed on inverted 6-inch pots and should have tobacco stems scattered between the pots as the best means to keep down aphis, which, if left undisturbed, will soon cripple the young foliage and buds. They cannot stand tobacco smoke when in bloom, for it ruins the flowers. Be careful in watering not to wet the flowers, but turn the water on gently and water each plant separately. A night temperature of 55° is what they require.

PRIMULAS.

For a cheap plant the different varieties of primulas (Sinensis, obconica, and Forbesi) are still valuable, for they stand the dwelling house atmosphere well, blooming freely for several months, and for this reason are popular with those who can not afford more expensive plants. Keep water away from the flowers and give them a temperature of about 50° at night. Plants from 4 to 5-inch pots, made up into pans with small ferns interspersed along the edge, are salable articles. They are rarely troubled with aphis or any other kind of insects, but if any pests do appear tobacco smoke does not harm them.

G.

Plant Notes at J. M. Keller's.

"Example is always more efficacious than precept." To nothing does this old saying apply more forcibly than to the occupation of plant growing. Inspiration comes in big waves to one when inspecting the finely finished productions of the accomplished grower and we are ready to believe, to quote again from the same author, that "few things are impossible to diligence and skill."

J. M. Keller, of Bay Ridge, is one of the the pioneers in decorative plant growing for the New York market. Although unassuming and quiet in manner, we have always found Mr. Keller disposed to give cheerfully and unreservedly of the fruit of his long experience for the benefit of his fellow gardeners through the medium of the AMERICAN FLORIST. Doubly interesting and instructive are the maxims of such a man when exemplified by the practical illustrations afforded in a stroll through the well stocked houses.

On a recent visit we were glad to note that the imported azaleas run very fine in quality this year and are as a rule much more fully furnished with buds than were those of last year's importation. This is an agreeable surprise, for the summer in the azalea growing section of Europe was cold and rainy. We noted especially a nice lot of that little gem of an azalea, Carl Enke, the dwarf pink now so pop la for mixed plant baskets and jardinieres; which a few years ago was regarded abroad as undesirable stock, but of which the American trade now calls for more than can be supplied. Mr. Keller, referring to the frequent failures of growers in blooming this pretty little subject, says that it will stand no forcing and the trouble is caused by ignorance or oversight of this fact. To insure blooming he advises careful watching to keep side growths from starting around the flower buds and prompt pinching-off when such do appear. This must be followed up religiously and attended to a dozen times during the winter if necessary.

Cypripedium insigne is blooming a month or more ahead of the average time. This is interesting and an explanation is not readily found as the plants were outside until October 1, after a cold and wet summer. Had the season been exceptionally hot so that the plants would have pe fe ted their growth and matured early then the early flowering would be easily accounted for.

Mr. Keller's system in poinsettia growing may be interesting to some. They are seen here even in late fall in all stages from the cutting bed up to plants six feet high. This is to supply the varying demands of buyers. The later the cuttings the smaller the flowering plant. The tallest plants occupy a solid bed and are intended to accommodate the call for heavy heads of cut bloom and afterwards will be used for stock from which to propagate, year-old plants being superior to old stock, the latter being regarded as undesirable as plants or for cuttings. The younger plants in their various stages are intended for pan stock. the demand for low effects for Christmas, in small pans, being very great. Mr. Keller believes in liberal feeding and the maintaining of the temperature at a minimum of 60°. Poinsettias do not like to get pot bound and when in pans or stinted pot room they must have ample nourishment to prevent shedding their leaves.

Speaking of Acacia armata, which has now taken a leading place among the higher grades of Easter plants, Mr. Keller states that fall imported plants give inferior results and cannot compare with those brought over in the spring and carried through the summer here, where they set buds much better than they do in Europe, if kept outdoors all summer. His experience is that it is not much use to try to hold over and develop plants that were unsalable last spring. Old plants of erica, however, should not be thrown away. Unsold plants should be cut back moderately and allowed to make their growth in the greenhouse before being put outside, which will be the case about the middle of June. The past season has proved a hard one for all the heaths, having been too wet. Plants of E. melanthera and cupressina from cuttings struck last spring are very uneven. Persoluta rosea looks rather better and is apparently fitted to withstand more water than the above-named species. Heaths of the fancy large-flowered sorts, such as Wilmoreana, blanda, etc., are better grown continuously under glass, and it is a mistake to put them outside. As to Cavendishii, that is too slow of growth for profitable raising here and the plants are best imported in full sizes.

Boronias have been kept outside with frame protection throughout the fall. This year's plants are in excellent condition, but of those left over last spring and planted out under identical conditions fully one-half are dead. Mr. Keller is unable to account for this peculiarity, which, however, is not a new experience.

A bench of hybrid Primula obconica from Ronsdorf's German seed is very interesting in the wide variety of coloring and foliage exhibited. The flowers are in all shades from white to crimson. The darker shades find the best market, the light tints being in but small demand. Many of the plants show a marked development of the so-called "fern-leaf" foliage common in the Chinese primrose. These plants have but recently been taken in from the frames where they have spent the summer under partial sash protection.

Cocos Weddelliana is having a good sale this year. Small plants when not good enough for sale as specimens are made up into nice little groups of three or four in a 6-inch pot. Thus arranged they are disposed of without difficulty.

Mr. Keller keeps his houses on the cool side always and refrains from fire heat as long as possible in the fall. This policy generally followed would produce harder stock, which would give more satisfaction to the buyers and we should hear less complaint of short-lived plants and the accompanying disappointment.

Growing Easter Lilies.

My observations in the cultivation of Lilium Harrisii and L. longiflorum lead me to think one-half of the disease and failure in growing is due to negligence or lack of proper care on the part of the grower. On the arrival of the bulbs at our houses we pot at once five to seven and seven to nine bulbs in 6-inch pots in a compost of thoroughly rotted cow manure, rotted turf and a little sand. Some of the smaller bulbs we put two in a pot. We place them in pits and in a shady location, giving one thorough watering, and no more unless they get dry, which does not often occur, as we keep them closely shaded with shutters until the growth commences to appear, when they are at once put in frames in the early fall months, in full sunlight, protected with glass at night if necessary. As it gets colder we remove to a cool house and place on benches near the glass, removing to lower benches as the tops rise. From December on we are very careful to maintain an even temperature of 50° at night and not over 70° in the day time. We find the plants do the best and are the healthiest when not exposed to lower temperature. We are careful never to give sudden checks. We transfer to warmer or colder houses as the growth demands to make them bloom at Easter, or any other time we want them in flower. We do all the retarding after the buds commence to appear.

Care in watering is very essential, always avoiding over watering, keeping a gentle moisture and giving frequent syringings on pleasant days. We give no liquid manure until the buds commence to form, and then very weak, as often an overdose burns the ends of the leaves. A gentle fumigation once a week and a little tobacco dust sprinkled on the tops keep off the greenfly. Don't wait until you can see them. Turn your pots around once a fortnight if you want straight stems. Our experience is that lilies require constant attention if you wish straight stems, good foliage and fine flowers. The Japan bulbs are potted and put under the carnation benches at a temperature of about 50° to 54°. They will root in the pots quicker and less disease results than when rooted in cooler temperature with this method of growing. We always have fine flowers of solid texture, straight stems and foliage down to the pot.

F. O. W.

The New Version.

An Irishman went into a florist's store and asked the clerk for a floral piece for a good friend that was dead. He was also anxious that a "foine" inscription should be put on the piece. The clerk asked him if he thought the inscription "May he rest in peace," would be appropriate.

"Well, now, not just that exactly," replied the Irishman. "But you know it is for Mulligan, who was blown up in the explosion at the stone yards yesterday, so if it is all the same to you I would like to have the inscription read, 'May he rest in pieces.'"—Boston Traveler.

ROCKFORD, ILL.—The thirty-seventh annual meeting of the Northern Illinois Horticultural Society was held here December 9–10.

BROCKTON, MASS.—C. S. Cooper has filed a voluntary petition in bankruptcy, with liabilities of $7,500; assets nominal. The greenhouses will be sold December 23 under foreclosure of mortgage.

The Retail Trade.

FLAT BOUQUET OF SIMPLE DESIGN.

The accompanying illustration shows a novel flat bouquet for funeral use made by Henry Morris, of Syracuse, N. Y. Mr. Morris says that this is a bouquet which people who are not in favor of floral display will buy, on account of its simplicity and daintiness. It consists of palm leaves, asparagus sprays and roses tied with lavender ribbon. The very best of everything is used, which makes quite an expensive bouquet.   A. J. B.

THE ARTIST.

Being a New Yorker, and somewhat of an observer, I never miss an opportunity to gaze into the windows of our flower stores, or floral palaces, as some of them may truly be called. The subject of window decoration is most important and we all strive to make them as beautiful as possible. I have noticed that the most attractive windows have generally the least material in them. The idea is not how much but how little may be used to get the best effect. We cannot put all our goods in the window, so let what we do use be of the very finest. I have often heard the remark; "Those are on their last legs, put them in the window." This is bad advice. Let the public see how good your stock is, not how bad.

One store on Broadway rarely has more than two or three large vases of flowers in the window, usually filled with American Beauty roses, or chrysanthemums with a few choice flowers to fill up corners. The vases are always in keeping with the flowers, and are often works of art. Ribbon is also used and is tied into good generous sashes or artfully intermingled with the flowers. Smilax is laid gracefully over the tiling to take away the bareness. Another store on this avenue gets splendid effects much in the same way, but depends more on mirror accessories, the window appearing almost bare at times except for a basket or two of fresh flowers artistically decorated with ribbon and perhaps a few pieces of "the latest thing" in Tiffany glassware placed here and there.

A window on Fifth avenue attracts much attention. The center is taken up by a huge tree stump about three feet high and eighteen inches in diameter. There is an immense piece of fungus growing from it. The trunk was cut several inches below the ground, giving it a very rustic and natural appearance. The center has been cut out and has been kept filled of late with a huge bunch of chrysanthemums. The remaining part of the window is filled with ferns and foliage plants, and a perfect carpet of Selaginella denticulata. Another pretty store is on Madison avenue, where I saw recently a unique display. It was filled with pretty opened parasols tastefully decorated with yellow chrysanthemums, and the effect was very good.

A flower shop which has recently been torn down is well worth a few lines here. The main window space was devoted to foliage and flowering plants, while one large window was taken up entirely by the ice box. This I am told was an original idea of the owner. It had many advantages. The entire stock of flowers could be seen from the avenue. They were kept in excellent condition and the arrangement proved to be a great drawing card.

OLEAN, N. Y.—Llewellyn has opened a branch store at 228 N. Union street.

A FLAT BOUQUET.

Chicago.

ALL KINDS OF STOCK IS SHORT.—GOOD CHRISTMAS OUTLOOK.—ALL FLOWERS BRING FAIR PRICES.—ANNIVERSARY OF GARDENERS' AND FLORISTS' UNION.— TRADE NOTES.

The situation of the local market may be expressed in a few words, as one dealer remarked, "if there were more flowers there would be more business." Trade has been as good as the incoming cut will permit, everything except the usual holiday decorative material being painfully short. It is clearly evident that the pick-ling process has already commenced. Carnations have not opened up a bit since last week and their shortage is still more noticeable. Liberty roses are also weak, although some dealers will have good cuts for Christmas. Except carnations, the demand just about cleaned up the stock each day this week. Clean up sales at satisfactory prices are common. The outlook for a brisk Christmas trade is encouraging, and the dealers expect to have their hands full. Shipping started out well on Monday, the early foreign holiday buyers getting in before the rush. Bouquet green is scarce and commands a stiff price. A slight increase of prices is noted all along the line in decorative material this year. Everyone is praying for increased stock as the little now coming in would be entirely inadequate to the expected heavy demand, which will be in force next week.

The third trade exhibition of holiday plants given by the Florists' Club will be held Wednesday evening, December 16, in the Atlas block. The show will be under the management of Frank Benthey, who is sparing no pains to make it a success. C. A. Samuelson, J. F. Kidwell and George Stollery will act as judges. Prizes have been offered by Peter Reinberg and Wietor Brothers for meritorious displays of specimen flowering plants, berried plants. decorative and foliage plants. The exhibition will be followed by a club meeting, and papers will be read by W. J. Smyth and J. S. Wilson. The next regular meeting of the club will be held January 6.

The Gardeners' and Florists' union has been in existence just one year. The members of the union appropriately celebrated the anniversary Wednesday evening, in their quarters, 106 Randolph street. An informal programme ,was carried out. The annual election of officers will occur Wednesday, December 23.

The Geo. Witthold Company's Christmas stock of decorative plants is unexcelled and they are enjoying a heavy patronage. The stock at their Edgebrook branch is coming on nicely for spring. They are executing many elaborate decorations in the retail stores.

The comparative scarcity and stiff prices of bouquet green will have the effect of putting smilax and asparagus into favor as the Christmas decorating material this year.

The bowlers are finally getting themselves into an organised; state. Until January, when the schedule begins in earnest, only desultory games will be played.

Amling is getting the fine cut of Weber & Brothers' Brides and Bridesmaids, which are coming in in splendid quality for the Christmas and spring trade.

E. F. Winterson Company is making a specialty of wild smilax and Christmas berries, their stock of which is quite extensive and of superior grade.

Peter Reinberg is enjoying a good run on his new Uncle John and Chatenay roses. The former has certainly made a hit.

The A. L. Randall Company is getting many early Christmas orders and they have good stock to fill them with.

The retail stores are taking on their Christmas dresses. Holly appears to be the favorite material used.

The scarcity of stock is an indication that much is already being pickled to spring at the eleventh hour.

Local glass factories are represented at an important meeting of the glass industry at Pittsburg this week.

Wietor Brothers' outlook for a fine Christmas crop of roses and carnations is particularly bright.

Matthew Weber has secured a building permit for five greenhouses, each 23½x120 feet.

Some nice sheet moss and Christmas berries are to be seen at Frank Garland's.

E. F. Winterson has entirely recovered from his recent indisposition.

John Lambros paid Milwaukee a business visit on Wednesday.

J. B. Deamud is out of the city for a few days on business.

Among the visitors this week were Mr. and Mrs. F. H. Holton. Milwaukee, Wis., and Prof. J. C. Blair, of Champaign, Ill.

New York.

BUSINESS SLACK.—STOCK IN GENERAL IS SCARCE.—FLOWERING PLANTS IN THE STORES.—NOTES OF THE TRADE.

Business at present is very slack. It has always been so a few weeks before the holidays. The supply of most flowers is light and with but little demand. Lilies are coming in more plentifully and bring very fair prices. Roman hyacinths are in in very limited quantities. Paper White narcissi are coming in very abundantly and no doubt they will sell well this Christmas, on account of the scarcity of Roman hyacinths. White carnations are also scarce, and the outlook so far is that there will be very few for the holidays. Flowering plants, such as azaleas, primroses, begonias and poinsettias are in most of the stores; no doubt this year will see a good sale for them if the prices of cut flowers are as high as in former years

Flower thieves are busy again. December 1 they visited L. Dupuy, of Whitestone, and deprived him of all the flowers he had, besides helping themselves to a bicycle. Whoever these miscreants are there is no doubt they are the same as visited Woodside establishments last year. They take the cuttings from the carnations after they are picked. Last fall one was arrested and pleaded guilty and is now serving a five year sentence.

Fred Smith and Miss Rose Eberhardt, both of Woodside, L. I., were married last Saturday evening. The bride was given away by her father, August H. Eberhardt. Alexander Smith was best man. After the ceremony supper was laid, in which a large company joined, with the good wishes of all for a happy married life.

E. Chanroux, of Flushing, L. I., died last Sunday, December 5. The deceased was a member of the Cut Flower Exchange and that association sent a beautiful floral piece in remembrance. He leaves a son, who will take care of the business.

August Copin, of Jefferson Market, was shot in the wrist by a next-door neighbor at his home in West Hoboken early in the morning of December 7. He had mistaken another house for his own and was taken for a burglar. He will lose his hand.

Arthur Herrington read a paper on the chrysanthemum at the American Institute December 9.

Visitors: Mrs. A. W. Williams, Pittsburg, Pa.; Robert Kift, Philadelphia; Paul Berkowits, of Bayersdorfer & Company, Philadelphia.

Philadelphia.

PLENTY OF GOOD STOCK FOR HOLIDAY TRADE.—OUTLOOK NOT GOOD FOR ACTIVE SEASON.—STILL SOME CHRYSANTHEMUMS.—GENERAL NOTES.

The prospects for Christmas are not much improved by early orders, and the concensus of opinion is that the volume of business will not exceed that of last season. Preparations for the holiday trade are going on, however, with all branches of the trade, and there will no doubt be plenty of stock for the demand. The growers who furnish blooming and other Christmas plants have many good things to offer. W. K. Harris has a first-class novelty in his new yellow primrose buttercup. It is a very showy plant, with

spikes of bloom crowding one another all over the pot. Each spike carries two or three whorls of flowers. It is in effect like a well flowered obconica, of a good brown color. It seems to be easy to grow, as it is in full flower in different temperatures. His other plants are holly trees, aucubas, full of red berries, also a house of Jerusalem cherries and peppers, oranges and lemons; Dracæna terminalis and made-up pans of the same and Boston ferns; Pandanus Veitchii, well colored and in various sizes; azaleas, nice showy plants in quantity, and a line of imported evergreens in pots. His stock cf Boston ferns in all sizes is fine.

Robt. Craig & Son are right in it with cyclamens, having a large quantity of well flowered plants. begonias, ardisias, well berried, and azaleas in quantity. Also Astilbe Japonica in good shape, a novelty at this time, and a fine lot of crotons.

Trade in the stores this week has been fair, but with plenty of room for improvement. Chrysanthemums still hang on and sell fairly well.

John Westcott has a fine lot of poinsettias, begonias, Gloire de Lorraine, callas, stevia, and his usual fine Jerusalem cherries.

The supply men say that red immortelles, bells, and other Christmas goods have sold very well.

Ziegenhalter has some ten thousand poinsettias; all nice plants, from 4 to 6-inch pots.

J. W. Colflesh has stevia, begonias, callas, and a choice lot of decorative plants.

Jacob Becker has a nice lot of azaleas very well flowered.

Griffin Bros. also have a nice lot of this plant.   K.

Boston.

There is no rush of business here this week, but a fair demand for about all the first-class flowers that come in. The prices received Thanksgiving week could not be maintained except on American Beauty, which have sold at from $5 and $6 per dozen for the best specials down to $1 a dozen for the smaller grade. Bride and Bridesmaid are in fair demand. This is not so much on account of demand as it is because the stock of the majority of the growers is off crop at this time. Carnations go slowly compared with a week ago. They are plentiful and chrysanthemums continue to come to the market. Lily of the valley, violets and Lilium Harrisii are moving satisfactorily, but of the latter only a limited supply is available.

The meeting of the Gardeners' and Florists' Club, held at Horticultural Hall, Tuesday evening, December 8, was very large and enthusiastic. Ten new members were admitted. Important changes in the constitution were proposed and will be acted upon at the next meeting. John K. M. L. Farquhar and Robert Cameron each read a paper on annuals, which caused a lively discussion. Jerome Suydam, of Flatbush, N. Y., exhibited two fine carnations, one unnamed, white, and Amaze, scarlet, and received honorable mention for them.

Visitors: J. D. Thompson, Joliet, Ill.; R. E. Moffis and Ernest Chamberlain, New Bedford, Mass.; T. J. Johnson, Providence, R. I.; John Scott, Brooklyn, N. Y.; Geo. Ferguson, Lenox, Mass.

SPRINGFIELD, MASS. — The Amateur Horticultural Society held an interesting meeting December 4.

St. Louis.

GOOD WESTERN TRADE.—GREEN IS SCARCE AS ELSEWHERE.—WORLD'S FAIR DECORATIONS IN PROGRESS.—NOTES.

Trade continues good and from reports it is much better than in former years. Stock is plentiful one day and scarce the next. Greens are offered at high prices, but in limited quantities. Carnations, excepting white, and roses are plentiful enough to meet the demand. Poinsettias in pans are seen in all the show windows, though stock of this kind is held back for holiday trade.

The American Association for the Advancement of Science, Dr. Wm. Trelease, of Missouri Botanic Garden, president, holds its annual meeting the latter part of December. At the same time the Society of Horticultural Science will hold its first meeting. The Plant and Animal Breeders' Association will also be in session. Prof. W. M. Hayes, of St. Paul, is acting secretary. Prof. S. A. Beach, of Geneva, N. Y., is secretary of the Society of Horticultural Science.

A Meyer, of South Jefferson avenue, believes in keeping up with the times. At present he is building a handsome show house, which will be fitted throughout with all the latest appliances. When completed the place will compare favorably with any in the city. Mr. Meyer is inclined to think that his locality does not warrant the building of such a structure, but trade will come to those who have the conveniences to take care of it. What will be left of Forest Park "after the fair" remains to be seen. The prevailing opinion is that the park can be gotten in as good shape as formerly, which may be true, but future generations will get the benefit of it. At present visitors going west on the park drives have to pass through the "lions' den" and then bump up against the World's Fair fence.

Swain Nelson & Sons and the Peterson Nursery Company, of Chicago, have just completed the installation of their exhibits at the horticultural grounds at the World's Fair. The exhibits are of herbaceous plants, shrubs and stems.

Wm. Schray & Sons and A. Jabolnsky are sending in some excellent Begonia Gloire de Lorraine. The plants are equal to any that the eastern growers offer St. Louis dealers.

Visitors: Wm. A. Bastian, with Kellogg, of Kansas City, Mo.

Washington.

BUSINESS EXPERIENCES LULL BEFORE THE HOLIDAYS.—STOCK NOT OVER PLENTIFUL.—FINE CROTONS IN GOVERNMENT GARDENS.—NOTES OF THE TRADE.

Though business is fair it ought to be better at this season. On account of mourning in several of the leading families of the official circle, and for other reasons not so readily understood, there has been but little entertaining. An occasional wedding, dinner or tea keeps something doing, but the masses seem to be quietly awaiting Christmas. In the meantime the florists are taking advantage of the lull and have their help busy on wreaths and decorative work. Stock even now is not over plentiful and will be scarce at Christmas. The local rose growers have very good American Beauty roses that retail at from $6 per dozen for medium stems to $10 for the longest. Bride and Bridesmaid are from $1.50 to $3 per dozen. There is a slight improvement in the quality of carnations, but the stems are short and too many blooms are sleepy. Some of the so-called fancies do

not seem to be much of an improvement on the old knockabouts, but they are held at $1.50 per dozen, the common kinds selling at 50 cents per dozen. Violets are $1 per bunch and from present indications will bring that price for some time to come. There are yet some good chrysanthemums.

Z. D. Blackistone's window decoration this week is a model of the White House made from wood placed in the White House in 1816 and taken out in 1902. There is also a good supply of souvenirs from White House wood at prices ranging from 25 cents up. The proceeds go to a charitable institution.

Those who are fond of striking effects in color should visit the house of crotons at the government propagating gardens. It is doubtful if a better collection of crotons can be found in any city. There are also a fine lot of marantas, all grown under the direction of Geo. H. Brown, landscape gardener.

Several dealers have received from Peterson, of Cincinnati, very fine Begonia Gloire de Lorraine in 7-inch pots. Geo. H. Cook has several in his show window banked with palms and ferns, cornucopias yielding Adiantum Farleyense and spice berries suspended over all. The effect is fine.

A landmark, a log house, on the Garden estate, was burned the morning after Thanksgiving. The house was very old but was well preserved and was once the family home, being the birthplace of Alex. B. Garden, the florist.

The weather is fine, which is a godsend to the growers, who look for a good Christmas stock of cut flowers. There has been some stiff freezing, 20° being about the lowest.

Gottlieb Tuppy, formerly with Henry Pfister, and Frank Fleury, formerly with Spitzer in the Grant Place flower store, are now with Geo. C. Shaffer.   S. E.

Buffalo.

TRADE IS GOOD OWING TO MUCH FUNERAL WORK.—SNOW MAKES GOOD SLEIGHING, AIDING BUSINESS.—STOCK IS PLENTIFUL.

Trade last week was good but it was mostly funeral work. The supply of stock has been very good but now you can see the effects of all growers laying back and saving up flowers.

S. A. Anderson had a varied lot of work one day last week for a funeral—a fish, an hour glass, a boat and a ship anchor—rather odd pieces for one day. As these notes are being written, I can look and see the "beautiful snow" falling and sleighs are out for the first time. If it will continue until Christmas and give us good sleighing business will certainly be good.

Recent visitors: Felix Meyers, of Robt. Craig & Son, Philadelphia; Harry Bunyard, of Clucas & Boddington, New York, and Ed. Fancourt, of Philadelphia. Robert Avery, of West Seneca, N. Y., has a fine lot of cyclamens that W. F. Kasting is handling for him.   BISON.

Cincinnati.

Trade the past week was fair with an increased supply and demand for carnations so the supply was not enough to fill orders. Quality is also improving and $4 and $5 per 100 is what the good ones bring. White carnations have the call and are scarce. Good violets are scarce and easily bring $1.50 per 100. There are enough roses for all orders with the exception of first-class Bridesmaid of which a few hundred more could

be used to good advantage every day. Valley has not been in active demand here of late and quite a lot of these find their way to the barrel. Paper White narcissi have made their appearance, the first coming in from George & Allan. A fine lot of pointsettia are also to be had. We also have the winter berries with us and these with holly and festooning remind one of the near approach of Christmas. This market will be very short on carnations for the holiday and good prices will prevail.

The regular monthly meeting of the Cincinnati Florists' Society will be held at the club rooms in the Jabez Elliott Flower Market December 12 and important business will be transacted.

Albert Heckman, Sr., will be found at his Covington, Ky., store hereafter and his son Albert Heckman, Jr., has taken his place at J. M. McCullough's Sons.   ALEX.

Milwaukee.

While stock has not been at all plentiful, yet there has been sufficient for all demands except an occasional late order. White carnations have been rather short lately and are in consequence holding right up to quoted prices. Valley is plentiful with a moderate demand. Beauties are in supply equal to the demand. There is plenty of green goods and some to spare. Holly has made its appearance and some good stock has been noted but it is mostly southern holly. Southern green is practically out of the market, but few crates being on hand and these are held at $9.00 per 100 pounds.

Fred. Kaiser has returned from his hunting trip and what is more important, he kindly sent the writer a few birds and they were extra fine.

Holton & Hunkel Company are now Milwaukee agents for Caldwell's K wality Kounts brand of wild smilax. Indications point to a shortage of carnations for Christmas. Prices on this item will surely be away up.

J. M. Fox is making lavish use of immortelle bells in his window for Christmas display.

Fred. Schmeling, who has been on the sick list for a few weeks, is about again.   H.

Richmond, Ind.

Councilman Neal reported to council December 7 that he understood an effort was being made to induce the E. G. Hill Company to remove its plant from the city. He stated that Indianapolis and New Castle were both trying to get the big greenhouses, and that as the company could not secure ground on which to enlarge its plant, the members of the company were seriously considering the idea of leaving the city. At the suggestion of Mr. Neal a special committee was appointed to confer with members of the company and see what could be done to induce them to remain in Richmond.

J. A. Evans, of the Quaker City Machine Company, has been awarded the contract to ventilate the government building at the St. Louis World's Fair.

TORONTO, ONT.—A. M. Ford, who opened a new retail store on King street, west, recently, reports that he is doing very well. Mr. Ford has had considerable experience in the business and the trade wish him all success in his venture.

THE AMERICAN FLORIST

NINETEENTH YEAR.

Subscription, $1.00 a year. To Europe, $2.00.
    Subscriptions accepted only from those
        in the trade.

Advertisements, on all except cover pages,
    10 Cents a Line, Agate; $1.00 per inch.
        Cash with Order.

No Special Position Guaranteed.

Discounts are allowed only on consecutive inser-
    tions, as follows—6 times, 5 per cent; 13 times,
    10 per cent; 26 times, 20 per cent;
        52 times, 30 per cent.

Cover space sold only on yearly contract at
    $1.00 per inch, net, in the case of the two
    front pages, regular discounts apply-
        ing only to the back pages.

The Advertising Department of the AMERICAN
FLORIST is for florists, seedsmen and nurserymen
and dealers in wares pertaining to those lines only.

Orders for less than one-half inch space not accepted.

Advertisements must reach us by Wednesday to
secure insertion in the issue for the following
Saturday.   Address

AMERICAN FLORIST CO., Chicago.

Swamped With Orders.

AMERICAN FLORIST CO.—Your last issue
brought more returns than I ever had
from any paper; practically swamped
with orders.   D. S. BEACH.
Bridgeport, Conn.

"M. S." should remember that unsigned
communications go to the waste-paper
basket.

IN the *Craftsman* for November there
is an appreciative article on the late
Frederick Law Olmsted, by Arthur
Spencer, with full-page portrait and
other illustrations. Copies may be had
of the United Crafts, Syracuse, N. Y., at
25 cents each.

Fort Smith Flower Show.

ED. AM. FLORIST.—In your report of
the exhibition of the Fort Smith flower
show you state that H. W. Buckbee won
the prize on the best twelve yellow chrysanthemums. This is an error, as the
prize for the best yellow was won by the
Muskogee Carnation Company with
their Col. Appleton.
        MUSKOGEE CARNATION CO.

Dyeing Lycopodium.

For dyeing dry or faded lycopodium a
mineral green is used; costing about $3
per pound. One half teaspoonful of the
dye to a wash boiler about three-fourths
full of hot water, thoroughly dissolved,
makes the solution in which the green
should be dipped. After dipping fifteen
or twenty bunches of the green add more
water and the same proportion of the
dye. Spread the bunches in a warm
place to dry.

Society of American Florists.

DEPARTMENT OF REGISTRATION.

Vaughan's Seed Store, Chicago and
New York, submits for registration the
following new cannas:
St. Louis (Seedling 801).—Robust
grower, five feet, three to five spikes;
foliage dark bronze; flower crimson-
scarlet; petals large, rounded, with
glossy surface; dry flowers fall off
promptly.
Milwaukee (Seedling 100).—Three and
one-half feet; foliage green, leaves pointed;
flowers rich, dark maroon, darker than
Duke of Marlboro.
        WM. J. STEWART, Sec'y.

Forcing Crimson Ramblers.

ED. AM. FLORIST:—Please inform me if
I should treat Crimson Rambler roses the
same as hydrangeas for Decoration day,
when they should be started and what
temperature suits them best.
        H. McC.

If the Crimson Ramblers were lifted
from the field they should be potted at
once and left outside in a cold frame until
about the middle of March. While outside in a dormant condition they should
be protected with sash or boards to
prevent them from freezing too hard, else
the long shoots are liable to winter kill.
About the middle of March bring them
indoors and start them slowly, say in a
temperature of 45° at night, gradually
raising the temperature in a few weeks
to 55°, which is high enough to bring
them into flower for Memorial day. The
same treatment will do for those grown
in pots all summer.   G.

Smilax and Asparagus.

ED. AM. FLORIST:—Please give me directions for growing smilax and asparagus
for next year. Should they be laid away
dormant for a while before planting?
        A. L.

Assuming that the asparagus are strong
plants in 4-inch or 5-inch pots at this
time, they will need another shift to a
size larger pot before planting them out
next June. There is nothing to be gained,
in fact only harm can result, from laying
them away and keeping them dormant
for a time before planting. Keep them
growing in good soil that has had plenty
of old cow manure added, in a temperature of 60°. It is not a good plan to
plant them into the bed before the first
of June, because the space can be used to
better advantage for other crops; the
first part of June is early enough to give
them a good start for the following
season. In preparing the bed (never plant
asparagus on benches) see that good
drainage in the shape of old brick bats
or gravel is provided, unless the soil is
naturally well drained. Use rather heavy
soil with a good supply of animal manure
added.

Smilax should be sown at the first of
the year for next year's crop. Of course,
if small plants in pots of the previous
year's sowing are on hand, they can be
shifted to a size larger and kept growing
in a moderately cool house until it is convenient to plant them out. Do not permit
them to run up into vines as long as they
are in pots, but keep the ends of the
shoots nipped so as to form a stronger
plant. If sown the first of the year,
however, they should be potted off when
two or three leaves are formed into
2½-inch pots and planted into the bed
or extremely low benches shortly after
June 1. As with the asparagus, there is
nothing at all to be gained by drying
them off at any time of the year. Keep
them growing in a temperature of 60°
and get as many crops as possible during
the year, and replant the bed at least
once in two years.   G.

Bureau of Soils Under Fire.

In the explanatory statement prefacing
a bulletin of Illinois Experiment Station,
on the "Present Status of Soil Investigation," by Cyril G. Hopkins, Director
Davenport has the following:
"This address was written for the purpose of calling attention to certain dis-
crepancies in the work of the different

prominent investigators in the subject of
soil fertility, especially such as have a
bearing upon investigations and conclusions touching soil conditions in Illinois.
The paper deals particularly with the
recently issued and much advertised Bulletin No. 22, from the Bureau of Soils,
United States Department of Agriculture,
on 'The Chemistry of the Soil as Related
to Crop Production,' which says that
practically all soils contain sufficient
plant food for good crop yields, and
that 'this supply will be indefinitely
maintained.' This is commonly understood and is certainly intended to mean
that the use of farm manure, the growing of clover and other leguminous crops,
as a source of nitrogen, or the application of bone meal or other fertilizers has
little or no tendency toward permanent
soil improvement, and that even the
effect which they do produce is due very
largely, if not entirely, to improved physical condition of the soil, which effect, the
Bureau of Soils believes, can be better
obtained by 'a simple rotation and
change of cultural methods,' and the
statement is added that 'the effect due to
cultivation is also more permanent than
the effect due to fertilizers.'

"This sudden and radical departure
from the established lines of agricultural
science struck at the very basis of soil
investigations in progress in this state,
and notice of these remarkable statements could not be avoided. The bulletin has been widely read and unfavor-
ably received by all who are capable of
judging of its merits. It has been welcomed by land agents with poor lands
for sale, and these are making the most
of this opportunity.

"After the publication of this bulletin
the offices of this experiment station
were at once flooded with letters from
the agricultural press and farmers alike
asking if these things could possibly
be true, and if all their ideas of soil fertility are erroneous. This address is
therefore published in order to answer a
mass of inquiries impossible to answer
by letter, and in order to prevent as much
as possible the evil consequences to Illinois soils that would certainly follow a
literal acceptance of the teachings of that
bulletin.

"It may be added that other papers on
the same subject were read at the same
meeting and that the tenor of the whole
discussion was to the effect that a serious mistake had been made by the
Bureau of Soils both in methods and conclusions.

"It is not a pleasant task to publish
matter aiming to set aside the conclusions
of any branch of government research,
but the circumstances surrounding this
station and the process of our work in soil
investigations make some general and
public statement imperative. Unpleasant though it is, it may yet be as well for
Americans to anticipate the criticism
that is certain to come in due time from
foreign investigators.

"This experiment station entertains
the hope that Illinois farmers will not
permit their ideas of the importance of
soil fertility to be disturbed by this
unfortunate incident, but that they will
go on treasuring the fertility in their
soils for economic use and not ignore or
waste the plant food required to make
crops."

Orange, N. J.

The regular monthly meeting and floral
show of the New Jersey Floricultural
society took place December 4 at its

rooms in Orange. The floral display was the last of the series in the competion for four silver cups which were offered by patrons of the society to the member receiving the highest number of points for the year in plants, flowers, fruits and vegetables. The judges varied at each meeting, those of this meeting being A. Caparn, Edwin Thomas and Mr. Hurrell. Malcolm MacRorie received the award for plants with 923 points; George Smith that for fruits with 600 points and Peter Duff the cup for flowers and vegetables with 904 and 850 points respectively. The presentation was made by Austin Colgate, representing John Crosby Brown, A. B. Jenkins, Wm. Runkle, O. D. Munn and Austin and Sydney Colgate, who were the contributors. The flower display was much the same as on previous evenings. Lager & Hurrell showed cattleyas, dendrobiums and cypripediums. Peter Duff had a vase of Pierpont Morgan rose of perfect form and remarkable for size, besides other roses and violets from the Brighthurst houses. The Morgan roses received 90 points. Dietrick Kindsgrab had begonias and cyclamens in pots and Malcolm MacRorie a phoenix. Lager & Hurrell received the first-class certificate. A first-class certificate was ordered to be given to John N. May for his new rose displayed at the November meeting and the society's prize of $25 won by Peter Duff at the American Chrysanthemum Society's show was ordered paid on receipt of the official information which for some reason had been delayed, though a letter from President Herrington mentioned it as on the way. The matter of this society's consolidation with other societies in this state was raised by Arthur Bodwin, and while decried by President Smith was left with a committee. In the annual election following the business meeting George Smith was unanimously re-elected president, Dietrick Kindsgrab vice-president, William Bennett secretary and Malcolm MacRorie treasurer. Wm. Ashmead, Edwin Thomas and Isaac Vance were elected to the arbitration committee. The meeting adjourned until January 8, when the matter of prices for the coming year will have been decided in committee, expression being asked from individual members by letter as to how the usefulness of the society may be increased during 1904. J. B. D.

MARION, O.—The twelfth annual chrysanthemum show of the Presbyterian church was given November 17.

Obituary.

DAVID COOK.

David Cook, a well known gardener, died at his home in Fishkill Landing, N. Y., last week, aged 72 years. For a number of years he had charge of J. Pierpont Morgan's summer place at Highland Falls. A widow and four children survive him.

DAVID L. TAYLOR.

David L. Taylor, one of the pioneer florists of the state, died at his home in Melrose, Mass., December 4, aged 81. He had been a resident of Melrose since 1847, when he started in the business on Emerson street. At one time his greenhouses were the most extensive in the United States, comprising some nineteen or more separate houses. He retired from active business about four years ago. Mr. Taylor was a native of Scotland, and leaves two sons and one daughter.

DANIEL M'INTYRE.

Daniel McIntyre died Saturday, December 5, at his home on the Hillsboro road, two miles from Nashville, Tenn. He was a native of Scotland and was a highly esteemed citizen. He was one of the pioneers in the floral business in this city. He came here thirty-five or forty years ago and engaged first as a gardener to private parties. He had a good knowledge of floriculture and in time established a place of his own. For many years he was engaged in growing flowers and was one of the most popular growers around the city. Before the days of special blooms, roses, carnations and the bulbous plants, when a flower was a flower, whether it was a geranium, a verbena or a jasmine, he was considered to be at the head of the trade. For a year or so he had a depot in an uptown drug store where fair specimens of flowers and fine plants were for sale. He was a great favorite with flower buyers and was noted particularly for his fine violets, his Marechal Niel and Lamarque roses. The funeral occurred Sunday, December 6. M. D.

THOMAS W. WEATHERED.

Thomas W. Weathered, who died December 4, was born in Stockport, Cheshire, England, on August 3, 1819. He came to the United States in 1840 and took a position as superintendent for R. H. Hoe in New York city. In 1849 he associated himself with Anthony Hitchings in the business of greenhouse heating on Crosby street. In 1859 he formed a partnership with Ed. Cherevoy and the Weathered & Cherevoy hot water boilers soon took a high place in the esteem of greenhouse men. Mr. Cherevoy died in 1870 and Mr. Weathered continued the business until 1888, when he retired leaving it to be conducted by his sons. Mr. Weathered was a great traveler. He went to California gold hunting with the famous "49ers" and it has been his custom annually up to the present year to make a pilgrimage to his old home in England. In business affairs he was the soul of honor and uprightness. Socially he was cheery and companionable and his disposition was kindly and considerate. Of a large family of children two sons and one daughter survive, the elder son being Chas. B. Weathered, the treasurer of the New York Florists' Club.

SITUATIONS, WANTS, FOR SALE.
One Cent Per Word.
Cash with the Adv.
Plant Advs. NOT admitted under this head.

Every paid subscriber to the AMERICAN FLORIST for the year 1903 is entitled to a five-line want ADV. (situations only) free, to be used at any time during the year.

Situation Wanted—As foreman or manager, 15 years' practical experience in wholesale and retail. Apply stating wages, size of place. etc.
FLORIST, Box 373, Trinidad, Col.

Situation Wanted—By gardener and florist; 21 years' experience in all branches. Private place or public institution preferred. Married.
5097 St. Anthony Ave., Merriam Park, Minn.

Situation Wanted—By young man of 26, with 5 years' experience in florist's work, besides other gardening experience. In or near Chicago preferred. I L, care American Florist.

Situation Wanted—As foreman, roses, carnations and general stock; ambitious, sober; life experience. State wages and give full particulars.
FOREMAN, 595 Pawtucket Ave., Pawtucket, R. I.

Situation Wanted—Hollander, single, speaks English, desires position on private place. 12 years' experience. Can furnish first-class references. Address
GARDENER, care American Florist.

INTERNATIONAL FLOWER DELIVERY.

PASSENGER STEAMSHIP MOVEMENTS.

The tabl s herewith give the scheduled time of depa ture of ocean steamships carrying first-class passengers from the principal American and foreign ports. covering the space of two weeks from date of this issue of the AMERICAN FLORIST. Much disappointment often res lts from attempts to forward flowers for steamer delivery by express. to the care of the ship's steward or otherwise. The carriers of these packages are not infrequently refused admission on board and even those delivered on board are not always certain to reach the parties for whom they were intended. Hence florists in interior cities having orders for the delivery of flowers to passengers on out-going steamers are advised to intrust the filing of such orders to some reliable florist in the port of departure, who understands the necessary details and formalities and has the facilities for attending to it properly. For the addresses of such firms we refer our readers to the advertisements on this page:

FROM	TO	STEAMER	*LINE	DAY	DUE ABOUT
New York......	Liverpool	Umbria	1	Sat. Dec. 19 6:00 a. m.	Dec. 26
New York......	"	Lucania	1	Sat. Dec. 26, 10:00 a. m.	Jan. 1
New York......	Glasgow	Corinthian	2	Thur. Dec. 24, 1:00 p. m.	Jan. 3
New York......	Hamburg	Graf Waldersee	3	Sat. Dec. 19, 6:00 a. m.	Jan. 1
New York......	Glasgow	Ethiopian	5	Sat. Dec. 19, Noon.	Dec. 29
New York......	London	Mesaba	6	Sat. Dec. 9, 9:00 a. m.	Dec. 19
New York......	"	Minneapolis	6	Sat. Dec. 26 10:0 a. m.	Jan. 5
New York......	Liverpool	Oceanic	7	Wed. Dec. 16, 4:00 p. m.	Dec. 23
New York......	"	Teutonic	7	Wed. Dec. 23, Noon.	Dec. 30
New York......	Southampton	New York	8	Sat. Dec. 19, 9:30 a. m.	Dec. 26
New York......	"	St. Paul	8	Sat. Dec. 26, 9:30 a. m.	Jan. 1
New York......	Antwerp	Kroonland	9	Sat. Dec. 19, 10:30 a. m.	Dec. 26
New York......	"	Zeeland	9	Sat. Dec. 26, 10:30 a. m.	Jan. 4
New York......	Havre	La Savoie	10	Thur. Dec. 17, 10:00 a. m.	Dec. 27
New York......	"	La Bretagne	10	Thur. Dec. 24, 10:00 a. m.	Jan. 2
New York......	Genoa	Nord America	12	Sat. Dec. 15, 11:00 a. m.	Feb. 1
New York......	"	Liguria	12	"ues. Dec. 22, 11.00 a. m.	Feb. 8
New York......	Bremen	Kaiser Wilh. II-	13	Tues. Dec. 15, 1:00 p. m.	Dec. 22
Boston	Liverpool	Bohemian	15	Sat. Dec. 16, 8:00 a. m.	Dec. 26
Boston	"	Canadian	15	Wed. Dec. 23, 1:00 p. m.	Jan. 2

*1 Cunard; 2 Allen-State; 3 Hamburg-American; 4 Scandinavian-American; 5 Anchor Line; 6 Atlantic Transport; 7 White Star; 8 American; 9 Red Star; 10 French; 11 Holland-American; 12 Italian Royal Mail; 13 North German Lloyd; 14 Fabre; 15 Dominion; 16 Leyland; 17 Occidental and Oriental; 18 Oceanic; 19 Allan; 20 Can. Pacific Ry.; 21 N. Pacific Ry.; 22 Hongkong-Seattle.

INTERNATIONAL FLOWER DELIVERY.

STEAMSHIPS LEAVE FOREIGN PORTS.

FROM	TO	STEAMER	*LINE	DAY	DUE ABOUT
Liverpool........	New York	Etruria	1	Sat. Dec. 10,	Dec. 16
Liverpool.......	"	Ivernia	1	Sat. Dec. 26,	Jan. 2
Liverpool.......	Boston	Saxonia	1	Tues. Dec. 15,	Dec. 22
Fiume	New York	Carpathia	1	Fri. Dec. 18,	
Glasgow.......	"	Laurentian	2	Sat. Dec. 19,	Dec. 29
Hamburg.......	"	Pennsylvania	3	Sat. Dec. 19,	Dec. 29
Hamburg.......	"	Patricia	3	Sat. Dec. 26,	Jan. 5
Glasgow.......	"	Furnessia	5	Sat. Dec. 26,	Jan. 5
London.........	"	Minnehaha	6	Thur. Dec. 17,	Dec. 26
London.........	"	Menominee	6	Thur. Dec. 24,	Jan. 3
Liverpool.......	"	Cedric	7	Wed. Dec. 16, 3:30 p. m.	Dec. 23
Liverpool.......	"	Majestic	7	Wed. Dec. 43, 3:30 p. m.	Dec. 30
Genoa	Boston	Romanic	7	Wed. Dec. 23,	
Southampton...	New York	Philadelphia	8	Sat. Dec. 19, Noon.	Dec. 26
Southampton...	"	St. Louis	8	Sat. Dec. 26 , Noon.	Jan. 2
Antwerp.......	"	Finland	9	Sat. Dec. 19, Noon	Dec. 26
Antwerp.......	"	Vaderland	9	Sat. Dec. 26, Noon	Jan. 4
Havre..........	"	La Touraine	10	Sat. Dec. 19.	Dec. 27
Havre..........	"	La Champagne	10	Sat. Dec. 26,	Jan. 2
Genoa..........	"	Sardegna	12	Mon. Dec. 14,	Dec. 24
Genoa..........	"	Citta di Milano	12	Mon. Dec. 21,	Dec. 31
Bremen........	"	Kronprinz Wilh.	13	Tues. Dec. 15,	Dec. 22
Bremen.	"	Brandenburg	13	Sat. Dec. 19,	Dec. 31
Bremen........	"	Neckar	13	Sat. Dec. 26,	Jan. 6
Naples........	"	Patria	14	Sat. Dec. 19,	
Liverpool.......	Boston	Cestrian	16	Sat. Dec. 19,	Dec. 28
Liverpool.......	"	Devonian	16	Sat. Dec 26,	Jan. 4

* See steamship list on opposite page.

THE SEED TRADE.

AMERICAN SEED TRADE ASSOCIATION.
S. F. Willard, Pres.; J. Charles McCullough,
First Vice-Pres.; C. E. Kendel, Cleveland, O.,
Sec'y and Treas.
Twenty-second annual convention St. Louis,
Mo., June, 1904.

VISITED CHICAGO: C. R. Kimberlin, of
J. M. Kimberlin, and W. J. Fosgate,
Santa Clara, Cal.

SANTA CLARA, CAL.—The Morse Seed
Company is surrounding its barnyard
with a high fence of new plank.

SANTA PAULA, CAL.—John Bodger &
Son will make extensive shipments of
lima beans to New Zealand this season.

VISITED BOSTON: Lester L. Morse, of
Santa Clara, Cal.; James B. Kidd, repre-
senting the Cox Seed Co., San Francisco,
Cal.

THE free seed scheme, at first a nuisance, is growing into a scandal, says the
Philadelphia Bulletin. It ought to be
abolished forthwith.

CHAS. P. BRASLAN, of the Braslan Seed
Growers Company, San Jose, Cal.,
expects to reach Chicago on his eastern
trip December 15.

IT is reported that the bank creditors
of D. Landreth & Sons were the parties
who prevented the carrying out of the
proposed compromise.

LEBANON, IND.—The Huntington &
Page Company, of Indianapolis, has
leased ninety acres of ground near here
and will use it as an onion farm.

LOS ANGELES, CAL.—The large warehouse of the Germain Seed and Plant
Company is pretty well filled up and all
the seed stock has not yet been stored.

THE recent troubles among contract-
ing seed growers and farmers in Nebraska
and Connecticut will probably result in
more binding contract arrangements in
the future.

SWEET CORN conditions continue
unsettled, but there is undoubtedly a
feeling of confidence in higher values.
The average germination is likely to be
lower than usual.

W. W. JOHNSON & SON, Ltd., of Boston,
England, are offering an extensive line of
novelties, mostly vegetables. The place
of honor is gi en to a new dwarf early
pea, Edward VII.

CALIFORNIA growers of seeds on contract who have recently covered the
country say that the business outlook in
their line does not compare favorably
with that of last December.

LOS ANGELES, CAL.—John R. Horne,
formerly with the Cox Seed Company, of
San Francisco, has accepted a position
as assistant manager with the Germain
Seed and Plant Company of this place.

VENTURA COUNTY, Cal., will make an
extensive display of beans at the St.
Louis World's Fair. That county is
credited with growing twenty-four per
cent of all the beans raised in the country.

NEW YORK.—John Scheepers, formerly
with C. Keur & Sons, of Hillegom, Holland, has formed a partnership with R.
Schoo & Co., wholesale bulb growers of

Hillegom and a plant firm of Boskoop,
Holland, locating American office at 136
Water street, this city.

BOUQUET GREEN prices remain firm at
$8 to $10 per 100-pound crate at wholesale. Fancy Delaware holly has not
appeared. Such cars as have arrived are
hardly of fair quality. The market is
glutted with southern holly of a very
poor quality in the hands of produce
commission houses.

Cleveland.

The Home Gardening Association here
is preparing to put flower seeds within
easy reach of school children for the purpose of prize gardening competitions, to
stimulate a desire for beautiful things.
Many shipments of beans and peas are
coming in daily, right from the fields. It
saves extra hauling and storing.
There is an early demand for sweet pea
seed for forcing under glass.　　O. G.

Situation of the Seed Growers.

ED. AM. FLORIST:—I note the AMERICAN
FLORIST and other similar publications
closely, and as yet there has been but
very little said concerning the situation
of the seed grower. The last two years
have been generally unsatisfactory to the
vine seed grower. Most growers were
unable to fill orders complete, and failed
to derive any benefit from the increased
values of seeds.
The cost of seed production is increasing, and the increased values of seeds certainly tempt one to cut out the contract
customers and sell his products on the
market. This will be done largely if the
dealers decline paying more for seed
another year. The seed famine for two
years in succession will practically clean
up all surpluses, and should we make full
crops next year would have no trouble
to sell our products on the market at
paying prices.
We would like to hear from the growers generally, and we would be pleased
also to have the views of others who
would care to express themselves.
　　　　　　　　　　　　D. H. GILBERT.

Financial Troubles in Holland.

A Holland nurseryman, under date of
November 14, writes the AMERICAN
FLORIST as follows: "We are now
going through a commercial crisis, which
of course does not fail to show its effects
in our line of business. Exceedingly low
stock markets account for it, I think.
The last couple of years money making
in American stocks was an easy and
apparently everybody's business until
now that the crash has come. The situation is best illustrated in a cartoon

showing the American eagle flying out
of the stock exchange in Amsterdam
holding in his claws a bag of gold representing Holland's national treasure.
Much bankruptcy has already followed
and amongst the unfortunates were
several banking institutions, unhappily
right in the bulb growing districts.
Credit was readily given for a number
of years, but many dealers and growers
will now have to settle up and bank on
their own resources for the future, and
I venture to say this will cause the disappearance of some of them. Perhaps
later on during the winter I will be able
to give the names of such firms as fall by
the wayside."

The Wise Men of Washington.

An example of the intelligent distribution of garden seeds by the Department
of Agriculture is described as follows by
the Sacramento, California, *Record-
Union* of November 26:

The annual haphazard distribution was interestingly illustrated in Santa Clara county last
year. For years Morse & Company have planted
hundreds of acres to lettuce for seed. The Morse
lettuce seed, raised in Santa Clara county, is
known on five continents. It grows very well in
Santa Clara county. However, last year about
every man, woman and child in that county
received as his share of the government distribution a package of Morse lettuce seed with the
request that it be planted, the results carefully
noted and report of the outcome of the "experiment" be sent the Department of Agriculture.
Perhaps the Department of Agriculture saw in
the growing of Morse lettuce seed a new industry
for Santa Clara county, but the community was
not particularly benefited by the incident. It is
not probable that the 3,00,000 pounds of seed to
be sent out this year will prove more beneficial
to the communities to which it is s at than was
the Morse lettuce seed sent last year to the county
of its origin.

THE NURSERY TRADE.

AM. ASSOCIATION OF NURSERYMEN.
N. W. HALE, Knoxville, Tenn., Pres.; FRANK
A. WEBER, St. Louis, Mo., Vice-Pres.; GEORGE C.
SEAGER, Rochester, N. Y., Sec'y.
Twenty-ninth annual convention, Atlanta, Ga.,
June, 1904.

WE are in receipt of the report of the
standing committees, American Park
and Outdoor Art Association, made at
the seventh annual meeting, held at
Buffalo, N. Y., July 7–9, 1903, covering
"Park Census," "Forest Reservations,"
"Local Improvement," and "Checking
Abuses of Public Advertising."

ORANGE, CAL.—The Jackson & Perkins
Company received a carload of moss
from the east November 23 to replace
that burned on the desert about a month
ago. About December 10 they will commence digging plants, for which work
they will need forty more men. They
will ship 250,000 rose plants this season.

Huntsville, Ala.

The Huntsville Wholesale Nursery Company has purchased the Motz farm of
eighty acres two miles from the city and
will establish thereon warehouses and
shipping headquarters.
The Alabama Nursery Company is
arranging to build a big warehouse on a
strip of land at Mercury, purchased by
the firm a few months ago.

Trade Mark Case Dismissed.

The big trade mark case brought by
Stark Brothers Nursery and Orchard
Company against James B. Wild &
Brothers, of Sarcoxie, Mo., for alleged
infringement of trade marks on the following named varieties of apples: Black
Ben Davis, Apple of Commerce, Champion and Senator, has been voluntarily
dismissed by the plaintiffs.

Springfield, Mass.

December 2 gave us a foot of snow
with continued cold weather which is a
little early for this section. However,
trade is good, there being a good demand
for cut flowers of all kinds, also funeral
work which is quite brisk. Chrysanthemums are gone and carnations and roses
are selling better. Carnations sold well
also while the chrysanthemums held
sway. Azaleas are in and sell on sight;
cyclamens, primrose and heather are
moving slowly but from the present outlook they will be in good demand for
Christmas trade. Holly has made its
appearance and is well berried. Store
men are on the jump getting things in
shape for the holiday trade.   A. B.

Oceanic, N. J.

The regular monthly meeting of the
Monmouth County Horticultural Society
was held at the Red Men's Hall, Oceanic,
December 4, with President Turner in
the chair. The discussion of the evening
was on "Sub-soiling," in which most of
the members took part. The nomination of officers took place and the following ticket was named: President, Wm.
Turner; vice-president, Geo. Hale; secretary, H. A. Kettel; financial secretary,
Geo. Kuhn; treasurer, W. W. Kennedy.
Three hundred and twenty-five dollars in
prize money was paid and a goodly balance left on hand. Geo. Hale treated the
boys to a box of cigars.   B.

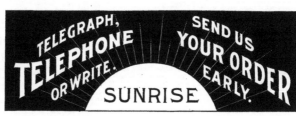

OUR PASTIMES.

Announcements of coming contests or other events of interests to our bowling, shooting and sporting readers are solicited and will be given place in this column.

Address all correspondence for this department to Wm. J. Stewart, 49 W. 28th St., New York. Robt. Kift, 1725 Chestnut St., Philadelphia, Pa.; or to the American Florist Co., Chicago, Ill.

At Chicago.

At a meeting of the Florists' Bowling club at Mussey's alleys, Tuesday evening, John Lambros tendered his resignation as secretary and was subsequently elected financial secretary and treasurer, this being a new office recently created by the club. When the annual election of officers took place several months ago, P. J. Hauswirth, the father of bowling amongst the Chicago florists, could not be prevailed upon to accept any office this year. At the last meeting, however, the club members insisted on him accepting the office of secretary, and he was unanimously elected. Mr. Hauswirth's extensive knowledge of bowling matters, both locally and nationally, insures the club that this important office will be well taken care of.

It was further decided to start a handicap match beginning the first week of January and to continue until April. This is with the object of getting a line on the members and to decide the team which will represent Chicago at St. Louis next August. Geo. Stollery was elected handicapper. Joseph Foerester was elected captain, this office to expire March 1.

The following are the scores of the games rolled Tuesday evening. Asmus,

with 172 in the first game, captured the high score:

Player	1st	2d	3d
E. Winterson		183	
Degnan	154	149	
Stevens	166		163
G. Stollery	167		199
F. Stollery	169		157
Esau	130		134
Kreitling		177	
Asmus	172	166	
Lambros	16		155
Conobros	105	125	
Huetner	128		155
Hauswirth		140	
Baxton		188	

Philadelphia Florists' Bowling League.

The standing of the teams in the Florists' League at the finish of the third week, which ended on Friday, remains practically the same as previously reported. The Dunhams, Kifts and Harrises are still the leaders of the first column, with a percentage of .667 each. The Eimermans head the list of the second column, followed by the Westcott and Moss teams. The features of the week were the excellent scores of George Moss for his team, Dr. Goebel for the Kift team and William Robertson for the Harris aggregation. The Westcotts put up a good fight on Friday, and would have won all three except for the unfortunate falling down of one man, added to the high average which was counted to the credit of the absentee on the opposing side. The Dunhams won two out of three in their match and stand a good chance to win out and capture the first prize. They have already met the teams who have proved the strongest in the tournament, and if they keep their nerve should be able to hold their own for the coming two weeks. The Kift and Harris teams play Monday night, the Dunhams and

Westcotts on Wednesday night and Moss and Eimerman on Friday night. Standing of the teams to date:

Team	W.	L.	P.C.		Team	W.	L.	P.C.
Dunham	6	3	.667		Eimerman	4	5	.444
Kift	6	3	.667		Moss	4	4	.333
Harris	6	3	.667		Westcott	2	7	.222

The Home of Chrysanthemum Stock. For Sale

WIETOR BROS.

Wholesale Growers of

Cut Flowers

51 Wabash Ave., CHICAGO.

 WITH one of the largest ranges of glass in the world devoted exclusively to cut flowers, we produce first grade stock in such large quantities that we can fill orders at all times.

BEAUTIES, ROSES, CARNATIONS.

Our stock was never finer than at present. Beauty is our specialty, of which we grow 60,000 plants. 75,000 Brides, Bridesmaids and Meteors; including Liberty and Ivory of choicest quality. 160,000 Carnation Plants on benches, all best sorts.

Buy of the Grower and get Fresh Stock at Fowest Market Rates......

CHRISTMAS PRICES.
Subject to Change without notice.

American Beauty

Extra long stem......per doz.			$12.00
Stems 36 inches	"		10.00
" 24 "	"		8.00
" 20 "	"		6.00
" 15 "	"		4.00
" 12 "	"		3.00
" 8 "	"		2.00
BRIDES. .... per 100, $12.00 to 15.00
BRIDESMAIDS .... " 12.00 to 15.00
METEORS .... " 12.00 to 15.00
GOLDEN GATES...... " 12.00 to 15.00
PERLES.................. " 8.00 to 10.00
IVORY.................. " 12.00 to 20.00
LIBERTY.................. " 10.00 to 20.00
Our selection... " 8.00
CARNATIONS,
Fancy .... " 8.00 to 10.00
Good.............. " 5.00 to 6.00

ALL OTHER STOCK AT LOWEST MARKET RATES.

CARNATIONS

————IN PLACING YOUR ORDERS FOR THE————

1904 Novelties, Remember the Two Greatest White Carnation Novelties ever offered the Trade

LADY BOUNTIFUL AND THE BELLE

FOR EARLINESS—We beat them all.   **FOR QUALITY**—We lead.
FOR QUANTITY—We have the Commercial White Carnations.

Growth and Habit are just right, none better—and when we say they are no. croppers, but early and continuous flowering we mean: They commence with the earliest, if not before all others and continue so without cessation throughout the entire season. They are easy doers, thriving well under ordinary conditions, and respond readily to good treatment. They are also easy propagators and will be found most satisfactory varieties in every way.

Our large stock still enables us to offer some February delivery.

| Price, per 100............................... | $ 12.00 |
| " per 1000............................... | 100.00 |
| 2,500 at ....$95.00 per 1000 |
| 5,000 at .... 90.00 per 1000 |

We also offer a set of 5 distinctly novel carnations. The combinations of colors are most beautiful and very attractive. For full descriptions and prices send for our descriptive price list.

We can also supply all the leaders of the 1904 Novelties at introducers' prices.

In making up your lists of 1904 wants, do not forget we can supply the best of the 1903 varieties in select, graded, well-rooted cuttings at prices consistent with well-grown stock.

ASPARAGUS COMORENSIS.

We have only a few hundred of the 3½-inch size left. Well grown stock, $12.00 per 100.

Send for our Descriptive List for 1904.

F. Dorner & Sons Co.,
LA FAYETTE, INDIANA.

Special Offer.

ROOTED CUTTINGS. Per 1000
GOV. WOLCOTT, finest white carnation...$25.00
ENCHANTRESS, finest light pink carnation 50 00
LAWSON... 20.00
Have 30 000 of the above to propagate from which insures good stock. Have also other standard varieties.

Chrysanthemum Special.
Stock plants of Liger, Richardson, Yellow Eaton, Chautauqua, Gold, per doz., $1.50; per 100, $10.00. Chadwick, Yellow Chadwick, Eaton and other standard varieties, 75c per doz.; $6.00 per 100, while they last.

POEHLMANN BROS. CO.

MORTON GROVE, ILL.

☞Don't forget we are headquarters for the best out American Beauties. Right in crop now.

BOSTON FERNS

2½-in., $4.00; 3-in., $8.00; 4-in., $15.00; 5-in., $25.00
6-in., $40.00; 7-in., $60.00; 8-in., $75.00 per 100.

PIERSONI FERNS, young plants from bench, $15.00 per 100; 3½-in., $30.00 per 100; 4-in., 50c each; 5-in., 75c each. Also bench-grown BOSTONS in all sizes. All stock extra fine. Cash with order.

DAVIS BROS., Geneva, Ill.

Need a Good Scarlet?

Take my word for it and order **Flamingo.** There is nothing better, nor more profitable in sight. I can also supply the following varieties: Albatross, Lady Bountiful, The Bell, Moonlight, Nelson Fisher, Mrs. Patten and Indianapolis, $12 00 per 100; $100.00 per 1000.

The Queen An excellent commercial white of last year's introduction, $5.00 per 100; $40.00 per 1 00.

S. S. SKIDELSKY,

708 North 16th St.,   PHILADELPHIA PA.

JOSEPH HEACOCK,

WYNCOTE, PA.

GROWER OF Areca Lutescens
Kentia Belmoreana
Kentia Forsteriana

For our prices see page 551, Nov. 7th issue.

Primroses...

Per 100
Chinese, Obconica Alba, Rosea, 2½-in. pots, $1.50
Asparagus Sprengeri, 3-in. pots............. 1 50
Pansy Plants, $3.00 per 1000............. .50

——CASH.——

JOS. H. CUNNINGHAM,   Delaware, Ohio.

A FINE LOT OF

FERNS.

Assorted Varieties, in 2¼ and 3-inch
pots at $2.00 per 100.........

WAGNER PARK CONSERVATORIES,

SIDNEY, OHIO.

Boston Ferns.

2½-in., $4.00 per 100; $35.00 per 1000.

Pierson Ferns.

2½-inch, $25.00 per 100.

The Conard & Jones Co., WEST GROVE, PA.

Crimson Ramblers FOR Easter

3 to 4 feet, fine, 50 for $9.00; $2.50 per dozen. Pink and White MME. COCHET and other FIELD ROSES, for potting up for Spring sales, 50 for $5.00. 5,000 forcing TOMATO PLANTS, Mayflower and Lorillard, $2.00 per 100; 500 for $8.00. Cash, please.

BENJ. CONNELL,   -   WEST GROVE, PA.

For Christmas Sales

Nephrolepis Piersoni.
4-inch pots, each............................$ .50
5-inch pots, each............................ .75
6-inch pots, each............................ 1.00

Nephrolepis Cordata Compacta.
4-inch pots, each............................$ .50
5-inch pots, each............................ .25
6-inch pots, each............................ .50

Nephrolepis Bostoniensis.
5-inch pots, each............................$ .25
6-inch pots, each............................ .50

Asparagus Plumosus Nanus.
2½-inch pots, per 100................. $ 5.00
3-inch pots, per 100................. 8.00
3½-inch pots, per 100................. 10.00

Begonia Incarnata.
In bloom ready for immediate sale.
4-inch pots, per 100.................$6.00

Primroses.
Daybreak, in bud and bloom, from 3½-inch pots, per 100.................$8.00

NATHAN SMITH & SON, Adrian, Mich.

CHRYSANTHEMUMS

THE FINEST NOVELTIES AND ALL THE LEADING PRIZE WINNERS.

MRS. H. W. BUCKBEE. Nive is X Mrs. Henry Robinson. A fine pure white for all purposes. C. S. A. Certificate, scoring 91 points.

ROCKFORD. Mrs. Henry Robinson X Col. D. Appleton. Incurved, yellow, fine habit, a grand commercial variety. At its best Oct. 30th. C. S. A. Certificate, scoring 88 points. ☞ Price of above, 50c each; $5 per doz; $35 per 100.

All the Best Australian and other Introductions

S. T. Wright, at $1.00 each. William Duckham, everybody's choice as the best 'mum to date, 75c each; $7.00 per doz.; $50 per 100. Maynell, Donald McLeod, Henry Barnes, Harrison Dick, Leila Filkins, Pantia Ralli, W. A. Etherington, Mrs. R. Hunt, Esther Edwards, at 50c each; $5.00 per dozen; $35.00 per 100.

H. W. Buckbee. The best commercial yellow for Thanksgiving, at 15c each; $1.25 per dozen; $8.00 per 100.
All of the leading commercial and exhibition varieties; prices on application; select young plants from 2-inch pots.
Orders are now being booked, and will be filled in rotation as received. Delivery after March 1st.

FOREST CITY GREENHOUSES,   **H. W. BUCKBEE,**
ROCKFORD SEED FARMS.   ROCKFORD, ILLINOIS.

Small Ferns for Fern Dishes.

Strong plants in 2¼-inch pots, $3.00 per 100; $25.00 per 1000.

Primula Obconica Grandiflora Alba, Rosea and Fimbriata.

Strong plants in 2¼ inch pots, $3.00 per 100; $25.00 per 1000. CASH.

OECHSLIN BROS.,   1688 W. Madison St., Chicago.

The F. R. WILLIAMS CO.

Wholesale Florists,

CLEVELAND,   -   OHIO.

Please mention the American Florist to advertisers.

Wired Toothpicks.

Price, per Box of 10,000. $1.50.

This quantity in two packages can be sent by
mail to distant states for 75 cents.
Box of 50,000, weight 30 pounds, $6.25 F. O. B.
Berlin. N. Y.

For Sale by the Leading Supply Dealers.

MANUFACTURED BY

W. J. COWEE, Berlin, N. Y.

SUCCESSFUL SELLERS..........
are the Successful growers who advertise in THE AMERICAN FLORIST.

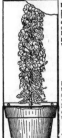

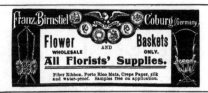

THE AMERICAN FLORIST

America is "the Prow of the Vessel; there may be more comfort Amidships, but we are the first to touch Unknown Seas."

Vol. XXI.　　　CHICAGO AND NEW YORK, DECEMBER 19, 1903.　　　No. 811.

THE AMERICAN FLORIST

NINETEENTH YEAR.

Copyright 1903, by American Florist Company
Entered as Second-Class Mail Matter.

PUBLISHED EVERY SATURDAY BY

AMERICAN FLORIST COMPANY,
334 Dearborn St., Chicago.

Eastern Office: 42 W. 28th St., New York.

Subscription, $1.00 a year. To Europe, $2.00.
Subscriptions accepted only from the trade.
Volumes half-yearly from August, 1901.

SOCIETY OF AMERICAN FLORISTS AND
ORNAMENTAL HORTICULTURISTS.

OFFICERS—JOHN BURTON, Philadelphia, Pa.,
president; C. C. POLLWORTH, Milwaukee, Wis.,
vice-president; WM. J. STEWART, 79 Milk Street,
Boston, Mass., secretary; H. B. BEATTY, Oil City,
Pa., treasurer.
OFFICERS-ELECT—PHILIP BREITMEYER, president; J. J. BENEKE, vice-president; secretary and
treasurer as before. Twentieth annual meeting
at St. Louis, Mo., August, 1904.

THE AMERICAN CARNATION SOCIETY.

Annual convention at Detroit, Mich., March 3,
1904. ALBERT M. HERR, Lancaster, Pa., secretary.

AMERICAN ROSE SOCIETY.

Annual meeting and exhibition, Philadelphia,
March, 1904. LEONARD BARRON, 136 Liberty St.,
New York, secretary.

CHRYSANTHEMUM SOCIETY OF AMERICA.

Annual convention and exhibition, November,
1904. FRED H. LEMON, Richmond, Ind., secretary.

THIS ISSUE 48 PAGES WITH COVER.

CONTENTS.

A day in New York........................789
Florists' plant notes......................793
The late Ernst G. Asmus (portrait)........790
Chicago Florists' Club exhibition.........791
Chrysanthemum Society of America.........791
The carnation—The Bride (illus.).........792
—Notes on varieties......................792
—Ventilation.............................792
Phalænopsis amabilis (illus.)............793
With the growers—A. N. Pierson (illus.)..794
—John Barr, Natick, Mass................794
—Robert Scott & Son, Sharon Hill, Pa....795
The retail trade—Decorative work of the day..796
—Florists' window screen (illus.)........796
Chicago..................................796
New York.................................797
Frank R. Traendly (portrait).............797
Philadelphia.............................797
Boston...................................798
St. Louis................................798
Washington...............................798
Toronto..................................799
Kansas City, Mo..........................799
Cleveland................................799
Cincinnati...............................799
San Francisco............................800
Obituary—Charles J. Woodruff............811
—Ernst G. Asmus.........................801
Council Bluffs, Iowa.....................801
The seed trade...........................802
The nursery trade........................812
Our pastimes.............................819
The allied trades........................80
Pittsburg................................82

A Day in New York.

Robt. Kift.

To do New York thoroughly one must be up with the lark in the morning. The wheels of trade are set moving when the gong sounds at 6 a. m. in the Growers' Market on the third floor of the Coogan building, Twenty-sixth street and Sixth avenue. The flowers arrive a short time before, being brought mainly from the Thirty-fourth street ferry in the company's van. Although the baskets and boxes may be in the stalls and the customers waiting there is a fine of $5 for selling before the bell rings. At the old Thirty-fourth street market when flowers were scarce much of the business was over by 6 a. m., and it was a great hardship for those who had a distance to come to get there before the best stock was gone. The present plan works admirably and all hands are suited. In about an hour everything is sold, as whether business is brisk or not there seems to be always enough customers to take up the stock at some price.

Smilax comes to the market in bunches of three strings together, not very heavy but nice stock. The price the morning of my visit was 25 cents per bunch, not rolled up but displayed spread out. On one side of the room is a row of ice boxes with W. Siebrecht at one end and Millang at the other. The latter sells on commission and appeared quite busy. Chas. Smith has the box next Millang and sells other stock as well as his own. Some double violets seen here were very nicely bunched and packed. Each bunch was wrapped in wax paper and packed in such a way as not to spoil its shape. While this is not new, yet it is not the plan everywhere and many violet growers would profit largely by adopting the same methods. Dealers in galax, leucothoe sprays and fern leaves seem to do a thriving business, while in one corner is fitted up a supply store in which can be purchased almost everything a retail florist needs. It seemed in the market as if as many more lights as are now in evidence would be an improvement. The illumination was bad.

On the floor below the New York Cut Flower Company opens up about 8 a. m. Here the class of goods handled is finer,

the bulk of the flowers being roses and choice carnations. Much of the stock comes packed in boxes which go to the retailers direct on regular orders with only the one handling. While Beauty, Bride, Bridesmaid and Liberty predominated, there were a number of other varieties. Mr. Dorrance sent in Killarney, Mme. Cusin, Nesbitt, Testout, Sunrise, Morgan and No. 6, a sulphur-colored flower. Asmus had a new cerise rose, also No. 6, Mme. Hoste and Jacob Becker's New Ideal in good shape. A great deal of stock is handled in this room every day. On Twenty-eighth street the business starts about 8 a. m., when the first express wagons begin to arrive. The commission houses handle a great deal of stock and are strong on violets, which are now magnificent. Thos. Young, Jr., with his chain of stores—his wholesale and retail establishments on Twenty-eighth street and his Fifth and Sixth avenue branches—is getting to be quite a factor in the business. His system must be perfect, as he is just as smiling as ever and seems not to have one added care.

At Small & Sons, on Broadway, a novelty in the shape of odd wooden boxes for plants is to be seen. It is called Russian ware, the construction and coloring being such as is seen in that country. They are very pretty and quaint looking. Small camelia plants in 6-inch pots, in blossom, are to be offered for the holiday trade and should sell.

The Fleischman store had its usual elegant appearance, aided by the many windows and brilliant lighting, together with the mirrors which reach from ceiling to floor. The wrapping stand is in front on one side, and on the other, just inside the door, is kept a pile of assorted cut flower boxes, an excellent idea. The window displays are never crowded, but yet are so attractive that they are nearly always surrounded with admirers.

George Stumpp, in the residence district on Fifth avenue, near Central park, has a model place. The wide windows on the front and side, the full length of the store, afford a grand chance for the decorator, and they are at all times filled with choice stock. Last week a fine lot of heaths, four or five feet tall, in full flower, made the front window exceedingly attractive. Inside the store, standing about in groups, were baskets of plants decorated with ribbons. As soon as the morning supply of roses is in all hands are set to dethorning the stems, which, while it takes time, is said to repay amply for the trouble. Violets are carefully handled here. Most of the stock is kept in the original shipping boxes until a couple of hours before it is wanted, when the blooms are placed in other boxes, each bunch in a separate glass, which stiffens them up. They are at their very best when offered for sale.

Wadley & Smyth have a very pretty store with a parlor effect further down the avenue. Their window is always tastefully decorated, nephrolepis and Parleyense ferns being largely used.

Thorley's Fifth avenue store has an elegant air that is quite in keeping with the aristocratic company with which it is surrounded. The feature here is the cool room, where the flowers are kept. There are no windows, but the inside is surrounded with mirrors. The door is opened, one steps in and the electric lights then flashed on reveal a wealth of choice stock of all kinds which, owing to the mirrors, seems without limit. It is all arranged in vases and jars resting on slats on the floor. The effect is fine.

Siebrecht & Son, on the corner below, are fitting up a magnificent store. They have secured a lease of twenty years on the ground and have erected a six-story building. It is said they have been offered $25,000 per year for the corner store, the one they are to occupy, which will give an idea of the value of property in that neighborhood.

The Rosary, on Thirty-fourth street, with the genial Mr. Troy in charge, has a fine location. With the greenhouse on the roof, only one story up, and the roomy basement and vault under the pavement, it is exceedingly well equipped for the business. A cibotium being fitted in a wire frame on top of a Dicksonia trunk was a happy thought. The cibotium will stand the house atmosphere while the Dicksonia dies and leaves an unsightly trunk. When this is capped with the other fern and the connection mossed up the deception is complete. There is much to be seen that is interesting to an outsider in a trip among the many beautiful stores of this great city, but one day is not enough, nor is there time enough at one sitting, to do justice even to that.

Arctic Flowers.

Professor Schei, the geologist who accompanied the recent Sverdurp expedition had an interesting paper before the Christiana Geographical Society concerning the vegetation found in Ellesmere in the arctic regions. It appears from the paper that there are whole meadows full of arctic flowers, as well as many so-called bird mountains, which might almost be described as botanical gardens. A slope discovered over one bay was completely covered with a violet colored carpet of saxifraga. Traces were found in stony debris which proved that there were formerly in those regions flowers which now only grow in warm climates like Australia.

EVANSVILLE, IND.—J. D. Carmody has notified the Board of Children's Guardians that he will give them a 6-acre lot as a site for the children's home. The ground is to be transferred without consideration.

Florists' Plant Notes.

FOR WEEK OF DECEMBER 19.

Stevias.—Do not fail to save about a dozen stock plants of stevia after the flowers have been cut. Place them in an odd corner in a cool house and do not think of taking any cuttings before March. A dozen stock plants will furnish all the cuttings required.

Bulbs.—Cover the bulbs outside with about four inches of stable manure to keep them from freezing too hard. It is true they can stand all the frost they are liable to get, but the additional covering makes it easier on the man who brings them inside to force. And then, too, hard freezing is liable to crack the pots and pans.

Spireas.—The clumps of Astilbe Japonica will soon arrive and can either be potted at once into 6-inch or 7-inch pots and stored

The Late Ernst G. Asmus.
(See obituary page 801.)

outside in a cold frame, or else the potting can be deferred until forcing time commences. We prefer to store the clumps in a cold frame, covering them with a few inches of soil or stable manure, and pot them as we bring them into heat, for the frost is apt to crack the pots. They can stand any amount of freezing and should not be brought into heat until twelve weeks before Easter unless a few are wanted before that date.

Lilies.—The Bermuda lilies intended for Easter flowering should be about four or five inches high by this time. If in this condition, keep them in a temperature of 55° to 60° at night, which ought to bring them along about right. Easter falls on April 3 next, which is quite early comparatively, so great judgment must be exercised to have them exactly on time, and it will probably be found necessary to change them around several times into different temperatures during the next three months. If any were started in 4-inch pots they should now be shifted to 5-inch. Use good soil with some leaf mould added. Look sharply for greenfly, which are liable to get down into the crown of the plants, from whence they are difficult to dislodge unless fumigation and syringing with tobacco water is regularly attended to. If they once get down into the crown they are safe

from the fumes of tobacco smoke; in this case dilute nicotine in water 200 times and apply with a hand syringe; or soak strong tobacco stems in warm water for twenty-four hours, using the water diluted with an equal quantity of clear water in the same way. This will drive them from their snug retreat into the open, where the smoke will do the rest.

Cinerarias.—Cinerarias for Easter should have their last shift into the flowering pots, 5-inch or 6-inch, at once. Use a good sandy soil with a third leaf mould added, and be sure to drain the pots well with charcoal or broken potsherds. They delight in frequent syringing, but should not be watered too copiously at the root. As the best preventive of greenfly, which find in the cineraria a dainty morsel, scatter fresh tobacco stems between the pots, renewing once a month. Give them plenty of room so as not to crowd the foliage. Those in bloom for Christmas must not have any more overhead syringing or the flowers will be ruined. Give them a light place in a temperature of about 40° to 45° at night, and do not smoke them too heavily at any time for the foliage burns easily; in fact with stems scattered between the pots, as suggested, no smoking will ever be necessary.   G.

A Vermont Florist.

Alexander Emslie opened a new flower store in the Otis block, Barre, on December 1. A McCray refrigerator will be installed and an up-to-date florist's store conducted. It is also the intention in the near future to keep a full line of seeds.

Mr. Emslie's growing plant increased in the period of four years, from a small 15x50 greenhouse to its present dimensions, about 18,000 square feet of glass. He will take charge of the store for the present himself; later changes will be made so he can devote his time to the growing end of the business.

Mr. Emslie is ably assisted by his three brothers, his twin brother Charles being in charge of the "Montpelier greenhouses" which were purchased from Ernest Jacobsen last summer. The other two brothers, George and William, are employed at the Barre establishment. Charles Simons, formerly with Mr. Jacobsen, is also employed at the Montpelier end.

At the greenhouses a general stock is grown, but carnations form the bulk of the crop. Bedding plants are grown extensively for spring trade which is very large. The establishment is built after Lord & Burnham construction, 16x24 glass, double thick being used throughout. A large Lord & Burnham 12-section hot water boiler was installed last fall. The heating capacity will carry an additional 5,000 feet of glass, which will be added as soon as possible, among the plans for next season being a rose house 30x100. A large vegetable business was formerly conducted but owing to the rapid growth of the flower business this has been given up.

The Barre greenhouses are situated on the Montpelier and Barre electric road, two miles from Barre and four from Montpelier. The Montpelier greenhouses are situated on State street in the center of the city. Mr. Emslie will be pleased to have any brother florists call at either of the establishments at any time.   C. R. B.

NYACK, N. Y.—A fire in Hard's greenhouses November 28 badly damaged one end of one greenhouse.

Chicago Florists' Club Exhibition.

The inclemency of the weather December 16 was not conducive to either an extensive exhibit or a large audience at the third exhibition given under the auspices of the Florists' Club. It was a trifle too cold for comfort, both for the plants themselves and the plant enthusiasts. The exhibition was devoted mainly to flowering and decorative plants, suitable for holiday sales. However, there were a number of exhibits of cut blooms of new varieties of roses, carnations and chrysanthemums. The hall, on the fifth floor of the Atlas building, was neatly decorated with festoons of laurel leaves, provided by Vaughan's Seed Store. The exhibits were staged on low tables in the center and around the east end of the room, being not sufficient to fill the entire floor space.

The exhibition, which was under the management of Frank Benthey, undoubtedly was of great benefit to the trade, as many well done specimens were shown.

The George Wittbold Company, which makes a specialty of plants of the holiday varieties, had a good exhibit of general basket displays, including Asparagus plumosus in dishes, Cocos Weddelliana, Latania Borbonica, Pandanus Veitchii and ferns.

Vaughan's Greenhouses had a beautiful display, the center of which was a number of European hollies heavily berried. One variegated holly was particularly attractive. The display included pepper plants, solanums, oranges, poinsettias, needle pines, and in ferns were fine specimens of the Anna Foster, Pierson and Boston.

Kidwell Brothers showed an extensive and meritorious display, which embraced many varieties of ferns, Pierson, Boston and pterises being included; also Asparagus plumosus, crotons, tulips in dishes, azaleas and baby primroses, all well done. Specimens of Dracæna Lindeni, D. Massangeana and camellias were also shown.

The Garfield Park Floral Company sent some exceptional azaleas, poinsettias, cyclamens and mignonette. One specimen of fringed cyclamen deserves special mention.

A. Peterson, of Cincinnati, sent four pots of exceedingly well done Begonia Gloire de Lorraine.

W. L. Palinsky had a display of good azaleas, Asparagus plumosus and Ficus elastica.

Leopold Koropp showed two artistically trimmed baskets of crotons, begonias and maidenhair ferns.

Kalous Brothers displayed a very fine specimen cyclamen.

In cut flower blooms, for which certificates of merit were provided by the club, the Chicago Carnation Company had a display of roses and carnations. Fifty Golden Gate roses exhibited by this concern were very large with stems four and one-half feet in length. In carnations were vases of fifty blooms each of the new Fiancee, Lawson, Harlowarden and Crusader.

Peter Reinberg had a vase of his new and undisseminated Uncle John rose. Marquisee's new Flamingo carnation was also shown, but the flowers were evidently frozen in transit.

Nathan Smith & Son, Adrian, Mich., sent the only chrysanthemum exhibit. For the season the flowers were exceptionally good. The variety shown was a new one called John Burton, while incurved, and a seedling of White Seedling 59-1-99×Superba. It is a chrysanthe-

mum of much promise, and scored 89 points.

The prizes were offered by Peter Reinberg and Wietor Brothers and these were awarded as follows, J. P. Kidwell and George Stollery acting as judges: Garfield Park Floral Company, certificate of merit and prizes of $15 and $5; J. A. Peterson, Cincinnati, O., certificate of merit and $10; W. L. Palinsky, $5; Kalous Brothers, $5; Vaughan's Greenhouses, honorable mention; Chicago Carnation Company, certificate of merit and $5 for Golden Gate roses; for carnations, $5; Peter Reinberg, certificate of merit for Uncle John rose; Nathan Smith & Son, Adrian, Mich., certificate of merit for John Burton chrysanthemum.

Chrysanthemum Society of America.

WORK OF COMMITTEES.

At New York, December 9, the following was shown:

Seedling, John Burton; light rose pink with silvery reverse, giving a shell pink appearance, Japanese incurved; shown by Nathan Smith & Son, Adrian, Mich.; scored 85 points commercial scale.

At Philadelphia, December 1, was shown the variety John Burton; an incurved Japanese, soft daybreak pink in color; shown by Nathan Smith & Son, Adrian, Mich.; scored 89 points, commercial scale. FRED. H. LEMON, Secy.

NATHAN SMITH & SON'S NEW LIGHT PINK CHRYSANTHEMUM, JOHN BURTON

(Scored 89 points at Chicago and Philadelphia.)

Nitrate Deposits of the Sahara.

The nitrate of soda industry, says Commercial Intelligence, is of enormous importance to Chili. There are nearly 100 works, producing about 1,400,000 metric tons of 2,204 pounds each annually, the estimated value of which is $54,504,800 in Europe. Can the African deposits described by travelers be compared with those of Chile? All the question of future prosperity lies here. If they exist, they are workable in spite of the distance from the coast, because the exit duty of $11.52 per ton exacted by Chile would compensate for heavier transport tariffs. Numbers of experts, according to E. Gauthier, are convinced that there are deposits, more extensive than those of South America, extending over all the west of the Sahara from Adar to the coast of the Atlantic and south of Morocco. This, he considers, is an explanation of M. Jacques Lebaudy's conduct, who is regarded as a business man.

TAYLORVILLE, ILL.—The Taylorville Floral Company, which has five houses, two for bedding plants, a rose, a carnation and a vegetable house, is growing plants almost entirely for home trade. There will be another range of houses erected here soon for vegetables.

The Carnation.

PETER FISHER says that Nelson Fisher, Enchantress and Mrs. M. A. Patten are all from the same seed pod, parentage Lawson and Bradt.

It is supposed that the Malmaison carnation was raised by Boupland, superintendent of the Empress Josephine's gardens. The empress is said to have been an ardent cultivator of carnations.

THE BRIDE.

This variety we have been growing for the past four years in several different kinds of soil, and find it equally good in all. It is an early, free and continuous producer. The flowers are pure white, averaging three to three and one-half inches with good stout stems carrying the flowers erect, averaging fourteen to sixteen inches long. This is by far the most prolific flowering white we have ever grown.   JOHN N. MAY.
[See illustration herewith.]

NOTES ON VARIETIES.

The following notes are made mostly from a few plants of each variety, planted together in one house. The house is run at a temperature of 50°, so no special treatment can be given any one variety, and no feeding has been done. Plants were benched from the field early in July.

The Bride.—Healthy, free, wiry grower; fine formed pure white flowers on stiff stems; looks like an "A1" commercial variety.

Alba.—Has given some good flowers but is too slow.

Harlowarden.—Fine, bold flowers, healthy, vigorous plants, and fairly free for so large a flower; the stem is too long and color a shade too dark.

Apollo.—Slow and diseased; has given some good flowers; seems to have all the faults of Crane.

Adonis.—Now showing a fine bloom; made no growth in field and could not be benched until late August, as plants were so small.

Marshall Field.—Has not done much; plants vigorous and healthy; stem good; flowers not so good as Bradt.

Enchantress.—Free grand grower, fine large flower, extra stem; easily the best of the 1903 varieties up to date; the only fault we have seen, so far, is a tendency to fade in the outer petals; this has been growing less since November 15.

Roosevelt.—No longer in it; Harry Fenn is much better.

Whitney.—Still the best in its class.

Nelson.—Not yet to be discarded by those who want quantity and reasonably good quality.

Mrs. Theo. Roosevelt.—Has done nothing with us, but has not had quite a fair show.

Cressbrook.—Outclassed.

Her Majesty.—Healthy plant, fair grower and fairly free; good flower but comes streaked with red.

Penelope.—Very early and has given some good flowers, but bursts badly and seems to lack substance; stem weak.

Wolcott.—Has given some grand flowers; bursts and is not free; probably would do much better with more heat.

Gov. Lowndes.—Sickly and straggly; has given a few good flowers.

Lawson.—Has not done so well as last year.

White Lawson.—All that Lawson ever had of good qualities, this has, with us, and the form is better; in our light soil the stem is long enough. (We have none for sale.)   W. N. RUDD.

VENTILATION.

A uniform state of purity in the atmosphere of a carnation house is necessary to the health of the plants, as much as proper ventilation is necessary to the well being of the tenants of a dwelling house. The amount of carbonic acid gas consumed by the plants in a house of carnations in full growth must deplete the air of this element in a very few hours, depriving the organs of the plants of the element necessary for the elaborate process of throwing off waste matter and building up new tissues. What such a state of affairs must lead to is easily seen. Therefore if we would promote the most perfect possible growth it is necessary to provide the means for admitting at all times a liberal supply of this life-giving fluid. We should aim to have the air in the greenhouse as nearly as possible as pure as the air out of doors. The regulation of the temperature during the day by means of adjusting the ventilators usually takes care of the ventilation, but during spells of adverse weather conditions, when the temperature outside is 10° or 15° below the normal indoor temperature, for instance, the purification of the atmosphere requires some extra attention. In cold weather it also becomes necessary to see that a thorough change of air is given at least every twenty-four hours. In old houses that are not very tight a strong wind may penetrate sufficiently to do away with the necessity of opening the ventilators for a few days in succession in extreme cases. But the newer and tighter the house the less can we depend upon natural conditions and must show the keenest judgment as to the needs of the plants. This may account for the fact that some florists can get better results from an old house than from a new one. The carnation is decidedly a fresh air loving plant and will not tolerate a restriction of the supply for a moment.

The ventilating sash should be so arranged that all parts of the house will be evenly supplied with air when they are open. This can only be accomplished by having the sash continuous, or at most only a small space between each sash. A row of sash on the south side of the house, or on the east side, if the house runs north and south, hinged at the top, is probably the most satisfactory arrangement for the roof ventilation.

Side ventilation at one or both sides of the house will supplement this to great advantage during the hot summer months. The small cost at which these adjustable sash can be put in can hardly be considered an item in the cost of construction. A good machine, of which there are several on the market, is necessary in these days of labor saving devices, to insure regular attention, for the roof at least. In houses longer than seventy-five feet it is well to have a machine for about every fifty lineal feet of sash, as the temperature often varies considerably in different parts of the house, rendering it necessary under same weather conditions to raise the sash much higher on one end of the house than on the other. Double strength pipe should be used for shafting, in order to do away as nearly as possible with difference in the height of the sash. The side ventilators being used only when they can be left open nearly all the time, can be worked just about as satisfactorily with an iron rod with holes drilled at intervals of two or three inches.

In regulating the temperature it should be the aim to imitate a natural day as nearly as possible, rising gradually up to the middle of the day and dropping gradually towards its close. Early in the morning when the sun exerts its first influence upon the temperature indoors, begin with a crack and at intervals of a half hour or so increase the supply, rising two or three degrees each time. This brings the temperature up to the normal day temperature about the latter part of the forenoon, where it should be held until about two o'clock, to be lowered again by the same process. Cold draughts should, of course, be avoided. In cold weather, 3:30 or 4 o'clock will find them closed again with the temperature about five degrees above the night temperature. After another drop of a degree or two it will be time to turn on the steam and come down slowly to the night temperature. On mild nights a crack of air on all night is very beneficial. The proper day temperature will depend upon the amount of sunshine and the temperature at which the house is kept at night. Ordinarily a rise of from 15° to 20° will be right when the sun is bright, and from 5° to 10° in cloudy weather—the brighter the weather the higher the temperature.   J.

JOHN N. MAY'S NEW CARNATION, THE BRIDE.

PHALAENOPSIS AMABILIS AT DR. SCHIFFMAN'S, ST. PAUL, MINN.

Phalaenopsis Amabilis.

The accompanying illustration shows a group of Phalaenopsis amabilis from a photograph recently taken at the establishment of Dr. Schiffmann, at St. Paul, Minn. Dr. Schiffmann has had much success in the cultivation of phalaenopsis and finds good demand for the blooms. P. Stuartiana is also in bloom at the present time. Dr. Schiffman has recently returned from Europe and will go to the orient next month, returning in May with a large collection of orchids, including about one thousand plants of P. Schilleriana and a number of Vanda Sanderiana.

Garden Competitions.

The Parisians have discovered with intelligence and good taste that the ordinary flower show has little to do with gardening as a branch of the arts. It is all very well, if one likes that sort of thing, to exhibit the largest and heaviest rose that ever gardener over-blew, and take a prize with it. If his ingenuity is perverse enough, he will next contrive some languid and pampered hybrid and take a prize with that, too, adding a third for some flower the color of which he has distorted from its natural hue. These are what the circus bills call feats of strength and agility, and they bear about the same relation to the art of gardening as the athletic stunts at the circus to the art of sculpture, according to the New York Commercial Advertiser. The crowd on the boards are ready with applause for the one, and the horticultural societies and florists' clubs with prizes for the other.

Real gardening, in the intelligent view, has little concern with the rarity or the cost of flowers, still less with abnormal traits in them. Gardening becomes an art when it so arranges flowers, shrubs, lawns and trees that they please the taste through the eye by their effects of line, mass, space and color. It is akin to the art of the painter with the ampler colors, the more brilliant lights and the broader spaces that nature gives the gardener. In the ordinary garden about the suburban or the country house, it is landscape architecture on a little scale. Even the very rich stand in awe of such a big phrase, but the humble commuter applies it when he plans his little garden in the autumn and lays it out next spring.

In France there must be prizes for every thing, and as soon as the Parisians discovered that flower shows do not reward real gardening, they found a way to do it themselves. Of course, they "instituted a competition" among the gardens of Neuilly, a prosperous, intelligent suburb like our Oranges. Thirty householders entered their gardens, and in an appointed week the jury visited them. Artists as eminent as Dagnan-Bouveret served on it, and it finally bestowed the prizes for "delicious" combinations of color, "beautifully arranged" beds, and the like. In one garden even the despised yellow daisies of our fields were so artistically disposed as to win a prize.

Here in America our rich occasionally have their names, with an incongruous Latin termination, fastened to some product of their gardener's ingenuity, and then boast vaguely of it. They should set their gardeners to the practice of the real art of gardening, and Newport and Lenox should "institute their competitions," like Neuilly. They would want to visit each other's gardens with the jury and make the occasion a function to which a discreet public might be admitted at a high price, as they are at a horse show, to provide a suitable number of admiring onlookers. The richer and more ambitious suburbs could do likewise in their own way, just as they now have their horse shows, and gratify every reasonable curiosity about each other's "grounds." The mere commuter in his turn would no longer have to be content with an "item" in the local paper when his garden happened to contain an abnormal carnation or an overloaded rose bush. He might win a week's competition, as at Neuilly, and be for seven days in his neighbors' eyes. Meanwhile, and not altogether accidentally, the true gardener might receive his merited deserts.

BALTIMORE, MD.—Leamon W. Leach has a new insecticide for which he claims much.

DENVER, COLO.—The Scott Floral Company (Phil Scott and E. J. Reynolds) announces that the new store, 839 Sixteenth street, corner of Champa street, will be occupied after January 1.

BLOOMINGTON, ILL.—"Business is very quiet," says F. A. Baller, "and the weather unusually severe. I have often noticed that when winter sets in unusually cold and stormy that we are very apt to have considerable respite later."

HOOPESTON, ILL.—The establishment of Andrew Peterson & Company is now in first-class shape. The carnations, roses and pot plants occupy houses 70x120 feet and the conservatory, 25x70 feet, is well filled with ornamental stock. The office, a neat brick structure, is a cozy, comfortable place and well equipped for business.

With the Growers.

A. N. PIERSON, CROMWELL, CONN.

W. R. Pierson.

The last of the crop of ten big chrysanthemum houses at the A. N. Pierson establishment has been cleared out, and now the lilies take possession. Everything is done on such a large scale here, there being over 500,000 feet of glass area, that one is not surprised when informed by Mr. Pierson that he has found it necessary to establish a dairy this fall with sixty-five cows as a starter in order to procure sufficient manure for use on the place.

Of carnations no less than 30,000 are planted. A new house 40x140 has been recently added to the carnation range. Wallace R. Pierson, who devotes his interest and time exclusively to carnation culture, advocates narrow benches and has been putting them in three and a half feet wide instead of five feet, as heretofore. He doesn't believe in field culture for carnation plants. A grand house of Queen Louise and one of Enchantress and Mrs. Lawson in the very pink of condition attest the wisdom of his practice.

There are so many rose houses in this establishment that it is doubtful whether the proprietor even can tell their exact number. All stock is grafted on the place, 135,000 having been grafted the past season. Here, as in the case of the carnations, tendency is to make the benches narrower and lower, three rows to a bench being considered sufficient in the case of American Beauty. Early planting is also one of Mr. Pierson's cardinal rules. The new rose, Franz Deegan, occupies an entire house and certainly makes a good impression with its rich wine-red growths and deep orange and yellow buds. Ashes find favor as a material in which to root roses on account of immunity from fungus of any sort.

One million seven hundred thousand lily of the valley and 500,000 bulbs of various kinds are forced here annually. A good proportion of the lily of the valley used is home grown. It requires three years cultivation in the field, with persistent weeding and generous mulching, so is no cheaper than the imported stock. Its advantage lies chiefly in the fact of its early maturing so the pips may be put in cold storage as early as October 1, thus securing good foliage on the early-forced lots, something impossible with the imported material. Mr. Pierson proposes henceforth to grow less of this stock and do it better, planting the rows fourteen inches apart instead of eight inches as heretofore and running the cultivator freely.

There is a house of Asparagus plumosus, 550 feet in length and two of Adiantum Farleyense 275 feet in length which are a sight worth going a long distance to see. The Farleyense is under the entire control of Mr. Schwartz who is remarkably expert in its handling.

The whole establishment is equipped with a double heating system, one outfit for steam and one for hot water. The circulation of the hot water is accelerated by steam pressure. A very frugal and seemingly profitable device is the construction of a little frame lean-to house against each ¾-span house, for propagating purposes, smilax growing, etc.

Mr. Pierson's storage rooms for cut flowers are cooled by upright cylinders of broken ice. Here are kept most flowers except carnations. Ice is deemed injurious to the keeping qualities of carnations. Many varieties of chrysanthemums are grown but Maud Dean and Major Bonnaffon are retained as pre-eminently money makers.

JOHN BARR, SOUTH NATICK, MASS.

The enterprise started here by John Barr under the title of Little South Floral Company has undergone a change of management and will henceforth be conducted under Mr. Barr's own name. Mr.

Barr was at the time of its inception gardener in charge of the extensive private estate of Mrs. B. P. Cheney and, with commendable judgment, retained his position until he could feel assured of the earning capacity of the new establishment. As is now generally known to the trade the place has already acquired a reputation in the dissemination of The Queen, one of the most useful white carnations ever put out, and in the Boston market the product of the houses is held in high estimation. Those who had the pleasure of seeing the wonderful exhibits of chrysanthemums, cyclamens and other specialties which won for Mr. Barr the highest honors year after year at the exhibitions of the Massachusetts Horticultural Society will understand why.

A new house 22x210 has been added the past season to the three of the original range and a new propagating house is now being built for the purpose of supplying the call for The Queen which promises to be very heavy again the coming season. The variety is now, as it has been all through the fall, a forest of buds already so tall that it will soon require the fourth tier of wires. Fair Maid is also a pleasing and profitable carnation as grown here being very prolific and retaining the favor of the trade. Among the dark varieties Harry Fenn is best liked and will supplant all others the coming season. There is a fine bunch of Stella, Dorner's beautiful variegated variety, which has done its full duty as a profitable carnation thus far. Morning Glory is so slow and so far inferior in all respects to Fair Maid that it will be grown no more here.

Mr. Barr has arranged to act as local disseminator of Totty's noted set of new chrysanthemums and will add chrysanthemums to carnations as a regular specialty of his business. He is jubilant over the fact that two of the most successful exhibitors at the recent Horticultural Society's chrysanthemum show, Messrs. Anderson, who staged the winning set of eight specimen plants and

UPPER SECTION OF A. N. PIERSON'S ESTABLISHMENT, CROMWELL, CONN.
A REAR VIEW OF THE LOWER PLACE.

Abrahams, who took six firsts with six entries, are both pupils of his.

ROBT. SCOTT & SON, SHARON HILL, PA.

The problem of raising and successfully blooming cape jasmines has discomfited many an ambitious grower, the discovery that all the flower buds had suddenly become blighted and yellow being his

Besides the gardenias there are other things of much interest to be seen there. All the popular varieties of roses are planted out for propagating purposes for Burpee's catalogue trade, and in fact everything in the plant line for that enterprising establishment is grown here. Mr. Scott was one of the introducers of Liberty rose, and takes pride in demonstrating the good qualities of that much

ence planted in solid beds, but whose "neck" proves to be too long and soft under winter forcing conditions.

A canna field outside was a gorgeous spectacle this fall, the most effective of all being Kate Grey, a tall orange of Italia type, remarkable for the size and abundance of its flowers. Another in the Italia section is Pennsylvania, a superb vermilion. Austria and McKinley also make a great showing. Gloriosa, an exceedingly dwarf variety with scarlet, gold bordered flowers, has proved the most popular catalogue variety the past season.

Mr. Scott has built a manure house. 35x50, which seems to be a very useful innovation, as under its cover the manure is saved from waste by rain-washings, and becoming dried and pulverized is in better condition for greenhouse use. It is constructed with cement bottom and sides and at one end is a water tank, seven feet deep, into which the manure can be conveniently thrown, and from which the manure water required for the greenhouses is pumped direct.

Ed. Schwartz, who now officiates as foreman for this establishment, has grown up on the place, having started with the firm as a boy.

CHRYSANTHEMUM MAUD DEAN.
(A. N. Pierson's, Cromwell, Conn., fall of 1903.)

first intimation that the apparently healthy plants had played him false, and that all his anticipations of a money-making crop of flowers were doomed; indeed, it is probably safe to assert that disappointment has oftener than otherwise been the outcome of the venture of gardenia growing.

Without assuming to make any predictions as to the results in flowers, and conceding that the critical period in their life is still to come, it is yet possible to refer to the gardenias at the Sharon Hill greenhouses of Robert Scott & Son in terms of superlative commendation. Mr. Scott himself is cautious enough to refrain from any forecast, but inasmuch as a first-class plant is the prime requirement, his success thus far is certainly significant. From cuttings struck last winter he now (late September) has fifteen hundred plants in 8-inch pots, two-and-a-half feet high and of equal width, with luxuriant foliage and sturdy stems, on the tips of which numerous flower buds are now developing.

A recent visit found Mr. Scott bending over his plants, peering intently into the tips of the twigs, looking for the "shoulders" which designate the rudimentary flower buds. Asked as to his method of culture, he stated that he never permits his plants to undergo the slightest check in their growth from the time of rooting. Starting in 2-inch pots, they are kept in the greenhouse at a high humidity and with a good bottom heat, shifted along to 4-inch, then 6-inch, then 8-inch, as quickly as the young roots reach the pots, and vigorous growth is encouraged in the young stages by plunging the pots in a hotbed and afterwards in sphagnum. They are syringed frequently, and when mealy bug makes its appearance it is treated to a sharp stream of water from a fine nozzle.

discussed variety. He asserts that the great secret of successful Liberty culture is never to let the plants get a check. A crop of buds a month ago was nipped off as there was then no sale for the blooms. A crop is now coming in from the high breaks, after which the plants will be cut back hard, then started later and kept growing rapidly, which course will bring in the main crop in January. Dickson's Killarney, a pretty rose with a pretty name, erstwhile known in New York as No. 19—the rose that was to make Mrs. Westinghouse famous—ranks with Maman Cochet, Papa Gontier and Kaiserin Augusta Victoria as an outdoor rose. Another of Dickson's production that promises well as a summer variety for cut flowers is Florence Pemberton, said to be the largest tea in existence.

Basket Campanulas.

By these I mean the group of which Campanula isophylla alba is such a well known type. Strange to say, no attempt appears to have been made to raise seedlings, the supposition being, apparently, that the plants were sterile; and yet I have this season raised some hundreds of seedlings from C. isophylla, from its white variety, and from the distinct C. Barrellierii, says a correspondent of Horticultural Advertiser, an English journal. Here let me state that I can not accept the statement of the "Dictionary of Gardening" that C. Barrelleirii is a synonym of C. fragilis; the former has a much more compact habit of growth, and also in flowering; C. fragilis throws its flower stems at considerable length; C. Barrelleirii not nearly so long; and while the blossoms of the latter are deeper in color, flatter, and with broader segments, those of C. fragilis are paler, more cupped and with narrower and more pointed segments, while the leaves are more deeply toothed on the edges. The two are flowering side by side on the shelf of my greenhouse, and I have C. isophylla alba, C. Mayii and C. Balchiniana, all flowering at the same time; the

PARTIAL VIEW OF ROBT. SCOTT & SON'S ESTABLISHMENT, SHARON HILL, PA.

FLORISTS' WINDOW SCREEN.

blossoms of the latter have a certain distinctness of character.

My seedlings are from seeds taken in 1901. The summer was hot and dry, and wishing to test whether the plant produced fertile seeds, I gathered some shoots, after flowering, from C. isophylla, from its white variety, and from C. Barrellierii, keeping each distinct by wrapping each securely in some newspapers. They were overlooked until this spring; I then rubbed out the seed, saved those from each sort separately and to my great surprise got many seedlings from each. Each sort has produced plants very like the seed parent, in general character; but from among the two blue varieties I have been able to select some plants with distinct woolly foliage, much more than is seen in C. Mayii. I have three or four at least whose leaves are densely covered with minute white hairs. I made no attempt at cross-fertilizing; the bees had an unrestricted range of the plants, and having a small plant of C. Mayii in flower at the same time, the woolly character in the progeny may have been derived from that.

Singular to state, one of my large plants of C. Barrellierii, the foliage of which is of bare deep green, this season put forth one strong shoot of distinctly woolly character, which I took off and attempted to root, but failed to do so. I have been informed upon authority which I could not but accept, that in cases the variegated leaved C. Balchiniana has sported to the woolly-leaved C. Mayii. I am told this could not possibly be. But I have learned enough of the family of campanulas to impress me with the fact that it is unwise to dogmatize about them. They have within them evident possibilities which should lead the most audacious among us not to be too positive in any statements we may make about them.

VANCOUVER, B. C.—The Vancouver Floral Company has added two more houses to its plant, one 20x80 and one 16x20. James Font has built three new houses, one 30x50, one 10x54 and one 10x40.

TRENTON, N. J. — The twenty-ninth annual meeting of the New Jersey State Horticultural Society will be held at the State house here on Thursday and Friday, January 7 and 8.

The Retail Trade.

THE elegance of a box of carnation flowers is greatly enhanced by the addition of a few sprays of carnation foliage. No other green can compare with it in association with carnations. It is a good plan to have a bunch of plants, of some rank growing sort, in an out-of-the-way corner for this purpose.

FLORISTS' WINDOW SCREENS.

The illustration herewith shows the skeleton of a florists' window screen, which is being offered by Franz Birnstiel, of Coburg, Germany. It is made in sections of various sizes with mirror in the center and is not very expensive. Receptacles for flowers and plants, vases, jardeniers, etc., are arranged on the frame work.

DECORATIVE WORK OF THE DAY.

At last the season seems to have fairly begun, and a few things that have come under my notice during the week may be of interest. At a tea given on Fifth avenue I saw a handsome bouquet of the new Breitmeyer rose, La Detroit, with long stems, and a large cluster of lily of the valley, tied with pale green ribbon. Another was made of mignonette and

Sunrise roses with orange ribbon, giving it quite an oriental appearance.

The young lady in whose honor the reception was given, instead of carrying the usual bouquet, had an arrangement of white flowers made as follows: A light garland of gardenias, lily of the valley and Adiantum cuneatum, about thirty inches long, tied at each end with long, loose bows of No. 5 white silk ribbon, and suspended along its full length was a shower of No. 2 white silk gauze. Lily of the valley and Adiantum cuneatum were attached to this by long careless bows in the same manner as in a shower bouquet. One of the loops is slipped over the left arm. the other end of the garland may be attached to the dress, or picked up in the right hand.

A wedding outfit sent out by a leading florist, the finest I have seen this winter, consisted of six large bouquets of cattleya interspersed with sprays of Laelia autumnalis, tied with ribbon, and a splendid bridal bouquet of lily of the valley and Dendrobium formosum giganteum.

At a dinner for forty I saw a very effective table decoration. In the center was a sunken fountain six feet across, illuminated by electricity, the basin filled with fish, and callas rising out of the water at the sides. The remainder of the table was covered with thick green moss and wild smilax, with bronze deer placed here and there, giving a wild woodland effect. The menus were printed on birch bark.

Another pretty dinner for a small party consisted of a center piece, comprised of corsages of violets and lily of the valley laid on a round basket or plateau. Gardenias for the gentlemen were also laid on, the spaces being filled in with lily of the valley and maidenhair fern. This is a very good arrangement for small tables.

THE ARTIST.

Chicago.

BUSINESS DULL, BUT AN ACTIVE HOLIDAY WEEK IS LOOKED FOR.—PLENTY OF GOOD STOCK IS EXPECTED FOR CHRISTMAS.—LINCOLN PARK TO BE EXTENDED.—GENERAL TRADE NOTES.

Local trade this week was not what could be termed flourishing, in fact at times it was practically at a standstill. Various forces conspired to bring about the dull condition of affairs. The usual distractions of the season preceding the Christmas holidays were aided and abetted by a spell of Arctic weather in

ADIANTUM FARLEYENSE AT A. N. PIERSON'S, CROMWELL, [CONN.

keeping the people away from the flower stores. Prices on the common run of stock are still within reach of every one, but the better grade of flowers, American Beauty, Liberty and all grades of carnations, have taken a decided step skyward. Stiff holiday prices promise to prevail in all grades, and from the outlook it appears that the demand will early clean up everything good on the market. Beauty is now coming in in good shape and quantity, and the only shortage is in medium lengths. The dark weather of last week did not have a beneficial effect on Brides and Bridesmaids, as they are not coming in so fast. All sorts of carnations, especially the colored, are moving fairly well and there will not be enough for Christmas. There appears to be plenty of violets and they are selling fairly well. Decorative material, holly, laurel leaves, spruce, etc., is now holding full sway and everything in this line is plentiful.

There was a good attendance at the regular meeting of the Florists' Club, December 16. W. A. Peterson, Adam Zender, Albert Woodward, J. F. Kidwell and F. S. Allen were elected members. The evening was devoted to routine business and the chairman of the executive committee announced that between January 1 and February 17 efforts would be made to have meetings in the various sections of the city, north, south and west. Dates and places of meetings will be made known later. All persons interested in the trade, non-members as well as members, are requested to attend, employes of trade firms being especially invited.

W. N. Rudd had a party of his local friends in the trade out at Mount Greenwood December 18. After a thorough inspection of the place, including the new carnation Phyllis, the visitors were royally entertained by the genial host, who also made the trip a pleasant one by securing a special car and serving refreshments enroute.

The cold weather of the present week set a record for a decade for the same time of the year. The mercury took a tumble without warning and coal is now king at the greenhouses. The heavy coat of snow over the glass proved a good protection from the cold Monday and but for this more damage would have resulted.

Lincoln Park is to be enlarged and improved by the addition of 250 acres of north shore property. Plans for the proposed improvement were considered formally for the first time at a conference of the park commissioners December 12. All favored the plan.

John Mangel is enjoying his usual thriving ante-Christmas trade. This week brought an unusual large number of wedding decorations. A bunch of orchids valued at $100 was sent the early part of the week to John F. Lee, St. Louis, Mo.

The Lincoln Park stock is in admirable shape for the holidays. Charles J. Strombach, head gardener, is taking a pardonable pride in the splendid collection of orchids to be seen there now. The park poinsettias are worthy of special mention.

The Florists' and Gardeners' Union will hold an important meeting Wednesday evening, December 23. The annual election of officers will take place and other business of importance be transacted.

George Reinberg is contemplating some important extensions and improvements at his greenhouses. A range of twelve rose houses will be built in the spring.

Charles W. McKellar, who recently returned from a holiday sojourn in the west, will re-enter the wholesale cut flower and commission business in this city about January 1.

The Florists' and Gardeners' Union has demanded from the commissioners of Lincoln Park an increase of wages for the eight members employed at the park. John Sterritt, with Weiland & Risch, Monday slipped on the ice and fell, severely wrenching his back. He was confined to his bed several days.

S. Peiser returned this week from a sojourn in San Francisco and other Pacific Coast points. He reports business on the coast in thriving condition.

Lawson and White Cloud carnations, with 2-foot stems, may be seen at Sinner Brothers. Their stock of Christmas folding bells is exhausted.

Many wholesale houses are sending out to their patrons uniquely contrived Christmas greetings in connection with their price lists.

'Frank H. Traendly.
(President-elect New York Florists' Club.)

J. B. Deamud has returned from a week's rabbit shooting on his Michigan farm. He claims a score of forty-seven rabbits.

F. Kennicott is convalescing from an attack of inflammatory rheumatism. He was out Tuesday for the first time in two weeks.

Vaughan's Seed Store is offering some European hollies in pots, variegated and plain, the latter exceptionally well berried.

Miss Annie Kreitling has had her name pleasantly interwoven with matrimonial rumors.

A trade visitor here this week was W.L. Morris, Des Moines, Ia.

New York.

FLORISTS' CLUB MEETING.—ELECTION OF OFFICERS.—GREENHOUSE THIEVES BUSY. — ADDITION TO CHARLES MILLANG'S PLACE.

The monthly meeting of the Florists' Club was held on the evening of December 14, forty members being present and President Troy in the chair. After the general routine of business had been transacted, election of officers for 1904

was held. The result was as follows: President, F. H. Traendly; vice-president, S. S. Butterfield; secretary, John Young; treasurer, C. B. Weathered; trustees, Alex. Wallace, W. J. Elliott, Theodore J. Lang. Each newly-elected officer then made a short speech. Mr. Lang started the ball rolling for a new bowling club and quite a good many of the members expressed a willingness to join. Mr. Lang promised to look up some good alleys and thought that we ought to have a strong team to send to St. Louis at the coming convention, and also to bring back a few cups. A committee was appointed to draw up suitable resolutions in behalf of the family of the late Thomas W. Weathered, also the family of the late Geo. T. N. Cottam. E. G. Hill, of Richmond, Ind., was present and made an interesting speech.

A surprise party was given to Victor L. Dorsai, of Woodside, on Tuesday, December 8, the occasion being his seventieth birthday. Among those present were Mr. and Mrs. John Donaldson, Mr. and Mrs. Charles Smith, Mr. and Mrs. Wm. Amos, Mr. and Mrs. Jos. Sklenka, Mr. and Mrs. Louis Dupuy.

The midnight visitors are still at it and on Tuesday night they visited the establishment of John Lymber, of Woodside, and made quite a haul, relieving that gentleman of carnations and other flowers, besides taking all the mignonette which he had been saving for the holidays.

John Hopkins, of Aqueduct, L. I., who has been under the weather for the last two weeks, had almost a fatal experience last week, chloride of lime being given to him by mistake. He luckily did not swallow any of it but the inside of his mouth was badly burned.

John Reimels possesses some new carnations, one red variety, a cross between Prosperity and Crane, and a pink one which resembles Albertina in color, a cross between Prosperity and Mrs. James Dean. This is the second year for both of them.

Alexander S. Burns of Woodside, who sued the New York and Queens County Railroad Company for injuries to his wife received in an accident on the road has received a verdict in his favor from a jury for $8,000.

Charles Millang is building a fine conservatory in the back of his store; he now occupies the entire length of the lot and will stock with flowering plants.

The Cut Flower Exchange had its monthly meeting December 5, at its office in the Coogan building. General business was transacted.

Otto Grundmann, of Secaucus, N. J., has a fine lot of Harrisii lilies which he is cutting from about 25,000 plants.

A dynamite explosion at Bronx Park yesterday (December 18) shattered much of the glass in the greenhouses.

Harold Eltzholtz, of Cedarhurst, has lost a suit for damages against his landlord.

Philadelphia.

LULL BEFORE THE HOLIDAY STORM.—NEW THEORY OF CAUSE OF BLACK SPOT.—NEW CORPORATION.—COLD WEATHER AFFECTS BUSINESS.

Things are quiet as is usual before the storm which it is hoped will break over the town next week. Take the season up to this time and there has been a falling off in the volume of trade to quite a considerable extent over that of last year. The effect of this is seen in the prices of flowers. Beauties in particular are not bringing as much by at least a third. Other stock is also lower but the difference is not so pronounced. It begins to look as if the Beauty demand has at last been supplied. The Christmas price will not reach above a dollar except possibly for some few specials which may bring an added quarter. Carnations are quoted at $4 to $8. Bells and wreaths are in evidence everywhere. There are quantities of holly about and most of it is very good. Lycopodium is scarce, however, and sells on sight at 15 cents per pound. All the flowering plants appear to be in good shape and will reach the standard of former years except possibly begonias which are not quite as good. The growers with an out-of-town trade are greatly worried on account of the severe weather which continues steadily and makes shipping of such tender stock very hazardous.

The Millbrook Lea Company, of Whatford, has been incorporated under the laws of Delaware with a capital stock of $100,-000. The company has 60,000 feet of glass in which a Lord & Burnham sectional boiler of large capacity has just been placed. J. S. Moull, whose business has been taken into the company, is manager. Carnations are the principal crop. They do unusually well here, the soil being largely impregnated with soapstone which the plants seem to like.

Jacob Becker has a theory as to the cause of black spot and rust on carnations. He thinks it is due in a measure to the use of iron stakes which corrode and give off an acid into the soil that is injurious to the roots of the plants and shows in the foliage when they take it up. Hereafter bamboo stakes for him, as a house of carnations tied up with them shows no sign of the dreaded spot.

The Lord & Burnham Company has placed a sample sectional boiler in its space at the market which should be a convenience to any one contemplating the purchase of a boiler.

Mr. Becker has a house of azaleas which are watered with tepid water, temperature about 85°. This he believes to be absolutely necessary to forcing the azaleas for Christmas.

John Walsh Young is sending in some very well colored Pandanus Veitchii.
K.

Boston.

CUT FLOWER BUSINESS VERY QUIET.—COLD WEATHER PREVAILS AND FROZEN SHIPMENTS REPORTED.—AMERICAN BEAUTY PRICES DROP.—FIRE AT FEINSTEIN'S.

Cut flower trade is practically at a standstill this week. Such buying as is being done is largely for holding purposes for Christmas, in anticipation of the impending advance in values. It has been very cold all through the week but with clear skies. As usual, more or less frozen shipments have been received. Last week saw a drop in value of American Beauty roses, they having proved unable to maintain the prices of the previous week. There is no question as to the scarcity of bright colored carnations for Christmas. These will probably bring a record price. The sale of green material is progressing and is developing unprecedented proportions. This does not apply to ground pine in any form. The New England trade has turned its back on this material and the question of its scarcity or abundance elsewhere fails to interest. Laurel has completely supplanted it for festooning, wreaths, etc., and is having an enormous sale. Even

holly wreaths have been forced to take a back seat. Loose holly has, however, more than held its own, and as the quality generally seen is excellent this year it is probable that the amount handled will surpass that in any former years. Holly at the city markets is piled up in cargo lots and buyers who are simple can get accommodated with cases at cut-rate prices. A recent experiment with the scales explains the secret, it being ascertained that this "catch-as-catch-can" material weighs all the way up to fifty pounds per case lighter than the standard cases handled by the wholesale flower people.

The sixth annual meeting of the Massachusetts Forestry Association was held December 10. Dr. H. P. Walcott was elected president and E. A. Start of Billerica, secretary and treasurer.

N. F. McCarthy & Co. are also busy. They have had some trouble with delayed holly shipments which they think will be fully compensated for when the quality is disclosed.

M. Feinstein, the North Station florist, suffered considerable damage from water and smoke in a disastrous fire in the building on Portland street in which his store is located.

Welch Brothers are doing a big holly business and report the cut flower shipping orders for Christmas as fully up to high-water mark of past years.

English mistletoe at Geo. A. Sutherland's is in remarkably fine condition, having come over without the slightest damage.

Visitors: H. F. A. Lange, Worcester; Wm. Appleton, Providence, R. I.

St. Louis.

MONTHLY MEETING OF FLORISTS' CLUB.—MANY WORLD'S FAIR NOTABLES ADDRESS MEETING.—NOTES OF THE FAIR.—TRADE AT A STANDSTILL, TOO COLD.

The monthly meeting of the Florists' Club, which was held on December 12, was well attended. The members of the club are becoming more enthused with each meeting—which is as it should be with the national convention not so very far off. New members are being constantly added to the roll; those who are inclined to be delinquent are receiving gentle reminders, and desirable recruits are being looked up. At this meeting John L. Koenig and Theo. Klockenkemper were elected members. J. W. Brenning and Henry Felter made application for membership. T. W. Brown, head gardener at the English exhibit at the World's Fair, addressed the club. He was later elected an honorary member. James Dunford read an interesting paper on "Stem Rot." An essay on "Greenhouse Heating," by Wm. Scott, of Buffalo, N. Y., was read by F. J. Fillmore. Max Herzog led a warm discussion on "Hot Water Heating." F. Dorner & Sons exhibited two vases of their new carnations, The Belle and Lady Bountiful. Both varieties were highly praised by the juding committee, Messrs. Winter, Steidel and Dunford. The new Breitmeyer rose was also on exhibition for the first time and received favorable comment. The resignation of Dr. Halstead, of Bellville, Ill., was accepted.

The fourteenth annual banquet given by the Missouri Botanical Garden to garden employes, florists and nurserymen in St. Louis and vicinity, on December 11, at the Mercantile Club, was a most enjoyable affair and of more than usual interest. Covers were set for seventy-five guests. After the dinner Dr.

Wm. Trelease, director of the garden, who officiated as toastmaster, announced that it was intended to have a change of programme each year, in fact something new, and for this occasion stereopticon views had been prepared by the speakers of the evening. Mr. Kessler, chief of the landscape department at the World's Fair, was then introduced. He spoke at length on what is being done in the landscape department. Views were shown of specimen trees and the grouping of shrubbery in the different parts of the grounds. The method of transplanting the big trees, some fifteen to twenty inches in diameter, was presented in detail. Mr. Kessler said that out of 300 trees planted only three had died.

After undergoing the rigors of a genuine old-fashioned blizzard, the worst in years, the florists find trade in a shaky condition. Prices remain the same, but the demand for flowers has fallen off considerably. Wholesale men say "there's nothing doing; it's too cold and people stay indoors." Stock is plentiful and of excellent quality.

M. Vachrat, head gardener to the city of Paris, France, who is in charge of the French garden at the Fair, was present and made a short address.

Otto Brening has entirely recovered from the indisposition of Thanksgiving week.

Mrs. H. C. Berning is seriously ill at her home.

Visitor: Wilbert Gullett, Lincoln, Ill.
F. K. B.

Washington.

PLENTY OF STOCK FOR HOLIDAYS.—BANQUETS MAKE BUSINESS.—RETAIL STORE DECORATIONS IN FORCE.

The show windows are being made attractive, red and green being everywhere prominent; while the growers are putting forth their best efforts to make a respectable showing of stock for Christmas. If the present bright weather continues there will be a better supply than was anticipated ten days ago. There is considerable poinsettia in sight and some azaleas will be in. Due Von Tholl tulips are on the market and are suitable for Christmas trade. Jerusalem cherries and peppers may also be seen in fair quantities. Good Liberty roses are now selling at $3 per dozen; good Testouts $3 per dozen; good Lawson carnations, $1 per dozen. Lawson holds its own against all comers. First-class violets, very few of which have come this way recently, have sold for $1.25 and $1.50 per bunch.

One of the most attractive show windows on Fourteenth street is that of Otto Bauer. A large Christmas bell adorns the centre with smaller bells surrounding, all in red. At night delicate shades of light from incandescent lamps in the bells give the whole a pleasing effect.

J. W. Small & Sons had a fine decoration in the banquet hall of the Arlington hotel at a dinner recently given by the Gridiron club, an organization of leading newspaper men.

The banquets and entertainments incidental to the meeting of the Republican national committee in this city last week made some business for the decorators.

Miss J. H. Ballenger, formerly with J. Louis Loose, is now in F. H. Kramer's store.

Philip Gauques, of the Botanical Gardens, is still in poor health.
S. E.

BROCKTON, MASS.—H. T. Crawford has been appointed receiver in the bankruptcy case of Charles S. Cooper.

Buffalo.

TRADE IS FAIR AND ACTIVE.—HOLIDAY BUSINESS LOOKED FOR.— CYCLAMEN EXHIBIT CLOSES.— NEUBECK'S NEW GREENHOUSE AND OFFICE.—REPORT OF THE.MELDRUM SHOW.

Trade the last week has been very good; several receptions called forth a large number of flowers, giving nearly all a chance to get busy. Funeral work was also quite active. Everyone is looking forward to a good Christmas trade. I made a call on L. H. Neubeck recently, and must say that he has the neatest and most up-to-date office and greenhouse to be found here. The store and office, while not large, are just what is wanted as the greenhouses are reached by ascending a few steps. The floors are cemented and all the woodwork is white and green. He has a very convenient private office.

A recent visitor was E. G. Hill, Richmond, Ind., who was going to Syracuse to see the Flamingo carnation at Marquisee's place; he also called on the trade and I believe did some selling. J. C. Peterson, of Cincinnati, Ohio, who has so much success with Begonia Gloire de Lorraine, was also a caller. Chas. H. Vick, New York State Superintendent of the St. Louis Fair, was also here in the interest of W. Hagermann & Co., New York.

The last meeting of the Florists' Club was well attended. Supt. Kettsch made a full report of the recent chrysanthemum show, showing that $926 was given in premiums. The H. A. Meldrum company was pleased with the success, and from a record kept there were 40,000 extra people in the store during the four days of the exhibition.

The exhibit of cyclamen between J. H. Rebstock and S. A. Anderson was decided in favor of Mr. Rebstock, his plants looking by far the best. Seven sent by Wm. Scott for display only were really more salable than either of the others as their size was what the majority of people would want.

F. G. Lewis, who put steam in his greenhouses at Lockport, N. Y., says nothing but steam for him. He still has his old houses heated with hot water.

Jerry Brookins, Orchard Park, has all his houses heated by steam as well as hot water. He says both were handy on Sunday and Monday.

Wm. Scott left Monday for Utica, N.Y., where he will give a talk on carnations before the Utica Florists' Club.

Severe weather with the temperature 8° above zero, kept all hustling to keep the houses warm.   BISON.

Toronto.

PRICES GO UP BUT DEMAND FOLLOWS STEADILY.—CARNATIONS GOOD AND PLENTIFUL BUT ROSES ARE SCARCE.—CHRISTMAS BELLS ARE RINGING.

Real wintry weather and good business is favoring us at present. Prices keep on their upper tendency, but even this does not prevent the continued demand for good stock. Good roses of all varieties are short; the second grade stock is more abundant. American Beauty is selling well and fortunately the stock keeps up to the high standard. Meteor is decidedly off and though the color is good the flowers are small. Bridesmaid and Bride only average a fair quality. Carnations are good and selling rapidly and if the stock holds its present fine quality there will be fine flowers for the holidays. Violets continue scarce though valley is getting more plentiful as also are callas. Christmas bells of all kinds, sizes and

descriptions are to be seen everywhere. There have been some very attractive windows the last week. Dunlop, displayed a very choice window of poinsettia and southern smilax; Chas. Tidy showed very fine Beauty and valley; Thos. Plumb, on Yonge street, had some very nice chrysanthemums and J. S. Simmers a good mixed window.

Chas. Turpe, in his new greenhouses has been doing exceedingly well with carnations and roses and intends to double his present capacity. Another of his specialties is mushrooms.

Grobba & Wandrey at Mimico intend putting up six new houses next summer for carnations. This firm will get away from growing of palms and ferns and go heavier into cut flowers.

Our violet specialist, Wm. Fendley, of Brampton, is cutting some very fine Princess of Wales, having stems fourteen inches long and very large flowers deeply colored.

Walter Muston, of the North Toronto Floral Company, has some very well grown Begonia Gloire de Lorraine. Geo. Hollis is cutting good Paper Whites and hyacinths. He has a stock of small ferns which find ready sale.

Wm. Jay & Son have a fine selection of plants that will be ready for the holidays. Lilium Harrisii is scarce. only a few stray blooms coming from J. H. Dunlop.

H. G. D.

Kansas City.

THANKSGIVING TRADE SHOWS AN INCREASE. —CHRYSANTHEMUMS SHOW A GAIN IN QUALITY. — PRICES AVERAGE GOOD. — TRADE NEWS.

While there was some complaint among the retailers as to the Thanksgiving trade not coming up to expectations, the majority of the downtown stores report an increase. Ideal weather conditions favored the foot-ball enthusiasts and several thousand yellow chrysanthemums were sold at good prices. Box trade for Thanksgiving was also very good. Taking it on an average the increase amounted to about fifteen per cent for this holiday. The quality of chrysanthemums offered this year was far ahead of last season and they commanded better prices, from $3 to $6 per dozen. The best American Beauty sold for $8 per dozen. Teas brought $2, fancy carnations $1.50, ordinary stock 75 cents. Violets were scarce at 50 cents per bunch of twenty-five. The week following Thanksgiving stock moved rather slowly. Were this a good market for supply, stock no doubt would have accumulated. Some days we wish it were, again we are glad it is not. Present indications are that there will be a large quantity of southern holly shipped in here. If so, prices will drop. The market will not stand many extra cars.

The air begins to scent of holly and pine. Early calls show signs of a heavy holiday business.

Arthur Newell, of Twelfth street, reports many funeral orders the last week.

Department stores have quit selling cut flowers, at least until after the holidays. Everton E. Law, of Butte, Mont., was a recent visitor.   W.

Cleveland.

The Cleveland Florists' Club held its stag banquet December 7 and in all ways it was a pronounced success. August Schmitt was toastmaster. About sixty

guests were present and the toasts, speeches and musical selections were highly appreciated.

There are plenty of flowers in the market of all kinds, roses, carnations, chrysanthemums, violets, Paper White narcissi, etc., and an almost equal demand for stock. We are waiting patiently for spring.

Soft coal slack and night watching will supplant natural gas, which is entirely too expensive for greenhouse men.

T. J. Kirchner is putting up two new houses, 20x85, on Quincy street.

Westman & Getz are showing some odd little fern dishes made of roots.

Wm Brinker received a car load of very fine Delaware holly.

Mr. and Mrs. Carl Hagenberger were in town Dec. 8.   O. G.

Cincinnati.

ENCOURAGING CHRISTMAS OUTLOOK. — PLENTY OF GOOD STOCK EXCEPT CARNATIONS, WHICH ARE SHORT.—TRADE NOTES.

Trade is holding up first rate and a nice lot of stock is coming in, and good prices prevail. The only shortage at present is in carnations, and the wholesale men are figuring where to get stock enough to fill orders for Christmas. Nearly every grower is cutting his stock and sending it in, for past experience has taught him not to hold back too much for the last minute. The market will be pretty well supplied with all kinds of stock except carnations for Christmas.

The regular monthly meeting of the Florists' Society did not take place, as there was no quorum present. Undoubtedly the disagreeable weather had much to do with keeping the boys away.

Thos. Windrum, Wm. Murphy, Richard Witterstaetter and W. K. Partridge will send in thousands of carnations, but not near enough to go around. We will also have chrysanthemums and violets.

Jos. Goldman and William Hull will send some of those fine Bride, Bridesmaid and Golden Gate.

Albert McCullough has returned from a month's fishing trip off the coast of Florida.

Peterson has Begonia Gloire de Lorraine in the usual fine shape.

Gus Meier and George Corbett, a fine lot of poinsettias, also roses.

George & Allan will have valley, Paper Whites and Romans.   A. O.

St. Paul.

Trade in the last week dropped off considerably owing to the unusually severe weather. Some of the stores report quite a bit of funeral work, but nothing else. The stock of the local growers is now improving, especially carnations, and the outlook for Christmas is much better than it was. A good many more blooming plants will be seen this year. There never have been enough for the demand in former years.

All the holly seen here this year has been unusually good. The commission men have lots of it and are offering it very low.

Henry Puvogel is still bringing in some good chrysanthemums, especially white, which come in very handy for funeral work.

A rumor has it that there will be a change in the firm of one of the leading florists the first of the year.

C. M. Figely, with E. H. Hunt, was a recent caller.   O.

THE AMERICAN FLORIST

NINETEENTH YEAR.

Subscription, $1.00 a year. To Europe, $2.00.
Subscriptions accepted only from those
in the trade.

Advertisements, on all except cover pages,
10 Cents a Line, Agate; $1.00 per inch.
Cash with Order.

No Special Position Guaranteed.

Discounts are allowed only on consecutive insertions, as follows—6 times, 5 per cent; 13 times,
10 per cent; 26 times, 20 per cent;
52 times, 30 per cent

Cover space sold only on yearly contract at
$1.00 per inch, net, in the case of the two
front pages, regular discounts applying only to the back pages.

The Advertising Department of the AMERICAN
FLORIST is for florists, seedsmen and nurserymen
and dealers in wares pertaining to those lines only.

Orders for less than one-half inch space not accepted.

Advertisements must reach us by Wednesday to
secure insertion in the issue for the following
Saturday. Address

AMERICAN FLORIST CO., Chicago.

SEND in your subscription now for the
ensuing year.

SUNSHINE is one the scarcest commodities in December.

READERS will oblige by sending reports
of Christmas trade as compared with
that of last year.

NARCISSUS VON SION cannot be forced
for the holidays. Leave them outside till
January and thus avoid disappointment
and loss.

DON'T store carnations in ice-cooled
rooms or close-aired vaults. If you do
they will go to sleep when exposed for
sale.

WE are in receipt of the report of the
nineteenth annual convention of the
Society of American Florists, held in
Milwaukee, Wis., August 18-21.

IN the advertisement of the George
Wittbold Company, issue of December
12, page 773, the prices of araucarias
should read per plant, not per dozen.

THE parties to whom "M. S." refers
gave their real names and addresses in
addition to initials. That is the least
that can be expected for gratuitous
service.

ADVERTISERS and correspondents will
kindly remember that we go to press one
day earlier next week and the week following on account of the holidays. Please
send news and advertisements early.

FALL-SOWN cyclamens make the best
plants, but it is not too late yet to sow
the seed if they have been overlooked,
and good plants can be had for Christmas, 1904. The demand for cyclamens
as holiday plants is on the increase.

DAVID S. BEACH, of Bridgeport, Conn.,
has sent us a specimen bloom of his
chrysanthemum, Santa Claus. Unfortunately it arrived in such a damaged
condition that we could not form any
just estimate of its character, but judging from its size and general appearance
it should be a valuable variety for late
bloom.

"KEEP from heat and frost," is the
customary instruction to the expressman
carrying cut flowers. But the shipper
should do his share by giving all the protection possible in the packing. For this
purpose there is nothing better than a
lining of many thicknesses of newspaper,

the edges lapped, a layer of cotton
between, and a layer of waxed paper
next to the flowers.

The Glass Situation.

The window glass situation is slowly
but surely working out to the improvement in values. The low prices that
were quoted by jobbers and manufacturers a month ago, according to the
Chicago Lumberman, are no longer available, and although there is an occasional
bargain offered, the general tone of the
glass market here is greatly improved
and it is likely to remain so during the
balance of the fire. Not all of the window
glass factories have yet started up, but
it is anticipated that most of them will
be in operation by the middle of this
month. The unsettled condition of the
wage question appears to have thus far
prevented the resumption of operations,
but now all is harmonious.

A Model Employer.

John Patterson, gardener to George
Foster Peabody, of Caldwell, Lake
George, N. Y., called on friends in Hartford, Conn., last week. Mr. Patterson
is on a lengthy pleasure trip to Boston,
St. Louis, Salt Lake City, Colorado
Springs, San Francisco, Pasadena, Alameda and Los Angeles. There he will turn
north to Vancouver, Seattle and Montreal. He will be gone about six weeks.
This trip is wholly at Mr. Peabody's
expense, he having provided Mr. Petter-
son with a first-class pass and a substantial purse for pocket money. Last year
Mr. Patterson went to Europe and his
employer paid all expenses, traveling and
personal.

If we had more employers like Mr.
Peabody that would appreciate the work
of their gardeners, it is difficult to say how
much more good work in gardening
would be done.   R. K.

Nashville.

STOCK IS PLENTIFUL.—GOOD HOLLY CUT
IN LARGE QUANTITY.—EVERGREEN GROW-
ERS REAP RICH HARVEST.

Already orders in large quantities are
being booked, giving an encouraging outlook for next week's trade. Prices will
be much higher than last year. The
streets are full of wagons of beautifully
berried holly cut within a radius of ten
to twenty miles from this city. It is
sold to the customer direct and does not
pass through the florists' hands. The
country dealers have become very expert
in the manufacture of holly wreaths, also
cedar and hemlock wreaths, and get good
prices for them.

Floral dealers in this city are looking
forward to an exceptionally large trade
during the holidays, and are fully prepared
to meet a large demand. The weather
for the past month has been unusually
cold for this latitude. Roses have hardly
been affected by the cloudy weather and
the Joy & Son Company reports it
will have good Beauty, Liberty, Bride
and Bridesmaid. Carnations have been
somewhat damaged by the cloudiness,
but a few bright days will bring them
out all right.

Owners of nearby farms are said to
have reaped a rich reward from the sale
of holiday evergreens, gathering in more
cash than was realized upon the corn or
the wheat crop, with much less labor.
Nor does the annual cutting seem to
diminish the supply, which very accom-
modatingly grows again from season to

season. The holly is very richly berried
this year.

The leading growers, and also the
smaller growers, will have plenty of bulbous blossoms, both as cut flowers and in
pots. Violets are scarce this year. There
will be a few poinsettias.

Geny Brothers have made a specialty
of carnation growing and have some of
the finest varieties grown.
                                    M. C. D.

San Francisco.

BUSINESS RATHER QUIET SINCE THANKSGIV-
ING.—STOCK HAS BEEN MUCH BENEFITED
BY SUNNY WEATHER AND IS SUFFICIENT
TO FILL DEMANDS.

Trade has been rather slow ever since
Thanksgiving day, with plenty of stock
to meet all demands. Attention is now
directed towards the coming of Christmas
and every one is busy preparing for that
busy time. Holly, red berries, etc., have
begun to arrive. Some fine cut poinsettias
from Los Angeles are in the market. They are
grown outdoors in the southern part of
the state, under a light covering. Those
seen so far have been of excellent quality
and size and retail at $3 to $3.50 per
dozen stems. Both roses and carnations
are getting more plentiful and of good
color. If the present fair weather continues indications point to a good supply
in all lines for the holidays.

A visit to E. W. McLellan's place found
everything in excellent condition. The
stock in all the rose and carnation houses
looks just right for a heavy Christmas
cut.

M. J. Shaw, manager of the San
Joaquin Floral Company, Stockton; Sidney Clack, Menlo Park, and J. Thompson, Santa Cruz, were recent callers.

J. B. Weish, 321 Geary street, has sold
his store to J. Eppstein, who for several
years has held a position in the conservatories in Golden Gate park.

Mrs. Charles Crockford, 560 Valencia
street, recently disposed of her seed business to W. Jacobson, from the east.
                                    ROMNEYA.

Albany, N. Y.

Arthur Cowee, the well known gladiolus specialist of Berlin, N. Y., is pleased
with the showing made the last season
both in the growth of bulbs and the flowers. Mr. Cowee reports many new, magnificent and striking varieties among the
seedlings. The stock of bulbs was the
largest and finest he ever harvested, and
orders are coming in so freely he feels
encouraged to increase his acreage the
coming season. In the spring of 1902
Mr. Cowee planted seventy-five acres of
his favorite bulb, and at that time the
amount was the largest in the world
devoted exclusively to gladioli.

J. D. Thompson, of the J. D. Thompson
Carnation Company, Joliet, Ill., was in
Albany about a week ago, and paid a
visit to Louis Menand, at Cemetery Station. Mr. Thompson was on his way to
New York. He complimented Mr.
Menand on his new greenhouse, which
has a number of novel features in its construction.   R. D.

Grand Rapids, Mich.

We had the most serious storm of the
season the first of the week. The greenhouses were completely snowed in and
the florists had hard work to keep the
glass clean so as to let the sun in
as much as possible. Carnations

and violets will be very scarce for Christmas, but there will be just about enough roses to go around. Christmas prices are: American Beauty, $12 per dozen; Bridesmaid and Liberty, $3 per dozen; carnations, 75 cents to $1.50 per dozen; violets, 50 cents per dozen.

Henry Smith's place begins to look right again. There is little evidence of the fire left. He has one house of Peru which is very fine. He considers this the best white carnation sent out for many years.

The Fifth Avenue Floral Company has quit business. Freeling & Mendels purchased the houses, boilers and pipe, and J. A. Creelman the stock and pots.

Wm. Cunningham's new place is a picture, everything in apple pie order. He is sending in fine Lawson.

Jas. Schols is busy picking violets. He will build two houses 16x120 for violets next spring.

Freeling & Mendels will erect four new houses early in the spring for carnations and roses.

The Stover Floral Company is shipping fine violets to the Chicago market.
N. B. S.

New Haven, Conn.

There was a rousing time at the bowling contest between the New Haven County Horticultural Society's bowling team and the team of the Hartford Florists' Club, at the alleys in New Haven Saturday night, December 12. Although the scores were rather poor on both sides, the Hartford boys playing at a great disadvantage on strange alleys, they beat their opponents 115 pins, New Haven getting only one game out of the three played. The prize was a fine ball. This was to be presented to the one having the highest average score, which proved to be a tie between Messrs. Norberg and Routier. These gentlemen will play off the tie on the home alleys on Thursday night, December 17. The Hartford team was finely entertained at the alleys, and afterwards at one of the leading hotels.
R. K.

Obituary.

CHARLES A. WOODRUFF.

Charles A. Woodruff, the well-known horticulturist, died December 13, at Ann Arbor, Mich. He was 77 years old and leaves a widow and son. He was the originator of the Woodruff and Ann Arbor white grapes.

ERNST G. ASMUS.

Ernst G. Asmus passed away at his home in West Hoboken, N. J., on Thursday afternoon, December 17, aged 59 years. Mr. Asmus had been in failing health for several months, a painful affection of the throat bringing about the fatal result. He was born at Hamburg, Germany, and came to this country when nine years of age. His father and his brother Rudolph established a flower business on Weavertown road, now known as Hudson boulevard, under the name of C. A. Asmus & Son. Rudolph retired to establish business for himself in 1862 and Ernst took his place in the firm. Soon afterwards Ernst separated and started in the same neighborhood on property belonging to Henry Kuhl adjoining Schutzen park. Afterwards he bought the estate of Peter Schup which, with the additional property afterward acquired, formed the foundation for the great business event-

ually developed. Here his career as a progressive commercial florist really began. He was a remarkably shrewd and able business man and accumulated a large competence in his business. The flowers from his place have always held a leading place as to high quality in the market of New York. He was a promoter and active worker in the affairs of the New York Cut Flower Company from its inception. He leaves a widow and three sons. One son, Adolph, attends to local business and another, Edward, has charge of the new house at Closter. The funeral will be held on Sunday at Trinity church, Hoboken, and burial at Hoboken cemetery, New Durham. All arrangements as to pall-bearers, etc., were in accordance with expressed wish of the deceased.

SITUATIONS, WANTS, FOR SALE.

One Cent Per Word.

Cash with the Adv.

Plant Advs. NOT admitted under this head.

Every paid subscriber to the AMERICAN FLORIST for the year 1903 is entitled to a five-line want ADV. (situations only) free, to be used at any time during the year.

Situation Wanted—A florist, 28 years old, Scandinavian, wants position. 10 years in the business. State salary, etc. Address
C A. care American Florist.

Situation Wanted—As foreman, roses, carnations and general stock; ambitious, sober; life experience. State wages and give full particulars. FOREMAN, 695 Pawtucket Ave., Pawtucket, R. I.

Situation Wanted—By gardener and florist; 21 years' experience in all branches. Private place or public institution preferred. Married man.
2297 St. Anthony Ave., Merriam Park, Minn.

Situation Wanted—Foreman, propagator and grower of roses, carnations, 'mums and the general routine of a commercial place. Thorough recommendations as to ability; age 35.
J S, care American Florist.

Situation Wanted—First-class grower of roses, carnations, 'mums, violets and general line of plants, also up in propagating, wants situation where No. 1 stuff is wanted. State wages.
GROWER, care American Florist.

Situation Wanted—By experienced grower of cut flowers and general stock; successful Beauty grower and propagator and can make designs. Best of references. Within 200 miles of Chicago preferred. Address L. G. BARBIER,
812 Runion Ave., Ft. Wayne, Ind.

Situation Wanted—as manager or foreman by practical man. First-class grower of cut flowers and plants. Capable of managing a large plant and handling help. Good wages expected. When answering state wages, extent of plant, amount of help, etc. First-class references.
No. 106, care American Florist.

Situation Wanted—By florist-gardener with 25 years' experience and 7 years in this country. Understands growing of vegetables, palms, ferns, roses, carnations, 'mums and general bedding stock. Wants position as head gardener or gentleman's place or as florist in a horticultural establishment. First-class reference.
E S, care American Florist.

Help Wanted—Competent man to take charge of southern nursery. Address
R C, care American Florist.

Help Wanted—Working foreman, for growing a general line of cut flowers, bedding plants, etc. Married man preferred. House with references and wages expected with house. Address
C. LOVERIDGE, Peoria, Ill.

Help Wanted—A grower to take full charge of a section of carnation houses. $18 per week to the right man. Single man preferred. About 8 miles from Cleveland. Stock is in fine condition. Address
M. BLOY, Manager of the Essex Greenhouses, North Olmstead, Ohio.

Help Wanted—Young lady-for store work, one with some knowledge of bookkeeping. Steady place and good home for right party. Address, stating experience, references and wages wanted. Position open February 1.
JOSE M. SMELY, Aurora, Ill.

Council Bluffs, Ia.

J. F. Wilcox's plant of six acres under glass is in fine shape. M. Stauch, the foreman, has eighteen houses 26x200 planted in Bride and Bridesmaid that are in excellent condition for Christmas. A new block of five houses 30x300 is planted to American Beauty, which will give a fine cut for the holidays. There are twelve houses 26x200 feet planted in carnations which are looking fine. Mr. Stauch has a pink seedling, very much like Lawson, but with a better stem which is declared to be promising.

I recently visited Joliet, Ill., and found the Chicago Carnation Company's plant in good shape. Fiancee is certainly a fine flower, also Reliance and Moonlight for white and Crusader for scarlet. Some unnamed seedlings looked promising. The J. D. Thompson Carnation Company's plant is the home of some excellent varieties, including Nelson Fisher and Mrs. M. A. Patten.　　　C. M. J.

Wholesale Flower Markets

MILWAUKEE, Dec. 17.		
Roses, Beauty, long per doz.	3.00	
" " med. "	1.50@ 2.00	
" " short "	.50@1.00	
" Bride, Bridesmaids	4.00@ 6.00	
" Meteor, Golden Gate	4.00@ 6.00	
" Perle		4.00
Carnations	2.00@ 3.00	
Smilax	15.00@12.50	
Asparagus		50.00
Violets	1.00@1.50	
Valley		3.00
Stevia	1.00@ 1.50	

PITTSBURG, Dec. 17.		
Roses, Beauty, specials	40.00@50.00	
" " extras	30.00@35.00	
" No. 1	18.00@25.00	
" ordinary	6.00@12.00	
" Bride, Bridesmaid	2.00@12.00	
" Meteor	4.00@10 00	
" Kaiserin, Liberties	4.00@15 00	
Carnations	3.00@ 5.00	
Lily of the valley	4.00@ 5.00	
Smilax	12.50@15.00	
Adiantum	1.00@ 1 50	
Asparagus, strings	40.00@50.00	
Asparagus Sprengeri	2.00@ 3.00	
Chrysanthemums	6.00@10.00	
Sweet Peas	1.00@ 1.50	
Violets	.50@ 1.0	
Lilies	12.00@16.00	
Mignonette	3.00@ 4.00	
Romans, Paper White		4.00

CINCINNATI, Dec. 17.		
Roses, Beauty	40.00@85.00	
" Bride, Bridesmaid	8.00@15.00	
" Liberty	15.00@25.00	
" Meteor, Golden Gate	15.00@18.00	
Carnations		4.00@ 6.00
Lily of the valley	3.00@ 4.00	
Asparagus		50.00
Smilax	12 50@15.00	
Adiantum	1.00@ 1.50	
Chrysanthemums	12.0@25.00	
Violets	2.00@ 3.00	
Narcissus		
Poinsettia	15.00@25.00	
Romans		4.00
Harrisii	per doz. 2.50	
Calla		15 00

ST. LOUIS, Dec. 17.		
Roses, Beauty, long stem	4.00@ 5 00	
" Beauty, medium stem		12.50
" Beauty, short stem	5.00@ 8.00	
" Liberty	3.00@ 8.00	
T. Bride, Bridesmaid	2.00@ 6.00	
" Golden Gate	3.00@ 6.00	
Carnations	2.00@ 5.00	
Smilax		12 50
Asparagus Sprengeri	1.00@ 3.00	
" Plumosus	15.00@30.00	
Ferns	per 1000, 1.75	
Violets, single	.75@ 1.00	
Valley	3.00@ 4.00	

DENVER, Dec. 16.		
Roses, Beauty, long		25.00
" " medium		15.00
" " short		8.00
" Liberty	4. @ 8 00	
" Chatenay	4. @ 7 00	
" Bride, Bridesmaid	3.00@ 4.00	
Carnations	3 00@ 4.00	
Smilax		20.00

INTERNATIONAL FLOWER DELIVERY.

PASSENGER STEAMSHIP MOVEMENTS.

The tables herewith give the scheduled time of departure of ocean steamships carrying first-class passengers from the principal American and foreign ports, covering the space of two weeks from date of this issue of the AMERICAN FLORIST. Much disappointment often results from attempts to forward flowers for steamer delivery by express, to the care of the ship's steward or otherwise. The carriers of these packages are not infrequently refused admission on board and even those delivered on board are not always certain to reach the parties for whom they were intended. Hence florists in interior cities having orders for the delivery of flowers to passengers on out-going steamers are advised to intrust the filling of such orders to some reliable florist in the port of departure, who understands the necessary details and formalities and has the facilities for attending to it properly. For the addresses of such firms we refer our readers to the advertisements on this page:

FROM	TO	STEAMER	*LINE	DAY	DUE ABOUT
New York	Liverpool	Lucania	1	Sat. Dec. 28, 10:00 a. m.	Jan. 1
New York	"	Etruria	1	Sat. Jan. 3, 8:00 p. m.	Jan. 8
Boston	"	Saxonia	1	Tues. Dec. 29, 6:00 a. m.	Jan. 8
New York	Glasgow	Corinthian	2	Thur. Dec. 24, 1:00 p. m.	Jan. 3
New York	Hamburg	Bluecher	3	Thur. Dec. 31, 10:00 a. m.	Jan. 10
New York	Glasgow	Anchoria	5	Sat. Jan. 3, Noon.	Jan. 12
New York	London	Minnespolis	6	Sat. Dec. 26, 10:00 a. m.	Jan. 5
New York	"	Minnehaha	6	Sat. Jan. 2, 8:00 a. m.	Jan. 12
New York	Liverpool	Teutonic	7	Wed. Dec. 23, Noon.	Dec. 30
New York	"	Cedric	7	Wed. Dec. 30, 1:00 p. m.	Jan. 6
Boston	"	Cymric	7	Tues. Dec. 24, 1:00 p. m.	Dec. 31
Boston	Medit. Ports	Republic	7	Sat. Jan. 3, 9:00 a. m.	
New York	Southampton	St. Paul	8	Sat. Dec. 26, Noon.	Jan. 1
New York	"	Philadelphia	8	Sat. Jan. 2, Noon.	Jan. 9
New York	Antwerp	Zeeland	9	Sat. Dec. 26, 10:30 a. m.	Jan. 5
New York	"	Finland	9	Sat. Jan. 2, 10:30 a. m.	Jan. 11
New York	Havre	La Bretagne	10	Thur. Dec. 24, 10:00 a. m.	Jan. 3
New York	"	La Touraine	10	Thur. Dec. 31, 10:00 a. m.	Jan. 7
New York	Rotterdam	Rotterdam	11	Wed. Dec. 30, 10:00 a. m.	Jan. 9
New York	Genoa	Liguria	12	Tues. Dec. 22, 11:00 a. m.	Jan. 3
New York	"	Città di Napoli	12	Tues. Dec. 29, 11:00 a. m.	Jan. 15
New York	Bremen	Main	13	Tues. Dec. 29, 1:00 p. m.	Jan. 8
Boston	Liverpool	Bohemian	16	Wed. Dec. 23, 1:00 p. m.	Jan. 8
Boston	"	Canadian	16	Wed. Dec. 30, 6:00 a. m.	Jan. 9

*1 Cunard; 2 Allen-State; 3 Hamburg-American; 4 Scandinavian-American; 5 Anchor Line; 6 Atlantic Transport; 7 White Star; 8 American; 9 Red Star; 10 French; 11 Holland-American; 12 Italian Royal Mail; 13 North German Lloyd; 14 Fabre; 15 Leyland; 17 Occidental and Oriental; 18 Oceanic; 19 Allan; 20 Can. Pacific Ry.; 21 N. Pacific Ry.; 22 Hongkong-Seattle.

INTERNATIONAL FLOWER DELIVERY.

STEAMSHIPS LEAVE FOREIGN PORTS.

FROM	TO	STEAMER	*LINE	DAY	DUE ABOUT
Liverpool	New York	Ivernia	1	Sat. Dec. 26,	Jan. 2
Liverpool	"	Umbria	1	Sat. Jan. 2,	Jan. 8
Flume	"	Aurania	1	Fri. Jan. 1,	
Glasgow	"	Numidian	2	Sat. Jan. 2,	Jan. 12
Hamburg	"	Patricia	3	Sat. Dec. 26,	Jan. 7
Hamburg	"	Pretoria	3	Sat. Jan. 2,	Jan. 14
Glasgow	"	Furnessia	3	Sat. Dec. 26,	Jan. 5
London	"	Menaba	6	Thur. Dec. 24,	Jan. 3
London	"	Minnetonka	6	Thur. Dec. 31,	Jan. 10
Liverpool	"	Majestic	7	Wed. Dec. 23, 3:30 p. m.	Dec. 30
Liverpool	"	Celtic	7	Wed. Dec. 30, 3:30 p. m.	Jan. 6
Genoa	Boston	Romanic	7	Wed. Dec. 23,	Jan. 10
Southampton	New York	St. Louis	8	Sat. Dec. 26, 9:30 a. m.	Jan. 1
Southampton	"	New York	8	Sat. Jan. 2, 9:30 a. m.	Jan. 9
Antwerp	"	Vaderland	9	Sat. Dec. 26, 4:30 a. m.	Jan. 4
Antwerp	"	Kroonland	9	Sat. Jan. 2, Noon	Jan. 11
Havre	"	La Champagne	10	Sat. Dec. 26,	Jan. 2
Havre	"	La Savoie	10	Sat. Jan. 2,	Jan. 10
Genoa	"	Sicilia	12	Mon. Dec. 23,	Jan. 14
Genoa	"	Lombardia	12	Mon. Jan. 4,	Jan. 20
Bremen	"	Rhein	13	Sat. Dec. 26, 7:00 a. m.	Jan. 6
Bremen	"	Neckar	13	Sat. Jan. 2, 7:00 a. m.	Jan. 11
Naples	"	Germanic	14	Wed. Dec. 30,	Jan. 10
Liverpool	Boston	Cestrian	16	Sat. Dec 26,	Jan. 5
Liverpool	"	Devonian	16	Sat. Jan. 2,	Jan. 12

* See steamship list on opposite page.

PLEASE MENTION US WHEN WRITING TO ADVERTISERS.

808   THE AMERICAN FLORIST.   Dec. 19,

THE SEED TRADE.

AMERICAN SEED TRADE ASSOCIATION.
S. F. Willard, Pres.; J. Charles McCullough,
First Vice-Pres.; C. E. Kendel, Cleveland, O.,
Sec'y and Treas.
Twenty-second annual convention St. Louis,
Mo., June, 1904.

DETROIT, MICH.—Lester L. Morse left here, homeward bound, December 17.

SWEET CORN growers continue to report greater shrinkage than first anticipated.

THE Hawaii Board of Agriculture proposes to supply purchasers with seeds at cost.

VISITED BOSTON: H. L. Faust, representing the Albert Dickinson Company, Chicago.

VISITED CHICAGO: Charles P. Braslan, San Jose, Cal.; L. L. Morse, Santa Clara, Cal.; Mr. Johns, Sioux City, Ia.

THE great scarcity of bouquet green has evidently increased the use of laurel wreathing for decorating in the leading cities of the central states.

D. M. FERRY & COMPANY, of Detroit, Mich., in their seed warehouses, find sheet iron as edgings for the floors and covers for suspicious openings, with water traps, the best remedies for mice.

PROSPECTS for contract growers certainly look bright, should they embark in the business of seed dealers. Sales of large lots of cucumber seed by them at $2 per pound show ability to sell to advantage.

SAN LUIS OBISPO, CAL.—Incorporation papers of the Haven Seed Company, of California, were signed November 30. The incorporators are L. W. Beckett, E. W. Clark, D. D. Barnard, E. M. Haven and Paul M. Gregg. E. M. Haven will assume active management of the seed farm to be located between this place and Arroyo Grande.

HAMILTON, N. Y.—Perhaps the most important civil case tried before the justice's court of this place in some time is that of Carpenter & Wilcox of Randallsville vs. Newell L. Douglass, of Earlville, in an action to recover damages alleged to have been occasioned by the purchase of pea seed, which proved untrue to name. Some very fine points of law are involved, especially the basis of damages, whether it shall be upon prices which ruled in Randallsville at the time or in New York, where the goods were disposed of.

Methods of Some Contract Growers.

How can contract seed growers object to seedsmen canvassing their territory for seed (unless they upset contracts) when many of these growers are picking up these same odd stocks and disposing of them to canners and others (not seedsmen) at less than seedsmen can quote? This is not true of all contract growers, some of whom make it a rule to offer their surplus to their own customers at contract value, but it is true of several. All of which means that seedsmen should have a list of growers who would positively agree to work on the lines last referred to, and to men who will do this in good faith should the legitimate seed trade turn their contract orders. During

the past two seasons more than one contract grower has in fact become a seed dealer or jobber and is not entitled to the seed dealers' business on a contract basis.

Minneapolis.

The Albert Dickinson Company, of Chicago, which now has offices in the Minneapolis Chamber of Commerce, will erect a seed elevator in Minneapolis. The company December 10 took out permits for buildings to cost $80,000, to be located in Guerney park, in southeast Minneapolis. The elevator and warehouse will be located at Twenty-fifth avenue and Dearborn street, and the power-house two blocks distant, at Twenty-seventh avenue and Belle street. The elevator will be iron-clad, 56x155 feet, two stories and basement and will cost $40,000. The warehouse will be 80x160 feet and cost $21,000. The power-house will be 36x95 feet, one story and basement and cost $19,000. The buildings will all be erected with a view of enlargement in the future.

Alma, Ill.

Trade has been fairly good in this county the last month. Chrysanthemums were rather dull in their season owing to the large quantities grown outdoors. No new houses have been built. The stock of plants and flowers is better than a year ago. Dorothy is proving one of the best bloomers among pink carnations.

W. S. Ross is devoting attention to bulbs, especially daffodils. He has also half an acre of sweet peas planted for next spring.   R.

ESTABLISHED 1877   26 Years in Business.

ALL READY

—FOR THE HOLIDAYS AT THE—

CITY HALL CUT FLOWER MARKET.

Special Stock from leading growers. American Beauty, Queen of Edgely, Bride, Bridesmaid, Golden Gate and Meteor Roses. All standard Carnations including, such specialties as Fair Maid and Lillian Pond of highest grade. Lily of the Valley, Paper Whites and Roman Hyacinths in unlimited supply. Violets, Chrysanthemums, Christmas Holly, Mistletoe, Laurel Festooning, Wreaths and other seasonable goods in our Florists' Supply Department.

Ready to quote prices now. Call us up by telephone early in the week. Largest Daily Receipts in New England.

WELCH BROS.
15 Province St., BOSTON, MASS.

THE NURSERY TRADE.

AM. ASSOCIATION OF NURSERYMEN.
N. W. HALE, Knoxville, Tenn., Pres.; FRANK A. WEBER, St. Louis, Mo., Vice-Pres.; GEORGE C. SEAGER, Rochester, N. Y., Sec'y. Twenty-ninth annual convention, Atlanta, Ga., June, 1904.

STORRS & HARRISON CO., Painesville, O., has been in the nursery business fifty years.

VISITED CHICAGO: Orlando Harrison of J. G. Harrison's Sons, Berlin, Ind., returning from the west.

PROF. C. S. SARGENT, of the Arnold Arboretum, who has made an extensive tour of Siberia and the orient, returned last week.

W. B. ROWE & SON, Worcester, England, are offering a new apple, Edward VII, of which high opinions have been expressed by British authorities.

HUNTSVILLE, Ala. — Stark Brothers' Nursery, seven miles south of Huntsville, will be discontinued in the first of the new year, according to recent reports.

CASEY, KY.—F. B. Hancock, who has defrauded a number of wholesale dealers, was sentenced to eighteen months in Atlanta penitentiary November 24.

ROCHESTER, N. Y.—Green's Nursery Company has been incorporated with a capital of $100,000. The incorporators are Chas. A. Green, Jennie C. Green and Robert C. Burleigh.

SPRINGFIELD, O.—Springfield men have organized a nursery company in Mississippi and a number of the stockholders left December 9 to look over the ground and arrange for business. The new company is to be known as the Good Nursery Company, and has a capital stock of $60,000. John M. Good is at the head of the enterprise, and he has interested with him Albert Hahn, L. Vinney, Edwin S. Houck, Ward Welsh and L. S. Job. They propose to purchase a plantation at about $37,000.

THE NEW APPLE. (The Apple of the Future.)

"EDWARD VII."

(Blenheim Orange × Golden Noble.)

Award of Merit (unanimous), Royal Horticultural Society, March 24th, 1903.

THE LATEST APPLE IN EXISTENCE.

The Fruit is solid, heavy and keeps well until June. It is excellent both for dessert and cooking purposes; in use mid-April to mid-June, and is certainly what we claim it to be, viz: the best late apple in existence.
The Tree is a regular and great bearer, upright in growth, short-jointed and a very late bloomer (in our early district it has not bloomed before the third week in May, so that it misses the May Frosts).

"THE GARDEN,"—March 28th 1903.
"Apple, EDWARD VII—This in an excellent late apple."

"THE GARDENERS' CHRONICLE," March 28th 1903.
"Messrs. W. B. Rowe & Son sent again a quantity of their fine late cooking apple, EDWARD VII, which received a unanimous Award of Merit, Mr. W. Crump, of Madresfield Court Gardens, testifying as to its abundant and early cropping qualities."

"THE GARDEN," April 18th, 1903.
"An excellent late apple; EDWARD VII is certainly one of the late apples of the future."

"THE GARDENING WORLD," May 9th, 1903
"Apple, EDWARD VII.—The photo, from which the illustration was prepared was taken from a specimen in our offices on the 24th ult., which shows that the fruit agrees with what the raisers represented it to be—namely, an apple in season during April and May. We noted the fruit on March 24th last, when exhibited at the Drill Hall, but from the appearance of the fruit at the time, we were afraid it would not keep. This impression has been dispelled by the fine condition of the specimen sent us on the above date."

PRICE: 1-year, 12 shillings and 6 pence; 2-year, 15 shillings; 3-year, 20 shillings; 4-year specimens in Bush and Standard Trees, at 25 shillings each.

To be obtained of all Nurserymen or direct from the raisers. Special quotation for a quantity.

W. B. ROWE & SON,

"Barbourne Nurseries," WORCESTER, ENGLAND.

Please mention the American Florist to advertisers.

PLEASE RENEW YOUR SUBSCRIPTION NOW.

OUR PASTIMES.

Announcements of coming contests or other events of interests to our bowling, shooting and sporting readers are solicited and will be given place in this column.

Address all correspondence for this department to Wm. J. Stewart, 42 W. 28th St., New York. Robt. Kift, 1725 Chestnut St., Philadelphia, Pa.; to the American Florist Co.. Chicago, Ill.

At New York.

Bowling interest is about to be revived and an effort made to put a good team in the field to represent New York at St. Louis next August. A meeting of bowlers is to be called for the first Monday in January, the place to be announced later. Those interested should address Theodore J. Lang, Thirty-eighth street and Sixth avenue, New York City.' .'' ...

At Chicago.

The Florists' Bowling Club held its last session of the year Tuesday evening at Mussey's alleys. The next meeting, which will take place in the first week of the new year, will be an important one, as the winter handicap tournament will be launched. The scores of the Tuesday evening games follow:

Player.	1st	2d	3d
Degnan	123	124	138
Buxton	13	133	
Huebner	129	147	128
Ess	115	107	
Kreitling	144		
G. Scott	128		
Balluff	141	131	166
Hauswirth	134	140	
Stephens	122	150	146
Asmus	166	147	

Several new members were taken into the club, and Edgar Sanders was elected an honorary member, the secretary being instructed to notify this well known gentleman of his election and say to him that all of the members hope to see him at the tournament at St. Louis next August. Mr. Sanders has always been a bowling enthusiast, and while not taking an active interest could always be found at the match games cheering the boys on to their best efforts.

At Philadelphia.

The match games are now nearly finished. The Dunham team has won eleven games and will carry win, but several teams may be tied for second place. The scores of the last games follow:

Player.			
Moss	168	127	137
Gibson	143	142	142
Dunlap	149	124	146
Polites	171	183	166
Bonsall	149	141	159
Total	775	727	749
Eimerman	197	143	146
Falck	148	188	194
Dungan	159	132	151
Baker	189	203	156
Connor			
Total	874	866	826
Dunham	175	141	190
Moore	153	104	170
Merlitz	169	110	115
Anderson	193	193	190
Watson	151	100	172
Total	841	710	897
Moss	216	162	168
Gibson	138	137	169
Dunlap	130	185	190
Polites	146	178	162
Bonsall	156	158	158
Total	797	820	797
Harris	173	153	197
Graham	116	151	153
Johnson	25.0	187	177
Baxter	117	158	168
Robertson	153	161	167
Total	759	810	791
Kift	168	123	135
Craig	177	123	158
Holmes	179	163	169
Goebel	185	145	159
Allen	136	139	146
Total	797	698	761
Westcott	155	155	131
Odelberger	147	119	214
McLester	143	142	143
Seaman	110	88	110
Yates	144	180	118
Total	608	654	711
Anderson	158	174	170
Merlitz	155	149	1 3
Moore	163	176	194
Dunham	172	177	173
Watson	133	152	157
Total	811	823	797

Harris	127	152	152
Johnson	190	183	164
Graham	145	126	192
Baxter	225	125	97
Robertson	137	178	146
Total	724	764	730
Eimerman	111	193	184
Falck	162	181	166
Dungan	152	145	167
Baker	112	162	210
Connor	142	215	180
Total	679	897	907

Philadelphia Florists' Bowling League.

The last tournament of the Florists' League was by long odds proved the best thing the Florists' Club has yet got up. The interest of the spectators is very keen and the rivalry among the teams is of a very ardent character. Notwithstanding the excitement and jollying which is part of the matches, the utmost good humor prevails and all have enjoyed the tournament very much. It is now certain that a new tournament, based on the same plan with slight modifications, will be inaugurated after the new year. There may be changes in the make-up of the teams, and perhaps in the captains, but otherwise the same system will prevail. It has been suggested that a ten per cent penalty should be put on absentee scores, so as to avoid any possible staying away where averages are high. It has also been thought advisable to reduce the value of the prizes, as it would seem that just as much fun can be gotten without going to so large an expense as has been incurred in the present tournament.

BOOKKEEPING and account forms for same by R. F. Tesson, as read at the Milwaukee convention has been printed in pamphlet form by the AMERICAN FLORIST and will be mailed FREE on request to any florist. Employers may have extra copies to distribute among their employes. The address is of much permanent value and well worth the study of our young men.

Carnation Cuttings.

Well Rooted. Ready Now.

	Per 100	Per 1000
Enchantress, light pink......	$ 6.00	$ 50.00
Harlowarden, crimson........	6.00	50.00
Her Majesty, white..........	5.00	45.00
Lillian Pond, white..........	5.00	45.00
Pres. McKinley, dark pink...	5.00	45.00
Sybil, dark pink.............	5.00	40.00
Dorothy Whitney, yellow.....	6.00	50.00
Gov. Wolcott, white..........	5.00	40.00
Alba, white	5.00	40.00
Estelle, scarlet..............	3.00	25.00
Mrs. T. W. Lawson, dark pink	2.50	20.00
Mrs. Higinbotham, light pink	4.00	30.00
Prosperity...................	2.50	20.00

NEW VARIETIES For January Delivery.

Crusader, best scarlet........	$10.00	80.00
Flamingo, fancy scarlet.......	12.00	100.00
White Lawson, pure white...	12.00	100.00
Reliance, white	10.00	80.00
Moonlight. white..............	10.00	75.00
Lady Bountiful, white.........	12.00	100.00

Send for price list of above and other varieties.

Chicago Carnation Co.
JOLIET, ILL.

Carnation Cuttings.

We are now booking orders for Carnation Cuttings. All orders will be filled strictly in rotation as received. Send in your orders at once and get the early plants.
We have the following varieties from which we can supply cuttings and will sell at the market prices for good stock:

Enchantress	Fair Maid	The Queen
Boston Market	Gov. Wolcott	Eldorado
Bradt	Prosperity	Manley
E. Sheppard	Adonis	Joost
	Lawson	Harlowarden
	Harry Fenn	Fragrance

All our plants are vigorous and healthy and having the best facilities for rooting we are prepared to fill large or small orders.
Long Distance Telephone.

BACKER & CO., Billerica, Mass.

Verbena King.

Hello! Say You! If you want to go to the World's Fair or want us to go, you will have to buy our fine Rooted Cuttings as they are money makers. Clean and healthy of the following: Verbenas, Heliotropes, Daisies, Coleus Kansas, Double White Petunias, Salvias, Ageratums, Mme. Sallerol Geraniums, Feverfew, red and yellow Alternanthera, all true to name. Satisfaction and safe arrival guaranteed. Write us your wants as our prices our right. We pay the express, too. Send for list to

C. Humfeld, Clay Center, Kas.

The Rooted Cutting Specialist.
That Cash or C. O. D. please.

GERANIUMS Rooted Cuttings.

Supply Unlimited.

Eight houses planted to stock plants. No cheap, under the bench cuttings, but every one a good one.

	Per 100	1000
S. A. Nutt, Frances Perkins. Buchner	$1.50	$10.00
Poitevine, and Jean Viaud..........	2.00	12.50
Castellane, Riccard, Soleil.........	2.00	15.00

Send for price list of Geraniums and Carnations.

ALBERT M. HERR,   Lancaster, Pa.

Grafted Roses

ALL OF THE LEADING VARIETIES.

The work of grafting has begun, and the best way, to secure good stock is to order it early.

Carnations.
Rooted cuttings of leading varieties

Chrysanthemums.
Clean and thrifty stock. All of the best kinds from 2½-in. pots and rooted cuttings,

Palms and Ferns.
Fourteen houses devoted to these alone.

Lily of the Valley
Every day in the year. Large stock for Christmas.

Asparagus Plumosus Nanus.

PRICE LIST FOR 1904 READY JANUARY 1.

A. N. PIERSON,   Cromwell, Conn.

Please mention the American Florist when writing

Lily of the Valley

ARRIVED IN FINE CONDITION. We offer a limited amount of the finest in the market for early forcing, $14.00 per 1000; $35.00 per case of 2,500. This stock is unsurpassed and nothing better to be had.

Bruns' Extra Fine Berlin Pips for early forcing are almost equally as good and always give satisfaction.
$12.00 per 1000; $30.00 per case of 2,500.
COLD STORAGE VALLEY, $15.00 per 1000.

Finest Cut Valley Always on Hand.

H. N. BRUNS,

Valley Specialist,

1409-1411 W. Madison St.,   CHICAGO.

SURPLUS BULBS

AT LOW PRICES TO CLOSE.

	Per 100	1000
WHITE ROMAN HYACINTHS, 13 ctm.....................................	2.00	15.00
SINGLE DUTCH HYACINTHS...	2.00	15.00
SINGLE EARLY TULIPS, Superfine Mixture.	.75	5.00
VON SION NARCISSUS, Single Nose Bulbs............................	1.50	12.50
LILY OF THE VALLEY PIPS, Selected Dresden.....................	1.75	15.00
Per case 2,500 pips................................$35.00		

R. & J. FARQUHAR & CO.,   6 and 7 So. Market Street, BOSTON, MASS.

ROOTED CARNATION CUTTINGS.

From strong, healthy plants.	100	1000
Enchantress	$6.00	$50.00
The Queen............................	6.00	50.00
Fair Maid............................	4.00	30.00
Gov. Wolcott........................	4.00	35.00
Boston Market.......................	4.00	35.00
Mrs. T. W. Lawson...................	3.00	25.00

HENRY A. STEVENS CO., Dedham, Mass.

Add to Your Bank Account

PLANT A FEW GARDENIAS.

First-class rooted cuttings, while they last, $6.00 per 100.

JOHN T. COCHRAN,   Claymont, Del.

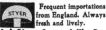

THE ALLIED TRADES.

Descriptive particulars—with drawings or photographs, if possible—of any new apparatus or device which may prove helpful to the trade are solicited for this department.

REED & KELLER's immortelle Christmas bells, etc., are proving very popular.

CLARK's wagon heaters, it is claimed, will heat a large florist's wagon continuously at an expense of one-quarter cent per hour for fuel. This is worthy of consideration these cold days.

REIMER & RADMER, agents of the Herendeen Manufacturing Company, recently installed Purman boilers and heating plants for F. Hesse, Heitmann & Baermann, John Arnold and Otto Eggebrecht, all of Milwaukee, Wis.

Lord's Frost-Proof Shipping Box.

The illustrations herewith show cross section of a new folding and frost-proof plant shipping box, and the same ready for shipment with additional cord to hold sides firmly in place. This box has been patented by the inventor, L. P. Lord, of Owatonna, Minn., who claims for it advantages as follows: 1. It is frost-proof, being made of double corrugated paper board. 2. Time used in packing plants reduced to a minimum, not more than ten minutes, saving labor. 3. Weight of package the least possible. 4. Safe from injury in shipment. 5. Easy to carry.

Kerr's Asparagus Stringer.

The illustration herewith shows a flat piece of tin and method of fastening string in same for training asparagus, smilax and such plants. The stringer is bent at the broad end so as to hook readily on wires strung across the house at the top and over the beds or benches at the bottom, two stringers being required for each string. It is claimed the patentee, George Kerr, of Winnipeg, Manitoba, that this is a very cheap and expeditious device. It is true that much time is taken up in the tedious work of stringing asparagus and smilax and these plants are now grown so extensively that the work of properly training them is a serious item in the expenses. If Mr. Kerr's device can show any material saving in labor it will be much appreciated by the growers.

Lenox, Mass.

The annual meeting of the Lenox Horticultural Society was held in the society's rooms December 5. In the last year two exhibitions have been held, and both were exceedingly well patronized. The officers for the ensuing year were all unanimously elected as follows: E. Jenkins, president; F. Heeremans, vice-president; S. Carlquist, treasurer; R. A. Schmid, secretary, and G. Foulsham assistant secretary. All are residents of Lenox. The regular meetings will be held as usual on the first and third Saturdays of each month at 7:30 p. m. Breitmeyer's new rose was exhibited in fine condition and was awarded a first-class certificate.

F. HEEREMANS, Sec'y.

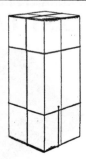

LORD'S FROST-PROOF MAILING BOX.

Pittsburg.

BUSINESS SHOWS NO IMPROVEMENT.—ROSE STOCK BELOW NORMAL.—OTHER FLOWERS ARE FINE AND PLENTIFUL.—BIG HOLIDAY TRADE IS LOOKED FOR.

There is little or no improvement in business over a week ago. Trade comes in spurts and the teas, weddings and funerals seem to be the basis of all the activity now, as the transient end of it has dropped considerably. Active preparations for the holidays have begun. The immortelle wreaths, bells and other novelties are making their appearance, and everyone seems to feel the holiday season is going to be a great success. The rose stock, both local and shipped, is still below normal, excepting American Beauty and Liberty. Double violets are higher priced, with no improvement in quality. Limited quantities of extra fancy Enchantress and Lawson carnations are coming in; Flamingo, Marquis and Scott are good; Roman hyacinths, bouvardias, pansies, lily of the valley, poinsettias, primulas and narcissi are fine and plentiful. Gardenias and cattleyas are scarce. Lilium Harrisii and green are scarce.

There was an interesting meeting of the Botanical Society at the Carnegie Institute December 3. The subject of discussion was, "Our Native Evergreens, Winter Berries and Christmas Flowers," and an extensive and interesting illustrative display was brought together. Incidentally President Falconer gave it

out that he had vainly tried to prevail upon John Dunbar, of Rochester, N. Y., to accept the position of superintendent of the local parks.

Randolph & McClements, I understand, was the first firm to use Breitmeyer's new rose, christened the Detroit. Over 500 of these beautiful flowers were used at the Johnston-Harris wedding Wednesday, December 9. The roses were made in six bouquets of about seven-dozen each for the bridesmaids. The flowers were a perfect match to the gowns.

The Pittsburg Florists' Exchange will acquire additional floor space about January 1. The present room will be converted into a refrigerator, and the new entrance will be on Wood street.

Mrs. J. Blicker, of Homestead, had over $500 worth of work Tuesday for the funeral of W. S. Bullock, one of the founders of Homestead.

Lowe & Roehrig have leased the building at 229 and 231 Diamond street for their Christmas greens.

W. C. Drews, of Braddock, reports unusual advance orders for Christmas greens.

P. J. Demas, of the Exchange, is still ill with influenza.

John Boldinger, of Ulum & Co., is on deck again.   E. L. M.

CASTILE, N. Y.—Ernst R. Oliver has secured a business interest in the establishment of Milo N. Wright. The greenhouses are being repaired, enlarged and new heating apparatus installed.

A FROST-PROOF
Shipping Box.

An entirely new Folding Box for plants. The lightest box made. Plants can be packed in one-third the time heretofore used and go safely in every way.

A MONEY SAVER

in time and express to every florist and nurseryman. Also very useful for delivering plants in cities, and to be used over and over.

You Need Them

Send for Descriptive Price List at once to

L. P. LORD,
OWATONNA,   MINNESOTA.

Kramer's Pot Hangers

Patent Applied for.

THE neatest, simplest, most convenient and only practical device for converting ordinary flower pots into hanging baskets. They fit all standard made pots from 3 to 10 inches in diameter. The illustration shows how they are attached. Just the thing for hanging up ferns, begonias, etc. You can make room and money by their use. Try them. For Sale by

Vaughan's Seed Store, Chicago and New York.
E. F. Winterson Co., Chicago.
C. C. Pollworth Co., Milwaukee, Wis.

Price with wire chain as shown in cut, $1.00 per dozen by express. Sample dozen by mail, $1.35.

I. N. KRAMER & SON,   Cedar Rapids, Iowa.

THOSE RED POTS
"STANDARDS"
FULL SIZE AND WIDE BOTTOMS.
BULB PANS AND AZALEA POTS.
DETROIT FLOWER POT M'F'Y.
HARRY BALSLEY,   DETROIT, MICH.
Rep.   490 Howard St.

GEO. KELLER & SON,
MANUFACTURERS OF
FLOWER POTS.
Before buying write for prices.
361-363 Herndon Street,
near Wrightwood Ave.,
CHICAGO, ILL.

HOLYOKE, MASS.—E. D. Howland read a paper on house plants and their care before the Holyoke Horticultural Society December 2.

ESTABLISHED 1866 **EMIL STEFFENS** SUCC'R. R.STEFFENS, AND STEFFENS BROS.
MANUFACTURER OF
FLORISTS' WIRE DESIGNS & SUPPLIES
335 EAST 21ST ST. NEW YORK CITY.

Standard Flower Pots
The WHILLDIN POTTERY COMPANY,
PHILADELPHIA, PA.   JERSEY CITY, N. J.   LONG ISLAND CITY, N. Y.
Traveling Representative, U. CUTLER RYERSON, 108 Third Ave., Newark, N. J.

LIGHTNING FLOWER POT WASHER

Washes all sizes of pots, clean as new, about as fast as you can handle them. **Strong Plants are only grown in Clean Pots.** Send for description. Sold direct $15.00 net F. O. B. Joliet.

C. E. FINLEY,   Joliet, Illinois.

RED POTS
SAMPLE POT AND PRICE LIST ON APPLICATION.
C. C. POLLWORTH CO., MILWAUKEE, WIS.
Please mention the American Florist when writing.

WRITE
A. F. KOHR, 1521-23 N. LEAVITT ST., CHICAGO, ILL.,
FOR PRICES OF
Standard Pots
which for strength and porosity combined are the best on the market.

FLOWER POTS
ALL KINDS.
STANDARD POTS SPECIALTY
List and SAMPLES FREE.
SWAHN'S POTTERY MF'G CO.,
P. O. Box 78.   MINNEAPOLIS, MINN.

Standard Flower... POTS
If your greenhouses are within 500 miles of the Capitol, write us, we can save you money......
W. H. ERNEST,
28th and M Streets,   WASHINGTON, D. C.

Red Standard Flower Pots
Price list and samples on application.
Paducah Pottery,
J. A. BAUER, Proprietor.
Paducah, Ky.

The Horticultural Trade Journal
THE LARGEST, BRIGHTEST AND BEST
Horticultural Trade paper in the British Isles. It contains MORE ADVERTISEMENTS, MORE ILLUSTRATIONS and MORE NEWS than any of its contemporaries. Read by the whole of the British trade and all the best European houses every week. Annual subscription, 75 cents. Specimen copy post free. Published weekly.
Horticultural Trade Journal Co., Padiham, Lancs., Eng.

ESTAB. 1765 A.H.HEWS&CO. NO. CAMBRIDGE MASS. L.I.CITY N.Y. CATALOGUE FREE

STANDARD FLOWER POTS!
Packed in small crates, easy to handle.

	Price per crate		Price per crate
1500 2-in.,	in crate, $4.88	120 7-in.,	in crate, $4.20
1500 2¼	" 5.25	60 8	" 3.00
1500 2½	" 6.00		HAND MADE.
1000 3	" 5.00	48 9-in.,	in crate, $3.60
800 3½	" 5.80	48 10	" 4.80
500 4	" 4.50	24 12	" 4.80
320 5	" 4.51	12 14	" 4.80
144 6	" 3.16	6 16	" 4.50

Seed pans, same price as pots. Send for price list of Cylinders for Cut Flowers, Hanging Baskets, Lawn Vases, etc. Ten per cent off for cash with order. Address
HILFINGER BROS. POTTERY, Fort Edward, N. Y.
Or AUGUST ROLKER & SONS, New York Agents,
31 Barclay Street, New York City.
Please mention the American Florist when writing.

SULPHO-TOBACCO SOAP
COMBINES THE STRONGEST
TOBACCO EXTRACT
with Sulphur and Alkali. Never fails to
KILL BUGS AND INSECTS
GREENHOUSE STOCK
kept healthy by using this popular Insecticide. Satisfaction guaranteed. Prices low. Write for sample cake.
Larkin Soap Co. BUFFALO, N.Y.
Please mention the American Florist when writing.

THE AMERICAN FLORIST

A WEEKLY JOURNAL FOR THE TRADE

America is "the Prow of the Vessel; there may be more comfort Amidships, but we are the first to touch Unknown Seas."

Vol. XXI. CHICAGO AND NEW YORK, DECEMBER 26, 1903. No. 812.

THE AMERICAN FLORIST

NINETEENTH YEAR.

Copyright 1903, by American Florist Company
Entered as Second-Class Mail Matter.

PUBLISHED EVERY SATURDAY BY

AMERICAN FLORIST COMPANY,
324 Dearborn St., Chicago.
Eastern Office: 42 W. 28th St., New York.

Subscription, $1.00 a year. To Europe, $2.00.
Subscriptions accepted only from the trade.
Volumes half-yearly from August, 1901.

THIS ISSUE 36 PAGES WITH COVER.

CONTENTS.

Palms and Ferns.

TEMPERATURE FOR PALMS.

Reference has been made at various times in this series of articles to the most suitable temperatures for various species of plants of these families, but it may possibly be more convenient for some inquirers to have the matter of tempera-ture referred to more at length, and in one article. The early setting in of winter brings this subject more before us, for with the severe frosts that have prevailed throughout the greater portion of the country during the latter part of November the heating apparatus has demanded more attention than is com-mon at that early date.

It has been frequently remarked that the palms of the trade are few in number from a varietal point of view, and at the present time the kentias are doubtless among the most important, from which it would seem quite proper that their requirements in regard to temperature should be first considered. In growing for trade purposes it is impracticable to make the closest possible distinctions in regard to temperature, nor is it necessary, for Kentia Belmoreana, K. Forsteriana and K. Canterburyana may all be grown in the same greenhouse, though as a matter of preference I would arrange the respective lots as follows, if such an arrangement may be made conveniently: K. Forsteriana at the warmest end of greenhouse, K. Belmoreana next in order and K. Canterburyana in the coolest por-tion, the latter growing naturally at a considerably higher elevation than the other two.

Such an arrangement having been made a thermometer hung in the center of the house ought not to exceed 60° to 62° at night during ordinary moderate weather, and if zero weather should be experienced I would much rather have the tempera-ture of the house drop to 56° by morn-ing than to bake the atmosphere in an attempt to maintain 62° or more. It is a perfectly natural proceeding for the temperature to fall gradually toward morning, and as such tends to preserving the health and vigor of the plants. The growing of kentias in a comparatively low temperature is a reasonable method and gives results in sturdy and stocky foliage that "looks well and wears well," as some of the shoe manufacturers say of their productions. It may also be offered as an evidence of the correctness of this view, the fact that although the past summer was an unusually cool one the growth of the kentias was never better

at that season. Latania Borbonica and Phœnix Canariensis will flourish under the same conditions as the kentias, and of these the phœnix may be given the cooler position if there be any choice. Rhapis flabelliformis and R. humilis make but little growth during the winter, nor do they require much heat, a night temperature of 50° being quite enough for their welfare, and giving their foliage that rustling stiffness so dear to the heart of the decorator, for he well knows that such plants will bear much use without injury. Areca lutescens and Cocos Wed-delliana did not make as much growth as usual in the past summer, these two being heat loving plants, from which we find that 65° to 68° is a satisfactory night temperature during the winter, allowing the temperature to fall on extremely cold nights to a minimum of 60°.

Too great stimulation by means of strong heat is not wise on the part of the areca grower during the months of December and January especially, else the foliage of this palm becomes too thin and grassy, and its lasting qualities are greatly reduced. There has also been some difficulty experienced with this palm when grown in an irregular tem-perature, such a condition sometimes resulting in the production of premature flower spikes even in very small plants, such an abnormal growth frequently ruining the plants altogether, or else checking their growth to such a degree as to render their recovery an unprofit-able process.

The abnormal flowering of Areca lutescens has been noted even among plants in 2-inch or 3-inch pots in some cases, though it seems to have been less prevalent of late years than was the case some ten or more years ago, possibly owing to the fact that comparatively few establishments of any pretentions are found at the present time without a night fireman, whereas only a few years ago the reverse of this was the rule, with the natural result that there were great variations between the evening and the morning temperature of the greenhouses.

Referring again to Cocos Weddelliana we may repeat that with the strong firing needful to maintain nearly 70° at night, there is always some danger from red spiders, one of the most troublesome pests to which this palm is exposed, and to prevent such a difficulty thorough syringing must be given and a moist atmosphere kept at all times.

Plants that are natives of the Malay Archipelago are usually decidedly trop ical in their habits, unless it be some that are found high up on the mountains, and Livistona rotundifolia seems to be one of those from the lowlands with a natural preference for heat and moisture this palm enjoying a temperature of 65° to 70° at night, with a possible preference for the latter figure. Seaforthia elegans and Ptychosperma Alexandræ both produce a more stocky growth and tougher foliage when grown in a reasonably cool house, and if the plants are larger than 4-inch pot size the conditions advised for the kentias will answer very well, though for very small plants I prefer a slightly higher temperature, it being always kept in mind that young stock or newly potted seedlings will be benefitted by a little extra heat, these juvenile plants being much more tender than are adults of the same species.

The common date palm, Phœnix dactylifera, is also capable of enduring a comparatively low temperature while resting from growth, though possibly not quite so hardy as *P.* Canariensis, a night temperature of 55° to 60° answering very well for this palm, but the much handsomer and more graceful P. rupicola grows better in a somewhat higher temperature, and in common with the other members of this genus is not inclined to make much growth during the winter.

P. reclinata grows well with P. rupicola, and the same conditions may be applied to P. sylvestris, the latter being also a very attractive palm of moderate growth, though but seldom seen among the trade collections of the present day.

The last three palms are best suited with a minimum night temperature of 60°. Cocos insignis, C. plumosa and C. flexuosa are occasionally found in trade collections, though in comparatively small numbers, as is also C. Romanzaffiana, and if the plants are small should be grown under the same conditions as Areca lutescens, but if they are well developed plants of decorative size will not need to be kept in a higher temperature than the kentias. Desmoncus, calamus, stevensonia, martinezia and most of the bactrises may also be considered among the tropical species of palms, and as such are most happy in a night temperature of close to 70°.

W. H. TAPLIN.

Joseph H. Hadkinson.

In appointing Joseph H. Hadkinson superintendent of floriculture at the World's Fair the management showed its appreciation of the work accomplished by Mr. Hadkinson on the seventy acres of land surrounding the palaces of agriculture and horticulture. When Mr. Hadkinson joined the World's Fair force of workers he was made the head gardener, on the recommendation of Frederic W. Taylor, chief of the departments of agriculture and horticulture. Most of his domain was a field of barren yellow clay. In less than a year he has converted this into immense gardens. There are great lawns and a six-acre rose garden. As superintendent of floriculture Mr. Hadkinson will be in charge of all the gardens and also the flowers displayed in the conservatories, which form a part of the palace of horticulture.

Mr. Hadkinson was born in Manchester, England. When a youth his parents emigrated to America and settled in Nebraska. He had studied in London, and in his new home he embarked in the nursery business. He gave that up to accept a position as instructor in horticulture in the University of Nebraska under Chief Taylor, who was then professor of agriculture at that institution. Mr. Hadkinson did the gardening at the Omaha exposition, and had charge of Nebraska's horticulture exhibit at the Pan-American exposition at Buffalo.

Florists' Plant Notes.

FOR WEEK OF DECEMBER 26.

Hydrangeas.—It is now time to place the hydrangeas, which are resting in a cool house, in a stronger heat to force them into flower for Easter. It takes about three months in a temperature of 60° at at night to have them on time. Keep them well watered as soon as the heat is applied and growth will commence almost immediately. Hydrangeas are "hard drinkers" and, once the buds are set, will require copious waterings at

Joseph H. Hadkinson.
(World's Fair Superintendent of Floriculture)

at least twice a day. Never allow them to wilt even slightly before watering, for this will spot the flowers and decrease their size. And then, too, the foliage is apt to be burned by the sun if they are permitted to wilt. Apply liquid manure twice a week after the buds are set; this will deepen the color of the flowers and darken the foliage. Allow plenty of room between the plants or the lower leaves will drop and the growth will be weak and drawn. Syringing must also be faithfully attended to as a preventive of red spider, but no water should ever touch the flowers after they are developed. Two-year-old plants that were grown in pots all summer require practically the same treatment, excepting that a shift to a size larger pot will be necessary after growth commences if they are in the least pot bound. Take a cutting or two from each plant some time during January. Strong bottom shoots should be selected for propagation. We believe it is a mistake to take any but the strongest cuttings, for no surer method of deteriorating the stock can be employed than the indiscriminate or careless selection of cuttings. The first season may show no apparent dete-

rioration; but let the practice be continued for several seasons in succession, and the flowers will lose their beautiful pink color and turn to a faded, murky hue, an aggravation alike to the grower and to the prospective buyer, besides increasing the number of plants that grow blind. These cuttings when rooted should be potted into 2½-inch pots, and about the first of April the strongest may be selected and shifted to 4-inch, which will make fine little plants with one large flower for each plant for Memorial Day. The rest may be kept cool and later planted out of doors. The plants for Memorial Day should be kept as near to 40° as possible for another two weeks. Water them sparingly, but do not discourage growth altogether; rather let them grow as the season advances into strong, stocky plants. About the middle of March the temperature can be raised ten degrees to start the plants into more rapid growth.

Bulbs.—The first of the year is a safe time to commence forcing Dutch bulbs, such as tulips, hyacinths, Narcissus Von Sion and others. When bringing them inside frozen, do not place them at once into the forcing temperature, but allow them to thaw out gradually in a cool shed for a day or two. Unless a part of a bench can be spared for forcing, tulips can just as well be grown under a warm bench for the first twelve days after forcing commences. Tack a piece of canvas or other heavy material in front to provide darkness, which is absolutely necessary to lengthen out the stems. A high temperature is also essential; 85° at night is not too high. While in this extreme temperature they should be copiously watered with warm water. After the first twelve days they are removed to a lighter place, gradually inuring them to the light to develop the foliage and flowers. Only the early varieties, such as Proserpine, Keizerskroon, La Reine, and a few others, should be forced thus early in the season. Leave the later varieties for later forcing. Von Sion can safely be forced from now on, but must not be subjected to such a high temperature or the buds will blast, nor is darkness necessary to lengthen the stems. Dutch hyacinths should be given a bench as soon as they are subjected to moderate heat; placing them under the bench will draw them up too much and weaken the stems, which detracts from their value as selling plants. In order to have a supply of bulbous stock continually on hand, it is necessary to bring a certain quantity of bulbs into heat every week; set apart a certain day each week for this purpose.

Lily of the Valley.—The recently imported valley pips can be forced successfully after the first of the year. Select a warm corner of a side bench where the temperature runs about 85° at night, in which to force them. After bringing them in from outdoors, thaw them out gradually by dipping the roots in cold water. Cut about an inch off the ends of the roots, so as to permit the pips to absorb the water better. A small quantity may be planted in pans or low pots of selling sizes, for the retail plant trade. For cutting, plant the pips in sand in boxes about twelve inches wide, eighteen inches long and six inches deep, leaving about two inches of space each way between the pips. They require no other stimulant than water, but of this they must have plenty. Keep them heavily shaded for the first two weeks, then gradually remove the shade until they can stand stronger light. When fully developed the boxes may be removed to

MAMMOTH VASES ON LAWN OF G. W. FIFIELD, LOWELL, MASS.

a cooler place where the flowers will last a long time. Perhaps a better plan than this, entailing less labor and expense, is to prepare a part of a bench into a frame a foot high made of one-inch boards, in three partitions, each division to be the length of a hotbed sash, which will hold about four hundred pips each. Every week one of the frames is planted up and as it takes just three weeks to force them, a continual supply of valley is always on hand. The sash are kept heavily shaded with boards or burlap for the first twelve days, alter which the shading is gradually removed. No water should ever touch the flowers after they are developed. · As soon as one batch is ready it is cut and the flowers are tied in bunches of twenty-five and placed in the ice box where they last a long time, when the frame is cleared and the sand prepared for another lot.   G.

Mammoth Vases.

The illustration herewith, shows two mammoth vases on the lawn of Geo. W. Fifield, Lowell, Mass., said to be the largest in the state. The gardener at this place, Frank Sladen, with his son, appears in the background.

DECORA, IA.—The business of H. H. Cadwell has been discontinued.

BROCKTON, MASS.—The greenhouses formerly belonging to Mr. Crawford and of late conducted by C. S. Cooper, were sold at auction on the morning of December 21.

The Carnation.

CULTURAL REMINDERS.

The beginning of a new year always opens a new chapter in the year's work. By that time things have settled down to a more stable condition. The inclement fall weather is past and the steady cold ushers in a different state of affairs. The air is less apt to be laden with moisture and clouds in zero weather than when it is warm. The heavy firing partially takes the place of sunshine, and the increasing amount of light consequent to the lengthening of the day awakens the plants to renewed activity. This is the springtime of the year for carnations under glass. It seems reasonable then that we should make liberal allowance for the increased needs of the plants. Nature supplies the stimulus to renewed ambitions; it is for us to supply the foundation upon which it should rest, in the way of more liberal feeding, an increasing supply of water and an abundance of fresh air. The heavy growth that begins about this time will exhaust the soil very quickly, and the result will soon be seen in smaller flowers and shorter and weaker stems. To those plants that have been in active growth for some time and give promise of keeping right up, a weekly application of liquid manure will be a benefit. This liquid may be made of fresh horse or cow manure, and we may also add some bone meal, chicken manure, or any other fertilizer in proportion to its strength. Some manures are much stronger than others, for which due

allowance must be made. The following will be found about right under normal conditions: Cow manure, one-half bushel to a barrel of water; horse manure, one bushel; chicken manure, a peck to the barrel. Two days' soaking will be sufficient, and after the liquid is drawn off the vessel may be filled the second time with water, which, after standing twenty-four hours, will be again ready for use. To this may safely be added two quarts of bone meal, bone and blood or wood ashes to the barrel. It is well to start in gradually, using the liquid about half the strength recommended, and working up to the maximum strength by degrees. As a top-dressing sheep manure may be used at the rate of a half to a cubic yard to a house 20x100, bone meal and wood ashes about a bushel to 1000 square feet of bench surface. This is not strong and an application of one of these fertilizers may be made at intervals of about a week in rotation. This is much better than applying in heavy doses at longer intervals. A light dusting of lime over the surface once a month will also be a benefit, more for its tendency to set free unavailable elements and its neutralizing effect than for the actual fertilizing elements it contains. It is, of course, important for every grower to study the needs of his own soil. Hard and fast lines cannot be followed in this any more than in other things. A rule is sometimes more valuable when broken than when adhered to. Some find chemical manures valuable. We have never tried them on a large enough scale to enable us to pass judgment upon them. Some soils will require heavier feeding than others. Heavy soils generally want less than light soils. The different varieties will also need careful study as to their wants. Good summer bloomers, such as Crocker, Joost, Dorothy, Hill, etc., will stand less than good winter blossoms, such as White Cloud, Lorna, Marquis and Nelson.

The elements most desirable to add to the soil at this time of the year are those that promote blooming qualities, strengthen the calyx and add firmness to the growth, rather than those that promote a heavy growth. Bone meal and bone and blood are rich in phosphoric acid and aid in the development of the flower. Wood ashes are rich in potash and stiffen the stems, strengthen the calyx and add stamina to the plant. Chicken manure produces about the same effect as bone meal. Horse, cow and sheep manure are rich in nitrogen and promote leaf growth, and are therefore more valuable later on, but may be used moderately now. Lime should be used by itself as a top-dressing, for if used with other fertilisers it is apt to liberate the fertilising elements and drive them into the air. Soot from soft coal gives a rich green color to the growth and intensifies the color of the flowers on most varieties. It may be used as a top-dressing the same strength as bone meal. Do not put on a heavy mulch of any kind for a couple of months yet. It is important to have the soil well under control at this season, and a heavy mulch would have the opposite effect. A dusting of lime over the soil on varieties that have been forced some for Christmas will help them back into normal condition.　　　J.

Christmas Stores of Chicago Retailers.

The retail florists of Chicago are generally well satisfied with the business of Christmas week. Nearly all of the stores were made attractive for the holidays. Holly, mistletoe, green, spruce, laurel, and the thousand and one varieties of decorative material so necessary for the holiday time were to be seen everywhere. The Fleischman store in the Palmer house block wore a beautiful holiday dress. The windows were uniquely decorated with immortelle bells, ferns in pots and holly wreaths. Many large poinsettias were disposed of, an unusually heavy demand favoring that bright colored plant this season.

So much business in the way of funeral work and other decorations came in the direction of P. J. Hauswirth last week that he had little time to decorate his own store at the Auditorium Annex on Michigan avenue. Something new in the way of Christmas wreaths was sent out by Mr. Hauswirth. Boxwood was the material used. He also used California peppers for holiday decorations with good effect.

O. J. Friedman's store at Michigan avenue and Van Buren street had a distinctive holiday appearance. A canopy of holly and laurel was erected over the sidewalk leading to the entrance. Some splendid heaths were sold to Christmas buyers. Mr. Friedman has been unusually busy lately. Among his late contracts is the decoration for the Standard Club's New Year's ball. He executed the elaborate decoration of the Young wedding at Grace church recently, using large quantities of chrysanthemums, lilies and smilax.

Charles A. Samuelson's place on Michigan avenue showed the results of the decorator's touch. The large windows showed a wealth of holly wreaths and Christmas bells. His primroses and fine poinsettias found a ready holiday sale.

The store of William J. Smyth, at Michigan avenue and Thirty-first street, was fixed up for the occasion. On tables ranged along the walls were placed a varied assortment of Christmas specialties. The windows were made attractive with holly wreaths and bells. Incandescent lights under poinsettia shades threw a charming effect over all. Mr. Smyth is well satisfied with the holiday business.

The Ernst Wienhoeber Company, whose store is located on the north side, did a large business this week. The salesroom, with its bright mirrors and fine cut flowers and plants, was very attractive. Cyclamens, seen here at their best, had a

Greenhouse Banana Plant.

large sale. The many Christmas day delivery orders filled by this company was proof ample of the ever-growing popularity of flowers as gifts.

John Mangel, as usual, had a very attractive display. He sold large quantities of extra fine holly. The interior of his cozy store on Wabash avenue was decorated under the direction of Mr. Lietch, who is a past master in this art. Arches covered with green and laurel suspended bells of immortelle. In the corner window was a mound of moss, in which were imbedded bunches of single and double violets.

The large, bright store of E. Asmus & Company, at Evanston, was artistically decorated. From the center of the ceiling to the corners were hung festoons of spruce and green. Fern dishes, Chinese primroses, cyclamens and palms constituted a large part of the Christmas business.

A. Lange, on Monroe street, enjoyed a

good holiday run of business. His windows presented a tempting appearance with lavish variety of good stock. Many fine poinsettias were sold.

Good decorative plants, such as palms, ferns, pandanuses, etc., were to be had in almost any quantity, while flowering plants of similar quality were quite scarce.

Society for Horticultural Science.

The following announcement and programme of the first gathering of the Society for Horticultural Science has been sent out from the office of the secretary, S. A. Beach, Geneva, N. Y.:

The first meeting with scientific programme of the Society for Horticultural Science will be held in St. Louis, December 28 and 29, in connection with the American Association for the Advancement of Science. Meetings will be held in room 221 of the Central High School building, corner of Grand and Finney avenues, December 28, 10 a. m. to 12 m., and 2 to 5 p. m.; and December 29, 9 a. m. to 12 m., and 2 to 5 p. m. The following programme, subject to change, has been prepared:

MONDAY FORENOON, DECEMBER 28.—"Co-ordination of Horticultural Work," by L. C. Corbett, horticulturist, United States department of agriculture; "The Mangosteen, Queen of tropical fruits," by D. G. Fairchild, agricultural explorer, department of agriculture; "Influence of wilt disease on watermelon cultivation in the south," by W. A. Orton, pathologist, department of agriculture; "Principles underlying the use of cover crops," by E. A. Emerson, Nebraska experiment station, and J. Craig, Cornell experiment station; "Principles underlying the practice of tillage," by A. R. Whitson, Wisconsin experiment station, and W. Paddock, Colorado experiment station.

MONDAY AFTERNOON.—A symposium on shading as a horticultural practice: "The shading of plants from the physiological standpoint," by L. C. Corbett, horticulturist, department of agriculture, and B. M. Duggar, Missouri experiment station; "Shading horticultural crops," by L. C. Corbett, horticulturist, department of agriculture; "A few facts obtained by growing vegetables in a cheese cloth enclosure in 1903," by W. T. Macoun, Canada experimental farms; "Shading strawberries," by V. A. Clark and O. M. Taylor, experiment station, Geneva, N. Y., presented by V. A. Clark; "Growing tobacco and pineapple under shade," by H. J. Webber, physiologist, in charge of plant breeding laboratory, department of agriculture.

TUESDAY FORENOON, DECEMBER 29.—Reports on recent progress in scientific horticulture in northeastern Europe, Germany, France, Great Britain and Ireland, and Canada.

[Only a part of these reports on horticultural progress abroad will be presented at the St. Louis meeting. The rest will probably be presented in 1904.]

TUESDAY AFTERNOON.—A joint session with the Plant and Animal Breeders' Association: "Mendel's Law," by F. A. Waugh, Massachusetts experiment station; "Seed selection according to specific gravity," by V. A. Clark, experiment station, Geneva, N. Y.; "Grape breeding: some correlations between size and specific gravity of the seed and its germination, with the vigor of the seedling," by S. A. Beach, experiment station, Geneva, N. Y.; "Breeding fruits for our Northwest," by N. E. Hansen, South Dakota experiment station; "Breeding oranges," by H. J. Webber, department of agriculture.

The society is being very favorably received, and the outlook is for an enthusiastic meeting.

Greenhouse Bananas.

The banana in fruit shown in the accompanying illustration has proved quite a drawing card for Joseph Harris, of Shamokin, Pa., and he thinks that it would pay other florists to grow a plant of this character for advertising purposes. The plant stands six feet high with leaves four to seven feet long, and there are 175 bananas in the bunch.

ROCHESTER, N. Y.—An elaborate programme has been prepared for the forty-ninth annual meeting of the Western New York Horticultural Society, to be held January 27 and 28.

PROPAGATING HOUSES OF HOOPES BROTHERS & THOMAS, WEST CHESTER, PA.

few instances this, it is to be feared, may be true, but judging from the trash imported nowadays under the original Japanese names and selected from water color hand paintings it is safe to assert that the least said the better. As soon as the smoke is cleared away we will see the peony question more clearly. In the meantime let us not forget the suggestion thrown out recently in reference to a peony exhibition, for it is well worth the attention of every one interested in the peony, and who is not? The plan of cold storage might be all right, but it is going to take a lot of time and trouble for some persons, and also a lot of cold storage space. Bringing together as many varieties as possible at a given point ought to aid in clearing up some of the disputes in nomenclature, and I hope it may be done.   GUESS.

British Trade Topics.

The dreary autumn days, with a superabundance of wet and an occasional fog, are now (November 14) brightened by the varied and prolific display of chrysanthemums, attesting to the increasing popularity of this attractive subject. In fact, owing to the mildness of the season the market has been glutted with the blooms, not only in the metropolis but in the provinces. November is the month for the chrysanthemum shows. The season has been a trying one for most growers owing to the excessive wet and the dreaded rust has caused sad havoc in many parts. Owing to the Royal Aquarium in London having been acquired by the Wesleyans to be converted into a place for religious observance, the National Chrysanthemum Society has been obliged to transfer its headquarters to the Crystal Palace, at Sydenham. This house of many windows is admirably adapted for a show, but it is not so central for London doers as the aquarium. I attended the November show of the society. Neither the quality nor quantity equaled the display at last year's show, but this was to be expected owing to the adverse climatic conditions. For all this, the show was of a varied and interesting character, attracting many visitors from all parts of the country.

One of the best displays was that of H. J. Jones, of Ryecroft nurseries, Lewisham, who is a noted raiser of the leading American and Australian novelties. Mr. Jones is a specialist in this branch, being well known as a judge, lecturer and the author of a work on chrysanthemums

The Work of Peony Enthusiasts.

It is enthusiasts and those who do things who make mistakes which give the calculating and the matter-of-fact, methodical persons their opportunity to draw attention to such mistakes and make "the necessary corrections, thus possibly unconsciously, or may be otherwise, though certainly indisputably, adding to this world's sum of knowledge and attracting more attention than could otherwise be the case. A case in point: Had it not been for the enthusiastic secretary of the peony committee making a few blunders, the opportunity for clearing the peony atmosphere would not have occurred. "The greatest thing that ever happened," said one enthusiast, rubbing his hands gleefully. "And such knowledge came from unexpected quarters," said another, quietly, with a smile. "Correct knowledge is generally in order and is always constitutional," said still another, who has pronounced ideas about things in general and plant nomenclature in particular. And this is especially so when we consider that the mother of so many special societies has been the means of much useful knowledge being so freely disseminated, as the national society was organized for just such purposes. If there were no mistakes made and to make there would be no necessity for corrections, consequently death to all animate and inanimate things would naturally follow. The struggle for existence makes life worth the living; it is life. Show us the person who never made a mistake and we will show you one who has done nothing.

I happen to know a man who, I believe, is neither a member of the peony·society nor the peony committee, nor has he friends connected with the official family of the Emperor of Japan, but who has imported apparently direct in unbroken cases through American agencies numerous varieties of peonies, both tree and herbaceous, at different times with no other than Japanese names attached. These were selected by the purchaser with great care from pictures that he was assured were hand painted, true representations from nature, which were very striking. It is presumed that many peony enthusiasts have seen similar

pictures. But whatever the cause, or the reason, the names attached to the pictures and those attached to the plants did not agree, those among the herbaceous varieties being by far the worst, for a greater lot of worthless varieties from an American's viewpoint would indeed be hard to find. Those among the tree varieties were not quite so bad, some of them proving to be grand, but they were so different from the pictures that it appeared as though no effort whatever had been made to send them true to name. If this be true, and I am afraid it is, what is the sense of honor among the Japanese? Is it discernible without a strong microscope? If the S. A. F. would send a committee on nomenclature direct to Japan to stay there for a year or two to look after these matters direct to stay in Japan, where they belong.

The varieties of the herbaceous section that have been raised from seed in England, France and especially · in America, so far as I have been able to observe, are far superior to those received direct from Japan. It has been intimated that many of our best varieties under English and French names are Japanese importations renamed. In a

INTERIOR OF E. A. ASMUS & COMPANY'S STORE, CHICAGO.

which has reached the thirteenth edition. His brilliant array of blooms was of the high standard associated with his culture and well merited the gold medal awarded. The newest varieties were well represented and included Mrs. J. Dunn, a new white Japanese slightly tinted with cream in the center, and Miss Jessie Dean, a single of a bright rose tint with white zone around disc, both of which received first-class certificates. Another gold medalist was H. Cannell, of Swanley and Lynsford, one of the founders of the society, who for many years has been in the front rank of exhibitors. He has a grand lot of chrysanthemums this fall at his Kentish home of flowers. Among the leading varieties to be seen in his show conservatory are Red Mme. Carnot, an Australian importation; Madame Paolo Radaelli, large white with pink shade; Lord Hopetoun, similar to F. Molyneux; Ethel Fitzroy, bronze with yellow stripe; General Hutton, a splendid yellow; Colonel Wetherall, a fine bronze. Brilliant cannas, for which Mr. Cannell is also famous, richly tinted pelargoniums and well colored apples were also contributed by him.

A superb group which was awarded first prize was arranged by Norman Davies, of Framfield nurseries, Sussex. Interspersed amongst crotons, palms and other foliage plants were some excellent specimens of F. S. Vallis, Bessie Godfrey. Calvat's Sun, Paolo Radaelli, Mrs. A. R. Knight, Marie Brunning, Miss Stofford others. W. J. Godfrey, of Exmouth, Devon, had a collection of some of his newest introductions and this was awarded a gold medal. Among the novelties I noticed that Messrs. Gregory & Evans, of Longlands nurseries, Sidney, Kent, showed their new white flowered heath, Erica gracilis nivalis, which was recently given a certificate by the Royal Horticultural Society. Jabez Ambrose, F. R. H. S., formerly with Messrs. Paul & Sons, and now in business as a nurseryman at Cheshunt, Herts, exhibited the new seedling grape, Melton Constable, raised by Mr. Shingler, head gardener to Lord Hastings, of Melton Constable. This new variety is likely to come to the front as a market grape and will take the place of some of the older sorts. Its chief advantage is that its fruit will hang in good condition until the end of February, while its attractive appearance will commend it to all market growers. It will be ready for distribution by Mr. Ambrose in July next year.

W. Wells, of Earlswood, Surrey, did not exhibit at this show, but on the same day he had a remarkably good collection of chrysanthemums at the Royal Horticultural Society's show at the Drill Hall, Westminster. Among the large-flowered section were W. R. Church, King of Yellows, Mrs. J. Seward, Cecil Cutts, Mrs. F. Hudson, Godfrey's Pride, Bessie Godfrey, W. Higgs, General Hutton, W. Duckham, T. C. Brock. His single-flowered Kitty Bourne, of golden tint, and W. A. Etherington, a Japanese of a pink shade, received awards of merit. At this meeting of the R. H. S. an interesting paper on "The advantages and evils of size in flowers, fruits and vegetables," was contributed by E. T. Cook, editor of the Garden, who emphasized the importance of regarding quality rather than size. He condemned the over-doubling of flowers, pointing out that many a flower was the better for a judicious degree of doubling, but when it was carried too far it turned what should be a handsome flower into a misshapen absurdity. This had been done in the case of zinnias.

Mr. Cook's contention was indorsed by many visitors, who recognize that some check is needed upon the increasing craze for size, irrespective of quality. Of the making of new horticultural books there is no end. Geo. Dungood, the Kentish fruit grower, and Owen Thomas, who was head gardener to Queen Victoria, are bringing out a comprehensive work dealing with the fruit garden, and they will be assisted by a number of well known experts.

The foreign flower trade in London has made rapid strides in the last twenty years, until the accommodations afforded at Covent Garden have been completely out-grown. A handsome new building has been erected by the Duke of Bedford for the requirements of this branch, and has been opened. The supply of French bloom is somewhat short at present owing to the bad season. As regards the new floral hall, in an interview I had the other day with J. Assbee, the superintendent, I learned that recently an official came over from New York to inspect the building with the view of a similar one being built on the other side. Mr. Assbee was away on his holiday at the time, but he has sent to America some information on the subject. From inquiries made among market nurserymen I find that the last season has been a bad one in the flower trade. Since the South African war trade generally has been lifeless and this depression has made itself felt among the florists. There is an increasing tendency for flowers to be dispensed with at funerals, as was the case at the obsequies of the late Marquis of Salisbury, and this, of course, makes a great difference to an expensive branch

of the trade. With the spread of palatial hotels in the metropolis there is a growing custom for dinner parties to be given at these places instead of at the private houses of the hosts, and this means a less demand for floral decorations.

A suggestion has been made for founding an orchid league by the admirers of Joseph Chamberlain, but this is not likely to become an accomplished fact owing to the dearness of the ex-colonial secretary's flavorite flower. Florists would welcome a movement for the adoption of some bloom which might give aid to trade in the way that the Primrose league has to thousands of street hawkers. Efforts are being made to popularize the wearing of roses on St. George's day, the great national festival. On this day at one London restaurant they present a rose to each diner—a custom which florists would like to see more extensively adopted. The observance of anniversaries by donning floral emblems has not made much headway in this country. As regards Primrose day, which is the chief flower wearing event of the year, the yellow blooms are obtained from the hedgerows and woodlands by hawkers and this, of course, has not benefited the florists. Politicians, for some inexplicable reason, have not taken kindly to floral emblems, and the primrose enjoys the monopoly in this direction.

BINGHAMTON, N. Y.,—Fire in the greenhouse of A. E. Fancher, November 28, caused a loss of $1,000, but if the plants freeze through the disabling of the heating apparatus the loss will amount to $5,000, with no insurance.

CATTLEYA DOWIANA, GROWN BY A. HALLSTROM, ST. PAUL.

Cattleya Dowiana.

Cattleya Dowiana is a native of Costa Rica, and as such, needs an abundance of heat and moisture during its growing season. I grow this cattleya during summer in our dendrobium and phalænopsis house, 65° at night. After flowering, which occurs before the bulbs are fully matured, they are removed to the cattleya house, where they are kept moderately moist until the pseudo-bulbs have obtained their full maturity. Then I keep them rather dry and cool, 50° to 56° at night, and during January and February as low as 45° to 48° during night. This low temperature seems not to injure, but rather tends to keep the plants dormant longer in the spring and counteracts the tendencies to make a second growth in the fall, which would otherwise weaken the plants. A mixture of fern roots and sphagnum, with a layer of charcoal and potsherds in the bottom of the crates, suits them. Crates are better than pots for this variety. A little weak liquid manure during the most active stage of growth improves them greatly. The photograph reproduced herewith was taken December 12.

AXEL HALLSTROM.

Heliotropes.

Some very fine varieties of heliotropes have been obtained from the continent during the past few years, says a correspondent of the Horticultural Advertiser (English), and while of vigorous growth they produce large and striking trusses of blooms. As pot plants they are delightful subjects for the greenhouse and they are well adapted for bedding purposes, though they should not be in too rich soil. Of the newest sorts Doctor Jenlin is very fine, and may be described as one of the darkest and finest blues; it is quite dark in color, the individual flowers being very large. Some might think Mme. Boucharlat to be of a darker shade, but the flowers are smaller than those of the preceding and do not form such large trusses. Lord Roberts has been shown a good deal during the past season; it is a variety of free growth with striking heads of bloom, but of a paler color than the two preceding. Perfection is the newest introduction; it is perhaps the largest and darkest of all, and yet highly pleasing in appearance. Etoile Celeste, pale silvery blue, is remarkable for its rich fragrance. And then there are such fine old varieties as Beauty of the Boudoir, President Garfield, Swanley Giant, and Vestal. White Lady is an excellent white and is popular with those who like this type of flower.

The Modern Plan.

Tess—I was passing that small florist's with Lord Britton yesterday and I hinted that I would like to have some of the lovely roses that were displayed in the window.

Jess—And did he send some to you?

Tess—Yes, they came this morning, C. O. D.—*Philadelphia Press.*

BOOKKEEPING and account forms for same by R. F. Tesson, as read at the Milwaukee convention has been printed in pamphlet form by the AMERICAN FLORIST and will be mailed FREE on request to any florist. Employers may have extra copies to distribute among their employes. The address is of much permanent value and well worth the study of our young men.

A BASKET OF ORCHIDS.

The Retail Trade.

THE USE OF ORCHIDS.

There is a steadily increasing demand for orchids from our customers and while a few years ago they were almost a rarity, the rich flowers are now to be seen daily in our best shops. But the demand is usually far greater than the supply, and to take a large order for them means many an anxious moment, especially at this season.

A very handsome wreath may be made entirely of Cypripedium insigne. These are used in profusion with a large bow of moss green ribbon. These wreaths are often relieved with a spray or cluster of white flowers or violets. Cypripediums are also used extensively for dinner decorations and are very fine for green and white effects. For funeral work a beautiful bunch can be made of Easter lilies, a large spray of cattleyas being inserted where the ribbon is tied, and the whole backed with four or five large cycas leaves.

A magnificent dinner given during the recent horse show is worth a description. Large wreaths of cattleyas and lily of the valley were laid on mirrors, which represented water, on which floated swans of white porcelain filled with lily of the valley. The corsages were of cattleyas and lily of the valley tied with No. 9 lavender ribbon, and the bouttonieres were of lily of the valley.

Cattleya Dowiana, the beautiful yellow orchid with rich crimson lip has been quite common this winter in New York and much sought after for bouquet work. The yellow orchids, Oncidium varicosum and others of that species are very effective for table decoration, especially in combination with American Beauty and Liberty roses or by themselves with Adiantum Farleyense.

Odontoglossum grande, the "baby orchid," is very short-lived as a cut flower, and seems to come between seasons, but is good as a pot plant. Vanda cœrulea, the beautiful blue orchid, is the fashionable flower of the season and for its size the most expensive, but it is unique in coloring. The finest corsage I have seen this season was made with this orchid, lily of the valley and Farleyense. Their great variety in form and coloring, will always keep orchids far in the lead as a floral acquisition. THE ARTIST.

Chicago.

SATISFACTORY HOLIDAY BUSINESS.—CARNATIONS NOT SCARCE AS EXPECTED.—HOLLY GLUT ON MARKET.—EVERETT'S LARGE STOCK FROZEN.—VISITORS.

The thaw of the early part of the week gave the dealers a scare, and for a time it looked as if all hopes for a flourishing Christmas business would be shattered. The cold returned, however, and Tuesday and Wednesday brought great activity. The local market was rather weak, but wholesalers had all they could do to keep up with their shipping orders. All rose stock was comparatively plentiful, the only shortage existing in American Beauty and red. The anticipated shortage of carnations did not materialize, all dealers being able to fill their orders with good fresh stock. There was probably more pickling of carnations than on any other item, and the picklers must have lost heavily, as there was plenty of good fresh stock to be had. Violets were a glut, and dealers who had prepared for a heavy demand in this line were glad to move them at any price, although violet quotations read from $1.25 to $2.00 per hundred. There were large supplies of good poinsettias on the market and all sold well. There was plenty of valley, calla, and other miscellaneous stock which did not sell as readily as last year.

It is the general opinion among whole-salers, commission men and retailers that this year's Christmas business fully equaled that of last year, while some say that it was much heavier.

Freezing Monday night caused a loss of several thousand dollars to A. B. Everett, whose greenhouse is located at Berteau and Oakley avenues, in Ravens-wood. His entire crop of carnations, to which about 27,000 feet of glass was devoted, was destroyed. The catastrophe was caused by the steam boiler giving out, and nothing could be done to save the plants. Workmen made repairs on the defective boiler the previous day, and it was thought to be in a safe condition.

The Fleischman people estimate that between one-quarter and one-half a million dollars' worth of cut flowers and plants are sold in New York City every Christmas week. They also say that American Beauty roses are selling at a much lower price in their Paris store than prevails here.

O. J. Friedman says that the time will soon be past when the grower can ask and receive one dollar each for American Beauty roses. Growers of Beauty are increasing at an alarming rate, he says, and the consequence will be that this favorite will lose both its tone and price.

Walter Kreitling was busy this week with special decorations. On Monday he had the table decorations for the Chicago club dinner. A huge kentia graced the center of the least board, and around this were banked ferns, poinsettias and boxwood sprigs.

The next meeting of the Florists' Club will be held Wednesday evening, January 6. The holiday business will be reviewed and prominent members of the trade will read papers regarding the stock marketed during the holidays.

E. Asmus & Company are sending to their customers in and about Evanston neat illustrated booklets on the care of plants. They contemplate holding a free flower show near Easter time.

The fakirs were selling holly wreaths at ten and fifteen cents each. The price is an indication of their poor quality. Water street holly, such as it was, could be purchased at almost any price.

The George Wittbold Company was busy this week filling orders for ferns and decorative plants. Ferns in birchbark dishes were sold in great numbers.

The Christmas tree seems to be as popular as ever. Captain Schuenemann easily disposed of a large cargo of good trees and received good prices.

Peter Reinberg's Chatenay roses enjoyed a heavy run for Christmas. The shipping force was kept busy nights keeping up with the orders.

Amling had fine Lawson and colored carnations in great quantity the fore part of the week, but they did not remain long on his counters.

E. Peiser, of Kennicott Brothers Company, thinks that this year's Christmas business, taken generally, will not equal that of last year.

Wietor Brothers had plenty of long stemmed American Beauty roses, but the mediums and shorts were rather scarce.

The E. F. Winterson Company made a specialty of holly and wreaths this week and their stock was entirely cleaned out.

Frank Garland had in store a large number of specimen Boston ferns in pots which sold well.

Bassett & Washburn had fine American Beauty roses and Lawson carnations for Christmas.

J. B. Deamud has been kept pretty lively with business since his return from the country.

Among the trade visitors in Chicago this week were Meyer Heller, Newcastle, Ind., and Edward Amerpohl, of the Janesville Floral Co., Janesville, Wis.

New York.

The market last week was very satisfactory. A slight change was felt Saturday, Beauty going as high as 60 cents. On Monday they went to 75 cents with good prospects of a further increase for Christmas. Carnations and violets are selling well. Growers predict a scarcity of carnations for the holidays. Paper White narcissi are plentiful, Roman hyacinths are holding out well but smilax is selling poorly. Lilies are about the same as last quoted. Poinsettias as cut flowers have sold slowly thus far. Numerous shipments of stored flowers came to the markets and the commission men during the four days preceding Christmas. This was the case especially with roses, of which the quantity of decayed and valueless stock was unprecedented and furnished a sad object lesson in the methods which are primarily responsible for the almost complete ruin of the Christmas cut flower business.

The funeral of Ernst G. Asmus Sunday was largely attended by the craft notwithstanding the bad weather. Several rich floral emblems were sent by friends. The directors of the New York Cut Flower Company sent a standing wreath of white roses, cattleyas, lilies and mignonette which stood six feet high. Dailledouze Brothers sent a wreath of white carnations and the American Rose Society a wreath of many kinds of roses, with a large bunch of American Beauty in the center.

John Donaldson of Elmhurst, L. I., has a remarkable crop of mushrooms coming up in his carnation benches, for which he finds a ready sale in the restaurants of New York. It is claimed they have a better flavor on account of being exposed to the sun. Mr. Donaldson says he never put any spawn in the benches and does not seem to know how to account for the crop. He picks from eight to twelve pounds a week.

Otto Andreæ, of Central Valley, sent in to Traendly & Schenck, for Christmas, shipments of Ulrich Brunner of strikingly fine quality, heavy flowers and stems three feet long. Mr. Andreæ is over ninety years of age but his pride and interest in his work remain unabated.

Charles Smith of Woodside, mourns the loss of his mother, who died at London, England, December 7, at the age of seventy-eight years.

Tulips in pans are seen in some store windows but are very dwarf, about three or four inches high.

Henry Schumann of Secaucus has four large benches of stevias that are fit for the holidays.

The regular monthly meeting of the Cut Flower Exchange will be held January 9.

Visitors: Augustus Tremper, Pascal Tremper, Orsan Burger, Wm. Burger and Stanton Rockefeller, all of Rhinebeck, N. Y.; Charles B. Stow, Kingston, N. Y.

SEDALIA, MO.—The greenhouses of Chas. Pfeiffer were considerably damaged by fire December 18.

Washington.

The sun for the last week has been kind to the fraternity in this section and there will be a better Christmas cut of roses in particular than was promised several weeks ago. There are more roses in sight than at the same time last year but not as many carnations. The local rose growers deserve credit both for the quantity of their flowers and the qualities that make for good commercial stock. The retailers who do not grow, are drawing largely on Philadelphia stock, which is good. The home growers of orchids, poinsettias, azaleas and other pot plants will make a very creditable showing.

The finishing touches have been given the store decorations. Among so many beautiful things it is hard to make a choice. J H Small & Sons have a finely decorated window. There is a chime of Christmas bells in red and white on a background of smilax and holly; beneath are poinsettias, Begonia Gloire de Lorraine and smaller plants banked with ferns. The shading of red and white lights in the evening makes a fine picture. Christmas prices for the best stock are as follows: Orchids (cut), cattleyas, $15 per dozen; cypripediums, $4 per dozen; vandas, $5 per dozen; roses, American Beauty, $10 to $18 per dozen; specials, $24 per dozen; Liberty, from $4 to $12 per dozen; carnations, from $1 to $2 50 per dozen for fancies; violets, $2 to $5 per 100; azaleas, $3 to $8, some fine ones being in sight.

Geo. H. Cooke has fine wreaths in red immortelles and ribbon and some novelties in plant combinations of crotons bordered with Boston ferns and Dracæna terminalis with ferns. These combinations are in 14-inch pans and are handsome. A lemon tree four feet high and bearing six large lemons was also noticed.

John Robertson has balls of moss decorated with berries that not only make a pretty decoration but also sell well. Extra fine Lawson, Crossbrook and Prosperity carnations, with stems from eighteen inches to two feet in length may be found here, grown by John Brown.

Geo. Field is sending in fine orchids and Testout roses. The American Rose Company, J. Louis Loose, Alex. B. Garden, Fred. Kramer, Clark Brothers, R. Bowdler and others have good stocks of cut flowers and plants.

At the A. Gude & Brother's range, of which Adolphus Gude is superintendent, there is a house of fine poinsettias, also a fine lot of Cypripedium insigne, azaleas and Adiantum Farleyense.

George C. Shaffer has two large bells in red suspended by long ties of red ribbon, with background of smilax and holly and a border of evergreen, orchids and azaleas forms the foreground.

E. G. Hill, of Richmond, Ind., who has been visiting points of intetest in the east, stopped here for some time. S. E.

Baltimore.

With Christmas only a few days off and lots of good roses in the market it looks as though there would be roses enough. Carnations are scarce, but it is due probably to the growers holding them back, as is usually the rule at this time. The Christmas prices are not put up until Wednesday. Poinsettias are plentiful and selling well. Violets are very scarce indeed, and a great many orders have been placed with out-of-town growers, but these seem to be of inferior quality. The prices posted at the Exchange on December 23, are as follows: American Beauty, $6 to $12 per dozen; Bride, $10 to $15 per 100; Bridesmaid, $10 to $15 per 100; Golden Gate, $10 to $15 per 100; violets, $1 25 to $1.50 per 100; carnations, $3 to $5 per 100; callas, $1.50 to $2.00 per dozen; smilax, 15 to 20 cents a string; poinsettias, $1.50 to $3 per dozen.

Halliday Brothers have a tasteful window decoration, a large bank of poinsettias overhung with Boston ferns and edged with some very choice orchids, the whole forming a most attractive arrangement. Mr. Halliday reports the usual dullness that the storekeepers are complaining of all over the city.

On entering Samuel Peast & Sons' store you would think Christmas in all its splendor had arrived. Bells are everywhere, from large red ones down to very small ones, all strung with the same bright ribbon, twined in and out with smilax.

Edwin A. Seidewitz reports an extra heavy cut at his greenhouses, both at Annapolis and Arlington, fully sufficient, he thinks, to supply his store for the holiday trade.   N. S.

Milwaukee.

RETAILERS HAVE BUSY WEEK.—PLENTY OF HOLLY SOLD AND NONE LEFT OVER.—BUSINESS EQUALS THAT OF LAST YEAR.

It is rather too early to make a careful estimate of this year's Christmas business, but present indications are that it will be equal to last year, with the possibility of a slight increase. There will be enough stock to fill all orders, with plenty of greens for all demands. Violets are in good demand, as well as lily of the valley, and there are large receipts of the latter. The trade in holly was very satisfactory this season, most all dealers being cleaned out, and only an occasional poor lot being left over. The sale of mistletoe was larger this year than any previous season.

Kapsalis & Lambros had a very heavy demand for their wreaths made of colored cape flowers. The wreaths made in this manner have a very attractive appearance, and are far cheaper than the immortelle wreaths.

M. A. McKenney & Co. had a very pretty window of Christmas flowering plants, and judging from the crowded condition of the store they had no complaint coming regarding their business.

Heitman & Baerman were right in it this Christmas with their Estelle and Crane carnations. Holton & Hunkel Co. is handling their stock.

Wm. Edlefsen says his trade was fully up to former years. He handled a large line of well grown flowering plants.

C. C. Pollworth Co. has been busy shipping out several cars of Delaware holly.

Visitors this week were J. E. Matthewson, Sheboygan; T. Hinchliffe, Racine; W. E. Macklin, Stevens Point; J. N. Johnson, Racine; Mrs. L. Clapp, Ripon, Wis.; Maude Cummings, Baraboo, Wis.   H.

ROSWELL, N. M.—D. S. Hersey, of Wichita, Kas., has been here recently prospecting with a view to locating in the floral business near this city.

Pittsburg.

CHRISTMAS PLANTS DISPLAYED EVERYWHERE AND BOUGHT LIBERALLY.—TRADE EXPECTED TO EXCEED LAST YEAR'S.—TEA ROSES ARE NOT UP TO STANDARD.—NEWS NOTES.

All the stores are beautifully decorated, red predominating. A noticeable feature is the display of so many azaleas, cyclamens, poinsettias, Peruvian pepper plants, crotons and dracænas. The report is that all plants are moving out nicely and will continue to do so. The sale of violets is large and all business will undoubtedly be equal to that of last Christmas if it does not exceed it. Roses will have to improve before Christmas, although American Beauty, Liberty and Morgan are up to the standard. Fine carnations are coming in, Enchantress and Mrs. Lawson being the most popular and best.

Transient trade the last few days has almost disappeared. This usually happens before all holidays, and at the busiest time the funeral work looms up. In a recent order for A. W. Mellon, Charles Siebert used 600 Liberty and 800 American Beauty roses, 268 sprays of Oncidium Rogersii, 200 Farleyense plants, 250 Enchantress carnations, fifty Anna Foster ferns and fifty yellow primrose plants.

Breitenstein & Flemm introduced a new Christmas feature in the form of Greek garlands made of red immortelles. They are attractive and very decorative.

Fred. Zieger, with R. M. Rebstock, of Buffalo, spent a few days here last week.

Walker & McLain, of Youngstown, O., report a satisfactory Christmas trade.

Dave Geddes is buying for everybody. It's a boy.

E. L. M.

Toronto.

The growers of this vicinity experienced the hardest weather they have had for years during the night of December 13. The thermometer was below zero and there was a heavy wind blowing all night and it was with difficulty that the houses were kept warm. Out of town growers even had it warmer than this vicinity and one box from Barrie had a note attached saying that it was 15° below zero and blowing a gale.

At J. H. Dunlop's I found him wearing "the smile that won't come off." He had just returned from his honeymoon. He showed me over his extensive range; roses here always predominate and they are certainly in good shape for the coming season, the plants at present showing many buds. His Franz Deegan, Baldwin and Ivory and also one house of Liberty are in very good shape. After the roses come the carnations, many of which are of the later introductions; Lilian Pond holds the laurels among the new comers and it is a splendid acquisition. Many of the other varieties look fine, and noticeable in the fancies is Stella the light penciling of which makes it very desirable. Prosperity is doing exceedingly well, but the much needed reds are a little off. The new boiler which has been installed with a new engine to pump back the returns, leaves it quite easy for him to keep up the temperature, and the entire place is a model of perfection.

H. G. Mills is cutting some good cypripediums; people are doing well with him and he is thinking of increasing his stock.

H. G. D.

Colorado Springs.

The Thanksgiving trade in this section was well up to the usual standard, making a clean sweep of all available stock in the cut flower line. Prices were raised about twenty-five per cent all around. The demand for carnations was enormous, both local and out of town. Roses were in fair crop but in little demand. At present things have settled down to the usual quiet preceding the holiday rush. There is just about enough business to keep up with the daily receipts of cut flowers, carnations excepted, which are still too few owing to the large demand from out of town. Violets are plentiful. We have seen about the last of the chrysanthemums, extra late varieties being little grown because there is little money in them. Roman hyacinths have made their appearance. Greens are plentiful. Roses are off crop. The weather has turned very cold again. There is an abundance of sunshine.

A trip among the growers showed most of them well stocked with Christmas plants. Poinsettias and cyclamens are unusually fine. Begonia Gloire de Lorraine is as popular as ever. This scarcity is evidenced by the high prices asked.

S. S.

Springfield, O.

The Aberfelda Floral Company was incorporated December 21 with a capital stock of $10,000 by Charles C. Leedle, Charles P. Brunner, Herman Voges, Jr., Forest S. Wolf and George D. Leedle. The incorporators have secured eleven and one-half acres of land a short distance south of the famous picnic resort, known as Aberfelda. The site has a frontage of about seven hundred feet, with a sidetrack on the main line of the Erie railway, which will permit the unloading of coal from the car directly into the boiler room. The company intends to begin at once the erection of a modern and an exceptionally substantial and durable greenhouse as early in the spring as the weather will permit. An excellent feature of this location for the peculiar purpose in view is the effective protection afforded against blizzards by the hills adjoining on the south, northeast and northwest, while the southern exposure to the sun is all that could be desired. All of the men identified with the new enterprise are successful business men.

Philadelphia.

Bayersdorfer & Company lost a valuable horse last Thursday, one of the handsome cob team in which they took so much pride. Mr. Bayersdorfer states that he had refused an offer of $750 for the pair only a few days before. The big warerooms on North Fourth street have been well depleted of seasonable goods by an unprecedented Christmas demand but the space cleared is already filled up with Easter stock which has begun to come in.

CLINTON, IA.—Theodore Ewoldt, who resides near Oakdale cemetery, has gone to St. Louis, where he was called by report of a serious accident to his brother.

GRAND RAPIDS, MICH.—Fire originating in a defective flue caused a small fire in one of the greenhouses of Robert Rattray, former city florist, 56 Lockwood street, December 18. The bedding plants, valued at $100, were a total loss; no insurance.

THE AMERICAN FLORIST

NINETEENTH YEAR.

Subscription, $1.00 a year. To Europe, $2.00.
Subscriptions accepted only from those
in the trade.

Advertisements, on all except cover pages,
10 Cents a Line, Agate; $1.00 per inch.
Cash with Order.

No Special Position Guaranteed.

Discounts are allowed only on consecutive insertions, as follows—6 times, 5 per cent; 13 times,
10 per cent; 26 times, 20 per cent;
52 times, 30 per cent.

Cover space sold only on yearly contract at
$1.00 per inch, net, in the case of the two
front pages, regular discounts applying only to the back pages.

The Advertising Department of the AMERICAN
FLORIST is for florists, seedsmen and nurserymen
and dealers in wares pertaining to those lines only.

Orders for less than one-half inch space not accepted.

Advertisements must reach us by Wednesday to
secure insertion in the issue for the following
Saturday. Address

AMERICAN FLORIST CO., Chicago.

When sending us change of address,
always send the old address at the same
time.

Leads Them All.

ED. AM. FLORIST:—Enclosed is a
renewal of my subscription to your
valuable paper, the best of all trade
papers.   W. J. GOWANS.
Los Angeles, Cal.

Pleased With Results.

AM. FLORIST CO.:—We are pleased with
the results of our advertising up to the
present time and believe we shall have
a large increase in our business next year.
STANDARD PUMP AND ENGINE CO.
Cleveland, O., December 10, 1903.

A HAPPY NEW YEAR TO ALL.

SEND in your subscription now for the
ensuing year.

READERS will oblige by sending reports
of Christmas trade as compared with
that of last year.

PAPER WHITE NARCISSI give best results
when brought along moderately in a cool
house with plenty of light.

WE are in receipt of very handsome cal-
endars for 1904 from Leo Niessen, Philadelphia, and George E. Dickinson, New
York.

Now that chrysanthemums are cleared
off, lilies should be given the right of way
in the house. Have the benches nice and
clean first.

DON'T try to get tulips in for Christmas. Tulips require time to develop and
the flowers obtained by rapid forcing are
of little value.

ADVERTISERS and correspondents will
kindly remember that we go to press one
day earlier next week on account of the
holiday. Please send news and advertisements early.

Diseased Lettuce.

ED. AM. FLORIST:—Can you give a
remedy for disease on lettuce, samples of
which you will find enclosed? A. J. S.

The lettuce leaves were infested with
several forms of fungi and with a bacterium. It is impossible from an examination of the material to determine definitely the cause of the disease when so
many organisms are present. The disease, however, is undoubtedly due to one

or more of these low forms of life. There
is very little that can be done to control
diseases of this kind on lettuce after they
have once gained a foothold. It is
always advisable before starting a crop
of lettuce to fumigate the greenhouse
thoroughly with sulphur, using the
flowers of sulphur, and heating just hot
enough to produce fumes without setting
the sulphur on fire. If the disease makes
its appearance on the lettuce, it may be
held in check somewhat by keeping the
temperature as low as possible without
injury to the plants, and by special care
in watering. It is better to use a sub-
irrigation method if it is possible to do
so, thus avoiding a soaking of the leaves
—a condition which is especially favorable for the development of fungi and
bacteria. Proper ventilation should of
course be given the house during the
growth and development of the plants.
    A. F. W.

Duty on Manetti Cuttings.

A protest filed by the American Express
Company against the action of the collector at Buffalo, in levying high duty on
rose cuttings, was decided favorably to
the importer by the Board of Classification of the United States General Appraisers at New York, December 19. The
board held that rose cuttings, being cuttings from Manetti, imported for the purpose of being potted and repotted, are
properly dutiable at twenty-five per cent
under paragraph 225 of the present tariff
law, as "cuttings of Manetti."

Special Express Rates.

The following inscription, printed on
the shipping tags of Robert Craig & Son,
Philadelphia, should be used by all florists sending plants by express:

This box is billed at special rate, twenty per
cent less than merchandise rates, by a special
arrangement agreed to by the Adams, American,
United States, National, Northern Pacific, Pacific,
Southern, and Wells, Fargo & Co.

Then, if not already enrolled as a member of the S. A. F., the florist availing
himself of this valuable concession should
promptly set himself right by forwarding
to Secretary W. J. Stewart the membership fee of $5 00, and thus recognize by
his support the benefits for which he is
indebted to the society, of which this is
only one.

Omaha.

The Nebraska Florists' Club held its
monthly meeting December 10. It was
well attended. The J. D. Thompson Carnation Company, of Joliet, Ill., displayed
two new carnations, Nelson Fisher and
Mrs. M. A. Patten. Both were much
admired on account their size and strong,
stiff and long stems. Afterwards they
were displayed in the show windows of
Hess & Swoboda for eight days, and for
keeping quality they cannot be beaten,
especially Mrs. M. A. Patten.

Business is very brisk and a big Christmas trade is expected. Flowers are
somewhat scarce on account of so much
dark weather. Violets especially were
never as scarce as at present.

J. F. Wilcox, of Council Bluffs, opened
his doors at his new home December 9
and received his many friends. GRIPPE.

Minneapolis.

Holiday business promises to break
records. There will be plenty of stock
except in carnations, nearly all growers
of the latter experiencing an off crop.
Prices for carnations will be nearly as

high as for teas. These with Beauty,
violets and poinsettias will be in plenty.
The growers are holding back their cut
flowers as usual, and some will be disappointed in trying to realize a fancy
price on inferior articles.

The Florists' Club took in eight new
members at its last meeting. The next
gathering will be in the club's new rooms
on Western avenue. The opening will be
hailed by a paper read by E. Nagel on a
subject of his own choosing. The green
dealers have witnessed an exceptionally
good trade this year. Holly has not
been up to the standard.

Charles M. Figeley, of E. H. Hunt,
Chicago, called on the trade last week.
    C. P. R.

Albany, N. Y.

The leaders of local society have begun
the season in real earnest, and with the
resumption of activity in the social world
has followed a revival of trade among
the florists. On Tuesday evening Mr.
and Mrs. Horace G. Young gave a com-
ing-out ball at the Ten Eyck in honor of
their daughter, Cornelia. The ballroom
was decorated for the occasion by flyres
with an abundance of laurel roping,
Christmas bells, mistletoe, holly, and
southern smilax. The guests partook of
supper at thirty-five small tables, which
were decorated with poinsettias. Last
week a considerable number of the
society matrons gave teas and dinners
for the debutantes, all of which furnished
ample work for the trade.

H. L. Menand, son of Louis Menand,
will on January 1 start out for himself
as a grower of decorative material for
the trade. Mr. Menand will have his
greenhouses at Menand's station, about
half a mile south of his father's place.
The young man has already two fine
beds of Asparagus Sprengeri, two of
Asparagus plumosus and two of smilax,
most of which stock is nearly ready for
market. The houses will comprise about
7,000 feet of glass.

Thomas Knight, with Julius Roehrs,
Rutherford, N. J., was a recent visitor.
    R. D.

Gainesville, Ga.

J. E. Jackson has added three houses
10x100 and they are filled with 2½-inch
pot roses, cut and propagated since
October 15. The cool, clear weather has
been good for the cuttings and he has
succeeded in striking about ninety-five
per cent. For next season Mr. Jackson
hopes to show a good climber from
Gruss an Teplitz. This variety is popular as a bedding rose in the southland.
The greatest trouble here is in getting
competent help. For some reason the
southern boy does not seem to care to be
a florist. The florists would rejoice it a
few of the good young men in this line
could be induced to emigrate from the
north, east and west.

Last month was the coldest November
ever known here. It kept the florists
hustling to keep up the temperature at
times. The first frost was about the
third week in October, followed by several more. The first of November it
dropped to 24° above and has been as
low as 14°. This, of course, ended the
outside flowers and caused the sale of
blooms to start up early, so trade has
been good.

Trade in carnations and roses is good.
Carnations, the last three weeks in
Atlanta, have been retailing at from 75
cents to $1 per dozen and roses from $1
to $1.50 per dozen.   J.

Syracuse, N. Y.

Christmas trade bids fair to be all that could be expected. Flowers are coming in freely and there will be no scarcity. The regular Christmas greens are having their usual demand. Carnations are selling well and are of good quality, bringing from 75 cents to $1.25 a dozen. Roses sell for $2.50 a dozen and upwards. Primroses and cyclamens range in price from 25 to 50 cents. There is a good demand for palms and plants for decorating purposes. The Boston fern does not diminish in popularity and brings anywhere from 75 cents to $5. Hyacinths and orchids are on the market and violets sell freely at from $2.50 to $3 a dozen.

At the Campbell greenhouses, 93 East Third street, Oswego, trade is especially good on carnations and roses. An innovation which is proving profitable is the permission to residents of nearby towns to telephone in their orders at the firm's expense.

Henry Morris departed from the usual practice the other day and made his first standing wreath of galax with a cluster of pink roses and a pink ribbon.

E. T. McQuivery, 813 Genesee street, Utica, has a fine stock of American Beauty roses, sweet peas and violets and reports a good business.

Frank Spencer Merritt, of Verona, a well known nurseryman, died December 18.   A. J. B.

New Bedford, Mass.

We have had a week of almost zero weather, which finished up with a rain storm and a warmer spell. There will be an immense quantity of evergreens sold this year. Plants and cut flowers likely will be scarce, although the very high prices asked check the demand. Retailers seem timid about stocking up.

The New Bedford Horticultural Society held its regular meeting December 8. There was an interesting talk by H. A. Jahn on hybridization of carnations, followed by a discussion. Five new members were elected. The next meeting will be the second Tuesday in January for the election of officers and the annual supper.

The Florists' Club held a smoker at the greenhouses of S. S. Peckham, Fairhaven, December 10. if there was any aphis on Mr. Peckham's premises it is probably now extinct. Refreshments were served by Mr. Peckham and his amiable wife.

    A. B. H.

Lowell, Mass.

The week before the grand rush finds everybody prepared to do a big business. The shops are well filled with everything necessary for Christmas trade. The shop windows never looked prettier. The market is flooded with green goods of every description of excellent quality. The first consignment of holly arrived last week. It has good, dark, glossy foliage and is well berried. Mistletoe is not so good. The weather for the last ten days has had a tendency to shorten up the supply of cut flowers, and growers are asking fancy prices for their blooms. The men who raise Fairmaid are asking $100 per 1000 for them. "Lucky is the man who has violets, for they are being snapped up at $25 per 1000. Fine poinsettias and azaleas are being shown by Potter, coming from Wm. Edgar, Waverly, Mass.

Chas. L. Marshall,

who fell from his windmill last week, is on the road to recovery.   A. M.

Hartford, Conn.

The entertainment committee is to send out circular letters to growers, importers and introducers inviting them to exhibit novelties, etc., at the club meetings. If exhibits are meritorious certificates or diplomas will be awarded. Exhibits should be addressed to the secretary, prepaid and reach him on the day of the meeting.

The Florists' Club team went to New Haven December 12 to bowl with New Haven Horticultural Society for a ball, put up as prize to the winning team.

At the meeting December 22 G. A. Parker, superintendent of Keeney park, will read a paper on Storr's college.

    R. K.

Dobb's Ferry, N. Y.

The regular meeting of the Dobb's Ferry Horticultural Association was held December 19. There was a large attendance. A prize given by Mr. McCord, of Tarrytown, for the best vase of roses was won by Mr. Keiling, gardener to Mr. McComb, with Bride and Bridesmaid which were exceptionally well grown. Thomas Lee was awarded honorable mention for a vase of Golden Gate. A prize was offered for the best foliage plant in pot not larger than six inches to be shown at the next meeting.

Eric, Pa.

The floral business heretofore carried on at 1108 State street and Twenty-sixth and Brown's avenue, by S. Alfred Baur, has been acquired and will hereafter be carried on by the Baur Floral Company. S. Alfred Baur has retired from said business and has no further interest therein. Armin J. Baur, late of Wm. Clark's, Colorado Springs, Col., takes over the management.

Columbus, O.

Everybody is busy getting ready for the anticipated Christmas rush, and the present demand is a good indication of a profitable business, providing stock is plenty. Carnations are above the average in quality and quantity this season, but there will not be enough grown in this section to supply the local market. Roses are doing as well as could be expected taking the weather into consideration. There will be many weak-stemmed ones.

The Underwood Brothers have a fine lot of poinsettias. John R. Hellenthal also has a good batch of these as well as a fine lot of stevias. His rose and carnation crop looks promising.

C. A. Roth has fine chrysanthemums which were held back for the Christmas trade and look as good as any November cut.

The Livingston Seed Company is making its usual run on holly and Christmas trees. CARL.

Wholesale Flower Markets

MILWAUKEE, Dec. 24.		
Roses, Beauty, long per doz.		12 00
" " med.	7.00@	9.00
" " short	4.00@	6.00
" Bride, Bridesmaids	12.00@	15.00
" Meteor, Golden Gate	12.00@	15.00
Perle	12.00@	15.00
Carnations	6.00@	8.00
Smilax	12.00@	15.00
Asparagus		50.00
Violets	2.00@	3.50
Valley		4 00
Stevia	1.50@	2.00

PITTSBURG, Dec. 24.		
Roses, Beauty, specials	40.00@	50.00
" " extras	30.00@	35.00
" " No. 1	18.00@	25.00
" " ordinary	6.00@	12.00
" Bride, Bridesmaid	3.00@	12.00
" Meteor	6.00@	10.00
" Kaiserin, Liberties	4.00@	15.00
Carnations	3.00@	8.00
Lily of the valley	4.00@	5.00
Smilax	12.50@	15.00
Adiantum	1 00@	1.50
Asparagus, strings	40.00@	60.00
Asparagus Sprengeri	2 00@	3.00
Chrysanthemums	6.00@	10.00
Sweet Peas	1.00@	1.50
Violets	5@	2.00
Lilies	12 00@	15.00
Mignonette	2.00@	4.00
Romans, Paper White		4.00

CINCINNATI, Dec. 24.		
Roses, Beauty	40.00@	85.00
" Bride, Bridesmaid	8.00@	15.00
" Liberty	15.00@	8.00
" Meteor, Golden Gate	15.00@	18.00
Carnations	4.00@	8.00
Lily of the valley	3.00@	4.00
Asparagus		50.00
Smilax	12 50@	15.00
Adiantum	1.00@	1.50
Chrysanthemums	12.00@	25.00
Violets	3.00@	3.00
Narcissus		4.00
Poinsettia	15.00@	25.00
Romans		4.00
Harrisii per doz.	2.50	
Calla		18 00

ST. LOUIS, Dec. 24.		
Roses, Beauty, long stem		12.00
" Beauty, medium stem	8 00@	10.00
" Beauty, short stem	1.50@	2.00
" Liberty	6 00@	15.00
" Bride, Bridesmaid	5.00@	8.00
" Golden Gate	6 00@	15.00
Carnations	6.00@	10.00
Smilax	12.50@	15.00
Asparagus Sprengeri	1.00@	3.00
" Plumosus	35.00@	75.00
Ferns per 1000, 1.75@	2.00	
Violets, single	1.50@	2.50
Valley	4.00@	5.00

DENVER, Dec. 23.		
Roses, Beauty, long		25.00
" " medium		15.00
" " short		8 00
" Liberty	4.00@	8.00
" Chatenay	4 00@	7.00
" Bride, Bridesmaid	4.00@	6 00
Carnations	3.00@	4.00
Smilax		20.00

BATTLE CREEK, MICH.—Trade has been very good here recently. C. C. Warburton expects to add a new house, 20x132 feet, early next spring.

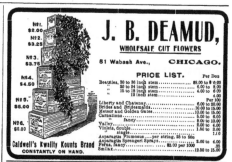

INTERNATIONAL FLOWER DELIVERY.

INTERNATIONAL FLOWER DELIVERY.

STEAMSHIPS LEAVE FOREIGN PORTS.

FROM	TO	STEAMER	*LINE	DAY	DUE ABOUT
Liverpool........	New York	Umbria	1	Sat. Jan. 2,	Jan. 8
Liverpool........	"	Lucania	1	Sat. Jan. 9,	Jan. 15
Fiume	"	Aurania	1	Fri. Jan. 1,	Jan. 11
Glasgow........	"	Siberian	2	Sat. Jan. 2,	Jan. 13
Hamburg........	"	Pretoria	3	Sat. Jan. 2,	Jan. 13
Hamburg........	"	Deutschland	3	Tues. Jan. 5,	Jan. 12
Hamburg........	"	Graf Waldersee	3	Sat. Jan. 9,	Jan. 19
Glasgow........	"	Ethiopia	5	Sat. Jan. 9,	Jan. 19
London........	"	Minnetonka	6	Thur. Dec. 31,	Jan. 10
London	"	Menominee	6	Thur. Jan. 7,	Jan. 17
Liverpool........	"	Celtic	7	Wed. Dec. 30, 3:30 p. m.	Jan. 6
Liverpool........	"	Teutonic	7	Wed. Jan. 6, 3:30 p. m.	Jan. 13
Southampton...	Boston	Cymric	7	Thurs. Jan. 7, 3:30 p. m.	Jan. 14
Southampton...	New York	New York	8	Sat. Jan. 2, Noon	Jan. 8
Antwerp.........	"	St. Paul	8	Sat. Jan. 9, Noon	Jan. 15
Havre	"	Kroonland	9	Sat. Jan. 9, 8:00 p. m.	Jan. 19
Havre	"	La Savoie	10	Sat. Jan. 2,	Jan. 12
Rotterdam.........	"	La Bretagne	10	Sat. Jan. 9,	Jan. 19
Genoa	"	Statendam	11	Sat. Jan. 2,	Jan. 12
Bremen........	"	Lombardia	12	Mon. Jan. 4,	Jan. 21
Genoa........	"	Neckar	13	Sat. Jan. 2, 8:00 a. m.	Jan. 6
Naples........	"	Prinzess Irene	13	Thurs. Jan. 7,	Jan. 20
Marseilles........	"	Germania	14	Wed. Dec. 30,	Jan. 14
		Neustria	14	Thurs. Jan. 7,	Jan. 14

* See steamship list on opposite page.

THE SEED TRADE.

AMERICAN SEED TRADE ASSOCIATION.
S. F. Willard, Pres.; J. Charles McCullough, First Vice-Pres.; C. E. Kendel, Cleveland, O., Sec'y and Treas.
Twenty-second annual convention St. Louis, Mo., June, 1904.

THE cry for wax beans is waxing louder.

J. CHARLES McCULLOUGH, of Cincinnati, is at Palm Beach, Fla.

ODD lots of sweet corn in the Nebraska districts are reported well taken up.

CINCINNATI, O.—Albert McCullough has returned from Florida, having been fishing off the coast for a month.

THERE has probably never been a year when so much holly was shipped and of such general mediocre quality.

REPRESENTATIVES of the United States Agricultural Department are negotiating for the purchase of a seed farm at Chico, Cal.

THE holly market is flat in Philadelphia and surplus stock was shipped to New York Christmas week. The quality was good.

OKLAHOMA CITY, OKLA.—Barteldes & Company are completing a new brick building of two stories and basement, 50x100 feet, at 429 Main street.

Holly and Bouquet Green.

The bulk bouquet green market at Chicago closed with stocks well cleaned up and prices firm. Holly, especially southern, was a glut, some cars being left on the track. The quality of the latter was poor. Not more than half of the eastern holly was first-class. For fancy stock the local florists paid $4 to $5 per case, while southern sold at $1 to $3 per case.

Philadelphia.

The following notice to the trade has been issued by the recently organized D. Landreth Seed Company, dated Bristol, Pa., December 17, 1903:

The D. Landreth Seed Company on December 12 purchased from the receiver, which sale was confirmed by Judge McPherson, of the United States District Court, the vegetable, flower and field seeds, merchandise not seeds, live stock, implements, growing contracts with seed farmers made by D. Landreth & Sons, and merchants' orders on file given to the travelers of D. Landreth & Sons, and are now, so far as is within their ability, on account of short crops, prepared to pack orders and make shipments from Bloomsdale farm, where all facilities exist for doing business. The seed stocks carried over of crop 1902 are just the same in quality as they were when the real proceedings took place, and the new crops of 1903 grown on the home farms, and procured under contract, are just the same quality as was originally intended they should be. We make this announcement that you may have the information direct from this office.

Methods of Some Contract Growers.

ED. AM. FLORIST:—In your issue of December 19, page 808, under the heading, "Methods of Some Contract Growers," we note remarks therein set forth with considerable pleasure and if jobbers will take some pains to know who is deserving of commendation or criticism along these lines, it will be of great help to the seed growing business. We have always maintained that once fairly met, no grower should dispose of his products outside of the regular line of his customers, unless for some very special reasons and those reasons such as

would not be liable in any way to interfere with the probable or possible trade of jobbers who contract with them. This, we think, should apply to any opportunity a grower may have outside of his own growing as much as to his own contract business and if an opportunity comes to his attention where it is possible to secure outside goods to an advantage it should be immediately made known to his general contract patrons, giving them opportunity to use if to their advantage or otherwise for grower and jobber alike to leave the goods unsought, and with this understanding on our part we read the article aforementioned with considerable interest.

THE JOHN H. ALLAN SEED CO.

The Government Seed Shop.

A successful attack on free seed distribution need not be expected for the reason that selfish interests will always keep the seed men from uniting, says the San Diego Tribune. Up to a few years ago they were almost a unit in opposing the distribution, when the contract was let in bulk and all who were not directly or indirectly interested in the contract fought the appropriation and the contractor. Now, however, the seeds are purchased by the department direct. The fact that seedsmen are divided is indicated by the assertion, by some of them, that the seeds are purchased largely from dealers who formerly were most active in their opposition to the distribution but who now have little to say. The seedsmen seem not to have been properly impressed with the spirit of the times. If they are not able to unite for offense, perhaps they could get together for division of spoils.

The Best Exhibition Sweet Peas.

In an audit of the great sweet pea show held in London last July, prepared by Charles H. Curtis for the National Sweet Pea Society of England, the following varieties, says the Gardeners' Magazine, were shown as first prize exhibits, the figures indicating number of times. Dorothy Eckford, 9; Lady Grisel Hamilton, 8; Lovely, 8; Duke of Westminster, 7; Hon. Mrs. E. Kenyon, 7; Jeannie Gordon, 7; Miss Willmott, 7; Prince of Wales, 7; Salopian, 7; Triumph, 7; Navy Blue, 6; Black Knight, 5; Coccinea, 5; Lady Mary Currie, 5; Lord Rosebery, 5; Prima Donna, 5; Agnes Johnston, 4; America, 4; Captain of the Blues, 4; George Gordon, 4; Gracie Greenwood, 4; King Edward VII., 4; Lottie Eckford, 4; Maid of Honor, 4; Othello, 4; Prince Edward of York, 4; Countess Cadogan, 3; Countess of Lathom, 3; Dorothy Tennant, 3; Duchess of Sutherland, 3; Mrs. Eckford, 3; Princess of Wales, 3; Admiration, 2; Countess of Radnor, 2; Dainty, 2; Duke of Clarence, 2; Emily Eckford, 2; Gaiety, 2; Her Majesty, 2; Lady M. Ormsby-Gore, 2; Lord Kenyon, 2; Lottie Hutchins, 2; Monarch, 2; Mrs. Walter P. Wright, 2; Royal Rose, 2; Sadie Burpee, 2; Apple Blossom, 1; Blanche Burpee, 1; Boreatton, 1; Captivation, 1; Colonist, 1; Countess of Aberdeen, 1; Countess of Powis, 1; Duchess of Westminster, 1; Duke of Sutherland, 1; Eliza Eckford, 1; Emily Henderson, 1; Golden Gate, 1; Gorgeous, 1; Gray Friar, 1; Hon. F. Bouverie, 1; Katherine Tracy, 1; Lady Nina Balfour, 1; Lemon Queen, 1; Maris, 1; Modesty, 1; Mrs. Fitzgerald, 1; Mrs. Joseph Chamberlain, 1; Pink Friar, 1; Queen Victoria, 1; Shahzada, 1.

South Pasadena, Cal.

GIANT PALMS GROWN AT E. H. RUST'S NURSERY.—REMARKABLE GROWTH BY SOME.—LAND PRICES SKY HIGH.—C. H. HOVEY'S ESTABLISHMENT.

At E. H. Rust's nurseries, Diamond and Linden streets, where Morton Biggs is foreman, palms seem to have the call. All the leading varieties are grown and in all sizes. Nearly all are grown on the ground, part under lath and part in the open. My attention was called to some large and valuable specimens of Cocos australis, C. compacta and Jubea spectabilis, for which from $50 to $100 apiece was asked. Araucaria excelsa is grown in the ground under lath. No loss is experienced in lifting it for removal. Mr. Rust has been working on a contract in the Westmoreland tract of 400 acres, putting out street trees, using in addition to other varieties something like 800 large plants of Washingtonia robusta, 100 Pinus Canariensis and 100 Pinus insignis or Monterey pine. I do not think Mr. Biggs took me for a tenderfoot, but he did try to dazzle my eyes with some remarkable growths. He planted a small Ficus repens in the lath house last spring. It is now twenty feet from root to tip. Buds of Gruss an Teplitz rose put in one month ago have some of them grown eight inches already. Mr. Rust employs several Japanese. He says they are better than white help.

C. H. Hovey is engaged in bulb growing. At Los Angeles he has charge of Mr. Rust's salesyard. He was feeling ill when I called because he sold a piece of acreage property near Los Angeles a year ago for a comparatively small price. Shortly afterward Huntington began to build an electric railway into that locality and now those acres are worth $2,000 apiece. The pace in and around Los Angeles is pretty swift, but how long will it last is the question. "Make hay while the sun shines," says the speculator, "and to-morrow we will make some more." "Yea," says Uncle Ben, "that's what you said in '87. Better make hay while the sun shines and get it under cover."

Mr. Hovey's specialties are freesias, yellow callas, tigridias and Gladiolus Childsii. He has about 75,000 Gladiolus Childsii. Of tigridias his stock reaches the 100,000 mark. But his pet is the yellow calla, Richardia Elliottiana. This must not be confounded with the old yellow calla. The amorphophallus, or snake plant, as it is called here, is a peculiar affair which must be seen to be appreciated.

R. H. A.

Paris, Tex.

Business is good here, all things considered. There are five small establishments in our city of 15,000 inhabitants. Miss Pearl Mauton has retired from the business, having married and taken a young man to cultivate in lieu of plants. Michael Robinus has built a greenhouse 20x60 at the entrance of Evergreen cemetery and it is well stocked with bedding plants. Our field roses were badly damaged by the first freeze in the middle of November. Being of young growth and in full bloom they were an easy prey to the frost. At this date, December 10, weather is very mild, almost springlike. We seldom have fire in our plant houses. Bedding and pot plants are the principal stock here.

W. D. H.

Long Beach, Cal.

The Alamitos Nursery, Junipero and Elliot streets, is owned by Mrs. C. C. Lowe and her son, H. N. Lowe. Here there is more glass than in any other Long Beach nursery. In the open ground is a good stock of palms and dracænas. Mr. Lowe shipped a car load of palms to Pomona in September. Several small glass and lath houses were filled with the usual assortment of house plants and ornamentals. There is a propagating house 6x70 and a carnation house 20x170 —both heated. The carnation house is yet something of an experiment. Actual experience is the only way to determine the best varieties to grow inside. San Francisco or eastern experience is of no value—conditions are so different here. Last year Genevieve Lord and Ethel Crocker did fairly well. This year the house is planted to Lord, Crocker, Queen Louise, Estelle, Lawson, Egypt, Mrs. Joost, Louise Faber (novelty 1903), Los Angeles and Allegra.

The Long Beach Nursery, 719 Locust avenue, is owned by G. A. Lindsay, who has just completed a small glass house planted to carnations which look healthy and bright. The varieties being tested are Evanston, Crocker, Los Angeles, Olympia and a new variety not yet named, which comes from the Japanese at Santa Monica. It is scarlet and Mr. Lindsay thinks it is very promising. Olympia is from Geo. Otto, of San Diego, and is somewhat on the style of Corbett, but is darker. Distillate will be used for heating. If the experiment is successful a large house will be put up next summer. Mr. Lindsay has a good assortment of ornamentals and finds palms to be one of the most profitable.

At the Fourth Street Nursery Albert Lenton has succeeded his father, S. Lenton, as proprietor. Mr. Lenton has been engaged in work on the university grounds at Berkeley until lately as a foreman. He is building a small cloth house to accommodate ferns, etc., in addition to the glass and lath houses already on the place. He expects to grow carnations, violets and ornamental stock.

The Signal Hill berry farm is owned by Elmo R. Meserve, who was formerly located in Los Angeles, but whose interests are all here now. He has eight acres in strawberries, mostly Brandywine, two acres or more in violets, some carnations and a lath house 60x220 planted to asparagus and smilax, principally the latter. Mr. Meserve has been trying to get a propagator, and intends to extend his carnation culture.

Rees & Compere, the well known bulb men, are proprietors of the Signal Hill nurseries and bulb farm on Cherry street. Mr. Compere has long been noted as a grower of freesia bulbs, and Mr. Rees is also a man of experience. They have about eight acres, all fenced and piped (2,500 feet of pipe).

J. B. Raine, whose place adjoins Mr. Meserve's, is mostly interested in small fruits, but he has a house 50x100 of Asparagus plumosus which he grows for cutting. R. H. A.

ESTHERVILLE, IA.—The greenhouses of Mrs. Jehu were considerably damaged by fire December 19. The loss is estimated at $2,500 with small insurance.

THE NURSERY TRADE.

AM. ASSOCIATION OF NURSERYMEN.

N. W. HALE, Knoxville, Tenn., Pres.; FRANK A. WEBER, St. Louis, Mo., Vice-Pres.; GEORGE C. SEAGER, Rochester, N. Y., Sec'y. Twenty-ninth annual convention, Atlanta, Ga., June, 1904.

OZONE PARK, N. Y.—Edwin Weber will retire from the Ozone Park Nurseries shortly, when the firm will consist of Chas. Iffinger and Chas. B. Knickman only.

HUNTSVILLE, ALA.—The Alabama Nursery Company is planning to erect a mammoth warehouse at the crossing of the Southern and St. Louis railroads at Mercury, Ala.

Western Wholesale Nurserymen.

The annual meeting of the Western Association of Nurserymen was held at Kansas City, Mo., December 15 and 16. The programme included the following papers: "Should this Association form a Fund to Punish Dishonest Dealers and Salesmen?" by A. Willis, Ottawa, Kas.; "Which is the Best Way to Handle Forest Tree Seedlings for Early Fall Delivery?" by J. Brown, Geneva, Neb.; "What Effect Will the Present High Price for Apple Seedlings Have on Apple Trees for the Year 1905?" by E. S Welch, Shenandoah, Ia.; "The Present Labor Situation," by F. H. Stannard, Ottawa, Kas.; "What Can We Do to Secure Better Transportation Facilities?" by J. H. Skinner, Topeka; "Is Not the System of Such Large Advances to Dealers and Salesmen Wrong and Unbusinesslike, and What Can We Do to Remedy It?" by J. W. Schuette, St. Louis.

The next meeting of the association will be held in Kansas City about the middle of July. The next annual convention will probably be held in Kansas City also. J. S. Butterfield, of Lee's Summit, Mo., was admitted to membership in the association. Officers for the ensuing year were elected as follows: F. H. Stannard, Ottawa, Kan., president; E. R. Taylor, Topeka, Kan., vice-president; E. J. Holman, Leavenworth, Kan., secretary-treasurer; Peter Youngers, Geneva, Neb., chairman; W. P. Stark, Louisiana, Mo.; D. S. Lake, Shenandoah, Ia.; E. F. Bernardin, Parsons, Kan.; R. J. Bagby, New Haven, Mo., executive committee.

THE NEW APPLE. (The Apple of the Future.)

"EDWARD VII."

(Blenheim Orange × Golden Noble.)

Award of Merit (unanimous), Royal Horticultural Society, March 24th, 1903.

THE LATEST APPLE IN EXISTENCE.

The Fruit is solid, heavy and keeps well until June. It is excellent both for dessert and cooking purposes; in use mid-April to mid-June, and is certainly what we claim it to be, viz: the best late apple in existence.

The Tree is a regular and great bearer, upright in growth, short-jointed and a very late bloomer (in our early district it has not bloomed before the third week in May, so that it misses the May Frosts).

"THE GARDEN,"—March 28th 1903.

"Apple, EDWARD VII—This is an excellent late apple."

"THE GARDENERS' CHRONICLE," March 28th 1903.

"Messrs. W. B. ROWE & SON sent again a quantity of their fine late cooking apple, EDWARD VII, which received a unanimous Award of Merit, Mr. W. Crump, of Madresfield Court Gardens, testifying as to its abundant and early cropping qualities."

"THE GARDEN," April 18th, 1903.

"An excellent late apple; EDWARD VII. is certainly one of the late apples of the future."

"THE GARDENING WORLD," May 9th, 1903

"Apple, EDWARD VII.—The photo, from which the illustration was prepared was taken from a specimen in our offices on the 9 th ult., which shows that the fruit agrees with what the raisers represented it to be—namely, an apple in season during April and May. We noted the fruit on March 24th last, when exhibited at the Drill Hall, but from the appearance of the fruit at the time, we were afraid it would not keep. This impression has been dispelled by the fine condition of the specimen sent us on the above date."

PRICE: 1-year, 12 shillings and 6 pence; 2-year, 15 shillings; 3-year, 20 shillings; 4-year specimens in Bush and Standard Trees, at 25 shillings each.

To be obtained of all Nurserymen or direct from the raisers. Special quotation for a quantity.

W. B. ROWE & SON,

"Barbourne Nurseries," WORCESTER, ENGLAND.

The Home of Chrysanthemum Stock. For Sale

OUR PASTIMES.

Announcements of coming contests or other events of interests to our bowling, shooting and sporting readers are solicited and will be given place in this column.
Address all correspondence for this department to Wm. J. Stewart, 48 W. 28th, 8'., New York. Robt. Kift, 1725 Chestnut St., Philadelphia, Pa.; to the American Florist Co., Chicago, Ill.

At St. Louis.

The Florists' bowling club rolled four interesting games Monday evening, December 15. The score follows:

Player	1st	2nd	3rd	4th
Kuehn	163	1*4	181	180
Beneke	189	185	145	164
Miller	155	148	173	165
O. R. Beneke	167	139	161	114
Meinhardt	127	119	97	157
Ellis	173	119	193	135
Warren	113	109	129	135

F. K. B.

Baltimore.

GARDENERS' CLUB TO OFFER PRIZES FOR BACK YARD GARDENS.—IDEA IS PRAISED. —CHANGES IN PARK MANAGEMENT.—NEW GENERAL SUPERINTENDENT.

There has been no change recently in the park superintendents of Baltimore except at Harlem park, J. W. Strickland being superseded by Charles Jones, formerly a gardener at Patterson park. All the other park superintendents, especially those of the large parks, are now known as district superintendents, having charge over all parks, squares, boulevards and monuments of their respective sections and are as follows:

Wm. R. Cassell, Druid Hill district.
Charles L. Seybold, Patterson district.
N. F. Flitton, Clifton district.
R. L. Sinclair, Carroll district.
J. F. Weasler, Riverside district.

Walter W. Crosby has been appointed general superintendent by the new park board and he will take charge January 1. Mr. Crosby is an engineer who graduated at a Massachusetts technical institution. The new park board has decided to reorganize the park department of Baltimore.

The proposition of the Gardeners' Club to offer prizes for back yard gardens and excellence in specified plants grown in city yards is a movement which must immediately win favor with those who are interested in beautifying the city, as well as all whose back yards are now, through neglect, dumps for the reception of endless varieties of useless truck cast off in the daily operation of house cleaning. It is admitted that there is little encouragement in the nature of things to beautify a 4x8 city yard, which is generally a playground for all the alley cats within speaking distance of this luxury, but patience and well-aimed bootjacks—who ever heard of anything else being thrown at a cat?—will work wonders in ridding the yard of the feline nuisance and the general result of a neatly kept, properly trimmed backyard garden is very pleasing, even though it be obtained at the cost of considerable trouble. To work in the yard is healthful exercise and in the encouragement to outdoor life which would be given by a series of prizes the average citizen would save enough in doctors' and medicine bills to pay for the plants, leaving the garden itself a clear profit. This would also encourage our brother florists and market gardeners during the months of April, May and June. We are sure with proper inducements the back yard garden will in the end become a profitable and enjoyable fad. Prizes should also be offered for window boxes and house plants, as they

are in the west—notably in Kansas City —where the campaign for city beautifying is characteristic of the best-kept communities. By all means let us have the garden contests in all large cities, and let everybody enter.

The new park board is preparing a bill for the state legislators asking for $1,000,000 to commence on the newly proposed boulevard system, the plans for which were executed by the Olmsted Brothers. It is proposed to first connect Druid Hill, Clifton and Patterson parks, and then ask for several additional millions to continue the boulevards and encircle the entire city. Several large parks will be established along the route.

THE AMERICAN FLORIST

America is "the Prow of the Vessel; there may be more comfort Amidships, but we are the first to touch Unknown Seas."

Vol. XXI.   CHICAGO AND NEW YORK, JANUARY 2, 1904.   No. 813.

THE AMERICAN FLORIST

NINETEENTH YEAR.

Copyright 1903, by American Florist Company
Entered as Second-Class Mail Matter.

PUBLISHED EVERY SATURDAY BY

AMERICAN FLORIST COMPANY,
324 Dearborn St., Chicago.
Eastern Office: 42 W. 28th St., New York.

Subscription, $1.00 a year.   To Europe, $2 00.
Subscriptions accepted only from the trade.
Volumes half-yearly from August, 1901.

SOCIETY OF AMERICAN FLORISTS AND
ORNAMENTAL HORTICULTURISTS.
OFFICERS—JOHN BURTON, Philadelphia, Pa.,
president; C. C. POLLWORTH, Milwaukee, Wis.,
vice-president; WM. J. STEWART, 79 Milk Street,
Boston, Mass., secretary; H. B. BEATTY, Oil City,
Pa., treasurer.
OFFICERS-ELECT—PHILIP BREITMEYER, president; J. J. BENEKE, vice-president; secretary and
treasurer as before. Twentieth annual meeting
at St. Louis, Mo., August, 1904.

THE AMERICAN CARNATION SOCIETY.
Annual convention at Detroit, Mich., March 2,
1904. ALBERT M. HERR, Lancaster, Pa., secretary.

AMERICAN ROSE SOCIETY.
Annual meeting and exhibition, Philadelphia,
March, 1904. LEONARD BARRON, 136 Liberty St.,
New York, secretary.

CHRYSANTHEMUM SOCIETY OF AMERICA.
Annual convention and exhibition, November,
1904. FRED H. LEMON, Richmond, Ind., secretary.

THE CHRISTMAS TRADE.

HE reports from representative correspondents show that business in general has increased quite satisfactorily over that of last year. There is no very marked change in the demand. Carnations seem to have been generally scarce and there is a growing demand for the colored varieties. Bulbous stock, at this season, is not improving in the public favor. The plant growers were fairly well patronized, especially where azaleas, poinsettias and similar subjects with bright flowers were offered. Cold storage stock no amount of counsel will prevent the storage of material for these special occasions, even when extra good prices are to be had during the preceding days and weeks. The experienced growers have learned that it is unwise to store their material, but every season seems to bring forth a fresh crop of the innocents. A number of the reports are given herewith:

MEADVILLE, PA.—Geo. W. Haas says that Christmas week was a record breaker, all cut flowers being in great demand and good prices paid. A heavy call for plants and holly, the commission men getting $3.25 per case for the latter.

MITCHELL, S. D.—E. C. Newbury conservatively estimates the increase in business over 1902 as fifteen per cent. Better prices, better quality and better demand was the situation in a nutshell. Begonia Gloire de Lorraine was in great demand.

ANDERSON, IND.—Stuart & Haugh say that business eclipsed that of Christmas, 1902. The demand was confined to carnations, roses and blooming plants. It was a great year for holly, there being tons of it. Carnation prices were very high.

LITTLE ROCK, ARK.—Business double that of Christmas, 1902, report J. W. Vestal & Son, although prices were the same and rose stock short. American Beauty roses were great sellers. Virtually no demand for bulbous stock and plant calls slow.

ST. JOSEPH, MO.—Could have used more carnations and violets, but roses were plentiful, says the Stuppy Floral Company. Plants were not as popular as last Christmas. Some white chrysanthemums were on the market, which sold for $3 to $4 per dozen.

BRIDGEPORT, CONN.—John Reck reports a nice increase in total sales, also higher prices in all lines than Christmas, 1902. Bulbous stock in poor demand. Red roses and carnations were the big sellers, and flowering plants sold well. Quality of all cut flowers splendid and everybody satisfied.

HAMILTON, ONT., CAN.—E. G. Brown reports this year's Christmas trade as slightly better than that of 1902. Roses, carnations and violets were scarce, and higher prices ruled all of these items. A significant demand for flowering and decorative plants observed. The call for bulbous stock was slow.

ROCHESTER, N. Y.—There was a satisfactory increase in holiday trade over last year. Carnation prices were higher, but all cut flowers equal to the demand. Roman hyacinths in pans sold well. Azaleas, cyclamens and poinsettias short in supply, according to J. B. Keller's Sons.

POUGHKEEPSIE, N. Y.—M. J. Lynch says that roses and violets were plentiful and of good quality. Carnations short and in great demand. The sale of flowering plants decreased, while the season was a record breaker in the sale of holly and greens. All prices about the same as last year.

RICHMOND, IND.—As reported by E. G. Hill & Co., the total Christmas sales this year were somewhat larger than 1902, and retail prices were ten per cent better. Carnations were scarce. High grade stock of all kinds was in demand almost exclusively, and there was a slow call for plants.

GRAND RAPIDS, MICH.—Although prices were generally better here this year than last, business was not increased. Henry Smith. Carnations were the scarce item and bulbous flowers were equal to the demand. Flowering plants sold well, cyclamens especially, and also ferns. All stock was of nice quality, and the best was well cleaned up.

WICHITA, KAS.—W. H. Culp & Company figure a ten per cent increase over 1902, although prices were on a level and carnations were not in good supply. The quality of Beauty roses was not up to standard. The popular tendency to consider cut flowers too high-priced helped the demand for plants.

DES MOINES, IA.—Little or no increase is noted here over the Christmas business of last year, says W. L. Morris. The prices on roses and carnations were much higher and the latter item was very scarce. There was a marked increase in the call for red roses. Holly and wreaths were sold at all kinds of prices.

KNOXVILLE, TENN.—With fully a fifty per cent increase over 1902, the Christmas business this year kept the local florists on the jump. Plenty of all stock for the demand, and of superior quality. Flowering plants and bulbous flowers proved good sellers. Prices about the same as last year, writes C. W. Crouch.

ROCKFORD, ILL.—Lower retail prices prevailed than Christmas, 1902. Lots of roses, carnations and violets left. Enchantress and red carnations had the call. Very little bulbous stock found buyers. C. W. Johnson says that fine cyclamens, begonias, poinsettias and azaleas were on the market, but their sale was not very active.

WINONA, MINN.—Edward · Kirchner reports a nice increase in Christmas business, with rose prices the same and carnations ruling twenty-five per cent higher than last year. The demand, however, was not equal to the supply. He states that most everyone asked for home-grown material, claiming that shipped flowers did not keep.

FARGO, N. D.—Twenty-eight degrees below zero on Christmas day! Under these conditions flower delivery was not easy, but the florists enjoyed a fair business notwithstanding, say Shotwell & Graves. There was plenty of everything to go around, at last year's price. Primroses and azaleas were in demand. Very little call for bulbous stock.

JACKSON, MISS.—W. J. Brown, Jr., is well satisfied with the Christmas business this year. Total sales and prices twenty per cent higher than 1902. Cut flowers in adequate supply and also bulbous stock, the latter selling well. The demand for flowering plants was immense, the writer selling every pot plant in bloom on his place.

DAYTON, O.—Carnations sold for less money than Christmas, 1902, and there was a sufficiency of everything. High grade roses and carnations were much sought after. The demand for plants seems to be on the wane. The fakirs sold roses at fifty cents per dozen. Holly and other greens are played out with the florists of this section, writes J. B. Heiss.

TOLEDO, O.—Here, too, an increase in holiday business is reported, according to G. A. Heinl, who estimates it as twenty-five per cent better than 1902. Carnations and violets were short. The quality of all flowers was far better than last year, the finest, Mr. Heinl thinks, that were sent out during thirty years in the business there. A good demand ruled for poinsettias.

PITTSFIELD, MASS.—Business and prices were on a par with last year. Everything short but roses, the latter, together with violets, not up to standard in quality. Everything in red had a ready call. In plants, the favorite proved to be

cyclamens, primroses and Begonia Gloire de Lorraine. Holly was plenty and could be purchased at from $2 to $5 per case, states John White.

PEORIA, ILL.—C. Loveridge says the business showed considerable increase over that of last year. Among cut flowers colored carnations were most in demand. Plants of azaleas, primroses and poinsettias sold well, but there was little call for palms. Holly sold well. More carnations could have been handled to advantage. Prices ruled somewhat higher than last year.

SPRINGFIELD, MO.—Florists here have no kick coming. A sixty per cent increase in Christmas business over 1902 is estimated by W. A. Chalfant. Roses, carnations and violets all short of the demand, and general quality not up to standard. Palms and ferns seemed popular. Our informant believes that the fancy carnation is gradually supplementing the rose as a popular holiday flower.

JACKSONVILLE, ILL.—Joseph Heinl estimates the Christmas business here as at least twenty-five per cent above that of last year, with prices also higher. The supply of roses and carnations was not equal to the demand, although the quality was not as good as last year. He also notes an increased demand for flowering plants, cyclamens, primroses and begonias selling well. Little demand for bulbous flowers, which were not plentiful.

LAFAYETTE, IND.—F. Dorner & Sons estimate this year's Christmas business as fifteen per cent better than last year. Carnations brought twenty-five per cent more in price. Carnations and violets not enough to go around. Bulbous flowers were used only in mixed boxes. Poinsettias had a heavy call, and large ferns and flowering plants were popular. A noticeable falling off in the sale of palms, but splendid demand for bouquet green, roping, etc.

BIRMINGHAM, ALA.—Prices averaged nearly fifty per cent higher than last Christmas and the total sales kept well apace, reports the Lindsay Floral Company. Could have sold three hundred per cent more roses and carnations.

Bulbous stock sold out clean, owing to carnation shortage. All flowers poor in quality as compared with last year. Decided increase in demand for flowering plants. Little quibbling over prices, buyers willing to pay any price.

DUBUQUE, IA.—The total receipts in Christmas sales were greater, although the average retail prices obtained were slightly lower than 1902. W. A. Hackett also informs us that the lighter varieties of roses and carnations were plentiful, reds exceedingly short. All bulbous flowers were extra good for the season, but there was an insignificant demand. The cheaper colored flowering plants had the call and sold in large quantities. The weather here has been remarkable. For delivering goods it was ideal up to Christmas eve. A cold wave then bowed itself in, chasing the mercury down to 17° below zero Saturday morning.

LINCOLN, NEB.—A fat increase in the total sales over the Christmas business of 1902 is noted here by C. H. Frey, at least twenty per cent better, he says. Good stock sold for higher prices, and the nice feature of it all was the supply of roses and carnations, which was adequate for the demand. Paper White narcissi sold well, as did lily of the valley, but singularly there was little call for Roman hyacinths. Carnations and violets had first call and all stock was fine. It was also a remarkable season for flowering and decorative plants. A blizzard arrived Christmas morning, but had little effect on the good business. All buyers of bouquet green registered a strenuous kick on the prices asked.

Cloth Propagating House.

The cloth house for carnation propagation shown in the accompanying engraving, made from a photograph taken on the grounds of the California Carnation Company, Loomis, Cal., cost $150. It is 25x100 feet, with propagating beds on the soil. It is kept empty all summer to dry out and in the fall the beds are dug up, leveled off and sand four inches deep put on. Plenty of water is used and three batches of cuttings can be rooted before the soil cools. The soil is a decomposed granite,

JOHN SCHEEPERS' FIELD OF TUBEROUS BEGONIAS AT HILLEGOM, HOLLAND.

CLOTH HOUSE FOR CARNATION PROPAGATION IN CALIFORNIA.

twelve feet deep. This gives the best of drainage. It is stated that 100,000 carnation cuttings are rooted in this house every seven days. The house holds 400,000 cuttings. It takes two men at $1.50 a day each to gather the cuttings, three girls at $1 a day to trim them and two more men to put them in the sand, water them, level the ground, etc. These seven hands put in from 15,000 to 20,000 cuttings a day. About 10,000 of each variety are inserted at a time. When rooted they are shipped, transplanted to glass houses or potted. Carnation plants are not housed in this locality except for fancy blooms. This method of growing rooted cuttings is very economical and the stock plants are always kept comparatively free from disease. Flora Hill, Crane and Lawson are said to be as good now as when introduced.

The Movable Greenhouse Bench.

The important thing in constructing and successfully conducting a commercial greenhouse today is economy of space. The grower who solves the problem of making use of the space in a greenhouse to the best advantage will come out financially in the lead. There are times when the florist is especially in need of room as for instance at Christmas, Easter and Decoration Day. In the spring also we find all florists using every square foot of space that can be pressed into service. To eliminate all waste of room is the purpose of a new device invented by H. Witte, of Baltimore, Md., who has perfected the idea of using the space of greenhouse walks for movable benches. Following is a short explanation of his device, which has been patented in the United States and Canada. We refer to one of its simplest forms as applied to a three-quarter-span greenhouse 25x100, suitable for roses, carnations, etc., having four benches built on stages.

The stationary benches in this house rest on joists running longitudinally, supported by iron pipes seven and one-half feet apart with suitable fittings and set in a concrete foundation. Underneath the second, third and fourth benches we find a number of frameworks on

wheels so arranged that racks fastened on the carriages are in mesh with an equal number of gear wheels which in turn are securely fastened by the thumb screws on a line of shafting which runs longitudinally through the whole house and has a crank at one end. If it is desired to move the shifting benches from underneath the stationary ones into the walks, the crank is turned three times forward, to clear the walk, and again three times backward. Each framework or car occupies a space of about fifteen feet longitudinally between the first and third post, the middle post being skipped. When the moving benches are withdrawn walk mounted on the frameworks moves into the back walk thus giving better access to the back bench. The cars can be coupled or uncoupled as they are needed. The system can be adopted to almost any commercial greenhouse, the

moving benches can if wanted be withdrawn underneath the side benches or underneath a center bench. The benches have been tested for four years and are excellent for all kind of bedding stuff, coleus, geraniums, alternantheras, ferns, begonias, etc. It has also been used for young roses and carnations and will be tested this winter especially for grafting cases for roses by running a line of heating pipes underneath so as not to interfere with the moving mechanism. Preliminary trials were favorable in this respect. The movable greenhouse bench received a certificate of merit from the Gardeners' Club of Baltimore. A working model of it was on exhibition at the recent chrysanthemum show there, receiving a special premium. It attracted particularly the smaller florist with limited means who wants a cheap arrangement for propagating in the spring. The device is installed at the greenhouses of the House of Refuge in Baltimore.

Florists' Plant Notes.

Astilbes.—Allow twelve weeks to force the astilbes into flower for Easter. It is possible to force them in less time if extreme heat is applied but this is not advisable. Pot the clumps firmly in good, heavy soil, in 6 or 7-inch pots, and for the first three weeks, if crowded for room, place them under a bench where light is not wholly excluded; but after that time they must have the full light. Give them plenty of room so as to allow the plants to develop symmetrically. They are rarely troubled with insects of any kind, and tobacco smoke must never get near them, for it burns the young foliage. If it becomes necessary to fumigate other plants in the same house, carry the astilbes out for the time, or else sprinkle them well and cover closely with newspapers to protect them from the smoke. The pots will soon be filled with a mass of live roots, which absorb the water like a sponge. Provide each plant with a saucer, and keep it filled with water, giving liquid manure twice a week. This will add materially to the size of the flowers.

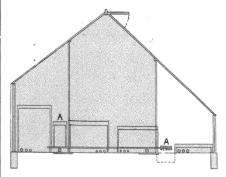

SECTION OF GREENHOUSE SHOWING MOVABLE BENCHES AT A.

Pansies.—Now is a good time to make a sowing of pansies if this was neglected last August. The fall pansies will grow stronger and come into bloom several weeks earlier than those sown now; nevertheless, the latter, while necessarily requiring more attention, will make fine stocky plants by Memorial Day, which, by the way, is the time when the larger part of the pansies are sold. Get the best strains from the best seedsmen, unless you saved your own seed last summer; sow a good mixture, besides separate varieties, and be sure to get plenty of Giant Yellow and Lord Beaconsfield. Prepare a place on a side bench with about three inches of good but not too heavy soil. Sow them in drills, not too thickly, and about the middle of March plant them outside in a frame about three inches apart. They require good protection from the cold with sash, and stable manure banked against the sides of the frames, so as to keep them growing without a check. Those that are being over-wintered outside should be well protected to prevent the ground from cracking too much.

Azaleas.—Any azaleas that failed to come into flower for Christmas should now be removed to a cooler house where they can come along more slowly. They should not be removed suddenly from a temperature of 70° to one of 40°, for this will check them too much and cause them to stand still altogether. There is always more or less demand for azaleas during the winter months, and this demand can be supplied by allowing a few to come along slowly, keeping the bulk of them cool for Easter. There is no excuse for not having azaleas in good shape for Easter, for all they require is a cool place of about 40° for the next two months, and about three weeks before the time they can, if necessary, be removed to a warmer house, which will bring them along about right. Keep the laterals that shoot up alongside the buds pinched off or they will blast.

Crimson Ramblers.—The crimson ramblers, to be forced for Easter, should now be gradually started into growth. It takes about twelve weeks to force them into flower properly, but everything depends upon starting them slowly. Begin with 40° and raise the temperature a few degrees every week, until the maximum of 58° at night is reached, which will bring them into flower nicely. As the temperature is raised and root action commences, more water is needed; frequent syringing is also necessary to

start them into growth. Liquid manure applied once a week after growth commences is also beneficial. The long shoots should be bent and tied in any desirable shape so as to induce even breaks.
G.

The Peony.

THE PEONY EXHIBITION.

The committee appointed at the last meeting of the Florists' Club of Philadelphia to look into the feasibility of holding a peony exhibition in Philadelphia some time during the early summer of 1904 is expected to report favorably. It is thought better to hold the same in conjunction with the June rose show, to be held by the Pennsylvania Horticultural Society, but unfortunately, owing to the uncertainty of weather conditions during the latter part of May and early in June, a date cannot well be agreed upon until quite close to the time for the rose show, so that it looks at this time as though a date for the peony show should be made independently of a time for the rose show. It would, of course, facilitate matters very materially if a date suitable to both could be hit upon. Cold storage may be had in the Reading Terminal Market, Twelfth and Market streets, Philadelphia, which is not far from Horticultural Hall and close to the center of the business parts of the city.

It looks as though, with united and well directed efforts on the parts of all who are in any way interested in the peony, that much in the way of straightening out some of the entanglements in nomenclature could be accomplished the first year if an intelligent effort is made, for no flower lends itself to the cold storage idea as does the peony, thus aiding the committee in its work. From a nomenclature viewpoint the tenuifolio and officinalis classes could be left out, but for decorative purposes, as part of the exhibition, they would add life and brilliancy to the coloring. There are mixtures among the officinalis types, as I know to my sorrow and loss, for I have received Pæonia officinalis rubra when P. officinalis rosea was ordered, and no effort whatever at restitution was made when attention to the mixture was called to the firm from which they were purchased. It may be true that the original rubra is to be preferred to the rosea for general purposes, but rosea was quoted at many times higher in price than is rubra. It is not often we find among

mixtures something superior to what we had purchased.

Some years ago a collection of five each was added to my collection from a reputable firm, and in due time flowered. Among them was a very fine and large double white variety, labeled E. Andre. A year or so later another firm announced the selling out of its peony stock, and among the varieties was E. Andre. The price quoted was suspiciously low, that when flowering time came around a request was made to send flowers for examination, which were in due course received and proved to be crimson in color. Eventually the "mixture" turned out to be none other than the celebrated Festiva Maxima, and what seems quite remarkable was the fact that Festiva Maxima did not appear in the firm's printed list, possibly because the stock on hand of this famous variety was limited in quantity; besides it is one of those good things which sells itself. It would be interesting to know the history of Festiva Maxima.

What is needed by the peony committee of the S. A. F. is valuable information about the names of peonies. Said committee cares not whence the information comes, so that same may be depended upon. It is proposed that exhibits correctly named will be invited from Europe. It is presumed to be out of the question to expect peony flowers to arrive in good condition, even if kept in cold storage, from faraway China and Japan. We will have to be satisfied for the present with the water color paintings.
EDWIN LONSDALE.

ED. AM. FLORIST:—Your correspondent "Guess" had better "guess again" when he assumes that the secretary of the S. A. F. Peony Association has made "mistakes." That individual has had to "stand pat" for some mistakes made by other people, but he is not aware of having made any himself. If the allusion refers to the spelling of the names in an address made before the Germantown Horticultural Society, the stenographer was mainly to blame, and in a lesser degree the labels in the Morris collection. And, moreover, it must not be forgotten by the critics that that address was not in any sense an official outgiving. If the allusion refers to the work the secretary did in connection with the "flower to add" proviso omitted by the mistake of the mover of the motion in Asheville, all that need be said is that the vote in Milwaukee legitimized everything, made

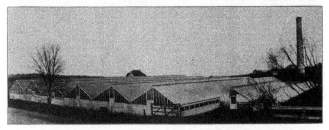

CARNATIONS AT THE W. L. ROCK FLOWER COMPANY'S, KANSAS CITY, MO.

all that had been done operative, and showed conclusively that the mud-slinging and vindictiveness of "the mutual admiration society" in New York had no influence whatever with any right thinking member of the S. A. F. The secretary made it quite clear that he considered the "power to add" proviso essential to calling the committee an association. The whole thing hinged on that point, and so soon as that point was settled at Milwaukee the fight was over. The place for the opposition to have marshaled its forces, if it had any, was right there and then. The S. A. F. does not do business through the newspapers, and it may be taken for granted that so long as the present secretary of the Peony Association is officially connected with the S. A. F. he doesn't propose to allow himself to be intimidated by a lot of half-veiled insinuations, downright misconstructions, or by any amount of ink-slinging or mud-slinging, all of which are mainly meant to gratify the personal animosity of one individual. These weapons are but boomerangs and carry with them their own punishment.

As for "Guess," he is evidently a friendly critic, but entirely mistaken as to the mistakes (?) of the secretary. Because of his evident friendliness his remarks deserve recognition, and are so accepted, as will be all criticisms and contributions of the same kind when offered in good faith as a help and not as a hindrance to the work of the association. But although "Guess" is evidently friendly, he will pardon the suggestion that in a discussion of this kind it is much the manlier part to sign one's name and not hide under a nom-de-plume. Be a man. Come out in the open. Don't hit from behind a hedge.

GEORGE C. WATSON.

Progressive Missourians.

The William L. Rock Flower Company, of Kansas City, was organized April 1, 1903, with a capital of $50,000 and a charter granted under the laws of Missouri. In the company was combined the wholesale business of the Rock-Heite Company (a co-partnership between W. L. Rock and Charles E.

Heite) and the retail business of W. L. Rock. Their plant consists of the ten acres of ground upon which they have built in the last two years eight modern greenhouses covering 50,000 square feet, a commodious potting shed, a boiler house with two 80 horse-power boilers, and a large stable with modern living rooms overhead accommodating twelve men. In the last year they have put up a brick stack at a cost of $1,200 with capacity of four 80 horse-power boilers.

Charles E. Heite, a grower of location, repute, has full management of the greenhouses. The firm grows principally carnations, roses, violets, lilies and chrysanthemums. This is the first season of growing roses. One house 28x200 was planted to Bride and Bridesmaid June 20. They have been in continuous bloom from August 25 until now, December 15, with the quality of the stock produced

above the average. From September 1 to December 1 the firm cut and sold (wholesale price) from this one house $767.96 worth of blooms and prospects are that a big crop will be cut until January 1.

Three 200-foot houses are devoted entirely to carnations, of which nearly all the latest varieties are grown with good success. One 200-foot house is devoted to ferns, Boston and Pierson; one 200-foot house to chrysanthemums and lilies; one to violets, and one to mixed plants, azaleas, etc. The entire plant is equipped with all the very latest devices and operated upon systematic lines. Neatness and cleanliness are a hobby with the owners. The whole output is handled at the firm's Walnut street store, sold to the retail trade under the management of W. L. Rock. Here, as at greenhouses, everything is neatness and cleanliness. Almost every convenience known to the retail florist has been installed.

The force consists of seven clerks, a cashier, a bookkeeper and Mr. Rock. Delivery is made by two two-horse wagons and one single horse wagon. The officers of the company are William L. Rock, president and treasurer; Louis Westevelt, secretary; Charles E. Heite, general manager. All are men under 38 years of age.

Here is a tribute by Mr. Rock to the AMERICAN FLORIST:

"Your paper is a very valuable helper. My success is largely attributed to reading the AMERICAN FLORIST and reading it thoroughly."

A Field Day at Philadelphia.

One of the most interesting events of the New Year for gardeners, florists and farmers will be the annual institute meeting at Horticultural Hall January 19, which is also the date of the regular monthly meeting of the Horticultural Society. It will be a combined institute meeting, society meeting and exhibition. The meetings will begin at 2 p. m. with an address of welcome by the chairman, Edwin Lonsdale. Ernst Hemming will be the first speaker at the afternoon

STORE OF THE W. L. ROCK FLOWER COMPANY, KANSAS CITY, MO.

session. His subject will be "The Old Fashioned Flower Garden," and those who remember his interesting talk on herbaceous plants before the Florists' Club are looking forward to hearing something very good from him on this new subject. J. H. Peachy, who is one of the institute lecturers, will speak on "The Making of a Farmer," and will no doubt also tell us how to keep the farmer on the farm once he's made. J. Otto Thilow has "Improvements in Vegetables of the Past Decade" for his subject. He is one of the chiefs of the great Dreer establishments, the connections of which are world wide and which have for nearly seventy years been the pioneers in the introduction of new and improved varieties of fruits, flowers and vegetables to the planters in this country. James Boyd, one of Philadelphia's fortunate business men who can snatch time enough from his factory or office for foreign travel, will tell what he saw in a recent trip through Syria and Egypt that is interesting to the lover of fine flowers or fine gardens, and as Mr. Boyd is an ardent plant lover, a keen observer and a man of deep knowledge of the literature and history of gardens past and present, his contribution on this occasion will be of more than passing interest and value. Other subjects for the afternoon session are "Lawns and Lawn Making," by Professor R. Carleton Ball, of Washington, and "Value of our Native Birds to the Farmer," by Professor Franklin Menges, of York, Pa. Adjournment will be at 5 p. m.

The evening session will open at 7:30 o'clock with a talk on "Soil Improvement," by Mr. Peachy, followed by J. Oglesby Paul on "Attractive Home Surroundings and their Value." Mr. Paul, as everyone knows, is the new landscape architect of Fairmount park and in the private practice of his art has earned an enviable reputation for so young a man. He is a pupil of the great Olmsted, whose fame as a creator of beautiful park and home surroundings is world-wide. Mr. Paul's talk will be one of the features of the meeting. It will be illustrated. Professor Menges will follow with "Insect Friends and Foes of the Farmer," after which Ex-Senator Harlan will give his famous address on "Alaska, Land of the Midnight Sun," which will be the great feature of the evening session.

The question box will, as usual, be open for anyone with problems to solve. Address G. C. Watson, Juniper and Locust streets, who has charge of this box. Mr. Watson reports having already received the following inquiries to be answered at the meeting:

"Isn't the English sparrow a much maligned bird?" Referred to Prof. Menges.
"Is Red Fescue a good grass for growing under trees?" Referred to R. Carleton Ball.
"Is bacteria culture for the farmer beyond the experimental stage?" Referred to J. H. Peachy.
"What is the best catch crop in case of a hay failure?" Referred to Professor Menges.
"What is the best time to trim evergreens?" Referred to J. Oglesby Paul.
"What is the best remedy for San Jose scale?" Referred to Professor Menges.

This field day of the gardening and farming interests in and around Philadelphia is a part of the regular work of the state department of agriculture and is arranged under the local auspices of the Pennsylvania Horticultural Society and the Florists' Club of Philadelphia. The executive committee consists of Edwin Lonsdale, chairman of committee for Philadelphia county, David Rust, representing the Horticultural Society, and George C. Watson, representing the Florists' Club. The reception committee consists of the following: William K.

Harris, W. Atlee Burpee, Robert Craig, Mrs. E. S. Starr, Jno. Westcott, J. Cheston Morris, Edward Campbell and Hewardson Brown.

The Rose.

AMERICAN BEAUTY—II.

After the Beauty is planted in the beds the watering will take constant attention. The supply should be regulated according to the condition of the plants. When they are developing a crop of blooms they will need more water than when off crop, also when they are going through a spell of cloudy weather or a check of any kind. The one source of trouble which must ever be guarded against is black spot. This is generally found to be more prevalent in the fall of the year than at any other time. To guard against this pest see that the ventilating is attended to properly, supplying plenty of fresh air whenever possible. On rainy, damp days, make use of a little steam to help dry out the house as well as to enable you to raise the ventilators sufficiently to supply pure air. Do not allow the benches to become sour and boggy, but regulate the watering so the plants will take up the supply readily at all times.

After the young stock has been planted it should be thoroughly watered and then be allowed to dry out well, which will start root action. For the first few weeks, or until the roots appear too near the surface, the top of the soil should be occasionally scraped up and kept fresh and loose. It is well to go through the house at least once a week and pick off all decayed and black spot foliage, thereby stopping the disease from spreading. The tying should be carefully done at all times. Never allow the plants to go without this attention until they become straggly and spindly from poor air and light. Unless the sun can reach each plant it will not dry off well after syringing, which is very harmful. In tying Beauty it will be found well to use two stakes instead of one as Bride and Bridesmaid are commonly tied. Place the second stake in line with the plant, about six inches from the center of the plant or the main stake. If this is done the plants may be tied so there will be no bunching of foliage and a free circulation of air is at all times possible.

The Beauty is a heavy feeder, consequently this will take considerable attention. Mulching generally gives the best satisfaction after the dark days are over. Feeding is generally necessary earlier than with other roses and liquid food gives satisfaction in the fall and early winter months as it is possible to regulate the supply much better than by mulching, Avoid overfeeding and any undue forcing as both are conducive to black spot and blind growth. The temperature of the house should be 58°—60° at night and 72°—75° on bright days, when it may be well ventilated. When a house begins to show much blind growth withhold the food supply somewhat and reduce the temperature and watering slightly. This will often bring buds on the long growth. When the blind shoots reach up too high they should be bent down and retied, always leaving sufficient length upright so that when the bud is cut there will be the proper amount of stem which is not crooked.

R. I.

TACOMA, WASH.—H. W. Manike is having much success this year with chrysanthemums and carnations.

The Late Ernst G. Asmus.

At a special meeting of the board of directors of the New York Cut Flower Company, held at its office on Tuesday, December 29, the following preamble and resolutions were adopted:

WHEREAS, Ernst G. Asmus, our friend, counsellor, and the first president of our organization, has been called from us by death, leaving a void, which to us, seems one that cannot be filled, and

WHEREAS, We, who have been associated with him in this organization, feel that it is but proper that we place on record, our estimate of his character and worth, and the sincere sorrow which each feels at parting with such a dear friend, able associate, and worthy co-laborer, therefore be it

RESOLVED, That the members of the board of directors of the New York Cut Flower Co., do hereby extend to the family their sincere sympathy at this bereavement, assuring them that by his death not only are we made mutually mourners for one beloved and respected, but that

In the death of Ernst G. Asmus, not only have we been deprived of the advice and assistance of one of our most useful members, but that rose growers of the whole country have lost one whose ambition, energy, and ability made him clearly among the first in his profession in the country; one ever alert to improve and advance the interest of the Rose; and largely through whose efforts the success of that flower has been advanced to the high standard it now holds,

RESOLVED, That this preamble and resolutions be placed in full on the minutes of this company, a copy of the same be published in the trade papers, and an engrossed copy be sent to the family.
EUGENE DAILLEDOUZE, Pres.
GEORGE W. HILLMAN, Sec'y.

The will of the late Ernst G. Asmus, was filed and admitted to probate, December 29. The estate is estimated to be worth from $150,000 to $200,000, consisting principally of realty and the horticultural business located on the Hudson Boulevard. The family home is left to the widow, Josephine Asmus, to hold so long as she remains a widow. In the event of her remarriage the estate is to be divided into equal parts among the three sons, Adolph, Grover and Edmund. The executors are directed to sell if advisable, any or all parts of the realty and to continue the business. In the event of the disposal of the estate the executors are directed to sell the business to the first son who shows a special aptitude for horticulture and expresses a desire to continue it. Bequests of $1,000 each are left to the sisters of the testator. The sum of $500 will be paid to Marcus Beck and also to Gus Rus, provided they will finish out twenty years of service with the family.

MECHANICSBURG, O.—Grant Matheny has leased S. L. Harper's place and will continue the business.

SPRINGFIELD, ILL.—A. C. Brown says business was very active during the holidays. A. C. Canfield cut some nice American Beauty roses from his new house. The Enchantress carnation looks well here wherever grown and is giving very general satisfaction. L. Unverzagt expects to go to a warmer climate after the first of the year for the benefit of his health.

OIL CITY, PA.—A reward of $25 has been offered for information leading to the conviction of the guilty persons who made an attempt a short time ago to destroy the Oil City greenhouses owned by P. S. Ingham, on East Bissell avenue. They set fire to the building in which Mr. Ingham was sleeping. Some time after midnight he was awakened by smelling smoke and upon investigation found fire had started on the outside of the building. It had not gained much headway and he experienced little difficulty in extinguishing it. He found that a quantity of refined oil had been poured on the side of the building before the match was applied.

Photo by G. M. Edmondson Co.

WEDDING DECORATIONS BY SMITH & FETTERS, CLEVELAND, O.

The Retail Trade.

S. S. PENNOCK, of Philadelphia, is handling some Virginia boxwood which some leading florists are finding very useful in designs and decorations, and it adds to the variety of green material which may be satisfactorily employed in this work.

A CLEVELAND WEDDING DECORATION.

The accompanying engraving shows the decoration furnished by Smith & Fetters, of Cleveland, O., at St. Paul's church in that city on the occasion of the wedding of Ruth Hanna, daughter of Senator Hanna, and Medill McCormick, of Chicago, last June. At the entrance of the church was a large arch, eighteen feet high, of white peonies and southern smilax. All pillars were wound with southern smilax and at the top of each was a huge tree of white peonies. Tall trees standing fifteen feet high of white peonies fixed on tall palms, were arranged on either side of the altar. Five hundred cathedral candles in arch-shaped standards were on the altar and each standard was showered with white peonies and Asparagus Sprengeri. A huge bunch of bridal wreath tied with white ribbons was at each pew, making a pathway of bridal wreathing to the altar, at the foot of which was placed a white enameled altar with kneeling cushion trimmed with white roses, making it appear a bower of white. Ten thousand white peonies were used and a force of fifteen persons worked two days to arrange the decorations.

CHRISTMAS PLANTS IN NEW YORK.

Each year sees the plant department of the retail florists' business at Christmas becoming more strongly intrenched in the favor of the public, following on lines identical with those of the Easter trade, and forcing the once-powerful cut flower trade from its strongholds on every side. The new and commendable interest in well-grown plants thus awakened is reviving the race of plant experts which for a generation seemed threatened with extinction, and we see now admirable examples of pretty and serviceable subjects carefully grown with a view to their giving satisfaction to their ultimate possessors. The varieties of plants easily brought into bloom for the Christmas holidays are limited as compared with the wealth of material available for Easter, and notwithstanding repeated experimenting on the part of the growers, the number of really good and popular things offered at Christmas increases with almost exasperating slowness. The predominant varieties this year are practically the same as one year ago—ardisias, poinsettias, ericas, cyclamens, primroses, oranges and, more abundant than all others, Azaleas Vervæneana, Simon Mardner and Deutsche Perle. Not so much trimming and bedecking is seen. Of course, no florist of any pretensions thinks of sending out a nice plant in a bare greenhouse pot; some covering is always given the pot, and a moderate touch of bright holly-red ribbon among the green foliage is too attractive to be omitted, but, as in the case of Easter plants, the stock now presented is so great an improvement over that of former days that the need of some artificial decking to hide blemishes and give finish to the subject is no longer felt, and Nature's own draping, when properly applied, is not easily improved upon. Receptacles for mixed plant combinations also show a marked advancement each season in artistic appropriateness, the many blendings of chip, braid, raffia and willow in tasteful green tints or scarlet and white affording a wide latitude for critical buyers. Among the new wares received with the greatest favor this year were a variety of designs in roughly-hewn wood, finished in antique weather-stained effects, introduced under the name of Russian boxes. They were offered in several shapes, but none more satisfactory than the plain oblong jardiniere.

BOULDER, COL.—Professor Ramaley, professor of biology in the state university, left here for San Francisco December 15, and from there will go to Japan to make a study of plant life in the Orient. He has secured a year's leave of absence. While there he will be the guest of the Japanese botanical society.

New York.

DETAILED REVIEW OF HOLIDAY BUSINESS.
—WORST WHOLESALE CONDITIONS IN
YEARS.—MARKET COMPLETELY OVER-
STOCKED.—RETAILERS WELL SATISFIED.
—ONLY CHOICE STOCK DEMANDED.

In speaking of the Christmas trade of
1903, we will speak first of the wholesale market and its outcome, as the
feature most deeply concerning the present and future welfare of the flower
grower, then of the retail trade and its
particular experiences.

The facts, as observed by those favored
with the best opportunities for drawing
rational conclusions, show that the
demand for flowers does not, and has not
for years, kept pace with the rapid
increase in production, and it is now
generally understood, although many
appear to purposely shut their eyes to
the unwelcome fact, that the production
of cut flowers for the wholesale markets
has reached such proportions that any
pronounced scarcity for any special holiday is not to be counted on. Notwithstanding this, it is undeniable that the
quantity of flowers held back by growers
from daily disposal and stored up for the
Christmas market, exceeded that of any
previous year, and that these goods,
bearing the unmistakable marks of age,
did seriously complicate the situation.
It does not describe the conditions properly to say that the market "went to
pieces," for it was not intact at any
time—in fact, was a hopeless wreck
before it started. Its stability was
ruined from the outset by the tremendous receipts and the apathy of buyers,
and it was barren of any spirit from
start to finish. It was most emphatically "a condition and not a theory"
that confronted the wholesalers, and
how to unload was their one problem,
the question of price being of minor
importance.

Taking up first the roses, it appears
that American Beauty was the one flower
in all the list that enjoyed a fairly well-
balanced condition of supply and demand,
but the tremendous overstock on all
other lines emboldened the retailers to
combat the attempt to exact the prices
of former years, the consequence being a
reduction of from twenty to fifty per
cent from quoted prices before sales could
be effected. Very few brought over $12
a dozen. In the other varieties of roses
top-grade flowers were the best sellers,
the short sizes not being wanted, because
of the cheapness of the better grades, and
stored stock of any kind was spurned at
sight. As might be expected, Bridesmaid
had the advantage, and there was little
call for Bride. Fifteen dollars for fresh
specials was the prevailing rate. From
these figures the prices ranged down to
almost nothing. Violets sustained the
most severe blow of all. The production
of violets for this market has been enor-
mously increased within the past year,
there being so many new growers that
they more than compensated for any
shortage of crop on the part of the older
ones. Consider, too, the headstrong
stupidity of the growers in limiting their
picking for a week or two previously in
order to swell the Christmas output, for
the record shows that 825 boxes of violets were received. As each box would
contain from ten to twenty-five hundred
or more, the gross receipts must have
been close to a million and a half. Buyers had it all their own way, and even
then it is estimated variously that from
one-quarter to one-third of the stock
remained unsold. But the quality was
grand.

Carnations were not in heavy supply,
although more abundant than had been
looked for. The best selling varieties
were such as Crane and Joost, white and
dark red being in the lightest demand.
Sales were fairly satisfactory, but were
hampered by the high prices, which were
the cause of more or less contention, and
a good many were eventually left over.
Of bulbous stock, it may be said that the
entire list shared in the general depression, Harrisii lilies suffering the most and
Paper White narcissi escaping fairly safe.
Poinsettias had a lively time, but green
material, in the greenhouse product,
stuck where it lighted and is still there.
In conclusion it may be said that, while
the total wholesale business may have
equaled that of last year, the amount of
stock left unsold or disposed of at a sacrifice will materially cut down the averages
on nearly all lines.

The joys of wholesaler and retailer,
unfortunately, do not run in parallel
lines. These two main divisions of the
flower business see through opposite ends
of the telescope, as it were. The retailers
are not doing much protesting, except on
the score of the advanced rates on a few
special things. They got along nicely all
through the week up to Thursday, without a thought on the problems that were
worrying the wholesalers, having all
they wanted to attend to in their holiday trade. Among the plants that
enjoyed the best general demand were
poinsettias, azaleas, ericas, orchids, primroses and Lorraine begonias in flowering
subjects, Dracæna terminalis, crotons
and Boston ferns in foliage plants, and
ardisias and imported holly in berried
plants. Red was the favorite color in
azaleas. Ardisias made a glorious record,
and the English hollies, with their glossy
foliage and crowding berries, were simply invincible. On the other hand,
oranges found a very poor market. The
buyers get more exacting as the years go
by, and anything shabby in the plant
line is promptly rejected. It would seem
that variety does not count for as much
now as perfection of growth, and one of
the characteristics most demanded is
tough and lasting constitution.

The best sellers in the cut flower line
were Beauty roses and special Bridesmaid
roses, scarlet and deep pink carnations.
The sale of violets at retail is reported as
having been much below the normal
Christmas trade. The weather was in
part responsible for this, being rather
inclement for street parading, but it is
worthy of note that the complaint of
falling demand comes mainly from the
heart of the fashionable district. The
same districts report a lack of enthusiasm in the holly and mistletoe line, but
the general demand for these things was
very fine and the market cleaned out in
good shape. English mistletoe, when in
good condition, went all right, but its
American namesake which, unfortunately, has no sentimental traditions
attached to it, fell behind.

Announcement is made by the manager
of the Herald Square Exhibition Hall,
where the Chrysanthemum Society of
America held its 1903 exhibition, that
the hall will be opened for an Easter
flower fair two weeks preceding Easter
Sunday.

Fred Lentz, with David Clarke's Sons,
had a diamond ring, a present from his
wife, stolen from him while on a crowded
horse car on the way to the Flower Market recently.

A. Knickman is about to open a new
store at 1552 Broadway, Brooklyn.

Chicago.

EVERYONE WELL PLEASED WITH HOLIDAY
BUSINESS.—RUSH NOT PHENOMENAL BUT
STEADY.—FINE SHIPPING BUSINESS IN
FORCE.—NEW CONSERVATORY PROMISED.
M'KELLAR IN BUSINESS AGAIN.

While there has been nothing phenomenal about the holiday business, yet every
one enjoyed a steady trade, enough, in
fact, to keep well apace with the limited
supply of cut flowers. The weather was
more than propitious for local trade and
wholesalers achieved results which the
most sanguine did not hope for a few
weeks ago. Especially gratifying this
year was the brisk plant trade, the result
no doubt of the limitations to the supply
of good rose and carnation stock. Plants,
especially the brighter colored, were
eagerly sought by the Christmas buyer,
and everything in that line was exceptionally choice in quality. While most of
the wholesalers declare that they filled
all of their regular customers' orders, yet
it is known that money went begging
for the better grades of roses and carnations. Since Christmas all rose and carnation prices have been reduced but little,
although the supply is opening up to
some extent. Good American Beauty
roses which were at a premium a week
ago are also accumulating a little more
rapidly. Violets remain a glut on the
market, and a number of plungers on
this item were hung up for thousands
during the Christmas week. Nobody
seemed to want violets, the rose and carnation buyers who could not be supplied
going over to decorative and flowering
plants. More poinsettias were seen than
for many moons. Holly piled up on the
market outrageously before Christmas,
and there were carloads of it left. Tulips
are appearing slowly, but their stems
have not yet reached maturity, in size
at least. One must seek long and diligently these days to discover any chrysanthemums.

Chas. W. McKellar this week bought
out the wholesale business of John Muno
and took active possession January 1.
The new proprietor will conduct a general wholesale and commission business
and will also deal in general florists' supplies, having rented additional floor
space in the Atlas block for that purpose.
Beside Muno's large cut he will receive
the consignments of many other growers. Henry Muno, the son of the former
proprietor, will remain with the new
firm. Mr. McKellar is assured of a large
patronage, he having a wide and favorable acquaintance among members of the
trade.

In the annual report of the commissioners of the West Park board, the largest
conservatory in Chicago is planned for
Garfield park. The new flower house
will occupy the ground space now taken
up by the race track and the cost will be
$150,000. President Frederick Bangs,
of the board, thinks that the conservatory will be built early in the spring.

At the next meeting of the Florists'
Club, Wednesday evening, January 6,
the Philadelphia seedsman, George C.
Watson, will give his views of the holiday business. Some other well known
men in the trade will present similar
topics.

Next week the local bowlers will take a
hitch in their suspenders and get to work.
A strenuous season on the alleys is anticipated in preparation for the national
florists' tournament at St. Louis.

When it comes to Lawson and White
Cloud carnations, Sinner Brothers will
yield the palm to no one for size and

quality of stock. They are handling a splendid variety of carnations.

In spite of the scarcity of bouquet green, some dealers had small quantities left over. It will have a good market, however, for some time to come, stores using it for decorations.

The A. L. Randall Company this week handled American Beauty roses with forty-two inch stems, coming from H. Bauske's greenhouses at Bowmanville.

George Reinberg has been shipping a nice lot of Bride and Bridesmaid. Several large consignments were shipped to Texas during the holiday week.

Peter Miller, who has been an employe of florists of this city and vicinity, committed suicide December 26 by throwing himself in front of a street car.

Many eastern violets are seen on the local retail market. Few are consigned to wholesalers or commisson men, the retailers getting them direct.

The stockholders of the Flower Growers' Market will hold a meeting to-day, (January 2) for the purpose of cleaning up their annual business.

On account of the holidays the Florists' Club held no meeting this week. The date of the next regular meeting is Wednesday, January 6.

The E. F. Winterson Company handled some remarkably fine Wisconsin violets during the holidays.

J. B. Deamud made a business trip to Des Moines, Ia., the fore part of the week.

Some nice American Beauty stock is seen at Weiland & Risch's these days.

A limited quantity of good daisies was handled this week by J. A. Budlong.

Poehlmann Brothers Company is getting in well grown Easter lilies.

Philadelphia.

TRADE GENERALLY SATISFIED WITH HOLIDAY BUSINESS.—BEAUTIES OFF CROP AND HIGH PRICED.—GREEN ALSO SCARCE.—GENERAL NOTES.

Christmas of 1903 is a thing of the past, and the Christmas trees that were not sold (and there were quantities of them) are being carted out to the dump for bonfire purposes. Take it altogether we believe the trade in general was satisfied. The volume of business was about the same as last year, which is very gratifying, as it was expected, on account of the rather dull fall, that there would be a falling off. The feature of the trade was the Beauty rose. For two weeks before, even within one week of Christmas, Beauties were very plentiful and could be bought for almost any figure, and it looked as if $9 per dozen would be the high figure for Christmas delivery. When, however, the time for delivery came it was seen the crops were off, and prices jumped to $15 per dozen for selected stock. All other roses were fairly plentiful and the range of prices was from $8 to $25. Carnations were in good demand, particularly Lawson and red, which were from $8 to $10. Joosts and other like sorts ranged from $4 to $6. Lycopodium green for wreaths was very scarce and 15 cents a pound was the price. Bells sold very well and were much in evidence at the windows.

The demand for cemetery flowers last week was very great, there being many choice and expensive pieces sent out to the cities of the dead. Holly wreaths were good sellers. Red immortelle designs, ivy pieces, galax and cut flowers in emblems and clusters were seen on every hand. In the mausoleums many expensive pieces were seen, in which

cypripediums and cattelyas were extensively used.

W. K. Harris, Jacob Becker and Robert Craig & Son were all much pleased with their Christmas trade. The Messrs. Craig say their business was much ahead of last season.

Fred Ehret handled a large quantity of Harry Foust's new white chrysanthemum. This was as fine as anything seen early in the season and brought $25 per hundred.

S. S. Pennock had a consignment of California pepper berries, which seemed to sell well. K.

Boston.

ALL SATISFIED WITH HOLIDAY BUSINESS.—HIGH GRADE STOCK IN DEMAND AND PLANTS SOLD WELL.—FIRE IN DINSMORE'S GREENHOUSES.

Christmas business was fully up to expectations and perhaps a little beyond, the talk of business depression having led us to plan conservatively, and so the outcome was a pleasure to all. The plant trade gave the cut flower specialty a close run for supremacy and the dealers express the opinion that a more moderate schedule of wholesale prices on the popular lines of plants, such as azaleas and poinsettias, would have resulted in a plant trade hitherto undreamed of. Colored azaleas in medium sizes had an immense sale; white roses were not wanted. Ericas were neither plenty, good, nor popular. Lorraine begonias seemed to fall off in popularity, but the number of palms, ferns and crotons sold was very large. A few pot covers of matting, etc., were disposed of but, in the main, plants were sold and delivered in the bare, unadorned greenhouse pots. As to cut flowers the most notable characteristic of this year's business was the absence of any sale for low-grade material. High-class stock was well cleaned up everywhere. The weather was mild and very favorable for the delivery of tender goods. Now to speak of the wholesalers. There is yet some shipping trade left for this market, fortunately, and for several days preceding the holidays the country orders held the market together in fairly good shape, as to really nice fresh stock, the proportion of which to the whole was much less than usual. Neither local nor country trade had any use, however, for low grade goods. The street men were busy with green goods, disdaining to touch flowers under any inducement, and so a big surplus composed mostly of low-grade Bride and Bridesmaid roses, white carnations of all grades, and violets, was held over to take its chances on the Saturday market. As to prices, a few American Beauty touched $12 a dozen, wholesale, but the majority of good blooms had to be sold at much lower prices. Carnations were from $4 to $6 a hundred, special favorites and novelties bringing nearly double these figures. A few Bridesmaid roses found buyers at $3 and $4 a dozen, but the prevailing price was from $12 to $16 a hundred. Bride, as usual at Christmas, was a poor seller.

John Barr reports very heavy orders for his white carnation The Queen. This splendid variety has made its friends everywhere and Mr. Barr has the largest stock in the country.

Robert Craig & Son will send out for I. Fassmore, the coming season, his white carnation Vesper. This is a very handsome flower, deeply fringed and of spicy fragrance.

Fire, resulting from an overheated

boiler, caused damage of about $100 to the establishment of Wm. Dinsmore, at Arlington on the night of December 18.

St. Louis.

HOLIDAY TRADE IS SATISFACTORY.—FAIR PRICES RULE.—LILY OF THE VALLEY AND BULBS ARE PLENTIFUL.—DEALERS CALL BUSINESS IMPROVEMENT OVER LAST YEAR.

Holiday trade conditions have been highly satisfactory to wholesaler, retailer and grower. Previous to Christmas the weather conditions put a damper on everything, as it was dull and cold, but the sun shone in time to brighten things up considerably, with the result that deliveries could be made on time and decorations attended to. All stock was of excellent quality and plentiful enough to meet the demand. Prices were reasonable. Lily of the valley and Roman hyacinths are abundant, extremely so.

G. B. McClure read a paper on "The Occurrence of Polypodium augustifolium ensiflorum in Florida" before the Fern chapter, which is holding a meeting in connection with the Association for the Advancement of Science.

Max Herzog and wife are still in a serious condition with pneumonia. Both were taken ill some time ago. Mrs. Herzog is slowly recovering while Mr. Herzog shows but little improvement.

Chas. Beyer says holiday business in his locality was better than in former years, especially in the cut flower trade. There was little demand for plants. He is busy with decorations.

F. J. Fillmore thinks trade is an improvement over last year. His roses are off crop just now, but from the number of breaks noticed he will have an immense yield.

Wm. Achway & Son have had a good trade. Their supply of Begonia Gloire de Lorraine was practically sold out early in the week.

Mrs. H. G. Berning is convalescent but by no means fully recovered from the effects of the operation performed some ten days ago. F. K. B.

Omaha, Neb.

Christmas trade was very good. Plants especially sold well and brought good prices. Azaleas, lilacs, cineraria, cyclamens and primroses were popular. Palms, ferns and araucarias went better than expected. Cut flowers sold at the same price as last Christmas with the exception of carnations and violets. Carnations sold from $1.50 to $2 per dozen and violets at $3 to $4 per hundred. All the cut flowers were good stock. Holly and greens sold better than in previous years. Holly was of good quality and by 4 o'clock Christmas eve the florists were all sold out.

December 23 the first Hollander showed up booking orders for next year.

GRIPPE.

Bay City, Mich.

Charles Williams, for the past seven years with Boehringer Brothers, has retired from the business and will reside to Grand Rapids, where he will reside with his daughter in the future. Mr. Williams, who is seventy-two years old, lost his wife November 27, the cause of death being inflammation of the bowels. The husband and wife had lived happily together for forty-seven years. Mr. Williams was highly esteemed by his employers, who much regret his departure.

THE AMERICAN FLORIST.

NINETEENTH YEAR.

Subscription, $1.00 a year. To Europe, $2.00.
Subscriptions accepted only from those
in the trade.

Advertisements, on all except cover pages,
10 Cents a Line, Agate; $1.00 per inch.
Cash with Order.

No Special Position Guaranteed.

Discounts are allowed only on consecutive insertions, as follows:—6 times, 5 per cent; 13 times,
10 per cent; 26 times, 20 per cent;
52 times, 30 per cent.

Space on front pages and back cover pages sold
only on yearly contract at $1.00 per inch, net.

The Advertising Department of the AMERICAN
FLORIST is for florists, seedsmen and nurserymen
and dealers in wares pertaining to those lines only.

Orders for less than one-half inch space not accepted.

Advertisements must reach us by Wednesday to
secure insertion in the issue for the following
Saturday. Address

AMERICAN FLORIST CO., Chicago.

When sending us change of address, always send
the old address at the same time.

SEND in your subscription now for the
ensuing year.

EASTER falls on April 3, nine days earlier
than last year.

"B. C." SHOULD refer to pages 575 and
576, issue of November 14, for information needed and send his full name and
address with all queries hereafter.

IN bunching Roman hyacinths, narcissi, freezias, or other bulbous flowers
for market, don't fail to mix in some of
their own foliage. It will materially
help the sale and the price.

FREEZIAS should have plenty of light
and should never be allowed to get dry.
When cutting the flowers take the entire
stem with foliage and in bunching for
market tie close down to the butt of the
stems.

IF Japanese fern balls have not done
well, let them dry off in a cool place for
a space of three months. Then start
them again, and it will be found that
they will come out much fuller and
evener.

WATCH the lilies carefully for greenfly.
An ounce of prevention is worth many
pounds of cure in this case, for the punc-
tures made by these insects ruin the
flowers, and the injury is often done
before the buds come in sight. Fumigate
constantly.

Temperature for Sweet Peas.

ED. AM. FLORIST:—Please advise me of
the proper temperature for sweet peas to
secure the best results.   E.

A carnation house temperature of 50°
to 52° is best suited to sweet peas.   G.

Fertilizers For Callas.

ED. AM. FLORIST:—What do you consider the best fertilizers for calla lilies in
pots?   ROCHELLE.

Callas can stand abundant feeding after
the first of the year. There is nothing
better than semi-weekly applications of
liquid cow manure. Other fertilizers,
such as bone meal and sheep manure,
applied more moderately, are also productive of good results.   G.

A Snub to 'Santa Claus.

Dismayed by the prospect of an overstocked market, the Christmas tree
dealers in Philadelphia saturated with
oil and burned up thirty car loads of
Christmas trees on December 17. This
radical procedure in the City of Brotherly

Love moves the New York Sun to comment as follows:

The Philadelphia Christmas tree dealers who
saturated 4,000 trees with oil and then burned
them in order to keep prices up by a more limited
supply deserve to be hanged on the trees that are
left till they almost gasp for breath. Are there
not 4,000 families in Philadelphia that can't
afford to buy Christmas trees at any price?

Why not send the surplus to the park
to keep the rhododendrons comfortable?

President Breitmeyer's Greeting.

TO THE READERS OF THE TRADE PAPERS
AND MEMBERS OF THE SOCIETY OF
AMERICAN FLORISTS AND ORNAMENTAL
HORTICULTURISTS:

I take great pleasure in wishing each
and every one a happy and most prosperous New Year.

I view with regret the result attained
in the profession during the year 1903,
especially the latter half, as not being up
to expectations, due to various causes.

It is my earnest desire that all of you
will use every effort to make the year
1904 a banner year in producing good
stock and realizing good and satisfactory
prices for the same.

As the president of the Society of
American Florists and Ornamental Horticulturists it is my duty to earnestly
request all readers of this greeting, especially non-members of our society, to
pause and reflect on the importance of
becoming members of the same. It is an
important matter, one of national
importance and most worthy of your
consideration.

Please send in your membership dues
to our secretary at once. Nothing would
please me more than a hearty and speedy
response.

In conclusion let us hope to meet all
old faces and as many new as the old
ones can induce to come to our convention at St. Louis.

With kind wishes, believe me,
            Yours sincerely,
            PHILIP BREITMEYER,
January 1, 1904.   President S. A. F.

Society of American Florists.

DEPARTMENT OF PLANT REGISTRATION.

M. H. Walsh, Woods Hole, Mass., submits for registration the following new
roses:

Minnehaha—A hybrid between Wichuraiana and Paul Neyron. Flowers
double, about two inches in diameter;
color pink; profuse bloomer; foliage
glossy, large, nine petioles to each leaf;
growth vigorous.

Hiawatha—A hybrid between Crimson
Rambler and Paul's Carmine Pillar.
Flowers single, shell shaped, in large
clusters remaining on the plant for fully
three weeks; petals crimson, tips scarlet,
base white; foliage very dark, glossy;
growth vigorous.
            WM. J. STEWART, Sec'y.

The Glass Market.

Up to the present time the manufacturers of window glass have not completed
their scheme about effecting a combination, and no agreements have been made
regarding the one selling agency, which
is to market the total output of glass by
the combination of manufacturers, says
the New York Oil, Paint and Drug
Reporter. All jobbers of glass will place
their contracts for new glass as individuals. No contracts have thus far been
made, and jobbers will hold aloof until
they are fully protected by the scheme to
be put into operation by the manufacturers. The statistical position of the

market here is very strong, and the
scarcity of glass is being felt. Prices
remained steady, with the exception of
some jobbers who continue to shade
prices to realise on their stocks. The
glass being sold now is the balance of
the old stock. As soon as the manufacturers of glass complete their arrangements, a rise in prices will be assured.

Dutch Hyacinths for Easter.

ED. AM. FLORIST:—What is the best
time to pot Dutch hyacinths to bloom
for Easter? Should they be potted in
soil or sand? Also, when should dwarf
sweet alyssum be planted to bloom about
the middle of May?   A SUBSCRIBER.

The best time to plant Dutch hyacinths for Easter is as soon as possible
after they arrive from Holland. To
defer potting those intended for later
forcing will shrivel the bulbs, and is
harmful in the extreme. If they are not
already potted do so at once and place
them outside in a cold frame and after a
thorough watering cover them with four
inches of soil and leave them there until
about twenty days before Easter. We
have experimented on a small scale with
planting bulbs in sand, but can see no
reason why the old common sense method
of planting them in soil should be changed.
Plant them in any old carnation soil that
has been used in the houses for a season.
Sow the dwarf sweet alyssum the latter
part of January to have them in bloom
for the middle of May.   G.

Catalogues Received.

J. D. Thompson Carnation Company,
Joliet, Ill., carnations; A. T. Cook, Hyde
Park, N. Y., seeds; California Rose Com-
pany, Los Angeles, Cal., roses; Sluis &
Groot, Enkhuizen, Holland, vegetable,
flower and agricultural seeds; King's
Acres Nurseries, Ltd., Hereford, Eng.,
nursery stock and roses; Storrie & Storrie, Dundee, Scotland, seeds and nursery
stock; Shatemuc Nurseries, Barrytown,
N. Y., hardy perennials; T. S. Hubbard
Company, Fredonia, N. Y., grape vines;
M. Herb, Naples, Italy, seeds and novel-
ties; L. A. Budlong Company, Chicago,
onion sets; Royal Palm Nurseries, Oneco,
Florida, nursery stock; The Storrs &
Harrison Company, Painesville, Ohio,
nursery stock, roses and bulbs; W. W.
Johnson & Son, Ltd., Boston, Eng.,
seeds and novelties; C. C. Morse & Company, Santa Clara, Cal., seeds; D. M.
Andrews, Boulder, Col., rare seeds;
Wilbur A. Christy, Kinsman, Ohio, glad-
ioli; Green's Greenhouses, Fremont, Neb.,
flowers; W. J. Foagate, Santa Clara,
Cal., seeds; C. H. Totty, Madison, N. J.,
chrysanthemums; John R. Box, West
Wickham, Kent, Eng., begonias; Haage
& Schmidt, Erfurt, Germany, seed novelties; Pape & Bermann, Quedlinburg, Germany, novelties; Thompson & Morgan,
Ipswich, Eng., hardy herbaceous plants;
Uberto Hillebrand, Pallanza, Italy,
seeds; Rogers Brothers, Chaumont, N.
Y., beans and peas; Vilmorin-Andrieux,
Paris, France, tree and shrub seeds;
Hasslach & Roumanille, St. Remy de
Provence, France, seeds; Chicago Flexible Shaft Company, Chicago, carriage
heater; Harrison & Sons, Leicester, Eng.,
seeds; Cragg, Harrison & Cragg, Heston, Hounslow, Middlesex, Eng., Nephrolepis Westoni; M. Crawford Company,
Cuyahoga Falls, Ohio, grapes; Wm.
Barron & Son, Borrowash, Derby, Eng.,
transplanting machines; Max Kornacker, Wehrden, a. d. Weser, Germany,
seeds; Reed & Keller, New York, Christmas bells.

Indianapolis.

HOLIDAY BUSINESS EQUALS FORMER YEARS.
—FLOWERING PLANTS IN FINE DEMAND.
—HIGH VIOLET PRICES.—GREENHOUSE
COMPELLED TO USE WOOD STOVES FOR
HEATING TEMPORARILY.

The volume of Christmas trade, according to our leading retail men, was about the same as last year. Up to Thursday noon it was very quiet around most of the down town stores, then the rush came which lasted until noon of Christmas day. During that time an immense amount of stock was disposed of. Though the supply proved equal to the demand, there was practically no surplus. Pot plants as usual were good property. Poinsettias and Begonia Gloire de Lorraine were not as much in favor as in former years, the best quality of azaleas and cyclamens being the leaders. Concerning roses, the demand as well as prices was the same as last year; while there was no increase in quantity in carnations, they were of better quality and consequently commanded higher prices. The sale of violets, meaning the best grade of double, increased about twenty-five per cent. A dollar for a bunch of twenty-five blooms was readily obtained.

The numerous cold waves that have struck Indianapolis have perceptibly diminished the coal pile. We are pleased to note, however, that coal is plentiful and reasonable in price. The 125-horsepower boiler of the Indianapolis Flower & Plant Company sprung a leak recently and wood stoves had to be employed to keep out Jack Frost until repairs could be made.

W. J. Hasselman's residence burned down December 25. The fire was caused by an overheated stove. The loss is estimated at $15,000.

Wm. Hartje has sold his place in Cambridge City and taken up his residence in Indianapolis.   J.

Findlay, O.

S. J. McMichael has acquired three and one-half acres additional of land and will extend his business considerably next spring.

At the Swan Floral Company's it is said that business is as good as could be expected at this time of the year.

E. J. Foster & Son are busy these days with roses and carnations in which they have had fine trade recently.

Barnd & Karg Company have some excellent stock and had a special sale of palms last week.

FORT MADISON, IA.—Carl Boll's establishment was visited by fire December 19 and a house of carnations practically destroyed. The total loss is estimated at about $2,500 with no insurance.

SITUATIONS, WANTS, FOR SALE.
One Cent Per Word.
Cash with the Adv.

Plant Advs. NOT admitted under this head.

Every paid subscriber to the AMERICAN FLORIST for the year 1903 is entitled to a five-line WANT ADV. (situations only) free, to be used at any time during the year.

Situation Wanted—By young American, 19 years of age. Completed florist in store or greenhouse. Address
W C D, care American Florist.

Situation Wanted—By all-around florist and gardener, well up in flowers, fruits and vegetables. Good references. Address
ALONE, care American Florist.

Situation Wanted—As foreman, roses, carnations and general stock; ambitious, sober; life experience. State wages and give full particulars.
FOREMAN, 596 Pawtucket Ave., Pawtucket, R. I.

Situation Wanted—Foreman, propagator and grower of roses, carnations, mums and the general routine of a commercial place. Thorough recommendations as to ability; age 35.
J S, care American Florist.

Situation Wanted—By all-around florist; good grower of pot plants; also Easter forced stock and carnations. 15 years' experience. Good reference. State wages. Address
A C, care American Florist.

Situation Wanted—By a young man as grafter. Have also practical experience in cut flowers and handling and shipping of young stock. Aged 26 years. Please state wages when writing.
C C, care American Florist.

Situation Wanted—As manager or foreman by practical man. First-class grower of cut flowers and plants. Capable of managing a large plant and handling help. Good wages expected. When answering state wages, extent of plant, amount of help, etc. First-class references.
No. 106, Care American Florist.

Situation Wanted—By young florist, 25 years of age, at present employed as rose-grower in large Chicago establishment; good grower of roses, carnations and general line of pot plants. Would like to take charge of greenhouse establishment. First-class references. Please state wages.
J M, care American Florist.

Situation Wanted—A man, 26 years old, wishes a position with a private family. Understands caring for driving horses. Vegetable, garden, lawn, fruit and shrubbery a specialty. Capable of taking charge of a fruit or vegetable farm. Good wages wanted and am willing to earn them. Would like job in greenhouse. Address
ARTHUR GOODNOUGH, Brandon, Vermont.

Situation Wanted—A gardening student, age 21, of the Royal Horticultural Society of London, England, seeks employment, such as will enable him to acquire a thorough knowledge of American methods of gardening. Resumeration of minor importance in comparison with facilities for obtaining experience and sound instruction. Unexceptionable references as to character and respectability will be furnished. Address
H, care R. & J. Farquhar & Co.,
7 South Market St. Boston.

Help Wanted—Good rose growers at once.
SOUTH PARK FLORAL CO., New Castle, Ind.

Help Wanted—A first-class grower of cut flowers. Write as to ability, also wages expected.
C. W. CROUCH, 311 Clinch St., Knoxville, Tenn.

Help Wanted—A young man with experience in growing roses. Give experience, also references. Wages $10 per week with increase as ability shown. ROSE GROWER, care American Florist.

Help Wanted—Young man with a thorough knowledge of growing roses and carnations. State experience and terms. Address
MAX RUDOLPH & CO.,
II W. 13th St., Cincinnati, O.

Help Wanted—Assistant for private place, must be good rose grower. Permanent position and good home for the right man. $30.00 per month and board. Single man. Address
C. UFFLER, Goranstown, Baltimore, Md.

Help Wanted—A man who thoroughly understands grafting, propagating and the care of young stock. Only an experienced man need apply to HARRY SLGMON, Supt.
Care The Floral Exchange, Inc., Edgely, Pa.

Help Wanted—A first-class grower and foreman. 25,000 sq. ft. of glass and two acres of ground to grow cut flowers and plant for store trade. Only experienced men should apply. Wages liberal. Reference please. Address
CONNECTICUT, care American Florist.

Help Wanted—Bright, energetic young man of good address for a Chicago retail store. Must be thoroughly up-to-date as a decorator and designer and a first-class salesman. Address with references as to character and ability, stating wages expected. Address
C R S, care American Florist.

Wanted—Annual Reports of the American Carnation Society for 1894, 1895 and 1901. Address
CARNATION, Care American Florist.

Wanted—To lease with option of buying a place of from 15,000 to 30,000 sq. feet of glass, establish trade preferred with necessary land, house, barns, etc. Must be in good condition and suitable for production of first-class stock.
M D, care American Florist.

For Sale—Greenhouses; good location for local and shipping business in Michigan. Well stocked. Reason for selling, on account of failing health.
H B, Care American Florist.

For Sale or Lease—Greenhouses. 7,000 feet of glass, 6 acres of ground. Good business. Splendid chance for a market gardener.
C. O. CONDE, Box 903, Marysville, O.

For Sale—Greenhouses. Good location for local and shipping business. Well stocked; winter coal laid in. Will sell cheap if sold at once. Selling on account of failing health.
JAS. RICHARDSON, London, O.

For Sale or Lease—Fine greenhouse establishment of 10,000 feet of glass, in good condition and well stocked, with or without dwelling. Fine opening for a single man. Stock reasonable.
X Y Z, care American Florist.

For Sale—Cheap; a well established florist business, 6,000 feet of glass, in a western Kentucky town of 20,000. No opposition whatever. Reason for selling, bad health. Full inspection. A splendid opportunity. Strictly business.
FLORIST, Henderson, Ky.

For Sale—At a great bargain for quick sale; greenhouses of about 3,500 feet of glass, hot water heat, first-class boiler, large enough to heat double the space, up-to-date ventilators, full of clean, healthy, paying stock. Can sell everything you raise. Will sell houses with or without land. Small amount of cash needed. Reason, old age and failing strength. Address
DES MOINES PLANT CO., 38th St., Des Moines, Ia.

WANTED.

Position as foreman or manager in an up-to-date establishment; either wholesale, retail or mailing. Am up in all branches, catalogue marking, building, heating and growing of fine stock. 3,000,000 plants grown the past season. Three years in last place. 40 years old and a hustler. Northern place preferred. Married, temperate and strictly business. Best of references as to ability and business qualities. Address LONE STAR, 614 No. Washington Ave., Dallas, Tex.

Situation Wanted.

A first-class maker-up, decorator and salesman at present employed by a leading New York retail florist in the above capacity and as buyer, will be at liberty after January 1, and desires a similar situation with good salary in the west.
Address   A McK, care E. C. Horan,
55 West 28th St., New York.

FOR SALE.

3 greenhouses, heated hot-water shed and 7 acres of land; house and stable. At Somerton Hills, 15 miles from Philadelphia. Will sell cheap.

Mrs. Geo. McFadden, 1428 Walnut St., Philadelphia.

A Man.

A competent party to take charge of our Greenhouse lumber business. Duties are: Drawing of plans, estimating and correspondence. A practical man of business ability wanted. State experience, salary and age.

Address   **GREENHOUSE,**
Care American Florist.

INTERNATIONAL FLOWER DELIVERY.

PASSENGER STEAMSHIP MOVEMENTS.

The tables herewith give the scheduled time of departure of ocean steamships carrying first-class passengers from the principal American and foreign ports, covering the space of two weeks from date of this issue of the AMERICAN FLORIST. Much disappointment often results from attempts to forward flowers for steamer-delivery by express, to the care of the ship's steward or otherwise. The carriers of these packages are not infrequently refused admission on board and even those delivered on board are not always certain to reach the parties for whom they were intended. Hence florists in interior cities having orders for the delivery of flowers to passengers on out-going steamers are advised to intrust the filling of such orders to some reliable florist in the port of departure, who understands the necessary details and formalities and has the facilities for attending to it properly. For the addresses of such firms we refer our readers to the advertisements on this page:

FROM	TO	STEAMER	*LINE	DAY	DUE ABOUT
New York	Liverpool	Ivernia	1	Sat. Jan. 9, 10:00 a. m.	
New York	"	Umbria	1	Sat. Jan. 16, 2:00 p. m.	
New York	Fiume	Carpathia	1	Tues. Jan. 12, Noon.	
New York	Glasgow	Mongolian	2	Thur. Jan. 7, 1:00 p. m.	
New York	Hamburg	Pennsylvania	3	Sat. Jan. 9, 9:30 a. m.	
New York	"	Patricia	3	Sat. Jan. 16, 4:00 p. m.	
New York	Genoa	Prinz Oskar	3	Tues. Jan. 5, 10:00 a. m.	
New York	Glasgow	Furnessia	5	Sat. Jan. 16, Noon.	
New York	London	Menaba	5	Sat. Jan. 9, 9:00 a. m.	
New York	"	Minnetonka	6	Sat. Jan. 16, 8:00 a. m.	
New York	Liverpool	Majestic	7	Wed. Jan. 6, 10:00 a. m.	Feb. 3
New York	"	Celtic	7	Wed. Jan. 13, 2:00 p. m.	
Boston	Alexandria	Romanic	7	Sat. Jan. 9, 1:00 a. m.	
New York	Southampton	St. Louis	8	Sat. Jan. 9, 9:30 a. m.	
New York	"	New York	8	Sat. Jan. 16, 9:30 a. m.	
New York	Antwerp	Vaderland	9	Sat. Jan. 9, 10:30 a. m.	
New York	Havre	La Champagne	10	Thur. Jan. 7, 10:00 a. m.	
New York	"	La Savoie	10	Thur. Jan. 14, 10:00 a. m.	
New York	Genoa	Sardegna	12	Tues. Jan. 5, 11:00 a. m.	
New York	"	Citta di Milano	12	Tues. Jan. 19, 11:00 a. m.	
New York	Rotterdam	Statendam	11	Tues. Jan. 19, 10:00 a. m.	
New York	Bremen	Kronprinz Wilh.	13	Tues. Jan. 5, 7:00 a. m.	Jan. 12
New York	"	Rhein	13	Tues. Jan. 12, 1:00 p. m.	Jan. 25
New York	Genoa	Hohenzollern	13	Tues. Jan. 5, 11:00 a. m.	Jan. 19
New York	Marseilles	Patria	14	Sat. Jan. 9,	
Boston	Liverpool	Cestrian	16	Wed. Jan. 6, Noon ·	
Boston	"	Devonian	16	Wed. Jan. 13, 6:00 a. m.	

*1 Cunard; 2 Allen-State; 3 Hamburg-American; 5 Scandinavian-American; 5 Anchor Line; 6 Atlantic Transport; 7 White Star; 8 American; 9 Red Star; 10 French; 11 Holland-American; 12 Italian Royal Mail; 13 North German Lloyd; 14 Fabre; 16 Leyland; 17 Occidental and Oriental; 19 Oceanic; 19 Allan; 20 Can. Pacific Ry.; 21 N. Pacific Ry.; 22 Hongkong-Seattle.

INTERNATIONAL FLOWER DELIVERY.

STEAMSHIPS LEAVE FOREIGN PORTS

FROM	TO	STEAMER	*LINE	DAY	DUE ABOUT
Liverpool	New York	Lucania	1	Sat. Jan. 9,	
Liverpool	"	Saxonia	1	Sat. Jan. 16,	
Glasgow	"	Numidian	2	Sat. Jan. 16,	
Hamburg	"	Deutschland	3	Tues. Jan. 5,	
Hamburg	"	Graf Waldersee	3	Sat. Jan. 9,	
Hamburg	"	Auguste Victoria	3	Sat. Jan. 16,	
Genoa	"	Prinz Adalbert	3	Tues. Jan. 12,	
Glasgow	"	Ethiopia	5	Sat. Jan. 9,	
London	"	Menominee	6	Thur. Jan. 7,	
London	"	Minneapolis	6	Thur. Jan. 14,	
Liverpool	"	Teutonic	7	Wed. Jan. 6, 3:30 p. m.	
Liverpool	"	Cedric	7	Wed. Jan. 13, 3:30 p. m.	
Alexandria	Boston	Republic	7	Thur. Jan. 21, 3:00 p. m.	Feb. 8
Liverpool	"	Cymric	7	Thur. Jan. 7, 3:30 p. m.	
Liverpool	"	Canopic	7	Thur. Jan. 14, 3:30 p. m.	
Southampton	New York	St. Paul	8	Sat. Jan. 9, Noon	
Southampton	"	Philadelphia	8	Sat. Jan. 16, Noon	
Antwerp	"	Kroonland	9	Sat. Jan. 9, 3:00 p. m.	
Antwerp	"	Zeeland	9	Sat. Jan. 16, Noon	
Havre	"	La Bretagne	10	Sat. Jan. 9,	
Havre	"	La Touraine	10	Sat. Jan. 16,	
Genoa	"	Lombardia	12	Mon. Jan. 4,	
Genoa	"	Nord America	12	Mon. Jan. 11,	
Rotterdam	"	Rotterdam	11	Sat. Jan. 16,	
Bremen	"	Hanover	13	Sat. Jan. 9, 7:00 a. m.	Jan. 22
Bremen	"	Kaiser Wilh. II	13	Tues. Jan. 12, 7:00 a. m.	Jan. 19
Bremen	"	Main	13	Sat. Jan. 16, 7:00 a. m.	Jan. 28
Genoa	"	Prinzess Irene	13	Thur. Jan. 7,	Jan. 20
Marseilles	"	Neustria	14	Thur. Jan. 7,	
Liverpool	Boston	Bohemain	16	Sat. Jan. 9,	
Liverpool	"	Canadain	16	Sat. Jan. 16,	

* See steamship list on opposite page.

ANNOUNCEMENT.

I am pleased to announce that after January 1, I will reopen in the Wholesale Cut Flower and Florists' Supply Business, at 51 Wabash Ave., Atlas Block, where I have purchased the wholesale business of John Muno.

Mr. Muno will continue to consign his entire crop to me consisting of choice Am. Beauties, Fancy Roses and Carnations. This together with crops of other flowers and decorative greens, etc., from other growers, will enable me to supply your immediate needs with first-class stock both in Cut Flowers and Supplies. Correspondence and consignments solicited from growers of first-class stock.

All outstanding accounts owing Mr. Muno should be made payable to John Muno, 51 Wabash Ave., care of Chas. W. McKellar. Mr. Henry Muno will remain in the employment of Chas. W. McKellar, and city accounts of John Muno can be settled with him personally. Mr. Muno takes this opportunity of thanking the trade for their liberal patronage to him, and wishing the trade in general a happy and prosperous New Year, and hoping that you will share at least a portion of your valued patronage with the new firm,

I Am, Yours Respectfully,

CHAS. W. McKELLAR,
51 Wabash Ave., ...CHICAGO.

SMILAX and BEAUTIES CHEAP.

500 Beauties, 3¼-inch pots, well branched, $6.00 per 100.
2,000 Smilax, 3½-inch, stocky plants, $2.00 per 100. Cash with order.

Quality of plants guaranteed.

ROSEMONT GARDENS, MONTGOMERY, ALA.
Please mention the American Florist when writing.

PLACE YOUR NAME.............
and your specialties before the purchasing florists of the entire country by advertising in

SEND ADVT. NOW. THE AMERICAN FLORIST.

PETER REINBERG

51 Wabash Ave., CHICAGO.

Wholesale Cut Flowers

LARGEST GROWER
IN THE WORLD.

Current Price List.

	Per Dos.
AM. BEAUTIES, long stems,	$6.00
" " 30-36-In. "	6.00
" " 30-84 "	$4.00 to 5.00
" " 15-18 "	3.00
" " Short stems.....	1.50 to 3.00
	Per 100
CHATENAY..................	$6.00 to 15.00
BRIDE........................	6.00 to 12.00
BRIDESMAID................	6.00 to 12.00
PERLE.......................	6.00 to 10.00
CARNATIONS...............	5.00
ROSES, OUR SELECTION......	5.00

All flowers are perfectly fresh and properly packed. No charge for P. and D. on orders over $5.

GALAX LEAVES, ETC., Fresh New Crop.

Galax Leaves, Green, per 1000..50c; Bronze....$.55
Cut Fancy Ferns, per 1000........ 1.00
Cut Dagger Ferns, per 1000....... 1.00
Leucothoe Sprays, per 1000...... 3.00
Rhododendron Sprays, per 1000.......... 5.00

Orders filled on short notice. Largest dealer in the U. S. Send cash with first order. Ask 70 prices on Native Shrubbery.

J. N. PRITCHARD, Elk Park, N. C.
Please mention the American Florist when writing.

THE SEED TRADE.

AMERICAN SEED TRADE ASSOCIATION.
S. F. Willard, Pres.; J. Charles McCullough, Firm Vice-Pres.; C. E. Kendel, Cleveland, O., Sec'y and Treas.
Twenty-second annual convention St. Louis, Mo., June, 1904.

THE Haven Seed Company's new address is Arroyo Grande, Cal.

BURPEE'S is the first of the general seed catalogues for 1904 to reach us.

VISITED CHICAGO.—James B. Kidd, representing the Cox Seed Company, San Francisco, Cal.

VISITED NEW ORLEANS.—Chas. P. Braslan, of the Braslan Seed Growers Company, San Jose, Cal.

CALIFORNIA seed growers are now looking for more rain, the rainfall up to this date being short of last year.

THE trade will be pleased to learn that S. E. Briggs, of the Steele-Briggs Seed Company, Toronto, Ont., is now able to be at his desk regularly.

A PRICE of 50 cents per pound on some sorts of onion seed is said to be forthcoming in some of the low priced catalogues in the mail trade.

POTATOES are reported as rotting in some of the warehouses of western potato specialists. It is thought that surplus stocks—if there are any—are pretty well out of farmers' hands.

THE Leonard Seed Company has installed a new onion set screener made by themselves somewhat after the Louisville patterns. The onion sets are revolved in a cylinder which grades them into three sizes, ¾-inch, 1-inch and over.

VAUGHAN'S SEED STORE, Chicago, is directly opposite the Iroquois theater, in which 600 lives were lost December 30, and was turned into an emergency hospital, employers and employes devoting all their energy to the work of rescue.

THE British government has taken the first step toward the adoption of the decimal system of weights. It has just been announced by the board of trade that, under a special order in council, it will sanction the use of a weight of 50 pounds, instead of the present standards of 112 pounds (called a hundredweight) and 56 pounds (called a half hundredweight). The fifty pounds is by this action made a legal standard of weight.

THERE is a boom in the English potato seed trade at present. Record prices have been made by Jno. Findlay's Northern Star, some samples of which are being exhibited in the window of Messrs. Carter & Company, seedsmen, in London. Jno. Findlay has brought out another remarkable disease-resister in El Dorado, which will not be put on the market until 1905. A proposal has been made for the establishment of a National Potato Society in London.

Properties of the Sweet Pea.

The properties of the sweet pea have been formulated by the National Sweet Pea Society of England as follows:

Form.—The standards must be erect, waved, or only slightly hooded. The standard, wings and keel to be in proportion to each other as will constitute a harmonious and well balanced flower.

Number of Blooms on a Stem.—No variety shall be recognized that has not at least three blooms on a stem, gracefully disposed.

Color.—Distinct and clear self colors are most to be desired, and therefore striped, watered and edged flowers will not be awarded certificates of merit unless they present quite new and remarkable combinations.

Dutch Competition.

An American bulb importer and shipper writes us regarding the article which appeared in our issue of November 21, page 650 on Dutch competition in England as follows:

"I have always made it a point never to trade with any Dutch establishment that makes a practice of visiting my customers. If a new house sent its representative to open connections with me, the first point about which I had to be satisfied was whether it was strictly wholesale or not. It seems a hard thing that business men in this country should have to stay here the year around and pay rents and wages and help to keep the country moving, and then have a Dutchman come along in the springtime and gather in all the business. The only remedy I can suggest is to put a tax on the annual crop of Dutch drummers who come to this country every year. I understand they have to pay something like $1,000 license before they are allowed to do any business in some European countries. I believe that is the only remedy for us in this country, and the tax should be made heavy enough to compensate the home trader for holding the fort the year around."

Office of
RALPH M. WARD & CO.
Importers and Exporters of
HORTICULTURAL PRODUCTS.
17 Battery Place, New York.

Correspondence Solicited.

THE NURSERY TRADE.

AM. ASSOCIATION OF NURSERYMEN.
N. W. HALE, Knoxville, Tenn., Pres.; FRANK
A. WEBER, St. Louis, Mo., Vice-Pres.; GEORGE C.
SEAGER, Rochester, N. Y., Sec'y.
Twenty-ninth annual convention, Atlanta, Ga.,
June, 1904.

ADRIAN, MICH.—The nursery of Spiel-
man Brothers is the oldest in Lenawee
county.

SAN FRANCISCO, CAL.—Brainard N.
Rowley, editor of the California Fruit
Grower, died November 20, aged fifty-
five years. Mr. Rowley was born in
Philadelphia. His son, Harry C. Rowley,
was closely associated with him during
the past nine years in the editorship and
business management of the paper.

HONOLULU, HAW.—C. J. Austin, superintendent at the government nursery,
made a report November 25 on the free
distribution of plants there. Since the
opening a few weeks previous a total of
2,665 plants have been distributed to 110
persons. By islands the distribution was;
Oahu, 2,182; Kauai, 208; Hawaii, 183;
Maui, 50, and Molokai, 42.

TACOMA, WASH.—State Horticulturist
A. Van Holderbeke was to-day called to
Colville, Stevens county, to settle a dispute over the inspection of a number of
fruit trees sent into the state by an eastern nursery, and which the county horticultural inspector has found to be infected
with insect pests. Agents of the nursery
dispute the finding. Mr. Van Holderbeke
says the rigid horticultural inspection
of nursery stock is proving an admirable
stay to the introduction of insect pests
into young orchards.

Manville, Fla.

W. H. Mann recently sold to Berkle-
man Brothers twenty acres of land on
which to plant a nursery.
During the late cold spell the mercury
reached 28°, but did but little damage, if
any, to the oranges.
The Interlachen Nursery has been shipping large quantities of stock to Cuba
this fall.
W. H. Mann has just shipped 5,000
orange trees to Mexico.

The Greening Golden Wedding.

Mr. and Mrs. John C. W. Greening, of
Monroe, Mich., celebrated the fiftieth
anniversary of their wedding December
26. Mr. Greening was the founder of
the Greening Brothers' Nursery Company
of Monroe. Special religious services

were held in the afternoon at the Trinity
Lutheran church in honor of the golden
wedding. The church was prettily decorated with palms, potted plants, American
Beauty roses, orange plants in bloom
and smilax, while each guest wore a bouquet of pink carnations, backed by a
golden maple leaf. At dinner later the
venerable couple sat at the head of the
table where they could look upon their
children, grandchildren and the invited
guests. Toasts were responded to by
Charles E., George A., Benjamin J., and
William J. Greening and Rev. Henry
Fincke.
Mr. and Mrs. Greening received the
congratulations of hundreds of friends.
They are both enjoying the best of
health. They have four children and
fifteen grandchildren. Mr. Greening was
born June 25, 1829, at Seebach, Prussia,
and at the age of 14 years was taken
from school and placed in the service of
Baron Von Berlepsch, one of the foremost

nurserymen then in Germany. Here he
learned the secrets of the business which
he afterwards followed so successfully.
In 1852 he emigrated to America, and
September 24, 1852, he arrived in Monroe almost penniless and without friends
or acquaintances. The following year
he married Miss Maria Schurtz, who had
been born in Bavaria. In their first years
of married life the young couple worked
very hard, he as gardener and she as servant. In 1856 the young German made
his first business venture, going into
partnership with Thomas Whelbley in a
one and one-half acre nursery. The firm
was dissolved in 1863, when Mr. Greening rented some land and began on a
small scale himself. In 1867 he purchased 16 acres of land at $100 an acre.
A heavy loss by fire in the following
spring set him back severely, but by persistent hard work the handicap was
overcome, and the business steadily built
up to its present size.

Pittsburg.

CHRISTMAS BUSINESS PUTS TO SHAME CALAMITY PREDICTORS.—CUT FLOWERS AND PLANTS ARE CLEANED UP AT GOOD PRICES.—PITTSBURG CUT FLOWER COMPANY LOSES IN BIG FIRE.

Christmas business "knocked the spots off" calamitious predictions. Garlands of boxwood and immortelles, wreaths of immortelles decorated with mistletoe or with California peppers, bells and other seasonable novelties were subject to great demand. Fine specimens of azaleas, cyclamens and poinsettias met with extraordinary sale. Violets were generally of high standard and quantities were sold. Fine roses were in demand and it seemed impossible to sell the cheaper grades. Liberty roses had the call. Beauty was not sought as in previous years, although a great number were sold. Red carnations as usual in holiday times were scarce. Enchantress and Mrs. Lawson, Scott and Adonis were exceedingly fine and were generally purchased without objection to the price.

The Pittsburg Cut Flower Company reports that the holiday season sales were gratifying in every respect with the exception of failure to move the cheaper grades of roses.

The Pittsburg Cut Flower Company's loss in the big storage house fire December 29 amounts to $250 to $300. The stock was stored in shipping boxes and uninsured.

With one or two exceptions stock from the east arrived in finer shape than ever before. In almost every instance the packing of the plants showed precaution. The Pittsburg Florists' Exchange had a remarkable run and sold nearly everything on hand. The shipping trade was very heavy.

The Pittsburg Rose and Carnation Company had a big cut of special Enchantress maid roses and of Enchantress carnations.

Many Boston ferns and palms were sold, also boxwood trees. John Bader made this end of the business hum. Geddes & Blind Brothers received many compliments for their window decoration, which was very effective. Breitenstein & Flemm showed some artistic arrangements of poinsettias and leucothoe wreaths.

The severely cold weather did not reach Pittsburg until the day after Christmas.

E. L. M.

Columbus, O.

All previous records were broken and every florist in the city is well pleased with the splendid Christmas trade. Had we full power to control the elements more favorable conditions could not have existed. It was owing to the favorable weather no doubt, that there was such a heavy demand for blooming plants and fortunately there was a good supply of these on hand which sold at satisfactory prices. The stock of cut flowers was generally good, with the exception of roses, which were slightly weak in stem, owing to so much heavy firing. The market was supplied with some of the finest carnations and violets ever known to the trade. Prices, ranging but little above former years, were about as follows: Beauties, $8 to $18; Bride and Bridesmaid $2 to $3; carnations $1 to $2; violets, $3.

DENISON, TEX.—Will B. Munson had a rushing trade, disposing of everything salable on the place. He had to refuse many orders.

Asparagus Plumosus Nanus.

WE ARE HEADQUARTERS ON THE SEED OF THIS.

OUR PASTIMES.

Announcements of coming contests or other events of interests to our bowling, shooting and sporting readers are solicited and will be given place in this column.
Address all correspondence for this department to Wm. J. Stewart, 43 W. 28th St., New York. Robt. Kift, 1725 Chestnut St., Philadelphia, Pa.; to the American Florist Co., Chicago, Ill.

At St. Louis.

The Florists' bowling club held an interesting and exciting meeting, Monday night, December 28. Two teams were chosen from among the club members present, and they played a match game with the following result:

FIRST TEAM.	1st.	2nd.	3rd.	T'l.
Beneke	158	174	148	480
Kefer	171	164	153	488
Miller	150	153	164	477
Ellis	170	167	159	496
Weber	117	169	159	435
Grand Total				2,376

SECOND TEAM.	1st.	2nd.	3rd.	T'l.
Kuehn	157	179	168	504
Ellison	184	166	209	559
Adles	192	208	158	545
G. E. Beneke	158	179	191	528
F. Weber	155	145	111	421
Grand Total				2,557

F. K. B.

At Philadelphia.

The last week of the Florists' League bowling tournament has resulted in a tie for second place between three of the teams. This is a strong vindication of the work of the committee in apportioning the teams. Four teams out of six finish almost neck and neck and many still are willing to bet for a second series on the two that are last in the race. The standing of the teams to date is as follows:

Teams.	Won.	Lost.	P. Ct.
Dunham	11	4	.733
Eimerman	9	6	.667
Kift	9	6	.667
Harris	9	6	.667
Moss	4	11	.250
Westcott	3	12	.250

A meeting of the committee was held on Saturday and arrangements made for rolling off the ties as follows: Eimerman vs. Harris, Monday, January 4; winner January 4 vs. Kift, Wednesday, January 6; loser January 4 vs. Kift, Friday, January 8. The best two games out of three decides the winner.

On New Year's day the club as usual held open house and a series of handicap sweepstakes was run off, commencing at 2 o'clock and continuing during the afternoon and evening. An informal lunch was served and the president, Commodore Westcott, brewed a bowl of his famous "Florists' Club punch" for the occasion. The arrangements were in charge of the following committee: William K. Harris, George Craig, David Rust, Robert Kift, Alex. Hanna, Charles Eimerman, George C. Watson, George Moss and John H. Dunham.

The new bowling series in the Florists' Club League tournament will not be arranged for until after the ties are rolled off. It is expected that there will be eight teams contesting in the second series instead of six, as there were many members disappointed at having been left out before.

DENVER, COL.—A. H. Bush, of Daniels & Fisher's, looks forward to a good holiday trade, but cannot say at this time whether it will exceed that of former years on account of numerous strikes in the mining trades.

Syracuse, N. Y.

TRADE IN 1903 THOUGHT TO HAVE EXCEEDED PREVIOUS YEAR.—MONEY IS PLENTIFUL AND GOOD HOLIDAY TRADE IS PROMISED.

As the end of the year approaches florists begin to consider whether they have made as much in 1903 as in 1902. The general opinion is that the balance will be in favor of the present year although it cannot be told with certainty until after the Christmas trade. From this distance it looks as if there would be a large volume of business during the holidays. Money seems to be a little more plentiful than at times this fall and the outlook in general is encouraging.

Mrs. Carrie E. Wells, of Fulton, has brought action against the well known seed man, Frank B. Mills, of Rose Hill, for $11,841.07. Mrs. Wells alleges that the Fulton Pulley Company made a contract with the defendant to furnish material for building the Marcellus Electric railroad and that the railroad company, in which Mr. Mills was interested, is insolvent and Mr. Mills is liable for the amount.

P. R. Quinlan & Company have now completed six greenhouses at Onondaga Valley which are used for growing carnations. Trade at their retail store in South Carolina street is reported to be good.

Henry Morris has in his windows the first of the calla lilies. "Business," said Mr. Morris, "is as usual at this time of the year and there is no cause for complaint."

Adah M. Boddy, formerly with Henry Burt, has opened a store at 112 West Genesee street and is advertising in the local dailies a full line of cut flowers, plants and palms.

Louis A. Guillaume, the Onondaga Valley carnation grower, has had a successful season and his stock is in good condition for the winter.

Chrysanthemums have practically disappeared, although some of the florists expect a few of the late crop for the holidays.

Gustav Bartholome has had a splendid trade at his greenhouse near Woodlawn cemetery.   A. J. B.

Montreal.

Joseph Bennett, superintendent of the Montreal Gardeners' and Florists' show, was presented with a case of cutlery December 7 in recognition of his valuable services. The occasion was the annual meeting of the Montreal Gardeners' and Florists' Club, held in Alexandra chambers. All the reports were of a satisfactory character, the treasurer's statement showing the recent chrysanthemum show brought in $659.29. The expenditure was $639.12, the prizes having amounted to $430.25. The annual dinner will be held on the third Monday in January. The election of officers resulted as follows:

President—R. W. Whiting.
First vice-president—A. Gibb.
Second vice-president—C. Craig.
Secretary-treasurer—W. H. Horobin.
Assistant secretary—Herbert Eddy.
Committee—J. Walsh. A. C. Wilshire, W. C. Hall, W. Alcock, J. Eddy and A. H. Walker.
    W. H. H.

Grows Better Every Issue.

AM. FLORIST Co.:—I am a little behind time, but your valuable paper is always on time, and gives better satisfaction every issue; $1 enclosed for renewal.
    G. J. LEARZAF.
Pittsburg, Pa., November 30, 1903.

Toronto.

ACTIVE HOLIDAY BUSINESS.—PLANT STOCK
WELL CLEANED UP.—ROSES COMMAND
HIGH FIGURE.

Everyone reports an increase in Christmas business over 1902. Roses had first call and always will have in this city when customers do not object to paying $4 per dozen for very ordinary stock. American Beauties were grand and excepting an occasional one, $15 per dozen was the top price realised. Meteor, Bridesmaid and Bride were scarce as the larger part of the stock cut was of second quality. In carnations, red was the most in demand and some Adonis were sold at $3 per dozen. Select Princess violets were sold at $3.50 per hundred wholesale and were not near enough, but the inferior qualities were hard to sell. There were quite a number of Begonia Gloire de Lorraine, most of which were left over. Azaleas were very popular and though in larger quantities than usual, they were easily disposed of. On nearly all plants the sales were considerably ahead. The stores never looked brighter and all good stock was well cleared up. Poinsettias seemed to be the favorite plants and Dunlop had purchased all that could be had and sold many pans, hampers, rustic baskets and bark arrangements. Christmas bells were sold in large quantities, those with the different green being the favorite decoration.   H. G. D.

BOOKS FOR FLORISTS.

The time is coming along when these are needed and opportunity at hand for reading them. Every one of the following should be in your library.

Send prices quoted and we send the books.

THE AMERICAN CARNATION (C. W. Ward).—A complete treatment of all the most modern methods of cultivating this most important flower. Illustrated. $3.50.

STEAM HEATING FOR BUILDINGS (Baldwin).—Contains valuable data and hints for steam fitters and those who employ this method of heating. The 350 pages are fully illustrated. $2.50.

HOW TO MAKE MONEY GROWING VIOLETS (Saltford).—This is by a practical grower who has made a success of the business. No grower of violets can afford to be without it. Price 25 cents.

GREENHOUSE CONSTRUCTION (Taft).—It tells the whole story about how to build, and heat a greenhouse, be it large or small, and that too in a plain, easily understood, practical way. It has 118 illustrations. $1.50.

HEATING AND VENTILATING BUILDINGS (Carpenter).—This book covers the entire subject most fully. In the preparation of heating and ventilating plans, it will be found a most valuable guide. $4.00.

THE GOLDFISH (Mulertt).—A number of florists find goldfish an attractive and paying addition to their business. The best advice is given in every department of the subject, including construction and care of the parlor aquarium, in this volume of 160 pages, handsomely illustrated. $2.00

FUMIGATION METHODS (Johnson).—A practical treatise on cheap and effective means of destroying insect pests. Handsomely bound and profusely illustrated; 250 pages. $1.00.

AMERICAN FLORIST CO.,
324 Dearborn Street,   CHICAGO.

Dallas, Tex.

CHRISTMAS TRADE EXCELLENT.—PRICES ARE HIGH AND DEMAND IS GOOD, SURPASSING PREVIOUS YEARS.—WEATHER WARM AND SPRINGLIKE.—RAILROAD MAN PLANS BIG GROWING ESTABLISHMENT.

The last week has been a busy one with the trade, the demand for flowers being far ahead of any former season. Prices for tea roses ranged from $2 to $4 a dozen; Beauty from $2 to $3 each; carnations, good flowers $2 and ordinary $1.50 a dozen; violets 75 cents per hundred. Bulbous stock was none too plenty and moved well at good prices, Roman hyacinths and narcissi selling from 50 cents to $1 per dozen, according to quality. Stevia was scarce and valley plenty, but not in very large demand. Flowering plants of all sorts were very scarce and what few there were sold quickly. Palms and ferns found a ready sale and many were disposed of at good prices. Greens of all kinds were in evidence and finer mistletoe you never saw than that sold on the street corners at any price the farmer could get. The weather Christmas day was fine and the whole population turned out in celebration. The sun shone brightly and the air was more like a warm May morning up north than Christmas day, yet the Texans called it ideal.

E. H. R. Green, the railroad magnate of Terrell, Tex., is building a large range of houses to grow cut flowers for the southern trade. He will erect some twenty houses the coming summer. There will also be a government experiment station conducted on his place. Mr. Green has several hundred acres of rich loamy soil, and an abundance of water.

F. W. Beach, manager for the Haskell Avenue Floral Company, has resigned his position.　　　　LONE STAR.

Cleveland.

GOOD NEW YEAR'S PROSPECTS.—DECORATIVE WORK IN FORCE.—SOCIETY DEBUTS MAKE BUSINESS.

Everything looks propitious for New Year's trade. The weather is cold and steady and the demand for cut flowers and plants shows an increase over last year's sales. Roses, carnations, violets, Roman hyacinths, Paper White narcissi and some valley are on the market, and prices are very high, but not disproportionately so, considering the good stock. Christmas roses were all that could be desired, from a wholesale point of view, but the miserable drizzling rains which set in Wednesday afternoon and continued all day Thursday had a very dampening effect on shoppers, and small retail dealers suffered accordingly. More ground pine and holly were used this year than any previous year.

Many of our florists report large decorations for New Year's, showing a gratifying revival of an old but exceedingly profitable custom, providing the weather is not too cold to permit plants to be hauled about without wrapping.

The debut of Miss Pearl White at the Colonial Club on the evening of December 29 was an elaborate affair. The J. M. Gasser Company had the decorations, which were exceptionally fine.

Mr. and Mrs. John Travers have resumed business at 952 Central avenue.

Miss Jane Eadie has been quite ill for some time.　　　　O. G.

BOULDER, COL.—S. Knudsen has added two new greenhouses to his establishment.

Goods That Every Florist Should Have.

Fancy Flower Baskets in novel shapes and rich material.

Cycas Leaves and Wreaths.

Accordeon-Pleated Water-Proof Crepe Paper. A sterling novelty for pot covering, etc. Also Velvet Two-Tone Crepe Paper, Plant Baskets and Pot Covers, Moss and Immortelle Wreaths.

Bohemian Glass Vases, Plain Glass Vases in novel shapes. Sell them with the flowers.

EVERYTHING RIGHT UP-TO-DATE.

H. Bayersdorfer & Co.

50-56 N. 4th St., PHILADELPHIA, PA.

Please mention the American Florist when writing

M. RICE & CO.,

Importers and Manufacturers,

Leading Florists' Supply House and Ribbon Specialists.

918 Filbert Street, **Philadelphia, Pa.**

Please mention the American Florist when writing.

FLORIST FOIL

Plain, Violet, Rose

MADE BY

The John J. Crooke Co.

155 Ave. D, NEW YORK. 149 Fulton St., CHICAGO.

Please mention the American Florist when writing.

TIN FOIL

Plain, Fancy, Printed & Mounted,

Manufactured by

The Conley Foil Co.

**521 to 541 West 25th St.,
NEW YORK.**

THE Gardeners' Chronicle.

A Weekly Illustrated Journal.

ESTABLISHED 1841.

The GARDENERS' CHRONICLE has been for over SIXTY YEARS THE LEADING JOURNAL of its class. It has achieved this position because, while specially devoting itself to supplying the daily requirements of gardeners of all classes, the information furnished is of such general and permanent value that the GARDENERS' CHRONICLE is looked up to as the STANDARD AUTHORITY on the subjects of which it treats.

Subscription to the United States, $4.20 per year. Remittances to be made payable to H. G. COVE.

OFFICE:— 41 Wellington St., Covent Garden, London, England.

Please Mention The American Florist When Writing.

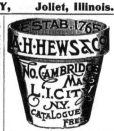

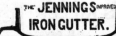

Milwaukee.

SLIGHT INCREASE IN HOLIDAY BUSINESS.— FLOWERING PLANTS COMING IN FAVOR.— DULLNESS NOTED IN CITY TRADE.

A careful canvas of the retail trade brings out the information that while Christmas trade was good, yet the increase was not near as large as in the past two seasons. However, everyone is satisfied with the amount of business done. A notable increase was in the amount of plants sold, there being a very heavy demand for flowering plants. Good holly wreaths were cleaned out early on Thursday and there is no doubt that far more could have been sold. While the demand for immortelle bells was good, there were quite a few left over. Last season it was impossible to get a bell the day before Christmas. New Year's business is good in the shipping line but thus far the city trade has been rather slow. The supply is rather limited but is the best seen thus far this season. Roses have fine color and of course there are no pickled carnations at present.

Currie Brothers are well pleased with their Christmas trade, the best they ever had. Their store was tastefully decorated with wild smilax and Christmas bells.

Adam Zender had a fine lot of long American Beauty roses which sold readily.

Albert and Ferdinand Loeffler had, as usual, a splendid lot of violets.

E. Haasch cleaned out a fine lot of extra fine cyclamens.   H.

Alameda, Cal.

Hayashi & Company have bought George Tyler's floral business on Everett street, as well as the depot at 150 Park street; and they also use the nursery at Buena Vista avenue and Park street. They are going to add extensively to the greenhouse equipment on Everett street so that they will have seven houses, with a total of 12,000 square feet of glass. They will install a steam heating plant, so that they will be able to produce cut flowers the year around. Their specialties will be carnations and chrysanthemums for the market. At the other nurseries they will provide stock for the depot on Park street, and also raise fruit trees, garden and house plants for the general market. At the depot they also maintain a bazar, where they handle a great variety of Japanese goods, which they import direct from Japan. This business has made great strides during the year, and it has added not a little to the reputation of Alameda as a place for the growth of chrysanthemums and carnations which they are able to produce in such great perfection. The members of this firm are H. Hayashi and T. Minami.

Lexington, Ky.

A deal was consummated December 12 whereby the Lakeview Greenhouses is consolidated with the business of the Honakers. Capt. J. D. Yarrington, former proprietor of the Lakeview establishment, will retire from the business entirely, and his entire stock of goods will be moved to Honaker's store. With these additions the firm of Honaker will have a total expanse of 100,000 feet of glass. A new section of greenhouses will be erected and new pipes and furnaces installed. By the consolidation of the two firms, the Honaker plant becomes one of the largest wholesale and retail concerns in the south.

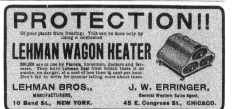

SAULT STE. MARIE, MICH.—Wm. E F. Weber reports trade steady with stock in fine condition. He will add some glass next spring.

La Detroit

THE AMERICAN FLORIST

A WEEKLY JOURNAL FOR THE TRADE

America is "the Prow of the Vessel; there may be more comfort Amidships, but we are the first to touch Unknown Seas."

Vol. XXI. CHICAGO AND NEW YORK, JANUARY 9, 1904. No. 814.

THE AMERICAN FLORIST

NINETEENTH YEAR.

Copyright 1903, by American Florist Company
Entered as Second-Class Mail Matter.
PUBLISHED EVERY SATURDAY BY

AMERICAN FLORIST COMPANY,
324 Dearborn St., Chicago.
Eastern Office: 42 W. 28th St., New York.

Subscription, $1.00 a year. To Europe, $2.00.
Subscriptions accepted only from the trade.
Volumes half-yearly from August, 1901.

SOCIETY OF AMERICAN FLORISTS AND
ORNAMENTAL HORTICULTURISTS.
OFFICERS—JOHN BURTON, Philadelphia, Pa.,
president; C. C. POLLWORTH, Milwaukee, Wis.,
vice-president; WM. J. STEWART, 79 Milk Street,
Boston, Mass., secretary; H. B. BEATTY, Oil City,
Pa., treasurer.
OFFICERS-ELECT—PHILIP BREITMEYER, president; J. J. BENEKE, vice-president; secretary and
treasurer as before. Twentieth annual meeting
at St. Louis, Mo., August, 1904.

THE AMERICAN CARNATION SOCIETY.
Annual convention at Detroit, Mich., March 2,
1904. ALBERT M. HERR, Lancaster, Pa., secretary.

AMERICAN ROSE SOCIETY.
Annual meeting and exhibition, Philadelphia,
March, 1904. LEONARD BARRON, 136 Liberty St.,
New York, secretary.

CHRYSANTHEMUM SOCIETY OF AMERICA.
Annual convention and exhibition, November,
1904. FRED H. LEMON, Richmond, Ind., secretary.

THIS ISSUE 40 PAGES WITH COVER.

AFTER THE HOLIDAYS.

HRISTMAS trade has, we trust, made deep inroads on the plant stock of our readers and left an abundance of much needed space for crowded material to spread out. The room vacated by the holiday azaleas, poinsettias, Lorraine begonias, cyclamens, ardisias and solanums will now be needed for the lilies and other Easter specialties, some of which should now be started off so that there may be no necessity for over-forcing later on.

The first of these to require attention are the hydrangeas, which should be brought at once from under the benches and from the cellars in which they have been resting and given a start in a temperature of 50° to 55°, to be followed two weeks later by a gradual advance to 65° and 70°. They will need frequent syringing under the foliage to keep down the red spider, to attacks of which hydrangeas are very subject. As Easter approaches the temperature in which they are grown may be raised or lowered according to progress, it being borne in mind that the flower heads should be about the size of half a dollar five or six weeks before Easter and should begin to show color at least two weeks before that event.

Lilies will need constant attention henceforth. They should be brought out from the close quarters where they have been busy making roots and given a chance to push ahead. It is the custom generally now to start the bulbs in 4-inch pots. This gives an opportunity to select them according to uniformity of height and habit for planting in large pots in groups of three or more. It is a good plan to make up a number of large pans of five, seven, or even more, 7-9 bulbs for special Easter demand, and these make a fine massive effect in the Easter show. It is also a good idea not to keep all the lilies for Easter. Some of them, especially the Harrisii, may be put into a temperature of 65° and brought into bloom in February and March, when they will be found very useful for many occasions and will in frequent cases bring a better price than they will at Easter and also leave the room vacant earlier. Those who force bulbs can use the recently acquired space for Roman

hyacinths, daffodils, Paper White narcissi, and tulips and palms. Boston ferns and similar subjects which have been crowded together to accommodate the Christmas stock will be benefitted by a chance for more air and light. Of course the azaleas that are wanted for Easter must still be kept in the cold, but it is well to use a part of the room recently vacated in the warm houses to bring in a succession of azaleas for use in January and February, as many decorations can not be acceptably done without color, and in such cases azaleas are exceedingly useful. Bougainvilleas may also be brought forward from the cool house to come in early. Bougainvilleas for forcing should have been kept very cool and dry all through the fall, a temperature of about 40° being about right. Those wanted for Easter should be left there a little while yet, the time required to bloom them being from six to eight weeks in a temperature of 60° to 70°. Crimson Rambler may now be started off in about a 50° heat.

American Beauty rose should be more generally grown for Easter, as no more acceptable subject can be found and the operation is simplicity itself. Beauty growers often throw out a house or two directly after the holidays to make room for young stock for the next year, especially if the plants have been kept at a high tension for cut flowers for two or three years. These plants can be bought cheap, and properly handled will make splendid subjects for pot culture for Easter sales. The plants should be cut back to varying heights, say from one to three-foot canes, planted one or two in a pot, and kept in a temperature not exceeding 45° until they are pretty well rooted, when heat may be gradually increased. Every shoot should produce a flower and it is possible to so control this and Magna Charta, which is the best of all roses for Easter blooming, so that the buds will be ready to open, not on Monday or Tuesday, but on Friday or Saturday before Easter, just when they are wanted, by a little moving around as they mature. Some growers prefer to cut both Beauty and Crimson Rambler back to mere stubs of the canes, liking the bushy effect thus obtained. It is well to have both kinds.

Belated Holiday Trade Reports.

FALL RIVER, MASS.—C. Warburton says that Christmas business did not reach standard. Cut flowers scarce and the trade went to plants of all kinds.

VICTORIA, B. C.—J. T. Higgins notes a twenty-five per cent increase over Christmas 1902. All cut flowers were short of the demand. Last year's prices ruled in all lines.

LOS ANGELES, CAL.—Lack of rain for a protracted season interfered with all business during the holidays. Stock was poor in quality and very scarce. A. F. Borden anticipates a serious drouth this year.

PORTLAND, ORE.—The florists totaled a nice thirty-five per cent increase in business over last Christmas, writes Martin & Forbes. Cut flowers short and all prices high. Flowering plants sold in large numbers.

UTICA, N. Y.—Wm. Mathews describes this year's business as much heavier than that of Christmas 1902. Cut flowers short and good call for bulbous stock and flowering plants. Many nice orchids on market.

FORT WORTH, TEX.—There were more calls for blooming plants than ever before, owing to the shortage of cut flowers. Business increased twenty per cent over Christmas 1902, but prices were about on a par.

MUNCIE, IND.—High prices cut down the sales. Carnations not in good supply. Begonia Gloire de Lorraine was a favorite. The money value of the Christmas business was about on a par with last year.

SAVANNAH, GA.—John Wolf notes that everyone made more money over Christmas 1902. All stock of superfine quality but woefully short. Buyers were eager to buy plants and were willing to pay the price.

PAWTUCKET, R. I.—Prices lower than last Christmas, but total sales greater. More blooming plants were sold than before, but bulbous stock buyers were very backward. Many elaborate church weddings.

DAVENPORT, IA.—J. T. Temple says that there was little increase in business over last Christmas. All stock short, but prices about the same. No demand for bulbous flowers. Poinsettias and azaleas sold well.

DOVER, N. H.—C. L. Howe says that this year's business was a great increase over that of Christmas 1902. Prices were twenty-five per cent better. Flowering plants proved very popular. Cut flowers short of demand.

BUTTE, MONT.—Law Brothers report a ten per cent increase over the Christmas business of 1902. Roses and carnations were short and bulbous stock was in poor supply. A good demand for fancy boxes of assorted flowers.

BAY CITY, MICH.—Christmas buyers did not get ahead of the supply and all cut flowers were of grand quality. Flowering plants and Boston ferns sold better than palms. Boehringer Brothers call attention to a phenomenal sale of holly.

HARRISBURG, PA.—Prices were lower than last Christmas and there were flowers enough of all kinds to go around. Poinsettias and mignonette were favorite sellers. Individual sales were smaller than the preceding Christmas, says G. Hanson.

WATERBURY, CONN.—Alexander Dallas sizes up this year's Christmas business as one-fourth heavier than 1902. Many more carnations could have been used to advantage. Flowering and berried plants were among the best Christmas sellers.

NEW ORLEANS, LA.—Very poor Christmas business, fully forty per cent lower than 1902, reports W. J. Virgin. Violets and carnations short of demand. No demand for plants and very slow call for bulbous stock. Heavy rain on Christmas day ruined the business.

LONDON, ONT.—Twenty-five per cent increase over Christmas 1902, say J. Gammage & Sons. Half of the cut flower buyers were turned away on the day before Christmas. Little demand for small plants. Good prices were paid willingly all along the line.

ATCHISON, KANS.—Christmas business was better than last year, says the Mangelsdorf Brothers Company. Carnations and violets very scarce and bulbous stock was an oversupply. Begonia Gloire de Lorraine was a good selling article.

CANTON, O.—In the opinion of Chas. Lindacher, there was an increase of at least fifteen per cent over that of last Christmas. Roses and carnations were sufficient for the demand and good prices prevailed. No increase noted in sale of bulbous flowers or plants.

A Pacific Coast Establishment.

John H. Sievers.

At 1251 Chestnut street, San Francisco, overlooking the Golden Gate and San Francisco Bay, is the nursery of John H. Sievers & Company, who have attained an enviable reputation as originators and introducers of many rare novelties in pelargoniums, tuberous begonias and especially carnations. John H. Sievers, the senior member of this firm, associated himself with F. A. Miller in the nursery and florist business in 1871. This partnership was subsequently dissolved in 1875, a rather eventful and disastrous year in business circles in San Francisco. Mr. Sievers, however, shortly made another start in business in his present location, growing a general assortment of plants and cut flowers. Roses were grown to quite an extent for several years and this firm held the first place as producers of fancy American Beauty and teas. This was also the home of the Rainbow rose, which sport from Papa Gontier was found in 1885 and introduced a few years later. Rose growing was gradually superseded and finally abandoned upon the advent of the improved carnation.

The first attempt at hybridizing the carnation was made in 1889, crossing the best then existing varieties with a few seedlings that were grown from seed imported from Germany. Experiments along these lines were carried on for several years until in 1895 some seventy varieties were noted. Fifty of these were catalogued in 1897. They were remarkable for their size, fragrance, range of color and prolific blooming. Many of them created favorable notice throughout the east, including the following varieties: Leslie Paul, Ethel Crocker, California Gold, Helen Dean, Harriet Bradford, John Carbone, Elsie Ferguson, John Hinkle and Lewis Bradbury. Several of these varieties are still retained and grown for cut blooms, comparing favorably with the recent eastern introductions. The California carnations should be grown in a night temperature of 55° in a soil to which very little fertilizers have been added, and should be kept on a sparing diet. This, I believe, is overlooked by many eastern growers trying these varieties, resulting in the plants going to grass

ESTABLISHMENT OF SIEVERS & BOLAND, SAN FRANCISCO, CAL.

EMPLOYES AND PELARGONIUMS AT SIEVERS & BOLAND'S, SAN FRANCISCO, CAL.

and bursting their calyxes.

Of the latest varieties originated by this firm and not yet disseminated the Hannah Hobart and A. B. Spreckles stand out preeminently in the lead. Cut blooms of the Hannah Hobart are ahead of any carnation in the San Francisco market, having never been wholesaled for less than $1 per dozen. It is of a deep shade of pink with well built up center from three and a half to four inches in occasionally four and a half inches in diameter. The habit of the plant is all that could be desired. It is a vigorous, strong grower, remarkably free from disease and an excellent bloomer. Next in merit comes the A. B. Spreckles, a scarlet of the highest order. Its flowers, three to three and a half inches in diameter, are borne on long wiry stems which come long from the commencement of flowering. This is the most fragrant carnation I have ever seen. The habit and productiveness are also excellent. But it is not alone in carnations that efforts have been rewarded with success. In hybridizing tuberous begonias and pelargoniums the most gratifying results have been obtained to which a number of varieties of superior merit can testify.

The greenhouses, twenty in number and containing nearly 60,000 square feet of glass, are heated by three sectional hot water boilers, coal being used as fuel in preference to oil, which was recently tried. Several houses are devoted to palms and ferns, one large house to orchids of the best commercial varieties. Poinsettias, azaleas, bulbs, etc., are grown in considerable quantities in their season. This establishment is in charge of Thos. E. Hooper, to whose able management a large share of the firm's present prosperity is due. ROMNEYA.

Holiday Impressions.

[A paper by Wm. J. Stewart, of Boston, Mass., read before the Chicago Florists' Club, January 6, 1904.]

GENTLEMEN:—In complying with your request for a few notes relative to the holiday trade of New York and Boston, I am pleased to be able to start with the premise that, notwithstanding the widespread financial depression and consequent leaning to economy in matters of luxury, the expenditures for the products of floriculture in this section during the recent holiday season are believed by competent judges to have fully equaled any past record.

Among the most significant feature of

the trade I would mention the evidences of steady advancement in the popularity of growing plants as holiday gifts, and the higher and more uniform quality displayed in the stock offered. To what extent the cut flower industry is, by its mistakes, directly responsible for a movement which means dispossession from its most cherished holding is not readily demonstrated, but there has been no lack of warning from year to year and it must now be evident to all that the absolute loss of confidence on the part of buyers in the integrity of the stock sold to them must have contributed not a little to the present conditions. However, we cannot look upon this drift of popular favor in the direction of living and growing objects, as other than natural, and it is gratifying to note in the cultural improvement seen in the holiday plants, a hopeful augury, for it tells us that the long wished for incentive to expert commercial plant growing in this country is now to be given and thereby glorious possibilities are opened up for the future of our art in the higher phases.

The headstrong tenacity of cut flower growers in adhering to discredited long-standing practices in the storing up and

valuing of their product and the utter collapse of the flower market in consequence, was another feature of the holiday experience in New York city. "Fortune makes him fool whom she makes her darling', and it needs no supernatural vision to see that the pickle-pot has been no small factor in the once imperious holiday cut flower's undoing. Fortunately for Boston, she fared rather better than did New York, because, owing to a number of reasons, she still enjoys a good suburban and country trade in cut flowers, and the outgoing shipments for the holidays and at other times tend materially to relieve and steady the usual market. Whether these local advantages are a permanent asset remains for the future to show.

The changes constantly going on progress so stealthily that it is impossible for us to distinguish where one condition ends or another begins, each period quietly disappearing into its successor, but, in shaping one's course for the future, if we are to achieve continued success, it is imperative that we clearly recognize that the conduct of any branch of the florists' business today is a widely different proposition from what it was a few years since.

Unfortunately, thus far the habit of imitation would seem to be a more conspicuous characteristic of the American floriculturist than the attribute of originality. Instances demonstrating the truth of this presumption will, no doubt, come readily to the mind of everyone. The bringing to light, by an enterprising fellow-florist, of any new or profitable line is the signal for a headlong rush from all sides to do the same thing. Production in certain fields has thus outstripped by far the demand therefor, and it is plain that until strenuousness is curtailed or else diverted to other lines, or some means of increasing the capacity of the market is put into operation, the trouble complained of in New York, and to some extent elsewhere also, are bound to intrude themselves with increasing frequency. So long, however, as the old operators hold out and continue to add to their productive capacity and newcomers still find room, under established methods of distribution, how can we

CARNATIONS AT SIEVERS & BOLAND'S, SAN FRANCISCO, CAL.

assume otherwise than that, despite all the protesting we hear, values have not yet fallen below the point of profit? We know this, that when that limit of depression has been touched, then the penalty of imprudent overdoing must be paid, and history will repeat itself in the survival of the fittest.

The Ginger Jar Opened in Chicago.

[A paper by George C. Watson, of Philadelphia, Pa., presented before the Chicago Florists' Club, January 6, 1904.]

GENTLEMEN:—Your esteemed president, Willis N. Rudd, has done me the distinguished honor of requesting a synopsis of my ideas of the holiday trade in Philadelphia, and I am quite overwhelmed. It is not only that we have crossed swords so often, he and I. His magnanimity is proverbial, although I never imagined it would stretch that far. But I have consulted what passes with me as a mind and it says "Go to. What does Chicago care about what is going on in the staid old Quaker City?"

That's true enough and I hardly see how it would interest you to know how many carnations old Bill Baker managed to get away with Christmas week, or how many poinsettias were left on the benches when Craig, Harris, Westcott and the rest of them got through; or whether Pennock did more business than Battles; or whether the market is going to knock out all the commission men; or if John Welsh Young is succeeding in his feat of riding the two horses "market" and "commission" on behalf of his paper; or if Kift is waking up as to the one horse he is having trouble with in guiding round the ring labeled "market;" or if Crawford is still as much in love with the charms of the free open-air life of the farm as ever; or if Herman Schoenfeld has stopped his underhand scheme of getting orders which the rest of us would like to do but don't know how; or if John Shellem's new and improved Carnot is to be a winner or otherwise; or if Wm. Didden with his Helen Reid new pink carnation will prove more of a sensation than Isaac Passmore's new white Vesper, the distribution of which has been intrusted to Craig; or if Hugh Graham is a bigger man than William Graham, or vice versa; or if Charles Fox is to trump with his Broad and Sansom street store the energy, ability, the big-wagons-in-the-center-of-the-city of John Habermehl of up-town fame; or if Bill Harris' mysterious yellow primrose is really so very mysterious after all; whether it was a good move to pass the old times by in the distribution of La Detroit; or whether George Rackham and Phil. Breitmeyer were really "safe" when they got on the rear platform of the Pullman that night in Philadelphia; whether Brother Nugent of New York was in Philadelphia eyes as narrow as the average New Yorker; all these and a thousand other ors, ifs and whethers I don't believe would stir your hearts one pulse beat, because you are too much interested, according to all accounts, in another matter much nearer and dearer to the hearts of Chicago.

That matter is the "union label." I am told you can't even bury your dead in Chicago unless the funeral is union from nails to clod. Good Lord, we used to think that when death closed our eyes all was peace—excepting, perhaps, the possibility of hell hereafter may have troubled some of us—but to think that we've got to die union or not die at all is enough to fill the bravest heart with despair.

There's an idea abroad in the east that all trains stop ten minutes for divorce in Chicago. It will be well to modify that notion hereafter according to union rules for if the sky-pilot and the rest of them can't show the proper badge—let the pillars of the universe shake—it will be no divorce.

Then again it may be proper to ask whether you can have a marriage in Chicago unless the bride and groom are both union, the flowers properly tagged with Amalgamated No. 4, the bridesmaid gifted with a walking card, the church clear of the boycott, and the presents labeled above the smallest suspicion of scab.

In fact there seems, to the unsophisticated imagination of the easterner, to be grave doubts as to whether a baby can be born in Chicago without the desire and consent of the union. The medieval precautions in connection with the birth of heirs to the effete monarchies of Europe pale into insignificance besides the necessities of the Chicago situation. If the prime minister and archbishop of the ancient order of United Midwives No. 43,344 and the serene High Muck-a-muck of the Registration Bureau No. 27, be not satisfied—God help the kid, that's all.

Our outspoken ex-president, John Burton, gave vent to his alarm over what a union might do if let loose among greenhouses. That was at Milwaukee last summer. He had visions of the poor-house and other nightmares seething in his brain; but these were nothing to the grim reality which confronts the unfortunate individual who has the misfortune to live in Chicago.

I am mighty glad I live in the cleanest, brightest, oldest, busiest, straightest, most corrupted old town in the union where the unions don't bother us! I'm glad we have had a good Christmas trade and sorry the cut flower men didn't succeed in boosting prices as they liked.

I'm mighty glad also we don't have to breathe the stockyard air of Chicago, the oil refineries of Cleveland, the smoke of Pittsburg, or participate in the madness of New York, the east winds of Boston or the racket of Buffalo, and I'm glad for a lot other reasons, too numerous to mention.

Having unburdened myself and cleared the way thus far I will proceed to do what your president asked me, namely, to tell you something about the Christmas trade in Philadelphia. I am quite convinced it is all foolishness, but here goes.

First on the list, green goods. A very large trade was done in these, the city hall being entirely given over to the dealers in this important branch of business. The mayor and other city officials remained on duty night and day and by their vigilance prevented a nefarious attempt to rig the market. A scheme to burn up some 1,400 carloads of Christmas trees was frustrated in time and the fire department came in for a grand ovation for their heroic efforts. The mayor pointed out that so long as he ruled there would be no effort spared to provide that prime necessity of modern civilization, cheap Christmas trees, and so highly are the efforts appreciated that there is a powerful boom on to run him for president against Mark Hanna next election.

I regret being unable to report a flourishing state of affairs in the cut flower end. Prices did not soar for some reason. One explanation was that there must have been a few carloads of cold-

storage peony blooms sent in from Chicago, as we have been told you can keep these in perfect condition anywhere from six days to six months. Another grievance of the cut flower men was "very little to cut." The explanation for that is probably neglect. I hear that many of the big fellows have been so busy bowling that they have had no time to go home to meals even, far less to look after their crops.

Plant trade was of the razzle dazzle order. On account of the conservative methods of the Pennsylvania railroad it was feared there would be great congestion in the traffic but President Cassett surprised them by digging a tunnel under the Schuylkill so as to clear enormous freights from Craig's, Harris', and other west Philadelphia growers, and by side-tracking a number of trains at German-town junction so as to relieve that section of the city the traffic was finally moved successfully with no untoward incident except perhaps the dumping of a few New York drummers in the "loop-skirts" of the city, whence they had to take a cab or walk in order to get to the center.

From the foregoing brief sketch you will dimly discern that we Philadelphians had a vociferous time and I trust you will be satisfied with my report. I've done the best I know how, or as the poet says, "I seen my duty and I done it."

Wishing you all loads of prosperity for 1904, I remain as ever, yours to command, etc., etc.

The Carnation.

AT PETER FISHER'S.

It is to be presumed that every aspiring carnation grower will be interested in what the distinguished originator of the "Lawson Pink" is doing. No sooner had that imposing variety made its memorable debut winning fame and fortune for those concerned therein, than Mr. Fisher was diligently at work trying to create something better. From the beginning he has held to the view that Lawson was but the precursor of a new race of commercial carnations which should eventually become as famous in its progeny as for itself. That he has met with success already is evidenced in the three later productions from this lineage—Enchantress, introduced last spring; Nelson Fisher and Mrs. M. A. Patten which are to be disseminated the coming season. These three varieties are the result of the same cross, viz.—Lawson pollen with Mrs. G. M. Bradt as seed parent. That rare characteristic of flourishing under widely-varying conditions of soil and environment which the Lawson has demonstrated seems to have been inherited by Enchantress as nobody who bought it has thus far expressed disapproval. The color of Lawson is here intensified; the form is greatly improved and there is no trouble early in the full with abbreviated stems such as the

Lawson invariably gives. Mr. Fisher's own faith in the variety is demonstrated in the beginning of a new house, 33x300, which will be finished in May and which he will plant exclusively with Nelson Fisher for cut flower purposes. The advance sales of the two introductions already amount to 160,000. To meet this and the anticipated further demand 6,000 plants of Mrs. Patten have been dismantled for propagating purposes and nearly 8,000 Nelson Fisher for the same use and Mr. Fisher is kept busy relentlessly snapping the heads off as they appear. Plants thus used for cutting purposes are not fed nor allowed to make a rank growth. The propagating house, where 70,000 cuttings are already in process of rooting, is run without bottom heat.

The seedling house is naturally a most interesting place in such an establishment. Mr. Fisher is working for the development of a deeper shade of color on the line of Enchantress. It appears in a number of seedlings but not with the other required points thus far. There is one white, No. 411, which Mr. Fisher, usually conservative in such comments, himself declares "will knock Gov. Wolcott silly." Also a fiery crimson, No. 113, with a giant's frame and constitution. Results from specific crosses are as odd and unexpected here as elsewhere, but it is certainly surprising to learn from Mr. Fisher that out of twenty-one seedlings, the issue from a cross of Lawson on Nelson Fisher, there were eighteen yellows!

NOTES ON NEWER VARIETIES.

We are not growing many of the late introductions among carnations this year but the following are notes on the behavior up-to-date of the new varieties we are trying:

Enchantress.—This variety has done extra well, better than any carnation on the place, new or old. It made a fine plant in the field, went right ahead when transplanted into the house and has been giving extra long stemmed fancy blooms all season. It sells before all others, is a good keeper, and at this date the plants are as full of bud and bloom as is possible to get any carnation. Altogether a magnificent variety.

Harlowarden.—This is a free, healthy grower, with fine large flower of good form. It would be much more valuable if dwarfer, the crop taking too long to mature owing to the stems being so long.

Gov. Wolcott.—We are growing this variety in a night temperature of 54° and under this treatment it is away ahead of the other whites with us. We get some burst flowers but not more than with the other whites grown, which are Flora Hill, Queen Louise, White Cloud, Glacier and Bon Homme Richard. It has a fine stem and the plants are full of buds and blooms.

Adonis.—This variety made the poorest plants of any in the field, but they are now grown fairly well, though our plants are still small. What blooms we are cutting are fine in color, good size, with long stiff stems. We shall have to grow more of it before passing judgment.

White Lawson.—We have a number of plants of this variety and believe it will prove as valuable as the variety whence it came. We notice that it seems to like a lower temperature than Mrs. Lawson. We have them growing on the end of a bench where it is rarely above 50° night temperature. The petals have a waxy texture with lots of substance and we

have not yet found a burst calyx. We cannot account for this as Mrs. Lawson plants grown in a little warmer part of the same house throw a number of burst calyxes.

Mrs. Higinbotham.—We are growing this a second season and it is so much ahead of last year that it is proving to be one of our best paying carnations. We have it growing in the same house as Mrs. Joost with a night temperature of 50°. It is equally as free as Joost, size of flower about the same, with stiff stem and the color takes well here.

We have six plants of Richmond Gem, sent us for trial. The flower is a little under the fancy size but the color is fine. It is an easy grower and we are never without a few blooms on these six plants.

C. W. JOHNSON.

Palms and Ferns.

PLANTS FOR THE HOLIDAY TRADE.

From time to time the rose growers of various localities have discussed the advisability of growing a different list of varieties to those that are the standbys of the trade generally, but the matter is usually settled by the majority returning to their first loves in the form of American Beauty, Brides and Bridesmaid and a very similar condition is found among those who devote their chief energies to the production of palms, ferns and other decorative stock. There are comparatively few changes made in the lists of decorative plants, with the exception that there occasionally appears a Pteris ovata fern, or a Scott fern, or a Fosterfern, or else some bright grower discovers a quicker or better method of growing some particular palm or other plant. And it is by no means easy to produce novelties in this class of plants that will prove to be just what the dealer is looking for, there being many points to be taken into consideration. Both palms and ferns are in demand at Christmas time, though the greater part of the trade at that time seems to be in plants of moderate size and medium price, for example, kentias that may be retailed at from $1.50 to $5 each; latanias in 6-inch and 8-inch pots and Boston ferns of about the corresponding sizes.

These plants, being selected for gifts by many of their purchasers, should always be shapely and well furnished and if possible to manage it there should be a special crop of such plants prepared for the holiday trade rather than to depend on the leavings after the fall rush of shipping trade is over. In order to have a special crop for this purpose it is necessary to pot them in the late summer and early fall that they may be well established by the time they are needed, a pot-bound plant enduring the trying conditions of a dwelling very much better than one that has been recently shifted. This is not only a good point for the dealer to remember in making his purchases, but it is also a good one to be impressed upon the customer, so many persons being afflicted with the idea that the pot of their favorite plant is not large enough, and consequently insisting on having it repotted long before there is any necessity for doing so. The best house-grown Kentia Forsteriana that I have ever seen gave such a poor point for over three years and only began to depreciate after the owner insisted upon having it repotted. It is during the period of strong fire heat in the palm houses that the troublesome pest of red spider is most likely to appear and as a precautionary

measure thorough syringing should be given every bright day, and in addition to this the paths and surface of the ground beneath the benches should always be kept moist, a thorough sprinkling with the hose under the benches and in all dry corners twice a day being a great help in promoting a healthy humidity in the atmosphere, the regular hosing overhead being preferably done in the morning.

But while the morning watering is the best at this season this is no reason for neglecting to give a thirsty plant a good drink at any time such a subject may be discovered, for much more injury will be done by permitting a plant to remain dry until the following morning than by giving it a good watering the last thing before closing up for the night, and the practice of the writer is to water at any period of the day rather than to allow it to wait until the next regular watering time. The common snail sometimes does some harm to the kentias, the point of attack being the tender young leaf that is just unfolding, leaves being frequently disfigured in this way during the winter and spring months on young and growing stock in 4-inch to 6-inch pots, the larger plants being less troubled by this pest, possibly on account of the greater distance from the ground at which the young leaves appear. Baiting with lettuce or cabbage leaves among the kentias is probably the easiest method of capturing the snails, and if the night man does not have too much firing to attend to, a little entomological research on his part may prove profitable in the palm houses.

The slack season that follows the holiday trade gives an opportunity for the recleaning of those plants that may have accumulated a new stock of insects and such will be found among every large collection, though a good pressure of water will help to keep the insects down to some extent. Well grown plants of Adiantum Farleyense and A. cuneatum are seldom found in greater supply than the market demands, so many of these ferns being used in high class decorations and also in the filling of fancy baskets and hampers. Farleyense seems to be about the only fern whose foliage is rich enough in texture and coloring to be used among the choicer orchid flowers and as the market for such flowers widens this most beautiful fern will also be more in demand. The sizes of A. Farleyense that are most used are those in 4-inch to 6-inch pots, but in A. cuneatum those in 4-inch pots are possibly the more useful, and plants that have been shifted from 3-inch pots in September will fill out nicely by midwinter, a stiff soil producing the most satisfactory plants for this purpose.

As a matter of fact the strong growing ferns that are used in the trade do not require elaborate formulas in soil preparation, and as we have noted before, these ferns may be grown in a good strong rose soil with plenty of well rotted stable manure, the chief precaution to observe in growing them being to avoid souring the soil by overwatering them just after they have been potted, and to give the commoner sorts that have been so often referred to a night temperature of 60°, while the more tender A. Farleyense should have a few degrees higher temperature. If a few adiantums of still finer foliage are called for, then grow some A. gracillimum, this form of A. cuneatum being the best of the fine leaved varieties, and much more satisfactory for trade use than that later introduction, A. Charlottæ. The adiantums of the Pacottei type, of which A. Pacottei and A. Legrandii are examples, are very pretty dwarf growing varieties, though somewhat tender in foliage, and a newer variety that apparently belongs to the same group is A. Bensoniana, this having some resemblance to A. Pacottei, but being possibly a stronger grower.

W. H. TAPLIN.

Florists' Plant Notes.

FOR WEEK OF JANUARY 9.

Bougainvilleas. Sanderiana.—The bougainvilleas which are now in a semi-dormant state in a cool house, can be placed in a few degrees higher temperature to bring them into flower for Easter. A temperature of 60° is about right. Extreme forcing is not advisable for the shoots are liable to grow blind. Give them plenty of syringing and water more freely as growth commences. The bougainvillea is valuable when in flower not only as a decorative plant, for its beautiful bracts hang for many weeks in a living room, but also as cut sprays. We have seen large specimens planted at the end of a greenhouse where they grew and flourished, producing immense bracts, invaluable for decorating purposes. Take some cuttings now for next year's stock. Only soft young growth should be selected for propagating, for the hard wood takes six months or more to root. Insert the cuttings in the warm end of of the propagating bed, and keep them well watered and sprinkled until rooted.

Poinsettias.—Place the old poinsettia plants that were left over from Christmas under a warm rose bench and withhold water entirely from them for the next three months. Immediately after flowering is their natural resting season, so let them remain perfectly dry under the benches until next April, when the soil is shaken out, the plants cut back and started into growth again. It is well to remember our experiences with poinsettias from one year to another. While ready sale was found for all sizes of poinsettias, we found that well grown plants in 6 and 8-inch pans were in greatest demand. Poinsettias are peculiar plants to handle after the bracts are developed. A common error, one which the writer noticed in visiting different establishments, was to force out the bracts fully in a warm temperature three or four weeks before the proper time; then removing them to a cooler temperature, where the invariable result was that all the leaves turned yellow. A poinsettia without its dark, handsome leaves is an abomination.

Asters—Make the first sowing of asters now. The Queen of the Market'strain is the one to sow for early flowering. Every two weeks hereafter until the middle of March another sowing should be made of the different strains, Comet, Victoria, Semple's and others, so as to have a succession of flowers from early summer until the early chrysanthemums' come around again next fall. Sow them in flats, not too thickly, and with ordinary care they will soon come up, and as soon as they are large enough to handle, transplant into flats about an inch and a half apart. For extremely early flowers, a bench of carnations that is not producing what it ought to may be devoted to asters without changing the soil, but be sure to give them plenty of headroom. Plant them about ten inches apart each way, and grow from four to six flowers on a plant. Growing them to single stems will of course produce the largest

flowers and the longest stems, but the difference in the price between the large and the ordinary sized flowers does not warrant the extra time and labor. Later on a frame or two can be planted up and covered with sash. These will also come into flower much earlier than those planted in the open ground.

Geraniums.—It is now time to give the geraniums propagated last September a shift to 3-inch pots. Many growers prefer to shift them at once into 4-inch, thus saving an extra potting. If the soil is well drained and watering is carefully done, this method may be all right; but in the writer's opinion, in these days of little sunshine when overwatering is too apt to be done, it is better to stick to the old way and shift to 3-inch now and 4-inch later on. Use quite heavy soil, but not too rich, adding some bone meal to the extent of a 4-inch pot full to a bushel of soil. Pot firmly and remove all yellow leaves. About two weeks after potting a cutting may be taken from the strongest plants, pinching the tops out of those that cannot afford to lose a cutting. This will make the plants more bushy. Give them plenty of room to prevent the plants from drawing up. Do not water too copiously at this time of the year, but rather induce a more sturdy growth by holding them slightly on the dry side. Excessive overhead watering or syringing at this time will rot the leaves. The cuttings taken off should be potted at once in sandy soil. There is still time to propagate from the old stock plants if it is desired to increase the stock of certain varieties. Propagated now they will make useful little plants in 3-inch pots, of which a limited quantity can be readily disposed of. The old plants should now be cleaned up and shifted into a size larger pot, and will make good plants for larger vases and variety beds.

G.

English Market Plants

Zonal Pelargoniums. – In the last few years these have come much more into use than formerly. The improved varieties we now have not only are suitable for window boxes and bedding but make good plants for all floral decorations, and for this purpose there is now quite a large trade. They must, of course, be well finished plants and of decided colors, and the semi-double varieties are favored more than the singles, though the singles also receive a good deal of attention. Taking the colors, scarlet, pink and salmon are most in demand. Whites are grown to some extent, but there are too many other good white flowers. White marguerites supply the white element for most purposes. King of Denmark (or Beaute Poitevine) is the favorite salmon. This is grown in very large quantities, but when it first came in many of the growers treated it too liberally. I remember seeing a house over 100 feet long, full of plants with enormous leaves and no bloom, and the grower told me it was no good. However, the same firm still grows it and does it well too. It may be the original vigor is somewhat exhausted, but growers have found it requires different treatment from the ordinary market sorts. It must be potted very firmly and well exposed to the light and air. There are several good scarlets, but F. V. Raspail and the improved variety still hold their own among the dark shades. The double Henry Jacoby is grown by some. Ville de Portiers is a good bright scarlet. Decorator is another name for this.

Captain Flayelle is a newer variety which came into the market in grand condition last season and we shall see it in larger quantities next spring. Mme. Alfred Erckener, is another useful semi-double scarlet. The semi-double pinks have been rather defective. Berthe de Presilly is free with large trusses and good color but the flowers do not open so well as could be desired. Pink Ras. pail, a new variety, should prove of value. It is a little wanting in color, but has a good truss and is very free. I am much taken with M. Anatole Raseleur, one of Bruant's recent novelties. I shall be much surprised if this does not take first place as a semi-double pink. It is a lovely shade of color with enormous truss and individual blooms of great size. It also has good foliage. In single pinks we have the most useful variety in Robert Hayes, or Millfield Rival. The last named is supposed to be an improvement but it would be difficult to sort them out if the two sorts got mixed. Mrs. Williams is another good pink. Of salmons, Lady Chesterfield has held its own for a good many years. Mrs. Charles Pearson has flowers of great size and is very free. Of the various shades of scarlet and red, Hall Caine, Gloriation (I think this is purely a market name) is a very fine deep scarlet, has been grown extensively for several years, and still remains a favorite. Henry Jacoby is also much in demand, and for some purposes Vesuvius and West Brighton Gem, the latter especially, are liked.

Although it does not require great cultural skill to produce the zonals in quantity there is a considerable difference in the quality of the different growers. So many growers try to do more than they have room for, and this means that they cannot finish well, while it is in the finish that most depends, it makes a considerable difference if the plants are kept short and sturdy from the start. To secure good stock for early spring work the cuttings should be put in by the end of August, and if they can be put in singly in small pots all the better. Those who grow tomatoes and vines can generally give them (the zonals) plenty of room and a light open position. They are potted on into their final pots (5-inch) during January and February. Grown on shelves up close to the glass they make short jointed sturdy plants. Some growers devote whole houses to them and grow them in beds, but the best I have seen have been grown on shelves in the vineries that are started late. As soon as there is a good show of buds the tips of the shoots are taken out. This throws more strength into the flower stems and larger trusses are secured. It requires a little judgment in giving the different kinds its use. Nitrate of soda is used by some for finishing the plants off with. Well finished plants make from 5 to 6 shillings per dozen, or a little more sometimes, but large contracts are made with some of the florists for delivery by van loads, and for these the prices generally rule about 5 shillings for best stuff, and 4 shillings for such as require different treatment from the ordinary market sorts. For town work the large sizes are frequently used for bedding instead of the ordinary bedding size from 3-inch pots. HORTUS.

WINONA, MINN.—Mrs. D. Voelker has disposed of her greenhouse on Huffstreet, owing to continued illness. Most of the stock was purchased by Chas. Siebrecht. Edward Kirchner bought the rafters and glass.

NEWS NOTES.

BRAINTREE, MASS.—G. H. Arnold is building a new greenhouse 30x175 feet.

NEW ALBANY, IND.—P. Walker & Company report exceptionally good business all through the holidays.

SPRINGFIELD, MASS.—Wm. P. Gale is a bankruptcy petitioner with debts to the amount of $961.22 and no assets.

MONTGOMERY, ALA.—The first annual meeting of the Alabama State Horticultural Society will be held in Mobile January 26 and 27.

BUFFALO, N. Y.—Fire broke out in R. A. Wien's greenhouse. 894 Jefferson street, at 3 a. m., December 20. The fire was caused by an overheated boiler. The damage was $200.

SIOUX FALLS, S. D.—Preparations are completed for the annual meeting of the South Dakota State Horticultural Society at Madison on January 19, 20 and 21.

NEW LONDON, CONN.—The park commissioners have engaged W. E. Arnold, of the Shady Hill Nursery Company, to lay out Riverside park, on the border of the Thames river.

PARKERSBURG, W. VA.—J. W. Dudley & Son, who have 100,000 square feet of glass, also have one of the finest stores in the state. Their Christmas business this year was double that of last.

BRATTLEBORO, VT.—The Christmas and New Year's trade was good. We could have sold a great many more carnations, although the price was twenty per cent better than 1902, says D. McGillivray.

GRAND RAPIDS, MICH.—Freyling & Mendels have bought the Van Hartesveldt place lately in bankruptcy and have torn down the material with which they will build three new houses the coming spring.

WINNIPEG, ONT.—H. E. Philpott reports Christmas trade this year double that of a year ago in cut flowers. He could not get enough plants, holly and wreathing to go around. He had a good supply of home grown white and yellow chrysanthemums for Christmas.

RICHMOND, VA.—In a lot of Enchantress carnations, M. A. Witty says he has discovered a pink sport of that variety of the shade seen in the center of Enchantress blooms, glistening like Mrs. Nelson. He says it is a lighter and more taking color than Mrs. Lawson.

LENOX, MASS.—Jacob Steibel, for the last two years superintendent of the Stoneover farm, owned by John E. Parsons, of New York, died December 30, aged 50 years. He was a member of the Lenox Horticultural Society. A widow, one son and four daughters survive him.

OMAHA, NEB.—The Nebraska Florists' Society has elected the following officers: S. R. Falconer, president; Wm. Ellsworth, vice-president; Geo. Swoboda, treasurer; J. H. Bath, secretary. The meetings are held the second Thursday of each month. The secretary's address is 109 South Sixteenth street, Omaha.

WEBB CITY, MO.—S. S. Brenneman has built two greenhouses 20x172. This gives him 25,000 square feet of glass, five houses in all. His principal crop is in carnations but he also grows roses and bedding plants. Holiday trade here was the best on record, carnations selling at $1 and roses at $1.50 per dozen.

Chicago.

THE BIG FIRE CAUSES GENERAL DEPRESSION.—FUNERALS CREATE A PHENOMENAL RUSH.—PRICES HAVE DECLINED.— FLORISTS' CLUB MEETS. — GENERAL TRADE NOTES.

Chicago is passing through a period of mourning. On the afternoon of December 30, in the Iroquois theater horror, the old year bequeathed to the new a legacy which will not blot from the minds of her people for many years. The new year was ushered in amid unspeakable grief and sorrow, for there were six hundred dead, and there were few families that did not count a relative or a friend among the victims. The Iroquois disaster wrought an unprecedented effect on the flower market, not only in Chicago but in nearby cities. The New Year's season, always one of celebration, dinners, fancy dress balls and elaborate decorations, gave place to funerals. Most of the large decorations which had been ordered of local retailers were countermanded, as soon as the society people awoke to the seriousness of the disaster. Things with retailers and wholesalers were in a state of collapse for awhile, until the campaign for funeral flowers broke out. The retail establishments were the centers of a wild stampede for flowers and every-thing white in sight was cleaned up at any price. Roses and carnations sold for Munchausen figures and when they were exhausted the overflow went to the lesser favorites and narcissi, hyacinths, valley and violets were used. The reaction set in Monday. From the cry of no stock to that of no demand, the transition was rapid and complete and the market is consequently in the dumps. The week is unanimously acknowledged to be the most listless and disheartening for many years, and to make matters worse, there is no promise that the conditions will be alleviated in the near future. The "oldest inhabitant" in the florists' business is getting out his hard time stories, but he is laughed to scorn by the disheartened dealer, whose feelings will not be assauged so easily. Prices in practically all lines have executed the toboggan stunt and carnations are ruling now from $2 to $4, where a week ago they were flirting with the double figure mark. The retailer must necessarily bear the brunt of the apathetic conditions, as the wholesaler still has his shipping trade, which really has not been so bad.

The last regular meeting of the Florists' Club was one of the most interesting that has been held for many a day. Papers on recent holiday trade, contributed by Wm. J. Stewart, secretary of the Society of American Florists, and George C. Watson, seer of Philadelphia, proved to be the entertaining features. Phil Hauswirth, in supplementing these essays, told the retailers and growers some wholesome truths, and he said some things of real value to every live florist in the city. Every florist that was not at the meeting will miss these facts. There are a few men in the trade of this city like Phil, Joe Curran and Gus Lange, who are doing good things in their line every day, and they are not afraid to tell about them to competitors or others. We are glad we have such men in our midst and trust no others of baser grade will ever afflict this industry.

John Starritt, head salesman for Weiland & Risch, is now receiving the congratulations of his numerous friends. He was married to Miss Lena

Daegling, of Oak Park. They have taken up their residence at 337 South. west avenue.

The directors of the Flower Growers' Market held their annual meeting Saturday, December 2. Beside the transaction of other business, Alexander Henderson and Walter Tonner were elected as directors to succeed Frank Beu and Mrs. Shaffer, whose terms have expired.

The local florists were singularly fortunate in the Iroquois theater catastrophe. To our knowledge not a relative or an employe of the craft attended the fatal matinee.

Mr. and Mrs. O. P. Bassett, accompanied by the latter's mother, will depart next week for Pasadena, Cal., where they will spend the balance of the winter.

Mrs. Helen M. Lee, mother of Mrs. Frank Benthey, died suddenly on January 2. She succumbed to a fatal stroke of apoplexy. The funeral occurred Tuesday.

Chas. W. McKellar is already pleased with business since he opened January 1. His office and salesroom have been completely refitted and refurnished.

Yellow tulips with long stems are being handled by Poehlmann Brothers Company. All their bulbous stock is of fine quality.

Frank Garland is fortunate this season with his tulips and narcissi. Of the latter 40,000 fine plants are coming into bloom.

Peter Reinberg is cutting his popular Sunrise roses in great numbers. The stock reflects great credit on the grower.

Wietor Brothers are busy handling an immense carnation cutting trade. Their stock is remarkably well grown.

Bassett & Washburn are getting in choice Liberty roses, which deserve an "extra select" label.

The florists are busy with their annual invoices and computing the profits (or losses) of 1903.

Andrew McAdams, who has been indisposed for several weeks, is convalescing.

Trade visitors this week were: J. A. Schindler, New Orleans, La.; Peter Hairens, New Castle, Ind.; J. W. Lyon, Belvidere, Ill.; Edward H. Stewart, Milwaukee, Wis.; Harry Venn, Canton, Ill.; Messrs. Hunkel and Baerman, Milwaukee.

New York.

COLD WEATHER CAUSES AN UNSTEADY MARKET.—PRICES IN ALL LINES LOWERING.—CUT FLOWER EXCHANGE HAS DIFFICULTY IN DELIVERING STOCK.—LONG ISLAND TRADE NOTES.

The weather the early part of the week was very unsteady on account of the cold weather, and prices were up one day and down another. Several shipments of flowers were frozen badly, especially roses and carnations. The growers who sell their stock at the Cut Flower Exchange had many of their flowers frozen last Tuesday on account of the length of time it takes to bring their goods from the train at Long Island City, thence by express wagons to their market. The thermometer registered 10° below zero Tuesday morning, and in some places a much lower temperature was recorded. Beauty roses have taken a downward course and the very best can now be had at $50. Bride and Bridesmaid are quoted at 18 cents for specials. Violets bring $1.25 for the best. Lily of the valley goes slowly but manages to clean out every day at some price. Carnations seem to hold up pretty well. Paper White narcissi are a glut and can be bought on some days as low as $1 per 100. Roman hyacinths are not going nearly so well as they should. It will be very hard for growers to get their money back out of the bulbs.

Since the above report was written, the market has taken a sudden downward turn and January 8 finds a heavy overstock in all lines with little demand. American Beauty specials are offered at $25. Lawson carnations at $3 and violets at 50 cents per bunch. All regular stocks are ruling about half of list quotations.

Cassidy & Sons, of Blissville, L. I., are erecting on the site of their buildings recently burned two greenhouses, each 22x90. This firm does a large business in the bedding plant line in Calvary Cemetery.

Mrs. John Donaldson, of Elmhurst, L. I., has been very sick with pneumonia for the last week, but is now reported as convalescing.

A. Knickman, of 163 Weirfield street, Brooklyn, has opened a store at 1552 Broadway.

John Dutcher, of Nyack, has thoroughly recovered from his recent severe illness.

Philadelphia.

EXTREME COLD MAKES DELIVERY DIFFICULT.—DECORATIONS IN HORTICULTURAL HALL.—FLORISTS' CLUB EXHIBITION.— MANY FINE DISPLAYS OF CARNATIONS.

The extremely cold weather of the past week has been a great detriment to the business, as all shipping orders, as well as local deliveries had to be sent out with the greatest care. Zero weather was recorded for two days and the mercury has not been above 25° for a week. Such unusual cold weather is making great inroads on the coal bins of the growers, and the expense from this item, it is thought, will equal that of last season.

The Wm. Graham Company had a fine decoration at Horticultural Hall Wednesday evening at which quantities of fine flowers were used. This firm will now have its hands full for some time to come as it has almost all the large engagements of the season.

The January meeting of the Florists' Club was a hummer and brim full of interest to the last minute. The exhibition of carnations was fine, there being many vases of fine blooms. C. W. Ward, of Queens, L. I., was the principal exhibitor with hundreds of extra choice flowers, mostly seedlings. Some of the blooms were up to John Thorpe's ideal, being four inches in diameter. They were a wonderful lot and attracted much favorable comment. Robert Craig & Son had four to five hundred fine blooms, consisting of vases of Prosperity, Enchantress, Harlowarden, McKinley, Mrs. Nelson, Vesper, and Adonis. John N. May had a vase of The Bride, a very fine white, the best of its color seen here yet; also a vase of his new rose, Gen. McArthur, a fine red, something after the old Pierre Guillot. Mr. Marquisee, of Syracuse, N. Y., had vases of Flamingo and Albatross, and the Chicago Carnation Company sent a vase of their new scarlet Crusader. S. J. Goddard, of Framingham, Mass., exhibited Queen, a good white. The Strafford Flower Farm had vases of Prosperity, Harry Fenn, May Naylor and Alpine. John Kuhn brought out his new deep pink seedling No. 100, surely a good thing. Wm. Didden had a fine pink seedling a little lighter than McKinley, which he called Helen Reid. Adolph Fahrenwold set up a vase of Liberty roses nearly as good as Beauty. Harry

Faust staged two vases of his new white chrysanthemum.

Mr. Ward made some very entertaining remarks about the carnations. His conclusions were that the best results were obtained by careful selection of stock from which to take cuttings so as to insure vigor. Varieties would not run out if this care was taken. He had some very fine Prosperity on the tables, showing great color, which were coming true because he had been careful to only propagate from plants bearing well colored flowers.

Mr. Craig gave a short history of the flower, speaking of its small and insignificant beginning. He said that quality was now what was wanted as there were more than enough grown, but it was only the perfect flowers that sold and repaid the grower.

Alfred Burton read an interesting paper on the advantages of an agricultural college education to the grower of plants and flowers. One in the same vein was also read by Robert Canning, of Amherst, Mass. Both essayists received the thanks of the club.   K.

Boston.

HEALTHY TRADE CONDITIONS PREVAIL.— WHITE FLOWERS AGAIN COMING INTO FAVOR.—NEW SOCIETY PRESIDENT INAUGURATED. — PROF. SARGENT'S ASIATIC TOUR ENDS.

The general condition of trade at present is healthy. The protracted spell of very cold weather has helped to diminish the product, already well reduced by the Christmas onslaught. Winter festivities have begun in earnest, a succession of assemblies, receptions, weddings and the like, serving to keep the retail end busy and maintain a steady call for material of good quality. The relatively small proportion of the latter as compared with the gross receipts is the most unsatisfactory feature of the rose market as seen at present. Undue exaltation of the desirability of a big crop "just right for Christmas" is, no doubt, at the bottom of the present preponderance of low-grade roses but the conditions will rapidly improve under the incentive of bright, clear weather, should we be blessed with such. Carnations are doing nicely both as to quality and sale. Valley has fallen back to normal level for mid-winter market. The white varieties, temporarily neglected in the Christmas desire for bright colors, have resumed their places in the front rank and bring full value. Conditions are not favorable for an immediate excessive influx of violets, so everything is running smoothly as regards this specialty. Smilax is gradually advancing in price and will command better figures from now on.

The meeting of the Massachusetts Horticultural Society last Saturday was of more than usual interest, being the first under the new management. President Wolcott's inaugural address was the most able paper which the society has had the privilege of listening to in a long time. Its tone was hopeful, its sentiments progressive and its recommendations thoroughly practical. The position which Dr. Wolcott has been called upon by the society to fill, is one of more than ordinary difficulty and his appeal to the members for their earnest cooperation during the coming year in the direction of a wise administration of the society's affairs, should meet with an unhesitating response. The exhibition at Horticultural Hall, January 2, brought

out a number of specimens of Primula sinensis, P. obconica and P. stellata from Mrs. J. L. Gardner, Wm. Thatcher gardener, and Geo. F. Fabyan, Jas. Stuart, gardener. The obconicas were especially noteworthy, showing the great improvement in size, form and color of flower from the intermixture of sinensis blood. Mr. Stuart's display also included six profusely-bloomed plants of Cattleya Percivaliana.

Prof. Charles S. Sargent has returned from his Asiatic exploring tour, begun early last summer. He is highly pleased over his success in securing a great deal of interesting material for the Arnold Arboretum. He pronounces it to have been the most satisfactory journey he ever made.

It is understood that the directors of the Massachusetts Horticultural Society have sent to President Herrington, of the Chrysanthemum Society of America, an invitation to hold the next annual meeting and exhibition of that association in Boston.

Julius Heurlein, of the Blue Hill Nursery, sailed on Tuesday, January 5, for France, expecting to be absent about a month.

Washington.

DECORATIONS AT PRESIDENT'S RECEPTION. —GEORGE FIELD HAS A NEW, LONG-STEMMED SPORT OF LA FRANCE.—MR. FIELD'S ORCHID HOUSES EXTENSIVE.— UNFAIR CONDUCT CHARGED TO PROMINENT FLORIST.

George Field, known to the craft as the disseminator of the American Beauty rose and now the orchid specialist of Washington, has a collection of cattleyas, vandas, dendrobiums and cypripediums that place him well up in the line of commercial orchid growers. There are eight houses devoted exclusively to orchid culture and enough varieties are grown to have blooms at all seasons, his crop going to the leading retail stores of Washington. Several houses of his range are devoted to roses. A promising sport of La France, as yet unnamed, is now interesting Mr. Field. He considers it much superior to the original both in size of flowers and growth, and the best sport from La France that has yet been shown. The petals are a deep pink, especially so on the back, while the length of stem makes it in that particular a close rival of American Beauty. It has been suggested that it be named Belle of Washington.

Fine stock may now be seen in the stores. Liberty roses from Philadelphia are extra fine. Several of the local growers are at last showing good carnations. Violets have also improved in quality. There is an abundance of Paper White narcissi, one overstocked dealer offering it at 25 cents per dozen retail. There are plenty of good azaleas to be had in 6-inch and 7-inch pots at from $1.50 to $2.50. Lilacs in pots are in several stores and find a ready sale, as they did at Christmas.

The New Year came in with ideal weather, but it only lasted one day. Saturday was wet and sleety changing to severe cold at night. Sunday morning the temperature was down to 6° above zero, with good "skating" on streets and sidewalks. The sun is again out, however, and the inroads on the coal piles at night are the only drawbacks to the growers.

New Year's day receptions made considerable business particularly in cut flowers. A great number of social events will occur this month and business is sure to be good. For the president's reception on New Year's day the White House was decorated throughout with palms, ferns, foliage plants and cut flowers from the government conservatories.

It is charged on the authority of persons of high standing and unquestioned veracity that a prominent Washington florist after being underbid on a wedding decoration made a futile attempt to get the job out of the hands of his business rival by offering to furnish the decoration for nothing providing he was paid for the bouquets.   S. E.

Cincinnati.

GAIN OF FIFTEEN PER CENT IN CHRISTMAS BUSINESS OVER LAST YEAR.—CUT FLOWERS AND PLANTS SELL WELL AT GOOD PRICES AND DEMAND CONTINUES ALL THE WEEK.—STOCK PLENTIFUL AND OF AN EXCELLENT QUALITY.

Christmas trade was satisfactory in all lines. Stock was very good, not much pickled stock coming into the market. The growers sending in this line of goods suffered accordingly. Roses and carnations were cleared out. All the commission houses had disposed of all their flowers when closing time arrived Christmas day. Reports from different sources regarding the amount of business done are very conflicting, some saying it was better than last year, others not as good, but taken as a whole the writer thinks there was an increase of about fifteen per cent. There was a good supply of violets both single and double, while the quality of roses was never better. There was a shortage of American Beauty, especially those of 18-inch to 24-inch stems. Extra select Bride and Bridesmaids brought $15 per 100, and there were not enough to go around.

On recommendation of the mayor boys at the House of Refuge are to be taught gardening. While admiring the flowers in the greenhouses on a tour of inspection the mayor exclaimed to Superintendent Allison: "Why don't you make florists out of some of the boys?" Superintendent Allison agreed. Mr. Critchell, the park superintendent, was told of the plan and approved of it.

Business since the holidays has been very good. Flowers of all kinds are in good demand, especially poinsettias, and these are being cut out very rapidly. By New Year it will be impossible to obtain any. Red roses and carnations are also very scarce. Smilax and other green goods are in good supply. Some sweet peas are to be had, but the supply is limited.

At College Hill last Sunday I called at the greenhouses of George Corbett and Max Rudolph & Company. At George Corbett's everything looked prosperous. His houses of carnations, especially the new one containing Lawson, is in elegant shape with thousands of buds. His violets are also good.

Lily of the valley did not sell as well as usual and had to be worked off Christmas day. There was a good demand for azaleas and palms, Begonia Gloire de Lorraine did not move as well as in previous years.

Ben George was under the impression that he had enough Paper Whites and Romans to go around, but when December 24 came he had to hustle to find enough for his orders.

Will Murphy said the supply of carnations, owing to the increase in amount of glass, was about equal to that of last year, but better prices prevailed.

The Rosebank had a fine lot of choice flowers. It had an exceptionally good run on violets, one commission house alone supplying nearly 7,000.

Max Rudolph said he had a fine crop of roses and carnations for the holiday trade, and the appearance of the place verifies this statement.

Gus Meier had a house of poinsettias containing 1,200 blooms, and these were all cut out inside of four days.   A. D.

St. Paul.

PLANTS AND MADE-UP POTS IN GREAT DEMAND FOR CHRISTMAS.—IMMORTELLE WREATHS AND BELLS CLEANED UP.—CUT FLOWERS ALL UNUSUALLY PLENTIFUL.—BUSINESS AS GOOD AS LAST YEAR.—TRADE NOTES.

The Christmas rush is now over and everyone in the trade is feeling happy and glad of it. From reports business was fully as good as last year. There was an increased demand for plants and made-up pots and baskets. Poinsettias were easily the favorites with Simon Mardoner azaleas and Gloire de Lorraine begonias following close. There was about the usual demand for palms and ferns. All the stores had good cyclamens which were well sold out. In cut flowers there was an increased call for Beauty at a good price. Better prices were realized on carnations than usual, ordinary flowers retailing at $2 per dozen and fancy at $3. The immortelle bells sold on sight and those that had them were sold out a day or two before Christmas. Plenty of cut flowers is rather unusual at Christmas here but this was the case, due to nice bright weather. Very few complaints about goods being frozen were heard, though the thermometer registered 10° Christmas morning. This shows that we all profited by last year's experience.

Gust. Colberg, for many years with L. L. May & Company will be with Aug. S. Swanson after January 1, he having acquired an interest in the Sixth Street store. We are sorry to hear that his youngest child is very ill and not expected to recover.

August S. Swanson had an unusually attractive window display on Sixth street with a fine lot of made up baskets, principally poinsettias.

Holm & Olson had their store well filled with fine plants and report sales nearly doubled, with cut flowers about the same as last year.

Alfred Clausen, of Albert Lea, Minn., the carnation grower, was a visitor.

L. L. May & Company had the usual large stock of plants in bloom.

Chas. Vogt did better than last year.   O.

Pittsburg.

SEVERE COLD HARD ON PLANTS IN SHIPMENT.—FLORISTS' CLUB HEARS PAPERS ON ROSES. — BREITMEYERS' EXHIBIT FROZEN.—NEW YEAR'S TRADE GOOD AND STOCK PLENTIFUL.

Roses were the subject for discussion at the Florists' Club meeting January 5. The meeting was well attended. T. P. Langhans illustrated the art of packing roses for shipment. Fred Burke outlined his methods in growing different varieties. Gustav Ludwig spoke on "Best Retailing Roses." Roses for private cultivators were discussed by David Fraser and pot roses and how to grow them by John Jones. J. Cook, of Baltimore, sent, under number, three varieties of roses,

red, pink and white, which seem to possess good qualities, but will hardly surpass the present standard varieties. Blind Brothers displayed some fine Bride and Bridesmaid, as did the Pittsburg Rose and Carnation Company. It is deeply regretted the shipment of La Detroit from Breitmeyer's Sons arrived frozen.

New Year's business was as usual, which means very good. At present the excessively cold weather makes business somewhat unstable. Flowers from the east suffered to a considerable extent in crossing the mountains, and even local conditions demanded extra heavy packing to resist the cold. Natural gas pressure at all the plants near here seems sufficient. Everything in flowers seems to be good and the supply liberal.

Mrs. E. A. Williams decorated the Pitts., burg club for the assembly ball on New Year's eve, and also supplied flowers at the Kennedy ball at the Schenley New Year's day.

L. I. Neff is to be congratulated on his recent window display of red tulips.

Geddes & Blind Brothers will build a new palm house, 20x90.

Syracuse, N. Y.

THERMOMETER HUGS THE ZERO MARK.—FLORISTS' EXPENSES INCREASE AND BUSINESS IS LESS.—HOLLY SCARCE IN HOLLY DAYS.—CALIFORNIA VIOLETS POPULAR.

For a week the thermometer has hugged the zero mark, going as low as 18° below, the coldest weather Syracuse has had for many years. This called a halt in business and increased the expenses of the florists, who have to keep shoveling the coal into their heaters to keep things from freezing up. As far as can be learned no serious damage was done by the cold. Had it not been for several large funerals business would have been very slow.

The holiday trade was as good as usual with no special features. The supply of holly for the first time in years ran out and none could be bought at any florist's store or grocery in the city. For several years back too much holly has been shipped in with the result that much of it was a loss to the retailers. Resolving not to be caught that way this year everybody ordered a great deal less than usual.

P. R. Quinlan & Company report a large demand for California violets, which are nearly as popular as the double variety. They brought $3.50 a hundred during the holidays. All the florists, used at the South Salina street store are being furnished from the new greenhouses at Onondaga valley.

All the florists are having difficulty in delivering their orders without having them frost bitten. Patent heaters, several folds of newspapers and other methods are being resorted to.   A. J. B.

Memphis, Tenn.

All florists here had a good increase in holiday trade over last year. Holly and mistletoe was fine and there was a good demand for holly wreaths, festooning and Christmas trees. All kinds of decorative material was cleaned up.

The Idlewild Greenhouses also had a very pretty display of azaleas, cyclamens, bulbous stock, decorative material and calla lilies.

The Memphis Floral Company had an attractive window of azaleas and bulbous stock.

The weather has been cold.   W. W.

THE AMERICAN FLORIST

NINETEENTH YEAR.

Subscription, $1.00 a year. To Europe, $2.00.
Subscriptions accepted only from those
in the trade.

Advertisements on all except cover pages,
10 Cents a Line, Agate; $1.00 per inch.
Cash with Order.

No Special Position Guaranteed.

Discounts are allowed only on consecutive insertions, as follows—6 times, 5 per cent; 13 times,
10 per cent; 26 times, 20 per cent;
52 times, 30 per cent.

Space on front pages and back cover page sold
only on yearly contract at $1.00 per inch, net.

The Advertising Department of the AMERICAN
FLORIST is for florists, seedsmen and nurserymen
and dealers in wares pertaining to those lines only.

Orders for less than one-half inch space not accepted.

Advertisements must reach us by Wednesday to
secure insertion in the issue for the following
Saturday. Address

AMERICAN FLORIST CO., Chicago.

When sending us change of address, always send
the old address at the same time.

Send in your subscription now for the
ensuing year.

BUCHARIS require little or no water
until they show flower. Then give an
abundance of water, with a little liquid
manure occasionally.

NEPHROLEPIS WESTONI is the name of
a new fern to be introduced in England
this season. It is described as a seedling
from N. exaltata or N. acuta, having the
tips of the pinnæ prettily crested.

IF the Pierson fern or any of the other
forms of nephrolepis are pale and
yellowish a table spoonful of Clay's
fertilizer applied to each plant occasionally will prove efficacious in inducing a
healthy green color.

LORRAINE BEGONIA will thrive and
bloom for many weeks in the dwelling house if it has been properly grown.
When it drops its blossoms in a week or
two under reasonably intelligent home
care it is "up to" the grower to explain.

LIKE all good things the salt water
remedy for red spider on carnations may
be overdone, as some growers have found
to their sorrow. A mixture of ground
tobacco and sulphur is a safer remedy in
the hands of inexperienced or careless
workmen.

MANY large dealers and shippers of
growing plants are now using double
thicknesses of a special corrugated paper
for frost-proof covering. The corruga-
tions insure an air space all around the
package than which there is no better
protection.

ROBERT CRAIG & SON, of Philadelphia,
Pa., found ready sale at Christmas for
Lorraine begonias in combination with
Pteris serrulata cristata in shallow pans.
A nicely variegated form of this begonia
has appeared here, the foliage being
mottled with light yellow.

Now is the time when the carnation
grower is apt to have more or less trouble
with bursting calyxes. The addition of
a little more heat, say 5°, will often
obviate it. A little nitrate of soda and
an occasional application of liquid
manure as a stimulant is also helpful
now.

AN observant and long-experienced
palm grower asserts that the majority of
growers make a mistake in keeping their
palms so heavily shaded and advocates
more light as conducive to health and
the "toughness" so essential in plants to
be used for general commercial decorative purposes.

ANCUBUS are rapidly coming to the
front as decorative plants for exposed
places, cold halls, etc., their tough green
or variegated foliage and bright berries
(on the female forms) standing considerable freezing without injury. They would
be especially acceptable as Christmas
subjects, were it not for the difficulty in
collecting the fruit so early in the season.

LILY OF THE VALLEY and Roman hyacinths often reach the wholesale market
with the lower bells water-soaked because
of careless handling after cutting. A
good plan with all such flowers is to
have a covering of wire netting for the
pans or other receptacles in which the
flowers are kept, with meshes large
enough to admit the stems but prevent
the flowers from sinking down into the
water.

Chrysanthemum Society of America.

WORK OF COMMITTEES.

John Burton was exhibited by Nathan
Smith & Son, Adrian, Mich., at Chicago,
December 16, 1903; color, daybreak pink;
Japanese incurved; scored, commercial
scale, 87 points.

The chairman of the Chicago committee reported that "in judging this chrysanthemum, the committee did not take
into consideration the lateness of the
variety, merely judging it on its merits.
If we had considered its lateness and
importance to the trade, it would
undoubtedly have scored at least 90."

FRED. H. LEMON, Sec'y.

Growing Asparagus Plumosus.

ED. AM. FLORIST:—Will you kindly ask
some of the readers of the AMERICAN
FLORIST to give a few hints on growing
Asparagus plumosus? The object is to
grow for short bunches, not strings.
Which would be better, a solid bed or
benches? Would the same treatment do
for Asparagus Sprengeri? F.

For suggestions on growing A. plumosus see answer to another correspondent
in last week's issue of this paper, page
756. At the risk of repitition, however,
let it be emphatically stated that solid
beds should always be used in preference
to benches, whether for strings or sprays,
for the same culture will do for both.
For A. Sprengeri, while the same treatment in a general way might give good
results, we have found it to be a better
plan to place the plants in very rich,
heavy soil in boxes about eight inches
wide, twelve deep and four feet long.
These boxes are elevated to a height of
about four feet, allowing the long
branches to hang over the sides. Place
them along the edge of a wide walk
where the overhanging branches will not
be broken off by passersby. The plants
will stand almost any quantity of feeding in the shape of liquid manure when
they are growing vigorously, and it is
not necessary to disturb them for three
or four years before replanting the boxes.
 G.

KANSAS CITY, MO.—Business at Christmas here was the best in history. Samuel
Murray says he never handled such stock
in plants and cut flowers. Ardisias,
cyclamens, azaleas, poinsettias, Lorraine
begonia, Chinese primroses, baby primroses, pans of hyacinths, etc., were in
demand. Baskets made up of poinsettias
and begonias sold well at good prices.
Pierson ferns went well. Prices on plants
were better than any previous year.
Beauties brought better prices.

Detroit.

CHRISTMAS TRADE SATISFACTORY.—CAR-
NATIONS SHORT, THROWING HEAVY
DEMAND TOWARD PLANTS. — AMERICAN
BEAUTY ROSES SCARCE.

Christmas trade, contrary to general
expectations, was very good, and generally better than the same period a year
ago. The most notable feature of the
Christmas trade this year was the tendency of customers to place their orders
early in the week. The weather was soft
and disagreeable the first days of the
week, but turned colder on Christmas
day after most deliveries had been made.
The trade of Monday and Tuesday
showed great activity. Anticipating a
shortage in the carnation supply, most
retailers prepared a large number of baskets of mixed plants and laid in a stock
of as many flowering plants as possible,
which, together with many Boston ferns
and palms, supplied a feature of the
trade. Ground pine was scarce and
little handled by the retailers. American
Beauty and other roses were very scarce,
the trade calling for many more than the
market afforded. Carnations were short
thirty to forty per cent of the demand.
The violet growers held back their stock
during the first days of the week, and the
accumulations for Thursday and Friday
were not entirely disposed of. The retail
price held most uniformly at $4 per hun-
dred. Poinsettias sold well, the supply
being about equal to the demand. There
was a slow, direct call for Easter lilies,
Roman hyacinths and Paper White narcissi, although, owing to the scarcity of
carnations, much of such stock was used
in boxes of assorted flowers. Azaleas
and other flowering plants met with
much favor, the demand far exceeding
the supply, except cyclamens. Many
Gloire de Lorraine begonias were sold,
but most dealers complain of them dropping their flowers.

The club meeting, January 6, brought
out an attendance of over forty members.
Much interest was shown and arrangements made for facilitating the work to
be connected with the coming carnation
meeting. President Rackham, of the
American Carnation Society, and President Flowerday, of the club, have
appointed several committees to look
after the various phases of the work.
Harmonie Hall, where the S. A. F. held
its convention over four years ago, has
been engaged for the meeting and exhibition. Herman Knope, who has charge
of Breitmeyers' Mack avenue greenhouses,
read a paper on chrysanthemums. His
essay was carefully prepared and fully
covered the essential points of the subject. After a discussion of the same a
vote of thanks was given the essayist.
James Hartshorne, of the Chicago Carnation Company, was present with an
exhibit of a vase of fifty blooms of the
new red carnation Crusader. An interesting feature of the evening was the
reading by Geo. A. Rackham of a steno-
graphic report of. the entire ceremonies
connected with the recent christening of
Breitmeyers' new rose, La Detroit.

Robert Klagge, of Mount Clemens, has
the material on the ground ready for the
erection of two greenhouses each 25x150
feet, to be used for summer roses.

The Jefferson avenue Flower Shop
established about three months ago has
discontinued business.

Visitors: James Hartshorne, Joliet, Ill.;
Arnold Ringier, Chicago; Chas. H. Vick,
representing Wm. Hagemann & Com-
gany, New York; C. W. Ward, representing
R. M. Ward & Company, New York.
 J. F. S.

Obituary.

THOMAS W. EMERSON.

Thomas W. Emerson, one of the oldest seedsmen of New England, died at his home in Salem Depot, N. H., December 28, at the age of seventy years. Mr. Emerson was born in Windham, N. H. When a young man he served as a clerk in the agricultural warehouse of Nourse, Mason & Co., the predecessors of the Ames Plow Company, after which he

The late Thos. W. Emerson.

established himself in the seed business in Boston, holding a position high in the trade for forty years. Five years ago he retired to his farm in New Hampshire on account of ill-health, his business some time previously having been incorporated as the T. W. Emerson Seed Company. He was the best known man in Boston in the specialty of field seeds, did an immense business therein, was a member of the Boston Chamber of Commerce, and was one of the most esteemed and popular men in the seed trade. One daughter, Mrs. Gardner Murphy, survives him.

Providence, R. I.

Flowers are plentiful, most at high prices. Roses have declined in value and wholesale at $3 to $8 per 100 for good flowers. Zero weather prevails, but no casualties have occurred to the greenhouse people.

At the inaugural ceremony at City Hall last week a great many floral baskets, bouquets and horseshoes were in evidence, most of this work falling to the suburban florists.

The Pocasset greenhouses eclipsed previous records by a most satisfactory chrysanthemum season.

J. G. Jensen has a good cut of chrysanthemums. He made a fine horseshoe for Inaugural day.

Pierson, of Norwood, has some of the best double violets of the year.

A. N. Pierson, of Cromwell, was in town last week.

W. Hazard is on the sick list, the result of overwork.

Howard Almy has installed a telephone, 337–3 West. M.

SITUATIONS, WANTS, FOR SALE.

One Cent Per Word.

Cash with the Adv.

Plant Advs. NOT admitted under this head.

Every paid subscriber to the AMERICAN FLORIST for the year 1903 is entitled to a five-line WANT adv. (situations only) free, to be used at any time during the year.

Situation Wanted—By young man as foreman at small place growing carnations, mums and general stock. Good experience, good reference. B O, care American Florist.

Situation Wanted—By young married man as manager of retail store; understands business thoroughly; can give best of references. N S L, care American Florist.

Situation Wanted—As foreman, roses, carnations and general stock; ambition, sober, life experience. State wages and give full particulars. FOREMAN, 595 Pawtucket Ave., Pawtucket, R. I.

Situation Wanted—By a thoroughly reliable and competent grower on a private or commercial place. 20 years' experience in greenhouses and outside work. Married. Reference. F. W. NORTH, Bangs, O.

Situation Wanted—By all-around florist and gardener, well up in flowers, fruits and vegetables. Good references. Alone. Address P. F. GARDENER, care Anna House, 102 N. Clark St., Chicago.

Situation Wanted—By all-around florist; good grower of pot plants; also Easter forced stock and carnations. 15 years' experience. Good reference. State wages. Address A C, care American Florist.

Situation Wanted—By an all-around florist, good grower of roses, carnations; age 35, single; with 20 years of experience. Please state wages and give full particulars. Address BEAUTY, care American Florist.

Situation Wanted—As head gardener on private place, park or institution. New place and the work preferred. Single, German, 30 years of age. Satisfactory references. Will be at liberty March 1st. Address W S, care American Florist.

Situation Wanted—By experienced man as head gardener on private place. In addition to landscape work, understands the care of plants and vegetables under glass and out of doors. Will be at liberty February 1st. Address K W, care American Florist.

Situation Wanted—As working foreman by expert grower of cut flowers and general stock; also designer. German, 36 years' experience. Thoroughly competent, sober and reliable. Please state wages. Address W. A., 19 Rice St., North Cambridge, Mass.

Situation Wanted—By young florist, 25 years of age, at present employed as rose-grower in large Chicago establishment; good grower of roses, carnations and general line of pot plants. Would like to take charge of greenhouse establishment. First-class references. Please state wages. J M, care American Florist.

Help Wanted—Good rose growers at once. SOUTH PARK FLORAL CO., New Castle, Ind.

Help Wanted—Up-to-date rose grower; steady employment; none other need apply. Address T. O'CONNOR, Blackstone Boulevard, Providence, R. I.

Help Wanted—An assistant florist. State experience and wages expected with board and room. Address I. L. PILLSBURY, Galesburg. Ill.

Help Wanted—Florist to assist in general greenhouse work. Also strong boy to learn the trade. Address FRANK BENZ, 2780 N. 40th Ave., Chicago.

Help Wanted—Young man for general help in rose growing. Also man for growing stove plants. State experience. Address J. A. PETERSON, McHenry Ave., Cincinnati, O.

Help Wanted—A first-class grower of American Beauty and Tea roses. A good situation and good wages to the man who can produce quality. Modern houses and every facility. Address ROSES, care American Florist.

Wanted—Annual Reports of the American Carnation Society for 1894, 1895 and 1901. Address CARNATION, care American Florist.

Help Wanted—Assistant for private place, must be good rose grower. Permanent position and good home for the right man. $30.00 per month and board. Single man. Address C. UPFLER, Goranstown, Baltimore, Md.

Help Wanted—Assistant florist for general greenhouse work; one that can take charge of 15,000 square feet of glass if needed. Must be of good ability and workmanship. $30.00 per month with board and room, five more if satisfactory from the 1st of April. Address H H, care American Florist.

Help Wanted—Bright, energetic young man of good address for a Chicago retail store. Must be thoroughly up-to-date as a decorator and designer and a first-class salesman. Address with references as to character and ability, stating wages expected. Address C R S, care American Florist.

Help Wanted—An up-to-date Beauty grower to take charge of new section of 30,000 feet of splendidly built houses. The best possible wages will be paid to grower of gilt-edged stock, and no other need apply. Married man from the West preferred. Address No. 1, care American Florist.

Help Wanted—One or two men. For gentlemens' places. They must be capable of growing vegetables and fruit, together with bedding plants. The care of greenhouse and conservatory, shrubbery and lawn work. Good wages for right men. Situations perm. ent. Inexperienced men need not apply. Address K N, care American Florist.

Wanted—To lease with option of buying a place of from 15,000 to 30,000 sq. feet of glass, wholesale trade preferred with necessary land, house, barns, etc. Must be in good condition and suitable for production of first-class stock. M D, care American Florist.

For Sale or Lease—Greenhouse, 7,000 feet of glass, without stock. Address WILLARD SMITH, Spokane, Wash.

For Sale—Greenhouses; good location for local and shipping business in Michigan. Well stocked. Reason for selling, on account of failing health. H B, care American Florist.

For Sale—Greenhouses. Good location for local and shipping business. Well stocked; winter coal laid in. Will sell cheap if sold at once. Selling on account of failing health. JAS. RICHARDSON, London, O.

For Sale or Lease—Fine greenhouse establishment of 10,000 feet of glass, in good condition and well stocked, with or without dwelling. Fine opening for a single man. Stock reasonable. X Y Z, care American Florist.

For Sale—At a great bargain for quick sale: greenhouses of about 3,500 feet of glass, hot water heat, first-class boiler, large enough to heat double the space, up-to-date ventilators, full of clean, healthy, paying stock. Can sell everything you raise. Will sell houses with or without land. Small amount of cash needed. Reason, old age and failing strength. Address DES MOINES PLANT CO., 38th St., Des Moines, Ia.

For Sale—Three greenhouses situated in West Tenn. About 10,000 square feet glass, well stocked with roses, carnations, palms, ferns and bedding plants. Heated by two Florence hot water heaters. About one and one-quarter acres of ground, 300 feet of old frames which belong to the plant. Everything in first-class condition. No competition. A good bargain. A change of climate necessary for family cause of sale. Address MRS. M. IRIS BROWN, Union City, Tenn.

WANTED.

Position as foreman or manager in an up-to-date establishment; either wholesale, retail or malling. Am up in all branches, catalogue marking, building, heating and growing of fine stock. 25,000 plants grown the past season. Three years in last place. 40 years old and a hustler. Northern place preferred. Married, temperate and strictly business. Best of reference as to ability and business qualities. Address LONE STAR, 611 No. Washington Ave., Dallas, Tex.

FOR SALE.

3 greenhouses. Located hot-water shed and 7 acres of land, house and stable. At Somerton Hills, 15 miles from Philadelphia. Will sell cheap.

Mrs. Geo. McFadden, 1428 Walnut St., Philadelphia.

First-Class Positions

Are regularly filled through advertising in this department. We receive almost daily inquiry for good men in all lines. Advertising rates given above.

INTERNATIONAL FLOWER DELIVERY.

PASSENGER STEAMSHIP MOVEMENTS.

The tables herewith give the scheduled time of departure of ocean steamships carrying first-class passengers from the principal American and foreign ports, covering the space of two weeks from date of this issue of the AMERICAN FLORIST. Much disappointment often results from attempts to forward flowers for steamer delivery by express, to the care of the ship's steward or otherwise. The carriers of these packages are not infrequently refused admission on board and even those delivered on board are not always certain to reach the parties for whom they were intended. Hence florists in interior cities having orders for the delivery of flowers to passengers on out-going steamers are advised to intrust the filling of such orders to some reliable florist in the port of departure, who understands the necessary details and formalities and has the facilities for attending to it properly. For the addresses of such firms we refer our readers to the advertisements on this page:

FROM	TO	STEAMER	*LINE	DAY	DUE ABOUT
New York	Liverpool	Umbria	1	Sat. Jan. 16, 2:00 p. m.	Jan. 22
New York	"	Lucania	1	Sat. Jan. 23, 9:00 a. m.	Jan. 29
New York	Glasgow	Siberian	2	Thur. Jan. 21, Noon.	Jan. 31
New York	Genoa	Deutschland	3	Tues. Jan. 19, 4:00 p. m.	Jan. 29
New York	Hamburg	Patricia	3	Sat. Jan. 16, 4:00 p. m.	Jan. 26
New York	"	Pretoria	3	Sat. Jan. 23, 8:00 a. m.	Feb. 2
New York	Glasgow	Furnessia	5	Sat. Jan. 16, Noon.	Jan. 26
New York	London	Minnetonka	6	Sat. Jan. 16, 5:00 a. m.	Jan. 26
New York	"	Menominee	6	Sat. Jan. 23, 9:00 a. m.	Feb. 2
New York	Liverpool	Celtic	7	Wed. Jan. 13, 2:00 p. m.	Jan. 20
New York	"	Teutonic	7	Wed. Jan. 20, 10:00 a. m.	Jan. 27
Boston	"	Cymric	7	Thur. Jan. 21, Noon.	Jan. 28
Boston	Alexandria	Romanic	7	Sat. Jan. 16, 9:00 a. m.	Feb. 3
New York	Southampton	New York	8	Sat. Jan. 16, 9:30 a. m.	Jan. 21
New York	"	St. Paul	8	Sat. Jan. 23, 9:30 a. m.	Jan. 29
New York	Antwerp	Kroonland	9	Sat. Jan. 23, 10:30 a. m.	Feb. 1
New York	Havre	La Savoie	10	Thur. Jan. 14, 10:00 a. m.	Jan. 24
New York	"	La Bretagne	10	Thur. Jan. 21, 10:08 a. m.	Jan. 31
New York	Rotterdam	Statendam	11	Tues. Jan. 19, 10:00 a. m.	Jan. 29
New York	Genoa	Citta di Milano	12	Tues. Jan. 16, 11:00 a. m.	Jan. 26
New York	"	Sicilia	12	Tues. Jan. 19, 11:00 a. m.	Feb. 3
New York	Bremen	Rhein	13	Tues. Jan. 16, 1:00 p. m.	Jan. 25
New York	Genoa	Prinsess Irene	13	Sat. Jan. 23, 11:00 a. m.	Feb. 5
New York	Naples	Germania	14	Tues. Jan. 19.	Jan. 29
Boston	Liverpool	Devonian	16	Wed. Jan. 13, 6:0 a. m.	Jan. 23
Boston	"	Winifredian	16	Wed. Jan. 20, 11:30 a. m.	Jan. 30

*1 Cunard; 2 Allen-State; 3 Hamburg-American; 4 Scandinavian-American; 5 Anchor Line; 6 Atlantic Transport; 7 White Star; 8 American; 9 Red Star; 10 French; 11 Holland-American; 12 Italian Royal Mail; 13 North German Lloyd; 14 Fabre; 16 Leyland; 17 Occidental and Oriental; 18 Oceanic; 19 Allan; 20 Can. Pacific Ry.; 21 N. Pacific Ry.; 22 Hongkong-Seattle.

INTERNATIONAL FLOWER DELIVERY.

STEAMSHIPS LEAVE FOREIGN PORTS

FROM	TO	STEAMER	*LINE	DAY	DUE ABOUT
Liverpool.........	New York	Saxonia	1	Sat. Jan. 16,	Jan. 23
Liverpool.........	"	Etruria	1	Sat. Jan. 23,	Jan. 29
Glasgow.........	"	Numidian	2	Sat. Jan. 16,	Jan. 26
Genoa............	"	Prinz Adalbert	2	Tues. Jan. 12,	Jan. 24
Genoa............	"	Palatia	2	Tues. Jan. 19,	Jan. 31
Hamburg.........	"	Auguste Victoria	3	Sat. Jan. 16,	Jan. 25
Hamburg.........	"	Bluecher	3	Sat. Jan. 23,	Feb. 2
Glasgow.........	"	Anchoria	5	Sat. Jan. 23,	Feb. 2
London...........	"	Minneapolis	6	Thur. Jan. 14,	Jan. 24
London...........	"	Minnehaha	6	Thur. Jan. 21,	Jan. 31
Liverpool.........	"	Cedric	7	Wed. Jan. 13, 3:00 p. m.	Jan. 20
Liverpool.........	"	Majestic	7	Wed. Jan. 20, 3:00 p. m.	Jan. 27
Liverpool.........	Boston	Canopic	7	Thur. Jan. 14, 3:30 p. m.	Jan. 21
Liverpool.........	"	Cret c	7	Thur. Jan. 21, 3:30 p. m.	Jan. 28
Alexandria	"	Republic	7	Thur. Jan. 21, 3:00 p. m.	Feb. 6
Southampton...	New York	Philadelphia	8	Sat. Jan. 16, Noon	Jan. 22
Southampton...	"	St. Louis	8	Sat. Jan. 23, Noon	Jan. 29
Antwerp.........	"	Zeeland	9	Sat. Jan. 16, Noon	Jan. 25
Antwerp.........	"	Finland	9	Sat. Jan. 23, 3:00 p. m.	Feb. 2
Havre	"	La Touraine	10	Sat. Jan. 16,	Jan. 23
Havre	"	La Champagne	10	Sat. Jan. 23,	Feb. 3
Rotterdam........	"	Rotterdam	11	Sat. Jan. 16,	Jan. 26
Genoa............	"	Nord America	12	Mon. Jan. 11,	Jan. 25
Genoa............	"	Liguria	12	Mon. Jan. 18,	Feb. 2
Bremen..........	"	Main	13	Sat. Jan. 16, 7:00 a. m.	Jan. 23
Bremen..........	"	Chemnitz	13	Sat. Jan. 23, 7:00 a. m.	Jan. 30
Genoa............	"	Hohenzollern	13	Thur. Jan. 21,	Feb. 2
Naples...........	"	Neustria	14	Tues. Jan. 12,	Jan. 24
Marseilles.......	"	Gal ia	14	Sat. Jan. 23,	Feb. 5
Liverpool........	Boston	Canadian	16	Sat. Jan. 16,	Jan. 26
Liverpool........	"	Cestrian	16	Sat. Jan. 23,	Feb. 2

See steamship list on opposite page.

The Seed Trade.

AMERICAN SEED TRADE ASSOCIATION.
S. F. Willard, Pres.; J. Charles McCullough,
First Vice-Pres.; C. E. Kendel, Cleveland, O.,
Sec'y and Treas.
Twenty-second annual convention St. Louis,
Mo., June, 1904.

A. H. Goodwin, of the Goodwin-Harries Company, Chicago, is now in Buffalo on business.

Currie Brothers, of Milwaukee, Wis., have the order to supply the state exhibit at the World's Fair.

Lima Beans seem to be a drug on the market, the Henderson variety particularly being in surplus.

H. W. Buckbee, of Rockford, Ill., reports a southern trade to date much in advance of last year.

The canners' convention, which will be held at Columbus, O., February 9, will attract many seedsmen and seed growers.

Onion sets that are keeping well should be in demand later, as many lots are full of soft stock requiring much hand picking.

Mail trade business in other lines is reported starting in good. Next week we expect some reports from the leading seedsmen in this line.

Gladiolus should be turned over when kept in the bins at least once a week to keep from sprouting. If they become troubled with greenfly sprinkle with tobacco dust once a week.

Thos. W. Emerson, of the T. W. Emerson Seed Company, Boston, Mass., died December 28 at his home in Salem Depot, N. H. For obituary and portrait see page 911.

Visited Chicago.—A. J. Brown, Grand Rapids, Mich.; B. Suzuki and O. Tsuji, Yokohama, Japan; Jos. A. Schindler, of Schindler & Company, New Orleans, La., enroute to Detroit, Mich.

It is reported that Detroit seed houses have cut the price on pickling cucumber seed below that usually asked by other seed houses and thereby secured considerable business that had been held back, hoping for a break in the market.

A Sign of Prosperity.

The accompanying engraving shows the new building recently erected by the Manitowoc Seed Company, Manitowoc, Wis. It is fireproof and is used for warehouse and wholesale seed purposes. The first floor is used for storage, shipping and receiving seeds. The second floor contains the bulk seed room, packing room and hand picking room. The third floor is used for milling and storing. With the elevators and complete machinery, the thorough, speedy and economical handling of seed peas is assured.

Old Seeds Versus Fresh Seeds.

In a paper read before the Paris Horticultural Congress in May last, the following conclusions are noted:

In the majority of cases fresh seeds give the best results, but with the following exceptions: With carrots, two-year-old seed gives less leafy plants and more highly colored roots. The use of three or four year old chicory seed tends to prevent premature greening. With cabbage, the use of two or three year old seed tends to produce better heads than fresh seed. With gherkins, pumpkins and melons, seed two or three years old is preferred; fresh seed produces too leafy vegetation. Likewise corn salad seed two or three years old is preferred to fresh seed. With radishes,

fresh seed is preferred for outdoor soil, since it produces more robust plants, but seed two or three years old is preferred under glass because it produces a less leafy product.

Commenting on these results, M. Bazin stated that fresh seed should always be preferred when it is wished to produce plants with a strong leaf growth, while for plants which it is desired should head well like cabbage, salads, melons, cucumbers, etc. it is preferable to use seeds two to three years old. With ornamental plants, particularly with balsams, seed more than a year old tends to produce double flowers to a much greater extent than fresh seed.

Milwaukee.

NEW YEAR'S TRADE IS FAIR.—STOCK IN SHORT SUPPLY—LARGE FUNERAL ORDERS AND DECORATIONS.—NEWS OF THE FLORISTS' CLUB.

Trade for New Year was fair, but I believe that the total amount of business done is not up to former years. Stock was not at all plentiful excepting white carnations and Bride roses, of which there was a slight surplus. On Friday and Saturday the demand was exceptionally heavy as large quantities of flowers were required for the funerals of the victims of the Iroquois theater and for the funeral of Capt. Pabst, the wealthy brewer. According to the best information there were more flowers at the last named funeral than have ever before been seen here at one time. Trade this week has been rather light, but this is generally the case immediately after the holidays. The high prices that have been prevailing have had a tendency to reduce the amount of business, but with more reasonable prices there is no doubt that business will keep right up from now on.

The Florists' Club held its regular meeting on Tuesday night. The officers for the coming year were installed. They are W. A. Kennedy, president; Fred. A. Holton, vice-president; Herman V. Hunkel, secretary; C. Dallwig, treasurer. The club decided to have a carnation meeting in February and several very liberal prizes will be offered. The club further appointed a committee to confer with the Manufacturers' and Merchants' associations to ascertain it there is no way by which those small words "please omit flowers" may be overcome. During a recent funeral large orders were countermanded as a result of this notice, and there is no doubt that considerable loss is incurred on this account.

Among the many floral testimonials at the Pabst funeral none attracted greater attention than a broken wheel, wrought of white blossoms. It was the wheel of the helmsman of a steamboat, with a portion of the rim and some of the spokes gone, the contribution of Charles Fischer and Oscar Mueller in recognition of the love that Captain Pabst had for the men who go down to the sea in ships.

Last Saturday Wm. Edlefsen had several very large designs, among others a five-foot wreath of violets and valley. Fred Schmeling had the misfortune to break his ankle by making a misstep when alighting from his cutter.

Mrs. Siekert, with Home Brothers, has been on the sick list for the last six weeks. Wm. Ellis has been kept busy with several good sized decorations.　H.

Des Moines, Ia.

The retail establishments of R. L. Blair and W. L. Morris have been consolidated, they with W. E. Kemble, of Oskaloosa, forming a stock company to be known as the Morris-Blair Floral Company. The new firm will occupy for the present Mr. Morris' store on Walnut street. Mr. Morris, being somewhat run down in health and needing a rest, will devote himself to growing stock for the company. Wm. Kemble will sell his surplus stock to the company. Mr. Blair will be in charge of the store business with able assistants.

R. L. B.

NEW STUCTURE OF THE MANITOWOC SEED COMPANY.

THE NURSERY TRADE.

AM. ASSOCIATION OF NURSERYMEN. N. W. HALE, Knoxville, Tenn., Pres.; FRANK A. WEBER, St. Louis, Mo., Vice-Pres.; GEORGE C. SEAGER, Rochester, N. Y., Sec'y. Twenty-ninth annual convention, Atlanta, Ga., June, 1904.

BRIDGEWATER, N. S.—The annual meeting of the Fruit Growers' Association of Nova Scotia will be held here January 27.

AUGUSTA, GA.—The Southern Orchard Planting Company has been incorporated with a capital of $100,000. J. Berry and A. M. French, incorporators.

DURANT, I. T.—What is to be the largest nursery farm in the Indian Territory is being put in on the Tone Sexton plantation adjoining Durant on the west.

OAKLAND, CAL.—The resolution authorizing the board of works to advertise for bids to plant American elm trees along Telegraph avenue has been favorably recommended by the public improvement committee of the city council.

SHREVEPORT, LA.—Downs & Company, seedsmen, nurserymen and florists, have purchased the Shreveport Nursery Company and are now the only firm here in the business. Trade has been very dull. There is a good demand for cut carnations and roses here and lots of mistletoe and holly are shipped north.

CHARLESTON, S. C.—Oliver L. Schlosser, 30 years of age, proprietor of the Millsdale nursery and an expert landscape gardener who came to this state from Chicopee, Mass., has mysteriously disappeared from his home in Greenville. He left there on December 15, promising to return in three days and has not been heard from since.

GUTHRIE, OKLA.—The Oklahoma Nursery purchased the William Murray farm just north of Guthrie, for $15,000, December 23. This is headquarters for the company in Oklahoma. A large plant will be erected for packing and shipping trees and a switch will be built to the farm from the Santa Fe and the Denver, Enid and Gulf railroads.

PHOENIX, ARIZ.—The last three years have nearly finished up the nursery business in this valley, most of the stock sold here being shipped in from the coast. The water supply here is too uncertain for nursery work. Nearly all the pumped water is full of alkali which kills young stock. We hope for better things with the completion of the reservoir, but that will be several years.

Atlanta, Ga.

State Entomologist Willman Newell, in a statement issued December 4, tells of the great increase in the fruit nurseries of Georgia and the number of trees grown in each. Since August he has inspected 191 nurseries and issued certificates to each. Only six nurseries contained trees which were infected with San Jose scale, and certificates were of course not issued to these. Mr. Newell says: "During the season of 1902 there were but 108 nurseries in the state, whereas since August 1, 1903, the state department of entomology has inspected and issued certificates to 191 nurseries, containing a total of 10,514,000 trees. The different fruit trees grown in these nurseries are as follows: Peach, 8,370,000; apple, 990,-000; pecan, 788,000; plum, 216,000; pear, 82,000; cherry, 40,000; grape, 15,000; china trees, 7,000; mulberries,

6,000. Total, 10,514,000. These figures do not include six nurseries, containing 236,000 trees, which were infested with San Jose scale.

"Of the total number of peach trees, 8,370,000, we estimate upon a safe basis that approximately one-third, or 2,790,-000, are available for planting the coming winter. Approximately 5,580,000 peach trees (dormant-budded, grafted and small June budded stock) will be carried through to next season by the nurserymen, all of which will be available for the season of 1904-'05. There will be between five and six million peach trees for sale by the Georgia nurseries next year. It seems very improbable that the planting of peach trees in commercial orchards will reach these enormous figures in 1904-'05, hence a large surplus of stock with correspondingly low prices may be expected. Of the 990,000 apple trees, probably one-fourth or 250,000 will be planted this winter."

Galveston, Tex.

J. D. Pruessner is building a new plant in a high portion of the city. He is just finishing a new house 20x100 and has also opened a store on Tremont street in which business for the holidays was excellent.

Trade has been fine for Christmas in cutflowers, as well as in plants. Plants in fancy baskets were very much in evidence.

W. A. Hawkins is pushing his cut flower business. He runs a store on Tremont street.

Mrs. Aichholz has gone to Germany for her health and left Mrs. Hansen in charge of the store.

Four thousand feet of the sea wall for the protection of the city have been finished.

Paul Poppe is growing a fine lot of plants and selling at wholesale to the trade.

Chas. Steding is doing a rushing retail business. P.

Buffalo.

MOST SATISFACTORY HOLIDAY TRADE.—INDIVIDUAL FLORISTS' REPORTS.—CARNATIONS NOT PLENTIFUL.—PAPERS READ AT FLORISTS' CLUB.

Trade for the holidays was very satisfactory to all. Poinsettias had the call above all other plants, azaleas coming next. Primroses and Begonia Gloire de Lorraine sold well, the latter bringing from $1.50 to $3 for good plants. Violets were sold by nearly all florists at $4 per hundred. The prices of cut flowers were nearly all as follows: Roses, Bride and Meteor, $3 and $4 per dozen; Perle, $2.50 to $3; Golden Gate, $3; carnations, $1 to $2; American Beauty, $15 to $18 per dozen; valley $1.50 per bunch; narcissi and Roman hyacinths, 75 cents per dozen; poinsettias and pans and single flowers sold beyond all expectations and the flowers were good. The reason attributed for the gradual dropping off of the cut flower trade is the high prices and, in many instances, poor quality. Carnations were not plentiful and at the prices offered one would take a plant at $1 in preference to carnations at the same price. Bells of all kinds were a glut on the market, while the immortelle wreaths sold well.

A call on the trade found the following reports on the Christmas business: Palmer & Son report an increase over last year; J. H. Rebstock's store trade from a cut flower point was not as good; plant trade far in excess of last year. R. M. Rebstock reports trade good in plants and a total increase of about twenty-five per cent; Byrne & Slattery's trade was beyond expectation. Plants and cut flowers sold well; L. H. Neubeck's trade was good, all stocks selling out; Wm. Scott's cash sales exceeded last year and charges fully as good; S. A. Anderson never had as good a trade. Plants sold far in advance of cut flowers.

For New Year's the trade in Buffalo is limited. The old time custom of entertaining is gone and the principal trade is in sending bunches, baskets, etc., to incoming city and county officials and the decorations in the several clubs. Funeral work was quiet for the week preceding Christmas but last week it was very brisk.

The next meeting of the Florists' Club will be enlivened by a paper on the retail store, by S. A. Anderson. A different paper will be read at each meeting by local and visiting growers and dealers, which we hope will add more life to the club.

W. F. Kasttog reports trade at home and shipping as very good but his holly arrived very late. BISON.

Hartford, Conn.

The Hartford Florists' Club had its regular meeting December 29. Holiday trade was reported as being very good. The chairman of the entertainment committee, R. Karlstrom, was instructed to prepare for the club's annual banquet, which will probably take place late in January or early in February.

Park Superintendent Theodore Wirth and his wife gave a Christmas party for a number of gardener friends with their families Christmas day. Mr. Scrivener, superintendent of Cedar Hill cemetery, acted the part of Santa Claus.

A small greenhouse belonging to Miss Alice Taintor, 28 Garden street, was burned down December 27 owing to an overheated furnace. The loss is estimated at about $300, covered by insurance.
R. K.

OUR PASTIMES.

Announcements of coming contests or other events of interests to our bowling, shooting and sporting readers are solicited and will be given place in this column. Address all correspondence for this department to Wm. J. Stewart, 42 W. 28th St., New York; Robt. Kift, 1725 Chestnut St., Philadelphia, Pa.; to the American Florist Co., Chicago, Ill.

At St. Louis.

The following are the scores of the last session of the Florists' Club bowling team. Beneke, of the first team, rolled over the 200 mark:

FIRST TEAM.

Player.	1st.	2nd.	3rd.	T'l.
Beneke	204	167	170	541
Miller	142	184	157	5 3
Adles	150	144	143	437
Meinhardt	136	135	164	435
Grand Total				1,906

SECOND TEAM.

Player.	1st.	2nd.	3rd.	T'l.
Kuehn	184	176	146	476
Ellison	183	139	170	492
Ellis	134	133	161	428
O. R. Beneke	146	126	171	443
Grand Total				1,839

At Chicago.

The bowlers held a meeting Thursday evening at Winterson's, which was attended by a large and enthusiastic membership. Matters pertaining to the good of the club were freely discussed and a plan outlined for the handicap games, which are to be rolled during the next few months. The resignation of Joseph Foerster as captain was accepted. Adjournment was then taken

to the Geroux alleys, where two games were rolled. Mrs. Phil Hauswirth is getting quite proficient in the art of bowling, having made the high scores of 167 and 197. Phil will have to get a "move on" if he expects to hold the medal in his family. The scores:

Player	1st	2d
G. Asmus	161	177
Stevens	182	140
Geo. Scott	198	161
Kil	136	151
Balluf	203	167
Kreitling	124	118
F. Stollery	147	169
G. Stollery	197	145
Hauswirth	129	119
Degnan	147	147
Winterson	153	
Chas. Benesch	66	
Mrs. Phil Hauswirth	167	197
Mrs. Geo. Asmus	100	133

Philadelphia Bowling Averages.

The tournament averages for the five weeks' series, November and December, were as follows:

Player.	Av.	Player.	Av.
Johnson	174	Goebel	153
Robertson	167	Kift	153
Connor	166	Graham	152
Yates	165	Zimerman	152
Bonsall	165	Mehortar	150
Moss	164	Adelberger	149
Anderson	164	Holme	149
Allen	163	Dungan	148
Falck	163	Craig	147
Polites	161	Gibson	145
Dunbar	161	Westnott	143
Watson	143	Baker	145
Moore	158	Merbitz	137
Dunlap	154	Baxter	129
Harris	153	Seaman	114

It is to be noted that the above are not the monthly averages of the members, but the averages for the tournament match games with every man tuned to

his finest pitch. Many a man can make a fine score when there's no stake up. It takes a series of match games to show the grit in a player's make-up. Consistent bowling also counts for something. For instance, the team that won the pennant in the above series were not up at the top among the averages, but were Messrs. Anderson, Dunham, Watson, Moore and Merbitz. They managed to get the pins when they needed them.

W.

Atlanta, Ga.

Holiday business here was twenty-five per cent better than last year. A better class of stock of all kinds was in the market than for some years past. C. J. Austin, of Mississippi, was in town this week in consultation with local people regarding the erection of a large range of glass to be devoted principally to roses and carnations for the wholesale trade. The new venture will probably be launched in Birmingham or Chattanooga. Chas. A. Hearl, an old Atlanta man, and erstwhile protege of Colon Egston will have charge of the establishment.

J. A.

PEORIA, ILL.—James C. Murray, the florist, is confined to his bed with illness and will not be able to be out for a month or two.

GREENSBURG, IND.—Through the failure of the heating apparatus to work properly the plants in two of Mrs. Dehimer's greenhouses, near this city, were destroyed by frost January 3. The loss will exceed $500.

REVIEW OF THE WORK OF THE CHRYSANTHEMUM SOCIETY OF AMERICA FOR 1903.

NAME.	Where shown.	Date.	EXHIBITED BY	Color.	Type.	POINTS SCORED.										
						Scale.	Color.	Form.	Fullness.	Stem, foliage.	Substance.	Size.	Distinctiveness.	Stem.	Foliage.	Total.
Rockford	Chic'go	Oct. 24	H. W. Buckbee, Rockford, Ill.	Yellow	Jap. Inc.	C	23	22	13	10	9	11				88
(a) H. W. Buckbee	Chic'go	"	"	Pure white	Jap. Ref.	C	26	23	14	8	9	12				91
(b) Sport of V-Morel	N. Y.	Nov. 21	F. Backofen, Paterson, N. J.	Pure white												
Seedling No. 3	Phila.	Nov. 7	Richard Rothe, Gar., Laverock, Pa.	White	Jap. Ref.	C	22	21	14	6	8	13				84
Seedling No. 3	Phila.	"	"	White	Jap. Ref.	C	14	19	9			13	12	6	8	84
Golden Age	Phila.	"	N. Smith & Son, Adrian, Mich.	Rich yellow	Jap. Ref.	C	23	21	13	8	8	13				86
Golden Age	Phila.	"	"	Rich yellow	Jap. Ref.	C	13	13	9			10	21	8	8	92
Golden Age	Cinci'ti	"	"	Deep yellow	Jap. Inc.	C	22	22	13	7	9	13				86
Golden Age	N. Y.	Nov. 11	"	Bright orange yellow	Jap. Ref.	C	25	16	12	9	9	10				81
Sunburst 1-02-01	N. Y.	"	"	Yellow	Jap. Inc.	C	23	19	15	7	9	13				86
Sunburst 1-02-01	Cinci'ti	Nov. 14	"	Deep yellow	Jap. Inc.	C	23	21	13	4	8	13				84
2-16-01	Cinci'ti	Nov. 28	"	Bright deep pink	Jap. Inc.	C	23	20	13	7	7	12				83
29-4-03	N. Y.	Nov. 11	"	Creamy white	Jap. Inc.	C	20	15	15	9	9	12				80
3-3-01	Boston	Nov. 28	"	Light pink		C	10	10	9				12	22	5	5	78
(c) Dr. Enguehard	Cinci'ti	Nov. 14	"	Bright pink	Jap.	C	23	23	15	10	10	14				95
Mrs. N. Smith	N. Y.	Nov. 11	"	Pure white		C	25	22	12	9	9	12				89
Miss Helen Frick	N. Y.	Nov. 28	"	Light rose pink, silvery reverse	Jap. Inc.	C										
Miss Helen Frick	Chic'go	Nov. 28	"	Pink		C	23	22	15	8	9	10				87
(d) John Burton	Phila.	Dec. 12	"	Pink	Jap. Inc.	C	23	23	14	8	9	12				89
John Burton	N. Y.	Dec. 9	"	Light rose pink	Jap. Inc.	C	21	20	14	5	10	15				85
John Burton	Chic'go	Dec. 16	"	Pink	Jap. Inc.	C	20	23	15	8	8	13				87
John Burton	Cinci'ti	Dec. 19	"	Very light pink	Jap. Inc.	C	18	22	15	9	10	12				86
Dr. Enguehard	Phila.	Nov. 21	F. R. Pierson, Tarrytown, N. Y.	Pink	Jap. Inc.	E	23	23	17	7	9	12				90
Dr. Enguehard	Phila.	"	"	Pink	Jap. Inc.	C	24	13	14	9		12	23	7	8	86
(e) Dr. Enguehard	Chic'go	"	"	Pink	Jap. Inc.	C	21	23	14	8	10	10				86
Dr. Enguehard	N. Y.	Nov. 14	"	Rose pink	Jap. Inc.	C	23	23	15	9	10	11				87
Madona	Cinci'ti	Nov. 7	H. W. Rieman, Indianapolis, Ind.	Light pink	Jap. Inc.	C	30	23	15	8	8	13				86
(f) Madona	Chic'go	"	"	Pink	Jap. Inc.	C	20	23	13	9	9	12				84
(g) Adelia	Chic'go	Nov. 14	"	White	Jap. Inc.	C	23	21	14	7	9	10				84
Adelia	Cinci'ti	"	"	White	Jap. Inc.	C	21	21	15	6	9	10				87
(h) American Beauty	N. Y.	Nov. 21	H. Molatsch. Rochester, N. Y.	Magenta	Jap. Inc.	C	20	23	14	9	8	10				88
Wm. J. Perraud	Chic'go	Oct. 24	E. G. Hill Co., Richmond, Ind.	Cream yellow	Jap. Inc.	C	15	22	12	9	9	13				80
China	Chic'go	"	"	Deep yellow	Chinese	E	14	14	9	6	10	10				80
(i) Lord Hopetoun	Chic'go	"	"	Red	Jap. Inc.	E	22	23	13	8	9	14				87
Ethel Fitzroy	Chic'go	"	"	Bronze gold	Jap. Inc.	E	14	13	9			15	23	5	7	86

REMARKS:—(a) Center incurved, outer petals reflexed. (b) Believed by the committee to be Eda Prass, not scored. (c) Imported by Nonin. (d) Soft daybreak pink, silvery reverse, giving a shell pink appearance. (e) Col. Appleton type, silvery reverse. (f) Type of Major Bonnaffon. (g) Ball shape. (h) Silvery reverse. (i) Color of George W. Childs.

FRED. H. LEMON, Sec

Kansas City, Mo.

FLORISTS EXPERIENCE PROSPEROUS HOLIDAY TRADE.—BLOOMING PLANTS IN FINE DEMAND.—CHRISTMAS PRICES.

The most essential factor, good weather, was with us during Christmas week. Delivery of plants was made up to noon of Christmas day without wrapping. Conservative estimates of the storemen place the increase for Christmas business at about twenty-five per cent. One notable feature was the increased sale and call for good blooming plants. Green stock sold as well as in former years. Holly was of indifferent quality, one case good, next case poor. California red peppers sold well. The average retail prices brought at Christmas follow: American Beauty roses from $4 to $20 per dozen, latter price slow sale; Bride, Bridesmaid, Perle, $2 to $5; Liberty, Chatenay and Sunrise, $2 to $6; poinsettias, $5 to $8 per dozen; violets, single $1, double $1.25 per bunch of twenty-five; carnations, 75 cents to $1 per dozen; fancy, $1.50 to $2.50 per dozen; narcissi, $1 per dozen; Romans, 75 cents; valley, $1 per dozen. At Rock's store was displayed a choice assortment of all the leading plants suitable for holiday trade, among which were a nice lot of well grown pot lilacs, cyclamens, azaleas, begonias, poinsettias and primroses, all sold before Christmas morning. Remarkable sales of red immortelle bells and red balls were made by this firm.

Kelloggs report a substantial increase in their store and also at their greenhouses at Pleasant Hill. They had a fine lot of azaleas which came in a week late.

New Year's trade averaged about the same as last year, the principal demand being for choice boxes of roses and bunches of violets.

Murray had a fine lot of Begonia Gloire de Lorraine, azaleas, poinsettias in pans and Roman hyacinths in pans which found ready sale. W.

HELENA, MONT.—Business has been somewhat backward here of late and chrysanthemums were much too plentiful to be profitable. Carnations sold well.

Lowell, Mass.

Never before have we experienced anything like the business done last week. The Christmas rush kept up until Friday noon, when everybody went home to get a much needed rest, having worked continually day and night for almost a week. Everything in bloom was offered for sale from a well grown azalea down to a geranium, and all found a ready market, especially azaleas, which brought good prices. Red bells suspended in the windows on red ribbons caught the public and sold quickly. Begonia Gloire de Lorraine lost none of its old time popularity. Poinsettias in pans fixed up with Porto Rican mets and tied with ribbon to match found ready sale. In fact, everything that bore a flower found a customer. There was an abundance of Christmas greens of all kinds. Holly was far better than a year ago. It had been feared there would be a shortage of flowers, but with a few good days before the rush the supply was far greater than expected, more than enough to fill the heavy demands. Carnations brought good figures. Ten dollars per 100 was the prevailing price for Lawson and Fairmaid, although some of the growers got $15 without trouble. No pickled or sleepy stock was offered for sale. Violets ran from $2 to $2.50 per 100 wholesale and sold like hot cakes. The demand for roses was better than last year and prices ran higher. Customers who were unwilling to loosen up $5 for a bunch of 100 violets readily bought a dozen Bridesmaid for the same figure.

What made the storemen happy was to find a channel to float out the surplus of flowers Saturday, when there were many funeral orders.   A. M.

Albany, N. Y.

Reports of Christmas trade made by the local florists are of a most encouraging character. Danker, of Maiden Lane, said his business was at least $100 better Christmas week than in the corresponding period of 1902. He sold 1,000 holly wreaths. Eyres reports that the demand was for plants, violets and carnations in the order named. Christmas bells and holly wreaths sold in unusually large numbers. W. C. King, 30 North Pearl street, made an encouraging report on cash sales. Messrs. Danker, Eyres and King each has a handsome calender which he is distributing to customers.   R. D.

Toronto.

EIGHTEEN BELOW ZERO DOESN'T HELP THE FLORISTS—CHRISTMAS PRICES PREVAIL FOR GOOD STOCK, WHICH IS SCARCE.—MANY FATALITIES IN FAMILIES OF THE CRAFT.

We have had extremely cold weather since January 1, ranging from zero to as low as 18° below, which has kept the growers busy at the fires. This is not the kind of weather to produce blooms, nor is it the kind for the retailers to sell flowers, and though there is not much doing good stock is hardly plentiful enough to fill orders. In the houses there is an excellent showing of buds and a few days' sun will see quantities of stock of all kinds abundant. Roses are good and still quoted at Christmas prices. Carnations are scarce, as the buds are not moving, and also retain their holiday figures. Violets are becoming more plentiful and have dropped to $2 per 100. Harrisii lilies are no longer a rarity, while callas, daffodils, hyacinths and narcissi are becoming more plentiful each day. The last year was the most successful in the local florists' history, and good reports of prosperity are numerous among the local craft.

James Rossiter, Jr., a son of the florist of that name, was killed last week. He was a fireman on a local railroad, and while attempting to look back at the end of his train from the cab window was struck by a passing engine.

Mrs. Lightfoot died of heart failure December 26. This is a large number of fatalities in so short a period, and the families of the deceased have the sympathy of the local florists.

Walter Muston was re-elected as councillor in North Toronto. He is evidently the right man in that place.

Grobba and Wandrey have some well grown lilacs and valley from this season's pips, which find ready sale.

Geo. Phillips, landscape gardener, and once prominent in the Florists' Club, died a few days ago.

D. J. Sinclair is suffering from rheumatism, and it is with difficulty that he gets around.   H. Y. D.

BAYSIDE, N. Y.—The greenhouses of Wm. Bell were totally destroyed by fire on the morning of January 6. There was no insurance. Deep sympathy is felt for Mr. Bell throughout the trade of New York, where Mr. Bell is held in the highest esteem.

Los Angeles, Cal.

Everyone reports a generally good holiday business. The outdoor stock was not as good as usual, but that grown indoors was especially fine. Outdoor carnations sold at 75 cents and $1 per dozen and none were left over. Outdoor roses sold for $2 and $3 per dozen. Hothouse carnations brought $1 to $1.50 per dozen, and roses as follows: American Beauty, twenty-inch stem, $5 and . $6; American Beauty, thirty-inch stem, $8 to $12; Bride and Bridesmaid, average, $4 per dozen. Potted plants were not in much demand. Pots of hyacinths and valley brought $1, azaleas $4, Boston ferns, Asparagus Sprengeri and A. plumosus, 5 and 6-inch pots, brought $1 to $1.50. Smilax was in great demand and brought on an average 12½ cents a string of six feet. Violets brought 50 cents per bunch of twenty-five for Princess from San Francisco and the same for a bunch of fifty Princess home grown. Probably 6,000 bunches were disposed of Christmas day alone.

The Grace Hill Nursery Company will build seven more 250-foot greenhouses this spring. They are making a pronounced success of carnations under glass, their favorites being Enchantress, Gov. Roosevelt, Lawson, Flora Hill, Louise, Manly and Estelle.

Dietrich & Huston are constantly enlarging their place and in the last year have built several moderate sized glass and lath houses.

Harry Turner, formerly of Cleveland, O., is working for the Grace Hill Nursery Company on Boyle Heights.

Bimo Mesure at Burnett is planting out five acres more of Princess violets this season, 120,000 plants.

The Ingleside Floral Company is producing some very nice American Beauty.

Miss Kaestner has opened a retail floral establishment at 631 South Broadway.

Gus. Smith has charge of the retail department of the E. J. Vawter Company.

E. J. Fry has opened a retail store at 646 South Broadway. POPPY.

Louisville, Ky.

Chas. Rayner, of Anchorage, Ky., met with a severe loss just before Christmas. The water got too low and burned the boilers so badly that he had difficulty in keeping his houses from freezing. The carnation houses got down to 32° and the rose houses to 45°. He has ordered a large new boiler at a cost, including installation, of $15,000.

At the meeting of the Society of Kentucky Florists the following officers were elected: Jacob Schulz, president; C. G. Walker, vice-president; Geo. Schulz, secretary; Jos. Coenen, financial secretary; C. H. Kinzman, treasurer.

August Baumer, formerly with Jacob Schulz, has leased a store room in the new Masonic Temple building and will commence business February 1. H. G. W.

Lenox, Mass.

The regular meeting of the Lenox Horticultural Society was held January 2, in the society's hall, with President B. Jenkins in the chair. General business was transacted and topics for the good of the society were discussed. On New Year's day the society attended the funeral of one of its esteemed members, Jacob Stiebel, superintendent to J. E. Parsons, of Lenox. G. F.

DANBURY, CONN.—W. G. Krober has sold his greenhouse stock to H. H. Tomlinson, who has leased the place for a period of three years from J. H. Ives. The latter will discontinue his store on Main street.

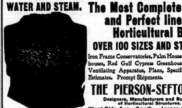

THE AMERICAN FLORIST

America is "the Prow of the Vessel; there may be more comfort Amidships, but we are the first to touch Unknown Seas."

Vol. XXI.   CHICAGO AND NEW YORK, JANUARY 16, 1904.   No. 815.

THE AMERICAN FLORIST

NINETEENTH YEAR.

Copyright 1903, by American Florist Company
Entered as Second-Class Mail Matter.

PUBLISHED EVERY SATURDAY BY

AMERICAN FLORIST COMPANY,
324 Dearborn St., Chicago.

Eastern Office: 42 W. 28th St., New York.

Subscription, $1.00 a year.   To Europe, $2.00.
Subscriptions accepted only from the trade.
Volumes half-yearly from August, 1901.

SOCIETY OF AMERICAN FLORISTS AND
ORNAMENTAL HORTICULTURISTS.
OFFICERS—JOHN BURTON, Philadelphia, Pa.,
president; C. C. POLLWORTH, Milwaukee, Wis.,
vice-president; WM. J. STEWART, 79 Milk Street,
Boston, Mass., secretary; H. B. BEATTY, Oil City,
Pa., treasurer.
OFFICERS-ELECT—PHILIP BREITMEYER, president; J. J. BENEKE, vice-president; secretary and
treasurer as before. Twentieth annual meeting
at St. Louis, Mo., August, 1904.

THE AMERICAN CARNATION SOCIETY.
Annual convention at Detroit, Mich., March 2,
1904. ALBERT M. HERR, Lancaster, Pa., secretary.

AMERICAN ROSE SOCIETY.
Annual meeting and exhibition, Philadelphia,
March, 1904. LEONARD BARRON, 136 Liberty St.,
New York, secretary.

CHRYSANTHEMUM SOCIETY OF AMERICA.
Annual convention and exhibition, November,
1904. FRED H. LEMON, Richmond, Ind., secretary.

THIS ISSUE 40 PAGES WITH COVER.

CONTENTS.

Palms and Ferns.

COMPARATIVE HARDINESS OF SOME PALMS.

To speak of the hardiness of a palm is to use a comparative term, from the fact that no palm should be called hardy in the sense that we dwellers in the temperate zone consider the hardiness of a tree such as an oak or a pine. But there are a number of palms that possess a considerable degree of hardiness, and that are used in some instances in great numbers for outdoor planting in localities where sharp frosts are by no means unknown, some portions of our southern states being much beautified by these noble plants, while from the center to the south of the state of California several species of palms are becoming, or have already become, quite a feature of the permanent planting for landscape effect. And there are also portions of the south of England, notably in Cornwall, where Chamærops humilis and Trachycarpus excelsus have both been growing outdoors for many years, though frequently exposed to a temperature several degrees below the freezing point. This does not seem so extraordinary in the case of Chamærops humilis when we take into consideration the fact that this palm is found growing wild in parts of southern Europe and also in northern Africa, but it sometimes startles the indoor cultivator to find that such a favorite with all palm growers as Kentia Belmoreana is planted out in southern California and has been several years.

There are some very handsome specimens of this palm in some of the gardens of Los Angeles, Cal., the plants in question having well developed trunks several feet (perhaps eight to ten feet) high and surmounted by a fine head of fronds, and all this notwithstanding the fact that there has been frost enough at times to freeze the ground to the depth of one inch. That this palm enjoys a reasonable amount of shade is again proved by some photographs in my possession, a specimen growing in the full sun for a greater number of years than one that is growing in the shade of a residence near by is much more dwarf than the latter and while the fully exposed plant may carry about the same number of fronds as the shade-grown plant, yet the foliage of the latter is much more luxuriant and the general effect of the plant is much more attractive. Several phœnixes are also used very largely for outdoor planting in that section of the country, both P. dactylifera and P. Canariensis being

found in specimens of large size and magnificent appearance, the latter species being considered the best for the purpose. It will also be remembered that our national government, through the medium of the agricultural department, has been investigating the question of planting orchards or groves of Phœnix dactylifera in Arizona with a view to the production of dates as a crop, though the experiment has not yet been of sufficient length to have permanent value. Another most impressive palm for outdoor use in California is the Coquito palm of Chili, Jubæa spectabilis, a species that is notable in being the most southern of American palms in its native habitat.

A large specimen of this species bears some resemblance to Phœnix Canariensis or P. dactylifera, but is more massive in appearance, having a trunk of great diameter proportionately and holding up its fronds in a more erect manner. The comparison between the phœnix and the jubæa will be better understood by an examination of a series of pictures which will appear later, for which I am indebted to Ernest Braunton, of Los Angeles, the photographs giving a better idea of the characteristic beauty of these fine specimens than could be had from a whole page of description. Several of the strong growing cocoses, for example C. plumosa, C. flexuosa and C. Romanzoffiana are also used in the gardens of southern California, the first named being considered the most satisfactory, being quite a rapid grower and extremely graceful in outline. Then there is the native species Washingtonia filifera, that is extremely abundant in some parts of that state, and that has been used to outline some of the avenues in the favored city of which we have spoken. Also the erythea, the only two species of which are natives of some of the islands on the Californian coast, and both of these palms are highly ornamental, though compara-tively slow in growth and dwarf in habit, thus making them very slow in forming a trunk or in reaching any great height. Seaforthias, Cocos australis, Livistona Chinensis and many other species are to be found in these famous gardens of California flourishing abundantly, those most successful in growing them find-ing that abundant moisture at the root is one great requisite for their welfare, a fact that has frequently been impressed upon the grower of palms under glass also.

Another example of the hardiness of some palms is found in the wide distribution of the best known of our eastern native palms; the emblem of South Carolina, and commonly known as the palmetto. This sabal is found, though sparingly, up along the coast of North Carolina, in a region where frost and snow are experienced to a greater or less extent every winter, the frosts injuring the foliage more or less and naturally dwarfing the growth, but not enough to kill the plants. Farther south this palm becomes more plentiful and more luxuriant in growth, but even down to the upper portions of Florida they often experience slight frosts, and with little injury. But with these strong growing palms there will be found great differences in behavior when exposed to severe frosts, the surroundings and exposure having much to do with it. The plant that is sheltered from the sun during severe weather will be much less liable to injury than one that stands in the full sunshine, and any plant that is to be planted outdoors permanently should have a course of preparation to harden it off.						W. H. TAPLIN.

Florists' Plant Notes.

Sweet Peas.—Now is a good time to make another sowing of sweet peas for indoor blooming. Start them in 4-inch pots, sowing about a half dozen seeds in a pot, and when they are three inches high plant them out on a bench or a bed, the latter preferred. Rich, heavy soil is necessary in which to grow them. Plant them in rows across the bed, leaving a space of two feet between the rows, and support the vines with chicken wire. Plenty of headroom is necessary, for they will grow fully five or six feet high. They can stand abundance of feeding in the shape of liquid manure after they are once fairly started and require frequent syringing to keep red spider in check. Blanche Ferry, Countess of Radnor, Blanche Burpee, as well as different colors of the later sorts, will force successfully at this time of the year, the later varieties producing fine stems a foot or more in length. Those that were sown in the fall should be producing heavily by this time. Keep them well picked and never allow them to go to seed, for this destroys the vitality of the vines. As soon as they have ceased to be profitable, throw them out before red spider gets a foothold.

Fuchsias.—Small plants of fuchsias propagated in November should be shifted along into larger pots. Use plenty of old hotbed manure in the soil, for they fairly revel in it. Half manure, if well rotted, is not too much. Give them plenty of room in a light place, moderately warm, so as not to draw the plants up. They will not require shade for six weeks more. Top the plants a week or two after shifting, growing from three to five branches to the plant. Several more lots of cuttings can be taken from the old stock plants, which will make fine little plants in 3-inch pots for spring sales, but after the middle of February it does not pay to propagate them for the plants will be too small to be of any use. The old stock plants should also be shifted along, as they will make large, useful plants for vases and veranda boxes in the spring.

Shrubs.—Give the rhododendrons more heat, if any are wanted for Easter. They are not in great demand at that time, although sale for a limited number is good shape can always be had. A temperature of 55° is sufficient to force them. They require plenty of water, especially

when in flower; otherwise the flowers wilt and are soon ruined. Acacias and ericas can be had in flower at any time now by applying a little more heat for a few weeks. Those for Easter had better be kept in a cool house for another six weeks, for late in the season they can be forced into flower in a short time by raising the temperature to 55°. It may be desirable to have a few plants of lilacs and Deutzia gracilis or D. Lemoinei in bloom for decorating the store window. It requires about six weeks in a temperature of 60° to force them into flower. Abundance of water and syringing is necessary. Those for Easter should be kept in a frame or pit, when they will not freeze too hard, until six weeks before Easter. Metrosideros, or bottle brush plant, of which a limited number find ready sale at Easter time because of their novel flowers, should be gradually given more heat. Do not force them too hard

Theodore Wirth.
Appointed Director S. A. F.
(See page 946.)

for they are liable to grow blind. Raising the temperature at night will bring them into flower in time for Easter.

Begonias.—The common bedding begonias which are now in a state of partial rest should have the soil partly shaken from the roots, repotted, and started into growth to make respectable plants for the spring trade. About a week or so before repotting, the plants should be trimmed down to a height of about six inches, which will induce them to form bushy plants. A batch of cuttings can be taken a few weeks after starting up the old plants. It is time now to sow the seed of Begonia Vernon, which is also useful for bedding. Use light soil, just pressing the seed into the surface of the soil with a pane of glass, and no covering with soil is needed. For the first few weeks keep the seed pan covered with a pane of glass until the seed germinates. If old stock plants are on hand, cuttings should also be taken at once, which will make good 4-inch stock for bedding. The different varieties of the rex family should also be propagated now. Growing them from seed is too slow, so leave that for the specialist. Leaf-propagation is the best method.						G.

ELMIRA, N. Y.—F. W. Durand will open a flower store at 117 West Water street.

The Carnation.

A NEW SCARLET.

The B. K. & B. Floral Company, of Richmond, Ind., is having flattering success with the new scarlet, Richmond Gem, illustrations of which appear in this issue. In point of size, color, stem and commercial value it is attracting much attention.

GAS INJURES CARNATION BLOOMS.

W. N. Rudd has been having some disagreeable experience with illuminating gas. It developed that as soon as carnation blooms were removed from the flower cellar for shipment they went to sleep, while blooms from the same lot which were not placed in the cellar would keep from seven to nine days. The cellar was well ventilated; both by flue and windows, and to all appearances the air was as fresh and pure as it could be outdoors, there being no smell of gas at any time. Removal of the stock to other quarters cured the trouble at once. The carnation seems especially sensitive to the effects of gas, and it is stated that sewer gas is almost as fatal as illuminating gas.

MRS. THOS. W. LAWSON.

This grand variety, the beginning of what we may hope to become an improved type of carnations, has brought with it its own set of peculiarities, and its importance among the list of commercial varieties fully justifies its treatment in a separate article. Most varieties have their own particular faults the analysis of which usually determines their value to the man who grows them. Most varieties, however, drop below the horizon of usefulness before a thorough knowledge of their wants becomes universal. It is seldom that a variety holds its place as long as Lawson has held its own. No carnation has yet held such a conspicuous position as Lawson, and the variety to displace is not yet in sight. "Is it as good as Lawson?" is a stereotyped phrase; no one thinks of asking whether a new aspirant is better. It is a pity that a course of treatment followed for the elimination of an evil should prove a detriment in some other particular. The tendency of this variety to burst a large proportion of its calyxes under ordinary conditions has led most growers to grow it at a temperature considerably higher than was thought advisable a few years ago. A temperature of 56° at night has become about the standard, and with plants lifted from the field it is necessary in order to reduce the tendency to split to a minimum. Plants grown indoors all summer are much less apt to split than those lifted from the field and may be grown two or three degrees cooler on that account. Anything gained in this way is appreciable, for an extremely high temperature has a tendency to fade the color and reduce the size of the bloom. In the cooler temperature there are also less apt to run down the vigor of the stock. Lawson has a very vigorous constitution, and like the true Yankees that we are we may expect that any strong point in a variety will be quickly taken advantage of. It often matters little at the time being whither the course pursued may lead in the end. In this way the strong constitution of this variety may prove its weakest point.

Considering the peculiarities of this variety, the selection of a suitable soil becomes an important item. A heavy soil usually aggravates a case of burst-

FULL SIZE BLOOMS OF CARNATION RICHMOND GEM.

ing calyxes. A very light soil combined with a high temperature weakens the stems and makes small flowers. A soil of a medium degree of heaviness is then the most plausible conclusion. Experiments have amply borne out the theory. The question of solid beds or raised benches also comes up for consideration here. The fact is quite well known that solid beds have a tendency to aggravate any evil resulting from dark weather, a a cool temperature and a general lack of activity in the surrounding conditions. We have always believed that a better paying crop of blooms can be grown on a raised bench than on a solid bed. Solid beds have their good points, but for midwinter work the value of a raised bench cannot be disputed. Probably the most serious defect in this variety is its habit of throwing short stems along time after being checked. Plants lifted from the field as late as latter August are apt to come short-stemmed until mid-winter. Much, of course, depends upon the care exercised in transplanting. Field grown plants are also more apt to produce the blooms in crops than those grown indoors all summer. Indoor culture has been tried almost everywhere, with the result that long stemmed flowers are cut very early in the season and that a uniform crop of high grade blooms extends through the months when flowers are most valuable. The lower temperature at which indoor grown plants can be grown during their flowering season is an important factor in the quality of the cut and the vigor of the stock.

Lawson is an exceedingly heavy grower and therefore will stand a rich soil and heavy feeding after it is well started. A maximum of exposure to the sun is of course desirable with any variety, but the flowers of this variety are easily scorched by the full glare of the sun. Therefore a light shade must be put on the glass very early in the season. The clear glass is hardly permissible after February 1. The question of shading requires judicious handling lest a too heavy coat be put on too early. More will be said of this later. J.

American Carnation Society.

DEPARTMENT OF-REGISTRATION. · · ·

The following new varieties have been registered by John E. Haines, Bethlehem, Pa.:

Juno, a bright scarlet, in size three inches and over, with well formed flower, which is fragrant and does not burst the calyx; stem long and strong, a free bloomer from September to June and a rapid grower.

Imperial, a pink variegated, stems from thirty to thirty-six inches long, size of flower three and one half inches, a free bloomer with hardy growth; blooms from September to June.

ALBERT M. HERR.

VASE OF CARNATION RICHMOND GEM.

CHRYSANTHEMUM DOROTHY · FAUST.

The Chrysanthemum.

CHRYSANTHEMUM COMMENTS.

The shows have given so much impetus to the exhibition varieties that a few words regarding their merits may be of some service to those interested. Of the French varieties which were certificated in the fall of 1902 a large portion will be disseminated in this country the coming season. The National Chrysanthemum Society of France has adopted a scale for judging seedlings quite similar to the one used in this country, viz.: Color, 35; size, 20; form, 15; fullness, 10; stem and foliage, 20. Varieties scoring 80 points or more are entitled to a certificate. Those which were certificated and will be catalogued the coming season are the following: M. Paul Labbe, 87 points; Mlle. Marthe Morel, 85; Etienne Bonnefond, 90; Henry II., 81; Mme. J. Perraud, 85; M. Paul Sahut, 86; M. Martignier, 89; Mlle. E. Chabanne, 89; Jean Calvat, 94; Mme. Henry Douillet, 93; Chrysanthemist Choulet, 94; Cinna, 82; Lt. Col. Ducroiset, 87; Pres. Viger, 96; Amateur A. Charvet, 91; Boccace, 84; M. F. Villermet, 83; Josephine Rousset, 92; Lohengrin, 85. Of the older French varieties, Rosalinde, by Calvat, 95 points; M. O. de Meulanacre, 92, and Marq. Vicounti Venosta, 98. The latter variety we notice in the American Florist of December 12 is referred to as immense in size and pure white. It may be possible that from crown buds this variety might be grown white, but from what we have seen of it it hardly seems probable, hence we conclude the color given is erroneous. It is described by Calvat in his catalogue of 1900 as lilac mauve. Wells & Company describe it as reddish purple. It has a decided purplish tinge, and has been well received throughout England and France

the last season, being prominent in many prize stands.

Dr. Enguehard (Nonin-1900) does not appear to be certificated by the French society. It has scored 95 points in this country, and will become very popular as soon as better known. It has many good qualifications, especially from a commercial standpoint. Mrs. F. W. Vallis, distributed by W. Wells & Company, is a new comer by a grower named Silsbury, on the Isle of Wight. It is an immense, long-petaled, drooping flower. We notice that in many of the foreign reports it is referred to as Mrs. F. S. Vallis. Which is correct we are unable to say, except it was originally disseminated

under the first name mentioned. Maynell, F. A. Cobbold, Donald McLeod, Harrison Dick, Wm. Duckham and S. T. Wright are among the best of the recent Australian productions. Among the recent English novelties the following have been successful at the exhibitions: Capt. Percy Scott, Mildred Ware, Cheltoni, Duchess of Sutherland, Godfrey's Pride, Lord Ludlow, Mrs. Greenfield, Geo. Penford, Mrs. J. I. Thornycroft, Sir H. Kitchener, Mrs. J. C. Neville, Mafeking Hero, Le Grand Dragon, Mrs. F. W. Vallis, Lily Mountford, Mrs. Geo. Mileham, Bessie Godfrey, Lord Salisbury, Mrs. Barkley, Matthew Smith, Henry Stowe, Mrs. Weeks, Miss Olive Miller and Mary Inglis. Among the many Australian varieties which met the favor in England and have not been largely grown in this country, we would include Mrs. Tom Rand, Sir Geo. White, J. M. Darcy, Marica, T. W. McNeice, Frank Hannaford, Gen. Hutton, Harry Plumeridge, Kimberly, Lord Alverstone, Lord Hopetoun, Mrs. C. J. Salter, Mrs. T. K. Bennett, Mrs. A. C. Milne Redhead, Ben Wells, Guy Hamilton, Mermaid, T. Carrington, Mrs. E. Thirkell, Nellie Pockett, Rev. W. Wilkes, W. R. Church and Henry Barnes. Miss Elsie Fulton has been well received abroad, and we grew it last season, but must agree with Wells & Company in pronouncing it synonomous with Princess Alice de Monaco. Both foliage and flower strongly indicate this.

Of the recent French varieties probably F. S. Vallis has created more sensation on the English showboards than any other variety. It is mentioned in nearly all the winning stands. From this source the following were also well received: Mme. Paolo Radaelli, Mme. Carnot, Calvat's Sun, M. Chenon de Lèche and Marq. Vicounti Venosta. Those who are interested in commercial varieties must bear in mind that most of the foregoing are exhibition sorts. A few of them doubtless possess commercial value which will be fully demonstrated when they are more generally grown. We notice W. J. Godfrey, the English specialist, has named a new variety Sunrise. It will be well to remember that this name was used by John N. May for an early bronze variety he disseminated in 1895.

CHRISTMAS CROP OF B. K. & B. FLORAL CO.'S CARNATION RICHMOND GEM.
(Photograph taken January 1. 1904.)

Miss Mary Hill, daughter of E. G. Hill, has again been favored, this time by M. Nonin, of Paris, who has named for her a new chrysanthemum, which scored 85 points at Lille, November 6. It is described as a Japanese incurved, rosy lilac, reverse white.

Since writing the above I have received Calvat's catalogue, and on further investigation find he is offering a new variety under the name of Marquise Viscounti Venosta, which is a pure white of the Morel type. The similarity of the two names will be rather confusing, the only difference is the final "e" on Marquise. Marquis Viscounti Venosta was one of the best "twelve blooms distinct" at the exhibition of the English National Chrysanthemum Society at Crystal Palace, November 10.   E. D. S.

A NEW WHITE VARIETY.

Dorothy Faust,the new late white chrysanthemum, is a novelty, being the very latest of them all. As a keeper it is a wonder. Flowers seen now are just as good as the best varieties of November. This variety originated with Harry Faust, of Werion, Pa. He thinks it is a sport from Bonnaffon, although it does not so much resemble that kind, appearing more like the early white Queen. A spring blooming sort is now in order, and this will complete the cycle and place the chrysanthemum in line with the carnation and the rose, a state of affairs which we hope will be deferred until the long-looked for blue variety makes its appearance. See accompanying illustration.   K.

A New Primrose.

This beautiful yellow primrose,Buttercup, of almost the exact color of a buttercup, may not be a new plant, but it certainly is newly found out, and now that it has been discovered is not likely to ever return to oblivion, as it has proved itself to be a variety of sterling merit. A plant in a 6-inch pot carries hundreds of blossoms, ranging in size from three quarters to an inch in diameter. These are borne on spikes which stand well alone. The foliage is something like obconica, but with the whole of the bloom distributed better up and down the stem. This latter might be a trifle stronger, as when in full flower the weight of the blossoms is apt to carry it over a little. Like many other sterling novelties this comes to the trade through the medium of W. K. Harris, of Philadelphia, who discovered its good qualities. He disposed of a stock of five thousand plants in the last two months. He says that it is the best thing sent out since Begonia Gloire de Lorraine. It grows readily from seed and is very easy to manage, requiring no special culture. The Buttercup is shown in the accompanying engraving.   K.

Wood Ashes as a Fertilizer.

An average sample of unleached wood ashes contains about seven per cent of potash and two per cent of phosphoric acid, which at current retail prices of these plant foods makes average wood ashes worth about 45 cents per hundred pounds, or $9 a ton, says A. M. Ten Eyck, in the Industrialist, published by the Kansas Agricultural College. Besides the actual fertilizing value by reason of the potash and phosphoric acid contained in the ashes, there is some value to ashes simply from the power which potash has to make the nitrogen of the soil available for plants by its chemical

W. K. HARRIS' NEW PRIMROSE BUTTERCUP.

action on the organic matter and humus in the soil. The potash in ashes exists in a readily soluble form, and is thus immediately available for plant food. Ashes also contain a little magnesia and a considerable amount of carbonate of lime, which is of some importance because of its effect in improving the texture of heavy soils. The farmer can better afford to pay $8 or $10 a ton for good wood ashes than the usual rates for almost any potash fertilizer.

Leached ashes have rarely more than one per cent of potash and one and a half per cent of phosphoric acid, which will make them worth about $3 or $4 per ton. Coal ashes are probably not worth 50 cents per ton as a fertilizer, but on heavy soils they may often be applied with profit just for their loosening effect, and they are valuable as a top dressing or mulch in fruit gardens. Sifted coal ashes absorb liquids, fix volatile ammonia and prevent offensive odors and are valuable as absorbents under hen roosts or in stables. Wood ashes should not be placed under hen roosts or in stables, because potash liberates ammonia and the quality of both the manure and the ashes as fertilizers is deteriorated.

On average soils, fruits and vegetables are benefited by liberal applications of wood ashes, and remarkable results have been obtained by the use of ashes on legume crops, especially clover and alfalfa. Ashes will not make so valuable a fertilizer for top dressing for wheat as when

used with the crops mentioned. Corn, Kafir corn and cane will doubtless be more benefited than wheat by the use of ashes as a fertilizer. However, if the soil is lacking in the potash element, a dressing of wood ashes will benefit almost any crop. Most of the soils of Kansas are well supplied with potash. If there is any part of the state in which this element of plant food is apt to be lacking in the soil it is in the eastern part, where the land is old and the plant foods have become exhausted to some extent. In the eastern and middle states it is more usual to apply ashes in orchards, or upon onion or cabbage fields.

Ashes are best applied in the spring, separately or in connection with phosphate fertilizers as a top dressing. For cultivated crops the ashes should be spread broadcast after the land has been harrowed and made practically ready for the crop, and cultivated in by light harrowing. On onions a light dressing is sometimes applied with good results when the plants are two or three weeks old, and I believe that no harm will come to the wheat by a light application of ashes this fall, or early next spring. There will tend to be some waste to the soluble potash if the ashes are applied late in the fall or during the winter, by surface drainage or leaching.

Ashes may be applied at the rate of fifty to one hundred bushels, or one or two tons to the acre. One ton of good wood ashes will contain about one hundred and forty pounds of potash and forty pounds of phosphoric acid, which is more of each of these elements than any ordinary crop will take from the soil in a single season. If leached ashes are used, the quantity applied should be increased.

I think it will be impossible to spread the ashes thin enough with the manure spreader. Spread in this way, there is likely to be not only a loss of fertilizer because of the too abundant supply, but there is also likely to result injury to the growing crop by reason of the presence of too much alkali. Ashes may be applied by sowing broadcast by hand, provided the hand is protected, or it is possible by care to spread them thinly enough from a wagon with a shovel. If the ashes are fine, and clean, it is possible to spread them with a revolving broadcast seeder.

In wood ashes we have the most serviceable and often the very cheapest fertilizer for peat and muck lands. Such soils are rich in nitrogen and usually poor in phosphoric acid and potash. The nitrogen is also in an unavailable condition, and by application of wood ashes, potash and phosphoric acid are not only supplied, but by the chemical action of the potash on the peat the nitrogen is brought into a condition available to the plant. I know of farmers who collect the ashes of neighboring villages. They usually furnish barrels into which residents prefer to put their ashes rather than throw them into the streets or door yards. I know of one instance in which a farmer located two and one-half miles from town collected ten tons of good ashes during the winter, which cost less than $5 per ton after the ashes were spread on the field.

Sawdust has no value as a fertilizer, but it may have some value in the physical effects which result when it is applied to light, sandy soils. It tends to make such soils hold water better, and when applied on the surface acts as a mulch to retain the water in the soil below. Such a combination of ashes and sawdust might be made so that the mixture could be applied with the manure spreader without getting on too heavy a dressing of ashes.

New York Florists' Club.

The opening meeting of the New York Florists' Club for 1904 on Monday evening, January 11, was a thoroughly live one and a good augury for a continuance of the prosperity which had characterized the previous year. On account of the absence of the retiring president, J. H. Troy, the duty of introducing F. H. Traendly, president-elect, devolved upon F. H. Traendly, retiring vice-president. After an ineffectual attempt to perform this Poo Bah act and gracefully shake hands with himself, this usually versatile gentleman finally called on Secretary Young to help him out, which request was duly and gracefully complied with, and after appropriate applause, President Traendly took his position and proceeded to read the following very concise and practical inaugural address:

In assuming the duties of president, I desire to thank you for the honor you have conferred upon me by selecting me as your presiding officer for the present year. The club is to be congratulated on its condition, having shown much progress during the past year as is shown by the treasurer's report. Among the suggestions I have to offer for the welfare of the club for the coming year is the establishing of special nights for the exhibition of different varieties of flow-

ers, devoting one date for carnations, another for roses, and so on through the list. I am fully aware that this is not a new suggestion, but trust the committee of award may be able to stimulate interest on these particular nights. I think the club will agree with me that something more interesting is needed than to attend the monthly meetings, to transact routine business and listen occasionally to an essay. It requires some courage to refer to a subject that recalls disagreeable memories, that of flower shows; yet I have in mind that a way might be devised to arrange to hold an exhibition on a small scale in a hall of moderate size, open to the public free, or by charging a nominal admission fee. I suggest that an advisory committee be appointed to consider the advisability of such a plan and report at an early date as to whether such an exhibition could be given without involving the club to any great extent financially, or, in fact, whether it would be at all practicable. I merely make the suggestion for what it is worth and to get an expression of your views on the subject of future shows. I would recommend to the board of trustees that it might be well to have the funds of the club deposited in a trust company, where it would be earning from two to two and one-half per cent a year, as every little helps.

That the summer outings are popular with our members, is shown by the success attending them for the past three years. If it is your wish to have another this summer, a committee should be appointed at once with power to go ahead and make arrangements and secure suitable grounds. I should also like to see the dinner committee get to work and complete arrangements for this event. Having served my apprenticeship with the entertainment committee, I feel that I am justified in venturing to advise the club to show a moderate liberality in an appropriation for the use of the committee. While the "canteen" serves its purpose, the committee should also bear in mind that something in the library line would also be welcome.

Unless the Florists' Club wants to be relegated to the ranks of the "has beens" as bowlers, it would be advisable for its athletic members to take an interest in the bowling club so that we may be creditably represented at the St. Louis convention this summer. I would impress upon you the importance of being on hand when the meetings are called to order at 7:30, that we may encourage out-of-town members to attend.

In conclusion let me ask your indulgence for any shortcomings on my part; I have the best interests of the club at heart and will, with your support and cooperation, endeavor to perform my duties to your satisfaction.

Following the president, Messrs. S. S. Butterfield, vice-president, John Young, secretary, and C. B. Weathered were severally called upon and each briefly expressed appreciation and promised loyal service. The secretary's annual report showed a gross membership of 237 at the present time and the report of the treasurer showed a gratifying increase in the cash on hand. Reports of the various standing committees were of the usual satisfactory nature and that of the trustees made special mention of the scrupulous correctness noted in the books of the treasurer and the neatness of the secretary's records, which it had been their duty to examine.

Mr. O'Mara, on behalf of the special committee appointed at the last meeting,

presented the following resolutions which were unanimously adopted:

T. W. WEATHERED.

WHEREAS, T. W. Weathered has been summoned hence by the immutable decree of the Almighty.

WHEREAS, While we bow in humble submission to His holy will, humbly acknowledging His wisdom and submitting to His all powerful will, yet we feel it to be our duty to extend our sympathy to those he left behind and voice our esteem for him as a Christian gentleman and citizen, therefore be it

Resolved, That the New York Florists' Club tender to his son, Chas. B. Weathered, our worthy treasurer, and through him to his remaining kindred, our heartfelt sympathy in their bereavement.

While the great loss is theirs, yet it falls upon us, too, as we have lost a life long friend, a wise counselor, a genial companion and a consistent friend of horticulture. We wish to testify at the close of his busy and useful life our appreciation of his genius as an inventor and his sterling worth as a man. His progressive spirit should be and is an inspiration to those of us who are left behind. His love for horticulture was part of his life and found expression in an ardent, helpful way through many years. In his life he set a high standard for all the Christian and civic virtues and has gone to his eternal reward, sincerely mourned by all who knew him, full of years and honors.

Resolved, That these resolutions be spread in full upon our records and that a copy of same be sent to Chas. B. Weathered.

GEO. N. COTTAM.

WHEREAS, God in His infinite wisdom has called unto Himself our friend and fellow member, George N. Cottam.

WHEREAS, We who have had the pleasure of his friendship and the benefit of his companionship for many years, feel it to be our duty and due to his memory to record our appreciation of his faithful services to this organization, therefore be it

Resolved, That in his death the New York Florists' Club has lost a valued member, and horticulture a gifted and ardent votary. We beg to tender to his family our sincere sorrow in their bereavement; knowing what our loss is, we can appreciate what it must be to them; to whom he was so dear. We will long bear in memory his genial disposition, which endeared him to us all. We will miss his practical knowledge and wide experience in all branches of horticulture. His unfailing good nature, his loyalty to this organization through the years of its existence, his enthusiasm for all that tended to its betterment made him a most valuable member, and his loss to us and to horticulture at large is a heavy one. He has left a record for usefulness to our organization which is creditable to his memory and an incentive to us.

Resolved, That these resolutions be spread in full upon our records and a copy of same be sent to his family.

An interesting discussion followed, on the recommendations contained in the president's address, during which it transpired that, notwithstanding previous experiences of a disheartening nature, the sentiment of the club was strongly in favor of some plan whereby public exhibitions of modest proportions might be presented. On the exhibition table were three vases of seedling carnations from the Cottage Gardens, all exceptionally fine flowers, one being No. 303, the scarlet which has created a sensation in the cut flower district. An invitation from the Morris County Gardeners' and Florists' Society to attend its smoker on the evening of January 13 was accepted.

W. H. Elliott, of Brighton, Mass., who was present as a visitor, complimented the club on the fine attendance and enthusiasm displayed and expressed his opinion that the "canteen" must have played a useful part in successfully warding off the paralysis so often experienced in organizations of this character. He applauded the disposition to inaugurate public exhibitions and in closing urged the members to give their united support to their officers and committees, not putting all the burden upon one or a few.

The following committees were then appointed:

On awards, P. O'Mara, Chas. Lenker, W. B. Siebrecht, J. Dowsett, A. L. Miller, John Birnie, A. B. Langjahr.

On entertainment, J. B. Nugent, Jr., Joseph Mands, Robt. Koehne.

ELABORATE GROUP OF FLOWERS AT ST. LOUIS, MO., FUNERAL.

On legislation, J. N. May, P. O'Mara. Chas. H. Allen.
On outing, W. J. Elliott. H. A. Bunyard, J. A. Shaw, J. Birnie, J. W. Rejuels, Alfred Zeller, Jos. A. Millang, L. W. Wheeler.
On dinner, L. Hafner, W. F. Sheridan, L. B. Craw.
To visit Cottage Gardens and report on carnation No. 303, J. Birnie, C. Lenker, A. L. Miller, W. H. Siebrecht.
On death of Ernst G. Asmus, John Young, S. C. Nash, Eugene Dailledouze.

New England Notes.

BAYSIDE, L. I.—A boiler explosion set fire to the greenhouses of William Bell, January 4, and damage to the extent of $8,000 resulted.

LOWELL, MASS.—Chas. L. Marshall fell from his windmill, on which he was at work, December 12, and was seriously injured, having a narrow escape from instant death.

HARTFORD, CONN.—Plans for the laying out and planting of the grounds about the Connecticut building at St. Louis have been prepared by Robert Karlstrom, of the Hartford park department.

SPRINGFIELD, MASS.—Plans have been perfected for a new horticultural building at· Amherst College, which it is hoped will receive the needed appropriation from the State Legislature. The estimated cost will be about $25,000.

NEW BEDFORD, MASS.—W. P. Pierce, of New Bedford, was surprised December 8, by a large party of friends, who presented him with a fine harness, blanket, and whip to complete the outfit of a new delivery wagon recently purchased.

NEW HAVEN, CONN.—Yale University sustained a severe loss in the destruction of the Forestry School building by fire the morning of December 12. The loss on the building is estimated at over $10,000 and many fine specimens difficult to replace were badly damaged.

The Retail Trade.

A FUNERAL GROUP.

The funeral of the late J. R. Butler, St. Louis, Mo., called for an extraordinary lot of cut flowers, as is shown by the accompanying engraving. The total value of the pieces is estimated at $2,000, the casket cover alone costing $350. In the latter six hundred roses were used.

A HOME WEDDING DECORATION.

A very pretty home wedding, which was a little out of the ordinary, took place at noon on Wednesday, December 30. Three rooms were decorated. The one in which the ceremony was performed was all in white, a shell canopy being used. This was tastefully decorated with dainty swainsona with a background of tall palms. The mantel was banked with Asparagus Parleyense, and two or three large vases of white roses, very loosely arranged. The large doorway, draped with southern smilax, was relieved with generous bunches of swainsona with extremely graceful effect. The next room was all in yellow, Franz Deegen roses and yellow carnations being used and the mirrors draped with Asparagus plumosus, with large masses of yellow roses on one side. The peculiar fragrance of the Franz Deegen roses was very noticeable. The dining room was filled with American Beauty roses. The one large table had a centre piece of Cypripedium insigne and swainsona with two vases of the same arrangement at each end. I noticed that no ribbon was used except on the posts which formed the aisle.

The decorations at a musical were very brilliant. The rooms throughout were decorated with palms and Asparagus plumosus with large vases of poinsettias placed in every available spot, giving a beautiful effect. A round table had a large center piece of poinsettias [fringed

with Asparagus Parleyense surrounded with small silver vases filled with lily of the valley.   THE ARTIST.

HINTS ON HOUSE DECORATION.

American ladies as a rule have good ideas as to the tasteful massing and harmony of color and form. The only exceptions are a few freaks who insist on doing whimsical or ridiculous things and, unhappily for the florist who would remonstrate but dare not, these plagues are as often found in the ranks of the most exclusive society as elsewhere. But usually the florist will find the lady of the house a good auxiliary in deciding upon what should be done. We saw at a reception not long ago, a basket filled with American Beauty and La France roses. Had the hostess been consulted beforehand we doubt if this ugly monstrosity of inharmonious color would have been brought forth and if she afterwards declined to pay for it, one could hardly have blamed her.

In a parlor decorated in pale blue and gold, American Beauty shines resplendent. Here, most shades of pink flowers may be used also, but light pink or Bridesmaid rose tints are in more perfect harmony if the prevailing tone approaches pale green. Against black, walnut or other dark background, Bridesmaid roses are out of keeping, but white or yellow flowers are grandly effective and Liberty roses are extremely rich. For mirror work nothing compares with asparagus and orchids. A very few orchids can be made to produce the maximum effect if skillfully used and for such a situation they are unrivaled.

It may be said that, generally speaking, extreme simplicity characterizes the work of the best artists at the present time. This does not, however, interlere necessarily with richness of effect or lavish expenditures. The greatly increased decorative beauty of the apartments in which elaborate affairs take place is, in part, responsible for the tendency to simplicity in the floral adornment of such places.

Chicago.

LITTLE IMPROVEMENT IN MARKET CONDITIONS.—SHIPPING KEEPS UP.—CARNATIONS BRING LOW PRICE.—FLORISTS' CLUB NEWS.—NO MEETING OF HORTICULTURAL SOCIETY.

It is difficult to discern much of an improvement over the market conditions of last week. Local trade is practically at a standstill, although the best of stock is offered at ridiculously low figures. The people are not buying flowers, however, and social events, theatres, etc., are doing but little to help the situation. Since the closing of all the playhouses in the city more than one line of business has suffered considerably and the florist is no exempt. Choice rose stock is not plentiful and the call for this item is sufficient to keep down the receipts. American Beauty is coming in in large quantities and are moved only by a great sacrifice of the market price. Carnations have not improved in price during the past week and are still quoted at $3 to $4 for the ordinary run of stock. The fancies bring from $8 to $10, but few of them are now sold. The market has not yet been able to shake the heavy supply of violets. Retailers are taking frantic measures to create a violet interest by practically giving them away. The eastern stock now coming to this market is excellent and holds a better price than local stock. The wholesalers are not complaining much about their department of the business. The fore part of the week saw an exhilerating activity in the shipping trade, but it eased up perceptably toward the end of the week.

The first allied trades meeting of the Florists' Club will be held Wednesday evening, January 20. Topics to be discussed will be pipe, fittings, glass and paint. Specialists and dealers will read papers on these lines. The club has arranged to hold meetings in different sections of the city during the balance of the winter. The first of these will occur at Matt Evert's hall, 2008 E. Ravenswood Park, opposite the Rose Hill depot, Saturday night, January 16. A large attendance is looked for. A party of down florists will meet at Wabash and Randolph streets and go to the meeting place in a body.

The Horticultural Society of Chicago was to have held a meeting Tuesday at the Great Northern hotel for the purpose of electing officers and transacting routine business. Not enough members were present, however, to constitute a quorum.

Nicholas Weiland, a brother of J. P. Weiland and an employe of Weiland and Risch, was married January 12 to Miss Katherine Feller, of Evanston. They will make their home at 723 Madison street, Evanston.

George Reinberg has the material on the ground for the erection of a range of eleven new houses, 25x260 feet. Work on the extension has already commenced. Four car loads of glass have been ordered.

The A. L. Randall Company is receiving some choice white lilacs from Emil Buettner. The company reports its shipping trade this week as far ahead of the same time last year.

Peter Reinberg this week supplied Fleischman with an order of 1,000 Uncle John roses for a decoration.

Frank Stollery has taken a booth in Flower Growers' market and is selling some nice decorative plants.

Amling is getting in and disposing of a nice lot of orchids. An increased demand for this specialty is opened.

Peter Wecker, formerly with George Reinberg, is now employed at the greenhouses of John Muno.

J. B. Deamud's violets deserve special mention. They are of exceptional size and color.

Fred Klingel, of Peter Reinberg's down town store, is confined to his home by illness.

Paul Dailledouze, of New York, is in town and staying at the Palmer House.

Bulbous stock of all descriptions is seen to good advantage at J. A. Budlong's.

Phil Hauswirth was a visitor at Jacksonville, Ill., this week on business.

Bentley & Company are handling rose stock that is hard to beat.

O. P. Bassett, of Bassett & Washburn, has gone to California.

New York.

SLUMP CONTINUES UNABATED.—SUPPLY OF STOCK HEAVY.—VIOLETS SELL RIDICULOUSLY LOW.—IMPORTANT SOCIETY MEETINGS.

The January slump in the cut-flower market continues unabated, and is as severe as ever experienced here. Prices in every line are way down, the demand being entirely inadequate for the daily supply and the buyers enjoying the privilege of making values about what they choose. If warm weather should be vouchsafed the street vendors would become available as mediums for the unloading of the surplus, but under present conditions they are of but little account except on violets. In the vicinity of Broadway the finest Rhinebeck products are being hawked by boys at adversity prices. Carnations are of high quality, but prices keep steadily falling from day to day. Narcissi of the trumpet varieties are getting plentiful, although the grades are small as yet.

Wm. Fogarty, at George M. Stumpps, received a gift of a "bouncing boy" 14½ pounds, from Mrs. Fogarty last Friday. Mother and new florist are doing well. Carl Woerner,of Flatbush,received a similar present on Wednesday from his wife. This boy is said to weigh eighteen pounds by Mr. Woerner's friends in the bowling club.

Chas. Miliang is making good use of the conservatory recently erected in the rear of his store. The plant buyers find it a great convenience when palms or ferns are wanted for hurry orders. A practical grower has been placed in charge,Mr.Miliang giving his own attention to the cut flower business.

The handsome cup donated by Moore, Hentz & Nash for the grower of the best American Beauty roses shown at the late exhibition, in Madison, N. J., was presented to the winner at the Morris County Gardeners' and Florists' Society's smoker on Wednesday evening.

On January 13 H. A. Siebrecht gave a talk on ornamental trees, shrubs and plants at the American Institute. In the meeting of the Horticultural Society of New York which followed, J. T. Withers read a paper on our native trees in landscape.

A few tulips blooming in low pans are seen in the windows. Although rather short stemmed as yet for cut flower purposes these early comers are very attractive in pan form.

George M. Stumpp has suffered a heavy

loss in specimen plants at his greenhouse from gas escaping from a leaky main. The gas company will be asked to settle.

The violet trains from Rhinebeck experienced a hard time during the recent stormy weather, being from two to fifteen hours late in arriving.

H. C. Steinhoff is sending lilac blooms of unprecedented beauty to this market. Some of them are of the newer double French varieties.

J. N. May has been confined to his home by illness for the past month and thus far is unable to attend to any business.

A. Herrington is preparing to sail for a visit to England on January 23. W. J. Elliott contemplates a trip to Bermuda.

W. E. Marshall is nursing a dislocated shoulder, the result of being thrown out of a sleigh when in Newport recently.

Killarney is making for itself a well-deserved popularity among the standard roses for the cut flower market.

Boston.

FLORISTS BRAVE STORM TO ATTEND INTERESTING SESSION OF THE CLUB.—AGGRESSIVE POLICY PROMISED FOR THIS YEAR.—HARDY GARDEN FLOWERS DISCUSSED BY R. O. ORPET.—VALUABLE POINTERS.

The monthly meeting of the Gardeners' and Florists' Club on Tuesday evening, January 12, was successful in spite of the stormy weather, there being about thirty gentlemen present. Thirteen new members were admitted. The new constitution and by-laws were adopted practically as presented by the committee, and the recommendations by the executive committee, reported by Mr. Sander, gave promise that a progressive policy is to be followed by the present administration. The special entertainment of the evening was an informal talk by E. O. Orpet, of Lancaster, on the subject of hardy garden flowers. Mr. Orpet is an interesting talker with a pleasing personality, which adds to the pleasure of listening to him. He referred to the wonderful up-growing of the spirit of horticulture in this country in the last few years, and congratulated the gardening fraternity on the revival, which means so much for their welfare. The American people, he said, are not yet a horticulturally-inclined race, but he believed the time would come when flowers and gardens would be appreciated here as abroad. He referred, approvingly, to the study of plant life in the public schools, and expressed his conviction that the more people take up horticulture as a hobby or pastime, the happier they will be. After reference to the necessity of proper preparation of the ground and other general cultural matters, he took up a few of the more desirable of the flowering perennials for individual comment, such as the narcissi, Mertensia Virginica, trilliums, columbines, Asclepias tuberosa, larkspurs, pæonias, gaillardias. Alstræmeria aurantiaca, German and Japanese irises, Aconitum autumnale, lilies, hardy grasses, etc. A discussion followed which brought out many interesting points. Mr. Orpet said there were no columbines to equal our native ones, Aquilegia Canadensis, A. cœrulea, A. chrysantha and A. longissima, but regretted that the latter was scarcely obtainable. With larkspurs he preferred to import plants of the finest varieties and raise stock from seed from these the first year. The double varieties, he said, could be depended upon to yield 80 per cent of double-flowering progeny. He had been rather disappointed in the Newport

Scarlet, which was inferior as a scarlet to nudicaule and cardinale, but unfortunately the two latter are not entirely hardy. He spoke a good word for the Shasta daisy, which, he said, is not fairly represented in the many forms now distributed under that name. Mr. Burbank he characterized as the cleverest living horticulturist. In the matter of lilies he expressed his belief that with auratums success is practically impossible in this country and that the so-called auratums which do succeed are not true auratums but hybrids of that species with speciosum. Among the best hardy lilies he enumerated auratum var. platyphyllum, Batmanniæ, tigrinum, Henryi, Canadense, superbum, the California pardalinum, pomponium speciosum and Thunbergianum. He suggested that the practice of pulling the dead lily stems up in the fall instead of cutting them down might be responsible for many failures in lily culture on account of the channel thus made for the passage of water to the heart of the bulbs.

Mr. Cameron stated that he gets best results with gaillardias by raising from seed each year. He recommended as worthy garden plants - Pentstemon diffusus, P. secundiflorus, P. ovatus and P. Digitalis and Lathyrus vernus. An amusing colloquy regarding the value of botany as a study for gardeners was precipitated. Messrs. Orpet, Sander, Cameron, Pettigrew and Stewart, particularly Mr. Orpet, said he regarded botany for young pupils as all nonsense; that gardeners did not need botany and could not afford to waste time on it, his experience being that a good gardener and a good botanist were rarely found in one individual. Mr. Sander agreed that the man who ran too much to botany was ge e al a mighty poor gardener, and seemed xed incidentally that there were many scientific men who thought themselves gardeners but were not. Mr. Pettigrew thought that the rudiments of structural botany and the physiology of plants should be of use to the gardener. Mr. Cameron and Mr. Stewart were unwilling to subscribe to the radical views of Messrs. Orpet and Sander. James Wheeler had a bunch of very fine violets on the exhibition table.

Philadelphia.

BUSINESS GENERALLY QUIET. — STREET MEN SELLING CARNATIONS AT A CENT APIECE. — GROWERS' MARKET GAINING GROUND. — HARRIS' NEW PRIMROSE POPULAR.

Business has been quiet this week. In some quarters it is described as very slow and it has been difficult to move the stock with any satisfaction. The street men have commenced to get their work in and while the price of carnations has been held firmly at from $1.50 to $3 for fresh stock, 12 cents per dozen has been the price on the street for flowers only one day old at that. Roses are coming in freely and while the quality is not large yet on account of the slow demand they are piling up and prices are lower. In fact, prices are fully twenty per cent lower all along the line.

W. K. Harris' new primrose, Buttercup, has made a great hit; for the last two weeks it has been at its best, being covered with its spikes of yellow blossoms. It is sure to become popular and will be in great demand next season. Pennock Brothers' window was fairly gorgeous with this plant last week. The body of the window was completely filled with a mound of these in full flower. The upper part was a shower of narrow baby ribbon in yellow to match the color of the flower.

The Growers' Market is getting along quietly, no great bustle, but steadily gaining ground. Manager Meehan is encouraged with the outlook, notwithstanding the present dullness, which tries such a system, when in its infancy, to the utmost.

The Philadelphia Carnation Company is sending in some very fine stock. Their houses are new and everything is now in great shape and a credit to Harry Crawford, who has the plant in charge.

Harris is sending in a few single narcissi. These are the first of what is likely to be the largest stock of these flowers in variety that has yet been sent to this market.

Fred. Ehret is still handling chrysanthemums. The new white variety, Dorothy Faust, is still in fine shape with a stock of some five hundred yet to cut.

Joseph Heacock was much pleased with a movement among his palms this week. A large number were shipped away. The stock is certainly grand at this time.

Much complaint has been made the past week over carnations going to sleep. Fresh flowers of one day are asleep before the close of the next.

Leo Niessen is handling some extra fine Liberty roses. He says they bring almost, if not quite, as much as the best Beauty roses.

This city is a great center for valley, one commission house, S. S. Pennock, handling 35,000 blooms at Christmas.

Blooming plants, particularly fine azaleas, now grace the windows and are in fair demand with the customers.

Ed. Reid is getting away with a choice lot of New York violets every day. They arrive in fine condition.

W. J. Baker had the first freesias of the season and they were grabbed up quickly. Francois Supoit, of Paoli, is sending in some fine lilacs which sell readily.

K.

Washington, D. C.

THE DUFFIELD-M'KENNA WEDDING. — ELABORATE BALL ROOM DECORATIONS. — CUT FLOWER BUSINESS INJURED BY COLD SNAP. — TRADE NOTES.

The social season being now at its height, business is good with the decorator. At the wedding, at the residence of Justice and Mrs. McKenna, of their eldest daughter, Isabel, to Pitts Duffield, of New York, the decorations were executed by Geo. H. Cooke. The ceremony took place in the window recess of the parlor, transformed into a bower of green, beneath a chime of white satin bells tied with white satin ribbon. An American Beauty rose served as a tongue for each bell. The bride carried a shower bouquet of lily of the valley and cypripediums; the bridesmaids carried bouquets of Liberty roses showered with lily of the valley. Over the doorways and mantel were double Roman wreaths decorated with white roses and cypripediums. The walls of each room on the first floor were sprayed with smilax. At the wedding breakfast, the library table reserved for President Roosevelt and the bridal party was decorated with lily of the valley and Adiantum Farleyense.

The dedicatory decoration of the new and spacious ballroom of the Willard hotel for the first bachelors' cotillion of the season, was by J. H. Small & Sons. The many window recesses were banked with palms and ferns and graceful drooping ferns were placed at every available point. Holly and smilax were arranged with striking effect around the chandeliers and along the balconies. The favor screens, flanked by groups of large palms, bore favors of red roses and white carnations. Other favors, which added color, were tiny beaded shoes and unique red lanterns.

The cold snap materially reduced the sales of cut flowers and pot plants. Most of the growers had on hand well flowered azaleas for which there was comparatively no sale. Now that milder weather prevails they are in better demand. Washington retail prices for good stock are: American Beauty roses $6 to $12 per dozen; Liberty roses $5 to $6 per dozen; other roses $2 and $3 per dozen; carnations 75 cents to $1.25 per dozen. The cold was extra hard on the violet trade, but good ones still bring $1 per bunch.

A. Gude & Brothers' store, just now, has a choice variety. Their American Beauty and other roses, orchids, azaleas, adiantums and other plants make a fine showing.

Alex. B. Garden, who follows photography as a diversion, has recently been taking snap shots of his houses of fine roses and azaleas.

Wm. E. Lacey, formerly with the American Rose Company, is now designer and decorator at C. Ponnett & Com. pany's store.

Fred. Michell, of Philadelphia, has been doing Washington. S. B.

St. Louis.

INFLUX OF GOOD STOCK IS STEADILY INCREASING BUT PRICES DISAPPOINT THE GROWERS. — BIG FUNERAL ORDER FILLED IN RUSH TIME. — SOME NOVEL FLORAL PIECES. — NOTES OF THE TRADE.

The Eggling Floral Company had a strenuous time filling orders for the J. R. Butler funeral recently. Calls for flowers worth $2,000 were received at a late hour. The casket cover alone was valued at $350. In it were used about six hundred roses. A noticeable piece was a large pillow of American Beauty and violets.

The dullness of the after holiday week was most noticeable. Stock is very scarce where abundant and of excellent quality. The number of fine roses, carnations and violets sent in here is steadily increasing. Prices are slightly lower than last week. The Weber & Sons Nursery Company will have an exhibit of trees, shrubs and herbaceous plants on the horticultural grounds at the World's Fair. A part of it is already installed.

The Michel Plant and Bulb Company will erect three new houses 20x120. The business is rapidly outgrowing its present quarters.

F. A. Weber left for a business trip in the east this week. He will visit Dreer's and other prominent establishments.

J. J. Beneke says holiday trade was good at his place on Olive street. He is busy filling orders for funeral work.

F. W. Ude, Jr., is marketing unusually fine Enchantress and Lawson carnations and California violets.

Mrs. E. G. Eggling is suffering from the effects of a severe sprain received early last week. F. K. B.

RIVERSIDE, CAL. — The California State Floral Society will hold an early spring show some time in March.

THE AMERICAN FLORIST

NINETEENTH YEAR.

Subscription, $1.00 a year. To Europe, $2.00.
Subscriptions accepted only from those
in the trade.

Advertisements, on all except cover pages,
10 Cents a Line, Agate; $1.00 per inch.
Cash with Order.

No Special Position Guaranteed.

Discounts are allowed only on consecutive insertions, as follows:—6 times, 5 per cent; 13 times,
10 per cent; 26 times, 20 per cent;
52 times, 30 per cent.

Space on front pages and back cover page sold
only on yearly contract at $1.00 per inch, net.

The Advertising Department of the AMERICAN
FLORIST is for florists, seedsmen and nurserymen
and dealers in wares pertaining to those lines only.

Orders for less than one-half inch space not accepted.

Advertisements must reach us by Wednesday to
secure insertion in the issue for the following
Saturday. Address

AMERICAN FLORIST CO., Chicago.
When sending us change of address, always send
the old address at the same time.

CYCLAMENS are good crop for Easter,
April 3.

AMONG the novel things for Christmas
seen at Robert Craig & Son's establishment in Philadelphia this season were
some astilbes from cold-storage roots as
finely flowered as the best ever done for
Easter. Mr. Craig says that despite the
very moderate Christmas call for white
flowers, these plants sold readily at
about double the usual Easter value.

MANY growers hitherto successful with
the little Otaheite orange trees, will be
obliged to abandon the cultivation of
these popular holiday plants unless some
remedy can be found for the peculiar
blight which has spread among them
within the past two or three years. The
loss this season has been heavy and no
effective means of combating the trouble
has, so far, been found.

Society of American Florists.

DEPARTMENT OF PLANT REGISTRATION.

The Conard & Jones Company, West
Grove, Pa., submits for registration a
new hybrid orchid-flowering canna,
Louisiana, a seedling of Pennsylvania.
The flower is a vivid scarlet, very large,
measuring seven inches or more across;
the foliage is large, glossy green, distinctly margined with a purple band. It
is an early and free bloomer.

John Scott, Brooklyn, N. Y., submits
Nephrolepis exaltata Scottii, a sport
from N. e. Bostoniensis. It is dwarf,
dense and compact in habit; the fronds
arching, rarely fertile; midrib reddish
brown and foliage leathery.

WM. J. STEWART, Sec'y.

NEW S. A. F. DIRECTOR.

Theodore Wirth is a native of Zurich,
Switzerland. After receiving a high
school education he chose gardening as
his profession, and was apprenticed to
Ulrich Stahl, Canton St. Gallen, from
which he emerged as a full-fledged gardener. He worked first at Zurich and
afterward at Paris, where he spent several years in the employ of the most celebrated plant specialists. Afterwards he
found a position with Beckwith & Sons
in London, and finally came to America
in 1886, where he was at first employed
in Orange, N. J., and afterward at Morn-
ingside Park, New York, under J. F. Huss.
By his ability he soon reached the position of assistant foreman. His next
assignment was the charge of the cemeteries of the Trinity corporation, after
which he laid out several private estates
at Central Island, the country place of

Col. Greggor at Locust Valley, Long
Island, and the beautiful school grounds
at Glen Cove. In 1895 he married the
daughter of Felix Mense, of Glen Cove.
In the spring of 1896 he was appointed
superintendent of the parks of Hartford,
Conn., and his management thereof has
brought him the highest credit as a landscape artist. Elizabeth park, the latest
addition to the system, is of his own
planning and has, with its greenhouses,
tastefully planted grounds and periodical
floral exhibitions, especially endeared
him to the public of Hartford. This season he has added to its attractions a
rose garden, one of the finest on the
American continent, comprising over
3,000 plants.

Mr. Wirth is a man of exceptional
ability. His selection as a member of
the executive board of the Society of
American Florists, assures for that body
an executive whose life has been intelligently and loyally devoted to the interests for which it stands, and in appointing him as a director Mr. Breitmayer
honors the society as well as Mr. Wirth.
As state vice-president for Connecticut
he was a faithful worker for the society's
interests and rendered valuable services
last year when the agitation of the oner-
ous express charges was in progress.
The gratifying results of that campaign
were in no small degree due to that gentleman's efforts. (See portrait page 938.)

Indianapolis.

E. G. HILL COMPANY HAS REMARKABLE
ROSE SEEDLINGS.—VISIT TO RICHMOND,
IND., GROWERS.—STATE FLORISTS' ASSO-
CIATION HOLDS ANNUAL MEETING.—
OFFICERS ELECTED.

John and Ed. Bertermann, H. W. Rieman, J. Hartje and H. Junge went to Richmond January 8. The time spent there
was so limited, however, that only two
places were visited, those of the B. K. &
B. Floral Company and the E. G. Hill
Company. Mr. Knopf, of the former
firm, showed his visitors around. He is
justly proud of his carnations. Almost
the whole time at the E. G. Hill plant
was spent among the new rose seedlings;
the progress Mr. Hill has made toward
producing valuable commercial varieties
is marvelous. The gem of all so far is
Ætna, of Liberty color, stronger in
growth and very fragrant, evidently as
active in midwinter as the leading rose.
Rosalind, Orr English and David Harum
show great promise. Bertermann Brothers recently marketed blooms of the latter
and the way they went at 50 cents
apiece, makes David Harum a very
tempting p o p o i o . Others in good
shape and much admired were Ideal,
Mildred Grant and Eaton.

The annual meeting of the Indiana
State Florists' Association was well
attended, and signs of renewed activity
were numerous. The election of officers
resulted as follows:

President, E. A. Nelson, Indianapolis.
Vice-president, H. Stewart, Anderson.
Second vice-president, H. Junge, Indianapolis.
Secretary, H. Huckriede, Indianapolis.
Treasurer, J. Heidenreich, Indianapolis.
Executive Committee: H. E. Haugh, Anderson,
chairman; John Rieman, A. Baur, H. Hatfield
and F. Alley.

Fred. Dorner was compelled to stay at
home on account of sickness.

Baur & Smith report heavy sales of
their carnation Indianapolis and John
Hartje's Moonlight. Of those exhibiting
at the Florists' Association meeting,
Baur & Smith were awarded a certificate
of merit for Indianapolis and John Hartje
a certificate of merit for Moonlight.

Honorable mention was given No. 79,
best described as an improved Enchantress. Favorable comment was given
No. 492, a pink of Dorothea shade.

Frank Harritt, the carnation grower,
lost his wife January 2.   J.

Lowell, Mass.

BUSINESS KEEPING UP IN SPITE OF ARCTIC
WEATHER.—THIRTY-FIVE BELOW ZERO
REGISTERED.—BULBOUS STOCK. BECOM-
ING A GLUT.

The cut-flower market is again in a
normal condition; prices for stock have
been lowered, which is something unusual
at this time of year. Some of the growers are kicking at the prices obtained.
Bulbous flowers are steadily on the
increase and Paper White narcissus
will soon become a drug if the supply
continues to increase much longer. The
violet supply is rapidly recuperating
from the severe cuts that it has been subjected to the last two months, in fact
the blooms are better now than they
were at Christmas. Lewis Smith is cutting violets that will cover a half dollar.

Last Monday was inauguration day
at the city hall but outside of a few bouquets and baskets sent to the new city
fathers by personal friends, the hall was
void of floral embellishments. Heretofore the custom has been to decorate
the municipal palace lavishly, the job
being split up so that everyone could
have a look into the city's treasury.

During the last week we experienced
the coldest weather in years. The mercury was down to 35° below zero, freezing up everything, and in some cases
where plants were to be used in decorations they were cut out. With these conditions existing the growers have been
on the jump throwing coal under the
boilers at $6 per ton. At present the
weather is a little easier, much to the joy
of the grower.

Business has kept up remarkably well
and bids fair to continue for some time
according to the social calendar, which
contains several social functions of great
importance. During the last week several society buds made their debut, amid
the fragrance of roses and violets, and
much stock of good quality was called
for.

John J. McMammon was installed last
Wednesday in the Massachusetts general
court, as a representative from the
Twenty-seventh Middlesex district.
    A. M.

Cincinnati.

GLUT OF VIOLETS AND SCARCITY OF GOOD
ROSES CHARACTERIZE MARKET. — FLO-
RISTS' SOCIETY PLANS EXHIBITION FEB-
RUARY 13.—SHORT STEMMED AMERICAN
BEAUTY IS TOO PLENTIFUL. — TRADE
CHANGES.

The usual after holiday dullness existed
last week and many flowers found their
way to the barrel. Violets, especially,
were a glut, thousands selling at 50 cents
per 100. Very good carnations are to be
had at $2 and $3 per 100. Good roses hold
up in price and it is hard to get enough
to fill orders. There is any amount of
poor roses. Romans and narcissi are
plentiful and there are a few short
stemmed tulips, but they do not sell well.
A lot of short stemmed American Beauties are being received which it is hard to
move at any price. Green goods are
plentiful with the exception of Asparagus
Sprengeri.

Miss Minerva Culton, for years stenographer to Albert McCullough, resigned her position with J. M. McCullough's Sons to accept a similar post with Hon. Wade H. Ellis, attorney general of Ohio.

At the monthly meeting of the Florists' Society January 9 it was decided to hold a display of roses, carnations and violets on Saturday, February 13.

Louis Villner, formerly with George & Allan, will open a retail flower store at 939 McMillan street, Walnut Hills.

Paul Dailledouze, of Flatbush, L. I., spent a few hours in town Tuesday on his way to the west.

George Corbett is cutting exceptionally fine Lawson carnations which bring top market prices.

We also hear of a new store to be opened in the Arcade shortly.

George & Allan have single daffodils, the first in the market. A. O.

NEW ALBANY, IND.—Anders Rasmussen is ill of typhoid fever.

ROCHESTER, N. Y.—The annual convention of the Western New York Horticultural Society will be held here, January 27-28, in the halls of the common council.

SITUATIONS, WANTS, FOR SALE.
One Cent Per Word.
Cash with the Adv.

Plant Advs. NOT admitted under this head.

Every paid subscriber to the AMERICAN FLORIST for the year 1903 is entitled to a five-line WANT ADV. (situations only) free, to be used at any time during the year.

Situation Wanted—By a single German of 30; life experience in cut flowers and pot plants near Chicago. State wages. Address
C B, care American Florist.

Situation Wanted—By young married man as manager of retail store; understands business thoroughly; can give best of references.
N B L, care American Florist.

Situation Wanted—As head gardener on private place or institution; 23 years' experience; age 37; married, two children. Address
3097 St. Anthony Ave., Merriam Park, Minn.

Situation Wanted—As forman, rose, carnations, and general stock; ambitious, sober; life experience. State wages and give full particulars.
FOREMAN, 595 Pawtucket Ave., Pawtucket, R. I.

Situation Wanted—By all-around florist and gardener, well-up in flowers, fruits and vegetables. Good reference. Address
F. F. GARDENER, care Anna House, 102 N. Clark St., Chicago.

Situation Wanted—By a grower of carnations, 'mums, bedding stuff, etc. Life experience in general routine of floriculture. Age 36, married. Best of reference. Southern states preferred.
C, care American Florist.

Situation Wanted—As working foreman by first-class cut flower grower, roses a specialty; understands grafting of roses under glass. Only first class place wanted; age 34, single.
P E, care American Florist.

Situation Wanted—By an all-around florist, good grower of roses, carnations; age 36, single; with 20 years of experience. Please state wages and give full particulars. Address
BEAUTY, care American Florist.

Situation Wanted—By a sober industrious man, 13 years' experience in pot and cut flower culture, capable of taking charge of a small place. Private or commercial; reference. Address
SUCCESS, care American Florist.

Situation Wanted—By a young man with 8 years' experience. Strictly sober and a good worker. Some experience in greenhouse building and steam fitting. Open for a position by the 20th inst. Address
LOCK BOX 243, Rankin, Ill.

Situation Wanted—By a thoroughly practical florist as grower; having good knowledge in growing carnations, roses, 'mums, ferns and bedding plants. 3 years. Good references as to abilities, sobriety and character. Address
D J, care American Florist

Situation Wanted—As working foreman by expert grower of cut flowers and general stock; also designer. German, 26 years' experience. Thoroughly competent, sober and reliable. Please state wages. Address
W..A.., 15 Rice St., North Cambridge, Mass.

Situation Wanted—As head gardener in private place, or foreman in florist establishment, by a thoroughly competent florist, 29 years old. 14 years' experience in Germany, England and America. First-class references. South California preferred. Address
G. O. L., Box 1207, Colorado Springs, Col.

Situation Wanted
As grower, designer and decorator.
Address   R N, care American Florist.

Help Wanted—Good rose growers at once.
SOUTH PARK FLORAL CO., New Castle, Ind.

Help Wanted—By an eastern seed house, a vegetable stock clerk. Address
STOCK, care American Florist.

Help Wanted—An assistant for greenhouse work. Private place. Wages $45.00.
JAMES HOLLOWAY, Glen Cove, N. Y.

Help Wanted—Up-to-date rose grower; steady employment; none other need apply. Address
T. O'CONNOR, Blackstone Boulevard, Providence, R. I.

Help Wanted—A man that understands growing ferns from the seed up. Also ornamental pot plants. Married man preferred. Good steady job for right man. Address
J. care American Florist.

Help Wanted—A first-class grower of American Beauty and Tea roses. A good situation and good wages to the man who can produce quality. Modern houses and every facility. Address
ROSES, care American Florist.

Help Wanted—Experienced man for general greenhouse work; must be good in propagating and the growing of bedding stock. State wages wanted per week without board. Address
J. A. BISSINGER, Lansing, Mich.

Help Wanted—Assistant for private place, must be good rose grower. Good chance for promotion and good home for the right man. $30.00 per month and board. Single man. Address
O. UPFLER, Germantown, Baltimore, Md.

Help Wanted—A smart man to act as agent for the U. S. for an up-to-date London firm of basket manufacturers and florist sundries. Address letters to H. M. HAMILTON, 3 York St., Covent Garden, London, W. C., (England.)

Help Wanted—Assistant for private place. Must be a good plantsman. Permanent position for the right man. $30.00 per week and no board. State wages. Address
ALFRED R. CROSS, North Cohasset, Mass.

Help Wanted—Gardener; good all-around man who thoroughly understands care of private greenhouse. Must be temperate. $35.00 per month with board and lodging. Address
Mrs. THOS. WILCE, 708 W. Harrison St., Chicago.

Help Wanted—An all-around florist; one who understands growing all kinds of plants for retail trade. Man who is willing to come to country town. Married man preferred. Wanted by Feb. 1. Reference. Address
B. S. BAKER, Warsaw, N. Y.

Help Wanted—First-class florist. Good grower of cut flowers, plants, etc., for retail trade where No. 1 stock is required. Only experienced and well recommended men need apply. Single preferred. Address
GEORGIA STREET NURSERY, Vancouver, B. C.

Help Wanted—Assistant florist for general greenhouse work; one that can take charge of 15,000 square-feet of glass if needed. Must be of good ability and workmanship. $30.00 per month and room. five more if satisfactory from the 1st of April. Address
H H, care American Florist.

Help Wanted—One or two men. For gentlemens' places. They must be capable of growing vegetables and fruit together with bedding plants. The care of greenhouse and conservatory, nursery and lawn work. Good wages for right men. Situations permanent. Inexperienced men need not apply. Address
K N, care American Florist.

Help Wanted—A man as grower of roses, carnations, 'mums, bedding stock and forcing bulbs. Must be capable of taking charge in absence of owner. Sober, honest and willing to work. Give reference and wages expected.
S. N. PENTECOST, 701-707 Republic St., Cleveland, O.

Help Wanted—Bright young lady for store work, in Camden, N. J. Must have some knowledge of designing, and first-class sales-lady. Address by letter only, stating experience, reference and wages wanted. Position open about March 1st.
SAMUEL H. GOWAN, West Collenswood, N. J.

Wanted—Annual Reports of the American Carnation Society for 1894, 1896 and 1901. Address
R H, care American Florist.

Wanted—To buy or rent by single industrious man, small retail florist place of about 3,000 to 6,000 square feet of glass. State of Iowa preferred. Send full particulars in first letter. Address
WEST, care American Florist.

For Sale or Lease—Greenhouse, 7,000 feet of glass, without stock. Address
WILLARD SMITH, Spokane, Wash.

For Sale—Greenhouses; good location for local and shipping business in Michigan. Well stocked. Reason for selling, on account of failing health.
H B, care American Florist.

For Sale—Greenhouses. Good location for local and shipping business. Well stocked; winter coal laid in. Will sell cheap if sold at once. Selling on account of failing health.
JAS. RICHARDSON, London, O.

For Sale or Lease—Fine greenhouse, establishment of 10,000 feet of glass, in good condition and well stocked, with or without dwelling. Fine opening for a single man. Stock reasonable.
X Y Z, care American Florist.

For Sale or Lease—Between 30,000 to 40,000 feet glass; barn, dwelling house; hot water heating, constant water supply, two acres for cultivation in Bronx Borough, New York city. Address
J. RINGLER, 728 3d Ave., New York.

For Sale—Four greenhouses. Chicago, 7,000 feet of glass, on leased ground. Well stocked with carnations and potted plants. Good retail trade and long lease. Price $3,500.00, part cash, balance on time. Address
J R F, care American Florist.

For Sale—Fine chance for an energetic man with small capital to acquire a well established retail florist business with best trade in city. Also greenhouses, 12,000 square feet, good location. Everything in running order. Will sell together or separate at a bargain. Cause for selling, poor health. Address
SCHLORAFF FLORAL CO., Erie, Pa.

For Sale—At a great bargain for quick sale: greenhouses of about 3,500 feet of glass, hot water heat; first-class boiler, large enough to heat double the space; up-to-date ventilators, full of clean, healthy, paying stock. Can sell everything you raise. Will sell houses with or without land. Small amount of cash needed. Reason, old age and failing strength. Address
DES MOINES PLANT CO., 38th St., Des Moines, Ia.

For Sale—Three greenhouses situated in West Tenn. About 10,000 square feet glass, well stocked with roses, carnations, palms, ferns and bedding plants. Heated by two Florence hot water heaters. About one and one-quarter acres of ground. 300 feet cold frames which belong to the plant. Everything in first-class condition. No competition. A good bargain. A change of climate necessary for family cause of sale. Address
MRS. M. Inis BROWN, Union City, Tenn.

WANTED.
Position as foreman or manager in an up-to-date establishment: either wholesale, retail or mailing. Am up in all branches, catalogue marking, building, heating and growing of the stock. 2,000,000 plants grown the past season. Three years in last place. 40 years old and a hustler. Northern place preferred. Married temperate and strictly business. Best of reference as to ability and business qualities. Address LONE STAR, 611 No. Washington Ave., Dallas, Tex.

FOR SALE.
3 greenhouses, heated hot-water shed and 7 acres of land, house and stable. At Somerton Hills, 15 miles from Philadelphia. Will sell cheap.
Mrs. Geo. McFadden, 1428 Walnut St., Philadelphia.

First-Class Positions
Are regularly filled through advertising in this department. We receive almost daily inquiry for good men in all lines. Advertising rates given above.

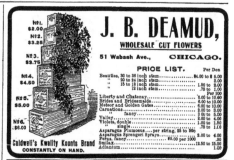

INTERNATIONAL FLOWER DELIVERY.

PASSENGER STEAMSHIP MOVEMENTS.

The tables herewith give the scheduled time of departure of ocean steamships carrying first-class passengers from the principal American and foreign ports, covering the space of two weeks from date of this issue of the AMERICAN FLORIST. Much disappointment often results from attempts to forward flowers for steamer delivery by express, to the care of the ship's steward or otherwise. The carriers of these packages are not infrequently refused admission on board and even those delivered on board are not always certain to reach the parties for whom they were intended. Hence florists in interior cities having orders for the delivery of flowers to passengers on out-going steamers are advised to intrust the filling of such orders to some reliable florist in the port of departure, who understands the necessary details and formalities and has the facilities for attending to it properly. For the addresses of such firms we refer our readers to the advertisements on this page.

FROM	TO	STEAMER	*LINE	DAY		DUE ABOUT
New York	Liverpool	Lucania	1	Sat.	Jan. 23, 9:00 a. m.	Jan. 30
New York	"	Saxonia	1	Sat.	Jan. 30, 2:00 p. m.	Feb. 6
New York	Plume	Aurania	1	Tues.	Jan. 26, 11:00 a. m.	
New York	Glasgow	Siberian	2	Sat.	Jan. 21, Noon.	Jan. 31
Portland	"	Hibernian	2	Sat.	Jan. 30,	Feb. 9
New York	Hamburg	Pretoria	3	Sat.	Jan. 23, 8:00 a. m.	Feb. 5
New York	"	Graf Waldersee	3	Sat.	Jan. 30, 4:00 p. m.	Feb. 9
New York	Genoa	Deutschland	3	Tues.	Jan. 19, 4:00 p. m.	Jan. 26
New York	Glasgow	Ethiopia	4	Sat.	Jan. 23, Noon.	Feb. 2
New York	London	Menominee	6	Sat.	Jan. 9, 9:00 a. m.	Feb. 2
New York	"	Minneapolis	6	Sat.	Jan. 30, 3:00 p. m.	Feb. 9
New York	Liverpool	Teutonic	7	Wed.	Jan. 20, 10:00 a. m.	Jan. 27
New York	"	Cedric	7	Wed.	Jan. 27, Noon.	Feb. 3
Boston	"	Cymric	7	Thur.	Jan. 21, Noon.	Jan. 28
Boston	Alexandria	Canopic	7	Sat.	Jan. 30, 7:00 a. m.	Feb. 17
Boston	Southampton	St. Paul	8	Sat.	Jan. 23, 9:30 a. m.	Jan. 29
New York	"	Philadelphia	8	Sat.	Jan. 30, 9:30 a. m.	Feb. 6
New York	Antwerp	Kroonland	9	Sat.	Jan. 23, 10:30 a. m.	Feb. 2
New York	"	Zeeland	9	Sat.	Jan. 30, 10:30 a. m.	Feb. 9
New York	Havre	La Bretagne	10	Thur.	Jan. 21, 10:00 a. m.	Jan. 31
New York	"	La Touraine	10	Thur.	Jan. 28, 10:00 a. m.	Feb. 7
New York	Rotterdam	Statendam	11	Tues.	Jan. 19, 10:00 a. m.	Jan. 31
New York	Genoa	Sicilia	12	Sat.	Jan. 19, 11:00 a. m.	Feb. 4
New York	"	Lombardia	12	Sat.	Jan. 26, 11:00 a. m.	Feb. 10
New York	Bremen	Kaiser Wilh. II	13	Tues.	Jan. 26, 10:00 a. m.	Feb. 2
New York	"	Hanover	13	Tues.	Jan. 26, 11:00 a. m.	Feb. 5
New York	Genoa	Princess Irene	13	Sat.	Jan. 23, 11:00 a. m.	Feb. 5
New York	Naples	Neckar	13	Sat.	Jan. 30, 11:00 a. m.	Feb. 12
New York	"	Germania	14	Tues.	Jan. 19,	Feb. 5
Boston	Liverpool	Winifredian	16	Sat.	Jan. 30, 11:30 a. m.	Jan. 30
Boston	"	Bohemain	16	Wed.	Jan. 27, 5:00 a. m.	Feb. 6

*1 Cunard; 2 Allen-State; 3 Hamburg-American; 4 Scandinavian-American; 5 Anchor Line; 6 Atlantic Transport; 7 White Star; 8 American; 9 Red Star; 10 French; 11 Holland-American; 12 Italian Royal Mail; 13 North German Lloyd; 14 Fabre; 16 Leyland; 17 Occidental and Oriental; 18 Oceanic; 19 Allan; 20 Can. Pacific Ry.; 21 N. Pacific Ry.; 22 Hongkong-Seattle.

THE SEED TRADE.

AMERICAN SEED TRADE ASSOCIATION.
S. F. Willard, Pres.; J. Charles McCullough,
First Vice-Pres.; C. E. Kendel, Cleveland, O.,
Sec'y and Treas.
Twenty-second annual convention St. Louis,
Mo., June, 1904.

THERE seem to be tuberose bulbs enough this year. to go around.

FANCY dark red onion sets are in demand but prices have not moved up much—yet.

CUCUMBER seed prices hold fairly steady at prices before mentioned, $1.50 to $1.75 per pound.

IT is reported that southern truckers have paid as high as $15 per bushel for Wardwell's wax beans.

THE bids for seeds for the United States Department of Agriculture were to be considered January 15.

VISITED CHICAGO.—A. Corneli, of the Schisler Corneli Seed Company, St. Louis, Mo.; W. H. Grenell, Saginaw, Mich.

FRANK J. RIES, of the Goodwin, Harries Seed Company, Chicago, left this week for an extended business trip through the west and south.

THE weather in the California seed districts continues very dry and unusually cold and while most of the crops are planted, nothing is growing.

SANTA CLARA, CAL.—Mrs. J. M. Kimberlin, wife of Prof. J. M. Kimberlin, the pioneer seed grower of Santa Clara county, died suddenly December 24, aged 72 years. She leaves a husband and six children.

London.

ROYAL HORTICULTURAL SOCIETY HOLDS LAST MEETING OF YEAR.—LATE CHRYS-ANTHEMUMS SHOWN.—THREE NEW CRO-TONS. — GARDENERS' GUILD, UNION OF WORKERS, IS PLANNED.

The Royal Horticultural Society's last meeting of the year, December 15, attracted a large number of visitors. There were also more trade growers and gardeners than usual. The Dahlia Society had a meeting the same date. There was an excellent exhibition. We have rarely had such a grand display of orchids in December. The usual trade growers made a good show and there were several fine groups from private collectors. The cypripediums and odon-toglossums were the most worthy of note. Of the latter some superb spotted varieties were shown and the cypripedi-ums included some beautiful new hybrids. Veitch & Sons again staged begonias, of which Winter Cheer was superbly flow-ered. Cannell & Sons were again in fine form with zonal pelargoniums in bloom. Wells & Company had a fine display of late chrysanthemums of various types, mostly of the decorative class. Elegans, a single variety with long fluted florets of a soft pink shade, was admired. There was also Mrs. J. Carter, cream, with the narrow, thread-like florets; Mrs. Swin-bourne, a pure white Japanese, with large, incurved florets; Miss Emily Fowler, a good yellow, and fine blooms of Mme. Paolo Radaelli. The last named was shown October 6 and has been seen in good condition at all shows since. The late blooms are deeper in color than those seen earlier in the season. Mr. Allman had a good collection of decorative varie-

ties. Sunstone, a pale amber, looks like a useful market variety, and Allmans, yellow, was honored with an award of merit. Cragg, Harrison & Cragg showed Heston White, a pure white sport from Mme. Felix Perrin, a flower of good sub-stance which will be useful for market work. The parent is extensively grown and in the market it is generally known as Framfield Pink, having first been grown by Norman Davis, of Framfield. D. W. Bull & Sons had a fine collection of choice palms, in healthy specimens and including some choice sorts not often seen, Livistona Woodfordii, Phœnix Ræbelenii, Kentia Sanderiana, and sev-eral distinct species of calamuses. These last named are very elegant, but they are not much appreciated for decorations on account of the formidable spines. F. S. Ware had a splendid collection of alpine and rock plants and hardy cacti. T. Rockford & Sons had three new crotons several plants of each being shown. Turnfordiensis, medium sized, with a rather broad leaves, bright yellow with a nar-row, irregular margin of green, gained an award of merit. It should make a useful market variety. Elegantissimus roseus, with long, narrow, drooping leaves, well variegated, the yellow chang-ing to a bright rosy tint, red stems, and leaf stalks, and Golden Gem, with rather larger leaves, pale yellow at the base, the other portion spotted, were the others. These are all found to stand exposure. Cutbush & Sons had a large group of ivies and evergreen shrubs. The Russell Company again showed hardy shrubs, Aucuba longifolia, well berried, looking very bright among the small, narrow, deep green leaves. E. Beckett showed an interesting collection of deciduous shrubs; the exhibit consisted of upwards of sixty sorts, the shoots being cut and shown in bunches. The various colors of the wood, bright red and other distinct shades, were very effective.

A meeting convened for the purpose of considering the question of forming an association among gardeners, to be called gardeners' guild, was well attended. Several letters were read, and various propositions made but no definite scheme was arrived at. After a rather lengthy discussion it was decided to adjourn the meeting until February, and a committee of seven with Owen Thomas as chairman and A. Dean as secretary was elected to meet previously and to formulate some definite lines on which such an associa-tion could be formed. It was suggested that the Royal Horticultural Society should be asked to cooperate in the mat-ter. It seems extremely unlikely that the dahlia, chrysanthemum and other special societies will be able to arrange with the R. H. S. to hold their shows and meetings in the new hall when it is completed.
A. H.

New Bedford, Mass.

Christmas trade was unexpectedly better than last year. Plants and flowers both sold well. The greatest demand in flowers was for carnations. E. H. Chamberlin and Wm. Pierce bought most of their plants and flowers in Boston. A. Jahn, S. S. Peckham, R. H. Wood-house and E. Y. Pierce report much better trade than last year. We have been having the coldest weather ever known here, with the thermometer in some places 15° below zero.
A. B. H.

THE NURSERY TRADE.

AM. ASSOCIATION OF NURSERYMEN.
N. W. HALE, Knoxville, Tenn., Pres.; FRANK
A. WEBER, St. Louis, Mo., Vice-Pres.; GEORGE C.
SEAGER, Rochester, N. Y., Sec'y.
Twenty-ninth annual convention, Atlanta, Ga.,
June, 1904.

HUNTSVILLE, TENN.—Maj. W. F. Heikes,
manager of the Huntsville nurseries, is
completing plans to erect a handsome
mansion in this city.

ATLANTA, GA.—Three million peach
trees and five hundred thousand apple
trees are to be planted in Georgia this
year, according State Entomologist Will-
mon Newell.

NEWARK, N. Y.—Certificates of incor-
poration have been filed by Emmons &
Company, with a capital of $5,000;
William C. Moore & Company, $5,000;
Knight & Bostwick, $5,000; and C. W.
Stuart & Company, $24,000. These
firms do a large nursery business.

GENEVA, N. Y.—The third annual convention of the New York Fruit Growers'
Association, in session here, closed January 7. These officers were elected: President, T. B. Wilson, of Halls Corners;
vice-presidents, J. T. Roberts, of Syracuse; J. B. Collamer, of Hilton; Albert
Wood, of Carlton Station and Ira Pease,
of Oswego; secretary, W. I. McKay, of
Geneva; treasurer, C. H. Darrow, of
Geneva. The next convention will be
held in Geneva.

LANSING, MICH.—State Forest Warden
Roth has forwarded his plan for the seed
beds of the forestry commission, and
there was a meeting of that body in this
city December 12 to discuss the report.
The plans were drawn by the forestry
bureau at Washington, and provide for
a permanent nursery in which to grow
seedlings of the kinds which are most
suitable to the Michigan reserve lands.
This nursery will be located in Roscom-
mon county, but the extent of it cannot
be estimated at this time. The planting
of the seed will begin as early as possible
in the spring. The warden is busily
engaged, and will continue so all winter,
in gathering the seed for this purpose.
White pine will be planted principally,
but Prof. Roth will try all kinds of coni-
ferous trees, as well as the Carolina poplar, catalpa, locust and similar varieties
which give promise of quick returns.
This is the first practical step to be taken
in the reforestation scheme which the
state commission has been formulating
during the last few years.

Cumberland, Md.

The Mountain Dale Orchard Company
of Maryland and W. Virginia, was
recently incorporated at Cumberland,
Md., with a capital stock of $20,000.
Officers: W. C. White (mayor of Cumberland), president; G. H. Hetsel, secretary-
treasurer; S. D. Moser, general manager.
Main office, Cumberland, Md. The company starts with an orchard of 25,000
peach, pear and plum trees from one to
four years old. About 50,000 additional
trees in variety will be planted in the
next two years. The company controls
or owns about 1,000 acres of land
adjoining the now famous Allegheny
peach orchards, near Paw Paw, W. Va.,
Hampshire county, and it is understood
has options on more of the contiguous
territory. It contemplates starting a
general nursery business.

OUR PASTIMES.

Announcements of coming contests or other events of interests to our bowling, shooting and sporting readers are solicited and will be given place in this column.
Address all correspondence for this department to Wm. J. Stewart, 43 W. 28th St., New York. Robt. Kift, 1725 Chestnut St., Philadelphia, Pa.; to the American Florist Co., Chicago, Ill.

At Flatbush, N. Y.

On Thursday evening, January 7, the Bowling Club held its annual games for "grab-bag" prizes with the usual good time and amusing results. Louis Schmuts found his destiny in his prize, a box of one hundred collar buttons, one button for each future year of his life.

At New York.

The New York bowlers have secured good practice alleys at Tenth avenue and Twenty-third street. The number of applicants for membership already in the hands of Captain Theo. J. Lang would indicate a well-grounded purpose to bring out the reserves and get on a war footing for the encounter at St. Louis next August.

At Colorado Springs, Col.

Colorado Springs had a visit from the Denver Florists' Bowling club last Saturday. The visitors were defeated by a margin of nearly 200 pins. Here is the story in figures:

DENVER.			
Player	1st	2d	3d
Benson	146	116	163
Kurth	118	137	141
Timmer	125	197	145
Berry	135	130	162
Glautber	140	152	136
Grand total			2012

COLORADO SPRINGS.			
Player	1st	2d	3d
Johnson	166	171	158
Vinson	131	178	176
Harris	124	138	179
Braidwood, Duff	100	92	156
Duntean	140	126	192
Grand total			2210

W. H. D.

At Chicago.

The bowlers met at the Geroux alleys, Tuesday evening and rolled six games with the following results. Owing to the fact that some of the members belong to teams in city leagues and who were playing on the same night it left a rather small attendance. However, since the handicap games start in soon it is expected that a full attendance will be assured hereafter. In our last week's notes we failed to give credit to Mrs. Walter Kreitling and her son Victor. Their scores were as follows:

Mrs. Kreitling	179	145
Victor Kreitling	217	232

Victor has challenged his father to roll a match and says he will give his "dad" fifty points and then "leave him in the shade." Walter is going into training for the event. The scores:

Player	1st	2d	3d	4th	5th	6th
Stevens	191	186	191	186	187	204
Asmus	131	181	178	169	161	181
Winterson	197	157	191	146	146	140
Ballyf	155	158	146	202	147	158
Hunber	158	145	123	141	186	137
Hauswirth			150	150	136	186

LENOX, MASS.—The officers-elect of the Lenox Horticultural Society were installed on December 19. The gain in membership during the year is twenty-six. A movement is on foot to create a fund for meeting and exhibition purposes.

Toronto.

WEATHER MODERATING AND BUSINESS IMPROVES.—GOOD STOCK ON THE MARKET.—PRICES AND GENERAL NOTES OF THE TRADE.

The weather has moderated considerably the last few days and with it trade has started to pick up. Funeral work is still a large factor. Roses are coming in in very fine shape and although there is not an over supply, there is enough to go around. Carnations still hold their quality and there are some very select fancies, Enchantress, Prosperity, Golden Beauty and Stella, which find ready sale. Violets are becoming very plentiful and the high prices at which they are still quoted find them hard to dispose of and a further reduction in the prices will be most favorable. Callas and Lilium Harrisii are in good demand. There are at present some very good flowering plants on the market, including some well grown azaleas, lilacs, cyclamens and ericas. Wednesday, January 13, saw the first drop in roses since the holidays. American Beauty are quoted at $30 to $40 per hundred; Bridesmaid, Bride, Meteor and Morgan $12 per hundred; Perle and Sunrise $10 per hundred; select carnations $6 per hundred; select valley $4; Princess violets $2; Paper White narcissi $3 per hundred, and lilies $15 per hundred.

J. Gard, of Pape avenue, has some fine bulbous stock; for the holidays he had some good violets and carnations, but since then the crop is a little off.

Grobba & Wandrey are bringing in

Lockport, N. Y.

Fire, January 8, destroyed the greenhouses owned by Frank B. Lewis and operated by his son, Clarence I. Lewis. The flames' origin is unknown, but is supposed to have been at the boiler. No night man was employed. The houses contained carnations and violets. The loss on buildings and stock was $3,000, with no insurance. Mr. Lewis will rebuild at once, work having started yesterday.

K. L.

Niles, O.

C. L. Adgate has sold his business to the Baltimore & Ohio railroad for a nice sum of money. He does not know as yet where he will locate. The railroad runs through his property.

Dana Miller, of C. L. Adgate's place, has started in the business with John Geddes, of Girard, Ohio, who has been in the trade quite a good many years.

some very fine tulips, red, white and yellow, and some nice Dutch hyacinths which are early for this season.

Harry Bunyard, representing Clucas & Boddington, but a short time will no doubt see others in his wake.

Our genial Thos. Manton is suffering from a cold. La Grippe is epidemic at present and a number of the craft are under its influence.

D. C. Nixon, publisher of the Canadian Florist, has been ill. H. G. D.

St. Paul, Minn.

Trade since the holidays has been good. Stock is plentiful, which has not been the case for several years at this season. Carnations are abundant. We have seen them sold for 50 cents a dozen. Wm. Speth, who had charge of Aug. Swanson's Sixth Street store, has accepted a position with Holm & Olson. Mr. Speth is noted for his window displays.

The Mrs. M. A. Patten and Nelson Fisher carnations which Holm & Olson have received are much admired by the local growers.

Carl Peterson, the "hyacinth king," is now bringing in Dutch hyacinths and tulips which sell readily.

J. A. Vandervoort, representing C. J. Speelman & Sons, was the first "Dutchman" to call this year.

Haugen & Swanson have fine violets. Their Princess of Wales are the largest seen here.　　　　　　　　　　　　O.

We Have Them

ROOTED CARNATION CUTTINGS, taken from flowering stems only. Well rooted and in perfect health. 25,000 Now Ready.

	Per 100	1000
Enchantress	$6.00	$50.00
The Queen	6.00	50.00
Fair Maid	4.00	30.00
Gov. Wolcott	4.00	30.00
Boston Market	4.00	30.00
Mrs. T. W. Lawson	3.00	20.00

SATISFACTION GUARANTEED.

HENRY A. STEVENS CO., DEDHAM, MASS.

NEW LARGE-FLOWERING CALLA

CALLA DEVONIENSIS.

Blooming Callas From Seed in One Year

The most beautiful and best Calla up to date without a doubt. It is equally valuable for pots and cut. It produces from 3 to 4 times as many flowers as the older sorts.

The seedlings come true and will bloom profusely the first year. This Calla came from England about 6 years ago and is a great improvement on C. Æthiopica. Its willingness to bloom is phenomenal while its culture is of the simplest.

One year old plants often produce from 6 to 8 flowers which are of great beauty. They are pure white large and are borne on stout stalks. They are also good keepers. If sown at intervals of 4 to 6 weeks this Calla can be had in bloom all the year.

100 seeds, 75c; 1000 seeds, $6.00.

Vaughan's Seed Store,
CHICAGO,　　　　NEW YORK,
84-86 Randolph St.　　14 Barclay St.

PLEASE mention the AMERICAN FLORIST every time you write to an advertiser.

CARNATION CUTTINGS

WELL ROOTED, CLEAN, HEALTHY AND POPULAR VARIETIES. ORDER NOW AND RECEIVE PROMPT SHIPMENT.

PINK.	Per 100	100)	RED.	Per 100	1000
Enchantress	$6.00	$50.00	Palmer	$2.00	$15.00
Morning Glory	2.00	15.00	Estelle	3.00	15.00
Higinbotham	1.50	12.50	Harlowarden	3.00	25.00
			WHITE.		
Lawson	1.60	12.50	Her Majesty	3.00	25.00
Guardian Angel	1.25	10.00	White Cloud	1.50	12.50
Cressbrook	1.50	12.50	Flora Hill	1.50	12.50

Rooted Rose Cuttings.

	Per 100	1000		Per 100	1000
Bride	$1.50	$12.50	La France	$2.00	$15.00
Bridesmaid	1.50	12.50	Meteor	1.50	12.50
Ivory	1.50	12.50	Liberty	3.00	25.00
Golden Gate	1.50	12.50			

WIETOR BROS., Wholesale Growers of Cut Flowers.
51-53 Wabash Avenue, CHICAGO.

Please mention the American Florist when writing.

NOW READY Carnations FOR SHIPMENT.

BEST AND MOST STRONGLY ROOTED CARNATIONS ON THE MARKET.

WHITE.	Per 100	1000	5000	PINK.	Per 100	1000	5000
Queen Louise	$1.00	$10.00	$40.00	Mrs. T. W. Lawson	1.60	12.50	60.00
Gov. Wolcott	1.20	10.00	40.00	Marquis	1.00	9.00	35.00
White Cloud	1.00	9.00	35.00	Mrs. Joost	1.20	10.00	40.00
SCARLET.				**VARIEGATED.**			
America	1.30	10.00	40.00	Armazindy	1.00	9.00	35.00
CRIMSON.				Prosperity	1.40	12.50	60.00
Gov. Roosevelt	1.20	11.00	50.00				

EXPRESS PREPAID TO ANY DESTINATION. SATISFACTION GUARANTEED OR YOUR MONEY BACK.

LOOMIS CARNATION CO.
LOCK BOX 115.　　　LOOMIS, CAL.
Please mention the American Florist when writing.

ROOTED CARNATION CUTTINGS.

Selected from perfectly healthy stock with the one idea of producing good strong plants. Most of the varieties are ready. New batches are coming in regularly for late orders.

	Per 100	1000		Per 100	1000
Enchantress	$5.00	$45.00	Lillian Pond	$4.00	
Gov. Wolcott	3.50	30.00	Harlowarden	6.00	
Lawson	2.00	17.50	Higinbotham	3.00	
Palmer	2.00	17.50	Joost	3.00	$17.50
Prosperity	3.50	30.00			

Stock 'mums of Merry Christmas, big clumps, 10c; $1.00 per dozen.

POEHLMANN BROS. COMPANY, Morton Grove, Ill.

Please mention the American Florist when writing.

Dallas, Tex.

H. Good, of Springfield, O., who was judge at the Waco show, spent a day with the craft and was shown the sights of Dallas by Messrs. Beach and Miller. He was somewhat surprised when he saw the rose fields of the Haskel Avenue Floral Company.

The Waco show was a decided success and was well patronized, many Dallas people going to view the grand display. There is talk of having a chrysanthemum show here next fall. There is no reason why Dallas should not make a success of one.

Otto Lang sprained his ankle badly trying to control a bronco. He is all right as a florist when he it comes to breaking in wild horses he is a failure. He has had several decorations of late that were unusually good.

Everybody is busy here and the stores are making good window displays. The Texas Seed and Floral Company has had much success with home-grown chrysanthemums and reports good trade both in seeds and cut flowers.

P. W. Beach, superintendent of the Haskell Avenue Floral Company, was ill in bed two weeks but is out and attending to business again.

Mrs. Henry Holtcamp and her daughter are having a fine trade in funeral work. They have the heaviest trade in this line and are artists.   LONE STAR.

Oceanic, N. J.

The meeting of the Monmouth County Horticultural society was held January 8. One new member was elected. The discussion of the evening was "The Forcing of Lilacs and Azaleas," in which most of the members took part. Two tables of flowers were shown. H. A. Kettel, gardener to James Loeb, had two varieties of tulips, some narcissi and Bride, Bridesmaid and Golden Gate roses in grand form. Wm. Turner, gardener to M. C. D. Borden, showed carnations, including Enchantress, Lawson, Roosevelt, Bradt, Prosperity, Queen, Lorna and Governor Wolcott. Mr. Turner has some of the best carnations in this vicinity and his Enchantress is exceptionally fine. N. Butterbach, gardener to C. N. Bliss, had Lawson, Prosperity, White Bradt and Manley carnations and a seedling, a soft pink, unique in shade, which scored ninety-five points and bids fair to surpass Lawson in shape, color and substance. Geo. H. Hale showed a big vase of poinsettias, not easily excelled. Mr. Hale was asked to give a few points on the culture of same, which were a benefit to every one present. The judges of the evening were W. W. Kennedy, John Kennedy and W. H. Griffiths. The society decided to hold its meetings twice a month during the winter as previously. The eighth annual ball of the society will be held February 12.   B.

ANOKA, MINN.—The Pratt Ford Company of this place incorporated January 9 with $50,000 capital. James W. Ford, of Owatonna, James W. Ford, Jr. of Anoka, and David D. Pratt, of Anoka, are the incorporators.

HARRISBURG, PA.—C. L. Schmidt reports that the holiday business completely overshadowed that of 1902, although prices were no higher. Roses and carnations were in ample supply, but the latter were not of standard quality. Carnations and violets are losing favor with the public owing to high prices.

Seasonable Plants for Forcing

Louisville.

The city has arranged to buy Central park, a plot of about twelve acres, which is laid out in walks and drives on undulating ground, covered with full grown forest trees. The price will be $275,000.

Nans & Neuner had garlands of green trimmed with small electric lights and an attractive display of very fine chrysanthemums and Gloire de Lorraine begonias.

Prof. E. L. Walker, of Fayetteville, Ark., is visiting relatives here. He will lay out the grounds of the Arkansas exhibit at the St. Louis World's Fair.

Christmas sales were about the same as last year. Plants and cut flowers sold about equally well. Holly sold well but there was an oversupply.

Mrs. C. W. Reimers had an attractive window display Christmas week, all red poinsettias and Christmas bells.

F. Walker & Company had a superior stock of violets and found ready sale for a large quantity.

Louis Risch, carnation specialist, had an excellent stock.

Jacob Schulz had a fine assortment of blooming plants.

C. W. Reimers had a good supply of poinsettias.   H. G. W.

Columbus, O.

The last week has been a busy one for the trade and wholesale prices on stock took a downward course and enabled the retailer to realize a living profit on all goods handled. Ohio's governor will be inaugurated this week. The inaugural promises to be one of the most brilliant affairs in the history of the Buckeye state. It is causing quite a stir in society and cannot fail to have a very favorable effect on business.

This winter is one of the severest known to even the oldest of our citizens. The mercury has often reached a lower point in this section of the country but for steady low temperature lasting from November 1 till now the season breaks all previous records.   CARL.

Springfield, Mass.

Not in many years has this city and vicinity experienced such severe weather as we had the last week, the mercury going down as low as 26° below zero. Little damage was done, fortunately, as coal was more plentiful and cheaper than a year ago. Business was slow during the cold snap but is now picking up. Cut flowers are more plentiful and reach the retailer on time. Pot plants are more plentiful and find ready sale. Funeral work is in good demand, helping to keep down any surplus stock.   A. B.

Pleased With Results.

AM. FLORIST CO.:—We are pleased with the results of our advertising up to the present time and believe we shall have a large increase in our business next year.

STANDARD PUMP AND ENGINE CO.

Cleveland, O., December 10, 1903.

Cannot Do Without It.

AMERICAN FLORIST CO.:—I send you my dollar for another year for the AMERICAN FLORIST, as I cannot do without it, there is so much valuable information in it.   G. P. MAHOOD.

Denison, Texas, December 26, 1903.

Albany, N. Y.

Governor Odell on Tuesday evening gave a dinner to the state officials and their wives. W. C. King furnished the table decorations of Liberty roses and Adiantum Farleyense. Last week Eyres furnished the decorations for the fashionable Dillon-Lintner wedding which took place in St. Peter's church. Carnations, poinsettias, Lilium Harrisii, southern smilax and laurel roping were used in abundance.

The opening of the new year found this section of country in the grip of an extraordinary cold spell, the like of which has not been known here for thirty years. On January 4 the minimum temperature recorded by the weather bureau was 23.8° below zero. Places to the north of Albany recorded temperatures even colder.

Louis Menand reports that his stock is doing finely at his new house on Cemetery avenue. R. D.

Ishpeming, Mich.

The Lutey Floral Company, of Houghton and Calumet, reports everything cleaned up at remunerative prices; never had a better Christmas.

Mrs. Stofford reports an excellent Christmas trade. While she had a large crop of carnations on the place they were not sufficient.

From the leading florists of the Upper Peninsula of Michigan I have obtained the following reports by telephone:

Trebelcock Brothers, at Ishpeming, say their Christmas trade eclipsed all previous records.

The Iron Cliffs greenhouses at Negaunee say that business was never better than this year. W. H. BALDWIN.

Little Neck, N. Y.

Wm. K. Vanderbilt is just beginning work on a magnificent Italian garden on his place at Success Lake. It is more than a mile from the house and is located on the southern slope of the ridge of hills crossing his estate. The gardens will be more than half a mile in extent and they are to be embellished with works of art imported from France and Italy. There also will be found rare trees and shrubs in great variety. About a quarter of a mile away from the gardens will be the greenhouses, covering several acres. Robert Hope, one of the best known gardeners in this vicinity, and who has made the places of W. Gould Brokaw, James Martin, Cord Meyer and Howard Gould beautiful, has been engaged by Mr. Vanderbilt.

Valuable and Convenient.

AMERICAN FLORIST COMPANY:—Your paper is certainly a very valuable one and very convenient in every way, Memphis, Tenn. OTTO SCHWILL.

Swamped With Orders.

AMERICAN FLORIST CO.—Your last issue brought more returns than I ever had from any paper; practically swamped with orders. D. S. BEACH.
Bridgeport, Conn.

Leads Them All.

ED. AM. FLORIST:— Enclosed is a renewal of my subscription to your valuable paper, the best of all trade papers. W. J. GOWANS.
Los Angeles, Cal.

FREMONT, NEB.—Business doubled is the way C. H. Green sizes up this year's Christmas business. Prices the same and all stock short, especially violets. Nobody wanted bulbous flowers, but bright-colored material was picked up fast and azaleas sold rapidly. A first-class Christmas trade and everybody feeling good.

972   THE AMERICAN FLORIST.   Jan. 16,

LANCASTER, PA.—The Pennsylvania State Horticultural Association will hold its forty-fifth annual meeting here, January 19–20.

THE AMERICAN FLORIST

America is "the Prow of the Vessel; there may be more comfort Amidships, but we are the first to touch Unknown Seas."

Vol. XXI.	CHICAGO AND NEW YORK, JANUARY 23, 1904.	No. 816.

THE AMERICAN FLORIST

NINETEENTH YEAR.

Copyright 1904, by American Florist Company
Entered as Second-Class Mail Matter.

PUBLISHED EVERY SATURDAY BY

AMERICAN FLORIST COMPANY,
324 Dearborn St., Chicago.
Eastern Office: 42 W. 28th St., New York.

Subscription, $1.00 a year.   To Europe, $2.00.
Subscriptions accepted only from the trade.
Volumes half-yearly from August, 1901.

SOCIETY OF AMERICAN FLORISTS AND
ORNAMENTAL HORTICULTURISTS.
OFFICERS—JOHN BURTON, Philadelphia, Pa.,
president; C. C. POLLWORTH, Milwaukee, Wis.,
vice-president; WM. J. STEWART, 79 Milk Street,
Boston, Mass., secretary; H. B. BEATTY, Oil City,
Pa., treasurer.
OFFICERS-ELECT—PHILIP BREITMEYER, president; J. J. BENEKE, vice-president; secretary and
treasurer as before. Twentieth annual meeting
at St. Louis, Mo., August, 1904.

THE AMERICAN CARNATION SOCIETY.
Annual convention at Detroit, Mich., March 9,
1904. ALBERT M. HERR, Lancaster, Pa., secretary.

AMERICAN ROSE SOCIETY.
Annual meeting and exhibition, Philadelphia,
March, 1904. LEONARD BARRON, 136 Liberty St.,
New York, secretary.

CHRYSANTHEMUM SOCIETY OF AMERICA.
Annual convention and exhibition, November,
1904. FRED H. LEMON, Richmond, Ind., secretary.

THIS ISSUE 40 PAGES WITH COVER.

Rhinebeck and Its Violet Growers.

IV.

In the Rhinebeck violet growing community, as a rule, a fairly uniform system
of cultivation is followed. On minor
matters one finds some divergence of
views as to the handling of the plants,
but, in general, each grower does about
as his neighbors do. The consensus of
views is that to attain the best results
and the fullest immunity from insects and
fungous troubles a moderately slow
growth is desirable. Observant growers
advise early planting as one means to
insure this, as there will then be no need
to hurry the plants under any circumstances, and, in the case of unseasonably
warm fall weather they are not caught
with big soft growth. Where excessive
growth and warm moist weather form a
combination it furnishes the most favorable kind of an opening for the dreaded
violet spot. Drip also makes spot inevitable, hence side ventilation is favored
because the liability for drip during the
night or in rainy weather is minimized.
It is customary to whitewash the glass
when planting, the wash being removed
from about the middle of November till
February 1. Overshading being another
fruitful cause of black spot the application of the wash must be done with
judgment it being borne in mind that
houses running east and west will need
the shade earlier than will those running
north and south. Prevention rather than
remedy should be the aim in combating
spot. Abundant ventilation is a cardinal
point and air is given freely all through
the fall until the thermometer touches
42°, when it must be shut off and, when
the atmosphere is damp, a little fire is
given even if the ventilators must be kept
open at the same time to hold the temperature in check. With good hard foliage,
scrupulous cleanliness always, careful
watching of atmospheric conditions,
plenty of pure air and judicious water-

ing there is little to be dreaded. Should
any spot appear the infected foliage and
in aggravated cases the entire plant is
promptly taken and burned. One grower
who had a grievous visitation of spot in
his houses last year tried bi-sulphide of
carbon as recommended for such attacks
but could see no difference afterwards
between the plants that had been treated
and those that had not and toward
spring they managed to grow out of the
trouble under the ordinary conditions
of culture. Some growers make a rule
of setting a double row of plants next to
the edge of each bench as a reserve to be
drawn upon for filling up any vacancies
that may be caused by disease. After the
holidays these, if not used, are then
removed.

A number of the growers pump their
water from the numerous creeks that
traverse this hilly territory. The water
from these sources has been credited with
remarkably beneficial properties in violet
culture, but the growers do not regard it
as an unmixed blessing, for the frequent
fogs arising from the creeks are full of
danger. The sandy yellow loam abundant in this section is preferred to black
soil for the beds. Good drainage is
essential and plenty of rubble is used
under the beds when necessary to secure
this. After planting the violets require a
very large amount of water. After the
first two weeks discrimination must be
exercised and water withheld when there
are manifestations of too rapid growth.
For a time watering is done broadcast,
but as soon as marketable flowers begin
to appear the wetting is done carefully
between the plants to avoid defacement
of the bloom. A light syringing once in
every two weeks is desirable to freshen
and clean the foliage and flowers, this
being done early on bright days. Mulching is done by some growers, but not by
all, and the material used varies with
the views of each grower. Some prefer
shavings as being cleanly under the
flowers, but there are elements of fungous
dangers in shavings. Some use chopped
up fibre or leaf mould and others dry
manure finely dessicated. Others think
it best to let the sun and air have access
to the soil. All recognise the necessity of
having the surface of the bed loosened up
once in two weeks. This is done with
a little steel fork, great care being required
in using the latter not to injure the surface feeding roots.

The pest most dreaded by Rhinebeck
growers has, however, not yet been
referred to. It is the aphis. Whethe
black or green fly it is the most destruc

ive enemy and the most difficult to overcome. The universal resort with the growers here is hydrocyanic-acid gas, tobacco in fumigation or any other form having been entirely abandoned. The earthenware jars in which the gas is generated are placed in the greenhouse paths about twenty-seven feet apart, the spacing being alternated in each path. The water and sulphuric acid having been placed in the crocks and the ventilators closed the cyanide of potassium in lumps wrapped in paper is hurriedly dropped in and the house vacated and the door locked. For a house 19½x152 feet twenty-four ounces of cyanide is the amount used and the time of exposure is from twenty to twenty-two minutes. This is a much smaller quantity than recommended by Prof. Galloway, and also a less exposure, but is the result of careful experimentation and it has been demonstrated that there is danger in a stronger application. This gassing is done every two weeks at the beginning of the season. It is considered very desirable to get the fight with the fly all over before picking time, as it spoils the color of the flowers on about three pickings after its application. If followed up faithfully early in the season it will be but rarely needed after regular pickings have begun. Some means of opening the ventilators from outside of the house after gassing is necessary on account of the deadly nature of the gas. The Chadborn automatic ventilator is especially adapted for this purpose as it is only necessary to shut off the water from the main to keep the houses closed and to let it on again to open all the sash.

The only other serious pests in the violet houses are the red spider and the grub. The first is exterminated by the frequent use of the syringe early in the season and the latter must be watched for in the manure and soil which should be well turned over outdoors for one winter before being used in the violet beds.

Bunching is an important part of the work of preparing the violet blooms for the wholesale market. The twine used in this work must be smooth enough not to adhere to the hands when wet and yet not hard enough to cut through the stems. The color is as nearly as possible that of the violets and must be absolutely fast.

Mainly Retrospective.

Some years ago a hue and cry went up about "consumption" among the roses grown for cut flowers in winter, but since cultural methods have been improved we hear no such complaints. We will go further and say that apparently the roses now grown seem to have a stronger constitution than they did when they were first introduced. I have in mind, particularly, American Beauty. There were never finer flowers of this standard variety in Philadelphia at Christmas time than there were last Christmas, and I feel safe in saying they were cut from the very stock originally received from George Field & Bros. of Washington, D. C., in the early eighties, no change of stock being deemed necessary nowadays.

As to the suggestion that smaller growers grow something that the larger owners, who grow roses and carnations by the acre under glass, would not think it worth while to take up, what is there to grow? Mignonette, sweet peas and such lines are soon overdone. A small quantity of grand roses and equally as grand carnations go a long way in these days.

The poinsettia is a revived favorite of the "seventies." It has been said it was in oversupply the past Christmas in some quarters, though strenuously denied in others. Just so soon as it is sold for less than it costs to grow it will be dropped. Wholesale prices in the holiday season just past were from $40 to $50 per 100, which are good paying figures. H. H. Battles, at his Thorn Hedge greenhouse establishment, Newtown Square, Pa., had ready to cut just at the right time about 6,000, many of which he used in his own retail business.

Of American Beauty, that grand old standby, there were not too many in Philadelphia, especially the last few hours before Christmas dawn. It seems there were too many of the higher quality of Beauty in New York to bring former high prices, and this is to be regretted, for it will work injury to growers elsewhere. But what may be to the disadvantage of one class of florists is to the direct advan-

H. M. Altick.

tage of the more numerous class, the retailer. History will repeat itself. In the seventies in and about Philadelphia every florist who started in business for himself started with the purpose of catering solely to the retail trade, but he very soon found in those early days—what giant strides has floriculture taken in the recent past—that his surplus was the better part of his business. He found the city retailer would pay better prices and more cheerfully than the retailer out of the business part of the town could get from his customers, and be gradually slid back where land was cheaper and railroad facilities good where the retail customer would not be so likely to bother him, because when a satisfactory connection had been made with a city retailer the latter needed most flowers when the grower could dispose of them in his own immediate locality easiest; thus causing a conflict of interest; but now the city retailer depends entirely on commission men and the larger growers for his supply which generally is unlimited, especially in the few leading varieties of roses. A retail trade will have to be encouraged by the smaller growers as self protection.

We hear occasionally a wail for a greater variety of flowers for winter, especially among roses, and many of the

leading retailers may be depended on to have some of all the roses grown for winter on hand; but most of them are satisfied with American Beauty, Brides, maid, the Bride, Meteor and Liberty. Now that the growing of Liberty is being better understood each year more of it will be grown and less of Meteor, Metcor may still remain the better summer rose, having more petals and delighting in hot weather. Thousands of dollars by some growers have been frittered away in the vain hope of striking something that would be likely to appeal to the popular fancy, but it has been money thrown away. There is the beautiful new rose La Detroit which finds numerous admirers, and I sincerely hope it may prove to be a winner, but it will take a mighty good pink rose to displace Bridesmaid; and an exceedingly fine white rose to put The Bride aside. Though Ivory finds favor in various parts of the country, yet The Bride when at its best is the most beautifully shaped white rose we have in the winter season, and so is Bridesmaid as a pink. Golden Gate has its friends and admirers, and Uncle John makes its parent to the rear, but it will take some time to do so. Golden Gate and Ivory are easy doers, and Uncle John, being a sport, as was Ivory, from Golden Gate, has that much to give it a start in the floral world, goes on its way thus far well recommended.

Our best and most popular roses are not free seeders, and that may be the reason they do not deteriorate, because it is understood the production of seed is one of the most trying in the existence of a plant's life, or perhaps it would be well to put it that seedlings superior to themselves are not so readily forthcoming, sports, and not seedlings, being the rule. In carnations it is different. Seed is produced quite freely, germinates easily, and in comparison with roses the percentage of improvement is large. La Purite, the cerise colored carnation, which held its own so long, has been relegated to the rear for some time, not so much perhaps because it had deteriorated, but because there were others of the same color superior. I am inclined to think, however, that a carnation does degenerate more than does a rose. It does seem as though plants which do not seed freely are more inclined to "sport," giving variety in that way, and are less likely to run out than those which follow the more natural course, reproduction by seed.

EDWIN LONSDALE.

H. M. Altick, S. A. F. Director.

H. M. Altick, recently appointed director of the Society of American Florists by President Breitmeyer, was born in Dayton, Ohio, February 6, 1864. He received a common school education, and started to earn his living at the age of fifteen years. He paid his own way through a commercial college, and kept books for twelve years, practicing for a time as an expert bookkeeper. He held a position as bookkeeper in one of Dayton's national banks for three and one-half years, where his health began to fail, which caused his resignation.

In 1893 he was one of the incorporators of the Highland Floral Company, of Dayton, Ohio, superintending the erection of a range of eight greenhouses, and afterward becoming secretary of the company. Like all new concerns having no experienced stockholders to manage, depending upon hired help to run the business, conditions became so unfavorable that in order to save his stock, which represented the savings of a lifetime, he

CRIMSON RAMBLER IN 7-INCH POT.　　　　　　NEW STOCK BEAUTY OF NICE.

assumed full control, became his own florist without previous practical experience, and with the aid of information gleaned from the trade papers as the foundation, and the experience that comes from practice, has demonstrated his ability as a first-class grower.

He has been a regular attendant at the S. A. F. conventions, being especially active in the shooting contests, where he has attained quite a reputation as a marksman. The florists' fund for the McKinley monument was originated by Mr. Altick, at the American Carnation Society convention in Brooklyn, N. Y., in 1903, and as chairman of the committee appointed for that purpose he is now busily engaged in agitating this popular movement, into which he has entered with tireless energy, giving much valuable time from his business to bring this canvass to a successful issue. At the Milwaukee convention Mr. Altick was elected as vice-president for Western Ohio for 1904.

In addition to the above Mr. Altick holds the office of justice of the peace in the township in which he resides, and the administering of justice, coupled with the active management of a range of greenhouses, would surely cause that gentleman to lead a very strenuous existence.

New Stock Beauty of Nice.

The illustration herewith shows the new stock, Beauty of Nice, which is offered this season by Ernst Benary, of Erfurt, Germany. This is a winter flowering variety, and it is claimed that it blooms satisfactorily from September to April. The flowers come sixty to seventy-five per cent double, and are of an attractive flesh pink shade.

Crimson Ramblers.

My method for forcing Crimson Ramblers for Easter, such as are herewith illustrated, is to dig good, strong, well-ripened plants from the field in the latter part of November, putting them up immediately so that they have no chance to get dry at the roots. Next I trim out the weak branches, place three stakes at equal distances in the pot and train the remaining strong branches around the sticks to form a symmetrical, basket-shaped plant. The plants are then placed in a cool house at about 40° night temperature, given a good soaking and syringed well on all bright days to make the canes break into good, even growth. As the plants make roots, the temperature is gradually raised to bring them in flower at the proper time. If the plants can be brought into flower in a temperature not exceeding 55° at night, they make better blooms and foliage than in higher temperature. P.

[The specimen herewith illustrated is from a batch of plants forced for Easter, 1903. The plant is in a 7-inch pot, about thirty-six inches high and bears forty clusters of blooms.—ED.]

RICHMOND, VA.—M. A. Whitty has a pink sport of Enchantress carnation. The shade is found in the center of Enchantress and glistens like that of Mrs. Nelson. It is said to be a lighter and more taking color than that of Mrs. Lawson.

HOQUIAM, WASH.—December was a mild month on Gray's Harbor. Very little rain fell and the days were as pleasant and warm as spring. Roses bloomed in many gardens. A dish of raspberries and some raspberry blossoms were picked in one garden.

McKinley Day.

We are in receipt of the following from Chairman H. M. Altick, of the committee on the McKinley memorial representing the American Carnation Society and Society of American Florists:

"I inclose printed matter as issued by the Carnation League of America, in reference to McKinley day, which I hope you may see fit to use in your next issue. The point I wish to impress is the financial benefit to the florists in the general reference to this memorial by all the leading papers throughout the United States, thus advertising our business free of charge and displaying it in that part of the paper which, as a rule, could not be bought at any price.

"I wish to impress upon my fellow florists that no line of business was ever placed under such obligations by a voluntary suggestion or placed in a position where it is so necessary to cater to public sentiment by substantial appreciation in so worthy a cause. A small sum from each florist will net a handsome fund and will add glory to our profession. Neglect to respond or selfishness may show to the world that we are incapable of receiving the lesson of unselfishness that is constantly taught by the beautiful and fragrant flowers surrounding us. Let us make the florists' McKinley fund a grand success, and in so doing elevate our chosen profession to a higher level."

The printed matter follows:

The Carnation League of America, instituted as an annual memorial to the late President William McKinley and dedicated to national patriotism, is a fixed institution and insures a perpetual observance of January 29, the anniversary of his birth, as McKinley day. To wear the late President's favorite flower, the carnation, in the lapel of the coat, in the hair, or at the throat, in silent memory of a departed public servant, is what is contemplated by this movement, in which the young and old of both sexes can have a part

The custom was first observed on January 29, 1903, with the greatest unanimity throughout the country, and by Americans all over the world. It is a simple, inexpensive act and full of patriotic sentiment. All through Mr. McKinley's life, both public and private, there ran a distinctive vein of sentiment, and a memorial of this sort is, therefore, peculiarly appropriate to him.

The custom will undoubtedly be observed the coming 29th of January more universally, if that is possible, than on the initial day, a year ago. Interest in the memorial has increased wonderfully during the past year, and Lewis G. Reynolds, of Dayton, Ohio, who suggested the idea, has received letters of the most unqualified approval from Americans everywhere.

No expectation is had of giving the movement the importance of local meetings and conventions, but in a quiet, unobtrusive way it can be made to wield an influence for good almost inexcusable and to foster a spirit of true patriotism worthy of our country and of the man whose memory it is proud to honor.

The Moore, Hentz & Nash Trophy.

The accompanying illustration shows the beautiful silver cup trophy awarded by Moore, Hentz & Nash, of New York, for the best American Beauty, Bride and Bridesmaid roses, exhibited at the Fort Madison, N. J., exhibition November 6–7, 1903. The prize, which was for the actual grower of the winning blooms, was awarded to Joseph Rusicka, grower for L. A. Noe, Madison, N. J. The presentation was made at the last meeting of the Morris County, Md., Florists' and Gardeners' Club.

Flower Carrying by Wagon.

ED. AMERICAN FLORIST:—You may have heard about a year ago that the florists of Madison, Chatham and Summit, N. J., undertook to a considerable extent to get their flowers to New York by wagons. And after a year's trial it may be interesting to know how well we have succeeded in assisting the United States Express Company in doing that kind of work.

You may remember that fifteen months since, all the transporting companies raised their rates on flowers and on empties. You may even remember that previous to 1892 they did not charge anything for returning empties, their receipts on shipments being considered sufficient remuneration. We send from here about 50,000 boxes annually.

Last winter a petition was circulated and signed by all the growers of this rose-growing region and presented to the Hon. Thos. C. Platt, president of the United States Express Company. Yielding to this and to the pressure from many other quarters, they rescinded the advance on shipments, but still have kept up the double rate for returning our empties.

Then the rough handling of our boxes, and the exposure to cold weather, have been other grievances which have given other parties a chance to step in and give us an improved service. A wagon express is now run regularly every night some twenty miles from here to New York, and carries the flowers from our very doors right up to Twenty-sixth street and Twenty-eight street, delivering them there promptly at seven o'clock in the morning. It saves half the handling and the flowers, too, get considerate handling.

The writer, during the circulation of this petition, was enabled to collect a considerable quantity of interesting data of which your readers might like to see a summary. The following statements relate only to a small area, all within three and a half miles from Chatham. All establishments beyond this distance, and every private or retailing place within it, are excluded from the enumeration. The district includes Madison

(and Afton) on one side, Murray Hill (and New Providence) on another, Summit on another and Short Hills, the farthest, (though seven miles by rail) is only three miles off in another quarter:

Town	Sq. Ft. of glass	Total exp. pd.	No. now used during the yr.	No.of men wz. end Jly. 1, '12	Estis. expens.
Madison	3814,100	$9 98.00	51	36	
Chatham	189,000	2 96 .91	15	11	
Summit	227,500	3,420.45	12	11	
Murr'y Hill	131,460	1,282.40	8	9	
Short Hills	110,00.0	1,016.60	4	4	
sq. ft.	1,672,'55	$16,370.38	90	62	

You will observe that the expense used to be at the rate of .01114-cent per foot. In view of the fact that more greenhouses have been built since then, and more are building, as well as because the rates have since been higher, this amount of $16,370 is less considerably than what is being paid annually since then.

The above figures afford many interesting facts. By adding one-fifth or one-fourth to the area the quantity of glass

The Moore, Hentz & Nash Trophy.

may be ascertained. If these greenhouses are assumed to have an average width of eighteen feet and then put end to end, they would reach fifteen and a half miles. The visitor who undertakes to walk up and back once through each house will have thirty-one miles to travel. Any one conversant with the output and cost per thousand feet may indulge his fancy as to what we are doing in number of flowers grown, etc. He may estimate the probable size of this winter's coal bill, the length of the hose in use and totals of many other items ad infinitum.

FRANK L. MOORE.

Philadelphia County Institute.

The county institute meeting of farmers, gardeners and florists of the Department of Agriculture of Pennsylvania was held in Horticultural hall, Philadelphia, January 19, under the auspices of the Pennsylvania Horticultural Society and the Florists' Club of Philadelphia.

In the absence of Mr. Lonsdale, from sickness, David Rust presided. Ernest Hemming discussed "The Old fashioned Flower Garden," giving some valuable hints for success with that now popular subject. His address will appear in full

in an early issue. Mr. Peachy, of Mifflin county, was sick, and his place was taken by the Hon. A. F. Schwarz, of Monroe county. His subject was "Market Gardening," and proved to be highly instructive. "Improvements in Vegetables of the Past Decade" was handled by J. Otto Thilow. His remarks were illustrated with charts, showing what had been accomplished in improving our standard garden vegetables. We hope to present this address also to our readers in an early issue. It is of great interest to every student of horticulture.

Other addresses given at the meeting, which we hope to publish for the benefit of our readers at an early date, were "Gardens of Syria and Egypt," by James Boyd, and "Attractive Home Surroundings and Their Value," by Oglesby Paul.

The latter was illustrated by some fifty stereopticon views, some foreign, but most of them American subjects, showing how some of the most charming garden effects had been produced with limited grounds but much care and enthusiasm. It seemed as if the New England states had furnished most of these small but quaint and picturesque spots, but other parts of the country were represented in views of large estates, where the real art of the landscape gardener had had free scope.

"Value of Our Native Birds to the Farmer" was ably discussed by Professor Menges, of York, Pa. His remarks were forceful and instructive, and except in the case of the sparrow were generally agreed to by those present.

"Lawns and Lawn Making" was assigned to Carleton Ball, assistant agrostologist of the Department of Agriculture, Washington. It was a good thing for Mr. Ball that his lecture came at the wind-up, when most people had to make a rush for their trains. He went straight back to the blue grass and red top of our forefathers, and condemned all the authorities on lawn grasses from Flint down. If the heckling Mr. Ball was in for had once started there would have been an all-night session sure, and it is doubtful if there would have remained enough of him to get back to Washington.

Ex-Senator Harlan spoke eloquently on the subject of "Alaska." It is now two years since Mr. Harlan was announced to speak on this subject. He has been special agent of the treasury department to our northern "land of the midnight sun," and his word painting and solid information was a revelation and worth waiting for so long.

Society for Horticultural Science.

The first annual meeting of the Society for Horticultural Science, to which reference has already been made in our columns, was held at St. Louis December 28–29 in connection with the convention of the American Association for the Advancement of Science. In the absence of the President, Prof. L. H. Bailey, Dr. B. T. Galloway, of the United States Department of Agriculture, presided.

Prof. L. C. Corbett, horticulturist of the United States Department of Agriculture, discussed the "Co-ordination of Horticultural Work," in the opening paper of the programme. He said that there is a class of horticultural problems waiting to be solved which are far-reaching and fundamental in character, such, for instance, as the determination of the specially adaptabilities of various economic plants and their varieties. To get wide and systematic information of this kind a uniform system of note-taking on varieties should be adopted. With this information at his command the seedsman could more intelligently recommend different varieties and strains for different localities. Prof. Corbett suggested that the Society for Horticultural Science, being of national scope, could be made an immensely important factor, in aiding in the accumulation of information of this character. Acting on this suggestion the society then added to its list of permanent committees one on the co-ordination of horticultural work.

D. G. Fairchild, agricultural explorer for the United States Department of Agriculture, spoke on the mangosteen, queen of tropical fruits. This choicest of tropical fruits is yet little grown outside of the Malay archipelago, but experiment has shown that it can be grown in very moist soil throughout a wide range in the tropics, including Hawaii. Mr. Fairchild believes that it could be successfully grown in Porto Rico and even in the everglades of Florida. The successful introduction of the industry into Porto Rico would be worth millions of dollars to the island. The mangosteen has a hard shell and is a fair shipper. Fruits have been in transit over twenty days without decaying.

Prof. R. A. Emerson, of the Nebraska experiment station, discussed the effects of cover crops on soil moisture and soil temperature. He said that cover crops prevent rapid freezing and thawing and hence lessen the danger of killing roots of trees. They withdraw water from the soil, thus causing trees to ripen their wood earlier. They hold the snow in winter, greatly lessening the depth to which the ground freezes. To hold snow crops which remain upright are preferable to those that mat down.

A feature of the programme was a many-sided discussion of shading as a horticultural practice. The practice of growing plants under a cloth cover has attracted much attention among horticulturists recently as a result of the striking experiments made by the United States Department of Agriculture in growing tobacco under cloth. Prof. Corbett opened the discussion with a comprehensive survey of shading in general as applied in horticulture. He pointed out that shading in the open is of two kinds, by lath screens and by cloth. The former lowered the temperature underneath on a warm, bright day, while the cloth cover increases it. Shading is especially adapted to crops grown for leafy parts or for shoots. It is not applicable to most root crops except especially radishes, sort of to crops grown for fruits. Dr. B. M. Duggar, of the Missouri experiment station, discussed shading from the standpoint of the plant physiologist. Shading increases the acid contents of plants and greatly reduces the amount of sugar, starch and other dry matter. Shading makes the leaves larger, thinner and softer and the stems weaker and more watery. Shading is especially effective in the growing of rhubarb and of asparagus.

P. H. Rolfs, in charge of the sub-tropical laboratory of the United States Department of Agriculture at Miami, Fla., spoke on shading pineapples and citrus, or shedding, as the practice is also called, from the use of wooden sheds. Shedding was originally practised as a protection against frosts, but has now proven to be valuable aside from this consideration. In the case of citrus the yields are not so great but the fruits are of unusually fine quality. High, tight

board windbreaks have produced still more beneficial results. In the case of the pineapples shading proved a positive benefit and increased the value of the crop twenty-five per cent. The general effects of shedding as applied to both citrus and pineapples is to equalize temperature and to conserve soil moisture to a most remarkable extent, with the result that the fruit is of increased size and of finer quality.

W. T. Macoun, of the Canada experimental farms, presented a report on results obtained in shading vegetables. All shaded vegetables grew better at first than did those not shaded, but only in a few cases did they continue to do so throughout the season. One noteworthy result of the use of cover is that it fully protects such plants as radishes and cauliflower from the attacks of the root maggott. It is concluded that a cheese-cloth enclosure may be of value in cities and towns where it is difficult to have a garden on account of injury done by dogs, cats and even young children.

V. A. Clark and O. M. Taylor, of the New York experiment station, at Geneva, reported an experiment in shading strawberries. In the cases of a few varieties the yields were much increased, sometimes even doubled, but in more cases the gain was inconsiderable or there was even an actual loss. These results were obtained with a very thin cheese cloth; using cloth one commercial grade heavier there was an average loss in yield with sixteen varieties of forty per cent. Shaded berries were about one-sixth heavier than others and it required only about two-thirds as many to make a quart. The chief gain in shading strawberries was found to be the cutting off of wind, whereby evaporation was reduced one-half.

C.

NEW LONDON, CONN.—The florists here were the victims of some unknown practical joker who ordered, by telephone, a number of floral designs to be sent to the railroad station January 4. No one was on hand to claim the goods.

SNAPSHOTS OF UNCLE JOHN THORPE.

Uncle John Thorpe.

The snapshots reproduced herewith of the veteran horticulturist, Uncle John Thorpe, show him with a look of anxiety upon his face as he receives a letter from one of his loved ones, and later smiling when he has opened the communication and finds that all is well.

Chicago.

NOT MUCH IMPROVEMENT IN LOCAL MARKET.—AMERICAN BEAUTY ROSES SCARCE.—SLIGHT STIFFENING IN ALL PRICES.—FLORISTS' CLUB HOLDS ROUSING MEET.—ING AT ROSE HILL.—OTHERS TO FOLLOW.

The general depression and stagnation which has characterized the local market for the last three weeks, has not shown much of an improvement and things on the Rialto are comparatively quiet. Shipping trade is running along consistently in small orders but the home market has been decidedly "off crop." Carnations have perceptibly shortened during the week. The fancies are in better demand than the lower grades, although white is enjoying a steady call. Long stemmed American Beauty roses are scarce, and the mediums hold about equal to the demand. The quality is not what the local dealers are accustomed to. There have been few choice Bride, Bridesmaid, Meteor, etc., on the market and all may be said to be off in color. The ice chests are overflowing with bulbous stock and Paper White narcissus is a heavy oversupply. Tulips are coming along nicely with good stems. Lilies may yet be called scarce, Harrisii particularly. Violets remain glued to the spot they assumed several weeks ago and are well nigh impossible to move. A big supply and demand of ferns and smilax is noted.

A "revival" meeting of the Florists' Club was held at Matthew Evert's hall, Rose Hill, Saturday evening, January 10. Over 100 members and friends attended and assisted in making it one of the most profitable and enthusiastic of the winter series. Pres. W. N. Rudd presided and, in the absence of Secretary Wienhoeber, John Degnan was appointed to that capacity. Among the many prominent members of the trade present was Paul Dailledouze, of Flatbush, L. I., who gave a highly interesting and instructive talk about the new carnations and roses he had met in his travels this season. He

⸪ SHOULD YOU CONTEMPLATE FAVORING ME WITH AN ORDER FOR CHRISTMAS, MAY I HAVE IT AT YOUR EARLIEST CONVENIENCE? FLOWERS HAVE TO BE HANDLED SO QUICKLY THAT THE LAST FEW DAYS TAX OUR ENERGIES TO THE UTMOST.

H. H. Battles
108 S. 12th St.
Phila.

THE BATTLES CHRISTMAS CARD.

spoke highly of E. G. Hill & Company's new red rose, and he suggested that he thought it might give Liberty a hard chase! He also made special mention of the following carnations: Flamingo, Indianapolis, Bountiful and Fiancee. Each one he said was a promising tomer. In conclusion he advised every one connected with the trade to become a member of his local club, a connection which he considered indispensable. The meeting was also addressed by J. C. Vaughan, Peter Reinberg, J. S. Wilson, Frank Benthey, Adam Zender, Phil. Hauswirth and many other growers, wholesalers and retailers. They all agreed that the Chicago Florists' Club was a most important adjunct of the trade. Eleven applicants were proposed for membership. The meeting wound up with a course of refreshments furnished by local members of the craft, and vocal music by the club quartette.

The regular meeting of the Florists' Club was held January 20 and although the weather was most inclement, the attendance was quite large. The business transacted was mostly of a routine character but some matters of unusual interest were discussed. It was decided that the next sectional meeting of the

club will be held on the northwest side, Thursday, January 28, at Metropolitan hall, 656 N. California avenue. The special subjects to come before the meeting come under the head of allied trades as follows: "Pipe Fittings and Valves," "Glass," and "Paints, Oils and Putty." The south side meeting will be held at the Drexel cafe, Thirty-ninth street and Cottage Grove avenue, Saturday, February 13. A committee of three, Phil. Hauswirth, James S. Wilson and George Stollery, was appointed to consider methods whereby the bowling interests may be brought under the supervision of the club. The following new members were elected: John Zeck, Geo. R. Scott, W. T. Hull, John Fichter, Fred Jones, John Dunn, J. W. Dunn, John Huebner, Chas. Stevens, C. Esse and J. G. Johnson. The appellate court this week affirmed the circuit court decree dismissing a bill filed by James Paganes and nine other flower dealers to enjoin the city of Chicago from interfering with them in the conduct of their business on the streets and sidewalks. The court declares the complainants cannot maintain the injunction sought.

At a recent meeting of the women's auxiliary of the American Park and Outdoor Art Association held in this city, Mrs. Wm. F. Grower was elected president. Announcement was made that the trees in Lincoln park are to be labeled for botanical study.

A serious fire was narrowly averted in the wholesale establishment of E. H. Hunt this week. A photographer was "snapping" the interior and the force of employes, when the powder and chem-

icals exploded, shattering the office windows. The report was heard several blocks.

Frank Potocka has succeeded Frank Lockyear as manager of the downtown store of Frank Garland. The latter is contemplating a change of location in the near future.

Phil. Hauswirth, in appearance as youthful as ever, now poses as a grandfather, Mrs. E. Hauswirth presenting his son with a baby girl January 20.

The Chicago Carnation Company, of Joliet, Ill., is to-day (Saturday) displaying an exhibit of new carnations at the Flower Growers' market.

Charles McKellar is getting in shipments of eastern orchids which are of grand quality and selling readily.

Wietor Brothers are cutting long Beauties, averaging 200 to 400 per day.

W. H. Hilton, of Woodlawn, is sojourning in Cuba for several weeks.

E. H. Hunt is getting in a cut of fine grown Lorraine tulips.

J. A. Budlong has been indisposed with the rheumatism.

Visitors: Henry W. Goetz, with John B. Goetz, Saginaw, Mich., H. A. Bunyard, with Clucas & Boddington, New York.

The Battles Christmas Blotter and Card.

The card and blotter herewith reproduced are an excellent example of tasteful and effective advertising for the high class trade. The special points to be noted are first, daintiness; second, the wording of the card. The latter is a marvel of restrained force—says a great deal in just the right way and says it in two sentences. That's what I call genius!
G. C. WATSON.

[It may be added that the full size of the blotter is 3x7¾ inches. The name and the word "flowers" are in red on the celluloid cover and the holly spray is green with red berries. The Santa Claus fastener is also colored. The type matter of the card is reproduced full size and the card itself is 2½x5¾ inches, printed in red.—ED.]

POUGHKEEPSIE, N. Y.—The annual banquet of the Dutchess County Horticultural Society was held January 13.

DELAWARE, O.—F. P. Vergou, a noted horticulturist and owner of the largest orchard in the state, was seriously injured in a runaway accident.

THE BATTLES CHRISTMAS BLOTTER.

Maltese Cross.   Standing Heart.

SOME DESIGNS BY THE C. A. DAHL CO., ATLANTA, GA.

The Retail Trade.

STANDING HEART.

This emblem of the "Heart of the Confederacy," sent by the governor of Georgia and his staff for the funeral of Gen. John B. Gordan, Atlanta, Ga., was made by the C. O. Dahl Company, of Atlanta. It was four feet high and made of white carnations on the edges and in the center, with a border of red carnations, white letters and a bow of red tulle.

MALTESE CROSS.

This emblem, the tribute of the Gate City Guard, one of the oldest military organizations in the south, at the funeral of Gen. John B. Gordon at Atlanta, Ga., was made of Bride roses on the border, outlined with pink carnations, with a border of white carnations on each side of the pink carnations. The center was made solid of pink carnations and the center of each of the four triangles was of Paper White narcissi. It was made by the C. A. Dahl Company, Atlanta.

A MISCHIEVOUS PRACTICE.

Because of the more extended publicity generally given to church decorations for large weddings, many florists make the mistake of competing for such work at prices far below those for which such jobs can profitably or creditably be done. Customers are usually aware of this and take full advantage of the unwise rivalry. They assume that at even the lowest figure they pay well for what they get, the vast areas of the edifices dwarfing the size of the material used and minimizing its effect so that they fail to realize the magnitude of the undertaking; thus we find people of otherwise sane ideas paying without any protest the estimate on the decoration of two or three rooms at the residence, but unwilling to expend much, if any, more for the work of properly adorning an edifice ten times as large.

The result of this endeavor to do something big for an inadequate price is not always creditable to the craft, and the man who refuses to take a job for less than it can be done and done properly, is a benefactor to his profession. How often one sees the pitiable evidences of an effort to make a cheap job presentable, the wherefore of which is the stinginess of the customer, aided and abetted by the injudicious eagerness of the florist to grasp everything. If the price obtainable is not sufficient to compensate for the use of good, fresh and well-proportioned palms, the florist will make a better reputation for himself by declining the work than by patching up a decoration with a lot of worn-out scrubs touched up with southern smilax and dried palm leaves stuck around in the tubs to conceal the defects.

Philadelphia.

COLD WEATHER CAUSES SHORTAGE AND BETTER PRICES.—AMERICAN BEAUTIES HAVE ADVANCED SLIGHTLY.—BUSINESS NOT EQUAL TO THAT OF LAST YEAR.—THE KETTLE CLUB BANQUET DECORATIONS.

At this writing prices are stiffening a trifle, as, owing to the intense cold weather of the past week, there is a shortage, more noticeable perhaps with Beauty roses, which fell for a few days last week to $4 per dozen, but have now advanced to $5 and $6. The business is fair for the season, some complaining and others expressing themselves satisfied, but the concensus of opinion is that it is not up to the volume of last year. There is considerable shipping trade to parties out of town, much of the demand calling for fancy stock. Niessen, Pennock and Reid have a large share of this business, and in spite of the extreme cold weather have had little trouble from this source. The trouble with the carnations still continues, flowers that are picked late one day and reach the stores the next morning go to sleep after one night's experience with the dealer. The growers declare they would keep with them for a week or longer if placed in water and stood around almost anywhere. The person who discovers the cause and provides a remedy will deserve much from the trade.

Macey, of Columbia avenue, has a vault under his front pavement, into which an open shaft admits fresh air as required, and he claims to have no trouble of this kind, and he has even raised ferns that were drowsy when received.

Supiot is sending in fine lilacs, and will The Wm. Graham Company had a fine decoration for the Kettle Club at the Union League last Wednesday night. A large square space in the banquet hall was surrounded by a tall hedge of Norway spruce, which was reached through a curved path hedged on both sides with the same trees. The table was set in the center of this space. Midway in the center ter of this, on the floor, the kettles of the club were suspended on a tripod of poles. It boiled over an electric fire in the center of fagots. The balance of the space was filled in with plants and smilax. The table was decorated with vases of Liberty roses. It was a beautiful decoration and one of the most unique ever made in this famous hall.

John H. Dunham, a well known member of the Philadelphia Florists' Club, gave a sauerkrout dinner to a select circle of his friends January 13. Deacon Harris was one of the guests, but he forgot to take his fiddle along, and that was a disappointment to Commodore Westcott, Judge Hanna, Corporal Eimerman, the Sage of the Ginger Jar, Nick Moore and others who were present. Mr. and Mrs. Dunham made good the omission, however, with various other features and were voted by all to be royal entertainers.

The Carnation League of America, organized to commemorate the late President McKinley, calls attention to the approach of the anniversary of his birth January 29, and urges all patriotic Americans to observe that day by wearing his favorite flower, the carnation, in the lapel or the coat, in the hair, or at the throat. Those who were caught short of stock on the same occasion last year will be glad to get this reminder so that preparations can be made in time.

Leo Niessen was married to Miss Madelaine Michell, daughter of Fred Michell, January 19. The ceremony was performed in St. Malachi's church, which was beautifully decorated for the occasion. The bride carried a shower bunch of valley and orange blossoms. A reception followed at the home of the bride's parents. Mr. and Mrs. Niessen are well known, and they have the best wishes of all the trade for a long and happy life.

Edward Campbell, the popular landscape architect of Armore, Pa., celebrated the twentieth anniversary of his marriage January 12 with a dinner and dance at his home. A number of prominent florists, nurserymen and seedsmen from Philadelphia and vicinity were guests.

Harris has large quantities for some time to come. Harris is also adding this to his list, and will have a continuous lot of choice flowers for the next two months.

Stephen Mortonson is sending to S. S. Pennock Liberties with stems four feet long, which are as fine as anything ever seen in this market.

Mrs. M. D. Young, of Ridge avenue, has sent out a pretty calendar which contains a beautiful photograph of the interior of her store.

MOLINE, ILL.— Wm. Kneese opened a store at Fifteenth street and Fourth avenue, January 18. Mr. Kneese has been in the florist business in Moline eighteen years.

New York.

FLAT MARKET WITH HEAVY SURPLUS.— LECAKES SAILS FOR EUROPE.—MAY BETTER.

In the National Arts Club, in West Thirty-fourth street, January 12, the American Society of Landscape Architects held its fifth annual dinner. Those present were from various cities in the United States, and were principally the architects in charge of public parks. Following the banquet the annual meeting was held, but only routine business was transacted. The officers elected were:

President—John C. Olmsted, of Boston.
Vice-President—Samuel Parsons, landscape architect department of parks of New York City.
Treasurer—C. N. Lowrie, of New York.
Secretary—Downing Vaux, of New York.

Business in cut flowers continues at low ebb as last reported, and a large unsalable surplus encumbers the market. The demand is exceedingly light on every line without exception, and prices very low and unstable. American Beauty roses run poor generally, but other varieties are of excellent quality. There is no sale for any but the better grade of carnations.

Deputy Collector Story has completed plans for the sale at public auction today of twenty-one large palms and several other plants seized by the customs authorities for violations of the laws, says the New York Commercial of January 16. The palms stand from six to twelve feet high and are in especially good condition.

Nicholas Lecakes sailed on a European trip last week and was given an enthusiastic send-off by his friends.

John Scheepers will handle the specialties of J. A. McDowell, of Mexico, and George W. David, of San Francisco.

John N. May is reported as improving.

Boston.

MARKET SHOWS SLIGHT IMPROVEMENT. —VERY COLD WEATHER IS EXPERIENCED. —HORTICULTURISTS DISCUSS THE GYPSY MOTH.—PARK SUPERINTENDENTS MEET.

After a week of the hardest experience which the cut flower trade has seen in many years, a slightly improved tone is noted in the wholesale market, and confidence in the immediate future is beginning to revive. The stagnation was complete for several days. This with zero weather just the wrong and unheard-of depths below zero as an occasional variation, has made the lot of the grower and wholesale dealer one far from enjoyable. Flowers in all lines are abundant despite the weather and there is not the slightest prospect of a scarcity in any line. There is nothing in sight that can have any material influence in advancing values beyond their present limits. All bulbous stock is abundant with very slow demand. This classification includes lily of the valley, Harrisii lilies, Roman hyacinths and the various sorts of narcissi.

On Saturday, January 10, a valuable exhibition of stereopticon views illustrating the ravages of the gypsy moth in neighboring towns was presented before the Massachusetts Horticultural Society by the Messrs. Farquhar. An interesting discussion regarding the best method of exterminating this pest which has already cost the State of Massachusetts a fortune was participated in by well-known specialists and a motion was passed approving the action of the Massachusetts Forestry Association in its efforts to facilitate the introduction of

parasites for the destruction of the moth. The schedule of the Saturday lectures for the rest of the season is arranged as follows:

JANUARY 23.
"The Plants of the East With Reference to the Flora of the Bible," by President H. H. Goodell, Agricultural College, Amherst.
JANUARY 30.
"Practical Nature Study in the Public Schools," by Mrs. Cora Stuart Jones, Roxbury.
FEBRUARY 6.
Paper followed by discussion. (Subject to be announced.)
FEBRUARY 13.
"My Experience and Observations in Horticulture," by Adin A. Hixon, Worcester.
FEBRUARY 20.
"Some Notes on Grafting," by William P. Rich, Boston.
FEBRUARY 27.
"The Study of Parasitic Fungi in the United States," by G. P. Clinton, S. D., New Haven, Conn.
MARCH 6.
"The Protection of our Native Plants," by Dr. Robert T. Jackson, Cambridge.
MARCH 13.
"Gladiolus," by Arthur Cowee, Berlin, N. Y.
MARCH 19.
"A Talk on Orchid Culture," by William N. Craig, North Easton.
MARCH 26.
"Peonies," by G. C. Watson, Philadelphia, Pa.

The executive committee of the Association of New England Park Superintendents met at the Quincy house, Boston, Wednesday evening, January 20. Those present included President G. A. Parker, Secretary Dunham, J. A. Pettigrew, W. J. Stewart, G. W. Amrhyn, New Haven; Theo. Wirth, Hartford; J. D. Pitts, Providence; T. W. Cook, New Bedford; J. W. Thompson, Watertown, N. Y.; B. V. Orthen, Manchester, N. H.; W. S. Manning, Newark, N. J. New Haven, Conn. was selected as location for the next convention, which will be held June 14, 15 and 16. It was decided to broaden the scope of the association and recommend change of name from New England to American. A sleigh ride as guests of Mr. Pettigrew was enjoyed by the visitors on Thursday. George A. Sutherland is very sick at the City hospital.

Visitors in town: Wm. Donald, Cold Spring Harbor, N. Y.; L. B. Craw, New York City; H. S. De Forest,, of Hitchings & Co.; Hon. C. W. Hoitt, Nashua, N. H.; G. X. Amrhyn, New Haven; Theodore Wirth, Hartford, Conn.

Detroit.

PREPARATION FOR CLUB EXHIBITION COMPLETED. — HARMONIE HALL, MEETING PLACE OF S. A. F. CONVENTION, WILL BE THE SCENE.—TRADE DEVOID OF INTERESTING FEATURES AND PRICES UNSATISFACTORY.

The club meeting Wednesday evening, January 20, had an audience of over thirty members. Letters pertaining to the coming carnation meeting consumed the entire time of the meeting. It is now definitely settled that the meeting, exhibition and banquet will be held in Harmonie Hall. The meeting will be held in the large dining hall on the second floor, where the proceedings of the S. A. F. convention were held four years ago. In the same hall the banquet connected with the carnation meeting will be held Thursday evening, March 3. The large auditorium on the top floor of the building, where the S. A. F. trade exhibit was held, will be devoted entirely to the carnation exhibition. The entertainment will be in charge of a committee composed of Robert Flowerday, Geo. A. Rackham, Philip Breitmeyer, Ed. Beard, Frank Holznagle and L. Bemb. Arrangements to regulate the admission of the public to the exhibition will be in the hands of Frank Beard, Geo. A. Rackham, Philip Breitmeyer and Frank Holznagle. President Rackham of the American Carnation Society, appointed J. F, Sullivan exhibition manager, with the assistance of G. H. Taepke. He also named Ed. Beard, Geo. Brown and Herman Knope to render assistance in that capacity. Indications already point to an extensive exhibit and a big attendance.

Trade since the holidays has been devoid of features of general interest. In common with the report from most other points, violets are in far greater supply than the demand, which has been spasmodic and uncertain. Unsatisfactory prices, to both growers and dealers, are being realized. The same is largely true of carnations, while the rose supply is about equal to the demand, which is fairly satisfactory. Continuous cold weather prevails and the growers complain of the excessive demands on their coal bins.

Wm. Bilger was a visitor to Chicago last week.

Visitors: J. F. Smith, representing Edwards & Docker, Phila.; A. L. Vaughan, Chicago; E. A. Fetters, Cleveland, Ohio.
J. F. S.

St. Louis.

A goodly number were in attendance at the monthly meeting of the Florists' Club, January 14. Several vases of carnations were on exhibition. President Beneke announced the exposition building had been secured for the exclusive use of the S. A. F. convention in August. During the life of the World's Fair numerous flower shows will be held on the grounds. President Beneke was requested to appoint a committee to confer with Mr. Hadkinson, who is in charge of the flower exhibits, in regard to the matter. Resolutions were adopted extending sympathy to Max Herzog, whose wife died of pneumonia recently. F. J. Fillmore led an interesting talk on roses. Walter Gillies read a paper on ferns.

From reports circulated about the wholesale houses and elsewhere local trade is practically at a standstill. About the only demand is for funeral work of which there appears to be considerable. American Beauty is offered in large quantities at $3 to $4. Carnations are abundant and call for from $1 to $4 per 100. Violets appear in almost unlimited quantities, the dealers offering them at almost any price. Paper White narcissus is on the markets at $2 to $3 per 100. Stevia is quoted at $1 per 100. If it were not for the shipping trade wholesalers would be carting the greater portion of their stock to the garbage box.

Geo. E. McClure, orchidist at the Missouri Botanical Garden, and Miss Ida Norton, librarian at the same institution, announce their marriage on February 1. They will go to Manhattan, Kas., for a week's visit at the home of the bride.

Max Herzog is much improved and indications are he will soon be out of danger.

Visitor: Mr. Anpleet, with Ionia Pottery Company. F. K. B.

Winona, Minn.

The greenhouses of Mrs. D. Voelker are not to be torn down, but have been leased for a term of years by the Winona Floral Company, which purchased all her stock with the exception of a few plants sold to Chas. Siebrecht.

Cleveland, O.

Fred Ehrbar, of the Ehrbar Floral Company, has purchased the entire stock and fixtures of Henry J. Piggott's Clark avenue store, and will manage it in connection with his store on Loraine street. His increased business demands opening another place to take care of south side customers.

The Cleveland Florists' Club has decided to have a banquet, which the wives and sweethearts of the members may attend. An appropriation has been made and a committee appointed to set the date and arrange for entertainment.

The Market Gardeners' Association held a meeting at their rooms on Woodland avenue. There was considerable discussion of a winter indoor market. Papers will be read on the subject at the next meeting.

The well known cut flower merchants, Bate Brothers and the F. R. Williams Floral Company, have decided to merge their business interests.

Henry Piggott finds his greenhouse business demands all his attention and will hereafter confine himself to that branch.

H. R. Carleton; of Willoughby, O., has appropriately named his new violet, Gov. Herrick.

Buffalo, N. Y.

The last two weeks everything has been almost at a standstill. A few receptions and dinners have called for a moderate lot of flowers. Stock is plentiful except carnations. Roses, violets, etc., are equal to the demand. Tulips, hyacinths and primroses are in good supply. Azaleas and Lilium Harrisii are plentiful.

We are waiting patiently for a weakening of the Buffalo Florists' Club, as we understood the new year was to be started with a series of talks, which it was hoped would put new life in the club. Cities half our size get speakers from abroad and entertain them while the Buffalo Florists' Club sleeps on.

S. A. Anderson has had a run on fine primulas at 25 cents. Palmer & Son, at their upper store, have sold cyclamens at 35 cents for good plants. It helps to enliven trade by having one thing at a bargain when business is quiet. Window displays have been only fair since the holidays.

The Florists' and Gardeners' Union, No. 10726, had its election and installation of officers January 13, when the following were named:

President, Jos. Streit.
Vice-Pres. Fred. Bartker.
Recording Secretary, John Schweichler.
Financial Secretary, Jos. Neubeck.
Treasurer, Henry Weber.
Sergeant-at-Arms, Carl Bauer.

The union is progressing well. New members are coming fast. At the last meeting six were elected and four applications received.

The board of trustees of Forest Lawn cemetery has undertaken the exclusive care and watering of vases in the cemetery. This was formerly done by the florists.

Walter Mott, of Jamestown, called January 19, looking younger than ever.
BISON.

St. Paul, Minn.

Business was better last week than the corresponding week of last year. Out of town orders are coming in well. Flowers are plentiful this season. Single Von Sion narcissi and tulips are coming in and are selling well.

John Monson was a caller last week

and had with him a new seedling rose which he expects to get rich on. It is a shell pink with a darker center and if it is anywhere near as good as he says it ought to win.

Visitors last week were: Chas. Vick, Wm. G. Schucht, L. Bauman and Chas. Schwake. O.

Obituary.

HUGH M'MICHAEL.

Hugh McMichael, of Wilmette, Ill., one of the best known men in the Chicago trade, died at his home, January 13, aged 37. He was a native of Newton Stewart, Scotland, and came to this country about fifteen years ago. The greenhouses will be leased and the stock sold on advantageous terms.

MRS. LUTHERA SIBLEY.

Mrs. Luthera Sibley, mother of Charles Sibley, died at her home in Athol, Mass., December 2, at the age of 77 years. She became a member of the S. A. F. in 1889 and continued an interested member of the society until last year, when ill health drew because of failing health. She was a woman not only of much ability, but of benevolence and kindness of heart, and was greatly beloved by her towns people.

WILLIAM J. REDDY.

William J. Reddy, one of the oldest florists of Syracuse, N. Y., died January 13. Mr. Reddy was born in England and worked at his profession in and around New York city for a number of years, after which he went to Syracuse and was employed by the late James J. Belden as private gardener. About twenty-five years ago he went to work for P. R. Quinlan in his greenhouses and was employed there until about three years ago, when his old age would not permit of his working longer. He was 70 years old and is survived by his widow, three daughters and one son, Robert Reddy, of Syracuse.

JOSIAH HOOPES.

Josiah Hoopes, a member of the firm of Hoopes Bro. & Thomas, nurserymen, West Chester, Pa., died January 16, aged 72 years. He had been ill for some time with pneumonia. The deceased, since his early boyhood, was an ardent lover of botany and his study of the native flowers and trees led him finally to adopt the nursery business as his profession. In the early fifties the present firm was organized and the business has grown until now it is one of the largest in the country. Mr. Hoopes wrote several works on evergreens, one of them, his "Book of Evergreens" being a practical treatise on the conifer or cone bearing plants of the world. It was published in 1868 and has had a large sale, having been translated into several languages. In addition to his duties at the nursery he took an interest in local public affairs and held many offices of trust. He leaves a wife and one son.
K.

THE AMERICAN FLORIST

NINETEENTH YEAR.

Subscription, $1.00 a year. To Europe, $2.00. Subscriptions accepted only from those in the trade.

Advertisements, on all except cover pages, 10 Cents a Line, Agate; $1.00 per inch. Cash with Order.

No Special Position Guaranteed.

Discounts are allowed only on consecutive insertions, as follows—6 times, 5 per cent; 13 times, 10 per cent; 26 times, 20 per cent; 52 times, 30 per cent.

Space on front pages and back cover page sold only on yearly contract at $1.00 per inch, net.

The Advertising Department of the AMERICAN FLORIST is for florists, seedsmen and nurserymen and dealers in wares pertaining to those lines only.

Orders for less than one-half inch space not accepted.

Advertisements must reach us by Wednesday to secure insertion in the issue for the following Saturday. Address

AMERICAN FLORIST CO., Chicago.

When sending us change of address, always send the old address at the same time.

CARNATION growers will remember that January 29, McKinley's birthday, is also carnation day.

J. D. THOMPSON figures that florists ought to have at least a ten per cent profit on their products.

THE violet foliage forwarded by "G. K." was received in such a dried-out condition that the disease could not be determined.

ADOLPHUS J. THOMPSON, of West Haven Conn., sends us some very good flowers of his new violet, which is said to be a sport of Farquhar, but of a very light, pleasing shade.

Chrysanthemum Mary Hill.

Upon further investigation I find the new chrysanthemum, Mary Hill, which I credited to Nonin of Paris, should be credited to Rozain-Boucharlat of Lyons. If you will make this change you will oblige   ELMER D. SMITH.

Society of American Florists.

Parties disseminating new plants of any class for the first time this season are respectfully requested to forward to the secretary names and descriptions thereof or a marked copy of a catalogue containing such descriptions so a full and accurate list of such novelties with the names of their introducers may be prepared for publication in the next annual report of the society.

WM. J. STEWART, Sec'y.
79 Milk street, Boston, Mass.

French Cannas for Early Spring.

ED. AM. FLORIST:—Will you kindly give directions for getting French cannas in flower for early spring sales? Also Rambler roses for Easter?   SUBSCRIBER.

Take strong, dormant cannas with good eyes, about March 1, and start them in sand on a bench, or in boxes, giving strong bottom heat, and when they have made a growth of six to eight inches high, lift and put into 4-inch pots and place in a house of 60° shade for a few days, after which give full sun. When well rooted shift into 5-inch pots, and by May 1 they will be strong, stocky plants with three to five shoots showing flower. I would recommend for this purpose such sorts as Florence Vaughan, Egandale, Mme. Crozy, David Harum, Queen Charlotte, Red Indian, King Humbert, Chicago, Beaute Poitevine and President McKinley.   JAS. S. WILSON.

Carnation Night at New York.

The next regular meeting of the New York Florists' Club, to be held on Monday evening, February 8, at the Grand Opera House Building, Twenty-third street and Eighth avenue, will be carnation night. This will be an excellent opportunity to all growers of carnation novelties and well-grown standard varieties to bring these before the club members; and a cordial invitation is extended to everyone interested, both members and non-members, to make a display and to be present on that occasion. Ladies are also respectfully invited to view the exhibition.

All carnations sent, on day of meeting, in care of Secretary John Young, 51 West Twenty-eighth street, will be taken care of and duly staged.

ALEX. WALLACE, Sec'y pro tem.

Carnation Adonis.

We notice Mr. Pierson's remarks concerning Adonis and wish to put in our oar for that variety. Considering the lateness of the delivery of Adonis last spring and a few other mishaps the variety evidently had with the dissemination the previous season in the field, we think it has done very well indeed. At any rate this is the impression we have of it now, judging from the behavior of the plants we have been able to save. Since housing the first batch of about 300 plants in August and about 500 September 20 we have scarcely lost a half dozen plants; and while the growth has not been rank it has been uniform and healthy, and seems "fast" enough to become a very profitable variety from early struck cuttings, and not later than the last of February. It easily surpasses any scarlet on the market now, and we look for a decided improvement next season. We do not wish to appear in the light of taking Mr. Pierson to task for his diagnosis of the variety, but merely present our observations for the benefit of the trade, not forgetting that a variety will not succeed everywhere.

H. WEBER & SONS.

A Warning to Rose Growers.

ED. AM. FLORIST:—As the time for the annual show of the American Rose Society in Philadelphia approaches I am compelled to ask, through your columns, of the rose growers of this country: What are you going to do to help the one flower that has been the foundation of your fortunes? Are you going to trust to the efforts of others, to do that which you should do yourselves? Do you expect others to do all the work and you reap whatever benefit may accrue? If you feel that way and think it will eventuate anything why, go ahead, and when too late find what a small hole you will have to crawl out of when asked why the Rose Society died. Are you any less interested in the rose than carnation men are in the carnation? Do you think the rose will take care of itself better than the carnation can? Do you think that because it is older, it can stand neglect better? Is this a good way, as business men, to advertise your wares? Is it that you think there are none who need education on the rose subject? Or do you think they will find others outside of our business who will prove efficient teachers? Can you afford this indifference? Can you sit down and let others pass you in the race? Brother rose growers, think of these questions. See if you are doing your business justice. And I trust you

will make up your mind to exhibit at this show and by being present aid the society and show others that you are sufficiently interested to devote a little time and some money in the cause of the rose. Respectfully yours,
BENJAMIN DORRANCE.
Dorranceton, Pa.

Pittsburg.

LONG COLD SPELL LOOSENS ITS CLUTCHES, —BUSINESS MERELY DRAGGING.—ROSES SCARCE AND PRICES FOR ALL GRADES HIGH.—OTHER FLOWERS GOOD.—GREAT FLOOD IS DEEMED INEVITABLE.

Pittsburg is slowly being released from the clutches of the long cold spell which began Christmas night, during which the mercury has ranged from 15° below zero to 40° above. The plants nearest the city have had little sunshine, because of the almost daily appearance of a fog. Business is merely dragging along. Roses continue scarce. In many houses they are off crop. Those available are high in price and the cheaper grades difficult to get. Carnations are now at their best, and are plentiful. Enchantress, Prosperity, Mrs. Lawson, Wolcott, Adonis and Nelson are especially fine. Tulips, daffodils, primulas, lily of the valley, sweet peas, lilacs, hyacinths, freesias and violets are all fine; Lilium Harrisii and ferns scarce.

A great flood seems inevitable. The flower stores on Pennsylvania avenue, Fifth and Sixth and Liberty streets will have water in their cellars, and possibly the storerooms. It is predicted that the coming flood will be a greater one than those of 1884 or 1891.

Howard Carney, of the Florists' Exchange, will go to New York and Philadelphia next week on business.

John Murchie, of Sharon, Pa., has a new white carnation, which he believes will withstand all criticisms.

The Pittsburg Rose & Carnation Co. will erect a new house, 30x350, for summer roses.

Mr. and Mrs. P. J. Deemas have returned from a visit to Chicago.

B. E. Blackley will open a store in Homestead about February 1.
E. L. M.

HINGHAM, MASS.—At the annual meeting of the Hingham Agricultural Society, December 8, U. S. Bates was elected president, Wm. H. Thomas, secretary and Reuben Sprague, treasurer.

SITUATIONS, WANTS, FOR SALE.
One Cent Per Word.
Cash with the Adv.

INTERNATIONAL FLOWER DELIVERY.

STEAMSHIPS LEAVE FOREIGN PORTS

FROM	TO	STEAMER	*LINE	DAY	DUE ABOUT
Liverpool.......	New York	Umbria	1	Sat. Jan. 30,	Feb. 7
Liverpool.......	"	Ivernia	1	Sat. Feb. 7,	Feb. 14
Fiume..........	"	Carpathia	1	Fri. Feb. 6,	
Glasgow........	"	Mongolian	2	Sat. Jan. 30,	Feb. 9
Genoa..........	"	Prinz Oskar	2	Tues. Feb. 2,	Feb. 19
Hamburg.......	"	Pennsylvania	3	Sat. Jan. 30,	Feb. 9
Hamburg.......	"	Patricia	3	Thur. Feb. 6,	Feb. 16
Glasgow........	"	Furnessia	5	Sat. Feb. 6,	Feb. 16
London.........	"	Mesaba	6	Thur. Jan. 28,	Feb. 7
London.........	"	Minnetonka	6	Thur. Feb. 4,	Feb. 14
Liverpool.......	"	Oceanic	7	Wed. Jan. 27, 3:30 p. m.	Feb. 2
Liverpool.......	"	Celtic	7	Wed. Feb. 3, 3:30 p. m.	Feb. 11
Liverpool.......	Boston	Cymric	7	Thur. Feb. 4, 3:30 p. m.	Feb. 13
Alexandria	"	Romanic	7	Thur. Feb. 4, 3:00 p. m.	Feb. 22
Southampton...	New York	New York	8	Sat. Jan. 30, Noon	Feb. 5
Southampton...	"	St. Paul	8	Sat. Feb. 6, Noon	Feb. 12
Antwerp........	"	Vaderland	8	Sat. Jan. 30, 11:00 a.m.	Feb. 9
Antwerp........	"	Kroonland	8	Sat. Feb. 6, 8:00 p. m.	Feb. 16
Havre	"	La Lorraine	10	Sat. Jan. 30,	Feb. 9
Havre	"	La Bretagne	10	Sat. Feb. 6,	Feb. 17
Rotterdam......	"	Statendam	11	Sat. Feb. 6,	Feb. 16
Genoa..........	"	Citta di Napoli	12	Mon. Jan. 25,	Feb. 9
Genoa..........	"	Sardegna	12	Mon. Feb. 1,	Feb. 18
Bremen.........	"	K. Wil. Der Grosse	13	Tues. Jan. 26, 8:00 a. m.	Feb. 2
Bremen.........	"	Rhein	13	Sat. Jan. 30, 8:00 a. m.	Feb. 10
Bremen.........	"	Koenigin Louise	13	Sat. Feb. 6, 8:00 a. m.	Feb. 16
Genoa..........	"	Lahn	13	Thur. Feb. 4,	Feb. 16
Liverpool.......	Boston	Devonian	14	Sat. Jan. 30,	Feb. 9
Liverpool.......	"	Winifredian	14	Sat. Feb. 6,	Feb. 16

* See steamship list on opposite page.

WILD SMILAX. ORDER DIRECT FROM HEADQUARTERS.
We carry the finest and most complete stock of Florists' Hardy Supplies, Dagger and Fancy Ferns, $1.50 per 1000, A No. 1 quality. Bronze and Green Galax, $1.00 per 1000, A No. 1 quality. Southern Wild Smilax, 50 pound case, $7.00. 25 pound case, $3.50 per case. Laurel Festooning, good and full, 5c and 6c per yard. Leucothoe Sprays, $1.00 per 100. Green Moss, $1.00 per bbl.; 75c per bag. Sphagnum Moss, $1.00 per bbl.; 50c per bag. Order by mail, telegraph or telephone will receive our personal and prompt attention. Long Dis. 'Phone 2618 Main.
HENRY M. ROBINSON, No. 11 Province St., BOSTON, MASS.

Chas. W. McKellar,

Wholesale Commission Florist
—AND DEALER IN—
ALL FLORISTS' SUPPLIES.

51 Wabash Ave., Chicago.

Long Distance 'Phone Central 3598.

Correspondence invited from growers of specialties in Cut Flowers.
Please mention the American Florist when writing.

Orchids!

Just arrived in superb condition, a large shipment of **DENDROBIUM NOBILE**, most useful for florists; also Dend. Chrysanthum and others. To arrive, Cattleya Triance and C. Gigas.

Lager & Hurrell, SUMMIT, N. J.
Orchid Growers and Importers.
Please mention the American Florist when writing.

A ll nurserymen, Seedsmen and Florists wishing to do business with Europe should send for the
"Horticultural Advertiser."
This is the British Trade Paper, being read weekly by all the Horticultural traders; it is also taken by over 1000 of the best continental houses. Annual subscription to cover cost of postage 75c. Money orders payable at Lowdham, Notts.
Address **EDITORS OF THE "H. A."**
Chilwell Nurseries   LOWDHAM Notts England.

WILD SMILAX Per case containing 50 lbs. $2.00. Good quality, first-class Smilax and prompt attention guaranteed.
F. & S. LEE, Marion, Ala.

GALAX...

Bronze or green, 75c per 1000. In 2,000 cts or more. **Leucothoe Sprays,** green, 90c per 1000. **Southern Smilax,** fresh stock, per 50-lb. case, $6.00; per 25-lb. case, $3.50. **Green Sheet Moss,** choice stock, $2.50 per barrel sack. **Spagnum Moss,** $1.75 per large bale.

FLORIST' SUPPLIES of Every DESCRIPTION.

Tel. 597 Madison   **L. J. KRESHOVER,**
Square.   110-112 W. 27th St., New York.
Please mention the American Florist when writing.

SMILAX and BEAUTIES CHEAP.

500 Beauties, 3½-inch pots, well branched, $6.00 per 100.
2,000 Smilax 3½-inch, stocky plants, $2.00 per 100. Cash with order.

Quality of plants guaranteed.

ROSEMONT GARDENS, MONTGOMERY, ALA.

ROBT. CRAIG & SON,
Roses, Palms
and Novelties in Decorative Plants.
Market and 49th Sts., Philadelphia, Pa.

IT IS NOT...

what you pay for the advertisement but what the advertisement pays you. It pays to advertise in the **American Florist.**

E. F. Winterson Co.

—Successors to—
McKellar & Winterson.

"Highest Quality"
AS WELL AS
"Under Grades"
IN
Roses, Carnations, Violets, Etc.,
AT LOWEST MARKET PRICES.
Get our Weekly Price List. It is true and worth your while.

HEADQUARTERS FOR
GALAX LEAVES AND ALL GREENS.

"SUPERIOR QUALITY" **Wild Smilax**
—(NONE BETTER.)—
ALWAYS ON HAND.

We carry the most complete line of Florists' Supplies in the West. Catalogue free. Address all correspondence to

45-47-49 Wabash Ave., CHICAGO.

Please mention the American Florist when writing.

PETER REINBERG

51 Wabash Ave., CHICAGO.
Wholesale Cut Flowers

LARGEST GROWER
IN THE WORLD.

Current Price List.

		Per Doz.
AM. BEAUTIES, long stems,		$5.00
" " 30-36-in. "	$2.00 to	4.00
" " 20-24 "		3.50
" " 15-18 "		1.50
" " Short stems.....	1.00 to	1.25

	Per 100
SUNRISE............................	$4.00 to $10.00
CHATENAY..........................	6.00 to 12.00
BRIDE..............................	5.00 to 8.00
BRIDESMAID........................	5.00 to 8.00
PERLE.............................	5.00 to 8.00
CARNATIONS........................	5.00 to 8.00
ROSES, OUR SELECTION......	4.00

All flowers are perfectly fresh and properly packed. No charge for P. and D. on orders over $5.

GALAX LEAVES, ETC.,

Fresh New Crop.

Galax Leaves, Green and Bronze, per 1000.....$ .60
Cut Fancy and Dagger Ferns, per 1000.......... 1.00
Leucothoe Sprays, green, per 1000.............. 2.00
  "   "   Red, per 1000.................. 6.00
Rhododendron Sprays, per 1000................. 5.00

Largest dealer in the U. S. Orders filled promptly. Send cash with order. Send 50c for a nice case, cut from the famous mountains of N. C. Nicely varnished, crooked or straight. Mention length desired and variety of wood—hickory, rhododendron, wahoo, poplar, striped maple, etc. Grand souvenir, besides useful. Try one or more.
J. N. PRITCHARD, Elk Park, N. C.

THE SEED TRADE.

AMERICAN SEED TRADE ASSOCIATION.
S. F. Willard, Pres.; J. Charles McCullough, First Vice-Pres.; C. E. Kendel, Cleveland, O., Sec'y and Treas.
Twenty-second annual convention St. Louis, Mo., June, 1904.

CUCUMBER seed of pickling sorts is holding firm and selling freely at $1.65 and upward per pound.

ALASKA peas have been sold below $2. The same of doubtful pedigree have been sold below $1 per bushel.

INDIANAPOLIS, IND.—The receiver for the Vail Seed Company paid a twenty-five per cent dividend December 24, 1903.

BOTH W. Atlee Burpee & Company and John Lewis Childs report mail trade starting in better than in 1903 at this date.

CONTRACT prices for bean growing are somewhat higher; scarce kinds difficult to grow may be given extra care as garden crops if prices justify.

KENTUCKY papers are making favorable mention of Representative Trimble's House bill regarding the adulteration of blue grass and other seeds.

SOME dealers believe that the prices of Stowell's evergreen sweet corn will weaken later, at the same time it must be admitted that their pedigree stock is scarce.

THE Connecticut State Grange, in a recent resolution, protests emphatically against the system of free seed distribution by the government, as at present conducted.

VISITED CHICAGO.—H. M. Wall, of the H. M. Wall Lithograph Company, New York; Fred. Barteldes, Lawrence, Kan.; W. H. Grenell, Saginaw, Mich.; H. A. Bunyard, with Clucas & Boddington, New York.

ANOKA, MINN.—The Pratt Ford Greenhouse Company of this place incorporated January 9 with $50,000 capital. James W. Ford of Owatonna, James W. Ford, Jr., of Anoka, and David D. Pratt of Anoka are the incorporators.

A MEETING of the executive committee of the American Seed Trade Association was held at the New Willard hotel, Washington, D. C., Wednesday, January 20, The National Board of Trade convened in the same city January 19. Albert McCullough and W. Atlee Burpee were delegates of the association to the latter meeting.

A CAREFUL observer says that canned vegetables because of their present general excellent quality, induce people to buy rather than raise their own. He says this is working against the seedsmen to-day more than the government free seed distribution. He also claims that many canners put up qualities fully equal to fresh vegetables from the home garden.

INDIANAPOLIS, IND.—William S. Gilbreath, for fifteen years associated with the Illinois Seed Company, of Chicago, and one year with the J. M. M'Cullough's Sons, Cincinnati, will open a seed house in Indianapolis under the name of the William S. Gilbreath Seed Company. He will conduct a general grass and field seed, grain and storage business. Mr. Gilbreath has a thorough knowledge of the business and a wide and favorable acquaintance in the trade.

The Philipps Seed Company.

A change has occurred in the Henry Philipps Seed & Implement Company, one of the seven brothers comprising the firm having withdrawn. Wm. T. Philipps, president of the old firm, sold his stock to his brothers and has organized a competing company. The new W. T. Philipps company is located at 519 Monroe street, and will be ready for business about Monday next. Its building is partially fitted out. The old firm continues at the old stand, and the six brothers comprising it are Herman, Henry J., Albert J., Charles J. S., Fred, and August J.—Toledo Times.

No Warranty Case.

In the case of Carpenter & Wilcox, of Randallsville, versus Newell L. Douglas, of Earlville, in which it is sought to recover damages alleged to have been occasioned by the purchase of pea seed which proved untrue to name, a decision was rendered in the justice court at Hamilton, N. Y., in favor of the complainant. The defendant, however, will appeal the case to a court of record. The action is based upon a warranty that Telephone peas were sold, and that they proved to be of nameless variety. The defense is that there was no warranty, and that the peas were sold with notice that the growers refused to warrant them as a variety or otherwise.

Underpaid Letters.

Considerable time and annoyance could be saved by concerns handling foreign correspondence, by exercising more care in the directing and stamping of letters and parcels post. In a recent consular report United States Consul Lathrop, at Bristol, England, calls attention to this trifle, which is a constant though small irritation. He saw on one merchant's desk in one morning's mail, twelve underpaid letters, on each of which the English postoffice collected double the deficiency. The American office boy, who stamps the outgoing letters, should be instructed that an increasing proportion of his employer's mail now goes to foreign countries and those letters or parcels should be stamped in full to avoid losing probably two weeks in the return and resending of the letter on account of the deficient postage. It is a trifle, though very annoying.

CLEVELAND, O.—The Cleveland Cut Flower Company has been incorporated by George Bate, F. R. Williams, H. A. Couse, E. S. Park and Iva M. Eaton with capital stock of $10,000.

Orange, N. J.

The annual installation dinner of the New Jersey Floricultural Society was held at its rooms in Orange January 16. The occasion drew forth the best of the club's well known horticultural talent and the Lawson, Enchantress, Harlowarden and Prosperity carnations which graced the tables shared attention with the after-dinner speeches. The central vase on the long table was filled with Euphorbia jacquiniflora whose slender, recurved branches and drooping lanceolate leaves hung in graceful curves over the sides. It was grown by Peter Duff.

The speaking was opened by an address of welcome by Pres. George Smith. Dr. J. M. W. Kitchen said "he had come fasting and with rheumatic pains in his back but there was now a contention of pains back and front." Mr. Macmillan, of Madison, spoke for the Morris County Gardeners' and Florists' Society. C. H. Totty's remarks were in memory of those who had passed away during the year. J. Austin Shaw and W. A. Manda spoke on the flourishing state of the society as manifested by the reports. They advised the formation of a "press committee" to carry out further the idea of informing and welcoming the public at future shows. Mr. Manda declared such shows as those held by the society to be a perpetual incentive to the public to grow flowers. Wm. Neil Cambell, of Vaughan's and Robert McArthur spoke. John Hays and Peter Duff, sang. Geo. Smith sang "The Tinker's Weddin', O!" Many other local celebrities added their oratory to the occasion and entertaining letters were received from many invited guests unable to be present.

The events which have brought the society more than ever before to the notice of both craft and general public were so recent as to render unnecessary any save brief remarks by President Geo. Smith in his report. The reports of Secretary Jos. A. Manda and Treasurer Malcolm MacRorie indicated general prosperity and a fair balance in the treasury in spite of increased expenditure caused by the society's activity. The installation exercises were conducted by J. B. Davis after the manner usually observed by the society and in which Ex-president Robert MacArthur, Peter Duff and John Hayes took part. In the business meeting, the rules were suspended to elect Harry May to membership by acclamation. A. Caparn and Robert McArthur were judges of exhibits for the evening. Exhibits were made by John Hayes, Peter Duff, George Smith and W. Ashmead.　　　J. B. DAVIS.

QUINCY, MASS.—Perry Green is growing sweet peas as a winter crop and had a fine cut for the holidays.

Jan. 23,

THE NURSERY TRADE.

AM. ASSOCIATION OF NURSERYMEN.
N. W. HALE, Knoxville, Tenn., Pres.; FRANK
A. WEBER, St. Louis, Mo., Vice-Pres.; GEORGE C.
SEAGER, Rochester, N. Y., Sec'y.
Twenty-ninth annual convention, Atlanta, Ga.,
June, 1904.

WM. A. PETERSON, of the Peterson Nursery, has been re-elected director of the State Bank of Chicago.

CLINTON, IA.—J. B. Cripps, a pioneer resident of Albion, and one of the best known and successful nurserymen of the state, is dead.

SAN FRANCISCO, CAL—The Calaveras big tree committee of the Outdoor Art League of California has forwarded a mammoth petition to President Roosevelt, asking him to aid in preserving the Calaveras groves of big trees. The petition carries 1,400,000 names of people in all parts of the United States.

SEATTLE, WASH.—State Horticulturist Van Holderbeke gives the following report of trees planted in nine counties and districts of the state during the past fall: Yakima 67,000, Walla Walla 7,470, Whitman 20,253, Wenatchee 23,040, Douglas 15,003, Thurston 23,740, Spokane 9,125, Chelan 23,040, Snohomish 42,411, Tacoma district, 22,750, or a total of 230,882 trees. The most of the planting was done during November.

Thompsonville, Conn.

In their own future home David William Brainard and Miss Frances Abbe Butler were united in marriage, January 12. The interior of the house was prettily decorated, southern smilax and white carnations being effectively used. In the parlor, where the ceremony took place, was artistically arranged a drapery of green, and on either side were banks of palms, surmounted by white carnations. In the upper rooms smilax and potted plants were used. The guests included only the near of kin and intimate friends. The bride was attired in a suit of gray, trimmed with lace and applique. She carried a shower bouquet of lily-of-the-valley. The ceremony was performed by Rev. A. V. S. Wallace. The recently-purchased home of Mr. and Mrs. Brainard is at the corner of Pease and Garden streets, only a few yards from Mr. Brainard's greenhouses. The groom is the oldest son of Mr. and Mrs. Charles Brainard. He is the local florist, and is a well known and highly respected young man. The bride is a daughter of Mr. and Mrs. Hermon Butler, of Windsor Locks. The bride and groom left for a wedding tour of a week.

Minneapolis, Minn.

S. T. Hopper has sold a half interest to H. B. Shamp and business will be conducted on a large scale under the name of Hopper & Shamp.

Trade has been rather quiet since Christmas but all the dealers are able to stand it. C. F. R.

Philadelphia Rambler.

The new forcing rose, strong field plants,
$15.00, $30.00 and $50.00 per 100.

CRIMSON RAMBLER.
Extra well branched, $8.00, $11.00 and $15.00
per 100.

The Conard & Jones Co., WEST GROVE,
PA.

Please mention the American Florist when writing.

OUR PASTIMES.

Announcements of coming contests or other events of interests to our bowling, shooting and sporting readers are solicited and will be given place in this column.
Address all correspondence for this department to Wm. J. Stewart, 49 W. 28th St., New York. Robt. Kift, 1725 Chestnut St., Philadelphia, Pa.; to the American Florist Co., Chicago, Ill.

NEW YORK.—The bowlers met on the new alleys January 18 and spent a very enjoyable evening, there being twelve in attendance.

At St. Louis.

The bowling club had a lively time Monday night. Two teams were organized from among the members present. The result follows:

Player	TEAM I.	1st	2d	3d	T'l
Beneke		187	180	183	590
Miller		146	159	142	427
Weber		186	172	169	478
Ellis		13	138	113	381
O. R. Beneke		147	168	141	456
Total		717	798	748	2262

Player	TEAM II.	1st	2d	3d	T'l
Kuehn		185	183	182	520
Adels		191	143	162	496
Meinhardt		116	167	221	495
Young		126	116	181	375
Weber, Jr.		130	122	125	387
Total		729	731	821	2275

F. K. B.

At Chicago.

The bowlers met at the Geroux alleys Tuesday evening. With the exception of Stevens the boys rolled an indifferent game, and some of the scores do not look well in print. The ladies are producing some fine games and next week the club expects to give prizes for the best lady bowler of the session. Stevens rolled a most consistent game, reaching the high score of 227 in the second frame. The scores follow:

Player	1st	2d	3d	4th
G. Asmus	149	177	162	168
J. Huebner	165	133	129	151
L. Kill	137	91	1	7
L. H. Winterson	143	146	132	134
J. P. Degnan	137	157	132	163
Scott	119			
E. F. Winterson	150	129	187	172
P. J. Hauswirth	166	126	163	135
Stevens	183	227	181	186
Asm	137	138	110	181
Balluff	129			
C. Kochman	104	130	120	
Victor Kreitling	189	197	148	

LADIES.	1st	2d	3d
Mrs. Hauswirth	135	151	169
Mrs. Winterson	159	114	94
Mrs. Asmus	115	116	99
Mrs. Kreitling	113	161	177
Miss Kreitling	89	115	166

Toronto.

BUSINESS IMPROVING STEADILY.—COLD WEATHER CONTINUES, KEEPING STOCK DOWN.—VIOLETS ARE MOVING BETTER.—GEORGE ALLAN GROWING GOOD CARNATIONS.

There is considerable improvement in the local trade, especially so in roses, the trade demanding almost everything that can be had. Funeral work has been much in demand and though transient trade is at a standstill all colors of flowers are being put into designs. The weather here remains decidedly cold. American Beauty roses are coming in in fairly large quantities, also Bridesmaid, Bride and Meteor, but the heavy demand keeps the market well cleaned up. Carnations average about the same quality that they did Christmas but the con-

tinued demand keeps the flowers picked close, and many are picked before they fully develop. Violets, which have proved a drug on the market for the last two weeks, are moving much faster. As the cut of bulbous stock increases cut flowers will no doubt be more plentiful in a few days.

Some good carnations are coming from George Allan, of Toronto Junction. Although he is a new man in this vicinity and even handicapped for room, the quality of the blooms he is producing leads us to believe that it will only be a matter of time until he is classed among the leaders in growing ability.

When smilax is in blossom it is certainly a very pretty and effective decoration for any florists' establishment. F. Brown, of Barrie, is sending in some choice strings at present which find ready sale. His violets are also good for this season.

Alex. McHardy, one of our progressive amateurs, is cutting some nice Cattleya Percivaliana alba which finds ready sale. Some nice bougainvilleas are coming from J. H. Dunlop's, which are very well grown and quite acceptable at this season.

Levi Schnur, representative for the Steele, Briggs Seed Company has just returned from a long eastern trip. He found prosperity in evidence in the many establishments, and found the florists well satisfied with the past season.

E. G. Belsmith, who in recent years had the monopoly of Toronto's ¿ wire works, especially in designs, has given up his local business and is now permanently located in the Dale Estate at Brampton.

W. E. Kennedy, manager of the George town Floral Company, Georgetown, Ont., was a visitor. He reported good business in his vicinity.　H. G. D.

Syracuse, N. Y.

GIRL FLORIST, DESPONDENT OVER BUSINESS TROUBLES, ATTEMPTS SUICIDE.—HENRY MORRIS A BANKRUPT.—EXTREMELY COLD WEATHER CAUSES DULL TRADE.

Ada M. Boddy, who recently opened a retail store in West Genesee street under the name of Lake View Rose garden, attempted to commit suicide by drinking carbolic acid. Miss Boddy is a negress, twenty-two years old. She had worked in Henry Burt's store since she was eleven years old, until a short time before the holidays, when she opened her own store. Business troubles caused her attempt. At Christmas time a large quantity of roses were not delivered by the express company and were spoiled. Bills began to come in and the outlook was dismal. Miss Boddy will undoubtedly recover. The store is still open, and the girl is said to have financial backing.

Henry Morris, of East Genesee street, has filed a petition in bankruptcy. His schedule shows debts of $1,518.92. Chester King has been appointed to conduct the business. Mr. Morris' retail store has always been on a paying basis, but the heavy burden he was carrying at his Elmwood greenhouses embarrassed him temporarily. It is thought some arrangement will be made whereby business may go on as formerly.

The coldest weather Syracuse has ever known prevailed here early this week. The thermometer was 32° below zero. Trade is consequently a little dull. Hyacinths, tulips and other bulbous stock are in demand. Florists have no difficulty in keeping their windows from freezing up so as to conceal the displays from view. There is considerable activity in social affairs, and several big funerals have helped out.　A. J. B.

Richmond, Ind.

At the annual meeting of the Richmond Florists' Club, held at the greenhouses of the B. K. & B. Floral Company, the following were elected officers for the ensuing year:

President, George B. Gause.
Vice-president, Chas. Knopf.
Secretary, H. C. Chessman.
Treasurer, John A. Kvass.

At the December meeting it was suggested that some member prepare a paper to read before the club at the January meeting. The president appointed Fred Lemon to prepare such a paper on his own subject and appoint some one to prepare the paper for the meeting in February.

There are many promising seedlings brought forward by the different florists id this vicinity, by the proprietors as well as the boys in the trenches. There have been several at the E. G. Hill Company recently, one of which will call E. G. "grandpapa." The three Fulle brothers are well represented. Ben H. Schroeder, foreman for Chessman & Schepman, has the latest, a twelve-pound boy. We concede them each and every one to score 99 points, and award each a certificate of merit.

Richmond is still "in the push," although there have not been many communications in the AMERICAN FLORIST of late from this point. All the retailers report an exceedingly heavy trade at good prices during the holidays. Everything was sold out. The wholesalers were unable to supply all demands. Good prices ruled.　H. C. C.

Catalogues Received.

J. W. Thorburn & Company, New York, seeds; W. Atlee Burpee & Company, Philadelphia, Pa., seeds; Weeber & Don, New York, seeds; Biltmore Nursery, Biltmore, N. C., nursery stock; Wm. Elliott & Sons, New York, seeds; R. & J. Farquhar & Company, Boston, Mass., seeds; F. Barteldes & Company, Lawrence, Kan., seeds; Iowa Seed Company, Des Moines, Iowa, seeds; John Lewis Childs, Floral Park, New York, seeds and plants; Texas Seed & Floral Company, Dallas, Tex., seeds and plants; J. M. McCullough's Sons, Cincinnati, O., seeds; Henry A. Dreer, Philadelphia, Pa., seeds, plants, bulbs, etc.; The McGregor Brothers Company, Springfield, O., seeds, plants, etc.; The Dingee & Conard Company, West Grove, Pa., roses, seeds, etc.; John Sharpe & Sons, Bardney, Lincoln, Eng., seeds; C. Petrick, Ghent, Belgium, plants; Sluis & Groot, Enkhuizen, Holland, vegetable, flower and agricultural seeds; The Storrs & Harrison Company, Painesville, O., seeds, trees, plants, etc.; Vaughan's Seed Store, Chicago, seeds and plants, bulbs, etc.; Nonne & Hoepker, Ahrensburg, Germany, seeds; Max Kornacker, Wehrden a. d. Weser, Germany, seeds, plants, etc.; A. N. Pierson, Cromwell, Conn., plants; Johnson & Stokes, Philadelphia, Pa., seeds, plants and bulbs; Arthur Cowee, Berlin, N. Y., gladioli; The Griffing Brothers Company, Jacksonville, Fla., nursery stock; Diggs & Beadles, Richmond, Va., seeds.

VAN WERT, O.—Edward Scharff has purchased an interest in the Van Wert greenhouses from his brother, Henry Scharff, and hereafter the firm will be known as Scharff Brothers. They will grow for the wholesale trade and expect to add 5,000 square feet of glass before next fall.

Providence, R. I.

The Florists' Club annual banquet was held Thursday evening, January 14. Gilb was the caterer and furnished as nice a supper as could be desired. The attendance was complete, all the old guard being present together with a number of new faces, an encouraging sign. President John Macrea, on behalf of the members, presented past President William Appleton with a silver-mounted gavel, suitably inscribed, which so took our former executive by surprise that it was some time before he was sufficiently recovered to sing an old folks' song, to the delight of all present. Toastmaster Wm. E. Chappell, gave everyone an opening wherewith to show his talent. John Benke favored the members with two solos in a pleasing manner. The subject of a general flower market was broached and seemed to meet with general favor. Messrs. Fitts and Southwick, of the park board, were present and spoke briefly but to the point. M.

ELIZABETH, N. J.—The twenty-ninth annual meeting of the New Jersey State Horticultural Society was concluded at the State House, January 8.